Lecture Notes in Computer Science 12170

More information about this series at http://www.springer.com/series/7410

Daniele Micciancio · Thomas Ristenpart (Eds.)

Advances in Cryptology – CRYPTO 2020

40th Annual International Cryptology Conference, CRYPTO 2020
Santa Barbara, CA, USA, August 17–21, 2020
Proceedings, Part I

 Springer

Editors
Daniele Micciancio 🆔
UC San Diego
La Jolla, CA, USA

Thomas Ristenpart 🆔
Cornell Tech
New York, NY, USA

ISSN 0302-9743 ISSN 1611-3349 (electronic)
Lecture Notes in Computer Science
ISBN 978-3-030-56783-5 ISBN 978-3-030-56784-2 (eBook)
https://doi.org/10.1007/978-3-030-56784-2

LNCS Sublibrary: SL4 – Security and Cryptology

This Springer imprint is published by the registered company Springer Nature Switzerland AG
The registered company address is: Gewerbestrasse 11, 6330 Cham, Switzerland

Preface

The 40th International Cryptology Conference (Crypto 2020), sponsored by the International Association of Cryptologic Research (IACR), was exceptional in many ways. The COVID-19 pandemic meant that for the first time in the conference's 40-year history, Crypto was not held at the University of California, Santa Barbara. Safety mandated that we shift to an online-only virtual conference.

Crypto 2020 received 371 submissions. Review occurred during what, for many countries, was the height thus far of pandemic spread and lockdowns. We thank the 54 person Program Committee (PC) and the 286 external reviewers for their efforts to ensure that, in the face of challenging work environments, illness, and death, we nevertheless were able to perform a standard double-blind review process in which papers received multiple independent reviews, authors were allowed a rebuttal, and papers were subsequently further reviewed and discussed. The two program chairs were not allowed to submit a paper, and PC members were limited to two submissions each. The PC ultimately selected 85 papers for acceptance, a record number for Crypto.

The PC selected four papers to receive recognition via awards, via a voting-based process that took into account conflicts of interest (including for the program chairs). Three papers were selected to receive a Best Paper award and were invited to the Journal of Cryptology: "Improved Differential-Linear Attacks with Applications to ARX Ciphers" by Christof Beierle, Gregor Leander, and Yosuke Todo; "Breaking the Decisional Diffie-Hellman Problem for Class Group Actions using Genus Theory" by Wouter Castryck, Jana Sotáková, and Frederik Vercauteren; and "Chosen Ciphertext Security from Injective Trapdoor Functions" by Susan Hohenberger, Venkata Koppula, and Brent Waters. One paper was selected to receive the Best Paper by Early Career Researchers award: "Handling Adaptive Compromise for Practical Encryption Schemes" by Joseph Jaeger and Nirvan Tyagi.

In addition to the regular program, Crypto 2020 included the IACR Distinguished Lecture by Silvio Micali on "Our Models and Us" and an invited talk by Seny Kamara on "Crypto for the People". Crypto 2020 carried forward the long-standing tradition of having a rump session, this year organized in a virtual format by Antigoni Polychroniadou, Bertram Poettering, and Martijn Stam.

The chairs would also like to thank the many people whose hard work helped ensure Crypto 2020 was a success:

- Leonid Reyzin (Boston University) – Crypto 2020 general chair.
- Sophia Yakoubov for helping with general chair duties, and Muthuramakrishnan Venkitasubramaniam, Tal Rabin, and Fabrice Benhamouda for providing valuable advice to the general chair.
- Carmit Hazay (Bar Ilan University) – Crypto 2020 workshop chair.
- Antigoni Polychroniadou, Bertram Poettering, and Martijn Stam – Crypto 2020 rump session chairs.

- Chris Peikert for his role in overseeing reviews and the Best Paper by Early Career Researchers award selection for which the program chairs were conflicted.
- Kevin McCurley and Christian Cachin for their critical assistance in setting up and managing a (new for Crypto) paper submission and review system.
- Kevin McCurley, Kay McKelly, and members of the IACR's emergency pandemic team for their work in designing and running the virtual format.
- Whitney Morris and Eriko Macdonald from UCSB event services for their help navigating the COVID-19 shutdown logistics.
- Anna Kramer and her colleagues at Springer.

July 2020   Daniele Micciancio
                                                                 Thomas Ristenpart

Organization

General Chair

Leonid Reyzin — Boston University, USA

Program Committee Chairs

Daniele Micciancio — UC San Diego, USA
Thomas Ristenpart — Cornell Tech, USA

Program Committee

Adi Akavia	University of Haifa, Israel
Martin Albrecht	Royal Holloway, University of London, UK
Roberto Avanzi	ARM, Germany
Lejla Batina	Radboud University, The Netherlands
Jeremiah Blocki	Purdue University, USA
David Cash	University of Chicago, USA
Melissa Chase	Microsoft Research, USA
Hao Chen	Microsoft Research, USA
Ilaria Chillotti	KU Leuven, Zama, Belgium
Henry Corrigan-Gibbs	EPFL, Switzerland, and MIT CSAIL, USA
Craig Costello	Microsoft Research, USA
Joan Daemen	Radboud University, The Netherlands
Thomas Eisenbarth	University of Lübeck, Germany
Pooya Farshim	University of York, UK
Sanjam Garg	UC Berkeley, USA
Daniel Genkin	University of Michigan, USA
Steven Goldfeder	Cornell Tech, USA
Shay Gueron	University of Haifa, Israel, and AWS, USA
Felix Günther	ETH Zurich, Switzerland
Tetsu Iwata	Nagoya University, Japan
Tibor Jager	Bergische Universitaet, Germany
Antoine Joux	CISPA – Helmholtz Center for Information Security, Germany
Jonathan Katz	George Mason Univeristy, USA
Eike Kiltz	Ruhr University Bochum, Germany
Elena Kirshanova	I.Kant Baltic Federal University, Russia
Venkata Koppula	Weizmann Institute of Science, Isarel
Anna Lysyanskaya	Brown University, USA
Vadim Lyubashevsky	IBM Research Zurich, Switzerland
Mohammad Mahmoody	University of Virginia, USA

Giulio Malavolta	Carnegie Mellon University and UC Berkeley, USA
Florian Mendel	Infineon Technologies, Germany
María Naya-Plasencia	Inria, France
Adam O'Neill	University of Massachusetts, USA
Olya Ohrimenko	The University of Melbourne, Australia
Claudio Orlandi	Aarhus University, Denmark
Elisabeth Oswald	University of Klagenfurt, Austria
Chris Peikert	University of Michigan, USA
Bertram Poettering	IBM Research Zurich, Switzerland
Antigoni Polychroniadou	JP Morgan AI Research, USA
Ananth Raghunathan	Google, USA
Mariana Raykova	Google, USA
Christian Rechberger	TU Graz, Austria
Alon Rosen	IDC, Israel
Mike Rosulek	Oregon State University, USA
Alessandra Scafuro	NC State University, USA
Dominique Schroeder	Florida Atlantic University, USA
Thomas Shrimpton	University of Florida, USA
Fang Song	Texas A&M University, USA
Marc Stevens	CWI Amsterdam, The Netherlands
Dominique Unruh	University of Tartu, Estonia
Michael Walter	IST, Austria
David Wu	University of Virginia, USA

Additional Reviewers

Masayuki Abe
Shweta Agrawal
Shashank Agrawal
Shweta Agrawal
Gorjan Alagic
Navid Alamati
Greg Alpar
Joel Alwen
Elena Andreeva
Gilad Asharov
Thomas Attema
Saikrishna Badrinarayanan
Shi Bai
Foteini Baldimtsi
Marshall Ball
James Bartusek
Carsten Baum
Asli Bay
Mihir Bellare

Fabrice Benhamouda
Sebastian Berndt
Ward Beullens
Ritam Bhaumik
Nina Bindel
Alex Block
Xavier Bonnetain
Charlotte Bonte
Carl Bootland
Jonathan Bootle
Raphael Bost
Christina Boura
Elette Boyle
Zvika Brakerski
Benedikt Bünz
Matteo Campanelli
Anne Canteaut
André Chailloux
Suvradip Chakraborty

Yilei Chen
Jie Chen
Nai-Hui Chia
Arka Rai Choudhuri
Kai-Min Chung
Michele Ciampi
Carlos Cid
Michael Clear
Ran Cohen
Kelong Cong
Aisling Connolly
Sandro Coretti
Daniele Cozzo
Tingting Cui
Benjamin Curtis
Jan Czajkowski
Dana Dachman-Soled
Alex Davidson
Leo De Castro
Luca De Feo
Thomas Debris
Jean Paul Degabriele
Cyprien Delpech de Saint Guilhem
Patrick Derbez
Apoorvaa Deshpande
Benjamin Diamond
Christoph Dobraunig
Nico Doettling
Benjamin Dowling
Yfke Dulek
Stefan Dziembowski
Christoph Egger
Maria Eichlseder
Daniel Escudero
Saba Eskandarian
Serge Fehr
Rex Fernando
Dario Fiore
Ben Fisch
Wieland Fischer
Nils Fleischhacker
Daniele Friolo
Georg Fuchsbauer
Tommaso Gagliardoni
Juan Garay
Romain Gay

Nicholas Genise
Rosario Gennaro
Marios Georgiou
Riddhi Ghosal
Satrajit Ghosh
Esha Ghosh
Koustabh Ghosh
Irene Giacomelli
Andras Gilyen
S. Dov Gordon
Rishab Goyal
Lorenzo Grassi
Matthew Green
Hannes Gross
Aldo Gunsing
Tim Güneysu
Mohammad Hajiabadi
Shai Halevi
Koki Hamada
Dominik Hartmann
Eduard Hauck
Carmit Hazay
Alexander Helm
Lukas Helminger
Julia Hesse
Dennis Hofheinz
Alex Hoover
Akinori Hosoyamada
Kathrin Hövelmanns
Andreas Hülsing
Ilia Iliashenko
Gorka Irazoqui
Joseph Jaeger
Eli Jaffe
Abhishek Jain
Aayush Jain
Samuel Jaques
Stanislaw Jarecki
Zhengfeng Ji
Zhengzhong Jin
Saqib Kakvi
Daniel Kales
Chethan Kamath
Akinori Kawachi
Mahimna Kelkar
Hamidreza Khoshakhlagh

Dakshita Khurana
Sam Kim
Michael Kim
Susumu Kiyoshima
Karen Klein
Dmitry Kogan
Markulf Kohlweiss
Ilan Komargodski
Daniel Kuijsters
Mukul Kulkarni
Ashutosh Kumar
Stefan Kölbl
Thijs Laarhoven
Russell W. F. Lai
Kim Laine
Virginie Lallemand
Changmin Lee
Tancrede Lepoint
Antonin Leroux
Gaëtan Leurent
Kevin Lewi
Baiyu Li
Xin Li
Xiao Liang
Feng-Hao Liu
Alex Lombardi
Julian Loss
Ji Luo
Fermi Ma
Bernardo Magri
Urmila Mahadev
Christian Majenz
Eleftheria Makri
Nathan Manohar
Sai Krishna Deepak Maram
Daniel Masny
Eleanor McMurtry
Sarah Meiklejohn
Bart Mennink
Peihan Miao
Tarik Moataz
Esfandiar Mohammadi
Hart Montgomery
Tal Moran
Andrew Morgan
Fabrice Mouhartem

Pratyay Mukherjee
Michael Naehrig
Samuel Neves
Ruth Francis Ng
Ngoc Khanh Nguyen
Valeria Nikolaenko
Ryo Nishimaki
Satoshi Obana
Sabine Oechsner
Jiaxin Pan
Omer Paneth
Lorenz Panny
Sunoo Park
Alain Passelègue
Valerio Pastro
Jacques Patarin
Kenneth Paterson
Alice Pellet–Mary
Zack Pepin
Ludovic Perret
Léo Perrin
Peter Pessl
Jeroen Pijnenburg
Benny Pinkas
Rachel Player
Oxana Poburinnaya
Eamonn Postlethwaite
Robert Primas
Willy Quach
Rahul Rachuri
Ahmadreza Rahimi
Divya Ravi
Ling Ren
Joost Renes
M. Sadegh Riazi
João L. Ribeiro
Silas Richelson
Doreen Riepel
Dragos Rotaru
Ron Rothblum
Adeline Roux-Langlois
Arnab Roy
Carla Ràfols
Paul Rösler
Simona Samardjiska
Yu Sasaki

John Schanck
Patrick Schaumont
Martin Schläffer
Jonas Schneider-Bensch
Peter Scholl
André Schrottenloher
Sven Schäge
Adam Sealfon
Gil Segev
Gregor Seiler
Okan Seker
Nicolas Sendrier
Sacha Servan-Schreiber
Karn Seth
Yannick Seurin
Siamak Shahandashti
Devika Sharma
Sina Shiehian
Omer Shlomovits
Omri Shmueli
Mark Simkin
Boris Škorić
Yongsoo Song
Pratik Soni
Florian Speelman
Nicholas Spooner
Akshayaram Srinivasan
Douglas Stebila
Damien Stehlé
Noah Stephens-Davidowitz
Younes Talibi Alaoui
Titouan Tanguy
Stefano Tessaro
Aravind Thyagarajan
Radu Titiu
Yosuke Todo

Ni Trieu
Rotem Tsabary
Daniel Tschudi
Vinod Vaikuntanathan
Thyla van der Merwe
Prashant Vasudevan
Marloes Venema
Muthuramakrishnan
  Venkitasubramaniam
Damien Vergnaud
Thomas Vidick
Fernando Virdia
Ivan Visconti
Satyanarayana Vusirikala
Riad Wahby
Xiao Wang
Brent Waters
Hoeteck Wee
Christian Weinert
Weiqiang Wen
Erich Wenger
Daniel Wichs
Luca Wilke
Keita Xagawa
Min Xu
Sophia Yakoubov
Rupeng Yang
Eylon Yogev
Yu Yu
Greg Zaverucha
Mark Zhandry
Tina Zhang
Fan Zhang
Yupeng Zhang
Vassilis Zikas

Contents – Part I

Hardware Security and Leakage Resilience

Outsourced Encryption

Constructions

Public Key Cryptography

Contents – Part II

Contents – Part III

Security Models

Handling Adaptive Compromise for Practical Encryption Schemes

Joseph Jaeger[1($\boxtimes$)] and Nirvan Tyagi[2]

[1] Paul G. Allen School of Computer Science & Engineering,
University of Washington, Seattle, USA
jsjaeger@cs.washington.edu
[2] Cornell Tech, New York City, USA
tyagi@cs.cornell.edu

Abstract. We provide a new definitional framework capturing the multi-user security of encryption schemes and pseudorandom functions in the face of adversaries that can adaptively compromise users' keys. We provide a sequence of results establishing the security of practical symmetric encryption schemes under adaptive compromise in the random oracle or ideal cipher model. The bulk of analysis complexity for adaptive compromise security is relegated to the analysis of lower-level primitives such as pseudorandom functions.

We apply our framework to give proofs of security for the BurnBox system for privacy in the face of border searches and the in-use searchable symmetric encryption scheme due to Cash et al. In both cases, prior analyses had bugs that our framework helps avoid.

Keywords: Symmetric cryptography · Ideal models · Adaptive security · Searchable symmetric encryption

1 Introduction

A classic question in cryptography has been dealing with adversaries that adaptively compromise particular parties, thereby learning their secrets. Consider a setting where parties use keys $k_1, \ldots, k_n$ to encrypt messages $m_1, \ldots, m_n$ to derive ciphertexts $\mathsf{Enc}(k_1, m_1), \ldots, \mathsf{Enc}(k_n, m_n)$. An adversary obtains the ciphertexts and compromises a chosen subset of the parties to learn their keys. What can we say about the security of the messages encrypted by the keys that remain secret? Surprisingly, traditional approaches to formal security analysis, such as using encryption schemes that provide semantic security [19], fail to suffice for proving these messages' confidentiality. This problem was first discussed in the context of secure multiparty computation [10], and it arises in a variety of important cryptographic applications, as we explain below.

In this work, we introduce a new framework for formal analyses when security in the face of adaptive compromise is desired. Our approach provides a modular route towards analysis using idealized primitives (such as random oracles or ideal ciphers) for practical and in-use schemes. This modularity helps

© International Association for Cryptologic Research 2020
D. Micciancio and T. Ristenpart (Eds.): CRYPTO 2020, LNCS 12170, pp. 3–32, 2020.
https://doi.org/10.1007/978-3-030-56784-2_1

us sidestep the pitfalls of prior ideal-model analyses that either invented new (less satisfying) ideal primitives, omitted proofs, or gave detailed but incorrect proofs. We exercise our framework across applications including searchable symmetric encryption (SSE), revocable cloud storage, and asymmetric password-authenticated key exchange (aPAKE). In particular, we provide full, correct proofs of security against adaptive adversaries for the Cash et al. [12] searchable symmetric encryption scheme that is used often in practice and the Burn-Box system [33] for dealing with compelled-access searches. We show that our new definitions imply the notion of equivocable encryption introduced to prove security of the OPAQUE [24] asymmetric password-authenticated key exchange protocol. More broadly, our framework can be applied to a wide variety of constructions [1,2,9,13,17,20,21,25–29,34].

Current approaches to the "commitment problem". Our motivating applications have at their core an adaptive simulation-based model of security. Roughly speaking, they ask that no computationally bound adversary can distinguish between two worlds. In the first world, the adversary interacts with the scheme whose security is being measured. In the second world, the "ideal" world, the adversary's queries are instead handled by a simulator that must make do with only limited information which represents allowable "leakage" about the queries the adversary has made so far. The common unifying factor between varying applications we consider is that the adversary can make queries resulting in being given a ciphertexts encrypting messages of its choosing, then with future queries adaptively choose to expose the secret keys underlying some of the ciphertexts. The leakage given to the simulator will not include the messages encrypted unless a query has been made to expose the corresponding key.

Proving security in this model, however, does not work based on standard assumptions of the underlying encryption scheme. The problem is that the simulator must commit to ciphertexts, revealing them to the adversary, before knowing the messages associated to them. Hence the commitment problem. Several prior approaches for proving positive security results exist.

One natural approach attempts to build special non-committing encryption schemes [10] that can be proven (in the standard model) to allow opening some a priori fixed ciphertext to a message. But these schemes are not practical, as they require key material at least as long as the underlying message. Another unsatisfying approach considers only non-adaptive security in which an attacker specifies all of its queries at the beginning of the game. This is one of the two approaches that were simultaneously taken by Cash et al. [12]. Here the simulator is given the leakage for all of these queries at once and generates a transcript of all of its response. This is unsatisfying because more is lost when switching from adaptive to non-adaptive security than just avoiding the commitment problem. It is an easy exercise to construct encryption schemes which are secure when all queries to it must be chosen ahead of time but are not secure even against key-recovery attacks when an adversary may adaptively choose its queries.

The primary approach used to avoid this is to use idealized models, which we can again split into two versions. The first is to use an idealized model of

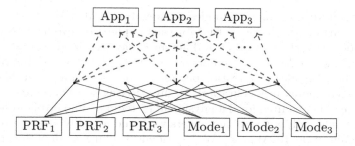

Fig. 1. Old state of affairs. Red dashed lines correspond to implications proved through programming in an ideal model proof. A different programming proof is needed to prove an application secure for each pair of PRF and symmetric encryption mode. (Color figure online)

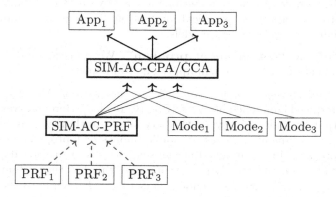

Fig. 2. New state of affairs. Red dashed lines correspond to implications proved through programming in an ideal model proof. New definitions are in bold boxes. Programming proofs are only needed to show each low level PRF construction meets SIM-AC-PRF. (Color figure online)

encryption. Examples of this include indifferentiable authenticated encryption [3] (IAE) or the ideal encryption model (IEM) of Tyagi et al. [33]. Security analyses in these models might not say much when one uses real encryption schemes, even when one is willing to use more established idealized models such as the ideal cipher model (ICM) or the random oracle model (ROM). One hope would be to use approaches such as indifferentiability [30] to modularly show that symmetric schemes sufficiently "behave like" ideal encryption, but this approach is unlikely to work for most encryption schemes used in practice [3].

The final approach, which is by far the most common in searchable symmetric encryption [1,2,9,12,13,17,20,21,25–29,34], is to fix a *particular encryption scheme* and prove security with respect to it in the ICM or ROM. Typically encryption schemes are built as modes of operations of an underlying pseudorandom function (PRF) and this function (or its constituent parts) is what is modeled as an ideal function. The downside of this is represented in Fig. 1. On the top, we have the applications one would like to prove secure, and on the bottom, we have the different modes of operation and PRFs that one might use. Using this approach means that for each application, we have to provide a separate ideal model proof for each different choice of a mode of operation and a PRF (represented by dotted red arrows in Fig. 1). If there are A applications, P PRFs, and M modes of operation one might consider using, then this requires $A \cdot P \cdot M$ ideal model proofs in total, an unsatisfying state of affairs.

Moreover, the required ideal analysis can be tedious[1] and error-prone. This is presumably why only a few of the papers we found actually attempt to provide the full details of the ROM proof. We have identified bugs in all of the proofs that did provide the details. The lack of a full, valid proof among the fifteen papers we considered indicates the need for a more modular framework to capture this use of the random oracle. Our work provides such a framework, allowing the random oracle details to be abstracted away as a proof that only needs to be provided once. This framework provides definitions for use by other cryptographers that are simple to use, apply to practical encryption schemes, and allow showing adaptive security in well-studied models.

Examples of the "commitment problem". We proceed by discussing the example applications where we will apply our framework.

Revocable cloud storage and the compelled access setting. We start with the recently introduced compelled access setting (CAS) [33]. Here one wants encryption tools that provide privacy in the face of an authority searching digital devices, e.g., government searches of mobile phones or laptops at border crossings. To protect against compelled access searches, the BurnBox tool [33] uses what they call revocable encryption. At its core, this has the system encrypt a user's files $m_1, \ldots, m_n$ with independent keys $k_1, \ldots, k_n$. Ciphertexts are stored on (adversarially visible) cloud storage. Before a search occurs, the user instructs the application to delete the keys corresponding to files that the user wishes to hide from the authority, thereby revoking their own access to them. The other keys and file contents are disclosed to the authority.

The formal security definition introduced by Tyagi et al. captures confidentiality for revoked files even in the face of adversarial choice of which files to revoke, meaning they want security in the face of adaptive compromises. This very naturally results in the commitment problem because the simulator can be forced to provide ciphertexts for files, but only later learn the contents of these files at the time of key revelation. At which point, it is supposed to give keys which properly decrypt these ciphertexts.

To address the commitment problem they introduced the IEM. This models symmetric encryption as perfect: every encryption query is associated to a freshly chosen random string as ciphertext, and decryption is only allowed on previously returned ciphertexts. Analyses in the IEM can commit to ciphertexts (when the adversary doesn't know the key) and later open them to arbitrary messages. In their implementation, they used AES-GCM for encryption which cannot be

---

[1] Even more-so because SSE protocols often *also* run into the commitment problem with a PRF and need to model that using a random oracle as well.

thought of as indifferentiable from the IEM. Hence their proof can ultimately only provide heuristic evidence for the security of their implemenation.

Symmetric searchable encryption. Our second motivating setting is symmetric searchable encryption (SSE), which has similar issues as that discussed above for BurnBox, but with added complexity. SSE handles the following problem: a client wants to offload storage of a database of documents to an untrusted server while maintaining the ability to perform keyword searches on the database. The keyword searches should not reveal the contents of the documents to the server. To enable efficient solutions, we allow queries to leak some partial information about documents. Security is formalized via a simulation-based definition [15], in which a simulator given only the allowed leakage must trick an adversary into believing it is interacting with the actual SSE construction. An adaptive adversary can submit keyword searches as a function of prior returned results. Proving security here establishes that the scheme only leaks what is allowed and nothing more. While the leakage itself has been shown to be damaging in various contexts [11,22], our focus here is on the formal analyses showing that leakage-abuse attacks are the best possible ones.

A common approach for SSE can be summarized at a high level as follows. The client generates a sequence of key pairs $(k_1, k'_1), \ldots, (k_n, k'_n)$ for keywords $w \in \{1, \ldots, n\}$ represented as integers for simplicity. The first key k_w in each pair is used to encrypt the identifiers of documents containing w. The latter key k'_w is used as a pseudorandom function (PRF) key to derive pseudorandom locations to store the encryption of the document identifiers. When the client later wants to search for documents containing w it sends the associated (k_w, k'_w) keys to the server. The server then uses k'_w to re-derive the pseudorandom locations of the ciphertexts and uses k_w to decrypt them.

To prove adaptive security, the simulator for such a protocol runs into the commitment problem because it must commit to ciphertexts of the document identifiers before knowing what the identifiers are. Perhaps less obviously, a simulator also runs into a commitment issues with the PRF. To ensure security the simulated locations of ciphertexts must be random, but then when responding to a search query the simulator is on the hook to find a key for the PRF that "explains" the simulated locations. Papers on SSE typically address these issue by modeling the PRF as a random oracle and fixing a specific construction of an encryption scheme based on a random oracle. As noted earlier, this has resulted in a need for many tedious and error-prone proofs.

Asymmetric password-authenticated key exchange and equivocable encryption. In independent and concurrent work, Jarecki et al. updated the ePrint version of [24] to introduce the notion of equivocable encryption and use it to prove security of their asymmetric password-authenticated key exchange protocol OPAQUE. The definition of equivocable encryption is essentially a weakened version of our confidentiality definition, considering only single-user security and allowing only a single encryption query; whereas we consider multi-user security and arbitrarily many adaptively chosen queries. Since their definition is implied by ours, our results will make rigorous their claim that "common encryption modes are equivocable under some idealized assumption".

A new approach. We introduce a new framework for analyzing security in adaptive compromise scenarios. Our framework has a simple, but powerful recipe: augment traditional simulation-based, property-based security definitions to empower adversaries with the ability to perform adaptive compromise of secret keys. For symmetric encryption, for example, we convert the standard simulation-based, multi-user indistinguishability under chosen plaintext attack (mu-IND-CPA) [4] to a game that includes the same adversarial powers, but adds an additional oracle for adaptively compromising individual user secret keys. Critical to our approach is (1) the use of simulators, which allows handling corruptions gracefully, and (2) incorporating handling of idealized models (e.g., the ROM or ICM). The latter is requisite for analyzing practical constructions.

We offer new definitions for multi-user CPA and CCA security of symmetric encryption, called SIM-AC-CPA (simulation-based security under adaptive corruption, chosen plaintext attack) and SIM-AC-CCA (chosen ciphertext attack). By restricting the classes of allowed simulators we can obtain stronger definitions (e.g., SIM-AC-$ which requires that ciphertexts look like random strings).

Symmetric encryption under adaptive compromise. We then begin exercising our framework by first answering the question: Are practical, in-use symmetric encryption schemes secure in the face of adaptive compromises? We give positive results here, in idealized models. Taking an encrypt-then-MAC scheme such as AES in counter mode combined with HMAC [5] as an example, we could directly show SIM-AC-CCA security while modeling AES as an ideal cipher and HMAC as a random oracle (c.f., [16]). But this would lead to a rather complex proof, and we'd have to do similarly complex proofs for other encryption schemes.

Instead, we provide simple, modular proofs by lifting the underlying assumptions made about primitives (AES and HMAC) to hold in adaptive compromise scenarios. Specifically, we introduce a new security notion for pseudorandom functions under adaptive compromise attacks (SIM-AC-PRF). This adapts the standard multi-user PRF notion to also give adversaries the ability to adaptively compromise particular keys. Then we prove that AES and HMAC each achieve this notion in the ICM and ROM, respectively. The benefit is that these proofs encapsulate the complexity of ideal model programming proofs in the simpler context of SIM-AC-PRF (as opposed to SIM-AC-CCA).

The workflow when using our framework is represented by Fig. 2. Here PRFs are individually shown to achieve SIM-AC-PRF security in an ideal model. Then modes of operation are proven secure under the assumption that they use a SIM-AC-PRF secure PRF. Then each application is proven secure under the appropriate assumption of the encryption scheme used. This decreases the total number of proofs required to $A + P + M$, significantly fewer than the $A \cdot P \cdot M$ required previously. Moreover, the complicated ideal model programming analysis (represented by red dashed arrows) is restricted to only appearing in the simplest of these proofs (analyzing of PRFs); it can then simply be "passed along" to the higher level proofs.

We can then show that for most CPA modes of operation (e.g., CBC mode or CTR mode), one can prove SIM-AC-CPA security assuming the underlying block cipher is SIM-AC-PRF. The core requirement is that the mode of operation enjoys a property that we call extraction security. This is a technical condition capturing the key security properties needed to prove that a mode of operation is SIM-AC-CPA assuming the underlying block cipher is SIM-AC-PRF. Moreover, we show that most existing (standard) proofs of IND-CPA security show, implicitly, the extraction security of the mode. Thus, we can easily establish adaptive compromise proofs given existing (standard) ones.

The above addresses only confidentiality. Luckily, integrity is inherited essentially for free from existing analysis. We generically show that SIM-AC-CPA security combined with the standard notion of ciphertext integrity implies SIM-AC-CCA security. Thus, one can prove encrypt-then-MAC is SIM-AC-CCA secure assuming the SIM-AC-CPA security of the encryption and the standard unforgeability security of the MAC. This is an easy adaptation of the standard proof [8] of encrypt-then-MAC.

Applying the framework to high-level protocols. Equipped with our new SIM-AC-CCA and SIM-AC-PRF security notions, we can return to our motivating task: providing positive security analyses of BurnBox and the Cash et al. SSE scheme.

We give a proof of BurnBox's CAS security assuming the SIM-AC-CPA security of the underlying symmetric encryption scheme. Our proof is significantly simpler than the original analysis, avoiding specifically the nuanced programming logic that led to the bug in the original analysis. For the Cash et al. scheme we apply our SIM-AC-PRF definition and a key-private version of our SIM-AC-CPA definition. Their adaptive security claim was accompanied only by a brief proof sketch which fails to identify an important detail that need to be considered in the ROM analysis (see the full version of this paper [23]). Our proof handles this detail cleanly while being ultimately of comparable complexity to their non-adaptive security proof.

Unfortunately, these settings and constructions are inherently complicated. So even with the simplification provided by our analysis techniques there is not space to fit their analysis in the body of our paper; it has instead been relegated to the full version of this work. We choose this organization because our main contribution is the definition abstraction which we believe will be of use for future work, rather than the particular applications we chose to exhibit its use.

Treatment of symmetric encryption. In this work, we focus on randomized encryption, over more modern nonce-based variants because this was the form of encryption used by the applications we identified. In the full version of this paper [23], we extend our definitions to nonce-based encryption. The techniques we introduce for analyzing randomized symmetric encryption schemes should extend to nonce-based encryption schemes.

Related works. A related line of work is that of selective-opening attacks [7] which studies the security of asymmetric encryption schemes against compromises in a multi-sender setting (where coins underlying encryption may be compromised) or multi-receiver setting (where secret decryption keys may be compromised). Selective-opening definitions are typically formulated to aim for standard model (or non-programmable random oracle model) achievability and hence do not suffice for the applications we consider in this work.

The full version of this paper is available on ePrint [23].

2 Preliminaries

A list T of length $n \in \mathbb{N}$ specifies an ordered sequence of elements $T[1]$, $T[2]$, $\dots, T[n]$. The operation $T.\mathsf{add}(x)$ appends x to this list by setting $T[n+1] \leftarrow x$. This making T a list of length $n + 1$. We let $|T|$ denote the length of T. The operation $x \leftarrow T.\mathsf{dq}()$ sets x equal to the last element of T and removes this element from T. In pseudocode lists are assumed to be initialized empty (i.e. have length 0). An empty list or table is denoted by $[\cdot]$. We sometimes use set notation with a list, e.g. $x \in T$ is true if $x = T[i]$ for any $1 \le i \le |T|$.

Let S and S' be two sets with $|S| \le |S'|$. Then $\mathsf{Inj}(S, S')$ is the set of all injections from S to S'. We will sometimes abuse terminology and refer to functions with co-domain $\{ S : S \subseteq \{0, 1\}^* \}$ as sets. For $n \in \mathbb{N}$ we define $[n] = \{1, \dots, n\}$.

The notation $y \leftarrow_{\$} A(x_1, x_2, \cdots : \sigma)$ denotes the (randomized) execution of A with state σ. Changes that A makes to its input variable σ are maintained after A's execution. For given $x_1, x_2, \dots$ and σ we let $[A(x_1, x_2, \cdots : \sigma)]$ denote the set of possible outputs of A given these inputs.

We define security notions using pseudocode-based games. The pseudocode "Require bool" is shorthand for "If not bool then return $\bot$". We will sometimes use infinite loops defining variable x_u for all $u \in \{0, 1\}^*$. Such code is executed lazily; the code is initially skipped, then later if a variable x_u would be used, the necessary code to define it is first run. The pseudocode "$\exists x \in X$ s.t. $p(x)$" for some predicate p evaluates to the boolean value $\bigvee_{x \in X} p(x)$. If this is true, the variable x is set equal to the lexicographically first $x \in X$ for which $p(x)$ is true.

We use an asymptotic formalism. The security parameter is denoted λ. Our work is generally written in a way to allow concrete security bounds to be extracted easily. In security proofs we typically explicitly state how we will bound the advantage of an adversary by the advantages of reduction adversaries we build (and possibly other terms). Reduction adversaries and simulators are explicitly given in code (from which concrete statements about their efficiency can be obtained by observation).

Let $f : \mathbb{N} \to \mathbb{N}$. We say f is negligible if for all polynomials p there exists a $\lambda_p \in \mathbb{N}$ such that $f(\lambda) \le 1/p(\lambda)$ for all $\lambda \ge \lambda_p$. We say f is super-polynomial if $1/f$ is negligible. We say f is super-logarithmic if 2^f is super-polynomial.

Ideal primitives. We will make liberal use of ideal primitives such as random oracles or ideal ciphers. An ideal primitive P specifies algorithms $\mathsf{P.Init}$ and $\mathsf{P.Prim}$. The initialization algorithm has syntax $\sigma_{\mathsf{P}} \leftarrow_{\$} \mathsf{P.Init}(1^\lambda)$. The stateful evaluation algorithm has syntax $y \leftarrow_{\$} \mathsf{P.Prim}(1^\lambda, x : \sigma_{\mathsf{P}})$. We sometimes us A^{P} as shorthand for giving algorithm A oracle access to $\mathsf{P.Prim}(1^\lambda, \cdot : \sigma_{\mathsf{P}})$. Adversaries are often given access to P via an oracle PRIM.

Ideal primitives should be *stateless*. By this we mean that after σ_P is output by P.Init, it is never modified by P.Prim (so we could have used the syntax $y \leftarrow_\$ \mathsf{P.Prim}(1^\lambda, x, \sigma_P)$). However, when written this way, ideal primitives are typically inefficient, e.g., for the random oracle model σ_P would store a huge random table. Our security results will necessitate that P be efficiently instantiated so we have adopted the stateful syntax to allow ideal primitives to be written in their efficient "lazily sampled" form. Despite this notational convenience, we will assume that any ideal primitive we reference is *essentially stateless*. By this, we mean that it could have been equivalently written to be stateless (if inefficient).[2]

The standard model is captured by the primitive $\mathsf{P_{sm}}$ for which $\mathsf{P_{sm}.Init}(1^\lambda)$ and $\mathsf{P_{sm}.Prim}(1^\lambda, x : \sigma_P)$ always returns the empty string ε.

We define a random oracle that takes arbitrary input and produce variable length outputs. It is captured by the primitive $\mathsf{P_{rom}}$ defined as follows.

$\mathsf{P_{rom}.Init}(1^\lambda)$	$\mathsf{P_{rom}.Prim}(1^\lambda, x : T)$
Return $[\cdot]$	$(x, l) \leftarrow x$
	If $T[x, l] = \bot$ then $T[x, l] \leftarrow_\$ \{0,1\}^l$
	Return $T[x, l]$

The ideal-cipher model is parameterized by a block-length $n : \mathbb{N} \to \mathbb{N}$ and captured by P^n_{icm} defined as follows.[3]

$\mathsf{P}^n_{icm}.Init(1^\lambda)$	$\mathsf{P}^n_{icm}.Prim(1^\lambda, x : (E, D))$
Return $([\cdot], [\cdot])$	$(op, K, y) \leftarrow x$
	If $op = +$ then
	$\quad$ If $E[K, y] = \bot$ then
	$\qquad z \leftarrow_\$ \{0,1\}^{n(\lambda)} \setminus \{ E[K, a] : a \in \{0,1\}^{n(\lambda)} \}$
	$\qquad E[K, y] \leftarrow z \,;\, D[K, z] \leftarrow y$
	$\quad$ Return $E[K, y]$
	Else
	$\quad$ If $D[K, y] = \bot$ then
	$\qquad z \leftarrow_\$ \{0,1\}^{n(\lambda)} \setminus \{ D[K, a] : a \in \{0,1\}^{n(\lambda)} \}$
	$\qquad D[K, y] \leftarrow z \,;\, E[K, z] \leftarrow y$
	$\quad$ Return $D[K, y]$

It stores tables E and D which it uses to lazily sample a random permutation for each K, with $E[K, \cdot]$ representing the forward evaluation and $D[K, \cdot]$ its inverse. It parses its input as a tuple (op, K, y) where $op \in \{+, -\}$ specifies the direction of evaluation and $K \in \{0,1\}^*$ and $y \in \{0,1\}^{n(\lambda)}$ specify the input.

Sometimes we construct a cryptographic primitive from multiple underlying cryptographic primitives which expect different ideal primitives. To capture this it will be useful to have a notion of combining ideal primitives. Let P' and P'' be ideal primitives. We define their cross product $\mathsf{P} = \mathsf{P}' \times \mathsf{P}''$ as follows.

---

[2] Without this restrictions an ideal primitive could behave in undesirable, contrived ways (e.g., on some special input outputting all prior inputs it has received).

[3] We will implicitly assume $n(\lambda)$ can be computed in time polynomial in λ. We make similar implicit assumptions for other functions that parameterize constructions of cryptographic primitives.

$$
\begin{array}{l|l}
\underline{\text{P.Init}(1^\lambda)} & \underline{\text{P.Prim}(1^\lambda, x : \sigma_P)} \\
\sigma'_P \leftarrow\!\!\!\text{\$ } \text{P}'.\text{Init}(1^\lambda) & (\sigma'_P, \sigma''_P) \leftarrow \sigma_P \\
\sigma''_P \leftarrow\!\!\!\text{\$ } \text{P}''.\text{Init}(1^\lambda) & (d, x) \leftarrow x \\
\text{Return } (\sigma'_P, \sigma''_P) & \text{If } d = 1 \text{ then } y \leftarrow\!\!\!\text{\$ } \text{P}'.\text{Prim}(1^\lambda, x : \sigma'_P) \\
 & \text{Else } y \leftarrow\!\!\!\text{\$ } \text{P}''.\text{Prim}(1^\lambda, x : \sigma''_P) \\
 & \sigma_P \leftarrow (\sigma'_P, \sigma''_P) \\
 & \text{Return } y
\end{array}
$$

By our earlier convention $A^{\text{P}' \times \text{P}''}$ is shorthand for giving algorithm A oracle access to $\text{P.Prim}(1^\lambda, \cdot\ : \sigma_P)$. In A's code, $B^{\text{P}'}$ denotes giving B oracle access to $\text{P.Prim}(1^\lambda, (1, \cdot)\ : \sigma_P)$ and $B^{\text{P}''}$ to denote giving B oracle access to $\text{P.Prim}(1^\lambda, (2, \cdot)\ : \sigma_P)$.

2.1 Standard Cryptographic Definitions

We recall standard cryptographic syntax and security notions.

Symmetric encryption syntax. A symmetric encryption scheme SE specifies algorithms SE.Kg, SE.Enc, and SE.Dec as well as sets SE.M, SE.Out, and SE.K representing the message, ciphertext, and key space respectively. The key generation algorithm has syntax $K \leftarrow\!\!\!\text{\$ } \text{SE.Kg}(1^\lambda)$. The encryption algorithm has syntax $c \leftarrow\!\!\!\text{\$ } \text{SE.Enc}^P(1^\lambda, K, m)$, where $c \in \text{SE.Out}(\lambda, |m|)$ is required. The deterministic decryption algorithm and has syntax $m \leftarrow \text{SE.Dec}^P(1^\lambda, K, c)$. Rejection of c is represented by returning $m = \bot$. Informally, correctness requires that encryptions of messages in $\text{SE.M}(\lambda)$ decrypt properly. We assume the boolean $(m \in \text{SE.M}(\lambda))$ can be efficiently computed.

Integrity of ciphertexts. Integrity of ciphertext security is defined by the game $G_{\text{SE}, P, \mathcal{A}_{\text{ctxt}}}^{\text{int-ctxt}}$ shown in Fig. 3. In the game, the attacker interacts with one of two "worlds" (determined by the bit b) via its oracles ENC, PRIM, EXP, and DEC. The attacker's goal is to determine which world it is interacting with.

Game $G_{\text{SE}, P, \mathcal{A}_{\text{ctxt}}}^{\text{int-ctxt}}(\lambda)$	$\text{ENC}(u, m)$	$\text{DEC}(u, c)$
For $u \in \{0,1\}^*$ do	Require $m \in \text{SE.M}(\lambda)$	Require $u \notin X$
$\quad K_u \leftarrow\!\!\!\text{\$ } \text{SE.Kg}(1^\lambda)$	$c \leftarrow\!\!\!\text{\$ } \text{SE.Enc}^P(1^\lambda, K_u, m)$	Require $c \notin C_u$
$\sigma_P \leftarrow\!\!\!\text{\$ } \text{P.Init}(1^\lambda)$	$C_u.\text{add}(c)$	$m_1 \leftarrow \text{SE.Dec}^P(1^\lambda, K_u, c)$
$b \leftarrow\!\!\!\text{\$ } \{0,1\}$	Return c	$m_0 \leftarrow \bot$
$b' \leftarrow\!\!\!\text{\$ } \mathcal{A}_{\text{ctxt}}^{\text{ENC,DEC,EXP,PRIM}}(1^\lambda)$		Return m_b
Return $(b = b')$	$\underline{\text{EXP}(u)}$	
	$X.\text{add}(u)$	
$\underline{\text{PRIM}(x)}$	Return K_u	
$y \leftarrow\!\!\!\text{\$ } \text{P.Prim}(1^\lambda, x : \sigma_P)$		
Return y		

Fig. 3. Game defining multi-user CTXT security of SE in the face of exposures.

The PRIM oracle gives the attacker access to the ideal primitive P. The encryption oracle ENC takes as input a user u and message m, then returns the encryption of that message using the key of that user, K_u. Recall that by our convention each K_u is not sampled until needed. The exposure oracle EXP takes in u and then returns K_u to the attacker. The decryption oracle DEC is the only oracle whose behavior depends on the bit b. It takes as input a user u and ciphertext c. When $b = 1$, it will return the decryption of c using K_u while when $b = 0$ it will always return $\perp$. Thus, the goal of the attacker it to forge a ciphertext which will decrypt to a non-$\perp$ value.

To prevent trivial attacker, we disallow querying a ciphertext to DEC$(u, \cdot)$ if it came from ENC$(u, \cdot)$ or if u was already exposed. This is captured by the "Require" statements in DEC using lists C_u and X (which store the ciphertexts returned by ENC$(u, \cdot)$ and the users that have been exposed, respectively).

We define the advantage function $\mathsf{Adv}^{\text{int-ctxt}}_{\mathsf{SE,P},\mathcal{A}_{\text{ctxt}}}(\lambda) = 2\Pr[\mathsf{G}^{\text{int-ctxt}}_{\mathsf{SE,P},\mathcal{A}_{\text{ctxt}}}(\lambda)] - 1$. We say SE is INT-CTXT secure with P if for all PPT $\mathcal{A}_{\text{ctxt}}$, the advantage $\mathsf{Adv}^{\text{int-ctxt}}_{\mathsf{SE,P},\mathcal{A}_{\text{ctxt}}}(\cdot)$ is negligible. INT-CTXT security is typically defined to only consider a single user and no exposures. Using a hybrid argument one can show that our definition of INT-CTXT security is implied by the more standard definition.

Function family. A family of functions F specifies algorithms F.Kg and F.Ev together with sets F.Inp and F.Out. The key generation algorithm has syntax $K \leftarrow_{\$} \mathsf{F.Kg}^{\mathsf{P}}(1^\lambda)$. The evaluation algorithm is deterministic and has the syntax $y \leftarrow \mathsf{F.Ev}(1^\lambda, K, x)$. It is required that for all $\lambda \in \mathbb{N}$ and $K \in [\mathsf{F.Kg}(1^\lambda)]$ that $\mathsf{F.Ev}(1^\lambda, K, x) \in \mathsf{F.Out}(\lambda)$ whenever $x \in \mathsf{F.Inp}(\lambda)$. It is assumed that random elements of F.Out(λ) can be efficiently sampled.

Game $\mathsf{G}^{\text{ow}}_{\mathsf{F,P},\mathcal{A}}(\lambda)$	PRIM(x)
$K \leftarrow_{\$} \mathsf{F.Kg}(1^\lambda) \,;\, \sigma_{\mathsf{P}} \leftarrow_{\$} \mathsf{P.Init}(1^\lambda)$	$y \leftarrow_{\$} \mathsf{P.Prim}(1^\lambda, x : \sigma_{\mathsf{P}})$
$x \leftarrow_{\$} \mathsf{F.Inp}(\lambda) \,;\, y \leftarrow \mathsf{F.Ev}^{\mathsf{P}}(\lambda, K, x)$	Return y
$x' \leftarrow_{\$} \mathcal{A}^{\text{PRIM}}(1^\lambda, K, y)$	
Return $(\mathsf{F.Ev}^{\mathsf{P}}(1^\lambda, K, x') = y)$	

Fig. 4. Game defining one-wayness of F.

One-wayness. The one-wayness of a family of functions F is given by the game G^{ow} shown in Fig. 4. The adversary is given a key K to F and the image y of a random point x in the domain. Its goal is to find a point with the same image. We define the advantage function $\mathsf{Adv}^{\text{ow}}_{\mathsf{F,P},\mathcal{A}}(\lambda) = \Pr[\mathsf{G}^{\text{ow}}_{\mathsf{F,P},\mathcal{A}}(\lambda)]$ and say F is OW secure with P if $\mathsf{Adv}^{\text{ow}}_{\mathsf{F,P},\mathcal{A}}(\cdot)$ is negligible for all PPT $\mathcal{A}$.

Security definitions. In the body of this paper we sometimes informally reference other security notions for symmetric encryption schemes (IND-CPA, IND-CCA, IND-KP, IND-\$) and function families (PRF, UF-CMA). These definitions are recalled in the full version of this paper [23].

3 New Security Definitions for Symmetric Primitives

In this section we provide our definitions for the security of symmetric crypto-graphic primitives (namely randomized encryption and pseudorandom functions) against attackers able to adaptively compromise users' keys.

3.1 Randomized Symmetric Encryption

We describe our security definitions for randomized symmetric encryption. We refer to them as SIM-AC-CPA and SIM-AC-CCA security. The definition of SIM-AC-CPA (resp. SIM-AC-CCA) security is a generalization of IND-CPA (IND-CCA) security to a multi-user setting in which some users' keys may be compromised by an attacker.

Consider game $\mathsf{G}^{\mathsf{sim\text{-}ac\text{-}cpa}}$ shown in Fig. 5. It is parameterized by a symmetric encryption scheme SE, simulator S, ideal primitive P, and attacker $\mathcal{A}_{\mathsf{cpa}}$. The attacker interacts with one of two "worlds" via its oracles ENC, EXP, and PRIM. The attacker's goal is to determine which world it is interacting with.

In the real world ($b = 1$) the encryption oracle ENC takes (u, m) as input and returns an encryption of m using u's key K_u. Oracle PRIM returns the output of the ideal primitive on input x. Oracle EXP returns u's key K_u to the attacker.

In the ideal world ($b = 0$), the return values of each of these oracles are instead chosen by a simulator S. In PRIM it is given the input provided to the oracle. In ENC it is given the name of the current user u and some leakage ℓ about the message m. If u has not yet been exposed ($u \notin X$) this leakage is just the length of the message. Otherwise the leakage is the message itself. The inputs and outputs of this oracle for a user u are stored in the lists M_u and C_u so they can be leaked to the simulator when EXP(u) is called.

We define $\mathsf{Adv}^{\mathsf{sim\text{-}ac\text{-}cpa}}_{\mathsf{SE},\mathsf{S},\mathsf{P},\mathcal{A}_{\mathsf{cpa}}}(\lambda) = 2\Pr[\mathsf{G}^{\mathsf{sim\text{-}ac\text{-}cpa}}_{\mathsf{SE},\mathsf{S},\mathsf{P},\mathcal{A}_{\mathsf{cpa}}}(\lambda)] - 1$. We say SE is SIM-AC-CPA secure with P if for all PPT $\mathcal{A}_{\mathsf{cpa}}$ there exists a PPT S such that $\mathsf{Adv}^{\mathsf{sim\text{-}ac\text{-}cpa}}_{\mathsf{SE},\mathsf{S},\mathsf{P},\mathcal{A}_{\mathsf{cpa}}}(\cdot)$ is negligible. Intuitively, this definition captures that ciphertexts reveal nothing about the messages encrypted other than their length unless the encryption key is known to the attacker. In the full version of this paper [23], we show that SIM-AC-CPA security is impossible in the standard model. The proof is a simple application of the ideas of Nielsen [31].

SIM-AC-CCA security extends SIM-AC-CPA security by giving $\mathcal{A}_{\mathsf{cca}}$ access to a decryption oracle which takes as input (u, c). In the real world, it returns the decryption of c using K_u. In the ideal world, the simulator simulates this. To prevent trivial attacks, the attacker is disallowed from querying (u, c) if c was returned from an earlier query ENC(u, m). We define $\mathsf{Adv}^{\mathsf{sim\text{-}ac\text{-}cca}}_{\mathsf{SE},\mathsf{S},\mathsf{P},\mathcal{A}_{\mathsf{cca}}}(\lambda) = 2\Pr[\mathsf{G}^{\mathsf{sim\text{-}ac\text{-}cca}}_{\mathsf{SE},\mathsf{S},\mathsf{P},\mathcal{A}_{\mathsf{cca}}}(\lambda)] - 1$. We say SE is SIM-AC-CCA secure with P if for all PPT $\mathcal{A}_{\mathsf{cca}}$ there exists a PPT S such that $\mathsf{Adv}^{\mathsf{sim\text{-}ac\text{-}cca}}_{\mathsf{SE},\mathsf{S},\mathsf{P},\mathcal{A}_{\mathsf{cca}}}(\cdot)$ is negligible.

Simplifications. It will be useful to keep in mind simplifications we can make to restrict the behavior of the adversary or simulator without loss of generally. They are applicable to all SIM-AC-style definitions we provide in this paper.

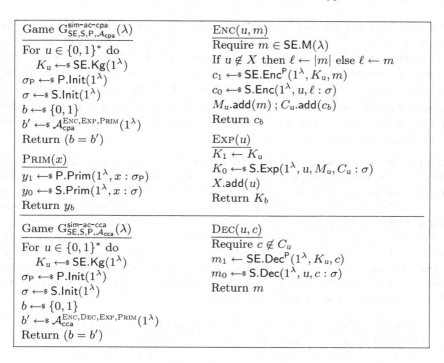

Fig. 5. Games defining SIM-AC-CPA and SIM-AC-CCA security of SE.

- If an oracle is deterministic in the real world, then we can assume that the adversary never repeats a query to this oracle or that the simulator always provides the same output to repeated queries.
- We can assume the adversary never makes a query to a user it has already exposed or that for such queries the simulator just runs the code of the real world (replacing calls to P with calls to S.Prim).
- We can assume the adversary always queries with $u \in [u_\lambda]$ for some polynomial $u_{(.)}$ or that the simulator is agnostic to the particular strings used to reference users.
- We can assume that adversaries never make queries that fail "Require" statements. (All requirements of oracles we provide will be efficiently computable given the transcripts of queries the adversary has made.)

Proving these are slightly more subtle to establish than analogous simplifications would be in non-simulation-based games because of the order that algorithms are quantified in our security definitions. They all follow the same pattern though, so we sketch the second of these.

Suppose SE is SIM-AC-CPA secure for all adversaries that never make a call $\text{ENC}(u, m)$ after having made a call $\text{EXP}(u)$, then we claim SE is SIM-AC-CPA secure. Let $\mathcal{A}$ be an arbitrary adversary. Then we build a wrapper adversary $\mathcal{A}'$ that simply forwards all of $\mathcal{A}$'s queries except for encryption queries made for a user that has already been exposed. In these cases $\mathcal{B}$ responds with the output of $\mathsf{SE.Enc}^{\mathrm{PRIM}(\cdot)}(1^\lambda, K_u, m)$ (or $\perp$ if $m \notin \mathsf{SE.M}(\lambda)$), where K_u is the key last returned from $\mathrm{EXP}(u)$. Let S' be a simulator for $\mathcal{A}'$. Then we construct S for $\mathcal{A}$ which responds exactly as S' would except in response to encryption queries made for a user that has already been exposed. In these cases S' responds with the output of $\mathsf{SE.Enc}^{\mathsf{S}'.\mathrm{Prim}(1^\lambda, \cdot : \sigma)}(1^\lambda, K_u, m)$, where K_u is the key it last returned for $\mathrm{EXP}(u)$. It is clear that $\mathsf{Adv}^{\mathsf{sim\text{-}ac\text{-}cpa}}_{\mathsf{SE,S,P},\mathcal{A}}(\lambda) = \mathsf{Adv}^{\mathsf{sim\text{-}ac\text{-}cpa}}_{\mathsf{SE,S',P},\mathcal{A}'}(\lambda)$ because the view of $\mathcal{A}$ is identical in the corresponding games.

Stronger security notions. It is common in the study of symmetric encryption primitives to study stronger security definitions than IND-CPA security. Most schemes instead aim directly for their output to be indistinguishable from random bits (IND-$). This implies IND-CPA security and additional nice properties such as forms of key-privacy.

We can capture such notions by placing restrictions on the behavior of the simulator. Let S be a simulator (for which we think of $\mathsf{S.Enc}$ as being undefined) which additionally defines algorithms $\mathsf{S.Enc}_1$ and $\mathsf{S.Enc}_2$ as well as set $\mathsf{S.Out}$. Then we define simulators $\mathsf{S}_k[\mathsf{S}]$ and $\mathsf{S}_\$[\mathsf{S}]$ to be identical to S except for the following encryption simulation algorithms.

$\underline{\mathsf{S}_k[\mathsf{S}].\mathsf{Enc}(1^\lambda, u, \ell : \sigma)}$	$\underline{\mathsf{S}_\$[\mathsf{S}].\mathsf{Enc}(1^\lambda, u, \ell : \sigma)}$
If $\ell \in \mathbb{N}$ then $c \leftarrow_\$ \mathsf{S.Enc}_1(1^\lambda, \ell : \sigma)$	If $\ell \in \mathbb{N}$ then $c \leftarrow_\$ \mathsf{S.Out}(\lambda, \ell)$
Else $c \leftarrow_\$ \mathsf{S.Enc}_2(1^\lambda, u, \ell : \sigma)$	Else $c \leftarrow_\$ \mathsf{S.Enc}_2(1^\lambda, u, \ell : \sigma)$
Return c	Return c

Checking $\ell \in \mathbb{N}$ acts as a convenient way of verifying if the user being queried has been exposed yet. Because $\mathsf{S.Enc}_1(1^\lambda, \ell : \sigma)$ is not given u in S_k, the output of S_k is distributed identically for any unexposed users. The class of key-anonymous simulators $\mathcal{S}_k$ is the set of all $\mathsf{S}_k[\mathsf{S}]$ for some S. Similarly, $\mathsf{S}_\$$ always outputs a random bitstring as the ciphertext for any unexposed user. The class of random-ciphertext simulators $\mathcal{S}_\$$ is the set of all $\mathsf{S}_\$[\mathsf{S}]$ for some S. Note that $\mathcal{S}_\$ \subset \mathcal{S}_k$.

We say SE is SIM-AC-KP secure with P if for all PPT $\mathcal{A}_{\mathsf{cpa}}$ there exists a PPT $\mathsf{S} \in \mathcal{S}_k$ such that $\mathsf{Adv}^{\mathsf{sim\text{-}ac\text{-}cpa}}_{\mathsf{SE,S,P},\mathcal{A}_{\mathsf{cpa}}}(\cdot)$ is negligible. We say that SE is SIM-AC-$ secure with P if for all PPT $\mathcal{A}_{\mathsf{cpa}}$ there exists a PPT $\mathsf{S} \in \mathcal{S}_\$$ such that $\mathsf{Adv}^{\mathsf{sim\text{-}ac\text{-}cpa}}_{\mathsf{SE,S,P},\mathcal{A}_{\mathsf{cpa}}}(\cdot)$ is negligible. It is straightforward to see that SIM-AC-$ security implies SIM-AC-KP security which in turn implies SIM-AC-CPA security. Standard counterexamples will show that these implications do not hold in the other direction.

It is sometimes useful to define security in an all-in-one style, introduced by Rogaway and Shrimpton [32], which simultaneously requires IND-$ security and INT-CTXT security. In our framework we can define $\mathcal{S}_\perp$ as the class of IND-CCA simulators which always return $\perp$ for decryption queries to unexposed users. Then we say SE is SIM-AC-AE secure with P if for all PPT $\mathcal{A}_{\mathsf{cca}}$ there exists a PPT $\mathsf{S} \in \mathcal{S}_\$ \cap \mathcal{S}_\perp$ such that $\mathsf{Adv}^{\mathsf{sim\text{-}ac\text{-}cca}}_{\mathsf{SE,S,P},\mathcal{A}_{\mathsf{cca}}}(\cdot)$ is negligible.

3.2   Pseudorandom Functions

Typically a symmetric encryption scheme will use a PRF as one of their basic building blocks. For modularity, it will be useful to provide a simulation-based security definition for PRFs in the face of active compromises. In Sect. 6, we show our PRF definition can be applied to construct a SIM-AC secure symmetric encryption scheme. Additionally, in the full version of this paper [23], we show that our definition is of independent use by using it to prove the adaptive security of a searchable symmetric encryption scheme introduced by Cash et al. [12].

Game $G^{\mathsf{sim\text{-}ac\text{-}prf}}_{\mathsf{F},\mathsf{S},\mathsf{P},\mathcal{A}_{\mathsf{prf}}}(\lambda)$	$\mathrm{Ev}(u,x)$
For $u \in \{0,1\}^*$ do	$y_1 \leftarrow \mathsf{F}.\mathsf{Ev}^{\mathsf{P}}(1^\lambda, K_u, x)$
$\quad K_u \leftarrow\!\!\text{\$}\ \mathsf{F}.\mathsf{Kg}(1^\lambda)$	If $u \notin X$ then
$\sigma_{\mathsf{P}} \leftarrow\!\!\text{\$}\ \mathsf{P}.\mathsf{Init}(1^\lambda)$	$\quad$ If $T_u[x] = \bot$ then $y_0 \leftarrow\!\!\text{\$}\ \mathsf{F}.\mathsf{Out}(\lambda)$
$\sigma \leftarrow\!\!\text{\$}\ \mathsf{S}.\mathsf{Init}(1^\lambda)$	$\quad$ Else $y_0 \leftarrow T_u[x]$
$b \leftarrow\!\!\text{\$}\ \{0,1\}$	Else
$b' \leftarrow\!\!\text{\$}\ \mathcal{A}^{\mathrm{Ev},\mathrm{Exp},\mathrm{Prim}}_{\mathsf{prf}}(1^\lambda)$	$\quad y_0 \leftarrow \mathsf{S}.\mathsf{Ev}(1^\lambda, u, x : \sigma)$
Return $b = b'$	$T_u[x] \leftarrow y_0$
$\mathrm{Prim}(x)$	Return y_b
$y_1 \leftarrow\!\!\text{\$}\ \mathsf{P}.\mathsf{Prim}(1^\lambda, x : \sigma_{\mathsf{P}})$	$\mathrm{Exp}(u)$
$y_0 \leftarrow\!\!\text{\$}\ \mathsf{S}.\mathsf{Prim}(1^\lambda, x : \sigma)$	$K_1 \leftarrow K_u$
Return y_b	$K_0 \leftarrow\!\!\text{\$}\ \mathsf{S}.\mathsf{Exp}(1^\lambda, u, T_u : \sigma)$
	$X.\mathsf{add}(u)$
	Return K_b

Fig. 6. Game defining multi-user PRF security of F in the face of exposures.

The game $G^{\mathsf{sim\text{-}ac\text{-}prf}}_{\mathsf{F},\mathsf{S},\mathsf{P},\mathcal{A}_{\mathsf{prf}}}$ is shown in Fig. 6. In the real world, Ev gives adversary $\mathcal{A}_{\mathsf{prf}}$ the real output of F. In the ideal world, Ev's output is chosen at random (and stored in the table T_u), unless u has already been exposed in which case simulator S chooses the output. The table T_u is given to S when an exposure of u happens so it can output a key consistent with prior Ev queries; we assume it is easy to iterate over all $(x, T_u[x])$ pairs for which $T_u[x]$ is not $\bot$. We define $\mathsf{Adv}^{\mathsf{sim\text{-}ac\text{-}prf}}_{\mathsf{F},\mathsf{S},\mathsf{P},\mathcal{A}_{\mathsf{prf}}}(\lambda) = 2\Pr[G^{\mathsf{sim\text{-}ac\text{-}prf}}_{\mathsf{F},\mathsf{S},\mathsf{P},\mathcal{A}_{\mathsf{prf}}}(\lambda)] - 1$. We say F is SIM-AC-PRF secure with P if for all PPT $\mathcal{A}_{\mathsf{prf}}$ there exists a PPT S such that $\mathsf{Adv}^{\mathsf{sim\text{-}ac\text{-}prf}}_{\mathsf{F},\mathsf{S},\mathsf{P},\mathcal{A}_{\mathsf{prf}}}(\cdot)$ is negligible.

4   Applications

The value of our definitions stems from their usability in proving the security of protocols constructed from symmetric encryption and pseudorandom functions. In this section, we discuss the application our definitions to simplify and modularize existing security results of Cash et al. [12] and Tyagi et al. [33], and how they imply the notion of equivocable encryption introduced by Jarecki et al. [24].

4.1   Asymmetric Password-Authenticated Key Exchange: OPAQUE

Password-authenticated key exchange (PAKE) protocols allow a client and a server with a shared password to establish a shared key resistant to offline guessing attacks. *Asymmetric* PAKE (aPAKE) further considers security in the case of server compromise, meaning that the server must store some secure representation of the password, rather than the password itself.

OPAQUE [24] is an aPAKE protocol currently being considered for standardization by the IETF. At a high level, OPAQUE is constructed from an oblivious pseudorandom function (OPRF) and an authenticated key exchange protocol (AKE). User key material for the AKE protocol is stored encrypted under an password-derived key from an OPRF. Key exchange proceeds in two steps: (1) the user rederives the encryption key by running the OPRF protocol with the server on their password, then (2) retrieves and decrypts the AKE keys from the server-held ciphertext and proceeds with the AKE protocol. The "commitment problem" arises when an adversary comprises the server state and then later compromises a user password.

Game $G_{SE,S,P,\mathcal{A}}^{eqv}(\lambda)$	$\text{PRIM}(x)$
$\sigma_P \leftarrow_\$ P.\text{Init}(1^\lambda)$	$y_1 \leftarrow_\$ P.\text{Prim}(1^\lambda, x : \sigma_P)$
$\sigma \leftarrow_\$ S.\text{Init}(1^\lambda)$	$y_0 \leftarrow_\$ S.\text{Prim}(1^\lambda, x : \sigma)$
$b \leftarrow_\$ \{0,1\}$	Return y_b
$(m, \sigma_\mathcal{A}) \leftarrow \mathcal{A}_1^{\text{PRIM}}(1^\lambda)$	
$K_1 \leftarrow_\$ SE.\text{Kg}(1^\lambda)$	
$c_1 \leftarrow_\$ SE.\text{Enc}^P(1^\lambda, K_1, m)$	
$c_0 \leftarrow_\$ S.\text{Enc}(1^\lambda, \|m\| : \sigma)$	
$K_0 \leftarrow_\$ S.\text{Exp}(1^\lambda, m : \sigma)$	
$b' \leftarrow_\$ \mathcal{A}_2^{\text{PRIM}}(1^\lambda, c_b, K_b, \sigma_\mathcal{A})$	
Return $(b = b')$	

Fig. 7. Game defining EQV security of SE.

Comparison to equivocable encryption. To prove security of their scheme, Jarecki et al. independently propose a weaker version of SIM-AC-CPA that they call equivocable encryption (EQV). Consider game G^{eqv} defined in Fig. 7. An encryption scheme SE is *equivocable* if for any PPT adversary $\mathcal{A} = (\mathcal{A}_1, \mathcal{A}_2)$, there exists a simulator S, such that the advantage function $\text{Adv}_{SE,S,P,\mathcal{A}}^{eqv}(\lambda) = 2\Pr[G_{SE,S,P,\mathcal{A}}^{eqv}(\lambda)] - 1$ is negligible. The [24] definition does not specify how to incorporate the ideal model, so we make a reasonable assumption.

Note that EQV is a weaker version of SIM-AC-CPA in that it allows for only one user and only one encryption query. Showing SIM-AC-CPA implies EQV can be done with a simple wrapper reduction in which the output of $\mathcal{A}_1$ from EQV is forwarded to the encryption oracle of SIM-AC-CPA. Since

EQV allows for only one encryption query, we can further show that EQV does not imply SIM-AC-CPA. Consider a scheme that uses a key $K = (K_1, K_2)$ and constructs ciphertexts as $(K_1, \mathsf{Enc}_{K_2}(m))$ unless $m = K_1$, in which case it is formed as $(K_2, \mathsf{Enc}_{K_2}(m))$. Such a scheme could be secure with respect to EQV but will not be secure in a game that allows multiple encryption queries. Interestingly, showing that our multi-user SIM-AC-CPA notion is implied by its single-user version through a hybrid argument is not straightforward due to managing inconsistencies in simulator state between hybrid steps. We have not been able to prove this result and leave it open for future work. Thus, even if EQV was extended to allow multiple encryption queries, it still may not be widely applicable to situations that require multiple users.

Ultimately, our work fills in the claim of Jarecki et al. that "common encryption modes are equivocable under some idealized assumption".

4.2   Searchable Symmetric Encryption

In the full version of this paper [23], we show that our symmetric encryption and PRF security definitions are useful for proving the security of searchable searchable symmetric encryption (SSE) schemes. An SSE scheme allows a client with a database of documents to store them in encrypted form on a server while still being able to perform keyword searches on these documents.

As a concrete example, we consider Cash et al. [12] which proved non-adaptive security of an SSE scheme when using a PRF and an IND-\$ secure encryption scheme and claimed adaptive security when the PRF is replaced with a random oracle and the encryption scheme is replaced with a specific random-oracle-based scheme. We will prove their adaptive result, this time assuming the family of functions is SIM-AC-PRF secure and the encryption scheme is SIM-AC-KP secure. This makes the result more modular because one is no longer restricted to use their specific choices of a PRF and encryption scheme constructed from a random oracle. As a concrete benefit of this, their choice of encryption scheme does not provide INT-CTXT security. To replace the scheme with one that does would require a separate proof while our proof allows the user to choice their favorite INT-CTXT secure scheme without requiring any additional proofs (assuming that scheme is SIM-AC-CPA secure).

Our proof is roughly as complex as their non-adaptive proof; it consists of three similar reductions to the security of the underlying primitives. Without our definitions, a full adaptive proof would have been a technically detailed (though "standard" and not conceptually difficult) proof because it would have to deal with programming the random oracle. Perhaps because of this, the authors of [12] only provided a sketch of the result, arguing that it follows from the same ideas as their non-adaptive proof plus programming the random oracle to maintain consistency. They claim, "[t]he only defects in the simulation occur when an adversary manages to query the random oracle with a key before it is revealed". This is technically insufficient; a defect also occurs if the same key is sampled multiple times by the simulator (analogously to parts of our proofs for Theorem 3 and Theorem 4). In our SSE proof, we need not address these details because programming the ideal primitive is handled by the assumed simulation security of the underlying primitives.

A large number of other works on SSE have used analogous techniques of constructing a PRF and/or encryption scheme from a random oracle to achieve adaptive security [1,2,9,12,13,17,20,21,25–29,34]. As we discuss in the full version of this paper [23], these papers all similarly elided the details of the random oracle programming proof and/or made mistakes in writing these details. The mistakes are individually small and not difficult to fix, but their prevalence indicates the value our definitions can provide to modularize and simplify the proofs in these works. We chose to analyze the Cash et al. scheme to highlight the application of our definitions because it was the simplest construction requiring both SIM-AC-PRF and SIM-AC-KP secure and because their thorough non-adaptive proof served as a useful starting point from which to build our proof.

4.3   Self-revocable Encrypted Cloud Storage: BurnBox

In the full version of this paper [23], we consider the BurnBox construction of a self-revocable cloud storage scheme proposed by Tyagi et al. [33]. Its goal is to help provide privacy in the face of an authority searching digital devices, e.g., searches of mobile phones or laptops at border crossings. In their proposed scheme a user stores encrypted version of their files on cloud storage. At any point in time they are able to temporarily revoke their own access to these files. Thereby an authority searching their device is unable to learn the content of these files despite their possession of all the secrets stored on the user's device.

Proving security of their scheme in their security model necessitates solving the "commitment problem." A simulator is forced to simulate the attacker's view by providing ciphertexts for files that it does not know the contents of, then later produce a plausible looking key which decrypts the files properly when told the contents. To resolve this issue in their security they modeled the symmetric encryption scheme in the ideal encryption model (which they introduced for this purpose). We are able to recover their result assuming the SIM-AC-CPA security of the encryption scheme. This provides rigorous justification for the use of practically-used encryption schemes which cannot necessarily be thought of as well modeled by the ideal encryption model (e.g. AES-GCM which they used in their prototype implementation). Moreover, the proof we obtain is simpler than the original proof of Tyagi et al. because we do not have to reason about the programming of the ideal encryption model. The original proof has a bug in this programming which we discuss in the full version of this paper [23].

5   Symmetric Encryption Security Results

In this section, we show that important existing results about the security of symmetric encryption schemes "carry over" to our new definitions. These results (together with our results in the next section) form the foundation of our claim that encryption schemes used in practice can be considered to achieve SIM-AC-AE security when their underlying components are properly idealized. First, we show that SIM-AC-CPA and INT-CTXT security imply SIM-AC-CCA security. Then we show that the classic Encrypt-then-MAC scheme achieves SIM-AC-CCA security. Each of these results are, conceptually, a straightforward extension of their standard proof. Finally, we show that random oracles and ideal ciphers are SIM-AC-PRF secure and ideal encryption [33] is SIM-AC-AE secure.

CPA and CTXT imply CCA. The following theorem captures that SIM-AC-CPA and INT-CTXT security imply SIM-AC-CCA security. Bellare and Namprempre [8] showed the analogous result for IND-CPA and IND-CCA security.

Theorem 1. *If* SE *is SIM-AC-CPA and INT-CTXT secure with* P*, then* SE *is SIM-AC-CCA secure with* P*.*

Proof (Sketch). Here we sketch the main ideas of the proof. The full details are provided in the full version of this paper [23].

The SIM-AC-CCA simulator we provide is parameterized by a SIM-AC-CPA simulator S_{cpa}. As state it stores σ of S_{cpa} and keeps each K_u that is has returned to exposure queries. For PRIM, ENC, and EXP queries it simply runs S_{cpa}. For DEC queries it does one of two things. If u has already been exposed it uses the key it previously returned to run the actual decryption algorithm (with oracle access to S_{cpa}'s emulation of P) and returns the result. Otherwise it assumes the adversary has failed at producing a forgery and simply returns $\perp$. (Note this means we have SIM-AC-AE security if SE is SIM-AC-$ secure.)

The SIM-AC-CPA security of SE ensures that the adversary cannot differentiate between the real and ideal world queries to PRIM, ENC, and EXP. The INT-CTXT security of SE does the same for the DEC queries. In the full proof we show that $\mathsf{Adv}^{\text{sim-ac-cca}}_{\mathsf{SE},\mathsf{S}_{cca},\mathsf{P},\mathcal{A}_{cca}}(\lambda) \leq \mathsf{Adv}^{\text{int-ctxt}}_{\mathsf{SE},\mathsf{P},\mathcal{A}_{ctxt}}(\lambda) + \mathsf{Adv}^{\text{sim-ac-cpa}}_{\mathsf{SE},\mathsf{S}_{cpa},\mathsf{P},\mathcal{A}_{cpa}}(\lambda)$.   □

Encrypt-then-MAC. Let SE be an encryption scheme. Let F be a family of functions for which $\mathsf{F.Inp}(\lambda) = \{0,1\}^*$. Then the Encrypt-then-MAC encryption scheme using SE and F is denoted EtM[SE, F]. Its message space is defined as $\mathsf{EtM[SE,F].M}(\lambda) = \mathsf{SE.M}(\lambda)$. If SE expects access to ideal primitive P_1 and F expects access to ideal primitive P_2 then EtM[SE, F] expects access to $P_1 \times P_2$. The key-generation algorithm EtM[SE, F].Kg returns $K = (K_{SE}, K_F)$ where K_{SE} was sampled with $\mathsf{SE.Kg}(1^\lambda)$ and K_F was sampled with $\mathsf{F.Kg}(1^\lambda)$. Algorithms EtM[SE, F].Enc, and EtM[SE, F].Dec are defined as follows.

$\mathsf{EtM[SE,F].Enc}^{P_1 \times P_2}(1^\lambda, K, m)$	$\mathsf{EtM[SE,F].Dec}^{P_1 \times P_2}(1^\lambda, K, (c_{SE}, \tau))$
$(K_{SE}, K_F) \leftarrow K$	$(K_{SE}, K_F) \leftarrow K$
$c_{SE} \leftarrow_\$ \mathsf{SE.Enc}^{P_1}(1^\lambda, K_{SE}, m)$	If $\tau \neq \mathsf{F.Ev}^{P_2}(1^\lambda, K_F, c_{SE})$ then return $\perp$
$\tau \leftarrow \mathsf{F.Ev}^{P_2}(1^\lambda, K_F, c_{SE})$	$m \leftarrow \mathsf{SE.Dec}^{P_1}(1^\lambda, K_{SE}, c_{SE})$
Return (c_{SE}, τ)	Return m

The following theorem establishes that the generic composition result of Bellare and Namprempre [8] holds with our simulation-based definitions of security. We sketch its straightforward proof in the full version of this paper [23].

Theorem 2. *Let* SE *be an encryption scheme. Let* F *be a family of functions for which* $F.\mathsf{Inp}(\lambda) = \{0,1\}^*$. *If* SE *is SIM-AC-CPA secure with* P_1 *and* F *is UF-CMA secure with* P_2, *then* $\mathsf{EtM}[SE, F]$ *is SIM-AC-CCA secure with* $P_1 \times P_2$.

Random oracles are good PRFs. We show that a SIM-AC-PRF secure family of functions can be constructed simply in the random oracle model. Consider R defined as follows. It is parameterized by a key-length function $R.kl : \mathbb{N} \to \mathbb{N}$ and output length function $R.ol : \mathbb{N} \to \mathbb{N}$. It has input set $R.\mathsf{Inp}(\lambda) = \{0,1\}^*$ and output set $R.\mathsf{Out}(\lambda) = \{0,1\}^{R.ol(\lambda)}$.

$$
\begin{array}{l|l}
\underline{R.\mathsf{Kg}(1^\lambda)} & \underline{R.\mathsf{Ev}^P(1^\lambda, K, x)} \\
K \leftarrow_{\$} \{0,1\}^{R.kl(\lambda)} & y \leftarrow P((K \parallel x, R.ol(\lambda))) \\
\text{Return } K & \text{Return } y
\end{array}
$$

Theorem 3. R *is SIM-AC-PRF secure with* P_{rom} *if* R.kl *is super-logarithmic.*

Concretely, in our proof we provide a simulator S_{prf} for which we show that,

$$
\mathsf{Adv}^{\text{sim-ac-prf}}_{R, S_{prf}, P_{rom}, \mathcal{A}_{prf}}(\lambda) \le \frac{u_\lambda^2 + p_\lambda u_\lambda}{2^{R.kl(\lambda)}}
$$

where u_λ is an upper bound on the number of users that $\mathcal{A}_{prf}$ queries to and p_λ is an upper bound on the number of PRIM queries that $\mathcal{A}_{prf}$ makes.

This theorem captures the random oracle programming implicit in the adaptive security claims of the numerous SSE papers we have identified that used a random oracle like a PRF to achieve adaptive security [1,2,9,12,13,17,20,21,25–29,34]. Of these works, most chose to elide the details of establishing that the adversary cannot detect the random oracle programming, likely considering them simple and/or standard. Despite this, we have identified bugs in all of the proofs that did provide more details. We discuss these bugs in more detail in the full version of this paper [23].

To be clear, we do not claim that any of the SSE schemes studied in these works are insecure. The prevalence of this issue speaks to the difficulty of properly accounting for the details in an ideal model programming proof. Our SIM-AC-PRF notion provides a convenient intermediate definition via which these higher-level protocols could have been proved secure without having to deal with the tedious details of a random oracle programming proof.

Proof (Sketch). Here we sketch the main ideas of the proof. The full details are provided in the full version of this paper [23]. The SIM-AC-PRF simulator works are follows. For PRIM queries it just emulates P_{rom} using a table T. For EV queries, it just runs R.Ev honestly with the key it previously returned for the given user. For EXP queries (on an unexposed user) it picks a random key for this user and sets T to be consistent with values in the table T_u it is given. This simulation is only detectable by an attacker that makes a query to the random oracle with some key that is later chosen by the simulator in response to an exposure or if the simulator happened to chose the same key for two different users.[4] These events happen with negligible probability.   □

Ideal ciphers are good PRFs. One of the most commonly used PRFs is AES so it would be useful to think of it as being SIM-AC-PRF secure; however, due to its invertible nature we cannot realistically model it as a random oracle and refer to the above theorem. Instead, AES is often modeled as an ideal cipher. Let B.kl : $\mathbb{N} \to \mathbb{N}$ be given and consider B defined as follows. It has input set B.Inp$(\lambda) = \{0,1\}^{n(\lambda)}$ and output set B.Out$(\lambda) = \{0,1\}^{n(\lambda)}$.

B.Kg(1^λ)	B.Ev$^P(1^\lambda, K, x)$
$K \leftarrow\!\!{}_{\$}\, \{0,1\}^{\text{B.kl}(\lambda)}$	$y \leftarrow P((+, K, x))$
Return K	Return y

The following establishes that an ideal cipher is SIM-AC-PRF secure.

Theorem 4. B *is SIM-AC-PRF secure with* $\mathsf{P}^n_{\text{icm}}$ *if* B.kl, n *are super-logarithmic.*

Concretely, in our proof we provide a simulator S_{prf} for which we show that,

$$\mathsf{Adv}^{\text{sim-ac-prf}}_{\mathsf{B},\mathsf{S}_{\text{prf}},\mathsf{P}^n_{\text{icm}},\mathcal{A}_{\text{prf}}}(\lambda) \leq \frac{u_\lambda^2 + p_\lambda u_\lambda}{2^{\text{B.kl}(\lambda)}} + \frac{q_\lambda^2}{2^{n(\lambda)+1}}$$

where u_λ is an upper bound on the number of users that $\mathcal{A}_{\text{prf}}$ queries to, p_λ is an upper bound on the number of PRIM queries that $\mathcal{A}_{\text{prf}}$ makes, and q_λ is an upper bound on the number of Ev queries that $\mathcal{A}_{\text{prf}}$ makes.

The proof of this theorem follows the same general pattern as the proof that a random oracle is SIM-AC-PRF secure (Theorem 3). It only needs to extend the ideas of this prior result slightly to apply a birthday bound so that we can treat the values of $\mathsf{P}^n_{\text{icm}}$ as being sampled with replacement. It works best to process this step last so we do not have to consider the order in which queries are made. The proof is given in the full version of this paper [23].

Ideal encryption model. In the full version of this paper [23], we recall the ideal encryption model used in the analysis of Tyagi et al. [33] and show that it gives a SIM-AC-AE secure encryption scheme. While doing so, we identify and show how to fix a bug in their proof which used this model.

6   Security of Modes of Operation

In the previous section, we showed that existing analysis of the integrity of a symmetric encryption scheme carries over to our simulation setting to lift SIM-AC-CPA security to SIM-AC-CCA security. It would be convenient to be able to

---

[4] The latter of these points is the subtle issue that does not have appear to have been identified in *any* of the SSE papers that were (implicitly) using a random oracle as a SIM-AC-PRF.

similarly prove that existing IND-CPA security of an encryption scheme suffices to imply SIM-AC-CPA security. Unfortunately, we cannot possibly hope for this to be the case. We know that IND-CPA security can be achieved in the standard model (assuming one-way functions exist), but SIM-AC-CPA security necessarily requires the use of ideal models.

For any typical encryption scheme we could figure out the appropriate way to idealize its underlying components and then write a programming proof to establish security. This would likely be detail intensive and prone to mistakes. We can improve on this by noting that typical symmetric encryption schemes are built as modes of operation using an underlying PRF. We can aim to prove security more modularly by assuming the SIM-AC-PRF security of the underlying family of functions. This alleviates the detail-intensiveness of the proof because the ideal model programming has already been handled in the assumption of SIM-AC-PRF security; it can simply be "passed" along to the new analysis.

In this section, we will show that we can do *even better* than that. We will restrict attention to modes of operation which are IND-\$ secure when built from a PRF and satisfy a special extractability property we define in Sect. 6.1 (which standard examples of models of operation do). Then, in Sect. 6.2, we establish a generic proof framework to elevate an existing IND-\$ security proof to a SIM-AC-\$ security proof, by showing that existing proofs of IND-\$ security tend to (implicitly) prove that the scheme satisfies our extractability property. Finally, in Sect. 6.3 we discuss how the techniques of this section can be extended to other constructions not captured by our formalism, but also note the existence of a (contrived) mode of operation which is IND-\$ secure with any secure PRF, but is never SIM-AC-\$ secure.

6.1 Modes of Operation and Extractability

We first need to have a formalism capturing what a mode of operation is. Our formalism does not capture all possible modes of operation, but does seem to capture most constructions that are of practical interest and would not be hard to modify to capture other constructions.

A mode of operation SE specifies efficient algorithms SE.Kg, SE.Enc, and SE.Dec as well as sets SE.M, SE.Out, SE.FInp, and SE.FOut. For any family of functions F with F.Inp = SE.FInp and F.Out = SE.FOut, it defines a symmetric encryption scheme SE[F] as follows.

$\underline{\text{SE[F].Kg}(1^\lambda)}$	$\underline{\text{SE[F].Enc}^{\text{P}}(1^\lambda, K, m)}$	$\underline{\text{SE[F].Dec}^{\text{P}}(1^\lambda, K, c)}$
$K_{\text{F}} \leftarrow_\text{\$} \text{F.Kg}(1^\lambda)$	$(K_{\text{SE}}, K_{\text{F}}) \leftarrow K$	$(K_{\text{SE}}, K_{\text{F}}) \leftarrow K$
$K_{\text{SE}} \leftarrow_\text{\$} \text{SE.Kg}(1^\lambda)$	$c \leftarrow_\text{\$} \text{SE.Enc}^{\text{F}^{\text{P}}_{K_{\text{F}}}}(1^\lambda, K_{\text{SE}}, m)$	$m \leftarrow \text{SE.Dec}^{\text{F}^{\text{P}}_{K_{\text{F}}}}(1^\lambda, K_{\text{SE}}, c)$
Return $(K_{\text{SE}}, K_{\text{F}})$	Return c	Return m

The superscript $\text{F}^{\text{P}}_{K_{\text{F}}}$ is shorthand for oracle access to $\text{F.Ev}^{\text{P}}(1^\lambda, K_{\text{F}}, \cdot)$. It is required that $\text{SE[F].M} = \text{SE.M}$. Moreover, for a given $\lambda \in \mathbb{N}$ the encryption of a message $m \in \text{SE.M}(\lambda)$ must always be in $\text{SE.Out}(\lambda, |m|)$.

Suppose we want to prove that SE is SIM-AC-\$ whenever F is SIM-AC-PRF. The natural way to do so is to build our simulator S from the encryption scheme from the given simulator S_F for F. In PRIM we can simply have S.Prim run S_F.Prim. In ENC the ciphertext is chosen at random if the user has not been exposed, otherwise we can simply run SE.Enc but use S_F.Ev in place of F_{K_F}. This just leaves EXP, here we are given a list of ciphertexts for the user and need to output a key to "explain" them. A natural approach is to randomly pick our own K_{SE} and use S_F.Exp to chose K_F. Doing so requires giving S_F a list of input and outputs to the family of function. Intuitively, it seems we want to be able to "extract" a list of input-outputs pairs for F that explain our ciphertexts.

Extractability. A mode of operation is extractable if it additionally specifies an efficient extraction algorithm SE.Ext satisfying a correctness and uniformity property we now define. The extraction algorithm SE.Ext has syntax $(y, r) \leftarrow_\$ \mathsf{SE.Ext}(1^\lambda, K_{SE}, c, m)$. The goal of this algorithm is to "extract" a sequence of responses y by F and a string of randomness r that explains how message m could be encrypted to ciphertext c when using key K_{SE}. We formally define correctness by the following game. It is assumed that SE.Ext provides outputs of the appropriate lengths to make this code well-defined. Extraction correctness of SE requires that $\Pr[G^{corr}_{SE,m}(1^\lambda)] = 1$ for all $\lambda \in \mathbb{N}$ and $m \in \mathsf{SE.M}(\lambda)$.

Game $G^{corr}_{SE,m}(1^\lambda)$	Distribution 1
$K_{SE} \leftarrow_\$ \mathsf{SE.Kg}(1^\lambda)$	$c \leftarrow_\$ \mathsf{SE.Out}(\lambda, \lvert m \rvert)$
$c \leftarrow_\$ \mathsf{SE.Out}(\lambda, \lvert m \rvert)$	$(y, r) \leftarrow_\$ \mathsf{SE.Ext}(1^\lambda, K_{SE}, c, m)$
$(y, r) \leftarrow_\$ \mathsf{SE.Ext}(1^\lambda, K_{SE}, c, m)$	Return (y, r)
$i \leftarrow 0$	Distribution 2
$c' \leftarrow \mathsf{SE.Enc}^{RF}(1^\lambda, K_{SE}, m; r)$	For $i = 1, \ldots, q(\lambda, \lvert m \rvert)$ do
Return $c = c'$	$\quad y[i] \leftarrow_\$ \mathsf{SE.Out}(\lambda)$
$\underline{RF(x)}$	$r \leftarrow_\$ \{0,1\}^{l(\lambda, \lvert m \rvert)}$
$i \leftarrow i + 1$	Return (y, r)
Return $y[i]$	

We will also require a uniformity property of SE.Ext. Specifically we require that its output be uniformly random whenever c is. Formally, there must exist $q, l : \mathbb{N} \times \mathbb{N} \to \mathbb{N}$ such that the two distributions on the right above are equivalent for all $\lambda \in \mathbb{N}$, $m \in \mathsf{SE.M}(\lambda)$, and $K_{SE} \in [\mathsf{SE.Kg}(1^\lambda)]$.[5]

Extraction security. A core step in our proof will require an additional property of SE which we will now define. Roughly, the desired property is that if SE.Ext is repeatedly used to explain randomly chosen ciphertexts an adversary cannot notice if it causes inconsistent values to be returned to SE.Enc.

Formally, consider the game $G^{ind\text{-}ac\text{-}ext}$ shown in Fig. 8. In it, a key is chosen for each user and then the adversary is given access to an encryption oracle. In this oracle a random ciphertext is sampled. Then SE.Ext is run to provide vector

---

[5] Computational relaxations of our uniformity and correctness property would suffice for our results, but seem to be unnecessary for any "natural" modes of operation.

Game $G_{SE,\mathcal{A}}^{\text{ind-ac-ext}}(\lambda)$	$\text{ENC}(u, m)$	$\text{RF}(u, x) \ //private$
For $u \in \{0,1\}^*$ do	Require $m \in \text{SE.M}(\lambda)$	$i \leftarrow i + 1$
$\quad K_{SE,u} \leftarrow\!\!\text{\$}\ \text{SE.Kg}(1^\lambda)$	Require $u \notin X$	If $T_u[x] \neq \bot$ then
$b \leftarrow\!\!\text{\$}\ \{0,1\}$	$c \leftarrow\!\!\text{\$}\ \text{SE.Out}(\lambda, \lvert m \rvert)$	$\quad$ If $b = 1$ then
$b' \leftarrow\!\!\text{\$}\ \mathcal{A}^{\text{ENC,EXP}}(1^\lambda)$	$(\boldsymbol{y}, r) \leftarrow\!\!\text{\$}\ \text{SE.Ext}(1^\lambda, K_{SE,u}, c, m)$	$\quad\quad \boldsymbol{y}[i] \leftarrow T_u[x]$
Return $(b = b')$	$i \leftarrow 0$	$T_u[x] \leftarrow \boldsymbol{y}[i]$
$\underline{\text{EXP}(u)}$	$c \leftarrow \text{SE.Enc}^{\text{RF}(u,\cdot)}(1^\lambda, K_{SE,u}, m; r)$	Return $T_u[x]$
$X.\text{add}(u)$	Return c	
Return $(K_{SE,u}, T_u)$		

Fig. 8. Game defining IND-AC-EXT security of SE. Note that the adversary is not given oracle access to the "private" oracle RF.

$\boldsymbol{y}$ and coins r which explain this ciphertext with respect to the queried message. Finally, SE.Enc is run with coins r and access to an oracle RF whose behavior depends on the chosen $\boldsymbol{y}$. The ciphertext it outputs is returned to the adversary.

When $b = 0$, this oracle simply returns the entries of $\boldsymbol{y}$, one at a time. The value returned for an input x is stored as $T_u[x]$. The behavior when $b = 1$ is similar except that if an input x to RF is ever repeated for a user u, then the value stored in $T_u[x]$ is used instead of the corresponding entry of $\boldsymbol{y}$. The attacker's goal is to distinguish between these two cases.

The adversary may choose to expose any user u, learning $K_{SE,u}$ and T_u. After doing so it is no longer able to make ENC queries to that user (as captured by the second "Require" statement in ENC). Note that by the uniformity of SE.Ext we could instead think of $\boldsymbol{y}$ and r as simply being picked at random without SE.Ext being run, but we believe the current framing is conceptually more clear.

We define $\text{Adv}_{SE,\mathcal{A}}^{\text{ind-ac-ext}}(\lambda) = 2 \Pr[G_{SE,\mathcal{A}}^{\text{ind-ac-ext}}] - 1$ and say that SE is IND-AC-EXT secure if $\text{Adv}_{SE,\mathcal{A}}^{\text{ind-ac-ext}}(\cdot)$ is negligible for all PPT $\mathcal{A}$. This notion will be used for an important step of the coming security proof. Of the properties required from an extraction algorithm it is typically the most difficult to verify.

Example Modes. As a simple example, we can consider counter-mode encryption. Let CTR.ol, CTR.il : $\mathbb{N} \rightarrow \mathbb{N}$ be fixed and the latter be super-logarithmic. Then CTR is defined as follows. Its key generation algorithm, CTR.Kg, always returns ε. Its sets are defined by

$$\text{CTR.M}(\lambda) = (\{0,1\}^{\text{CTR.ol}(\lambda)})^*, \quad \text{CTR.Out}(\lambda, l) = \{0,1\}^{l + \text{CTR.il}(\lambda)}$$
$$\text{CTR.FInp}(\lambda) = \{0,1\}^{\text{CTR.il}(\lambda)}, \quad \text{CTR.FOut}(\lambda) = \{0,1\}^{\text{CTR.ol}(\lambda)}.$$

Algorithms CTR.Enc, CTR.Dec, and CTR.Ext are defined below where $+$ is addition modulo $2^{\text{CTR.il}(\lambda)}$ with elements of $\{0,1\}^{\text{CTR.il}(\lambda)}$ interpreted as integers.

$\mathrm{CTR.Enc}^O(1^\lambda, K_{\mathsf{SE}}, m)$	$\mathrm{CTR.Dec}^O(1^\lambda, K_{\mathsf{SE}}, c)$	$\mathrm{CTR.Ext}(1^\lambda, K, c, m)$
$c_0 \leftarrow_{\$} \{0, 1\}^{\mathrm{CTR.il}(\lambda)}$	$c_0 \parallel c' \leftarrow c$	$r \leftarrow c_0$
For $i = 1, \ldots, \lvert m \rvert_{\mathrm{CTR.ol}(\lambda)}$	For $i = 1, \ldots, \lvert c' \rvert_{\mathrm{CTR.ol}(\lambda)}$	For $i = 1, \ldots, \lvert m \rvert_{\mathrm{F.ol}(\lambda)}$
$\quad c_i \leftarrow m_i \oplus O(c_0 + i)$	$\quad m_i \leftarrow c_i \oplus O(c_0 + i)$	$\quad \boldsymbol{y}[i] \leftarrow m_i \oplus c_i$
Return c	Return m	Return $(\boldsymbol{y}, r)$

It is clear that CTR.Ext is correct and that its outputs are distributed uniformly when c is picked at random. The IND-AC-EXT security of CTR follows from the probabilistic analysis done in existing proofs of security for CTR, such as the proof of Bellare, Desai, Jokipii, and Rogaway [6]. The standard analysis simply bounds the probability that any of the values $r_1 + 1, \ldots, r_1 + l_1, r_2 + 1, \ldots, r_2 + l_2, \ldots, r_q + 1, \ldots, r_q + l_q$ collide when the r_i's are picked uniformly and the l_i's are adaptively chosen (before the corresponding r_i is chosen).

Other IND-AC-EXT secure modes of operation include cipher-block chaining (CBC), cipher feedback (CFB), and output feedback (OFB).

6.2 Extractability Implies SIM-AC-\$ Security

Finally, we can state the main result of this section, that IND-AC-EXT security of an extractable mode of operation implies SIM-AC-\$ security.

Theorem 5. *Let* SE *be an extractable mode of operation which is IND-AC-EXT secure. Then* SE[F] *is SIM-AC-\$ secure with* P *whenever* F *is SIM-AC-PRF secure with* P *and satisfies* F.Inp = SE.FInp *and* F.Out = SE.FOut.

The full proof is given in the full version of this paper [23]. It considers a sequence of games which transition from the real world of $\mathsf{G}^{\mathsf{sim\text{-}ac\text{-}cpa}}$ to the ideal world (using a simulator we specify). In the first transition we use the security of F to replace SE's oracle access to it with oracle access to a lazily-sampled random function (or simulation by a given simulator $\mathsf{S}_{\mathsf{prf}}$ if the corresponding user has been exposed). Next we modify the game so that (for unexposed users) ciphertexts are chosen at random and then explained by SE.Ext. Then SE.Enc is run with the chosen random coins and oracle access to this explanation (except for whenever a repeat query is made) to produce a modified ciphertext which is returned. The uniformity of SE.Ext ensures this game is identical to the prior game. Then we apply the IND-AC-EXT security of SE so that the oracle given to SE.Enc is not kept consistent on repeated queries. The correctness of SE.Ext gives that the output of SE.Enc is equal to the c that was sampled at random. We provide simulator $\mathcal{S}_{\$}$ that simulates this game perfectly. It runs $\mathsf{S}_{\mathsf{prf}}$ whenever the game would. On an exposure it generate the table T_u for $\mathsf{S}_{\mathsf{prf}}$ by running SE.Ext on ciphertexts to obtain explanatory outputs of the PRF.

Concretely, in the proof we construct adversaries $\mathcal{A}_{\mathsf{prf}}$ and $\mathcal{A}_{\mathsf{ext}}$ along with simulator $\mathsf{S}_{\mathsf{cpa}}$ for which we show

$$\mathsf{Adv}^{\mathsf{sim\text{-}ac\text{-}cpa}}_{\mathsf{SE}[\mathsf{F}], \mathsf{S}_{\$}[\mathsf{S}_{\mathsf{cpa}}], \mathsf{P}, \mathcal{A}_{\mathsf{cpa}}}(\lambda) \leq \mathsf{Adv}^{\mathsf{sim\text{-}ac\text{-}prf}}_{\mathsf{F}, \mathsf{S}_{\mathsf{prf}}, \mathsf{P}, \mathcal{A}_{\mathsf{prf}}}(\lambda) + \mathsf{Adv}^{\mathsf{ind\text{-}ac\text{-}ext}}_{\mathsf{SE}, \mathcal{A}_{\mathsf{ext}}}(\lambda).$$

In the full version of this paper [23], we show that a variant of IND-AC-EXT security without exposures (which we call IND-EXT) necessarily holds if SE[F] is single-user IND-\$ secure for all single-user PRF secure F's. Moreover, we identify that the typical way that IND-EXT security is shown in security proofs for SE is by proving a slightly stronger property which *will* suffice to imply IND-AC-EXT security. Thereby, one can obtain a SIM-AC-\$ security proof from a IND-\$ security proof by using the information theoretic core of the existing proof.

6.3   Extensions and a Counter-Example Construction

Simple extensions. For encryption schemes not covered by our formalism, it will often be easy to extend the underlying ideas to cover the scheme. Suppose SE uses two distinct function families as PRFs, one could extend our mode of operation syntax to cover this by giving two separate PRF oracles to the encryption and decryption oracles. Then security would follow if there is an extraction algorithm satisfies analogous properties which explains outputs for both of the oracles. The proof would just require an additional step in which the second SIM-AC-PRF is replaced with simulation, as in our transition between games G_0 and G_1.

One can analogously prove the SIM-AC-\$ security of the Encrypt-then-PRF construction, where instead of a second SIM-AC-PRF function family we have a SIM-AC-\$ encryption scheme. From random ciphertexts it is straightforward to extract the required output of the function family and encryption scheme.

We can also extend the analysis to cover GCM when its nonces chosen uniformly at random. It is not captured by our current syntax because the encryption algorithm always applies the PRF to the all-zero string to derive a sub-key for a hash function. It is straightforward to extend our extraction ideas to allow consistency on this PRF query while maintaining our general proof technique.

Non-extractable counterexample. We showed our general security result for extractable modes of operations and described how to extend it for some simple variants. One might optimistically hope that SIM-AC-\$ security would hold for any IND-\$ secure mode of operation (when a SIM-AC-PRF secure function family is used). Unfortunately, we can show that this is not the case. We can provide an example mode of operation which is IND-\$ secure when using a PRF, but not SIM-AC-CPA secure for any choice of function family. It will be clear that this mode of operation is not extractable, as required by our earlier theorem.

Fix $n : \mathbb{N} \to \mathbb{N}$. Let G be a function family that is OW secure with P_{sm} and for which $G.Kg(1^\lambda)$ always returns ε and $G.Ev(1^\lambda, \varepsilon, \cdot)$ is always a permutation on $\{0,1\}^{n(\lambda)}$. Such a G us a one-way permutation on n-bits. From G we construct our counterexample CX. It has sets $CX.Out(\lambda, l) = \{0,1\}^{l+n(\lambda)}$ and $CX.M(\lambda) = CX.FInp(\lambda) = CX.FOut(\lambda) = \{0,1\}^{n(\lambda)}$. Key generation is given by $CX.Kg = G.Kg$. Encryption and decryption are given as follows.

$CX.Enc^O(1^\lambda, K_{SE}, m)$	$CX.Dec^O(1^\lambda, K_{SE}, c)$
$c_0 \leftarrow^\$ \{0,1\}^{n(\lambda)}$	$c_0 \,\|\, c_1 \leftarrow c$
$y \leftarrow G.Ev^\varepsilon(1^\lambda, \varepsilon, O(c_0))$	$y \leftarrow G.Ev^\varepsilon(1^\lambda, \varepsilon, O(c_0))$
$c_1 \leftarrow y \oplus m$	$m \leftarrow y \oplus c_1$
Return c	Return m

Above, the superscript ε is used as shorthand for the oracle that always returns ε. Note that this is exactly the behavior of G's expected ideal primitive P_{sm}. This counterexample uses the ideas originally introduced by Fischlin et al. [18] to construct non-programmable random oracles by exploiting a one-way permutation. The construction is not extractable because doing so would require being able to invert the one-way permutation. The following theorem formally establishes that this is a counterexample.

Theorem 6. *Fix* $n : \mathbb{N} \to \mathbb{N}$. *Let* G *be a one-way permutation on* n-*bits. Let* F *be a family of functions with* $F.\mathsf{Out}(\lambda) = F.\mathsf{Inp}(\lambda) = \{0,1\}^{n(\lambda)}$ *and* P *be an ideal primitive. Then* CX[F] *is IND-\$ secure with* P *if* F *is PRF secure with* P. *However,* CX[F] *is not SIM-AC-CPA secure with* P.

Proof (Sketch). That CX[F] is IND-\$ secure when F is PRF secure follows from, e.g., the standard security proof for CTR plus the observation that a permutation applied to a PRF is still a PRF. For the negative result, let S be any simulator and consider the following SIM-AC-CPA adversary $\mathcal{A}_{cpa}$ and OW adversary $\mathcal{A}$.

$\mathcal{A}_{cpa}^{\text{ENC,EXP,PRIM}}(1^\lambda)$	$\mathcal{A}^{\text{PRIM}}(1^\lambda, K, y)$
$m \leftarrow^{\$} \{0,1\}^{n(\lambda)}$	$\sigma \leftarrow S.\mathsf{Init}(1^\lambda)$
$c_0 \parallel c_1 \leftarrow \text{ENC}(1, m)$	$c_0 \parallel c_1 \leftarrow^{\$} S.\mathsf{Enc}(1^\lambda, 1, n(\lambda) : \sigma)$
$y \leftarrow c_1 \oplus m$	$m \leftarrow c_1 \oplus y$
$(K_{SE}, K_F) \leftarrow \text{EXP}(1)$	$M.\mathsf{add}(m) \, ; \, C.\mathsf{add}(c_0 \parallel c_1)$
$x \leftarrow F.\mathsf{Ev}^{\text{PRIM}}(1^\lambda, K_F, c_0)$	$(K_{SE}, K_F) \leftarrow^{\$} S.\mathsf{Exp}(1^\lambda, 1, M, C : \sigma)$
If $G.\mathsf{Ev}^\varepsilon(1^\lambda, \varepsilon, x) = y$ then return 1	$x \leftarrow F.\mathsf{Ev}^{S.\mathsf{Prim}(1^\lambda, \cdot : \sigma)}(1^\lambda, K_F, c_0)$
Return 0	Return x

Adversary $\mathcal{A}_{cpa}$ queries for the encryption of a random message. Then it exposes the corresponding users and uses the given key to calculate the input-output pair this claims for G. If indeed, this is a valid pair it returns 1, otherwise it returns 0. When $b = 1$, note that $\mathcal{A}_{cpa}$ will always return 1. Intuitively, when $b = 0$, adversary $\mathcal{A}_{cpa}$ should almost never return 1 because from the perspective of the simulator S it looks like y was chosen at random, so finding a pre-image for it requires breaking the security of G.

This intuition is captured by the adversary $\mathcal{A}$. It simulates the view S would see when run for $\mathcal{A}$, except instead of picking m at random it waits until after running S.Enc and sets $m \leftarrow c_1 \oplus y$ where y is the G image it was given as input. Note that y is a uniformly random string because G is a permutation and S is only given the length of the message at this point. Thus, this re-ordering of the calculation of m does not change the view of S. By asking S for the appropriate key and running F.Ev, the adversary obtains a potential pre-image for y.

Simple calculations give $\mathsf{Adv}_{SE,S,P,\mathcal{A}_{cpa}}^{\text{sim-ac-cpa}}(\lambda) = 1 - \mathsf{Adv}_{G,P,\mathcal{A}}^{\text{ow}}(\lambda)$. The latter advantage is negligible from the security of G, so the former is non-negligible. □

Extensions to PRFs. It is often useful to construct a PRF H with large input domains from a PRF F with smaller input domains. The smaller PRF F is often thought of as being reasonably modeled by a random oracle or ideal cipher. If the larger construction H is an indifferentiable construction of a random oracle [14, 30], then we can apply Theorem 3 to obtain the SIM-AC-PRF security of H.

In the case that H is not indifferentiable, one can often use techniques similar to the above to lift a PRF security proof for H to a SIM-AC-PRF security proof for H whenever F is SIM-AC-PRF secure. Implicit in the existing security proof there will often be a way of "explaining" a random output of H with random outputs by F. On exposure queries, the simulator for H would extract these explanations and feed them to the existing simulator for F to obtain the key to output. For primitive queries, it would just run the F simulator and for evaluation queries after exposure it would just run H using the F simulator in place of F.

Acknowledgments. We thank Thomas Ristenpart for insightful discussions and helpful contributions in the earlier stage of this project. Jaeger was supported in part by NSF grant CNS-1717640, NSF grant CNS-1719146, and a Sloan Research Fellowship. Tyagi was supported in part by NSF grant CNS-1704296.

References

1. Asharov, G., Naor, M., Segev, G., Shahaf, I.: Searchable symmetric encryption: optimal locality in linear space via two-dimensional balanced allocations. In: Wichs, D., Mansour, Y. (eds.) 48th ACM STOC, Cambridge, MA, USA, 18–21 June 2016, pp. 1101–1114. ACM Press (2016)
2. Asharov, G., Segev, G., Shahaf, I.: Tight tradeoffs in searchable symmetric encryption. In: Shacham, H., Boldyreva, A. (eds.) CRYPTO 2018, Part I. LNCS, vol. 10991, pp. 407–436. Springer, Cham (2018). https://doi.org/10.1007/978-3-319-96884-1_14
3. Barbosa, M., Farshim, P.: Indifferentiable authenticated encryption. In: Shacham, H., Boldyreva, A. (eds.) CRYPTO 2018, Part I. LNCS, vol. 10991, pp. 187–220. Springer, Cham (2018). https://doi.org/10.1007/978-3-319-96884-1_7
4. Bellare, M., Boldyreva, A., Micali, S.: Public-key encryption in a multi-user setting: security proofs and improvements. In: Preneel, B. (ed.) EUROCRYPT 2000. LNCS, vol. 1807, pp. 259–274. Springer, Heidelberg (2000). https://doi.org/10.1007/3-540-45539-6_18
5. Bellare, M., Canetti, R., Krawczyk, H.: Keying hash functions for message authentication. In: Koblitz, N. (ed.) CRYPTO 1996. LNCS, vol. 1109, pp. 1–15. Springer, Heidelberg (1996). https://doi.org/10.1007/3-540-68697-5_1
6. Bellare, M., Desai, A., Jokipii, E., Rogaway, P.: A concrete security treatment of symmetric encryption. In: 38th FOCS, Miami Beach, Florida, 19–22 October 1997, pp. 394–403. IEEE Computer Society Press (1997)
7. Bellare, M., Hofheinz, D., Yilek, S.: Possibility and impossibility results for encryption and commitment secure under selective opening. In: Joux, A. (ed.) EUROCRYPT 2009. LNCS, vol. 5479, pp. 1–35. Springer, Heidelberg (2009). https://doi.org/10.1007/978-3-642-01001-9_1
8. Bellare, M., Namprempre, C.: Authenticated encryption: relations among notions and analysis of the generic composition paradigm. In: Okamoto, T. (ed.) ASIACRYPT 2000. LNCS, vol. 1976, pp. 531–545. Springer, Heidelberg (2000). https://doi.org/10.1007/3-540-44448-3_41

9. Bost, R.: Σοφος: forward secure searchable encryption. In: Weippl, E.R., Katzenbeisser, S., Kruegel, C., Myers, A.C., Halevi, S. (eds.) ACM CCS 2016, Vienna, Austria, 24–28 October 2016. ACM Press (2016)
10. Canetti, R., Feige, U., Goldreich, O., Naor, M.: Adaptively secure multi-party computation. In: 28th ACM STOC, Philadephia, PA, USA, 22–24 May 1996, pp. 639–648. ACM Press (1996)
11. Cash, D., Grubbs, P., Perry, J., Ristenpart, T.: Leakage-abuse attacks against searchable encryption. In: Ray, I., Li, N., Kruegel, C. (eds.) ACM CCS 2015, Denver, CO, USA, 12–16 October 2015, pp. 668–679. ACM Press (2015)
12. Cash, D., et al.: Dynamic searchable encryption in very-large databases: data structures and implementation. In: NDSS 2014, San Diego, CA, USA, 23–26 February 2014. The Internet Society (2014)
13. Cash, D., Tessaro, S.: The locality of searchable symmetric encryption. In: Nguyen, P.Q., Oswald, E. (eds.) EUROCRYPT 2014. LNCS, vol. 8441, pp. 351–368. Springer, Heidelberg (2014). https://doi.org/10.1007/978-3-642-55220-5_20
14. Coron, J.-S., Dodis, Y., Malinaud, C., Puniya, P.: Merkle-Damgård revisited: how to construct a hash function. In: Shoup, V. (ed.) CRYPTO 2005. LNCS, vol. 3621, pp. 430–448. Springer, Heidelberg (2005). https://doi.org/10.1007/11535218_26
15. Curtmola, R., Garay, J.A., Kamara, S., Ostrovsky, R.: Searchable symmetric encryption: improved definitions and efficient constructions. In: Juels, A., Wright, R.N., De Capitani di Vimercati, S. (eds.) ACM CCS 2006, Alexandria, Virginia, USA, 30 October–3 November 2006, pp. 79–88. ACM Press (2006)
16. Dodis, Y., Ristenpart, T., Steinberger, J., Tessaro, S.: To hash or not to hash again? (In)differentiability results for H^2 and HMAC. In: Safavi-Naini, R., Canetti, R. (eds.) CRYPTO 2012. LNCS, vol. 7417, pp. 348–366. Springer, Heidelberg (2012). https://doi.org/10.1007/978-3-642-32009-5_21
17. Etemad, M., Küpçü, A., Papamanthou, C., Evans, D.: Efficient dynamic searchable encryption with forward privacy. PoPETs 2018(1), 5–20 (2018)
18. Fischlin, M., Lehmann, A., Ristenpart, T., Shrimpton, T., Stam, M., Tessaro, S.: Random Oracles with(out) programmability. In: Abe, M. (ed.) ASIACRYPT 2010. LNCS, vol. 6477, pp. 303–320. Springer, Heidelberg (2010). https://doi.org/10.1007/978-3-642-17373-8_18
19. Goldwasser, S., Micali, S.: Probabilistic encryption. J. Comput. Syst. Sci. 28(2), 270–299 (1984)
20. Hahn, F., Kerschbaum, F.: Searchable encryption with secure and efficient updates. In: Ahn, G.-J., Yung, M., Li, N. (eds.) ACM CCS 2014, Scottsdale, AZ, USA, 3–7 November 2014, pp. 310–320. ACM Press (2014)
21. Hu, S., Cai, C., Wang, Q., Wang, C., Luo, X., Ren, K.: Searching an encrypted cloud meets blockchain: a decentralized, reliable and fair realization. In: IEEE INFOCOM 2018 - IEEE Conference on Computer Communications, pp. 792–800, April 2018
22. Islam, M.S., Kuzu, M., Kantarcioglu, M.: Access pattern disclosure on searchable encryption: ramification, attack and mitigation. In: NDSS 2012, San Diego, CA, USA, 5–8 February 2012. The Internet Society (2012)
23. Jaeger, J., Tyagi, N.: Handling adaptive compromise for practical encryption schemes. Cryptology ePrint Archive, Report 2020/765 (2020). http://eprint.iacr.org/2020/765
24. Jarecki, S., Krawczyk, H., Xu, J.: OPAQUE: an asymmetric PAKE protocol secure against pre-computation attacks. In: Nielsen, J.B., Rijmen, V. (eds.) EUROCRYPT 2018, Part III. LNCS, vol. 10822, pp. 456–486. Springer, Cham (2018). https://doi.org/10.1007/978-3-319-78372-7_15

25. Kamara, S., Papamanthou, C.: Parallel and dynamic searchable symmetric encryption. In: Sadeghi, A.-R. (ed.) FC 2013. LNCS, vol. 7859, pp. 258–274. Springer, Heidelberg (2013). https://doi.org/10.1007/978-3-642-39884-1_22
26. Kamara, S., Papamanthou, C., Roeder, T.: Dynamic searchable symmetric encryption. In: Yu, T., Danezis, G., Gligor, V.D. (eds.) ACM CCS 2012, Raleigh, NC, USA, 16–18 October 2012, pp. 965–976. ACM Press (2012)
27. Kim, K.S., Kim, M., Lee, D., Park, J.H., Kim, W.-H.: Forward secure dynamic searchable symmetric encryption with efficient updates. In: Thuraisingham, B.M., Evans, D., Malkin, T., Xu, D. (eds.) ACM CCS 2017, Dallas, TX, USA, 31 October–2 November 2017, pp. 1449–1463. ACM Press (2017)
28. Li, J., et al.: Searchable symmetric encryption with forward search privacy. IEEE Trans. Dependable Secure Comput., 1 (2019, early access). https://ieeexplore.ieee.org/document/8621026
29. Liu, Q., Tian, Y., Wu, J., Peng, T., Wang, G.: Enabling verifiable and dynamic ranked search over outsourced data. IEEE Trans. Services Comput., 1 (2019, early access). https://ieeexplore.ieee.org/document/8734776
30. Maurer, U., Renner, R., Holenstein, C.: Indifferentiability, impossibility results on reductions, and applications to the random Oracle methodology. In: Naor, M. (ed.) TCC 2004. LNCS, vol. 2951, pp. 21–39. Springer, Heidelberg (2004). https://doi.org/10.1007/978-3-540-24638-1_2
31. Nielsen, J.B.: Separating random Oracle proofs from complexity theoretic proofs: the non-committing encryption case. In: Yung, M. (ed.) CRYPTO 2002. LNCS, vol. 2442, pp. 111–126. Springer, Heidelberg (2002). https://doi.org/10.1007/3-540-45708-9_8
32. Rogaway, P., Shrimpton, T.: A provable-security treatment of the key-wrap problem. In: Vaudenay, S. (ed.) EUROCRYPT 2006. LNCS, vol. 4004, pp. 373–390. Springer, Heidelberg (2006). https://doi.org/10.1007/11761679_23
33. Tyagi, N., Mughees, M.H., Ristenpart, T., Miers, I.: BurnBox: self-revocable encryption in a world of compelled access. In: Enck, W., Felt, A.P. (eds.) USENIX Security 2018, Baltimore, MD, USA, 15–17 August 2018, pp. 445–461. USENIX Association (2018)
34. Zuo, C., Sun, S.-F., Liu, J.K., Shao, J., Pieprzyk, J.: Dynamic searchable symmetric encryption schemes supporting range queries with forward (and backward) security. In: Lopez, J., Zhou, J., Soriano, M. (eds.) ESORICS 2018, Part II. LNCS, vol. 11099, pp. 228–246. Springer, Cham (2018). https://doi.org/10.1007/978-3-319-98989-1_12

Overcoming Impossibility Results in Composable Security Using Interval-Wise Guarantees

Daniel Jost$^{(\boxtimes)}$ ⓘ and Ueli Maurer$^{(\boxtimes)}$

Department of Computer Science, ETH Zurich, 8092 Zurich, Switzerland
{dajost,maurer}@inf.ethz.ch

Abstract. Composable security definitions, at times called simulation-based definitions, provide strong security guarantees that hold in any context. However, they are also met with some skepticism due to many impossibility results; goals such as commitments and zero-knowledge that are achievable in a stand-alone sense were shown to be unachievable composably (without a setup) since provably no efficient simulator exists. In particular, in the context of adaptive security, the so-called "simulator commitment problem" arises: once a party gets corrupted, an efficient simulator is unable to be consistent with its pre-corruption outputs. A natural question is whether such impossibility results are unavoidable or only artifacts of frameworks being too restrictive.

In this work, we propose a novel type of composable security statement that evades the commitment problem. Our new type is able to express the composable guarantees of schemes that previously did not have a clear composable understanding. To this end, we leverage the concept of system specifications in the Constructive Cryptography framework, capturing the conjunction of several interval-wise guarantees, each specifying the guarantees between two events. We develop the required theory and present the corresponding new composition theorem.

We present three applications of our theory. First, we show in the context of symmetric encryption with adaptive corruption how our notion naturally captures the expected confidentiality guarantee—the messages remain confidential until either party gets corrupted—and that it can be achieved by any standard semantically secure scheme (negating the need for non-committing encryption). Second, we present a composable formalization of (so far only known to be standalone secure) commitment protocols, which is instantiable without a trusted setup like a CRS. We show it to be sufficient for being used in coin tossing over the telephone, one of the early intuitive applications of commitments. Third, we reexamine a result by Hofheinz, Matt, and Maurer [Asiacrypt'15] implying that IND-ID-CPA security is not the right notion for identity-based encryption, unmasking this claim as an unnecessary framework artifact.

1 Introduction

1.1 A Plea for Composable Security

Common security definitions found in the literature are game-based, i.e., they require that an adversary cannot win a game that exports certain oracles to

© International Association for Cryptologic Research 2020
D. Micciancio and T. Ristenpart (Eds.): CRYPTO 2020, LNCS 12170, pp. 33–62, 2020.
https://doi.org/10.1007/978-3-030-56784-2_2

the adversary. The goal of such a security game is to capture the adversary's potential attacks in a minimal manner. However, the mapping of the game's interface to potential attacks in the real-world use of the cryptographic protocol is commonly not straight-forward. Thus, it is often a-priori unclear which game-based security notion is required in order for the protocol to be secure in a specific application. Rather, that aspect is often informally considered and passed down outside the security definitions, becoming "folklore" over the years.

Composable frameworks, such as [4,11,16,21], on the other hand, provide operational security definitions instead. The way they formalize security is based around comparing the execution of the protocol in the real world to an idealized world that intrinsically has the desired security properties. Importantly, this definition is with respect to any environment, thereby ensuring that the security guarantees not only do not exclude any attacks but also hold irrespective of other protocols (or multiple instances of the same one) being executed. For instance, the composable security definition of a symmetric encryption scheme *is* the construction of a secure communication channel from an authentic one and a key, with different assumed and constructed channels leading to different notions (e.g., whether replaying is possible). Hence, for a given application it is now trivial to decide whether a certain scheme suffices.

Finally, composable frameworks facilitate modularity. First, they are based on defining components with clean abstraction boundaries (e.g., a secure channel) that abstract away the details of how that module has been constructed (or otherwise obtained). This idealized module can then be used by a higher-level protocol with the security of the combined overall protocol following directly from the composition theorem. Thus, the security of complex protocols can be neatly proven by composing it from smaller sub-protocols.

1.2   Obstacles for Composable Security

While the clear semantics, modularity, and high security guarantees suggest that all protocols should be proven secure in a composable framework rather than in an ad-hoc game-based manner, composable definitions are still not prevalent with the majority of new research still carried out using game-based definitions.

One of the main reasons hindering adoption might be that many primitives are known to be impossible to achieve in the plain UC model, such as zero knowledge [4] and commitments [5]. Furthermore, Lindell has shown [12] that impossibility results are not specific to the UC model but inherent to any kind of similar model based around the existence of an efficient simulator. As a consequence, respective protocols have to rely on additional setup assumptions, such as a common reference string, and are also generally less efficient.

One particular obstacle composable definitions often face is the so-called "simulator commitment problem", which mainly arises when considering adaptive security. In a nutshell, it describes the simulator's inability to explain some of its previous choices the moment a party gets corrupted. More concretely, consider the example of two parties securing their communication using symmetric encryption. The intuition is that the adversary does not learn the messages until either of the parties gets corrupted, thereby revealing the key. Before, the adversary should learn at most the length. As a result, the simulator, in the first phase, has to output a fake ciphertexts independent of the real messages. For any semantically secure encryption scheme he can actually do so. This, however, commits him on those fake ciphertexts. At the moment a party gets corrupted, the simulator then needs to be able to explain those ciphertexts by outputting a matching encryption key. Even if he learns all the previous messages, he will not be able to do so for regular encryption schemes. Note, however, that the commitment problem is not restricted to adaptive corruptions only. Similar issues also arise, for instance, in the context of password-based security [7] or identity-based encryption [8], where it has been shown that due to this commitment problem the standard game-based notions do not induce the expected corresponding composable statements.

On a general level, this raises the fundamental question whether such impossibility results actually indicate a security issue, and hence protocols not satisfying the stronger composable definitions should not be used, or whether they present an artifact of the framework. Especially for the commitment problem, the common understanding is that the latter is true. Furthermore, the obstacles are often dealt with by either reverting to composable security with static corruptions only, or by simply retracting to game-based definitions. As a result, there is a clear need for a better composable security notion that lets us settle this question and remedy the issue of the spurious impossibilities.

1.3   Existing Attempts to Overcome the Obstacles

A number of approaches have been proposed in order to circumvent the aforementioned issues of composable security.

First, Canetti and Krawczyk proposed the notion of non-information oracles [6] within the UC-framework. A non-information oracle is essentially a game-based definition embedded into an ideal functionality. For instance, rather than saying that an encryption scheme should realize a secure channel that only leaks the length, the respective functionality leaks the output of the non-information oracle, which is required to satisfy a CPA-like definition. While this circumvents the commitment problem, there are two drawbacks. First, it weakens composition by requiring explicit reductions to the embedded games in the security proof of the higher-level protocols using the functionality. Second, for each ideal functionality a different type of non-information oracle needs to be defined, without providing any generic template. As a consequence, the question of the "right" non-information oracle re-arises, just like when defining a security game.

Second, a line of work considers super-polynomial simulators [3,20,22]. The initial proposal by Pass [20] considered sub-exponential simulators and polynomially bounded environments. This implies, however, that the simulator cannot be absorbed into the environment, ceding some of the most fundamental composition properties of the UC-framework. The later works by Prabhakaran and Sahai [22] and Broadnax et al. [3] empower the simulator in a more controlled manner, preserving most natural composition properties. Their adoption, however, still suffers from being rather technical, and moreover, still quite limited in the number of issues they can overcome. For instance, when considering a PRG whose seed might leak, even an all powerful simulator will not be able to explain a truly randomly chosen output with an appropriate seed.

Finally, Backes, Dürmuth, Hofheinz, and Küsters [1] proposed an approach where the real-world resource would just disallow certain activation sequences by the environment that were otherwise impossible to simulate. While this avoids the complications of the other approaches, it scarifies the evident semantics of composable security notions by excluding certain—deemed artificial—attacks. A similar approach has recently been used by Jost, Maurer and Mularczyk in [10].

1.4 Contributions

Interval-wise guarantees. In this work, we propose an alternative solution to the simulator-commitment problem that is aimed at expressing the guarantees of regular schemes within a composable framework. More concretely, we introduce a novel type of construction notion within the Constructive Cryptography (CC) framework that avoids the commitment problem while providing a number of distinct benefits. First, it provides a clean semantics of how the guarantees should be interpreted. Second, it holds in any environment, just as any statement in the CC framework. Third, it is equipped with a composition theorem.

Since the commitment problem usually occurs at a very specific point of the protocol execution, such as when a party gets corrupted, where the security guarantees of the protocol anyway inherently change, our novel construction notion is centered around the very natural idea of formalizing guarantees that hold in a certain interval (between two events). That is, our notion for instance allows to formalize separate security guarantees before and after the corruption event. In contrast to existing simulation-based notions, we thereby only require the simulation to work within each interval, not forcing the simulation to be consistent between the intervals (which causes the initial commitment issues). We discuss how the security guarantees provided by our notion should be interpreted, when stronger notions might still be desirable, and how our notion fits into the space of static versus adaptive security.

Theory extensions. On a technical level, we leverage the specification-based approach of the CC framework, where proving a protocol π to be secure corresponds to modeling the assumed real-world specification $\mathcal{R}$, and showing that the resulting specification $\pi\mathcal{R}$ is contained in an ideal specification $\mathcal{S}$, i.e, $\pi\mathcal{R} \subseteq \mathcal{S}$.

We formalize interval-wise guarantees as a novel type of specifications within the CC framework. We carefully consider the subtleties arising when defining such specifications and show how they interact with the other aspects of the framework. Finally, we present the respective composition theorem, that actually supersedes all the existing ones, and in particular allows to syntactically combine multiple such interval-wise construction statements, or an interval-wise one with a regular construction statement.

Applications. As a third contribution, we apply our methodology to several examples. First, we consider the encrypt-then-MAC paradigm in a setting where the keys can adaptively leak to the adversary, stylizing adaptive passive corruptions. Using our interval-wise guarantees, we obtain a simple composable security definition thereof without the need for non-committing encryption. More concretely, we consider the following three properties. First, we require the messages to be confidential as long as neither the encryption nor the authentication key leaked. (An IND-CPA secure scheme cannot guarantee confidentiality without authenticity.) In our definition, this is phrased as the construction of a secure channel *up to that point*. Second, between the exposure of the encryption key and the authentication key, we require communication to still be authentic, i.e., an authenticated channel to be constructed. Finally, after the encryption key has been exposed, we still require correctness.

As a second application, we show a composable formalization of information-theoretically binding commitment schemes realizable in the plain model. We then show how, based on such a commitment scheme, Blum's protocol constructs a composable coin-toss notion. Applying composition then directly implies that this formalization can be achieved in the plain model as well. While the resulting specification is obviously too weak to serve as a common reference string, it guarantees unbiasedness. Hence, it is provides a good enough type of randomness resource whenever unbiasedness is sufficient, in particular formalizing and formally validating the intuitive-level argumentation about flipping a coin over the telephone of the corresponding papers of that time.

Finally, we consider the composable guarantees of identity-based encryption. We revisit the result by Hofheinz, Matt, and Maurer [8] that shows the standard ind-id-cpa notion to be too weak when considering a traditional composable statement based on the existence of a single simulator, even when considering *static corruptions*, due to the commitment problem. Furthermore, the authors have shown that the same weaker construction that actually can be achieved, could also be achieved by a weaker game-based notion ind-id1-cpa, modeling so-called lunch-time attacks. We refute their results in the following way: Based on interval-wise guarantees we formalize a composable specification of IBE that corresponds exactly to the standard ind-id-cpa notion.

1.5 Outline

In Sect. 3, we provide a introduction to our notion, before presenting the technical details in Sect. 4. In Sect. 5 we present a novel composable definition of perfectly binding commitments and its application to coin tossing. In the full version [9], we moreover revisit composable security of identity-based encryption.

2 Preliminaries: Constructive Cryptography

This work builds upon some more recent aspect of the Constructive Cryptography (CC) framework [13,16]. We therefore revisit the key aspects thereof, follows the exposition introduced in [16], with some adaptations from [10].

2.1   Resources, Converters, and the Interaction Model

At its heart, the Constructive Cryptography framework views cryptography as a resource theory, in which parties use certain resources (e.g., communication channels and a shared secret key) to construct another resource via a protocol.

Global events. In this work, we use the version of Constructive Cryptography introduced in [10] that enriches the interaction model by a notion of globally observable events. Formally, events are a generalization of monotone binary outputs (MBO) introduced by Maurer et al. [15]. Roughly, an MBO is a value that can change from 0 to 1 but not back, which can be interpreted as a single event happening once the MBO changes to 1. An event then just corresponds to a named MBO and the *global event history* $\mathcal{E}$ is a list of event names without duplicates (to model that every event can occur at most once). For an event name n, we denote by $\mathcal{E} \xleftarrow{+} \mathcal{E}_n$ the act of appending n to $\mathcal{E}$ (or leaving it unchanged if it is already contained). Moreover, we use $\mathcal{E}_n$ as a short-hand notation to denote that n is in the list $\mathcal{E}$, and say that the event happened. Finally, we denote by $\mathcal{E}_{n_1} \prec \mathcal{E}_{n_2}$ that the event n_1 precedes the event n_2 in the event history.

Resources. A resource[1] R is a reactive system that interacts in the following two ways with the rest of the world: First, it allows interaction at one or several named *communication interfaces*, in the following just called interfaces, at which it can be queried an input x, and must answer with an output y at the same interface. Second, during an activation, the resource R can depend on the global event history $\mathcal{E}$, and can furthermore append events from a predefined set of names. We call this set of names the events controlled by R.

Formally, resources are modeled as random systems [14], where the interface address, the actual input x, and the current state of the event history are encoded as part of the input. Analogously, the answer y and the new state of the event history are encoded as part of the output, under the constraint that the old state of the event history is a prefix of the new one. For the sake of this paper, a reader unfamiliar with the CC framework might however just think of a resource as the behavior of an oracle machine, where each interface corresponds to an oracle and the event history being similar to the "directory" ITI used in the recent version of UC [4]. Note, however, that a resource only defines the behavior of the system and not its description, i.e., two different (pseudo-code descriptions of) ITMs having the same input-output behavior denote the same resource.

A set of resources can be viewed as a single one, with the interface set of the composed resource being the union. For resources $R_1, \ldots, R_n$ (with disjoint interface sets) we denote by $[R_1, \ldots, R_n]$ the *parallel composition*.

Converters and protocols. In the Constructive Cryptography framework, *converters* express the local action executed by one party. A converter expects

---

[1] The analogon to *functionalities* in the UC framework [4].

to be connected to a given number of interfaces at the "inside", and emulates a certain set of interfaces at the "outside". Upon an input at an outside interface, the converter is allowed to make a bounded number of oracle queries to the inside interfaces, before returning a value at the queried interface.

For a converter π and a resource R, let $\mathcal{I}$ denote a tuple describing an injective mapping from π's inside interfaces to interfaces of R. We then denote by $R' := \pi^{\mathcal{I}}R$ the resource obtained from connecting the converter accordingly. The resource R' no longer exposes those interfaces but the ones emulated by π instead. Converter attachment satisfies the natural property of *composition order independence*, stating that the composition order does not matter—only the final system does.

Proposition 1. *Let π_1 and π_2 be two converters, let R be a resource and let $\mathcal{I}_1$ and $\mathcal{I}_2$ be such that they assign* disjoint *interfaces. Then, $\pi_1^{\mathcal{I}_1}\pi_2^{\mathcal{I}_2}R = \pi_2^{\mathcal{I}_2}\pi_1^{\mathcal{I}_1}R$. Moreover, if S is another resource such that the interface sets of R and S are disjoint, then we have $\pi_1^{\mathcal{I}_1}[R, S] = [\pi_1^{\mathcal{I}_1}R, S]$.*

We define a *protocol* to be a set of converter-connection pairs, i.e,. $\pi := \{(\pi_1, \mathcal{I}_1), \ldots, (\pi_n, \mathcal{I}_n)\}$ with pairwise disjoint $\mathcal{I}_i$'s. Moreover, we say that π is a protocol for a resource R, if R has all the required interfaces for the protocol application to be well-defined, and write πR to denote its application.

The environment (distinguisher). The distinguisher D is a special type of environment that first interacts with a resource R by making queries to the resource's interfaces. Between two such queries it can access the global event history and append events to it, except the ones controlled by R. Note that activations are atomic, i.e., at any moment in time either the resource or the distinguisher is activated, but not both. Finally, the distinguisher ends the interaction with the resource by outputting a bit. The advantage of D is then defined as

$$\Delta^{\mathsf{D}}(\mathsf{R}, \mathsf{S}) := \Pr[\mathsf{D}^{\mathcal{E}}(\mathsf{S}) = 1] - \Pr[\mathsf{D}^{\mathcal{E}}(\mathsf{R}) = 1],$$

where we use the syntax $\mathsf{D}^{\mathcal{E}}(\cdot)$ to make explicit that the distinguisher has oracle access to the global event history $\mathcal{E}$.

2.2 Constructions

Specifications. It is natural to consider only certain desired (or assumed) properties of a system and deliberately not specify others. Some of those choices are intrinsic to the mathematical model we use, such as only considering the input-output behavior and ignoring the physical aspects. Other properties can be purposefully ignored by considering specifications of systems that simply leave out those aspects, focusing only on the relevant properties. Following [17], we model specifications as sets of resources $\mathcal{R}$ that all have the same interface set. For each property, such as confidentiality, one has in mind, one can consider the set $\mathcal{R}$ of resources satisfying that property. Vice versa, each set of resources $\mathcal{R}$ can be interpreted as the set of properties common to all elements. For instance, authenticated communication might be modeled as the set of all communication channels that are authentic—not specifying the level of confidentiality by including both confidential as well as non-confidential channels.

Constructions as subsets. In provable security one typically considers the execution of a protocol π that makes use of some assumed specification $\mathcal{R}$, such as a communication network or a public-key infrastructure. In short, one wants to show that the specification $\pi\mathcal{R} := \{\pi\mathsf{R} \mid \mathsf{R} \in \mathcal{R}\}$ satisfies the desired security properties. As explained in the previous section, those properties are formalized as a specification $\mathcal{S}$, and thus proving security means proving $\pi\mathcal{R} \subseteq \mathcal{S}$. Note that obviously the guarantees given by $\mathcal{S}$ are generally weaker than the ones by $\pi\mathcal{R}$. The purpose of such a statement is, however, that the security properties are in $\mathcal{S}$ both more explicit and simpler to analyze. In other words, the goal is to distill out the relevant properties and abstract away the others.

Traditionally, the statement $\pi\mathcal{R} \subseteq \mathcal{S}$ is read as the protocol π constructing the specification $\mathcal{S}$ from the specification $\mathcal{R}$, or in UC-jargon the protocol securely realizing the specification $\mathcal{S}$ in the $\mathcal{R}$-hybrid model. Hence, as a shorthand notation we introduce the following construction notion.

Definition 1. *Let $\mathcal{R}$ and $\mathcal{S}$ be specifications, and let π be a protocol for $\mathcal{R}$. Then, we say that π constructs $\mathcal{S}$ from $\mathcal{R}$, denoted $\mathcal{R} \xrightarrow{\pi} \mathcal{S}$, if and only if $\pi\mathcal{R} \subseteq \mathcal{S}$, i.e.,*

$$\mathcal{R} \xrightarrow{\pi} \mathcal{S} \; :\Longleftrightarrow \; \pi\mathcal{R} \subseteq \mathcal{S}.$$

In slight abuse of notation, we write $\mathsf{R} \xrightarrow{\pi} \mathsf{S}$ in lieu of $\{\mathsf{R}\} \xrightarrow{\pi} \{\mathsf{S}\}$ for singleton specifications.

This construction notion is associated with the usual composition properties of Constructive Cryptography: sequential and parallel composition—which form the equivalence of the universal composition theorem of the UC-framework.

Theorem 1. *Let $\mathcal{R}$, $\mathcal{S}$, and $\mathcal{T}$ be arbitrary specifications, and let π and π' be arbitrary protocols for $\mathcal{R}$ and $\mathcal{S}$, respectively. Then, we have*

1. $\mathcal{R} \xrightarrow{\pi} \mathcal{S} \wedge \mathcal{S} \xrightarrow{\pi'} \mathcal{T} \implies \mathcal{R} \xrightarrow{\pi' \circ \pi} \mathcal{T}$,
2. $\mathcal{R} \xrightarrow{\pi} \mathcal{S} \implies [\mathcal{R}, \mathcal{T}] \xrightarrow{\pi} [\mathcal{S}, \mathcal{T}]$.

Proof. The first property follows directly from the transitivity of the subset relation, $\pi'(\pi\mathcal{R}) \subseteq \pi'\mathcal{S} \subseteq \mathcal{T}$, and the second property follows from Proposition 1: $\pi[\mathcal{R}, \mathcal{T}] = [\pi\mathcal{R}, \mathcal{T}] \subseteq [\mathcal{S}, \mathcal{T}]$.

The specifications $\pi\mathcal{R}$ and $\mathcal{S}$ are often referred to as real- and ideal-world, respectively, according to the so-called real-world/ideal-world paradigm on which most composable frameworks [4,11,16,21] are based. Following that paradigm, security statement affirm that the real word is "just-as-good" as the ideal world, meaning that for all parties, no matter whether honest or adversarial, it does not make a difference whether they live in the real (where an arbitrary element of $\pi\mathcal{R}$ is present), or in the ideal world (where some element of $\mathcal{S}$ is present). Hence, if the honest parties are content with the guarantees they get from the ideal specification, they can safely execute the protocol in the real world instead.

The (in)existence of a simulator. Simulation-based security turned out to be one of the most fundamental concepts in cryptography and is closely linked with the real-world/ideal-world paradigm. It not only forms the foundation of semantic security, zero knowledge, and the security of MPC, but also of virtually every composable framework. Whereas the former definitions tend to require an after-the-fact simulation of the transcript, composable frameworks get their stronger guarantees from requiring on-line simulation, where an adaptive environment interacts with the simulator. The common understanding of those security definitions is then that the simulator "translates" the attacks from the real-world adversary to the ideal world such that they achieve the same effect.

While the initial version of the Constructive Cryptography framework also hard-coded the existence of a simulator (with respect to the dummy adversary), starting from [17], the simulator is no longer an integral part of the construction notion. Rather, employing a simulator is just one way of defining an ideal specification, σS that makes the achieved security properties obvious. For instance, the specification of confidential channels can then be written as the specification S of channels that only leak the message length, combined with an arbitrary simulator. From this description it is apparent that for any resource in the combined specification σS, only the length is leaked.

If one restricts oneself to specifications of this type, then the following more specific composition theorem can be deduced.

Proposition 2. *Let $\mathcal{R}$, S, and $\mathcal{T}$ be specifications, and let π and π' be protocols for $\mathcal{R}$ and S, respectively. For any simulators σ (for S) and σ' (for $\mathcal{T}$), such that the set of interfaces controlled by the simulators are disjoint from the ones controlled by the protocols, we have*

1. $\mathcal{R} \xrightarrow{\pi} \sigma S \wedge S \xrightarrow{\pi'} \sigma'\mathcal{T} \implies \mathcal{R} \xrightarrow{\pi'\circ\pi} \sigma\sigma'\mathcal{T}$,
2. $\mathcal{R} \xrightarrow{\pi} \sigma S \implies [\mathcal{R}, \mathcal{T}] \xrightarrow{\pi} \sigma[S, \mathcal{T}]$.

Proof. By composition order invariance we have $\pi'\sigma S = \sigma\pi'S \subseteq \sigma\sigma'\mathcal{T}$, implying $S \xrightarrow{\pi'} \sigma'\mathcal{T} \implies \sigma S \xrightarrow{\pi'} \sigma\sigma'\mathcal{T}$. The first property then follows directly from combining this with Theorem 1. The second property follows from Theorem 1 and Proposition 1 as well: $\pi[\mathcal{R}, \mathcal{T}] = [\pi\mathcal{R}, \mathcal{T}] \subseteq [\sigma S, \mathcal{T}] = \sigma[S, \mathcal{T}]$. ☐

2.3 Relaxations

The basic construction notion does not take into account statistical errors or computational assumptions. Those aspects are formalized by so-called relaxations, as introduced in [17]. On an abstract level, a relaxation is a mapping from specifications to weaker, so-called relaxed, specifications. For our purpose, where we instantiate specifications by sets of resources, we can define a relaxation as a function mapping a single resource to a set of resources.

Definition 2. *Let Θ denote the set of all resources. A relaxation ϕ is a function $\phi\colon \Theta \to 2^\Theta$ (where 2^Θ denotes the power set of Θ) such that $\mathsf{R} \in \phi(\mathsf{R})$ for all $\mathsf{R} \in \Theta$. In addition, for a specification $\mathcal{R}$, we define $\mathcal{R}^\phi := \bigcup_{\mathsf{R}\in\mathcal{R}} \phi(\mathsf{R})$ as a shorthand notation.*

A concrete relaxation thereby formalizes some notion of resources being "almost-as-good" in some context. That is, if we were happy with constructing a resource specification $\mathcal{S}$, then we should also be happy with $\mathcal{S}^\phi$, if we believe the weakening ϕ to be justifiable in the given context. For instance, one could consider the relaxation that maps the resource R to the set of all computationally indistinguishable resources from R under some computational assumption. Hence, if we believe the computational assumption to be valid, we should be as content with the relaxed specification as with the original one.

Abstracting away irrelevant properties is a core paradigm of any modular analysis. Applied to Constructive Cryptography, this means that ideally we should be able to "forget" relaxations. That is, if one shows that one protocol constructs $\mathcal{S}^\phi$ (from some assumed resources), one should be able to compose it with another statement that assumes $\mathcal{S}$ instead. On the most abstract level, it is easy to see that the following rules apply to any relaxation.

Proposition 3. *For any specifications $\mathcal{R}$ and $\mathcal{S}$, and any relaxation ϕ, we have*

1. *$\mathcal{R} \subseteq \mathcal{R}^\phi$,*
2. *$\mathcal{R} \subseteq \mathcal{S} \implies \mathcal{R}^\phi \subseteq \mathcal{S}^\phi$,*
3. *$(\mathcal{R} \cap \mathcal{S})^\phi \subseteq \mathcal{R}^\phi \cap \mathcal{S}^\phi$,*
4. *$(\mathcal{R} \cup \mathcal{S})^\phi = \mathcal{R}^\phi \cup \mathcal{S}^\phi$.*

Proof. All properties trivially follow from $R \in \phi(R)$. $\qquad\qquad\qquad\qquad\qquad$ □

The reduction relaxation. We now introduce the most fundamental relaxation, which captures computational security based on explicit reductions. This is defined as a function ϵ that maps distinguishers to their respective performance in $[0,1]$, where $\epsilon(D)$ typically refers to the winning probability of a modified distinguisher D' (the reduction) on the underlying computational problem.

Definition 3. *Let ϵ be a function that maps distinguishers to a value in $[0,1]$. Then, the induced relaxation on a resource R, denoted R^ϵ, is defined as*

$$R^\epsilon := \left\{ S \mid \forall D : |\Delta^D(R, S)| \leq \epsilon(D) \right\}.$$

We call such a relaxation generally an ϵ-relaxation or reduction relaxation.

We now discuss several properties that ϵ-relaxations have. First, the errors just add up, as expressed by the following theorem.

Theorem 2. *Let $\mathcal{R}$ be an arbitrary specification, and let ϵ_1 and ϵ_2 be arbitrary ϵ-relaxations. Then we have $\left(\mathcal{R}^{\epsilon_1}\right)^{\epsilon_2} \subseteq \mathcal{R}^{\epsilon_1 + \epsilon_2}$.*

Proof. This follows directly from the triangle inequality of the distinguishing advantage. $\qquad\qquad\qquad\qquad\qquad\qquad\qquad\qquad\qquad\qquad\qquad\qquad\qquad\qquad$ □

Second, they naturally commute with protocol application and parallel composition of additional resources, i.e., the relaxation can be "pulled out". In such a step, however, the additional resource or converter has to be explicitly accounted for in the reduction.

Theorem 3. *The ϵ-relaxation is compatible with protocol application in the following sense that $\pi\left(\mathcal{R}^\epsilon\right) \subseteq (\pi\mathcal{R})^{\epsilon_\pi}$, for $\epsilon_\pi(\mathsf{D}) := \epsilon(\mathsf{D}\pi(\cdot))$, where $\mathsf{D}\pi(\cdot)$ denotes the distinguisher that first attaches π to the given resource and then executes D. Moreover, it is compatible with parallel composition, i.e., $[\mathcal{R}^\epsilon, \mathcal{S}] \subseteq [\mathcal{R}, \mathcal{S}]^{\epsilon_\mathcal{S}}$, for $\epsilon_\mathcal{S}(\mathsf{D}) := \sup_{\mathsf{S} \in \mathcal{S}} \epsilon(\mathsf{D}[\cdot, \mathsf{S}])$, where $\mathsf{D}[\cdot, \mathsf{S}]$ denotes the distinguisher that emulates S in parallel to the given resource and then lets D interact with them.*

Proof. The proof can be found in the full version [9]. $\qquad\square$

The composition theorem with ϵ-relaxations then follows directly from these compatibility results. The following corollary phrases the corresponding result—which in older version of Constructive Cryptography used to be called *the* composition theorem, thereby hard-coding computational security.

Corollary 1. *For any specifications $\mathcal{R}$, $\mathcal{S}$, and $\mathcal{T}$, any protocols π and π', and any ϵ-relaxation ϵ and ϵ', we have*

1. *$\mathcal{R} \xrightarrow{\pi} \mathcal{S}^\epsilon \wedge \mathcal{S} \xrightarrow{\pi'} \mathcal{T}^{\epsilon'} \implies \mathcal{R} \xrightarrow{\pi'\circ\pi} \mathcal{T}^{\epsilon_{\pi'}+\epsilon'}$,*
2. *$\mathcal{R} \xrightarrow{\pi} \mathcal{S}^\epsilon \implies [\mathcal{R}, \mathcal{T}] \xrightarrow{\pi} [\mathcal{S}, \mathcal{T}]^{\epsilon_\mathcal{T}}$,*

where ϵ_π and $\epsilon_\mathcal{S}$ are defined as in Theorem 3, respectively.

Proof. The proof can be found in the full version [9]. $\qquad\square$

3 Interval-Wise Guarantees: Motivation and Intuition

In this section, we outline the general approach, and its motivation, proposed in this work, before we deep dive into the technicalities in Sect. 4. In particular, we believe that the conceptual contributions are of interest independent from the exact mathematical formalization.

3.1 A Motivating Example

Consider two parties, Alice and Bob, who want to communicate securely over the Internet. If they have a pre-shared secret key available, e.g. from running a key agreement protocol, then it is well known that the encrypt-then-MAC paradigm achieves the desired goal. Assuming independent keys for the encryption and MAC scheme, this construction is secure if the underlying encryption scheme is IND-CPA secure and the MAC scheme is weakly unforgeable.

What, however, if we assume that in reality the keys to not be one hundred percent secure? Intuitively one should expect the scheme to remain secure until either of the keys leak to an adversary, and the security properties then to gracefully downgrade accordingly. More concretely, there is little reason to doubt the following security guarantees should be provided by the scheme:

1. until either of the keys leak, the scheme should provide both confidentiality and authenticity;

2. if only the encryption key leaked so far, then the scheme should still provide authenticity;
3. once the MAC key leaked, the scheme should at least still provide correctness, i.e., allow the parties to communicate in the absence of an active network attack.

(Note that if first the MAC key gets exposed, then a scheme that is only IND-CPA secure might not provide full confidentiality.)

3.2   A Naive Attempt

While the encrypt-then-MAC paradigm has composably proven to be sound in a context where both parties are honest and the keys are secure (e.g. [6, 18]), extending those results to deal with key exposures has turned out to be surprisingly strenuous.

Intuitively, one might model the achieved security guarantees as an *secure channel with downgradable security*, which waives confidentiality and authenticity once the respective keys leaked. The protocol should then construct such a channel from an insecure channel and two leakable keys[2], for authentication and encryption, respectively. See Fig. 1 for a formal definition of the respective resources InsecCh, AuthKey, and EncKey (for the assumed resources), and SecCh for the secure channel with downgradable security. Following the paradigm of modularity, one might try to formalize and prove this in two steps and first consider authentication only, as modeled by a downgradable authenticated channel AuthCh (c.f. Fig. 1 as well). Indeed, one can show the following construction.

Proposition 4. *Let* AuthCh *denote the authenticated channel that degrades its security once the respective key is leaked, as formally defined in Fig. 1, and let* π_{MAC} *denote the simple protocol that applies a MAC scheme to the messages. Then, there exists a simulator* σ_{MAC} *such that*

$$[\text{AuthKey}, \text{InsecCh}] \xrightarrow{\pi_{MAC}} (\sigma_{MAC}\text{AuthCh})^{\epsilon_{MAC}},$$

where ϵ_{MAC} *denotes a simple reduction to the MAC-forgery game.*

Proof. This is a well-known result, which has for instance been sketched in [13].

However, once we turn our attention towards the second construction step— using encryption to achieve confidentiality—we run into the so-called simulator commitment problem of composable security, as expressed by the following proposition.

---

[2] In CC, the adversary by definition only has access to interfaces statically assigned to him. Hence, adaptive corruptions are modeled by introducing explicit memory and computation resources with an adversarial interface, granting the adversary access once the party is corrupted. For simplicity, we here consider directly leaking key resources instead. Assuming secure erasure, this is equivalent to passive corruptions.

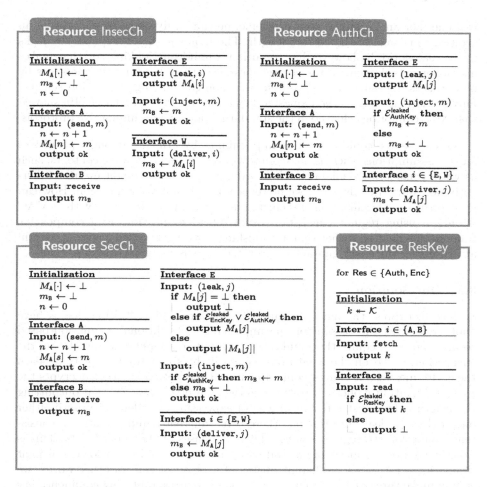

Fig. 1. The resources involved in the encrypt-then-MAC example. Observe how the authenticated and the secure channel degrade their guarantees once the respective keys have been leaked.

Proposition 5. *Let* SecCh *denote a secure channel that degrades the respective guarantees once the keys have been exposed, as depicted in Fig. 1, and let* π_{ENC} *be the protocol that applies a symmetric encryption scheme. For any (efficient) simulator* σ_{ENC}, *and (an efficiency preserving) reduction* ϵ_{CPA} *to the IND-CPA game, we have*

$$[\mathsf{EncKey}, \mathsf{AuthCh}] \xrightarrow{\pi_{ENC}} (\sigma_{ENC}\mathsf{SecCh})^{\epsilon_{CPA}},$$

i.e., IND-CPA security does not suffice.

Proof (Sketch). In the first phase, the simulator has to produce, without knowing the message, fake ciphertexts $c_1, c_2, \ldots, c_n$ that look indistinguishable from the real one. For an IND-CPA secure scheme, he can easily do so by encrypting an arbitrary message of the correct length. The moment the encryption key leaks in the real world, he however has to output a uniformly looking key that makes his ciphertexts decrypt to the correct messages. Even knowing the messages by now, this is infeasible unless we assume a non-committing encryption scheme. Furthermore, as long as the requested key is shorter than n, Nielsen [19] showed that NCE cannot be achieved in the standard model by non-interactive protocols.

Of course one could avoid this impossibility by utilizing stronger primitives and/or assumptions, such as non-committing encryption. In some contexts, such as when considering deniability, their stronger guarantees might even be inherently necessary. In this work, we however pose the following question: How can we express the aforementioned security guarantees, that the encrypt-then-MAC paradigm using regular encryption intuitively does provide, in a composable framework? That is, rather than establishing a stronger security notion, we aim at expressing the exact guarantees provided by existing game-based notions.

3.3   Our Solution

So how to express the natural properties that are achieved? First, let us have another look at the reason for the impossibility: traditional simulation-based security notions require the simulator to commit to a ciphertext, emulating the encryption, based on the length only. Even if the simulator later gets to learn the entire message, it cannot come up with an encryption key that decrypts the previously output ciphertext to this message. Observe, however, that outputting the length only is just a technical way of expressing confidentiality until either one of the keys leak. In principle, there is no inherent requirement for a consistent simulation strategy across the different phases of the experiments. This is exactly what our proposal of interval-wise guarantees builds on: allowing disjoint simulation strategies for different phases of a protocol run. In other words, we simply make three disjoint security statements, one guaranteeing confidentiality and authenticity until either key is leaked, one only guaranteeing authenticity between the exposure of the encryption key and the MAC key, and one guaranteeing correct delivery of messages afterwards. Given the specification centric approach of Constructive Cryptography, this can be phrased as

$$\pi_{\mathsf{ENC}}\pi_{\mathsf{MAC}}[\mathsf{AuthKey}, \mathsf{EncKey}, \mathsf{InsecCh}] \subseteq \mathcal{S}_1 \cap \mathcal{S}_2 \cap \mathcal{S}_3,$$

where $\mathcal{S}_1$ to $\mathcal{S}_3$ are specifications formalizing the respective guarantees.

Phrasing separate statements can trivially be done in any framework, but also comes with a number of drawbacks. First, having to specify three constructions of unconnected, potentially differently described, specifications incurs a certain cognitive overhead, making the overall achieved security more demanding to understand. Second, and more severely, one loses some compositional properties. In particular, the analysis of another protocol building on top of those guarantees would require to make the exact same case distinction.

To overcome those drawbacks, we phrase each guarantee as an appropriate *interval-wise relaxation* of the same underlying resource: the downgradable secure channel. That is, we phrase security as

$$\pi_{\mathsf{ENC}}\pi_{\mathsf{MAC}}[\mathsf{AuthKey}, \mathsf{EncKey}, \mathsf{InsecCh}] \subseteq \mathsf{SecCh}^{\phi_1} \cap \mathsf{SecCh}^{\phi_2} \cap \mathsf{SecCh}^{\phi_3},$$

where ϕ_1 to ϕ_3 formalize the interval-wise relaxations. Another protocol can then simply assume the overly idealized downgradable secure channel SecCh, with our novel composition theorem taking care of devising the appropriate overall security statement. We formalize this type of relaxation and the corresponding composition theorem in the next section, i.e., Sect. 4.

Translating the approach to another composable framework, such as UC, might be feasible but non-trivial. First, one might try to formalize a single interval-wise guarantee as a different corruption model, where for instance the adversary simply does not get the encryption key to securely realize a functionality analogon to SecCh. To then compose this step with a SecCh-hybrid statement, one would probably require some compiler translating the statement. We, thus, believe that formalizing our results in CC that allows for arbitrary specifications is both simpler and more natural.

A remark on adaptive versus static security. Our security statement makes a static case separation on the intervals considered. This might raise the question as to how this differs from simply considering static corruptions only. We would like to stress that our statement is about a real-world system, where the environment gets to adaptively (depending on all the outputs it sees) choose when the appropriate keys are leaked. Hence, our notion lies somewhere in between the traditional notions of static and adaptive security.

To which extent our notion suffices in practice, and when a stronger traditional adaptive statement is required, is in our opinion an interesting open research problem. On the one hand, fully adaptively secure notions, without doubt, play a crucial role as a technical tool in many cryptographic constructions. On the other hand, very few cases are known where the overall security of an application actually seems to be meaningfully impacted by adaptiveness. For instance, consider the folklore example of an MPC protocol where an adversary knows which party she has to corrupt based on some observed value during the execution. Nevertheless, for a polynomially sized adversary structure (i.e., choices which parties to corrupt), the adversary could still guess upfront, implying that even traditional static security would suffice. This is for instance the case if there are only logarithmically (or constant) many parties overall.

Moreover, even if there super-polynomially many choices, it could still be that our interpretation of the static result is wrong: if we distinguish n static cases, and in each one of them a certain property is violated with probability ϵ, then all we can say is that by the union bound the probability of a property being violated is bounded by $n\epsilon$. Hence, concluding from ϵ being negligible that the protocol is overall secure, might simply not be sound in the first place.

A remark on stronger security guarantees. The primary goal of this work is to express the security guarantee of certain schemes in a composable framework, for which so far this has not been possible. This does not contradict stronger security notions, such as non-committing encryption, being of use as well. For instance, insisting that the simulator can explain the ciphertexts (in the traditional notion) formalizes that the ciphertexts are never of any value—in a broader sense than confidentiality. This might play an important role in advanced properties such as deniability, or e.g. in a scenario where an adversary wants to prove to another party that he managed to wiretap the channel before the transmitted message and the corresponding encryption key are publicly announced. Phrasing that no adversary can succeed requires the simulator to work beyond the public announcement, and achieving it requires non-committing encryption. Otherwise, committing to the ciphertext ahead of the public announcement should convince the other party.

4   Interval-Wise Guarantees: Definitions

In this section, we formalize interval-wise guarantees as a type of relaxation and provide the corresponding composition theorem. In the spirit of modularity, we proceed in several steps. First, we introduce one relaxation that waives all guarantees after a certain point, and second, the complementary one that waives all guarantees before a certain event. Third, we combine those relaxations and show that it fits well into the existing theory. Finally, we present the resulting construction notion and phrase the motivating example therein.

4.1   Guarantees up to Some Point

As we have seen in the motivational example, the confidentiality of the messages should be guaranteed *until* the key is leaked. To phrase this, we, on a high level, only require that the simulator works up to this event. We formalize this as a novel type of relaxation consisting of all systems behaving equally up to this point. To this end, for a resource R, we consider the modified resource that halts once a certain predicate on the global event history is satisfied.

Definition 4. *Let* R *denote a resource, and let* $P(\mathcal{E})$ *denote a monotone predicate on the global event history. That is, if* $\mathcal{E}$ *is a prefix of* $\mathcal{E}'$ *then* $P(\mathcal{E}) \rightarrow P(\mathcal{E}')$. *Then, we denote by* $\mathrm{until}_P(\mathsf{R})$ *the resource that behaves like* R *but halts the moment* $P(\mathcal{E})$ *becomes true. That is, it no longer triggers any further events and all subsequent (including the one for the query that triggered the condition) answers are the special symbol* $\perp$.

Getting back to our example, consider the resource $\mathrm{until}_P(\mathsf{SecCh})$ for $P(\mathcal{E}) :=$ $\mathcal{E}_{\mathsf{AuthKey}}^{\mathsf{leaked}} \vee \mathcal{E}_{\mathsf{EncKey}}^{\mathsf{leaked}}$, depicted in Fig. 2. Since this resource no longer produces any output once either event occurred, it clearly never leaks the messages to Eve and removes Eve's capability of injecting messages. Hence, the resulting resource closely matches the expected secure channel when ignoring key exposures.

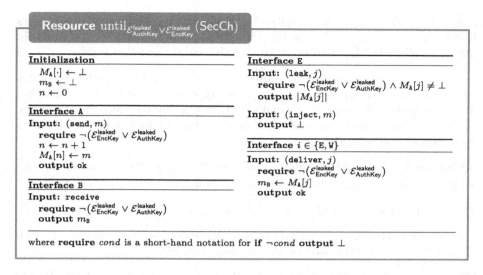

Fig. 2. The secure channel from Fig. 1 when halted once either key leaks. In contrast to the original one, this resource never leaks the actual messages.

We now define the according relaxation, which maps a system to the set of all systems that behave equivalently up to some event.

Definition 5. *Let P be a monotone predicate on the global event history, indicating until when the behavior must be the same as the one of the resource R. Then, the induced relaxation on a resource R, denoted $R^{P]}$, is defined as*

$$R^{P]} := \big\{ S \mid \mathrm{until}_P(R) = \mathrm{until}_P(S) \big\}$$

We call such a relaxation generally an until-relaxation.

As with the ϵ-relaxation, the statements only become reusable and thus truly composable if we understand how the until-relaxation interacts with the other elements of the framework. For this, first observe that equality up to some point is monotone, i.e., if two resources are equivalent up to some point, they are also equivalent up to every earlier point. This furthermore implies that two until-relaxations add up in the natural manner, as follows.

Theorem 4. *Let R and S be two resources, and let P_1 and P_2 be two monotone predicates. Then, we have*

$$\mathrm{until}_{P_1}(R) = \mathrm{until}_{P_1}(S) \implies \mathrm{until}_{P_1 \vee P_2}(R) = \mathrm{until}_{P_1 \vee P_2}(S).$$

In particular, for every specification $\mathcal{R}$, we have $\mathcal{R}^{P_1]} \subseteq \big(\mathcal{R}^{P_1]}\big)^{P_2]} \subseteq \mathcal{R}^{P_1 \vee P_2]}$.

Proof. The first property follows directly from the definition of the until() projection. In order to prove the second property, let $S \in \big(\mathcal{R}^{P_1]}\big)^{P_2]}$. Then, there exists $\mathsf{T} \in \mathcal{R}^{P_1]}$ such that $\mathrm{until}_{P_2}(\mathsf{S}) = \mathrm{until}_{P_2}(\mathsf{T})$. Moreover, there exists $\mathsf{R} \in \mathcal{R}$ such that $\mathrm{until}_{P_1}(\mathsf{T}) = \mathrm{until}_{P1}(\mathsf{R})$. By the first property we, thus, obtain $\mathrm{until}_{P_1 \vee P_2}(\mathsf{S}) = \mathrm{until}_{P_1 \vee P_2}(\mathsf{T}) = \mathrm{until}_{P_1 \vee P_2}(\mathsf{R})$, concluding the proof.   □

Furthermore, on a positive note, the relaxation is compatible with both protocol application and parallel composition, as expressed by the following theorem. Those compatibility properties—analogously to Corollary 1—also directly imply sequential and parallel composition properties. For the lack of use, we however omit explicitly stating them.

Theorem 5. *The until-relaxation is compatible with protocol attachment, i.e.,* $\pi(\mathcal{R}^{P]}) \subseteq (\pi\mathcal{R})^{P]}$ *and with parallel composition, i.e.,* $[\mathcal{R}^{P]}, \mathcal{S}] \subseteq [\mathcal{R}, \mathcal{S}]^{P]}$.

Proof. A proof is presented in the full version [9].

Unfortunately, however, the until-relaxation does not commute directly with the ϵ-relaxation, as expressed by the following theorem.

Theorem 6. *There exist specifications* $\mathcal{R}$ *and* $\mathcal{S}$, *a monotone predicate* P, *and a function* ϵ *mapping distinguishers to values in* $[0, 1]$ *such that*

$$(\mathcal{R}^{P]})^\epsilon \nsubseteq (\mathcal{R}^\epsilon)^{P]} \qquad \text{and} \qquad (\mathcal{S}^\epsilon)^{P]} \nsubseteq (\mathcal{S}^{P]})^\epsilon.$$

Proof. The proof can be found in the full version [9].

This not only raises the question which order actually corresponds to the intuitive interpretation of such a combination—the set of all systems which behave equally until the condition is triggered assuming the assumption of ϵ is valid—but also restricts reuse of such statement. That is, if one construction assumes $\mathcal{S}^{P]}$ to obtain $\mathcal{T}$, and another one constructs $\mathcal{S}^\epsilon$ instead, then adjusting the former construction to assume $\mathcal{S}^\epsilon$ instead is non-trivial. As a consequence, we will introduce a combined relaxation in Sect. 4.3, resolving both issues.

4.2 Guarantees From Some Point On

In this section, we now consider the complementing type of guarantees: guarantees that only hold from a certain point on. Formalizing such guarantees in a model where an adaptive environment interacts with the resource is, however, quite delicate. In this work, we thus opt for a rather simple (and restricted) version of it, where we use again a monotone condition on the global event history. We then define the projection that disables access to a system R before that condition is met. Clearly, the condition must rely on "external" events only (the ones not controlled by R), i.e., satisfying it must not require accessing the resource itself.

Definition 6. *Let* $P(\mathcal{E})$ *denote a monotone predicate on the global event history. For a resource* R, *let* $\mathrm{from}_P(\mathsf{R})$ *denote the resource that behaves like* R, *except that it only accepts queries once* $P(\mathcal{E})$ *is true (and before only returns* $\perp$*).*

For instance, the resource $\mathrm{from}_{\mathcal{E}_{\mathsf{EncKey}}^{\mathsf{leaked}}}(\mathsf{SecCh})$ only answers queries once the environment triggered the event $\mathcal{E}_{\mathsf{EncKey}}^{\mathsf{leaked}}$. Thus, in contrast to SecCh, this resource always leaks the full message of the adversary, in line with our intuition that it describes the behavior after the key has been exposed.

Based on this projection, we now introduce the corresponding relaxation.

Definition 7. *Let $P(\mathcal{E})$ be a monotone predicate, indicating from which point on the behavior must be the same as the one of the resource R. Then, the induced relaxation on a resource R, denoted $\mathsf{R}^{[P}$, is defined as*

$$\mathsf{R}^{[P} := \big\{ \mathsf{S} \mid \mathrm{from}_P(\mathsf{R}) = \mathrm{from}_P(\mathsf{S}) \big\}$$

We call such a relaxation generally a from-relaxation.

The way the from-relaxation interacts with the other elements of the theory is analogous to the until-relaxation. First, two from-relaxations add up naturally: if we relax the guarantees offered by a specification to only hold from the moment P_1 is satisfied, and then further relax them to only hold once P_2 is satisfied, then the guarantees only hold once $P_1 \wedge P_2$ is satisfied.

Theorem 7. *Let R and S be two resources, and let P_1 and P_2 be monotone predicates on the global event history. Then, we have*

$$\mathrm{from}_{P_1}(\mathsf{R}) = \mathrm{from}_{P_1}(\mathsf{S}) \implies \mathrm{from}_{P_1 \wedge P_2}(\mathsf{R}) = \mathrm{from}_{P_1 \wedge P_2}(\mathsf{S}).$$

In particular, for every specification $\mathcal{R}$, we have $\mathcal{R}^{[P_1} \subseteq \big(\mathcal{R}^{[P_1}\big)^{[P_2} \subseteq \mathcal{R}^{[P_1 \wedge P_2}$.

Proof. The proof is analogous to the one of Theorem 4.

Second, the relaxation is compatible with protocol application and parallel composition, which moreover implies that it graciously interacts with the basic construction notion.

Theorem 8. *The from-relaxation is compatible with protocol application, i.e., $\pi\big(\mathcal{R}^{[P}\big) \subseteq \big(\pi\mathcal{R}\big)^{[P}$ and with parallel composition, i.e., $\big[\mathcal{R}^{[P}, \mathcal{S}\big] \subseteq \big[\mathcal{R}, \mathcal{S}\big]^{[P}$.*

Proof. The proof is analogous to the one of Theorem 5.

Analogously to the until-relaxation, the from-relaxation, however, does not commute with the ϵ-relaxation.

Theorem 9. *There exist specifications $\mathcal{R}$ and $\mathcal{S}$, a monotone predicate $P(\mathcal{E})$, and a function ϵ mapping distinguishers to values in $[0, 1]$ such that*

$$\big(\mathcal{R}^{[P}\big)^{\epsilon} \not\subseteq \big(\mathcal{R}^{\epsilon}\big)^{[P} \quad \text{and} \quad \big(\mathcal{S}^{\epsilon}\big)^{[P} \not\subseteq \big(\mathcal{S}^{[P}\big)^{\epsilon}.$$

Proof. A proof can be found in the full version [9] of this report.

Finally, consider the interaction between the from- and the until-relaxation. While the from-projection and the until-projection commute, i.e.,

$$\mathrm{from}_{P_1}\big(\mathrm{until}_{P_2}(\mathsf{R})\big) = \mathrm{until}_{P_2}\big(\mathrm{from}_{P_1}(\mathsf{R})\big),$$

it is an interesting open question whether the two respective relaxations actually commute. As a consequence, we introduce a combined from-until relaxation in the next subsection.

4.3   The Interval-Wise Relaxation

As we have seen, the ϵ-relaxation commutes neither with the until-relaxation nor the from-relaxation, and its unclear whether the from- and until-relaxations do. This impedes modularity and reusability of the statements and also deteriorates their intuitive semantics: if for instance we want to express that a system behaves like a certain ideal up to some point, and under certain computational assumptions, which order of the relaxations is the right one and should be proven? To alleviate those issues, in this section, we introduce two combined relaxations that build on the atomic ones introduced in the previous section. We then show that they both have natural semantics and clean properties.

First, we consider a relaxation that combines the from- and until-relaxation, thereby alleviating the issue that those relaxations might not commute.

Definition 8. *Let $P_1(\mathcal{E})$ and $P_2(\mathcal{E})$ be two monotone predicates, indicating from when until when the resource must behave like* R. *We then define the following relaxation*

$$\mathsf{R}^{[P_1,P_2]} := \left\{ \mathsf{S} \mid \mathrm{until}_{P_2}(\mathrm{from}_{P_1}(\mathsf{R})) = \mathrm{until}_{P_2}(\mathrm{from}_{P_1}(\mathsf{S})) \right\}.$$

While this combined relaxation apparently neither corresponds to $\left(\mathsf{R}^{[P_1]}\right)^{P_2]}$ nor $\left(\mathsf{R}^{P_2]}\right)^{[P_1}$, it interestingly corresponds to the transitive closure thereof. Taking the transitive closure, moreover, also restores symmetry, i.e., $\mathsf{S} \in \mathsf{R}^{[P_1,P_2]} \Leftrightarrow \mathsf{R} \in \mathsf{S}^{[P_1,P_2]}$, lost by each of the two individual combinations. Overall, this indicates that the combined relaxation best corresponds to the intuition of the "almost-as-good" relation it should intuitively represent.

Theorem 10. *For any resource* R *and any monotone predicates P_1 and P_2, we have*

$$\mathsf{R}^{[P_1,P_2]} = \bigcup_{n \in \mathbb{N}} \left(\bigcup \{ \mathsf{R}^{\phi_1 \cdot \phi_2 \cdots \phi_n} \mid \forall i \leq n : \phi_i \in \{P_2], [P_1\} \} \right)$$
$$= \left(\left(\mathsf{R}^{[P_1}\right)^{P_2]}\right)^{[P_1} = \left(\left(\mathsf{R}^{P_2]}\right)^{[P_1}\right)^{P_2]},$$

where $\mathsf{R}^{\phi_1 \cdot \phi_2 \cdots \phi_n}$ is a shorthand notation for first applying ϕ_1, then ϕ_2, until ϕ_n.

Proof. The proof can be found in the full version [9].

We can now leverage this alternative definition to directly derive properties about the combined relaxations based on the proven properties of the two underlying ones. In particular, we can show that two such relaxations add up in the expected manner and are compatible with both protocol application as well as parallel composition.

Theorem 11. *For every specification $\mathcal{R}$, and all monotone predicates P_1, P_2, P_1', and P_2', we have $\left(\mathcal{R}^{[P_1,P_2]}\right)^{[P_1',P_2']} \subseteq \mathcal{R}^{[P_1 \wedge P_1', P_2 \vee P_2']}$.*

Proof. This follows directly by combining Theorems 4, 7 and 10.

Theorem 12. *The combined relaxation is both compatible with protocol application, i.e.,* $\pi\big(\mathcal{R}^{[P_1,P_2]}\big) \subseteq \big(\pi\mathcal{R}\big)^{[P_1,P_2]}$ *and with parallel composition, i.e.,* $\big[\mathcal{R}^{[P_1,P_2]}, \mathcal{S}\big] \subseteq \big[\mathcal{R}, \mathcal{S}\big]^{[P_1,P_2]}$.

Proof. By Theorem 10 we have that $\mathcal{R}^{[P_1,P_2]} = \Big(\big(\mathsf{R}^{[P_1]}\big)^{P_2]}\Big)^{[P_1}$. Using the compatibility of the from-relaxation and until-relaxation, i.e., Theorems 5 and 8, directly implies the desired properties.   □

As we have seen, neither the until- nor the from-relaxation commute with the computational ϵ-relaxation, and the same holds true for the from-until-relaxation as well. As a consequence, neither $(\mathsf{R}^{[P_1,P_2]})^\epsilon$ nor $(\mathsf{R}^\epsilon)^{[P_1,P_2]})$ seems to capture the set of all systems that behave like $\mathcal{R}$ in the interval $[P_1, P_2]$ assuming that the computational problem encoded in ϵ is hard. In the spirit of the combined from-until relaxation, we solve this issue by introducing a combined relation. Since the ϵ relaxation is not idempotent, but the epsilons add up, taking the transitive closure, however, does not match the desired relaxation but the following restricted version of transitive closure does.

Definition 9. *For two monotone predicates P_1 and P_2, and a function ϵ mapping distinguishers to values in $[0,1]$, we define the following relaxation:*

$$\mathsf{R}^{[P_1,P_2]:\epsilon} := \Big(\big(\mathsf{R}^{[P_1,P_2]}\big)^\epsilon\Big)^{[P_1,P_2]},$$

and call such a relaxation an interval-wise relaxation.

We now prove that the interval-wise relaxation has all the desired properties.

Theorem 13. *Let P_1 and P_2 be two monotone predicates, and let ϵ be a function mapping distinguishers to values in $[0,1]$. Then, for any specification $\mathcal{R}$ we have*

$$\big(\mathcal{R}^{[P_1,P_2]:\epsilon}\big)^{[P_1',P_2']:\epsilon'} \subseteq \mathcal{R}^{[P_1\wedge P_1', P_2\vee P_2']:\epsilon_{[P_1\wedge P_1', P_2\vee P_2']} + \epsilon'_{[P_1\wedge P_1', P_2\vee P_2']}},$$

where $\epsilon_{[P_1\wedge P_1', P_2\vee P_2']}(D) := \epsilon(\mathsf{D} \circ \mathrm{until}_{P_2\vee P_2'} \circ \mathrm{from}_{P_1\wedge P_1'})$, i.e., the performance of the distinguisher interacting with the projected resource, and analogously for $\epsilon'_{[P_1\wedge P_1', P_2\vee P_2']}$.

Proof. The proof can be found in the full version [9].

Theorem 14. *The interval-wise relaxation is compatible with protocol application, i.e.,* $\pi\big(\mathcal{R}^{[P_1,P_2]:\epsilon}\big) \subseteq \big(\pi\mathcal{R}\big)^{[P_1,P_2]:\epsilon_\pi}$ *and with parallel composition, i.e.,* $\big[\mathcal{R}^{[P_1,P_2]:\epsilon}, \mathcal{S}\big] \subseteq \big[\mathcal{R}, \mathcal{S}\big]^{[P_1,P_2]:\epsilon_\mathcal{S}}$.

Proof. By definition we have $\mathsf{R}^{[P_1,P_2]:\epsilon} := \Big(\big(\mathsf{R}^{[P_1,P_2]}\big)^\epsilon\Big)^{[P_1,P_2]}$. Using the compatibility of the ϵ-relaxation and the from-until-relaxation, i.e., Theorems 3 and 12, directly implies the result.

4.4   The Resulting Construction Notion

Based on the interval-wise relaxation, we now introduce our new construction notion. To this end, let Ω denote a set of tuples $(P_1, P_2, \epsilon, \boldsymbol{\sigma})$, where P_1 and P_2 are monotone predicates on the global event history, ϵ is a function mapping distinguishers to values in $[0, 1]$, and $\boldsymbol{\sigma}$ denotes a simulator. We then consider constructions of the following type:

$$\mathcal{R} \xrightarrow{\pi} \bigcap_{(P_1, P_2, \epsilon, \sigma) \in \Omega} (\boldsymbol{\sigma} \mathcal{S})^{[P_1, P_2]:\epsilon}.$$

That is, each element in Ω describes a time-interval in which the elements in $\pi \mathcal{R}$ can be abstracted as elements in $\mathcal{S}$—with respect to the simulator $\boldsymbol{\sigma}$ and error ϵ.

Application to the running example. In our example, we want to phrase that the symmetric encryption protocol constructs the secure channel from the authenticated one and the key in the corresponding intervals.

Proposition 6. *Let* $\pi_{\mathsf{ENC}} = (\pi_{\mathsf{enc}}, \pi_{\mathsf{dec}})$ *denote the protocol securing communication using a symmetric encryption scheme. Then, for the resources in Fig. 1, there exist (efficient) simulators* $\boldsymbol{\sigma}_1$, $\boldsymbol{\sigma}_2$, *and* $\boldsymbol{\sigma}_3$ *such that*

$$[\mathsf{EncKey}, \mathsf{AuthCh}] \xrightarrow{\pi_{\mathsf{ENC}}} \bigcap_{(P_1, P_2, \epsilon, \sigma) \in \Omega} (\boldsymbol{\sigma} \mathsf{SecCh})^{[P_1, P_2]:\epsilon}$$

for

$$\Omega := \big\{ \big(\mathsf{true}, \mathcal{E}^{\mathsf{leaked}}_{\mathsf{EncKey}} \vee \mathcal{E}^{\mathsf{leaked}}_{\mathsf{AuthKey}}, \epsilon_{\mathsf{CPA}}, \boldsymbol{\sigma}_1\big), \big(\mathcal{E}^{\mathsf{leaked}}_{\mathsf{EncKey}}, \mathsf{false}, 0, \boldsymbol{\sigma}_2\big),$$
$$\big(\mathcal{E}^{\mathsf{leaked}}_{\mathsf{AuthKey}}, \mathsf{false}, 0, \boldsymbol{\sigma}_3\big) \big\},$$

where ϵ_{CPA} *denotes a simple reduction from distinguishing the secure and authenticated channel (without key leakage) to the IND-CPA game.*

Proof. A proof sketch is presented in the full version [9] of this report.

Composition. Finally, we finish the section by stating the composition guarantees of this type of construction statement. It follows directly from the properties proven about the interval-wise relaxation in Theorems 13 and 14.

Theorem 15. *Let* $\mathcal{R}$, $\mathcal{S}$, *and* $\mathcal{T}$ *be arbitrary specifications, let* π *and* π' *be arbitrary protocols, and let* Ω *and* Ω' *be arbitrary interval-wise guarantees. Then, we have*

$$\mathcal{R} \xrightarrow{\pi} \bigcap_{(P_1, P_2, \epsilon, \sigma) \in \Omega} (\boldsymbol{\sigma} \mathcal{S})^{[P_1, P_2]:\epsilon} \quad \wedge \quad \mathcal{S} \xrightarrow{\pi'} \bigcap_{(P_1', P_2', \epsilon', \sigma') \in \Omega'} (\boldsymbol{\sigma}' \mathcal{T})^{[P_1', P_2']:\epsilon'}$$

$$\implies \mathcal{R} \xrightarrow{\pi' \circ \pi} \bigcap_{\substack{(P_1, P_2, \epsilon, \sigma) \in \Omega \\ (P_1', P_2', \epsilon', \sigma') \in \Omega'}} (\boldsymbol{\sigma} \boldsymbol{\sigma}' \mathcal{T})^{[P_1 \wedge P_1', P_2 \vee P_2']:\tilde{\epsilon}},$$

where $\tilde{\epsilon} := (\epsilon_{\pi'})_{[P_1 \wedge P_1', P_2 \vee P_2']} + (\epsilon'_{\sigma})_{[P_1 \wedge P_1', P_2 \vee P_2']}$. Furthermore, we have

$$\mathcal{R} \xrightarrow{\pi} \bigcap_{(P_1, P_2, \epsilon, \sigma) \in \Omega} (\sigma \mathcal{S})^{[P_1, P_2]:\epsilon} \implies [\mathcal{R}, \mathcal{T}] \xrightarrow{\pi} \bigcap_{(P_1, P_2, \epsilon, \sigma) \in \Omega} (\sigma [\mathcal{S}, \mathcal{T}])^{[P_1, P_2]:\epsilon_\mathcal{T}}.$$

Proof. The proof is stated in the full version [9]. □

Note that this construction notion subsumes all those previously introduced in this work. In particular, instantiating $P_1 = \texttt{true}$, $P_2 = \texttt{false}$, $\epsilon(\mathsf{D}) = 0$, and $\sigma = \mathsf{id}$, i.e., the identity converter, yields $(\mathsf{id}\mathcal{S})^{[\texttt{true}, \texttt{false}]:0} = \mathcal{S}$. As a consequence, the above composition theorem also allows to combine constructions according to each of the notions introduced in this work. For instance, in our example, we can compose the construction of AuthCh from Proposition 4 (according to the standard notion) with the interval-wise construction of SecCh from Proposition 6.

5 Application to Commitments and Coin-Tossing

In this section, we present a composable formalization of (perfectly binding) commitments that can be constructed in the plain model. To this end, we formalize the properties of commitment schemes—correctness, binding, and hiding—each as individual specifications. Thereby, hiding is formalized using the interval-wise guarantees introduced in the previous section. We then apply Blum's coin-tossing protocol on top of it. While, obviously, the resulting specifications are not sufficient to be used as a CRS, we show that it is unbiased.

5.1 Information-Theoretically Binding Commitments

While UC commitments [5] provide clean and strong guarantees, unfortunately they intrinsically require setup assumptions such as a common reference string. Nevertheless, for many protocols, regular commitments only satisfying the classical game-based properties seem to suffice. This raises the question: can we formalize a weaker yet composable security notion for (non-interactive) commitments?

In Constructive Cryptography, the security of a commitment scheme is formalized using three different constructions [16], for each set of potentially dishonest parties (ignoring the case of both parties being dishonest). Typically, this is presented as one construction parametrized in the set of honest parties, where the ideal specification consists of a filtered resource. That is, for each party P, a filter ϕ_P is specified that when connected to the resource limits the honest party's capabilities. However, there is no fundamental reason for those three construction statements' specifications to be of some unified type. As a result, we henceforth focus on specifying each property—hiding, binding, and correctness—individually, starting with correctness.

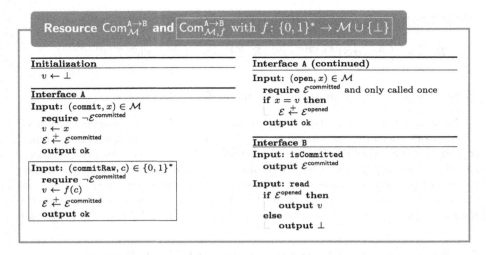

Fig. 3. The commitment resources for message space $\mathcal{M}$. In the basic version, Alice has to specify the value at the time of commitment, whereas in the unfiltered version she additionally has the ability to commit to $f(c)$.

Definition 10. *Let* $\pi_{\mathsf{com}} = (\pi_{\mathsf{com}}^{\mathsf{A}}, \pi_{\mathsf{com}}^{\mathsf{B}})$ *denote a non-interactive commitment protocol where* A *commits a value* $m \in \mathcal{M}$ *towards* B. *The scheme is said to be (perfectly)* correct *if*

$$\left[\mathsf{Ch}_1^{\mathsf{A} \to \mathsf{B}}, \mathsf{Ch}_2^{\mathsf{A} \to \mathsf{B}}\right] \xrightarrow{\pi_{\mathsf{com}}} \mathsf{Com}_{\mathcal{M}}^{\mathsf{A} \to \mathsf{B}},$$

where $\mathsf{Com}_{\mathcal{M}}^{\mathsf{A} \to \mathsf{B}}$ *denotes the commitment resource defined in Fig. 3, and* $\mathsf{Ch}_1^{\mathsf{A} \to \mathsf{B}}$ *and* $\mathsf{Ch}_2^{\mathsf{A} \to \mathsf{B}}$ *denote two single-message communications channels[3] from* A *to* B.

Now we proceed to formalize the hiding property. On an intuitive level, (computational) hiding of a non-interactive commitment scheme requires that the commitment string must not reveal any information about the committed value to the receiver B, until the commitment is opened. Clearly, we can directly apply our notion from Sect. 4 and formalize this using an interval-wise relaxation.

Definition 11. *Let* $\pi_{\mathsf{com}} = (\pi_{\mathsf{com}}^{\mathsf{A}}, \pi_{\mathsf{com}}^{\mathsf{B}})$ *denote a non-interactive commitment protocol. Then, the scheme is said to be (computationally)* hiding *if*

$$\left[\mathsf{Ch}_1^{\mathsf{A} \to \mathsf{B}}, \mathsf{Ch}_2^{\mathsf{A} \to \mathsf{B}}\right] \xrightarrow{\pi_{\mathsf{com}}^{\mathsf{A}}} \left(\sigma_{\mathsf{com}}^{\mathsf{B}} \mathsf{Com}_{\mathcal{M}}^{\mathsf{A} \to \mathsf{B}}\right)^{[\mathsf{true}, \mathcal{E}^{\mathsf{opened}}]:\epsilon},$$

for some simulator $\sigma_{\mathsf{com}}^{\mathsf{B}}$ *and some computational assumption encoded in* ϵ.

---

[3] That is, a channel that allows the sender to input a single message once. For simplicity, assume that the channel has guaranteed immediate delivery, i.e., whenever the sender has input a message, the receiver can fetch it.

The situation is more challenging with binding. The UC formalization, and analogously $\mathsf{Com}_{\mathcal{M}}^{A\to B}$, requires that the adversary inputs the value to which it commits to in the initial phase, in order to formalize that it then cannot be altered anymore. This, however implies that the simulator must be able to extract the value from the commitment string, fundamentally contradicting the hiding property in the plain model. Since such a formalization is just one (albeit convenient) manner to specify that the value is fixed at the end of the commitment phase, we circumvent this impossibility in another manner. To this end, we consider perfect (or information-theoretically secure) commitments only, where the commitment string uniquely determines the committed value. We leverage this considering a resource $\mathsf{Com}_{\mathcal{M},f}^{A\to B}$, depicted in Fig. 3, which allows the dishonest A to input an arbitrary string x in order to commit to the value $v = f(x)$. Here, $f\colon \{0,1\}^* \to \mathcal{M} \cup \{\bot\}$ denotes an arbitrary function that maps the commitment string either to a message m, or to $\bot$ indicating that it is malformed.

Definition 12. *Let* $\boldsymbol{\pi}_{\mathsf{com}} = (\pi_{\mathsf{com}}^A, \pi_{\mathsf{com}}^B)$ *denote a non-interactive commitment protocol where* A *commits a value* $m \in \mathcal{M}$ *towards* B*. Then, the scheme is said to be* perfectly binding *if there exists an efficient simulator* σ_{com}^A *such that*

$$\left[\mathsf{Ch}_1^{A\to B}, \mathsf{Ch}_2^{A\to B}\right] \xrightarrow{\pi_{\mathsf{com}}^B} \left\{\sigma_{\mathsf{com}}^A \mathsf{Com}_{\mathcal{M},f}^{A\to B} \mid f\colon \{0,1\}^* \to \mathcal{M} \cup \{\bot\}\right\},$$

where $\mathsf{Com}_{\mathcal{M},f}^{A\to B}$ *denotes the extended commitment resource defined in Fig. 3.*

As a side note, note that the resource $\mathsf{Com}_{\mathcal{M}}^{A\to B}$ can trivially be expressed as a filtered version of $\mathsf{Com}_{\mathcal{M},f}^{A\to B}$, where the filter ϕ_A removes access to the `commitRaw` oracle. That is, we obviously have $\phi_A \mathsf{Com}_{\mathcal{M},f}^{A\to B} = \mathsf{Com}_{\mathcal{M}}^{A\to B}$ for every function f.

Remark 1. Observe that the function f is not necessary efficiently computable. Actually, for a hiding scheme, f cannot be efficiently computable. This, however, does not imply that the overall specification has to contain resources that are not efficiently implementable, as clearly the real-world resource is efficient, and yet corresponds to $\sigma^A \mathsf{Com}_{\mathcal{M},f}^{A\to B}$ for an inefficient f. In other words, the decomposition, containing the inefficient resource, is just one way of describing an overall efficient resource. The specification could, thus, be restricted to consist of only efficient resources, which we did not make explicit here focusing only on the security properties. This is somewhat reminiscent of the solution proposed by Broadnax et al. [3] to deal with inefficient simulators in a manner that retains the expected composition guarantees.

ElGamal commitments. We briefly consider a variant of ElGamal commitments as a concrete instantiation of the above formalized notion. Let $\mathbb{G} = \langle g \rangle$ denote a cyclic group of order n with generator g.

- To commit to a message $m \in \mathbb{G}$, $((g^a, g^b, m \cdot g^{ab}), (a, b)) \leftarrow \mathrm{Commit}(m)$ for $a, b \in \mathbb{Z}_n$ uniformly at random. That is, the commitment string is $(g^a, g^b, m \cdot g^{ab})$ and the opening value (a, b).

– Open$((c, A, B), (a, b)) := c \cdot g^{-ab}$ if $A = g^a$ and $B = g^b$, and $\perp$ otherwise.

Proposition 7. *Let* $\pi_{\mathsf{EIG\text{-}com}}$ *denote the protocol, i.e., the pair of converters, implementing the aforementioned ElGamal commitment scheme. Then,* $\pi_{\mathsf{EIG\text{-}com}}$ *satisfies correctness, hiding (under the DDH assumption), and binding according to Definitions 10 to 12, respectively.*

Proof (Sketch). It is easy to see that the our correctness condition holds. Furthermore, with the simulator $\sigma^{\mathsf{B}}_{\mathsf{com}}$ outputting a random triple of group elements as commitment string, hiding holds under the DDH assumption, i.e., for ϵ encoding an appropriate reduction to the DDH problem. Finally, consider the function f that maps $(U, V, W) \in \mathbb{G}^3$ to $W \cdot g^{-\mathrm{DL}_g(U) \cdot \mathrm{DL}_g(V)}$ and all other bit-strings to $\perp$. For this function, it is easy to see that a simulator $\sigma^{\mathsf{A}}_{\mathsf{com}}$ exists such that the construction that formalizes binding holds. $\qquad\square$

5.2   Coin-Tossing

In this section, we consider Blum's simple coin-tossing protocol [2]. The protocol assumes to have a commitment resource from Alice to Bob, and a communication channel in the reverse direction, at its disposal. It then proceeds as follows: Alice chooses $X \in \{0, 1\}$ uniformly at random and commits to it. Once Bob is sure that Alice committed, he chooses $Y \in \{0, 1\}$ uniformly at random and sends it over to Alice (in clear). Finally, Alice opens the commitment and both parties output $Z = X \oplus Y$.

Clearly, this protocol does not provide fairness—even when instantiated with a UC-secure commitment. This is due to the fact that both parties can always choose to abort the protocol by not responding, and in particular Alice can do so *after* she has seen the result. When instantiating the commitment with the resource constructed in the last section, one even obtains a weaker resource. Note that this is inherent for our construction being in the plain model, as otherwise it could be used as the bit of a CRS, contradicting well-known impossibility results.

In a nutshell, the resource obtained by our construction guarantees that the output is not biased, but does not exclude that during the opening phase, one of the parties learns some trapdoor allowing it to distinguish it from a uniformly random value. For example, our formalization would allow the resulting bit to be the first bit of a PRG's output, while leaking the seed during the opening phase. Note that such a coin toss resource is still useful, for instance for lotteries. First, if the resulting bit is just used to determine which party gets some good, then bias-resistance is obviously good enough irrespective of the fact that the parties might be aware that the result is only pseudo-random. Second, in a simple lottery where people's preferences are obvious, fairness can be achieved by declaring the party that caused the abort to have lost.

The coin-toss resource. The ideal specification is expressed in terms of the resources $\mathsf{CT}^{\mathsf{A,B}}_{\mathcal{M}}$ and $\mathsf{CT}^{\mathsf{A,B}}_{\mathcal{M},f}$, where the former denotes a restricted version of

---

Resource $\mathsf{CT}_{\mathcal{M}}^{A,B}$ **and** $\boxed{\mathsf{CT}_{\mathcal{M},f}^{A,B}}$ **with** $f: \{0,1\}^* \to \mathcal{M} \cup \{\bot\}$

Initialization
  $Z \twoheadleftarrow \mathcal{M}$
  initiated, responded, released $\leftarrow$ false

Interface A
Input: init
  require $\neg \mathcal{E}^{\text{committed}}$
  initiated $\leftarrow$ true
  $\mathcal{E} \overset{+}{\leftarrow} \mathcal{E}^{\text{committed}}$
  output ok

Input: read
  require responded
  output Z

  Input: (getLeakage, c) $\in \mathcal{M}$
  require only called once
  output $f(c)$

Interface A (continued)
Input: release
  require responded and only called once
  $\mathcal{E} \overset{+}{\leftarrow} \mathcal{E}^{\text{opened}}$
  released $\leftarrow$ true
  output ok

Interface B
Input: isInitiated
  output initiated

Input: respond
  require initiated
  responded $\leftarrow$ true
  output ok

Input: read
  require released
  output Z

Fig. 4. The coin-toss resources for coin space $\mathcal{M}$. In the unfiltered version, Alice additionally has the capability to once obtain a leakage to $f(c)$, where f is a parameter of the resource. Note that neither version provides fairness, as Alice can always chooses to not release the value after having seen it.

the latter. The resource $\mathsf{CT}_{\mathcal{M}}^{A,B}$ initially draws an element $Z \in \mathcal{M}$ uniformly at random. In order for the coin-toss Z to become available to the parties, A has to initiate it, and B has to respond afterwards. From this point on, A can obtain Z and then decide whether the value should also be released to B. In the resource $\mathsf{CT}_{\mathcal{M},f}^{A,B}$, A furthermore can query once a leakage $f(c)$, of some potentially inefficient function f. A formal definition of the resources can be found in Fig. 4.

The constructions. First, consider correctness. It is easy to see that the following construction holds, i.e., two honest parties actually get to agree on a uniform random bit.

Proposition 8. *Let* $\boldsymbol{\pi}_{\mathsf{CT}} := (\pi_{\mathsf{CT}}^{A}, \pi_{\mathsf{CT}}^{B})$ *denote the pair of converters implementing Blum's protocol. Then, we have*

$$\left[\mathsf{Com}_{\{0,1\}}^{A \to B}, \mathsf{Ch}^{B \to A}\right] \xrightarrow{\boldsymbol{\pi}_{\mathsf{CT}}} \mathsf{CT}_{\{0,1\}}^{A,B},$$

and thus

$$\left[\mathsf{Ch}_1^{A \to B}, \mathsf{Ch}_2^{A \to B}, \mathsf{Ch}^{B \to A}\right] \xrightarrow{\boldsymbol{\pi}_{\mathsf{CT}} \circ \boldsymbol{\pi}_{\mathsf{com}}} \mathsf{CT}_{\{0,1\}}^{A,B},$$

for any commitment scheme $\boldsymbol{\pi}_{\mathsf{com}}$ *satisfying Definition 10 (correctness).*

Second, consider the guarantee for an honest initiator A.

Proposition 9. *Let* $\pi_{\mathsf{CT}} := (\pi^{\mathsf{A}}_{\mathsf{CT}}, \pi^{\mathsf{B}}_{\mathsf{CT}})$ *denote the pair of converters implementing Blum's protocol. Then, there exists an efficient simulator* $\sigma^{\mathsf{B}}_{\mathsf{CT}}$ *such that*

$$\left[\mathsf{Com}^{\mathsf{A}\to\mathsf{B}}_{\{0,1\}}, \mathsf{Ch}^{\mathsf{B}\to\mathsf{A}}\right] \xrightarrow{\ \pi^{\mathsf{A}}_{\mathsf{CT}}\ } \sigma^{\mathsf{B}}_{\mathsf{CT}}\mathsf{CT}^{\mathsf{A},\mathsf{B}}_{\{0,1\}},$$

and thus, for any commitment scheme π_{com} *satisfying Definition 11 (hiding), we have*

$$\left[\mathsf{Ch}^{\mathsf{A}\to\mathsf{B}}_{1}, \mathsf{Ch}^{\mathsf{A}\to\mathsf{B}}_{2}, \mathsf{Ch}^{\mathsf{B}\to\mathsf{A}}\right] \xrightarrow{\ \pi^{\mathsf{A}}_{\mathsf{CT}}\circ\pi^{\mathsf{A}}_{\mathsf{com}}\ } \left(\sigma^{\mathsf{B}}_{\mathsf{com}}\sigma^{\mathsf{B}}_{\mathsf{CT}}\mathsf{CT}^{\mathsf{A},\mathsf{B}}_{\{0,1\}}\right)^{[\mathsf{true},\mathcal{E}^{\mathsf{opened}}]:\tilde{\epsilon}},$$

with $\tilde{\epsilon} := \left(\epsilon_{\sigma^{\mathsf{B}}_{\mathsf{CT}}}\right)_{[\mathsf{true},\mathcal{E}^{\mathsf{opened}}]}$.

Proof. Recall that $\mathsf{Com}^{\mathsf{A}\to\mathsf{B}}_{\{0,1\}}$ only reveals the value X to Bob after he sent his value Y. Hence, X and Y are independent and with X chosen uniform at random by Alice, implying that $Z = X \oplus Y$ is a uniform random value. Hence, using the simple simulator $\sigma^{\mathsf{B}}_{\mathsf{CT}}$ that simulates the output of the commitment resource as $X := Z \oplus Y$, it is easy to see that the construction actually achieves the coin-toss resource perfectly. □

Note that this implies that the output Z that Alice obtains looks indistinguishable from a uniform random value until the value is released for the dishonest party. Hence, while it is not guaranteed that the dishonest party does not learn some trapdoor afterwards, the value Z is at least unbiased.

Finally, consider the security guarantees for an honest party B against a potentially dishonest party A. To this end, we turn to the unfiltered resources $\mathsf{Com}^{\mathsf{A}\to\mathsf{B}}_{\{0,1\},f}$ and $\mathsf{CT}^{\mathsf{A},\mathsf{B}}_{\{0,1\},f}$, where the latter once allows Alice to obtain $f(c)$ for a c of her choice.

Proposition 10. *Let* $\pi_{\mathsf{CT}} := (\pi^{\mathsf{A}}_{\mathsf{CT}}, \pi^{\mathsf{B}}_{\mathsf{CT}})$ *denote the pair of converters implementing Blum's protocol. Then, there exists an efficient simulator* $\sigma^{\mathsf{A}}_{\mathsf{CT}}$ *such that*

$$\left\{\left[\mathsf{Com}^{\mathsf{A}\to\mathsf{B}}_{\{0,1\},f}, \mathsf{Ch}^{\mathsf{B}\to\mathsf{A}}\right] \mid f\colon \{0,1\}^* \to \{0,1,\perp\}\right\}$$

$$\xrightarrow{\ \pi^{\mathsf{B}}_{\mathsf{CT}}\ } \left\{\sigma^{\mathsf{A}}_{\mathsf{CT}}\mathsf{CT}^{\mathsf{A},\mathsf{B}}_{\{0,1\},f} \mid f\colon \{0,1\}^* \to \{0,1,\perp\}\right\},$$

and thus, for any commitment scheme π_{com} *satisfying Definition 12 (binding), we have*

$$\left[\mathsf{Ch}^{\mathsf{A}\to\mathsf{B}}_{1}, \mathsf{Ch}^{\mathsf{A}\to\mathsf{B}}_{2}, \mathsf{Ch}^{\mathsf{B}\to\mathsf{A}}\right] \xrightarrow{\ \pi^{\mathsf{B}}_{\mathsf{CT}}\circ\pi^{\mathsf{B}}_{\mathsf{com}}\ } \left\{\sigma^{\mathsf{A}}_{\mathsf{com}}\sigma^{\mathsf{A}}_{\mathsf{CT}}\mathsf{CT}^{\mathsf{A},\mathsf{B}}_{\{0,1\},f} \mid f\colon \{0,1\}^* \to \{0,1,\perp\}\right\}.$$

Proof. Consider the real-world system resulting from attaching Bob's converter only, for some function f. Interacting with this resource, the environment can input a commitment string C at Alice's interface, then see Bob's bit Y at Alice's channel interface, and finally see the resulting bit $Z = f(C) \oplus Y$ as the output of Bob's converter. In the following, consider the ideal-world system with the same function f as in the real world. It is now easy to see that a simulator can easily replicate the real-world behavior by getting Z from the resource, querying the leakage-oracle on C getting $f(C)$, and then setting $Y = Z \oplus f(C)$. □

As a final note, observe that formalizing Bob's security guarantees for the commitment resource in terms of an interval-wise relaxation, rather than introducing the unfiltered resource $CT^{A,B}_{\{0,1\},f}$, would not work. This is due to the fact that in the real world Y (requiring the additional capabilities to simulate) is output at Alice's interface before Bob sees Z. Hence, simulating only until Alice sends Y would not give any guarantees on Bob's output. In summary, this demonstrates Constructive Cryptography's advantage of being able to consider different types of statements within one (meta-)framework.

6 Conclusion and Future Work

We have demonstrated that considering new types of resource specifications can lead to security notions that are composable, yet do not suffer the artificial impossibilities exhibited by the classical simulation-based definitions. We have introduced a type of specification that formalizes guarantees that hold in a certain time-interval (between two events), which has clean semantics, comes with a natural syntactical composition theorem, and integrates well with the existing Constructive Cryptography framework.

While our novel type of relaxation does not resolve every issue of composable security, we ultimately believe that all (meaningful) security statements can be expressed as an as assumed specification being contained in an ideal one. Further work is, hence, needed to identify additional types of specifications that allow to express more properties—while retaining strong syntactical composition rules and clear semantics.

References

1. Backes, M., Dürmuth, M., Hofheinz, D., Küsters, R.: Conditional reactive simulatability. In: Gollmann, D., Meier, J., Sabelfeld, A. (eds.) ESORICS 2006. LNCS, vol. 4189, pp. 424–443. Springer, Heidelberg (2006). https://doi.org/10.1007/11863908_26
2. Blum, M.: Coin flipping by telephone a protocol for solving impossible problems. SIGACT News **15**(1), 23–27 (1983). https://doi.org/10.1145/1008908.1008911
3. Broadnax, B., Döttling, N., Hartung, G., Müller-Quade, J., Nagel, M.: Concurrently composable security with shielded super-polynomial simulators. In: Coron, J.-S., Nielsen, J.B. (eds.) EUROCRYPT 2017. LNCS, vol. 10210, pp. 351–381. Springer, Cham (2017). https://doi.org/10.1007/978-3-319-56620-7_13
4. Canetti, R.: Universally composable security: a new paradigm for cryptographic protocols. In: 42nd IEEE Symposium on Foundations of Computer Science - FOCS 2001, pp. 136–145. IEEE Computer Society (2001)
5. Canetti, R., Fischlin, M.: Universally composable commitments. In: Kilian, J. (ed.) CRYPTO 2001. LNCS, vol. 2139, pp. 19–40. Springer, Heidelberg (2001). https://doi.org/10.1007/3-540-44647-8_2
6. Canetti, R., Krawczyk, H.: Universally composable notions of key exchange and secure channels. In: Knudsen, L.R. (ed.) EUROCRYPT 2002. LNCS, vol. 2332, pp. 337–351. Springer, Heidelberg (2002). https://doi.org/10.1007/3-540-46035-7_22

7. Demay, G., Gaži, P., Maurer, U., Tackmann, B.: Per-session security: password-based cryptography revisited. In: Foley, S.N., Gollmann, D., Snekkenes, E. (eds.) ESORICS 2017. LNCS, vol. 10492, pp. 408–426. Springer, Cham (2017). https://doi.org/10.1007/978-3-319-66402-6_24

8. Hofheinz, D., Matt, C., Maurer, U.: Idealizing identity-based encryption. In: Iwata, T., Cheon, J.H. (eds.) ASIACRYPT 2015. LNCS, vol. 9452, pp. 495–520. Springer, Heidelberg (2015). https://doi.org/10.1007/978-3-662-48797-6_21

9. Jost, D., Maurer, U.: Overcoming impossibility results in composable security using interval-wise guarantees. Cryptology ePrint Archive, Report 2020/092 (2020). https://eprint.iacr.org/2020/092

10. Jost, D., Maurer, U., Mularczyk, M.: A unified and composable take on ratcheting. In: Hofheinz, D., Rosen, A. (eds.) TCC 2019. LNCS, vol. 11892, pp. 180–210. Springer, Cham (2019). https://doi.org/10.1007/978-3-030-36033-7_7

11. Kuesters, R., Tuengerthal, M., Rausch, D.: The iitm model: a simple and expressive model for universal composability. Cryptology ePrint Archive, Report 2013/025 (2013). https://eprint.iacr.org/2013/025

12. Lindell, Y.: General composition and universal composability in secure multiparty computation. J. Cryptology **22**(3), 395–428 (2009)

13. Maurer, U.: Constructive cryptography – a new paradigm for security definitions and proofs. In: Mödersheim, S., Palamidessi, C. (eds.) TOSCA 2011. LNCS, vol. 6993, pp. 33–56. Springer, Heidelberg (2012). https://doi.org/10.1007/978-3-642-27375-9_3

14. Maurer, U.: Indistinguishability of random systems. In: Knudsen, L.R. (ed.) EUROCRYPT 2002. LNCS, vol. 2332, pp. 110–132. Springer, Heidelberg (2002). https://doi.org/10.1007/3-540-46035-7_8

15. Maurer, U., Pietrzak, K., Renner, R.: Indistinguishability amplification. In: Menezes, A. (ed.) CRYPTO 2007. LNCS, vol. 4622, pp. 130–149. Springer, Heidelberg (2007). https://doi.org/10.1007/978-3-540-74143-5_8

16. Maurer, U., Renner, R.: Abstract cryptography. In: Innovations in Computer Science - ICS 2011, pp. 1–21. Tsinghua University (2011)

17. Maurer, U., Renner, R.: From indifferentiability to constructive cryptography (and back). In: Hirt, M., Smith, A. (eds.) TCC 2016. LNCS, vol. 9985, pp. 3–24. Springer, Heidelberg (2016). https://doi.org/10.1007/978-3-662-53641-4_1

18. Maurer, U., Tackmann, B.: On the soundness of authenticate-then-encrypt: formalizing the malleability of symmetric encryption. In: Keromytis, A.D., Shmatikov, V. (eds.) Proceedings of the 17th ACM Conference on Computer and Communication Security, pp. 505–515. ACM, October 2010

19. Nielsen, J.B.: Separating random oracle proofs from complexity theoretic proofs: the non-committing encryption case. In: Yung, M. (ed.) CRYPTO 2002. LNCS, vol. 2442, pp. 111–126. Springer, Heidelberg (2002). https://doi.org/10.1007/3-540-45708-9_8

20. Pass, R.: Simulation in quasi-polynomial time, and its application to protocol composition. In: Biham, E. (ed.) EUROCRYPT 2003. LNCS, vol. 2656, pp. 160–176. Springer, Heidelberg (2003). https://doi.org/10.1007/3-540-39200-9_10

21. Pfitzmann, B., Waidner, M.: A model for asynchronous reactive systems and its application to secure message transmission. In: Proceedings 2001 IEEE Symposium on Security and Privacy - S&P 2001, pp. 184–200, May 2001. https://doi.org/10.1109/SECPRI.2001.924298

22. Prabhakaran, M., Sahai, A.: New notions of security: achieving universal composability without trusted setup. In: Proceedings of the Thirty-Sixth Annual ACM Symposium on Theory of Computing, STOC 2004, pp. 242–251. ACM, New York (2004). https://doi.org/10.1145/1007352.1007394

Indifferentiability for Public Key Cryptosystems

Mark Zhandry[1,2](✉) and Cong Zhang[3](✉)

[1] Princeton University, Princeton, USA
mzhandry@princeton.edu
[2] NTT Research, Palo Alto, USA
[3] Rutgers University, New Brunswick, USA
cz200@cs.rutgers.edu

Abstract. We initiate the study of indifferentiability for public key encryption and other public key primitives. Our main results are definitions and constructions of public key cryptosystems that are indifferentiable from ideal cryptosystems, in the random oracle model. Cryptosystems include:
- Public key encryption;
- Digital signatures;
- Non-interactive key agreement.

Our schemes are based on relatively standard public key assumptions. By being indifferentiable from an ideal object, our schemes automatically satisfy a wide range of security properties, including any property representable as a single-stage game, and can be composed to operate in higher-level protocols.

Keywords: Indifferentiability · Composition · Public key encryption · Random oracle model · Ideal cipher model

1 Introduction

When designing a cryptographic system, it is difficult to predict how it will be used in practice and what security properties will be required of it. For example, if the larger system produces certain error messages, this can lead to chosen ciphertext attacks [6]. Perhaps a message is encrypted using random coins which themselves are derived from the message, as is used for de-duplication [28]. Maybe the secret key itself will be encrypted by the system, as is sometimes used in disk encryption. Or perhaps there was bad randomness generation on the hardware device, leading to secret keys or encryption randomness that is low-entropy or correlated across many instances.

Cryptographers have devised different security models to capture each of the scenarios above and more, each requiring different constructions to satisfy. However, seldom are these different security models considered in tandem, meaning that each application scenario may require a different scheme. Even worse, there are many potential security models that have yet to be considered; after all, it is

© International Association for Cryptologic Research 2020
D. Micciancio and T. Ristenpart (Eds.): CRYPTO 2020, LNCS 12170, pp. 63–93, 2020.
https://doi.org/10.1007/978-3-030-56784-2_3

difficult to predict the various applications devised by software developers that may deviate from the existing provably secure uses.

With the above in mind, our goal is to develop a *single* construction for a given cryptographic concept that simultaneously captures any reasonable security property and can be composed to work in any reasonable larger protocol. As such, only a single instance of the scheme needs to be developed and then deployed in a variety of use cases, even those that have not yet been discovered.

Ideal Hash Functions: The Random Oracle Model. Our inspiration will be the random oracle model (ROM) [4], a common heuristic used in cryptography. Here, a hash function is assumed to be so well designed that the only reasonable attacks simply evaluate the hash function as a black box and gain nothing by trying to exploit the particular design. To capture this, the hash function is modeled as a truly random function, accessible by making queries to the function.

A random oracle truly is the "ideal" hash function: it is trivially one-way and collision resistant, the standard security notions for hash functions. But it is also much stronger: it is correlation intractable [7], a good extractor even for computational sources, and much more. When used in a larger system, random oracles can yield provably secure schemes even when standard security properties for hash functions are insufficient. In fact, the most efficient schemes in practice are often only known to be secure using random oracles. As such, the ROM is ubiquitous in cryptography.

Other idealized models have been studied before. Examples include the ideal cipher model [25], the generic group model [26], and more recently ideal *symmetric* key encryption [2]. However, no prior work considers idealized models for public key cryptosystems.

Ideal Public Key Cryptosystems. In this work, we define and construct the first ideal *public key* cryptosystems such as public key encryption and digital signatures. By being ideal, our schemes will immediately satisfy a wide class of security properties, including most studied in the literature. Our schemes will be proven to be ideal in the random oracle model using Maurer's indifferentiability framework [20], under general computational assumptions. We also show that certain classic relations among cryptographic objects also hold in the ideal setting, while discussing cases where such relations fail.

Our goal comes with interesting challenges: on one hand, public key schemes tend to require number-theoretic structure in order to attain the necessary functionality. On the other hand, ideal schemes by definition have essentially no structure. Therefore, our results require novel techniques, including bringing indifferentiability into the public key setting.

1.1   What Is an Ideal Public Key Scheme?

Now, we turn to our results. Our first result is to define, precisely, what an "ideal" public key cryptosystem is. For simplicity, in the following discussion, we will consider the case of two-party non-interactive key exchange (NIKE). Such a scheme consists of two algorithms. KEYGEN is a key generation algorithm run by each of two users. We will adopt the convention that the input to KEYGEN is the user's secret key SK, and the output is the corresponding public key PK. The two users then exchange their public keys. They then run SHAREDKEY to extract a common shared key. SHAREDKEY will take as input the public key for one user and the secret key for the other, and output a shared key K. The correctness requirement is that both users arrive at the same key:

$$\text{SHAREDKEY}(\text{PK}_1, \text{SK}_2) = \text{SHAREDKEY}(\text{PK}_2, \text{SK}_1),$$

whenever $\text{PK}_1 = \text{KEYGEN}(\text{SK}_1)$ and $\text{PK}_2 = \text{KEYGEN}(\text{SK}_2)$.

Any NIKE scheme will have the syntax above and the same correctness requirement. On the other hand, any given NIKE scheme may have additional structural properties that make it insecure in certain settings. For example, if multiple shared keys are generated using the same public key PK for a given user, the resulting shared keys may be correlated in some algebraic way. In order to be secure in the widest variety of settings, an ideal NIKE scheme should therefore not have any such additional structure over the minimum needed to ensure correctness.

In the case of existing idealized models, the idealization is simply a uniformly random choice of procedures subject to the mandatory correctness requirements. For example, a hash function has no correctness requirement except for determinism; as such its idealization is a random oracle. Likewise, a block cipher must be a (keyed) permutation, and the decryption functionality must be its inverse. As such, the ideal cipher is a random keyed permutation and its inverse.

Therefore, the natural way to model an ideal NIKE scheme is to have all algorithms be random functions. Of course, the correctness requirement means that there will be correlations between the algorithms. We take an ideal NIKE scheme to be two oracles KEYGEN, SHAREDKEY such that:

- KEYGEN(SK) is a random injection;
- SHAREDKEY(PK, SK) is a random function, except that $\text{SHAREDKEY}(\text{PK}_1, \text{SK}_2) = \text{SHAREDKEY}(\text{PK}_2, \text{SK}_1)$ whenever $\text{PK}_1 = \text{KEYGEN}(\text{SK}_1)$ and $\text{PK}_2 = \text{KEYGEN}(\text{SK}_2)$[1].

We emphasize that all functions are public and visible to the attacker and the formal definition for ideal NIKE is given in Sect. 3.1.

1.2 Indifferentiability

Of course, just like a random oracle/generic group/ideal cipher, ideal NIKE cannot exist in the real world. This then begs the question: how do we design and rigorously argue that a NIKE scheme is so well designed that it can be treated as an ideal NIKE scheme in applications?

---

[1] By the injectivity of KEYGEN, this is still a well-defined function.

Barbosa and Farshim [2] offer one possible answer. They build a symmetric key encryption scheme from a hash function. Then, they show, roughly, that if the hash function is ideal (that is, a random oracle), then so is their scheme. Our goal in this work will be to do the same for public key schemes: to build an ideal NIKE scheme assuming that a hash function H is a random oracle.

As in [2], formal justification of ideal security requires care. Suppose we have a construction of an ideal NIKE scheme (KEYGEN, SHAREDKEY) in the random oracle model, meaning each of the algorithms makes queries to a random function H. In the case where H is *hidden* to the adversary, such a construction is almost trivial, and would essentially reduce to building symmetric key encryption from a PRF. However, Maurer, Renner, and Holenstein [20] observed that this is *not* enough, since H is a *public* function and the adversary can query H as well.

Clearly, any construction (KEYGEN, SHAREDKEY) will now be distinguishable from the idealized algorithms, since the adversary can evaluate the algorithms for himself by making queries to H, and checking if the results are consistent with the oracles provided. Instead, what is needed is the stronger notion of *indifferentiability*, which says that when (KEYGEN, SHAREDKEY) are ideal, it is possible to *simulate* H by a simulator S which can make queries to (KEYGEN, SHAREDKEY). In the real world, (KEYGEN, SHAREDKEY) are constructed from H per the specification. In the ideal world, (KEYGEN, SHAREDKEY) are the idealized objects, and H is simulated by making queries to the ideal objects. Indifferentiability requires that the two worlds are indistinguishable to an adversary that gets access to all the oracles.

Maurer, Renner, and Holenstein shows that indifferentiability has many desirable properties: it composes well and will be *as good as* the ideal object in many settings (see Sect. 1.3 below for some limitations).

Therefore, our goal will be to build NIKE which is indifferentiable from ideal NIKE in the random oracle model. As indifferentiability has mostly been used in the symmetric key setting, this will require new techniques to bring indifferentiability into the public key world. Indeed, most works on indifferentiability build ideal objects with minimal correctness requirements: none in the case of random oracles, and bijectivity/injectivity in the case of ideal ciphers/symmetric key encryption. The case of public key cryptosystems requires significantly more structure for correctness. In fact, we face an immediate theoretical barrier: Impagliazzo and Rudich [17] demonstrate that a random oracle is incapable of constructing something as structured as public key encryption, even ignoring the strong indifferentiability requirement.

Instead, we will obtain our needed structure using public key tools. However, public key tools come with *too much* structure: every term has an algebraic meaning which is not present in the idealized setting. Therefore, our goal will actually be to employ a novel combination of public key techniques *together with* random oracles in order to eliminate this extra structure. The result will be an indifferentiable NIKE scheme.

1.3   Discussion

Limitations. Before giving our constructions in detail, we briefly discuss limitations. Most importantly, idealized cryptosystems do not exist in the real world. Even more, Canetti, Goldreich, and Halevi [7] demonstrate that no concrete instantiation in the standard model is "as good as" an ideal object. Therefore, idealizations of cryptographic primitives are only heuristic evidence for security.

Nevertheless, the counter-examples are usually somewhat contrived, and do not apply in typical real-world settings. Indeed, in the case of hash functions, significant resources have been invested in analyzing their security, and the best attacks typically treat the hash function as a random oracle[2]. As such, the random oracle appears to be a reasonable approximation to the real world in most settings. By building schemes from such strong hash functions and proving security using indifferentiability, such schemes are essentially "as good as" the ideal schemes, assuming the underlying hash function is ideal.

In fact, the random oracle model is widely used for the construction of new cryptosystems, as it allows security to be justified where no obvious concrete security property for hash functions would suffice. In these cases, the system is typically proven to satisfy the single security property considered. In our case, we are able to rely on the same heuristic treatment of hash functions, and attain ideal security.

Now, Ristenpart, Shacham, and Shrimpton [22] demonstrate the limitations of the indifferentiability framework. In particular, they show that indifferentiability is *insufficient* for proving security properties defined by *multi-stage* games. While this potentially precludes certain applications, indifferentiability is still sufficient to prove many security properties such as CCA-security, key-dependent-message and circular security in restricted settings (see [2] for discussion), bounded leakage resilience, and more. We also note that if all but one of the stages are independent of the ideal primitives, then indifferentiability is sufficient. This captures, for example, the usual modeling of deterministic public key encryption in the random oracle model [3]. Even more, in the case where multiple stages depend on the ideal primitives, Mittelbach [21] shows that indifferentiability is sufficient in some settings.

We leave as an interesting direction for future work building ideal public key schemes that can be proven secure in stronger models of indifferentiability such as reset indifferentiability [22] or context-restricted indifferentiability [19].

1.4   Constructing Ideal NIKE

We now turn to our constructions. Our goal will be to combine a *standard model* NIKE (keygen, sharedkey)—one with concrete mild security properties that are easy to instantiate—with random oracles to obtain an ideal model NIKE (KEYGEN, SHAREDKEY).

---

[2] There are actually several exceptions, for instance, the length-extension attacks against various Merkle-Damgard-based hash functions, such as MD5.

Making KEYGEN *indifferentiable.* First, we will focus just on KEYGEN, which on its own must be indifferentiable from a random injection. Of course, we could just set KEYGEN to be a random oracle[3], but we want to somehow incorporate keygen so that it can provide the structure needed when we turn to construct SHAREDKEY. Nevertheless, a random oracle (or some other idealized object) is needed somewhere in the construction. As a first attempt, we could consider defining KEYGEN(SK) = H(keygen(SK)), hashing the output of keygen to eliminate any structure on the public keys. This, unfortunately, does not work. For example, keygen may not be collision resistant, and any collision for keygen will therefore give a collision for KEYGEN. The resulting KEYGEN would then clearly be distinguishable from a random function without even making queries to H.

Attack 1. Even if we assume keygen was collision resistant, the scheme would still not be indifferentiable. Indeed, the attacker can query KEYGEN(SK), evaluate pk = keygen(SK) for itself, and then query H on pk. The simulator now has to simulate H, and for indifferentiability to hold it must know how to set H(pk) = KEYGEN(SK). However, the simulator only gets to see pk and somehow must query KEYGEN on SK. Extracting SK from pk involves breaking the original NIKE, which is presumably intractable.

A different approach would be to define KEYGEN(SK) = keygen(H(SK)). The problem here is that keygen may output very structured public keys, which are clearly distinguishable from random. One possibility is to assume keygen has pseudorandom public keys; that is, that keygen applied to uniformly random coins gives a pseudorandom output.

Attack 2. However, we still have a problem. Indeed, suppose the adversary queries KEYGEN(SK), which in the ideal world will give a random string. Then the adversary queries H(SK). In the ideal world, the simulator must set H(SK) = r such that keygen(r) = KEYGEN(SK). This may be flat out impossible (in the case where the range of keygen is sparse), and at a minimum requires inverting keygen, again breaking the security of the NIKE scheme.

A third approach which does work is to combine the two: KEYGEN(SK) = H_1(keygen(H_0(SK))). Now both H_0, H_1 are random oracles that are simulated by the simulator. This actually gives indifferentiability: when the adversary queries H_0(SK), the simulator will program H_0(SK) = r for a randomly chosen r. Then it will program H_1(keygen(r)) = KEYGEN(SK) by querying KEYGEN. The only way a problem can arise is if the input keygen(r) was already programmed in H_1. All that we need to exclude such a possibility is that keygen is well-spread: that the distribution of outputs given a uniformly random input has high min-entropy. This follows easily from the security of the NIKE protocol.

The takeaway from the above discussion is that inputs and outputs for a standard-model scheme must be processed by idealized objects; this is the only way that the simulator can obtain enough information to be indifferentiable.

---

[3] By having the random oracle be sufficiently expanding, it will be an injection with high probability.

Making SHAREDKEY *Indifferentiable.* Next, we move to define SHAREDKEY in a way to make the joint oracles (KEYGEN, SHAREDKEY) indifferentiable from an ideal NIKE protocol.

Unfortunately, we immediately run into problems. We somehow need to design the shared-key algorithm SHAREDKEY to take as input one public key $PK_1 = H_1(\mathsf{keygen}(H_0(SK_1)))$, as well as another secret key SK_2. It will output a shared key K. Importantly, we need to maintain the correctness requirement that $\mathsf{SHAREDKEY}(PK_1, SK_2) = \mathsf{SHAREDKEY}(PK_2, SK_1)$ whenever $PK_1 = \mathsf{KEYGEN}(SK_1)$ and $PK_2 = \mathsf{KEYGEN}(SK_2)$.

Guided by Impagliazzo and Rudich's [17] barrier, we cannot rely on the functionalities of the random oracles H_0, H_1 for this. Instead, we must use the functionality provided by (keygen, sharedkey). However, sharedkey expects output from keygen, and this value has been completely scrambled by the hash function H_1, which is un-invertible. Therefore, SHAREDKEY has no way to apply sharedkey in a meaningful way.

So we need some way to preserve the structure of the output keygen while still allowing for an indifferentiability proof. But at the same time, we cannot just expose the output of keygen in the clear, as explained above.

Our solution is to replace H_1 with a random *permutation* P such that *both* P and P^{-1} are publicly accessible (we discuss instantiating the random permutation below). We then have that

$$\mathsf{KEYGEN}(SK) = P^{-1}(\mathsf{keygen}(H_0(SK))).$$

Then we can define $\mathsf{SHAREDKEY}(PK, SK) = \mathsf{sharedkey}(P(PK), H_0(SK))$. Note that, defining SHAREDKEY in this way achieves the desired correctness guarantee, which follows simply from the correctness of (keygen, sharedkey).

Attack 3. However, by allowing the permutation P to be invertible, we have invalidated our indifferentiability proof above for KEYGEN. Suppose for example that keygen's outputs are easily distinguishable from random. Then an attacker can compute $PK = \mathsf{KEYGEN}(SK)$, and then query P on either PK or a random string r. In the case of a random string, $P(r)$ will itself be essentially a random string. On the other hand, $P(PK)$ will be an output of keygen, and hence distinguishable from random. The problem is that the simulator defining P only gets to see r and has no way to know whether r came from KEYGEN or was just a random string. Therefore, the attacker can fool the simulator, leading to a distinguishing attack.

To avoid this problem, we will assume the standard-model NIKE protocol has *pseudorandom public keys*. In this case, the simulator will *always* respond to a P using a fresh random output of keygen. In the case where the query to P was on a random r, the result will look random to the adversary. On the other hand, if the query was on a $PK = \mathsf{KEYGEN}(SK)$, the simulator is ready to program any subsequent $H_0(SK)$ query to satisfy $P(PK) = \mathsf{keygen}(H_0(SK))$.

Attack 4. Many more problems still arise, similar to the problems above faced when trying to define $\mathsf{KEYGEN}(SK) = \mathsf{keygen}(H(SK))$. Namely, the adversary could first call the query $k = \mathsf{SHAREDKEY}(\mathsf{PK'}, \mathsf{SK})$, which in the ideal world will give a random string. Then the adversary makes queries to P, H_0 and computes $\mathsf{sharedkey}(P(\mathsf{PK'}), H_0(\mathsf{SK}))$ for itself. In the ideal world, the simulator must set $P(\mathsf{PK'}) = r$ and $H_0(\mathsf{SK}) = s$ such that $\mathsf{sharedkey}(r, s) = k$. But this involves inverting $\mathsf{sharedkey}$ on k, which may be computationally infeasible. Worse yet, the adversary could do this for $\mathsf{PK'_1}, \ldots, \mathsf{PK'_\ell}$ and $\mathsf{SK_1}, \ldots, \mathsf{SK_\ell}$, obtaining ℓ^2 different random and independent $k_{i,j}$ values from $\mathsf{SHAREDKEY}$ by considering all possible $\mathsf{PK'_i}, \mathsf{SK_j}$ pairs. The simulator then needs to somehow find $r_1, \ldots, r_\ell, s_1, \ldots, s_\ell$ such that $\mathsf{sharedkey}(r_i, s_j) = k_{i,j}$, where $k_{i,j}$ are each random independent strings. This is clearly impossible for large enough ℓ, since it would allow for compressing an $O(\ell^2)$-bit random string into $O(\ell)$ bits.

Our solution is to apply one more hash function, this time to the output of sharedkey: $\mathsf{SHAREDKEY}(\mathsf{PK_1}, \mathsf{SK_2}) = H_1(\mathsf{sharedkey}(P(\mathsf{PK_1}), H_0(\mathsf{SK_2})))$. Now, all we need is that $\mathsf{sharedkey}(r_i, s_j)$ are all distinct for different i, j pairs, which follows with high probability from the security of the NIKE scheme. Then we can simply program $H_1(\mathsf{sharedkey}(r_i, s_j)) = k_{i,j}$.

Attack 5. This construction unfortunately is still insecure: the adversary first samples $\mathsf{sk_1}$ and $\mathsf{SK_2}$, then it queries $\mathsf{PK_2} = \mathsf{KEYGEN}(\mathsf{SK_2})$, $\mathsf{pk_2} = P(\mathsf{PK_2})$, then calculates $k = \mathsf{sharedkey}(\mathsf{pk_2}, \mathsf{sk_1})$ and queries $H_1(k)$. After that, the adversary calculates $\mathsf{pk_1} = \mathsf{keygen}(\mathsf{sk_1})$, and queries $\mathsf{PK_1} = P^{-1}(\mathsf{pk_1})$. Next it calls $k' = \mathsf{SHAREDKEY}(\mathsf{PK_1}, \mathsf{SK_2})$ and finally tests $k' \overset{?}{=} H_1(k)$. In the real world, the test always passes, while to achieve indifferentiability, the simulator has to output a proper $H_1(k)$. Unfortunately, until the query $H_1(k)$, simulator knows nothing of $(\mathsf{sk_1}, \mathsf{SK_2})$ (it only has $\mathsf{KEYGEN}(\mathsf{SK_2})$), which means that it cannot program $H_1(k)$ to be k'. Therefore test fails with overwhelming probability in the ideal world. To get prevent this attack, we present our final construction:

$$\mathsf{SHAREDKEY}(\mathsf{PK_1}, \mathsf{SK_2}) = H_1(\{\mathsf{PK_1}, \mathsf{PK_2}\}, \mathsf{sharedkey}(P(\mathsf{PK_1}), H_0(\mathsf{SK_2}))),$$

where $\mathsf{PK_2} = \mathsf{KEYGEN}(\mathsf{SK_2}) = P^{-1}(\mathsf{keygen}(H_0(\mathsf{SK_2})))$[4]. How does this help? We note that, in the final construction, by including $\mathsf{PK_1}, \mathsf{PK_2}$ in the H_1 queries, we force the adversary to query $\mathsf{PK_1} = P^{-1}(\mathsf{pk_1})$ before the H_1 query. This allows the simulator to program P^{-1} in a way that allows it to correctly answer the later H_1 query. In particular, it samples $\mathsf{SK_1}$ itself and responds to the P^{-1} query with $\mathsf{PK_1} = \mathsf{KEYGEN}(\mathsf{SK_1})$. Afterward, when then adversary makes the query $H_1(\{\mathsf{PK_1}, \mathsf{PK_2}\}, k)$, the simulator will respond with $\mathsf{SHAREDKEY}(\mathsf{PK_2}, \mathsf{SK_1})$, which is always identical to $\mathsf{SHAREDKEY}(\mathsf{PK_1}, \mathsf{SK_2})$.

Attack 6. Even with our final construction, we must be careful. Suppose that it was possible for the adversary to choose a public key $\mathsf{pk^*}$ such that it can guess the value of $\mathsf{sharedkey}(\mathsf{pk^*}, \mathsf{sk})$ for a random (hidden) sk, then there is *still* an attack. Namely, the adversary queries $\mathsf{PK^*} = P^{-1}(\mathsf{pk^*})$ and $\mathsf{PK} = \mathsf{KEYGEN}(\mathsf{SK})$ for a random SK. It then guesses the value t_0^* of $\mathsf{sharedkey}(\mathsf{pk^*}, H_0(\mathsf{SK}))$, without

---

[4] Here, $\{\mathsf{PK_1}, \mathsf{PK_2}\}$ means the un-ordered set containing $\mathsf{PK_1}$ and $\mathsf{PK_2}$, so that $\{\mathsf{PK_1}, \mathsf{PK_2}\} = \{\mathsf{PK_2}, \mathsf{PK_1}\}$.

ever actually querying H_0, then it randomly samples an additional string t_1^* such that the simulator fails to distinguish t_0^* from t_1^* with high probability. Finally, it flips a coin b, and queries $k = H_1(\{\mathsf{PK}^*, \mathsf{PK}\}, t_b^*)$; if $b = 0$ it checks that the result is equal to $\mathsf{SHAREDKEY}(\mathsf{PK}^*, \mathsf{SK})$ and else it checks that the result is *not* equal to $\mathsf{SHAREDKEY}(\mathsf{PK}^*, \mathsf{SK})$. In the real world, if $b = 0$, this check will pass as long as the guess t_0^* is correct, and if $b = 1$, it will pass as long as no collision occurs. On the other hand, in the ideal world, although the simulator can simulate $k = H_1(\{\mathsf{PK}^*, \mathsf{PK}\}, t_0^*)$ correctly without knowing SK (the technique in Attack 5), it doesn't know the query corresponds to t_0^* or t_1^*. As a result, the check would fail with a noticeable probability. Our solution is to add another security requirement for the NIKE scheme, which we call *entropic shared keys*, insisting that for any pk^* of the adversary's choosing, the adversary *cannot* guess $\mathsf{sharedkey}(\mathsf{pk}^*, \mathsf{sk})$ except for negligible probability.

Attack 7. One last attack strategy: the attacker could first query $\mathsf{PK}_1 = \mathsf{KEYGEN}(\mathsf{SK}_1), \mathsf{PK}_2 = \mathsf{KEYGEN}(\mathsf{SK}_2), k = \mathsf{SHAREDKEY}(\mathsf{PK}_1, \mathsf{SK}_2)$. Then, it could query $r_1 = P(\mathsf{PK}_1), r_2 = P(\mathsf{PK}_2)$. Finally, it could treat r_1, r_2 as the messages in the standard-model NIKE protocol, and guess the shared key t for the protocol. Then it could query H_1 on t (and $\{\mathsf{PK}_1, \mathsf{PK}_2\}$). In the real world, the result $H_1(\{\mathsf{PK}_1, \mathsf{PK}_2\}, t)$ would be equal to k, so the simulator in the ideal world needs to be able to set $H_1(\{\mathsf{PK}_1, \mathsf{PK}_2\}, t) = k$. At this point, the simulator has $\mathsf{PK}_1, \mathsf{PK}_2, t$. But the simulator has no knowledge of SK_1 or SK_2. Therefore it has no way of guessing the correct input to $\mathsf{SHAREDKEY}$ to obtain k, as doing so requires recovering either SK_1 or SK_2 by inverting KEYGEN.

Of course, this attack requires the adversary to guess the shared key t from the public messages r_1, r_2 in the standard-model NIKE scheme, which should be impossible. One difficulty is that, in our construction, the adversary implicitly has access to a kind of verification oracle for the standard-model NIKE, which allows it to input r_1, r_2 as well as a guess k' for k, and learn if the guess was correct. One of the r_1, r_2 can even be chosen by the adversary. To see how such an oracle arises, imagine the adversary queried $\mathsf{KEYGEN}(sk_1)$ to get PK_1 and $P(\mathsf{PK}_1)$ to get r_1. Then for an r_2 of its choice, it queries $P^{-1}(r_2)$ to get PK_2. Next, it queries $\mathsf{SHAREDKEY}(\mathsf{PK}_2, \mathsf{SK}_1)$ to get K, and $H_1(\mathsf{PK}_2, \mathsf{PK}_1, k')$ to get K'. The correctness of our algorithms implies that $K' = K$ if and only if $k' = k$.

Thus, if our NIKE scheme is only secure against passive attacks, it might be vulnerable to this attack vector. Concretely, if the underlying standard-model NIKE is the isogeny-based scheme of [18], then the active attack of [16] can be mounted against our scheme. Instead, we will require a stronger notion of NIKE security for the standard-model scheme, which we call *semi-active unpredictable shared keys*. Here, we require that the shared key is unpredictable, even if the adversary is given the verification oracles as described above. Such NIKE can easily be constructed under standard assumptions.

While we have protected against certain natural attacks, we need to argue indifferentiability against all possible attacks. To do so we use a careful simulation strategy for H_0, H_1, P, P^{-1}, and prove indifferentiability through a careful sequence of hybrids. In essence, each step in the hybrid argument corresponds roughly to one of the attack strategies discussed above, and our proof shows that these attacks do not work, demonstrating the indistinguishability of the hybrids.

Constructing P, P^{-1}. Our random permutation P, P^{-1} can easily be instantiated using the ideal cipher model in the setting where the key space contains only a single element. We note that indifferentiable ideal ciphers can be constructed from random oracles [10].

Therefore, all we need for our construction is three random oracles. Multiple random oracles can easily be built from a single random oracle by prefixing the oracle index to the input. Finally, an indifferentiable random oracle of any domain/range can be constructed from a fixed-size random oracle [8].

The Role of P in the Proof. It is natural to wonder what role P plays in the actual security of our scheme. After all, since P^{-1} is publicly invertible using P, the adversary can easily undo the application of P^{-1} to the output of KEYGEN. So it may seem that P is a superfluous artifact of the proof.

There are multiple ways to address this question. One answer is that without P, there would be no way to have a computationally efficient simulator as discussed above. One could consider an inefficient simulator, but this would correspond to a weaker notion of indifferentiability. This notion of indifferentiability would be useless when composing with protocols that have computational rather than statistical security. What's more, we would actually be unable to prove even this weaker form. Indeed, our proof crucially relies on the computational security of the standard-model NIKE protocol. Since the inefficient simulator would essentially have to break the security of the NIKE protocol, it would be impossible to carry out the proof.

A higher-level answer is that by including P—which is under full control of the simulator—the simulator gets to learn extra information about what values the adversary is interested in. In particular, in order to relate the ideal oracles to the standard-model scheme, the adversary must always send a query to the simulator. This extra information provided by making such queries is exactly what the simulator needs for the proof to go through. This is a common phenomenon in random-oracle proofs, where hashing sometimes has no obvious role except to provide a reduction/simulator with necessary information.

Yet another answer is that, if P is omitted, the scheme is actually insecure in some settings. For example, an ideal NIKE satisfies the property that an adversary, given Alice's secret key and *half* of Bob's public key, cannot compute the shared key between Alice and Bob. Now, consider the case where the standard model NIKE does *not* satisfy this requirement. Then if we do not include P, our construction does not satisfy the requirement either. Instead, by including P, an adversary who gets half of Bob's ideal public key cannot invert the permutation to recover *any* information about the corresponding standard-model public key. It then follows that the adversary cannot guess the shared key.

1.5   Extending to Other Idealized Cryptosystems

We now turn our attention to extending the above results to other cryptosystems. First, we use our ideal NIKE scheme to construct ideal public key encryption (PKE). Note that ideal public key encryption is in particular CCA secure, whereas the standard way to turn a NIKE scheme into a PKE scheme is never CCA secure. In order to make the scheme CCA secure, a natural starting point is the Fujisaki-Okamoto (FO) transform [15]. While this transformation applied to our ideal NIKE certainly achieves CCA security, it unfortunately is not indifferentiable when applied to our NIKE. The reasons are several-fold, and should come as no surprise given that FO was never designed to achieve indifferentiability.

For starters, recall from our NIKE discussion that all inputs and outputs of the algorithms need to be passed through ideal objects under the simulator's control. In the FO transformation, this is not the case. Another reason why FO does not give indifferentiability is that the FO transform allows for encryption randomness to be recovered during decryption; in fact, this is a crucial feature of the CCA security proof. On the other hand, such encryption schemes cannot be ideal, since ideal encryption schemes guarantee that the encryption randomness is hidden even to the decrypter[5].

To overcome these issues, we first show a careful transformation from our ideal NIKE into ideal *deterministic* public key encryption (DPKE). By focusing first on DPKE, we side-step the randomness issue. Our transformation is inspired by the FO transform, but in order to ensure that all inputs/outputs are passed through oracles under the simulator's control, we employ our random permutation trick again.

Finally, we turn to convert ideal DPKE into ideal PKE. The usual conversion (simply including the encryption randomness as part of the message) does not suffice, again because the usual conversion allows the decrypter to recover the encryption randomness. We instead essentially hide the randomness by hashing with a random oracle. This, however, requires care in order to enable a complete indifferentiability proof.

Ideal Signatures. Finally, we investigate constructing ideal signatures. While in the standard model signatures can in principle be built from one-way functions and therefore random oracles, we observe that the situation for ideal signatures is much more challenging. For example, an ideal signature scheme will be *unique*, meaning for any message/public key, only a single signature will verify. On the other hand, constructing unique signatures even under standard security notions is difficult, and the only known constructions require strong number-theoretic tools such as bilinear maps.

We instead assume a building block as a standard-model signature scheme with unique signatures, as well as some other mild security properties which can

---

[5] One can define a different idealization of PKE where the ideal decryption functionality *does* output the encryption randomness. However, this stronger functionality corresponds to weaker security guarantees.

be easily instantiated using bilinear maps. We show that such a scheme can, in fact, be turned into ideal signatures using similar ideas to the above.

1.6   Instantiations

Our NIKE schemes require a standard-model NIKE. Unfortunately, we cannot use a truly arbitrary standard model NIKE, as in addition to the semi-active unpredictable shared keys, we also need pseudorandom public keys and entropic shared keys. As such, we need to make sure such a scheme can be instantiated. Our other results similarly require standard-model schemes where various outputs of the schemes are pseudorandom bit strings.

We note that the entropic shared key requirement is satisfied by all constructions we are aware of and the semi-active unpredictable shared keys can be achieved on cryptographic groups or bilinear maps [14], under doubly-strong CDH assumption. On the other hand, the requirement of pseudorandom public keys is slightly non-trivial. Many number-theoretic constructions have public keys that are elements in $\mathbb{Z}_q^k$ for some modulus k; even if the public keys are pseudorandom in these sets, there may be no way to represent a random element of $\mathbb{Z}_q^k$ as a random bit string (which we need in order to apply the ideal permutation P), since $q^k = |\mathbb{Z}_q^k|$ may be far from a power of 2.

However, it will usually be easy to map such public keys to random strings in $\{0,1\}^n$ for some integer n. For example, in the case $k = 1$, suppose we are given a (pseudo)random element $\mathsf{pk} \in \mathbb{Z}_q$. Let n be some integer such that $n \geq \lambda + \log_2 q$ for a security parameter λ. Let $t = \lfloor 2^n/q \rfloor$ be the largest integer such that $tq \leq 2^n$. Then we can extend pk into a random element pk' in $\mathbb{Z}_{tq}$ by setting $\mathsf{pk}' = \mathsf{pk} + aq$, where a is a random integer in $\mathbb{Z}_t$. Finally, we note that a random integer in $\mathbb{Z}_{tq}$ is distributed exponentially close (in λ) to a random integer in $\mathbb{Z}_{2^n}$.

We can similarly handle the case $k > 1$ by bijecting public keys into $\mathbb{Z}_{q^k}$ in the standard way. Such conversions can be applied to Diffie-Hellman key agreement. The result that we attain our NIKE results under doubly-strong-CDH, whereas our signature scheme requires CDH in bilinear map groups. The full details can be found in [27].

2   Background

NOTATION. Throughout this paper, $\lambda \in \mathbb{N}$ denotes the security parameter. We let $\mathbb{N}$ be the set of non-negative integers, including zero and $\{0,1\}^*$ denote the set of all finite-length bit strings, including the empty string ϵ ($\{0,1\}^0 = \epsilon$). For two bit strings, X and Y, $X||Y$ denotes string concatenation and (X,Y) denotes a uniquely decodable encoding of X and Y. The length of a string X is denoted by $|X|$.

For a finite set $\mathcal{S}$, we denote $s \leftarrow \mathcal{S}$ the process of sampling s uniformly from $\mathcal{S}$. For a probabilistic algorithm A, we denote $y \leftarrow A(x; R)$ the process of running

A on inputs x and randomness R, and assigning y the result. We let $\mathcal{R}_A$ denote the randomness space of A; we require $\mathcal{R}_A$ to be the form $\mathcal{R}_A = \{0,1\}^r$. We write $y \leftarrow A(x)$ for $y \leftarrow A(x, R)$ with uniformly chosen $R \in \mathcal{R}_A$, and we write $y_1, \ldots, y_m \leftarrow A(x)$ for $y_1 \leftarrow A(x), \ldots, y_m \leftarrow A(x)$ with fresh randomness in each execution. If A's running time is polynomial in λ, then A is called probabilistic polynomial-time (PPT). We say a function $\mu(n)$ is negligible if $\mu \in o(n^{-\omega(1)})$, and is non-negligible otherwise. We let $\mathsf{negl}(n)$ denote an arbitrary negligible function. If we say some $p(n)$ is poly, we mean that there is some polynomial q such that for all sufficiently large n, $p(n) \leq q(n)$. We say a function $\rho(n)$ is noticeable if the inverse $1/\rho(n)$ is poly. We use boldface to denote vector, i.e. $\boldsymbol{m}$; we denote $\boldsymbol{m}_i$ as the i-th component of $\boldsymbol{m}$ and $|\boldsymbol{m}|$ as the length of $\boldsymbol{m}$.

RANDOM ORACLE MODEL (ROM). Random oracle model is an idealized model proposed by Bellare and Rogaway [4]. ROM formalizes a model (a theoretical black box) which responds to any unique query with a truly random string, and if the query is repeated, the response would be consistent. More concretely, a random oracle model has a publicly accessible hash function $H : \{0,1\}^* \to \{0,1\}^n$ such that:

1. for any x, every bit of $H(x)$ is truly random;
2. for any $x \neq y$, $H(x)$ and $H(y)$ are independent.

IDEAL CIPHER MODEL (ICM). The ideal cipher model is another idealized model which is firstly proposed by Shannon [25] and then formalized by Black [5]. This model also responds to any unique query with a truly random string. While, instead of having a publicly accessible random function, ideal cipher model has a publicly accessible ideal cipher $E : \{0,1\}^k \times \{0,1\}^n \to \{0,1\}^n$. Specifically, E is an ideal cipher along with a k-bit key and n-bit input/output such that:

1. for any pair (k, x), every bit of $E(k, x)$ is truly random;
2. for any fix key k, $E(k, *)$ is a random permutation;
3. for any $k_1 \neq k_2$ and (x, y), $E(k_1, x)$ and $E(k_2, y)$ are independent.

Moreover, any adversary interacting with an ideal cipher model would be given access to both the cipher and its inverse. The following definitions in this part highly rely on [2] and we roughly use its text here.

GAMES. An n-adversary game $\mathcal{G}$ is a Turing machine, denoted as $\mathcal{G}^{\Sigma, \mathcal{A}_1, \ldots, \mathcal{A}_n}$, where Σ is a system and $\mathcal{A}_i$ are adversarial algorithms that can keep full local state but might only communicate with each other through $\mathcal{G}$. If we say a n-adversary game $\mathcal{G}_n$ is reducible to an m-adversary game $\mathcal{G}_m$, we mean that, for any $(\mathcal{A}_1, \ldots, \mathcal{A}_n)$, there are $(\mathcal{A}'_1, \ldots, \mathcal{A}'_m)$ such that for any system Σ we have that $\mathcal{G}_n^{\Sigma, \mathcal{A}_1, \ldots, \mathcal{A}_n} = \mathcal{G}_m^{\Sigma, \mathcal{A}'_1, \ldots, \mathcal{A}'_m}$. A game $\mathcal{G}$ is called a n-stage game [22] if $\mathcal{G}$ is an n-adversary game and it cannot be reducible to any m-adversary game, where $m < n$. In particular, for any single-stage game $\mathcal{G}_{\Sigma, \mathcal{A}}$, we can trivially rewrite it as $\overline{\mathcal{A}}^{\overline{\mathcal{G}}^\Sigma}$, where $\overline{\mathcal{G}}$ is an oracle machine and $\overline{\mathcal{A}}$ is an adversarial algorithm, and $\overline{\mathcal{A}}$ is compatible with this oracle machine $\overline{\mathcal{G}}$. Moreover, we say two games are equivalent if they are reducible in both directions.

RANDOM FUNCTIONS. Let $\mathcal{X}$ and $\mathcal{Y}$ be two finite sets, we denote $\mathcal{F}[\mathcal{X} \rightarrow \mathcal{Y}]$ to be the set of all functions that map from $\mathcal{X}$ to $\mathcal{Y}$. If we say a function $F : \mathcal{X} \rightarrow \mathcal{Y}$ is a random function, we mean that F is uniformly sampled from $\mathcal{F}[\mathcal{X} \rightarrow \mathcal{Y}]$. Moreover, if F grants oracle accesses to all parties (honest and adversarial) in a black-box manner, then we treat F as an idealized model.

RANDOM INJECTIONS. Similarly, let $\mathcal{X}$ and $\mathcal{Y}$ be two sets such that $|\mathcal{X}| \leq |\mathcal{Y}|$, we define $\mathcal{I}[\mathcal{X} \rightarrow \mathcal{Y}]$ to be the set of all injections that map from $\mathcal{X}$ to $\mathcal{Y}$. If we say a function $F : \mathcal{X} \rightarrow \mathcal{Y}$ is a random injection, we mean that F is uniformly sampled from $\mathcal{I}[\mathcal{X} \rightarrow \mathcal{Y}]$.

LAZY SAMPLERS. Lazy samplers are algorithmic procedures, to simulate various ideal objects along with arbitrary domain and range, by lazily sampling function at each point. Those ideal objects include: random oracle model, ideal cipher model, random functions and random injections [24].

2.1 Public Key Primitives

In this part, we recall the definitions of the public key primitives that we consider in our work.

NON-INTERACTIVE KEY EXCHANGE (NIKE) [11]. NIKE is a cryptographic primitive which enables two parties, who know the public keys of each other, to agree on a symmetric shared key without requiring any interaction. It consists of two algorithms: NIKE.keygen and NIKE.sharedkey together with a shared key space $\mathcal{SHK}$.

- NIKE.keygen: Given input a secret key sk, the algorithm outputs a public key pk;
- NIKE.sharedkey Given inputs a public key pk_1 and a secret key sk_2, the algorithm outputs a shared key $shk \in \mathcal{SHK}$.

For correctness, we require that, for any two key pairs $(pk_1, sk_1), (pk_2, sk_2)$, the system satisfies:

$$\mathsf{NIKE.sharedkey}(pk_1, sk_2) = \mathsf{NIKE.sharedkey}(pk_2, sk_1).$$

PUBLIC KEY ENCRYPTION (PKE) [11]. A public-key encryption scheme consists of three algorithms: PKE.keygen, PKE.enc, PKE.dec together with a message space $\mathcal{M}$. Formally,

- PKE.keygen Given input a secret key sk, the algorithm outputs a public key pk;
- PKE.enc Given inputs a public key pk and $m \in \mathcal{M}$, the algorithm outputs a ciphertext $c = \mathsf{PKE.enc}(pk, m)$;
- PKE.dec Given inputs a secret key sk and a ciphertext c, the algorithm outputs either a plaintext m or $\perp$.

For correctness, we require that, for any key pair $(\mathsf{pk}, \mathsf{sk})(\mathsf{pk} = \mathsf{PKE.keygen}(\mathsf{sk}))$ and $\mathsf{m} \in \mathcal{M}$, the scheme satisfies:

$$\mathsf{PKE.dec}(\mathsf{sk}, \mathsf{PKE.enc}(\mathsf{pk}, \mathsf{m})) = \mathsf{m}.$$

DIGITAL SIGNATURE [23]. A digital signature scheme consists of three algorithms: $\mathsf{Sig.keygen}, \mathsf{Sig.sign}, \mathsf{Sig.ver}$ along with a message space $\mathcal{M}$. Formally,

- $\mathsf{Sig.keygen}$ Given input a sign key sk, the algorithm outputs a verification key vk;
- $\mathsf{Sig.sign}$ Given inputs a sign key sk and a message $\mathsf{m} \in \mathcal{M}$, the algorithm outputs a signature $\sigma = \mathsf{Sig.sign}(\mathsf{sk}, \mathsf{m})$;
- $\mathsf{Sig.ver}$ Given inputs a signature σ, a message and a verification key vk, outputs either 1 or 0.

For correctness, we require that, for any key pair $(\mathsf{sk}, \mathsf{vk})(\mathsf{vk} = \mathsf{Sig.keygen}(\mathsf{sk}))$ and $\mathsf{m} \leftarrow \mathcal{M}$, the signature scheme satisfies:

$$\mathsf{Sig.ver}(\mathsf{Sig.sign}(\mathsf{sk}, \mathsf{m}), \mathsf{m}, \mathsf{vk}) = 1.$$

2.2 Indifferentiability

For indifferentiability, significant parts of the discussion in this section is based on [2]. In [20], Maurer, Renner and Holenstein (MRH) propose the indifferentiability framework, which formalizes a set of necessary and sufficient conditions for one system to securely be replaced with another one in a wide class of environments. This framework has been used to prove the structural soundness of a number of cryptographic primitives, which includes hash functions [8,12], blockciphers [1,10,13], domain extenders [9] and authenticated encryption with associated data [2]. In the following, we first recall the definition of indifferentiability.

A random system $\Sigma := (\Sigma.\mathsf{hon}, \Sigma.\mathsf{adv})$ is accessible via two interfaces $\Sigma.\mathsf{hon}$ and $\Sigma.\mathsf{adv}$, where $\Sigma.\mathsf{hon}$ provides a honest interface through which the system can be accessed by all parties and $\Sigma.\mathsf{adv}$ models the adversarial access to the inner working part of Σ. Typically, a system implements either some ideal objects $\mathcal{F}$, or a construction $C^{\mathcal{F}'}$, which applies some underlying ideal objects $\mathcal{F}'$.

Definition 1 (Indifferentiability [2,20]). *Let Σ_1 and Σ_2 be two systems and S be a simulator. The indifferentiability advantage of a differentiator $\mathcal{D}$ against (Σ_1, Σ_2) with respect to S is*

$$\mathrm{Adv}^{\mathrm{indif}}_{\Sigma_1, \Sigma_2, S, \mathcal{D}}(1^\lambda) := \Pr[\mathrm{Real}_{\Sigma_1, \mathcal{D}}] - \Pr[\mathrm{Ideal}_{\Sigma_2, S, \mathcal{D}}],$$

where games $\mathrm{Real}_{\Sigma_1, \mathcal{D}}$ and $\mathrm{Ideal}_{\Sigma_2, S, \mathcal{D}}$ are defined in Fig. 1. We say Σ_1 is indifferentiable from Σ_2, if there exists an efficient simulator S such that for any probabilistic polynomial time differentiator $\mathcal{D}$, the advantage above is negligible. Moreover, we say Σ_1 is weakly indifferentiable from Σ_2, if for any probabilistic polynomial time differentiator $\mathcal{D}$, there exists an efficient simulator $S_{\mathcal{D}}$ such that the advantage above is negligible.

$\mathrm{Real}_{\Sigma_1,\mathcal{D}}$:	$\mathrm{HonestR}(X)$	$\mathrm{Ideal}_{\Sigma_2,\mathcal{S},\mathcal{D}}$:	$\mathrm{HonestI}(X)$
$b \leftarrow \mathcal{D}^{\mathrm{HonestR},\mathrm{AdvR}}$	Return $\Sigma_1.\mathrm{hon}(X)$.	$b \leftarrow \mathcal{D}^{\mathrm{HonestI},\mathrm{AdvI}}$	Return $\Sigma_2.\mathrm{hon}(X)$.
Return b.	$\underline{\mathrm{AdvR}(X)}$	Return b.	$\underline{\mathrm{AdvI}(X)}$
	Return $\Sigma_1.\mathrm{adv}(X)$.		Return $\mathcal{S}^{\Sigma_2.\mathrm{hon}(\cdot)}(X)$.

Fig. 1. Indifferentiability of Σ_1 and Σ_2, where $\mathcal{S}$ is the simulator and $\mathcal{D}$ is the adversary.

In the rest of the paper, we also use the notations in [2] and consider the definition above to two systems with interfaces as:

$$(\Sigma_1.\mathrm{hon}(X), \Sigma_1.\mathrm{adv}(x)) := (\mathrm{C}^{\mathcal{F}_1}(X), \mathcal{F}_1(x));$$
$$(\Sigma_2.\mathrm{hon}(X), \Sigma_2.\mathrm{adv}(x)) := (\mathcal{F}_2(X), \mathcal{F}_2(x)),$$

where $\mathcal{F}_1$ and $\mathcal{F}_2$ are two ideal objects sampled from their distributions and $\mathrm{C}^{\mathcal{F}_1}$ is a construction of $\mathcal{F}_2$ by calling $\mathcal{F}_1$.

Next, we recall composition theorem for indifferentiability. In [20], MRH give out the composition theorem for indifferentiability, and then Ristenpart, Shacham and Shrimpton (RSS) [22] propose a game-based version for the theorem.

Theorem 2 (Indifferentiability Composition [2,22]). *Let $\Sigma_1 := (\mathrm{C}^{\mathcal{F}_1}, \mathcal{F}_1)$ be a system that is indifferentiable from $\Sigma_2 := (\mathcal{F}_2, \mathcal{F}_2)$ along with simulator $\mathcal{S}$. Let $\mathcal{G}$ be a single-stage game. Then for any adversary $\mathcal{A}$, there exists an adversary $\mathcal{B}$ and a differentiator $\mathcal{D}$ such that*

$$\Pr[\mathcal{G}^{\mathrm{C}^{\mathcal{F}_1},\mathcal{A}^{\mathcal{F}_1}}] \leq \Pr[\mathcal{G}^{\mathcal{F}_2,\mathcal{B}^{\mathcal{F}_2}}] + \mathrm{Adv}_{\Sigma_1,\Sigma_2,\mathcal{S},\mathcal{D}}^{\mathrm{indif}}.$$

However, RSS prove that the composition theorem above does not extend to multi-stage games as the simulator has to keep the local state for consistency. While, Barbosa and Farshim [2] observe that if allowing some relaxations on the games, we could rewrite some multi-stage games as equivalent to single-stage games. Essentially, for an n-adversary game $\mathcal{G}_n^{\mathrm{C}^{\mathcal{F}},\mathcal{A}_1,...,\mathcal{A}_n}$, if only one adversary (say $\mathcal{A}_1$) can call the ideal objects $\mathcal{F}$ directly and the rest can only call $\mathrm{C}^{\mathcal{F}}$, then $\mathcal{G}_n$ can be rewritten as a single-stage game, because the game $\mathcal{G}_n$ itself, of course, has access to $\mathrm{C}^{\mathcal{F}}$. Then in [2], BF formalize this observation in the following theorem.

Theorem 3 (Multi-stage Game Composition [2]). *Let $\Sigma_1 := (\mathrm{C}^{\mathcal{F}_1}, \mathcal{F}_1)$ be a system that is indifferentiable from $\Sigma_2 := (\mathcal{F}_2, \mathcal{F}_2)$ along with simulator $\mathcal{S}$. Let $\mathcal{G}$ be an n-adversary game and $\mathcal{A} := (\mathcal{A}_1, \ldots, \mathcal{A}_n)$ be a n-tuple of adversaries where $\mathcal{A}_1$ can access $\mathcal{F}_1$ but $\mathcal{A}_i$ ($i > 1$) can only access $\mathrm{C}^{\mathcal{F}_1}$. Then there is an n-adversary $\mathcal{B}$ and a differentiator $\mathcal{D}$ such that*

$$\Pr[\mathcal{G}^{\mathrm{C}^{\mathcal{F}_1},\mathcal{A}_1^{\mathcal{F}_1},\mathcal{A}_2^{\mathrm{C}^{\mathcal{F}_1}},...,\mathcal{A}_n^{\mathrm{C}^{\mathcal{F}_1}}}] = \Pr[\mathcal{G}^{\mathcal{F}_2,\mathcal{B}_1^{\mathcal{F}_2},...,\mathcal{B}_n^{\mathcal{F}_2}}] + \mathrm{Adv}_{\Sigma_1,\Sigma_2,\mathcal{S},\mathcal{D}}^{\mathrm{indif}}.$$

Remark. Barbosa and Farshim [2] give a strong motivation for the relaxation imposed on the class of games above. To our best of knowledge, the related-key attack (key-dependent message attack) game is not known to be equivalent to any single-stage game. As a result, it would be insufficient to prove a system is related-key attack secure as follows: 1) there is another system, say Σ_2, such that Σ_1 is indifferentiable from Σ_2; 2) Σ_2 is related-key attack secure. However, if allowing the relaxation, the proof follows trivially, hence from a practical point of view (by adding this specific relaxation on games), composition extends well beyond 1-adversary games.

3   Indifferentiable NIKE

In this section, we propose the notion of "ideal NIKE" and then build an indifferentiable non-interactive key exchange scheme from simpler ideal primitives and a standard-model NIKE scheme.

3.1   What Is Ideal NIKE?

In this part we give the rigorous description of ideal NIKE, formally:

Definition 4 (Ideal NIKE). *Let $\mathcal{X}, \mathcal{Y}, \mathcal{W}$ be three sets such that $|\mathcal{X}| \geq 2^{\omega(\log \lambda)}, |\mathcal{Y}| \geq 2^{\omega(\log \lambda)}, |\mathcal{W}| \geq 2^{\omega(\log \lambda)},$ $|\mathcal{X}| \leq |\mathcal{Y}|$ and $|\mathcal{X}| \times |\mathcal{Y}| \leq |\mathcal{W}|$. We denote $\mathcal{F}[\mathcal{X} \rightarrow \mathcal{Y}]$ as the set of all injections that map $\mathcal{X}$ to $\mathcal{Y}$ and $\mathcal{G}[\mathcal{X} \times \mathcal{Y} \rightarrow \mathcal{W}]$ as the set of the functions that map $\mathcal{X} \times \mathcal{Y}$ to $\mathcal{W}$. We define $\mathcal{T}$ as the set of all function pairs (F, G) such that: 1) $F \in \mathcal{F}, G \in \mathcal{G}$; 2) $\forall x, y \in \mathcal{X}, G(x, F(y)) = G(y, F(x))$; 3) $G(x_1, y_1) = G(x_2, y_2) \Rightarrow (x_1 = x_2 \wedge y_1 = y_2) \vee (y_1 = F(x_2) \wedge y_2 = F(x_1))$.*

We say that a NIKE scheme $\Pi_{\mathsf{NIKE}} = (\mathsf{IKE.KEYGGEN}, \mathsf{NIKE.SHAREDKEY})$, associated with secret key space $\mathcal{X}$, public key space $\mathcal{Y}$ and shared key space $\mathcal{W}$, is an ideal NIKE if $(\mathsf{NIKE.KEYGEN}, \mathsf{NIKE.SHAREDKEY})$ is sampled from $\mathcal{T}$ uniformly.

It's trivial to note that, due to an information-theoretic argument, an ideal NIKE achieves related-key attack security, leakage-resiliency and so forth. Next, we show how to construct an indifferentiable NIKE scheme from simpler primitives.

3.2   Construction

In this section, we build an indifferentiable NIKE scheme from simpler ideal primitives (namely random oracles and ideal ciphers) along with a standard-model (that is, *non-ideal*) NIKE scheme.

Building Blocks. Our scheme consists of several building blocks:

– A standard-model NIKE scheme $\Pi_{\mathsf{SM-NIKE}} = (\mathsf{keygen}, \mathsf{sharedkey})$ with secret key space $\mathcal{X}$, public key space $\mathcal{Y}$, and shared key space $\mathcal{Z}$;

- $H_0 := \{0,1\}^* \to \mathcal{X}$ is a random oracle whose co-domain matches the secret key space of Π.
- $H_1 := \{0,1\}^* \to \mathcal{W}$ is a random oracle, where $|\mathcal{X}| \times |\mathcal{Y}| \leq |\mathcal{W}|$;
- $P := \mathcal{Y} \to \mathcal{Y}$ is a random permutation on the public key space of Π, and P^{-1} is P's inverse.

Note that, the random permutations typically operate on bit strings, which means $\mathcal{Y} = \{0,1\}^n$ for some natural number $n \geq \omega(\log \lambda)$. Moreover, the shared key space in the standard model NIKE $\mathcal{Z}$ and in our construction $\mathcal{W}$ might be not equivalent, because it's unnecessarily correct that $|\mathcal{X}| \times |\mathcal{Y}| \leq |\mathcal{Z}|$. And if not, then setting $\mathcal{W} = \mathcal{Z}$ would give a differentiator directly, by just checking whether $|\mathcal{X}| \times |\mathcal{Y}| \leq |\mathcal{W}|$.

Construction. Now we are ready to build an indifferentiable NIKE scheme, denoted as $\Pi_{\mathsf{NIKE}} = (\mathsf{NIKE.KEYGEN}, \mathsf{NIKE.SHAREDKEY})$, from the building blocks above. Formally,

- $\mathsf{NIKE.KEYGEN}(\mathsf{SK})$: Given input SK, the algorithm runs $\mathsf{keygen}(H_0(\mathsf{SK}))$, and outputs the public key $\mathsf{PK} = P^{-1}(\mathsf{keygen}(H_0(\mathsf{SK})))$;
- $\mathsf{NIKE.SHAREDKEY}(\mathsf{PK}_1, \mathsf{SK}_2)$: Given inputs $(\mathsf{PK}_1, \mathsf{SK}_2)$, the algorithm computes $\mathsf{PK}_2 = \mathsf{NIKE.KEYGEN}(\mathsf{SK}_2)$ and $\mathsf{sharedkey}(P(\mathsf{PK}_1), H_0(\mathsf{SK}_2))$. If $\mathsf{PK}_1 \leq \mathsf{PK}_2$, then it outputs the shared key as

$$\mathsf{SHK} = H_1(\mathsf{PK}_1, \mathsf{PK}_2, \mathsf{sharedkey}(P(\mathsf{PK}_1), H_0(\mathsf{SK}_2))),$$

else, it outputs

$$\mathsf{SHK} = H_1(\mathsf{PK}_2, \mathsf{PK}_1, \mathsf{sharedkey}(P(\mathsf{PK}_1), H_0(\mathsf{SK}_2))).$$

Correctness of the scheme easily follows, and what's more interesting is its indifferentiability. Next, we prove our scheme is indifferentiable from an ideal NIKE. Before that, we first specify the security properties of the standard-model NIKE.

Property 1. SEMI-ACTIVE UNPREDICTABLE SHARED KEY. We say the shared key, for a NIKE scheme, is semi-active unpredictable, if there is ϵ_1 such that for any PPT adversary $\mathcal{A}$, the advantage

$$\mathrm{Adv}_{\mathcal{A}} := \Pr[\mathcal{A}^{\mathcal{O}_1, \mathcal{O}_2}(\mathsf{pk}_1, \mathsf{pk}_2) = \mathsf{sharedkey}(\mathsf{pk}_1, \mathsf{sk}_2)] \leq \epsilon_1 = \mathsf{negl}(\lambda),$$

where $\mathsf{pk}_i = \mathsf{keygen}(\mathsf{sk}_i), \mathsf{sk}_i \leftarrow \mathcal{X}$ and $\mathcal{O}_i$ is a predicate oracle such that takes $(\mathsf{pk}_i, \mathsf{shk})$ as input and outputs a bit (the public key pk here might be malicious). Concretely, the oracle $\mathcal{O}_i$ outputs "1" iff $\mathsf{shk} = \mathsf{sharedkey}(\mathsf{sk}_i, \mathsf{pk})$. This is the standard security game for NIKE schemes against active adversary, except that we relax the notion on two pieces: 1) we only require unpredictability of the shared key, rather than indistinguishability from random; 2) the oracles take both public key pk and shared key shk as input and tell whether shk is a valid shared key, rather than taking the public key pk, and outputting the corresponding shared key shk.

The next two properties are mild additional security properties that are not usually required for NIKE schemes, but are achieved by most natural schemes. We require these properties in order to prove the ideal security of our construction.

Property 2. ENTROPIC SHARED KEYS. We say the shared key, for a NIKE scheme is entropic, if there is ϵ_2 s.t. for any PPT adversary $\mathcal{A}$, the advantage

$$\Pr[\mathsf{shk}^* = \mathsf{sharedkey}(\mathsf{pk}^*, \mathsf{sk}) : (\mathsf{pk}^*, \mathsf{shk}^*) \leftarrow \mathcal{A}, \mathsf{sk} \overset{\$}{\leftarrow} \mathcal{X}] \leq \epsilon_2 = \mathsf{negl}(\lambda),$$

Note that the entropic shared keys property tells us that if the adversary only knows one public key (even it's chosen by the adversary), it cannot predict the shared key if the other secret key is random and hidden. In other words, this property guarantees that there is no way to make the shared key have low min-entropy.

Property 3. PSEUDORANDOM PUBLIC KEYS. We say the public key, for a NIKE scheme, is pseudorandom, if there is ϵ_3 s.t. for any PPT adversary $\mathcal{A}$, the advantage

$$\mathrm{Adv}_{\mathcal{A}} := |\Pr[\mathcal{A}(\mathsf{keygen}(\mathsf{sk}))] - \Pr[\mathcal{A}(R)]| \leq \epsilon_3 = \mathsf{negl}(\lambda),$$

where $\mathsf{sk} \leftarrow \mathcal{X}, R \leftarrow \mathcal{Y}$. We immediately observe that as $\mathcal{Y} = \{0,1\}^n$, our standard-model NIKE must have public keys that are pseudorandom bit strings. And we say a NIKE scheme is Good if it satisfies the three properties above.

Theorem 5. (Indifferentiable NIKE). Π_{NIKE} *is indifferentiable from an ideal NIKE if* $\Pi_{\mathsf{SM-NIKE}}$ *is* Good. *More precisely, there exists a simulator* $\mathcal{S}$ *such that for all* $(q_{H_0}, q_{H_0}, q_{H_0}, q_{H_0})$-*query PPT differentiator* $\mathcal{D}$ *with* $q_{H_0} + q_P + q_{P^{-1}} + q_{H_1} \leq q$, *we have*

$$\mathrm{Adv}^{\mathsf{indif}}_{\Pi_{\mathsf{NIKE}}, \mathcal{S}, \mathcal{D}} \leq (8q^2 + 9q)\sqrt{2\epsilon_3 + \frac{1}{|\mathcal{X}|}} + \frac{4q^2 + 5q}{|\mathcal{Y}|} + \frac{q^2}{|\mathcal{W}|} + 4q^2\epsilon_1 + (q^2 + 11q)\epsilon_2 + 9q\epsilon_3.$$

The simulator makes at most q *queries to its oracles.*

Proof Sketch. According to the definition of indifferentiability, we immediately observe that any PPT adversary has two honest interfaces (NIKE.KEYGEN, NIKE.SHAREDKEY) (below we will denote (NKG, NSK) for ease) and four adversarial interfaces (H_0, P, P^{-1}, H_1). Therefore, we need to build an efficient simulator $\mathcal{S}$ that can simulate the four adversarial interfaces H_0, P, P^{-1} and H_1 properly, which means, for any PPT differentiator $\mathcal{D}$, the view of $\mathcal{D}$ in the real game is computationally close to the view in the ideal game. In the following, we illustrate the description of our simulator (similar form as in [2]) in Fig. 2 and then we give the high-level intuition of our proof strategy (here we only give the proof sketch and the intuition of the simulator, and please refer to [27] for full details).

We immediately observe that, our simulator makes at most q queries to (NKG, NSK), and it keeps four tables and the size of each table is at most q,

Algo.$\mathcal{S}.H_0(\mathsf{SK})$:

if $\exists(\mathsf{SK},\mathsf{sk},\mathsf{pk},\mathsf{PK}) \in T_{H_0}$,
    return sk;
if $\exists(*,\mathsf{sk},\mathsf{pk},\mathsf{PK}) \in T_P$ s.t. $\mathsf{PK} = \mathsf{NKG}(\mathsf{SK})$,
    return sk;
$\mathsf{sk} \twoheadleftarrow \mathcal{X}$,
$T_{H_0} \leftarrow T_{H_0} \cup (\mathsf{SK},\mathsf{sk},\mathsf{keygen}(\mathsf{sk}),\mathsf{NKG}(\mathsf{SK}))$,
    return sk.

Algo.$\mathcal{S}.P(\mathsf{PK})$

if $\exists(*,\mathsf{sk},\mathsf{pk},\mathsf{PK}) \in T_P$,
    return pk;
if $\exists(\mathsf{SK},*,\mathsf{pk},\mathsf{PK}) \in T_{P-1}$,
    return pk;
if $\exists(\mathsf{SK},\mathsf{sk},\mathsf{pk},\mathsf{PK}) \in T_{H_0}$,
    return pk;
$\mathsf{sk} \twoheadleftarrow \mathcal{X}$, $T_P \leftarrow T_P \cup (*,\mathsf{sk},\mathsf{keygen}(\mathsf{sk}),\mathsf{PK})$,
    return $\mathsf{keygen}(\mathsf{sk})$.

Algo.$\mathcal{S}.P^{-1}(\mathsf{pk})$:

if $\exists(\mathsf{SK},*,\mathsf{pk},\mathsf{PK}) \in T_{P-1}$, return PK;
if $\exists(*,\mathsf{sk},\mathsf{pk},\mathsf{PK}) \in T_P$, return PK;
if $\exists(\mathsf{SK},\mathsf{sk},\mathsf{pk},\mathsf{PK}) \in T_{H_0}$, return PK;
$\mathsf{SK} \twoheadleftarrow \mathcal{X}$, $T_{P-1} \leftarrow T_{P-1} \cup (\mathsf{SK},*,\mathsf{pk},\mathsf{NKG}(\mathsf{SK}))$, return $\mathsf{NKG}(\mathsf{SK})$.

Algo.$\mathcal{S}.H_1(\mathsf{PK}_1,\mathsf{PK}_2,\mathsf{shk})$:

if $\exists(\mathsf{PK}_1,\mathsf{PK}_2,\mathsf{shk},\mathsf{SHK}) \in T_{H_1}$, return SHK;
$\mathsf{w} \twoheadleftarrow \mathcal{W}$,
if $\mathsf{PK}_1 > \mathsf{PK}_2$, $T_{H_1} \leftarrow T_{H_1} \cup (\mathsf{PK}_1,\mathsf{PK}_2,\mathsf{shk},\mathsf{w})$, return w;
else if $\exists(\mathsf{SK}_1,\mathsf{sk}_1,\mathsf{pk}_1,\mathsf{PK}_1) \in T_{H_0}, (\mathsf{SK}_2,\mathsf{sk}_2,\mathsf{pk}_2,\mathsf{PK}_2) \in T_{H_0}$,
        if $\mathsf{shk} = \mathsf{sharedkey}(\mathsf{sk}_1,\mathsf{pk}_2)$, return $\mathsf{NSK}(\mathsf{SK}_1,\mathsf{SK}_2)$;
        else $T_{H_1} \leftarrow T_{H_1} \cup (\mathsf{PK}_1,\mathsf{PK}_2,\mathsf{shk},\mathsf{w})$, return w.
    if $\exists(\mathsf{SK}_1,\mathsf{sk}_1,\mathsf{pk}_1,\mathsf{PK}_1) \in T_{H_0}, (*,\mathsf{sk}_2,\mathsf{pk}_2,\mathsf{PK}_2) \in T_P$,
        if $\mathsf{shk} = \mathsf{sharedkey}(\mathsf{sk}_1,\mathsf{pk}_2)$, return $\mathsf{NSK}(\mathsf{SK}_1,\mathsf{SK}_2)$;
        else $T_{H_1} \leftarrow T_{H_1} \cup (\mathsf{PK}_1,\mathsf{PK}_2,\mathsf{shk},\mathsf{w})$, return w.
    if $\exists(\mathsf{SK}_1,\mathsf{sk}_1,\mathsf{pk}_1,\mathsf{PK}_1) \in T_{H_0}, (\mathsf{SK}_2,*,\mathsf{pk}_2,\mathsf{PK}_2) \in T_{P-1}$,
        if $\mathsf{shk} = \mathsf{sharedkey}(\mathsf{sk}_1,\mathsf{pk}_2)$, return $\mathsf{NSK}(\mathsf{SK}_1,\mathsf{SK}_2)$;
        else $T_{H_1} \leftarrow T_{H_1} \cup (\mathsf{PK}_1,\mathsf{PK}_2,\mathsf{shk},\mathsf{w})$, return w.
    if $\exists(\mathsf{SK}_2,\mathsf{sk}_2,\mathsf{pk}_2,\mathsf{PK}_2) \in T_{H_0}, (*,\mathsf{sk}_1,\mathsf{pk}_1,\mathsf{PK}_1) \in T_P$,
        if $\mathsf{shk} = \mathsf{sharedkey}(\mathsf{sk}_2,\mathsf{pk}_1)$, return $\mathsf{NSK}(\mathsf{SK}_2,\mathsf{SK}_1)$;
        else $T_{H_1} \leftarrow T_{H_1} \cup (\mathsf{PK}_1,\mathsf{PK}_2,\mathsf{shk},\mathsf{w})$, return w.
    if $\exists(\mathsf{SK}_2,\mathsf{sk}_2,\mathsf{pk}_2,\mathsf{PK}_2) \in T_{H_0}, (\mathsf{SK}_1,*,\mathsf{pk}_1,\mathsf{PK}_1) \in T_{P-1}$,
        if $\mathsf{shk} = \mathsf{sharedkey}(\mathsf{sk}_2,\mathsf{pk}_1)$, return $\mathsf{NSK}(\mathsf{SK}_2,\mathsf{SK}_1)$;
        else, $T_{H_1} \leftarrow T_{H_1} \cup (\mathsf{PK}_1,\mathsf{PK}_2,\mathsf{shk},\mathsf{w})$, return w.
    if $\exists(\mathsf{SK}_1,*,\mathsf{pk}_1,\mathsf{PK}_1) \in T_{P-1}, (*,\mathsf{sk}_2,\mathsf{pk}_2,\mathsf{PK}_2) \in T_P$,
        if $\mathsf{shk} = \mathsf{sharedkey}(\mathsf{sk}_2,\mathsf{pk}_1)$, return $\mathsf{NSK}(\mathsf{SK}_1,\mathsf{SK}_2)$;
        else, $T_{H_1} \leftarrow T_{H_1} \cup (\mathsf{PK}_1,\mathsf{PK}_2,\mathsf{shk},\mathsf{w})$, return w.
    if $\exists(\mathsf{SK}_2,*,\mathsf{pk}_2,\mathsf{PK}_2) \in T_{P-1}, (*,\mathsf{sk}_1,\mathsf{pk}_1,\mathsf{PK}_1) \in T_P$,
        if $\mathsf{shk} = \mathsf{sharedkey}(\mathsf{sk}_1,\mathsf{pk}_2)$, return $\mathsf{NSK}(\mathsf{SK}_2,\mathsf{SK}_1)$;
        else, $T_{H_1} \leftarrow T_{H_1} \cup (\mathsf{PK}_1,\mathsf{PK}_2,\mathsf{shk},\mathsf{w})$, return w.
    $T_{H_1} \leftarrow T_{H_1} \cup (\mathsf{PK}_1,\mathsf{PK}_2,\mathsf{shk},\mathsf{w})$, <u>return w.</u>

Fig. 2. Simulator for NIKE in terms of four sub-simulators associated with two oracles $(\mathsf{NKG},\mathsf{NSK})$. These four sub-simulators share four tables $(T_{H_0},T_P,T_{P-1},T_{H_1})$ as joint state (which are initialized empty). The commands, e.g. "$\exists(\mathsf{SK},\mathsf{sk},\mathsf{pk},\mathsf{PK}) \in T_{H_0}$", go through the table in some well-defined order.

referring to $\mathcal{S}$ is efficient. In the following, we present the intuitive idea that why $\mathcal{S}$ works. Note that, in the real game, H_0, H_1 are random oracles, P is a random permutation associated with its inverse P^{-1}. Hence, the responses of a proper simulator should follow the following rules:

1. The responses of H_0, H_1 are computational close to uniform distribution;
2. The responses of P, P^{-1} are computational close to a random permutation;
3. There do not exist $(\mathsf{PK}_1 \neq \mathsf{PK}_2), (\mathsf{pk}_1 \neq \mathsf{pk}_2)$ such that $P^{(}\mathsf{PK}_1) = P^{(}\mathsf{PK}_2)$ or $P^{-1}(\mathsf{pk}_1) = P^{-1}(\mathsf{pk}_2)$;
4. $\mathsf{NKG}(\mathsf{SK}) = P^{-1}(\mathsf{keygen}(H_0(\mathsf{SK})))$;
5. $\mathsf{NSK}(\mathsf{SK}_1, \mathsf{PK}_2) = \mathsf{NSK}(\mathsf{SK}_2, \mathsf{PK}_1) = H_1(\{\mathsf{PK}_1, \mathsf{PK}_2\}^6, \mathsf{sharedkey}(\mathsf{sk}_1, \mathsf{pk}_2))$.

Next, we illustrate why and how $\mathcal{S}$ achieves these five rules.

Rule 1. Easy to note that the response of any H_0 query $(H_0(\mathsf{SK}))$ is well-formed. Roughly, $\mathcal{S}$ responds to it using T_{H_0}, T_P (the second term of the corresponding tuple) or with a random string $\mathsf{sk} \in \mathcal{X}$. Moreover, note that the second term in every tuple from table T_{H_0} or T_P is uniformly sampled, referring to $H_0(\mathsf{SK})$ is uniformly distributed. For H_1 query, say $H_1(\mathsf{PK}_1, \mathsf{PK}_2, \mathsf{shk})$, the simulator responds to it with either $\mathsf{NSK}(\mathsf{SK}_1, \mathsf{PK}_2)$ (if the tests pass) or a random string $\mathsf{w} \in \mathcal{W}$. And we note that $(\mathsf{NKG}, \mathsf{NSK})$ is an ideal NIKE, which means that $\mathsf{NSK}(\mathsf{SK}_1, \mathsf{PK}_2)$ is uniformly distributed.

Rule 2. For P query, say $P(\mathsf{PK})$, the simulator responds to the query in four cases: 1) using T_P; 2) using $T_{P^{-1}}$; 3) using T_{H_0}; 4) randomly sampling a secret key and outputting the corresponding public key. Easy to note that, in case 1, 3, and 4, $\mathcal{S}$ always returns a random public key, and due to the pseudo-random public keys, we have that the response is computational close to uniform. For Case 2, note that if $\mathsf{PK} \in \mathsf{T_{P\text{-}1}}$, then we know that the adversary has made a query $P^{-1}(\mathsf{pk})$ previously. For that P^{-1} query, $\mathcal{S}$ samples $\mathsf{SK} \in \mathcal{X}$ and responds to it with $\mathsf{PK} = \mathsf{NKG}(\mathsf{SK})$. As $(\mathsf{NKG}, \mathsf{NSK})$ is an ideal NIKE, we have that PK is close to uniform in $\mathcal{Y}$ and the response of $P^{-1}(\mathsf{pk})$ is well distributed. As a result, when making a query $P(\mathsf{PK})$, pk is the proper answer. Moreover, P^{-1} is P's inverse, which means the responses of P^{-1} are also well-distributed.

Rule 3. This rule indicates that P and P^{-1} must be bijective. For $\mathcal{S}$, note that there are four bad cases that break the rule:

1. pk-collision: $\mathcal{A}$ makes a query $P(\mathsf{pk}^*)$ with response PK_1^*, and then it makes another query $P^{-1}(\mathsf{PK}_2^*)$ with response pk^*;
2. PK-collision: $\mathcal{A}$ makes a query $P(\mathsf{PK}^*)$ with response pk_1^*, and then it makes another query $P(\mathsf{pk}_2^*)$ with response $\mathsf{NKG}(\mathsf{SK}^*) = \mathsf{PK}^*$;
3. Guessed-$H_0(\mathsf{SK})$-on-pk*: adversary makes a query $P^{-1}(\mathsf{PK}^*)$ with response $\mathsf{keygen}(\mathsf{sk}^*)$, and $\mathcal{A}$ also makes a query $H_0(\mathsf{SK})$ such that $\mathsf{keygen}(H_0(\mathsf{SK}^*)) = \mathsf{keygen}(\mathsf{sk}^*)$ and $\mathsf{NKG}(\mathsf{SK}) \neq \mathsf{PK}^*$;
4. Guessed-SK*-on-PK*: $\mathcal{A}$ makes a query $P(\mathsf{pk}^*)$ with response $\mathsf{NKG}(\mathsf{SK}^*)$, and $\mathcal{A}$ also makes a query $H_0(\mathsf{SK}^*)$ such that $\mathsf{keygen}(H_0(\mathsf{SK}^*)) \neq \mathsf{pk}^*$.

---

[6] If $\mathsf{PK}_1 \leq \mathsf{PK}_2$, $\{\mathsf{PK}_1, \mathsf{PK}_2\} = (\mathsf{PK}_1, \mathsf{PK}_2)$, and else $\mathsf{PK}_1 \leq \mathsf{PK}_2 = (\mathsf{PK}_2, \mathsf{PK}_1)$.

For case 1, due to pseudorandom random public keys, it occurs with negligible probability. For case 2, as NKG is ideal NIKE oracle, collision never happens except with negligible probability.

For case 3, as the simulator samples sk^*, which is independent of $\mathcal{A}$'s view, the probability of $\mathcal{A}$ outputs a proper SK ($H_0(\mathsf{SK}) = \mathsf{sk}^*$) is bounded by pseudorandom public keys. Analogously, in case 4 $\mathcal{A}$ cannot guess SK^* correctly except for negligible probability.

Rule 4. Note that if the adversary first makes a query $H_0(\mathsf{SK})$, then the equation holds for certain when it requests P^{-1}. Hence, the only chance that $\mathcal{A}$ violates this rule is case 3 in Rule 3 occurs, referring to Rule 4 holds as long as Rule 3 holds.

Rule 5. Firstly, we note that the responses of H_1 queries are independent of the ones of H_0, P, P^{-1} queries, and the only consistency $\mathcal{S}$ has to preserve is the equation in this rule. Immediately observe that, if and only if, the inputs of the H_1 are in a good form (say, $\mathsf{PK}_1 = \mathsf{PK}_2$ and shk is a valid shared key of pk_1 and pk_2), the response should be consistent to NSK-oracle (if the inputs are not in a good form, then the response is independent of NSK-oracle with high probability).

Easy note that, except for the last case (associated with underline), $\mathcal{S}$ responds to H_1 queries properly: $\mathcal{S}$ calls NSK-oracle when the input is within good form and otherwise returns a string $\mathsf{w} \in \mathcal{W}$. While, for the last one, the simulator just responds with w without checking whether the inputs are good or not. Hence, we hope that, for the last case, either the inputs are not in a good form or $\mathsf{NSK}(\mathsf{SK}_1, \mathsf{PK}_2)$ is independent of $\mathcal{A}$'s view. In fact, there are three bad cases that might break it:

1. A known secret key and another random public key: $\mathcal{A}$ chooses sk_1 and makes a query $P^{-1}(\mathsf{keygen}(\mathsf{sk}_1))$ with response $\mathsf{PK}_1 = \mathsf{NKG}(\mathsf{SK}_1)$, while $\mathsf{PK}_2 \notin T_P \cup T_{P^{-1}} \cup T_{H_0}$;
2. Two known secret keys in $T_{P^{-1}}$: Adversary chooses $\mathsf{sk}_1, \mathsf{sk}_2$ and makes queries $P^{-1}(\mathsf{keygen}(\mathsf{sk}_1)), P^{-1}(\mathsf{keygen}(\mathsf{sk}_2))$ with responses $\mathsf{NKG}(\mathsf{SK}_1), \mathsf{NKG}(\mathsf{SK}_2)$;
3. Two known public keys without secret key keys: $\mathcal{A}$ chooses $\mathsf{SK}_1, \mathsf{SK}_2$ and makes queries $P(\mathsf{NKG}(\mathsf{SK}_1)), P(\mathsf{NKG}(\mathsf{SK}_2))$ with responses $\mathsf{pk}_1 = \mathsf{keygen}(\mathsf{sk}_1), \mathsf{pk}_2 = \mathsf{keygen}(\mathsf{sk}_2)$.

For case 1, we note that PK_2 never appears in tables $T_P, T_{P^{-1}}$ and T_{H_0}, which means $P(\mathsf{PK}_2)$ is independent of $\mathcal{A}$'s view. Hence, the probability that shk is a valid shared key is bounded by the entropic shared keys (illustrated in Attack 6), which is negligible.

For case 2, we observe that $\mathcal{A}$ chooses the two secret keys itself; hence shk would be a valid shared key if $\mathcal{A}$ wants. However, SK_1 and SK_2 are independent of $\mathcal{A}$'s view, which refers to that $\mathsf{NSK}(\mathsf{SK}_1, \mathsf{PK}_2)$ is also independent of $\mathcal{A}$'s view.

For case 3, $\mathcal{A}$ knows pk_1 and pk_2 while the corresponding secret keys sk_1 and sk_2 are independent of $\mathcal{A}$'s view. Meanwhile, the adversary might implement $(\mathsf{NKG}, \mathsf{NSK})$ into oracles and use those oracles as an additional helper to predict the shared key (illustrated in Attack 7). Fortunately, $(\mathsf{NKG}, \mathsf{NSK})$ is an ideal

NIKE; thus the only thing the adversary can do is *equality test*, which means the oracles adversary implements is the best helper it can count on. Hence, the probability that shk is a valid shared key is bounded by the semi-active unpredictable shared keys.

4 Indifferentiable Public Key Encryption

In this section, we propose the notion of "ideal PKE" and then build an indifferentiable public key encryption scheme from ideal NIKE and random oracles. Roughly, our strategy consists of two steps: first, we construct an indifferentiable deterministic public key encryption (DPKE) from an ideal NIKE, and then build an indifferentiable PKE from an ideal DPKE.

4.1 What Is Ideal PKE?

In this part, we give the rigorous description of ideal PKE, formally:

Definition 6 (Ideal PKE). *Let $\mathcal{X}, \mathcal{Y}, \mathcal{M}, \mathcal{R}, \mathcal{C}$ be five sets such that: 1) $|\mathcal{X}| \geq 2^{\omega(\log \lambda)}, |\mathcal{Y}| \geq 2^{\omega(\log \lambda)}, |\mathcal{R}| \geq 2^{\omega(\log \lambda)}$ and $|\mathcal{C}| \geq 2^{\omega(\log \lambda)}$; 2) $|\mathcal{X}| \leq |\mathcal{Y}|$; 3) $|\mathcal{Y}| \times |\mathcal{M}| \times |\mathcal{R}| \leq |\mathcal{C}|$. We denote $\mathcal{F}[\mathcal{X} \to \mathcal{Y}]$ as the set of all injections that map $\mathcal{X}$ to $\mathcal{Y}$; $\mathcal{E}[\mathcal{Y} \times \mathcal{M} \times \mathcal{R} \to \mathcal{C}]$ as the set of all injections that map $\mathcal{Y} \times \mathcal{M} \times \mathcal{R}$ to $\mathcal{C}$ and $\mathcal{D}[\mathcal{C} \times \mathcal{X} \to \mathcal{M} \cup \perp]$ as the set of all functions that map $\mathcal{X} \times \mathcal{C}$ to $\mathcal{M} \cup \perp$. We define $\mathcal{T}$ as the set of all function tuples (F, E, D) such that:*

- *$F \in \mathcal{F}, E \in \mathcal{E}$ and $D \in \mathcal{D}$;*
- *$\forall x \in \mathcal{X}, m \in \mathcal{M}$ and $r \in \mathcal{R}$, $D(x, E(F(x), m, r)) = m$;*
- *$\forall x \in \mathcal{X}, c \in \mathcal{C}$, if there is no $(m, r) \in \mathcal{M} \times \mathcal{R}$ such that $E(F(x), m, r) = c$, then $D(x, c) = \perp$.*

We say that a PKE scheme $\Pi_{\mathsf{PKE}} = (\mathsf{PKE.KEYGEN}, \mathsf{PKE.ENC}, \mathsf{PKE.DEC})$, associated with secret key space $\mathcal{X}$, public space $\mathcal{Y}$, message space $\mathcal{M}$, nonce space space $\mathcal{R}$, and ciphertext space $\mathcal{C}$, is an ideal PKE if Π_{PKE} is sampled from $\mathcal{T}$ uniformly. Moreover, if the nonce space is empty, then we say such a scheme is an ideal DPKE.

4.2 Construction for Deterministic PKE

In this section, we build an indifferentiable *deterministic* PKE (DPKE) from simpler ideal primitives (namely random oracles and ideal ciphers) along with an ideal NIKE. We firstly present our first attempt of the construction and then illustrate a differentiator to break it (this attack also indicates a difficulty of building indifferentiable PKE). Next, we give our solution to get rid of the attack and establish the proof.

First Attempt to Build an Indifferentiable DPKE. Given an ideal NIKE Π_{NIKE}, a natural way to build an indifferentiable DPKE is the following: 1) convert this ideal NIKE into a PKE scheme; 2) apply the Fujisaki-Okamoto transformation [15], which combines with a random oracle to give at least CCA-2 security. The hope is that this transformation would give us an indifferentiable DPKE. Specifically, let $\Pi_{\mathsf{NIKE}} = (\mathsf{NKG}, \mathsf{NSK})$ be an ideal NIKE, associated with secret key space $\mathcal{X}$, public key space $\mathcal{Y}$ and shared key space $\mathcal{Z}$, and we denote $\mathsf{sk}, \mathsf{pk}, \mathsf{shk}$ to be the secret key, public key and shared key of Π_{NIKE}, respectively. For an easy exposition, we always denote the inputs of component primitives (for instance, in the standard model NIKE in Sect. 3 or the ideal NIKE in this section) as the lower-case and inputs of the target primitives as the upper-case. Let $H_0, H_1 := \{0,1\}^* \to \mathcal{X}; H_2 := \{0,1\}^* \to \mathcal{Z}; H_3 := \{0,1\}^* \to \mathcal{M}$, then applying FO-transform, we have the following DPKE scheme: $\Pi_{\mathsf{DPKE}} = (\mathsf{DPKE.KEYGEN}, \mathsf{DPKE.ENC}, \mathsf{DPKE.DEC})$.

- DPKE.KEYGEN(SK): On inputs secret key SK, the algorithm outputs public key $\mathsf{PK} = \mathsf{NKG}(H_0(\mathsf{SK}))$;
- DPKE.ENC(PK, M): On inputs public key PK and message M, the algorithm computes $\delta = H_2(\mathsf{PK}\|\mathsf{M})$, and outputs ciphertext C as

$$\mathsf{C} = (\mathsf{C}_1, \mathsf{C}_2, \mathsf{C}_3) = (\mathsf{NKG}(H_1(\mathsf{PK}\|\mathsf{M})), \delta \oplus \mathsf{NSK}(\mathsf{PK}, H_1(\mathsf{PK}\|\mathsf{M})), H_3(\mathsf{PK}, \delta) \oplus \mathsf{M});$$

- DPKE.DEC(SK, C): On inputs secret key SK and ciphertext $\mathsf{C} = (\mathsf{C}_1, \mathsf{C}_2, \mathsf{C}_3)$, the algorithm computes:

$$\mathsf{PK} = \mathsf{DPKE.KEYGEN}(\mathsf{SK}); \mathsf{A}_1 = \mathsf{NSK}(\mathsf{C}_1, H_0(\mathsf{SK}));$$
$$\mathsf{A}_2 = \mathsf{C}_2 \oplus \mathsf{A}_1; \mathsf{A}_3 = \mathsf{C}_3 \oplus H_3(\mathsf{PK}\|\mathsf{A}_2).$$

Then it tests whether $\mathsf{C} \overset{?}{=} \mathsf{DPKE.ENC}(\mathsf{PK}\|\mathsf{M})$. If yes, then outputs A_3, else aborts.

Correctness easily follows, but this scheme is not indifferentiable. Next we present a differentiator to break it.

Differentiator for FO Transform. Due to definition, $\mathcal{D}$ has three honest interfaces (DPKE.KEYGEN, DPKE.ENC, DPKE.DEC) (below, we will denote (DKG, DE, DD) for short) and six adversarial interfaces (H_0, H_1, H_2, H_3, NKG, NSK), and we build $\mathcal{D}$ as in Fig. 3:

Differentiator $\mathcal{D}$:
$\mathsf{SK} \overset{\$}{\leftarrow} \mathcal{X}, \mathsf{M} \overset{\$}{\leftarrow} \mathcal{M}; \mathsf{A} \leftarrow \mathsf{DKG}(\mathsf{SK}), (\mathsf{B}_1, \mathsf{B}_2, \mathsf{B}_3) \leftarrow \mathsf{DE}(\mathsf{A}, \mathsf{M});$
$\mathsf{Q}_1 \leftarrow H_0(\mathsf{SK}), \mathsf{Q}_2 \leftarrow \mathsf{NSK}(\mathsf{B}_1, \mathsf{Q}_1), \mathsf{Q}_3 = H_3(\mathsf{A}, \mathsf{Q}_2 \oplus \mathsf{B}_2);$
Return $1(\mathsf{Q}_3 = \mathsf{B}_3 \oplus \mathsf{M})$

Fig. 3. Differentiator for FO-transform.

We immediately observe that, in the real game, A and $(\mathsf{B}_1, \mathsf{B}_2, \mathsf{B}_3)$ are the corresponding public key and ciphertext, respectively. Moreover, due to Π_{NIKE}'s correctness, we have

$$\mathsf{NSK}(\mathsf{PK}, H_1(\mathsf{PK}\|\mathsf{M})) = \mathsf{NSK}(\mathsf{C}_1, H_0(\mathsf{sk})) = \mathsf{NSK}(\mathsf{B}_1, \mathsf{Q}_1).$$

which means that $\mathcal{D}$ always outputs 1. However, in the ideal game, the simulator knows nothing of queries to the honest interfaces, and the only information it has is: $(\mathsf{SK}, \mathsf{A}, \mathsf{B_1}, \mathsf{B_2})$ (other information such like $\mathsf{H_0}(\mathsf{SK}), \mathsf{NSK}(\mathsf{B_1}, \mathsf{Q_1})$ and $\mathsf{H_3}(\mathsf{A}, \mathsf{Q_2} \oplus \mathsf{B_2})$ are simulated by $\mathcal{S}$ itself). Therefore, without decryption oracle, M is independent of simulator's view. And the decryption oracle always aborts except $\mathcal{S}$ hands in a valid ciphertext, which consists of three elements $(\mathsf{B_1}, \mathsf{B_2}, \mathsf{B_3})$. Moreover, in the ideal world, the honest interface DPKE.ENC is a random injection, hence $\Pr[\mathcal{S} \text{ outputs a valid } \mathsf{B_3}] \leq \frac{\mathrm{poly}(\lambda)}{|\mathcal{M}|}$.

Our Solution. To prevent the attack above, the only hope is $\mathcal{S}$ can always output a valid ciphertext itself. Our trick is, instead of using random oracles, we use an ideal cipher model P, with inverse. Specifically, let $\mathcal{Z} = \mathcal{Y} \times \mathcal{M}$ (we specify the shared key space of Π_{NIKE} to be $\mathcal{Y} \times \mathcal{M}$ and $|\mathcal{X}| \leq |\mathcal{M}|$), and $P := \mathcal{Z} \to \mathcal{Z}$. Now, we denote $\delta = P(\mathsf{PK}\|\mathsf{M})$, and modify the ciphertext as $C = (\mathsf{NKG}(\mathsf{H_1}(\mathsf{PK}\|\mathsf{M})), \delta \oplus \mathsf{NSK}(\mathsf{PK}, \mathsf{H_1}(\mathsf{PK}\|\mathsf{M})))$. Formally:

- DPKE.KEYGEN(SK): On inputs secret key SK, the algorithm outputs public key $\mathsf{PK} = \mathsf{NKG}(H_0(\mathsf{SK}))$;
- DPKE.ENC(PK, M): On inputs public key PK and message M, the algorithm computes $\delta = P(\mathsf{PK}\|\mathsf{M})$, and outputs ciphertext C as

$$\mathsf{C} = (\mathsf{C_1}, \mathsf{C_2}) = (\mathsf{NKG}(H_1(\mathsf{PK}\|\mathsf{M})), \delta \oplus \mathsf{NSK}(\mathsf{PK}, \mathsf{H_1}(\mathsf{PK}, \mathsf{M})));$$

- DPKE.DEC(SK, C): On inputs secret key SK and ciphertext $\mathsf{C} = (\mathsf{C_1}, \mathsf{C_2})$, the algorithm computes:

$$\mathsf{PK} = \mathsf{DPKE.KEYGEN}(\mathsf{SK}); \mathsf{A_1} = \mathsf{NSK}(\mathsf{C_1}, H_0(\mathsf{SK}));$$
$$\mathsf{A_2} = \mathsf{C_2} \oplus \mathsf{A_1}; \mathsf{A_3} = P^{-1}(\mathsf{A_2}), \mathsf{A_4} = \mathsf{A_3}/\mathsf{PK}.$$

Then it tests whether $\mathsf{C} \overset{?}{=} \mathsf{DPKE.ENC}(\mathsf{A_3})$. If yes, then outputs $\mathsf{A_4}$[7], else aborts.

In our new setting, we immediately observe that the ciphertext only consists of *two* elements, which means $\mathcal{S}$ can always hand in the valid ciphertext to the decryption oracle. As a result, our new scheme prevents the attack above. Apparently, this is *only* an evidence that our new scheme prevents this specific differentiator. And to prove it's an indifferentiable DPKE, we need to show that our scheme can prevent all kind of efficient differentiators.

Theorem 7 (Indifferentiable DPKE). Π_{DPKE} *is indifferentiable from an ideal DPKE if* $\Pi_{\mathsf{NIKE}} = (\mathsf{NKG}, \mathsf{NSK})$ *is an ideal NIKE. More precisely, there exists a simulator $\mathcal{S}$ such that for all* $(q_{H_0}, q_{H_1}, q_P, q_{P^{-1}}, q_{\mathsf{NKG}}, q_{\mathsf{NSK}})$-*query PPT differentiator $\mathcal{D}$ with* $q_{H_0} + q_{H_1} + q_P + q_{P^{-1}} + q_{\mathsf{NKG}} + q_{\mathsf{NSK}} \leq q$, *we have*

$$\mathrm{Adv}^{\mathrm{indif}}_{\Pi_{\mathsf{DPKE}}, \mathcal{S}, \mathcal{D}} \leq \frac{11q^2}{|\mathcal{X}|} + \frac{20q^2}{|\mathcal{Y}|}.$$

The simulator makes at most q^2 *queries to its oracles.*

---

[7] We note that $\mathsf{A_3} = \mathsf{PK}\|\mathsf{M}$, and by $\mathsf{A_3}/\mathsf{PK}$, we mean removing PK from $\mathsf{A_3}$.

4.3 Construction for PKE

In this section, we complete the construction by building an indifferentiable PKE from ideal DPKE and random oracles. Similarly as in Sect. 4.2, we firstly present two attempts and then illustrate the corresponding differentiators to break the schemes. Then we give the modified solution to get rid of those attacks and complete the proof.

First Attempt to Build an Indifferentiable PKE. Immediately to observe that we cannot build our scheme in the trivial way, say, treating the random nonce as part of the message and discarding it in the decryption procedure, because this construction loss the information of the randomness and that would induce a differentiator which trivially tests the validity of the randomness. To prevent it, we again apply the hash technique ($H_0 := \{0,1\}^* \to \mathcal{R}$); we first hash the nonce and then use the hashed value as the randomness. Specifically,

- PKE.KEYGEN(SK) = DKG(SK);
- PKE.ENC(PK, M, R) = DE(PK, M$\|H_0$(PK, M, R));
- PKE.DEC(SK, C): On inputs a secret key SK and a ciphertext C, the algorithm runs DD(SK, C). If DD aborts then the algorithm aborts, else let (M$\|$str) = DD(C, SK), it outputs M.

However, the scheme would not achieve indifferentiability if the random oracle is not well-designed, and the following we give out a differentiator to break our first attempt in Fig. 4:

Differentiator $\mathcal{D}$:
SK $\xleftarrow{\$} \mathcal{X}$, M $\xleftarrow{\$} \mathcal{M}$; r $\xleftarrow{\$} \mathcal{R}$; A $\leftarrow$ PKG(SK), B $\leftarrow$ DE(A, M$\|$r), Q$_1$ $\leftarrow$ PD(sk, B),
Return $1(\mathsf{Q}_1 \neq \perp)$

Fig. 4. Differentiator for non-well-designed random oracle.

Easy to note that, in real game, $\Pr[\mathcal{D} = 1] = 1$. Meanwhile, in ideal game, we claim that, with noticeable probability, the decryption would abort. In fact, the decryption procedure outputs M if and only if there exists a nonce R $\in \mathcal{R}$ such that H_0(PK, M, R) = r. Moreover, R, r $\in \mathcal{R}$, and H_0 is a random oracle, we have that $\Pr[\forall \mathsf{R} \in \mathcal{R}, H_0(\mathsf{PK}, \mathsf{M}, \mathsf{R}) \neq r] \approx 1/e$, referring to $\Pr[\mathcal{D} = 1] \leq 1 - 1/e \approx 0.6$.

Our Solution. To prevent this attack, we have to shorten the size of H_0's range, to make sure that every element in H_0's range has pre-image with high probability. Meanwhile, to make sure the ciphertext space is sufficiently large, we also need to pad some dummy strings. Specifically, let Π_{DPKE} be an ideal DPKE, associated with secret key space $\mathcal{X}$, public key space $\mathcal{Y} = \{0,1\}^{n_1}$, message space $\mathcal{M} = \{0,1\}^{n_2+2n_3}$, and ciphertext space $\mathcal{C}$, and let $H_0 := \{0,1\}^* \to \{0,1\}^{n_3}$, where $n_2 > 0$ and $n_1, n_3 \geq \omega(\log \lambda)$, then we build our scheme as:

- PKE.KEYGEN(SK) = DKG(SK):
- PKE.ENC(PK, M, R): On inputs public key PK, message $M \in \{0,1\}^{n_2}$ and nonce $R \in \{0,1\}^{2n_3}$, the algorithm outputs ciphertext:

$$C = DE(PK, M||H_0(PK, M, R)||\underbrace{0\ldots0}_{n_3});$$

- PKE.DEC(SK, C): On inputs secret key SK and ciphertext C, the algorithm runs $A = D_{DPKE}(SK, C)$. If $A = \perp$ or the last n_3 bits are not 0^{n_3}, then it aborts, else the algorithm outputs the first n_2 bits.

Correctness follows easily, and the rest is to show its indifferentiability.

Theorem 8 (Indifferentiable PKE). Π_{PKE} *is indifferentiable from an ideal PKE if* $\Pi_{\mathsf{DPKE}} = (DKG, DE, DD)$ *is an ideal DPKE. More precisely, there exists a simulator such that for all* $(q_{H_0}, q_{DKG}, q_{DE}, q_{DD})$*-query PPT differentiator* $\mathcal{D}$ *with* $q_{H_0} + q_{DKG} + q_{DE} + q_{DD} \leq q$, *we have*

$$\mathrm{Adv}^{\mathrm{indif}}_{\Pi_{\mathsf{PKE}}, \mathcal{S}, \mathcal{D}} \leq 3q(\frac{1}{e})^{2n_3} + \frac{6q^2}{2^{n_3}} + \frac{3q^2}{|\mathcal{C}|} + \frac{q}{|\mathcal{Y}| \times |\mathcal{M}|}.$$

The simulator makes at most q^2 *queries to its oracles.*

5 Indifferentiable Digital Signatures

In this section, we extend our result to the digital signature scheme. We propose the notion of "Ideal Signature", and then build an indifferentiable signature scheme from simpler ideal primitives (random oracle model and ideal cipher model) and a stand-model signature scheme.

5.1 What Is "Ideal Signature"?

In this part, we give the rigorous description of ideal signature, formally:

Definition 9 (Ideal Signature). *Let* $\mathcal{X}, \mathcal{Y}, \mathcal{M}, \Sigma$ *be four sets such that:* 1) $|\mathcal{X}| \geq 2^{\omega(\log \lambda)}, |\mathcal{Y}| \geq 2^{\omega(\log \lambda)}, |\mathcal{M}| \geq 2^{\omega(\log \lambda)}$ *and* $|\Sigma| \geq 2^{\omega(\log \lambda)}$; 2) $|\mathcal{X}| \leq |\mathcal{Y}|$; 3) $|\mathcal{X}| \times |\mathcal{M}| \leq |\Sigma|$. *We denote* $\mathcal{F}[\mathcal{X} \to \mathcal{Y}]$ *as the set of all injections that map* $\mathcal{X}$ *to* $\mathcal{Y}$; $\mathcal{S}[\mathcal{X} \times \mathcal{M} \to \Sigma]$ *as the set of all injections that map* $\mathcal{X} \times \mathcal{M}$ *to* Σ *and* $\mathcal{V}[\mathcal{Y} \times \mathcal{M} \times \Sigma \to \{0,1\}]$ *as the set of all functions that map* $\mathcal{Y} \times \mathcal{M} \times \Sigma$ *to a bit. We define* $\mathcal{T}$ *as the set of all function tuples* (F, S, V) *such that:*

- $F \in \mathcal{F}, S \in \mathcal{S}$ *and* $V \in \mathcal{V}$;
- $\forall x \in \mathcal{X}, m \in \mathcal{M}, V(F(x), m, S(x, m)) = 1$;
- $\forall x \in \mathcal{X}, m \in \mathcal{M}$ *and* $\sigma \in \Sigma$, *if* $\sigma \neq \mathsf{sign}(x, m)$, *then* $V(F(x), m, \sigma) = 0$;
- $\forall x \in \mathcal{X}, m \in \mathcal{M}$ *and* $\sigma_1, \sigma_2 \in \Sigma, V(F(x), m, \sigma_1) = V(F(x), m, \sigma_2) = 1 \Rightarrow$ $\sigma_1 = \sigma_2$.

We say that a digital signature scheme $\Pi_{\mathsf{Sig}} = (\mathsf{Sig.KEYGEN}, \mathsf{Sig.SIGN}, \mathsf{Sig.VER})$, *associated with secret key space* $\mathcal{X}$, *public key space* $\mathcal{Y}$, *message space* $\mathcal{M}$ *and signature space* Σ, *is an ideal digital signature, if* Π_{Sig} *is sampled from* $\mathcal{T}$ *uniformly.*

5.2   Construction

In this section, we build our indifferentiable signature scheme from random oracle model and a standard-model signature scheme.

Difficulty of Building an Indifferentiable Signature. To achieve indifferentiability, we note that the signature σ would be masked by an idealized primitive, say $\Sigma = P^{-1}(\sigma)$ as above. In the verification algorithm, the scheme inverts Σ and uses σ to proceed. Unfortunately, this P-technique is insufficient here. In fact, given Σ (it is either a valid signature or a random string), the simulator cannot call Ver (the ideal signature) for help, as it does not know the public key and message. So the simulator cannot respond to $P(\Sigma)$ properly. To get rid of this difficulty, we would apply an ideal cipher model (E, E^{-1}) instead, where we set $(\mathsf{PK}, \mathsf{M})$ as its secret key. How does it help? We note that we force the adversary to hand it the public key and message to the simulator when inverting Σ; as a result, the simulator can call Ver and simulate $E(\Sigma)$ properly. Concretely,

Building Blocks. Our scheme will consist of several building blocks:

- A standard-model signature scheme $\Pi_{\mathsf{SM-Sig}} = (\mathsf{keygen}, \mathsf{sign}, \mathsf{ver})$ with secret key space $\mathcal{X}$, public key space $\mathcal{Y} = \{0,1\}^{n_1}$, message space $\mathcal{M} = \{0,1\}^{n_2}$ and signature space $\mathcal{Z} \subset \{0,1\}^{n_3}$;
- $H_0 := \{0,1\}^* \to \mathcal{X}; H_1 := \{0,1\}^* \to \mathcal{M}$;
- $P := \{0,1\}^{n_1} \to \{0,1\}^{n_1}$ is a random permutation and P^{-1} is P's inverse,
- $E := \{0,1\}^{n_1+n_2} \times \{0,1\}^{n_3} \to \{0,1\}^{n_3}$ is an ideal cipher model, where $\{0,1\}^{n_1+n_2}$ is its key space and E^{-1} is its inverse.

Construction. Now we are ready to build an indifferentiable signature scheme, denoted as $\Pi_{\mathsf{Sig}} = (\mathsf{Sig.KEYGEN}, \mathsf{Sig.SIGN}, \mathsf{Sig.VER})$, from the building blocks above. Formally,

- $\mathsf{Sig.KEYGEN}(\mathsf{SK})$: On inputs secret key SK, the algorithm outputs public key $\mathsf{PK} = P^{-1}(\mathsf{keygen}(H_0(\mathsf{SK})))$;
- $\mathsf{Sig.SIGN}(\mathsf{SK}, \mathsf{M})$: On inputs secret key SK and message M, the algorithm computes $\mathsf{PK} = \mathsf{Sig.KEYGEN}(\mathsf{SK})$ and outputs the signature

$$\Sigma = E^{-1}((\mathsf{PK}\|\mathsf{M}), \mathsf{sign}(H_0(\mathsf{SK}), H_1(\mathsf{M}))),$$

- $\mathsf{Sig.VER}(\mathsf{PK}, \mathsf{M}, \Sigma)$: On inputs public key PK, message M and the signature σ, the algorithm outputs a bit $b = \mathsf{ver}(P(\mathsf{PK}), H_1(\mathsf{M}), E((\mathsf{PK}\|\mathsf{M}), \Sigma))$.

Correctness easily follows, and the rest is to prove its indifferentiability. Before that, we specify several security properties of the standard-model signature.

Property 1 UNIQUENESS. We say a signature achieves uniqueness, if $\forall (\mathsf{pk}, \mathsf{sk}) \leftarrow \mathsf{keygen}, \mathsf{m} \in \mathcal{M}, \sigma_1, \sigma_2 \in \Sigma$, we have,

$$\mathsf{ver}(\mathsf{pk}, \mathsf{m}, \sigma_1) = \mathsf{ver}(\mathsf{pk}, \mathsf{m}, \sigma_2) = 1 \Rightarrow \sigma_1 = \sigma_2.$$

Property 2 RANDOM-MESSAGE ATTACK (RMA). We say a signature scheme is RMA-secure if there is ϵ_1 such that for any PPT adversary $\mathcal{A}$, the advantage

$$\text{Adv}_{\mathcal{A}} := \Pr[\text{ver}(\text{pk}, m^*, \sigma^*) = 1 : \sigma^* \leftarrow \mathcal{A}^{\text{sign}(\text{sk}, m_1, \ldots, m_q)}(\text{pk}, m^*)] \leq \epsilon_1 = \text{negl}(\lambda),$$

where $(\text{pk}, \text{sk}) \leftarrow \text{keygen}, (m^*, m_1, \ldots, m_q) \xleftarrow{\$} \mathcal{M}$ and m^* was not previously signed.

Property 3 PSEUDORANDOM PUBLIC KEY. We say the public key is pseudorandom, if there is ϵ_2 such that for any PPT adversary $\mathcal{A}$, $r \leftarrow \mathcal{X}, R \leftarrow \mathcal{Y}$.

$$\text{Adv}_{\mathcal{A}} := |\Pr[\mathcal{A}(\text{keygen}(r))] - \Pr[\mathcal{A}(R)]| \leq \epsilon_2 = \text{negl}(\lambda).$$

We say a signature scheme is Good if it satisfies the three properties above.

Theorem 10 (Indifferentiable Signatures). Π_{Sig} *is indifferentiable from an ideal digital signature if* $\Pi_{\text{SM-Sig}}$ *is* Good. *More preciously, there exists a simulator* $\mathcal{S}$ *such that for all* $(q_{H_0}, q_{H_1}, q_P, q_{P^{-1}}, q_E, q_{E^{-1}})$-*query PPT differentiator* $\mathcal{D}$ *with* $q_{H_0} + q_{H_1} + q_P + q_{P^{-1}} + q_E + q_{E^{-1}} \leq q$, *we have*

$$\text{Adv}_{\Pi_{Sig}, \mathcal{S}, \mathcal{D}}^{\text{indif}} \leq 15q^2 \sqrt{2\epsilon_2 + \frac{1}{|\mathcal{X}|}} + \frac{6q^2}{|\mathcal{Y}|} + \frac{8q}{|\mathcal{Z}|} + \frac{2q^2}{|\mathcal{M}|} + 6q^2\epsilon_1 + 3q^2\sqrt{\epsilon_2}.$$

The simulator makes at most q^2 *queries to its oracles.*

Acknowledgments. We thank Prof. Martin Albrecht for navigating the revisions of our paper as a shepherd. We thank the anonymous reviewers of Eurocrypt'2020 for pointing out a proof flaw in our earlier version. Mark Zhandry is supported by the Defense Advanced Research Projects Agency through the ARL under Contract W911NF-15-C-0205 and NSF grant 1616442. The views expressed are those of the authors and do not reflect the official policy or position of the Department of Defense or the National Science Foundation.

References

1. Andreeva, E., Bogdanov, A., Dodis, Y., Mennink, B., Steinberger, J.P.: On the indifferentiability of key-alternating ciphers. In: Canetti, R., Garay, J.A. (eds.) CRYPTO 2013. LNCS, vol. 8042, pp. 531–550. Springer, Heidelberg (2013). https://doi.org/10.1007/978-3-642-40041-4_29
2. Barbosa, M., Farshim, P.: Indifferentiable authenticated encryption. In: Shacham, H., Boldyreva, A. (eds.) CRYPTO 2018. LNCS, vol. 10991, pp. 187–220. Springer, Cham (2018). https://doi.org/10.1007/978-3-319-96884-1_7
3. Bellare, M., Boldyreva, A., O'Neill, A.: Deterministic and efficiently searchable encryption. In: Menezes, A. (ed.) CRYPTO 2007. LNCS, vol. 4622, pp. 535–552. Springer, Heidelberg (2007). https://doi.org/10.1007/978-3-540-74143-5_30
4. Bellare, M., Rogaway, P.: Random oracles are practical: a paradigm for designing efficient protocols. In: Proceedings of the 1st ACM Conference on Computer and Communications Security, pp. 62–73. ACM (1993)

5. Black, J.: The ideal-cipher model, revisited: an uninstantiable blockcipher-based hash function. In: Robshaw, M. (ed.) FSE 2006. LNCS, vol. 4047, pp. 328–340. Springer, Heidelberg (2006). https://doi.org/10.1007/11799313_21
6. Bleichenbacher, D.: Chosen ciphertext attacks against protocols based on the RSA encryption standard PKCS #1. In: Krawczyk, H. (ed.) CRYPTO 1998. LNCS, vol. 1462, pp. 1–12. Springer, Heidelberg (1998). https://doi.org/10.1007/BFb0055716
7. Canetti, R., Goldreich, O., Halevi, S.: The random oracle methodology, revisited. J. ACM **51**(4), 557–594 (2004)
8. Coron, J.-S., Dodis, Y., Malinaud, C., Puniya, P.: Merkle-Damgård revisited: how to construct a hash function. In: Shoup, V. (ed.) CRYPTO 2005. LNCS, vol. 3621, pp. 430–448. Springer, Heidelberg (2005). https://doi.org/10.1007/11535218_26
9. Coron, J.-S., Dodis, Y., Mandal, A., Seurin, Y.: A domain extender for the ideal cipher. In: Micciancio, D. (ed.) TCC 2010. LNCS, vol. 5978, pp. 273–289. Springer, Heidelberg (2010). https://doi.org/10.1007/978-3-642-11799-2_17
10. Coron, J.-S., Holenstein, T., Künzler, R., Patarin, J., Seurin, Y., Tessaro, S.: How to build an ideal cipher: the indifferentiability of the Feistel construction. J. Cryptol. **29**(1), 61–114 (2016). https://doi.org/10.1007/s00145-014-9189-6
11. Diffie, W., Hellman, M.: New directions in cryptography. IEEE Trans. Inf. Theory **22**(6), 644–654 (1976)
12. Dodis, Y., Ristenpart, T., Shrimpton, T.: Salvaging Merkle-Damgård for practical applications. In: Joux, A. (ed.) EUROCRYPT 2009. LNCS, vol. 5479, pp. 371–388. Springer, Heidelberg (2009). https://doi.org/10.1007/978-3-642-01001-9_22
13. Dodis, Y., Stam, M., Steinberger, J., Liu, T.: Indifferentiability of confusion-diffusion networks. In: Fischlin, M., Coron, J.-S. (eds.) EUROCRYPT 2016. LNCS, vol. 9666, pp. 679–704. Springer, Heidelberg (2016). https://doi.org/10.1007/978-3-662-49896-5_24
14. Freire, E.S.V., Hofheinz, D., Kiltz, E., Paterson, K.G.: Non-interactive key exchange. In: Kurosawa, K., Hanaoka, G. (eds.) PKC 2013. LNCS, vol. 7778, pp. 254–271. Springer, Heidelberg (2013). https://doi.org/10.1007/978-3-642-36362-7_17
15. Fujisaki, E., Okamoto, T.: Secure integration of asymmetric and symmetric encryption schemes. J. Cryptol. **26**(1), 80–101 (2011). https://doi.org/10.1007/s00145-011-9114-1
16. Galbraith, S.D., Petit, C., Shani, B., Ti, Y.B.: On the security of supersingular isogeny cryptosystems. In: Cheon, J.H., Takagi, T. (eds.) ASIACRYPT 2016. LNCS, vol. 10031, pp. 63–91. Springer, Heidelberg (2016). https://doi.org/10.1007/978-3-662-53887-6_3
17. Impagliazzo, R., Rudich, S.: Limits on the provable consequences of one-way permutations. In: Goldwasser, S. (ed.) CRYPTO 1988. LNCS, vol. 403, pp. 8–26. Springer, New York (1990). https://doi.org/10.1007/0-387-34799-2_2
18. Jao, D., De Feo, L.: Towards quantum-resistant cryptosystems from supersingular elliptic curve isogenies. In: Yang, B.-Y. (ed.) PQCrypto 2011. LNCS, vol. 7071, pp. 19–34. Springer, Heidelberg (2011). https://doi.org/10.1007/978-3-642-25405-5_2
19. Jost, D., Maurer, U.: Security definitions for hash functions: combining UCE and indifferentiability. In: Catalano, D., De Prisco, R. (eds.) SCN 2018. LNCS, vol. 11035, pp. 83–101. Springer, Cham (2018). https://doi.org/10.1007/978-3-319-98113-0_5
20. Maurer, U., Renner, R., Holenstein, C.: Indifferentiability, impossibility results on reductions, and applications to the random oracle methodology. In: Naor, M. (ed.) TCC 2004. LNCS, vol. 2951, pp. 21–39. Springer, Heidelberg (2004). https://doi.org/10.1007/978-3-540-24638-1_2

21. Mittelbach, A.: Salvaging indifferentiability in a multi-stage setting. In: Nguyen, P.Q., Oswald, E. (eds.) EUROCRYPT 2014. LNCS, vol. 8441, pp. 603–621. Springer, Heidelberg (2014). https://doi.org/10.1007/978-3-642-55220-5_33

22. Ristenpart, T., Shacham, H., Shrimpton, T.: Careful with composition: limitations of the indifferentiability framework. In: Paterson, K.G. (ed.) EUROCRYPT 2011. LNCS, vol. 6632, pp. 487–506. Springer, Heidelberg (2011). https://doi.org/10.1007/978-3-642-20465-4_27

23. Rivest, R.L., Shamir, A., Adleman, L.: A method for obtaining digital signatures and public-key cryptosystems. Commun. ACM **21**(2), 120–126 (1978)

24. Rogaway, P., Shrimpton, T.: A provable-security treatment of the key-wrap problem. In: Vaudenay, S. (ed.) EUROCRYPT 2006. LNCS, vol. 4004, pp. 373–390. Springer, Heidelberg (2006). https://doi.org/10.1007/11761679_23

25. Shannon, C.E.: Communication theory of secrecy systems. Bell Syst. Tech. J. **28**(4), 656–715 (1949)

26. Shoup, V.: Lower bounds for discrete logarithms and related problems. In: Fumy, W. (ed.) EUROCRYPT 1997. LNCS, vol. 1233, pp. 256–266. Springer, Heidelberg (1997). https://doi.org/10.1007/3-540-69053-0_18

27. Zhandry, M., Zhang, C.: Indifferentiability for public key cryptosystems. Cryptology ePrint Archive, Report 2019/370 (2019). https://eprint.iacr.org/2019/370

28. Zhu, B., Li, K., Patterson, H.: Avoiding the disk bottleneck in the data domain deduplication file system. In: Proceedings of the 6th USENIX Conference on File and Storage Technologies, FAST 2008, pp. 18:1–18:14. USENIX Association, Berkeley (2008)

Quantifying the Security Cost of Migrating Protocols to Practice

Christopher Patton$^{(\boxtimes)}$ and Thomas Shrimpton$^{(\boxtimes)}$

Florida Institute for Cybersecurity Research,
Computer and Information Science and Engineering,
University of Florida, Gainesville, FL, USA
{cjpatton,teshrim}@ufl.edu

Abstract. We give a framework for relating the concrete security of a
"reference" protocol (say, one appearing in an academic paper) to that
of some derived, "real" protocol (say, appearing in a cryptographic standard). It is based on the indifferentiability framework of Maurer, Renner,
and Holenstein (MRH), whose application has been exclusively focused
upon non-interactive cryptographic primitives, e.g., hash functions and
Feistel networks. Our extension of MRH is supported by a clearly defined
execution model and two composition lemmata, all formalized in a modern pseudocode language. Together, these allow for precise statements
about game-based security properties of cryptographic objects (interactive or not) at various levels of abstraction. As a real-world application,
we design and prove tight security bounds for a potential TLS 1.3 extension that integrates the SPAKE2 password-authenticated key-exchange
into the handshake.

Keywords: Real-world cryptography · Protocol standards · Concrete
security · Indifferentiability

1 Introduction

The recent effort to standardize TLS 1.3 [44] was remarkable in that it leveraged provable security results as part of the drafting process [40]. Perhaps the
most influential of these works is Krawczyk and Wee's OPTLS authenticated
key-exchange (AKE) protocol [35], which served as the basis for an early draft
of the TLS 1.3 handshake. Core features of OPTLS are recognizable in the final
standard, but TLS 1.3 is decidedly not OPTLS. As is typical of the standardization process, protocol details were modified in order to address deployment
and operational desiderata (cf. [40, §4.1]). Naturally, this raises the question of
what, if any, of the proven security that supported the original AKE protocol
is inherited by the standard. The objective of this paper is to answer a general
version of this question, quantitatively:

> *Given a reference protocol $\tilde{\Pi}$ (e.g., OPTLS), what is the cost, in terms
> of concrete security [7], of translating $\tilde{\Pi}$ into some real protocol Π (e.g.,
> TLS 1.3) with respect to the security notion(s) targeted by $\tilde{\Pi}$?*

© International Association for Cryptologic Research 2020
D. Micciancio and T. Ristenpart (Eds.): CRYPTO 2020, LNCS 12170, pp. 94–124, 2020.
https://doi.org/10.1007/978-3-030-56784-2_4

Such a quantitative assessment is particularly useful for standardization because real-world protocols tend to provide relatively few choices of security parameters; and once deployed, the chosen parameters are likely to be in use for several years [33].

A more recent standardization effort provides an illustrative case study. At the time of writing, the CFRG[1] was in the midst of selecting a portfolio of password-authenticated key-exchange (PAKE) protocols [10] to recommend to the IETF[2] for standardization. Among the selection criteria [51] is the suitability of the PAKE for integration into existing protocols. In the case of TLS, the goal would be to standardize an extension (cf. [44, §4.2]) that specifies the usage of the PAKE in the handshake, thereby enabling defense-in-depth for applications in which (1) passwords are available for use in authentication, and (2) sole reliance on the web PKI for authentication is undesirable, or impossible. Tight security bounds are particularly important for PAKEs, since their security depends so crucially on the password's entropy. Thus, the PAKE's usage in TLS (i.e., the real protocol Π) should preserve the concrete security of the PAKE itself (i.e., the reference protocol $\tilde{\Pi}$), insofar as possible.

The direct route to quantifying this gap is to re-prove security of the derived protocol Π and compare the new bound to the existing one. This approach is costly, however: particularly when the changes from $\tilde{\Pi}$ to Π seem insignificant, generating a fresh proof is likely to be highly redundant. In such cases it is common to instead provide an informal security argument that sketches the parts of the proof that would need to be changed, as well as how the security bound might be affected (cf. [35, §5]). Yet whether or not this approach is reasonable may be hard to intuit. Our experience suggests that it is often difficult to estimate the significance of a change before diving into the proof.

Another difficulty with the direct route is that the reference protocol's concrete security might not be known, at least with respect to a specific attack model and adversarial goal. Simulation-style definitions, such as those formalized in the UC framework [20], define security via the inability of an environment (universally quantified, in the case of UC) to distinguish between attacks against the real protocol and attacks against an ideal protocol functionality. While useful in its own right, a proof of security relative to such a definition does not immediately yield concrete security bounds for a *particular* attack model or adversarial goal.

This work articulates an alternative route in which one argues security of Π by reasoning about the *translation* of $\tilde{\Pi}$ into Π itself. Its *translation framework* (described in §2 and introduced below) provides a formal characterization of translations that are "safe", in the sense that they allow security for Π to be argued by appealing to what is already known (or assumed) to hold for $\tilde{\Pi}$. The framework is very general, and so we expect it to be broadly useful. In this work we will demonstrate its utility for standards development by applying it to the design and analysis of a TLS extension for SPAKE2 [3], one of the PAKEs

---

[1] Cryptography Forum Research Group.
[2] Internet Engineering Task Force.

considered by the CFRG for standardization. Our result (Theorem 1) precisely quantifies the security loss incurred by this usage of SPAKE2, and does so in a way that directly lifts existing results for SPAKE2 [1,3,6] while being largely agnostic about the targeted security notions.

THE FULL VERSION [42]. This article is the extended abstract of our paper. The full version includes all deferred proofs, as well as additional results, remarks, and discussion.

Overview. Our framework begins with a new look at an old idea. In particular, we extend the notion of *indifferentiability* of Maurer, Renner, and Holenstein [38] (hereafter MRH) to the study of cryptographic protocols.

Indifferentiability has become an important tool for provable security. Most famously, it provides a precise way to argue that the security in the random oracle model (ROM) [12] is preserved when the random oracle (RO) is instantiated by a concrete hash function that uses a "smaller" idealized primitive, such as a compression function modeled as an RO. Coron et al. [26] were the first to explore this application of indifferentiability, and due to the existing plethora of ROM-based results and the community's burgeoning focus on designing replacements for SHA-1 [53], the use of indifferentiability in the design and analysis of hash functions has become commonplace.

Despite this focus, the MRH framework is more broadly applicable. A few works have leveraged this, e.g.: to construct ideal ciphers from Feistel networks [27]; to define security of key-derivation functions in the multi-instance setting [11]; to unify various security goals for authenticated encryption [4]; or to formalize the goal of domain separation in the ROM [8]. Yet all of these applications of indifferentiability are about cryptographic primitives (i.e., objects that are non-interactive). To the best of our knowledge, ours is the first work to explicitly consider the application of indifferentiability to protocols. That said, we will show that our framework unifies the formal approaches underlying a variety of prior works [17,31,41].

Our conceptual starting point is a bit more general than MRH. In particular, we define indifferentiability in terms of the *world* in which the adversary finds itself, so named because of the common use of phrases like "real world", "ideal world", and "oracle worlds" when discussing security definitions. Formally, a world is a particular kind of *object* (defined in §2.1) that is constructed by connecting up a *game* [15] with a *scheme*, the former defining the security goal of the latter. The scheme is embedded within a *system* that specifies how the adversary and game interact with it, i.e., the scheme's execution environment.

Intuitively, when a world and an adversary are executed together, we can measure the probability of specific events occurring as a way to define adversarial success. Our MAIN$^\psi$ security experiment, illustrated in the left panel of Fig. 1, captures this. The outcome of the experiment is 1 ("true") if the adversary A "wins", as determined by the output w of world W, and predicate ψ on the transcript tx of the adversary's queries also evaluates to 1. Along the lines of "penalty-style" definitions [47], the transcript predicate determines whether

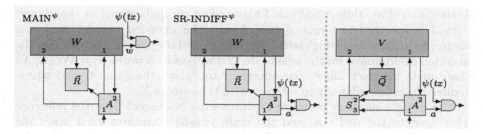

Fig. 1. Illustration of the MAIN$^\psi$ (Definition 1) and SR-INDIFF$^\psi$ (Definition 3) security experiments for worlds W, V, resources $\vec{R}, \vec{Q}$, adversary A, simulator S, and transcript predicate ψ.

or not A's attack was valid, i.e., whether the attack constitutes a trivial win. (For example, if W captures IND-CCA security of an encryption scheme, then ψ would penalize decryption of challenge ciphertexts.)

SHARED-RESOURCE INDIFFERENTIABILITY AND THE LIFTING LEMMA. Also present in the experiment is a (possibly empty) tuple of *resources* $\vec{R}$, which may be called by both the world W and the adversary A. This captures embellishments to the base security experiment that may be used to prove security, but are not essential to the definition of security itself. An element of $\vec{R}$ might be an idealized object such as an RO [12], ideal cipher [27], or generic group [43]; it might be used to model global trusted setup, such as distribution of a common reference string [22]; or it might provide A (and W) with an oracle that solves some hard problem, such as the DDH oracle in the formulation of the Gap DH problem [39].

The result is a generalized notion of indifferentiability that we call *shared-resource indifferentiability*. The SR-INDIFF$^\psi$ experiment, illustrated in the right panel of Fig. 1, considers an adversary's ability to distinguish some *real* world/resource pair $W/\vec{R}$ (read "W with $\vec{R}$") from a *reference* world/resource pair $V/\vec{Q}$ when the world and the adversary share access to the resources. The real world W exposes two interfaces to the adversary, denoted by subscripts W_1 and W_2, that we will call the *main* and *auxiliary* interfaces of W, respectively. The reference world V also exposes two interfaces (with the same monikers), although the adversary's access to the auxiliary interface of V is mediated by a *simulator* S. Likewise, the adversary has direct access to resources $\vec{R}$ in the real experiment, and S-mediated access to resources $\vec{Q}$ in the reference experiment.

The auxiliary interface captures what changes as a result of translating world $V/\vec{Q}$ into $W/\vec{R}$: the job of the simulator S is to "fool" the adversary into believing it is interacting with $W/\vec{R}$ when in fact it is interacting with $V/\vec{Q}$. Intuitively, if for a given adversary A there is a simulator S that successfully "fools" it, then this should yield a way to translate A's attack against $W/\vec{R}$ into an attack against $V/\vec{Q}$. This intuition is captured by our "lifting" lemma (Lemma 1, §2.3), which says that if $V/\vec{Q}$ is MAIN$^\psi$-secure and $W/\vec{R}$ is indifferentiable from $V/\vec{Q}$ (as captured by SR-INDIFF$^\psi$), then $W/\vec{R}$ is also MAIN$^\psi$-secure.

GAMES AND THE PRESERVATION LEMMA. For all applications in this paper, a world is specified in terms of two objects: the intended security goal of a scheme, formalized as a (single-stage [45]) game; and the system that specifies the execution environment for the scheme. In §2.4 we specify a world $W = \mathbf{Wo}(G, X)$ whose main interface allows the adversary to "play" the game G and whose auxiliary interface allows it to interact with the system X.

The world's auxiliary interface captures what "changes" from the reference experiment to the real one, and the main interface captures what stays the same. Intuitively, if a system X is indifferentiable from Y, then it ought to be the case that world $\mathbf{Wo}(G, X)$ is indifferentiable from $\mathbf{Wo}(G, Y)$, since in the former setting, the adversary might simply play the game G in its head. Thus, by Lemma 1, if Y is secure in the sense of G, then so is X. We formalize this intuition via a simple "preservation" lemma (Lemma 2, §2.4), which states that the indifferentiability of X from Y is "preserved" when access to X's (resp. Y's) main interface is mediated by a game G. As we show in §2.4, this yields the main result of MRH as a corollary (cf. [38, Theorem 1]).

UPDATED PSEUDOCODE. An important feature of our framework is its highly expressive pseudocode. MRH define indifferentiability in terms of "interacting systems" formalized as sequences of conditional probability distributions (cf. [38, §3.1]). This abstraction, while extremely expressive, is much harder to work with than conventional cryptographic pseudocode. A contribution of this paper is to articulate an abstraction that provides much of the expressiveness of MRH, while preserving the level of rigor typical of game-playing proofs of security [15]. In §2.1 we formalize *objects*, which are used to define the various entities that run in security experiments, including games, adversaries, systems, and schemes.

EXECUTION ENVIRONMENT FOR eCK-PROTOCOLS. Finally, in order define indifferentiability for cryptographic protocols we need to precisely specify the system X (i.e., execution environment) in which the protocol runs. In §3.1 we specify the system $X = \mathbf{eCK}(\Pi)$ that captures the interaction of the adversary with protocol Π in the extended Canetti-Krawczyk (eCK) model [37]. The auxiliary interface of X is used by the adversary to initiate and execute sessions of Π and corrupt parties' long-term and per-session secrets. The main interface of X is used by the game in order to determine if the adversary successfully "attacked" Π.

Note that our treatment breaks with the usual abstraction boundary. In its original presentation [37], the eCK model encompasses both the execution environment and the intended security goal; but in our setting, the full model is obtained by specifying a game G that codifies the security goal and running the adversary in world $W = \mathbf{Wo}(G, \mathbf{eCK}(\Pi))$. As we discuss in §3.1, this allows us to use indifferentiability to prove a wide range of security goals without needing to attend to the particulars of each goal.

Case Study: Design of a PAKE Extension for TLS. Our framework lets us make precise statements of the following form: "protocol Π is G-secure if protocol $\tilde{\Pi}$ is G-secure and the execution of Π is indifferentiable from the execution of $\tilde{\Pi}$." This allows us to argue that Π is secure by focusing on what changes from $\tilde{\Pi}$

to Π. In §3.2 we provide a demonstration of this methodology in which we design and derive tight security bounds for a TLS extension that integrates SPAKE2 [3] into the handshake. Our proposal is based on existing Internet-Drafts [5,36] and discussions on the CFRG mailing list [18,55].

Our analysis (Theorem 1) unearths some interesting and subtle design issues. First, existing PAKE-extension proposals [5,54] effectively replace the DH key-exchange with execution of the PAKE, feeding the PAKE's output into the key schedule instead of the usual shared secret. As we will discuss, whether this usage of the output is "safe" depends on the particular PAKE and its security properties. Second, our extension adopts a "fail closed" posture, meaning if negotiation of the PAKE fails, then the client and server tear down the session. Existing proposals allow them to "fail open" by falling back to standard, certificate-only authentication. There is no way to account for this behavior in the proof of Theorem 1, at least not without relying on the security of the standard authentication mechanism. But this in itself is interesting, as it reflects the practical motivation for integrating a PAKE into TLS: it makes little sense to fail open if one's goal is to reduce reliance on the web PKI.

PARTIALLY SPECIFIED PROTOCOLS. TLS specifies a complex protocol, and most of the details are irrelevant to what we want to prove. The *Partially Specified Protocol (PSP)* framework of Rogaway and Stegers [46] offers an elegant way to account for these details without needing to specify them exhaustively. Their strategy is to divide a protocol's specification into two components: the protocol core (PC), which formalizes the elements of the protocol that are essential to the security goal; and the specification details (SD), which captures everything else. The PC, fully specified in pseudocode, is defined in terms of calls to an SD oracle. Security experiments execute the PC, but it is the *adversary* who is responsible for answering SD-oracle queries. This formalizes a very strong attack model, but one that yields a rigorous treatment of the standard *itself*, rather than a boiled down version of it.

We incorporate the PSP framework into our setting by allowing the world to make calls to the adversary's auxiliary interface, as shown in Fig. 1. In addition, the execution environment **eCK** and world-builder **Wo** are specified so that the protocol's SD-oracle queries are answered by the adversary.

Related Work. Our formal methodology was inspired by a few seemingly disparate results in the literature, but which fit fairly neatly into the translation framework. Recent work by the authors [41] considers the problem of secure *key-reuse* [31], where the goal is design cryptosystems that safely expose keys for use in multiple applications. They formalize a condition (GAP1, cf. [41, Def. 5]) under which the G-security of a system X implies that G-security of X holds even when X's interface is exposed to additional, insecure, or even malicious applications. This condition can be formulated as a special case of SR-INDIFF$^{\psi}$ security, and their composition theorem (cf. [41, Theorem 1]) as a corollary of our lifting lemma. The lifting lemma can also be thought of as a computational analogue of the main technical tool in Bhargavan et al.'s treatment of downgrade resilience (cf. [17, Theorem 2]). We discuss this connection in detail in the full version.

THE UC FRAMEWORK. MRH point out (cf. [38, §3.3]) that the notion of indifferentiability is inspired by ideas introduced by the UC framework [20]. There are conceptual similarities between UC (in particular, the generalized UC framework that allows for shared state [21]) and our framework, but the two are quite different in their details. We do not explore any formal relationship between frameworks, nor do we consider how one might modify UC to account for things that are naturally handled by ours (e.g., translation and partially specified behavior [46]). Such an exploration would make interesting future work.

PROVABLE SECURITY OF SPAKE2. The SPAKE2 protocol was first proposed and analyzed in 2005 by Abdalla and Pointcheval [3], who sought a simpler alternative to the seminal encrypted key-exchange (EKE) protocol of Bellovin and Merritt [16]. Given the CFRG's recent interest in SPAKE2 (and its relative SPAKE2+ [25]), there has been a respectable amount of recent security analysis. This includes concurrent works by Abdalla and Barbosa [1] and Becerra et al. [6] that consider the forward secrecy of (variants of) SPAKE2, a property that Abdalla and Pointcheval did not address. Victor Shoup [49] provides an analysis of a variant of SPAKE2 in the UC framework [20], which has emerged as the de facto setting for studying PAKE protocols (cf. OPAQUE [32] and (Au)CPace [30]). Shoup observes that the usual notion of UC-secure PAKE [23] cannot be proven for SPAKE2, since the protocol on its own does not provide key confirmation. Indeed, many variants of SPAKE2 that appear in the literature add key confirmation in order to prove it secure in a stronger adversarial model (cf. [6, §3]).

A recent work by Skrobot and Lancrenon [50] characterizes the general conditions under which it is secure to compose a PAKE protocol with an arbitrary symmetric key protocol (SKP). While their object of study is similar to ours—a PAKE extension for TLS might be viewed as a combination of a PAKE and the TLS record layer protocol—our security goals are different, since in their adversarial model the adversary's goal is to break the security of the SKP.

2 The Translation Framework

This section describes the formal foundation of this paper. We begin in §2.1 by defining objects, our abstraction of the various entities run in a security experiment; in §2.2 we define our base experiment and formalize shared-resource indifferentiability; in §2.3 we state the lifting lemma, the central technical tool of this work (we defer a proof to the full version); and in §2.4 we formalize the class of security goals to which our framework applies.

NOTATION. When X is a random variable we let $\Pr[X = v]$ denote the probability that X is equal to v; we write $\Pr[X]$ as shorthand for $\Pr[X = 1]$. We let $x \leftarrow y$ denote assignment of the value of y to variable x. When $\mathcal{X}$ is a finite set we let $x \twoheadleftarrow \mathcal{X}$ denote random assignment of an element of $\mathcal{X}$ to x according to the uniform distribution.

A *string* is an element of $\{0,1\}^*$; a *tuple* is a finite sequence of symbols separated by commas and delimited by parentheses. Let ε denote the empty string, $(\,)$ the empty tuple, and $(z,)$ the singleton tuple containing z. We sometimes (but not always) denote a tuple with an arrow above the variable (e.g., $\vec{x}$). Let $|x|$ denote the length of a string (resp. tuple) x. Let x_i and $x[i]$ denote the i-th element of x. Let $x \parallel y$ denote concatenation of x with string (resp. tuple) y. We write $x \preceq y$ if string x is a prefix of string y, i.e., there exists some r such that $x \parallel r = y$. Let $y \% x$ denote the "remainder" r after removing the prefix x from y; if $x \npreceq y$, then define $y \% x = \varepsilon$ (cf.[19]). When x is a tuple we let $x.z = (x_1, \ldots, x_{|x|}, z)$ so that z is "appended" to x. We write $z \in x$ if $(\exists\, i)\, x_i = z$. Let $[i..j]$ denote the set of integers $\{i, \ldots, j\}$; if $j < i$, then define $[i..j]$ as $\emptyset$. Let $[n] = [1..n]$.

For all sets $\mathcal{X}$ and functions $f, g : \mathcal{X} \to \{0,1\}$, define function $f \wedge g$ as the map $[f \wedge g](x) \mapsto f(x) \wedge g(x)$ for all $x \in \mathcal{X}$. We denote a group as a pair $(\mathcal{G}, *)$, where $\mathcal{G}$ is the set of group elements and $*$ denotes the group action. Logarithms are base-2 unless otherwise specified.

2.1 Objects

Our goal is to preserve the expressiveness of the MRH framework [38] while providing the level of rigor of code-based game-playing arguments [15]. To strike this balance, we will need to add a bit of machinery to standard cryptographic pseudocode. Objects provide this.

Each object has a *specification* that defines how it is used and how it interacts with other objects. We first define specifications, then describe how to *call* an object in an experiment and how to *instantiate* an object. Pseudocode in this paper will be typed (along the lines of Rogaway and Stegers [46]), so we enumerate the available types in this section. We finish by defining various properties of objects that will be used in the remainder.

Specifications. The relationship between a specification and an object is analogous to (but far simpler than) the relationship between a class and a class instance in object-oriented programming languages like Python or C++. A specification defines an ordered sequence of *variables* stored by an object—these are akin to attributes in Python—and an ordered sequence of *operators* that may be called by other objects—these are akin to methods. We refer to the sequence of variables as the object's *state* and to the sequence of operators as the object's *interface*.

We provide an example of a specification in Fig. 2. (We give a detailed description of the syntax in the full version.) Spec **Ro** is used throughout this work to model functions as random oracles (ROs) [12]. It declares seven variables, $\mathcal{X}$, $\mathcal{Y}$, q, p, T, i, and j, as shown on lines 1–2 in Fig. 2. (We will use shorthand for line references in the remainder, e.g., "2:1–2" rather than "lines 1–2 in Fig. 2".) Each variable has an associated type: $\mathcal{X}$ and $\mathcal{Y}$ have type **set**, q, p, i, and j have type **int**, and T has type **table**. Variable declarations are denoted by the keyword "var", while operator definitions are denoted by the keyword "op". Spec **Ro** defines three operators: the first, the SETUP-operator (2:3), initializes the RO's

```
spec Ro:                                    9  op (SET, M object):
  1  var X, Y set, q, p int                10    var x elem_X, y elem_Y
  2  var T table, i, j int                 11    if j ≥ p then ret ⊥
  3  op (SETUP): T ← []; i, j ← 0          12    j ← j + 1; ((x, y), σ) ← M()
  4  op (x elem_X):                        13    T[x] ← y
  5    if i ≥ q then ret ⊥                 14    ret ((x, y), σ)
  6    if T[x] = ⊥ then
  7      i ← i + 1; T[x] ⟵$ Y
  8    ret T[x]
```

Fig. 2. Specification of a random oracle (RO) object. When instantiated, variables X and Y determine the domain and range of the RO, and integers q and p determine, respectively, the maximum number of distinct RO queries, and the maximum number of RO-programming queries (via the SET-operator), (cf. Definition 6).

state; the second operator (2:4–8) responds to standard RO queries; and the third, the SET-operator (2:9–14), is used to "program" the RO [29].

Calling an Object. An object is *called* by providing it with oracles and passing arguments to it. An oracle is always an interface, i.e., a sequence of operators defined by an object. The statement "$out \leftarrow obj^{\mathbf{I}_1,\dots,\mathbf{I}_m}(in_1,\dots,in_n)$" means to invoke one of obj's operators on input of $in_1,\dots,in_n$ and with oracle access to interfaces $\mathbf{I}_1,\dots,\mathbf{I}_m$ and set variable out to the value returned by the operator. Objects will usually have many operators, so we must specify the manner in which the responding operator is chosen. For this purpose we will adopt a convention inspired by "pattern matching" in functional languages like Haskell and Rust. A pattern is comprised of a tuple of literals, typed variables, and nested tuples. A value is said to *match* a pattern if they have the same type and the literals are equal. For example, value val matches pattern (_ elem_X) if val has type elem_X. (The symbol "_" contained in the pattern denotes an anonymous variable.) Hence, if object R is specified by **Ro** and x has type elem_X, then the expression "$R(x)$" calls R's second operator (2:4–8). We write "$val \sim pat$" if the value of variable val matches pattern pat.

Calls to objects are evaluated as follows. In the order in which they are defined, check each operator of the object's specification if the input matches the operator's pattern. If so, then execute the operator until a return statement is reached and assign the return value to the output. If no return statement is reached, or if val does not match an operator, then return ⊥.

Let us consider an illustrative example. Let Π be an object that implements Schnorr's signature scheme [48] for a group $(\mathcal{G}, \cdot)$ as specified in Figure 3. The expression $\Pi(\text{GEN})$ calls Π's first operator, which generates a fresh key pair. If

```
spec Schnorr:
  1  op (GEN): s ⟵$ Z_{|G|}; PK ← g^s; ret (PK, s)     4  op^H (s int, SIGN, msg str):
  2  op^H (PK elem_G, VERIFY, msg str, (x, t int)):     5    r ⟵$ Z_{|G|}; t ← H(g^r, msg)
  3    ret t ≡ H(g^x · PK^t, msg) (mod |G|)             6    ret (r − st, t)
```

Fig. 3. Specification of Schnorr's signature scheme.

$s \in \mathbb{Z}$ and $msg \in \{0,1\}^*$, then expression $\Pi_s^H(\textsf{SIGN}, msg)$ evaluates the third operator, which computes a signature (x,t) of message msg under secret key s (we will often write the first argument as a subscript). The call to interface oracle $\mathcal{H}$ on line 3:5 is answered by object H. (Presumably, H is a hash function with domain $\mathcal{G} \times \{0,1\}^*$ and range $\mathbb{Z}_{|\mathcal{G}|}$.) If $PK \in \mathcal{G}$, $msg \in \{0,1\}^*$, and $x, t \in \mathbb{Z}$, then expression $\Pi_{PK}^H(\textsf{VERIFY}, msg, (x,t))$ evaluates the second operator. On an input that does not match any of these patterns—in particular, one of (\textsf{GEN}), (_ $\textbf{elem}_\mathcal{G}$, \textsf{VERIFY}, _ $\textbf{str}$, (_, _ $\textbf{int}$)), or (_$\textbf{int}$, \textsf{SIGN}, _ $\textbf{str}$)—the object returns $\bot$. For example, $\Pi^{\mathbf{I}_1,\dots,\mathbf{I}_m}(\textsf{foo bar}) = \bot$ for any $\mathbf{I}_1, \dots, \mathbf{I}_m$.

It is up to the caller to ensure that the correct number of interfaces is passed to the operator. If the number of interfaces passed is less than the number of oracles named by the operator, then calls to the remaining oracles are always answered with $\bot$; if the number of interfaces is more than the number of oracles named by the operator, then the remaining interfaces are simply ignored by the operator.

EXPLANATION. We will see examples of pattern matching in action throughout this paper. For now, the important takeaway is that calling an object results in one (or none) of its operators being invoked: which one is invoked depends on the type of input and the order in which the operators are defined.

Because these calling conventions are more sophisticated than usual, let us take a moment to explain their purpose. Theorem statements in this work will often quantify over large sets of objects whose functionality is unspecified. These conventions ensure that doing so is always well-defined, since any object can be called on any input, regardless of the input type. We could have dealt with this differently: for example, in their adaptation of indifferentiability to multi-staged games, Ristenpart et al. require a similar convention for functionalities and games (cf. "unspecified procedure" in [45, §2]). Our hope is that the higher level of rigor of our formalism will ease the task of verifying proofs of security in our framework.

Instantiating an Object. An object is instantiated by passing arguments to its specification. The statement "$obj \leftarrow \textbf{Object}(in_1, \dots, in_m)$" means to create a new object obj of type **Object** and initialize its state by setting $obj.var_1 \leftarrow in_1$, $\dots, obj.var_m \leftarrow in_m$, where $var_1, \dots, var_m$ are the first m variables declared by **Object**. If the number of arguments passed is less than the number of variables declared, then the remaining variables are uninitialized. For example, the statement "$R \leftarrow \textbf{Ro}(\mathcal{X}, \mathcal{Y}, q, p, [], 0, 0)$" initializes R by setting $R.\mathcal{X} \leftarrow \mathcal{X}$, $R.\mathcal{Y} \leftarrow \mathcal{Y}$, $R.q \leftarrow q$, $R.p \leftarrow p$, $R.T \leftarrow []$, $R.i \leftarrow 0$, and $R.j \leftarrow 0$. The statement "$R \leftarrow \textbf{Ro}(\mathcal{X}, \mathcal{Y}, q, p)$" sets $R.\mathcal{X} \leftarrow \mathcal{X}$, $\mathcal{R}.\mathcal{Y} \leftarrow \mathcal{Y}$, $R.q \leftarrow q$, and $R.p \leftarrow p$, but leaves T, i, and j uninitialized. Object can also be copied: the statement "$new \leftarrow obj$" means to instantiate a new object new with specification **Object** and set $new.var_1 \leftarrow obj.var_1, \dots, new.var_n \leftarrow obj.var_n$, where $var_1, \dots, var_n$ is the sequence of variables declared by obj's specification.

Types. We now enumerate the types available in our pseudocode. An object has type **object**. A set of values of type **any** (defined below) has type **set**; we let $\emptyset$ denote the empty set. A variable of type **table** stores a table of key/value pairs, where keys and values both have type **any**. If T is a table, then we let T_k and $T[k]$ denote the value associated with key k in T; if no such value exists, then $T_k = \bot$. We let $[\,]$ denote the empty table.

When the value of a variable x is an element of a computable set $\mathcal{X}$, we say that x has type **elem**$_\mathcal{X}$. We define type **int** as an alias of **elem**$_\mathbb{Z}$, type **bool** as an alias of **elem**$_{\{0,1\}}$, and type **str** as an alias of **elem**$_{\{0,1\}^*}$. We define type **any** recursively as follows. A variable x is said to have type **any** if: it is equal to $\bot$ or $(\,)$; has type **set**, **table**, or **elem**$_\mathcal{X}$ for some computable set $\mathcal{X}$; or it is a tuple of values of type **any**.

Specifications declare the type of each variable of an object's state. The types of variables that are local to the scope of an operator need not be explicitly declared, but their type must be inferable from their initialization (that is, the first use of the variable in an assignment statement). If a variable is assigned a value of a type other than the variable's type, then the variable is assigned $\bot$. Variables that are declared but not yet initialized have the value $\bot$. For all $\mathbf{I}_1, \ldots, \mathbf{I}_m, in_1, \ldots, in_n$ the expression "$\bot^{\mathbf{I}_1, \ldots, \mathbf{I}_m}(in_1, \ldots, in_n)$" evaluates to $\bot$. We say that $x = \bot$ or $\bot = x$ if variable x was previously assigned $\bot$. For all other expressions, our convention will be that whenever $\bot$ is an input, the expression evaluates to $\bot$.

Properties of Operators and Objects. An operator is called *deterministic* if its definition does not contain a random assignment statement; it is called *stateless* if its definition contains no assignment statement in which one of the object's variables appears on the left-hand side; and an operator is called *functional* if it is deterministic and stateless. Likewise, an object is called deterministic (resp. stateless or functional) if each operator, with the exception of the SETUP-operator, is deterministic (resp. stateless or functional). (We make an exception for the SETUP-operator in order to allow trusted setup of objects executed in our experiments. See §2.2 for details.)

RESOURCES. Let $t \in \mathbb{N}$. An operator is called *t-time* if it always halts in t time steps regardless of its random choices or the responses to its queries; we say that an operator is *halting* if it is t-time for some $t < \infty$. Our convention will be that an operator's runtime includes the time required to evaluate its oracle queries. Let $\vec{q} \in \mathbb{N}^*$. An operator is called *$\vec{q}$-query* if it makes at most $\vec{q}_1$ calls to its first oracle, $\vec{q}_2$ to its second, and so on. We extend these definitions to objects, and say that an object is t-time (resp. halting or $\vec{q}$-query) if each operator of its interface is t-time (resp. halting or $\vec{q}$-query).

EXPORTED OPERATORS. An operator f_1 is said to *shadow* operator f_2 if: (1) f_1 appears first in the sequence of operators defined by the specification; and (2) there is some input that matches both f_1 and f_2. For example, an operator with pattern $(x \; \mathbf{any})$ would shadow an operator with pattern $(y \; \mathbf{str})$, since y is of type **str** and **any**. An object is said to export a *pat-type*-operator if its specification defines a non-shadowed operator that, when run on an input matching pattern *pat*, always returns a value of type *type*.

---

procedure **Real**$^{\Phi}_{W/\vec{R}}(A)$:

1 $A(\mathsf{SETUP})$; $W(\mathsf{SETUP})$
2 for $i \leftarrow 1$ to u do $R_i(\mathsf{SETUP})$
3 $tx \leftarrow ()$; $a \leftarrow A_1^{\mathbf{W_1},\mathbf{W_2},\mathbf{R}}(\mathsf{OUT})$
4 $w \leftarrow W_1(\mathsf{WIN})$; ret $\Phi(tx, a, w)$

procedure **W**(i, x):

5 $y \leftarrow W_i^{\mathbf{A_2},\mathbf{R}}(x)$; $tx \leftarrow tx \cdot (i, x, y)$; ret y

procedure **A**(i, x):

6 if $S = \bot$ then ret $A_i^{\mathbf{W_1},\mathbf{W_2},\mathbf{R}}(x)$ // Real
7 ret $A_i^{\mathbf{W_1},\mathbf{S_2},\mathbf{S_3}}(x)$ // Ref

procedure Ref $^{\Phi}_{W/\vec{R}}(A, S)$:

8 $S(\mathsf{SETUP})$; $A(\mathsf{SETUP})$; $W(\mathsf{SETUP})$
9 for $i \leftarrow 1$ to u do $R_i(\mathsf{SETUP})$
10 $tx \leftarrow ()$; $a \leftarrow A_1^{\mathbf{W_1},\mathbf{S_2},\mathbf{S_3}}(\mathsf{OUT})$
11 $w \leftarrow W_1(\mathsf{WIN})$; ret $\Phi(tx, a, w)$

procedure **R**(i, x):

12 ret $R_i(x)$

procedure **S**(i, x):

13 ret $S_i^{\mathbf{W_2},\mathbf{R}}(x)$

Fig. 4. Real and reference experiments for world W, resources $\vec{R} = (R_1, \ldots, R_u)$, adversary A, and simulator S.

2.2   Experiments and Indifferentiability

This section describes our core security experiments. An experiment connects up a set of objects in a particular way, giving each object oracle access to interfaces (i.e., sequences of operators) exported by other objects. An object's *i-interface* is the sequence of operators whose patterns are prefixed by literal i. We sometimes write i as a subscript, e.g., "$X_i(\cdots)$" instead of "$X(i, \cdots)$" or "$X(i, (\cdots))$". We refer to an object's 1-interface as its *main* interface and to its 2-interface as its *auxiliary* interface.

A *resource* is a halting object. A *simulator* is a halting object. An *adversary* is a halting object that exports a $(1, \mathsf{OUT})$-**bool**-operator, which means that on input of (OUT) to its main interface, it outputs a bit. This operator is used to in order to initiate the adversary's attack. The attack is formalized by the adversary's interaction with another object, called the *world*, which codifies the system under attack and the adversary's goal. Formally, a world is a halting object that exports a functional $(1, \mathsf{WIN})$-**bool**-operator, which means that on input of (WIN) to its main interface, the world outputs a bit that determines if the adversary has won. The operator being functional means this decision is made deterministically and in a "read-only" manner, so that the object's state is not altered. (These features are necessary to prove the lifting lemma in §2.3.)

MAIN Security. Security experiments are formalized by the execution of procedure **Real** defined in Fig. 4 for adversary A in world W with shared resources $\vec{R} = (R_1, \ldots, R_u)$. In addition, the procedure is parameterized by a function Φ. The experiment begins by "setting up" each object by running $A(\mathsf{SETUP})$, $W(\mathsf{SETUP})$, and $R_i(\mathsf{SETUP})$ for each $i \in [u]$. This allows for trusted setup of each object before the attack begins. Next, the procedure runs A with oracle access to procedures $\mathbf{W_1}$, $\mathbf{W_2}$, and $\mathbf{R}$, which provide A with access to, respectively, W's main interface, W's auxiliary interface, and the resources $\vec{R}$.

Figure 1 illustrates which objects have access to which interfaces. The world W and adversary A share access to the resources $\vec{R}$. In addition, the world has access to the auxiliary interface of A (4:5), which allows us to formalize security properties in the PSP setting [46]. Each query to $\mathbf{W_1}$ or $\mathbf{W_2}$ by A

is recorded in a tuple tx called the *experiment transcript* (4:5). The outcome of the experiment is $\Phi(tx, a, w)$, where a is the bit output by A and w is the bit output by W. The MAIN$^\psi$ security notion, defined below, captures an adversary's advantage in "winning" in a given world, where what it means to "win" is defined by the world itself. The validity of the attack is defined by a function ψ, called the *transcript predicate*: in the MAIN$^\psi$ experiment, we define Φ so that $\mathbf{Real}^\Phi_{W/\vec{R}}(A) = 1$ holds if A wins and $\psi(tx) = 1$ holds.

Definition 1 (MAIN$^\psi$ security). Let W be a world, $\vec{R}$ be resources, and A be an adversary. Let ψ be a transcript predicate, and let $\mathrm{win}^\psi(tx, a, w) := (\psi(tx) = 1) \wedge (w = 1)$. The MAIN$^\psi$ advantage of A in attacking $W/\vec{R}$ is

$$\mathbf{Adv}^{\mathrm{main}^\psi}_{W/\vec{R}}(A) := \Pr\left[\mathbf{Real}^{\mathrm{win}^\psi}_{W/\vec{R}}(A)\right].$$

Informally, we say that $W/\vec{R}$ is ψ-*secure* if the MAIN$^\psi$ advantage of every efficient adversary is small. Note that advantage for indistinguishability-style security notions is defined by normalizing MAIN$^\psi$ advantage (e.g., Definition 11 in the full version). □

This measure of advantage is only meaningful if ψ is efficiently computable, since otherwise a computationally bounded adversary may lack the resources needed to determine if its attack is valid. Following Rogaway-Zhang (cf. computability of "fixedness" in [47, §2]) we will require $\psi(tx)$ to be efficiently computable given the entire transcript, except the response to the last query. Intuitively, this exception ensures that, at any given moment, the adversary "knows" whether its next query is valid before making it.

Definition 2 (Transcript-predicate computability). Let ψ be a transcript predicate. Object F *computes* ψ if it is halting, functional, and $F(\bar{tx}) = \psi(tx)$ holds for all transcripts tx, where $\bar{tx} = (tx_1, \ldots, tx_{q-1}, (i_q, x_q, \bot))$, $q = |tx|$, and $(i_q, x_q, \_) = tx_q$. We say that ψ is *computable* if there is an object that computes it. We say that ψ is t-time computable if there is a t-time object F that computes it. Informally, we say that ψ is efficiently computable if it is t-time computable for small t. □

SHORTHAND. In the remainder we write "$W/\vec{R}$" as "W/H" when "$\vec{R} = (H,)$", i.e., when the resource tuple is a singleton containing H. Similarly, we write "$W/\vec{R}$" as "W" when $\vec{R} = (\,)$, i.e., when no shared resources are available. We write "win" instead of "win$^\psi$" whenever ψ is defined so that $\psi(tx) = 1$ for all transcripts tx. Correspondingly, we write "MAIN" for the security notion obtained by letting $\Phi = \mathrm{win}$.

SR-INDIFF Security. The **Real** procedure executes an adversary in a world that shares resources with the adversary. We are interested in the adversary's ability to distinguish this "real" experiment from a "reference" experiment in which we change the world and/or resources with which the adversary interacts. To that end, Fig. 4 also defines the **Ref** procedure, which executes an adversary in a fashion similar to **Real** except that a simulator S mediates the adversary's

```
spec NoDeg:  // W points to W₁; W′ to W₂; R to resources
 1  var M, SD object
 2  op (SETUP): M(SETUP); SD(SETUP)
 3  op^{W,W′,R} (1, x any): ret M^{W,W′,R}(x)
 4  op^{W,W′,R} (2, x any): ret SD^{R}(x)
```

Fig. 5. Specification of n.d. (non-degenerate) adversaries.

access to the resources and the world's auxiliary interface. In particular, A's oracles $\mathbf{W}_2$ and $\mathbf{R}$ are replaced with $\mathbf{S}_2$ and $\mathbf{S}_3$ respectively (4:7 and 10), which run S with access to $\mathbf{W}_2$ and $\mathbf{R}$ (4:13). SR-INDIFF$^\psi$ advantage, defined below, measures the adversary's ability to distinguish between a world $W/\vec{R}$ in the real experiment and another world $V/\vec{Q}$ in the reference experiment.

Definition 3 (SR-INDIFF$^\psi$ security). Let W, V be worlds, $\vec{R}, \vec{Q}$ be resources, A be an adversary, and S be a simulator. Let ψ be a transcript predicate and let $\text{out}^\psi(tx, a, w) := (\psi(tx) = 1) \wedge (a = 1)$. Define the SR-INDIFF$^\psi$ advantage of adversary A in differentiating $W/\vec{R}$ from $V/\vec{Q}$ relative to S as

$$\mathbf{Adv}^{\text{sr-indiff}^\psi}_{W/\vec{R}, V/\vec{Q}}(A, S) := \Pr\left[\mathbf{Real}^{\text{out}^\psi}_{W/\vec{R}}(A)\right] - \Pr\left[\mathbf{Ref}^{\text{out}^\psi}_{V/\vec{Q}}(A, S)\right].$$

By convention, the runtime of A is the runtime of $\mathbf{Real}^{\text{out}^\psi}_{W/\vec{R}}(A)$. Informally, we say that $W/\vec{R}$ is ψ-indifferentiable from $V/\vec{Q}$ if for every efficient A there exists an efficient S for which the SR-INDIFF$^\psi$ advantage of A is small. □

SHORTHAND. We write "out" instead of "out$^\psi$" when ψ is defined so that $\psi(tx) = 1$ for all tx. Correspondingly, we write "SR-INDIFF" for the security notion obtained by letting $\Phi = \text{out}$.

Non-Degenerate Adversaries. When defining security, it is typical to design the experiment so that it is guaranteed to halt. Indeed, there are pathological conditions under which $\mathbf{Real}^\Phi_{W/\vec{R}}(A)$ and $\mathbf{Ref}^\Phi_{W/\vec{R}}(A, S)$ do not halt, even if each of the constituent objects is halting (as defined in §2.1). This is because infinite loops are possible: in response to a query from adversary A, the world W is allowed to query the adversary's auxiliary interface A_2; the responding operator may call W in turn, which may call A_2, and so on. Consequently, the event that $\mathbf{Real}^\Phi_{W/\vec{R}}(A) = 1$ (resp. $\mathbf{Ref}^\Phi_{W/\vec{R}}(A, S) = 1$) must be regarded as the event that the real (resp. reference) experiment halts and outputs 1. Defining advantage this way creates obstacles for quantifying resources of a security reduction, so it will be useful to rule out infinite loops.

We define the class of *non-degenerate (n.d.) adversaries* as those that respond to main-interface queries using all three oracles—the world's main interface, the world's aux.-interface, and the resources—but respond to aux.-interface queries using only the resource oracle. To formalize this behavior, we define n.d. adversaries in terms of an object that is called in response to main-interface queries, and another object that is called in response to aux.-interface queries.

Definition 4 (Non-degenerate adversaries). An adversary A is called *non-degenerate (n.d.)* if there exist a halting object M that exports an (OUT)-**bool**-operator and a halting, functional object SD for which $A = \mathbf{NoDeg}(M, SD)$ as specified in Fig. 5. We refer to M as the *main algorithm* and to SD as the *auxiliary algorithm.*   □

Observe that we have also restricted n.d. adversaries so that the main and auxiliary algorithms do not share state; and we have required that the auxiliary algorithm is functional (i.e., deterministic and stateless). These measures are not necessary, strictly speaking, but they will be useful for security proofs. Their purpose is primarily technical, as they do not appear to be restrictive in a practical sense. (They do not limit the primary application considered in this work (§3.2). Incidentally, we note that Rogaway and Stegers make similar restrictions in [46, §5].)

2.3   The Lifting Lemma

The main technical tool of our framework is its lifting lemma, which states that if $V/\vec{Q}$ is ψ-secure and $W/\vec{R}$ is ψ-indifferentiable from $V/\vec{Q}$, then $W/\vec{R}$ is also ψ-secure. This is a generalization of the main result of MRH, which states that if an object X is secure for a given application and X is indifferentiable from Y, then Y is secure for the same application. In §2.4 we give a precise definition of "application" for which this statement holds.

THE RANDOM ORACLE MODEL (ROM). The goal of the lifting lemma is to transform a ψ-attacker against $W/\vec{R}$ into a ψ-attacker against $V/\vec{Q}$. Indifferentiability is used in the following way: given ψ-attacker A and simulator S, we construct a ψ-attacker B and ψ-differentiator D such that, in the real experiment, D outputs 1 if A wins; and in the reference experiment, D outputs 1 if B wins. Adversary B works by running A in the reference experiment with simulator S: intuitively, if the simulation provided by S "looks like" the real experiment, then B should succeed whenever A succeeds.

This argument might seem familiar, even to readers who have no exposure to the notion of indifferentiability. Indeed, a number of reductions in the provable security literature share the same basic structure. For example, when proving a signature scheme is unforgettable under chosen message attack (UF-CMA), the first step is usually to transform the attacker into a weaker one that does not have access to a signing oracle. This argument involves exhibiting a simulator that correctly answers the UF-CMA adversary's signing-oracle queries using only the public key (cf. [14, Theorem 4.1]): if the simulation is efficient, then we can argue that security in the weak attack model reduces to UF-CMA. Similarly, to prove a public-key encryption (PKE) scheme is indistinguishable under chosen ciphertext attack (IND-CCA), the strategy might be to exhibit a simulator for the decryption oracle in order to argue that IND-CPA reduces to IND-CCA.

Given the kinds of objects we wish to study, it will be useful for us to accommodate these types of arguments in the lifting lemma. In particular, Lemma 1 considers the case in which one of the resources in the reference experiment is an RO that may be "programmed" by the simulator. (As we discuss in the full version (§A), this capability is commonly used when simulating signing-oracle queries.) In our setting, the RO is programmed by passing it an object M via its SET-operator (2:9–14), which is run by the RO in order to populate the table. Normally we will require M to be an entropy source with the following properties.

Definition 5 (Sources). Let $\mu, \rho \geq 0$ be real numbers and $\mathcal{X}, \mathcal{Y}$ be computable sets. An $\mathcal{X}$-*source* is a stateless object that exports a ( )-**elem**$_{\mathcal{X}}$-operator. An $(\mathcal{X}, \mathcal{Y})$-*source* is a stateless object that exports a ( )-(**elem**$_{\mathcal{X} \times \mathcal{Y}}$, **any**)-operator. Let M be an $(\mathcal{X}, \mathcal{Y})$-source and let $((X, Y), \Sigma)$ be random variables distributed according to M. (That is, run $((x, y), \sigma) \leftarrow M( )$ and assign $X \leftarrow x$, $Y \leftarrow y$, and $\Sigma \leftarrow \sigma$.) We say that M is (μ, ρ)-*min-entropy* if the following conditions hold:

(1) For all x and y it holds that $\Pr\left[X = x\right] \leq 2^{-\mu}$ and $\Pr\left[Y = y\right] \leq 2^{-\rho}$.
(2) For all y and σ it holds that $\Pr\left[Y = y\right] = \Pr\left[Y = y \mid \Sigma = \sigma\right]$.

We refer to σ as the *auxiliary information* (cf. "source" in [9, §3]).   □

A brief explanation is in order. When a source is executed by an RO, the table T is programmed with the output point (x, y) so that $T[x] = y$. The auxiliary information σ is returned to the caller (2:14), allowing the source to provide the simulator a "hint" about how the point was chosen. Condition (1) is our min-entropy requirement for sources. We also require condition (2), which states that the range point programmed by the source is independent of the auxiliary information.

Definition 6 (The ROM). Let $\mathcal{X}, \mathcal{Y}$ be computable sets where $\mathcal{Y}$ is finite, let $q, p \geq 0$ be integers, and let $\mu, \rho \geq 0$ be real numbers. A *random oracle from $\mathcal{X}$ to $\mathcal{Y}$ with query limit* (q, p) is the object $R = \mathbf{Ro}(\mathcal{X}, \mathcal{Y}, q, p)$ specified in Fig. 2. This object permits at most q unique RO queries and at most p RO-programming queries. If the query limit is unspecified, then it is $(\infty, 0)$ so that the object permits any number of RO queries but no RO-programming queries. Objects program the RO by making queries matching the pattern (SET, M **object**). An object that makes such queries is called (μ, ρ)-$(\mathcal{X}, \mathcal{Y})$-*min-entropy* if, for all such queries, the object M is always a (μ, ρ)-min-entropy $(\mathcal{X}, \mathcal{Y})$-source. An object that makes no queries matching this pattern is *not RO-programming (n.r.)*.   □

To model a function H as a random oracle in an experiment, we revise the experiment by replacing each call of the form "$H(\cdots)$" with a call of the form "$\mathcal{R}_i(\cdots)$", where i is the index of the RO in the shared resources of the experiment, and $\mathcal{R}$ is the name of the resource oracle. When specifying a cryptographic scheme whose security analysis is in the ROM, we will usually skip this rewriting step and simply write the specification in terms of $\mathcal{R}_i$-queries: to obtain the standard model experiment, one would instantiate the i-th resource with H instead of an RO.

We are now ready to state and prove the lifting lemma. Our result accommodates indifferentiability arguments in which the RO might be programmed by the simulator.

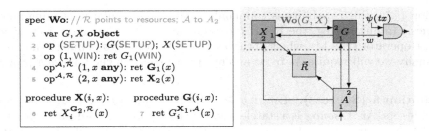

Fig. 6. Left: Specification **Wo** for building a world from a security game G and system X. Right: Who may call whom in experiment $\mathbf{Real}_{W/\vec{R}}^{\Phi}(A)$, where $W = \mathbf{Wo}(G, X)$.

Lemma 1 (Lifting). *Let $\vec{I} = (I_1, \ldots, I_u), \vec{J} = (J_1, \ldots, J_v)$ be resources; let $\mathcal{X}, \mathcal{Y}$ be computable sets, where $\mathcal{Y}$ is finite; let $N = |\mathcal{Y}|$; let $\mu, \rho \geq 0$ be real numbers for which $\log N \geq \rho$; let $q, p \geq 0$ be integers; let R and P be random oracles for $\mathcal{X}, \mathcal{Y}$ with query limits $(q + p, 0)$ and (q, p) respectively; let W, V be n.r. worlds; and let ψ be a transcript predicate. For every t_A-time, (a_1, a_2, a_r)-query, n.d. adversary A and t_S-time, (s_2, s_r)-query, (μ, ρ)-$(\mathcal{X}, \mathcal{Y})$-min-entropy simulator S, there exist n.d. adversaries D and B for which*

$$\mathbf{Adv}_{W/\vec{J}}^{MAIN^{\psi}}(A) \leq \Delta + \mathbf{Adv}_{V/\vec{I}\cdot R}^{main^{\psi}}(B) + \mathbf{Adv}_{W/\vec{J}, V/\vec{I}\cdot P}^{sr\text{-}indiff^{\psi}}(D, S),$$

where $\Delta = p\left[(p+q)/2^{-\mu} + \sqrt{N/2^{\rho} \cdot \log(N/2^{\rho})}\right]$, D is $O(t_A)$-time and $(a_1 + 1, a_2, a_r)$-query, and B is $O(t_A t_S)$-time and $(a_1, a_2 s_2, (a_2 + a_r)s_r)$-query.

We leave the proof to the full version of this paper. Apart from dealing with RO programmability, which accounts for the Δ-term in the bound, the proof is essentially the same argument as the sufficient condition in [38, Theorem 1] (cf. [45, Theorem 1]). The high min-entropy of domain points programmed by the simulator ensures that RO-programming queries are unlikely to collide with standard RO queries. However, we will need that range points are statistically close to uniform; otherwise the Δ-term becomes vacuous. Note that $\Delta = 0$ whenever programming is disallowed.

2.4   Games and the Preservation Lemma

Lemma 1 says that indifferentiability of world W from world V means that security of V implies security of W. This starting point is more general than the usual one, which is to first argue indifferentiability of some system X from another system Y, then use the composition theorem of MRH in order to argue that security of Y for some application implies security of X for the same application. Here we formalize the same kind of argument by specifying the construction of a world from a system X and a game G that defines the system's security.

A *game* is a halting object that exports a functional $(1, \mathsf{WIN})$-**bool**-operator. A *system* is a halting object. Figure 6 specifies the composition of a game G and system X into a world $W = \mathbf{Wo}(G, X)$ in which the adversary interacts with G's main interface and X's auxiliary interface, and G interacts with X's main interface. The system X makes queries to G's auxiliary interface, and G in turn makes queries to the adversary's auxiliary interface. As shown in right hand side of Fig. 6, it is the game that decides whether the adversary has won: when the real experiment calls $W_1(\mathsf{WIN})$ on line 4:4, this call is answered by the operator defined by **Wo** on line 6:3, which returns $G_1(\mathsf{WIN})$.

Definition 7 (G^ψ **security**). Let ψ be a transcript predicate, G be a game, X be a system, $\vec{R}$ be resources, and A be an adversary. We define the G^ψ advantage of A in attacking $X/\vec{R}$ as

$$\mathbf{Adv}_{X/\vec{R}}^{G^\psi}(A) := \mathbf{Adv}_{\mathbf{Wo}(G,X)/\vec{R}}^{\mathrm{main}^\psi}(A).$$

We write $\mathbf{Adv}_{X/\vec{R}}^{G}(A)$ whenever $\psi(tx) = 1$ for all tx. Informally, we say that $X/\vec{R}$ is G^ψ-secure if the G^ψ advantage of any efficient adversary is small.   □

World **Wo** formalizes the class of systems for which we will define security in this paper. While the execution semantics of games and systems seems quite natural, we remark that other ways of capturing security notions are possible. We are restricted only by the execution semantics of the real experiment (Definition 1). Indeed, there are natural classes of security definitions we cannot capture, including those described by multi-stage games [45].

For our particular class of security notions we can prove the following useful lemma. Intuitively, the "preservation" lemma below states that if a system X is ψ-indifferentiable from Y, then $\mathbf{Wo}(G,X)$ is ψ-indifferentiable from $\mathbf{Wo}(G,Y)$ for any game G. We leave the simple proof to the full version. The main idea is that B in the real (resp. reference) experiment can precisely simulate A's execution in its real (resp. reference) experiment by using G to answer A's main-interface queries.

Lemma 2 (Preservation). *Let ψ be a transcript predicate, X, Y be objects, and $\vec{R}, \vec{Q}$ be resources. For every $(g_1, \_)$-query game G, t_A-time, (a_1, a_2, a_r)-query, n.d. adversary A, and simulator S there exists an n.d. adversary B such that*

$$\mathbf{Adv}_{W/\vec{R},V/\vec{Q}}^{\mathrm{sr\text{-}indiff}^\psi}(A, S) \leq \mathbf{Adv}_{X/\vec{R},Y/\vec{Q}}^{\mathrm{sr\text{-}indiff}^\psi}(B, S),$$

where $W = \mathbf{Wo}(G, X)$, $V = \mathbf{Wo}(G, Y)$, and B is $O(t_A)$-time and $(a_1 g_1, a_2, a_r)$-query.

3   Protocol Translation

In this section we consider the problem of quantifying the security cost of *protocol translation*, where the real system is obtained from the reference system by modifying the protocol's specification. As a case study, we design and prove secure a TLS extension for SPAKE2 [3], which, at the time of writing, was one of the PAKEs considered by the CFRG for standardization.

We define security for PAKE in the extended Canetti-Krawczyk (eCK) model of LaMacchia et al. [37], a simple, yet powerful model for the study of authenticated key exchange. The eCK model specifies both the execution environment of the protocol (i.e., how the adversary interacts with it) and its intended goal (i.e., key indistinguishability [13]) in a single security experiment. Our treatment breaks this abstraction boundary.

Recall from the previous section that for any transcript predicate ψ, game G, and systems X and $\tilde{X}$, we can argue that X is G^ψ-secure (Definition 7) by proving that X is ψ-indifferentiable from $\tilde{X}$ (Definition 3) and assuming $\tilde{X}$ itself is G^ψ-secure. In this section, the system specifies the execution environment of a cryptographic protocol for which the game defines security. In §3.1 we specify a system $\mathbf{eCK}(\Pi)$ that formalizes the execution of protocol Π in the eCK model. Going up a level of abstraction, running an adversary A in world $W = \mathbf{Wo}(G, \mathbf{eCK}(\Pi))$ in the MAIN$^\psi$ experiment (Definition 1) lets A execute Π via W's auxiliary interface and "play" the game G via W's main interface. The environment $\mathbf{eCK}$ surfaces information about the state of the execution environment, which G uses to determine if A wins. Finally, transcript predicate ψ is used to determine if the attack is valid based on the sequence of W_1- and W_2-queries made by A.

3.1   eCK-Protocols

The eCK model was introduced by LaMacchia et al. [37] in order to broaden the corruptive powers of the adversary in the Canetti-Krawczyk setting [24]. The pertinent change is to restrict the class of protocols to those whose state is deterministically computed from the player's static key (i.e., its long-term secret), ephemeral key (i.e., the per-session randomness), and the sequence of messages received so far. This results in a far simpler formulation of session-state compromise. We embellish the syntax by providing the party with an *initial input* at the start of each session, allowing us to capture features like per-session configuration [17].

Definition 8 (Protocols). An *(eCK-)protocol* is a halting, stateless object Π, with an associated finite set of *identities* $\mathcal{I} \subseteq \{0,1\}^*$, that exports the following operators:

- (SGEN)-(pk, sk **table**): generates the static key and corresponding public key of each party so that (pk_i, sk_i) is the public/static key pair of party $i \in \mathcal{I}$.
- (EGEN, i **str**, α **any**)-(ek **any**): generates an ephemeral key ek for party i with input α. The ephemeral key constitutes the randomness used by the party in a given session.
- (SEND, i **str**, sk, ek, α, π, in **any**)-(π', out **any**): computes the outbound message out and updated state π' of party i with static key sk, ephemeral key ek, input α, session state π, and inbound message in. This operator is deterministic.

```
spec eCK: // 𝒜 points to 𝒜₂; ℛ to res.        20  op^{𝒜,ℛ} (2, INIT, s, i str, a any):
  1  var Π object, r int                        21    Init(active, s, i, a)
  2  var pk, sk, ek, α, π table; atk any        22  op^{𝒜,ℛ} (2, SEND, s, i str, in any):
  3  op (SETUP):                                 23    ret Send(s, i, in)
  4    Π(SETUP); r ← Π(MOVES)                    24  op^{𝒜,ℛ} (2, EXEC, s₁, i₁, s₀, i₀ str, a₁, a₀ any):
  5    pk, sk, ek, α, π ← []; atk ← ( )          25    Init(passive, s₁, i₁, a₁)
  6                                              26    Init(passive, s₀, i₀, a₀)
  7  // Main interface                           27    out ← ⊥; tr ← ( )
  8  op^{𝒜,ℛ} (1, INIT):                         28    for j ← 1 to r + 1 do γ ← j (mod 2)
  9    (pk, sk) ← Π^{𝒜,ℛ}(SGEN); ret pk          29      out ← Send(s_γ, i_γ, out)
 10  op^{𝒜,ℛ} (1, GAME ST, x, s, i str):         30      tr ← tr . out
 11    ret Π^{𝒜,ℛ}(GAME ST, x, i, π_s^i)         31    ret tr
 12  op (1, ATTACK ST): ret atk
 13                                              procedure Init(t, s, i, a):  // t ∈ {active, passive}
 14  // Auxiliary interface                      32    ek_s^i ← Π^{𝒜,ℛ}(EGEN, i, a)
 15  op (2, PK, i str): ret pk_i                 33    α_s^i ← a; π_s^i ← ⊥
 16  op (2, SK, i str):                          34    atk ← atk . (t, s, i)
 17    atk ← atk . (SK, i); ret sk_i
 18  op (2, EK, s, i str):                       procedure Send(s, i, in):
 19    atk ← atk . (EK, s, i); ret ek_s^i        35    (π_s^i, out) ← Π^{𝒜,ℛ}(SEND, i, sk_i, ek_s^i, α_s^i, π_s^i, m)
                                                 36    ret out
```

Fig. 7. Execution environment for two-party eCK-protocols.

- (MOVES)-(r **int**): indicates the maximum number of moves (i.e., messages sent) in an honest run of the protocol. This operator is deterministic.   □

The execution environment for eCK-protocols is specified by **eCK** in Fig. 7. The environment stores the public/static keys of each party (tables pk and sk) and the ephemeral key (ek), input (α), and current state (π) of each session. As usual, the adversary is responsible for initializing and sending messages to sessions, which it does by making queries to the auxiliary interface (7:14–31). Each session is identified by a pair of strings (s, i), where s is the *session index* and i is the identity of the party incident to the session. The auxiliary interface exports the following operators:

- (INIT, s, i **str**, a **any**): initializes session (s, i) on input a by setting $\alpha_s^i \leftarrow a$ and $\pi_s^i \leftarrow \bot$. A session initialized in this way is said to be under *active attack* because the adversary controls its execution.
- (SEND, s, i **str**, in **any**)-(out **any**): sends message in to a session (s, i) under active attack. Updates the session state π_s^i and returns the outbound message out.
- (EXEC, s_1, i_1, s_0, i_0 **str**, a_1, a_0 **any**)-(tr **any**): executes an honest run of the protocol for initiator session (s_1, i_1) on input a_1 and responder session (s_0, i_0) on input a_0 and returns the sequence of exchanged messages tr. A session initialized this way is said to be under *passive attack* because the adversary does not control the protocol's execution.
- (PK, i **str**)-(pk **any**), (SK, i **str**)-(sk **any**), and (EK, s, i **str**)-(ek **any**): returns, respectively, the public key of party i, the static key of party i, and the ephemeral key of session (s, i).

Whenever the protocol is executed, it is given access to the adversary's auxiliary interface (see interface oracle $\mathcal{A}$ on lines 7:9, 11, 32, and 35). This allows us to formalize security goals for protocols that are only partially specified [46]. In world $\mathbf{Wo}(G, X)$, system $X = \mathbf{eCK}(\Pi)$ relays Π's $\mathcal{A}$-queries to G: usually game G will simply forward these queries to the adversary, but the game must explicitly define this. (See the definition of KEY-IND security below in the full version for an example.)

The attack state (atk) records the sequence of actions carried out by the adversary. Specifically, it records whether each session is under active or passive attack (7:34), whether the adversary knows the ephemeral key of a given session (7:19), and which static keys are known to the adversary (7:17). These are used by the game to decide if the adversary's attack was successful. In addition, the game is given access to the $game\ state$, which surfaces any artifacts computed by a session that are specific to the intended security goal: examples include the session key in a key-exchange protocol, the session identifier (SID) or partner identifier (PID) [10], or the negotiated mode [17]. The game state is exposed by the protocol's GAME␣ST-interface (e.g., lines 8:8–13). All told, the main interface (7:7–12) exports the following operators:

- (INIT)-(pk **any**): initializes each party by running the static key generator and returns the table of public keys pk.
- (ATTACK ST)-(atk **any**): returns the attack state atk to the caller.
- (GAME ST, x, s, i **str**)-(val **any**): provides access to the game state.

ATTACK VALIDITY. For simplicity, our execution environment allows some behaviors that are normally excluded in security definitions. Namely, (1) the adversary might initialize a session before the static keys have been generated, or try to generate the static keys more than once; or (2) the adversary might attempt to re-initialize a session already in progress. The first of these is excluded by transcript predicate ϕ_{init} and the second by ϕ_{sess}, both defined below.

Definition 9 (Predicates ϕ_{init} and ϕ_{sess}). Let $\phi_{\mathrm{init}}(tx) = 1$ if $|tx| \geq 1$, $tx_1 = (1, \mathrm{INIT})$, and for all $1 < \alpha \leq |tx|$ it holds that $tx_\alpha \neq (1, \mathrm{INIT})$. Let $\phi_{\mathrm{sess}}(tx) = 0$ iff there exist $1 \leq \alpha < \beta \leq |atk|$ such that $atk_\alpha = (t_\alpha, s_\alpha, i_\alpha)$, $atk_\beta = (t_\beta, s_\beta, i_\beta)$, $(s_\alpha, i_\alpha) = (s_\beta, i_\beta)$, and $t_\alpha, t_\beta \in \{\mathsf{passive}, \mathsf{active}\}$, where atk is the attack state corresponding to transcript tx. □

3.2 Case Study: PAKE Extension for TLS 1.3

In order to support the IETF's PAKE-standardization effort, we choose one of the protocols considered by the CFRG and show how to securely integrate it into the TLS handshake. By the time we began our study, the selection process had narrowed to four candidates [52]: SPAKE2 [3], OPAQUE [32], CPace [30], and AuCPace [30]. Of these four, only SPAKE2 has been analyzed in a game-based security model (the rest have proofs in the UC-framework [20]) and as such is the only candidate whose existing analysis can be lifted in our setting. Thus, we choose it for our study.

Existing proposals for PAKE extensions [5,54] allow passwords to be used either in lieu of certificates or alongside them in order to "hedge" against failures of the web PKI. Barnes and Friel [5] propose a simple, generic extension for TLS 1.3 [44] (`draft-barnes-tls-pake`) that replaces the standard DH key-exchange with a 2-move PAKE. This straight-forward approach is, arguably, the best option in terms of computational overhead, modularity, and ease-of-implementation. Thus, our goal will be to instantiate `draft-barnes-tls-pake` with SPAKE2. We begin with an overview of the extension and the pertinent details of TLS. We then describe the SPAKE2 protocol and specify its usage in TLS. We end with our security analysis.

Usage of PAKE with TLS 1.3 (`draft-barnes-tls-pake`). The TLS handshake begins when the client sends its "ClientHello" message to the server. The server responds with its "ServerHello" followed by its parameters "EncryptedExtensions" and "CertificateRequest" and authentication messages "Certificate", "CertificateVerify", and "Finished". The client replies with its own authentication messages "Certificate", "CertificateVerify", and "Finished". The Hellos carry ephemeral DH key shares signed by the parties' Certificates, and the signatures are carried by the CertificateVerify messages. Each party provides key confirmation by computing a MAC over the handshake transcript; the MACs are carried by the Finished messages.

The DH shared secret is fed into the "key schedule" [44, §7.1] that defines the derivation of all symmetric keys used in the protocol. Key derivation uses the *HKDF* function [34], which takes as input a "salt" string, the "initial key material (IKM)" (i.e., the DH shared secret), and an "information" string used to bind derived keys to the context in which they are used in the protocol. The output is used as a salt for subsequent calls to *HKDF*. The first call is $salt \leftarrow HKDF(0^k, psk, \text{derived})$, where $k \geq 0$ is a parameter of TLS called the hash length and psk is the pre-shared key. (If available, otherwise $psk = 0^k$.) Next, the parties derive the client handshake-traffic key $K_1 \leftarrow HKDF(salt, dhe, info_1)$, the server handshake-traffic key $K_0 \leftarrow HKDF(salt, dhe, info_0)$, and the session key $K \leftarrow HKDF(salt, dhe, \text{derived})$. Variable dhe denotes the shared secret. Each information string encodes both Hellos and a string that identifies the role of the key: c hs traffic for the client and s hs traffic for the server. The traffic keys are used for encrypting the parameter and authentication messages and computing the Finished MACs, and the session key is used for encrypting application data and computing future pre-shared keys.

EXTENSIONS. Protocol extensions are typically comprised of two messages carried by the handshake: the *request*, carried by the ClientHello; and the *response*, carried by the ServerHello or by one of the server's parameter or authentication messages. Usually the request indicates support for a specific feature and the response indicates whether the feature will be used in the handshake. In `draft-barnes-tls-pake`, the client sends the first PAKE message in an extension request carried by its ClientHello; if the server chooses to negotiate usage of the PAKE, then it sends the second PAKE message as an extension response carried by its ServerHello. When the extension is used, the PAKE specifies the values of psk and dhe in the key schedule.

```
spec SPake2-AP_G^{C,S}:                      14  // Client sends KEX1
 1  var PW object, N_1, N_0 elem_G            15  op (SEND, c elem_C, sk, ek int, ⊥, ⊥, ⊥):
 2  op (SETUP): N_1, N_0 ←$ G                 16    X_1^* ← g^{ek} · N_1^{sk}
 3  op (MOVES): ret 2                         17    ret ((wait, X_1^*), (c, X_1^*))
 4  op-'^R (SGEN): pk ← []                    18  // Client on KEX0
 5    for i ∈ C ∪ S do pk_i ← (N_1, N_0)      19  op-'^R (SEND, c elem_C, sk, ek int, ⊥,
 6    ret (pk, PW^R())                        20      (wait, X_1^* elem_G), (s elem_S, X_0^* elem_G)):
 7  op (EGEN, ...): ek ←$ Z_{|G|}; ret ek     21    Z ← (X_0^* · N_0^{-sk})^{ek}
 8  op (GAME ST, x, i str,                    22    ikm ← (c, s, X_1^*, X_0^*, sk, Z)
 9      (st, j, K str, X_1^*, X_0^* elem_G)): 23    K ← R_1(ikm)
10    if st ≠ done then ret ⊥                 24    ret ((done, s, K, X_1^*, X_0^*), ⊥)
11    if x = sid then ret (X_1^*, X_0^*)      25  // Server on KEX1 sends KEX0
12    if x = pid then ret j                   26  op-'^R (SEND, s elem_S, sk table, ek int, ⊥, ⊥
13    if x = key then ret K                   27      (c elem_C, X_1^* elem_G)):
                                              28    X_0^* ← g^{ek} · N_0^{sk_c}; Z ← (X_1^* · N_1^{-sk_c})^{ek}
                                              29    ikm ← (c, s, X_1^*, X_0^*, sk_c, Z)
                                              30    K ← R_1(ikm)
                                              31    ret ((done, c, K, X_1^*, X_0^*), (s, X_0^*))
                                              32  op (SEND, ...): ret (fail, ⊥)  // Invalid message
```

Fig. 8. Protocol $\mathbf{SPake2\text{-}AP}_{\mathbb{G}}^{\mathcal{C},\mathcal{S}}$, where $\mathbb{G} = (\mathcal{G}, \cdot)$ is a prime-order, cyclic group with generator g and $\mathcal{S}, \mathcal{C} \subseteq \{0,1\}^*$ are finite, disjoint, non-empty sets. Object PW is a symmetric password generator for $\mathcal{S}, \mathcal{C}, \mathcal{P}$ for some dictionary $\mathcal{P} \subseteq \mathbb{Z}_{|\mathcal{G}|}$.

At first brush, it may seem "obvious" that the security of the extension follows immediately from the security of the PAKE, since the PAKE is run without modification. There are two important points to note here. The first is that the extension is underspecified: the output of a PAKE is generally a single session key, so it is up to the implementer to decide how the session key is mapped to the inputs of the key schedule (i.e., *psk* and *dhe*). The second point is that the PAKE is not only used to derive the session key (used to protect application data), but also to encrypt handshake messages and compute MACs. As a result, whether this usage is secure or not depends on the concrete protocol and how it is implemented in the extension.

The SPAKE2 Protocol. SPAKE2 is the eCK-protocol $\mathbf{SPake2\text{-}AP}_{\mathbb{G}}^{\mathcal{C},\mathcal{S}}(PW)$ in Fig. 8 (cf. [1, Figure 1]). (Refer to the full version for a detailed explanation.) Sets $\mathcal{C}$ and $\mathcal{S}$ denote the clients and servers respectively. Key derivation is carried out by a call to $\mathcal{R}_1$. To obtain the concrete protocol, one would use the hash function H to instantiate the first resource in the experiment. However, since all existing analyses model H as an RO [1,3,6], we will also use an RO. (See Theorem 1 below.)

The protocol is parameterized by an object PW used to generate the static keys. Syntactically, we require that PW halts and outputs a table sk for which $sk[s][c] = sk[c] \in \mathcal{P}$ for all $(c, s) \in \mathcal{C} \times \mathcal{S}$ and some set $\mathcal{P} \subseteq \mathbb{Z}_{|\mathcal{G}|}$, called the *dictionary*. We refer to such an object as a *symmetric password generator for $\mathcal{C}, \mathcal{S}, \mathcal{P}$*. Following Bellare et al. [10], each client c is in possession of a single password $sk[c] \in \mathcal{P}$, used to authenticate to each server; and each server s is in possession of a table $sk[s]$ that stores the password $sk[s][c]$ shared

```
spec SPake2-TLS_G^{C,S}:  // A points to A_2 (via a game); R to resources
 1  var PW, en object, const_1, const_0 str
 2  op (MOVES): ret 3                              procedure KDF(ikm, c, s, hello_1, hello_0):
 3  op–'^R (SGEN): pk ← []                        54  var info_1, info_0, info, salt str
 4    N_1 ← R_2(const_1); N_0 ← R_2(const_0)       55  info_1 ← A(c hs traffic, hello_1, hello_0)
 5    for i ∈ C ∪ S do pk_i ← (N_1, N_0)           56  info_0 ← A(s hs traffic, hello_1, hello_0)
 6    ret (pk, PW^R())                             57  info  ← A(derived,       c, s)
 7  op^A (EGEN, i elem_{C∪S}, a any):              58  salt  ← A(salt,          c, s)
 8    var ρ elem_N, r str                          59  if |{info_1, info_0, info}| ≠ 3 ∨
 9    ρ ← A(rnd, i, a); if ρ ≠ ⊥ then r ←$ {0,1}^ρ 60    ⊥ ∈ {info_1, info_0, info, salt}
10    ek ←$ Z_{|G|}; ret (ek, r)                   61    then ret (⊥, ⊥, ⊥)
11  op (GAME ST, x, i str,                         62  K_1 ← R_1(salt, en_1(ikm), info_1)
12    (st, j, K str, X_1^*, X_0^* elem_G, …)):     63  K_0 ← R_1(salt, en_1(ikm), info_0)
13    if st ∉ {done, s wait} then ret ⊥            64  K  ← R_1(salt, en_1(ikm), info)
14    if x = sid  then ret (X_1^*, X_0^*)          65  ret (K_1, K_0, K)
15    if x = pid  then ret j
16    if x = key  then ret K
17
18  // Client sends HELLO1
19  op^{A,R} (SEND, c elem_C, sk, (ek int, r any), a any, ⊥, ⊥):
20    var hello_1 str
21    N_1 ← R_2(const_1); X_1^* ← g^{ek} · N_1^{sk}
22    hello_1 ← A(c hello, r, a, c, X_1^*); if A(c kex, hello_1) ≠ (c, X_1^*) then ret (fail, A(proto err))
23    ret ((c wait, X_1^*, hello_1), hello_1)
24  // Client on (HELLO0, AUTH0) sends AUTH1
25  op^{A,R} (SEND, c elem_C, sk, (ek int, r any), a any,
26    (c wait, X_1^* elem_G, hello_1 str), (hello_0, auth_0 str)):
27    var s elem_S, X_0^* elem_G, auth_1 str
28    (s, X_0^*) ← A(s kex, hello_0); if ⊥ ∈ {s, X_0^*} then ret (fail, A(proto err))
29    N_0 ← R_2(const_0); Z ← (X_0^* · N_0^{-sk})^{ek}; ikm ← (c, s, X_1^*, X_0^*, sk, Z)
30    tr ← hello_1 ∥ hello_0; (K_1, K_0, K) ← KDF(ikm, c, s, hello_1, hello_0)
31    if K_1 = ⊥ then ret (fail, A(proto err))
32    if A(s verify, K_0, (a, tr), auth_0) ≠ 1 then ret (fail, A(verify err))
33    tr ← tr ∥ auth_0; auth_1 ← A(c auth, K_1, (a, tr), r)
34    ret ((done, s, K, X_1^*, X_0^*), auth_1)
35
36  // Server on HELLO1 sends (HELLO0, AUTH0)
37  op^{A,R} (SEND, s elem_S, sk table, (ek int, r any), a any, ⊥, hello_1 str):
38    var c elem_C, X_1^* elem_G, hello_0, auth_0 str
39    (c, X_1^*) ← A(c kex, hello_1); if ⊥ ∈ {c, X_1^*} then ret (fail, A(proto err))
40    N_1 ← R_2(const_1); Z ← (X_1^* · N_1^{-sk_c})^{ek}; ikm ← (c, s, X_1^*, X_0^*, sk_c, Z)
41    N_0 ← R_2(const_0); X_0^* ← g^{ek} · N_0^{sk_c}
42    hello_0 ← A(s hello, r, a, s, X_0^*); if A(s kex, hello_0) ≠ (s, X_0^*) then ret (fail, A(proto err))
43    tr ← hello_1 ∥ hello_0; (K_1, K_0, K) ← KDF(ikm, c, s, hello_1, hello_0)
44    if K_1 = ⊥ then ret (fail, A(proto err))
45    auth_0 ← A(s auth, K_0, (a, tr), r); tr ← tr ∥ auth_0
46    ret ((s wait, c, K, X_1^*, X_0^*, K_1, tr), (hello_0, auth_0))
47  // Server on AUTH1
48  op^{A,R} (SEND, s elem_S, sk table, (ek int, r any), a any,
49    (s wait, c, K str, X_1^*, X_0^* elem_G, K_1, tr str), auth_1 str):
50    if A(c verify, K_1, (a, tr), auth_1) ≠ 1 then ret (fail, A(verify err))
51    ret ((done, c, K, X_1^*, X_0^*), ⊥)
52
53  op^A (SEND, …): ret (fail, A(unexpected message))
```

Fig. 9. Protocol **SPake2-TLS**$_G^{C,S}$, where PW, $\mathbb{G} = (\mathcal{G}, \cdot)$, g, $\mathcal{C}$, and $\mathcal{S}$ are as defined in Fig. 8. Object en is a $(\{0,1\}^* \times \{0,1\}^* \times \mathcal{G} \times \mathcal{G} \times \mathbb{Z}_{|\mathcal{G}|} \times \mathcal{G})$-encoder, where $\mathcal{G}$ is a represented set (Definition 10).

with each client c. Generally speaking—and for SPAKE2 in particular [1, 3, 6]—passwords are assumed to be uniformly and independently distributed over the dictionary $\mathcal{P}$. We call such a generator *uniform*.

Securely Instantiating draft-barnes-tls-pake with SPAKE2. In Fig. 9 we define a protocol $\mathbf{SPake2}\text{-}\mathbf{TLS}_{\mathbb{G}}^{\mathcal{C},\mathcal{S}}(PW, const_1, const_0)$ that partially specifies the usage of SPAKE2 in TLS. We say "partially" because most of the details of TLS are provided by calls to interface oracle $\mathcal{A}$, which are answered by the adversary's auxiliary interface in the real experiment. Calls to $\mathcal{R}_1$ and $\mathcal{R}_2$ are answered by, respectively, an RO for *HKDF* and an RO for a function $H_{\mathbb{G}}$, defined below. Before being passed to *HKDF*, the input is first encoded using an object en with the following properties.

Definition 10 (Encoders and represented sets). A *represented set* is a computable set $\mathcal{X}$ for which $\bot \notin \mathcal{X}$ (cf. "represented groups" in [2, §2.1]). Let $\mathcal{X}$ be a represented set. An $\mathcal{X}$-*encoder* is a functional, halting object en that exports the following operators:

- $(1, x \ \mathbf{elem}_{\mathcal{X}})\text{-}(M \ \mathbf{str})$: the encoding algorithm, returns the encoding M of x as a string.
- $(0, M \ \mathbf{str})\text{-}(x \ \mathbf{elem}_{\mathcal{X} \cup \{\bot\}})$: the decoding algorithm, returns the element x of $\mathcal{X}$ encoded by string M (or $\bot$ if M does not encode an element of $\mathcal{X}$).

Correctness requires that $en_0(en_1(x)) = x$ for every $x \in \mathcal{X}$. ☐

The Hellos carry the SPAKE2 key-exchange messages. The first is encoded by the client on line 9:22 and decoded by the server on line 39, and the second is encoded by the server on line 42 and decoded by the client on line 28. Value ikm (the input to H in SPAKE2) is passed to procedure **KDF** (54–65), which is used to derive the traffic and session keys. Oracle $\mathcal{A}$ (which points to the adversary's aux. interface in the security experiment) chooses the salt and information strings, subject to the constraint that the information strings are distinct.

We refer to the ClientHello as HELLO1 and to the ServerHello as HELLO0. Our spec lumps all other handshake messages into two: AUTH0 for the server's parameter and authentication messages (EncryptedExtensions...Finished); and AUTH1 for the client's authentication messages (Certificate...Finished). This consolidates all traffic-key dependent computations into four $\mathcal{A}$-queries: AUTH0 is computed on line 9:45 and verified on line 32 and AUTH1 is computed on line 33 and verified on line 50. In the full version we include a detailed explanation of Fig. 9 and design rationale for the extension. One notable feature is that instead of relying on trusted setup to generate the public parameters $N_1, N_0 \in \mathbb{G}$, we pick two distinct constants $const_1, const_0 \in \{0,1\}^*$ and compute the parameters as $N_1 \leftarrow H_{\mathbb{G}}(const_1)$ and $N_0 \leftarrow H_{\mathbb{G}}(const_0)$, where $H_{\mathbb{G}} : \{0,1\}^* \to \mathcal{G}$ is a hash function suitable for the given group $\mathbb{G} = (\mathcal{G}, \cdot)$ (e.g., a suitable "hash-to-curve" algorithm [28]).

SECURITY. We now derive the concrete security of this usage of SPAKE2. Our analysis is in the *weak corruption model* of Bellare et al. [10], which assumes that only static keys (i.e., passwords) and not ephemeral keys can be revealed to the attacker. This is without loss of generality, as all existing analyses of SPAKE2 assume the same corruption model [1,3,6]. Our proof also uses the GDH assumption [39], defined below.

Definition 11 (Predicate ϕ_{wc}). Let $\phi_{\mathrm{wc}}(tx) = (\nexists\,\alpha)\,tx_\alpha \sim (2, \mathsf{EK}, \dots)$.   □

Definition 12 (The GDH problem). Let $\mathbb{G} = (\mathcal{G}, \cdot)$ be a cyclic group with generator $g \in \mathcal{G}$. A *DDH oracle for* $\mathbb{G}$ is a halting object *DDH* for which $DDH(X, Y, Z) = 1$ holds if and only if $\log_g X \cdot \log_g Y = \log_g Z$ for all $X, Y, Z \in \mathcal{G}$. Define $\mathbf{Adv}_{\mathbb{G}}^{\mathrm{gdh}}(A) := \Pr\left[\, x, y \xleftarrow{} \mathbb{Z}_{|\mathcal{G}|} : A^{DDH}(g^x, g^y) = g^{xy} \,\right]$ to be the advantage of an adversary A in solving the GDH problem for $\mathbb{G}$. Informally, we say the GDH problem is hard for $\mathbb{G}$ if the advantage of every efficient adversary is small.   □

Let $k \geq 0$ be an integer; let $const_1, const_0$ be distinct strings; let $\mathbb{G} = (\mathcal{G}, \cdot)$ be a prime-order cyclic group; let $\mathcal{C}, \mathcal{S} \subseteq \{0,1\}^*$ be finite, disjoint, non-empty sets; let $\mathcal{P} \subseteq \mathbb{Z}_{|\mathcal{G}|}$ be a dictionary; and let PW be a uniform, symmetric password-generator for $\mathcal{C}, \mathcal{S}, \mathcal{P}$. Define $\mathcal{T}$ to be the set $\{0,1\}^* \times \{0,1\}^* \times \mathcal{G} \times \mathcal{G} \times \mathbb{Z}_{|\mathcal{G}|} \times \mathcal{G}$. Let $\Pi = \mathbf{SPake2\text{-}TLS}_{\mathbb{G}}^{\mathcal{C},\mathcal{S}}(PW, const_1, const_0)$, $\tilde{\Pi} = \mathbf{SPake2\text{-}AP}_{\mathbb{G}}^{\mathcal{C},\mathcal{S}}(PW)$, $X = \mathbf{eCK}(\Pi)$, and $\tilde{X} = \mathbf{eCK}(\tilde{\Pi})$. Let $\psi = \phi_{\mathrm{init}} \wedge \phi_{\mathrm{sess}} \wedge \phi_{\mathrm{wc}}$. The following says that for any game G, the G^ψ-security of X (in the ROM for *HKDF* and $H_{\mathbb{G}}$) follows from the G^ψ-security of $\tilde{X}$ (in the ROM for H) under the GDH assumption.

Theorem 1. *Let F be an RO from $(\{0,1\}^*)^3$ to $\{0,1\}^k$, R be an RO from $\{0,1\}^*$ to $\mathcal{G}$, and H be an RO from $\mathcal{T}$ to $\{0,1\}^k$. Let DDH be a DDH oracle for $\mathbb{G}$. For every game G and t_A-time, n.d. adversary A making q_r resource queries, q_s SEND-queries, and q_e EXEC-queries, there exist an n.d. adversary B and GDH-adversary C such that*

$$\mathbf{Adv}_{X/(F,R)}^{G^\psi}(A) \leq \mathbf{Adv}_{\tilde{X}/(H,DDH)}^{G^\psi}(B)$$

$$+ 2q_e \mathbf{Adv}_{\mathbb{G}}^{\mathrm{gdh}}(C) + \frac{2q_s}{|\mathcal{P}|} + \frac{(q_s + 2q_e)^2}{2|\mathcal{G}|},$$

where: DDH is t_{DDH}-time; B runs in time $O(\hat{T})$ and makes at most q_s SEND-queries, q_e EXEC-queries, $O(\hat{Q})$ DDH-queries, and q_r H-queries; C runs in time $O(\hat{T})$ and makes at most $O(\hat{Q})$ DDH-queries; $\hat{T} = t_A(t_A + q_r \cdot t_{DDH})$; and $\hat{Q} = q_r(q_s + q_e)$.

We leave the proof to the full version but sketch the main ideas here. The claim is proved by first applying Lemma 1, then applying Lemma 2 so that we can argue security using the ψ-indifferentiability of $X/(F,R)$ from $\tilde{X}/(H, DDH)$. The bound reflects the loss in security that results from using the PAKE to derive the traffic keys. The GDH-advantage term is used to bound the probability that derivation of one of these keys during an honest run of the protocol (via EXEC) coincides with a previous RO query; the $2q_s/|\mathcal{P}|$-term is used to bound the probability of the same event occurring during an active attack (via SEND). The simulator kills a session if the SID ever collides with another session other than the partner, which accounts for the final term.

Given a non-degenerate, ψ-differentiator D, the goal is to exhibit an efficient simulator S and GDH-adversary C that yield the result. Recall that S gets two oracles in the reference experiment: one for the aux. interface of $\tilde{X}$, which is used to execute the reference protocol $\tilde{\Pi}$; and another for resources (H, DDH). Its job is to simulate aux./resource queries for $X/(F, R)$. The central problem it must solve is that the adversary has direct access to the main interface of $\tilde{X}$, which provides it with the game and attack state. Hence, the adversary needs to use its own oracles in a way that ensures the game and attack state are consistent with the adversary's view of the execution.

Refer to S's oracles as $\mathcal{X}$ and $\mathcal{R}$. Its strategy is to "embed" a run of the reference protocol into each simulation of the real one so that each EXEC- or SEND-query from the adversary is mapped to an EXEC- or SEND-query to $\mathcal{X}$. RO queries are simulated by S itself, except that $\mathcal{R}_1$ (points to H) is called whenever the query coincides with the derivation of a session key. The DDH oracle (pointed to by $\mathcal{R}_2$) is used to determine if this is the case. The difficult part is simulating computation of the traffic keys without knowing the password and/or shared secret. In a nutshell, the strategy is to "guess" that the adversary has not yet made an RO query that coincides with these, generate fresh keys, then back-patch the RO simulation in order to ensure consistency going forward.

Acknowledgements. Funding for this work was provided by NSF grant CNS-1816375. We thank the anonymous reviewers of CRYPTO 2020 for their useful comments.

References

1. Abdalla, M., Barbosa, M.: Perfect forward security of SPAKE2. Cryptology ePrint Archive, Report 2019/1194 (2019). https://eprint.iacr.org/2019/1194
2. Abdalla, M., Bellare, M., Rogaway, P.: The oracle Diffie-Hellman assumptions and an analysis of DHIES. In: Naccache, D. (ed.) CT-RSA 2001. LNCS, vol. 2020, pp. 143–158. Springer, Heidelberg (2001). https://doi.org/10.1007/3-540-45353-9_12
3. Abdalla, M., Pointcheval, D.: Simple password-based encrypted key exchange protocols. In: Menezes, A. (ed.) CT-RSA 2005. LNCS, vol. 3376, pp. 191–208. Springer, Heidelberg (2005). https://doi.org/10.1007/978-3-540-30574-3_14
4. Barbosa, M., Farshim, P.: Indifferentiable authenticated encryption. In: Shacham, H., Boldyreva, A. (eds.) CRYPTO 2018. LNCS, vol. 10991, pp. 187–220. Springer, Cham (2018). https://doi.org/10.1007/978-3-319-96884-1_7
5. Barnes, R., Friel, O.: Usage of PAKE with TLS 1.3. Internet-Draft draft-barnes-tls-pake-04, Internet Engineering Task Force (2018). https://datatracker.ietf.org/doc/html/draft-barnes-tls-pake-04
6. Becerra, J., Ostrev, D., Škrobot, M.: Forward secrecy of SPAKE2. In: Baek, J., Susilo, W., Kim, J. (eds.) ProvSec 2018. LNCS, vol. 11192, pp. 366–384. Springer, Cham (2018). https://doi.org/10.1007/978-3-030-01446-9_21

7. Bellare, M., Desai, A., Jokipii, E., Rogaway, P.: A concrete security treatment of symmetric encryption. In: Proceedings 38th Annual Symposium on Foundations of Computer Science, pp. 394–403 (1997). https://doi.org/10.1109/SFCS.1997.646128

8. Bellare, M., Davis, H., Günther, F.: Separate your domains: NIST PQC KEMs, oracle cloning and read-only indifferentiability. Cryptology ePrint Archive, Report 2020/241 (2020). https://eprint.iacr.org/2020/241

9. Bellare, M., Keelveedhi, S., Ristenpart, T.: Message-locked encryption and secure deduplication. In: Johansson, T., Nguyen, P.Q. (eds.) EUROCRYPT 2013. LNCS, vol. 7881, pp. 296–312. Springer, Heidelberg (2013). https://doi.org/10.1007/978-3-642-38348-9_18

10. Bellare, M., Pointcheval, D., Rogaway, P.: Authenticated key exchange secure against dictionary attacks. In: Preneel, B. (ed.) EUROCRYPT 2000. LNCS, vol. 1807, pp. 139–155. Springer, Heidelberg (2000). https://doi.org/10.1007/3-540-45539-6_11

11. Bellare, M., Ristenpart, T., Tessaro, S.: Multi-instance security and its application to password-based cryptography. In: Safavi-Naini, R., Canetti, R. (eds.) CRYPTO 2012. LNCS, vol. 7417, pp. 312–329. Springer, Heidelberg (2012). https://doi.org/10.1007/978-3-642-32009-5_19

12. Bellare, M., Rogaway, P.: Random oracles are practical: a paradigm for designing efficient protocols. In: Proceedings of the 1st ACM Conference on Computer and Communications Security, CCS 1993, pp. 62–73. ACM, New York (1993)

13. Bellare, M., Rogaway, P.: Entity authentication and key distribution. In: Stinson, D.R. (ed.) CRYPTO 1993. LNCS, vol. 773, pp. 232–249. Springer, Heidelberg (1994). https://doi.org/10.1007/3-540-48329-2_21

14. Bellare, M., Rogaway, P.: The exact security of digital signatures-how to sign with RSA and Rabin. In: Maurer, U. (ed.) EUROCRYPT 1996. LNCS, vol. 1070, pp. 399–416. Springer, Heidelberg (1996). https://doi.org/10.1007/3-540-68339-9_34

15. Bellare, M., Rogaway, P.: Code-based game-playing proofs and the security of triple encryption. Cryptology ePrint Archive, Report 2004/331 (2004). https://eprint.iacr.org/2004/331

16. Bellovin, S.M., Merritt, M.: Encrypted key exchange: password-based protocols secure against dictionary attacks. In: Proceedings 1992 IEEE Computer Society Symposium on Research in Security and Privacy, pp. 72–84 (1992). https://doi.org/10.1109/RISP.1992.213269

17. Bhargavan, K., Brzuska, C., Fournet, C., Green, M., Kohlweiss, M., Zanella-Béguelin, S.: Downgrade resilience in key-exchange protocols. In: 2016 IEEE Symposium on Security and Privacy, pp. 506–525 (2016). https://doi.org/10.1109/SP.2016.37

18. Bhargavan, K.: Review of the balanced PAKE proposals. Mail to IRTF CFRG, September 2019 (2019). https://mailarchive.ietf.org/arch/msg/cfrg/5VhZLYGpzU8MWPlbMr2cf4Uc-nI

19. Boldyreva, A., Degabriele, J.P., Paterson, K.G., Stam, M.: Security of symmetric encryption in the presence of ciphertext fragmentation. In: Pointcheval, D., Johansson, T. (eds.) EUROCRYPT 2012. LNCS, vol. 7237, pp. 682–699. Springer, Heidelberg (2012). https://doi.org/10.1007/978-3-642-29011-4_40

20. Canetti, R.: Universally composable security: a new paradigm for cryptographic protocols. Cryptology ePrint Archive, Report 2000/067 (2000). https://eprint.iacr.org/2000/067

21. Canetti, R., Dodis, Y., Pass, R., Walfish, S.: Universally composable security with global setup. In: Vadhan, S.P. (ed.) TCC 2007. LNCS, vol. 4392, pp. 61–85. Springer, Heidelberg (2007). https://doi.org/10.1007/978-3-540-70936-7_4

22. Canetti, R., Fischlin, M.: Universally composable commitments. Cryptology ePrint Archive, Report 2001/055 (2001). https://eprint.iacr.org/2001/055

23. Canetti, R., Halevi, S., Katz, J., Lindell, Y., MacKenzie, P.: Universally composable password-based key exchange. In: Cramer, R. (ed.) EUROCRYPT 2005. LNCS, vol. 3494, pp. 404–421. Springer, Heidelberg (2005). https://doi.org/10.1007/11426639_24

24. Canetti, R., Krawczyk, H.: Analysis of key-exchange protocols and their use for building secure channels. In: Pfitzmann, B. (ed.) EUROCRYPT 2001. LNCS, vol. 2045, pp. 453–474. Springer, Heidelberg (2001). https://doi.org/10.1007/3-540-44987-6_28

25. Cash, D., Kiltz, E., Shoup, V.: The Twin Diffie-Hellman problem and applications. In: Smart, N. (ed.) EUROCRYPT 2008. LNCS, vol. 4965, pp. 127–145. Springer, Heidelberg (2008). https://doi.org/10.1007/978-3-540-78967-3_8

26. Coron, J.-S., Dodis, Y., Malinaud, C., Puniya, P.: Merkle-Damgård revisited: how to construct a hash function. In: Shoup, V. (ed.) CRYPTO 2005. LNCS, vol. 3621, pp. 430–448. Springer, Heidelberg (2005). https://doi.org/10.1007/11535218_26

27. Coron, J.S., Holenstein, T., Künzler, R., Patarin, J., Seurin, Y., Tessaro, S.: How to build an ideal cipher: the indifferentiability of the Feistel construction. J. Cryptol. 29(1), 61–114 (2016). https://doi.org/10.1007/s00145-014-9189-6

28. Faz-Hernandez, A., Scott, S., Sullivan, N., Wahby, R.S., Wood, C.A.: Hashing to elliptic curves. Internet-Draft draft-irtf-cfrg-hash-to-curve-07, Internet Engineering Task Force (2020). https://datatracker.ietf.org/doc/html/draft-irtf-cfrg-hash-to-curve-07

29. Fischlin, M., Lehmann, A., Ristenpart, T., Shrimpton, T., Stam, M., Tessaro, S.: Random oracles with(out) programmability. In: Abe, M. (ed.) ASIACRYPT 2010. LNCS, vol. 6477, pp. 303–320. Springer, Heidelberg (2010). https://doi.org/10.1007/978-3-642-17373-8_18

30. Haase, B., Labrique, B.: AuCPace: Efficient verifier-based PAKE protocol tailored for the IIoT. Cryptology ePrint Archive, Report 2018/286 (2018). https://eprint.iacr.org/2018/286

31. Haber, S., Pinkas, B.: Securely combining public-key cryptosystems. In: Proceedings of the 8th ACM Conference on Computer and Communications Security, CCS 2001, pp. 215–224. ACM, New York (2001)

32. Jarecki, S., Krawczyk, H., Xu, J.: OPAQUE: an asymmetric PAKE protocol secure against pre-computation attacks. Cryptology ePrint Archive, Report 2018/163 (2018). https://eprint.iacr.org/2018/163

33. Kotzias, P., Razaghpanah, A., Amann, J., Paterson, K.G., Vallina-Rodriguez, N., Caballero, J.: Coming of age: a longitudinal study of TLS deployment. In: Proceedings of the Internet Measurement Conference 2018, IMC 2018, pp. 415–428. Association for Computing Machinery, New York (2018). https://doi.org/10.1145/3278532.3278568

34. Krawczyk, D.H., Eronen, P.: HMAC-based extract-and-expand key derivation function (HKDF). RFC 5869 (2010). https://rfc-editor.org/rfc/rfc5869.txt

35. Krawczyk, H., Wee, H.: The OPTLS protocol and TLS 1.3. In: 2016 IEEE European Symposium on Security and Privacy, pp. 81–96 (2016). https://doi.org/10.1109/EuroSP.2016.18

36. Ladd, W., Kaduk, B.: SPAKE2, a PAKE. Internet-Draft draft-irtf-cfrg-spake2-10, Internet Engineering Task Force (2020). https://datatracker.ietf.org/doc/html/draft-irtf-cfrg-spake2-10

37. LaMacchia, B., Lauter, K., Mityagin, A.: Stronger security of authenticated key exchange. In: Susilo, W., Liu, J.K., Mu, Y. (eds.) ProvSec 2007. LNCS, vol. 4784, pp. 1–16. Springer, Heidelberg (2007). https://doi.org/10.1007/978-3-540-75670-5_1

38. Maurer, U., Renner, R., Holenstein, C.: Indifferentiability, impossibility results on reductions, and applications to the random oracle methodology. In: Naor, M. (ed.) TCC 2004. LNCS, vol. 2951, pp. 21–39. Springer, Heidelberg (2004). https://doi.org/10.1007/978-3-540-24638-1_2

39. Okamoto, T., Pointcheval, D.: The gap-problems: a new class of problems for the security of cryptographic schemes. In: Kim, K. (ed.) PKC 2001. LNCS, vol. 1992, pp. 104–118. Springer, Heidelberg (2001). https://doi.org/10.1007/3-540-44586-2_8

40. Paterson, K.G., van der Merwe, T.: Reactive and proactive standardisation of TLS. In: Chen, L., McGrew, D., Mitchell, C. (eds.) SSR 2016. LNCS, vol. 10074, pp. 160–186. Springer, Cham (2016). https://doi.org/10.1007/978-3-319-49100-4_7

41. Patton, C., Shrimpton, T.: Security in the presence of key reuse: Context-separable interfaces and their applications. Cryptology ePrint Archive, Report 2019/519 (2019). https://eprint.iacr.org/2019/519

42. Patton, C., Shrimpton, T.: Quantifying the security cost of migrating protocols to practice. Cryptology ePrint Archive, Report 2020/573 (2020). https://eprint.iacr.org/2020/573

43. Pollard, J.M.: Kangaroos, monopoly and discrete logarithms. J. Cryptol. **13**(4), 437–447 (2000). https://doi.org/10.1007/s001450010010

44. Rescorla, E.: The Transport Layer Security (TLS) protocol version 1.3. RFC 8446 (2018). https://rfc-editor.org/rfc/rfc8446.txt

45. Ristenpart, T., Shacham, H., Shrimpton, T.: Careful with composition: limitations of the indifferentiability framework. In: Paterson, K.G. (ed.) EUROCRYPT 2011. LNCS, vol. 6632, pp. 487–506. Springer, Heidelberg (2011). https://doi.org/10.1007/978-3-642-20465-4_27

46. Rogaway, P., Stegers, T.: Authentication without elision: Partially specified protocols, associated data, and cryptographic models described by code. In: 2009 22nd IEEE Computer Security Foundations Symposium, pp. 26–39 (2009)

47. Rogaway, P., Zhang, Y.: Simplifying game-based definitions. In: Shacham, H., Boldyreva, A. (eds.) CRYPTO 2018. LNCS, vol. 10992, pp. 3–32. Springer, Cham (2018). https://doi.org/10.1007/978-3-319-96881-0_1

48. Schnorr, C.P.: Efficient signature generation by smart cards. J. Cryptol. **4**(3), 161–174 (1991). https://doi.org/10.1007/BF00196725

49. Shoup, V.: Security analysis of SPAKE2+. Cryptology ePrint Archive, Report 2020/313 (2020). https://eprint.iacr.org/2020/313

50. Skrobot, M., Lancrenon, J.: On composability of game-based password authenticated key exchange. In: 2018 IEEE European Symposium on Security and Privacy, pp. 443–457 (2018). https://doi.org/10.1109/EuroSP.2018.00038

51. Smyshlyaev, S.: Overview of existing PAKEs and PAKE selection criteria. IETF 104 (2019). https://datatracker.ietf.org/meeting/104/materials/slides-104-cfrg-pake-selection

52. Smyshlyaev, S.: Round 2 of the PAKE selection process. Mail to IRTF CFRG, September 2019 (2019). https://mailarchive.ietf.org/arch/msg/cfrg/-a1sW3jK_5avmb98zmFbCNLmpAs

53. Stevens, M., Bursztein, E., Karpman, P., Albertini, A., Markov, Y.: The first collision for full SHA-1. In: Katz, J., Shacham, H. (eds.) CRYPTO 2017. LNCS, vol. 10401, pp. 570–596. Springer, Cham (2017). https://doi.org/10.1007/978-3-319-63688-7_19
54. Sullivan, N., Krawczyk, D.H., Friel, O., Barnes, R.: Usage of OPAQUE with TLS 1.3. Internet-Draft draft-sullivan-tls-opaque-00, Internet Engineering Task Force (2019). https://datatracker.ietf.org/doc/html/draft-sullivan-tls-opaque-00, Work in progress
55. Tackmann, B.: PAKE review. Mail to IRTF CFRG, October 2019 (2019). https://mailarchive.ietf.org/arch/msg/cfrg/1sNu9USxo1lnFdzCL5msUFKBjzM

Symmetric and Real World Cryptography

The Memory-Tightness of Authenticated Encryption

Ashrujit Ghoshal$^{(\boxtimes)}$, Joseph Jaeger$^{(\boxtimes)}$, and Stefano Tessaro$^{(\boxtimes)}$

Paul G. Allen School of Computer Science & Engineering,
University of Washington, Seattle, USA
{ashrujit,jsjaeger,tessaro}@cs.washington.edu

Abstract. This paper initiates the study of the provable security of authenticated encryption (AE) in the memory-bounded setting. Recent works – Tessaro and Thiruvengadam (TCC '18), Jaeger and Tessaro (EUROCRYPT '19), and Dinur (EUROCRYPT '20) – focus on confidentiality, and look at schemes for which trade-offs between the attacker's memory and its data complexity are inherent. Here, we ask whether these results and techniques can be lifted to the full AE setting, which additionally asks for integrity.

We show both positive and negative results. On the positive side, we provide tight memory-sensitive bounds for the security of GCM and its generalization, CAU (Bellare and Tackmann, CRYPTO '16). Our bounds apply to a restricted case of AE security which abstracts the deployment within protocols like TLS, and rely on a new memory-tight reduction to corresponding restricted notions of confidentiality and integrity. In particular, our reduction uses an amount of memory which linearly depends on that of the given adversary, as opposed to only imposing a constant memory overhead as in earlier works (Auerbach et al., CRYPTO '17).

On the negative side, we show that a large class of black-box reductions cannot generically lift confidentiality and integrity security to a joint definition of AE security in a memory-tight way.

Keywords: Provable security · Symmetric cryptography ·
Time-memory trade-offs · Memory-tightness

1 Introduction

Cryptographic attacks aim to use as little *memory* as possible. While some attacks are memoryless (e.g., for collision finding), others are subject to a *trade-off* – as the available memory decreases, the time and data complexities increase. A security proof (especially one in the spirit of *concrete* security) should tell us precisely *how* memory affects other complexity metrics. However, this is technically challenging, and consequently, security proofs ignored memory until recently.

This paper continues an ongoing line of works introducing memory limitations in provable security, and initiates the study of (nonce-based) *authenticated encryption* (AE) in the memory-bounded setting. Recent works [6,10,16]

© International Association for Cryptologic Research 2020
D. Micciancio and T. Ristenpart (Eds.): CRYPTO 2020, LNCS 12170, pp. 127–156, 2020.
https://doi.org/10.1007/978-3-030-56784-2_5

have shown memory-sensitive proofs of security for symmetric encryption, showing that trade-offs between memory and data complexities are inherent. These results, however, only deal with *confidentiality* of encryption – and one of the main contributions of this paper is to highlight the challenges of lifting them to the more complex setting of AE.

We discuss definitional aspects, and then shift our focus to *memory-tight reductions* [1] in the AE setting. We prove both *positive* and *negative* results. We introduce a new technique for memory-tight reductions to obtain tight memory-sensitive bounds for the AE-security of GCM in a setting that corresponds to its usage for establishing a secure channel. We also show that restricting AE security to specific settings is inherent for memory-tight reductions – indeed, we show that the common approach of lifting confidentiality and integrity guarantees into a combined notion of AE security (or of CCA security) fails in its most general form, at least with respect to a broad class of security reductions.

1.1 Context: Time-Memory Trade-Offs for AE

Let us start by setting the context and highlighting some of the challenges. First off, existing results [6,10] can be combined to analyze the INDR security[1] of nonce-based encryption. For example, consider a toy scheme[2] SE based on a block cipher E with block length n which encrypts $M \in \{0,1\}^n$ with key K as

$$\mathsf{SE.E}(K, N, M) = \mathrm{E}_K(N) \oplus M .$$

Here, N is the nonce and INDR security should hold as long as no two messages are encrypted with the same nonce. One can show that for every adversary $\mathcal{A}$ with time, data, and memory complexities t, q, and S, respectively,

$$\mathsf{Adv}_{\mathsf{SE}}^{\mathsf{indr}}(\mathcal{A}) \leqslant O\left(\frac{q \cdot S \cdot \log(q)}{2^n}\right) + \mathsf{Adv}_{\mathrm{E}}^{\mathsf{prp}}(\mathcal{B}) , \tag{1}$$

where $\mathcal{B}$ is an adversary against the security of E as a pseudorandom permutation (PRP), which has time and memory complexities (roughly) t and S, respectively, and makes q queries. In particular, if $S < 2^{n/2}$, then SE achieves beyond-birthday security $q > 2^{n/2}$ with respect to data complexity.

OUR GOAL, IN MORE DETAIL. However, INDR security is rarely sufficient on its own – we want *fully secure* AE schemes which also satisfy (ciphertext) *integrity* (or CTXT security, for short). Following [15], we adopt a *single* AE security definition that incorporates *both* INDR and CTXT, by measuring indistinguishability of two oracle pairs $(\mathrm{ENC}_b, \mathrm{DEC}_b)$ for $b \in \{0,1\}$. For $b = 1$, ENC_1 returns real ciphertexts, and DEC_1 decrypts properly. For $b = 0$, instead, ENC_0 returns random ciphertexts, and DEC_0 decrypts only previous outputs from ENC_0. It is

---

[1] Which measures the indistinguishability of ciphertexts from truly random ones.

[2] Our discussion can easily be extended to many schemes following the format of counter-mode encryption.

important to use a combined definition, as it captures settings such as chosen-ciphertext attacks and padding-oracle attacks [17], which use a decryption oracle to break confidentiality.[3]

LIFTING TRADE-OFFS. We want to prove a bound analogous to that of (1) for AE security, preserving in particular the existing space-time trade-off. The usual approach is to prove INDR and CTXT *individually*, and then combine them to show AE security. This makes sense because (1) we *know* how to prove tight trade-offs for INDR security, and (2) we may be able to prove stronger bounds on CTXT easily, even without memory restrictions. The classical statement (originally in [15]) is that for every adversary $\mathcal{A}$,

$$\mathsf{Adv}_{\mathsf{SE}}^{\mathsf{ae}}(\mathcal{A}) \leqslant \mathsf{Adv}_{\mathsf{SE}}^{\mathsf{indr}}(\mathcal{B}) + \mathsf{Adv}_{\mathsf{SE}}^{\mathsf{ctxt}}(\mathcal{C}) \,,$$

for suitable adversaries $\mathcal{B}$ and $\mathcal{C}$, with similar time and query complexities as those of $\mathcal{A}$. However, this is only helpful towards our goal if the reduction is *memory-tight*, in the sense Auerbach et al. (ACKF) [1], i.e., $\mathcal{B}$ and $\mathcal{C}$'s memory costs must not noticeably exceed those of $\mathcal{A}$. This is fundamental to preserve a time-memory trade-off like the one from (1).

Unfortunately, the standard proof is not memory-tight with respect to the INDR adversary $\mathcal{B}$, as it needs to simulate DEC_0 which requires remembering prior ciphertexts. In a nutshell, we will show that the lack of memory-tightness is inherent, *but* the definition can be restricted enough for interesting deployment scenarios to actually allow for a memory-tight reduction.

DEFINITIONAL ISSUES. Several "without loss of generality" definitional equivalences are false in the memory-bounded setting. For example, INDR security holds as long as nonces do not repeat, but there are options to formalize this, e.g.: (A) The game enforces this by answering encryption queries repeating a nonce with $\bot$, unless the same message is re-encrypted, or (B) The adversary never repeats a nonce. If we do not care about memory, these two definitions are indeed equivalent, but if we do, then they are not. Indeed, the bound in (1) for our toy scheme can only be true for (B) – it is not hard to see that otherwise we can mount a memory-less distinguishing attack with $q \approx 2^{n/2}$ queries. (The attack also works if $\bot$ is returned even if we re-encrypt the same message.) We discuss definitions in detail in Sect. 3.

1.2 Positive Results

We provide a novel memory-tight reduction for the common case where AE is used to establish a secure communication *channel*, as in TLS. The key point is that in this setting, only certain restricted adversarial interactions can occur in the AE security game, i.e.:

(1) Nonces are *implicit* – they are incremented as a counter.

---

[3] While we target such a single definition of AE, we stress that our results would extend to considering CCA security as a target.

(2) The receiver *aborts upon the first decryption failure*. In particular, messages *need* to be delivered in the same order as they are encrypted.

Our memory-tight reduction is for an abstraction of this setting we refer to as a *channel*. (Although, for this introduction, we stick with the more conventional language of AE.) We apply our reduction to prove (tight) memory-sensitive bounds for a channel instantiated with the CAU scheme by Bellare and Tackmann [4], an abstraction of GCM [11].

THE SECURITY GAME. When restricting AE security to this setting, we can assume that the adversary $\mathcal{A}$ can encrypt messages $M_1, M_2, \ldots$ and obtains ciphertexts $C_1, C_2, \ldots$ via an *encryption oracle* ENC_b, for $b \in \{0, 1\}$. When $b = 1$, the C_i's are actual encryptions of the M_i's (with increasing nonces), whereas when $b = 0$, they are truly random ciphertexts. The adversary is also given access to a *decryption* oracle DEC_b. If $b = 1$, this just applies the decryption algorithm of the AE scheme, using increasing nonces. If decryption fails, DEC_b responds to this and any future queries with $\bot$. For $b = 0$, the oracle responds with $M_1, M_2, \ldots$ as long as it is supplied the ciphertexts $C_1, C_2, \ldots$ *in the order they have been produced by* ENC_0. If the ciphertexts come in the wrong order, DEC_0 responds to this and any future queries with $\bot$. The goal here is to distinguish $(\text{ENC}_0, \text{DEC}_0)$ and $(\text{ENC}_1, \text{DEC}_1)$.

PROOF IDEA. In this channel setting, to obtain a memory-tight reduction from AE security to CTXT and INDR security, we first use CTXT security to replace the oracles $(\text{ENC}_1, \text{DEC}_1)$ with $(\text{ENC}_1, \text{DEC}_0)$. (This step is easily seen to be memory-tight.) Next, we aim to use INDR security to replace ENC_1 with ENC_0. The catch here is that when doing so, we need to simulate the DEC_0 oracle in the INDR security game (which does not provide one). Again, this seems to require remembering all prior ciphertexts, thus preventing memory-tightness.

A key observation, however, is that ciphertexts are only accepted when arriving with the right order. For this reason, we will show (via an information-theoretic argument) that our reduction only needs to store the δ oldest ciphertexts which have not been delivered yet, for some δ – the key point here is that δ can be chosen to depend (roughly linearly) on the memory of the adversary used by the reduction, so the overall memory of the constructed adversary is of the same magnitude of that of the AE adversary.

This is in contrast to existing memory-tight reductions in the literature which are (near) "memory-less", i.e., the reduction adds a small memory overhead, *independent* of the memory of the adversary. Our reduction is the first example where the reduction uses memory in addition to that of the adversary, but the size of this memory is bounded in terms of the adversary's memory complexity.

APPLICATION TO CAU. We apply our memory-tight reduction to show bounds for CAU (and hence GCM) in the communication channel setting. We refer to the resulting channel as NCH, and it is based on a block cipher E. We show that for every adversary $\mathcal{A}$, there exists $\mathcal{B}$ such that

$$\text{Adv}_{\text{NCH}}^{\text{ch-ae}}(\mathcal{A}) \leqslant 4 \cdot \text{Adv}_{\text{E}}^{\text{prp}}(\mathcal{B}) + O\left(\frac{pqS}{2^n}\right), \tag{2}$$

where $O(\cdot)$ hides a small constant, q and S are the data and memory complexities of $\mathcal{A}$, and p is an upper bound on the length of ciphertexts. Further, $\mathcal{B}$ makes $q \cdot p$ queries, and has time complexity similar to that of $\mathcal{A}$. Instrumental to our result here is Dinur's Switching Lemma [6]. The main challenge is to prove a bound for CTXT security – our proof relies once again on similar techniques to our memory-tight reduction.

1.3   Negative Results

A meaningful question is whether we can give a memory-tight reduction beyond the setting of channels, and reduce AE security to INDR and CTXT security in the most general sense. Here, we show that this is unlikely by giving impossibility results for black-box reductions.

We consider reductions to INDR and CTXT which are restricted, but note that all prior impossibility results on memory-tight reductions [1,8,18] make similar or stronger restrictions. In particular, we require the reductions to simulate their encryption oracles "faithfully" to an AE adversary, i.e., if they answer an encryption query with a ciphertext C, the same query (1) has been asked to the encryption oracle available to the reduction and (2) it has returned C. This restriction is natural, and we are not aware of any reductions evading it.

STRAIGHTLINE REDUCTIONS. Our first result builds an (inefficient) adversary $\mathcal{A}$ against AE security which no straightline reduction can use to (1) break CTXT security (regardless of the memory available to the reduction) or, more importantly, to (2) break INDR security (unless the reduction uses an amount of memory proportional to the query complexity of the adversary). Moreover, $\mathcal{A}$ uses little memory, and thus our result implies impossibility even for "weakly memory-tight reductions" which adapt their memory usage (such as the one we give in this paper). This is unlike recent works [8,18], which only rule out reductions with memory independent of that of the adversary.

At a high level, $\mathcal{A}$ forces the reduction to complete a memory-hard task before being useful. If the reduction succeeds, $\mathcal{A}$ executes an (inefficient) procedure to break INDR security. (And importantly, this procedure does not help in breaking CTXT security!) More in detail, the first part of $\mathcal{A}$'s execution consists of *challenge rounds*. In each of these rounds, $\mathcal{A}$ encrypts random plaintexts $M_1, \ldots, M_u$, which result in ciphertexts $C_1, \ldots, C_u$, and also picks a random index $i^* \in [u]$. It then asks for the decryption of C_{i^*}, and checks whether the response equals M_{i^*}. If so, it moves to the next round, if not it aborts by doing something useless. Only if all rounds are successful $\mathcal{A}$ proceeds to break INDR security. We use techniques borrowed from the setting of random oracles with auxiliary input (AI-ROM) [5] to prove that the probability that all rounds are successful decays exponentially as long as the reduction's memory does not fit all of $M_1, \ldots, M_u$.

FULL REWINDING. The restriction to straightline reductions seem too restrictive: After all, a reduction could (1) wait for a decryption query C_{i^*}, then (2) rewind the adversary to re-ask $M_1, M_2, \ldots$ until M_{i^*} is asked. The caveat is that our definition of INDR security does not allow for *re-asking* encryption queries (again, as pointed out above, such a notion would prevent us from using the results of [6,10]). Therefore, if we assume that all the reduction can do is remember (say) S plaintext-ciphertext pairs, the above adversary $\mathcal{A}$ will fail to pass a challenge round with probability at least $1 - S/u$.

Still, this does not mean that rewinding cannot help when allowing more general adversarial strategies. While handling arbitrary rewinding appears to be out of reach, we make partial progress by extending our proof (and our construction of $\mathcal{A}$) to show that "full" rewinding (i.e., re-running $\mathcal{A}$ from the beginning) does not help. This is the same rewinding model considered in prior memory-tightness lower bounds [1]. However, in those results, one obtains a rewinding-memory trade-offs (in that reducing memory would require more rewinding). Here, our result is absolute, in the sense that if memory is too small, no amount of rewinding can help.

Paper overview. In Sect. 2, we introduce our notation, basic definitions and cover some cryptographic background necessary for the paper. In Sect. 3, we recall the standard definitions for the security notions of nonce-based encryption. We point out several nuances while defining security in the memory bounded setting. We conclude the section by giving a time-memory tradeoff for the INDR security of CAU. In Sect. 4, we show that memory-tight reductions can be given for the combined confidentiality and integrity security of cryptographic channels. Using the result from Sect. 3, we prove the security of a channel based on CAU. The resulting channel can be viewed as (a simplification of) the channel obtained when using GCM in TLS 1.3. In Sect. 5, we give impossibility results (for a natural restricted class of black-box reductions) for giving a memory-tight reduction from AE security to INDR and CTXT security. This establishes that our move to the channel setting for Sect. 4 was necessary for our positive result.

2   Definitions

Let $\mathbb{N} = \{0, 1, 2, \dots\}$. For $D \in \mathbb{N}$, let $[D] = \{1, 2, \dots, D\}$. If S and S' are finite sets, then $\mathsf{Fcs}(S, S')$ denotes the set of all functions $F : S \to S'$ and $\mathsf{Perm}(S)$ denotes the set of all permutations on S. Picking an element uniformly at random from S and assigning it to s is denoted by $s \leftarrow\!\!\$\, S$. The set of finite vectors with entries in S is S^* or $(S)^*$. Thus $\{0, 1\}^*$ is the set of finite length strings.

If $x \in \{0, 1\}^*$ is a string, then $|x|$ denotes its bitlength. If $n \in \mathbb{N}$ and $x \in \{0, 1\}^*$, then $|x|_n = \max\{1, \lceil |x|/n \rceil\}$. We let $x_1 \dots x_\ell \leftarrow_n x$ denote setting $\ell \leftarrow |x|_n$ and parsing x into ℓ blocks of length n (except x_ℓ which may have $|x_\ell| < n$). We let $x[: n]$ denote the first n bits of x and $x[i : n]$ denote the i-th (exclusive) through n-th (inclusive) bits of x. We adopt the convention that if $|x| < |x'|$ then $x \oplus x' = x \oplus x'[: |x|]$. The empty string is ε.

We will make use of queues which operate in first-in, first-out order. If Q is a queue then $Q.\mathsf{add}(M)$ adds M to the back of the queue and $M \leftarrow Q.\mathsf{dq}()$ removes the first element of the queue and assigns it to M. If the queue is empty, then M is assigned the value $\perp \notin \{0,1\}^*$ which is used to represent rejection or uninitialized values.

Algorithms are randomized when not specified otherwise. If $\mathcal{A}$ is an algorithm, then $y \leftarrow \mathcal{A}^{O_1, \cdots}(x_1, \ldots; r)$ denotes running $\mathcal{A}$ on inputs $x_1, \ldots$ with coins r and access to the oracles $O_1, \ldots$ to produce output y. Performing this execution with a random r is denoted $y \leftarrow_s \mathcal{A}^{O_1, \cdots}(x_1, \ldots)$. The set of all possible outputs of $\mathcal{A}$ when run with inputs $x_1, \ldots$ is $[\mathcal{A}(x_1, \ldots)]$. The notation $y \leftarrow O(x_1, \ldots)$ is used for calling oracle O with inputs $x_1, \ldots$ and assigning its output to y. (Note, the code run by the oracle is not necessarily deterministic.)

We make regular use of pseudocode games inspired by the code-based framework of [3]. Examples of games can be found in Fig. 1. We let $\Pr[\mathsf{G}]$ denote the probability that a game G outputs $\mathtt{true}$. Booleans are implicitly initialized to $\mathtt{false}$, integers to 0, and all other types to $\perp$.

COMPLEXITY CONVENTIONS. When measuring the efficiency of an adversary we follow the standard convention used in studying memory-tightness [1] on measuring the local complexity of an adversary and not included the complexity of whatever game it interacts with. We primarily focus on the worst-case runtime (i.e. how much computation it performs in between making oracle queries) and memory complexity (i.e. how many bits of state it stores for local computation) of adversaries. Note that while these exclude the time and memory used within whatever oracles the adversary may call, we do include the time and memory used to write down an oracle query and receive the response.

2.1   Cryptographic Background

FUNCTION FAMILY. A function family is an efficiently computable function $\mathsf{F} : A \times B \to C$, where A, B, and C are sets. A hash function is a family of functions. We often write $F_K(\cdot)$ in place of $F(K, \cdot)$.

PSEUDORANDOM FUNCTION/PERMUTATION. Let $\mathsf{E} : \{0,1\}^k \times \{0,1\}^n \to \{0,1\}^m$ be a function family. If $n = m$ and $\mathrm{E}_K(\cdot)$ is a permutation for each $K \in \{0,1\}^k$, then we say that E is a block-cipher. The primary security notions of interest for such functions are PRF and PRP security. The former is typically more useful in applications, but when E is a block-cipher we prefer to assume PRP security and use that to deduce PRF security.

These security notions are defined by games shown in Fig. 1. In $\mathsf{G}^{\mathsf{prp}}$, the adversary is given access to either $\mathrm{E}_K(\cdot)$ for a random key or a random permutation $P : \{0,1\}^n \to \{0,1\}^n$. Game $\mathsf{G}^{\mathsf{prf}}$ is defined similarly except a random function $F : \{0,1\}^n \to \{0,1\}^m$ is used in place of the permutation. For $x \in \{\mathsf{prp}, \mathsf{prf}\}$, we define the advantage of $\mathcal{A}$ by $\mathsf{Adv}_{\mathsf{E}}^x(\mathcal{A}) = \Pr[\mathsf{G}_{\mathsf{E},1}^x(\mathcal{A})] - \Pr[\mathsf{G}_{\mathsf{E},0}^x(\mathcal{A})]$.

SWITCHING LEMMA. A classic result in cryptography is the "switching lemma" which bounds how well an adversary can distinguish between a random function and a random permutation. Consider the game $\mathsf{G}_{D,b}^{\mathsf{sl}}$ shown in Fig. 1. In it, the adversary is given oracle access to either a random function or a random

Game $G^{prp}_{E,b}(\mathcal{A})$	Game $G^{prf}_{E,b}(\mathcal{A})$	Game $G^{sl}_{D,b}(\mathcal{A})$
$K \leftarrow\!\!\text{\textdollar}\; \{0,1\}^k$	$K \leftarrow\!\!\text{\textdollar}\; \{0,1\}^k$	$F \leftarrow\!\!\text{\textdollar}\; \mathsf{Fcs}([D],[D])$
$P \leftarrow\!\!\text{\textdollar}\; \mathsf{Perm}(\{0,1\}^n)$	$F \leftarrow\!\!\text{\textdollar}\; \mathsf{Fcs}(\{0,1\}^n,\{0,1\}^m)$	$P \leftarrow\!\!\text{\textdollar}\; \mathsf{Perm}([D])$
$b' \leftarrow\!\!\text{\textdollar}\; \mathcal{A}^{\text{EVAL}_b}$	$b' \leftarrow\!\!\text{\textdollar}\; \mathcal{A}^{\text{EVAL}_b}$	$b' \leftarrow\!\!\text{\textdollar}\; \mathcal{A}^{\text{EVAL}_b}$
Return $b' = 1$	Return $b' = 1$	Return $b' = 1$
Oracle $\text{EVAL}_b(x)$	Oracle $\text{EVAL}_b(x)$	Oracle $\text{EVAL}_b(x)$
$y_1 \leftarrow \text{E}_K(x)$	$y_1 \leftarrow \text{E}_K(x)$	$y_1 \leftarrow F(x)$
$y_0 \leftarrow P(x)$	$y_0 \leftarrow F(x)$	$y_0 \leftarrow P(x)$
Return y_b	Return y_b	Return y_b

Fig. 1. Security games for PRF and PRP security of E and the switching lemma.

Game $G^{axu}_H(\mathcal{X})$
$((A_1,C_1),(A_2,C_2)),Z) \leftarrow\!\!\text{\textdollar}\; \mathcal{X}$
$L \leftarrow\!\!\text{\textdollar}\; \{0,1\}^k$
If $(A_1,C_1) = (A_2,C_2)$ then return **false**
Return $\text{H}_L(A_1,C_1) \oplus \text{H}_L(A_2,C_2) = Z$

Fig. 2. Security game for AXU security of H.

permutation with domain/range $[D]$ and is trying to figure out which. We define $\mathsf{Adv}^{sl}_D(\mathcal{A}) = \Pr[G^{sl}_{D,b}(\mathcal{A})] - \Pr[G^{sl}_{D,b}(\mathcal{A})]$.

The classic switching lemma shows $\mathsf{Adv}^{sl}_D(\mathcal{A}) \in O(q^2/D)$ where q is the number of queries made by $\mathcal{A}$. In general, bounding the memory-complexity of the attacker cannot be used to meaningfully improve this bound because a low-memory collision-finding attack (e.g., using Pollard's ρ-method [12,13]) achieves advantage $\mathsf{Adv}^{sl}_D(\mathcal{A}) \in \Omega(q^2/D)$. However, as originally observed by Jaeger and Tessaro we *can* obtain better results when restricting attention to adversaries that never repeat any queries.

Let $\mathsf{Adv}^{sl}_D(q,S)$ denote the maximal value of $\mathsf{Adv}^{sl}_D(\mathcal{A})$ for all $\mathcal{A}$ that are S-bounded and make q non-repeating queries to their oracle. Jaeger and Tessaro [10] showed that $\mathsf{Adv}^{sl}_D(q,S) \leq \sqrt{Sq/D}$ under a combinatorial conjecture. Later, Dinur [6] improved this to show that $\mathsf{Adv}^{sl}_D(q,S) \in O(Sq\log(q)/D)$.

An immediate application of the switching lemma is that if $\mathcal{A}$ is an S-bounded adversary which makes q non-repeating queries to its oracle, then $|\mathsf{Adv}^{prf}_E(\mathcal{A}) - \mathsf{Adv}^{prp}_E(\mathcal{A})| \leq \mathsf{Adv}^{sl}_D(q,S)$ for any block-cipher E whose range has size D.

AXU HASH FUNCTION. Let $H : \{0,1\}^k \times (\{0,1\}^* \times \{0,1\}^*) \to \{0,1\}^n$ be a hash function. Its almost XOR-universal (AXU) security is defined by the game G^{axu}_H shown in Fig. 2. In it, an adversary $\mathcal{X}$ attempts to guess the xor of the output of H on two distinct inputs of its choosing for a random key L. We define $\mathsf{Adv}^{axu}_H(\mathcal{X}) = \Pr[G^{axu}_H(\mathcal{X})]$. Typically one makes use of a c-AXU hash which for all $\mathcal{X}$ satisfy $\mathsf{Adv}^{axu}_H(\mathcal{X}) \leq c \cdot (N_1 + N_2)/2^n$ where N_1 (resp. N_2) is the maximum block length of any A (resp. C) output by $\mathcal{X}$. Note this is unconditional, so we will not have to worry about memory complexity when reducing to AXU security.

3   Nonce-Based Encryption and Memory-Boundedness

In this section we recall known definitions and results for nonce-based encryption [14]. We carefully consider how these change when we move to the memory-bounded setting. For example, as was previously noted by Auerbach, et al. [1], definitions which are tightly equivalent when the memory usage of adversaries is not bounded do not necessarily remain so with bounds on memory. So we will consider several variants of the definitions we are recalling and try to reason about which is the "correct" one to use. We additionally note some results which can be extended to give appealing time-memory tradeoffs in the memory-bounded setting and some for which this does not seem to be possible.

In Sect. 3.1, we discuss INDR security which measures the indistinguishability of ciphertexts from truly random ones. This security notion requires that the adversary be disallowed from repeating nonces. We discuss three conventions for capturing this which are tightly equivalent when ignoring memory restrictions, but observe they are no longer tightly equivalent with these restrictions. Based on these discussions, the rest of the paper focuses on the restricted class of adversaries that will never repeat nonces in their queries to encryption oracles. In Sect. 3.2, we discuss CTXT (integrity of ciphertexts) and AE security (combined INDR and CTXT) security. For these, the adversary must be disallowed from trivially winning by forwarding ciphertexts from its encryption oracle to its decryption oracle. Again we discuss several conventions for this which are tightly equivalent when ignoring memory restrictions. Based on these discussions, the rest of the paper will use the convention that if an adversary queries (N, C) to its decryption oracle after receiving C from an encryption query for (N, M), the oracle will respond with M. With our chosen conventions, it does not appear to be possible to prove that AE security is implied by INDR and CTXT security with a memory-tight reduction. The rest of the paper will focus on this (im)possibility. Section 4 shows it *is* possible in the restricted setting of secure channels while Sect. 5 shows it is not possible for general nonce-based encryption if the reduction behaves in a black-box manner.

Finally, in Sect. 3.3 we recall the CAU scheme by Bellare and Tackmann [4], an abstraction of GCM [11]. Following existing proofs [4,9,11] and using [6,10], we show that INDR security of CAU can be proven by a memory-tight reduction to PRP security with an appealing time-memory tradeoff and we informally discuss why such reductions seem impossible for CTXT or AE security.

SYNTAX AND CORRECTNESS. A (nonce-based) encryption scheme NE is defined by algorithms NE.Kg, NE.D, and NE.E. Additionally it is associated with message space $\mathsf{NE.M} \subseteq \{0,1\}^*$ and nonce space NE.N.

The syntax of the algorithms is shown in Fig. 3. The key generation algorithm NE.Kg takes no input and returns key K. The encryption algorithm NE.E takes key K, nonce $N \in$ NE.N, and message $M \in$ NE.M. It returns ciphertext C. The decryption algorithm NE.D takes key K, nonce $N \in$ NE.N, and ciphertext C. It returns message $M \in$ NE.M $\cup \{\bot\}$. When $M = \bot$, the ciphertext is rejected as invalid.

We additionally assume there is a ciphertext-length function NE.cl $: \mathbb{N} \to \mathbb{N}$ such that for any $K \in$ [NE.Kg], $N \in$ NE.N, and $M \in$ NE.M we have $|C| =$ NE.cl$(|M|)$ whenever $C \leftarrow$ NE.E(K, N, M). Typically, a nonce-based encryption scheme also takes associated data as input which is authenticated during encryption. Associated data does not meaningfully effect our results, so we have omitted it for simplicity of notation.

NE Syntax
$K \leftarrow_\$ $ NE.Kg
$C \leftarrow$ NE.E(K, N, M)
$M \leftarrow$ NE.D(K, N, C)

Fig. 3. Syntax of nonce-based encryption scheme.

Correctness of an encryption scheme requires for all $K \in$ [NE.Kg], $N \in$ NE.N, and $M \in$ NE.M that NE.D$(K, N,$ NE.E$(K, N, M)) = M$.

3.1 Indistinguishability from Random (INDR) Security

The first security notion we will consider requires that ciphertexts output by the encryption scheme cannot be distinguished from ciphertexts chosen at random.

DEFINITIONS. Consider the game $\mathsf{G}^{\mathsf{indr}}_{\mathsf{NE},b}$ shown in Fig. 4. Here an adversary $\mathcal{A}$ is given access to an encryption oracle ENC to which it can query a pair (N, M) and receive back either the encryption of message M with nonce N $(b = 1)$ or a random string of the appropriate length $(b = 0)$. The adversary outputs a bit trying to guess which of these two views it was given. We define $\mathsf{Adv}^{\mathsf{indr}}_{\mathsf{NE}}(\mathcal{A}) = \Pr[\mathsf{G}^{\mathsf{indr}}_{\mathsf{NE},1}(\mathcal{A})] - \Pr[\mathsf{G}^{\mathsf{indr}}_{\mathsf{NE},0}(\mathcal{A})]$.

In defining security we must address how to handle the possibility of $\mathcal{A}$ making multiple queries with the same nonce. Encryption schemes are typically designed under the assumption that the same nonce will not be used multiple times and may become completely insecure in the face of such nonce repetition. The primary convention we will adopt is to restrict attention to adversaries that will never repeat nonces in their encryption queries. We use the phrase "nonce-respecting INDR" to refer to security with respect to such adversaries.

An alternate approach would be to modify the code of the game to respond appropriately to queries where nonces repeat. One version of this, which we will refer to as INDR-R, would restrict attention to adversaries that will only repeat nonces when they also repeat the message queried to encryption. For this the game would be modified to keep track of all encryption queries that have been made so far. When it receives a repeated (N, M) pair, it simply returns the same C that it returned last time it saw that pair. A second version of this, which we will refer to as INDR-B, makes no restriction on the queries of the adversary. Instead, the game is modified to return $\bot$ whenever the adversary makes a query with a nonce it has already used.

Game $\mathsf{G}^{indr}_{\mathsf{NE},b}(\mathcal{A})$	Game $\mathsf{G}^{ctxt\text{-}w}_{\mathsf{NE},b}(\mathcal{A})$	Oracle $\mathrm{DEC}^w_b(N,C)$
$K \leftarrow^\$ \mathsf{NE.Kg}$	$K \leftarrow^\$ \mathsf{NE.Kg}$	If $M[N,C] \neq \bot$ then
$b' \leftarrow \mathcal{A}^{\mathrm{ENC}_b}$	$b' \leftarrow \mathcal{A}^{\mathrm{ENC}_1,\mathrm{DEC}^w_b}$	Return $M[N,C]$ if $w=1$
Return b'	Return b'	Return $\diamond$ if $w=2$
		Return $\bot$ if $w=3$
Oracle $\mathrm{ENC}_b(N,M)$	Game $\mathsf{G}^{ae\text{-}w}_{\mathsf{NE},b}(\mathcal{A})$	$M_1 \leftarrow \mathsf{NE.D}(K,N,C)$
$C_1 \leftarrow \mathsf{NE.E}(K,N,M)$	$K \leftarrow^\$ \mathsf{NE.Kg}$	$M_0 \leftarrow \bot$
$C_0 \leftarrow^\$ \{0,1\}^{\mathsf{NE.cl}(|M|)}$	$b' \leftarrow \mathcal{A}^{\mathrm{ENC}_b,\mathrm{DEC}^w_b}$	Return M_b
$M[N,C_b] \leftarrow M$	Return b'	
Return C_b		

Fig. 4. Games defining INDR, CTXT-w, and AE-w security of NE for $w \in \{1,2,3\}$.

DISCUSSION. When memory is not an issue, all of these variants would be equivalent. Proving this follows by noting that an adversary can just remember all prior queries it has made and thus never need to repeat. This proof strategy is no longer available to us when we want to preserve the memory usage of adversaries. We focus on nonce-respecting INDR because it hits the sweet spot of being strong enough for common applications, yet weak enough that we know how to give provable time-memory trade-offs.

Because nonce-respecting INDR considers a strictly smaller class of adversaries than the other two and all of the games behave identically for this class of adversary it is tightly implied by the others. In fact, using ideas from [6,10] we can see that nonce-respecting INDR is strictly weaker. The toy encryption scheme SE considered in the introduction built from a block-cipher with block length n is vulnerable to low-memory collision-finding attacks with advantage $\Omega(q^2/2^n)$ in the INDR-R and INDR-B settings, but no attacks can have advantage better than $O(qs/2^n)$ in the nonce-respecting INDR setting. Here q and s refer to the number of queries and amount of memory used by the attackers, respectively. This underlies why the ideas of Jaeger and Tessaro [10] can be used to prove nonce-respecting INDR (but not INDR-R or INDR-B) time-memory trade-offs for natural counter-mode based encryption schemes. In most common uses of nonce-based encryption the nonces are incremented as a counter or picked uniformly at random. In the former case, nonces clearly never repeat so nonce-respecting INDR suffices (we will see this formally in Sect. 4). Nonces may repeat in the latter case, but we can follow [6,10] here and replace the uniform random values with random, non-repeating values so again nonce-respecting INDR suffices.

3.2 Security Beyond Confidentiality

INDR security only guarantees confidentiality of the messages against passive attackers. However, in practice, attackers may actively modify ciphertexts in transit. As such, it is important to consider security definition that take this into account. We will consider integrity definitions and authenticated encryption definitions which simultaneously asked for integrity and confidentiality.

DEFINITIONS. Consider the other two games shown in Fig. 4. We will first focus on $G_{NE,b}^{ae-w}$ which defines three variants of authenticated encryption security parameterized by $w \in \{1, 2, 3\}$. In this game, the adversary is given access to an encryption oracle and a decryption oracle. Its goal is to distinguish between a "real" and "ideal" world. In the real world ($b = 1$) the oracles uses NE to encrypt messages and decrypt ciphertexts. In the ideal world ($b = 0$) encryption returns random messages of the appropriate length and decryption returns $\bot$. For simplicity, we will restrict attention nonce-respecting adversaries which do not repeat nonces across encryption queries (as in nonce-respecting INDR security). Note there is no restriction placed on nonces used for decryption queries. Integrity of ciphertext security is defined by $G_{NE,b}^{ctxt-w}$ which behaves similarly except the adversary is always given access to the real encryption algorithm.

The decryption oracle needs to prevent trivial attacks. If the adversary receives C from a query of $\text{ENC}(N, M)$ and then queries $\text{DEC}(N, C)$ it would receive M in the real world and $\bot$ in the ideal world, making them easy to distinguish. We must adopt some convention for how the oracles behave when such a query is made to prevent this type of trivial attack. Towards this, the decryption oracle is parameterized by the value $w \in \{1, 2, 3\}$ corresponding to three different security notions. In all three, we use a table $M[\cdot, \cdot]$ to detect when the adversary forwards encryption queries on to its decryption oracle. When $w = 1$, the decryption oracle returns $M[N, C]$ in this case. When $w = 2$, it returns a special symbol $\diamond$. When $w = 3$, it returns the symbol $\bot$ which is also used by the encryption scheme to represent rejection. For $x \in \{ae, ctxt\}$ and $w \in \{1, 2, 3\}$ we define the advantage of an adversary $\mathcal{A}$ by $\text{Adv}_{NE}^{x-w}(\mathcal{A}) = \Pr[G_{NE,1}^{x-w}(\mathcal{A})] - \Pr[G_{NE,0}^{x-w}(\mathcal{A})]$. The corresponding security notions are referred to as AE-w and CTXT-w.

DISCUSSION. When memory usage is not an issue, the choice of w does not matter. We can without loss of generality assume that the adversary never makes one of these trivial attack queries because it could simply store the table $M[\cdot, \cdot]$ for itself and simulate any such queries.[4] It's not clear that this equivalence holds if we do not assume that storing $M[\cdot, \cdot]$ is "free" for the adversary.

The only memory-tight implication we are aware of between these is that security for $w = 2$ tightly implies security for $w = 3$. This follows because an adversary with access to DEC_b^2 can simulate DEC_b^3 with low memory. If DEC_b^2 returns $M = \diamond$ the adversary returns $\bot$, otherwise it does not modify M. All of the other implications we might want to show seem to require remembering all prior encryption queries to properly simulate DEC.

Ultimately, for heuristic reasons, we believe that $w = 1$ is the "correct" choice and will focus on it in our later sections. The typical motivation behind chosen-ciphertext security notions is that in practice an attacker can often observe the behavior of the decrypting party to learn something about the message they received. There is no reason to think an attacker should only be able to do that for ciphertexts that have been modified, but not ciphertexts that have been unmodified. This is best captured by $w = 1$. The $w = 2$ definition seems

---

[4] Restricting attention to adversaries which never make trivial attack queries is, indeed, a fourth way one could define security.

to posit that the adversary can distinguish between ciphertexts it forwarded on and ciphertexts that it modified (whether they were accepted or rejected) by observing the decrypting party's behavior. The $w = 3$ definition seems to posit that the adversary cannot learn anything about ciphertexts it forwards on unmodified, but can learn about other modified ciphertexts by observing the decrypting party's behavior.

REVISITING A CLASSIC RESULT. A classic result, which has been shown for numerous styles of encryption, is that confidentiality and integrity together imply authenticated encryption [15]. However, this becomes more difficult for nonce-based encryption when we consider memory-tightness.

The classic proof that INDR and CTXT-1 security imply AE-1 security first replaces real decryption with $\perp$ via a reduction to CTXT-1 security and then replace real encryption with random using INDR security. However, in this second step the reduction adversary would have to simulate the oracle DEC_0^1 which seems to require storing the table $M[\cdot, \cdot]$.[5] This potentially requires using much more memory than the AE-1 adversary, losing the benefit of time-memory trade-offs for INDR-R. The rest of the paper is dedicated to understanding this reduction. In Sect. 4.2, we make it memory tight when restricting attention to secure channels which only accept ciphertexts if they are received in order. In Sect. 5, we give negative results showing that for nonce-based encryption this reduction cannot be made memory tight (using a black-box reduction).

3.3 Security of the CAU Encryption Scheme

We conclude this section by considering the specific encryption scheme CAU for which we can prove INDR security with a time-memory tradeoff. We will use this scheme in Sect. 4 to show a time-memory tradeoff for the authenticated encryption security of a channel instantiated with it.

One of the most widely deployed encryption schemes is Galois Counter-Mode (GCM) [11]. Bellare and Tackmann [4] generalized it to the scheme CAU which constructs an encryption scheme from a block cipher E and hash function H. Using the techniques of Jaeger and Tessaro [10] we obtain a proof of security for its nonce-respecting INDR security with an appealing time-memory tradeoff.

CONSTRUCTION. We recall the CAU construction of an encryption scheme. Fix a key length $\text{CAU.kl} \in \mathbb{N}$, a block length $n = \text{CAU.bl} \in \mathbb{N}$, and a nonce length $\text{CAU.nl} < \text{CAU.bl}$. Then let E be a function family with E : $\{0,1\}^{\text{CAU.kl}} \times \{0,1\}^{\text{CAU.bl}} \to \{0,1\}^{\text{CAU.bl}}$ and H be a function family with H : $\{0,1\}^{\text{CAU.bl}} \times (\{0,1\}^* \times \{0,1\}^*) \to \{0,1\}^{\text{CAU.bl}}$. The scheme constructed from E and H is denoted $\text{CAU}[E, H]$. Its message space $\text{CAU}[E, H].M$ is the set of all strings of length at most $n \cdot (2^{n-\text{CAU.nl}} - 1)$ and its nonce space $\text{CAU}[E, H].N$ is the set $\{0,1\}^{\text{CAU.nl}}$.

The algorithms of $\text{CAU}[E, H]$ are shown in Fig. 5. The code uses $\text{pad}(\cdot)$ to denote the padding function which on input N outputs $N||0^{n-\text{CAU}[E,H].\text{nl}-1} || 1$.

---

[5] The standard reduction *would* be memory tight for $w = 3$.

Algorithm CAU[E, H].E(K, N, M)	Algorithm CAU[E, H].D$(K, N, T \parallel C)$
$Y \leftarrow \text{pad}(N)$	$L \leftarrow E_K(0^n); Y \leftarrow \text{pad}(N)$
$M_1 \ldots M_\ell \leftarrow_n M$	$C_1 \ldots C_\ell \leftarrow_n C$
For $i = 1, ..., \ell$ do	$T' \leftarrow H_L(A, C) \oplus E_K(Y)$
$\quad C_i \leftarrow M_i \oplus E_K(Y + i)$	If $T \neq T'$ then return $\bot$
$C \leftarrow C_1 \ldots C_\ell$	For $i = 1, ..., \ell$ do
$L \leftarrow E_K(0^n)$	$\quad M_i \leftarrow C_i \oplus E_K(Y + i)$
$T \leftarrow H_L(A, C) \oplus E_K(Y)$	$M \leftarrow M_1 \ldots M_\ell$
Return $T \parallel C$	Return M

Fig. 5. Encryption scheme CAU parameterized by function family E (typically a block cipher) and hash function H. In the code, $\text{pad}(N) = N \parallel 0^m \parallel 1$ for the appropriate choice of m and $M_1 \ldots M_\ell \leftarrow_n M$ splits M into n-bit blocks.

Since our simplified notation does not use associated data we instead assume there is a fixed associated data string A used with every message.

The encryption algorithm parses the input message into ℓ blocks of length n (except for the last, which may be shorter) and pads the nonce to a string Y of length n. It encrypts the message using counter-mode encryption with $Y + 1$ as the first counter. This gives it a partial ciphertext C. The authentication is inspired by a Carter-Wegman MAC. A key L for the hash function is obtained as $L \leftarrow E_K(0^n)$. This key is used to compute the tag T as $T \leftarrow H_L(A, C) \oplus E_K(Y)$ and then $T \parallel C$ is the full ciphertext output by encryption.

The decryption algorithm parses the input ciphertext as $T \parallel C$. It computes the correct tag T' for C by setting $L \leftarrow E_K(0^n)$ and $T \leftarrow H_L(A, C) \oplus E_K(Y)$ (as was done in encryption). If $T \neq T'$ the ciphertext is rejected by returning $M = \bot$. Otherwise the message M is obtained by counter-mode decrypting C.

INDR SECURITY OF CAU. The following theorem formalizes that CAU is nonce-respecting INDR secure assuming E is a secure PRF.

Theorem 1. *Let $\mathcal{A}$ be an adversary against the nonce-respecting INDR security of CAU[E, H] that makes at most q oracle queries, each at most $p \cdot$ CAU.bl bits long. Then we can construct a $\mathcal{A}_{\text{prf}}$ such that*

$$\text{Adv}_{\text{CAU[E,H]}}^{\text{indr}}(\mathcal{A}) \leqslant \text{Adv}_{\text{E}}^{\text{prf}}(\mathcal{A}_{\text{prf}}) .$$

Adversary $\mathcal{A}_{\text{prf}}$ has runtime essentially that of $\mathcal{A}$, makes at most $q(p + 1) + 1$ queries to its oracle, has memory/time complexity essentially that of $\mathcal{A}$ and never repeats queries to its oracle.

It is important that $\mathcal{A}_{\text{prf}}$ never repeats queries because it allows us to apply the time-memory switching lemma from Sect. 2. This give us roughly,

$$\text{Adv}_{\text{CAU[E,H]}}^{\text{indr}}(\mathcal{A}) \in \text{Adv}_{\text{E}}^{\text{prp}}(\mathcal{A}_{\text{prf}}) + O(S \cdot pq \cdot \log(pq)/2^n)$$

where S is a bound on the memory complexity of $\mathcal{A}$. For variants other than nonce-respecting INDR it would not be clear how to prevent $\mathcal{A}_{\text{prf}}$ from repeating queries without storing the prior queries of $\mathcal{A}$.

Proof (Sketch). One constructs $\mathcal{A}_{\mathsf{prf}}$ to first set $L \leftarrow \text{EVAL}(0^n)$. Then it runs $\mathcal{A}$ and simulates encryption queries by running CAU.E while using its EVAL oracle in place of E_K. It does not recompute L each time because it has already computed it. Its final output is whatever $\mathcal{A}$ outputs. One can verify that the view of $\mathcal{A}$ when simulated by $\mathcal{A}_{\mathsf{prf}}$ is "real" encryptions when $b = 1$ and random strings when $b = 0$, so the claimed advantage bound follows.   □

CTXT/AE SECURITY OF CAU. It does not appear to be possible to give a similar time-memory trade-off for the CTXT or AE security of CAU. The standard analysis of either of these first uses PRF security to replace the output of E with random. It then argues that the adversary's view is independent of the $\mathrm{H}_L(A, C)$ values produced in encryption so that it can apply the security of H. For $x = \mathsf{ae}$ or $x = \mathsf{ctxt}$ this would give a bound of the form,

$$\mathsf{Adv}_{\mathsf{CAU}[\mathrm{E,H}]}^{x\text{-}1}(\mathcal{A}) = \mathsf{Adv}_{\mathrm{E}}^{\mathsf{prf}}(\mathcal{A}_{\mathsf{prf}}) + \mathsf{Adv}_{\mathrm{H}}^{\mathsf{axu}}(\mathcal{X}) \ .$$

However, this PRF adversary $\mathcal{A}_{\mathsf{prf}}$ needs to simulate a decryption oracle to $\mathcal{A}$. The natural ways of doing this (remembering all prior encryption queries or using EVAL to run decryption) either require significant use of memory or repeating queries to EVAL. This prevents us from applying the switching lemmas of [6,10] to get appealing time-memory tradeoffs when E is a PRP.

In Sect. 4.3, we will use a new technique for memory-tight reductions to prove that using CAU in a channel can provide (the channel equivalent of) CTXT security (and thus AE security from Sect. 4.2).

4   Memory-Tight Reductions for Cryptographic Channels

In this section we show that memory-tight reductions can be given for the combined confidentiality and integrity security of cryptographic channels. These are a form of stateful encryption which provide the guarantee that messages cannot be duplicated or reordered, in addition to the typical confidentiality and integrity goals of encryption.

4.1   Syntax and Security Notions

SYNTAX AND CORRECTNESS. A (cryptographic) channel CH specifies algorithms CH.Sg, CH.S, and CH.R along with message space $\mathsf{CH.M} \subseteq \{0,1\}^*$. The syntax of these algorithms is shown in Fig. 6. The state generation algorithm CH.Sg takes no input. It returns sender state σ^s and receiver state σ^r. The sending algorithm CH.S takes a sender state σ^s and message $M \in \mathsf{CH.M}$. It returns updated sender state σ^s and a ciphertext C. The receiving algorithm CH.R takes a receiver state σ^r and a ciphertext C. It returns updated receiver state σ^r and a message $M \in \mathsf{CH.M} \cup \{\bot\}$. When $M = \bot$, this represents the receiver rejecting the message as invalid.

A channel is expected to never again return $M \neq \bot$ after if it has rejected a message. This models the behavior of protocols such as TLS which are assumed

CH Syntax	Game $\mathsf{G}^{\text{ch-corr}}_{\text{CH},b}(\mathcal{A})$	Oracle $\text{EncDec}_b(M_0)$
$(\sigma^s, \sigma^r) \leftarrow\!\!\text{\$}\, \mathsf{CH.Sg}$	$(\sigma^s, \sigma^r) \leftarrow\!\!\text{\$}\, \mathsf{CH.Sg}$	$(\sigma^s, C) \leftarrow\!\!\text{\$}\, \mathsf{CH.S}(\sigma^s, M_0)$
$(\sigma^s, C) \leftarrow\!\!\text{\$}\, \mathsf{CH.S}(\sigma^s, M)$	$b' \leftarrow\!\!\text{\$}\, \mathcal{A}^{\text{EncDec}}$	$(\sigma^r, M_1) \leftarrow \mathsf{CH.R}(\sigma^r, C)$
$(\sigma^r, M) \leftarrow \mathsf{CH.R}(\sigma^r, C)$	Return $b' = 1$	Return M_b

Fig. 6. Left: Syntax of channel algorithms. **Right:** Channel correctness game.

to be run over a reliable transport layer and has been the standard notion for channels since the work of Bellare, Kohno, and Namprempre [2]. When a protocol (e.g. QUIC or DTLS) is run over an unreliable transport layer, then a *robust* channel is used instead [7]. We leave memory-tight proofs of security for robust channels as an interesting direction for future work.

We typically assume there is a ciphertext-length function $\mathsf{CH.cl} : \mathbb{N} \to \mathbb{N}$ such that for any $M \in \mathsf{CH.M}$ and state σ^s, we have $\Pr[|C| = \mathsf{CH.cl}(|M|) : (\sigma^s, C) \leftarrow\!\!\text{\$}\, \mathsf{CH.S}(\sigma^s, M)] = 1$.

Correctness requires that if the receiver is given the ciphertexts sent by the sender in order and without modification then the receiver will output the same sequence of messages that were sent. One way to formalize this is via the game $\mathsf{G}^{\text{ch-corr}}_{\text{CH},b}$ shown in Fig. 6. We define $\mathsf{Adv}^{\text{ch-corr}}_{\text{CH}}(\mathcal{A}) = \Pr[\mathsf{G}^{\text{ch-corr}}_{\text{CH},1}(\mathcal{A})] - \Pr[\mathsf{G}^{\text{ch-corr}}_{\text{CH},0}(\mathcal{A})]$. Perfect correctness requires that $\mathsf{Adv}^{\text{ch-corr}}_{\text{CH}}(\mathcal{A}) = 0$ for all (even unbounded) $\mathcal{A}$. This implies that the M_1 output by $\mathsf{CH.R}$ always equals M_0.

SECURITY DEFINITIONS. We consider indistinguishability from random, integrity of ciphertext, and authenticated encryption security for channels just like we did for nonce based encryption.

Authenticated encryption security of a channel CH is defined by game $\mathsf{G}^{\text{ch-ae}}_{\text{CH},b}$ defined in Fig. 7. In it the adversary is given access to an encryption oracle and a decryption oracle. The adversary's goal is to distinguish between a "real" and "ideal" world. In the real world ($b = 1$) the oracles use CH to encrypt messages and decrypt ciphertexts. In the ideal world ($b = 0$) encryption returns random messages of the appropriate length and decryption returns $\bot$. In both worlds, as long as the adversary's queries to decryption have consisted of the outputs of encryption in the correct order, the oracles are considered in sync and decryption just returns the appropriate message that was queried to encryption.[6] After the first time the adversary queries something else, the oracles are out of sync and will never be in sync again (so DEC will always return M_b).

Authenticated encryption security is a combined confidentiality and integrity notion. We can also define separate notions. INDR security is defined by the game $\mathsf{G}^{\text{ch-indr}}_{\text{CH},b}$ which is the same as $\mathsf{G}^{\text{ch-ae}}_{\text{CH},b}$ except the adversary is only given oracle access to ENC_b. CTXT security is defined by the game $\mathsf{G}^{\text{ch-ctxt}}_{\text{CH},b}$ which is the same as $\mathsf{G}^{\text{ch-ae}}_{\text{CH},b}$ except the adversary is given oracle access to ENC_1 and

---

[6] This matches the convention of CTXT-1 and AE-1 for encryption schemes. We believe it to be "correct" for the same reasons discussed for those definitions.

Game $\mathsf{G}^{\mathsf{ch\text{-}ae}}_{\mathsf{CH},b}(\mathcal{A})$	Game $\mathsf{G}^{\mathsf{ch\text{-}ctxt}}_{\mathsf{CH},b}(\mathcal{A})$	Oracle $\mathrm{DEC}_b(C)$
$\mathsf{sync} \leftarrow \mathbf{true}$	$\mathsf{sync} \leftarrow \mathbf{true}$	$(\sigma^r, M_1) \leftarrow \mathsf{CH.R}(\sigma^r, C)$
$(\sigma^s, \sigma^r) \leftarrow\!\!\$\ \mathsf{CH.Sg}$	$(\sigma^s, \sigma^r) \leftarrow\!\!\$\ \mathsf{CH.Sg}$	$M_0 \leftarrow \perp$
$b' \leftarrow\!\!\$\ \mathcal{A}^{\mathrm{ENC}_b, \mathrm{DEC}_b}$	$b' \leftarrow\!\!\$\ \mathcal{A}^{\mathrm{ENC}_1, \mathrm{DEC}_b}$	$M' \leftarrow \mathbf{M.dq}()$
Return $b' = 1$	Return $b' = 1$	$C' \leftarrow \mathbf{C.dq}()$
Game $\mathsf{G}^{\mathsf{ch\text{-}indr}}_{\mathsf{CH},b}(\mathcal{A})$	Oracle $\mathrm{ENC}_b(M)$	If sync then
$\mathsf{sync} \leftarrow \mathbf{true}$	$(\sigma^s, C_1) \leftarrow\!\!\$\ \mathsf{CH.S}(\sigma^s, M)$	If $C = C'$ then
$(\sigma^s, \sigma^r) \leftarrow\!\!\$\ \mathsf{CH.Sg}$	$C_0 \leftarrow\!\!\$\ \{0,1\}^{\mathsf{CH.cl}(|M|)}$	Return M'
$b' \leftarrow\!\!\$\ \mathcal{A}^{\mathrm{ENC}_b}$	$\mathbf{M.add}(M); \mathbf{C.add}(C_b)$	$\mathsf{sync} \leftarrow \mathbf{false}$
Return $b' = 1$	Return C_b	Return M_b

Fig. 7. Games defining the INDR, CTXT, and AE security of a channel.

Game $\mathsf{G}^{\mathsf{it}}_{L,\delta}(\mathcal{A}_1, \mathcal{A}_2)$
$R \leftarrow\!\!\$\ \{0,1\}^L$
$(i, \sigma) \leftarrow\!\!\$\ \mathcal{A}_1(R)$
$r \leftarrow\!\!\$\ \mathcal{A}_2(i, \sigma, R[: i-1])$
Return $r = R[i : i + \delta]$

Fig. 8. Information theoretic game in which $\mathcal{A}$ tries to remember a δ bit sequence in an L-bit random string.

DEC_b. These games are given explicitly in Fig. 7. We define the advantage of $\mathcal{A}$ by $\mathsf{Adv}^x_{\mathsf{CH}}(\mathcal{A}) = \mathsf{Pr}[\mathsf{G}^x_{\mathsf{CH},1}(\mathcal{A})] - \mathsf{Pr}[\mathsf{G}^x_{\mathsf{CH},0}(\mathcal{A})]$ for $x \in \{\mathsf{ch\text{-}ae}, \mathsf{ch\text{-}indr}, \mathsf{ch\text{-}ctxt}\}$.

4.2 Confidentiality and Integrity Imply Authenticated Encryption

We will show that INDR security plus CTXT security imply AE security using a memory-tight reduction. While the normal proof that INDR and CTXT security suffice to imply AE security is not particularly difficult, it uses a non-memory tight reduction to INDR security. Making the proof memory tight will require more involved analysis.

INFORMATION THEORETIC LEMMA. Before proceeding to the proof, we first will provide a simple information theoretic lemma that will be a useful subcomponent of that proof. Consider the game $\mathsf{G}^{\mathsf{it}}_{L,\delta}$ shown in Fig. 8. In it, an adversary is given a length L string R and tries to choose an index i for which it is able to remember the next δ-bits of the string using state σ. We say that an adversary $(\mathcal{A}_1, \mathcal{A}_2)$ is S-bounded if $|\sigma| = S$ always. We define $\mathsf{Adv}^{\mathsf{it}}_{L,\delta}(\mathcal{A}_1, \mathcal{A}_2) = \mathsf{Pr}[\mathsf{G}^{\mathsf{it}}_{L,\delta}(\mathcal{A}_1, \mathcal{A}_2)]$.

Lemma 1. *Let* $L, \delta, S \in \mathbb{N}$. *Let* $(\mathcal{A}_1, \mathcal{A}_2)$ *be an* S-*bounded adversary. Then*

$$\mathsf{Adv}^{\mathsf{it}}_{L,\delta}(\mathcal{A}_1, \mathcal{A}_2) \leqslant L \cdot 2^S / 2^\delta \ .$$

Proof. Let $L, \delta, S, \mathcal{A}_1, \mathcal{A}_2$ be defined as in the theorem statement. Without loss of generality we can assume that $\mathcal{A}_1$ and $\mathcal{A}_2$ are deterministic. Then for any fixed choice of i and σ, the probability that $\mathcal{A}_2(i, \sigma, R[: i - 1]) = R[i : i + \delta]$ will be exactly $1/2^\delta$. Then we can calculate as follows.

$$
\begin{aligned}
\Pr[\mathsf{G}^{\mathsf{it}}_{L,n}(\mathcal{A}_1, \mathcal{A}_2)] &\leqslant \Pr_R[\exists i, \sigma \text{ s.t. } R[i : i + \delta] = \mathcal{A}_2(i, \sigma, R[: i - 1])] \\
&\leqslant \sum_{i,\sigma} \Pr[R[i : i + \delta] = \mathcal{A}_2(i, \sigma, R[: i - 1])] \\
&= \sum_{i,\sigma} 1/2^\delta \leqslant L \cdot 2^S / 2^\delta .
\end{aligned}
$$

The last inequality follows from there being at most $L \cdot 2^\delta$ choices for (i, σ).
□

SECURITY RESULT. Now we can proceed to our security result showing that AE security can be implied by INDR and CTXT security in a memory-tight manner. The technical crux of the result is the reduction adversary $\mathcal{A}_\delta$ which simulates the view of an AE adversary $\mathcal{A}$ to attack the INDR security of the channel. In our theorem statement this reduction adversary is parameterized by a variable δ which determines how much local memory it uses. Using Lemma 1, our concrete advantage bound is expressed in terms of δ and establishes that the reduction can be successful with this value not much larger than the local memory of $\mathcal{A}$.

Theorem 2. *Let* CH *be a cryptographic channel. Let* $\mathcal{A}$ *be an adversary with memory complexity* S *and making at most* q *queries to its* ENC *oracle, each of which returns a ciphertext of length at most* x. *Then for any* $\delta \in \mathbb{N}$ *we can build an adversary* $\mathcal{A}_\delta$ *(described in the proof) such that*

$$
\mathsf{Adv}^{\mathsf{ch\text{-}ae}}_{\mathsf{CH}}(\mathcal{A}) \leqslant \mathsf{Adv}^{\mathsf{ch\text{-}ctxt}}_{\mathsf{CH}}(\mathcal{A}) + 2 \cdot \mathsf{Adv}^{\mathsf{ch\text{-}indr}}_{\mathsf{CH}}(\mathcal{A}_\delta) + 2q \cdot x \cdot 2^S / 2^\delta .
$$

Adversary $\mathcal{A}_\delta$ *has running time approximately that of* $\mathcal{A}$ *and uses about* $S + 2\delta$ *bits of state.*

Setting $\delta = S + \log(qx) + \kappa$ makes the last term about $1/2^\kappa$ while limiting the memory usage of $\mathcal{A}_\delta$ to only $2S + 2\log(qx) + 2\kappa$.

The standard way of proving that INDR security and CTXT security imply AE security would first use CTXT security to transition from a world in which $\mathcal{A}$ is given oracle access to $(\text{ENC}_1, \text{DEC}_1)$ to a world in which $\mathcal{A}$ is given oracle access to $(\text{ENC}_1, \text{DEC}_0)$. Then INDR security would be used to transition to $\mathcal{A}$ being given oracle access to $(\text{ENC}_0, \text{DEC}_0)$. The issue in our setting with this proof arises in the second step. The INDR reduction adversary needs to simulate DEC_0 for $\mathcal{A}$. The natural way of doing so requires storing the entirety of the tables $\mathbf{M}$ and $\mathbf{C}$ which means that $\mathcal{A}_\delta$ may use much more memory than $\mathcal{A}$.

Our proof of Theorem 2 follows this same general proof flow, but uses a more involved analysis for the reduction to INDR security. In particular, we make use of the following insight: If $\mathcal{A}$ has memory complexity S but cannot distinguish the ciphertexts it see from random (because of INDR security), then from Lemma 1 it cannot remember many more than S of the ciphertext bits that it has received from ENC but not yet forwarded to DEC.

If $\mathcal{A}$ ever queries a ciphertext which is not the next ciphertext in $\mathbf{C}$, then DEC_0 oracle will never again return anything other than $\perp$. Because we can assume that $\mathcal{A}$ will be unable to remember too many bits of ciphertext, we can just have our reduction adversary $\mathcal{A}_\delta$ remember a few more bits of ciphertext than $\mathcal{A}$ can. If the total length of ciphertext that $\mathcal{A}$ has received from its encryption oracle, but not forwarded on to its decryption oracle ever exceeds the amount that $\mathcal{A}_\delta$ will store, then $\mathcal{A}_\delta$ assumes $\mathcal{A}$ must have forgotten some intermediate ciphertext before that point, allowing the reduction to cease storing future ciphertexts because sync will be `false` before that point.

Proof. We will construct INDR adversaries $\mathcal{A}'_\delta$, $\mathcal{A}''_\delta$, and S-bounded adversary $(\mathcal{A}_1, \mathcal{A}_2)$ and show that

$$\text{Adv}_{\text{CH}}^{\text{ch-ae}}(\mathcal{A}) \leqslant \text{Adv}_{\text{CH}}^{\text{ch-ctxt}}(\mathcal{A}) + \text{Adv}_{\text{CH}}^{\text{ch-indr}}(\mathcal{A}'_\delta) + 2\text{Adv}_{q\cdot x,\delta}^{\text{it}}(\mathcal{A}_1, \mathcal{A}_2) + \text{Adv}_{\text{CH}}^{\text{ch-indr}}(\mathcal{A}''_\delta)$$

The stated theorem then follows by applying Lemma 1 and constructing the adversary $\mathcal{A}_\delta$ which runs either $\mathcal{A}'_\delta$ or $\mathcal{A}''_\delta$ (chosen at random) and outputs whatever that adversary does. The resulting $\mathcal{A}_\delta$ will satisfy the efficiency constraints stated in the theorem statement. We will prove this bound via a sequence of transformations that slowly change $\mathsf{G}_{\text{CH},1}^{\text{ch-ae}}$ to $\mathsf{G}_{\text{CH},0}^{\text{ch-ae}}$.

CTXT TRANSITION. Let $\mathsf{G}_0 = \mathsf{G}_{\text{CH},1}^{\text{ch-ae}}(\mathcal{A})$ and $\mathsf{G}_1 = \mathsf{G}_{\text{CH},0}^{\text{ch-ctxt}}(\mathcal{A})$. Because $\mathsf{G}_{\text{CH},1}^{\text{ch-ae}}(\mathcal{A})$ and $\mathsf{G}_{\text{CH},1}^{\text{ch-ctxt}}(\mathcal{A})$ are identical games we have that $\Pr[\mathsf{G}_0] - \Pr[\mathsf{G}_1] = \text{Adv}_{\text{CH}}^{\text{ch-ctxt}}(\mathcal{A})$.

TRANSITION TO LIMITED MEMORY GAME. Next we want to transition to a version of G_1 that stores a bounded amount of local state. Consider the games G_2 and G_3 shown in Fig. 9. The tables $\mathbf{M}_2$ and $\mathbf{C}_2$ track the messages and ciphertexts as in the real game. Because of this $\Pr[\mathsf{G}_1] = \Pr[\mathsf{G}_2]$.

In the transition to G_3 we are going to stop using these tables and instead solely rely on the tables $\mathbf{M}$ and $\mathbf{C}$. With these tables, if the total number of bits of ciphertexts that would be stored in $\mathbf{C}$ exceeds δ then we permanently stop adding elements to these tables – we assume that the adversary will cause sync to be set to `false` at some point earlier in the game. Note that up until this point the tables $(\mathbf{M}_2, \mathbf{C}_2)$ and $(\mathbf{M}, \mathbf{C})$ are used identically. The two games only differ in the boxed code in DEC which returns M_2 if the adversary has queried a ciphertext stored in $\mathbf{C}_2$ that was not stored in $\mathbf{C}$. Hence, these games are identical-until-bad so the fundamental lemma of game playing [3] gives,

$$\Pr[\mathsf{G}_3] - \Pr[\mathsf{G}_2] \leqslant \Pr[\mathsf{G}_3 \text{ sets bad}].$$

We want to apply Lemma 1 to bound the probability that bad is set. To do so we need to be able to treat the ciphertexts as random strings. Thus we defer the analysis of the probability that it occurs until after applying INDR security.

INDR TRANSITION. Now consider the game G_4. It is identical to G_3 except that the ciphertexts returned by ENC are chosen at random instead of using CH. We

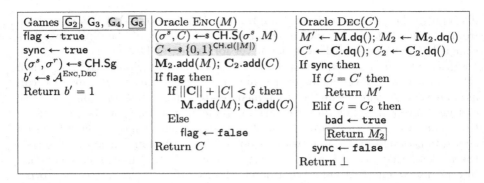

Fig. 9. Hybrid games for proof of Theorem 2. Highlighted code is only included in highlighted games. Boxed code is only included in boxed games.

can transition to this game using a reduction to INDR security. It is important here that our reduction adversary will not need to use too much memory because of the way that we have limited the memory needed for G_3.

Consider the adversaries $\mathcal{A}_\delta$ and $\mathcal{A}'_\delta$ shown in Fig. 10. Highlighted code is only included in the latter adversary.

Adversary $\mathcal{A}'_\delta$ uses its ENC oracle to present $\mathcal{A}$ with a view identical to G_3 if $b = 1$ and identical to G_4 if $b = 0$. Note here that the tables $(\mathbf{M}_2, \mathbf{C}_2)$ do not effect the view of $\mathcal{A}$ in either of these game, allowing $\mathcal{A}_\delta$ not to have to store them. We have that $\Pr[\mathsf{G}_{\mathsf{CH},1}^{\mathsf{ch-indr}}(\mathcal{A}'_\delta)] = \Pr[\mathsf{G}_3]$ and $\Pr[\mathsf{G}_{\mathsf{CH},0}^{\mathsf{ch-indr}}(\mathcal{A}'_\delta)] = \Pr[\mathsf{G}_4]$. In other words, $\mathsf{Adv}_{\mathsf{CH}}^{\mathsf{ch-indr}}(\mathcal{A}'_\delta) = \Pr[\mathsf{G}_3] - \Pr[\mathsf{G}_4]$.

Adversary $\mathcal{A}''_\delta$ instead uses its INDR oracle to simulate the view of $\mathcal{A}$, but returns 1 if the flag bad would have been set. Because this can only be set by the first ciphertext not stored in $\mathbf{C}$ we only need to be able to simulate the games up until that point. So we store this extra ciphertext and put an $*$ in $\mathbf{C}$ so that in DEC we know when we have reached the relevant point. We have that $\Pr[\mathsf{G}_{\mathsf{CH},1}^{\mathsf{ch-indr}}(\mathcal{A}''_\delta)] = \Pr[\mathsf{G}_3 \text{ sets bad}]$ and $\Pr[\mathsf{G}_{\mathsf{CH},0}^{\mathsf{ch-indr}}(\mathcal{A}''_\delta)] = \Pr[\mathsf{G}_4 \text{ sets bad}]$. In other words, $\Pr[\mathsf{G}_3 \text{ sets bad}] \leqslant \mathsf{Adv}_{\mathsf{CH}}^{\mathsf{ch-indr}}(\mathcal{A}''_\delta) + \Pr[\mathsf{G}_4 \text{ sets bad}]$.

FINAL TRANSITION. The final transition is from G_4 to G_5. These two games are identical-until-bad as can be seen in DEC. Because of this we have that

$$\Pr[\mathsf{G}_4] - \Pr[\mathsf{G}_5] \leqslant \Pr[\mathsf{G}_4 \text{ sets bad}].$$

Using all of $\mathbf{M}_2$ and $\mathbf{C}_2$ instead of just $\mathbf{M}$ and $\mathbf{C}$ makes G_5 identical to $\mathsf{G}_{\mathsf{CH},0}^{\mathsf{ch-ae}}$.

BOUNDING PROBABILITY OF bad. We conclude by bounding the probability G_4 sets bad via a reduction to our information theoretic analysis. Consider the S-bounded $(\mathcal{A}_1, \mathcal{A}_2)$ that behaves as follows. First, $\mathcal{A}_1$ internally simulates the view of $\mathcal{A}$ in G_4 using the coins for $\mathcal{A}$ which maximize the probability of bad and using the bits of R as the ciphertext bits returned by encryption. If $\mathcal{A}$ causes flag to be set to $\mathtt{false}$, $\mathcal{A}_1$ will halt and output the current state of $\mathcal{A}$ as σ with i chosen so the next δ bits of $\mathbf{C}$ and c are the values of R for $\mathcal{A}_2$ to guess.

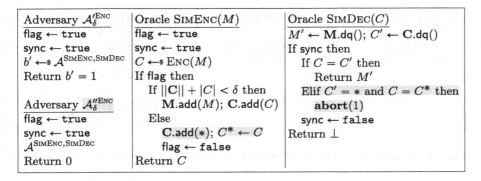

Fig. 10. INDR adversaries for proof of Theorem 2. Highlighting indicates code that is only used by adversary $\mathcal{A}'_\delta$.

Then $\mathcal{A}_2$ will resume executing $\mathcal{A}$ using σ. When $\mathcal{A}$ makes encryption queries it will just make up its own responses. When $\mathcal{A}$ makes a decryption query for a ciphertext C then $\mathcal{A}_2$ will concatenate it into its guess r. It just assumes this was the correct next ciphertext that should have been stored in $\mathbf{C}$ (otherwise $\mathcal{A}$ would fail in setting bad). To determine which M to return for this query, $\mathcal{A}_2$ re-runs $\mathcal{A}$ from the beginning using the same coins $\mathcal{A}_1$ used. It uses its given prefix of R and the current value of r to respond to encryption queries until it reaches the encryption query corresponding to the current decryption query. Whatever message $\mathcal{A}$ queried for this encryption query is then returned for the decryption query. Once r is δ bits long, $\mathcal{A}_2$ outputs that as its guess.

We can see that when bad would be set in G_4, the view of $\mathcal{A}$ is perfectly simulated up until that point and $\mathcal{A}_2$ will guess r correctly. This gives us $\Pr[G_4 \text{ sets bad}] \leqslant \mathsf{Adv}^{\mathsf{it}}_{q\cdot x, \delta}(\mathcal{A}_1, \mathcal{A}_2)$ as desired.

Combining all the bounds we have shown completes the proof. □

4.3 AE Security of a TLS 1.3-Like Channel

We have shown that the AE security of a channel can be reduced to its constituent INDR and CTXT security in a way that preserves memory complexity. This is, of course, only meaningful if we have channels for which we can give provable time-memory tradeoffs for their INDR and CTXT security. Using the ideas of Jaeger and Tessaro [10] it is easy to give such examples for INDR security.

Using the ideas from proof of Theorem 2 we will prove the security of a channel based on GCM (or more generally CAU). The resulting channel can be viewed as a (simplified) version of the channel obtained by using GCM in TLS 1.3.

THE CONSTRUCTION. The construction we consider is a straightforward construction of a channel from a nonce-based encryption scheme NE by using a counter for the nonce. The INDR security of this channel follows easily from the nonce-respecting INDR security of NE. Proving integrity of the channel from

NCH[NE].Sg	NCH[NE].S$((K, N), M)$	NCH[NE].R$((K, N), C)$

$K \leftarrow_\$ $ NE.Kg
$N \leftarrow_\$ $ NE.N
Return $((K, N), (K, N))$
	$N \leftarrow N + 1$
	$C \leftarrow$ NE.E(K, N, M)
	Return $((K, N), C)$
		If $N = \bot$ then
		  Return $((\bot, \bot), \bot)$
		$N \leftarrow N + 1$
		$M \leftarrow$ NE.D(K, N, C)
		If $M = \bot$ then
		  Return $((\bot, \bot), \bot)$
		Return $((K, N), M)$

Fig. 11. Algorithms of channel NCH[NE] constructed from encryption scheme NE.

the integrity of NE is possible, but of limited applicability since we do not have examples of encryption schemes with proven time-memory tradeoffs for integrity. We will instead only show integrity for the specific case that NE = CAU.

The channel NCH[NE] is parameterized by an encryption scheme NE. It has NCH[NE].M = NE.M. We assume that NE.N can be interpreted as a cyclic group written using additive notation. Its algorithms are shown in Fig. 11. State generation sets the state of both parties equal to a shared random key and nonce. Encryption increments the nonce and uses NE to encrypt the message with the current nonce. Decryption increments the nonce and uses NE to decrypt the ciphertext with the current nonce. If the ciphertext is rejected ($M = \bot$), the receiver will replace its state with $\bot$'s. Henceforth it will reject all ciphertexts it receives (via the first line which checks if $N = \bot$ already holds.

INDR SECURITY. The INDR security of NCH[NE] follows easily from nonce-respecting INDR security of NE. This is captured by the following theorem.

Theorem 3. *Let $\mathcal{A}$ be an adversary against the INDR security of NCH[NE] that makes less than $|$NE.N$|$ oracle queries. Then we can construct $\mathcal{B}$ such that*

$$\mathsf{Adv}^{\mathsf{ch\text{-}indr}}_{\mathsf{NCH[NE]}}(\mathcal{A}) \leqslant \mathsf{Adv}^{\mathsf{indr}}_{\mathsf{NE}}(\mathcal{B}) .$$

Adversary $\mathcal{B}$ has complexity comparable to that of $\mathcal{A}$ and is nonce-respecting.

Proof (Sketch). Adversary $\mathcal{B}$ picks N at random and then starts executing $\mathcal{A}$. Whenever $\mathcal{A}$ makes a ENC(M) query, $\mathcal{B}$ increments N, queries $C \leftarrow$ ENC(N, M), and returns C to $\mathcal{A}$. Adversary $\mathcal{B}$ outputs whatever $\mathcal{A}$ does. Verifying the claims made about this adversary is straightforward.   □

CTXT SECURITY. For CTXT security we need to focus our attention on the particular construction of NCH[NE] obtained when using the encryption scheme NE = CAU[E, H] for some function families E and H.

In our proof, we will take advantage of the fact that the adversary can essentially only make a single forgery attempt. If it fails at this attempt, then the state of the decryption algorithm can be erased and it will henceforth always return $\bot$. Because CAU uses a Carter-Wegman style MAC we have to first use the PRF security of E to hide the values of $H_L(A, C)$ used in encryption queries. To get our desired state-aware results we need to make sure that our PRF reduction does not use much more memory than the original adversary. This creates an issue similar to what we saw in Sect. 4 where it can be difficult to simulate the values returned by DEC. This issue is resolved by adjusting the proof technique used to establish Theorem 2 where we exploit the fact that ciphertexts look random to assume that $\mathcal{A}$ cannot remember too many ciphertexts.

Theorem 4. *Let* NE = CAU[E, H] *for some* E *and* H. *Let* $\mathcal{A}$ *be a nonce-respecting adversary against the* CTXT *security of* NCH[NE] *with memory complexity* S *that makes at most* $q \leqslant 2^{\mathsf{CAU.nl}} - 1$ *encryption queries, each of which returns a ciphertext of length at most* x. *Then for any* $\delta \in \mathbb{N}$ *we can construct an adversary* $\mathcal{A}_{\mathsf{prf}}$ *such that*

$$\mathsf{Adv}^{\mathsf{ch\text{-}ctxt}}_{\mathsf{NCH[NE]}}(\mathcal{A}) \leqslant 2 \cdot \mathsf{Adv}^{\mathsf{prf}}_{\mathrm{E}}(\mathcal{A}_{\mathsf{prf}}) + \mathsf{Adv}^{\mathsf{axu}}_{\mathrm{H}}(\mathcal{X}) + q \cdot x \cdot 2^S/2^\delta \ .$$

Adversary $\mathcal{A}_{\mathsf{prf}}$ *has running time approximately that of* $\mathcal{A}$ *and uses about* $S + 2\delta$ *bits of state. It makes at most* $q(x/n + 2) + 1$ *non-repeating queries to its oracle.*

The proof is given in the full version. As with Theorem 1, the PRF adversary we give never repeats queries so we can apply the switching lemma to obtain a bound using PRP security of E. Here it is important that the memory of $\mathcal{A}_{\mathsf{prf}}$ is not much more than that of $\mathcal{A}$. Assuming $|A| < p$, setting $\delta \approx S + n$, and assuming $S > n$ we can combine all of our theorems so far to obtain a bound of

$$\mathsf{Adv}^{\mathsf{ch\text{-}ae}}_{\mathsf{NCH[NE]}}(\mathcal{A}) \leqslant 4 \cdot \mathsf{Adv}^{\mathsf{prf}}_{\mathrm{E}}(\mathcal{B}) + O\left(\frac{Spq \log(pq) + c(p + q)}{2^n}\right)$$

for a $\mathcal{B}$ with comparable efficiency to $\mathcal{A}$ and assuming H is c-AXU.

5   Negative Results for Memory-Tight AE Reductions

In this section we give impossibility results for giving a memory-tight reduction (for a natural restricted class of black-box reductions) from AE-1 security to nonce-respecting INDR and CTXT-1 security. This establishes that our restriction to the channel setting for Sect. 4 was necessary for our positive results.

BLACK-BOX REDUCTIONS. A reduction $\mathcal{R}$ maps an adversary $\mathcal{A}$ to an adversary $\mathcal{R}[\mathcal{A}]$. We consider reductions that run an AE-1 adversary $\mathcal{A}$ in a black-box manner as shown in Fig. 12. It starts with initial state σ output by $\mathcal{R}.\mathsf{Init}$. The parameter $\mathcal{R}.\mathsf{rew}$ determines how many times $\mathcal{R}$ will perform a full rewind of $\mathcal{A}$. Then it runs $\mathcal{A}$ while simulating its encryption and decryption oracles. For every encryption query, $\mathcal{R}$ runs $\mathcal{R}.\mathsf{SimEnc}$ with the query and its state as input to produce the updated state, a flag rf, and a ciphertext. If the flag rf is true, then $\mathcal{R}$ starts running $\mathcal{A}$ from the beginning again. Otherwise, it answers with the query answer $\mathcal{R}.\mathsf{SimEnc}$ returned. Decryption queries are handled analogously. If $\mathcal{R}$ did not rewind $\mathcal{A}$ before $\mathcal{A}$ finished its execution, then it runs $\mathcal{R}.\mathsf{Upd}$ on $\mathcal{A}$'s

Reduction $\mathcal{R}[\mathcal{A}]^O$	Oracle $\text{REnc}(N, M)$
$\sigma \twoheadleftarrow \mathcal{R}^O.\text{Init}$	$(\sigma, \text{rf}, C) \twoheadleftarrow \mathcal{R}^O.\text{SimEnc}(\sigma, N, M)$
$i \leftarrow 0$	If rf then goto NEXT
While $i \leqslant \mathcal{R}.\text{rew}$ do	Return C
$\quad b \twoheadleftarrow \mathcal{A}^{\text{REnc,RDec}}$	Oracle $\text{RDec}(N, C)$
$\quad \sigma \twoheadleftarrow \mathcal{R}^O.\text{Upd}(\sigma, b)$	$(\sigma, \text{rf}, M) \twoheadleftarrow \mathcal{R}^O.\text{SimDec}(\sigma, N, C)$
$\quad$ NEXT: $i \leftarrow i + 1$	If rf then goto NEXT
Return $\mathcal{R}^O.\text{Fin}(\sigma)$	Return M

Fig. 12. Syntax of a black-box reductions $\mathcal{R}$ running AE-1 adversary $\mathcal{A}$. We represent the oracles $\mathcal{R}$ has access to collectively as O.

output to updates its state and starts running $\mathcal{A}$ from the beginning if has not already rewinded $\mathcal{R}.\text{rew}$ times. Finally, $\mathcal{R}$ outputs whatever $\mathcal{R}.\text{Fin}(\sigma)$ returns. The following definition captures some restrictions we will place on reductions.

Definition 1. *Let $\mathcal{R}$ be a reduction using the syntax from Fig. 12. It is full-rewinding if $\mathcal{R}.\text{rew} > 0$ or straightline if $\mathcal{R}.\text{rew} = 0$. It is nonce-respecting if $\mathcal{R}[\mathcal{A}]$ is nonce-respecting when $\mathcal{A}$ is nonce-respecting. It is faithful if $\mathcal{R}[\mathcal{A}]$ answers encryption queries of $\mathcal{A}$ consistent with its own encryption oracle, i.e., $\mathcal{R}$ responds with C on an encryption query made on (N, M), only if it previously queried its own encryption oracle with (N, M) and received C as the answer.*

ADDITIONAL NOTATION. We fix an understood nonce-based encryption scheme NE for which we assume that $\{0,1\}^{\text{ml}} \subseteq \text{NE.M}$. We also assume $\mathbb{N} \times \mathbb{N} \subseteq \text{NE.N}$ and we use $\text{N} = \text{NE.N}$ as shorthand. We assume that $[\text{NE.Kg}] = \{0,1\}^{\text{kl}}$. We let $\text{C} = \{0,1\}^{\text{NE.cl(ml)}}$. We also introduce some new notation for the complexity of an algorithm $\mathcal{A}$. First, $\text{Mem}(\mathcal{A})$ is defined as the number of bits of memory that $\mathcal{A}$ uses. The total number of queries to its oracles is $\text{Query}(\mathcal{A})$, and the number of computation steps $\text{Time}(\mathcal{A})$. For a reduction $\mathcal{R}$ we use $\text{Mem}(\mathcal{R})$ to denote the number of bits of memory that $\mathcal{R}$ uses in addition any memory of the adversary it runs.

Game $\text{G}^{\text{it-chl-}r}_{u,m}(\mathcal{D}_1, \mathcal{D}_2)$
$\sigma \leftarrow \perp$
For $i \in [r]$ do
$\quad$ For $j \in [u]$ do
$\quad\quad M_j \twoheadleftarrow \{0,1\}^m$
$\quad \sigma \leftarrow \mathcal{D}_1(\sigma, M_1, \dots, M_u)$
$\quad j^* \twoheadleftarrow [u]$
$\quad (\sigma, M) \leftarrow \mathcal{D}_2(\sigma, j^*)$
$\quad$ If $M_{j*} \neq M$ then return **false**
Return **true**

Fig. 13. Information theoretic game played by adversary $(\mathcal{D}_1, \mathcal{D}_2)$.

INFORMATION THEORETIC LEMMA. We give a lemma that will be a useful sub-component of our proofs. It pertains to game $\text{G}^{\text{it-chl-}r}_{u,m}$ in Fig. 13. It is an r-round game, played by a two-stage adversary $(\mathcal{D}_1, \mathcal{D}_2)$. In each round, $\mathcal{D}_1$ gets

state σ from the prior round, along with u random strings $M_1, \ldots, M_u$ each
of length m. Adversary $\mathcal{D}_1$ outputs state σ which is input to $\mathcal{D}_2$ along with a
randomly sampled index j^* from $[u]$. Then $\mathcal{D}_2$ outputs a string M and state
σ that is passed to $\mathcal{D}_1$ in the next round. If $M = M_{j^*}$, we say that $(\mathcal{D}_1, \mathcal{D}_2)$
has answered the challenge of this round correctly. If $(\mathcal{D}_1, \mathcal{D}_2)$ answers all the
r challenges correctly, the game returns true. Otherwise it returns false. We
define $\mathsf{Adv}_{u,m}^{\mathsf{it\text{-}chl\text{-}}r}(\mathcal{D}_1, \mathcal{D}_2) = \Pr[\mathsf{G}_{u,m}^{\mathsf{it\text{-}chl\text{-}}r}(\mathcal{D}_1, \mathcal{D}_2)]$. Adversary $(\mathcal{D}_1, \mathcal{D}_2)$ is S-bounded
if the state output by $\mathcal{D}_1$ is at most S bits long. We can prove the following.

Lemma 2. *If $(\mathcal{D}_1, \mathcal{D}_2)$ is S-bounded, then*

$$\mathsf{Adv}_{u,m}^{\mathsf{it\text{-}chl\text{-}}r}(\mathcal{D}_1, \mathcal{D}_2) \leqslant \left(\frac{2(S+m)}{u} + \frac{3}{2^m} \right)^r .$$

The proof, deferred to the full version, goes via a reduction to the $r = 1$ case
which is analyzed using techniques from the AI-ROM setting [5].

5.1 Memory Lower Bound for Straightline Reductions

Our first theorem shows that it is not possible to give memory-tight, straightline
reductions proving the AE-1 security of an encryption scheme from its INDR
and CTXT-1 security. (As the theorem statement is somewhat complicated, we
will describe how to interpret it below.)

Theorem 5 (Impossibility for straightline reductions). *Let NE be a
nonce-based encryption scheme. Fix $u, r \in \mathbb{N}$ and define the nonce-respecting
adversary $\mathcal{A}$ as shown in Fig. 15. Let $\mathcal{R}$ be a straightline, nonce-respecting, faithful black-box reduction from AE-1 to nonce-respecting INDR with $\mathsf{Mem}(\mathcal{R}) = S$.
Let $\mathcal{R}'$ be a straightline, nonce-respecting, faithful reduction from AE-1 to
CTXT-1. Then, we can construct adversaries $\mathcal{C}$ and $\mathcal{W}$ such that,*

(i) $\mathsf{Adv}_{\mathsf{NE}}^{\mathsf{ae\text{-}1}}(\mathcal{A}) \geqslant 1 - \dfrac{2^{\mathsf{kl}}}{2^{2\mathsf{NE.cl(ml)}}}$,

(ii) $\mathsf{Adv}_{\mathsf{NE}}^{\mathsf{indr}}(\mathcal{R}[\mathcal{A}]) \leqslant 2 \cdot \left(\dfrac{2(S + \log r + \mathsf{kl}) + 2\mathsf{ml}}{u} + \dfrac{3}{2^{\mathsf{ml}}} \right)^r + 4 \cdot \mathsf{Adv}_{\mathsf{NE}}^{\mathsf{indr}}(\mathcal{C})$,

(iii) $\mathsf{Adv}_{\mathsf{NE}}^{\mathsf{ctxt\text{-}1}}(\mathcal{R}'[\mathcal{A}]) \leqslant \mathsf{Adv}_{\mathsf{NE}}^{\mathsf{ctxt\text{-}1}}(\mathcal{R}'[\mathcal{W}])$.

*Moreover, $\mathcal{A}$ satisfies $\mathsf{Query}(\mathcal{A}) = (u+1) \cdot r + 2$ and $\mathsf{Mem}(\mathcal{A}) \leqslant 2\mathsf{kl} + 2\mathsf{ml} +
2\mathsf{NE.cl(ml)} + 2\log|\mathsf{N}| + \log u \cdot r$. Also $\mathcal{C}$ and $\mathcal{W}$ satisfy $\mathsf{Query}(\mathcal{C}) < \mathsf{Query}(\mathcal{R}) +
\mathsf{Query}(\mathcal{A})$, $\mathsf{Time}(\mathcal{C}) \in O(\mathsf{Query}(\mathcal{A}) + \mathsf{Time}(\mathcal{R}))$, and $\mathsf{Query}(\mathcal{W}) = \mathsf{Query}(\mathcal{A})$ and
$\mathsf{Time}(\mathcal{W}) \in O(\mathsf{Query}(\mathcal{A}))$.*

To interpret this theorem, assume that the parameters of NE are such that
the advantage of $\mathcal{A}$ is essentially one. Hence, a successful pair of reductions $\mathcal{R}$
and $\mathcal{R}'$ would need at least one of $\mathcal{R}[\mathcal{A}]$ or $\mathcal{R}'[\mathcal{A}]$ to have high advantage. For
memory-tight $\mathcal{R}$ and $\mathcal{R}'$ we expect there to be linear functions f_1 and f_2 such

$$
\begin{array}{|ll|}
\hline
\textbf{Games } \mathsf{G}_b^0,\ \mathsf{G}^1 & \text{Oracle } \mathrm{ENC}_b(N, M) \\
\hline
b \leftarrow 1 & C_0 \leftarrow\!\!\$\ \mathsf{C} \\
K^* \leftarrow\!\!\$\ \mathsf{NE.Kg}();\ \sigma \leftarrow\!\!\$\ \mathcal{R}^{\mathrm{ENC}_b}.\mathrm{Init} & C_1 \leftarrow \mathsf{NE.E}(K^*, N, M) \\
\text{For } i \in [r] \text{ do} & \boxed{C_1 \leftarrow \mathsf{NE.E}(K^*, N, 0^{\mathsf{ml}})} \\
\quad j^* \leftarrow\!\!\$\ [u] & \text{Return } C_b \\
\quad \text{For } j \in [u] \text{ do} & \\
\qquad M_j \leftarrow\!\!\$\ \{0,1\}^{\mathsf{ml}};\ N_j \leftarrow (i, j) & \\
\qquad (\sigma, \cdot, C_j) \leftarrow\!\!\$\ \mathcal{R}^{\mathrm{ENC}_b}.\mathrm{SIMENC}(\sigma, N_j, M_j) & \\
\qquad (\sigma, \cdot, M) \leftarrow\!\!\$\ \mathcal{R}^{\mathrm{ENC}_b}.\mathrm{SIMDEC}(\sigma, N_{j*}, C_{j*}) & \\
\qquad \text{If } M \neq M_{j*} \text{ then return } \mathtt{false} & \\
\text{Return } \mathtt{true} & \\
\hline
\end{array}
$$

Fig. 14. Games G^1 and G_1^0 for $b \in \{0,1\}$. Highlighted code is only included in G^1.

$$
\begin{array}{|l|l|}
\hline
\text{Adversaries } \mathcal{A}^{\mathrm{ENC,DEC}},\ \boxed{\mathcal{S}^{\mathrm{ENC,DEC}}},\ \mathcal{W}^{\mathrm{ENC,DEC}} & \text{Adversaries } \mathcal{B}^{\mathrm{ENC}},\ \mathcal{E}^{\mathrm{ENC}} \\
\hline
\text{For } i \in [r] \text{ do} & M_1 \leftarrow\!\!\$\ \{0,1\}^{\mathsf{ml}} \\
\quad j^* \leftarrow\!\!\$\ [u] & M_2 \leftarrow\!\!\$\ \{0,1\}^{\mathsf{ml}} \\
\quad \text{For } j \in [u] \text{ do} & N_1 \leftarrow (0,1);\ N_2 \leftarrow (0,2) \\
\qquad M_j \leftarrow\!\!\$\ \{0,1\}^{\mathsf{ml}} & C_1 \leftarrow \mathrm{ENC}(N_1, M_1) \\
\qquad N_j \leftarrow (i, j) & C_2 \leftarrow \mathrm{ENC}(N_2, M_2) \\
\qquad C_j \leftarrow \mathrm{ENC}(N_j, M_j) & \text{For } K \in \{0,1\}^{\mathsf{kl}} \text{ do} \\
\quad M \leftarrow \mathrm{DEC}(N_{j*}, C_{j*}) & \quad \mathsf{eq}_1 \leftarrow (\mathsf{NE.E}(K, N_1, M_1) = C_1) \\
\quad \text{If } M \neq M_{j*} \text{ then return } 1 & \quad \mathsf{eq}_2 \leftarrow (\mathsf{NE.E}(K, N_2, M_2) = C_2) \\
\mathsf{bad} \leftarrow \mathtt{true} & \quad \text{If } \mathsf{eq}_1 \text{ and } \mathsf{eq}_2 \text{ then return } 1 \\
\text{Return } \mathcal{B}^{\mathrm{ENC}};\ \boxed{\text{Return } 0;}\ \text{Return } \mathcal{E}^{\mathrm{ENC}} & \text{Return } 0;\ \text{Return } 1 \\
\hline
\end{array}
$$

Fig. 15. Adversaries against the AE-1 security of NE. Boxed code is only included in $\mathcal{S}$. Highlighted code is only included in $\mathcal{A}$ and $\mathcal{B}$.

that their local computation time and memory usage when interacting with an adversary $\mathcal{A}$ would be bounded by $f_1(q_{\mathcal{A}})$ and $f_2(s_{\mathcal{A}})$ where $q_{\mathcal{A}} = \mathsf{Query}(\mathcal{A})$ and $s_{\mathcal{A}} = \mathsf{Mem}(\mathcal{A})$.

Suppose this was the case. Then we can fix upper bounds for $\log(u)$ and $\log(r)$, determining the memory usage of $\mathcal{A}$ and hence $f_1(s_{\mathcal{A}}) = S$. Now we can pick reasonable u and r such that, $2 \cdot \left(\frac{2(S + \log r + \mathsf{kl}) + 2\mathsf{ml}}{u} + \frac{3}{2^{\mathsf{ml}}} \right)^r$ is very small (by say making the inside of the parenthesis less than $1/2$ and setting $r = 128$). Then, for one of the reductions to have high advantage, one of $\mathcal{C}$ or $\mathcal{R}'[\mathcal{W}]$ would have to have high advantage. But the efficiencies of these are bounded as small functions of the query complexity of $\mathcal{A}$ (rather than its local runtime) so cannot be too large. But then assuming security of NE prevents any of them from having high advantage.

Proof. Consider the adversary $\mathcal{A}$ in Fig. 15 against AE-1 security of NE. Note that it is nonce-respecting. It has a challenge phase followed by an invocation of $\mathcal{B}$. Each iteration of the challenge phase consists of $\mathcal{A}$ making u encryption queries with unique nonces and making one decryption query on one of the u ciphertexts it received as answers chosen uniformly at random with its corresponding nonce. If the answer of the decryption query is not consistent with the prior encryption query, $\mathcal{A}$ returns 1. There are r iterations of the challenge phase. If these are all passed, $\mathcal{A}$ runs adversary $\mathcal{B}$ (shown on the right) with its ENC oracle and outputs whatever $\mathcal{B}$ outputs. From the code of $\mathcal{A}$ we can see that it makes $r \cdot u + 2$ encryption queries, r decryption queries, and satisfies

$$\mathsf{Mem}(\mathcal{A}) \leqslant 2\mathsf{kl} + 2\mathsf{ml} + 2\mathsf{NE.cl}(\mathsf{ml}) + 2 \log |\mathsf{N}| + \log u \cdot r .$$

To prove the theorem we need to separately establish the three advantage claims (and corresponding statements about the efficiency of various algorithms). For the first claim, note that $\mathsf{Adv}_{\mathsf{NE}}^{\mathsf{ae\text{-}1}}(\mathcal{A}) = \mathsf{Adv}_{\mathsf{NE}}^{\mathsf{ae\text{-}1}}(\mathcal{B})$ because M will always equal M_{j^*} when $\mathcal{A}$ is playing $\mathsf{G}_{\mathsf{NE},b}^{\mathsf{ae\text{-}1}}$. The simple analysis giving the needed bound on $\mathsf{Adv}_{\mathsf{NE}}^{\mathsf{ae\text{-}1}}(\mathcal{B})$ is deferred to the full version.

For the third claim, consider adversary $\mathcal{W}$ defined as shown in Fig. 15. It is identical to $\mathcal{A}$, except that it calls $\mathcal{E}$, which is similar to $\mathcal{B}$ but always returns 1. Because $\mathcal{R}'$ is faithful, $\mathcal{B}$ would never return 0 when run by $\mathcal{R}'[\mathcal{A}]$ playing $\mathsf{G}_{\mathsf{NE},b}^{\mathsf{ctxt\text{-}1}}$ so $\mathsf{Adv}_{\mathsf{NE}}^{\mathsf{ctxt\text{-}1}}(\mathcal{R}'[\mathcal{A}]) = \mathsf{Adv}_{\mathsf{NE}}^{\mathsf{ctxt\text{-}1}}(\mathcal{R}'[\mathcal{W}])$ holds trivially.

We spend the rest of the proof establishing the second claim. Consider the adversary $\mathcal{S}$ in Fig. 15. It behaves identically to $\mathcal{A}$ until the flag bad is set. Using the Fundamental Lemma of Game Playing [3], we can obtain for $b \in \{0, 1\}$

$$\left| \mathsf{Pr}\left[\mathsf{G}_{\mathsf{NE},b}^{\mathsf{indr}}(\mathcal{R}[\mathcal{A}]) \right] - \mathsf{Pr}\left[\mathsf{G}_{\mathsf{NE},b}^{\mathsf{indr}}(\mathcal{R}[\mathcal{S}]) \right] \right| \leqslant \mathsf{Pr}\left[\mathcal{R}[\mathcal{A}] \text{ sets bad in } \mathsf{G}_{\mathsf{NE},b}^{\mathsf{indr}} \right] .$$

Consider the games G_b^0 for $b \in \{0, 1\}$ in Fig. 14. In it, we assume that $\mathcal{R}$ always outputs $\mathsf{rf} = \mathtt{false}$ since it is straightline. Note that G_b^0 simulates the challenge phase of $\mathcal{A}$ and the game $\mathsf{G}_b^{\mathsf{indr}}$ to $\mathcal{R}$ perfectly, so it returns $\mathtt{true}$ whenever $\mathcal{R}[\mathcal{A}]$ would set bad is set in $\mathsf{G}_b^{\mathsf{indr}}$. From this we can show

$$\mathsf{Adv}_{\mathsf{NE}}^{\mathsf{indr}}(\mathcal{R}[\mathcal{A}]) \leqslant \mathsf{Adv}_{\mathsf{NE}}^{\mathsf{indr}}(\mathcal{R}[\mathcal{S}]) + \mathsf{Pr}\left[\mathsf{G}_0^0 \right] + \mathsf{Pr}\left[\mathsf{G}_1^0 \right] . \qquad (3)$$

Now consider the game G^1 defined in the same figure. It is identical to either G_b^0 except that it answers all encryption queries with the encryption of the message 0^{ml}. We now state two lemmas which give bounds on both $\mathsf{Pr}\left[\mathsf{G}_b^0\right]$'s via G^1. First, in Lemma 3, we use that the INDR security of NE implies G^1's encryption oracle is indistinguishable from those in either G_b^0 to transition to G^1. Next, in Lemma 4 we give a bound on $\mathsf{Pr}\left[\mathsf{G}^1\right]$ which was obtained by using $\mathcal{R}$ to construct an adversary for $\mathsf{G}_{u,\mathsf{ml}}^{\mathsf{it\text{-}chl\text{-}}r}$ and bounding its advantage with Lemma 2. The proofs of these lemmas are deferred to the full version.

Lemma 3. *There exist adversaries $\mathcal{C}_1$ and $\mathcal{C}_2$ such that*

$$\mathsf{Pr}\left[\mathsf{G}_1^0 \right] \leqslant \mathsf{Pr}\left[\mathsf{G}_0^0 \right] + \mathsf{Adv}_{\mathsf{NE}}^{\mathsf{indr}}(\mathcal{C}_1),$$
$$\mathsf{Pr}\left[\mathsf{G}_0^0 \right] \leqslant \mathsf{Pr}\left[\mathsf{G}^1 \right] + \mathsf{Adv}_{\mathsf{NE}}^{\mathsf{indr}}(\mathcal{C}_2)$$

where G_b^0 *and* G^1 *are defined as in Fig. 14. Moreover* $\mathsf{Query}(\mathcal{C}_1) < \mathsf{Query}(\mathcal{R}) + \mathsf{Query}(\mathcal{A})$ *and* $\mathsf{Time}(\mathcal{C}_1) \in O(\mathsf{Query}(\mathcal{A}) + \mathsf{Time}(\mathcal{R}))$. *Adversary* $\mathcal{C}_2$*'s complexity is the same.*

Lemma 4. *If* $\mathcal{R}$ *is a straightline, nonce-respecting, faithful black-box reduction from* AE-1 *to nonce-respecting* INDR *with* $\mathsf{Mem}(\mathcal{R}) = S$. *Then,*

$$\Pr\left[\mathsf{G}^1\right] \leqslant \left(\frac{2(S + \log r + \mathsf{kl}) + 2\mathsf{ml}}{u} + \frac{3}{2^{\mathsf{ml}}}\right)^r$$

where G^1 *is defined as in Fig. 14.*

Applying these lemmas to Eq. 3 gives

$$\mathsf{Adv}_{\mathsf{NE}}^{\mathsf{indr}}(\mathcal{R}[\mathcal{A}]) \leqslant 2 \cdot \left(\frac{2(S + \log r + \mathsf{kl}) + 2\mathsf{ml}}{u} + \frac{3}{2^{\mathsf{ml}}}\right)^r$$
$$+ \mathsf{Adv}_{\mathsf{NE}}^{\mathsf{indr}}(\mathcal{R}[\mathcal{S}]) + 2 \cdot \mathsf{Adv}_{\mathsf{NE}}^{\mathsf{indr}}(\mathcal{C}_1) + \mathsf{Adv}_{\mathsf{NE}}^{\mathsf{indr}}(\mathcal{C}_2) .$$

To complete the proof, we combine the three INDR adversaries $\mathcal{R}[\mathcal{S}]$, $\mathcal{C}_1$, and $\mathcal{C}_2$. Let $\mathcal{C}$ be the INDR randomly chooses one of $\mathcal{R}[\mathcal{S}]$, $\mathcal{C}_1$, or $\mathcal{C}_2$ (with probabilities $1/4$, $1/2$, and $1/4$, respectively) then runs the adversary it chose, outputting whatever that adversary does. Simple calculations give

$$4 \cdot \mathsf{Adv}_{\mathsf{NE}}^{\mathsf{indr}}(\mathcal{C}_2) = \mathsf{Adv}_{\mathsf{NE}}^{\mathsf{indr}}(\mathcal{R}[\mathcal{S}]) + 2 \cdot \mathsf{Adv}_{\mathsf{NE}}^{\mathsf{indr}}(\mathcal{C}_1) + \mathsf{Adv}_{\mathsf{NE}}^{\mathsf{indr}}(\mathcal{C}_2) .$$

The claimed complexity of $\mathcal{C}$ follows from that of $\mathcal{R}[\mathcal{S}]$, $\mathcal{C}_1$, and $\mathcal{C}_2$.   □

5.2   Memory Lower Bound for Full-Rewinding Reductions

We can extend our result to cover full-rewinding reductions as captured by the following theorem. Its interpretation works similarly to that of Theorem 5.

Theorem 6 (Impossibility for full-rewinding reductions). *Let* NE *be a nonce-based encryption scheme. Fix* $u, r, c \in \mathbb{N}$. *We can construct a nonce-respecting adversary* $\mathcal{A}$ *such that for all full-rewinding, nonce-respecting, restricted reductions* $\mathcal{R}$ *from* AE-1 *to nonce-respecting* INDR *with* $\mathsf{Mem}(\mathcal{R}) = S$ *and all full-rewinding, nonce-respecting, restricted reductions* $\mathcal{R}'$ *from* AE-1 *to* CTXT-1 *there exist adversaries* $\mathcal{C}$ *and* $\mathcal{W}$ *such that,*

(i) $\mathsf{Adv}_{\mathsf{NE}}^{\mathsf{ae}\text{-}1}(\mathcal{A}) \geqslant 1 - \dfrac{2^{\mathsf{kl}}}{2^{2\mathsf{NE.cl(ml)}}}$,

(ii) $\mathsf{Adv}_{\mathsf{NE}}^{\mathsf{indr}}(\mathcal{R}[\mathcal{A}]) \leqslant 2 \cdot \left(\dfrac{2(S + \log r + \mathsf{kl}) + 2\mathsf{ml}}{u} + \dfrac{3}{2^{\mathsf{ml}}}\right)^r + \dfrac{2^{S+1}}{2^{c \cdot \mathsf{NE.cl(ml)}}} +$
$\ 6 \cdot \mathsf{Adv}_{\mathsf{NE}}^{\mathsf{indr}}(\mathcal{C})$,

(iii) $\mathsf{Adv}_{\mathsf{NE}}^{\mathsf{ctxt}\text{-}1}(\mathcal{R}'[\mathcal{A}]) \leqslant \mathsf{Adv}_{\mathsf{NE}}^{\mathsf{ctxt}\text{-}1}(\mathcal{R}'[\mathcal{W}])$.

Moreover, $\mathcal{A}$ satisfies $\mathsf{Query}(\mathcal{A}) = c + (u+1) \cdot r + 2$ *and* $\mathsf{Mem}(\mathcal{A}) \leqslant 2kl + 2ml + 2\mathsf{NE.cl}(ml) + 2\log|N| + \log u \cdot r$. *Also* $\mathcal{C}$ *and* $\mathcal{W}$ *satisfy* $\mathsf{Query}(\mathcal{C}) < \mathsf{Query}(\mathcal{R}) + \mathsf{Query}(\mathcal{A})$, $\mathsf{Time}(\mathcal{C}) \in O(\mathsf{Query}(\mathcal{A}) + \mathsf{Time}(\mathcal{R}))$, $\mathsf{Query}(\mathcal{W}) = \mathsf{Query}(\mathcal{A})$, *and* $\mathsf{Time}(\mathcal{W}) \in O(\mathsf{Query}(\mathcal{A}))$.

For interests of space, the proof of this result has been deferred to the full version. We give a very brief intuition about how this impossibility proof proceeds. We define a new adversary that is similar to $\mathcal{A}$ used for the proof of Theorem 5, but has an additional "buffer" phase before the challenge phase. In the buffer phase, it makes c encryption queries on a fixed message 0^{ml} using different nonces. The key idea is that if the reduction rewinds the adversary after going past the buffer phase and still manages to pass the challenge phase, it must have remembered the c ciphertexts. Because these c ciphertexts look random (from the INDR security of NE), the memory of the reduction has to grow with c. This rules out low memory reductions that pass the challenge phase after rewinding the adversary after going past the buffer phase. As in the previous section, we can show that if a reduction cannot pass the challenge phase, it cannot have a high advantage of breaking INDR security. If the reduction does not rewind after going past the buffer phase, we can bound its advantage analogously to the straightline reduction case.

6   Conclusions

Our work gives memory-sensitive bounds for the security of a particular construction of a channel and shows the difficulty of providing such bounds for encryption schemes. It leaves open a number of interesting questions including: (i) whether memory-sensitive bounds can be given for other practical examples of channels, (ii) whether analogous results can be shown for any robust channels [7], and (iii) whether memory-sensitive bounds can be extended to the multi-user setting.

Acknowledgements. This work was partially supported by NSF grants CNS-1719146, CNS-1553758 (CAREER), and by a Sloan Research Fellowship.

References

1. Auerbach, B., Cash, D., Fersch, M., Kiltz, E.: Memory-tight reductions. In: Katz, J., Shacham, H. (eds.) CRYPTO 2017, Part 1. LNCS, vol. 10401, pp. 101–132. Springer, Cham (2017). https://doi.org/10.1007/978-3-319-63688-7_4
2. Bellare, M., Kohno, T., Namprempre, C.: Breaking and provably repairing the ssh authenticated encryption scheme: a case study of the encode-then-encrypt-and-mac paradigm. ACM Trans. Inf. Syst. Secur. (TISSEC) **7**(2), 206–241 (2004)
3. Bellare, M., Rogaway, P.: The security of triple encryption and a framework for code-based game-playing proofs. In: Vaudenay, S. (ed.) EUROCRYPT 2006. LNCS, vol. 4004, pp. 409–426. Springer, Heidelberg (2006). https://doi.org/10.1007/11761679_25

4. Bellare, M., Tackmann, B.: The multi-user security of authenticated encryption: AES-GCM in TLS 1.3. In: Robshaw, M., Katz, J. (eds.) CRYPTO 2016, Part I. LNCS, vol. 9814, pp. 247–276. Springer, Heidelberg (2016). https://doi.org/10.1007/978-3-662-53018-4_10

5. Coretti, S., Dodis, Y., Guo, S., Steinberger, J.: Random oracles and non-uniformity. In: Nielsen, J.B., Rijmen, V. (eds.) EUROCRYPT 2018, Part I. LNCS, vol. 10820, pp. 227–258. Springer, Cham (2018). https://doi.org/10.1007/978-3-319-78381-9_9

6. Dinur, I.: On the streaming indistinguishability of a random permutation and a random function. In: Canteaut, A., Ishai, Y. (eds.) EUROCRYPT 2020, Part II. LNCS, vol. 12106, pp. 433–460. Springer, Cham (2020). https://doi.org/10.1007/978-3-030-45724-2_15

7. Fischlin, M., Günther, F., Janson, C.: Robust channels: handling unreliable networks in the record layers of QUIC and DTLS 1.3. Cryptology ePrint Archive, Report 2020/718 (2020). https://eprint.iacr.org/2020/718

8. Ghoshal, A., Tessaro, S.: On the memory-tightness of hashed ElGamal. In: Canteaut, A., Ishai, Y. (eds.) EUROCRYPT 2020, Part II. LNCS, vol. 12106, pp. 33–62. Springer, Cham (2020). https://doi.org/10.1007/978-3-030-45724-2_2

9. Iwata, T., Ohashi, K., Minematsu, K.: Breaking and repairing GCM security proofs. In: Safavi-Naini, R., Canetti, R. (eds.) CRYPTO 2012. LNCS, vol. 7417, pp. 31–49. Springer, Heidelberg (2012). https://doi.org/10.1007/978-3-642-32009-5_3

10. Jaeger, J., Tessaro, S.: Tight time-memory trade-offs for symmetric encryption. In: Ishai, Y., Rijmen, V. (eds.) EUROCRYPT 2019, Part I. LNCS, vol. 11476, pp. 467–497. Springer, Cham (2019). https://doi.org/10.1007/978-3-030-17653-2_16

11. McGrew, D.A., Viega, J.: The security and performance of the Galois/Counter Mode (GCM) of operation. In: Canteaut, A., Viswanathan, K. (eds.) INDOCRYPT 2004. LNCS, vol. 3348, pp. 343–355. Springer, Heidelberg (2004). https://doi.org/10.1007/978-3-540-30556-9_27

12. Pollard, J.M.: A Monte Carlo method for factorization. BIT Numer. Math. **15**(3), 331–334 (1975)

13. Quisquater, J.-J., Delescaille, J.-P.: How easy is collision search. New results and applications to DES. In: Brassard, G. (ed.) CRYPTO 1989. LNCS, vol. 435, pp. 408–413. Springer, New York (1990). https://doi.org/10.1007/0-387-34805-0_38

14. Rogaway, P.: Nonce-based symmetric encryption. In: Roy, B., Meier, W. (eds.) FSE 2004. LNCS, vol. 3017, pp. 348–358. Springer, Heidelberg (2004). https://doi.org/10.1007/978-3-540-25937-4_22

15. Rogaway, P., Shrimpton, T.: A provable-security treatment of the key-wrap problem. In: Vaudenay, S. (ed.) EUROCRYPT 2006. LNCS, vol. 4004, pp. 373–390. Springer, Heidelberg (2006). https://doi.org/10.1007/11761679_23

16. Tessaro, S., Thiruvengadam, A.: Provable time-memory trade-offs: symmetric cryptography against memory-bounded adversaries. In: Beimel, A., Dziembowski, S. (eds.) TCC 2018, Part I. LNCS, vol. 11239, pp. 3–32. Springer, Cham (2018). https://doi.org/10.1007/978-3-030-03807-6_1

17. Vaudenay, S.: Security flaws induced by CBC padding - applications to SSL, IPSEC, WTLS. In: Knudsen, L.R. (ed.) EUROCRYPT 2002. LNCS, vol. 2332, pp. 534–545. Springer, Heidelberg (2002). https://doi.org/10.1007/3-540-46035-7_35

18. Wang, Y., Matsuda, T., Hanaoka, G., Tanaka, K.: Memory lower bounds of reductions revisited. In: Nielsen, J.B., Rijmen, V. (eds.) EUROCRYPT 2018, Part I. LNCS, vol. 10820, pp. 61–90. Springer, Cham (2018). https://doi.org/10.1007/978-3-319-78381-9_3

Time-Space Tradeoffs and Short Collisions in Merkle-Damgård Hash Functions

Akshima[1(✉)], David Cash[1(✉)], Andrew Drucker[1(✉)], and Hoeteck Wee[2,3(✉)]

[1] University of Chicago, Chicago, USA
{akshima,davidcash}@uchicago.edu, andy.drucker@gmail.com
[2] CNRS, ENS and PSL, Paris, France
wee@di.ens.fr
[3] NTT Research, Palo Alto, USA

Abstract. We study collision-finding against Merkle-Damgård hashing in the random-oracle model by adversaries with an arbitrary S-bit auxiliary advice input about the random oracle and T queries. Recent work showed that such adversaries can find collisions (with respect to a random IV) with advantage $\Omega(ST^2/2^n)$, where n is the output length, beating the birthday bound by a factor of S. These attacks were shown to be optimal.

We observe that the collisions produced are very long, on the order of T blocks, which would limit their practical relevance. We prove several results related to improving these attacks to find shorter collisions. We first exhibit a simple attack for finding B-block-long collisions achieving advantage $\tilde{\Omega}(STB/2^n)$. We then study if this attack is optimal. We show that the prior technique based on the bit-fixing model (used for the $ST^2/2^n$ bound) provably cannot reach this bound, and towards a general result we prove there are qualitative jumps in the optimal attacks for finding length 1, length 2, and unbounded-length collisions. Namely, the optimal attacks achieve (up to logarithmic factors) on the order of $(S+T)/2^n$, $ST/2^n$ and $ST^2/2^n$ advantage. We also give an upper bound on the advantage of a restricted class of short-collision finding attacks via a new analysis on the growth of trees in random functional graphs that may be of independent interest.

1 Introduction

This work considers the security of random-oracle-based hash functions against *preprocessing* adversaries which have a bounded amount of arbitrary auxiliary information on the random oracle to help them. Attacks in this model were first considered by Hellman [11], who gave a heuristic time-space tradeoff for inverting cryptographic functions. We would like to understand the power of these attacks in the context of finding collisions in hash functions, and in particular, salted hash functions based on the widely used Merkle-Damgård paradigm.

FINDING SHORT COLLISIONS. In this work, we focus on understanding the best attacks for finding *short* collisions, as motivated by real-world applications. Concretely, we put forth and study the following conjecture:

© International Association for Cryptologic Research 2020
D. Micciancio and T. Ristenpart (Eds.): CRYPTO 2020, LNCS 12170, pp. 157–186, 2020.
https://doi.org/10.1007/978-3-030-56784-2_6

STB conjecture: The best attack with time T and space S for finding collisions of length B in salted MD hash functions built from hash functions with n-bit outputs achieves success probability $\Theta((STB + T^2)/2^n)$.

The birthday attack achieves $O(T^2/2^n)$, and we will describe an attack that achieves $O(STB/2^n)$. Short of proving circuit lower bounds, we cannot hope to rule out better attacks, except in idealized models, where we treat the underlying hash function as a random oracle.

THE AI-RO MODEL. We use the *auxiliary-input random oracle* (AI-RO) model introduced by Unruh [15], which was originally motivated by dealing with the non-uniformity of adversaries that is necessary for some applications of the random-oracle model [1]. In the AI-RO model, two parameters S, T are fixed, and adversaries are divided into two stages $(\mathcal{A}_1, \mathcal{A}_2)$: The first has unbounded access to a random function h, and computes an S-bit *auxiliary input* (or advice string) σ for $\mathcal{A}_2$. Then the second stage accepts σ as input, and gets T queries to an oracle computing h, and attempts to accomplish some goal involving the function h. We think of the adversaries as information-theoretic and ignore run-time.

Salted-collision resistance of MD hash functions at the AI-RO model was first studied by Coretti, Dodis, Guo and Steinberger (CDGS) [3]. They proved the STB conjecture in the setting $B = T$, showing an attack with success probability $ST^2/2^n$ and proving its optimality.

OUR RESULTS IN A NUTSHELL. We study the STB conjecture in the AI-RO model, studying both upper bounds (better attacks) and lower bounds (ruling out better attacks). Our contributions are as follows:

- *Upper bounds.* We present an attack with success probability $O(STB/2^n)$. The attack exploits the existence of expanding depth-B trees of size $O(B)$ in random functional graphs defined by h.

- *Limitations of prior lower bounds.* We show that the CDGS [3] techniques cannot rule out attacks with success probability ST^2/N, even for $B = 2$. In particular, the crux of the CDGS technique is a $O(ST/N)$ bound in an intermediate idealized model (that translates to an AI-RO bound with a multiplicative loss of T), and we provide a matching attack with $B = 2$ in this intermediate model.

- *A lower bound for $B = 2$.* We present new techniques to prove the STB conjecture for $B = 2$ in the AI-RO model. That is, the optimal attack achieves success probability $\Theta((ST + T^2)/N)$ for $B = 2$. This is the main technical contribution of this work. Interestingly, this means that for $B = 2$, if the space $S \leq T$, then there is no better attack than the birthday attack!

- *Bounding low-depth trees.* We rule out the existence of expanding depth-B trees of size $\tilde{O}(B^2)$ in random functional graphs, which shows that simple extensions of our attack cannot achieve success probability better than STB/N.

1.1   Prior Works

COLLISION-RESISTANCE IN THE AI-RO. We consider salted collision resistance following Dodis, Guo and Katz [6], in order to rule out trivial attacks where the adversary hardwires a collision on h. Assume, as we shall for the rest of the paper, that the function has the form $h : [N] \times [M] \to [N]$, where $[N] = [2^n]$ and $[M] = [2^m]$, which we identify with $\{0,1\}^n$ and $\{0,1\}^m$ respectively. In salted collision-resistance in the AI-RO model, the second-stage adversary gets as input a random "salt" $a \in [N]$ (along with σ), and must find $\alpha \neq \alpha' \in [M]$ such that $h(a, \alpha) = h(a, \alpha')$. The prior work obtained a bound of $O(S/N + T^2/N)$ on the success probability of any adversary, which is optimal (their result actually covers a wider parameter range and different forms of h that are not relevant for our results here). These results were interestingly proven via *compression arguments* [9,10], where it is shown that an adversary that is successful too often can be used to compress uniformly random strings, which is impossible (cf. [14] for other applications of encoding arguments in computer science and combinatorics).

In order to better model in-use hash functions, the aforementioned work of Coretti, Dodis, Guo and Steinberger examined salted-collision-finding against an MD hash function built from a random oracle h [3]. In their setting the first stage adversary works as before, but the second adversary only needs to find a collision in the iterated MD function built from h, starting at a random salt; We give precise definitions in the next section. That work showed that finding these collisions is substantially easier, giving an attack and matching lower bound of $O(ST^2/N)$. This was surprising in a sense, as it shows there exists an $S = T \approx 2^{60}$ attack against a hash function with 180-bit output, well below the birthday attack with $T \approx 2^{90}$.

A closer look at this attack reveals that the collisions it finds are very long (on the order of T blocks), so in our example the colliding messages each consist of 2^{60} blocks. While technically violating collision-resistance, this adversary is not damaging in any widely-used application we are aware of, as the colliding messages are several petabytes long. Addressing whether or not this attack, or the lower bound, can be improved to find shorter collisions is the starting point for our work.

The results of [3] did not use compression. Instead they applied a tightening of the remarkable and powerful *bit-fixing* (or *presampling*) method of Unruh [15], which we briefly recall here. In the bit-fixing random oracle (BF-RO) model, the adversary no longer receives an advice string. Instead the first stage adversary can fix, a priori, some bits P of the table of h. Then the rest of h is sampled, and the second stage attempts to find a salted collision as before. Building on Unruh's results, Coretti et al. showed (very roughly) that a bound of $O((T + P)T/N)$ on the advantage of any adversary in the BF-RO implies a bound of $O(ST^2/N)$ in the AI-RO. Moreover, the BF-RO bound was very easily proved, resulting in a simple and short proof.

1.2 This Work

Motivated by real-world hash functions like SHA-256, where $N = 2^n = 2^{256}$, $M = 2^{512}$, we are interested in parameter settings with $B \ll T$, such as $S = 2^{70}$, $T = 2^{95}$ and $B = 2^{18}$, which corresponds to computing a 256-bit digest of a 16 MB message using SHA-256. Here, (ignoring constants) the CDG bound is meaningless, since $ST^2/N > 1$, whereas the corresponding attack achieves constant advantage when $T = B \approx 2^{93}$, collisions which are several yottabytes ($= 10^{24}$ bytes) long.

We first observe that Hellman's attack (or an easy modification of the attack in [3]) can find length-B collisions with success probability roughly STB/N. We make this formal in Sect. 3.

While the attack was easy to modify for short collisions, proving that it is optimal is an entirely different matter with significant technical challenges. In order to explain them, we recall the approach of [3] used to prove the $O(ST^2/N)$ bound for salted MD. They used a technical approach (with tighter parameters) first developed by Unruh [15], which connects the AI-RO model to the *bit-fixing random oracle (BF-RO)* model (we defer the definition to the next section). Their work transfers lower bounds in the BF-RO model to lower bounds in the AI-RO model.

We show that the BF-to-AI template inherently cannot give a lower bound for finding short collisions, *because finding short collisions in the BF-RO model is relatively easy.* That is, the lower bound of the form we would need for BF-RO model simply does not hold. In the notation introduced above, we would need to show that no adversary finding length-2 collisions can do better than $O((P + T)/N)$ advantage, but we give a simple attack in BF-RO model that finds length-2 collisions with advantage $\Omega(PT/N)$. Thus another approach is required.

OUR LOWER BOUND TECHNIQUE. Given that the BF-to-AI technique cannot distinguish between short and long collision finding, we must find another approach. There are two options from the literature: The previously-mentioned compression arguments, and another lesser-known but elegant method of Impagliazzo using concentration inequalities.

Compression arguments which were previously observed [3] to be difficult (or "intractable") to apply to the setting of salted MD collision finding despite working in the original non-MD setting [6]. Given that compression was already difficult in this setting, it does not seem promising to extend it to the harder problem of short collisions.

To address these difficulties, we introduce a new technique that first applies a variant of the "constructive" Chernoff bound of Impagliazzo and Kabanets [13] to prove time-space tradeoff lower bounds. The concentration-based approach to time-space tradeoff lower bounds was, to our knowledge, first introduced by Impagliazzo in an unpublished work, and then later elucidated in an appendix [12] (there an older work of Zimand [17] is also credited). The high-level idea is to first prove that any adversary (with no advice) can succeed on any fixed $U \in [N]$ of $\Omega(S)$ of inputs with probability $\varepsilon^{\Omega(S)}$. (In some sense bounding every sufficiently large "moment of the adversary"). The argument continues by applying a concentration bound to the random variable that counts the number of winning inputs for this adversary, showing that it wins on a $O(\varepsilon)$-fraction of inputs except with probability $2^{-\Omega(S)}$. In a final elegant step, one shows that every advice string is likely to be bad via a union bound over all possible 2^S advice strings, to get a final bound of ε.

The technique of Impagliazzo gives a direct and simple proof for the optimal bound on inverting a random permutation. There are two issues in applying it to short MD collisions however. First, as we formally show later, it provably fails for salted MD hashing. The issue is that the adversary may simply succeed with probability greater than ε^S on some subsets U (see Sect. 7), so the first step cannot be carried out.

We salvage the technique by showing it is sufficient to bound the adversary's average advantage for *random* subsets U rather than *all* subsets. In the language of probability, we use a concentration bound that only needs *average* of the moments to be bounded by $\varepsilon^{\Omega(S)}$, rather than all of the moments; see Theorem 1.

So far we have been able to reduce the problem of proving a lower bound in AI-RO model to the problem of bounding the probability that an adversary with no advice can succeed on every element of a random subset of inputs. For the problems we considered, even this appeared to be complicated. To tame the complexity of these bounds, we apply compression arguments; Note that we are only proving the simpler bound needed for the Impagliazzo technique, but using compression, when previously compression was used for the problem directly. Our variation has the interesting twist that we can not only compress the random function (as other work did), but also the random subset U on which the adversary is being run. This turns out to vastly simplify such arguments.

APPLICATIONS OF OUR TECHNIQUE. We first apply our technique to reprove the $O(ST^2/N)$ bound for (non-short) collision finding against salted MD hash functions. We then turn to the question of short collisions. Proving a general bound (perhaps $O(STB/N)$) for finding length-B collisions appears to be very difficult, so we start by examining the first new case of $B = 2$.

We show that there are qualitative gaps between finding length-1 collisions, length-2 collisions, and arbitrary-length collisions. Specifically, while for length-1 collisions we have $\varepsilon = O((S + T^2)/N)$, we show that length-2 collisions are easier when $S > T$, as the optimal bound is $O((ST + T^2)/N)$. For arbitrary-length collisions there is another gap, where the optimal bound is $O(ST^2/N)$. Our bound for length-2 collisions uses our new compression approach used above.

It appears that we could, in principle, obtain similar bounds for other small length bounds like 3 and 4, but these proofs would be too long and complex for us to write down; Going to arbitrary length bounds seems to be out of reach, but there is no inherent obstruction in applying our technique to the general case with new ideas.

BOUND FOR A RESTRICTED CLASS OF ATTACKS. Given the difficulty of proving the general case, we instead consider ruling out the class of attacks that gives optimal attacks in the known cases. Roughly speaking, these attacks use auxiliary information consisting of S collisions at well-chosen points in the functional graph. In the online phase, the attack repeatedly tries to "walk" to these points by taking one "randomizing" step followed by several steps with zero-blocks.

For this class of attacks, we show that the best choice of collision points will result in $\varepsilon = O(STB/N)$. This result requires carefully analyzing the size of large, low-depth trees in random functional graphs, a result that may be of independent interest.

1.3   Discussion

ON THE NON-EXISTENCE OF NON-UNIFORM ATTACKS. A common argument against studying lower bounds for non-uniform attacks[1] is that we have no nontrivial examples of better-than-generic non-uniform attacks on real-world hash functions like SHA,-1 and that the complexity of the non-uniform advice may anyway be prohibitive. Our STB conjecture, if true, would explain the non-existence of these attacks: for small B, S where $SB \leq T$, non-uniform attacks do not achieve any advantage over the birthday attack!

OTHER RELATED WORK. In addition to Hellman's seminal work, we mention that time-space trade-offs and lower bounds for other problems, including inverting random functions and permutations and problems in the generic-group model, and other models have been investigated [2,4,5,7,16].

ACKNOWLEDGEMENTS. We thank an anonymous reviewer at CRYPTO 2020 for suggesting an improvement to Theorem 8. Previously the theorem only gave a bound of $O(STB^2/N)$. The first two authors were supported in part by NSF CNS-1453132.

2   Preliminaries

NOTATION. For non-negative integers N, k we write $[N]$ for $\{1, 2, \ldots, N\}$ and $\binom{[N]}{k}$ for the collection of size-k subsets of $[N]$. For a set X, we write X^+ for tuples of 1 or more elements of X. Random variables will be written in bold, and we write $\mathbf{x} \xleftarrow{\$} X$ to indicate that $\mathbf{x}$ is a uniform random variable on X.

MERKLE-DAMGÅRD (MD) HASHING. We consider an abstraction of plain MD hashing, where a variable-length hash function is constructed from a fixed-length compression function that is modeled as a random oracle. For integers N, M and a function $h : [N] \times [M] \to [N]$, Merkle-Damgård hashing is defined $\mathrm{MD}_h :$ $[N] \times [M]^+ \to [N]$ recursively by $\mathrm{MD}_h(a, \alpha) = h(a, \alpha)$ for $\alpha \in [M]$, and

$$\mathrm{MD}_h(a, (\alpha_1, \ldots, \alpha_B)) = h(MD_h(a, (\alpha_1, \ldots, \alpha_{B-1})), \alpha_B)$$

for $\alpha_1, \ldots, \alpha_B \in [M]$. We refer to elements of $[M]$ as *blocks*.

---

[1] An AI-adversary with S bits of advice and T queries can be compiled into a circuit of size roughly $O(S + T)$.

Game AI-CR$_{h,a}(\mathcal{A})$	Game BF-CR$_{h,a}(\mathcal{B}, \mathcal{L})$

$\sigma \leftarrow \mathcal{A}_1(h)$
 $\alpha, \alpha' \leftarrow \mathcal{A}_2^h(\sigma, a)$
 If $\alpha \neq \alpha'$ and $\mathrm{MD}_h(a, \alpha) = \mathrm{MD}_h(a, \alpha')$
    Then Return 1
 Else Return 0
	$\alpha, \alpha' \leftarrow \mathcal{B}^{h_\mathcal{L}}(a)$
	 If $\alpha \neq \alpha'$ and $\mathrm{MD}_{h_\mathcal{L}}(a, \alpha) = \mathrm{MD}_{h_\mathcal{L}}(a, \alpha')$
	    Then Return 1
	 Else Return 0

Fig. 1. Games AI-CR$_{h,a}(\mathcal{A})$ and BF-CR$_{h,a}(\mathcal{B}, \mathcal{L})$.

2.1 Collision Resistance Definitions

We recall definitions for collision resistance against preprocessing and against bit-fixing.

AUXILIARY-INPUT SECURITY. We formalize auxiliary-input security [15] for salted MD hashing as follows.

Definition 1. *For a pair of algorithms* $\mathcal{A} = (\mathcal{A}_1, \mathcal{A}_2)$, *a function* $h : [N] \times [M] \to [N]$, *and* $a \in [N]$ *we define game* AI-CR$_{h,a}(\mathcal{A})$ *in Fig. 1. We define the auxiliary-input collision-resistance advantage of* $\mathcal{A}$ *against Merkle-Damgård as*

$$\mathbf{Adv}_{\mathrm{MD}}^{\mathrm{ai\text{-}cr}}(\mathcal{A}) = \Pr[\mathrm{AI\text{-}CR}_{\mathbf{h},\mathbf{a}}(\mathcal{A}) = 1],$$

where $\mathbf{h} \xleftarrow{\$} \mathsf{Func}([N] \times [M], [N])$, $\mathbf{a} \xleftarrow{\$} [N]$ *are independent.*

We say $\mathcal{A} = (\mathcal{A}_1, \mathcal{A}_2)$ *is an* (S, T)-AI *adversary if* $\mathcal{A}_1$ *outputs* S *bits and* $\mathcal{A}_2$ *issues* T *queries to its oracle (for any inputs and oracles). We define the* (S, T)-*auxiliary-input collision resistance of Merkle-Damgård, denoted* $\mathbf{Adv}_{\mathrm{MD}}^{\mathrm{ai\text{-}cr}}(S, T)$, *as the maximum of* $\mathbf{Adv}_{\mathrm{MD}}^{\mathrm{ai\text{-}cr}}(\mathcal{A})$ *taken over all* (S, T)-AI *adversaries* $\mathcal{A}$.

We note that in our formalization, the games in the figures are not randomized, but just defined for any h and a. In the definition we use the games to define random variables by applying the game as a function to random variables $\mathbf{h}$ and $\mathbf{a}$. This has the advantage of being explicit about sample spaces when applying compression arguments.

We also consider bounded-length collisions as follows.

Definition 2. *We say a pair of algorithms* $\mathcal{A} = (\mathcal{A}_1, \mathcal{A}_2)$ *is an* (S, T, B)-AI *adversary if* $\mathcal{A}_1$ *outputs* S *bits,* $\mathcal{A}_2$ *issues* T *queries to its oracle, and the outputs of* $\mathcal{A}_2$ *each consist of* B *or fewer blocks.*

We define the (S, T, B)-*auxiliary-input collision resistance of MD, denoted* $\mathbf{Adv}_{\mathrm{MD}}^{\mathrm{ai\text{-}cr}}(S, T, B)$, *as the maximum of* $\mathbf{Adv}_{\mathrm{MD}}^{\mathrm{ai\text{-}cr}}(\mathcal{A})$ *taken over all* (S, T, B)-AI *adversaries* $\mathcal{A}$.

BIT-FIXING SECURITY. We recall the bit-fixing model of Unruh [15]. When $f : X \to Y$ is a function on some domain and range, and $\mathcal{L}$ is a list $(x_i, y_i)_{i=1}^{|\mathcal{L}|}$ where $x_i \in X$ and $y_i \in Y$ for all $i \in 1, \ldots, |\mathcal{L}|$ and all the x_i are distinct, we define $f_\mathcal{L}$

as follows:

$$f_{\mathcal{L}}(x) = \begin{cases} y_i & \text{if } \exists (x_i, y_i) \in \mathcal{L} \text{ such that } x = x_i \\ f(x) & \text{otherwise.} \end{cases}$$

In other words, $\mathcal{L}$ is a list of input/output pairs, and $f_{\mathcal{L}}$ is just f, but with outputs overwritten by the tuples in $\mathcal{L}$.

Definition 3. *Let $h : [N] \times [M] \to [N]$, and $a \in [N]$. For an adversary $\mathcal{B}$ and a list $\mathcal{L}$ of input/output pairs for h we define* $\mathsf{BF\text{-}CR}_{h,a}(\mathcal{B}, \mathcal{L})$ *in Fig. 1. We define the* bit-fixing collision-resistance advantage *of $(\mathcal{B}, \mathcal{L})$ against Merkle-Damgård as*

$$\mathbf{Adv}_{\mathrm{MD}}^{\mathrm{bf\text{-}cr}}(\mathcal{B}, \mathcal{L}) = \Pr[\mathsf{BF\text{-}CR}_{h,a}(\mathcal{B}, \mathcal{L}) = 1],$$

where $h \xleftarrow{\$} \mathsf{Func}([N] \times [M], [N])$, $\mathbf{a} \xleftarrow{\$} [N]$ *are independent.*

We say $(\mathcal{B}, \mathcal{L})$ is an (P, T)-BF adversary if $\mathcal{L}$ has at most P entries and $\mathcal{B}$ issues T queries to its oracle (for any inputs and oracles). We define the (P, T)-bit-fixing collision resistance of MD, denoted $\mathbf{Adv}_{\mathrm{MD}}^{\mathrm{bf\text{-}cr}}(P, T)$, as the maximum of $\mathbf{Adv}_{\mathrm{MD}}^{\mathrm{bf\text{-}cr}}(\mathcal{B}, \mathcal{L})$ taken over all (P, T)-BF adversaries $(\mathcal{B}, \mathcal{L})$.

As with AI security, we also consider bounded-length collision resistance against BF adversaries.

Definition 4. *We say $(\mathcal{B}, \mathcal{L})$ is an (P, T, B)-BF adversary if $\mathcal{L}$ has at most P entries, $\mathcal{B}$ issues T queries to its oracle (for any inputs and oracles) and the outputs of $\mathcal{B}$ each consist of B or fewer blocks. We define the (P, T, B)-bit-fixing collision resistance of MD, denoted $\mathbf{Adv}_{\mathrm{MD}}^{\mathrm{bf\text{-}cr}}(P, T, B)$, as the maximum of $\mathbf{Adv}_{\mathrm{MD}}^{\mathrm{bf\text{-}cr}}(\mathcal{B}, \mathcal{L})$ taken over all (P, T, B)-BF adversaries $(\mathcal{B}, \mathcal{L})$.*

CHERNOFF BOUNDS. We will use the following variant of the Chernoff-type bound proved by Impagliazzo and Kabanets [13]. It essentially says that if the uth moments of a sum are bounded on average, then we can conclude the sum is tightly concentrated, up to some dependence on u. Note that $\mathbf{X}_1, \dots, \mathbf{X}_N$ are not assumed independent.

Theorem 1. *Let $0 < \delta < 1$ and let $\mathbf{X}_1, \cdots, \mathbf{X}_N$ be $0/1$ random variables, $\mathbf{X} = \mathbf{X}_1 + \cdots \mathbf{X}_N$, and let $\mathbf{U}$ be an independent random subset of $[N]$ of size u. Assume*

$$\Pr[\bigwedge_{i \in \mathbf{U}} \mathbf{X}_i] \leq \delta^u.$$

Then

$$\Pr[\mathbf{X} \geq \max\{6\delta N, u\}] \leq 2^{-u}.$$

In their original version, instead of a random set $\mathbf{U}$ it was required that the first inequality hold for all sets U of size u (so all u^{th} moments must be bounded). It is easy to show that our weaker condition is still sufficient, and the proof of this version is almost identical and given in the appendix (Sect. 8) only for completeness.

We will also apply the following standard multiplicative Chernoff bound in Sect. 8.

Theorem 2. *Let $0 < \delta < 1$ and let $\mathbf{X}_1, \cdots, \mathbf{X}_N$ be independent $0/1$ random variables and put $\mathbf{X} = \mathbf{X}_1 + \cdots \mathbf{X}_N$. Then*

$$\Pr[\mathbf{X} \geq (1 + \delta) \cdot E[\mathbf{X}]] \leq \exp\left(\frac{-\delta^2 \cdot E[\mathbf{X}]}{2 + \delta}\right).$$

3   Bounded-Length Auxiliary-Input Attack

Coretti et al. [2] gave an $\Omega(ST^2)$ attack where the adversary gets S-bit advice and T oracle queries to find (unbounded length) collisions against MD^h. It is easy to adapt the attack to find length B collisions with advantage $\Omega(STB)$.

   We describe this attack and its analysis in the full version.

Theorem 3. *For any positive integers S, T, B such that $B \leq T < N/4$, $STB \leq N/2$ and $M \geq N$,*

$$\mathbf{Adv}_{\mathrm{MD}}^{\mathrm{ai\text{-}cr}}(S, T, B) \geq \frac{STB - 96S}{48N \log N}.$$

4   Length 2 Collisions Are Relatively Easy in the BF Model

Unruh in [15] proved a remarkable general relationship between the AI-RO and BF-RO models that was sharpened by Coretti et al. [2]. We recall their theorem now, and then show that this method, when applied to salted MD hashing, is insensitive to the length of collisions found and hence cannot give the improved bound we seek in the AI-RO model. We note that the second part of this theorem was not stated there, but follows exactly from their proof.

Theorem 4. *For any positive integers S, T, P and $\gamma > 0$ such that $P \geq (S + \log \gamma^{-1})T$,*

$$\mathbf{Adv}_{\mathrm{MD}}^{\mathrm{ai\text{-}cr}}(S, T) \leq 2\mathbf{Adv}_{\mathrm{MD}}^{\mathrm{bf\text{-}cr}}(P, T) + \gamma.$$

Moreover, for any positive integer B,

$$\mathbf{Adv}_{\mathrm{MD}}^{\mathrm{ai\text{-}cr}}(S, T, B) \leq 2\mathbf{Adv}_{\mathrm{MD}}^{\mathrm{bf\text{-}cr}}(P, T, B) + \gamma.$$

   The following is a simple extension of an attack of [3], which shows that finding even just length-2 collisions in the BF model is much easier than finding length-1 collisions, and in fact is as easy as finding general length collisions.

Theorem 5. *For all positive integers P, T such that $PT \leq 2N$, there exists a $(P, T, 2)$-BF adversary $(\mathcal{B}, \mathcal{L})$ such that*

$$\mathbf{Adv}_{\mathrm{MD}}^{\mathrm{bf\text{-}cr}}(\mathcal{B}, \mathcal{L}) \geq \left(1 - \frac{1}{e}\right)\frac{PT}{2N}.$$

Proof. We construct a $(P, T, 2)$-BF adversary $(\mathcal{B}, \mathcal{L})$ to prove the theorem. We assume P is even for simplicity of notation. To define the list $\mathcal{L}$, let $\alpha, \alpha' \in [M], a_1, \ldots, a_{P/2}, y \in [N]$ be some arbitrary points, and let $\mathcal{L}$ consist of the P entries

$$((a_1, \alpha), y), \ ((a_1, \alpha'), y), \ \ldots \ ((a_{P/2}, \alpha), y), \ ((a_{P/2}, \alpha'), y).$$

Adversary $\mathcal{B}$ does the following on input a and oracle $h_{\mathcal{L}}$: Let $\alpha_1, \cdots, \alpha_T \in [M]$ be arbitrary distinct points. For $j = 1, \ldots, T$, query (a, α_j) to the oracle $h_{\mathcal{L}}$. If the output is an element of $\{a_1, \ldots, a_{P/2}\}$, then output colliding messages $\alpha_j \| \alpha$ and $\alpha_j \| \alpha'$.

We lower bound $\mathbf{Adv}_{\mathrm{MD}}^{\mathrm{bf\text{-}cr}}(\mathcal{B}, \mathcal{L})$. Let E be the event that the output of some query made by $\mathcal{B}$ is in the set $\{a_1, \ldots, a_{P/2}\}$. Clearly, when E happens, our adversary wins the game. Thus

$$\mathbf{Adv}_{\mathrm{MD}}^{\mathrm{bf\text{-}cr}}(\mathcal{B}, \mathcal{L}) \geq 1 - \Pr[\neg E] \geq 1 - \left(1 - \frac{P}{2N}\right)^T \geq 1 - e^{-PT/2N} \geq \left(1 - \frac{1}{e}\right)\frac{PT}{2N}$$

where the last inequality holds because $0 \leq \frac{PT}{2N} \leq 1$. $\square$

This adversary shows that applying Theorem 4 can at best give $\mathbf{Adv}_{\mathrm{MD}}^{\mathrm{ai\text{-}cr}}(S, T, 2) = O(ST^2/N)$, which we show to be suboptimal in Sect. 6, where using compression techniques we prove a bound of $\tilde{\mathrm{O}}\,(ST/N)$.

5   Unbounded Length Collision AI Bound

In this section we give a different proof of the $O(ST^2)$ bound of Coretti et al. [2], formalized as follows.

Theorem 6. *For any positive integers S, T,*

$$\mathbf{Adv}_{\mathrm{MD}}^{\mathrm{ai\text{-}cr}}(S, T) \leq \frac{192e(S + \log N)T^2 + 1}{N}.$$

Following Impagliazzo [13], we proceed by analyzing an adversary without auxilliary input "locally."

Definition 5. *For a pair of algorithms $\mathcal{A} = (\mathcal{A}_1, \mathcal{A}_2)$ and positive integer u we define*

$$\mathbf{Adv}_{\mathrm{MD}}^{u\text{-}ai\text{-}cr}(\mathcal{A}) = \Pr[\forall a \in \mathbf{U} \ : \ \mathsf{AI\text{-}CR}_{\mathbf{h}, a}(\mathcal{A}) = 1],$$

where $\mathbf{h} \xleftarrow{\$} \mathsf{Func}([N] \times [M], [N])$, and $\mathbf{U} \xleftarrow{\$} \binom{[N]}{u}$ are independent.

Lemma 1. *For any positive integers S, T, u, and $\hat{\sigma} \in \{0, 1\}^S$, let $\mathcal{A} = (\mathcal{A}_1, \mathcal{A}_2)$ be an adversary where $\mathcal{A}_1$ always outputs $\hat{\sigma}$, and $\mathcal{A}_2$ issues T queries to its oracle. Then*

$$\mathbf{Adv}_{\mathrm{MD}}^{u\text{-}ai\text{-}cr}(\mathcal{A}) \leq \left(\frac{32euT^2}{N}\right)^u.$$

This lemma is proved below. We first prove the theorem using the lemma.

Proof of Theorem 6. Let $\mathcal{A} = (\mathcal{A}_1, \mathcal{A}_2)$ be an (S, T)-AI adversary. We need to bound $\mathbf{Adv}_{\mathrm{MD}}^{\mathrm{ai\text{-}cr}}(\mathcal{A})$ as in the theorem. Call h *easy for adversary* $\mathcal{A}$ if

$$\Pr[\mathsf{AI\text{-}CR}_{h,a}(\mathcal{A}) = 1] \geq \frac{192e(S + \log N)T^2}{N}.$$

We will first show that h is unlikely to be easy for $\mathcal{A}$, no matter how $\mathcal{A}_1$ computes its S advice bits. Below, for each $\hat{\sigma} \in \{0, 1\}^S$ let $\mathcal{A}_{\hat{\sigma}}$ be $\mathcal{A}$, except with $\mathcal{A}_1$ replaced by an algorithm that always outputs $\hat{\sigma}$.

Fix some $\hat{\sigma} \in \{0, 1\}^S$. For each $a \in [N]$ let $\mathbf{X}_a$ be an indicator random variable for the event that $\mathsf{AI\text{-}CR}_{h,a}(\mathcal{A}_{\hat{\sigma}}) = 1$. By Lemma 1 we have $\Pr[\bigwedge_{a \in \mathbf{U}} \mathbf{X}_a] \leq \delta^u$ for any u and $\delta = 32euT^2/N$. Then by Theorem 1 with $u = S + \log N$, we have

$$\Pr[\mathbf{h} \text{ is easy for } \mathcal{A}_{\hat{\sigma}}] = \Pr[\sum_{a=1}^{N} \mathbf{X}_a \geq 192euT^2] \leq 2^{-(S + \log N)}.$$

Let E be the event that there exists $\hat{\sigma} \in \{0, 1\}^S$ such that $\mathbf{h}$ is easy for $\mathcal{A}_{\hat{\sigma}}$. By a union bound over $\hat{\sigma} \in \{0, 1\}^S$,

$$\Pr[E] \leq 2^S 2^{-(S + \log N)} = 1/N.$$

Finally we have

$$\Pr[\mathsf{AI\text{-}CR}_{\mathbf{h},\mathbf{a}}(\mathcal{A}) = 1] \leq \Pr[\mathsf{AI\text{-}CR}_{\mathbf{h},\mathbf{a}}(\mathcal{A}) = 1 | \neg E] + \Pr[E]$$

$$\leq \frac{192e(S + \log N)T^2}{N} + \frac{1}{N}.$$

The last inequality holds because for each $h \notin E$,

$$\Pr[\mathsf{AI\text{-}CR}_{h,\mathbf{a}}(\mathcal{A}) = 1] \leq \max_{\hat{\sigma} \in \{0,1\}^S} \Pr[\mathsf{AI\text{-}CR}_{h,\mathbf{a}}(\mathcal{A}_{\hat{\sigma}}) = 1] \leq \frac{192e(S + \log N)T^2}{N}.$$

Since this holds for any (S, T)-AI adversary $\mathcal{A}$, we obtain the lemma. $\square$

5.1   Proof of Lemma 1

COLLIDING CHAINS. We start with some useful definitions and a simplifying lemma.

Definition 6. *Let* $h : [N] \times [M] \to [N]$. *A list of elements* $(x_0, \alpha_0), \ldots, (x_\ell, \alpha_\ell)$ *from* $[N] \times [M]$ *is called an* MD-chain *(for h) when* $h(x_i, \alpha_i) = x_{i+1}$ *for* $i = 0, \ldots, \ell - 1$. *We say two chains* $(x_0, \alpha_0), \ldots (x_\ell, \alpha_\ell)$ *and* $(x'_0, \alpha'_0), \ldots (x'_{\ell'}, \alpha'_{\ell'})$ *collide (for h) if* $h(x_\ell, \alpha_\ell) = h(x'_{\ell'}, \alpha'_{\ell'})$.

We will treat chains as strings (over $[N] \times [M]$) and speak of prefixes and suffixes with their usual meaning.

Lemma 2. *Let C, C' be distinct non-empty colliding chains for h. Then C, C' contain prefixes $\tilde{C}, \tilde{C}'$ respectively, $\tilde{C} = (x_0, \alpha_0), \ldots (x_\ell, \alpha_\ell)$ and $\tilde{C}' = (x'_0, \alpha'_0), \ldots (x'_{\ell'}, \alpha'_{\ell'})$, such that either $(x_\ell, \alpha_\ell) \neq (x'_{\ell'}, \alpha'_{\ell'})$ or one of $\tilde{C}, \tilde{C}'$ is a strict suffix of the other.*

Proof. Induction on the maximum length of C, C'. For length 1 this is obvious. For the inductive step, suppose neither is a strict suffix of the other, and that the final entries are equal. Then we can remove the final entries from both chains to get two non-empty shorter chains and apply the inductive hypothesis.   □

PROOF OF LEMMA 1. We prove the lemma by compression. Let $\mathbf{U} \xleftarrow{\$} \binom{[N]}{u}$ and $\mathbf{h} \xleftarrow{\$} \mathsf{Func}([N] \times [M], [N])$ be independent. Let $\mathcal{A} = (\mathcal{A}_1, \mathcal{A}_2)$ be an (S, T)-AI adversary where $\mathcal{A}_1$ always outputs some fixed string $\hat{\sigma}$. Observe that if, for all $a \in \mathbf{U}$, $\mathcal{A}_2$ never queries a point of $\mathbf{h}$ with input salt $a' \in \mathbf{U}, a \neq a'$ among the T queries it makes for input a, and also that the chains produced for each a are disjoint from the chains for a', then it is relatively simple to carry out a compression argument, by storing two pointers $[T]$ to compress an entry in $[N]$ (which would translate to a bound of $(T^2/N)^u$). But of course $\mathcal{A}$ might "cross up" queries for the different salts. If we tried to prove a version of the lemma for *all* $U \subseteq \binom{[N]}{u}$ (as was done in the original context of the appendix in [12]) rather than a random $\mathbf{U}$, then the adversary could be specialized for the set U; In Sect. 7 we give an attack that finds collisions of $B = 2$ for a fixed subset with greater probability than the upper bound on the advantage of attacking a random subset of same size.

Also, when we choose $\mathbf{U}$ at random, a fixed $\mathcal{A}$ can't be specialized for the set, and the "crossed up" queries between salts are unlikely. Formally, if $\mathcal{A}$ queries a salt $a' \in \mathbf{U}$ while attacking $a \in \mathbf{U}$, we take advantage of this by *compressing an entry of the random set* $\mathbf{U}$ when a crossed-up query occurs. Very roughly, this requires a pointer in $[T]$ and saves a factor N/S (because we are omitting one entry from an (unordered) set of size about S). The net compression is then about ST/N per crossed-up query. The details are a bit more complicated, as this compression actually experiences a smooth trade-off as more such queries are compressed and the set shrinks. We handle the case when the chains for $a \neq a'$ intersect via a simpler strategy that also results in ST/N factors.

Once the crossed-up queries are handled, the proof effectively reduces to the simpler case without crossed-up queries.

Proof. For the rest of the proof we fix some $\mathcal{A} = (\mathcal{A}_1, \mathcal{A}_2)$, where $\mathcal{A}_1$ always outputs some fixed $\hat{\sigma}$. Let

$$\mathcal{G} = \{(U, h) \mid \forall a \in U : \mathsf{AI\text{-}CR}_{h,a}(\mathcal{A}) = 1\} \subseteq \binom{[N]}{u} \times \mathcal{H}.$$

Let

$$\varepsilon = \mathbf{Adv}^{u\text{-}ai\text{-}cr}_{\mathrm{MD}}(\mathcal{A}).$$

So $|\mathcal{G}| = \varepsilon\binom{N}{u}N^{MN}$. We define an injection

$$f : \mathcal{G} \to \{0,1\}^L$$

with L satisfying

$$\frac{2^L}{\binom{N}{u}N^{MN}} \leq \left(\frac{32euT^2}{N}\right)^u.$$

Pigeonhole then immediately gives the bound on ε.

For $(U, h) \in \mathcal{G}$, $f(U, h)$ outputs an L-bit encoding, where L will be determined below, of

$$(F, U_{\mathsf{Fresh}}, \mathsf{Pred}, \mathsf{Cases}, \mathsf{Coll}, \tilde{h}),$$

where the first output F is an integer between 1 and u, U_{Fresh} is a subset of U of size F, Pred is a set of pointers, Cases is a list of elements in $\{1a, 1b, 2\}$, and Coll is a list of pairs of pointers, and the last output $\tilde{h}$ is h but rearranged and with some entries deleted. We now define these outputs in order.

FRESH SALTS AND PREDICTION QUERIES. Fix some $(U, h) \in \mathcal{G}$, and let $U = \{a_1, \ldots, a_u\}$, where the a_i are in lexicographic order. Let $\mathsf{Qrs}(a_i) \in ([N] \times [M])^T$ denote the queries $\mathcal{A}_2$ makes to its oracle when run on input $(\hat{\sigma}, a_i)$. Let us abuse notation by writing $a_i \notin \mathsf{Qrs}(a_j)$ to mean that a_i is not the first component of any entry in $\mathsf{Qrs}(a_j)$ (in other words, the salt a_i is not queried when $\mathcal{A}_2$ runs on a_j).

We define $U_{\mathsf{Fresh}} \subseteq U$ inductively by

$$a_i \in U_{\mathsf{Fresh}} \iff \forall 1 \leq j < i : a_j \in U_{\mathsf{Fresh}} \implies a_i \notin \mathsf{Qrs}(a_j).$$

The set U_{Fresh} trivially contains a_1. For $i > 1$, $a_i \in U_{\mathsf{Fresh}}$ if no prior salt in U_{Fresh} causes $\mathcal{A}_2$ to query a_i. Conversely, for any $a_i \in U \setminus U_{\mathsf{Fresh}}$, there is a prior salt $a_j \in U_{\mathsf{Fresh}}$ such that $a_i \in \mathsf{Qrs}(a_j)$.

Let us denote the size of U_{Fresh} by F, and let us write $U_{\mathsf{Fresh}} = \{a'_1, \ldots, a'_F\}$ where the a'_j are in lexicographic order. From now on we will only need to deal with the queries issued when the adversary is run on fresh salts. Let $Q_j = \mathsf{Qrs}(a'_j)$ for $j = 1, \ldots, F$ and

$$Q_{\mathsf{Fresh}} = Q_1 \| \cdots \| Q_F \in ([N] \times [M])^{FT}.$$

Going forward, we will sometimes use indices from $[FT]$ to point to queries in Q_{Fresh} and sometimes indices from $[T]$ to point to queries in Q_j for some j.

For each $a \in U \setminus U_{\mathsf{Fresh}}$, there exists a minimum $t_a \in [FT]$ such that $Q_{\mathsf{Fresh}}[t_a]$ is a query with input salt a. We define $\mathsf{Pred} \subseteq [FT]$, the *prediction queries*, to be

$$\mathsf{Pred} = \{t_a \mid a \in U \setminus U_{\mathsf{Fresh}}\} \subseteq [FT].$$

We have $|\mathsf{Pred}| = u - F$.

NEW AND OLD QUERIES. Call an index $r \in [FT]$ *new* if $Q_{\mathsf{Fresh}}[r]$ does not appear earlier in Q_{Fresh} (more precisely, if $s < r$ implies $Q_{\mathsf{Fresh}}[s] \neq Q_{\mathsf{Fresh}}[r]$). For $j \in [F]$

we will speak of an index $t \in [T]$ being *new* in Q_j, technically meaning that $(j-1)T + t \in [FT]$ is new. Since we assume that the queries in Q_j are distinct, $Q_j[t]$ being new is equivalent to $Q_j[t]$ not appearing in $Q_1 \| \cdots \| Q_{j-1}$. When a query is not new, we say it is *old*.

Claim. Let $Q_{\mathsf{Fresh}} = Q_1 \| \cdots \| Q_F \in ([N] \times [M])^{FT}$ be defined as above. Then for each j, at least one of the following cases holds:

1. (a) There exists $s_j \in [T]$ such that s_j is new in Q_j and $h(Q_j[s_j]) = a'_j$,
   (b) There exists $s'_j < s_j \in [T]$ such that s_j and s'_j are new in Q_j and $h(Q_j[s_j]) = h(Q_j[s'_j])$
2. There exists $s_j \in [T]$ and $s'_j \in [FT]$ such that s_j is new in Q_j, s'_j points to query in $Q_1 \| \ldots \| Q_{j-1}$, and $h(Q_j[s_j])$ equals the input salt of $Q_{\mathsf{Fresh}}[s'_j]$.

These cases are depicted in Fig. 2.

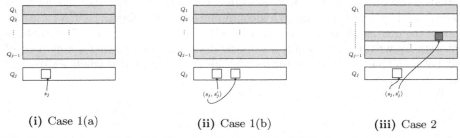

(i) Case 1(a)   (ii) Case 1(b)   (iii) Case 2

Fig. 2. Cases from Claim 5.1. Box denotes an index. White box denotes query at the index is new.

Proof of claim. For each j, Q_j contains a pair of colliding chains that both start from a'_j. Either some query in the chains is old, or else all the queries in both chains are new.

Suppose first that some query is old, and focus on the chain containing the old query. Since a'_j is fresh, this old query cannot be the first query of the chain. Thus, starting from the beginning of this chain, we eventually reach a query that is new but the next query is old. Because these queries form a chain, this new query will output the old query's input salt. So we take s_j to point to this new query in Q_j, and s'_j to point to the earlier query in $Q_1 \| \cdots \| Q_{j-1}$, and Case 2 of the claim holds.

Now suppose that all queries in the chains are new. By Lemma 2, we can assume without loss of generality that either the last queries of the chains are distinct, or that one chain is a strict suffix of the other. If the chains have distinct final queries, then we can take s_j, s'_j to point to these distinct (new) queries in Q_j and Case 1b of the claim holds. If one chain is a strict suffix of the other, then the longer chain must contain a (new) query that outputs a'_j, since both chains start with salt a'_j. Then Case 1a of the claim holds. $\qquad\square$

DEFINITION OF f. On input (U, h), $f(U, h)$ first computes U_{Fresh} and Pred as defined above. It then computes $\mathsf{Q}_{\mathsf{Fresh}}$, and Q_j for each $j = 1, \ldots, F$. It initializes: (1) Array Cases and Coll, each of size F, the latter of which will hold entries from domains depending on cases, (2) $\tilde{h}$ to be the table of h, but sorted to contain the responses for $\mathsf{Q}_{\mathsf{Fresh}}$, followed by the rest of the table in lexicographic order.

For $j = 1, \ldots, F$, f examines Q_j and determines which of the cases in the claim occurs. It sets $\mathsf{Cases}[j] \in \{1a, 1b, 2\}$ and performs one of the following:

Case 1a: Set $\mathsf{Coll}[j] \leftarrow s_j \in [T]$ and delete the entry corresponding to $\mathsf{Q}_j[s_j]$ from $\tilde{h}$.

Case 1b: Set $\mathsf{Coll}[j] \leftarrow (s_j, s_j') \in [T] \times [T]$ and delete the entry corresponding to query $\mathsf{Q}_j[s_j]$ from $\tilde{h}$.

Case 2: Set $\mathsf{Coll}[j] \leftarrow (s_j, s_j') \in [T] \times [FT]$ and delete the entry corresponding to query $\mathsf{Q}_j[s_j]$ from $\tilde{h}$.

This completes the description of f. After this process, $\tilde{h}$ consists of the responses to the queries of $\mathcal{A}_2$ when it is run on the salts in U_{Fresh}, except for the deleted queries, followed by the remaining outputs of h in lexicographic order. Since at least one case always holds by the claim, and we delete exactly one new query from each Q_j, we have $\tilde{h} \in [N]^{MN-F}$.

ANALYSIS OF f. We first argue that the output length of f is not too long, and later that is it injective. Let the number of salts in U_{Fresh} having compression type 1a, 1b and 2 be δ_1, δ_1' and δ_2, respectively. Then $F = \delta_1 + \delta_1' + \delta_2$. We set the output length L to the maximum of the following expression, over $1 \leq F \leq u$, and $\delta_1 + \delta_1' + \delta_2 = F$, rounded to the next integer:

$$\log \left(u \cdot 2^{2F} \binom{N}{F} \binom{FT}{u-F} T^{\delta_1} T^{2\delta_1'} (FT^2)^{\delta_2} N^{MN-F} \right).$$

This formula is explained by considering the outputs of f in turn:

- F and U_{Fresh} account for $\log u + \log \binom{N}{F}$ bits together,
- Pred needs $\log \binom{FT}{u-F}$ bits,
- Cases is an array of size F, storing a ternary value in each entry, and thus less than $2F$ bits total,
- Coll stores $\delta_1 \log T + \delta_1' \log T^2 + \delta_2 \log FT^2$ bits,
- $\tilde{h}$ stores $(MN - F) \log N$ bits.

We have

$$\frac{2^L}{\binom{N}{u} N^{MN}} \leq \max_{F = \delta_1 + \delta_1' + \delta_2} u \cdot 2^{2F} \cdot \frac{\binom{N}{F}\binom{FT}{u-F}}{\binom{N}{u}} \cdot \left(\frac{T^{\delta_1} \cdot (T^2)^{\delta_1'} \cdot (FT^2)^{\delta_2}}{N^F} \right).$$

We bound the middle term by

$$\frac{\binom{N}{F}\binom{FT}{u-F}}{\binom{N}{u}} \leq \left(\frac{eN}{F} \right)^F \left(\frac{u}{N} \right)^u \left(\frac{eFT}{u-F} \right)^{u-F} = \left(\frac{eu}{F} \right)^F \left(\frac{euFT}{N(u-F)} \right)^{u-F}$$

$$\leq \left(e2^{u/F} \right)^F \left(\frac{e2^{u/(u-F)}FT}{N} \right)^{u-F} \leq (4e)^u \left(\frac{FT}{N} \right)^{u-F}.$$

Assuming f is injective, by pigeonhole we have $2^L \geq \varepsilon \binom{N}{u} N^{MN}$. Plugging this in and using $F \leq u \leq 2^u$, we obtain

$$\varepsilon \leq \max_{F=\delta_1+\delta_1'+\delta_2} (32e)^u \left(\frac{FT}{N}\right)^{u-F} \left(\frac{T}{N}\right)^{\delta_1} \left(\frac{T^2}{N}\right)^{\delta_1'} \left(\frac{FT^2}{N}\right)^{\delta_2} \leq \left(\frac{32euT^2}{N}\right)^u.$$

It remains to show that f is injective, i.e. that (U, h) is determined by $f(U, h) = (F, U_{\mathsf{Fresh}}, \mathsf{Pred}, \mathsf{Cases}, \mathsf{Coll}, \tilde{h})$. The inversion algorithm works as follows:

1. Decode the binary input by reading off F from the first $\log u$ bits. The size of U_{Fresh}, Pred, and Cases are determiend by F. Then Coll can be parsed out using Cases, and finally $\tilde{h}$ can be parsed out easily.
2. Initialize h and $\mathsf{Q}_{\mathsf{Fresh}}$ to be empty tables.
3. For each $a_j' \in U_{\mathsf{Fresh}}$ (in lexicographic order) the j-th entry of Cases indicates the type of tuple of pointers stored in the j-th entry of Coll. Run $\mathcal{A}_2$ on a_j'. Respond to queries using the entries of $\tilde{h}$ in order (except if the query is a repeat) and populating the entries of h and $\mathsf{Q}_{\mathsf{Fresh}}$ except when one of the following happens:
   (a) For $\mathsf{Cases}[j] = 1\mathrm{a}$, when $\mathsf{Q}_j[s_j]$ is queried, respond to the query with a_j'.
   (b) For $\mathsf{Cases}[j] = 1\mathrm{b}$, when $\mathsf{Q}_j[s_j]$ is queried, respond with $h(\mathsf{Q}_j[s_j'])$ (using the partial table for h).
   (c) For $\mathsf{Cases}[j] = 2$, when $\mathsf{Q}_j[s_j]$ is queried, respond with the input salt of query $\mathsf{Q}_{\mathsf{Fresh}}[s_j']$.
   After responding, continue running $\mathcal{A}_2$ on a_j' and populating the tables.
4. After running $\mathcal{A}_2$ on all of the salts in U_{Fresh}, populate the rest of h using the remaining entries of $\tilde{h}$ in order.
5. Finally, examine the queries $\mathsf{Q}_{\mathsf{Fresh}}$, and form U by adding the salts pointed to by the indices of Pred to U_{Fresh}. (More formally, output $U = U_{\mathsf{Fresh}} \cup \{\text{input salt of } \mathsf{Q}_{\mathsf{Fresh}}[t] : t \in \mathsf{Pred}\}$.)

We first argue inversion replies to the queries issued by $\mathcal{A}_2$ on a_j' correctly, for each $a_j' \in U_{\mathsf{Fresh}}$. For queries that are not deleted from $\tilde{h}$, these are simply copied from $\tilde{h}$. By construction and Claim 5.1, the queries that were deleted will be copied correctly. Finally, once $\mathsf{Q}_{\mathsf{Fresh}}$ is correctly computed, we have that U is correctly recovered. □

6   Length 2 Collision AI Bound

We next prove an upper bound on the advantage of an adversary producing collisions of length at most 2.

Theorem 7. *For any positive integers* S, T,

$$\mathbf{Adv}_{\mathsf{MD}}^{\mathrm{ai\text{-}cr}}(S, T, 2) \leq 6 \cdot (2^9 e^3) \max\left\{\left(\frac{(S + \log N)T}{N}\right), \left(\frac{T^2}{N}\right)\right\} + \frac{1}{N}.$$

We prove this theorem in exactly the same fashion as Theorem 6, where an adversary is analyzed without auxiliary input "locally," as in the lemma below.

Proving the theorem from this lemma is similar to before, and omitted here but given in the full version.

Lemma 3. *For any positive integers S, T, u, and $\hat{\sigma} \in \{0,1\}^S$, let $\mathcal{A} = (\mathcal{A}_1, \mathcal{A}_2)$ be an adversary where $\mathcal{A}_1$ always outputs $\hat{\sigma}$, and $\mathcal{A}_2$ issues T queries to its oracle and attempts to output a collision of length at most 2. Then*

$$\mathbf{Adv}_{\mathrm{MD}}^{u\text{-ai-cr}}(\mathcal{A}) \leq (2^9 e^3)^u \max\left\{ \left(\frac{uT}{N}\right)^u, \left(\frac{T^2}{N}\right)^u \right\}.$$

6.1   Proof for Lemma 3

INTUITION. At a high level this proof is similar to that of Lemma 1. The primary difference is that we must avoid the ST^2 factors that come from chains hitting old edges. This turns out to be quite subtle, as the adversary may have generated some structures involving collisions in early queries and later hit them. But if we try to compress these structures preemptively, we find they are not profitable (i.e. the required pointers are bigger than the savings). In our proof, however, this strategy is actually a gambit: We make some losing moves up front, and then later are able to compress multiple edges and eventually profit. Looking forward, this happens for either version of Case 4 in Fig. 4, where the early edges are blue. There it is not profitable to compress the second blue edge on its own, but we later get a super-profit by compressing one or two black edges, resulting in a net compression.

We now proceed with the formal compression proof. Let $\mathcal{A} = (\mathcal{A}_1, \mathcal{A}_2)$ be an adversary as specified in the lemma. Let

$$\mathcal{G} = \{(U, h) \mid \forall a \in U : \mathsf{AI\text{-}CR}_{h,a}(\mathcal{A}) = 1\} \subseteq \binom{[N]}{u} \times \mathcal{H}.$$

and $\varepsilon = \mathbf{Adv}_{\mathrm{MD}}^{u\text{-ai-cr}}(\mathcal{A})$, so $|\mathcal{G}| = \varepsilon\binom{N}{u}N^{MN}$. We define an injection

$$f : \mathcal{G} \to \{0,1\}^L$$

with L satisfying

$$\frac{|\{0,1\}^L|}{\binom{N}{u}N^{MN}} \leq (2^9 e^3)^u \left(\frac{\max\{T^2, uT\}}{N}\right)^u.$$

Pigeonhole again immediately gives the bound on ε.

For $(U, h) \in \mathcal{G}$, $f(U, h)$ outputs an L-bit encoding, where L will be determined below, of

$$(F, U_{\mathsf{Fresh}}, \mathsf{Pred}, \mathsf{Cases}, \mathsf{Coll}, \mathsf{Loops}, \mathsf{Bulbs}, \mathsf{Diamonds}, \tilde{h}),$$

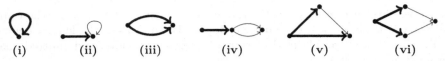

Fig. 3. Types of queries *used* to obtain colliding chains for $B = 2$. Bold arrows indicate that the query is necessarily new.

which we define below. The first, second and third outputs F, U_{Fresh} and Pred are computed *exactly* as in the proof of Lemma 1, and in particular $U_{\mathsf{Fresh}} \subseteq U$ and $\mathsf{Pred} \subseteq [FT]$, $|\mathsf{Pred}| = u - F$, where $|U_{\mathsf{Fresh}}| = F$.

In order to describe the remaining outputs of f, we need some definitions. Write $U_{\mathsf{Fresh}} = \{a'_1, \cdots, a'_F\}$ and let $\mathsf{Q}_{\mathsf{Fresh}}$ and Q_j be defined exactly as in the proof of Lemma 1. Without loss of generality, for each $j \in [F]$, we assume that an adversary makes distinct queries in Q_j. In other words, for each fresh salt a'_j, $\mathsf{Qrs}(a'_j)$ contains distinct queries.

USED QUERIES AND THEIR ARRANGEMENTS. For $j = 1, \ldots, F$ Q_j contains a pair of colliding chains of length at most 2, so their union is formed from at most 4 "used" entries of Q_j. Note that one entry of Q_j could appear multiple times in the colliding chains (for instance, if there is a self loop, or both chains start with the same edge).

For any pair of colliding chains, we can always find a subset of queries corresponding to one of the arrangements in Fig. 3 (ignore colors and dashed versus solid lines for now). This subset will be strict sometimes. For instance, in case (iii), the adversary may have opted to add the same query to the end of both chains, or even to add another pair of colliding queries; In these cases we only consider the queries shown in the diagram, and if two such cases are possible we choose one arbitrarily.

We define the *used* queries in Q_j, denoted Used_j, to be the subset of $[T]$ that are indices of the queries corresponding to our chosen pair of colliding chains. We have that $1 \le |\mathsf{Used}_j| \le 4$.

NEW, REUSED, AND UNUSED-OLD QUERIES. For any $j \in [F]$, a query in Q_j is said to be *new* if it does not appear in $\mathsf{Q}_1 || \cdots || \mathsf{Q}_{j-1}$. If query is not new, it is said to be *old*. If a query in Q_j is old, and that query appears amongst the queries pointed to by Used_k for some $k < j$ (i.e. the query equals $\mathsf{Q}_k[s]$ for some $s \in \mathsf{Used}_k$), then we say the query is *reused* and otherwise it is *unused-old*.

Claim. Let $\mathsf{Q}_{\mathsf{Fresh}}$, Q_j, and Used_j be $j = 1, \ldots, F$ be defined as above. Then for each j, at least one of the following cases (which are depicted in Fig. 4) holds:

1. [Used_j **contains only new queries.**]
   (a) There exists $s_j \in [T]$ such that $\mathsf{Q}_j[s_j]$ is new and $h(\mathsf{Q}_j[s_j]) = a'_j$,
   (b) There exists $s_j^1 \neq s_j^2 \in [T]$ such that $\mathsf{Q}_j[s_j^1]$ and $\mathsf{Q}_j[s_j^2]$ are new, and $h(\mathsf{Q}_j[s_j^1]) = h(\mathsf{Q}_j[s_j^2])$

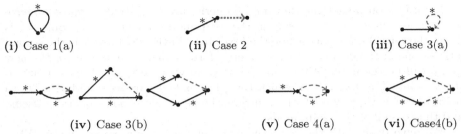

(i) Case 1(a)   **(ii)** Case 2   **(iii)** Case 3(a)

(iv) Case 3(b)   **(v)** Case 4(a)   **(vi)** Case4(b)

Fig. 4. Cases in Claim 6.1. Red dotted arrow represents a *reused* old query. Blue dashed arrow represents an *unused-old* query. '*' marks the queries that will be compressed by f. (Color figure online)

2. [**Used$_j$ contains at least one reused query.**] There exists $s_j \in [T]$ and $t_j \in [F]$ such that $Q_j[s_j]$ is new and $h(Q_j[s_j])$ equals input salt of some query in Q_{t_j} pointed to by Used_{t_j}.
3. [**Used$_j$ contains exactly 1 unused old query.**]
   (a) There exists $s_j \in [T]$ and $u_j \in [FT]$ such that $Q_j[s_j]$ is new, u_j is new (in its respective Q_k, $k < j$) and $h(Q_j[s_j])$ and $h(Q_{\mathsf{Fresh}}[u_j])$ both equal the input salt of query $Q_{\mathsf{Fresh}}[u_j]$,
   (b) There exists $s_j^1 \neq s_j^2 \in [T]$ and $u_j \in [FT]$ such that $Q_j[s_j^1], Q_j[s_j^2]$ are new, and $h(Q_j[s_j^1])$ equals the input salt of $Q_{\mathsf{Fresh}}[u_j]$, and $h(Q_j[s_j^2]) = h(Q_{\mathsf{Fresh}}[u_j])$.
4. [**Used$_j$ contains exactly 2 unused old queries.**]
   (a) There exists $s_j \in [T]$ and $u_j^1 < u_j^2 \in [FT]$ such that $Q_j[s_j]$ is new, u_j^2 is new (in its respective $Q_k, k < j)^2$, the input salt of queries $Q_{\mathsf{Fresh}}[u_j^1]$ and $Q_{\mathsf{Fresh}}[u_j^2]$ are equal, $h(Q_j[s_j])$ equals their common input salt, and $h(Q_{\mathsf{Fresh}}[u_j^2]) = h(Q_{\mathsf{Fresh}}[u_j^1])$,
   (b) There exists $s_j^1 \neq s_j^2 \in [T]$, $u_j^1 < u_j^2 \in [FT]$ such that $Q_j[s_j^1], Q_j[s_j^2]$ are new, u_j^2 is new (in its respective $Q_k, k < j$), $h(Q_j[s_j^1])$ equals the input salt of query $Q_{\mathsf{Fresh}}[u_j^1]$, $h(Q_j[s_j^2])$ equals the input salt of query $Q_{\mathsf{Fresh}}[u_j^2]$, and $h(Q_{\mathsf{Fresh}}[u_j^2]) = h(Q_{\mathsf{Fresh}}[u_j^1])$.

Proof of claim. Fix $j \in [F]$ and consider Used_j. The queries in Q_j corresponding to Used_j fall into one of the cases in Fig. 3. Since a_j' is fresh, the queries with input salt a_j' must be new (otherwise a_j' would be predicted). Thus the bold edges in the figure must be new queries. The other queries can be *new*, *reused* or *unused-old*.

Suppose all of the queries of Q_j in Used_j are new. For cases (ii)–(vi) in Fig. 3 there are 2 distinct queries that have the same output, so we take s_j^1, s_j^2 to point to these queries in Q_j and case 1(b) holds. In the remaining case (i), the output of the query is a_j', so we take s_j to point at the relevant query in Q_j and case 1(a) of the claim holds.

---

[2] Query at u_j^1 is not compressed, so it does not matter whether it is new or not.

From now on we assume that not all queries are new. Next, suppose an edge in Used_j is reused, say appearing in the used queries for Q_k, $k < j$. Since a'_j is fresh, the reused query cannot be the first query in the chain, so it is the second edge of one of the chains. As these queries form a chain, the output of the new query will be the input of the reused query. So we take $t_j = k$ (i.e. to point to the kth-salt a'_k in U_{Fresh} from which the query is being reused), and $s_j \in [T]$ to point to the new query in Q_j that outputs the input salt of some query in Used_k, and thus case 2 of the claim holds.

We have dealt with the case where the old query is a reused query. What remains is if the old query is unused-old. There are either 1 or 2 unused-old queries and we handle these separately.

Suppose there exists exactly one query in the colliding chains that is unused-old. Again this query has to be the last edge of the chain. Since the chain has length 2, we are in case (ii) or (iv)–(vi) of Fig. 3. In case (ii), we have that case 3(a) of the claim holds as we can take $u_j \in [FT]$ to point to the loop. Otherwise we can find queries pointed to by s_j, s'_j in Q_j and $u_j \in [FT]$ such that case 3(b) holds.

Finally suppose are exactly two unused-old queries in the colliding chains. Then we must be in case (iv) or (vi) of Fig. 3. By inspection we can find the required pointers, and either case 4(a) or (b) holds.   □

DEFINITION OF f. On input (U, h), $f(U, h)$ first computes U_{Fresh} and Pred (and F) as before. It then computes $\mathsf{Q}_{\mathsf{Fresh}}$, and Q_j and Used_j for each $j = 1, \ldots, F$. It initializes: (1) Array Cases and Coll, each of size F, which will hold entries from domains depending on cases, (2) A list Loops which will hold elements of $[FT]$ (i.e. "large pointers") (3) A set Bulbs which will hold elements of $[FT]$ (i.e. "large pointers") (4) A list $\mathsf{Diamonds}$ which will hold elements of $[FT] \times [FT]$, (i.e. pairs of "large pointers") (5) $\tilde{h}$ to be the table of h, but sorted to contain the responses for $\mathsf{Q}_{\mathsf{Fresh}}$, followed by the rest of the table in lexicographic order.

The computation of f next populates the sets $\mathsf{Loops}, \mathsf{Bulbs}$, and $\mathsf{Diamonds}$. Specifically, for $j = 1, \ldots, F$, it checks which case holds; If case 3a, 4a, or 4b holds, then it does the following:

Case 3a: Add u_j to Loops and delete the entry corresponding to $\mathsf{Q}_{\mathsf{Fresh}}[u_j]$ from $\tilde{h}$,

Case 4a: Add u_j^1 and u_j^2 to Bulbs, and delete the entry corresponding to $\mathsf{Q}_{\mathsf{Fresh}}[u_j^2]$ from $\tilde{h}$,

Case 4b: Add the pair (u_j^1, u_j^2) to $\mathsf{Diamonds}$ and delete the entry corresponding to $\mathsf{Q}_{\mathsf{Fresh}}[u_j^2]$ from $\tilde{h}$.

There is a subtlety in Case 4a: It may be that two bulbs are hanging off of the same vertex, when the adversary produces two Case-(iv) (from Fig. 3) collisions with the same intermediate node. In this case our algorithm will put the second collision into Case 2 and not 4a, even though strictly speaking there was no reused edge - only a reused node (which Case 2 allows). This ensures that the queries in Bulbs will be partitioned into pairs with the same input salts, which our inversion algorithm will leverage.

We have now defined all of the outputs of f except for Cases, Coll and $\tilde{h}$, which we define now. For $j = 1, \ldots, F$, f examines Q_j and determines which of the cases above occurs for Used_j. It sets $\mathsf{Cases}[j] \in \{1a, 1b, 2, 3a, 3b, 4a, 4b\}$ and performs one of the following (see Fig. 5):

Case 1a: Set $\mathsf{Coll}[j] \leftarrow s_j \in [T]$ and delete the entry corresponding to $Q_j[s_j]$ from $\tilde{h}$.

Case 1b: Set $\mathsf{Coll}[j] \leftarrow (s_j^1, s_j^2) \in [T] \times [T]$ and delete the entry corresponding to query $Q_j[s_j^2]$ from $\tilde{h}$.

Case 2: Compute $v_j \in [4]$ to point to which of the (at most) four used queries in Q_{t_j} is reused, and then set $\mathsf{Coll}[j] \leftarrow (s_j, t_j, v_j) \in [T] \times [F] \times [4]$ and delete the entry corresponding to $Q_j[s_j]$ from $\tilde{h}$.

Case 3b: Set $\mathsf{Coll}[j] \leftarrow (s_j^1, s_j^2, u_j)$ and delete entries corresponding to queries $Q_j[s_j^1]$ and $Q_j[s_j^2]$ from $\tilde{h}$.

Case 4a: Compute v_j, index of u_j^1 in Bulbs. Set $\mathsf{Coll}[j] \leftarrow (s_j, v_j) \in [T] \times [|\mathsf{Bulbs}|]$ and delete the entry corresponding to query $Q_j[s_j]$ from $\tilde{h}$.

Case 4b: Set $\mathsf{Coll}[j] \leftarrow (s_j^1, s_j^2) \in [T] \times [T]$, and delete the entries corresponding to queries $Q_j[s_j^1]$ and $Q_j[s_j^2]$ from $\tilde{h}$.

Thus, $\tilde{h}$ consists of the query responses for $\mathcal{A}_2$ when run on the salts in U_{Fresh}, except for the queries indicated to be deleted by compressor, followed by the remaining outputs of h in lexicographic order. This completes the description of f.

ANALYSIS OF f. We first argue the output length of f is not too long, and later that it is injective. Let the number of salts in U_{Fresh} having compression type 1(a) and 1(b) be δ_1 and δ_1' respectively, compression type 2 be δ_2, compression type 3(b) to be δ_3 and compression type 4(a) be $\delta_4 = |\mathsf{Bulbs}|/2$. Let $|\mathsf{Bulbs}| = n_b$, $|\mathsf{Loops}| = n_\ell$ and $|\mathsf{Diamonds}| = n_d$. Then $F = \delta_1 + \delta_1' + \delta_2 + n_\ell + \delta_3 + \delta_4 + n_d$.

Claim. The number of entries deleted from $\tilde{h}$ by f is equal to $\delta_1 + \delta_1' + \delta_2 + n_\ell + 2\delta_3 + \frac{n_b}{2} + \delta_4 + 3n_d$.

Proof. Observe that f does the following:

- deletes 1 entry from $\tilde{h}$ for each index added to Loops. So, n_ℓ entries deleted from $\tilde{h}$ when f populates Loops.
- deletes 1 entry from $\tilde{h}$ for each pair of indices added to Bulbs. So, $n_b/2$ entries deleted from $\tilde{h}$ when f populates Bulbs.
- deletes 1 entry from $\tilde{h}$ for each pair of indices added to Diamonds. So, n_d entries deleted from $\tilde{h}$ when f populates Diamonds.
- for every fresh salt of type 1a, 1b, 2 and 4a one entry corresponding to a new query among the queries of the salt is deleted from $\tilde{h}$. Thus, $\delta_1, \delta_1', \delta_2$ and δ_4 entries will be deleted by f from $\tilde{h}$ due to fresh salts belonging to Case 1a, 1b, 2 and 4a, respectively.

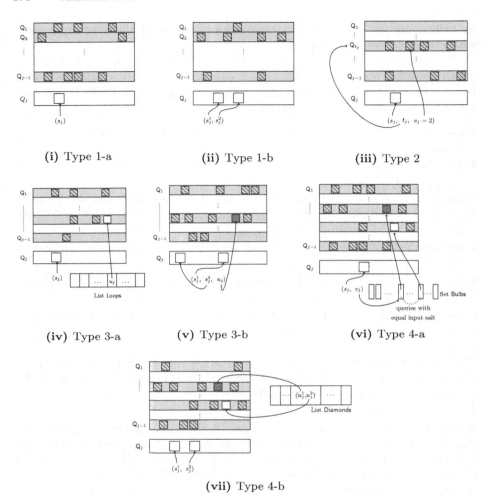

(i) Type 1-a   **(ii)** Type 1-b   **(iii)** Type 2

(iv) Type 3-a   **(v)** Type 3-b   **(vi)** Type 4-a

(vii) Type 4-b

Fig. 5. Compression of different cases for $B = 2$ by f. Boxes denote an index. Boxes with blue stripes denote used queries in Q_j. White box denotes query at the index is new (and gets compressed). (Color figure online)

– for every salt of type 3b and 4b, entries corresponding to two queries that are new in Qrs of salt are deleted from $\tilde{h}$, thus $2\delta_3$ and $2n_d$ entries are deleted by f from $\tilde{h}$ for fresh salts undergoing compression of type 3b and 4b, respectively.

This totals to $\delta_1 + \delta_1' + \delta_2 + n_\ell + 2\delta_3 + \frac{n_b}{2} + \delta_4 + 3n_d$ entries being deleted. Therefore, to prove the claim, we need to show that f deletes the entry of any query exactly once from $\tilde{h}$. To this end, we proceed in 3 steps as follows:

Claim. Any query belongs to at most one of **Loops**, **Bulbs** or **Diamonds**.

Proof. We prove the above claim by contradiction. Let's assume there exists a query q that belongs in both Loops and Bulbs. Without loss of generality, we can assume that the query's first occurrence is at index $i \in [FT]$, it is added in Loops for some fresh salt a'_j of type 3a and added to Bulbs for some fresh salt a'_k of type 4a such that $j, k \in [F]$ and $j < k$. However, as index i is added to Loops, query q becomes a used query in Q_j. When q is used in Q_k, it will be a reused query and hence a'_k should be of type 2 instead of type 4a and q would not be added to Bulbs, contradicting our assumption.

We can similarly show that no query can simultaneously be in Loops and Diamonds or Bulbs and Diamonds, thus proving the claim. □

For every $j \in [F]$ and for any value of Cases[j], f deletes an entry corresponding to a new query in Q_j from $\tilde{h}$ while populating Cases[j] and Coll[j]. Lets assume there exists $j, k \in [F]$ such that $j < k$ and f deletes some query q while populating Cases and Coll for both a'_j and a'_k. Then q should be a new query both in queries of a'_j and queries of a'_k for it to be deleted. However, this is not possible by the definition of new queries.

Claim. If f adds a query to one of Loops, Bulbs and Diamonds, then it never deletes its entry from $\tilde{h}$ while populating Cases and Coll.

Proof. Lets assume otherwise that f adds some query q to Loops for some salt a'_j of type 3a and for some $k \in [F]$, it deletes the entry corresponding to q from $\tilde{h}$ while populating Cases[k] and Coll[k]. This means, q should be a used query in both Q_j and Q_k. However, it can be a new query in at most one of Q_j and Q_k and has to be an old query in the queries of the other salt depending on whether $j < k$ or $j > k$. Thus, q would be a reused query in one of Q_j or Q_k. If $j < k$, then q is a reused query among the used queries of a'_k. This means a'_k would be of type 2 (as it is not a new query and not the first query in the chain). This means, q would not be deleted while processing Cases[k] and Coll[k]. This contradicts our assumption. When $j > k$, then q would be a reused query among the queries for a'_j and then a'_j should not be of type 3a, again contradicting our assumption. Similarly, we can prove when a'_j is of type 4a or 4b. This proves the above claim. □

We set the output length of L via the following equation, where the maximum is taken over $1 \leq F \leq u$ and the $\delta_i, \delta'_1, n_\ell, n_b, n_d$ summing to F:

$$2^L = \max \binom{N}{u} N^{MN} \cdot u \cdot 2^{3F} \cdot \frac{\binom{N}{F}\binom{FT}{u-F}}{\binom{N}{u}} \cdot \left(\frac{T}{N}\right)^{\delta_1} \cdot \left(\frac{T^2}{N}\right)^{\delta'_1} \cdot \left(\frac{4FT}{N}\right)^{\delta_2}$$
$$\cdot \left(\frac{FT}{N}\right)^{n_\ell} \cdot \left(\frac{FT \cdot T^2}{N^2}\right)^{\delta_3} \cdot \frac{\binom{FT}{n_b}(T \cdot n_b)^{\delta_4}}{N^{n_b/2+\delta_4}} \cdot \left(\frac{(FT)^2 T^2}{N^3}\right)^{n_d}$$

Then using Stirling's approximation, we bound $\dfrac{\binom{N}{F}\binom{FT}{u-F}}{\binom{N}{u}} \leq (4e)^u \left(\dfrac{FT}{N}\right)^{u-F}$ exactly as before. Next, using $n_b/2 = \delta_4 \leq F$ and $T^2 \leq N$ we simplify,

$$\frac{\binom{FT}{n_b} \cdot (T \cdot n_b)^{\delta_4}}{N^{n_b/2+\delta_4}} \leq \left(\frac{eFT}{n_b \cdot N}\right)^{n_b} \cdot (T \cdot n_b)^{n_b/2} = \left(\frac{2e^2 F^2 T^2 \cdot T \cdot n_b}{2n_b^2 N^2}\right)^{n_b/2}$$

$$\leq \left(\frac{e^2 2^{2F/n_b} FT^2 \cdot T}{2N^2}\right)^{n_b/2} \leq (2e^2)^F \left(\frac{FT}{N}\right)^{n_b/2} \left(\frac{T^2}{N}\right)^{n_b/2}$$

$$\leq (2e^2)^u \left(\frac{FT}{N}\right)^{\delta_4} \cdot \left(\frac{T^2}{N}\right)^{n_b/2}$$

Thus, putting everything together and simplifying using $F \leq u \leq 2^u$, and assuming f is injective, we obtain:

$$\frac{2^L}{\binom{N}{u} N^M N} \leq 2^{4u} \cdot (4e)^u \cdot (2e^2)^u \cdot \left(\frac{FT}{N}\right)^{u-F} \cdot \left(\frac{T^2}{N}\right)^{\delta_1+\delta_1'} \cdot \left(\frac{4FT}{N}\right)^{\delta_2} \cdot$$

$$\left(\frac{FT}{N}\right)^{n_\ell} \left(\frac{FT \cdot T^2}{N^2}\right)^{\delta_3} \left(\frac{FT}{N}\right)^{\delta_4} \left(\frac{T^2}{N}\right)^{n_b/2} \left(\frac{(FT)^2 T^2}{N^3}\right)^{n_d}$$

$$\leq (2^9 e^3)^u \cdot \left(\frac{uT}{N}\right)^{u-F+\delta_2+n_\ell+\delta_3+\delta_4+2n_d} \left(\frac{T^2}{N}\right)^{\delta_1+\delta_1'+\delta_3+n_b/2+n_d}$$

$$\leq (2^9 e^3)^u \cdot \max\left\{\left(\frac{T^2}{N}\right)^u, \left(\frac{uT}{N}\right)^u\right\}$$

Next, we need to prove the assumption that f is injective. In other words, it needs to be shown that given $f(U, h) = (F, U_{\mathsf{Fresh}}, \mathsf{Pred}, \mathsf{Cases}, \mathsf{Coll}, \mathsf{Loops}, \mathsf{Bulbs}, \mathsf{Diamonds}, \tilde{h})$, (U, h) can be uniquely determined. The inversion algorithm works as follows:

1. Parse the inputs, starting with F, as with the previous proof.
2. Initialize h and $\mathsf{Q}_{\mathsf{Fresh}}$ to be empty tables and array $U = U_{\mathsf{Fresh}}$.
3. For each $a'_j \in U_{\mathsf{Fresh}}$ (in lexicographic order), the j-th entry of Cases indicates the type of tuple of pointers stored in the j-th entry of Coll. Run $\mathcal{A}_2$ on a'_j and respond to queries using the entries of $\tilde{h}$ in order (except if the query is a repeat) and populating the entries of h and $\mathsf{Q}_{\mathsf{Fresh}}$ except when one of the following happens:
   (a) For $\mathsf{Cases}[j] = 1a$, when $\mathsf{Q}_j[s_j]$ is queried, respond to the query with a'_j. If $\mathsf{Cases}[j] = 1b$ continue until it reaches query at index s_j^2 in Q_j. To respond to this query, return the output of the query $\mathsf{Q}_j[s_j^1]$.
   (b) For $\mathsf{Cases}[j] = 2$, when $\mathsf{Q}_j[s_j]$ is queried, return the input salt of query $\mathsf{Q}_{t_j}[\mathsf{Used}_{t_j}[v_j]]$.
   (c) For $\mathsf{Cases}[j] = 3b$, if query pointed by s_j^1 in Q_j is made, return the input salt of the query pointed by u_j. If query pointed by s_j^2 in Q_j is made, return the output of the query pointed by u_j.

(d) For Cases$[j] = 4a$, when $Q_j[s_j]$ is queried, return the input salt of the query at index v_j in the set Bulbs.

(e) For Cases$[j] = 4b$, when $Q_j[s_j^1]$ or $Q_j[s_j^2]$ is queried, return the input salt of first and second query in the first unused element of list Diamonds, respectively.

(f) The query is in Loops, then respond to the query with the input salt of the query.

(g) The query is in Bulbs and there is a prior query with the same input salt in Bulbs, then respond to the query with the output of this prior query.

(h) The second query of an element in Diamonds, then respond to the query with the output of the first query of the same element in Diamonds.

After responding, continue running $\mathcal{A}_2$ on a_j' and populating the tables.

4. After running $\mathcal{A}_2$ on all of the salts in U_{Fresh}, populate the rest of h using the remaining entries of $\tilde{h}$ in order.

5. Finally, examine the queries Q_{Fresh}, and form U by adding the salts of queries in Q_{Fresh} indexed by the elements of Pred to U_{Fresh}.

We first argue inversion replies to the queries issued by $\mathcal{A}_2$ on a_j' correctly, for each $a_j' \in U_{\mathsf{Fresh}}$. For queries that are not deleted from $\tilde{h}$, these are simply copied from $\tilde{h}$. By construction, the queries that were deleted will be copied correctly. Finally, once Q_{Fresh} and Q are correctly computed, we have that U is correctly recovered. □

7 Modification of Impagliazzo and Kabanets' Result Is Necessary

Here we show that the approach of [12] provably cannot work for the problem of short MD collisions. This modification is necessary because we can show that there exists an adversary that can achieve a better advantage on a fixed set U as compared to the bound we prove for a random set $\mathbf{U}$. We start with a definition for this case and then state and prove our counterexample attack.

Definition 7. *For a pair of algorithms $\mathcal{A} = (\mathcal{A}_1, \mathcal{A}_2)$ and set $U \subseteq [N]$ we define*

$$\mathbf{Adv}_{\mathrm{MD}}^{U\text{-ai-cr}}(\mathcal{A}) = \Pr[\forall a \in U \; : \; \mathsf{AI\text{-}CR}_{\mathbf{h},a}(\mathcal{A}) = 1],$$

where $\mathbf{h} \xleftarrow{\$} \mathsf{Func}([N] \times [M], [N])$.

Lemma 4. *For any positive integers S, T, u such that $uT^2 = \theta(N)$, any set U of size u and $\hat{\sigma} \in \{0,1\}^S$, there exists adversary $\mathcal{A} = (\mathcal{A}_1, \mathcal{A}_2)$ such that $\mathcal{A}_1$ always outputs $\hat{\sigma}$, and $\mathcal{A}_2$ issues T queries to its oracle and always outputs collision of length at most 2. Then*

$$\mathbf{Adv}_{\mathrm{MD}}^{U\text{-ai-cr}}(\mathcal{A}) = \left(\Omega\left(\frac{T^2}{N}\right) \right)^{c \cdot u}$$

where c is a constant smaller than 1.

Proof. We construct such an adversary $\mathcal{A} = (\mathcal{A}_1, \mathcal{A}_2)$ to prove the lemma. When $\mathcal{A}_2$ makes x queries to its oracle on input $(a, \hat{\sigma})$, we denote the queries as $\mathsf{Qrs}(a) \in ([N] \times [M])^x$. For every $i \in [x], \mathsf{Qrs}(a)[i]$ denotes the ith query and satisfies $\mathsf{Qrs}(a)[i] = (a, \cdot)$.

Our proposed $\mathcal{A}_2$ tries to reduce the size of set of salts for which it needs to find collisions. $\mathcal{A}_2$ does that by finding pairs of salts in the given set that have the same output after hashing with 1 block messages. We formally describe the $\mathcal{A}_2$ next.

- Given: a fixed set $U = \{a_1, \ldots, a_u\}$, $\mathcal{A}_2$ makes t distinct, arbitrary queries on every $a_i \in U$, denoted $\mathsf{Qrs}(a_i)$.
- Set $U' = \emptyset$
- for j in 2 to u:
  1. for i in 1 to $j - 1$:
     (a) If $\{h(\mathsf{Qrs}(a_i)[1]), \ldots, h(\mathsf{Qrs}(a_i)[t])\} \cap \{h(\mathsf{Qrs}(a_j)[1]), \ldots, h(\mathsf{Qrs}(a_j)[t])\}$ $\neq \emptyset$ and a_i is not already merged:
         - mark a_i and a_j as merged
         - insert some element from $\{h(\mathsf{Qrs}(a_i)[1]), \ldots, h(\mathsf{Qrs}(a_i)[t])\} \cap \{h(\mathsf{Qrs}(a_j)[1]), \ldots, h(\mathsf{Qrs}(a_j)[t])\}$ in U'
         - break
- Insert non-merged salts from U in U'.
- for every node in U': find collisions using t queries

Next we analyze this adversary $\mathcal{A}$ for the case where $uT^2 = \theta(N)$. Observe $\mathcal{A}$ makes a total of $uT = ut + u't$ queries. This implies $t = \frac{uT}{u+u'} \geq \frac{T}{2}$. Thus, $ut^2 = \theta(N)$ holds true in that case.

Let $E_{i,j}$ be an indicator variable that

$$\{h(\mathsf{Qrs}(a_i)[1]), \ldots, h(\mathsf{Qrs}(a_i)[t])\} \cap \{h(\mathsf{Qrs}(a_j)[1]), \ldots, h(\mathsf{Qrs}(a_j)[t])\} \neq \emptyset.$$

In words, $E_{i,j}$ indicates that there is a repeated output in queries for a_i and a_j. Then

$$\Pr[a_i, a_j \text{ can be merged}] \geq \Pr\left[E_{i,j} \cap \overline{E}_{1,i} \cap \cdots \cap \overline{E}_{i,j-1}\right]$$

$$= \Pr\left[E_{i,j} | \overline{E}_{1,i} \cap \cdots \cap \overline{E}_{i,j-1}\right] \cdot \Pr\left[\overline{E}_{1,i} \cap \cdots \cap \overline{E}_{i,j-1}\right]$$

$$= \frac{t^2}{N} \times \left(1 - \frac{t^2}{N}\right)^{j-1} \geq \frac{t^2}{N} \cdot \left(1 - \frac{(j-1)t^2}{N}\right)$$

$$\geq \frac{t^2}{N} \cdot \left(1 - \frac{ut^2}{N}\right) = \Omega\left(\frac{t^2}{N}\right)$$

Then, the expected number of merged nodes is:

$$\sum_{j=2}^{u} \sum_{i=1}^{j-1} \Pr[a_i, a_j \text{ can be merged}] = \sum_{j=2}^{u} \sum_{i=1}^{j-1} \Omega\left(\frac{t^2}{N}\right) = \Omega\left(\frac{u^2 t^2}{N}\right) = \Omega(u)$$

using that $ut^2 = \theta(N)$. Thus, we can say $\mathbb{E}[\|\mathbf{U}'\|] = c_1 \cdot u$ for some constant $c_1 < 1$. This implies, by Markov's inequality we can get

$$\Pr\left[|\mathbf{U}'| \geq c_2 \cdot c_1 u\right] \leq \frac{c_1 u}{c_2 \cdot c_1 u} = \frac{1}{c_2}$$

for some constant $c_2 > 1$ that satisfies $c_2 \cdot c_1 < 1$. Then, the probability that adversary can find collisions of length 2 for every salt in U is $\left(\Omega\left(\frac{T^2}{N}\right)\right)^{c_2 \cdot c_1 \cdot u}$. $\qquad\square$

This probability is strictly greater than that for finding collisions on every salt in a random set of size u, $\left(O\left(\frac{uT+T^2}{N}\right)\right)^u$ (bound shown in Lemma 3) for $t \geq u$. To be able to prove Theorem 7 without modifying Impagliazzo and Kabanets' technique, we need the bound $\left(O\left(\frac{uT+T^2}{N}\right)\right)^u$ on the advantage of finding collisions on fixed u-sized set to hold true, which does not.

8 Impossibility of Improving Zero-Walk AI Attacks

The attack in Sect. 3 and the attack of Corretti et al. follow the same template: The first unbounded phase can find collisions for some salts $a_1, \ldots, a_s$, and then the second phase tries to "walk" to these salts by querying a fixed message repeatedly. The bounded-length version needs to restart the walk to obey the length bound.

A obvious improvement to these attacks would be to examine the functional graph[3] for the function $h_0(\cdot) := h(\cdot, 0)$ and select $a_1, \ldots, a_s$ that are especially likely to be reached by the random walking stage. It is tempting to conjecture such an attack is optimal for the bounded case, as it was for the unbounded case, and we are not aware of a better attack.

In this section we formalize the approach in these attacks and show that these "zero walk" attacks cannot do much better than the basic attack in Sect. 3. Concretely, we will show that these attacks can do no better (up to logarithmic factors) than $O(STB/N)$ advantage. The bound of known attacks and our bound matches up to logarithmic factors.

At the heart of this bound is a delicate concentration inequality for the size of bounded-depth trees in random functional graphs, which may be of independent interest: Essentially, we show that with high probability, in the functional graph for a random $f : [N] \to [N]$, all of the directed depth-D trees will have at most $\tilde{O}(D^2)$ nodes. Typical results in this area (cf. [8]) only give asymptotic expectations.

Below we formalize the notion of zero-walk adversaries and then state and prove our bound.

Definition 8. *An (S, T, B)-AI adversary $A = (A_1, A_2)$ is said to be a* zero-walk *adversary if it has the following form:*

---

[3] The functional graph for $f : [N] \to [N]$ is defined to have vertex set $[N]$ and edges directed from a to $f(a)$ for all $a \in [N]$.

1. *The first stage $\mathcal{A}_1$ always produces a bit-encoded output of the form $\sigma = \{(a_1, \alpha_1, \alpha_1'), \ldots, (a_s, \alpha_s, \alpha_s')\}$ where $s = S/\lceil(\log N + 2\log M)\rceil$, $a_i \in [N]$, $\alpha_i, \alpha_i' \in [M]$.*
2. *The second stage $\mathcal{A}_2$, on input a and $\sigma = \{(a_1, \alpha_1, \alpha_1'), \ldots, (a_s, \alpha_s, \alpha_s')\}$ and given oracle h, does the following:*
   If $a \in \{a_1, \ldots, a_s\}$, say $a = a_k$, then output α_k and α_k'.
   Else: For i in $1, \ldots, \lfloor T/B \rfloor$:
   (a) Choose $\hat{\alpha}_i \xleftarrow{\$} [M]$. Query $c_0 \leftarrow h(a, \hat{\alpha}_i)$.
   (b) For j in $1, \ldots, B-1$:
       If $c_{j-1} \in \{a_1, \ldots, a_s\}$, say $c_j = a_k$, then output $\hat{\alpha}_i \| 0^{j-1} \| \alpha_k$ and $\hat{\alpha}_i \| 0^{j-1} \| \alpha_k'$.
       Else: Query $c_j \leftarrow h(c_{j-1}, 0)$.

Theorem 8. *For any positive integers S, T, B such that $B \leq T$, $SB \geq T$ and any zero-walk (S, T, B)-AI adversary $\mathcal{A}$,*

$$\mathbf{Adv}_{\mathrm{MD}}^{\mathrm{ai\text{-}cr}}(\mathcal{A}) = O\left(\frac{STB\ln(NB)}{N}\right).$$

This theorem follows easily from Lemma 5 which we state now, but the proof of that lemma is technical. For a function $f \in \mathsf{Func}([N], [N])$, an element $a \in [N]$, and non-negative integer g, we define $f^{-g}(a) = \bigcup_{i=0}^{g}\{a' \in [N] : f^i(a') = a\}$, where we define f^0 to be the identity function. Note that $f^{-g}(a)$ includes all of the elements that iterate to a in g *or fewer* steps, so we have in particular that $a \in f^{-g}(a)$ for any $g \geq 0$. We say that an element $a \in [N]$ is (r, B')-*rich for f* if $|f^{-B'}(a)| \geq r$.

Lemma 5. *Let $\mathbf{f} \xleftarrow{\$} \mathsf{Func}([N], [N])$. Define $r = \lceil 1000(B')^2 \ln(NB')\rceil + 1$ and let ε be the probability that there exists $a \in [N]$ that is (r, B')-rich for $\mathbf{f}$. Then*

$$\varepsilon < 1/N.$$

The proof of this lemma is technical and given in the full version. We remark that lemma is easier to prove if we settle for a weaker result with r proportional to $\tilde{\Omega}(B'^3)$.

Proof of Theorem 8. Let C be a constant to be fixed later. Let $\mathcal{A}$ be zero-walk adversary, and write $\mathbf{h}_0(\cdot)$ for $\mathbf{h}(0, \cdot)$. Let E be the event that there exist $a_1, \ldots, a_s$ such that $\bigcup_{i=1}^{s} \mathbf{h}_0^{-(B-2)}(a_i)$ has size at least $CSB^2\ln(NB)$. Then

$$\Pr[\mathsf{AI\text{-}CR}_{\mathbf{h},\mathbf{a}}(\mathcal{A}) = 1] \leq \Pr[\mathsf{AI\text{-}CR}_{\mathbf{h},\mathbf{a}}(\mathcal{A}) = 1 | \neg E] + \Pr[E]$$

$$\leq \left(\sum_{i \in [\lfloor T/B \rfloor]} \frac{CSB^2\ln(NB)}{N}\right) + \frac{1}{N} = O\left(\frac{STB\ln(NB)}{N}\right).$$

The first probability bound holds because for a fixed h, we have that $\mathcal{A}$ wins only if one of its T chosen c_0 values lies in $\bigcup_{i=0}^{s} \mathbf{h}_0^{-(B-2)}(a_i)$, which has size at most $CSB^2\ln(NB)$ when E does not hold; We simply apply a union bound over the $\lfloor T/B \rfloor$ choices of c_0. The second probability bound is by Lemma 5, with $B' = B - 2$ and the constant C set appropriately. $\qquad\square$

References

1. Bellare, M., Rogaway, P.: Random oracles are practical: a paradigm for designing efficient protocols. In: Denning, D.E., Pyle, R., Ganesan, R., Sandhu, R.S., Ashby, V. (eds.) ACM CCS 93: 1st Conference on Computer and Communications Security, Fairfax, Virginia, USA, 3–5 November 1993, pp. 62–73. ACM Press (1993)
2. Coretti, S., Dodis, Y., Guo, S.: Non-uniform bounds in the random-permutation, ideal-cipher, and generic-group models. In: Shacham, H., Boldyreva, A. (eds.) CRYPTO 2018. LNCS, vol. 10991, pp. 693–721. Springer, Cham (2018). https://doi.org/10.1007/978-3-319-96884-1_23
3. Coretti, S., Dodis, Y., Guo, S., Steinberger, J.: Random oracles and non-uniformity. In: Nielsen, J.B., Rijmen, V. (eds.) EUROCRYPT 2018. LNCS, vol. 10820, pp. 227–258. Springer, Cham (2018). https://doi.org/10.1007/978-3-319-78381-9_9
4. Corrigan-Gibbs, H., Kogan, D.: The discrete-logarithm problem with preprocessing. In: Nielsen, J.B., Rijmen, V. (eds.) EUROCRYPT 2018. LNCS, vol. 10821, pp. 415–447. Springer, Cham (2018). https://doi.org/10.1007/978-3-319-78375-8_14
5. De, A., Trevisan, L., Tulsiani, M.: Time space tradeoffs for attacks against one-way functions and prgs. In: Rabin, T. (ed.) CRYPTO 2010. LNCS, vol. 6223, pp. 649–665. Springer, Heidelberg (2010). https://doi.org/10.1007/978-3-642-14623-7_35
6. Dodis, Y., Guo, S., Katz, J.: Fixing cracks in the concrete: random oracles with auxiliary input, revisited. In: Coron, J.-S., Nielsen, J.B. (eds.) EUROCRYPT 2017. LNCS, vol. 10211, pp. 473–495. Springer, Cham (2017). https://doi.org/10.1007/978-3-319-56614-6_16
7. Fiat, A., Naor, M.: Rigorous time/space tradeoffs for inverting functions. In: 23rd Annual ACM Symposium on Theory of Computing, New Orleans, LA, USA, 6–8 May 1991, pp. 534–541. ACM Press (1991)
8. Flajolet, P., Odlyzko, A.M.: Random mapping statistics. In: Quisquater, J.-J., Vandewalle, J. (eds.) EUROCRYPT 1989. LNCS, vol. 434, pp. 329–354. Springer, Heidelberg (1990). https://doi.org/10.1007/3-540-46885-4_34
9. Gennaro, R., Gertner, Y., Katz, J., Trevisan, L.: Bounds on the efficiency of generic cryptographic constructions. SIAM J. Comput. **35**(1), 217–246 (2005)
10. Gennaro, R., Trevisan, L.: Lower bounds on the efficiency of generic cryptographic constructions. In: 41st Annual Symposium on Foundations of Computer Science, Redondo Beach, CA, USA, 12–14 November 2000, pp. 305–313. IEEE Computer Society Press (2000)
11. Hellman, M.: A cryptanalytic time-memory trade-off. IEEE Trans. Inf. Theory **26**(4), 401–406 (1980)
12. Impagliazzo, R.: Relativized separations of worst-case and average-case complexities for np. In: Proceedings of the 2011 IEEE 26th Annual Conference on Computational Complexity, CCC 2011, pp. 104–114. IEEE Computer Society (2011)
13. Impagliazzo, R., Kabanets, V.: Constructive proofs of concentration bounds. In: Serna, M., Shaltiel, R., Jansen, K., Rolim, J. (eds.) APPROX/RANDOM -2010. LNCS, vol. 6302, pp. 617–631. Springer, Heidelberg (2010). https://doi.org/10.1007/978-3-642-15369-3_46
14. Morin, P., Mulzer, W., Reddad, T.: Encoding arguments. ACM Comput. Surv. **50**(3), 46:1–46:36 (2017)
15. Unruh, D.: Random oracles and auxiliary input. In: Menezes, A. (ed.) CRYPTO 2007. LNCS, vol. 4622, pp. 205–223. Springer, Heidelberg (2007). https://doi.org/10.1007/978-3-540-74143-5_12

16. Yao, A.C.-C.: Coherent functions and program checkers (extended abstract). In: 22nd Annual ACM Symposium on Theory of Computing, Baltimore, MD, USA, 14–16 May 1990, pp. 84–94. ACM Press (1990)
17. Zimand, M.: How to privatize random bits. Technical report, University of Rochester (1996)

Appendix: Proof of Theorem 1

Proof. Define the r.v. $\mathbf{Z}$ by

$$\mathbf{Z} = |\{U \subseteq [N] : |U| = u, \sum_{i \in U} \mathbf{X}_i = u\}|.$$

Then

$$\mathbb{E}\left[\mathbf{Z}\right] \le \binom{N}{u} \delta^u \le \left(\frac{e\delta N}{u}\right)^u.$$

We first handle the case where $6\delta N \ge u$. Observe that if $\sum_{i=1}^{N} \mathbf{X}_i \ge 6\delta N$, then $\mathbf{Z} \ge \binom{6\delta N}{u}$, and by Markov's inequality we have

$$\Pr[\sum_{i=1}^{N} \mathbf{X}_i \ge 6\delta N] \le \Pr[\mathbf{Z} \ge \binom{6\delta N}{u}] \le \left(\frac{e\delta N}{u}\right)^u \cdot \binom{6\delta N}{u}^{-1}$$

$$\le \left(\frac{e\delta N}{u}\right)^u \cdot \left(\frac{u}{6\delta N}\right)^u = (e/6)^u < 2^{-u}.$$

In the other case, where $u > 6\delta N$, we have $\mathbb{E}\left[\mathbf{Z}\right] \le 2^{-u}$, and Markov's gives

$$\Pr[\sum_{i=1}^{N} \mathbf{X}_i \ge u] \le \Pr[\mathbf{Z} \ge 1] \le 2^{-u}.$$

$\square$

The Summation-Truncation Hybrid: Reusing Discarded Bits for Free

Aldo Gunsing$^{(\boxtimes)}$ and Bart Mennink$^{(\boxtimes)}$

Digital Security Group, Radboud University, Nijmegen, The Netherlands
aldo.gunsing@ru.nl, b.mennink@cs.ru.nl

Abstract. A well-established PRP-to-PRF conversion design is truncation: one evaluates an n-bit pseudorandom permutation on a certain input, and truncates the result to a bits. The construction is known to achieve tight $2^{n-a/2}$ security. Truncation has gained popularity due to its appearance in the GCM-SIV key derivation function (ACM CCS 2015). This key derivation function makes four evaluations of AES, truncates the outputs to $n/2$ bits, and concatenates these to get a $2n$-bit subkey.

In this work, we demonstrate that truncation is wasteful. In more detail, we present the Summation-Truncation Hybrid (STH). At a high level, the construction consists of two parallel evaluations of truncation, where the truncated $(n - a)$-bit chunks are not discarded but rather summed together and appended to the output. We prove that STH achieves a similar security level as truncation, and thus that the $n - a$ bits of extra output is rendered for free. In the application of GCM-SIV, the current key derivation can be used to output $3n$ bits of random material, or it can be reduced to three primitive evaluations. Both changes come with no security loss.

Keywords: PRP-to-PRF · Truncation · Sum of permutations · Efficiency · GCM-SIV

1 Introduction

The vast majority of symmetric cryptographic schemes is built upon a pseudorandom permutation, such as AES [21]. Such a function gets as input a key and bijectively transforms its input to an output such that the function is hard to distinguish from random if an attacker has no knowledge about the key. The approach is natural: the design as well as the analysis of pseudorandom permutations has faced ample research. Yet, in many encryption modes [3], message authentication codes [4,10,18,65], authenticated encryption schemes [24,29,49] and other applications of pseudorandom permutations [45], the underlying primitive is only used *in forward direction*. Here, one does not make use of the invertibility of the permutation, and even stronger: the fact that one uses a pseudorandom permutation instead of a pseudorandom function comes at a security penalty.

© International Association for Cryptologic Research 2020
D. Micciancio and T. Ristenpart (Eds.): CRYPTO 2020, LNCS 12170, pp. 187–217, 2020.
https://doi.org/10.1007/978-3-030-56784-2_7

A prominent example of this is the Wegman-Carter nonce-based message authentication code from 1981 [18,65]:

$$\mathsf{WC}^{F,H}(\nu,m) = F(\nu) \oplus H(m)\,,$$

where F is a pseudorandom function transforming a nonce ν to an n-bit output and H a universal hash function transforming an arbitrary length message m to an n-bit output. Provided that F and H are sufficiently strong and the nonce is never repeated, this construction is known to achieve 2^n security [65]. However, given the thorough understanding in pseudorandom permutation design, Shoup suggested to instantiate Wegman-Carter using a pseudorandom permutation P, leading to a construction now known as the Wegman-Carter-Shoup construction [61]:

$$\mathsf{WCS}^{P,H}(\nu,m) = P(\nu) \oplus H(m)\,.$$

This construction, however, is known to only achieve approximately $2^{n/2}$ birthday bound security in the size of P [11,47,61]. This bound may be fine for sufficiently large pseudorandom permutations like the AES, but with the use of legacy ciphers and with the rise of lightweight pseudorandom permutations [1,2,15,16,23,28,35,43,60,66] whose widths could get down to 64 or even 32 bits, birthday attacks are a practical thread as recently demonstrated by McGrew [48] and Bhargavan and Leurent [12].

This and comparable examples (e.g., counter mode encryption [3] and GCM authenticated encryption [49]) showcase the value and need for pseudorandom functions. Unfortunately, we have little understanding in how to design dedicated pseudorandom functions, the only two notable exceptions to date being SURF [9] and AES-PRF [52] (see also Sect. 1.1.3). With respect to generic constructions, the well-established PRP-PRF switch dictates that a pseudorandom permutation behaves like a pseudorandom function up to the birthday bound, $2^{n/2}$ where n is the primitive width [6,8,19,25,34,36]. This switch allows one to obtain a pseudorandom function by simply taking a pseudorandom permutation, but yet, it incurs a loss in the security bound that is comparable to the loss in moving from Wegman-Carter to Wegman-Carter-Shoup.

1.1 Beyond Birthday Bound PRP-to-PRF Conversion

Various methods to transform a PRP into a PRF have been proposed that achieve security beyond the birthday bound on the block size of the underlying primitive. This work will mostly be concerned with two of them: the sum of permutations and truncation.

1.1.1 Sum of Permutations

The sum of two independent n-bit permutations P_1, P_2,

$$\mathsf{SoP}^{P_1,P_2}(x) = P_1(x) \oplus P_2(x)\,, \tag{1}$$

was first introduced by Bellare et al. [7]. Closely following this introduction, Lucks [46] proved around $2^{2n/3}$ security and Bellare and Impagliazzo [5] around $2^n/n$ security. An intensive line of research of Patarin [56–58] yielded around optimal 2^n security, up to constant, following the mirror theory. Dai et al. [22] proved around 2^n security using their rather compact and elegant chi-squared method.

The two independent permutations can be simulated using a single one through domain separation [5, 46]:

$$\mathsf{SoSP}^P(x) = P(x\|0) \oplus P(x\|1)\,. \tag{2}$$

The scheme achieves a similar level of security as SoP [22, 57].

A generalization worth describing is the CENC construction of Iwata [37]. CENC offers a tradeoff between counter mode and the sum of permutations. It is determined by a parameter $w \geqslant 1$ and uses $P(x\|0)$ to mask w subsequent blocks $P(x\|1), \dots, P(x\|w)$. Iwata proved $2^{2n/3}$ security [37]. Iwata et al. [38] argued that, in fact, optimal 2^n security of CENC directly follows from Patarin's mirror theory. Bhattacharya and Nandi [14] re-confirmed this bound using the chi-squared method.

1.1.2   Truncation

The idea of truncation consists of simply discarding part of the output of an n-bit permutation P:

$$\mathsf{Trunc}_a^P(x) = \mathsf{left}_a(P(x))\,, \tag{3}$$

where $0 \leqslant a \leqslant n$. The idea dates back to Hall et al. [34], who proved $2^{n-a/2}$ security for a specific selection of parameters a. Bellare and Impagliazzo [5] and Gilboa and Gueron [26] improved the scope of the proof to tight $2^{n-a/2}$ security for all parameter choices. The first documented solution for the problem, however, dates back to 1978, when Stam [62], derived it in a non-cryptographic context. (See also Gilboa et al. [27].) Bhattacharya and Nandi [13] recently transformed Stam's analysis to the chi-squared method and derived the identical $2^{n-a/2}$ bound. Mennink [50] considered a general treatment of truncation with pre- and post-processing and related the generalized scheme with historical results of Stam from 1986 [63].

1.1.3   Other Approaches

We briefly elaborate on two more recent approaches on beyond birthday bound secure PRP-to-PRF conversion. Cogliati and Seurin [20] introduced Encrypted Davies-Meyer:

$$\mathsf{EDM}^{P_1,P_2}(x) = P_2(P_1(x) \oplus x)\,, \tag{4}$$

where P_1 and P_2 are two n-bit permutations. They proved security up to around $2^{2n/3}$. Dai et al. [22] proved security of the construction up to around $2^{3n/4}$

using the chi-squared method and Mennink and Neves [51] proved security up to around $2^n/n$ using the mirror theory.

Mennink and Neves [51] proposed its dual version Encrypted Davies-Meyer Dual:

$$\mathsf{EDMD}^{P_1,P_2}(x) = P_2(P_1(x)) \oplus P_1(x). \tag{5}$$

They proved that EDMD^{P_1,P_2} is at least as secure as SoP^{P_1,P_2}. In other words, the construction is known to achieve around 2^n security. Mennink and Neves [52] subsequently used the construction to design a dedicated PRF based on the AES [21]. Bernstein's SURF [9], dating back to 1997, follows the same idea.

1.2 Truncation in GCM-SIV

GCM is a well-established authenticated encryption scheme [40,49]. It follows the nonce-based encrypt-then-MAC paradigm, where encryption is performed in counter mode and the associated data and ciphertext are subsequently authenticated using the GHASH universal hash function.

GCM is vulnerable to nonce misuse attacks. Gueron and Lindell introduced GCM-SIV, a nonce misuse resistant authenticated encryption scheme. Several variants of GCM-SIV exist [29,32,33,39], and we will focus on the most recent one. It follows the nonce misuse resistant SIV mode of Rogaway and Shrimpton [59] and uses individual ingredients of GCM. In the context of this work, we are particularly interested in the key derivation function of GCM-SIV [33]. This key derivation function is based on an ($n = 128$)-bit block cipher E and it derives either 256 bits of key material (if E is instantiated with AES-128) or 384 bits of key material (if E is instantiated with AES-256) based on key k and nonce ν as follows:

$$\begin{cases} \mathsf{left}_{n/2}(E_k(\nu\|0)) \| \cdots \| \mathsf{left}_{n/2}(E_k(\nu\|3)), & \text{for 256-bit subkey,} \\ \mathsf{left}_{n/2}(E_k(\nu\|0)) \| \cdots \| \mathsf{left}_{n/2}(E_k(\nu\|5)), & \text{for 384-bit subkey.} \end{cases} \tag{6}$$

This key derivation was in fact introduced in a follow-up version of GCM-SIV [33] after weaknesses were discovered in the original mechanism [55]. The key derivation of (6) has actually been disputed over time. Iwata and Seurin [41] advocated for the sum of permutations instead, and Bose et al. [17] noted that one can even just leave block ciphers in, as bijectivity in the key derivation function do not matter in the bigger picture of GCM-SIV. Despite this disputation, GCM-SIV enjoys strong support from the practical community. GCM-SIV is considered for standardization by the IETF-CFRG [30,31] and NIST [54]. Therefore, it is a legitimate question to investigate the exact behavior of the key derivation function within GCM-SIV.

1.3 Summation-Truncation Hybrid

Besides the difference in security guaranteed between truncation and the sum of permutations, $2^{n-a/2}$ versus 2^n, the former has another drawback: $n - a$ bits are truncated *and simply discarded*. We will demonstrate that this practice

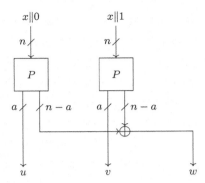

Fig. 1. Summation-Truncation Hybrid STH_a of (7).

is wasteful: one can make more economical use of the discarded randomness *without any sacrification of security*!

Before heading to the main contribution, let us first consider what we can do with the discarded part of truncation *if we focused on a single truncation call*. In other words, we compute $y = P(x)$, output $\mathsf{left}_a(y)$ and discard $\mathsf{right}_{n-a}(y)$. We wish to make more economical use of $\mathsf{right}_{n-a}(y)$. One way of doing so is to simply add the value with $\mathsf{left}_a(y)$; another way of doing so might be to split $\mathsf{right}_{n-a}(y)$ in two pieces, add the results, and append that value to the output of the truncation. It appears that, regardless of the adopted approach, one arrives at a generalized truncation function in the terminology of Mennink [50, 63]. His result describes that, whatever post-processing is applied to P, security of the scheme is tightly determined at $2^{n-a'/2}$, where a' is the output size of the generalized truncation function. (In the former example, $a' = a$, whereas in the latter example, $a' = a + (n - a)/2 = (n + a)/2$.) In other words, security of the construction does not increase and it might even decrease if the truncated data is attempted to be used more economically.

A next step is to look at *two* subsequent truncation calls, as appear, e.g., in the GCM-SIV key derivation (6). We present the Summation-Truncation Hybrid STH, that at a high level consists of two parallel evaluations of truncation, where the truncated parts are not discarded but rather summed together and appended to the output. In detail, if P is an n-bit permutation and a is a parameter satisfying $0 \leqslant a \leqslant n$, the Summation-Truncation Hybrid is a pseudorandom function that maps $n - 1$ bits of input to $n + a$ bits of output as follows:

$$\mathsf{STH}_a^P(x) = \mathsf{left}_a(P(x\|0)) \,\|\, \mathsf{left}_a(P(x\|1)) \,\|\, \mathsf{right}_{n-a}\left(P(x\|0) \oplus P(x\|1)\right) . \quad (7)$$

The function is depicted in Fig. 1.

Clearly, STH_a is exactly as expensive as two evaluations of Trunc_a, but differs in that it outputs $n - a$ bits *for free*. This may give a significant efficiency gain for repeated evaluations of truncation, for instance in the GCM-SIV key derivation in (6). Concretely, considering the case of GCM-SIV with 128-bit keys, it suffices to make three permutation calls instead of four, and for the case of 256-bit keys

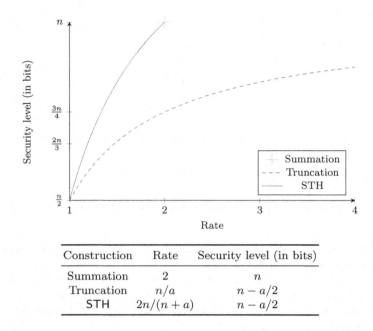

Fig. 2. Comparison between the efficiency and security of summation, truncation and the Summation-Truncation Hybrid. The rate denotes the average number of input bits needed for every output bit. Lower is more efficient.

Construction	Rate	Security level (in bits)
Summation	2	n
Truncation	n/a	$n - a/2$
STH	$2n/(n+a)$	$n - a/2$

it suffices to make four permutation calls instead of six. We go into more detail for GCM-SIV in Sect. 7.

We also consider a variant of STH based on two permutations without domain separation. In detail, if P_1 and P_2 are n-bit permutations and a is a parameter satisfying $0 \leqslant a \leqslant n$, the Summation-Truncation Hybrid 2 is a pseudorandom function that maps n bits of input to $n + a$ bits of output as follows:

$$\mathsf{STH2}_a^{P_1,P_2}(x) = \mathsf{left}_a(P_1(x)) \parallel \mathsf{left}_a(P_2(x)) \parallel \mathsf{right}_{n-a}(P_1(x) \oplus P_2(x)) . \quad (8)$$

Its properties are very similar to the ones of the original STH.

1.4 Security of Summation-Truncation Hybrid

In Sect. 3 we formally prove that the security of STH_a is determined by the security of truncation, i.e., that q evaluations of STH_a are approximately as secure as $2q$ bits of truncation, *despite the $q(n-a)$ bits of free random output*. A comparison between the efficiency and security of truncation, summation and STH is shown in Fig. 2.

The core idea of the proof consists of separating the truncation and the summation. This is not directly possible, as both parts share some secret information: the random permutation. The separation, at a high level, is performed by getting rid of this shared secret so that one only has to reason based on public information.

In more detail, in the proof we first execute the truncation part of the construction, based on the secret permutation. Then, we select a *new* secret permutation for the summation. On the upside, this trick makes it possible to reason about the truncation and summation parts *independently*. On the downside, replacing the secret permutation half-way gives rise to a different construction than the original one, of course. To remedy this, the new permutations is not selected from the set of all possible permutations, but rather from those that are *compatible* with the output generated by the truncation. This set is solely based on public information, i.e., information known by the adversary, as we do give the output of the truncation.

As a bonus, as truncation gives information about the outputs of the permutation directly, we see that this set of compatible permutations is easy to reason about. We demonstrate that choosing such a random permutation is the same as choosing a *family of permutations* with the indices equal to the outputs of the truncation. As we can now replace the truncation with a random function, relying on the extensive state of the art on truncation [5,13,26,34,62], these indices even become uniformly distributed, which makes them nice to handle.

This transition then brings us to the final part of the proof, that generalizes security of the sum of permutations with just a single permutation to the sum of permutations based on an arbitrary family of permutations. The analysis relies on the chi-squared method and generalizes the proof of Dai et al. [22], with the catch that we not only consider a family of permutations, but rather that the selection of permutations from this family is uniformly distributed as it depends on the outputs of the random function (that replaced the truncation).

2   Preliminaries

Let $n, a, b \in \mathbb{N}$ with $n \geqslant a, b$. We denote by $\{0,1\}^n$ the set of bit strings of length n. If $x \in \{0,1\}^n$, $\mathsf{left}_a(x)$ returns the a leftmost bits and $\mathsf{right}_b(x)$ the b rightmost bits of x, in such a way that

$$x = \mathsf{left}_a(x) \parallel \mathsf{right}_{n-a}(x) \, .$$

For $n, m \in \mathbb{N}$, we denote by $\mathsf{Perm}[n]$ the set of all permutations on $\{0,1\}^n$ with $I_n \in \mathsf{Perm}[n]$ the identity permutation, and by $\mathsf{Func}[n, m]$ the set of all functions from $\{0,1\}^n$ to $\{0,1\}^m$.

If $\mathcal{X}$ is a finite set, $x \xleftarrow{\$} \mathcal{X}$ denotes the event of uniformly randomly drawing x from $\mathcal{X}$. For two distributions μ, ν over a finite event space Ω, the statistical distance between μ and ν is defined as

$$\|\mu - \nu\| = \sum_{x \in \Omega} \max(0, \mu(x) - \nu(x))$$
$$= \max_{A \subseteq \Omega} |\mu(A) - \nu(A)| \, .$$

A randomized algorithm $\mathcal{O}$ introduces its variables as random variables, so $\mathbb{P}_{\mathcal{O}}\left[x = a\right]$ denotes the probability that the variable x in algorithm $\mathcal{O}$ is equal to a. As a shorthand we denote $\mathbb{P}_{\mathcal{O}}\left[a\right]$ and $\mathbb{P}_{\mathcal{O}}\left[A\right]$, with a a single value and A a set of values, for the probabilities that algorithm $\mathcal{O}$ returns the value a or a value in the set A, respectively. Just $\mathbb{P}_{\mathcal{O}}$ denotes the distribution of the return value of algorithm $\mathcal{O}$. For a random variable X with distribution μ, we denote its expectation by $\mathbb{E}_{\mu}\left[X\right]$. If the distribution is clear from the context, we write just $\mathbb{E}\left[X\right]$.

A distinguisher $\mathcal{D}$ is an algorithm that is given access to an oracle $\mathcal{O}$ to which it can make a certain amount of queries, and afterwards it outputs $b \in \{0, 1\}$.

We briefly state an elementary property of conditional expectation.

Lemma 1. *Suppose that* $\mathbb{E}\left[Y \mid X\right] = \mathbb{E}\left[Y\right]$. *Then* $\mathbb{E}\left[X \cdot Y\right] = \mathbb{E}\left[X\right] \cdot \mathbb{E}\left[Y\right]$.

Proof. By the law of total expectation we have

$$
\begin{aligned}
\mathbb{E}\left[X \cdot Y\right] &= \mathbb{E}\left[\mathbb{E}\left[X \cdot Y \mid X\right]\right] \\
&= \mathbb{E}\left[X \cdot \mathbb{E}\left[Y \mid X\right]\right] \\
&= \mathbb{E}\left[X \cdot \mathbb{E}\left[Y\right]\right] \\
&= \mathbb{E}\left[X\right] \cdot \mathbb{E}\left[Y\right] . \qquad \square
\end{aligned}
$$

2.1   Block Ciphers

Let $\kappa, n \in \mathbb{N}$. A block cipher $E : \{0,1\}^{\kappa} \times \{0,1\}^{n} \rightarrow \{0,1\}^{n}$ is a permutation on n-bit strings for every fixed key $k \in \{0,1\}^{\kappa}$. Denote by $\mathsf{Perm}[n]$ the set of all permutations on $\{0,1\}^{n}$. The security of a block cipher is measured by the distance between E_k for secret key from a random permutation $P \xleftarrow{\$} \mathsf{Perm}[n]$. The advantage of a distinguisher $\mathcal{D}$ in breaking the PRP (pseudorandom permutation) security of E is defined as

$$
\mathbf{Adv}_E^{\mathrm{prp}}(\mathcal{D}) = \left\| \mathbb{P}\left[\mathcal{D}^{E_k} = 1\right] - \mathbb{P}\left[\mathcal{D}^{P} = 1\right] \right\| , \tag{9}
$$

where the probabilities are taken over the random drawing of $k \xleftarrow{\$} \{0,1\}^{\kappa}$, $P \xleftarrow{\$} \mathsf{Perm}[n]$, and the randomness used by $\mathcal{D}$. Distinguisher $\mathcal{D}$ is usually bound by a query complexity q and a time complexity t. The maximum over all such distinguishers is denoted by $\mathbf{Adv}_E^{\mathrm{prp}}(q, t)$.

2.2   Pseudorandom Functions

Let $n, m \in \mathbb{N}$. Let $F^P \in \mathsf{Func}[n, m]$ be a function from $\{0,1\}^n$ to $\{0,1\}^m$ that is instantiated with a permutation $P \in \mathsf{Perm}[n]$. The security of F is measured by the distance between F^P for secret and uniformly randomly drawn $P \xleftarrow{\$} \mathsf{Perm}[n]$ from a random function $R \xleftarrow{\$} \mathsf{Func}[n, m]$. The advantage of a distinguisher $\mathcal{D}$ in breaking the PRF (pseudorandom function) security of F is defined as

$$
\mathbf{Adv}_F^{\mathrm{prf}}(\mathcal{D}) = \left\| \mathbb{P}\left[\mathcal{D}^{F^P} = 1\right] - \mathbb{P}\left[\mathcal{D}^{R} = 1\right] \right\| . \tag{10}
$$

For $q \in \mathbb{N}$, we define by $\mathbf{Adv}_F^{\mathrm{prf}}(q)$ the maximum advantage over all distinguishers $\mathcal{D}$ making q queries to the oracle.

2.3 Truncation

Our security analysis will, in part, rely on the PRF security of truncation of (3). We copy the result of Stam [62], translated to cryptographic terminology [13,50].

Lemma 2 (Truncation [13,50,62]). *Let $n, a, q \in \mathbb{N}$ such that $0 \leqslant a \leqslant n$. We have:*

$$\mathbf{Adv}_{\mathrm{Trunc}_a}^{\mathrm{prf}}(q) \leqslant \left(\binom{q}{2} / 2^{2n-a} \right)^{1/2} . \tag{11}$$

3 Summation-Truncation Hybrid

Let $n, a \in \mathbb{N}$ such that $0 \leqslant a \leqslant n$, and write $b = n - a$. Let $P \in \mathsf{Perm}[n]$ be a permutation. We define the Summation-Truncation Hybrid $\mathsf{STH}_a^P \in \mathsf{Func}[n - 1, n + a]$ as follows:

$$\mathsf{STH}_a^P(x) = \mathsf{left}_a(P(x\|0)) \, \| \, \mathsf{left}_a(P(x\|1)) \, \| \, \mathsf{right}_b \left(P(x\|0) \oplus P(x\|1) \right) . \tag{12}$$

The function is depicted in Fig. 1. As expressed in this figure, we refer to the first a bits as u, the second a bits as v, and the final b bits as w, and write $y = u\|v\|w$.

Clearly, STH_a is equivalent to SoP for $a = 0$. If $a = n$, STH_a consists of a concatenation of two block cipher evaluations. For general a, one evaluation of STH_a *with the last b bits discarded* is equivalent to a double evaluation of Trunc_a. As we will show, however, there is no reason to discard these b bits. Stated differently, q evaluations of STH_a are roughly as secure as $2q$ evaluations of Trunc_a, although the former outputs significantly more random data.

Theorem 1. *Let $n, a, q \in \mathbb{N}$ such that $0 \leqslant a \leqslant n$, and write $b = n - a$. Assume that $b \geqslant \max(n/12, 10)$. We have:*

$$\mathbf{Adv}_{\mathsf{STH}_a}^{\mathrm{prf}}(q) \leqslant 3 \left(\frac{q}{2^{n-a/3}} \right)^{3/2} + \frac{1}{\sqrt{2\pi}} \left(\frac{q}{2^{n-5}} \right)^{2^{b-2}} + \frac{q}{2^n} + \mathbf{Adv}_{\mathsf{Trunc}_a}^{\mathrm{prf}}(2q) . \tag{13}$$

The dominating bound of Theorem 1 is, in fact, $\mathbf{Adv}_{\mathsf{Trunc}_a}^{\mathrm{prf}}(2q)$, and therefore, security of STH_a is only marginally worse than that of Trunc_a, even though it is much more efficient. We prove Theorem 1 in Sect. 4.

Remark 1. In Theorem 1, as well as in Lemma 2, we focus on PRF security in the information-theoretic setting, where the underlying primitive is a secret random permutation. One can easily transfer these results to a complexity-theoretic setting where P is defined as a block cipher instance E_k for secret key. More detailed, the bound of Trunc_a (Lemma 2) carries over with an additional loss of $\mathbf{Adv}_E^{\mathrm{prp}}(q, t)$, and the bound of STH_a carries over with an additional loss of $\mathbf{Adv}_E^{\mathrm{prp}}(2q, t)$, where the time complexity is bounded by t.

We also consider a variant of STH based on two independent random permutations without domain separation. Let $n, a \in \mathbb{N}$ such that $0 \leqslant a \leqslant n$, and write $b = n - a$. Let $P_1, P_2 \in \mathsf{Perm}[n]$ be two permutations. We define $\mathsf{STH2}_a^{P_1, P_2} \in \mathsf{Func}[n, n + a]$ as follows:

$$\mathsf{STH2}_a^{P_1, P_2}(x) = \mathsf{left}_a(P_1(x)) \,\|\, \mathsf{left}_a(P_2(x)) \,\|\, \mathsf{right}_b(P_1(x) \oplus P_2(x)) \,. \quad (14)$$

We get a similar bound as for the original STH.

Theorem 2. *Let $n, a, q \in \mathbb{N}$ such that $0 \leqslant a \leqslant n$, and write $b = n - a$. Assume that $b \geqslant \max(n/12, 10)$. We have:*

$$\mathbf{Adv}_{\mathsf{STH2}_a}^{\mathrm{prf}}(q) \leqslant 3 \left(\frac{q}{2^{n-a/3}}\right)^{3/2} + \frac{1}{\sqrt{2\pi}} \left(\frac{q}{2^{n-5}}\right)^{2^{b-2}} + 2\mathbf{Adv}_{\mathsf{Trunc}_a}^{\mathrm{prf}}(q) \,. \quad (15)$$

We prove Theorem 2 in Sect. 6.

One might also be interested in creating a larger instance of the hybrid. One approach would be to consider applying other functions than summation on the discarded parts. For example, one could apply the generalized CENC construction [37] on top of them. This could lead to other interesting results and might improve the efficiency as well, but this is left for potential future work.

4   Proof of Theorem 1

Let $n, a, q \in \mathbb{N}$ such that $0 \leqslant a \leqslant n$, and write $b = n - a$. As of now, we will drop subscript a to STH for brevity. Consider any distinguisher $\mathcal{D}$ making q queries to its oracle. Without loss of generality, $\mathcal{D}$ is deterministic and does not make pointless queries, i.e., $x_i \neq x_j$ for all $i \neq j$. Our goal is to bound the distance between STH^P for a random permutation $P \xleftarrow{\$} \mathsf{Perm}[n]$ on the one hand and a random function $R \xleftarrow{\$} \mathsf{Func}[n - 1, n + a]$ on the other hand:

$$\mathbf{Adv}_{\mathsf{STH}}^{\mathrm{prf}}(\mathcal{D}) = \left\| \mathbb{P}\left[\mathcal{D}^{\mathsf{STH}^P} = 1\right] - \mathbb{P}\left[\mathcal{D}^R = 1\right] \right\| \,. \quad (16)$$

We will bound (16) in multiple steps. The first step (Sect. 4.1) will be to show that, without loss of generality, we can move to a non-adaptive setting and argue based on probabilities of transcripts to occur. Then, the second step (Sect. 4.2) consists of transforming the real world STH^P into a world that separates the Trunc and SoP parts within STH. Then, the third step (Sect. 4.3) replaces that Trunc part by a random function, at the cost of $\mathbf{Adv}_{\mathsf{Trunc}}^{\mathrm{prf}}(2q)$. Then, the fourth step (Sect. 4.4) operates on the ideal world R: it transforms it into a world that does not output strings of the form $u\|u\|0^b$ for $u \in \{0, 1\}^a$, noting that these never occur in the real world we were left with in the third step. Finally, the fifth step (Sect. 4.5) bounds the remaining two worlds using the chi-squared method.

4.1   Moving Towards Transcripts

As a first step, we note that the input adaptivity does not help and it suffices to simply consider the probability of transcripts to occur in the real world and in the ideal world. Let $\mathcal{O}_1$ be an oracle that generates transcripts as lists of random strings, Algorithm 1, and $\mathcal{O}_2 = \mathsf{NSTH}$ (Non-adaptive STH) be an oracle that generates transcripts as results of STH^P with random $P \xleftarrow{\$} \mathsf{Perm}[n]$ and fixed inputs $x_i = i$, Algorithm 2.

We will show that the advantage of attacker $\mathcal{D}$ in distinguishing the two worlds of (16) is at most the statistical distance between world $\mathcal{O}_1$ and world $\mathcal{O}_2$. Suppose we get a transcript τ from any of the two oracles $\mathcal{O}_1$ or $\mathcal{O}_2$, we will use it to simulate $\mathcal{D}$'s oracles as follows. If $\mathcal{D}$ makes query x_i, we respond with $u_i\|v_i\|w_i$ from the transcript. Denote by A the set of all transcripts τ for which $\mathcal{D}$ returns 1. Note that we can cleanly define this, as $\mathcal{D}$ is deterministic and its decision only depends on τ; moreover, the fact that world $\mathcal{O}_2$ uses fixed inputs for P does not matter as it is a random permutation. Then, the advantage of $\mathcal{D}$ is at most

$$(16) \leqslant |\mathbb{P}_{\mathcal{O}_1}[A] - \mathbb{P}_{\mathcal{O}_2}[A]| \leqslant \|\mathbb{P}_{\mathcal{O}_1} - \mathbb{P}_{\mathcal{O}_2}\| . \tag{17}$$

Henceforth, it is sufficient to restrict our focus to the statistical distance between $\mathcal{O}_1$ and $\mathcal{O}_2$.

Algorithm 1 $\mathcal{O}_1 = R_1$
1: **function** R_1
2:     **for** $i \leftarrow 1$ to q **do**
3:         $u_i \xleftarrow{\$} \{0,1\}^a$
4:         $v_i \xleftarrow{\$} \{0,1\}^a$
5:         $w_i \xleftarrow{\$} \{0,1\}^b$
6:     $\boldsymbol{u} = (u_1, \ldots, u_q)$
7:     $\boldsymbol{v} = (v_1, \ldots, v_q)$
8:     $\boldsymbol{w} = (w_1, \ldots, w_q)$
9:     **return** $\tau = (\boldsymbol{u}, \boldsymbol{v}, \boldsymbol{w})$

Algorithm 2 $\mathcal{O}_2 = \mathsf{NSTH}$
1: **function** NSTH
2:     $P \xleftarrow{\$} \mathsf{Perm}[n]$
3:     **for** $i \leftarrow 1$ to q **do**
4:         $u_i \leftarrow \mathsf{left}_a(P(i\|0))$
5:         $v_i \leftarrow \mathsf{left}_a(P(i\|1))$
6:         $U_i \leftarrow \mathsf{right}_b(P(i\|0))$
7:         $V_i \leftarrow \mathsf{right}_b(P(i\|1))$
8:         $w_i = U_i \oplus V_i$
9:     $\boldsymbol{u} = (u_1, \ldots, u_q)$
10:     $\boldsymbol{v} = (v_1, \ldots, v_q)$
11:     $\boldsymbol{w} = (w_1, \ldots, w_q)$
12:     **return** $\tau = (\boldsymbol{u}, \boldsymbol{v}, \boldsymbol{w})$

4.2   Permutation-Separated STH

We define a variant of $\mathcal{O}_2$, namely $\mathcal{O}_3 = \mathsf{PSTH}$ (Permutation-separated STH), in Algorithm 3. This oracle "separates" the Trunc part and the SoP part within NSTH. In more detail, it first calls internal procedure PTrunc that draws a random permutation $P \xleftarrow{\$} \mathsf{Perm}[n]$ and outputs the lists $\boldsymbol{u}$ and $\boldsymbol{v}$. Then, it calls internal procedure PSoP that takes the two lists $(\boldsymbol{u}, \boldsymbol{v})$ and returns a list $\boldsymbol{w}$ using a random permutation P'. This permutation is randomly drawn from a set

---

Algorithm 3 $\mathcal{O}_3 = \mathsf{PSTH}$

1: **function** PSTH
2:     $(\boldsymbol{u}, \boldsymbol{v}) \leftarrow \mathsf{PTrunc}$
3:     $\boldsymbol{w} \leftarrow \mathsf{PSoP}(\boldsymbol{u}, \boldsymbol{v})$
4:     **return** $\boldsymbol{\tau} = (\boldsymbol{u}, \boldsymbol{v}, \boldsymbol{w})$

1: **function** PTrunc
2:     $P \xleftarrow{\$} \mathsf{Perm}[n]$
3:     **for** $i \leftarrow 1$ to q **do**
4:         $u_i \leftarrow \mathsf{left}_a(P(i\|0))$
5:         $v_i \leftarrow \mathsf{left}_a(P(i\|1))$
6:     $\boldsymbol{u} = (u_1, \dots, u_q)$
7:     $\boldsymbol{v} = (v_1, \dots, v_q)$
8:     **return** $(\boldsymbol{u}, \boldsymbol{v})$

1: **function** PSoP$(\boldsymbol{u}, \boldsymbol{v})$
2:     **if** $\mathsf{Perm}_{\mathrm{comp}}(\boldsymbol{u}, \boldsymbol{v}) \neq \varnothing$ **then**
3:         $P' \xleftarrow{\$} \mathsf{Perm}_{\mathrm{comp}}(\boldsymbol{u}, \boldsymbol{v})$
4:     **else**
5:         $P' \leftarrow I_n$
6:     **for** $i \leftarrow 1$ to q **do**
7:         $U_i \leftarrow \mathsf{right}_b(P'(i\|0))$
8:         $V_i \leftarrow \mathsf{right}_b(P'(i\|1))$
9:         $w_i = U_i \oplus V_i$
10:    $\boldsymbol{w} = (w_1, \dots, w_q)$
11:    **return** $\boldsymbol{w}$

$\mathsf{Perm}_{\mathrm{comp}}(\boldsymbol{u}, \boldsymbol{v}) \subseteq \mathsf{Perm}[n]$ defined as the set of all permutations from $\mathsf{Perm}[n]$ for which PTrunc would return $(\boldsymbol{u}, \boldsymbol{v})$. Note that in our analysis this set will never be empty, so the 'else' branch will never be taken and is included solely to complete the algorithm.

We will prove that any transcript $\boldsymbol{\tau}$ is equally likely in $\mathcal{O}_2$ and $\mathcal{O}_3$. Consider any valid transcript $\boldsymbol{\tau}$, and define by $\mathsf{Perm}_{\mathrm{result}}(\boldsymbol{\tau}) \subseteq \mathsf{Perm}[n]$ the set of all permutations that give result $\boldsymbol{\tau} = (\boldsymbol{u}, \boldsymbol{v}, \boldsymbol{w})$ when used in $\mathcal{O}_2 = \mathsf{NSTH}$. Then,

$$\mathbb{P}_{\mathcal{O}_2}[\boldsymbol{\tau}] = \mathbb{P}_{\mathsf{NSTH}}[\boldsymbol{\tau}] = \frac{|\mathsf{Perm}_{\mathrm{result}}(\boldsymbol{\tau})|}{|\mathsf{Perm}[n]|}.$$

On the other hand, for $\mathcal{O}_3 = \mathsf{PSTH}$, we first have to get the right $(\boldsymbol{u}, \boldsymbol{v})$:

$$\mathbb{P}_{\mathsf{PTrunc}}[(\boldsymbol{u}, \boldsymbol{v})] = \frac{|\mathsf{Perm}_{\mathrm{comp}}(\boldsymbol{u}, \boldsymbol{v})|}{|\mathsf{Perm}[n]|}.$$

Next, we have to get the right $\boldsymbol{w}$. As $\mathsf{Perm}_{\mathrm{result}}(\boldsymbol{\tau}) \subseteq \mathsf{Perm}_{\mathrm{comp}}(\boldsymbol{u}, \boldsymbol{v})$, this probability is equal to:

$$\mathbb{P}_{\mathsf{PSoP}(u,v)}[\boldsymbol{w}] = \frac{|\mathsf{Perm}_{\mathrm{result}}(\boldsymbol{\tau})|}{|\mathsf{Perm}_{\mathrm{comp}}(\boldsymbol{u}, \boldsymbol{v})|}.$$

The randomnesses in PTrunc and PSoP are independent, hence the two probabilities are independent as well. This means that the probability of getting τ in $\mathcal{O}_3 = \mathsf{PSTH}$ is equal to their product. In other words:

$$
\begin{aligned}
\mathbb{P}_{\mathcal{O}_3}[\tau] = \mathbb{P}_{\mathsf{PSTH}}[\tau] &= \mathbb{P}_{\mathsf{PSTH}}\left[\tau \mid (u, v) \leftarrow \mathsf{PTrunc}\right] \cdot \mathbb{P}_{\mathsf{PTrunc}}\left[(u, v)\right] \\
&\quad + \mathbb{P}_{\mathsf{PSTH}}\left[\tau \mid (u, v) \not\leftarrow \mathsf{PTrunc}\right] \cdot \left(1 - \mathbb{P}_{\mathsf{PTrunc}}\left[(u, v)\right]\right) \\
&= \mathbb{P}_{\mathsf{PSoP}(u,v)}[w] \cdot \mathbb{P}_{\mathsf{PTrunc}}\left[(u, v)\right] + 0 \\
&= \frac{|\mathrm{Perm}_{\mathrm{result}}(\tau)|}{|\mathrm{Perm}_{\mathrm{comp}}(u, v)|} \cdot \frac{|\mathrm{Perm}_{\mathrm{comp}}(u, v)|}{|\mathrm{Perm}[n]|} \\
&= \frac{|\mathrm{Perm}_{\mathrm{result}}(\tau)|}{|\mathrm{Perm}[n]|} \\
&= \mathbb{P}_{\mathsf{NSTH}}[\tau] = \mathbb{P}_{\mathcal{O}_2}[\tau]\,.
\end{aligned}
$$

We have henceforth obtained that

$$
\|\mathbb{P}_{\mathcal{O}_2} - \mathbb{P}_{\mathcal{O}_3}\| = 0\,. \tag{18}
$$

4.3   Isolating Truncation Advantage

Next, we define $\mathcal{O}_4 = \mathsf{RSTH}$ (Random function-based STH) in Algorithm 4. The algorithm is identical to $\mathcal{O}_3 = \mathsf{PSTH}$, but with the function PTrunc replaced by a random function S. Note that S is written as separate procedure; this is done to suit further analysis in Sect. 4.5.

Algorithm 4 $\mathcal{O}_4 = \mathsf{RSTH}$

1: **function** RSTH
2:     $(u, v) \leftarrow S$
3:     $w \leftarrow \mathsf{PSoP}(u, v)$ ▷ See Algorithm 3
4:     **return** $\tau = (u, v, w)$

1: **function** S
2:     **for** $i \leftarrow 1$ to q **do**
3:         $u_i \xleftarrow{\$} \{0, 1\}^a$
4:         $v_i \xleftarrow{\$} \{0, 1\}^a$
5:     $u = (u_1, \ldots, u_q)$
6:     $v = (v_1, \ldots, v_q)$
7:     **return** (u, v)

The only difference between $\mathcal{O}_3 = \mathsf{PSTH}$ and $\mathcal{O}_4 = \mathsf{RSTH}$ is in the generation of (u, v): in the former, they are generated as a truncated permutation, whereas in the latter they are generated as a random function. Therefore, we immediately have:

$$
\|\mathbb{P}_{\mathcal{O}_3} - \mathbb{P}_{\mathcal{O}_4}\| \leqslant \|\mathbb{P}_{\mathsf{PTrunc}} - \mathbb{P}_S\| = \mathbf{Adv}_{\mathsf{Trunc}}^{\mathrm{prf}}(2q)\,. \tag{19}
$$

4.4 Discarding the Zero

We proceed on the other end of (17). We turn $\mathcal{O}_1 = R_1$ into $\mathcal{O}_0 = R_0$ that operates identically except that it never returns $w_i = 0^b$ when $u_i = v_i$. The oracle is given in Algorithm 5. As before, we write T as a separate procedure to suit further analysis in Sect. 4.5.

Algorithm 5 $\mathcal{O}_0 = R_0$

1: **function** R_0
2:     $(\boldsymbol{u}, \boldsymbol{v}) \leftarrow S$
3:     $\boldsymbol{w} \leftarrow T(\boldsymbol{u}, \boldsymbol{v})$
4:     **return** $\boldsymbol{\tau} = (\boldsymbol{u}, \boldsymbol{v}, \boldsymbol{w})$

1: **function** $T(\boldsymbol{u}, \boldsymbol{v})$
2:     **for** $i \leftarrow 1$ to q **do**
3:         **if** $u_i \neq v_i$ **then**
4:             $w_i \xleftarrow{\$} \{0,1\}^b$
5:         **else**
6:             $w_i \xleftarrow{\$} \{0,1\}^b \setminus \{0^b\}$
7:     **return** $\boldsymbol{w} = (w_1, \ldots, w_q)$

We look at the statistical distance between $\mathbb{P}_{\mathcal{O}_1}$ and $\mathbb{P}_{\mathcal{O}_0}$. Let bad_1 be the set of transcripts $\boldsymbol{\tau} = (\boldsymbol{u}, \boldsymbol{v}, \boldsymbol{w})$ such that $u_i = v_i$ and $w_i = 0^b$ for some i. As $\mathbb{P}_{\mathcal{O}_0}[\boldsymbol{\tau}] = 0$ for $\boldsymbol{\tau} \in \mathsf{bad}_1$ and $\mathbb{P}_{\mathcal{O}_1}[\boldsymbol{\tau}] \leqslant \mathbb{P}_{\mathcal{O}_0}[\boldsymbol{\tau}]$ for $\boldsymbol{\tau} \notin \mathsf{bad}_1$ we see, where A can be any set of transcripts, that

$$\|\mathbb{P}_{\mathcal{O}_1} - \mathbb{P}_{\mathcal{O}_0}\| = \max_A |\mathbb{P}_{\mathcal{O}_1}[A] - \mathbb{P}_{\mathcal{O}_0}[A]|$$
$$= \mathbb{P}_{\mathcal{O}_1}[\mathsf{bad}_1]$$
$$\leqslant \sum_{i=1}^{q} \mathbb{P}_{\mathcal{O}_1}[u_i = v_i, w_i = 0^b]$$
$$= \frac{q}{2^n}. \tag{20}$$

4.5 Final Step

Looking back, Eqs. (17), (18), (19), and (20) have transformed our original goal (16) into

$$\mathbf{Adv}_{\mathsf{STH}}^{\mathrm{prf}}(\mathcal{D}) \leqslant \|\mathbb{P}_{\mathcal{O}_0} - \mathbb{P}_{\mathcal{O}_4}\| + \frac{q}{2^n} + \mathbf{Adv}_{\mathsf{Trunc}}^{\mathrm{prf}}(2q). \tag{21}$$

We now look at the worlds $\mathcal{O}_0$ and $\mathcal{O}_4$. Noting that in both worlds $\boldsymbol{u}$ and $\boldsymbol{v}$ are generated identically, we can parameterize these worlds. We define $\mathcal{O}_0^{\boldsymbol{u}, \boldsymbol{v}} =$

$T(\boldsymbol{u}, \boldsymbol{v})$ and $\mathcal{O}_4^{\boldsymbol{u},\boldsymbol{v}} = \mathsf{PSoP}(\boldsymbol{u}, \boldsymbol{v})$, so that in both cases $\boldsymbol{u}$ and $\boldsymbol{v}$ are generated by S and $\boldsymbol{w}$ by $\mathcal{O}_b^{\boldsymbol{u},\boldsymbol{v}}$ for $b \in \{0, 4\}$. This means that

$$
\begin{aligned}
\|\mathbb{P}_{\mathcal{O}_0} - \mathbb{P}_{\mathcal{O}_4}\| &= \sum_{\boldsymbol{u},\boldsymbol{v}} \sum_{\boldsymbol{w}} \max(0, \mathbb{P}_{\mathcal{O}_0}[(\boldsymbol{u}, \boldsymbol{v}, \boldsymbol{w})] - \mathbb{P}_{\mathcal{O}_4}[(\boldsymbol{u}, \boldsymbol{v}, \boldsymbol{w})]) \\
&= \sum_{\boldsymbol{u},\boldsymbol{v}} \sum_{\boldsymbol{w}} \max(0, \mathbb{P}_{\mathcal{O}_0^{\boldsymbol{u},\boldsymbol{v}}}[\boldsymbol{w}] - \mathbb{P}_{\mathcal{O}_4^{\boldsymbol{u},\boldsymbol{v}}}[\boldsymbol{w}]) \cdot \mathbb{P}_S[(\boldsymbol{u}, \boldsymbol{v})] \\
&= \sum_{\boldsymbol{u},\boldsymbol{v}} \left\| \mathbb{P}_{\mathcal{O}_0^{\boldsymbol{u},\boldsymbol{v}}} - \mathbb{P}_{\mathcal{O}_4^{\boldsymbol{u},\boldsymbol{v}}} \right\| \cdot \mathbb{P}_S[(\boldsymbol{u}, \boldsymbol{v})] \\
&= \mathbb{E}_{\boldsymbol{u},\boldsymbol{v}} \left[\left\| \mathbb{P}_{\mathcal{O}_0^{\boldsymbol{u},\boldsymbol{v}}} - \mathbb{P}_{\mathcal{O}_4^{\boldsymbol{u},\boldsymbol{v}}} \right\| \right],
\end{aligned}
$$

with $\boldsymbol{u}$ and $\boldsymbol{v}$ drawn uniformly. The remaining task boils down to bounding the distance between PSoP of Algorithm 3 and random function T of Algorithm 5.

For this, we first define $C_{\boldsymbol{u},\boldsymbol{v}}(i)$ and $C'_{\boldsymbol{u},\boldsymbol{v}}(i)$ as the number of previous elements in $\boldsymbol{u}, \boldsymbol{v}$ equal to u_i and v_i, respectively, as follows:

$$
\begin{aligned}
C_{\boldsymbol{u},\boldsymbol{v}}(i) &= |\{j \mid j < i, u_j = u_i\}| + |\{j \mid j < i, v_j = u_i\}|, \\
C'_{\boldsymbol{u},\boldsymbol{v}}(i) &= |\{j \mid j < i, u_j = v_i\}| + |\{j \mid j < i, v_j = v_i\}|.
\end{aligned}
$$

In our derivation we want to assume that these values stay below 2^{b-2}. We define bad_2 as the set of all $(\boldsymbol{u}, \boldsymbol{v})$ such that $C_{\boldsymbol{u},\boldsymbol{v}}(i) \geqslant 2^{b-2}$ or $C'_{\boldsymbol{u},\boldsymbol{v}}(i) \geqslant 2^{b-2}$ for some i. We want to discard the bad cases while still reasoning about $\boldsymbol{u}$ and $\boldsymbol{v}$ as uniformly random values. For this, we use the following lemma.

Lemma 3. *Let f be a non-negative function such that $\left\| \mathbb{P}_{\mathcal{O}_0^{\boldsymbol{u},\boldsymbol{v}}} - \mathbb{P}_{\mathcal{O}_4^{\boldsymbol{u},\boldsymbol{v}}} \right\| \leqslant f(\boldsymbol{u}, \boldsymbol{v})$ for $(\boldsymbol{u}, \boldsymbol{v}) \notin \mathsf{bad}_2$. Then*

$$
\mathbb{E}_{\boldsymbol{u},\boldsymbol{v}} \left[\left\| \mathbb{P}_{\mathcal{O}_0^{\boldsymbol{u},\boldsymbol{v}}} - \mathbb{P}_{\mathcal{O}_4^{\boldsymbol{u},\boldsymbol{v}}} \right\| \right] \leqslant \mathbb{E}_{\boldsymbol{u},\boldsymbol{v}}[f(\boldsymbol{u}, \boldsymbol{v})] \tag{22}
$$

$$
+ \mathbb{P}_{\boldsymbol{u},\boldsymbol{v}}[(\boldsymbol{u}, \boldsymbol{v}) \in \mathsf{bad}_2]. \tag{23}
$$

Note that in $\mathbb{E}_{\boldsymbol{u},\boldsymbol{v}}[f(\boldsymbol{u}, \boldsymbol{v})]$ the values $\boldsymbol{u}, \boldsymbol{v}$ are still drawn uniformly.

Proof. For $(\boldsymbol{u}, \boldsymbol{v}) \notin \mathsf{bad}_2$ we have that $\left\| \mathbb{P}_{\mathcal{O}_0^{\boldsymbol{u},\boldsymbol{v}}} - \mathbb{P}_{\mathcal{O}_4^{\boldsymbol{u},\boldsymbol{v}}} \right\| \leqslant f(\boldsymbol{u}, \boldsymbol{v})$. On the other hand, for $(\boldsymbol{u}, \boldsymbol{v}) \in \mathsf{bad}_2$ we get $\left\| \mathbb{P}_{\mathcal{O}_0^{\boldsymbol{u},\boldsymbol{v}}} - \mathbb{P}_{\mathcal{O}_4^{\boldsymbol{u},\boldsymbol{v}}} \right\| \leqslant 1 \leqslant f(\boldsymbol{u}, \boldsymbol{v}) + 1$. Together, this means that $\left\| \mathbb{P}_{\mathcal{O}_0^{\boldsymbol{u},\boldsymbol{v}}} - \mathbb{P}_{\mathcal{O}_4^{\boldsymbol{u},\boldsymbol{v}}} \right\| \leqslant f(\boldsymbol{u}, \boldsymbol{v}) + \mathbf{1}_{\mathsf{bad}_2}(\boldsymbol{u}, \boldsymbol{v})$, where $\mathbf{1}_{\mathsf{bad}_2}$ is the indicator function of bad_2, which is 1 for $(\boldsymbol{u}, \boldsymbol{v}) \in \mathsf{bad}_2$ and 0 otherwise. By taking the expectation on both sides this results in

$$
\begin{aligned}
\mathbb{E}_{\boldsymbol{u},\boldsymbol{v}} \left[\left\| \mathbb{P}_{\mathcal{O}_0^{\boldsymbol{u},\boldsymbol{v}}} - \mathbb{P}_{\mathcal{O}_4^{\boldsymbol{u},\boldsymbol{v}}} \right\| \right] &\leqslant \mathbb{E}_{\boldsymbol{u},\boldsymbol{v}}[f(\boldsymbol{u}, \boldsymbol{v}) + \mathbf{1}_{\mathsf{bad}_2}(\boldsymbol{u}, \boldsymbol{v})] \\
&= \mathbb{E}_{\boldsymbol{u},\boldsymbol{v}}[f(\boldsymbol{u}, \boldsymbol{v})] + \mathbb{P}_{\boldsymbol{u},\boldsymbol{v}}[(\boldsymbol{u}, \boldsymbol{v}) \in \mathsf{bad}_2].
\end{aligned}
$$

$\square$

We derive bounds for (22) with suitable f and (23) separately.

4.5.1 Bounding (22)

As a first step we have to find a non-negative function f such that $\left\|\mathbb{P}_{\mathcal{O}_0^{u,v}} - \mathbb{P}_{\mathcal{O}_4^{u,v}}\right\| \leqslant f(u,v)$ for $(u,v) \notin \mathsf{bad}_2$. The following theorem gives such function.

Theorem 3. Let $a, b, q \in \mathbb{N}$ and let $u = (u_1, \ldots, u_q)$ and $v = (v_1, \ldots, v_q)$ be vectors of length q with elements in $\{0,1\}^a$ such that $C_{u,v}(i), C'_{u,v}(i) < 2^{b-2}$ for all i. Let $\mathcal{O}$ and $\mathcal{R}$ be as in Algorithm 6. Then

$$\|\mathbb{P}_{\mathcal{O}} - \mathbb{P}_{\mathcal{R}}\| \leqslant \sqrt{\frac{4}{2^{3b}} \sum_{i=1}^{q} C_{u,v}(i) \cdot C'_{u,v}(i)}.$$

Algorithm 6 $\mathcal{O}$
1: **function** $\mathcal{O}$
2:     **for** $k \in \{0,1\}^a$ **do**
3:         $P_k \xleftarrow{\$} \mathsf{Perm}[b]$
4:     **for** $i \leftarrow 1$ to q **do**
5:         $U_i \leftarrow P_{u_i}(\langle C_{u,v}(i)\rangle_{b-1}\|0)$
6:         $V_i \leftarrow P_{v_i}(\langle C'_{u,v}(i)\rangle_{b-1}\|1)$
7:         $w_i \leftarrow U_i \oplus V_i$
8:     **return** $w = (w_1, \ldots, w_q)$

Algorithm 7 $\mathcal{R}$
1: **function** $\mathcal{R}$
2:     **for** $i \leftarrow 1$ to q **do**
3:         **if** $u_i \neq v_i$ **then**
4:             $w_i \xleftarrow{\$} \{0,1\}^b$
5:         **else**
6:             $w_i \xleftarrow{\$} \{0,1\}^b \setminus \{0^b\}$
7:     **return** $w = (w_1, \ldots, w_q)$

Here $\langle x \rangle_n$ is the encoding of x as a n-bit string.

The proof of Theorem 3 will be given in Sect. 5.

It is obvious that $\mathcal{R}$ equals $\mathcal{O}_0^{u,v}$. We will next show that $\mathcal{O}$ generates the same distribution as $\mathcal{O}_4^{u,v}$, by looking at the distribution of U_i given all previous values (the analysis is symmetrical for the values V_i).

In world $\mathcal{O}$, the value is generated by the permutation P_{u_i} with the input $\langle C_{u,v}(i)\rangle_{b-1}\|0$. Note that we can encode $C_{u,v}(i)$ as a $b-1$-bit string, as we assume that $C_{u,v}(i) < 2^{b-2} < 2^{b-1}$. The output value of P_{u_i} will be distributed uniformly from $\{0,1\}^b$ minus its previously generated values. These values, in turn, are U_j and V_j such that $u_j = u_i$ or $v_j = u_i$, respectively, for $j < i$. Note that we do get a new value, as $\langle C_{u,v}(i)\rangle_{b-1}\|0$ is different from $\langle C_{u,v}(j)\rangle_{b-1}\|0$ or $\langle C'_{u,v}(j)\rangle_{b-1}\|1$ for such j.

In world $\mathcal{O}_4^{u,v}$, the value is generated by the single permutation P' selected from the set $\mathsf{Perm}_{\mathrm{comp}}(u,v)$ with the new input $i\|0$. Note that $\mathsf{Perm}_{\mathrm{comp}}(u,v)$ is never empty as we assume that $C_{u,v}(i), C'_{u,v}(i) < 2^{b-2} < 2^b$ for all i, hence there always exists a permutation that would generate u and v. We know that the first a bits of the output of P' have to be equal to u_i. This means that previously generated values of P' do not matter as long as their first a bits are different. Again, for the last b bits we know that they cannot be equal to U_j or V_j with $u_j = u_i$ or $v_j = u_i$, respectively, for $j < i$. Furthermore, the value is uniformly chosen from the remaining elements in the set $\{0,1\}^b$, as P' is selected uniformly from $\mathsf{Perm}_{\mathrm{comp}}(\boldsymbol{u}, \boldsymbol{v})$.

This means that the distribution of all U_i's is the same in both worlds. As the analysis of all V_i's is similar, both $\mathcal{O}$ and $\mathcal{O}_4^{\boldsymbol{u},\boldsymbol{v}}$ have the same distribution.

We will now use Theorem 3 to bound (22). As the property $\mathbb{E}\left[X\right]^2 \leqslant \mathbb{E}\left[X^2\right]$ implies that $\mathbb{E}\left[\sqrt{X}\right] \leqslant \sqrt{\mathbb{E}\left[X\right]}$, we get

$$
\mathbb{E}_{\boldsymbol{u},\boldsymbol{v}}\left[f(\boldsymbol{u},\boldsymbol{v})\right] \leqslant \sqrt{\mathbb{E}_{\boldsymbol{u},\boldsymbol{v}}\left[\frac{4}{2^{3b}} \sum_{i=1}^{q} C_{\boldsymbol{u},\boldsymbol{v}}(i) \cdot C'_{\boldsymbol{u},\boldsymbol{v}}(i)\right]}
$$

$$
= \sqrt{\frac{4}{2^{3b}} \sum_{i=1}^{q} \mathbb{E}_{\boldsymbol{u},\boldsymbol{v}}\left[C_{\boldsymbol{u},\boldsymbol{v}}(i) \cdot C'_{\boldsymbol{u},\boldsymbol{v}}(i)\right]}. \tag{24}
$$

Although $C_{\boldsymbol{u},\boldsymbol{v}}(i)$ and $C'_{\boldsymbol{u},\boldsymbol{v}}(i)$ are not independent, we will show that their *expectations* are independent, i.e. that $\mathbb{E}_{\boldsymbol{u},\boldsymbol{v}}\left[C'_{\boldsymbol{u},\boldsymbol{v}}(i) \mid C_{\boldsymbol{u},\boldsymbol{v}}(i)\right] = \mathbb{E}_{\boldsymbol{u},\boldsymbol{v}}\left[C'_{\boldsymbol{u},\boldsymbol{v}}(i)\right]$. First of all, as $\boldsymbol{u}$ and $\boldsymbol{v}$ are distributed uniform, every u_j and v_j has a probability of $1/2^a$ of being equal to u_i or v_i for $j < i$, hence

$$
\mathbb{E}_{\boldsymbol{u},\boldsymbol{v}}\left[C_{\boldsymbol{u},\boldsymbol{v}}(i)\right] = \mathbb{E}_{\boldsymbol{u},\boldsymbol{v}}\left[C'_{\boldsymbol{u},\boldsymbol{v}}(i)\right] = \frac{2(i-1)}{2^a}.
$$

Next, we have to compute $\mathbb{E}_{\boldsymbol{u},\boldsymbol{v}}\left[C'_{\boldsymbol{u},\boldsymbol{v}}(i) \mid C_{\boldsymbol{u},\boldsymbol{v}}(i)\right]$. In this case we condition over the event that $u_i = v_i$. If this is the case, we know the value of $C'_{\boldsymbol{u},\boldsymbol{v}}(i)$ exactly, as it is equal to $C_{\boldsymbol{u},\boldsymbol{v}}(i)$. On the other hand, if $u_i \neq v_i$, we know that there are $C_{\boldsymbol{u},\boldsymbol{v}}(i)$ less candidates, but also that every candidate has a higher probability $1/(2^a - 1)$ of being equal to v_i. This gives the following result:

$$
\begin{aligned}
\mathbb{E}_{\boldsymbol{u},\boldsymbol{v}}\left[C'_{\boldsymbol{u},\boldsymbol{v}}(i) \mid C_{\boldsymbol{u},\boldsymbol{v}}(i)\right] &= \mathbb{P}_{\boldsymbol{u},\boldsymbol{v}}\left[u_i = v_i\right] \cdot \mathbb{E}_{\boldsymbol{u},\boldsymbol{v}}\left[C'_{\boldsymbol{u},\boldsymbol{v}}(i) \mid C_{\boldsymbol{u},\boldsymbol{v}}(i), u_i = v_i\right] \\
&\quad + \mathbb{P}_{\boldsymbol{u},\boldsymbol{v}}\left[u_i \neq v_i\right] \cdot \mathbb{E}_{\boldsymbol{u},\boldsymbol{v}}\left[C'_{\boldsymbol{u},\boldsymbol{v}}(i) \mid C_{\boldsymbol{u},\boldsymbol{v}}(i), u_i \neq v_i\right] \\
&= \frac{1}{2^a} \cdot C_{\boldsymbol{u},\boldsymbol{v}}(i) + \left(1 - \frac{1}{2^a}\right) \cdot \frac{2(i-1) - C_{\boldsymbol{u},\boldsymbol{v}}(i)}{2^a - 1} \\
&= \frac{1}{2^a} \cdot C_{\boldsymbol{u},\boldsymbol{v}}(i) + \frac{2^a - 1}{2^a} \cdot \frac{2(i-1) - C_{\boldsymbol{u},\boldsymbol{v}}(i)}{2^a - 1} \\
&= \frac{1}{2^a} \cdot C_{\boldsymbol{u},\boldsymbol{v}}(i) + \frac{1}{2^a} \cdot (2(i-1) - C_{\boldsymbol{u},\boldsymbol{v}}(i)) \\
&= \frac{2(i-1)}{2^a} \\
&= \mathbb{E}_{\boldsymbol{u},\boldsymbol{v}}\left[C'_{\boldsymbol{u},\boldsymbol{v}}(i)\right].
\end{aligned}
$$

By Lemma 1 this means that we have $\mathbb{E}_{u,v}\left[C_{u,v}(i) \cdot C'_{u,v}(i)\right] = \mathbb{E}_{u,v}\left[C_{u,v}(i)\right] \cdot \mathbb{E}_{u,v}\left[C'_{u,v}(i)\right]$, so

$$(24) = \sqrt{\frac{4}{2^{3b}} \sum_{i=1}^{q} \mathbb{E}_{u,v}\left[C_{u,v}(i)\right] \cdot \mathbb{E}_{u,v}\left[C'_{u,v}(i)\right]}$$

$$= \sqrt{\frac{4}{2^{3b}} \sum_{i=1}^{q} \left(\frac{2(i-1)}{2^a}\right)^2}$$

$$\leqslant \sqrt{\frac{4}{2^{3b}} \frac{4 \cdot q^3}{3 \cdot 2^{2a}}}$$

$$\leqslant \sqrt{6 \cdot \frac{q^3}{2^{3n-a}}}$$

$$\leqslant 3 \left(\frac{q}{2^{n-a/3}}\right)^{3/2}.$$

This finishes the first part of the bound.

4.5.2   Bounding (23)

We now look at (23). The event $(u, v) \in \mathsf{bad}_2$ occurs when a 2^{b-2}-collision occurs inside (u, v). As u and v are chosen uniformly, the probability of getting a t-collision is bounded by

$$\frac{(2q)^t}{2^{a(t-1)} \cdot t!},$$

where we later substitute $t = 2^{b-2}$. By Stirling's approximation, which says that

$$t! \geqslant \sqrt{2\pi t} \left(\frac{t}{e}\right)^t \geqslant \sqrt{2\pi} \left(2^{-3/2} \cdot t\right)^t,$$

we get that

$$(23) \leqslant \frac{1}{\sqrt{2\pi}} \cdot \frac{(2q)^t}{2^{a(t-1)}} \cdot \left(\frac{1}{2^{-3/2} \cdot t}\right)^t$$

$$= \frac{2^a}{\sqrt{2\pi}} \cdot \left(\frac{2q}{2^a}\right)^t \cdot \left(\frac{1}{2^{-3/2} \cdot t}\right)^t$$

$$= \frac{2^a}{\sqrt{2\pi}} \cdot \left(\frac{2q}{2^{a-3/2} \cdot t}\right)^t. \tag{25}$$

From the assumption that $b \geqslant n/12$ and $b \geqslant 10$ (hence $b \leqslant 2^b/96$), we get that $a \leqslant n \leqslant 12b \leqslant 2^b/8 = t/2$, so

$$(25) \leqslant \frac{1}{\sqrt{2\pi}} \left(\frac{2q}{2^{a-2} \cdot t}\right)^t. \tag{26}$$

Finally, by substituting $t = 2^{b-2}$ we get

$$(26) = \frac{1}{\sqrt{2\pi}} \left(\frac{2q}{2^{a-2} \cdot 2^{b-2}} \right)^{2^{b-2}}$$

$$= \frac{1}{\sqrt{2\pi}} \left(\frac{q}{2^{n-5}} \right)^{2^{b-2}}.$$

This finishes the second part of the bound.

5   Proof of Theorem 3

Let $a, b, q \in \mathbb{N}$ and let $\boldsymbol{u} = (u_1, \ldots, u_q)$ and $\boldsymbol{v} = (v_1, \ldots, v_q)$ be vectors of length q with elements in $\{0, 1\}^a$ such that $C_{\boldsymbol{u},\boldsymbol{v}}(i), C'_{\boldsymbol{u},\boldsymbol{v}}(i) < 2^{b-2}$ for all i. Let $\mathcal{O}$ and $\mathcal{R}$ be as in Algorithm 6. We denote their outputs by $\boldsymbol{w} = (w_1, \ldots, w_q)$. Further, for $i \in \{0, \ldots, q\}$ denote $\boldsymbol{w}_i = (w_1, \ldots, w_i)$.

We will rely on the chi-squared method by Dai et al. [22]. For each $i = 1, \ldots, q$ and each $\boldsymbol{w}_{i-1}$, define

$$\chi^2(\boldsymbol{w}_{i-1}) = \sum_w \frac{\left(\mathbb{P}_{\mathcal{O}}\left[w_i = w \mid \boldsymbol{w}_{i-1} \right] - \mathbb{P}_{\mathcal{R}}\left[w_i = w \mid \boldsymbol{w}_{i-1} \right] \right)^2}{\mathbb{P}_{\mathcal{R}}\left[w_i = w \mid \boldsymbol{w}_{i-1} \right]}. \tag{27}$$

The chi-squared method gives the following bound [22]:

Lemma 4 (Chi-Squared Method).   *Consider two systems $\mathcal{O}, \mathcal{R}$. Suppose that for any vector $\boldsymbol{w}_i$, $\mathbb{P}_{\mathcal{R}}\left[\boldsymbol{w}_i\right] > 0$ whenever $\mathbb{P}_{\mathcal{O}}\left[\boldsymbol{w}_i\right] > 0$. Then,*

$$\|\mathbb{P}_{\mathcal{O}} - \mathbb{P}_{\mathcal{R}}\| \leqslant \left(\frac{1}{2} \sum_{i=1}^q \mathbb{E}_{\mathcal{O}}\left[\chi^2(\boldsymbol{w}_{i-1}) \right] \right)^{1/2}.$$

Our proof of Theorem 3 is related to that of Dai et al. [22], where they look at both the SoSP construction of (2) for a single permutation and the SoP construction of (1) based on two different permutations. In our terminology, these correspond to the case of $\boldsymbol{u} = \boldsymbol{v} = (0^a, \ldots, 0^a)$ and $\boldsymbol{u} = (0^a, \ldots, 0^a)$, $\boldsymbol{v} = (1^a, \ldots, 1^a)$, respectively. Our analysis, thus, carefully combines and generalizes these approaches. An additional difficulty arises from the fact that the different cases *depend on* the values of $\boldsymbol{u}$ and $\boldsymbol{v}$, that may be arbitrary.

In the chi-squared method we have to reason over $\mathbb{P}_{\mathcal{O}}\left[w_i = w \mid \boldsymbol{w}_{i-1} \right]$. However, in our case it is difficult to do this directly, as the conditional probability does not give information about the intermediate values U_j and V_j for $j < i$, but only about their sum $w_j = U_j \oplus V_j$. The following lemma shows that we can assume this extra information without increasing the bound. Intuitively, this is similar to the fact that giving an adversary more information does not lower its advantage.

Lemma 5. *Let Z_{i-1} be a random variable in world $\mathcal{O}$ (but not necessarily in world $\mathcal{R}$). Then,*

$$\mathbb{E}_{\mathcal{O}}\left[\chi^2(\boldsymbol{w}_{i-1})\right] \leqslant \sum_w \mathbb{E}_{\mathcal{O}}\left[\frac{\left(\mathbb{P}_{\mathcal{O}}\left[w_i = w \mid \boldsymbol{w}_{i-1}, Z_{i-1}\right] - \mathbb{P}_{\mathcal{R}}\left[w_i = w \mid \boldsymbol{w}_{i-1}\right]\right)^2}{\mathbb{P}_{\mathcal{R}}\left[w_i = w \mid \boldsymbol{w}_{i-1}\right]}\right].$$

Proof. Recall that

$$\chi^2(\boldsymbol{w}_{i-1}) = \sum_w \frac{\left(\mathbb{P}_{\mathcal{O}}\left[w_i = w \mid \boldsymbol{w}_{i-1}\right] - \mathbb{P}_{\mathcal{R}}\left[w_i = w \mid \boldsymbol{w}_{i-1}\right]\right)^2}{\mathbb{P}_{\mathcal{R}}\left[w_i = w \mid \boldsymbol{w}_{i-1}\right]}.$$

Let $\boldsymbol{w}_{i-1}$ and w be fixed and write $p = \mathbb{P}_{\mathcal{R}}\left[w_i = w \mid \boldsymbol{w}_{i-1}\right]$. Then

$$\frac{1}{p}\left(\mathbb{P}_{\mathcal{O}}\left[w_i = w \mid \boldsymbol{w}_{i-1}\right] - p\right)^2$$

$$= \frac{1}{p}\left(\sum_z \mathbb{P}_{\mathcal{O}}\left[Z_{i-1} = z \mid \boldsymbol{w}_{i-1}\right] \cdot \mathbb{P}_{\mathcal{O}}\left[w_i = w \mid \boldsymbol{w}_{i-1}, Z_{i-1} = z\right] - p\right)^2$$

$$= \frac{1}{p}\left(\mathbb{E}_{\mathcal{O}}\left[\mathbb{P}_{\mathcal{O}}\left[w_i = w \mid \boldsymbol{w}_{i-1}, Z_{i-1}\right] \,\middle|\, \boldsymbol{w}_{i-1}\right] - p\right)^2$$

$$= \frac{1}{p}\mathbb{E}_{\mathcal{O}}\left[\mathbb{P}_{\mathcal{O}}\left[w_i = w \mid \boldsymbol{w}_{i-1}, Z_{i-1}\right] - p \,\middle|\, \boldsymbol{w}_{i-1}\right]^2$$

$$\leqslant \frac{1}{p}\mathbb{E}_{\mathcal{O}}\left[\left(\mathbb{P}_{\mathcal{O}}\left[w_i = w \mid \boldsymbol{w}_{i-1}, Z_{i-1}\right] - p\right)^2 \,\middle|\, \boldsymbol{w}_{i-1}\right]$$

$$= \mathbb{E}_{\mathcal{O}}\left[\frac{1}{p}\left(\mathbb{P}_{\mathcal{O}}\left[w_i = w \mid \boldsymbol{w}_{i-1}, Z_{i-1}\right] - p\right)^2 \,\middle|\, \boldsymbol{w}_{i-1}\right].$$

Furthermore, by taking the expectation on both sides we get

$$\mathbb{E}_{\mathcal{O}}\left[\frac{\left(\mathbb{P}_{\mathcal{O}}\left[w_i = w \mid \boldsymbol{w}_{i-1}\right] - \mathbb{P}_{\mathcal{R}}\left[w_i = w \mid \boldsymbol{w}_{i-1}\right]\right)^2}{\mathbb{P}_{\mathcal{R}}\left[w_i = w \mid \boldsymbol{w}_{i-1}\right]}\right]$$

$$\leqslant \mathbb{E}_{\mathcal{O}}\left[\mathbb{E}_{\mathcal{O}}\left[\frac{\left(\mathbb{P}_{\mathcal{O}}\left[w_i = w \mid \boldsymbol{w}_{i-1}, Z_{i-1}\right] - \mathbb{P}_{\mathcal{R}}\left[w_i = w \mid \boldsymbol{w}_{i-1}\right]\right)^2}{\mathbb{P}_{\mathcal{R}}\left[w_i = w \mid \boldsymbol{w}_{i-1}\right]} \,\middle|\, \boldsymbol{w}_{i-1}\right]\right]$$

$$= \mathbb{E}_{\mathcal{O}}\left[\frac{\left(\mathbb{P}_{\mathcal{O}}\left[w_i = w \mid \boldsymbol{w}_{i-1}, Z_{i-1}\right] - \mathbb{P}_{\mathcal{R}}\left[w_i = w \mid \boldsymbol{w}_{i-1}\right]\right)^2}{\mathbb{P}_{\mathcal{R}}\left[w_i = w \mid \boldsymbol{w}_{i-1}\right]}\right].$$

The proof is completed by combining both equations. □

In our case we take $Z_i = (\boldsymbol{U}_i, \boldsymbol{V}_i)$ with $\boldsymbol{U}_i = (U_1, \ldots, U_i)$ and $\boldsymbol{V}_i = (V_1, \ldots, V_i)$. Note that in this case we can ignore $\boldsymbol{w}_i$, as its value is fixed given Z_i.

We now reformulate $\mathbb{P}_{\mathcal{O}}\left[w_i = w \mid \boldsymbol{U}_{i-1}, \boldsymbol{V}_{i-1}\right]$. Given $\boldsymbol{U}_{i-1}$ and $\boldsymbol{V}_{i-1}$, we look at the probability that $U_i \oplus V_i = w$ for an arbitrary w. For this, we define:

$$S_i = \{U_j | j < i, u_j = u_i\} \cup \{V_j | j < i, v_j = u_i\},$$
$$S_i' = \{U_j | j < i, u_j = v_i\} \cup \{V_j | j < i, v_j = v_i\}.$$

We write $s_i = |S_i|$, $s'_i = |S'_i|$, and $D_{i,w} = |S_i \cap (S'_i \oplus w)|$.

In order for $U_i \oplus V_i$ to be equal to w, the variable U_i must take a value from $\{0,1\}^b \setminus (S_i \cup (S'_i \oplus w))$. The number of choices for this is exactly

$$2^b - |S_i \cup (S'_i \oplus w)| = 2^b - |S_i| - |S'_i \oplus w| + |S_i \cap (S'_i \oplus w)|$$
$$= 2^b - s_i - s'_i + D_{i,w}. \tag{28}$$

Moreover, the choice of V_i is fixed to $U_i \oplus w$.

We claim that, regardless of whether u_i and v_i are equal or distinct,

$$\mathbb{E}_{\mathcal{O}} \left[\frac{(\mathbb{P}_{\mathcal{O}}\,[w_i = w \mid \boldsymbol{U}_{i-1}, \boldsymbol{V}_{i-1}] - \mathbb{P}_{\mathcal{R}}\,[w_i = w \mid \boldsymbol{w}_{i-1}])^2}{\mathbb{P}_{\mathcal{R}}\,[w_i = w \mid \boldsymbol{w}_{i-1}]} \right] \leqslant \frac{8 s_i s'_i}{2^{4b}}. \tag{29}$$

The proof of (29) will be given in Sect. 5.2 (for the case where $u_i = v_i$) and in Sect. 5.3 (for the case where $u_i \neq v_i$). The two proofs will rely on some probabilistic analysis of $D_{i,w}$, given in Sect. 5.1.

Before getting there, however, we first complete the proof under the hypothesis that (29) holds. Note that s_i and s'_i do not depend on the specific values of U_j or V_j, they only depend on the value of $\boldsymbol{u}$ and $\boldsymbol{v}$. In fact $s_i = C_{\boldsymbol{u},\boldsymbol{v}}(i)$ and $s'_i = C'_{\boldsymbol{u},\boldsymbol{v}}(i)$, which means that

$$\|\mathbb{P}_{\mathcal{O}} - \mathbb{P}_{\mathcal{R}}\|^2$$
$$\leqslant \frac{1}{2} \sum_{i=1}^{q} \mathbb{E}_{\mathcal{O}} \left[\chi^2(\boldsymbol{w}_{i-1}) \right]$$
$$\leqslant \frac{1}{2} \sum_{i=1}^{q} \sum_{w} \mathbb{E}_{\mathcal{O}} \left[\frac{(\mathbb{P}_{\mathcal{O}}\,[w_i = w \mid \boldsymbol{U}_{i-1}, \boldsymbol{V}_{i-1}] - \mathbb{P}_{\mathcal{R}}\,[w_i = w \mid \boldsymbol{w}_{i-1}])^2}{\mathbb{P}_{\mathcal{R}}\,[w_i = w \mid \boldsymbol{w}_{i-1}]} \right]$$
$$\leqslant \frac{4}{2^{4b}} \sum_{i=1}^{q} \sum_{w} s_i s'_i$$
$$\leqslant \frac{4}{2^{3b}} \sum_{i=1}^{q} C_{\boldsymbol{u},\boldsymbol{v}}(i) \cdot C'_{\boldsymbol{u},\boldsymbol{v}}(i).$$

5.1 Expectation and Variance of $D_{i,w}$

The value $D_{i,w}$ counts the number of elements $g \in \{0,1\}^b$ such that $g \in S_i$ and $g \oplus w \in S'_i$. Our goal is to derive two bounds, one on its expected value $\mathbb{E}\,[D_{i,w}]$ and one on its variance $\mathbf{Var}\,[D_{i,w}]$, with the randomness chosen over the sets S_i and S'_i which are chosen uniform from $\{0,1\}^b$ without replacement. Note that this corresponds with world $\mathcal{O}$. We will, again, do so for the two different cases: equal permutations (for which S_i and S'_i are identical) in Sect. 5.1.2 and different permutations (for which S_i and S'_i are independent) in Section 5.1.3. The proofs share common analysis, which is first given in Section 5.1.1.

The proof is based on Lemma 4 of Bhattacharya and Nandi [13], that considers a variant of SoP where a single output is summed with multiple other outputs, but where all outputs are still from the same permutation. We look at the special case where it is summed with just one value, but extend the analysis to the case of different independent permutations.

5.1.1 General Analysis

Let I_g be the random variable that is 1 if $g \in S_i$ and $g \oplus w \in S_i'$, and 0 otherwise. Note that $D_{i,w} = \sum_{g \in \{0,1\}^b} I_g$. For the expectation we have that

$$\mathbb{E}[I_g] = \mathbb{P}[g \in S_i, g \oplus w \in S_i']$$
$$= \mathbb{P}[g \in S_i]\,\mathbb{P}[g \oplus w \in S_i' \mid g \in S_i]\,,$$

where we have to compute this value separately for equal and different permutations. For the expectation of $D_{i,w}$ we simply find

$$\mathbb{E}[D_{i,w}] = \sum_g \mathbb{E}[I_g]\,.$$

We now look at the variance of $D_{i,w}$. We use the following property:

$$\mathbf{Var}[D_{i,w}] = \mathbf{Var}\left[\sum_g I_g\right]$$
$$= \sum_g \mathbf{Var}[I_g] + \sum_{g \neq g'} \mathbf{Cov}(I_g, I_{g'})\,, \tag{30}$$

where

$$\mathbf{Cov}(I_g, I_{g'}) = \mathbb{E}[I_g I_{g'}] - \mathbb{E}[I_g]\mathbb{E}[I_{g'}]$$
$$= \mathbb{E}[I_g]\,\mathbb{P}[I_{g'} = 1 \mid I_g = 1] - \mathbb{E}[I_g]\mathbb{E}[I_{g'}]\,.$$

First, we will argue that $\mathbf{Cov}(I_g, I_{g'}) \leqslant 0$ whenever $g' \neq g \oplus w$. Indeed, if this condition is satisfied, we have that g', $g' \oplus w$, g and $g \oplus w$ are mutually distinct, and thus that

$$\mathbb{P}[I_{g'} = 1 \mid I_g = 1] = \mathbb{P}[g' \in S_i, g' \oplus w \in S_i' \mid g \in S_i, g \oplus w \in S_i']$$
$$\leqslant \mathbb{P}[g' \in S_i, g' \oplus w \in S_i']$$
$$= \mathbb{E}[I_{g'}]\,.$$

For the derivation of the inequality, we have used the following observation. On the one hand, for equal permutations, S_i and S_i' are identical, so the inequality is satisfied as the probability of having two specific elements in a set of fixed size decreases when it is known that two other elements are already in it. On the other hand, for different permutations, S_i and S_i' are independent, so the inequality boils down to two independent cases with one element instead of two. Henceforth, we obtained that $\mathbf{Cov}(I_g, I_{g'}) \leqslant 0$ whenever $g' \neq g \oplus w$.

Having eliminated the case of $\mathbf{Cov}\,(I_g, I_{g'})$ for $g' \neq g \oplus w$, we can proceed as follows for the second term of (30):

$$\sum_{g \neq g'} \mathbf{Cov}\,(I_g, I_{g'}) \leqslant \sum_g \mathbf{Cov}\,(I_g, I_{g \oplus w})$$

$$= \sum_g \mathbb{E}\,[I_g]\,\mathbb{P}\,[I_{g \oplus w} = 1 \mid I_g = 1] - \mathbb{E}\,[I_g]\,\mathbb{E}\,[I_{g \oplus w}]$$

$$\leqslant \sum_g \mathbb{E}\,[I_g] - \mathbb{E}\,[I_g]\,\mathbb{E}\,[I_{g \oplus w}]$$

$$= \sum_g \mathbb{E}\,[I_g^2] - \mathbb{E}\,[I_g]^2$$

$$= \sum_g \mathbf{Var}\,[I_g]\,.$$

Concluding,

$$\mathbf{Var}\,[D_{i,w}] \leqslant 2 \sum_g \mathbf{Var}\,[I_g]$$

$$= 2 \sum_g \mathbb{E}\,[I_g]\,(1 - \mathbb{E}\,[I_g])$$

$$\leqslant 2 \sum_g \mathbb{E}\,[I_g]$$

$$= 2 \cdot \mathbb{E}\,[D_{i,w}]\,.$$

5.1.2 Equal Permutations

In this case we have that S_i and S_i' are identical. This means that for $w \neq 0^b$

$$\mathbb{P}\,[g \in S_i]\,\mathbb{P}\,[g \oplus w \in S_i' \mid g \in S_i] = \frac{s_i(s_i - 1)}{2^b(2^b - 1)}\,.$$

Hence, we have obtained:

$$\mathbb{E}_{\mathcal{O}}\,[D_{i,w}] = \frac{s_i(s_i - 1)}{2^b - 1}\,, \tag{31}$$

$$\mathbf{Var}_{\mathcal{O}}\,[D_{i,w}] \leqslant \frac{2s_i(s_i - 1)}{2^b - 1} \leqslant \frac{2s_i s_i'}{2^b}\,. \tag{32}$$

5.1.3 Different Permutations

Now S_i and S_i' are independent, and hence

$$\mathbb{P}\,[g \in S_i]\,\mathbb{P}\,[g \oplus w \in S_i' \mid g \in S_i] = \frac{s_i s_i'}{2^{2b}}\,.$$

Hence, we have obtained:

$$\mathbb{E}_{\mathcal{O}}\left[D_{i,w}\right] = \frac{s_i s_i'}{2^b}, \tag{33}$$

$$\mathbf{Var}_{\mathcal{O}}\left[D_{i,w}\right] \leqslant \frac{2 s_i s_i'}{2^b}. \tag{34}$$

5.2 (29) for Equal Permutations

From (28) the number of valid choices for U_i and V_i is equal to $2^b - 2s_i + D_{i,w}$, as $s_i = s_i'$ for equal permutations. Furthermore, the total number of possible choices is $2^b - s_i$ for U_i and $2^b - s_i - 1$ for V_i. This means that

$$\begin{aligned}
\mathbb{P}_{\mathcal{O}}\left[w_i = w \mid \boldsymbol{U}_{i-1}, \boldsymbol{V}_{i-1}\right] &= \frac{2^b - 2s_i + D_{i,w}}{(2^b - s_i)(2^b - s_i - 1)} \\
&= \frac{(2^b - 1) - s_i - (s_i - 1) + D_{i,w}}{((2^b - 1) - (s_i - 1))((2^b - 1) - s_i)}.
\end{aligned}$$

As 0^b is not possible in our modified ideal world, we have that $\mathbb{P}_{\mathcal{R}}\left[w_i = w \mid \boldsymbol{w}_{i-1}\right] = 1/(2^b - 1)$, which results in

$$\begin{aligned}
&\left(\mathbb{P}_{\mathcal{O}}\left[w_i = w \mid \boldsymbol{U}_{i-1}, \boldsymbol{V}_{i-1}\right] - \mathbb{P}_{\mathcal{R}}\left[w_i = w \mid \boldsymbol{w}_{i-1}\right]\right)^2 \\
&= \left(\frac{(2^b - 1) - s_i - (s_i - 1) + D_{i,w}}{((2^b - 1) - (s_i - 1))((2^b - 1) - s_i)} - \frac{1}{2^b - 1}\right)^2 \\
&= \left(\frac{D_{i,w} - s_i(s_i - 1)/(2^b - 1)}{(2^b - s_i)(2^b - s_i - 1)}\right)^2 \\
&\leqslant \frac{4(D_{i,w} - s_i(s_i - 1)/(2^b - 1))^2}{2^{4b}},
\end{aligned}$$

using that $s_i < 2^{b-2}$. We know from (31–32) that $\mathbb{E}_{\mathcal{O}}\left[D_{i,w}\right] = s_i(s_i - 1)/(2^b - 1)$ and $\mathbf{Var}_{\mathcal{O}}\left[D_{i,w}\right] \leqslant 2s_i^2/2^b$ for any $w \in \{0,1\}^b \setminus \{0^b\}$, hence

$$\begin{aligned}
&\mathbb{E}_{\mathcal{O}}\left[\frac{\left(\mathbb{P}_{\mathcal{O}}\left[w_i = w \mid \boldsymbol{U}_{i-1}, \boldsymbol{V}_{i-1}\right] - \mathbb{P}_{\mathcal{R}}\left[w_i = w \mid \boldsymbol{w}_{i-1}\right]\right)^2}{\mathbb{P}_{\mathcal{R}}\left[w_i = w \mid \boldsymbol{w}_{i-1}\right]}\right] \\
&\leqslant \frac{4}{2^{3b}} \cdot \mathbb{E}_{\mathcal{O}}\left[D_{i,w} - \frac{s_i(s_i - 1)}{2^b - 1}\right] \\
&= \frac{4}{2^{3b}} \cdot \mathbf{Var}_{\mathcal{O}}\left[D_{i,w}\right] \\
&\leqslant \frac{8 s_i s_i'}{2^{4b}}.
\end{aligned}$$

5.3 (29) for Different Permutations

From (28) the number of valid choices for U_i and V_i is equal to $2^b - s_i - s_i' + D_{i,w}$. Furthermore, the total number of possible choices is $2^b - s_i$ for U_i and $2^b - s_i'$

for V_i. This means that

$$\mathbb{P}_{\mathcal{O}}\left[w_i = w \mid \boldsymbol{U}_{i-1}, \boldsymbol{V}_{i-1}\right] = \frac{2^b - s_i - s_i' + D_{i,w}}{(2^b - s_i)(2^b - s_i')}.$$

As $u_i \neq v_i$, all values in $\{0,1\}^b$ are possible in the ideal world, hence $\mathbb{P}_{\mathcal{R}}\left[w_i = w \mid \boldsymbol{w}_{i-1}\right] = 1/2^b$. This results in

$$\left(\mathbb{P}_{\mathcal{O}}\left[w_i = w \mid \boldsymbol{U}_{i-1}, \boldsymbol{V}_{i-1}\right] - \mathbb{P}_{\mathcal{R}}\left[w_i = w \mid \boldsymbol{w}_{i-1}\right]\right)^2$$

$$= \left(\frac{2^b - s_i - s_i' + D_{i,w}}{(2^b - s_i)(2^b - s_i')} - \frac{1}{2^b}\right)^2$$

$$= \left(\frac{D_{i,w} - s_i s_i'}{(2^b - s_i)(2^b - s_i')}\right)^2$$

$$\leqslant \frac{4(D_{i,w} - s_i s_i'/2^b)^2}{2^{4b}},$$

using that $s_i, s_i' < 2^{b-2}$. We know from (33–34) that $\mathbb{E}_{\mathcal{O}}\left[D_{i,w}\right] = s_i s_i'/2^b$ and $\mathbf{Var}_{\mathcal{O}}\left[D_{i,w}\right] \leqslant 2 s_i s_i'/2^b$ for any $w \in \{0,1\}^b$, hence

$$\mathbb{E}_{\mathcal{O}}\left[\frac{\left(\mathbb{P}_{\mathcal{O}}\left[w_i = w \mid \boldsymbol{U}_{i-1}, \boldsymbol{V}_{i-1}\right] - \mathbb{P}_{\mathcal{R}}\left[w_i = w \mid \boldsymbol{w}_{i-1}\right]\right)^2}{\mathbb{P}_{\mathcal{R}}\left[w_i = w \mid \boldsymbol{w}_{i-1}\right]}\right]$$

$$\leqslant \frac{4}{2^{3b}} \cdot \mathbb{E}_{\mathcal{O}}\left[\left(D_{i,w} - \frac{s_i s_i'}{2^b}\right)^2\right]$$

$$= \frac{4}{2^{3b}} \cdot \mathbf{Var}_{\mathcal{O}}\left[D_{i,w}\right]$$

$$\leqslant \frac{8 s_i s_i'}{2^{4b}}.$$

6   Proof of Theorem 2

The proof of Theorem 2 is very similar to the proof of Theorem 1, but with a few minor differences. First of all, the steps 4.1 and 4.2 remain basically the same and can be modified in a straightforward way. The step 4.3 is slightly different, as truncation is applied to two different permutations. This leads to the term $2\mathbf{Adv}_{\mathsf{Trunc}}^{\mathsf{prf}}(q)$ instead of the old $\mathbf{Adv}_{\mathsf{Trunc}}^{\mathsf{prf}}(2q)$. Furthermore, the step 4.4 becomes obsolete as we do not have to limit the range in the case of two independent permutations. This means that the term $q/2^n$ vanishes. Finally, the final step 4.5 remains roughly the same. In fact, as there are two independent permutations, $\boldsymbol{u}$ and $\boldsymbol{v}$ can be viewed separately. We might be able to use this information to improve some constants, but the gain is limited to those. We do not go into such detail and just reuse the old ones.

7   Application to GCM-SIV

GCM-SIV is a nonce misuse resistant authenticated encryption scheme of Gueron and Lindell, for which various versions exist [29, 32, 33, 39]. We consider the most recent one, that is also specified in internet draft IETF RFC [44]. It is built on top of a block cipher $E : \{0, 1\}^\kappa \times \{0, 1\}^n \rightarrow \{0, 1\}^n$, and the internet draft considers an instantiation with AES-128 (where $\kappa = n = 128$) or AES-256 (where $\kappa = 256$ and $n = 128$).

If E is instantiated with AES-128, the first step of an evaluation of GCM-SIV is to derive two 128-bit subkeys $k_1 \parallel k_2 \in \{0, 1\}^{256}$ based on key k and nonce ν as in (6):

$$
\begin{aligned}
k_1 &= \mathsf{left}_{n/2}(E_k(\nu\|0)) \parallel \mathsf{left}_{n/2}(E_k(\nu\|1)), \\
k_2 &= \mathsf{left}_{n/2}(E_k(\nu\|2)) \parallel \mathsf{left}_{n/2}(E_k(\nu\|3)).
\end{aligned}
\tag{35}
$$

Then, the associated data, message, and nonce are properly fed to the GHASH universal hash function (keyed with k_1), its outcome is encrypted using E_{k_2}, and the resulting value is set as tag. This tag is, subsequently, set as input to counter mode based on E_{k_2} to obtain a keystream that is added to the plaintext to obtain the ciphertext. If E, on the other hand, is instantiated with AES-256, the procedure is the same but with a 128-bit and a 256-bit subkey $k_1 \parallel k_2 \in \{0, 1\}^{384}$ as derived in (6):

$$
\begin{aligned}
k_1 &= \mathsf{left}_{n/2}(E_k(\nu\|0)) \parallel \mathsf{left}_{n/2}(E_k(\nu\|1)), \\
k_2 &= \mathsf{left}_{n/2}(E_k(\nu\|2)) \parallel \cdots \parallel \mathsf{left}_{n/2}(E_k(\nu\|5)).
\end{aligned}
\tag{36}
$$

We refer to [52, Fig. 3] for a clean picture of this algorithm.

The isolated character of the key derivation function in GCM-SIV is also well-reflected in the security bound of GCM-SIV. The security bound of GCM-SIV as outlined by Mennink and Neves [52, Theorem 3], which is in turn taken from Iwata and Seurin [41], consists of two separated terms:

– A term upper bounding the PRF security of the key derivation function, namely

$$
\mathbf{Adv}^{\mathrm{prf}}_{\mathsf{Trunc}_{n/2}}(c \cdot q) + \mathbf{Adv}^{\mathrm{prp}}_{E}(c \cdot q, t),
\tag{37}
$$

where q is the number of invocations of the key derivation function, and where $c = 4$ for the 128-bit keyed variant and $c = 6$ for the 256-bit keyed variant;
– A term that describes the security of GCM-SIV as an authenticated encryption scheme once k_1 and k_2 are uniformly random. This term is irrelevant for current discussion.

Now, if we would replace the truncation in the key derivation of GCM (Eqs. (35) and (36)) by STH, we would get

$$
\begin{aligned}
k_1 &= \mathsf{left}_{n/2}(E_k(\nu\|0)) \parallel \mathsf{left}_{n/2}(E_k(\nu\|1)), \\
k_2 &= \mathsf{right}_{n/2}(E_k(\nu\|0) \oplus E_k(\nu\|1)) \parallel \mathsf{left}_{n/2}(E_k(\nu\|2))
\end{aligned}
$$

for the 128-bit keyed variant, and

$$k_1 = \mathsf{left}_{n/2}(E_k(\nu\|0)) \;\|\; \mathsf{left}_{n/2}(E_k(\nu\|1)),$$
$$k_2 = \mathsf{right}_{n/2}(E_k(\nu\|0) \oplus E_k(\nu\|1)) \;\|$$
$$\mathsf{left}_{n/2}(E_k(\nu\|2)) \;\|\; \mathsf{left}_{n/2}(E_k(\nu\|3)) \;\|\; \mathsf{right}_{n/2}(E_k(\nu\|2) \oplus E_k(\nu\|3))$$

for the 256-bit keyed variant. When we use STH, we see that for the derivation of a 256-bit subkey the underlying block cipher E is called three times instead of four times, and for the derivation of a 384-bit subkey it is called four times instead of six times. As for security, the original bound of Iwata and Seurin [41] (see also [52, Theorem 3]) carries over with (37) replaced by

$$\mathbf{Adv}^{\mathrm{prf}}_{\mathsf{STH}_{n/2}}(2 \cdot q) + \mathbf{Adv}^{\mathrm{prp}}_{E}(c \cdot q, t),$$

where $c = 3$ for the 128-bit keyed variant and $c = 4$ for the 256-bit keyed variant. As the PRF security of $\mathsf{STH}_{n/2}$ (Theorem 1) is similar to the PRF security of truncation (Lemma 2), there is no significant loss in security. In particular, when we allow for a maximum advantage of 2^{-32}, we are able to derive approximately 2^{64} different keys for both instantiations, even when $t \gg 2^{64}$. Hence the security does not reduce when using the more efficient STH version.

We conclude by noting that this only discusses the key derivation *in isolation*. As bijectivity in the key derivation is not an issue in the bigger picture of GCM-SIV, one can get away by simply taking untruncated block ciphers [17]. However, there are many more applications where replacing block cipher evaluations by STH truly lead to security gains, most notably Wegman-Carter and counter mode encryption, as also outlined in Sect. 1.

Acknowledgments. The authors would like to thank the anonymous reviewers of CRYPTO 2020 for their valuable feedback. Aldo Gunsing is supported by the Netherlands Organisation for Scientific Research (NWO) under TOP grant TOP1.18.002 SCALAR.

References

1. Beaulieu, R., Shors, D., Smith, J., Treatman-Clark, S., Weeks, B., Wingers, L.: The SIMON and SPECK families of lightweight block ciphers. Cryptology ePrint Archive, Report 2013/404 (2013)

2. Beierle, C., et al.: The SKINNY family of block ciphers and its low-latency variant MANTIS. In: Robshaw, M., Katz, J. (eds.) CRYPTO 2016, Part II. LNCS, vol. 9815, pp. 123–153. Springer, Heidelberg (2016). https://doi.org/10.1007/978-3-662-53008-5_5

3. Bellare, M., Desai, A., Jokipii, E., Rogaway, P.: A concrete security treatment of symmetric encryption. In: FOCS 1997, pp. 394–403. IEEE Computer Society (1997)

4. Bellare, M., Guérin, R., Rogaway, P.: XOR MACs: new methods for message authentication using finite pseudorandom functions. In: Coppersmith, D. (ed.) CRYPTO 1995. LNCS, vol. 963, pp. 15–28. Springer, Heidelberg (1995). https://doi.org/10.1007/3-540-44750-4_2

5. Bellare, M., Impagliazzo, R.: A tool for obtaining tighter security analyses of pseudorandom function based constructions, with applications to PRP to PRF conversion. Cryptology ePrint Archive, Report 1999/024 (1999)

6. Bellare, M., Kilian, J., Rogaway, P.: The security of cipher block chaining. In: Desmedt, Y.G. (ed.) CRYPTO 1994. LNCS, vol. 839, pp. 341–358. Springer, Heidelberg (1994). https://doi.org/10.1007/3-540-48658-5_32

7. Bellare, M., Krovetz, T., Rogaway, P.: Luby-Rackoff backwards: increasing security by making block ciphers non-invertible. In: Nyberg, K. (ed.) EUROCRYPT 1998. LNCS, vol. 1403, pp. 266–280. Springer, Heidelberg (1998). https://doi.org/10.1007/BFb0054132

8. Bellare, M., Rogaway, P.: The security of triple encryption and a framework for code-based game-playing proofs. In: Vaudenay [64], pp. 409–426

9. Bernstein, D.J.: SURF: Simple Unpredictable Random Function (1997). https://cr.yp.to/papers.html#surf

10. Bernstein, D.J.: How to stretch random functions: the security of protected counter sums. J. Cryptol. 12(3), 185–192 (1999). https://doi.org/10.1007/s001459900051

11. Bernstein, D.J.: Stronger security bounds for Wegman-Carter-Shoup authenticators. In: Cramer, R. (ed.) EUROCRYPT 2005. LNCS, vol. 3494, pp. 164–180. Springer, Heidelberg (2005). https://doi.org/10.1007/11426639_10

12. Bhargavan, K., Leurent, G.: On the practical (in-)security of 64-bit block ciphers: collision attacks on HTTP over TLS and OpenVPN. In: Weippl, E.R., Katzenbeisser, S., Kruegel, C., Myers, A.C., Halevi, S. (eds.) ACM CCS 2016, pp. 456–467. ACM (2016)

13. Bhattacharya, S., Nandi, M.: A note on the chi-square method: a tool for proving cryptographic security. Cryptogr. Commun. 10(5), 935–957 (2018). https://doi.org/10.1007/s12095-017-0276-z

14. Bhattacharya, S., Nandi, M.: Revisiting variable output length XOR pseudorandom function. IACR Trans. Symmetric Cryptol. 2018(1), 314–335 (2018)

15. Bogdanov, A., et al.: PRESENT: an ultra-lightweight block cipher. In: Paillier, P., Verbauwhede, I. (eds.) CHES 2007. LNCS, vol. 4727, pp. 450–466. Springer, Heidelberg (2007). https://doi.org/10.1007/978-3-540-74735-2_31

16. Borghoff, J., et al.: PRINCE – a low-latency block cipher for pervasive computing applications. In: Wang, X., Sako, K. (eds.) ASIACRYPT 2012. LNCS, vol. 7658, pp. 208–225. Springer, Heidelberg (2012). https://doi.org/10.1007/978-3-642-34961-4_14

17. Bose, P., Hoang, V.T., Tessaro, S.: Revisiting AES-GCM-SIV: multi-user security, faster key derivation, and better bounds. In: Nielsen, Rijmen [53], pp. 468–499

18. Brassard, G.: On computationally secure authentication tags requiring short secret shared keys. In: Chaum, D., Rivest, R.L., Sherman, A.T. (eds.) CRYPTO '82, pp. 79–86. Plenum Press, New York (1982)

19. Chang, D., Nandi, M.: A short proof of the PRP/PRF switching lemma. Cryptology ePrint Archive, Report 2008/078 (2008)

20. Cogliati, B., Seurin, Y.: EWCDM: an efficient, beyond-birthday secure, noncemisuse resistant MAC. In: Robshaw, M., Katz, J. (eds.) CRYPTO 2016, Part I. LNCS, vol. 9814, pp. 121–149. Springer, Heidelberg (2016). https://doi.org/10.1007/978-3-662-53018-4_5

21. Daemen, J., Rijmen, V.: The Design of Rijndael: AES - The Advanced Encryption Standard. Information Security and Cryptography. Springer, Heidelberg (2002). https://doi.org/10.1007/978-3-662-04722-4

22. Dai, W., Hoang, V.T., Tessaro, S.: Information-theoretic indistinguishability via the chi-squared method. In: Katz, Shacham [42], pp. 497–523

23. De Cannière, C., Dunkelman, O., Knežević, M.: KATAN and KTANTAN — a family of small and efficient hardware-oriented block ciphers. In: Clavier, C., Gaj, K. (eds.) CHES 2009. LNCS, vol. 5747, pp. 272–288. Springer, Heidelberg (2009). https://doi.org/10.1007/978-3-642-04138-9_20

24. Dworkin, M.: NIST SP 800–38A: Recommendation for Block Cipher Modes of Operation: Methods and Techniques (2001)

25. Freedman, D.: A remark on the difference between sampling with and without replacement. J. Am. Stat. Assoc. **72**(359), 681–681 (1977)

26. Gilboa, S., Gueron, S.: The advantage of truncated permutations. CoRR abs/1610.02518 (2016)

27. Gilboa, S., Gueron, S., Morris, B.: How many queries are needed to distinguish a truncated random permutation from a random function? J. Cryptol. **31**(1), 162–171 (2018)

28. Gong, Z., Nikova, S., Law, Y.W.: KLEIN: a new family of lightweight block ciphers. In: Juels, A., Paar, C. (eds.) RFIDSec 2011. LNCS, vol. 7055, pp. 1–18. Springer, Heidelberg (2012). https://doi.org/10.1007/978-3-642-25286-0_1

29. Gueron, S., Langley, A., Lindell, Y.: AES-GCM-SIV: specification and analysis. Cryptology ePrint Archive, Report 2017/168 (2017)

30. Gueron, S., Langley, A., Lindell, Y.: AES-GCM-SIV: Nonce Misuse-Resistant Authenticated Encryption. Internet-Draft draft-irtf-cfrg-gcmsiv-09, Internet Engineering Task Force, November 2018

31. Gueron, S., Langley, A., Lindell, Y.: AES-GCM-SIV: Nonce Misuse-Resistant Authenticated Encryption. Request for Comments (RFC) 8452, April 2019. http://tools.ietf.org/html/rfc8452

32. Gueron, S., Lindell, Y.: GCM-SIV: full nonce misuse-resistant authenticated encryption at under one cycle per byte. In: Ray, I., Li, N., Kruegel, C. (eds.) ACM CCS 2015, pp. 109–119. ACM (2015)

33. Gueron, S., Lindell, Y.: Better bounds for block cipher modes of operation via nonce-based key derivation. In: Thuraisingham, B.M., Evans, D., Malkin, T., Xu, D. (eds.) ACM CCS 2017, pp. 1019–1036. ACM (2017)

34. Hall, C., Wagner, D., Kelsey, J., Schneier, B.: Building PRFs from PRPs. In: Krawczyk, H. (ed.) CRYPTO 1998. LNCS, vol. 1462, pp. 370–389. Springer, Heidelberg (1998). https://doi.org/10.1007/BFb0055742

35. Hong, D., et al.: HIGHT: a new block cipher suitable for low-resource device. In: Goubin, L., Matsui, M. (eds.) CHES 2006. LNCS, vol. 4249, pp. 46–59. Springer, Heidelberg (2006). https://doi.org/10.1007/11894063_4

36. Impagliazzo, R., Rudich, S.: Limits on the provable consequences of one-way permutations. In: Goldwasser, S. (ed.) CRYPTO 1988. LNCS, vol. 403, pp. 8–26. Springer, New York (1990). https://doi.org/10.1007/0-387-34799-2_2

37. Iwata, T.: New blockcipher modes of operation with beyond the birthday bound security. In: Robshaw, M. (ed.) FSE 2006. LNCS, vol. 4047, pp. 310–327. Springer, Heidelberg (2006). https://doi.org/10.1007/11799313_20

38. Iwata, T., Mennink, B., Vizár, D.: CENC is optimally secure. Cryptology ePrint Archive, Report 2016/1087 (2016)

39. Iwata, T., Minematsu, K.: Stronger security variants of GCM-SIV. IACR Trans. Symmetric Cryptol. **2016**(1), 134–157 (2016)

40. Iwata, T., Ohashi, K., Minematsu, K.: Breaking and repairing GCM security proofs. In: Safavi-Naini, R., Canetti, R. (eds.) CRYPTO 2012. LNCS, vol. 7417, pp. 31–49. Springer, Heidelberg (2012). https://doi.org/10.1007/978-3-642-32009-5_3

41. Iwata, T., Seurin, Y.: Reconsidering the security bound of AES-GCM-SIV. IACR Trans. Symmetric Cryptol. **2017**(4), 240–267 (2017)
42. Katz, J., Shacham, H. (eds.): CRYPTO 2017, Part III. LNCS, vol. 10403. Springer, Cham (2017). https://doi.org/10.1007/978-3-319-63697-9
43. Lim, C.H., Korkishko, T.: mCrypton – a lightweight block cipher for security of low-cost RFID tags and sensors. In: Song, J.-S., Kwon, T., Yung, M. (eds.) WISA 2005. LNCS, vol. 3786, pp. 243–258. Springer, Heidelberg (2006). https://doi.org/10.1007/11604938_19
44. Lindell, Y., Langley, A., Gueron, S.: AES-GCM-SIV: Nonce Misuse-Resistant Authenticated Encryption. Internet-Draft draft-irtf-cfrg-gcmsiv-05, Internet Engineering Task Force, May 2017
45. Luby, M., Rackoff, C.: How to construct pseudorandom permutations from pseudorandom functions. SIAM J. Comput. **17**(2), 373–386 (1988)
46. Lucks, S.: The sum of PRPs is a secure PRF. In: Preneel, B. (ed.) EUROCRYPT 2000. LNCS, vol. 1807, pp. 470–484. Springer, Heidelberg (2000). https://doi.org/10.1007/3-540-45539-6_34
47. Luykx, A., Preneel, B.: Optimal forgeries against polynomial-based MACs and GCM. In: Nielsen, Rijmen [53], pp. 445–467
48. McGrew, D.: Impossible plaintext cryptanalysis and probable-plaintext collision attacks of 64-bit block cipher modes. Cryptology ePrint Archive, Report 2012/623 (2012)
49. McGrew, D.A., Viega, J.: The security and performance of the galois/counter mode (GCM) of operation. In: Canteaut, A., Viswanathan, K. (eds.) INDOCRYPT 2004. LNCS, vol. 3348, pp. 343–355. Springer, Heidelberg (2004). https://doi.org/10.1007/978-3-540-30556-9_27
50. Mennink, B.: Linking stam's bounds with generalized truncation. In: Matsui, M. (ed.) CT-RSA 2019. LNCS, vol. 11405, pp. 313–329. Springer, Cham (2019). https://doi.org/10.1007/978-3-030-12612-4_16
51. Mennink, B., Neves, S.: Encrypted Davies-Meyer and its dual: towards optimal security using mirror theory. In: Katz, Shacham [42], pp. 556–583
52. Mennink, B., Neves, S.: Optimal PRFs from blockcipher designs. IACR Trans. Symmetric Cryptol. **2017**(3), 228–252 (2017)
53. Nielsen, J.B., Rijmen, V. (eds.): EUROCRYPT 2018, Part I. LNCS, vol. 10820. Springer, Cham (2018). https://doi.org/10.1007/978-3-319-78381-9
54. NIST: Block Cipher Techniques - Modes Development (2020). https://csrc.nist.gov/projects/block-cipher-techniques/bcm/modes-develoment
55. NSA IA: Key Recovery Attacks on AES-GCM-SIV (2017). https://mailarchive.ietf.org/arch/msg/cfrg/k2mpWgod4mbdOxsvN6EtXHb0BAg
56. Patarin, J.: A proof of security in $O(2^n)$ for the Xor of two random permutations. In: Safavi-Naini, R. (ed.) ICITS 2008. LNCS, vol. 5155, pp. 232–248. Springer, Heidelberg (2008). https://doi.org/10.1007/978-3-540-85093-9_22
57. Patarin, J.: Introduction to mirror theory: analysis of systems of linear equalities and linear non equalities for cryptography. Cryptology ePrint Archive, Report 2010/287 (2010)
58. Patarin, J.: Security in $O(2^n)$ for the Xor of two random permutations - proof with the standard H technique-. Cryptology ePrint Archive, Report 2013/368 (2013)
59. Rogaway, P., Shrimpton, T.: A provable-security treatment of the key-wrap problem. In: Vaudenay [64], pp. 373–390
60. Shibutani, K., Isobe, T., Hiwatari, H., Mitsuda, A., Akishita, T., Shirai, T.: *Piccolo*: an ultra-lightweight blockcipher. In: Preneel, B., Takagi, T. (eds.) CHES 2011.

LNCS, vol. 6917, pp. 342–357. Springer, Heidelberg (2011). https://doi.org/10. 1007/978-3-642-23951-9_23

61. Shoup, V.: On fast and provably secure message authentication based on universal hashing. In: Koblitz, N. (ed.) CRYPTO 1996. LNCS, vol. 1109, pp. 313–328. Springer, Heidelberg (1996). https://doi.org/10.1007/3-540-68697-5_24

62. Stam, A.J.: Distance between sampling with and without replacement. Stat. Neerl. **32**(2), 81–91 (1978)

63. Stam, A.J.: A note on sampling with and without replacement. Stat. Neerl. **40**(1), 35–38 (1986)

64. Vaudenay, S. (ed.): EUROCRYPT 2006. LNCS, vol. 4004. Springer, Heidelberg (2006). https://doi.org/10.1007/11761679

65. Wegman, M.N., Carter, L.: New hash functions and their use in authentication and set equality. J. Comput. Syst. Sci. **22**(3), 265–279 (1981)

66. Wu, W., Zhang, L.: LBlock: a lightweight block cipher. In: Lopez, J., Tsudik, G. (eds.) ACNS 2011. LNCS, vol. 6715, pp. 327–344. Springer, Heidelberg (2011). https://doi.org/10.1007/978-3-642-21554-4_19

Security Analysis of NIST CTR-DRBG

Viet Tung Hoang[1](✉) and Yaobin Shen[2](✉)

[1] Department of Computer Science, Florida State University, Tallahassee, FL, USA
tvhoang@cs.fsu.edu
[2] Department of Computer Science and Engineering, Shanghai Jiao Tong University,
Shanghai, China
yb_shen@sjtu.edu.cn

Abstract. We study the security of CTR-DRBG, one of NIST's recommended Pseudorandom Number Generator (PRNG) designs. Recently, Woodage and Shumow (Eurocrypt' 19), and then Cohney et al. (S&P' 20) point out some potential vulnerabilities in both NIST specification and common implementations of CTR-DRBG. While these researchers do suggest counter-measures, the security of the patched CTR-DRBG is still questionable. Our work fills this gap, proving that CTR-DRBG satisfies the robustness notion of Dodis et al. (CCS'13), the standard security goal for PRNGs.

Keywords: Provable security · Random number generator

1 Introduction

Cryptography ubiquitously relies on the assumption that high-quality randomness is available. Violation of this assumption would often lead to security disasters [9,12,20], and thus a good Pseudorandom Number Generator (PRNG) is a fundamental primitive in cryptography, in both theory and practice. In this work we study the security of CTR-DRBG, the most popular standardized PRNG.[1]

A TROUBLED HISTORY. CTR-DRBG is one of the recommended designs of NIST standard SP 800-90A, which initially included the now infamous Dual-EC. While the latter has received lots of scrutiny [8,9], the former had attracted little attention until Woodage and Shumow [31] point out vulnerabilities in a NIST-compliant version. Even worse, very recently, Cohney et al. [12] discover that many common implementations of CTR-DRBG still rely on table-based AES and thus are susceptible to cache side-channel attacks [5,18,24,25].

While the attacks above are catastrophic, they only show that (i) some insecure options in the overly flexible specification of CTR-DRBG should be deprecated, and (ii) developers of CTR-DRBG implementation should be mindful of misuses such as leaky table-based AES, failure to refresh periodically,

---

[1] A recent study by Cohney et al. [12] finds that CTR-DRBG is supported by 67.8% of validated implementations in NIST's Cryptographic Module Validation Program (CMVP). The other recommended schemes in NISP SP 800-90A, Hash-DRBG and HMAC-DRBG, are only supported by 36.3% and 37.0% of CMVP-certified uses, respectively.

© International Association for Cryptologic Research 2020
D. Micciancio and T. Ristenpart (Eds.): CRYPTO 2020, LNCS 12170, pp. 218–247, 2020.
https://doi.org/10.1007/978-3-030-56784-2_8

or using low-entropy inputs. Following these counter-measures will thwart the known attacks, but security of CTR-DRBG remains questionable. A full-fledged provable-security treatment of CTR-DRBG is therefore highly desirable—Woodage and Shumow consider it an important open problem [31].

PRIOR PROVABLE SECURITY. Most prior works [7,30] only consider a simplified variant of CTR-DRBG that takes no random input, and assume that the initial state is truly random. These analyses fail to capture scenarios where the PRNG's state is either compromised or updated with adversarial random inputs. Consequently, their results are limited and cannot support security claims in NIST SP 800-90A.

A recent Ph.D. thesis of Hutchinson [23] aims to do better, analyzing security of CTR-DRBG via the robustness notion of Dodis et al. [15]. But upon examining this work, we find numerous issues, effectively invalidating the results. A detailed discussion of the problems in Hutchinson's analysis can be found in Appendix A.

CONTRIBUTIONS. In this work, we prove that the patched CTR-DRBG satisfies the robustness security of Dodis et al. [15]. Obtaining a good bound for CTR-DRBG requires surmounting several theoretical obstacles, which we will elaborate below.

An important stepping stone in proving robustness of CTR-DRBG is to analyze the security of the underlying randomness extractor that we name *Condense-then-Encrypt* (CtE); see Fig. 2 for the code and an illustration of CtE. The conventional approach [15,29,31] requires that the extracted outputs be pseudorandom. However, CtE oddly applies CBCMAC multiple times on the *same* random input (with different constant prefixes), foiling attempts to use existing analysis of CBCMAC [14].

To address the issue above, we observe that under CTR-DRBG, the outputs of CtE are used for deriving keys and IVs of the CTR mode. If we model the underlying blockcipher of CTR as an ideal cipher then the extracted outputs only need to be *unpredictable*. In other words, CtE only needs to be a good *randomness condenser* [27]. In light of the Generalized Leftover Hash Lemma [1], one thus needs to prove that CtE is a good almost-universal hash function, which is justified by the prior CBCMAC analysis of Dodis et al. [14]. As an added plus, aiming for just unpredictability allows us to reduce the min-entropy threshold on random inputs from 280 bits to 216 bits.

Still, the analysis above relies on the CBCMAC result in [14], but the latter implicitly *assumes* that each random input is sampled from a set of equal-length strings. (Alternatively, one can view that each random input is sampled from a general universe, but then its exact length is revealed to the adversary.) This assumption may unnecessarily limit the choices of random sources for CtE or squander entropy of random inputs, and thus removing it is desirable. Unfortunately, one cannot simply replace the result of [14] by existing CBCMAC analysis for variable-length inputs [4], as the resulting unpredictability bound for CtE will be poor. Specifically, we would end up with an inferior term $\sqrt{q} \cdot p/2^{64}$ in bounding the unpredictability of p extracted outputs against q guesses.

To circumvent the obstacle above, we uncover a neat idea behind the seemingly cumbersome design of CtE. In particular, given a random input I, CtE first condenses it to a key $K \leftarrow \mathsf{CBCMAC}(0 \parallel I)$ and an initialization vector $\mathrm{IV} \leftarrow \mathsf{CBCMAC}(1 \parallel I)$, and then uses CBC mode to encrypt a constant string under K and IV. To predict the CBC ciphertext, an adversary must guess both K and IV simultaneously. Apparently, the designers of CtE intend to use the iteration of CBCMAC to undo the square-root effect in the Leftover Hash Lemma [14,19] that has plagued existing CBCMAC analysis [14]. Still, giving a good unpredictability bound for (K, IV) is nontrivial, as (i) they are derived from the same random input I, and (ii) prior results [4], relying on analysis of ordinary collision on CBCMAC, can only be used to bound the marginal unpredictability of either K or IV. We instead analyze a *multi-collision* property for CBCMAC, and thus can obtain a tighter bound on the unpredictability of (K, IV). Concretely, we can improve the term $\sqrt{q} \cdot p/2^{64}$ above to $\sqrt{qL} \cdot \sigma/2^{128}$, where L is the maximum block length of the random inputs, and σ is their total block length.[2]

Even with the good security of CtE, obtaining a strong robustness bound for CTR-DRBG is still challenging. The typical approach [15,17,31] is to decompose the complex robustness notion into simpler ones, *preserving* and *recovering*. But this simplicity comes with a cost: if we can bound the recovering and preserving advantage by ϵ and ϵ' respectively, then we only obtain a loose bound $p(\epsilon + \epsilon')$ in the robustness advantage, where p is the number of random inputs. In our context, the blowup factor p will lead to a rather poor bound.

Even worse, as pointed out by Dodis et al. [15], there is an adaptivity issue in proving recovering security of PRNGs that are built on top of a universal hash H. In particular, here an adversary, given a uniform hash key K, needs to pick an index $i \in \{1, \ldots, p\}$ to indicate which random input I_i that it wants to attack, and then predicts the output of $H_K(I_i)$ via q guesses. The subtlety here is that the adversary can *adaptively* pick the index i that depends on the key K, creating a situation similar to selective-opening attacks [3,16]. Dodis et al. [15] give a simple solution for this issue, but their treatment leads to another blowup factor p in the security bound. In Sect. 6.1 we explore this problem further, showing that the blowup factor p is inherent via a counter-example. Our example is based on a contrived universal hash function, so it does not imply that CTR-DRBG has inferior recovering security per se. Still, it shows that if one wants to prove a good recovering bound for CTR-DRBG, one must go beyond treating CtE as a universal hash function.

Given the situation above, instead of using the decomposition approach, we give a direct proof for the robustness security via the H-coefficient

---

[2] For a simple comparison of the two bounds, assume that $\sigma \lesssim 2^{18} \cdot p$, meaning that a random input is at most $4\,\mathrm{MB}$ on average, which seems to be a realistic assumption for typical applications. The standard NIST SP 800-90A dictates that $L \leq 2^{28}$. Then our bound $\sqrt{qL} \cdot \sigma/2^{128}$ is around $\sqrt{q} \cdot p/2^{96}$. If we instead consider the worst case where $\sigma \approx Lp$, then our bound is around $\sqrt{q} \cdot p/2^{86}$.

technique [10, 26]. We carefully exercise the union bound to sidestep pesky adaptivity pitfalls and obtain a tight bound.[3]

LIMITATIONS. In this work, we assume that each random input has sufficient min entropy. This restriction is admittedly limited, failing to show that CTR-DRBG can slowly accumulate entropy in multiple low-entropy inputs, which is an important property in the robustness notion. Achieving full robustness for CTR-DRBG is an important future direction. Still, our setting is meaningful, comparable to the notion of Barak and Halevi [2]. This is also the setting that the standard NIST SP 800-90A assumes. We note that Woodage and Shumow [31] use the same setting for analyzing HMAC-DRBG, and Hutchinson [23] for CTR-DRBG.

SEED-DEPENDENT INPUTS. Our work makes a standard assumption that the random inputs are independent of the seed of the randomness extractor.[4] This assumption seems unavoidable as deterministic extraction from a general source is impossible [11]. In a recent work, Coretti et al. [13] challenge the conventional wisdom with meaningful notions for *seedless* extractors and PRNGs, and show that CBCMAC is *insecure* in their model. In Sect. 7, we extend their ideas to attack CTR-DRBG. We note that this is just a theoretical attack with a contrived sampler of random inputs, and does not directly translate into an exploit of real-world CTR-DRBG implementations.

Ruhault [28] also considers attacking CTR-DRBG with a seed-dependent sampler. But his attack, as noted by Woodage and Shumow [31], only applies to a variant of CTR-DRBG that does not comply with NIST standard. It is unclear how to use his ideas to break the actual CTR-DRBG.

2 Preliminaries

NOTATION. Let ε denote the empty string. For an integer i, we let $[i]_t$ denote a t-bit representation of i. For a finite set S, we let $x \leftarrow_\$ S$ denote the uniform sampling from S and assigning the value to x. Let $|x|$ denote the length of the string x, and for $1 \le i < j \le |x|$, let $x[i:j]$ denote the substring from the i-th bit to the j-th bit (inclusive) of x. If A is an algorithm, we let $y \leftarrow A(x_1, \ldots ; r)$ denote running A with randomness r on inputs $x_1, \ldots$ and assigning the output to y. We let $y \leftarrow_\$ A(x_1, \ldots)$ be the result of picking r at random and letting $y \leftarrow A(x_1, \ldots ; r)$.

CONDITIONAL MIN-ENTROPY AND STATISTICAL DISTANCE. For two random variables X and Y, the *(average-case) conditional min-entropy* of X given Y is

$$H_\infty(X \mid Y) = -\log\left(\sum_y \Pr[Y = y] \cdot \max_x \Pr[X = x \mid Y = y]\right) .$$

---

[3] Using the same treatment for recovering security still ends up with the blowup factor p, as it is inherent.

[4] In the context of CtE, the seed is the encoding of the ideal cipher. In other words, we assume that the sampler of the random inputs has no access to the ideal cipher.

The *statistical distance* between X and Y is

$$\mathsf{SD}(X, Y) = \frac{1}{2} \sum_z |\Pr[X = z] - \Pr[Y = z]| .$$

The statistical distance $\mathsf{SD}(X, Y)$ is the best possible advantage of an (even computationally unbounded) adversary in distinguishing X and Y.

SYSTEMS AND TRANSCRIPTS. Following the notation from [22], it is convenient to consider interactions of a distinguisher A with an abstract system $\mathbf{S}$ which answers A's queries. The resulting interaction then generates a transcript $\tau = ((X_1, Y_1), \ldots, (X_q, Y_q))$ of query-answer pairs. It is known that $\mathbf{S}$ is entirely described by the probabilities $\mathsf{p_S}(\tau)$ that correspond to the system $\mathbf{S}$ responding with answers as indicated by τ when the queries in τ are made.

We will generally describe systems informally, or more formally in terms of a set of oracles they provide, and only use the fact that they define corresponding probabilities $\mathsf{p_S}(\tau)$ without explicitly giving these probabilities. We say that a transcript τ is valid for system $\mathbf{S}$ if $\mathsf{p_S}(\tau) > 0$.

THE H-COEFFICIENT TECHNIQUE. We now describe the H-coefficient technique of Patarin [10,26]. Generically, it considers a deterministic distinguisher A that tries to distinguish a "real" system $\mathbf{S}_1$ from an "ideal" system $\mathbf{S}_0$. The adversary's interactions with those systems define transcripts X_1 and X_0, respectively, and a bound on the distinguishing advantage of A is given by the statistical distance $\mathsf{SD}(X_1, X_0)$.

Lemma 1. [10,26] *Suppose we can partition the set of valid transcripts for the ideal system into good and bad ones. Further, suppose that there exists $\epsilon \geq 0$ such that $1 - \frac{\mathsf{p_{S_1}}(\tau)}{\mathsf{p_{S_0}}(\tau)} \leq \epsilon$ for every good transcript τ. Then,*

$$\mathsf{SD}(X_1, X_0) \leq \epsilon + \Pr[X_0 \text{ is bad}] .$$

3   Modeling Security of PRNGs

In this section we recall the syntax and security notion of Pseudorandom Number Generator (PRNG) from Dodis et al. [15].

SYNTAX. A PRNG with state space State and seed space Seed is a tuple of deterministic algorithms $\mathcal{G} = (\mathsf{setup}, \mathsf{refresh}, \mathsf{next})$. Under the syntax of [15], setup is instead probabilistic: it takes no input, and returns $seed \leftarrow_\$ \mathsf{Seed}$ and $S \leftarrow_\$ \mathsf{State}$. However, as pointed out by Shrimpton and Terashima [29], this fails to capture real-world PRNGs, where the state may include, for example, counters. Moreover, real-world setup typically gets its coins from an entropy source, and thus the coins may be non-uniform. Therefore, following [29,31], we instead require that the algorithm $\mathsf{setup}(seed, I)$ take as input a seed $seed \in \mathsf{Seed}$ and a string I, and then output an initial state $S \in$ State; there is no explicit requirement on the distribution of S.

Next, algorithm refresh($seed, S, I$) takes as input a seed $seed$, a state S, and a string I, and then outputs a new state. Finally algorithm next($seed, S, \ell$) takes as input a seed $seed$, a state S, and a number $\ell \in \mathbb{N}$, and then outputs a new state and an ℓ-bit output string. Here we follow the recent work of Woodage and Shumow [31] to allow variable output length.

DISTRIBUTION SAMPLERS. A *distribution sampler* $\mathcal{D}$ is a stateful, probabilistic algorithm. Given the current state s, it will output a tuple (s', I, γ, z) in which s' is the updated state, I is the next randomness input for the PRNG $\mathcal{G}$, $\gamma \geq 0$ is a real number, and z is some side information of I given to an adversary attacking $\mathcal{G}$. Let p be an upper bound of the number of calls to $\mathcal{D}$ in our security games. Let s_0 be the empty string, and let $(s_i, I_i, \gamma_i, z_i) \leftarrow \$ \mathcal{D}(s_{i-1})$ for every $i \in \{1, \ldots, p\}$. For each $i \leq p$, let

$$\mathcal{I}_{p,i} = (I_1, \ldots, I_{i-1}, I_{i+1}, \ldots, I_p, \gamma_1, \ldots, \gamma_p, z_1, \ldots, z_p) \ .$$

We say that sampler $\mathcal{D}$ is *legitimate* if $H_\infty(I_i \mid \mathcal{I}_{p,i}) \geq \gamma_i$ for every $i \in \{1, \ldots, p\}$. A legitimate sampler is λ-*simple* if $\gamma_i \geq \lambda$ for every i.

In this work, we will consider only simple samplers for a sufficiently large min-entropy threshold λ. In other words, we will assume that each random input has sufficient min entropy. This setting is somewhat limited, as it fails to show that the PRNG can slowly accumulate entropy in multiple low-entropy inputs. However, it is still meaningful—this is actually the setting that the standard NIST SP 800-90A assumes. We note that Woodage and Shumow [31] also analyze the HMAC-DRBG construction under the same setting.

ROBUSTNESS. Let $\lambda > 0$ be a real number, A be an adversary attacking $\mathcal{G}$, and $\mathcal{D}$ be a legitimate distribution sampler. Define

$$\mathsf{Adv}^{\mathrm{rob}}_{\mathcal{G},\lambda}(A, \mathcal{D}) = 2 \Pr\Big[\mathbf{G}^{\mathrm{rob}}_{\mathcal{G},\lambda}(A, \mathcal{D}) \Big] - 1 \ ,$$

where game $\mathbf{G}^{\mathrm{rob}}_{\mathcal{G},\lambda}(A, \mathcal{D})$ is defined in Fig. 1.

Informally, the game picks a challenge bit $b \leftarrow \$ \{0, 1\}$ and maintains a counter c of the current estimated amount of accumulated entropy that is initialized to 0. It runs the distribution sampler $\mathcal{D}$ on an empty-string state to generate the first randomness input I. It then calls the setup algorithm on a uniformly random seed to generate the initial state S, and increments c to γ. The adversary A, given the seed and the side information z and entropy estimation γ of I, has access to the following:

(i) An oracle REF() to update the state S via the algorithm refresh with the next randomness input I. The adversary learns the corresponding side information z and the entropy estimation γ of I. The counter c is incremented by γ.

Game $\mathbf{G}_{\mathcal{G},\lambda}^{\text{rob}}(A, \mathcal{D})$	procedure REF()
$b \twoheadleftarrow \{0,1\}$; $s \leftarrow \varepsilon$; $seed \twoheadleftarrow$ Seed	$(s, I, \gamma, z) \twoheadleftarrow \mathcal{D}(s)$
$c \leftarrow 0$; $(s, I, \gamma, z) \twoheadleftarrow \mathcal{D}(s)$;	$S \leftarrow \text{refresh}(seed, S, I)$; $c \leftarrow c + \gamma$
$S \leftarrow \text{setup}(seed, I)$; $c \leftarrow c + \gamma$	return (γ, z)
$b' \twoheadleftarrow A^{\text{REF,ROR,GET,SET}}(seed, \gamma, z)$	
return $(b' = b)$	

procedure RoR(1^ℓ)	procedure GET()	procedure SET(S^*)
$(R_1, S) \leftarrow \text{next}(seed, S, \ell)$	$c \leftarrow 0$	$S \leftarrow S^*$; $c \leftarrow 0$
if $(c < \lambda)$ then $c \leftarrow 0$; return R_1	return S	
$R_0 \twoheadleftarrow \{0,1\}^\ell$; return R_b		

Fig. 1. Game defining robustness for a PRNG $\mathcal{G} = (\text{setup}, \text{refresh}, \text{next})$ against an adversary A and a distribution sampler $\mathcal{D}$, with respect to an entropy threshold λ.

(ii) An oracle GET() to obtain the current state S. The counter c is reset to 0.
(iii) An oracle SET() to set the current state to an adversarial value S^*. The counter c is reset to 0.
(iv) An oracle RoR(1^ℓ) to get the next ℓ-bit output. The game runs the next algorithm on the current state S to update it and get an ℓ-bit output R_1, and also samples a uniformly random string $R_0 \twoheadleftarrow \{0,1\}^\ell$. If the accumulated entropy is insufficient (meaning $c < \lambda$) then c is reset to 0 and R_1 is returned to the adversary. Otherwise, R_b is given to the adversary.

The goal of the adversary is to guess the challenge bit b, by outputting a bit b'. The advantage $\mathsf{Adv}_{\mathcal{G},\lambda}^{\text{rob}}(A, \mathcal{D})$ measures the normalized probability that the adversary's guess is correct.

EXTENSION FOR IDEAL MODELS. In many cases, the PRNG is based on an ideal primitive Π such as an ideal cipher or a random oracle. One then can imagine that the PRNG uses a huge seed that encodes Π. In the robustness notion, the adversary A would be given oracle access to Π but the distribution sampler $\mathcal{D}$ is assumed to be independent of the seed, and thus has no access to Π. This extension for ideal models is also used in prior work [6,31].

Some PRNGs, such as CTR-DRBG or the Intel PRNG [29], use AES with a constant key K_0. For example, $K_0 \leftarrow \text{AES}(0^{128}, 0^{127} \| 1)$ for the Intel PRNG, and $K_0 \leftarrow \text{0x00010203} \cdots$ for CTR-DRBG. An alternative treatment for ideal models in this case is to let both $\mathcal{D}$ and A have access to the ideal primitive, but pretend that K_0 is truly random, independent of $\mathcal{D}$. This approach does not work well in our situation because (i) the constant key of CTR-DRBG does not look random at all, and (ii) allowing $\mathcal{D}$ access to the ideal primitive substantially complicates the robustness proof of CTR-DRBG. We therefore avoid this approach to keep the proof simple.

4   The Randomness Extractor of **CTR-DRBG**

A PRNG is often built on top of an internal (seeded) randomness extractor Ext : Seed $\times$ $\{0,1\}^*$ $\rightarrow$ $\{0,1\}^s$ that takes as input a seed *seed* $\in$ Seed and a random input $I \in \{0,1\}^*$ to deterministically output a string $V \in \{0,1\}^s$. For example, the Intel PRNG [29] is built on top of CBCMAC, or HMAC-DRBG on top of HMAC. In this section we will analyze the security of the randomness extractor of **CTR-DRBG**, which we call *Condense-then-Encrypt* (CtE). We shall assume that the underlying blockcipher is AES.[5]

4.1   The CtE Construction

The randomness extractor CtE is based on two standard components: CBCMAC and CBC encryption. Below, we first recall the two components of CtE, and then describe how to compose them in CtE.

THE CBCMAC CONSTRUCTION. Let $\pi : \{0,1\}^n \rightarrow \{0,1\}^n$ be a permutation. For the sake of convenience, we will describe CBCMAC with a general IV; one would set IV $\leftarrow 0^n$ in the standard CBCMAC algorithm. For an initialization vector IV $\in \{0,1\}^n$ and a message $M = M_1 \cdots M_t$, with each $|M_i| = n$, we recursively define

$$\mathsf{CBCMAC}^{\mathrm{IV}}[\pi](M_1 \cdots M_t) = \mathsf{CBCMAC}^{R}[\pi](M_2 \cdots M_t)$$

where $R \leftarrow \pi(\mathrm{IV} \oplus M_1)$, and in the base case of the empty-string message, let $\mathsf{CBCMAC}^{\mathrm{IV}}[\pi](\varepsilon) = \mathrm{IV}$. In the case that $\mathrm{IV} = 0^n$, we simply write $\mathsf{CBCMAC}[\pi](M)$ instead of $\mathsf{CBCMAC}^{\mathrm{IV}}[\pi](M)$.

THE CBC ENCRYPTION CONSTRUCTION. In the context of CtE, the CBC encryption is only used for full-block messages. Let $E : \{0,1\}^k \times \{0,1\}^n \rightarrow \{0,1\}^n$ be a blockcipher. For a key $K \in \{0,1\}^k$, an initialization vector $\mathrm{IV} \in \{0,1\}^n$, and a message $M = M_1 \cdots M_t$, with each $|M_i| = n$, let

$$\mathsf{CBC}_K^{\mathrm{IV}}[E](M_1 \cdots M_t) = C_1 \cdots C_t \ ,$$

where $C_1, \ldots, C_t$ are defined recursively via $C_0 \leftarrow \mathrm{IV}$ and $C_i \leftarrow E_K(C_{i-1} \oplus M_i)$ for every $1 \le i \le t$. In our context, since we do *not* need decryptability, the IV is *excluded* in the output of CBC.

THE CtE CONSTRUCTION. Let $E : \{0,1\}^k \times \{0,1\}^n \rightarrow \{0,1\}^n$ be a blockcipher, such that k and n are divisible by 8, and $n \le k \le 2n$—this captures all choices of AES key length. Let pad : $\{0,1\}^* \rightarrow (\{0,1\}^n)^+$ be the padding scheme that first appends the byte 0x08, and then appends 0's until the length is a multiple

---

[5] While **CTR-DRBG** does support 3DES, the actual deployment is rare: among the CMVP-certified implementations that support **CTR-DRBG**, only 1% of them use 3DES [12].

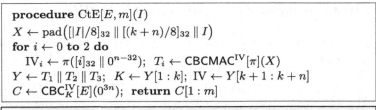

procedure $\text{CtE}[E, m](I)$
$X \leftarrow \text{pad}\big([|I|/8]_{32} \parallel [(k+n)/8]_{32} \parallel I\big)$
for $i \leftarrow 0$ **to** 2 **do**
$\quad \text{IV}_i \leftarrow \pi([i]_{32} \parallel 0^{n-32}); \quad T_i \leftarrow \text{CBCMAC}^{\text{IV}}[\pi](X)$
$Y \leftarrow T_1 \parallel T_2 \parallel T_3; \quad K \leftarrow Y[1:k]; \quad \text{IV} \leftarrow Y[k+1:k+n]$
$C \leftarrow \text{CBC}_K^{\text{IV}}[E](0^{3n}); \quad \textbf{return } C[1:m]$

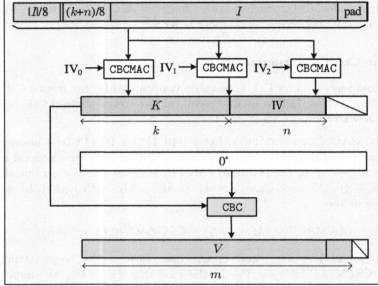

Fig. 2. The $\text{CtE}[E, m]$ construction, built on top of a blockcipher $E : \{0,1\}^k \times \{0,1\}^n \rightarrow \{0,1\}^n$. Here the random input I is a byte string. For an integer i, we let $[i]_t$ denote a t-bit representation of i, and the permutation π is instantiated from E with the k-bit constant key $\text{0x00010203}\cdots$.

of n. Note that $\text{pad}(X) \neq \text{pad}(Y)$ for any $X \neq Y$. For the sake of convenience, we shall describe a more generalized construction $\text{CtE}[E, m]$, with $m \leq 3n$. The code of this construction is shown in Fig. 2. The randomness extractor of CTR-DRBG corresponds to $\text{CtE}[E, k + n]$; we also write $\text{CtE}[E]$ for simplicity.

4.2 Security of CtE

SECURITY MODELING. In modeling the security of a randomness extractor Ext, prior work [14, 29, 31] usually requires that $\text{Ext}(seed, I)$ be pseudorandom for an adversary that is given the seed S, provided that (i) the random input I has sufficiently high min entropy, and (ii) the seed S is uniformly random. In our situation, following the conventional route would require each random input to have at least 280 bits of min entropy for CTR-DRBG to achieve birthday-bound security. However, for the way that CtE is used in CTR-DRBG, we only need the

---

Game $\mathbf{G}_{\mathsf{Cond}}^{\mathrm{guess}}(A, \mathcal{S})$

$(I, z) \leftarrow_\$ \mathcal{S}; \quad seed \leftarrow_\$ \mathsf{Seed}; \quad V \leftarrow \mathsf{Cond}(seed, I)$

$(Y_1, \ldots, Y_q) \leftarrow_\$ A(seed, z); \quad \mathbf{return} \ (V \in \{Y_1, \ldots, Y_q\})$

Fig. 3. Game defining security of a condenser Cond against an adversary A and a source $\mathcal{S}$.

n-bit prefix of the output to be *unpredictable*, allowing us to reduce the min-entropy threshold to 216 bits. In other words, we only need $\mathsf{CtE}[E, n]$ to be a good *condenser* [27].

We now recall the security notion for randomness condensers. Let Cond : $\mathsf{Seed} \times \{0,1\}^* \rightarrow \{0,1\}^n$ be a deterministic algorithm. Let $\mathcal{S}$ be a λ-*source*, meaning a stateless, probabilistic algorithm that outputs a random input I and some side information z such that $H_\infty(I \mid z) \geq \lambda$. For an adversary A, define

$$\mathsf{Adv}_{\mathsf{Cond}}^{\mathrm{guess}}(A, \mathcal{S}) = \Pr[\mathbf{G}_{\mathsf{Cond}}^{\mathrm{guess}}(A, \mathcal{S})]$$

as the *guessing advantage* of A against the condenser Cond on the source $\mathcal{S}$, where game $\mathbf{G}_{\mathsf{Cond}}^{\mathrm{guess}}(A, \mathcal{S})$ is defined in Fig. 3. Informally, the game measures the chance that the adversary can guess the output $\mathsf{Cond}(seed, I)$ given the seed $seed \leftarrow_\$ \mathsf{Seed}$ and some side information z of the random input I.

When the condenser Cond is built on an ideal primitive Π such as a random oracle or an ideal cipher, we only consider sources independent of Π. Following [14], instead of giving A oracle access to Π, we will give the adversary A the entire (huge) encoding of Π, which can only help the adversary. In other words, we view the encoding of Π as the seed of Cond, and as defined in game $\mathbf{G}_{\mathsf{Cond}}^{\mathrm{guess}}(A, \mathcal{S})$, the adversary A is given the seed.

To show that $\mathsf{CtE}[E, n]$ is a good condenser, we will first show that it is an almost universal (AU) hash, and then apply a Generalized Leftover Hash Lemma of Barak et al. [1]. Below, we will recall the notion of AU hash.

AU HASH. Let Cond : $\mathsf{Seed} \times \mathsf{Dom} \rightarrow \{0,1\}^n$ be a (keyed) hash function. For each string X, define its *block length* to be $\max\{1, |X|/n\}$. For a function $\delta : \mathbb{N} \rightarrow [1, \infty)$, we say that Cond is a δ-*almost universal* hash if for every distinct strings X_1, X_2 whose block lengths are at most ℓ, we have

$$\Pr_{seed \leftarrow_\$ \mathsf{Seed}}[\mathsf{Cond}(seed, X_1) = \mathsf{Cond}(seed, X_2)] \leq \frac{\delta(\ell)}{2^n} .$$

The following Generalized Leftover Hash Lemma of Barak et al. [1] shows that an AU hash function is a good condenser.

Lemma 2 (Generalized Leftover Hash Lemma). [1] *Let* Cond : $\mathsf{Seed} \times \mathsf{Dom} \rightarrow \{0,1\}^n$ *be a* δ-*AU hash function, and let* $\lambda > 0$ *be a real number. Let* $\mathcal{S}$

be a λ-source whose random input I has at most ℓ blocks. For any adversary A making at most q guesses,

$$\mathsf{Adv}^{\mathrm{guess}}_{\mathrm{Cond}}(A, \mathcal{S}) \le \frac{q}{2^n} + \sqrt{\frac{q}{2^\lambda} + \frac{q \cdot (\delta(\ell) - 1)}{2^n}} \ .$$

DISCUSSION. A common way to analyze CBCMAC-based extractors is to use a result by Dodis et al. [14]. However, this analysis is restricted to the situation in which either (i) the length of the random input is fixed, or (ii) the side information reveals the exact length of the random input. On the one hand, while the assumption (i) is true in Linux PRNG where the kernel entropy pool has size 4,096 bits, it does not hold in, say Intel PRNG where the system keeps collecting entropy and lengthening the random input. On the other hand, the assumption (ii) may unnecessarily squander entropy of random inputs by intentionally leaking their lengths. Given that CTR-DRBG is supposed to deal with a generic source of potentially limited entropy, it is desirable to remove the assumptions (i) and (ii) in the analysis.

At the first glance, one can deal with variable input length by using the following analysis of Bellare et al. [4] of CBCMAC. Let $\mathrm{Perm}(n)$ be the set of permutations on $\{0,1\}^n$. Then for any distinct, full-block messages X_1 and X_2 of at most $\ell \le 2^{n/4}$ blocks, Bellare et al. show that

$$\Pr_{\pi \,\overset{\$}{\leftarrow}\, \mathrm{Perm}(n)}[\mathsf{CBCMAC}[\pi](X_1) = \mathsf{CBCMAC}[\pi](X_2)] \le \frac{2\sqrt{\ell}}{2^n} + \frac{64\ell^4}{2^{2n}} \ . \tag{1}$$

However, this bound is too weak for our purpose due to the square root in Lemma 2. In particular, using this formula leads to an inferior term $\frac{\sqrt{q \cdot p}}{2^{n/2}}$ in bounding the unpredictability of p extracted outputs against q guesses.

To improve the concrete bound, we observe that to guess the output of $\mathsf{CtE}[E, n]$, the adversary has to guess both the key and IV of the CBC encryption simultaneously. Giving a good bound for this joint unpredictability is nontrivial, since the key and the IV are derived from the *same* source of randomness (but with different constant prefixes). This requires us to handle a *multi-collision* property of CBCMAC.

SECURITY ANALYSIS OF CtE. The following Lemma 3 gives a multi-collision property of CBCMAC that CtE needs;

Lemma 3 (Multi-collision of CBCMAC). *Let $n \ge 32$ be an integer. Let $X_1, \ldots, X_4$ be distinct, non-empty, full-block messages such that*

(i) X_1 and X_2 have the same first block, and X_3 and X_4 have the same first block, but these two blocks are different, and
(ii) the block length of each message is at most ℓ, with $4 \le \ell \le 2^{n/3-4}$.

Then for a truly random permutation $\pi \leftarrow^\$ \mathrm{Perm}(n)$, *the probability that both* $\mathsf{CBCMAC}[\pi](X_1) = \mathsf{CBCMAC}[\pi](X_2)$ *and* $\mathsf{CBCMAC}[\pi](X_3) = \mathsf{CBCMAC}[\pi](X_4)$ *happen is at most* $64\ell^3/2^{2n}$.

Armed with the result above, we now can show in Lemma 4 below that $\mathrm{CtE}[E, n]$ is a good AU hash. Had we used the naive bound in Eq. (1), we would have obtained an inferior bound $\frac{2\sqrt{\ell}}{2^n} + \frac{64\ell^4}{2^{2n}}$.

Lemma 4. *Let* $n \geq 32$ *and* $k \in \{n, n+1, \ldots, 2n\}$ *be integers. Let* $E : \{0,1\}^k \times \{0,1\}^n \to \{0,1\}^n$ *that we model as an ideal cipher. Let* $\mathrm{CtE}[E, n]$ *be described as above. Let* I_1, I_2 *be distinct strings of at most* ℓ *blocks, with* $\ell + 2 \leq 2^{n/3-4}$. *Then*

$$\Pr\big[\mathrm{CtE}[E, n](I_1) = \mathrm{CtE}[E, n](I_2)\big] \leq \frac{1}{2^n} + \frac{64(\ell + 2)^3}{2^{2n}} \, ,$$

where the randomness is taken over the choices of E.

Proof. Recall that in $\mathrm{CtE}[E, n](I_b)$, with $b \in \{1, 2\}$, we first iterate through CBCMAC three times to derive a key K_b and an IV J_b, and then output $E(K_b, J_b)$. Let Y_b and Z_b be the first block and the second block of $K_b \parallel J_b$, respectively. We consider the following cases:

Case 1: $(Y_1, Z_1) \neq (Y_2, Z_2)$. Hence $(K_1, J_1) \neq (K_2, J_2)$. If $K_1 = K_2$ then since E is a blockcipher, $E(K_1, J_1) \neq E(K_2, J_2)$. Suppose that $K_1 \neq K_2$. Without loss of generality, assume that K_1 is not the constant key in CBCMAC. Since E is modeled as an ideal cipher, $E(K_1, J_1)$ is a uniformly random string, independent of $E(K_2, J_2)$, and thus the chance that $E(K_1, J_1) = E(K_2, J_2)$ is $1/2^n$. Therefore, in this case, the probability that $\mathrm{CtE}[E, n](I_1) = \mathrm{CtE}[E, n](I_2)$ is at most $1/2^n$.

Case 2: $(Y_1, Z_1) = (Y_2, Z_2)$. It suffices to show that this case happens with probability at most $64(\ell + 2)^3/2^{2n}$. For each $a \in \{0, 1\}$, let $P_a \leftarrow [a]_{32} \parallel 0^{n-32}$. For $b \in \{1, 2\}$, let

$$U_b \leftarrow \mathrm{pad}\big([|I_b|/8]_{32} \parallel [(k + n)/8]_{32} \parallel I_b\big) \, .$$

Let π be the permutation in CBCMAC. Note that $Y_b \leftarrow \mathsf{CBCMAC}[\pi](P_0 \parallel U_b)$ and $Z_b \leftarrow \mathsf{CBCMAC}[\pi](P_1 \parallel U_b)$ for every $b \in \{1, 2\}$. Applying Lemma 3 with $X_1 = P_0 \parallel U_1$, $X_2 = P_0 \parallel U_2$, $X_3 = P_1 \parallel U_1$, and $X_4 = P_1 \parallel U_2$ (note that these strings have block length at most $\ell + 2$), the chance that $Y_1 = Y_2$ and $Z_1 = Z_2$ is at most $64(\ell + 2)^3/2^{2n}$. $\square$

Combining Lemma 2 and Lemma 4, we immediately obtain the following result, establishing that $\mathrm{CtE}[E, n]$ is a good condenser.

Theorem 1. *Let* $n \geq 32$ *and* $k \in \{n, n+1, \ldots, 2n\}$ *be integers. Let* $E : \{0,1\}^k \times \{0,1\}^n \to \{0,1\}^n$ *that we model as an ideal cipher. Let* $\mathrm{CtE}[E, n]$ *be described as above. Let* $\mathcal{S}$ *be a* λ-*source that is independent of* E *and outputs random inputs of at most* ℓ *blocks. Then for any adversary* A *making at most* q *guesses,*

$$\mathsf{Adv}^{\mathrm{guess}}_{\mathrm{CtE}[E,n]}(A, \mathcal{S}) \leq \frac{q}{2^n} + \frac{\sqrt{q}}{2^{\lambda/2}} + \frac{8\sqrt{q(\ell + 2)^3}}{2^n} \, .$$

procedure $\mathrm{XP}[E](I)$
$X \leftarrow \mathrm{pad}\big([|I|/8]_{32} \parallel [(k+n)/8]_{32} \parallel I\big)$
for $i \leftarrow 0$ to 2 do
$\quad \mathrm{IV}_i \leftarrow \pi([i]_{32} \parallel 0^{n-32}); \quad T_i \leftarrow \mathsf{CBCMAC}^{\mathrm{IV}_i}[\pi](X)$
$Y \leftarrow T_1 \parallel T_2 \parallel T_3; \quad K \leftarrow Y[1:k]; \quad \mathrm{IV} \leftarrow Y[k+1:k+n]$
$C \leftarrow E(K, \mathrm{IV})$ //Output of $\mathrm{CtE}[E,n](I)$
return $C \oplus K[1:n]$

Fig. 4. The $\mathrm{XP}[E]$ construction, built on top of a blockcipher $E : \{0,1\}^k \times \{0,1\}^n \to \{0,1\}^n$. Here the random input I is a byte string. For an integer i, we let $[i]_t$ denote a t-bit representation of i, and the permutation π is instantiated from E with the k-bit constant key $\mathrm{0x00010203}\cdots$.

ANOTHER REQUIREMENT OF CtE. In proving security of CTR-DRBG, one would encounter the following situation. We first derive the key $J \leftarrow \mathrm{CtE}[E](I)$ on a random input I, and let K be the key of CBC encryption in $\mathrm{CtE}[E](I)$. The adversary then specifies a mask P. It wins if $K = J \oplus P$; that is, the adversary wins if it can predict $K \oplus J$. To bound the winning probability of the adversary, our strategy is to show that even the n-bit prefix of $K \oplus J$ is hard to guess. In particular, we consider a construction *Xor-Prefix* (XP) such that $\mathrm{XP}[E](I)$ outputs the n-bit prefix of $K \oplus J$, and then show that $\mathrm{XP}[E]$ is a good condenser.

The code of $\mathrm{XP}[E]$ is given in Fig. 4. Informally, $\mathrm{XP}[E](I)$ first runs $\mathrm{CtE}[E,n](I)$ to obtain an n-bit string C, and then outputs $C \oplus K[1:n]$, where K is the key of CBC encryption in $\mathrm{CtE}[E,n](I)$.

The following result shows that $\mathrm{XP}[E]$ is a good AU hash.

Lemma 5. *Let $n \geq 32$ and $k \in \{n, n+1, \ldots, 2n\}$ be integers. Let $E : \{0,1\}^k \times \{0,1\}^n \to \{0,1\}^n$ that we model as an ideal cipher. Let $\mathrm{XP}[E]$ be described as above. Let I_1, I_2 be distinct strings of at most ℓ blocks, with $\ell + 2 \leq 2^{n/3-4}$. Then*

$$\Pr\big[\mathrm{XP}[E](I_1) = \mathrm{XP}[E](I_2)\big] \leq \frac{1}{2^n} + \frac{64(\ell+2)^3}{2^{2n}} \ ,$$

where the randomness is taken over the choices of E.

Proof. Recall that in $\mathrm{XP}[E](I_b)$, with $b \in \{1,2\}$, we first iterate through CBCMAC to derive a key K_b and an IV J_b, and then output $E(K_b, J_b) \oplus K_b[1:n]$. Let Y_b and Z_b be the first block and the second block of $K_b \parallel J_b$, respectively. We consider the following cases:

Case 1: $(Y_1, Z_1) \neq (Y_2, Z_2)$. Hence $(K_1, J_1) \neq (K_2, J_2)$. If $K_1 = K_2$ then since E is a blockcipher, $E(K_1, J_1) \neq E(K_2, J_2)$ and thus

$$E(K_1, J_1) \oplus K_1[1:n] \neq E(K_2, J_2) \oplus K_2[1:n] \ .$$

Suppose that $K_1 \neq K_2$. Without loss of generality, assume that K_1 is not the constant key in CBCMAC. Since E is modeled as an ideal cipher, the string

$E(K_1, J_1) \oplus K_1[1:n]$ is uniformly random, independent of $E(K_2, J_2) \oplus K_2[1:n]$, and thus the chance that these two strings are the same is $1/2^n$. Therefore, in this case, the probability that $\mathrm{XP}[E](I_1) = \mathrm{XP}[E](I_2)$ is at most $1/2^n$.

Case 2: $(Y_1, Z_1) = (Y_2, Z_2)$. It suffices to show that this case happens with probability at most $64(\ell + 2)^3/2^{2n}$. For each $a \in \{0,1\}$, let $P_b \leftarrow [b]_{32} \parallel 0^{n-32}$. For $b \in \{1,2\}$, let

$$U_b \leftarrow \mathrm{pad}\big([|I_b|/8]_{32} \parallel [(k+n)/8]_{32} \parallel I_b\big) \ .$$

Let π be the permutation in CBCMAC. Note that $Y_b \leftarrow \mathrm{CBCMAC}[\pi](P_0 \parallel U_b)$ and $Z_b \leftarrow \mathrm{CBCMAC}[\pi](P_1 \parallel U_b)$ for every $b \in \{1,2\}$. Applying Lemma 3 with $X_1 = P_0 \parallel U_1$, $X_2 = P_0 \parallel U_2$, $X_3 = P_1 \parallel U_1$, and $X_4 = P_1 \parallel U_2$ (note that these strings have block length at most $\ell + 2$), the chance that $Y_1 = Y_2$ and $Z_1 = Z_2$ is at most $64(\ell + 2)^3/2^{2n}$. $\qquad\square$

Combining Lemma 2 and Lemma 5, we immediately obtain the following result, establishing that $\mathrm{XP}[E]$ is a good condenser.

Lemma 6. *Let $n \geq 32$ and $k \in \{n, n+1, \ldots, 2n\}$ be integers. Let $E : \{0,1\}^k \times \{0,1\}^n \rightarrow \{0,1\}^n$ that we model as an ideal cipher. Let $\mathrm{XP}[E]$ be described as above. Let $\mathcal{S}$ be a λ-source that is independent of E and outputs random inputs of at most ℓ blocks. Then for any adversary A making at most q guesses,*

$$\mathrm{Adv}_{\mathrm{XP}[E]}^{\mathrm{guess}}(A, \mathcal{S}) \leq \frac{q}{2^n} + \frac{\sqrt{q}}{2^{\lambda/2}} + \frac{8\sqrt{q(\ell+2)^3}}{2^n} \ .$$

5 The CTR-DRBG Construction

The CTR-DRBG construction is based on the randomness extractor CtE in Sect. 4 and the Counter (CTR) mode of encryption. Below, we will first recall the CTR mode before describing CTR-DRBG.

THE COUNTER MODE. Let $E : \{0,1\}^k \times \{0,1\}^n \rightarrow \{0,1\}^n$ be a blockcipher. For a key $K \in \{0,1\}^k$, an IV $\in \{0,1\}^n$, and a message M, let $r \leftarrow \lceil |M|/n \rceil$, and let

$$\mathrm{CTR}_K^{\mathrm{IV}}[E](M) = M \oplus Y[1:|M|] \ ,$$

in which $Y \leftarrow Y_1 \parallel \cdots \parallel Y_r$ and each $Y_i \leftarrow E(K, \mathrm{IV} + i \bmod 2^n)$. Since we do *not* need decryptability, the IV is *excluded* in the output of CTR.

THE CTR-DRBG CONSTRUCTION. The code of CTR-DRBG[E] is given in Fig. 5. Recall that here we model E as an ideal cipher, and thus the algorithms of CTR-DRBG are given oracle access to E instead of being given a seed.

REMARKS. The specification of CTR-DRBG in NIST 800-90A is actually very flexible, allowing a wide range of options that do not conform to the specification in Fig. 5:

procedure setup$^E(I)$	procedure refresh$^E(S,I)$	procedure next$^E(S,\ell)$
$X \leftarrow \mathrm{CtE}[E](I)$	$X \leftarrow \mathrm{CtE}[E](I)$	$K \leftarrow S[1:k];\ V \leftarrow S[k+1:k+n]$
$K \leftarrow 0^k;\ \mathrm{IV} \leftarrow 0^n$	$K \leftarrow S[1:k]$	$r \leftarrow n \cdot \lceil \ell/n \rceil$
$S \leftarrow \mathrm{CTR}_K^{\mathrm{IV}}[E](X)$	$V \leftarrow S[k+1:k+n]$	$P \leftarrow \mathrm{CTR}_K^V[E](0^{r+k+n})$
return S	$S \leftarrow \mathrm{CTR}_K^V[E](X)$	$R \leftarrow P[1:\ell]$
	return S	$S \leftarrow P[r+1:r+k+n]$
		return (R,S)

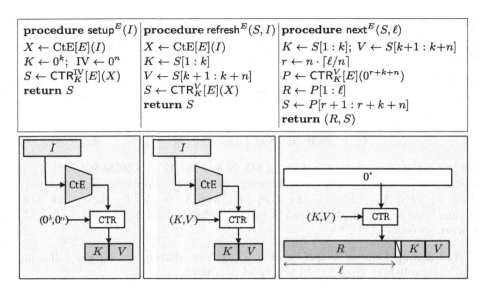

Fig. 5. The CTR-DRBG construction. Each picture illustrates the algorithm right on top of it. The state S consists of an n-bit string V and a k-bit string K.

- **Bypassing randomness extraction:** The use of CtE to extract randomness is actually *optional*, but if CtE is not used then the random inputs are required to be uniformly random. In practice, it is unclear how to enforce the full-entropy requirement. In fact, as Woodage and Shumow [31] point out, OpenSSL implementation of CTR-DRBG allows one to turn off the use of CtE, yet directly use raw random inputs. Bypassing CtE, coupled with the negligence of properly sanitizing random inputs, may lead to security vulnerabilities, as demonstrated via an attack of Woodage and Shumow. We therefore suggest making the use of CtE mandatory.
- **Use of nonces:** Procedures setup and refresh may take an additional nonce as input. This extension allows one to run multiple instances of CTR-DRBG on the *same* source of randomness, provided that they are given different nonces. In this work we do not consider multi-instance security.
- **Use of additional inputs:** Procedure next may take an additional random input. If CtE is used, this extension is simply a composition of refresh and the basic next (without additional inputs). Therefore, without loss of generality, we can omit the use of addition inputs in next.

6   Security Analysis of CTR-DRBG

6.1   Results and Discussion

Consider an adversary A attacking CTR-DRBG that makes at most q oracle queries (including ideal-cipher ones) in which each next query is called to output at most B blocks, and the total block length of those outputs is at most s. Let $\mathcal{D}$ be a λ-simple distribution sampler. Assume that under A's queries, $\mathcal{D}$ produces at most p random inputs, in which the i-th random input has maximum block length ℓ_i. Let

$$L = \max\{\ell_1, \ldots, \ell_p\}$$

be the maximum block length of the random inputs, and let

$$\sigma = \ell_1 + \cdots + \ell_p$$

be their maximum total block length. The following Theorem 2 gives a bound on the robustness of CTR-DRBG on simple samplers.

Theorem 2. *Let $E : \{0,1\}^k \times \{0,1\}^n \to \{0,1\}^n$ be a blockcipher. Let $\mathcal{G}$ be the construction CTR-DRBG$[E]$ as described above. Let $\mathcal{D}$ be a λ-simple distribution sampler and A be an adversary attacking $\mathcal{G}$ whose accounting of queries is given above. Then*

$$\mathsf{Adv}_{\mathcal{G},\lambda}^{\mathrm{rob}}(A,\mathcal{D}) \leq \frac{2(B+3)(s+3p)}{2^n} + \frac{6q(q+1)}{2^k} + \frac{6p(q+1)}{2^n} + \frac{12p \cdot \sqrt{q}}{2^{\lambda/2}}$$
$$+ \frac{48(\sqrt{q}+1) \cdot \sqrt{L+2} \cdot (\sigma+2p)}{2^n} \ .$$

INTERPRETING OUR BOUND. Under NIST SP 800-90A, $L \leq 2^{28}$ and $B \leq 2^{12}$. Assuming that $q, p \leq 2^{45}$ and $s, \sigma \leq 2^{50}$, if the min-entropy threshold λ is at least 216, the adversary's advantage is at most 2^{-32}. This is comparable to what conventional blockcipher-based constructions (such as CBCMAC) offer.[6]

CAVEAT. Under our security notion, if an adversary can learn the state of CTR-DRBG, the outputs of next are compromised until refresh is called. Thus Theorem 2 does not contradict the recent (side-channel) attack of Cohney et al. [12] on common implementations of CTR-DRBG. Our results indicate that such an attack can be mitigated by calling refresh frequently, assuming that each random input has sufficient min entropy. This is consistent with the recommendation of Cohney et al., and thus our work can be viewed as a theoretical justification for their counter-measures.

SECURITY RECOMMENDATION. NIST SP 800-90A only requires that random inputs have min entropy of at least 128 bits. This threshold is too low, even for the modest goal of using CtE to extract randomness from p random inputs. We therefore recommend increasing the min-entropy threshold to at least 216 bits. On the other hand, the standard only requires calling refresh after producing

---

[6] We choose the bound 2^{-32} in this example because this is a failure probability that NIST standards usually accept. For instance, NIST 800-38B requires CBCMAC implementation to rekey after 2^{48} messages so that the probability of IV collision in CBCMAC under a single key is below 2^{-32}.

2^{48} bits for the outputs. We suggest reducing this limit to, say 2^{24} to force implementations to refresh more frequently.

OBSTACLES IN THE PROOF OF THEOREM 2. A common way to prove robustness of a PRGN is to decompose the complex notion of robustness into two simpler notions: *preserving* and *recovering* [15,17,31]. In particular, if we can bound the recovering and preserving advantages by ϵ and ϵ' respectively, then this gives a bound $p(\epsilon + \epsilon')$ on robustness. However, if one uses the decomposition approach above to deal with CTR-DRBG then one would run into the following issues.

First, at best one can only obtain a birthday bound $B^2/2^n$ for the preserving and recovering security: a birthday security is unavoidable since under these two notions, the adversary has to distinguish a CTR output with a truly random string. Combining this birthday bound with the blowup factor p leads to an inferior bound $B^2 p/2^n$.

Next, there lies a trap in proving recovering security of any PRNG that is built on top of an AU hash function H. In particular, under the recovering notion, the adversary needs to pick an index $i \in \{1, \ldots, p\}$ to indicate which random input I_i that it wants to attack, and then predicts the output of $H_K(I_i)$ via q guesses. At the first glance, one can trivially use the Generalized Leftover Hash Lemma to bound the guessing advantage of each I_j as δ; the recovering advantage should be also at most δ. However, this argument is wrong, because here the adversary can *adaptively* pick the index i after seeing the hash key K. The correct bound for the recovering advantage should be $p \cdot \delta$. This subtlety is somewhat similar to selective-opening security on encryption schemes [3,16].

To understand the adaptivity issue above, consider the following counter-example. Let $H : \{0,1\}^t \times \text{Dom} \to \{0,1\}^n$ be a hash function, and let $p = 2^t$. Let $\text{Dom}_1, \ldots, \text{Dom}_p$ be a partition of Dom. Suppose that we have p random inputs $I_1 \in \text{Dom}_1, \ldots, I_p \in \text{Dom}_p$, each of at least λ min entropy. Assume that if the key K is a t-bit encoding of an integer i and the input X belongs to Dom_i then H misbehaves, outputting 0^n; otherwise it is a good cryptographic hash function that we can model as a (keyed) random oracle. Then H is still a good condenser: for each fixed $i \in \{1, \ldots, p\}$ and for a uniformly random key $K \leftarrow_\$ \{0,1\}^t$, the chance that one can predict $H_K(I_i)$ after q guesses is at most $\frac{1}{2^t} + \frac{q}{2^\lambda} + \frac{q}{2^n}$. Now, under the recovering notion, the adversary can choose the index i after seeing the key K. If the adversary chooses i as the integer that K encodes, then $H(K, I_i) = 0^n$, and thus the adversary can trivially predict $H(K, I_i)$.

The subtlety above also arises in the proof of a theoretical PRNG by Dodis et al. [15]. These authors are aware of the adaptivity issue, and give a proper treatment of the recovering bound at the expense of a blowup factor p. The counter-example above suggests that this factor p is inherent, and there is no hope to improve the recovering advantage.

To cope with the issues above, instead of using the decomposition approach, we give a direct proof for the robustness security via the H-coefficient technique. By considering all CTR outputs at once, we can replace the term $B^2 p/2^n$ by a

```
procedure CTR_K^V[E](M)
m ← ⌈|M|/n⌉
if c ≥ λ then Keys ← Keys ∪ {K}
for i ← 1 to m do
    P_i ← E(K, V + i)
    if c ≥ λ then Queries ← Queries ∪ {(K, V + i, P_i)}
P ← P_1 ⋯ P_m;   C ← P[1 : |M|] ⊕ M;   return C
```

Fig. 6. The extended code of procedures CTR of $\mathbf{S}_{\mathrm{real}}$. The code maintains two lists Keys and Queries that are initialized to $\emptyset$. Here c is the global counter estimating min entropy of the state of $\mathbf{S}_{\mathrm{real}}$.

better one $Bs/2^n$. Likewise, a direct proof helps us to avoid the blowup factor p in bounding the guessing advantage of the extracted randomness $\mathrm{CtE}(I_i)$.

TIGHTNESS OF THE BOUND. Our bound is probably not tight. First, the term $p \cdot \sqrt{q}/2^{\lambda/2}$ is from our use of the Generalized Leftover Hash Lemma to analyze the guessing advantage of $\mathrm{CtE}[E, n]$. It is unclear if a dedicated analysis of the guessing advantage of CtE can improve this term. Next, the term $pq/2^n$ is an artifact of our analysis in which we only consider the unpredictability of the n-bit prefix of each CTR key instead of the entire key. It seems possible to improve this to $pq/2^k$, leading to a better security bound if the underlying blockcipher is either AES-192 or AES-256. Finally, the term $\sqrt{qL} \cdot \sigma/2^n$ is the result of our multi-collision analysis of CBCMAC, but the bound in Lemma 3 is rather loose. We leave this as an open problem to improve our bound.

6.2   Proof of Theorem 2

SETUP. Since we consider computationally unbounded adversaries, without loss of generality, assume that A is deterministic. Let $\mathbf{S}_{\mathrm{real}}$ and $\mathbf{S}_{\mathrm{ideal}}$ be the systems that model the oracles accessed by A in game $\mathbf{G}_{\mathcal{G},\lambda}^{\mathrm{rob}}(A, \mathcal{D})$ with the challenge bit $b = 1$ and $b = 0$ respectively. For bookkeeping purpose, the system $\mathbf{S}_{\mathrm{real}}$ also maintains two ordered lists Keys and Queries that are initialized to be $\emptyset$. Those lists shall be updated within procedure CTR of $\mathbf{S}_{\mathrm{real}}$; the extended code of CTR is shown in Fig. 6. Informally, Keys keeps track of CTR keys whose min-entropy counter is at least λ, and Queries maintains the corresponding ideal-cipher queries of CTR.

A HYBRID ARGUMENT. We will now create a hybrid system $\mathbf{S}_{\mathrm{hybrid}}$. The hybrid system will implement $\mathbf{S}_{\mathrm{real}}$, but each time it's asked to run CTR, if the min-entropy level c is at least the threshold λ, our hybrid system will use a fresh, uniformly random string instead of the CTR output. In particular, the outputs of RoR of $\mathbf{S}_{\mathrm{hybrid}}$, when $c \geq \lambda$, are uniformly random strings. The code of procedure CTR of $\mathbf{S}_{\mathrm{hybrid}}$ is shown in Fig. 7. It also maintains the lists Keys and

---

procedure $\mathsf{CTR}_K^V[E](M)$

$m \leftarrow \lceil |M|/n \rceil$

if $c \geq \lambda$ **then** $\mathsf{Keys} \leftarrow \mathsf{Keys} \cup \{K\}$

for $i \leftarrow 1$ **to** m **do**

    if $c \geq \lambda$ **then** $P_i \leftarrow\!\!\$ \{0,1\}^n$; $\mathsf{Queries} \leftarrow \mathsf{Queries} \cup \{(K, V+i, P_i)\}$

    else $P_i \leftarrow E(K, V+i)$

$P \leftarrow P_1 \cdots P_m$; $C \leftarrow P[1:|M|] \oplus M$; **return** C

Fig. 7. The extended code of procedures CTR of $\mathbf{S}_{\mathrm{hybrid}}$.

Queries. To avoid confusion, we shall write $\mathsf{Keys}(\mathbf{S})$ and $\mathsf{Queries}(\mathbf{S})$ to refer to the corresponding lists of system $\mathbf{S} \in \{\mathbf{S}_{\mathrm{real}}, \mathbf{S}_{\mathrm{hybrid}}\}$.

For any systems $\mathbf{S}_1$ and $\mathbf{S}_0$, let $\Delta_A(\mathbf{S}_1, \mathbf{S}_0)$ denote the distinguishing advantage of the adversary A against the "real" system $\mathbf{S}_1$ and "ideal" system $\mathbf{S}_0$. We now construct an adversary A^* of about the same efficiency as A such that

$$\Delta_{A^*}(\mathbf{S}_{\mathrm{real}}, \mathbf{S}_{\mathrm{hybrid}}) = \Delta_A(\mathbf{S}_{\mathrm{ideal}}, \mathbf{S}_{\mathrm{hybrid}}) \ .$$

Adversary A^* runs A and provides the latter with access to its oracles. However, for each RoR query, if $c \geq \lambda$ (which A^* can calculate), instead of giving A the true output, A^* will instead give A a uniformly random string of the same length. Finally, when A outputs its guess b', adversary A^* will output the same guess. Adversary A^* perfectly simulates the systems $\mathbf{S}_{\mathrm{ideal}}$ (in the real world) and $\mathbf{S}_{\mathrm{hybrid}}$ (in the hybrid world) for A, and thus achieves the same distinguishing advantage.

Below, we will show that

$$\Delta_A(\mathbf{S}_{\mathrm{real}}, \mathbf{S}_{\mathrm{hybrid}}) \leq \frac{(B+3)(s+3p)}{2^n} + \frac{3q(q+1)}{2^k} + \frac{3p(q+1)}{2^n} + \frac{6p \cdot \sqrt{q}}{2^{\lambda/2}}$$
$$+ \frac{24(\sqrt{q}+1) \cdot \sqrt{L+2} \cdot (\sigma + 2p)}{2^n} \ . \tag{2}$$

Since this bound applies to *any* adversary of the same accounting of queries, it applies to adversary A^* as well, meaning that

$$\Delta_{A^*}(\mathbf{S}_{\mathrm{real}}, \mathbf{S}_{\mathrm{hybrid}}) \leq \frac{(B+3)(s+3p)}{2^n} + \frac{3q(q+1)}{2^k} + \frac{3p(q+1)}{2^n} + \frac{6p \cdot \sqrt{q}}{2^{\lambda/2}}$$
$$+ \frac{24(\sqrt{q}+1) \cdot \sqrt{L+2} \cdot (\sigma + 2p)}{2^n} \ . \tag{3}$$

By the triangle inequality,

$$\begin{aligned}
\mathsf{Adv}_{\mathcal{G},\lambda}^{\mathrm{rob}}(A, \mathcal{D}) &= \Delta_A(\mathbf{S}_{\mathrm{real}}, \mathbf{S}_{\mathrm{ideal}}) \\
&\leq \Delta_A(\mathbf{S}_{\mathrm{real}}, \mathbf{S}_{\mathrm{hybrid}}) + \Delta_A(\mathbf{S}_{\mathrm{hybrid}}, \mathbf{S}_{\mathrm{ideal}}) \\
&= \Delta_A(\mathbf{S}_{\mathrm{real}}, \mathbf{S}_{\mathrm{hybrid}}) + \Delta_{A^*}(\mathbf{S}_{\mathrm{real}}, \mathbf{S}_{\mathrm{hybrid}}) \ . \tag{4}
\end{aligned}$$

From Eqs. (2), (3), and (4),

$$\mathsf{Adv}^{\mathrm{rob}}_{\mathcal{G},\lambda}(A,\mathcal{D}) \leq \frac{2(B+3)(s+3p)}{2^n} + \frac{6q(q+1)}{2^k} + \frac{6p(q+1)}{2^n} + \frac{12p \cdot \sqrt{q}}{2^{\lambda/2}}$$
$$+ \frac{48(\sqrt{q}+1) \cdot \sqrt{L+2} \cdot (\sigma + 2p)}{2^n} .$$

We now justify Eq. (2) by the H-coefficient technique.

DEFINING BAD TRANSCRIPTS. Recall that when A interacts with a system $\mathbf{S} \in \{\mathbf{S}_{\mathrm{real}}, \mathbf{S}_{\mathrm{hybrid}}\}$, the system $\mathbf{S}$ maintains a $(k+n)$-bit state $S = (K, V)$. This state starts as $(K_0, V_0) = (0^k, 0^n)$, and then setup is called to update the state to (K_1, V_1). The queries of A will cause it to be updated to $(K_2, V_2), (K_3, V_3)$, and so on. When the adversary A finishes querying $\mathbf{S}$, we'll grant it all states (K_i, V_i), all random inputs I_j and their extracted randomness $\mathsf{CtE}[E](I_j)$, the list Queries, and triples $(J, X, E(J, X))$ for any $J \in \{0,1\}^k \backslash \mathsf{Keys}(\mathbf{S})$ and $X \in \{0,1\}^n$. This extra information can only help the adversary. A transcript is *bad* if one of the following conditions happens:

(i) There are different triples $(J, X_1, Y_1), (J, X_2, Y_2) \in \mathsf{Queries}(\mathbf{S})$ that are generated under the same call of CTR (meaning that $X_1 \neq X_2$) such that $Y_1 = Y_2$.[7] This cannot happen in $\mathbf{S}_{\mathrm{real}}$ but may happen in $\mathbf{S}_{\mathrm{hybrid}}$.

(ii) The transcript contains a query (J, X) of A to E/E^{-1} such that $J \in \mathsf{Keys}(\mathbf{S})$. In other words, the adversary somehow managed to guess a secret key of the CTR mode before it is granted extra information.

(iii) There are distinct i and j, with $K_j \in \mathsf{Keys}(\mathbf{S})$, such that $K_i = K_j$. That is, there is a collision between the keys K_i and K_j, in which K_j is the secret keys for CTR mode that we want to protect. The other key K_i may either be a secret CTR key, or a compromised key that the adversary knows.

(iv) There is some key $K_i \in \mathsf{Keys}(\mathbf{S})$ that is also the constant key in CBCMAC.

(v) There is some key $J \in \mathsf{Keys}(\mathbf{S})$ that is derived from I_j and there is an index $i \neq j$ such that J is also the key of CBC encryption in $\mathsf{CtE}[E](I_i)$.

(vi) There is some key $J \in \mathsf{Keys}(\mathbf{S})$ that is derived from I_j such that J is also the key of CBC encryption in $\mathsf{CtE}[E](I_j)$.

If a transcript is not bad then we say that it's *good*. Let $\mathcal{T}_{\mathrm{real}}$ and $\mathcal{T}_{\mathrm{hybrid}}$ be the random variables of the transcript for $\mathbf{S}_{\mathrm{real}}$ and $\mathbf{S}_{\mathrm{hybrid}}$ respectively.

PROBABILITY OF BAD TRANSCRIPTS. We now bound the chance that $\mathcal{T}_{\mathrm{hybrid}}$ is bad. Let Bad_i be the event that $\mathcal{T}_{\mathrm{hybrid}}$ violates the i-th condition. By the union bound,

$$\Pr[\mathcal{T}_{\mathrm{hybrid}} \text{ is bad}] = \Pr[\mathrm{Bad}_1 \cup \cdots \cup \mathrm{Bad}_6] \leq \sum_{i=1}^{6} \Pr[\mathrm{Bad}_i] .$$

---

[7] One can tell whether two triples in Queries($\mathbf{S}$) belong to the same call of CTR since the list Queries($\mathbf{S}$) is ordered, and the lengths of the messages of CTR are known.

We first bound $\Pr[\mathrm{Bad}_1]$. Suppose that $\mathsf{Queries}(\mathbf{S}_{\mathrm{hybrid}})$ are generated from Q calls of CTR, and let $P_1, \ldots, P_Q$ be the corresponding CTR outputs. Let $T_1, \ldots, T_Q$ be the block length of $P_1, \ldots, P_Q$. Note that $Q, T_1, \ldots, T_Q$ are random variables, but since $k \leq 2n$, we have $T_i \leq B + 3$ for every i, and $T_1 + \cdots + T_Q \leq s + 3p$. The event Bad_1 happens if among T_i blocks of some P_i, there are two duplicate blocks. Since the blocks of each P_i are uniformly random,

$$\Pr[\mathrm{Bad}_1] \leq \mathbf{E}\Big(\sum_{i=1}^{Q} \frac{T_i^2}{2^n}\Big) \leq \mathbf{E}\Big(\sum_{i=1}^{Q} \frac{T_i \cdot (B+3)}{2^n}\Big) \leq \frac{(B+3)(s+3p)}{2^n} \ .$$

Next, we shall bound $\Pr[\mathrm{Bad}_2]$. Note that the keys in $\mathsf{Keys}(\mathbf{S}_{\mathrm{hybrid}})$ can be categorized as follows.

- **Strong keys:** Those keys are picked uniformly at random.
- **Weak keys:** Those keys K_i are generated via

$$K_i \leftarrow \mathsf{CTR}_{K_{i-1}}^{V_{i-1}}[E]\big(\mathsf{CtE}[E](I)\big)[1:k]$$

for a random input I of $\mathcal{D}$.

For a strong key, the chance that the adversary can guess it using q ideal-cipher queries is at most $q/2^k$. Since there are at most q strong keys, the chance that one of the strong keys causes Bad_2 to happen is at most $q^2/2^k$. For each $j \leq p$, let $\mathsf{Hit}_2(j)$ be the event that the key derived from the random input I_j is a weak key, and it causes Bad_2 to happen. From the union bound,

$$\Pr[\mathrm{Bad}_2] \leq \frac{q^2}{2^k} + \Pr[\mathsf{Hit}_2(1) \cup \cdots \cup \mathsf{Hit}_2(p)] \leq \frac{q^2}{2^k} + \sum_{j=1}^{p} \Pr[\mathsf{Hit}_2(j)] \ .$$

We now bound each $\Pr[\mathsf{Hit}_2(j)]$. Let J be the key derived from the random input I_j and assume that J is weak. Since $J \in \mathsf{Keys}(\mathbf{S}_{\mathrm{hybrid}})$, the next state of $\mathbf{S}_{\mathrm{hybrid}}$ is generated (as shown in Fig. 7) by picking a uniformly random string, and thus subsequent queries give no information on J. In addition, recall that the n-bit prefix of J is the xor of $\mathsf{CtE}[E, n](I_j)$ with a mask P_j. If we grant P_j to the adversary then it only increases $\Pr[\mathsf{Hit}_2(j)]$. The event $\mathsf{Hit}_2(j)$ happens only if the adversary can somehow guess $\mathsf{CtE}[E, n](I_j)$ via q choices of its ideal-cipher queries. But anything that the adversary receives is derived from the blockcipher E, the side information z_j and the entropy estimation γ_j of I_j, the other (I_i, γ_i, z_i) with $i \neq j$. Thus from Theorem 1,

$$\Pr[\mathsf{Hit}_2(j)] \leq \frac{q}{2^n} + \frac{\sqrt{q}}{2^{\lambda/2}} + \frac{8\sqrt{q(\ell_j + 2)^3}}{2^n}$$

$$\leq \frac{q}{2^n} + \frac{\sqrt{q}}{2^{\lambda/2}} + \frac{8\sqrt{q(L+2)} \cdot (\ell_j + 2)}{2^n} \ .$$

Summing up over all events $\mathsf{Hit}_2(1), \ldots, \mathsf{Hit}_2(p)$,

$$\Pr[\mathrm{Bad}_2] \leq \frac{q^2}{2^k} + \frac{pq}{2^n} + \frac{p \cdot \sqrt{q}}{2^{\lambda/2}} + \frac{8\sqrt{q(L+2)} \cdot (\sigma + 2p)}{2^n} \ .$$

We now bound $\Pr[\mathsf{Bad}_3]$. For a strong key, the chance that it collides with one of the other q keys in the system in at most $q/2^k$. Since there are at most q strong keys, the chance that some strong key causes Bad_3 to happen is at most $q^2/2^k$. For each $j \leq p$, let $\mathsf{Hit}_3(j)$ be the event that the key derived from the random input I_j is a weak key, and it causes Bad_3 to happen. From the union bound,

$$\Pr[\mathsf{Bad}_3] \leq \frac{q^2}{2^k} + \Pr[\mathsf{Hit}_3(1) \cup \cdots \cup \mathsf{Hit}_3(p)] \leq \frac{q^2}{2^k} + \sum_{j=1}^{p} \Pr[\mathsf{Hit}_3(j)] \ .$$

We now bound each $\Pr[\mathsf{Hit}_3(j)]$. The event $\mathsf{Hit}_3(j)$ happens only if the environment somehow can "guess" $\mathsf{CtE}[E,n](I_j)$ via q choices of its other keys, using just information from the blockcipher E, the side information z_j and the entropy estimation γ_j of I_j, the other (I_i, γ_i, z_i) with $i \neq j$. Thus from Theorem 1,

$$\Pr[\mathsf{Hit}_3(j)] \leq \frac{q}{2^n} + \frac{\sqrt{q}}{2^{\lambda/2}} + \frac{8\sqrt{q(\ell_j + 2)^3}}{2^n}$$

$$\leq \frac{q}{2^n} + \frac{\sqrt{q}}{2^{\lambda/2}} + \frac{8\sqrt{q(L + 2)} \cdot (\ell_j + 2)}{2^n} \ .$$

Summing up over all events $\mathsf{Hit}_3(1), \ldots, \mathsf{Hit}_3(p)$,

$$\Pr[\mathsf{Bad}_3] \leq \frac{q^2}{2^k} + \frac{pq}{2^n} + \frac{p \cdot \sqrt{q}}{2^{\lambda/2}} + \frac{8\sqrt{q(L + 2)} \cdot (\sigma + 2p)}{2^n} \ .$$

Bounding $\Pr[\mathsf{Bad}_4]$ is similar to handling Bad_3, but now the environment has just a *single* choice, instead of q choices. Thus

$$\Pr[\mathsf{Bad}_4] \leq \frac{q}{2^k} + \frac{p}{2^n} + \frac{p}{2^{\lambda/2}} + \frac{8\sqrt{(L + 2)} \cdot (\sigma + 2p)}{2^n} \ .$$

Bounding $\Pr[\mathsf{Bad}_5]$ is similar to handling Bad_3, but now the environment has p choices instead of q ones. Thus

$$\Pr[\mathsf{Bad}_5] \leq \frac{pq}{2^k} + \frac{p^2}{2^n} + \frac{p^{1.5}}{2^{\lambda/2}} + \frac{8\sqrt{p(L + 2)} \cdot (\sigma + 2p)}{2^n} \ .$$

Finally, consider Bad_6. Again, the chance that some strong key causes Bad_6 to happen is at most $q/2^k$. For each $j \leq p$, let $\mathsf{Hit}_6(j)$ be the event that the key derived from the random input I_j is a weak key, and it causes Bad_6 to happen. From the union bound,

$$\Pr[\mathsf{Bad}_6] \leq \frac{q}{2^k} + \Pr[\mathsf{Hit}_6(1) \cup \cdots \cup \mathsf{Hit}_6(p)] \leq \frac{q}{2^k} + \sum_{j=1}^{p} \Pr[\mathsf{Hit}_6(j)] \ .$$

We now bound each $\Pr[\mathsf{Hit}_6(j)]$. The event $\mathsf{Hit}_6(j)$ happens only if the environment somehow can "guess" $\mathsf{XP}[E](I_j)$ via a *single* choice of the CTR mask, using just information from the blockcipher E, the side information z_j and the entropy estimation γ_j of I_j, the other (I_i, γ_i, z_i) with $i \neq j$. From Lemma 6 with a single guess,

$$\Pr[\mathsf{Hit}_6(j)] \leq \frac{1}{2^n} + \frac{1}{2^{\lambda/2}} + \frac{8\sqrt{(\ell_j + 2)^3}}{2^n} \leq \frac{1}{2^n} + \frac{1}{2^{\lambda/2}} + \frac{8\sqrt{(L+2)} \cdot (\ell_j + 2)}{2^n} .$$

Summing up over all events $\mathsf{Hit}_6(1), \ldots, \mathsf{Hit}_6(p)$,

$$\Pr[\mathsf{Bad}_6] \leq \frac{q}{2^k} + \frac{p}{2^n} + \frac{p}{2^{\lambda/2}} + \frac{8\sqrt{(L+2)} \cdot (\sigma + 2p)}{2^n} .$$

Summing up, and taking into account that $q \geq p$,

$$\Pr[\mathcal{T}_{\mathrm{hybrid}} \text{ is bad}] \leq \frac{(B+3)(s+3p)}{2^n} + \frac{3q(q+1)}{2^k} + \frac{3p(q+1)}{2^n} + \frac{6p \cdot \sqrt{q}}{2^{\lambda/2}}$$
$$+ \frac{24(\sqrt{q}+1) \cdot \sqrt{L+2} \cdot (\sigma + 2p)}{2^n} . \tag{5}$$

TRANSCRIPT RATIO. Let τ be a good transcript such that $\Pr[\mathcal{T}_{\mathrm{hybrid}} = \tau] > 0$. We now prove that

$$1 - \frac{\Pr[\mathcal{T}_{\mathrm{real}} = \tau]}{\Pr[\mathcal{T}_{\mathrm{hybrid}} = \tau]} \leq 0 . \tag{6}$$

If $\mathcal{T}_{\mathrm{real}}$ is good then $\mathsf{Queries}(\mathbf{S}_{\mathrm{real}})$ and the granted triples (K, X, Y) at the end of the game (with all $K \in \{0,1\}^n \backslash \mathsf{Keys}(\mathbf{S}_{\mathrm{real}})$ and $X \in \{0,1\}^n$), would contain all adversary's queries to E/E^{-1} and $\mathbf{S}_{\mathrm{real}}$'s queries to E in its setup, next, refresh procedures. Since A is deterministic, when $\mathcal{T}_{\mathrm{real}}$ is good, it is completely determined from $\mathcal{D}$'s outputs, $\mathsf{Queries}(\mathbf{S}_{\mathrm{real}})$, and the granted triples (K, X, Y) at the end of the game. Let $\mathsf{Queries}(\tau)$ and $\mathsf{Keys}(\tau)$ be the value of $\mathsf{Queries}(\mathbf{S})$ and $\mathsf{Keys}(\mathbf{S})$ for $\mathbf{S} \in \{\mathbf{S}_{\mathrm{real}}, \mathbf{S}_{\mathrm{hybrid}}\}$ indicated by τ. Thus the event that $\mathcal{T}_{\mathrm{real}} = \tau$ can be factored into the following sub-events:

– Inputs: The distribution sampler $\mathcal{D}$ outputs as instructed in τ.
– Prim: The blockcipher E agrees with the granted queries (K, X, Y) in τ, with $K \in \{0,1\}^n \backslash \mathsf{Keys}(\tau)$. That is, for any such triple (K, X, Y), if we query $E(K, X)$, we'll get the answer Y.
– $\mathsf{Coll}_{\mathrm{real}}$: The blockcipher E agrees with the triples in $\mathsf{Queries}(\tau)$. Note that for any $(K, X, Y) \in \mathsf{Queries}(\tau)$, we have $K \in \mathsf{Keys}(\tau)$.

Due to the key separation in Prim and $\mathsf{Coll}_{\mathrm{real}}$ and due to the fact that $\mathcal{D}$ has no access to E,

$$\Pr[\mathcal{T}_{\mathrm{real}} = \tau] = \Pr[\mathsf{Inputs}] \cdot \Pr[\mathsf{Prim}] \cdot \Pr[\mathsf{Coll}_{\mathrm{real}}] .$$

Likewise, if $\mathcal{T}_{\mathrm{hybrid}}$ is good then the granted triples (K, X, Y) at the end of the game (with all $K \in \{0,1\}^n \backslash \mathsf{Keys}(\mathbf{S}_{\mathrm{hybrid}})$ and $X \in \{0,1\}^n$), would contain all adversary's queries to E/E^{-1} and $\mathbf{S}_{\mathrm{hybrid}}$'s queries to E in its setup, next, refresh procedures. Thus if $\mathcal{T}_{\mathrm{hybrid}}$ is good then it is completely determined from $\mathcal{D}$'s outputs, $\mathsf{Queries}(\mathbf{S}_{\mathrm{hybrid}})$, and the granted triples (K, X, Y) at the end of the game. Hence the event that $\mathcal{T}_{\mathrm{hybrid}} = \tau$ can be factored into Inputs, Prim and the following sub-event:

– $\mathsf{Coll}_{\mathsf{ideal}}$: For any triple $(K, X, Y) \in \mathsf{Queries}(\tau)$, if we pick $Z \leftarrow\!\!\$ \, \{0,1\}^n$, we'll have $Z = Y$. This random variable Z stands for the uniformly random block that $\mathbf{S}_{\mathsf{hybrid}}$ samples when it is supposed to run $E(K, X)$ (but actually does not do) under procedure CTR on key $K \in \mathsf{Keys}(\tau)$.

Then

$$\Pr[\mathcal{T}_{\mathsf{hybrid}} = \tau] = \Pr[\mathsf{Inputs}] \cdot \Pr[\mathsf{Prim}] \cdot \Pr[\mathsf{Coll}_{\mathsf{ideal}}] \ .$$

Therefore,

$$\frac{\Pr[\mathcal{T}_{\mathsf{real}} = \tau]}{\Pr[\mathcal{T}_{\mathsf{hybrid}} = \tau]} = \frac{\Pr[\mathsf{Coll}_{\mathsf{real}}]}{\Pr[\mathsf{Coll}_{\mathsf{ideal}}]} \ .$$

Now, suppose that $\mathsf{Queries}(\tau)$ contains exactly r keys, and the i-th key contains exactly t_i tuples. Since τ is good, for any two tuples (K, X, Y) and (K, X', Y') of the i-th key, we have $X \neq X'$ and $Y \neq Y'$. Thus on the one hand,

$$\Pr[\mathsf{Coll}_{\mathsf{real}}] = \prod_{i=1}^{r} \frac{1}{2^n (2^n - 1) \cdots (2^n - t_i + 1)} \ .$$

On the other hand,

$$\Pr[\mathsf{Coll}_{\mathsf{ideal}}] = \prod_{i=1}^{r} \frac{1}{(2^n)^{t_i}} \ .$$

Hence

$$\Pr[\mathsf{Coll}_{\mathsf{ideal}}] \leq \Pr[\mathsf{Coll}_{\mathsf{real}}] \ ,$$

and thus

$$\frac{\Pr[\mathcal{T}_{\mathsf{real}} = \tau]}{\Pr[\mathcal{T}_{\mathsf{hybrid}} = \tau]} = \frac{\Pr[\mathsf{Coll}_{\mathsf{real}}]}{\Pr[\mathsf{Coll}_{\mathsf{ideal}}]} \geq 1$$

as claimed.

WRAPPING IT UP. From Lemma 1 and Eqs. (5) and (6), we conclude that

$$\Delta_A(\mathbf{S}_{\mathsf{real}}, \mathbf{S}_{\mathsf{hybrid}}) \leq \frac{(B + 3)(s + 3p)}{2^n} + \frac{3q(q + 1)}{2^k} + \frac{3p(q + 1)}{2^n} + \frac{6p \cdot \sqrt{q}}{2^{\lambda/2}}$$
$$+ \frac{24(\sqrt{q} + 1) \cdot \sqrt{L + 2} \cdot (\sigma + 2p)}{2^n}$$

as claimed.

7 Breaking CTR-DRBG with a Seed-Dependent Sampler

In this section, we show that if the underlying blockcipher is AES-128 then CTR-DRBG is *insecure* in the new security model of Coretti et al. [13].

SEEDLESS PRNGS. A seedless PRNG that is built on top of an ideal primitive Π is a tuple of deterministic algorithms $\mathcal{G} = (\mathsf{setup}, \mathsf{refresh}, \mathsf{next})$, any of which has oracle access to Π. Algorithm $\mathsf{setup}^{\Pi}(I)$, on a random input I, outputs a state S.

Game $\mathbf{G}^{\mathrm{res}}_{\mathcal{G},\Pi}(A)$	procedure $\mathrm{REF}(I)$	procedure $\mathrm{RoR}(1^\ell)$
$b \leftarrow\!\!\$ \{0,1\};\ \ s \leftarrow \varepsilon;\ \ (I,s) \leftarrow\!\!\$ A^{\Pi}(s)$	$S \leftarrow \mathsf{refresh}^{\Pi}(S,I)$	$(R_1, S) \leftarrow \mathsf{next}^{\Pi}(S,\ell)$
$S \leftarrow \mathsf{setup}^{\Pi}(I);\ \ b' \leftarrow\!\!\$ A^{\mathrm{REF},\mathrm{RoR},\Pi}(s)$		$R_0 \leftarrow\!\!\$ \{0,1\}^\ell$
return $(b' = b)$		return R_b

Fig. 8. Game defining resilience for a seedless PRNG $\mathcal{G} = (\mathsf{setup}, \mathsf{refresh}, \mathsf{next})$ that is built on top of an ideal primitive Π.

Next, algorithm $\mathsf{refresh}^{\Pi}(S, I)$ takes as input a state S and a string I and then outputs a new state. Finally algorithm $\mathsf{next}^{\Pi}(S, \ell)$ takes as input a state S and a number $\ell \in \mathbb{N}$, and then outputs a new state and an ℓ-bit output string. Note that the description of CTR-DRBG in Fig. 5 also conforms to this syntax.

SECURITY MODELING. Instead of using the full notion of Coretti et al. [13], we levy some additional restrictions on the adversary to simplify the definition and to make our attack more practical. In particular, we (i) strip away the adversary's ability to read or modify the PRNG's state, (ii) require that each random input must have sufficient min entropy, and (iii) forbid the adversary from calling next when the accumulated entropy is insufficient. The simplified notion, which we call *resilience*, is described in Fig. 8. Define

$$\mathsf{Adv}^{\mathrm{res}}_{\mathcal{G},\Pi}(A) = 2\Pr\!\left[\mathbf{G}^{\mathrm{res}}_{\mathcal{G},\Pi}(A)\right] - 1$$

as the advantage of A breaking the resilience of $\mathcal{G}$. Informally, the game begins by picking a challenge bit $b \leftarrow\!\!\$ \{0,1\}$. In the first phase, the adversary A, given just oracle access to Π, outputs a random input I and keeps some state s. The game then runs $\mathsf{setup}^{\Pi}(I)$ to generate an initial state S for the PRNG. In the second phase, the adversary, in addition to Π, is given the following oracles:

(i) An oracle $\mathrm{REF}(I)$ to update the state S via $S \leftarrow \mathsf{refresh}^{\Pi}(I)$.
(ii) An oracle $\mathrm{RoR}(1^\ell)$ to get the next ℓ-bit output. The game runs the next algorithm on the current state S to update it and get an ℓ-bit output R_1, and also samples a uniformly random string $R_0 \leftarrow\!\!\$ \{0,1\}^\ell$. It then returns R_b to the adversary.

The goal of the adversary is to guess the challenge bit b, by outputting a bit b'.

To avoid known impossibility results [11], one needs to carefully impose restrictions on the adversary A. Consider game $\mathbf{G}^{\mathrm{res}}_{\mathcal{G},\Pi}(A)$ in which the challenge bit $b = 0$. Note that this game is independent of the construction $\mathcal{G}$: one can implement the oracle $\mathrm{REF}(I)$ to do nothing, and oracle $\mathrm{RoR}(1^\ell)$ to return $R \leftarrow\!\!\$ \{0,1\}^\ell$. Let s_i and L_i be the random variables for the adversary's state and its current list of queries/answers to Π right before the adversary makes the i-th query to RoR, respectively. Let $\mathcal{I}_i$ be the list of random inputs before the adversary makes the i-th query to RoR. We say that A is λ-*legitimate* if $H_\infty(I \mid s_i, L_i) \geq \lambda$, for any $i \in \mathbb{N}$ and any $I \in \mathcal{I}_i$.

THE ATTACK. We adapt the ideas of the CBCMAC attack in [13] to attack CTR-DRBG, assuming that the key length and block length of the underlying blockcipher are the same. In other words, our attack only applies if the underlying blockcipher is AES-128. Still, it works for any fixed entropy threshold $\lambda > 0$.

Let $E : \{0,1\}^k \times \{0,1\}^n \to \{0,1\}^n$ be the underlying blockcipher of CTR-DRBG, and let π be the permutation in CBCMAC. Pick an arbitrary integer $m \geq \lambda$. For each $a \in \{0,1\}$, let

$$U_a \leftarrow [a]_{32} \parallel 0^{n-32} \parallel [(mn + n - 64)/8]_{32} \parallel [n/4]_{32} \ ,$$

and let

$$B_a \leftarrow \mathsf{CBCMAC}[\pi]\big(U_a \parallel 0^{n-64}\big) \ .$$

For each integer $i \geq 0$ and any string $x \in \{0,1\}^n$, define $\pi^i(x)$ recursively via $\pi^i(x) \leftarrow \pi\big(\pi^{i-1}(x)\big)$ and $\pi^0(x) \leftarrow x$. In the first phase, for each $i \in \{0, \dots, m-1\}$, the adversary A picks $M_i \leftarrow_\$ \{\pi^i(B_0) \oplus \pi^i(B_1), 0^n\}$. It then outputs

$$I \leftarrow 0^{n-64} \parallel M_0 \parallel \cdots \parallel M_{m-1} \ ,$$

and also outputs the empty string as its state s. In the second phase, A queries $\mathsf{RoR}(1^n)$ to get an answer Y. Next, recall that in the real world (where the challenge bit $b = 1$), to set up the initial state, $\mathsf{setup}(I)$ first derives

$$K \leftarrow \mathsf{CBCMAC}[\pi](U_0 \parallel I \parallel P); \ \ \mathrm{IV} \leftarrow \mathsf{CBCMAC}[\pi](U_1 \parallel I \parallel P) \ ,$$

where $P \leftarrow \mathsf{pad}(\varepsilon)$, and then runs $\mathsf{CBC}_K^{\mathrm{IV}}[E](0^{2n})$. Our adversary aims to predict two possible pairs (K_0, V_0) and (K_1, V_1) for (K, IV), and then compare Y with the corresponding RoR outputs Z_0 and Z_1. Specifically, A

> **for** $a \in \{0,1\}$ **do**
> $\quad P \leftarrow \mathsf{pad}(\varepsilon); \ K_a \leftarrow \pi\big(\pi^m(B_a) \oplus P\big); \ V_a \leftarrow \pi\big(\pi^m(B_{1-a}) \oplus P\big)$
> $\quad R_a \leftarrow \mathsf{CBC}_{K_a}^{V_a}[E](0^{2n}); \ J_a \leftarrow R_a[1:n], V_a^* \leftarrow R_a[n+1:2n]$
> $\quad Z_a \leftarrow \mathsf{CTR}^E(J_a, V_a^*, 0^n)$
> **if** $Y \in \{Z_0, Z_1\}$ **then return** 1 **else return** 0

In summary, A makes $2m$ queries to π in the first phase, and $2m + 4$ queries to π and 6 queries to E in the second phase. Let L be the list of queries and answers to π and E. Since the state s of A right before it queries RoR is the empty string, in the ideal world, we have $H_\infty(I \mid s, L) = m \geq \lambda$, and thus the adversary is λ-legitimate.

We now analyze the adversary's advantage. In the ideal world, the answer Y is a uniformly random string, independent of Z_0 and Z_1, and thus the chance that $Y \in \{Z_0, Z_1\}$ is 2^{1-n}. As a result, the chance that A outputs 1 in the ideal world is 2^{1-n}. In the real world, we claim that A's prediction of (K, V) is correct. Consequently, the chance that it outputs 1 in the real world is 1, and thus $\mathsf{Adv}^{\mathrm{res}}_{\mathcal{G}, \Pi}(A) = 1 - 2^{1-n}$.

To justify the claim above, note that $K \leftarrow \mathsf{CBCMAC}[\pi](B_0, M_0 \cdots M_{m-1} \| P)$ and $\mathrm{IV} \leftarrow \mathsf{CBCMAC}[\pi](B_1, M_0 \cdots M_{m-1} \| P)$. From the definition of CBCMAC, the two CBCMAC calls above can be rewritten as follows:

$X_0 \leftarrow B_0;\ Y_0 \leftarrow B_1$
for $i = 0$ **to** $m - 1$ **do** $X_{i+1} \leftarrow \pi(X_i \oplus M_i);\ Y_{i+1} \leftarrow \pi(Y_i \oplus M_i)$
$K \leftarrow \pi(X_m \oplus P);\ \ \mathrm{IV} \leftarrow \pi(Y_m \oplus P)$

We will prove by induction that in the code above, $\{X_i, Y_i\} = \{\pi^i(B_0), \pi^i(B_1)\}$ for every $i \in \{0, \ldots, m\}$; the claim above corresponds to the special case $i = m$. The statement is true for the base case $i = 0$, from the definition of X_0 and Y_0. Assume that our statement is true for $i < m$, we now prove that it also holds for $i + 1$. Since $M_i \in \{\pi^i(B_0) \oplus \pi^i(B_1), 0^n\}$, from the inductive hypothesis, $\{X_i \oplus M_i, Y_i \oplus M_i\} = \{\pi^i(B_0), \pi^i(B_1)\}$. As $X_{i+1} \leftarrow \pi(X_i \oplus M_i)$ and $Y_{i+1} \leftarrow \pi(X_i \oplus M_i)$, our statement also holds for $i + 1$.

DISCUSSION. The key idea of the attack above is to craft a random input I such that it is easy to learn both the key K and the initialization vector IV of CBC in $\mathsf{CtE}[E](I)$. This attack can be extended for a general key length $k \in \{n, \ldots, 2n\}$, but now the adversary can only learn just K and the $(2n - k)$-bit prefix of IV. Still, the adversary can make 2^{k-n} guesses to determine the remaining $k - n$ bits of IV. This leads to a theoretical attack of about 2^{64} operations for AES-192, but for AES-256, the cost (2^{128} operations) is prohibitive. We leave it as an open problem to either extend our attack for CTR-DRBG with AES-256, or to prove that it is actually resilient.

Acknowledgments. We thank Stefano Tessaro for insightful discussions, Yevgeniy Dodis for suggesting the study of CTR-DRBG in the seedless setting, and CRYPTO reviewers for useful feedback. Viet Tung Hoang was supported in part by NSF grants CICI-1738912 and CRII-1755539. Yaobin Shen was supported in part by National Key Research and Development Program of China (No. 2019YFB2101601, No. 2018YFB0803400), 13th five-year National Development Fund of Cryptography (MMJJ20170114), and China Scholarship Council (No. 201806230107). Much of this work was done while Yaobin Shen was visiting Florida State University.

A   Problems in Hutchinson's Analysis of CTR-DRBG

In this section, we describe the issues in Hutchinson's analysis of CTR-DRBG [23]. For convenience, we shall use the notation and terminology in Sect. 4.

First, under CTR-DRBG, one uses CBCMAC to extract randomness multiple times from basically the *same* random input (with different constant prefixes). Conventional analysis of CBCMAC [14] via the Leftover Hash Lemma [19] only implies that each of the corresponding outputs is *marginally* pseudorandom, but in the proof of his Lemma 5.5.4, Hutchinson incorrectly concludes that they are *jointly* pseudorandom.

Next, in the proof of his Lemma 5.5.14, Hutchinson considers a multicollision

$$\mathsf{CBCMAC}[\pi](M_1) = \mathsf{CBCMAC}[\pi](M_1^*), \ldots, \mathsf{CBCMAC}[\pi](M_r) = \mathsf{CBCMAC}[\pi](M_r^*)$$

with $r \in \{2,3\}$ and a truly random permutation $\pi : \{0,1\}^n \to \{0,1\}^n$. Assume that each individual collision $\mathsf{CBCMAC}[\pi](M_i) = \mathsf{CBCMAC}[\pi](M_i^*)$ happens with probability at most ϵ. Hutchinson claims (without proof) that the multicollision happens with probability at most ϵ^3, but this is obviously wrong for $r = 2$. While one may try to salvage the proof by changing the multicollision probability to ϵ^r, proving such a bound is difficult.

Next, in several places, his probabilistic reasoning is problematic. For instance, in the proof of his Lemma 5.5.14, he considers $X_1 \leftarrow \mathsf{CBC}_{K_1}^{\mathrm{IV}_1}[E](0^{3n})$ and $X_2 \leftarrow \mathsf{CBC}_{K_2}^{\mathrm{IV}_2}[E](0^{3n})$, for $K_1 \neq K_2$ and $\mathrm{IV}_1 \neq \mathrm{IV}_2$, and $E : \{0,1\}^k \times \{0,1\}^n \to \{0,1\}^n$ is modeled as an ideal cipher. He claims that

$$\Pr[X_1 = X_2] \leq \frac{1}{2^{3n}} \cdot \left(\frac{18}{2^n}\right)^3 ,$$

but this collision probability is actually around $\frac{1}{2^{3n}}$, which is much bigger than the claimed bound.

In addition, while Hutchinson appears to consider random inputs of a general block length L, he actually uses $L = 3$ in the proof of his Lemma 5.5.4, and the resulting incorrect bound propagates to other places.

Finally, even if all the bugs above are fixed, Hutchinson's approach is doomed to yield a weak bound

$$\frac{p^2}{2^{(\lambda-n)/2}} + \frac{\sigma p}{2^{n/2}} ,$$

assuming that we have p random inputs, each of at least $\lambda \geq n$ bits of min entropy, and their total block length is at most σ. This poor bound is due to: (i) the decomposition of robustness to two other notions (preserving and recovering) that leads to a p-blowup, and (ii) the unnecessary requirement that CBCMAC on random inputs yield pseudorandom (instead of just unpredictable) outputs.

References

1. Barak, B., et al.: Leftover hash lemma, revisited. In: Rogaway, P. (ed.) CRYPTO 2011. LNCS, vol. 6841, pp. 1–20. Springer, Heidelberg (2011). https://doi.org/10.1007/978-3-642-22792-9_1
2. Barak, B., Halevi, S.: A model and architecture for pseudo-random generation with applications to /dev/random. In: Atluri, V., Meadows, C., Juels, A. (eds.) ACM CCS 05, pp. 203–212. ACM Press, November 2005
3. Bellare, M., Hofheinz, D., Yilek, S.: Possibility and impossibility results for encryption and commitment secure under selective opening. In: Joux, A. (ed.) EUROCRYPT 2009. LNCS, vol. 5479, pp. 1–35. Springer, Heidelberg (2009). https://doi.org/10.1007/978-3-642-01001-9_1

4. Bellare, M., Pietrzak, K., Rogaway, P.: Improved security analyses for CBC MACs. In: Shoup, V. (ed.) CRYPTO 2005. LNCS, vol. 3621, pp. 527–545. Springer, Heidelberg (2005). https://doi.org/10.1007/11535218_32
5. Bernstein, D.J.: Cache-timing attacks on AES (2005)
6. Bertoni, G., Daemen, J., Peeters, M., Van Assche, G.: Sponge-based pseudorandom number generators. In: Mangard, S., Standaert, F.-X. (eds.) CHES 2010. LNCS, vol. 6225, pp. 33–47. Springer, Heidelberg (2010). https://doi.org/10.1007/978-3-642-15031-9_3
7. Campagna, M.: Security bounds for the NIST codebook-based deterministic random bit generator. Cryptology ePrint Archive, Report 2006/379 (2006). https://eprint.iacr.org/2006/379
8. Checkoway, S., et al.: A systematic analysis of the Juniper Dual EC incident. In: Proceedings of the 2016 ACM SIGSAC Conference on Computer and Communications Security, pp. 468–479. ACM (2016)
9. Checkoway, S., et al.: On the practical exploitability of dual EC in TLS implementations. In: Proceedings of the 23rd USENIX Security Symposium, pp. 319–335, August 2014
10. Chen, S., Steinberger, J.: Tight security bounds for key-alternating ciphers. In: Nguyen, P.Q., Oswald, E. (eds.) EUROCRYPT 2014. LNCS, vol. 8441, pp. 327–350. Springer, Heidelberg (2014). https://doi.org/10.1007/978-3-642-55220-5_19
11. Chor, B., Goldreich, O.: Unbiased bits from sources of weak randomness and probabilistic communication complexity (extended abstract). In: 26th FOCS, pp. 429–442. IEEE Computer Society Press, October 1985
12. Cohney, S., et al.: Pseudorandom black swans: cache attacks on CTR DRBG. In: IEEE Security and Privacy 2020 (2020)
13. Coretti, S., Dodis, Y., Karthikeyan, H., Tessaro, S.: Seedless fruit is the sweetest: random number generation, revisited. In: Boldyreva, A., Micciancio, D. (eds.) CRYPTO 2019. LNCS, vol. 11692, pp. 205–234. Springer, Cham (2019). https://doi.org/10.1007/978-3-030-26948-7_8
14. Dodis, Y., Gennaro, R., Håstad, J., Krawczyk, H., Rabin, T.: Randomness extraction and key derivation using the CBC, cascade and HMAC modes. In: Franklin, M. (ed.) CRYPTO 2004. LNCS, vol. 3152, pp. 494–510. Springer, Heidelberg (2004). https://doi.org/10.1007/978-3-540-28628-8_30
15. Dodis, Y., Pointcheval, D., Ruhault, S., Vergnaud, D., Wichs, D.: Security analysis of pseudo-random number generators with input: /dev/random is not robust. In: Sadeghi, A.R., Gligor, V.D., Yung, M. (eds.) ACM CCS 13, pp. 647–658. ACM Press, November 2013
16. Dwork, C., Naor, M., Reingold, O., Stockmeyer, L.J.: Magic functions. In: 40th FOCS, pp. 523–534. IEEE Computer Society Press, October 1999
17. Gaži, P., Tessaro, S.: Provably robust sponge-based PRNGs and KDFs. In: Fischlin, M., Coron, J.-S. (eds.) EUROCRYPT 2016, Part I. LNCS, vol. 9665, pp. 87–116. Springer, Heidelberg (2016). https://doi.org/10.1007/978-3-662-49890-3_4
18. Gullasch, D., Bangerter, E., Krenn, S.: Cache games - bringing access-based cache attacks on AES to practice. In: 2011 IEEE Symposium on Security and Privacy, pp. 490–505. IEEE Computer Society Press, May 2011
19. Håstad, J., Impagliazzo, R., Levin, L.A., Luby, M.: A pseudorandom generator from any one-way function. SIAM J. Comput. 28(4), 1364–1396 (1999)
20. Heninger, N., Durumeric, Z., Wustrow, E., Halderman, J.A.: Mining your Ps and Qs: detection of widespread weak keys in network devices. In: Proceedings of the 21st USENIX Security Symposium, pp. 205–220, August 2012

21. Hoang, V.T., Shen, Y.: Security analysis of NIST CTR-DRBG. Cryptology ePrint Archive, Report 2020/619 (2020). https://eprint.iacr.org/2020/619

22. Hoang, V.T., Tessaro, S.: Key-alternating ciphers and key-length extension: exact bounds and multi-user security. In: Robshaw, M., Katz, J. (eds.) CRYPTO 2016, Part I. LNCS, vol. 9814, pp. 3–32. Springer, Heidelberg (2016). https://doi.org/10.1007/978-3-662-53018-4_1

23. Hutchinson, D.: Randomness in cryptography: theory meets practice. Ph.D. thesis, Royal Holloway, University of London (2018)

24. Neve, M., Seifert, J.-P.: Advances on access-driven cache attacks on AES. In: Biham, E., Youssef, A.M. (eds.) SAC 2006. LNCS, vol. 4356, pp. 147–162. Springer, Heidelberg (2007). https://doi.org/10.1007/978-3-540-74462-7_11

25. Osvik, D.A., Shamir, A., Tromer, E.: Cache attacks and countermeasures: the case of AES. In: Pointcheval, D. (ed.) CT-RSA 2006. LNCS, vol. 3860, pp. 1–20. Springer, Heidelberg (2006). https://doi.org/10.1007/11605805_1

26. Patarin, J.: The "Coefficients H" technique. In: Avanzi, R.M., Keliher, L., Sica, F. (eds.) SAC 2008. LNCS, vol. 5381, pp. 328–345. Springer, Heidelberg (2009). https://doi.org/10.1007/978-3-642-04159-4_21

27. Raz, R., Reingold, O.: On recycling the randomness of states in space bounded computation. In: 31st ACM STOC, pp. 159–168. ACM Press, May 1999

28. Ruhault, S.: SoK: security models for pseudo-random number generators. IACR Trans. Symm. Crypt. **2017**(1), 506–544 (2017)

29. Shrimpton, T., Terashima, R.S.: A provable-security analysis of intel's secure key RNG. In: Oswald, E., Fischlin, M. (eds.) EUROCRYPT 2015, Part I. LNCS, vol. 9056, pp. 77–100. Springer, Heidelberg (2015). https://doi.org/10.1007/978-3-662-46800-5_4

30. Shrimpton, T., Terashima, R.S.: Salvaging weak security bounds for blockcipher-based constructions. In: Cheon, J.H., Takagi, T. (eds.) ASIACRYPT 2016, Part I. LNCS, vol. 10031, pp. 429–454. Springer, Heidelberg (2016). https://doi.org/10.1007/978-3-662-53887-6_16

31. Woodage, J., Shumow, D.: An analysis of NIST SP 800-90A. In: Ishai, Y., Rijmen, V. (eds.) EUROCRYPT 2019. LNCS, vol. 11477, pp. 151–180. Springer, Cham (2019). https://doi.org/10.1007/978-3-030-17656-3_6

Security Analysis and Improvements
for the IETF MLS Standard
for Group Messaging

Joël Alwen[3(✉)], Sandro Coretti[2(✉)], Yevgeniy Dodis[1(✉)],
and Yiannis Tselekounis[1(✉)]

[1] New York University, New York, USA
{dodis,tselekounis}@cs.nyu.edu
[2] IOHK, Hong Kong, People's Republic of China
sandro.coretti@iohk.io
[3] Wickr Inc., San Francisco, USA
jalwen@wickr.com

Abstract. Secure messaging (SM) protocols allow users to communicate securely over untrusted infrastructure. In contrast to most other secure communication protocols (such as TLS, SSH, or Wireguard), SM sessions may be long-lived (e.g., years) and highly asynchronous. In order to deal with likely state compromises of users during the lifetime of a session, SM protocols do not only protect authenticity and privacy, but they also guarantee *forward secrecy (FS)* and *post-compromise security (PCS)*. The former ensures that messages sent and received before a state compromise remain secure, while the latter ensures that users can recover from state compromise as a consequence of normal protocol usage.

SM has received considerable attention in the two-party case, where prior work has studied the well-known double-ratchet paradigm, in particular, and SM as a cryptographic primitive, in general. Unfortunately, this paradigm does not scale well to the problem of secure *group* messaging (SGM). In order to address the lack of satisfactory SGM protocols, the IETF has launched the message-layer security (MLS) working group, which aims to standardize an eponymous SGM protocol. In this work we analyze the *TreeKEM* protocol, which is at the core of the SGM protocol proposed by the MLS working group.

On a positive note, we show that TreeKEM achieves PCS in isolation (and slightly more). However, we observe that the current version of TreeKEM does not provide an adequate form of FS. More precisely, our work proceeds by formally capturing the exact security of TreeKEM as a so-called *continuous group key agreement (CGKA)* protocol, which we

S. Coretti—Work partially done at NYU and supported by NSF grants 1314568 and 1319051.

Y. Dodis—Partially supported by gifts from VMware Labs, Facebook and Google, and NSF grants 1314568, 1619158, 1815546.

Y. Tselekounis—Work done at NYU and supported by NSF grants 1314568 and 1319051.

D. Micciancio and T. Ristenpart (Eds.): CRYPTO 2020, LNCS 12170, pp. 248–277, 2020.
https://doi.org/10.1007/978-3-030-56784-2_9

believe to be a primitive of independent interest. To address the insecurity of TreeKEM, we propose a simple modification to TreeKEM inspired by recent work of Jost *et al.* (EUROCRYPT '19) and an idea due to Kohbrok (MLS Mailing List). We then show that the modified version of TreeKEM comes with almost no efficiency degradation but achieves *optimal* (according to MLS specification) CGKA security, including FS and PCS. Our work also lays out how a CGKA protocol can be used to design a full SGM protocol.

1   Introduction

Secure messaging. End-to-end Secure Messaging (SM) allows people to exchange messages without compromising their authenticity nor privacy. To further their applicability the protocols in this work are designed for the, so called, *asynchronous* setting. In the context of (secure) messaging "asynchronous" means that no assumptions are made about the online/offline behavior of participants. E.g. at times no participant at all may be online. Some participants may be offline for long periods while others are online only irregularly. It may even be that for the duration of a session no more than a single participant is online simultaneously nor should they rely on any particular user being online to perform operations.[1] Thus, protocols for the asynchronous setting must eschew interactive communication (which greatly increases the difficulty of achieving strong security properties). In other words all protocol operations (e.g. creating a new session, adding/removing participants to an existing session and sending a messages in a session) must always be performed by sending out a *single* packet to enact the desired operation. In fact, (due to desired constraints on bandwidth) all protocols in this work actually send out the same packet to all participants as a single broadcast.

In contrast to common secure communication protocols such as TLS, IPSEC and SSH, SM protocols are designed for settings where sessions may exist for long periods of time. SM protocols are therefore expected to satisfy so-called *forward secrecy (FS)* and *post-compromise security (PCS)* (a.k.a. backward secrecy). The former means that even when a participant's key material is compromised, past messages (delivered before the compromise) remain secure. Conversely, PCS means that once the compromise ends, the participants will eventually recover full security as a side effect of continued normal protocol usage.

The rigorous design and analysis of *two-party* asynchronous SM protocols has received considerable attention in recent years. This is in no small part due to advent of the *double ratchet paradigm*, introduced by Marlinspike and Perrin [27]. Forming the cryptographic core of a slew of popular messaging applications (e.g., Signal, who first introduced it, as well as WhatsApp, Facebook Messenger, Skype, Google Allo, Wire, and more), double ratchet protocols are now regularly used by over a billion people worldwide.

---

[1] Classic insecure examples of such messaging applications are SMS and eMail.

However, double ratchet protocols are inherently designed for the case where only two users communicate with each other. In order to employ them for groups with more than two users, there is thus little or no alternative to running double ratchets between all pairs of users (at least to distribute and update key material). Unfortunately, that means the double ratchet paradigm does not scale well in settings with a large number of users. In particular, the communication complexity to update key material (an operation crucial to providing PCS) grows *linearly* in the group size. In fact, this poor performance holds for *all*, currently deployed, SM protocols enjoying some form of FS and PCS (i.e., including non-double ratchet based ones [20]).

This begs the natural question of how to build secure asynchronous *group* messaging protocols (SGM) that enjoy similar security properties to the two-party ones but whose efficiency scales (say) logarithmically in the group size.

Message layer security and TreeKEM. In order to address the lack of satisfactory SGM protocols, the IETF has launched the message-layer security (MLS) working group, which aims to standardize an eponymous SGM protocol [5,29]. Following in the footsteps of the double ratchet, the MLS protocol promises to be widely deployed and heavily used. Indeed, the working group already includes various messaging companies (Cisco, Facebook, Google, Wickr, Wire, Twitter, etc.) whose combined messaging user base includes everything from government agencies, political organizations, and NGOs, to companies both large and small— not to mention a major part of the world's consumer population.

The heart of the MLS standard is the so-called TreeKEM protocol. TreeKEM continuously generates fresh, shared, and secret randomness used by the participating parties to evolve the group key material. Each new group key is used to initiate a fresh symmetric hash ratchet that defines a stream of nonce/key pairs used to symmetrically encrypt/decrypt higher-level application messages (such as texts in a chat) using an AEAD (authenticated encryption with associated data). A stream is used until the next evolution of the group key at which point a new stream is initiated.

So not only is TreeKEM the most novel and intricate part of the MLS draft, but understanding it is also central to understanding the security and efficiency properties of full MLS protocol itself. In particular, TreeKEM is crucially involved in achieving PCS and FS.

1.1   Contributions

Continuous group key agreement. This paper makes progress in the formal study of secure group-messaging protocols (SGMs) by studying the security of the latest version of the TreeKEM protocol. First, our work defines the notion of *continuous group key agreement (CGKA)* and casts TreeKEM as a CGKA protocol. CGKA protocols provide methods for adding as well as removing group members and, most crucially, for performing *updates*. Each update operation is initiated by an arbitrary user and results in a new so-called *update secret*. Update secrets are high-entropy random values that the parties use to refresh their group key material in the higher-level protocols (e.g., in the SGM). In an update operation, the initiator also suitably encrypts information about the update secret for other group members.

Our security definition for CGKA protocols requires that (i) users obtain the same update secrets (correctness), (ii) update secrets look random to an attacker observing the protocol messages, (iii) past update secrets remain random even if the state of a party is compromised by the attacker (FS), and (iv) parties can recover from state compromise (PCS). All of these properties are captured by a single, fairly intuitive security game.

We argue that the formal security properties of CGKA are phrased in such a way that it is a suitable building block for full SGM protocols. In particular, CGKA is inspired by the modularization of Alwen *et al.* [2], who constructed a secure two-party messaging protocol (based on the double-ratchet paradigm) by combining three primitives: continuous key agreement (CKA), forward secure authenticated encryption with associated data (FS-AEAD), and a so-called PRF-PRNG, which is a two-input hash function that is a pseudo-random function (resp. generator) with respect to its first (resp. second) input. CGKA is therefore to be seen as the multi-user analogue of CKA and is tailored to be used in conjunction with a PRF-PRNG and the multi-user version of FS-AEAD. Specifically, the update secret is run through the PRF-PRNG in order to obtain new keys for the multi-user FS-AEAD. Due to the already quite high complexity of CGKA itself, this work focuses exclusively on CGKA and sketches how it can be used in a higher-level protocol to obtain a full SGM protocol.

TreeKEM has poor forward secrecy. Having defined the notion of CGKA, we analyze the latest version of TreeKEM w.r.t. the new definition. By doing so, we observe that there are serious issues with TreeKEM's forward secrecy, stemming from the fact that its users do not erase old keys sufficiently fast. Specifically, note that in order to efficiently perform updates (with packet sizes logarithmic in the number of users), TreeKEM arranges all group members at the leaves of a binary tree and uses public-key encryption (PKE) to encrypt information about update secrets, denoted by I, to specific subsets of members (determined by their position in the tree). After processing the update, however, parties do not erase or modify the PKE secret keys used to decrypt the update information, since they might need them to process future updates. Hence, corrupting any party other than the update initiator will completely reveal I to an attacker, thereby violating FS. In fact, we show that in a group with n members, in order for I to remain secret upon state compromise of an arbitrary user, even in the best case at least $\Omega(n/\log(n))$ many additional updates are required before the compromise in the best case. This can rise to $\Omega(n)$ many updates in the worst case (depending on the order of updates). Even worse, unless the sibling (in the tree) of I's initiator performs an update, I is never forward secret regardless of who else updates.

Our work formally captures the exact type of FS achieved by TreeKEM by providing an appropriate weakening of the CGKA security definition and proving that TreeKEM satisfies it. On a positive note, even the weakened definition provides PCS, i.e., TreeKEM's update secrets are at least backward secure.

Fixing TreeKEM. In order to remedy TreeKEM's issues with FS, we devise a new type of public-key encryption (PKE) (based on work by Jost *et al.* [24] and a suggestion by Konrad Kohbrok on the MLS mailing list [26]) and show that using it in lieu of the (standard) PKE within TreeKEM results in a protocol with *optimal* FS. Specifically, with the new flavor of PKE, *public and secret keys suitably change with every encryption and decryption*, respectively. This kind of key evolution ensures that after decryption, the (evolved) secret key leaks no information about the original message, thereby thwarting the above attack. We also provide a very efficient instantiation of the new PKE notion, thereby ending up with a practical fix and *going from very loose to optimal security at negligible cost*, albeit under the following assumption about the order in which messages are delivered to all participants.

Global ordering of messages. Our main CGKA security definitions encode the assumption that the delivery server (which caches protocol messages until users come online again) delivers CGKA messages in the same order to all users in a session. Having said that, the delivery server (which we modeled formally as the adversary) may still drop or delay messages at will, as well as decide on the delivery order between users arbitrarily (as long as each user eventually gets the same order of protocol messages). We remark that this assumptions is made explicitly in the MLS design spec. (cf. Section 11 of version 8 [5]) albeit only in terms of conditions required to guarantee functionality, not security. Moreover, the TreeKEM protocol was designed with that in mind. (It is worth noting that the assumption could also be practically realized in the public bulletin board model, e.g., using a block-chain protocol.)

Of course, an alternative approach would have been to remove the assumption from our security definitions. The correctness and security implications of doing this are somewhat subtle; for example, it is inevitable that the current group can easily be split into disjoint sub-groups, who might not even be aware of each other, simply thinking that people in other subgroups are offline rather than "split". We discuss these issues in Sect. 7, pointing out that the "right" security level desired in this case is not yet settled and agreed upon in the MLS community (for good reasons rather than lack of effort, as we explain in Sect. 7). We also note that it is relatively trivial for a higher level protocol building on the CGKA (such as MLS) to ensure users only accept CGKA messages in the same order as intended by their sender. E.g. MLS ensures this by having sender and receivers of CGKA packets necessarily agree on the hash of the preceding transcript in order to authenticate and decrypt new CGKA packets.

Given this state of affairs, we feel that we are justified to follow the current MLS guidelines, by building the global ordering of messages assumption into our model, so that we can: (1) achieve the strongest possible security (including FS, PCS and guaranteed agreement), as well as (2) analyze TreeKEM in the security model *it was designed for.* However, in Sect. 7 we discuss what happens in TreeKEM (and our improved version) when the order delivery assumption does not hold, including the following two security guarantees: (1) Compromising user ID, who was removed from the perspective of sub-group A, should not compromise the security of A, even if ID "split" to a different subgroup B prior to removal from A; (2) Compromising user ID, who updated its state after "splitting" from A, should not compromise the security of A.

Adaptive security. The security of both TreeKEM and the improved version mentioned above is proved w.r.t. a *non-adaptive* attacker, i.e., an attacker that is required to announce all corruptions at the beginning (as opposed to being able to corrupt on-the-fly depending on values and messages produced by the protocol).

The difficulty in handling adaptive security is inherent for any cryptographic protocol where keys can encrypt others keys, and the attacker might ask to selectively corrupt some subset of keys. Prominent examples include multicast and generalized selective decryption [16,30], constraint PRFs [17], and Yao's garbled circuits [23], among many others. In each of these setting, going from non-adaptive to adaptive security naively would result in exponential security loss in some natural parameter n for the corresponding setting.

A major breakthrough in improving the state of provable security security against adaptive attackers in such settings came from a series of works, starting with Panjwani [30], and culminating with a very clever and general reduction technique of Jafargholi *et al.* [22]. These highly non-trivial works which showed that in certain cases, one can get adaptive security at the multiplicative reduction factor of "only" $n^{\log n} \ll 2^n$. While these provable, yet "super-polynomial", reductions are still far from being usable in the real world, they are substantially better than the trivial exponential security loss mentioned above, and serve as further evidence that the corresponding protocols are likely secure "in the real world" — a view commonly shared by the majority of practitioners.

Fortunately, we managed to adapt the same non-trivial reduction technique to the setting of TreeKEM, showing the slightly super-polynomial security even in the adaptive setting. As mentioned above, this is the best we can do using the current state-of-the-art in adaptive security in all the "selective decryption" applications we know.

In the full version of the paper [3] we discuss several research directions related to SM.

1.2 Related Work

The double ratchet paradigm was introduced by Marlinspike and Perrin [27], based on the OTR (off-the-record) protocol [7], and an early analysis was performed by Cohn-Gordon *et al.* [10]. An important line of work [6,13,21,24,31] formally studied two-party secure messaging. In particular, Jost *et al.* [24] introduced the notion of updatable PKE which is related to the one used in this paper. However, in our setting a simpler definition suffices, although we use the same efficient construction as [24]. Alwen *et al.* [2] provided a modular design for double-ratchet algorithms and formal definition of secure messaging in the two-party setting. In the group setting, Cremers *et al.* [11] note TreeKEM's disadvantages w.r.t. PCS for multiple groups, and Weider [36] suggests Causal TreeKEM, a variant that requires less ordering of protocol messages. TreeKEM was suggested in [4,32]. The most influential precursor to TreeKEM, the asynchronous ratchet tree (ART) protocol, was introduced by Cohn-Gordon *et al.* [9], focusing on adaptive security (informally sketched) for static groups. ART uses an older technique called "Tree-based DH groups" [33,35,38] which is also used by [25] to build key agreement. However, TreeKEM and ART differ significantly from [25], as we discuss in the full version [3]. Besides MLS, several other end-to-end secure group messaging protocols have been proposed and even deployed [14,18–20,34,37]. Also, TreeKEM is related to schemes for (symmetric-key) broadcast encryption [12,15] and multicast encryption [8,28,38]. A more detailed comparison between protocols and notions can be found in the full version [3]. Finally, the recent follow-up work of [1] also analyzes TreeKEM's security and introduces a new CGKA construction improving on TreeKEM. However, beyond this high-level similarity the results are relatively orthogonal, using different security models, and focusing on complementary aspects of TreeKEM, such as efficiency and adaptive reduction tightness.

2   Preliminaries

This section introduces some general notation and basic concepts around binary trees. Definitions of PRGs and CPA-secure public-key encryption can be found in the full version [3].

Notation. For a positive integer a, $[a]$ denotes the set $\{1, 2, \ldots, a\}$. For an integer n, $\mathsf{mp2}(n)$ is the maximum power of 2 smaller than n, dividing n. Security games in this work involve *dictionaries*. The value stored with key x in a dictionary D is denoted by $D[x]$. The statement $D[\cdot] \leftarrow y$ (for any type of y) initializes a dictionary D in which the default initial value for each key is y. This work considers rooted binary trees, in which all nodes have between 0 and 2 unique children. The *height* of τ is the length of the longest path from the root to any leaf.[2] A node with no children is called a *leaf*; all other nodes are called *internal*. A tree τ is *full* if it has height h and 2^h leaves. For an integer $h \geq 0$, denote by FT_h the full binary tree of height h. For two leaf nodes ℓ and ℓ' in some tree, let $\mathsf{LCA}(\ell, \ell')$ be the least common ancestor of ℓ and ℓ', i.e., the node where the paths from these leaves to the root meet.

3   Continuous Group Key Agreement

The purpose of *continuous group key-agreement (CGKA)* is to continuously provide members of a messaging group with fresh secret random values, which they use to refresh their key material (in a higher-level protocol). This section formally defines the syntax of CGKA schemes and presents a security notion that simultaneously captures correctness, key indistinguishability, forward secrecy, as well as post-compromise security.

---

[2] In particular, the tree of height 0 consists of a single node, the root.

3.1 CGKA Syntax

A CGKA scheme provides algorithms to create a group, add as well as remove users, perform updates, and process protocol messages.

Definition 1. *A continuous group key-agreement (CGKA)* scheme CGKA = (init, create, add, rem, upd, proc) *consists of the following algorithms:*

- Initialization: init *takes an ID* ID *and outputs an initial state* γ.
- Group creation: create *takes a state* γ, *a list of IDs* G = $(ID_1, \ldots, ID_n)$, *and outputs a new state* γ' *and a control message* W.
- Add: add *takes a state* γ *an ID* ID', *and outputs a new state* γ *as well as control messages* W *and* T.
- Remove: rem *takes a state* γ *and an ID* ID' *and outputs a new state* γ' *and a control message* T.
- Update: upd *takes a state* γ *and outputs a new state* γ' *and a control message* T.
- Process: proc *takes a state* γ *and a control message* T *and outputs a new state* γ' *and an update secret* I.

The basic usage of a CGKA scheme is as follows: Generally, once a group is established using create, any group member, referred to as the *sender*, may call any of the algorithms to add or remove members or to perform updates. Each time, such a call results in a new so-called *epoch*. It is implicitly the task of a server connecting the parties to then relay the resulting *control* messages to all current group members (including the sender). Observe that there are two types of control messages: *welcome* messages W, which are sent to parties *joining* a group, and normal control messages T, which are intended for parties already in the group. Whenever the server delivers a control message to a group member, they process it using proc. Algorithm proc also outputs an *update secret* I, where the intention is that $I \neq \bot$ if and only if the control message corresponds to an update.

3.2 CGKA Security

Informally, the basic properties that any CGKA scheme must satisfy are the following: *Correctness:* All group members output the same update secret I in update epochs. *Privacy:* The update secrets look random given the transcript of control messages. *Forward secrecy (FS):* If the state of any group member is leaked at some point, all previous update secrets remain hidden from the attacker. *Post-compromise security (PCS):* After every group member whose state was leaked performs an update (that is processed by the group) update secrets become secret again.

These properties are captured by the security game presented in this section (cf. Fig. 1). In the game the attacker is given access to various oracles to drive the execution of a CGKA protocol. It is important to note that the capabilities of the attacker and restrictions on the order in which the attacker may call the oracles is motivated by how a CGKA protocol would be used in a higher-level protocol. Most importantly, the attacker will not be allowed to modify or inject any control messages. The corresponding design choices are justified in Sect. 3.3.

Epochs. The main oracles to drive the execution are the oracles to create groups, add users, remove users, and to deliver control messages, i.e., **create-group**, **add-user**, **remove-user**, **send-update**, and **deliver**. The first four oracles allow the adversary to instruct parties to initiate new epochs, whereas the deliver oracle makes parties actually proceed to the next epoch. The server connecting the parties is trusted to provide parties with a consistent view of which operation takes place in each epoch. That is, while multiple parties may initiate a new epoch, the attacker is forced to pick a single operation that defines the new epoch; the corresponding sender is referred to as the *leader* of the epoch. Observe that the parties may advance at various speeds and therefore be in epochs arbitrarily far apart.

The game forces the attacker to initially, i.e., in epoch 1, create a group. Thereafter, any group member may add new parties, remove current group members, or perform an update. The attacker may also corrupt any party at any point (thereby learning that party's secret state) and challenge the update secret in any epoch where the leader performed an update operation. Furthermore, the adversary can instruct parties to stop deleting old secrets. There will be restrictions checked at the end of the execution of the game to ensure that the attacker's challenge/corruption/no-deletion behavior does not lead to trivial attacks.

Initialization. The **init** oracle sets up the game and all the variables needed to keep track of the execution. The random bit b is used for real-or-random challenges, and the dictionary γ keeps track of all the users' states. For every epoch, the dictionaries lead, $\mathbf{I}$, and $\mathbf{G}$ record the leader, the update secret, and the group members, respectively, and ep records which epoch each user is currently in. The array ctr counts all new operations initiated by a user in their current epoch. Moreover, D keeps track of which parties delete their old values and which do not. Dictionary chall is used to ensure that the adversary can issue at most a single challenge per (update) epoch. Finally, M records all control messages produced by parties; the adversary has read access to M (as indicated by the keyword **pub**).

Initiating operations and choosing epoch leaders. As mentioned above, the attacker must choose a leader in every epoch, i.e., a sender whose control message is ultimately processed by all group members. More precisely, for each user ID currently in some epoch t, ctr[ID] can be thought of as a (local) "version number" that counts the various operations initiated by ID in epoch t. The counter is incremented each time ID initiates a new operation. The resulting control messages for users ID_i are stored in M with key $(t+1, \mathsf{ID}, \mathsf{ID}_i, \mathsf{ctr[ID]})$, representing the number of the next epoch, the sender, the recipient, and the (local) version number of the operation. Similarly, dictionary $\mathbf{G}$ stores the new group that would result from the operation with key $(t+1, \mathsf{ID}, \mathsf{ctr[ID]})$.

For every epoch t, the first control message $M[t, \mathsf{ID}, \mathsf{ID}', c]$ delivered via **deliver**, for some users ID and ID' and version number c, determines that ID

Oracles of Security Game for CGKA

init
  $b \leftarrow\!\!{\$} \ \{0,1\}$
  $\forall \mathsf{ID} : \gamma[\mathsf{ID}] \leftarrow \mathsf{init}(\mathsf{ID})$
  $\mathsf{lead}[\cdot], \mathbf{I}[\cdot], \mathbf{G}[\cdot] \leftarrow \epsilon$
  $\mathsf{ep}[\cdot], \mathsf{ctr}[\cdot] \leftarrow 0$
  $D[\cdot] \leftarrow \mathsf{true}$
  $\mathsf{chall}[\cdot] \leftarrow \mathsf{false}$
  pub $M[\cdot] \leftarrow \epsilon$

create-group $(\mathsf{ID}_0, \mathsf{ID}_1, \ldots, \mathsf{ID}_n)$
  $t \leftarrow \mathsf{ep}[\mathsf{ID}]$
  req $t = 0$
  $c \leftarrow \ ++ \ \mathsf{ctr}[\mathsf{ID}_0]$
  $(\gamma[\mathsf{ID}_0], W) \leftarrow$
    $\mathsf{create}(\gamma[\mathsf{ID}_0], \mathsf{ID}_1, \ldots, \mathsf{ID}_n)$
  for $i = 0, \ldots, n$
    $|\quad M[t+1, \mathsf{ID}_0, \mathsf{ID}_i, c] \leftarrow W$
  $\mathbf{G}[t+1, \mathsf{ID}, c] \leftarrow \{\mathsf{ID}_0, \mathsf{ID}_1, \ldots, \mathsf{ID}_n\}$

reveal (t)
  req $\mathbf{I}[t] \notin \{\epsilon, \bot\} \wedge \neg\mathsf{chall}[t]$
  $\mathsf{chall}[t] \leftarrow \mathsf{true}$
  return $\mathbf{I}[t]$

chall (t)
  req $\mathbf{I}[t] \notin \{\epsilon, \bot\} \wedge \neg\mathsf{chall}[t]$
  $I_0 \leftarrow \mathbf{I}[t]$
  $I_1 \leftarrow \mathcal{K}$
  $\mathsf{chall}[t] \leftarrow \mathsf{true}$
  return I_b

add-user $(\mathsf{ID}, \mathsf{ID}')$
  $t \leftarrow \mathsf{ep}[\mathsf{ID}]$
  req $t > 0 \wedge \mathsf{ID}' \notin \mathbf{G}[t]$
  $c \leftarrow \ ++ \ \mathsf{ctr}[\mathsf{ID}]$
  $(\gamma[\mathsf{ID}], W, T) \leftarrow$
    $\mathsf{add}(\gamma[\mathsf{ID}], \mathsf{ID}')$
  $M[t+1, \mathsf{ID}, \mathsf{ID}', c] \leftarrow (W, T)$
  for $\tilde{\mathsf{ID}} \in \mathbf{G}[t]$
    $|\quad M[t+1, \mathsf{ID}, \tilde{\mathsf{ID}}, c] \leftarrow T$
  $\mathbf{G}[t+1, \mathsf{ID}, c] \leftarrow \mathbf{G}[t] \cup \{\mathsf{ID}'\}$

remove-user $(\mathsf{ID}, \mathsf{ID}')$
  $t \leftarrow \mathsf{ep}[\mathsf{ID}]$
  req $t > 0 \wedge \mathsf{ID}' \notin \mathbf{G}[t] > 0$
  $c \leftarrow \ ++ \ \mathsf{ctr}[\mathsf{ID}]$
  $(\gamma[\mathsf{ID}], T) \leftarrow \mathsf{rem}(\gamma[\mathsf{ID}], \mathsf{ID}')$
  for $\tilde{\mathsf{ID}} \in \mathbf{G}[t]$
    $|\quad M[t+1, \mathsf{ID}, \tilde{\mathsf{ID}}, c] \leftarrow T$
  $\mathbf{G}[t+1, \mathsf{ID}, c] \leftarrow \mathbf{G}[t] \setminus \{\mathsf{ID}'\}$

send-update (ID)
  $t \leftarrow \mathsf{ep}[\mathsf{ID}]$
  req $t > 0$
  $c \leftarrow \ ++ \ \mathsf{ctr}[\mathsf{ID}]$
  $(\gamma[\mathsf{ID}], T) \leftarrow \mathsf{upd}(\gamma[\mathsf{ID}])$
  for $\tilde{\mathsf{ID}} \in \mathbf{G}[t]$
    $|\quad M[t+1, \mathsf{ID}, \tilde{\mathsf{ID}}, c] \leftarrow T$
  $\mathbf{G}[t+1, \mathsf{ID}, c] \leftarrow \mathbf{G}[t]$

deliver $(t, \mathsf{ID}, \mathsf{ID}', c)$
  req $\mathsf{lead}[t] \in \{\epsilon, (\mathsf{ID}, c)\} \wedge$
    $(t = \mathsf{ep}[\mathsf{ID}'] + 1 \vee \mathsf{added}(t, \mathsf{ID}, \mathsf{ID}', c))$
  $T \leftarrow M[t, \mathsf{ID}, \mathsf{ID}', c]$
  $(\gamma[\mathsf{ID}'], I) \leftarrow \mathsf{proc}(\gamma[\mathsf{ID}'], T)$
  if $\mathsf{lead}[t] = \epsilon$
    $|\quad \mathsf{lead}[t] \leftarrow (\mathsf{ID}, c)$
    $|\quad \mathbf{I}[t] \leftarrow I$
    $|\quad \mathbf{G}[t] \leftarrow \mathbf{G}[t, \mathsf{ID}, c]$
  else if $I \neq \mathbf{I}[t]$
    $|\quad$ **win**
  if $\mathsf{removed}(t, \mathsf{ID}')$
    $|\quad \mathsf{ep}[\mathsf{ID}'] \leftarrow -1$
  else
    $|\quad \mathsf{ep}[\mathsf{ID}'] ++$
  $\mathsf{ctr}[\mathsf{ID}'] \leftarrow 0$

corr (ID)
  return $\gamma[\mathsf{ID}]$

no-del (ID)
  $|\quad D[\mathsf{ID}] \leftarrow \mathsf{false}$

Fig. 1. Oracles for the CGKA security game for a scheme $\mathsf{CGKA} = (\mathsf{init}, \mathsf{create}, \mathsf{add}, \mathsf{rem}, \mathsf{upd}, \mathsf{proc})$. The functions added and $\mathsf{removed}$ are defined in the text.

is the leader and c the version that was chosen by the server. Correspondingly, the game records $\mathsf{lead}[t] \leftarrow (\mathsf{ID}, c)$ and sets the group membership to $\mathbf{G}[t] \leftarrow \mathbf{G}[t, \mathsf{ID}, c]$.

In general, whenever a party ID' processes any control message, the counter $\mathsf{ctr}[\mathsf{ID}']$ is reset to 0 as all operations initiated by ID' in its current epoch are now obsolete (either processed by ID or rejected by the server in favor of some other operation). Note that the sender of an operation also sends a control message addressed to themselves to the server. The server confirms an operation by returning that message back to the sender.

Group creation. The oracle **create-group** causes ID_0 to create a group with members $\{\mathsf{ID}_0, \ldots, \mathsf{ID}_n\}$. This is only allowed if ID_0 is currently in epoch 0, which is enforced by the **req** statement. Thereafter, ID_0 calls the group creation algorithm and sends the resulting welcome messages to all users involved (including itself).

Adding and removing users and performing updates. For all three oracles **add-user**, **remove-user** and **send-update**, the **req** statement checks that the call makes sense (e.g., checking that a party added to the group is not currently a

---

Safety Predicate

safe $(\mathbf{q}_1, \ldots, \mathbf{q}_q)$
  for (i, j) *s.t.* $\mathbf{q}_i = \mathbf{corrupt}(\mathsf{ID})$ *for some* ID *and* $\mathbf{q}_j = \mathbf{chall}(t^*)$ *for some* t^*
    if $\mathsf{q2e}(\mathbf{q}_i) \leq t^*$ *and* $\nexists\, k$ *s.t.* $0 < \mathsf{q2e}(\mathbf{q}_i) < \mathsf{q2e}(\mathbf{q}_k) \leq t^*$ *and* $\mathbf{q}_k \in \{\mathbf{send\text{-}update}(\mathsf{ID}), \mathbf{remove\text{-}user}(*, \mathsf{ID})\}$
      | return 0
    if $\mathsf{q2e}(\mathbf{q}_i) > t^*$ *and* $\exists k$ *s.t.* $\mathsf{q2e}(\mathbf{q}_k) \leq t^*$ *and* $\mathbf{q}_k = \mathbf{no\text{-}del}(\mathsf{ID})$
      | return 0
  return 1

Fig. 2. The safety predicate determines whether a sequence of oracle calls $(\mathbf{q}_1, \ldots, \mathbf{q}_q)$ allows the attacker to trivially win the CGKA security game.

group member). Subsequently, the oracles call the corresponding CGKA algorithms (add, rem, and upd, respectively) and store the resulting control messages in M.

Delivering control messages. The oracle **deliver** is called with the same four arguments $(t, \mathsf{ID}, \mathsf{ID}', c)$ that are used as keys for the M array. The **req** statement at the beginning checks that (1) either there is no leader for epoch t yet or version c of ID is the leader already and (2) the recipient ID' is currently either in epoch $t - 1$ or a newly added group member, which is checked by predicate added defined by $\mathsf{added}(t, \mathsf{ID}, \mathsf{ID}', c) := \mathsf{ID}' \notin \mathbf{G}[t-1] \wedge \mathsf{ID}' \in \mathbf{G}[t, \mathsf{ID}, c]$. If the checks are passed, the appropriate control message is retrieved from M and run through proc on the state of ID'. If there is no leader for epoch t yet, the game sets the leader as explained above and also records the update secret $\mathbf{I}[t]$ output by proc. In all future calls to **deliver**, the values I output by process will be checked against $\mathbf{I}[t]$, and, in case of a mismatch, the instruction **win** reveals the secret bit b to the attacker; this ensures correctness. Finally, the epoch counter for ID' is incremented—or set to -1 if the operation just processed removes ID' from the group. This involves a check via predicate removed defined by $\mathsf{removed}(t, \mathsf{ID}') := \mathsf{ID}' \in \mathbf{G}[t-1] \wedge \mathsf{ID}' \notin \mathbf{G}[t]$.

Challenges, corruptions, and deletions. In order to capture that update secrets must look random, the attacker is allowed to issue a challenge for any epoch corresponding to an update operation. When calling **chall**(t) for some t, the oracle first checks that t indeed corresponds to an update epoch and that a leader already exists. Similarly, using **reveal**, the attacker can simply learn the update secret of an epoch. It is also ensured that for each epoch, the attacker can make at most one call to either **chall** or **reveal**.

To formally model forward secrecy and PCS, the attacker is also allowed to learn the current state of any party by calling the oracle **corrupt**. Finally, the attacker can instruct a party ID to stop deleting old values by calling **no-del**(ID). Subsequently, the game will *implicitly* store all old states of ID (instead of overriding them) and leak it to the attacker when he calls **corrupt**.[3] The game also sets the corresponding flag.

---

[3] Modeling no-deletions explicitly would clutter Fig. 1 quite a bit.

Avoiding trivial attacks. In order to ensure that the attacker may not win the CGKA security game with trivial attacks (such as, e.g., challenging an epoch t's update secret and leaking some party's state in epoch t), at the end of the game, the predicate **safe** is run on the queries $q_1, \ldots, q_q$ in order to determine whether the execution was devoid of such attacks. The predicate tests whether the attacker can trivially compute the update secret in a challenge epoch t^* using the state of a party ID in some epoch t and the control messages observed on the network. This is the case if either (1) ID has not performed an update or been removed before epoch t^* or (2) ID stopped deleting values at some point up to epoch t^* and was corrupted thereafter. The predicate is depicted in Fig. 2. The figure uses the function $q2e(q)$, which returns the epoch corresponding to query q. Specifically, for $q \in \{\mathbf{corrupt}(\mathsf{ID}), \mathbf{no\text{-}del}(\mathsf{ID})\}$, if ID is member of the group when q is made, $q2e(q)$ is the value of $ep[\mathsf{ID}]$ (when the query is made), otherwise, $q2e(q)$ returns $\bot$. For $q \in \{\mathbf{send\text{-}update}(\mathsf{ID}), \mathbf{remove\text{-}user}(\mathsf{ID}, \mathsf{ID}')\}$, $q2e(q)$, is the epoch for which ID initiates the operation. If q is not processed by any user we set $q2e(q) = \bot$.[4]

Observe that the predicate **safe** can in general be replaced by any other predicate P, potentially weakening the resulting security notion.

Advantage. In the following, a (t, c, n)-*attacker* is an attacker $\mathcal{A}$ that runs in time at most t, makes at most c challenge queries, and never produces a group with more than n members. For any adversary $\mathcal{A}$ for which the safety predicate evaluates to true on the queries made by it, $\mathcal{A}$ wins the CGKA security game if he correctly guesses the random bit b in the end. The advantage of $\mathcal{A}$ with safety predicate P against a CGKA scheme CGKA is defined by $\mathsf{Adv}^{\mathsf{CGKA,P}}_{\mathsf{cgka\text{-}na}}(\mathcal{A}) :=$ $|\Pr[\mathcal{A} \text{ wins}] - \frac{1}{2}|$.

Definition 2 (Non-adaptive CGKA security). *A continuous group key-agreement protocol CGKA is* non-adaptively $(t, c, n, \mathsf{P}, \varepsilon)$-secure *if for all* (t, c, n)-*attackers,* $\mathsf{Adv}^{\mathsf{CGKA,P}}_{\mathsf{cgka\text{-}na}}(\mathcal{A}) \leq \varepsilon$.

3.3 Explanation of Assumptions in Definition

CGKA in higher-level protocol. Syntax and security of CGKA protocols are defined in such a way that they can be used by a higher-level protocol—in particular a full secure group-messaging (SGM) scheme (e.g., the entire MLS protocol)—in a modular fashion. As explained below, this modularity allows to assume that the parties are connected by authenticated channels and messages are delivered in order in the CGKA security definition.

Authenticated channels. Any sensible SGM security definition allows the attacker to *inject*, i.e., forge and/or replay, protocol messages at will. However, this behavior is easy to defend against by having group members sign all messages they send. In particular, CGKA control messages can be authenticated this way.

---

[4] Any boolean expression containing $\bot$ is false.

Therefore, the CGKA security game may assume that channels are authenticated since any injections of control messages can be taken care of by the corresponding security reduction.

The only time this is problematic is when the attacker learns some user's singing keys via state leakage. However, authenticity can be recovered in a generic way by using ephemeral signature keys as part of the higher-level protocol. That is, users periodically sample fresh signature keys and publish the public key as well as a signature on it using their previous secret key. Of course this requires that the attacker remain *passive*, i.e., that he not inject, during the time window between compromise and key update. While this is arguably not the strongest adversarial model one might consider, observe that not making such an assumption[5] would essentially require security against *insider attacks* (attacks in which group members deviate from the protocol arbitrarily). This is an interesting and important issue, but it is outside the scope of this paper (not to mention much if not all of the academic literature on SGM). Nor is defending against any such attack part of MLS's goals.[6] In fact, it is not clear whether completely defending against insider attacks can result in a practical protocol at all. We believe the study of SGM secure against insider attacks to be one of the main open problems in the area.

Message ordering. Any SGM protocol using CGKA as a component (and authenticating CGKA control messages as described above) may additionally ensure that CGKA messages are delivered in order by, e.g., transcript hashing: Group members keep a running hash value h, which is updated as $h_{new} \leftarrow H(h_{old}||T)$ each time a CGKA control message T is sent. In addition, h_{old} is sent along with T, and T is only processed by a party if h_{old} matches the local running hash. Therefore, while the full SGM security definition allows the attacker to reorder messages, CGKA security need not consider out-of-order messages (as this can be handled by the security reduction).

In Sect. 7 we discuss security in the presence of group splitting attacks.

4   TreeKEM

4.1   Overview

The TreeKEM CGKA protocol is based on so-called (binary) *ratchet trees (RTs)*. In a TreeKEM RT, group members are arranged at the leaves, and all nodes have an associated public-key encryption (PKE) key pair, except for the root. The tree invariant is that each user knows all secret keys on their *direct path*, i.e., on the path from their leaf node to the root. In order to perform an update—the most crucial operation of a CGKA—and produce a new update secret I, a party

---

[5] Note that this assumption is universal in the 2-party SM literature.

[6] In particular, its well understood that an insider in an MLS session can, at the very least, perform denial of service attacks on group members by sending out malformed packets.

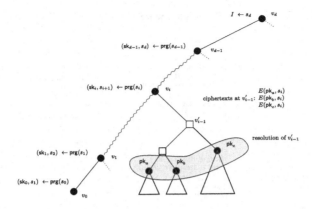

Fig. 3. An update operation initiated by the party at leaf v_0. First, a random "seed value" s_0 is chosen. Thereafter, a PRG is applied iteratively at every level i of v_0's direct path in order to derive (i) a PKE secret key sk_i for that level (from which a public key can be computed using the key generation algorithm) and (ii) a seed s_{i+1} for the next level. Every seed s_i is encrypted using the public key of the corresponding co-path node v'_{i-1}. Sometimes, such a node can be blank, in which case s_i must be encrypted using the public keys of each node in the *resolution*, which is the smallest set of nodes covering all leaves in the subtree of v'_{i-1}. This ensures that all these nodes are able to compute the keys from v_i upward. The update secret I produced by such an update is the seed value s_d at the root.

first generates fresh key pairs on every node of their direct path. Then, for every node v' on its *co-path*—the sequence of siblings of nodes on the direct path—it encrypts specific information under the public key of v' that allows each party in the subtree of v' to learn all new secret keys from v's parent up to the root (cf. Fig. 3 and Sect. 4.4).

Before presenting the formal description of TreeKEM in Sect. 4.4, basic concepts around ratchet trees are explored in Sect. 4.3. Moreover, Sect. 4.2 quickly discusses the simple PKI model used in this work.

4.2   PKI

The TreeKEM protocol requires a public-key infrastructure (PKI) where parties can register ephemeral keys. The MLS documents [5,29] lay out explicitly how users are to generate, authenticate, distribute, and verify each others initialization keys. For simplicity and in order not to detract from the essential components of TreeKEM, this work models the PKI by providing protocol algorithms and attackers with access to the following PKI functionality: (1) Any user ID may request a *fresh* (encryption) public key pertaining to some other user ID'. That is, when ID calls get-pk(ID'), the PKI functionality generates a fresh key pair (pk, sk) and returns pk to ID. The PKI also records the triple (pk, sk, ID') and passes the information (pk, ID') to the attacker. (2) Any user ID' may request secret keys corresponding to public keys associated with them.

TreeKEM

TK-init (ID)
  ME ← ID
  τ ← ⊥
  ctr ← 0
  τ'[·], conf[·] ← ⊥

TK-create (G)
  ctr ++
  ID₀ ← ME
  (pk₀, sk₀) ← PKEG
  for i = 1, . . . , |G|
  | pkᵢ ← get-pk(G.i)
  G' ← (ID₀, G)
  pk' ← (pk₀, pk)
  τ'[ctr] ← INIT(G', pk', 0, sk₀)
  W ← (create, G', pk')
  conf[ctr] ← W
  return W

TK-add (ID')
  ctr ++
  pk' ← get-pk(ID')
  τ'[ctr] ← ADDID(τ, ID', pk')
  τ'[ctr] ← BLANK(τ'[ctr], ID')
  W ← (wel, PUB(τ'[ctr]))
  T ← (add, ME, ID', pk')
  conf[ctr] ← T
  return (W, T)

TK-rem (ID')
  ctr ++
  τ'[ctr] ← BLANK(τ, ID')
  τ'[ctr] ← REMID(τ'[ctr], ID')
  T ← (rem, ME, ID')
  conf[ctr] ← T
  return T

TK-upd
  ctr ++
  (τ'[ctr], U) ← UPGEN(τ, ME)
  T ← (up, ME, U)
  conf[ctr] ← T
  return T

TK-proc (T, IK)
  if ∃j : T = conf[j]
  | τ ← τ'[j]
  else
  | proc(T)
  ctr ← 0
  τ'[·], conf[·] ← ⊥
  return (τ.I)

---

proc (T = (create, G, pk))
  let j s.t. G.IDⱼ = ME
  skⱼ ← get-sk(pk.j)
  τ ← INIT(G, pk, j, skⱼ)

proc (T = (add, ID, ID', pk'))
  τ ← ADDID(τ, ID', pk')
  τ ← BLANK(τ, ID')

proc (T = (wel, τ̄))
  τ ← τ̄
  τ.ME.sk ← get-sk(τ.ME.pk)

proc (T = (rem, ID, ID'))
  τ ← BLANK(τ, ID')
  τ ← REMID(τ, ID')

proc (T = (up, ID, U))
  τ ← UPPRO(τ, ID, ME, U)

Fig. 4. The TreeKEM protocol operations. The functions ADDID, REMID, and BLANK are defined in Sect. 4.3, while UPGEN and UPPRO are defined in Sect. 4.4.

Specifically, when ID' calls get-sk(pk), if a triple (pk, sk, ID') is recorded, the PKI functionality returns sk to ID'. Note in particular that the PKI ensures that every public key is only used once. Of course, in practice such a PKI functionality would actually be implemented by having users generate key pairs themselves and registering them with the PKI. However, the above formalization simplifies the description of the protocols.

4.3 Ratchet Trees

Basics. The following are some basic concepts around TreeKEMs ratchet trees.

LBBTs. An RT in TreeKEM is a so-called *left-balanced binary tree (LBBT)*. In a nutshell, an LBBT on n nodes (is defined recursively and) has a maximal full binary tree as its left child and an LBBT on the remaining nodes as its right child:

Definition 3 (Left-Balanced Binary Tree). *For $n \in \mathbb{N}$ the* left-balanced binary tree (LBBT) *on n nodes* LBBT_n *is the binary tree constructed as follows: The tree* LBBT_1 *is a single node. Let* $x = \mathsf{mp2}(n)$.[7] *Then, the root of* LBBT_n *has the full subtree* FT_x *as the left subtree and* LBBT_{n-x} *as the right subtree.*

---

[7] Recall that $\mathsf{mp2}(n)$ is the maximum power of two dividing n.

Observe that LBBT_n has exactly n leaves and that every internal node has two children. In an RT, nodes are *labeled* as follows: *Root:* The root is labeled by an *update secret I*. *Internal nodes:* Internal nodes are labeled by a *key pair* $(\mathsf{pk}, \mathsf{sk})$ for the PKE scheme Π. *Leaf nodes:* Leaf nodes are labeled like internal nodes, except that they additionally have an *owner* ID.

Labels are referred to using dot-notation (e.g., $v.\mathsf{pk}$ is v's public key). As a shorthand, $\tau.\mathsf{ID}$ is the leaf node with label ID. Any subset of a node's labels may be undefined, which is indicated by the special symbol $\perp$. Furthermore, a node v may be *blank*. A blank node has all of its labels set to $\perp$. As explained below, all internal nodes in a freshly initialized RT are blank, and, moreover, blanks can result from adding and removing users to and from a group, respectively.

Paths and blanking. As hinted at the beginning of this section, it will be useful to consider the following types of paths: the *direct path* $\mathsf{dPath}(\tau, \mathsf{ID})$, which is the path from the leaf node labeled by ID to the root; the *co-path* $\mathsf{coPath}(\tau, \mathsf{ID})$, which is the sequence of siblings of nodes on the direct path $\mathsf{dPath}(\tau, \mathsf{ID})$. Furthermore, given an ID ID and an RT τ, the function $\tau' \leftarrow \mathrm{BLANK}(\tau, \mathsf{ID})$ blanks all nodes on $\mathsf{dPath}(\tau, \mathsf{ID})$.

Resolutions and representatives. A crucial notion in TreeKEM is that of a resolution. Intuitively, the resolution of a node v is the smallest set of non-blank nodes that covers all leaves in v's subtree.

Definition 4 (Resolution). *Let τ be a tree with node set V. The resolution $\mathsf{Res}(v) \subseteq V$ of a node $v \in V$ is defined recursively as follows: If v is not blank, then $\mathsf{Res}(v) = \{v\}$, else if v is a blank leaf, then $\mathsf{Res}(v) = \emptyset$, otherwise, $\mathsf{Res}(v) := \cup_{v' \in C(v)} \mathsf{Res}(v')$, where $C(v)$ are the children of v.*

Each leaf ℓ' in the subtree τ' of some node v' has a representative in τ':

Definition 5 (Representative). *Consider a tree τ and two leaf nodes ℓ and ℓ'.*

1. *Assume ℓ' is non-blank and in the subtree rooted at v'. The representative $\mathsf{Rep}(v', \ell')$ of ℓ' in the subtree of v' is the first filled node on the path from v' (down) to ℓ.*
2. *Consider the least common ancestor $w = \mathsf{LCA}(\ell, \ell')$ of ℓ and ℓ'. Let v be the child of w on the direct path of ℓ, and v' that on the direct path of ℓ'. The representative $\mathsf{Rep}(\ell, \ell')$ of ℓ' w.r.t. ℓ is defined to be the representative $\mathsf{Rep}(v', \ell')$ of ℓ' in the subtree of v'.*

It is easily seen that $\mathsf{Rep}(v', \ell') \in \mathsf{Res}(v')$.

Simple RT operations. The following paragraphs describe how RTs are initialized as well as how they grow and shrink. The proofs of Lemmas 1 and 2 below can be found in the full version [3].

RT initialization. Given lists of users $G = (\mathsf{ID}_0, \mathsf{ID}_1, \ldots, \mathsf{ID}_n)$ and public keys $\mathbf{pk} = (\mathsf{pk}_0, \mathsf{pk}_1, \ldots, \mathsf{pk}_n)$ as well as an integer j and a secret key sk_j, a new RT is initialized as the left-balanced binary tree LBBT_{n+1} where all the internal nodes as well as the root are blanked, the label of every leaf i is set to $(\mathsf{ID}_i, \mathsf{pk}_i, \bot)$, and the secret key at leaf j is additionally set to sk_j. In the following, the above operation is denoted by $\textsc{Init}(G, \mathbf{pk}, j, \mathsf{sk}_j)$.

Adding IDs to the RT. Given an RT τ, the procedure $\tau' \leftarrow \textsc{AddID}(\tau, \mathsf{ID}, \mathsf{pk})$, sets the labels of the first blank leaf of τ to $(\mathsf{ID}, \mathsf{pk}, \bot)$, and outputs the resulting tree, τ'. If there is no blank leaf in the tree $\tau = \mathsf{LBBT}_n$, method $\textsc{AddLeaf}(\tau)$ is called, which adds a leaf z to it, resulting in a new tree $\tau' = \textsc{AddLeaf}(\tau)$: If n is a power of 2, create a new node r' for τ'. Attach the root of τ as its left child and z as its right child. Otherwise, let r be the root of τ, and let τ_L and τ_R be r's left and right subtrees, respectively. Recursively insert z into τ_R to obtain a new tree τ'_R, and let τ' be the tree with r as a root, τ_L as its left subtree and τ'_R as its right subtree.

Lemma 1. *If $\tau = \mathsf{LBBT}_n$, then $\tau' = \mathsf{LBBT}_{n+1}$.*

Removing an ID. The procedure $\tau' \leftarrow \textsc{RemID}(\tau, \mathsf{ID})$ blanks the leaf labeled with ID and truncates the tree such that the rightmost non-blank leaf is the last node of the tree. Specifically, the following recursive procedure $\textsc{Trunc}(v)$ is called on the rightmost leaf v of τ, resulting in a new tree $\tau' \leftarrow \textsc{Trunc}(\tau)$:[8] If v is blank and not the root, remove v as well as its parent and place its sibling v' where the parent was. Then, execute $\textsc{Trunc}(v')$. If v is non-blank and the root, execute $\textsc{Trunc}(v'')$ on the rightmost leaf node in the tree. Otherwise, do nothing.

Lemma 2. *If $\tau = \mathsf{LBBT}_n$, then $\tau' = \mathsf{LBBT}_y$ for some $0 < y \leq n$. Furthermore, unless $y = 1$, the rightmost leaf of τ' is non-blank.*

Public copy of an RT. Given an RT τ, $\tau' \leftarrow \textsc{Pub}(\tau)$ creates a public copy, τ', of the RT by setting all secret-key labels to $\bot$.

4.4   TreeKEM Protocol

This section now explains the TreeKEM protocol in detail by describing all the algorithms involved in the scheme, which is depicted in Fig. 4. For simplicity, the state γ is not made explicit; it consists of the variables initialized by init. TreeKEM makes (black-box) use of the following cryptographic primitives: a pseudo random generator prg, and a CPA-secure public-key encryption scheme $\Pi = (\mathsf{PKEG}, \mathsf{Enc}, \mathsf{Dec})$. TreeKEM as described here is slightly different from TreeKEM as described in the current MLS draft [5]. These differences are elaborated on in the full version [3]. Essentially, they are small efficiency improvements that do not affect security.

---

[8] Overloading function $\textsc{Trunc}$ for convenience here.

Initialization. The initialization procedure TK-init expects as input an ID ID and initializes several state variables: Variable ME remembers the ID of the party running the scheme and τ will keep track of the RT used. The other variables are used to keep track of all the operations (creates, adds, removes, and updates) initiated by ME but not confirmed yet by the server. Specifically, each time a party performs a new operation, it increases ctr and stores the potential next state in $\tau'[\text{ctr}]$. Moreover, conf[ctr] will store the control message the party expects from the server as confirmation that the operation was accepted. These variables are reset each time proc processes a control message (which can either be one of the messages in conf or a message sent by another party).

Group creation. Given lists of users $G = (\text{ID}_1, \ldots, \text{ID}_n)$, TK-create initializes a new ratchet tree by first creating a new PKE key pair $(\text{pk}_0, \text{sk}_0)$, fetching public keys $\mathbf{pk} = (\text{pk}_1, \ldots, \text{pk}_n)$ corresponding to the IDs in G from the PKI, and then calling INIT with[9] $G' = (\text{ID}_0, G)$ and $\mathbf{pk}' = (\text{pk}_0, \mathbf{pk})$ as well as 0 and sk_0. The welcome message simply consists of G' and $\mathbf{pk}'$.

Adding a group member. To add new group member ID', add first obtains a corresponding public key pk' from the PKI and then updates the RT by calling ADDID (described above) followed by BLANK, which removes all keys from the new party's leaf up to the root. This ensures that the new user does not know any secret keys used by the other group members before he joined. The welcome message for the new user simply consists of a public copy of the current RT (specifically, PUB sets the sender's secret-key label to $\bot$), and the control message for the remaining group members of the IDs of the sender and the new user as well as the latter's public key.

Removing a group member. A group member ID' is removed by first blanking all the keys from the leaf node of ID' to the root. This prevents parties from using keys known to ID' in the future. User ID' is subsequently removed from the tree by calling REMID. The control message for the remaining group members consists of the IDs of the sender and the removed user.

Performing an update. A user ME performs an update by choosing new key pairs on their direct path as follows:

- *Compute path secrets*: Let $v_0 = v, v_1, \ldots, v_d$, be the nodes on the direct path of the ME's leaf node v. First, ME chooses a uniformly random s_0. Then, they compute $\text{sk}_i \| s_{i+1} \leftarrow \text{prg}(s_i)$, for $i = 0, \ldots, d - 1$.
- *Update RT labels*: For $i = 0, \ldots, d - 1$, ME computes $\text{pk}_i \leftarrow \text{PKEG}(\text{sk}_i)$ and updates the PKE label of v_i to $(\text{pk}_i, \text{sk}_i)$.
- *Root node*: For the root node, ME sets $I := s_d$.

---

[9] Here we slightly abuse vector notation.

The above operation is denoted by $\tau' \leftarrow \text{PROPUP}(\tau, v, s_0)$. Having computed the new keys on its direct path, ME proceeds as follows:

- *Encrypt path secrets*: Let $v'_0, \ldots, v'_{d-1}$ be the nodes on the co-path of v (i.e., v'_i is the sibling of v_i). For every value s_i and every node $v_j \in \text{Res}(v'_{i-1})$, ME computes $c_{ij} \leftarrow \text{Enc}(v_j.\text{pk}, s_i)$.
- *Output*: All ciphertexts c_{ij} are concatenated to an overall ciphertext $\mathbf{c}$ (in some canonical order[10]). Let $U \leftarrow (\text{PK}, \mathbf{c})$, where $\text{PK} := (\text{pk}_0, \ldots, \text{pk}_{d-1})$ be the update information for the remaining group members.

The entire update process described above is denoted by $(\tau', U) \leftarrow \text{UPGEN}(\tau, \text{ID})$. The control message for this operation simply consists of ME's ID and U.

Notation. It will also be convenient to refer to the set of secret keys $\text{RecKeys}(s_i) := \{\text{sk}_i, \ldots, \text{sk}_{d-1}, s_d\}$ that can be recovered from path secret s_i. Moreover, let $\text{PKeys}(s_i) := \{\text{sk} \mid s_i \text{ is encrypted under PK corresponding to sk}\}$ be the set of secret keys such that s_i is encrypted under the corresponding public keys.

Processing control messages. When processing a control message T, a user first checks whether T corresponds to an operation they initiated. If so, they simply adopt the corresponding RT in $\tau'[\cdot]$.

Whenever T was sent from another user, depending on the type of the control message, proc operates as follows:

- $T = (\text{create}, G, \mathbf{pk})$: In this case, simply determine the position j of ME in the G list, retrieve the appropriate secret key sk_j from the PKI, and initialize the RT via $\tau \leftarrow \text{INIT}(G, \mathbf{pk}, j, \text{sk}_j)$.
- $W = (\text{wel}, \tilde{\tau})$: Simply adopt $\tilde{\tau}$ as the current RT τ and set the secret key at ME's node to the key $\text{get-sk}(\tau.\text{ME.pk})$ retrieved from the PKI.
- $T = (\text{add}, \text{ID}, \text{ID}', \text{pk}')$: Add the new user ID' to the RT and blank all nodes in the direct path of the new user.
- $T = (\text{rem}, \text{ID}, \text{ID}')$: Blank all nodes on the direct path of user ID' and remove ID' from the RT.
- $T = (\text{up}, \text{ID}, U)$: A user ID' at some leaf ℓ' receiving $U = (\text{PK}, \mathbf{c})$, issued by the user with id ID at leaf v, recovers the update information as follows: Let $w := \text{Rep}(v, \ell')$. The user with ID', uses $w.\text{sk}$ to decrypt c_{ij} (for the appropriate j) and obtain s_i. Finally, update the ratchet tree by overriding the public-key labels on the v-root-path by the keys in PK, and by then producing a new tree $\tau' \leftarrow \text{PROPUP}(\tau, \text{LCA}(v, \ell'), s_i)$. The entire process just described is denoted by $\tau' \leftarrow \text{UPPRO}(\tau, \text{ID}, \text{ID}', U)$.

Irrespective of whether T was created by ME or another user, after processing it, TK-proc resets the variables pertaining to keeping track of ME's unconfirmed operations.

---

[10] For the sake of concreteness, consider the order obtained by first sorting the c_{ij} by i and then by j, using the natural ordering for resolutions obtained by first considering the left child and then the right child (cf. Definition 4).

5   Security of TreeKEM

Ideally, a CGKA scheme satisfies Definition 2 w.r.t. the safety
predicate **safe**. However, this is
not the case for TreeKEM. Specifically, while TreeKEM achieves
post-compromise security (PCS), it
only provides a very weak notion
of forward secrecy. We first illustrate this with a simple example
in Sect. 5.1 and then proceed to
characterize the exact security of
the TreeKEM protocol in Sect. 5.2,
using a predicate **tkm**. While precise (cf. Sect. 4.4), predicate **tkm**
is quite unintuitive and cumbersome. To that end, we show that
a scheme secure w.r.t. **tkm** is also
secure w.r.t. to the slightly weaker
but more intuitive predicates **fsu**

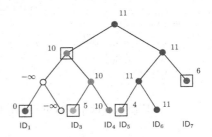

Fig. 5. A ratchet tree showing only the epoch numbers of secret keys; empty nodes are blank. This tree was created by (say) the following sequence of 11 operations: initialization with eight parties $ID_1, \ldots, ID_8$; updates by ID_5, ID_2, ID_5, ID_3, and ID_7; removal of ID_8; update by ID_2; removal of ID_2; updates by ID_4 and ID_6. The boxed nodes contain keys from which the attacker can compute the update secret of epoch 11.

and **pcs**; the former captures a notion of forward security while the latter captures PCS without guaranteeing forward secrecy.

5.1   TreeKEM Is Not Forward Secret

On an intuitive level, the reason the TreeKEM protocol fails to be forward secret
is that after processing the messages generated by an update operation, parties
must keep the secret keys used to decrypt the update information since they
might be needed for processing future updates. Therefore, corrupting any party
other than the update initiator completely reveals the update secret of the previous epoch, and *potentially keys of older epochs* as well, violating forward secrecy.

In order to better understand this issue, imagine that for every secret key
that appears in the ratchet tree, the epoch number in which it was created is
recorded; for keys retrieved from the PKI, epoch 0 is assigned. At any point
during the game, the annotated ratchet tree will be of the following type: each
node is either blank or has a secret key whose epoch number equals the maximum
of the epoch numbers of its children (where, for simplicity, the epoch number is
$-\infty$ for blank nodes). An example of a ratchet tree annotated with these epoch
numbers is given in Fig. 5.

Consider the security of the update secret I produced in epoch 11 against
future corruptions. As per TreeKEMs definition, information about I is
encrypted under the public keys of all nodes on the co-path of ID_6. The nodes on
said co-path are the epoch-4 key at ID_5's leaf, the epoch-6 key at ID_7's leaf, and
highest epoch-10 key in the tree. The latter key, however, can also be recovered
from the initial key of ID_1 or the epoch-5 key at ID_3's leaf (since those keys are on

---

Predicate tkm

$\mathbf{tkm}\,(\mathbf{q}_1,\ldots,\mathbf{q}_q)$

    $(\mathcal{V},\mathcal{E}) \leftarrow \mathsf{KG}(\mathbf{q}_1,\ldots,\mathbf{q}_q)$

    for (i,j) *s.t.* $\mathbf{q}_i = \mathbf{corr}(\mathsf{ID})$ *for some* ID *and* $t = \mathsf{q2e}(\mathbf{q}_i)$, $\mathbf{q}_j = \mathbf{chall}(t^*)$ *for some* t^*

      if $\mathsf{I}[t^*] \in \mathcal{K}_{\mathsf{ID}}^t$

        return 0

    return 1

Fig. 6. The predicate **tkm** for the TreeKEM protocol.

the co-path of ID_4, who performed the update in epoch 10). These "dangerous" keys are highlighted by boxes in Fig. 5.

Observe now that if the attacker corrupts any party ID *after* epoch 11 but before a boxed key known to ID is overridden by an update, he can compute I. In particular, each of the parties in $\{\mathsf{ID}_1, \mathsf{ID}_3, \mathsf{ID}_5, \mathsf{ID}_7\}$ must execute an update before they are corrupted in order for I to remain secure (as these parties are the only ones that can override the corresponding boxed leaf keys).

5.2 Capturing TreeKEM's Security

In order to capture the security level achieved by the TreeKEM protocol exactly, this section defines a safety predicate **tkm** based on the notion of a *key graph*. The key graph records the relationships among secret keys in an execution of the protocol. That is, it keeps track of which keys can be computed given which other keys (learned via state compromise). Specifically, given a sequence of oracle queries $Q = (\mathbf{create\text{-}group}, \mathbf{q}_1, \ldots, \mathbf{q}_t)$ the key graph $(\mathcal{V}_t, \mathcal{E}_t) \leftarrow \mathsf{KG}(Q)$ is defined as follows:

- **create-group**$(\mathsf{ID}_1, \ldots, \mathsf{ID}_n)$: The **create-group** operation defines $(\mathcal{V}_0, \mathcal{E}_0)$ as follows: (1) $\mathcal{V}_0 \leftarrow \{\mathsf{sk}_{\mathsf{ID}_1}, \ldots, \mathsf{sk}_{\mathsf{ID}_n}\}$, i.e., $\mathcal{V}_0$ consists of the secret keys of all users in the initial group. (2) $\mathcal{E}_0 \leftarrow \emptyset$.
- $\mathbf{q}_i = \mathbf{send\text{-}update}(\mathsf{ID})$: Let $\mathsf{sk}_0, \ldots, \mathsf{sk}_{d-1}$ and $s_0, \ldots, s_d$ be the secret keys and path secrets generated by the update operation. Compute[11] (i) $\mathcal{V}_i \leftarrow \mathcal{V}_{i-1} \cup \{\mathsf{sk}_0, \ldots, \mathsf{sk}_{d-1}, s_d\}$, (ii) For $j = 1, \ldots, d$, $K_j \leftarrow \{(\mathsf{sk}, \mathsf{sk}') \mid \mathsf{sk} \in \mathsf{PKeys}(s_j), \mathsf{sk}' \in \mathsf{RecKeys}(s_j)\}$, (iii) Set $\mathcal{E}_i \leftarrow \mathcal{E}_{i-1} \cup \left(\bigcup_{j \in [d]} K_j\right)$.
- $\mathbf{q}_i = \mathbf{add\text{-}user}(\mathsf{ID}, \mathsf{ID}')$: Set $\mathcal{V}_i \leftarrow \mathcal{V}_{i-1} \cup \{\mathsf{sk}_{\mathsf{ID}'}\}$.

The queries **remove-user**, **deliver**, do not make any modifications to the key graph, but they indirectly affect the way it evolves.

Let $(\mathcal{V}, \mathcal{E})$ be the key graph defined by executing a sequence of operations of the TreeKEM protocol. For a user with ID ID and an epoch t, $\mathcal{K}_{\mathsf{ID}}^t$ consists of the following elements: (1) The private keys in the state of ID in epoch t. (2) The private keys in $\mathcal{V}$ that are are reachable from the above keys in the key graph $(\mathcal{V}, \mathcal{E})$.

Having defined TreeKEM's key graph, admissible adversaries are now captured via the predicate **tkm** in Fig. 6. The predicate essentially makes sure that the

---

[11] See Sect. 4.4, for a definition of the sets PKeys and $\mathsf{RecKeys}$.

PCS and FSU Predicates

$\mathbf{pcs}\ (\mathbf{q_1}, \ldots, \mathbf{q}_q)$
    if $\exists (i, j)$, *s.t.* $\mathbf{q}_i = \mathbf{corr}(\mathsf{ID})$ *for some* ID, $\mathbf{q}_j = \mathbf{chall}(t^*)$ *for some* t^*, *and* $\mathsf{q2e}(\mathbf{q}_i) > t^*$
    | return 0
    return $\mathbf{safe}(\mathbf{q_1}, \ldots, \mathbf{q}_q)$

$\mathbf{fsu}\ (\mathbf{q_1}, \ldots, \mathbf{q}_q)$
    for (i, j) *s.t.* $\mathbf{q}_i = \mathbf{corr}(\mathsf{ID})$ *for some* ID, $\mathbf{q}_j = \mathbf{chall}(t^*)$ *for some* t^*
    | if $t^* < \mathsf{q2e}(\mathbf{q}_i)$ *and* $\nexists k$ *s.t.* $\mathbf{q}_k = \mathbf{send\text{-}update}(\mathsf{ID})$ *s.t.* $t^* < \mathsf{q2e}(\mathbf{q}_k) \leq \mathsf{q2e}(\mathbf{q}_i)$
    | | return 0
    return $\mathbf{safe}(\mathbf{q_1}, \ldots, \mathbf{q}_q)$

Fig. 7. The PCS predicate **pcs** and the FS-with-updates predicate **fsu**.

attacker does not learn any keys from which a challenged update secret is reachable (Fig. 7).

More intuitive predicates. Since predicate **tkm** is very specific to TreeKEM, the security level achieved by TreeKEM is perhaps understood more easily by considering the following two predicates: (1) The *PCS predicate*, denoted **pcs**, captures PCS only, i.e., without any kind of forward secrecy. This is achieved by excluding corruptions after any challenge (on top of the normal safety predicate). (2) The notion of limited forward secrecy (FS) captured here is *FS with updates (FSU)*. Specifically, when the state of a party ID is leaked, then all keys *before* the most recent update by ID remain secret.

In the following lemma, we establish relations between the these predicates and **tkm**. The proof of the lemma can be found in the full version [3].

Lemma 3. *For any sequence of queries Q, if $\mathbf{pcs}(Q) = 1$ or $\mathbf{fsu}(Q) = 1$, then $\mathbf{tkm}(Q) = 1$.*

In the full version [3], we also show that the formalization introduced above is necessary for evaluating and proving security for the TreeKEM protocol.

5.3 Proof of Security of TreeKEM

This section presents the following security result for the TreeKEM protocol and provides high-level intuition for the security proof. The details of the proof can be found in the full version [3].

Theorem 1 (Non-adaptive security of TreeKEM). *Assume that prg is a $(t_{\mathsf{prg}}, \varepsilon_{\mathsf{prg}})$-secure pseudo-random generator, Π is a $(t_{\mathsf{cpa}}, \varepsilon_{\mathsf{cpa}})$-CPA-secure public-key encryption scheme. Then, TreeKEM is a $(t, c, n, \mathsf{P}, \varepsilon)$-secure CGKA protocol, for $\mathsf{P} \in \{\mathbf{tkm}, \mathbf{pcs}, \mathbf{fsu}\}$, $\varepsilon = 2cn(\varepsilon_{\mathsf{prg}} + \varepsilon_{\mathsf{cpa}})$, and $t \approx t_{\mathsf{prg}} \approx t_{\mathsf{cpa}}$.*

Proof intuition. Consider an execution of the (single-challenge) CGKA game with the TreeKEM scheme. Recall that an update operation by a node at depth d produces, for a uniformly random s_0, the values $s_0 \xrightarrow{\mathsf{prg}} (\mathsf{sk}_0, s_1) \xrightarrow{\mathsf{prg}} (\mathsf{sk}_1, s_2) \xrightarrow{\mathsf{prg}}$

$\ldots \xrightarrow{\text{prg}} (\text{sk}_{d-1}, s_d)$ where $I = s_d$ is the update secret. In the example tree in Fig. 5, assume that the update secret $I = s_3$ created in epoch 11 is challenged. Observe that the last update (by ID_6) encrypts information about I under the keys at the nodes on ID_6's co-path. These keys stem from epochs 4, 6, and 10, respectively. To use the CPA security of said keys to argue that no information about I is obtained by the attacker, one has to recursively check under which other keys information about them has been encrypted. For example, in epoch 10, information was encrypted using a key from epoch 5 and the initial key of ID_1 (who has never performed an update).

Therefore, the proof proceeds in a series of hybrids that fake ciphertexts and replace PRG outputs by random values in a bottom-up fashion, i.e., beginning with the nodes at the greatest depths. In the example of Fig. 5, the hybrids would be the following (highlighting the differences in each step):

- H_d^{c}: Is identical to the original CGKA experiment.
- H_d^{p}: When the updates in epochs 4, 5, 10, and 11 are computed, the output of the first application of the PRG is replaced by a uniformly random value, i.e., instead of computing $(\text{sk}_0, s_1) \leftarrow \text{prg}(s_0)$, sk_0 and s_1 are simply chosen randomly. The rest of the update is computed normally. The security of this step follows from that of the PRG.
- H_{d-1}^{c}: When the updates in epochs 10 and 11 are computed, instead of encrypting s_1 under the corresponding key on the co-path, the all-zero string is encrypted. This step is safe by the CPA security of the PKE in use and the fact that the secret keys at depth d produced by the updates in epochs 4, 5, 10, and 11 are chosen randomly.
- H_{d-1}^{p}: When the updates in epochs 6, 10, and 11 are computed, all PRG computations at depth $d - 1$ are replaced by choosing uniformly random values. That is, instead of applying the PRG, the values (sk_0, s_1) (in the case of epoch 6) and (sk_1, s_2) (in the case of epoch 10 and 11) are chosen randomly. The security of this step follows from that of the PRG and by observing that encryptions of s_1 have been replaced by dummy encryptions in the previous hybrid.
- H_{d-1}^{c}: When the updates in epochs 10 and 11 are computed, instead of encrypting s_2 under the corresponding keys on the resolution of the co-path nodes, the all-zero string is encrypted. This step is safe by the CPA security of the PKE in use and the fact that the secret key at depth $d - 1$ produced by the update in epoch 6 and the initial key of ID_1 are chosen randomly.
- H_{d-2}^{p}: Similarly to H_{d-1}^{p}, values (sk_2, s_3) are chosen randomly when computing updates in epochs 10 and 11.
- H_{d-3}^{c}: In epoch 11, the encryption of s_3 is replaced by a dummy encryption. Observe that in H_{d-3}^{c}, the adversary is now not provided with any information about $s_3 = I$ in update 11. Hence, its advantage in the final hybrid is 0.

Adaptive security for TreeKEM. Due to space limitations, adaptive security is discussed in the full version [3], where we derive that TreeKEM is adaptively secure with security loss factor of $O(n^{\log n})$.

6 Optimal Forward Secrecy

The level of security satisfied by the TreeKEM protocol is limited, as shown in Sect. 5. In order to achieve better security, this section presents a modified version of TreeKEM that is secure even w.r.t. to predicate **safe**. The new version of the protocol is based on a suggestion by Kohbrok [26] on the MLS mailing list and uses so-called *updatable public-key encryption (UPKE)* (cf. Jost *et al.* [24]). In this work we use a variant of UPKE, which we formally present in Sect. 6.2; a construction of a slightly stronger variant can be found in the full version [3].

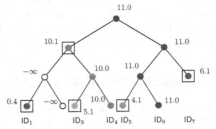

Fig. 8. A ratchet tree showing only the epoch and version numbers of secret keys; empty nodes are blank. This tree was created by (say) the following sequence of 11 operations: initialization with eight parties $ID_1, \ldots, ID_8$; updates by ID_5, ID_2, ID_5, ID_3, and ID_7; removal of ID_8; update by ID_2; removal of ID_2; updates by ID_4 and ID_6. The boxed nodes contain keys under whose earlier versions information leading to update secret of epoch 11 was encrypted.

6.1 Fixing TreeKEM

In a nutshell, the new TreeKEM protocol uses UPKE instead of normal PKE. On an intuitive level, the encryption algorithm of a UPKE scheme outputs a new public key (to be used for future encryptions) along with the ciphertext. Similarly, the decryption algorithm outputs a corresponding new secret key. This is done in such a fashion that even given the new version of the secret key, no information about the plaintexts encrypted under older versions is revealed.

In order to better understand how this solves the issue with TreeKEM's subpar forward secrecy (FS), consider the example execution of the TreeKEM protocol depicted in Fig. 8 (which was already used in Sect. 5). Once more, imagine that for every secret key that appears in the ratchet tree, the epoch number in which it was created is recorded, where keys retrieved from the PKI and used when the group is created, are assigned epoch 0. Imagine further that, in addition to the epoch number, the *version* number of each key is recorded. More precisely, a UPKE key generated by an update operation has version 0, and with every plaintext encrypted under it, the version number is incremented by 1. For example, in Fig. 8, the initial key of ID_1 has been used by four different update operations.

It is now easy to see how UPKE solves the FS issue: While in the plain version, the boxed keys could be used to recover the update secret I of epoch 11, in the new TreeKEM, the information that would allow recovery of I was encrypted under the second most recent version of the boxed keys. However, UPKE now guarantees that the most recent version of any boxed key obtained upon corruption of a corresponding user after epoch 11 reveals no information about I. For example, information about epoch 11's update secret was encrypted under version 0 of the highest epoch-10 key. In turn, information about the latter key was encrypted under version 3 of the key at ID_1's leaf. As a result of these encryptions the two keys are now at versions 1 and 4, respectively. Thus, even if, say, ID_1 is compromised after epoch 11, the new key versions reveal no useful information about epoch 11's update secret.

6.2 Updatable Public-Key Encryption

Below we define a variant of UPKE in which the public (resp. private) key update functionality is implemented by the encryption (resp. decryption) operation. This is how our UPKE notion deviates from that of [24], in which the key update operations are implemented by independent functionalities.

Definition 6. *An* updatable public-key encryption *(UPKE) scheme is a triple of algorithms* $\mathsf{UPKE} = (\mathsf{PKEG}, \mathsf{Enc}, \mathsf{Dec})$ *with the following syntax:*

- Key generation: PKEG *receives a uniformly random key* sk_0 *and outputs a fresh initial public key* $\mathsf{pk}_0 \leftarrow \mathsf{PKEG}(\mathsf{sk}_0)$.
- Encryption: Enc *receives a public key* pk *and a message* m *and produces a ciphertext* c *and a new public key* pk'.
- Decryption: Dec *receives a secret key* sk *and a ciphertext* c *and outputs a message* m *and a new secret key* sk'.

Correctness. A UPKE scheme must satisfy the following correctness property. For any sequence of randomness and message pairs $\{r_i, m_i\}_{i=1}^q$,

$$\mathsf{P}\left[\begin{array}{l} \mathsf{sk}_0 \leftarrow \mathcal{SK}; \mathsf{pk}_0 \leftarrow \mathsf{PKEG}(\mathsf{sk}_0); \text{ For } i \in [q], (c_i, \mathsf{pk}_i) \leftarrow \mathsf{Enc}(\mathsf{pk}_{i-1}, m_i; r_i); \\ (m'_i, \mathsf{sk}_i) \leftarrow \mathsf{Dec}(\mathsf{sk}_{i-1}, c_i) : m_i = m'_i \end{array} \right] = 1.$$

The notion of CPA security that we define below is along the lines of CPA-secure PKE, with the only difference being that for honestly generated ciphertexts the adversary receives access to the randomness that produced them. In this way we capture protocol executions in which prior to the challenge epoch, the adversary receives access to the ciphertexts generated by users (by observing the network), as well as to the randomness used by corrupted users to encrypt path secrets prior to the challenge epoch.

IND-CPA security for UPKE. For any adversary $\mathcal{A}$ with running time t we consider the IND-CPA security game:

- Sample $\mathsf{sk}_0 \leftarrow \mathcal{SK}$, $\mathsf{pk}_0 \leftarrow \mathsf{PKEG}(\mathsf{sk}_0)$, $b \leftarrow \{0, 1\}$.
- $\mathcal{A}$ receives pk_0 and for $i = 1, \ldots, q$, $\mathcal{A}$ outputs m_i and receives $(c_i, \mathsf{pk}_i, r_i)$ such that $(c_i, \mathsf{pk}_i) \leftarrow \mathsf{Enc}(\mathsf{pk}_{i-1}, m_i; r_i)$, for uniformly random r_i
- $\mathcal{A}$ outputs (m_0^*, m_1^*)
- For $i = 1, \ldots, q$, compute $(m_i, \mathsf{sk}_i) \leftarrow \mathsf{Dec}(\mathsf{sk}_{i-1}, c_i)$
- Compute $(c^*, \mathsf{pk}^*) \leftarrow \mathsf{Enc}(\mathsf{pk}_q, m_b^*)$, $(\cdot, \mathsf{sk}^*) \leftarrow \mathsf{Dec}(\mathsf{sk}_q, c^*)$
- $b' \leftarrow \mathcal{A}(\mathsf{pk}^*, \mathsf{sk}^*, c^*)$

$\mathcal{A}$ wins the game if $b = b'$. The advantage of $\mathcal{A}$ in winning the above game is denoted by $\mathsf{Adv}_{\mathrm{cpa}}^{\mathsf{UPKE}}(\mathcal{A})$.

Definition 7. *An updatable public-key encryption scheme* UPKE *is* (t, ε)-*CPA-secure if for all t-attackers* $\mathcal{A}$, $\mathsf{Adv}_{\mathrm{cpa}}^{\mathsf{UPKE}}(\mathcal{A}) \leq \varepsilon$.

6.3   An Optimally Secure Protocol

The new TreeKEM protocol presented in the this section uses UPKE CPA-secure encryption in place of standard CPA-secure encryption. Using UPKE when a user issues an update operation not only updates the PKE keys in its direct path but also the PKE keys of all nodes in the resolution of the co-path nodes. The new TreeKEM protocol is presented by highlighting the differences to TreeKEM.

The initialization, group creation, user addition/removal operations of the protocol are identical to those of TreeKEM. The only difference is the use of UPKE. The *update* and *process* operations work as shown next.

Performing an update. A user performs an update as follows:

- Compute path secrets: Let $v_0 = v, v_1, \ldots, v_d$, be the nodes along the direct path of the node v who issues an update. For uniformly random s_0 compute $\mathsf{sk}_i \| s_{i+1} \leftarrow \mathsf{prg}(s_i)$, for $i = 0, \ldots, d - 1$.
- Update the RT labels along the direct path: For $i = 0, \ldots, d - 1$, compute $\mathsf{pk}_i \leftarrow \mathsf{PKEG}(\mathsf{sk}_i)$ and the PKE label of v_i is updated to $(\mathsf{pk}_i, \mathsf{sk}_i)$.
- Root node: For the root, set $I := s_d$.

Up to now, the computation is identical to the one in the TreeKEM protocol.

- Encrypt path secrets and update public keys: Let $v'_0, \ldots, v'_{d-1}$, be the nodes on the co-path of v (i.e., v'_i is the sibling of v_i). For every value s_i and every node $v_j \in \mathsf{Res}(v'_{i-1})$, compute $(c_{ij}, \mathsf{pk}_{ij}) \leftarrow \mathsf{Enc}(v_j.\mathsf{pk}, s_i)$ and set the public key of v_j to pk_{ij}.
- Output: All ciphertexts c_{ij} are concatenated to an overall ciphertext $\mathbf{c}$ and all keys pk_{ij} are stored in $\bar{\mathsf{PK}}$. Return $U \leftarrow (\mathsf{PK}, \bar{\mathsf{PK}}, \mathbf{c})$, where $\mathsf{PK} := (\mathsf{pk}_0, \ldots, \mathsf{pk}_{d-1})$. This extended update process is denoted by

$$(\tau', U) \leftarrow \mathrm{ExtUpGen}(\tau, \mathsf{ID}).$$

Processing control messages. Processing control messages is similar to the TreeKEM protocol. The main difference is in the way the users process the output of the public key encryption scheme. In particular, for any node of the ratchet tree, v, when processing the output of the encryption operation under the public key of v, $(c, \mathsf{pk}'_v) \leftarrow \mathsf{Enc}(\mathsf{pk}_v, s)$, users compute $(s, \mathsf{sk}'_v) \leftarrow \mathsf{Dec}(v.\mathsf{sk}, c)$, process the path secret s as in TreeKEM, but in addition they set the public and secret key of v to pk'_v and sk'_v, respectively.

6.4   Security of the New TreeKEM

The modified version of the TreeKEM protocol satisfies optimal security, i.e., security w.r.t. the predicate **safe**. The proof of Theorem 2 can be found in the full version [3].

Theorem 2 (Non-adaptive security of Modified TreeKEM). *Assume that* prg *is a* $(t_{prg}, \varepsilon_{prg})$-*secure pseudo-random generator,* Π *is a* $(t_{cpa}, \varepsilon_{cpa})$-*CPA-secure updatable public-key encryption scheme. Then, the protocol of Sect. 6.3 is a* $(t, c, n, \textbf{safe}, \varepsilon)$-*secure CGKA protocol, for* $\varepsilon = 2cn(\varepsilon_{prg} + \varepsilon_{cpa})$ *and* $t \approx t_{prg} \approx t_{cpa}$.

Adaptive security for Modified TreeKEM. Due to space limitations, adaptive security is discussed in the full version [3], where we argue that Modified TreeKEM is adaptively secure with security loss factor of $O(n^{\log n})$.

7   Group Splitting

Group splitting occurs when the attacker, who (in any reasonable SGM definition) has full control over message delivery, does not properly resolve race conditions for control messages. For example, if two group members A and B having processed the same set of protocol messages, both produce an update, the attacker may choose to deliver A's update to a subset $\mathcal{A}$ of parties and B's update to the set $\mathcal{B}$ of remaining parties. The two sets of parties are now potentially in incompatible (yet not independent) states and any state compromise of users in $\mathcal{A}$ can potentially compromise the secrets generated by users in $\mathcal{B}$. This can only be avoided if each CGKA protocol operation updates all the key material in the users' states, so that, after processing the updates, the users in $\mathcal{A}$ (resp. $\mathcal{B}$) do not share common private keys with users in $\mathcal{B}$ (resp. $\mathcal{A}$), and therefore, they cannot process protocols messages generated by users in that group. Clearly, if we aim for practical efficiency, this is not a tenable solution as it requires complexity linear in the size of the group. Thus, we believe it is essential to make a compromise between efficiency and security against splitting attacks.

The security properties that suggested below constitute a reasonable trade-off between security and efficiency, since they only require "touching" a $O(\log n)$ keys in the users' states.

1. *Group re-merging:* Either by accident or by design, groups could potentially end up in compatible states again if they process a suitable set of protocol messages. This is not necessarily a problem, but it is in general undesirable as it contradicts detection of group-splitting attacks that could potentially affect the higher level protocol. Re-merging can easily be avoided by using the transcript-hashing technique outlined above.

2. *Security in split groups:* Should compromising users in $\mathcal{B}$ help break security of users in $\mathcal{A}$? Such a requirement seems quite strong considering the fact that all group members will still believe that the group has not split and consists of all parties in $\mathcal{A} \cup \mathcal{B}$. However, the security of users in $\mathcal{A}$ should be maintained in either one in the following two cases:

   (a) Security for $\mathcal{A}$ is guaranteed once all compromised users from $\mathcal{B}$ have been removed in $\mathcal{A}$'s view of the group. (Not providing this guarantee would imply that former group members might still be able to learn group keys after they have left the group.)
   (b) Security for $\mathcal{A}$ is guaranteed if all users compromised in $\mathcal{B}$ performed an update sometime prior to compromise but after they split from $\mathcal{A}$. (Not providing this guarantee would mean that under the right circumstances even when all compromised user have updated PCS might still not be achieved.)

It is not hard to see that TreeKEM and modified TreeKEM satisfy 2.(a) and 2.(b). For TreeKEM, after users in $\mathcal{A}$ remove a user that, according to their view, belongs to $\mathcal{A}$ (but he is actually a member of $\mathcal{B}$ due to split), all future protocol operations are independent of the secret keys that that the removed user knows. Therefore, he cannot process those messages. A similar argument holds for 2.(b): if users compromised in $\mathcal{B}$ have issued an update sometime prior to compromise, then all their secret keys have been updated, and control messages generated by users in $\mathcal{A}$ require the erased keys in order to be processed. Similar arguments hold for the modified TreeKEM.

References

1. Alwen, J., et al.: Keep the dirt: tainted treekem, an efficient and provably secure continuous group key agreement protocol. Cryptology ePrint Archive, Report 2019/1489 (2019). https://eprint.iacr.org/2019/1489
2. Alwen, J., Coretti, S., Dodis, Y.: The double ratchet: security notions, proofs, and modularization for the signal protocol. In: Ishai, Y., Rijmen, V. (eds.) EUROCRYPT 2019, Part I. LNCS, vol. 11476, pp. 129–158. Springer, Cham (2019). https://doi.org/10.1007/978-3-030-17653-2_5
3. Alwen, J., Coretti, S., Dodis, Y., Tselekounis, Y.: Security analysis and improvements for the IETF MLS standard for group messaging. Cryptology ePrint Archive, Report 2019/1189 (2019). https://eprint.iacr.org/2019/1189
4. Barnes, R.: Subject: [MLS] remove without double-join (in TreeKEM). MLS Mailing List. Mon, 06 August 2018 13:01 UTC (2018). https://mailarchive.ietf.org/arch/msg/mls/Zzw2tqZC1FCbVZA9LKERsMIQXik
5. Barnes, R., Beurdouche, B., Millican, J., Omara, E., Cohn-Gordon, K., Robert, R.: The Messaging Layer Security (MLS) Protocol. Internet-Draft draft-ietf-mls-protocol-08, Internet Engineering Task Force, November 2019. Work in Progress
6. Bellare, M., Singh, A.C., Jaeger, J., Nyayapati, M., Stepanovs, I.: Ratcheted encryption and key exchange: the security of messaging. In: Katz, J., Shacham, H. (eds.) CRYPTO 2017, Part III. LNCS, vol. 10403, pp. 619–650. Springer, Cham (2017). https://doi.org/10.1007/978-3-319-63697-9_21

7. Borisov, N., Goldberg, I., Brewer, E.A.: Off-the-record communication, or, why not to use PGP. In: Proceedings of the 2004 ACM Workshop on Privacy in the Electronic Society, WPES 2004, 28 October 2004, pp. 77–84 (2004)
8. Canetti, R., Garay, J.A., Itkis, G., Micciancio, D., Naor, M., Pinkas, B.: Multicast security: a taxonomy and some efficient constructions. In: IEEE INFOCOM 1999, New York, NY, USA, 21–25 March 1999, pp. 708–716 (1999)
9. Cohn-Gordon, K., Cremers, C., Garratt, L., Millican, J., Milner, K.: On ends-to-ends encryption: asynchronous group messaging with strong security guarantees. In: Lie, D., Mannan, M., Backes, M., Wang, X. (eds.) ACM CCS 2018, pp. 1802–1819. ACM Press, October 2018
10. Cohn-Gordon, K., Cremers, C., Dowling, B., Garratt, L., Stebila, D.: A formal security analysis of the signal messaging protocol. In: 2017 IEEE European Symposium on Security and Privacy, EuroS&P 2017, pp. 451–466 (2017)
11. Cremers, C., Hale, B., Kohbrok, K.: Revisiting post-compromise security guarantees in group messaging. Cryptology ePrint Archive, Report 2019/477 (2019). https://eprint.iacr.org/2019/477
12. Dodis, Y., Fazio, N.: Public key broadcast encryption for stateless receivers. In: Feigenbaum, J. (ed.) DRM 2002. LNCS, vol. 2696, pp. 61–80. Springer, Heidelberg (2003). https://doi.org/10.1007/978-3-540-44993-5_5
13. Durak, F.B., Vaudenay, S.: Bidirectional asynchronous ratcheted key agreement with linear complexity. In: Attrapadung, N., Yagi, T. (eds.) IWSEC 2019. LNCS, vol. 11689, pp. 343–362. Springer, Cham (2019). https://doi.org/10.1007/978-3-030-26834-3_20
14. eQualit.ie. (n + 1)sec (2016). https://learn.equalit.ie/wiki/Np1sec
15. Fiat, A., Naor, M.: Broadcast encryption. In: Stinson, D.R. (ed.) CRYPTO 1993. LNCS, vol. 773, pp. 480–491. Springer, Heidelberg (1994). https://doi.org/10.1007/3-540-48329-2_40
16. Fuchsbauer, G., Jafargholi, Z., Pietrzak, K.: A quasipolynomial reduction for generalized selective decryption on trees. In: Gennaro, R., Robshaw, M. (eds.) CRYPTO 2015, Part I. LNCS, vol. 9215, pp. 601–620. Springer, Heidelberg (2015). https://doi.org/10.1007/978-3-662-47989-6_29
17. Fuchsbauer, G., Konstantinov, M., Pietrzak, K., Rao, V.: Adaptive security of constrained PRFs. In: Sarkar, P., Iwata, T. (eds.) ASIACRYPT 2014, Part II. LNCS, vol. 8874, pp. 82–101. Springer, Heidelberg (2014). https://doi.org/10.1007/978-3-662-45608-8_5
18. Goldberg, I., Ustaoglu, B., Van Gundy, M., Chen, H.: Multi-party off-the-record messaging. In: Al-Shaer, E., Jha, S., Keromytis, A.D. (eds.) Proceedings of the 2009 ACM Conference on Computer and Communications Security, CCS 2009, Chicago, Illinois, USA, 9–13 November 2009, pp. 358–368. ACM (2009)
19. NCC Group: Olm cryptographic review - 1 November 2016 version 2 (2016). https://www.nccgroup.trust/globalassets/our-research/us/public-reports/2016/november/ncc_group_olm_cryptogrpahic_review_2016_11_01.pdf
20. Howell, C., Leavy, T., Alwen, J.: Wickr messaging protocol: technical paper (2018). https://wickr.com/wickrs-messaging-protocol/
21. Jaeger, J., Stepanovs, I.: Optimal channel security against fine-grained state compromise: the safety of messaging. In: Shacham, H., Boldyreva, A. (eds.) CRYPTO 2018, Part I. LNCS, vol. 10991, pp. 33–62. Springer, Cham (2018). https://doi.org/10.1007/978-3-319-96884-1_2
22. Jafargholi, Z., Kamath, C., Klein, K., Komargodski, I., Pietrzak, K., Wichs, D.: Be adaptive, avoid overcommitting. In: Katz, J., Shacham, H. (eds.) CRYPTO 2017, Part I. LNCS, vol. 10401, pp. 133–163. Springer, Cham (2017). https://doi.org/10.1007/978-3-319-63688-7_5

23. Jafargholi, Z., Wichs, D.: Adaptive security of Yao's garbled circuits. In: Hirt, M., Smith, A. (eds.) TCC 2016-B, Part I. LNCS, vol. 9985, pp. 433–458. Springer, Heidelberg (2016). https://doi.org/10.1007/978-3-662-53641-4_17

24. Jost, D., Maurer, U., Mularczyk, M.: Efficient ratcheting: almost-optimal guarantees for secure messaging. In: Ishai, Y., Rijmen, V. (eds.) EUROCRYPT 2019, Part I. LNCS, vol. 11476, pp. 159–188. Springer, Cham (2019). https://doi.org/10.1007/978-3-030-17653-2_6

25. Kim, Y., Perrig, A., Tsudik, G.: Group key agreement efficient in communication. IEEE Trans. Comput. **53**(7), 905–921 (2004)

26. Kohbrok, K.: Subject: [MLS] improve FS granularity at a cost. MLS Mailing List. Thu, 24 January 2019 09:51 UTC (2019). https://mailarchive.ietf.org/arch/msg/mls/WRdXVr8iUwibaQu0tH6sDnqU1no

27. Marlinspike, M., Perrin, T.: The double ratchet algorithm, November 2016. https://whispersystems.org/docs/specifications/doubleratchet/doubleratchet.pdf

28. Mittra, S.: Iolus: a framework for scalable secure multicasting. In: Proceedings of ACM SIGCOMM, Cannes, France, 14–18 September 1997, pp. 277–288 (1997)

29. Omara, E., Beurdouche, B., Rescorla, E., Inguva, S., Kwon, A., Duric, A.: The Messaging Layer Security (MLS) Architecture. Internet-Draft draft-ietf-mls-architecture-03, Internet Engineering Task Force, September 2019. Work in Progress

30. Panjwani, S.: Tackling adaptive corruptions in multicast encryption protocols. In: Vadhan, S.P. (ed.) TCC 2007. LNCS, vol. 4392, pp. 21–40. Springer, Heidelberg (2007). https://doi.org/10.1007/978-3-540-70936-7_2

31. Poettering, B., Rösler, P.: Towards bidirectional ratcheted key exchange. In: Shacham, H., Boldyreva, A. (eds.) CRYPTO 2018, Part I. LNCS, vol. 10991, pp. 3–32. Springer, Cham (2018). https://doi.org/10.1007/978-3-319-96884-1_1

32. Rescorla, E.: Subject: [MLS] TreeKEM: an alternative to ART. MLS Mailing List. Thu, 03 May 2018 14:27 UTC (2018). https://mailarchive.ietf.org/arch/msg/mls/WRdXVr8iUwibaQu0tH6sDnqU1no

33. Steer, D.G., Strawczynski, L., Diffie, W., Wiener, M.: A secure audio teleconference system. In: Goldwasser, S. (ed.) CRYPTO 1988. LNCS, vol. 403, pp. 520–528. Springer, New York (1990). https://doi.org/10.1007/0-387-34799-2_37

34. Open Whisper Systems: The signal application (2020). https://github.com/signalapp

35. Wallner, D., Hardner, E., Agee, R.: Key management for multicast: issues and architectures. IETF RFC2676 (1999). https://tools.ietf.org/html/rfc2627

36. Weidner, M.: Group messaging for secure asynchronous collaboration. M.Phil. dissertation (2019). https://mattweidner.com/acs-dissertation.pdf. Advisors: Beresford, A., Kleppmann, M

37. Whatsapp: Encryption overview 2017, 19 December 2017. https://www.whatsapp.com/security/WhatsApp-Security-Whitepaper.pdf

38. Wong, C.K., Gouda, M., Lam, S.S.: Secure group communications using key graphs. IEEE/ACM Trans. Netw. **8**(1), 16–30 (2000)

Universally Composable Relaxed Password Authenticated Key Exchange

Michel Abdalla[1,2]([⊠])([iD]), Manuel Barbosa[3]([⊠])([iD]), Tatiana Bradley[4]([⊠])([iD]),
Stanisław Jarecki[4]([⊠])([iD]), Jonathan Katz[5]([⊠]), and Jiayu Xu[5]([⊠])([iD])

[1] DIENS, École normale supérieure, CNRS, PSL University, Paris, France
michel.abdalla@ens.fr
[2] INRIA, Paris, France
[3] FCUP and INESC TEC, Porto, Portugal
mbb@fc.up.pt
[4] University of California, Irvine, USA
{tebradle,sjarecki}@uci.edu
[5] Department of Computer Science, George Mason University, Fairfax, USA
jkatz2@gmail.com, jxu27@gmu.edu

Abstract. Protocols for *password authenticated key exchange* (PAKE)
allow two parties who share only a weak password to agree on a cryptographic key. We revisit the notion of PAKE in the universal composability
(UC) framework, and propose a relaxation of the PAKE functionality of
Canetti et al. that we call *lazy-extraction PAKE* (lePAKE). Our relaxation allows the ideal-world adversary to *postpone* its password guess
until after a session is complete. We argue that this relaxed notion still
provides meaningful security in the password-only setting. As our main
result, we show that several PAKE protocols that were previously only
proven secure with respect to a "game-based" definition of security can
be shown to UC-realize the lePAKE functionality in the random-oracle
model. These include SPEKE, SPAKE2, and TBPEKE, the most efficient PAKE schemes currently known.

1 Introduction

Protocols for *password authenticated key exchange* (PAKE) allow two parties
who share only a weak password to agree on a cryptographically strong key
by communicating over an insecure network. PAKE protocols have been studied extensively in the cryptographic literature [8–10,13,14,16,26], and are compelling given the widespread use of passwords for authentication. Even though
the current practice is to implement password-based authentication by using
TLS to set up a secure channel over which the password is sent, there are many
arguments in favor of using PAKE protocols in conjunction with TLS [23]. Continued interest in PAKE is indicated by the fact that several PAKE protocols
are currently under active consideration for standardization by the IETF [29].

Defining security for PAKE protocols is made challenging by the fact that
a password shared by the parties may have low entropy, and so can be guessed

© International Association for Cryptologic Research 2020
D. Micciancio and T. Ristenpart (Eds.): CRYPTO 2020, LNCS 12170, pp. 278–307, 2020.
https://doi.org/10.1007/978-3-030-56784-2_10

by an adversary with noticeable probability. This must somehow be accounted for in any security definition. Roughly speaking, the security guaranteed by a PAKE protocol is that an attacker who initiates Q *online* attacks—i.e., actively interferes in Q sessions of the protocol—can make at most Q password guesses (i.e., at most one per session in which it interferes) and can succeed in impersonating a party only if one of those guesses was correct. In particular, this means that *offline* attacks, in which an adversary merely eavesdrops on executions of the protocol, should not help the adversary in any way.

Two paradigms of PAKE security. In the cryptographic literature there are two leading paradigms for defining the above intuition. The first is the so-called "game-based" definition introduced by Bellare et al. [8]. Here, a password is chosen from a distribution with min-entropy κ, and the security experiment considers an interaction of an adversary with multiple instances of the PAKE protocol using that password. A PAKE protocol is considered secure if no probabilistic polynomial-time (PPT) attacker can distinguish a real session key from a random session key with advantage better than $Q \cdot 2^{-\kappa}$ plus a negligible quantity.

A second approach uses a "simulation-based" definition [10,13]. The most popular choice here is to work in the universal composability (UC) framework [12], and this is what we assume here. This approach works by first defining an appropriate ideal functionality for PAKE; a PAKE protocol is then considered secure if it realizes that functionality in the appropriate sense. Canetti et al. [13] pursued this approach, and defined a PAKE functionality that explicitly allows an adversary to make password guesses; a random session key is generated unless the adversary's password guess is correct. As argued by Canetti et al. [13], this approach has a number of advantages. A definition in the UC framework is better suited for handling general correlations between passwords, e.g., when a client uses unequal but related passwords with different servers, or when an honest party uses different but closely related passwords due to mistyping. It also ensures security under arbitrary protocol composition, which is useful for arguing security of protocols that use PAKE as a subroutine, e.g., for converting symmetric PAKE to asymmetric PAKE [15,21] or strong asymmetric PAKE [23]. This is especially important in the context of PAKE standardization, because strong asymmetric PAKE protocols can strengthen the current practice of password-over-TLS authentication while achieving optimal security against server compromise.

Is there an inherent price for simulation-based security? Simulation-based security for PAKE is a desirable target. Unfortunately, the current state-of-the-art [11,13,25,28] suggests that this notion is more difficult to satisfy than the game-based definition. In particular, the most efficient UC PAKE protocol [11] is roughly a factor of two less efficient than the most efficient game-based PAKEs[1] such as SPEKE [20,22,31], SPAKE2 [7], or TBPEKE [33].

---

[1] Variants of EKE [9] shown to be universally composable [4,11] may appear to be exceptions, but EKE requires an ideal cipher defined over a cryptographic group, and it is not clear how that can be realized efficiently.

Perhaps surprisingly, we show here that this "gap" can be overcome; in particular, we show that *the SPEKE, SPAKE2, and TBPEKE protocols—which were previously only known to be secure with respect to the game-based notion of security—can be shown to be universally composable* (in the random-oracle model). The caveat is that we prove universal composability with respect to a relaxed version of the PAKE functionality originally considered by Canetti et al. [13]. At a high level, the main distinction is that the UC PAKE functionality of Canetti et al. requires an attacker conducting an online attack against a session to make its password guess *before* that session is completed, whereas the relaxed functionality we consider—which we call *lazy-extraction PAKE* (lePAKE)—allows the attacker to delay its password guess until *after* the session completes. (However, the attacker is still limited to making a single password guess per actively attacked session.) On a technical level, this relaxed functionality is easier to realize because it allows the simulator to defer extraction of an attacker's password guess until a later point in the attacker's execution (see further discussion below). Nevertheless, the lazy-extraction PAKE functionality continues to capture the core properties expected from a PAKE protocol. In particular, as a sanity check on the proposed notion, we show that lePAKE plus key confirmation satisfies the game-based notion of PAKE with *perfect forward secrecy* (PFS) [5,6,8].

Implications for PAKE standardization. Recently, the Crypto Forum Research Group (CFRG), an IRTF (Internet Research Task Force) research group focused on applications of cryptographic mechanisms, initiated a PAKE selection process with the goal of providing recommendations for password-based authenticated key establishment for the IETF. Originally, four candidates were under consideration by the CRFG in the symmetric PAKE category; the final decision was between SPAKE2 and CPace, and the latter was ultimately selected. Our results validate the security of SPAKE2 and the proof we provide for TBPEKE will be adapted to cover CPace and included in the full version [2].

1.1   Technical Overview

The fundamental reason for an efficiency gap between known protocols achieving game-based PAKE and simulation-based PAKE is that the UC PAKE functionality, as defined by Canetti et al. [13] and used in all subsequent work, requires the adversary's password guesses to be (straight-line) *extractable* from the adversary's messages to the honest parties. Recall that for a PAKE to be UC secure there must exist an efficient simulator which simulates PAKE protocol instances given access to the ideal PAKE functionality, which in particular requires the simulator to specify a unique explicit password guess for each PAKE instance which the real-world adversary actively attacks. (The ideal PAKE functionality then allows the simulator, and hence the real-world adversary, to control the session key output by this instance *if* the provided password guess matched the password used by that PAKE instance, and otherwise the session key is random and thus secure.) The fact that the simulator must specify this explicit password before the attacked PAKE instance terminates, requires the simulator to online extract the password guess committed to in adversary's messages. Moreover, this extraction must be performed straight-line, because universal composibility prohibits rewinding the adversary.

Unfortunately, online extraction cannot be done for many efficient game-based PAKE's listed above, because in these protocols each party sends a single protocol message which forms a *perfectly hiding* commitment to the password. Specifically, if g generates group of prime order p then in SPAKE2 each party sends a message of the form $X = g^z \cdot P_i{}^{pw}$ where $z \leftarrow_R \mathbb{Z}_p$, P_1, P_2 are random group elements in the CRS, and $i = 1$ or 2 depending on the party's role. In TBPEKE, this message has the form $X = (P_1 \cdot P_2^{H(pw)})^z$, and in SPEKE it is $X = H(pw)^z$ where H is a hash onto the group. These commitments are binding under the discrete logarithm hardness assumption (the first two are variants of the Pedersen commitment [32] and the third one requires the random-oracle model), and they are equivocable, i.e., the simulator can "cheat" on messages sent on behalf of the honest parties, but they are perfectly hiding and thus not extractable. These commitments can be replaced with extractable ones, but it is not clear how to do so without increasing protocol costs (or resorting to ideal ciphers over a group).

PAKE with post-execution input extraction. However, in all the above schemes the final session key is computed by hashing the protocol transcript and the Diffie-Hellman key established by this PAKE interaction, e.g. $Z = g^{z_1 \cdot z_2}$ in SPAKE2 or $Z = (H(pw))^{z_1 \cdot z_2}$ in SPEKE. Since this final hash is modeled as a random oracle (RO), an adversary who learns any information on the session key must query this RO hash on the proper input. If the information in this hash query suffices for the simulator to identify the unique password to which this query corresponds, then a protocol message *together with the final hash inputs* do form an extractable commitment to the unique password guess the adversary makes on the attacked session.

However, the hash used in the final session key derivation is a local computation each party does in a "post-processing" stage which can be executed after the counterpart terminates the protocol. Therefore a simulator which extracts a password guess from the adversary's protocol message(s) and this local hash computation might extract it after the attacked session terminates. By the rules of the PAKE functionality of Canetti et al. [13], such extraction would happen too late, because the PAKE functionality allows the simulator to test a password guess against a session but does so only when this session is still active (and has not been attacked previously e.g. on a different password guess). Indeed, it would seem counter-intuitive to allow the ideal-world adversary, i.e., the simulator, to provide the unique effective password guess *after* the attacked session completes. Nevertheless, this is exactly how we propose to relax the UC PAKE functionality in order to accommodate protocols where input-extraction is possible, but succeeds only from the adversary's post-processing computation.

The relaxation we propose, the *lazy-extraction* PAKE, will require the ideal-world adversary to "interrupt" a fresh session while it is active in order to then perform the post-execution password test (we will call such tests "late" password tests). This models the UC PAKE requirement that an adversary can use an honest PAKE session as a password-testing oracle only if it actively attacks that session, and in particular it still holds that passively observed sessions do not provide any avenue for an attack. (To keep the new elements of the lazy-extraction PAKE model clear we use separate terms, resp. RegisterTest and LateTestPwd, for this new type of online session interruption and for the late password test, see Sect. 2.) Moreover, even if the adversary chooses this "lazy-extraction attack" route, the functionality still allows for only a *single* password test on an actively attacked session. This requirement effectively commits a (computationally bounded) real-world adversary to a unique password guess on each actively attacked session, because an adversary who performs the local computation related to more than one password test would not be simulatable in the model where the ideal-world adversary can submit at most one such test to the lazy-extraction PAKE functionality.

Explicit authentication and perfect forward security. To test the proposed lazy-extraction UC PAKE notion we show two further things. First, we show that any lazy-extraction UC PAKE followed by a key confirmation round upgrades lazy-extraction UC PAKE to PAKE with explicit (mutual) authentication (PAKE-EA) [17], but it also realizes a stronger variant of lazy-extraction PAKE functionality which we call the *relaxed* UC PAKE. In the relaxed PAKE model, the adversary can still make a (single) late password test on an actively attacked session but such sessions are guaranteed to terminate with an abort. Hence, the attacker cannot use a late password test to compromise a session. Intuitively, if a lazy-extraction PAKE is followed by a key confirmation and the attacker delays its late password test until after the key confirmation is sent, then the key confirmation must fail and its counterpart will abort on such session. Hence, the "late password test" reveals if the tested passworded was correct but it cannot reveal a key of an active session.

Secondly, we show that any relaxed UC PAKE satisfies the game-based notion of PAKE with perfect forward secrecy (PFS) [5,6,8]. (A similar test was done by Canetti et al. with regard to the original UC PAKE notion [13].) Intuitively, since the lazy-extraction attack avenue against a relaxed PAKE cannot be used to compromise keys of any active session, it follows that all active sessions, i.e., all sessions which terminate with a session key as opposed to an abort, are as secure in the relaxed UC PAKE model as they are in the original UC PAKE model of Canetti et al. In particular, they are secure against future password compromise.

Related and concurrent work. Jarecki et al. [24] recently introduced the relaxed UC PAKE model in the context of the *asymmetric* PAKE (aPAKE) functionality [15], and showed that this relaxation is necessary to prove security of the OPAQUE protocol proposed in [23]. As discussed above, the lazy-extraction PAKE model goes further than the relaxed PAKE model, and this further relaxation appears to be necessary in order to model protocols like SPEKE, SPAKE2, and TBPEKE as universally composable PAKEs. (See Section 2 for the precise specifications of the lazy-extraction PAKE and the relaxed PAKE models.)

Hasse and Labrique [18] have recently argued that CPace [19] realizes a variant of the lazy-extraction UC PAKE functionality, but the variant of this notion they consider seems unsatisfactory, e.g. it appears not to imply security of passively observed sessions, and it appears to be not realizable as stated (see Sect. 2 for discussion). They also argue that adding a key-confirmation step suffices to convert such protocol into a standard UC PAKE, while we show that the result is still only a *relaxed* UC PAKE.[2]

In concurrent work, Shoup [34] analyzes the UC security of two variants of SPAKE2 in the symmetric (PAKE) and asymmetric (aPAKE) settings. Both variants include built-in key confirmation and the protocol flows are simplified so that only the initiator uses the password for *blinding* its first message. Shoup shows these protocols UC secure with respect to revised ideal functionalities for PAKE and aPAKE, under a slightly weaker assumption than the one required by our modular proof, namely strong Diffie-Hellman [3] instead of Gap CDH. (Strong DH is a variant of Gap CDH where the DDH oracle can be queried on triples whose first element is fixed.) The revised UC PAKE functionality considered in [34] appears equivalent to the relaxed UC PAKE functionality which we show is realized by SPAKE2 with key confirmation.

1.2 Publication Note

The work of Abdalla and Barbosa [1], which provides a game-based security analysis of SPAKE2, has been merged with the current paper. However, since the focus of the present work is on the UC security analysis of practical PAKE schemes, we omit specific game-based security analyses of SPAKE2 here and refer the reader to [1] for these analyses.

1.3 Paper Overview

In Sect. 2, we introduce the two relaxations of the UC PAKE functionality, namely the lazy-extraction UC PAKE and relaxed UC PAKE functionalities, respectively abbreviated as lePAKE and rPAKE, together with the extension of the latter to explicit (mutual) authentication. In Sect. 3, we show that SPAKE2 scheme of [7] is a secure lePAKE under the Gap CDH assumption. In Sect. 4, we show that any lePAKE protocol followed by a key confirmation round is a secure rPAKE-EA, i.e., rPAKE with explicit authentication. In Sect. 5, we show that every rPAKE-EA protocol satisfies the game-based notion of PAKE with perfect forward secrecy, and that every lePAKE protocol by itself already satisfies weak forward secrecy. In Sect. 6, we also include the proof that TBPEKE [33] is a secure lePAKE protocol under appropriate assumptions, and we explain that this proof extends to similar results regarding SPEKE [20,22,31] and other variants of TBPEKE.

---

[2] In [18] this is explicitly claimed not for CPace itself but for its asymmetric (aPAKE) version called AuCPace.

2   Relaxations of UC PAKE

In Fig. 1, we present the PAKE functionality as defined by Canetti et al. [13], and compare it with two relaxations that we refer to as *relaxed PAKE* (rPAKE) and *lazy-extraction PAKE* (lePAKE). We explain at a high level the differences between these various formulations. In the original PAKE functionality $\mathcal{F}_{\mathsf{PAKE}}$, after a party initiates a session (but before the party generates a key) the attacker may try to guess the password used in that session by making a single TestPwd query. If the attacker's password guess is correct, the session is marked compromised; if not, the session is marked interrupted. When a session key is later generated for that session, the attacker is given the ability to choose the key if the session is marked compromised, but a random key is chosen otherwise. Importantly, the attacker is only allowed to make a password guess for a session *before* the key is generated and the session terminates.

In both the relaxed PAKE functionality $\mathcal{F}_{\mathsf{rPAKE}}$ and the lazy-extraction PAKE functionality $\mathcal{F}_{\mathsf{lePAKE}}$, the attacker is given the ability to make a password guess for a session even *after* a session key is generated and that session has completed. Formally, this is allowed only if the attacker makes a RegisterTest query before the session key is generated; this indicates the attacker's intention to (possibly) make a password guess later, and models active interference with a real-world protocol execution. (Of course, the attacker also has the option of making a password guess before a key is generated as in the original $\mathcal{F}_{\mathsf{PAKE}}$.) Having made a RegisterTest query for a session, the attacker may then make a LateTestPwd query to that session after the session key K is generated. $\mathcal{F}_{\mathsf{rPAKE}}$ and $\mathcal{F}_{\mathsf{lePAKE}}$ differ in what happens next:

First, in $\mathcal{F}_{\mathsf{rPAKE}}$, the attacker is only told whether or not its password guess is correct, but learns nothing about K in either case. Secondly, in $\mathcal{F}_{\mathsf{lePAKE}}$, the attacker is given K if its password guess is correct, and given a random key otherwise.[3]

It is easy to see that both $\mathcal{F}_{\mathsf{rPAKE}}$ and $\mathcal{F}_{\mathsf{lePAKE}}$ are relaxations of $\mathcal{F}_{\mathsf{PAKE}}$, in the sense that any protocol realizing $\mathcal{F}_{\mathsf{PAKE}}$ also realizes $\mathcal{F}_{\mathsf{rPAKE}}$ and $\mathcal{F}_{\mathsf{lePAKE}}$. Although, as defined, $\mathcal{F}_{\mathsf{lePAKE}}$ and $\mathcal{F}_{\mathsf{rPAKE}}$ are incomparable, the version of $\mathcal{F}_{\mathsf{lePAKE}}$ in which the attacker is additionally notified whether its password guess is correct (cf. Footnote (See Footnote 3)) is a strict relaxation of $\mathcal{F}_{\mathsf{rPAKE}}$.

Following the work of Groce and Katz [17], we also consider PAKE functionalities that incorporate explicit (mutual) authentication, which we refer to as PAKE-EA.[4] Intuitively, in a PAKE-EA protocol a party should abort if it did not establish a matching session key with its intended partner. As in the case of PAKE, the original PAKE-EA functionality introduced by Groce and

---

[3] Note that here the attacker is not explicitly notified whether its password guess is correct. While it is arguably more natural to notify the attacker, we obtain a slightly stronger functionality by omitting this notification. .

[4] Although Canetti et al. [13] informally suggest a way of modeling explicit authentication in PAKE, the functionality they propose seems unacceptably weak in the sense that it does not require a party to abort even when an attacker successfully interferes with its partner's session.

<u>Session initiation</u>

On (NewSession, $sid, \mathcal{P}, \mathcal{P}', pw$, role) from $\mathcal{P}$, ignore this query if record $\langle sid, \mathcal{P}, \cdot, \cdot, \cdot \rangle$ already exists. Otherwise record $\langle sid, \mathcal{P}, \mathcal{P}', pw$, role$\rangle$ marked **fresh** and send (NewSession, $sid, \mathcal{P}, \mathcal{P}'$, role) to $\mathcal{A}$.

<u>Active attack</u>

- On (TestPwd, $sid, \mathcal{P}, pw^*$) from $\mathcal{A}$, if $\exists$ a **fresh** record $\langle sid, \mathcal{P}, \mathcal{P}', pw, \cdot \rangle$ then:
  - If $pw^* = pw$ then mark it **compromised** and return "correct guess";
  - If $pw^* \neq pw$ then mark it **interrupted** and return "wrong guess".
- On (RegisterTest, $sid, \mathcal{P}$) from $\mathcal{A}$, if $\exists$ a **fresh** record $\langle sid, \mathcal{P}, \mathcal{P}', \cdot, \cdot \rangle$ then mark it **interrupted** and flag it **tested**.
- On (LateTestPwd, $sid, \mathcal{P}, pw^*$) from $\mathcal{A}$, if $\exists$ a record $\langle sid, \mathcal{P}, \mathcal{P}', pw, \cdot, K \rangle$ marked **completed** with flag **tested** then remove this flag and do:
  - If $pw^* = pw$ then return $\boxed{K}$ "correct guess" to $\mathcal{A}$;
  - If $pw^* \neq pw$ then return $\boxed{K^\$ \leftarrow_R \{0,1\}^\kappa}$ "wrong guess" to $\mathcal{A}$.

<u>Key generation</u>

On (NewKey, $sid, \mathcal{P}, K^*$) from $\mathcal{A}$, if $\exists$ a record $\langle sid, \mathcal{P}, \mathcal{P}', pw$, role$\rangle$ not marked **completed** then do:

- If the record is **compromised**, or either $\mathcal{P}$ or $\mathcal{P}'$ is corrupted, then set $K := K^*$.
- If the record is **fresh** and $\exists$ a **completed** record $\langle sid, \mathcal{P}', \mathcal{P}, pw$, role$', K' \rangle$ with role$' \neq$ role that was **fresh** when $\mathcal{P}'$ output (sid, K'), then set $K := K'$.
- In all other cases pick $K \leftarrow_R \{0,1\}^\kappa$.

Finally, append K to record $\langle sid, \mathcal{P}, \mathcal{P}', pw$, role$\rangle$, mark it **completed**, and output (sid, K) to $\mathcal{P}$.

Fig. 1. UC PAKE variants: The original PAKE functionality $\mathcal{F}_{\mathsf{PAKE}}$ of Canetti et al. [13] is the version with all gray text omitted. The relaxed PAKE functionality $\mathcal{F}_{\mathsf{rPAKE}}$ includes the gray text but omits the boxed portions; the lazy-extraction PAKE functionality $\mathcal{F}_{\mathsf{lePAKE}}$ includes the gray text but omits the dashed portions.

Session initiation

On (NewSession, $sid, \mathcal{P}, \mathcal{P}', pw, \mathsf{role}$) from $\mathcal{P}$, ignore this query if record $\langle sid, \mathcal{P}, \cdot, \cdot, \cdot \rangle$ already exists. Otherwise record $\langle sid, \mathcal{P}, \mathcal{P}', pw, \mathsf{role} \rangle$ marked **fresh** and send (NewSession, $sid, \mathcal{P}, \mathcal{P}', \mathsf{role}$) to $\mathcal{A}$.

Active attack

- On (TestPwd, $sid, \mathcal{P}, pw^*$) from $\mathcal{A}$, if $\exists$ a **fresh** record $\langle sid, \mathcal{P}, \mathcal{P}', pw, \cdot \rangle$ then:
  - If $pw^* = pw$ then mark it **compromised** and return "correct guess";
  - If $pw^* \neq pw$ then mark it **interrupted** and return "wrong guess".
- On (RegisterTest, $sid, \mathcal{P}$) from $\mathcal{A}$, if $\exists$ a **fresh** record $\langle sid, \mathcal{P}, \mathcal{P}', \cdot, \cdot \rangle$ then mark it **interrupted** and flag it **tested**.
- On (LateTestPwd, $sid, \mathcal{P}, pw^*$) from $\mathcal{A}$, if $\exists$ a record $\langle sid, \mathcal{P}, \mathcal{P}', pw, \cdot, K \rangle$ marked **completed** with flag **tested** then remove this flag and do:
  - If $pw^* = pw$ then return "correct guess" to $\mathcal{A}$.
  - If $pw^* \neq pw$ then return "wrong guess" to $\mathcal{A}$.

Key generation and explicit authentication

- On (GetReady, $sid, \mathcal{P}$) from $\mathcal{A}$, if $\exists$ a record $\langle sid, \mathcal{P}, \mathcal{P}', pw, \mathsf{role} \rangle$ marked **fresh** then re-label it **ready**.
- On (NewKey, $sid, \mathcal{P}, K^*$) from $\mathcal{A}$, if $\exists$ a record $\langle sid, \mathcal{P}, \mathcal{P}', pw, \mathsf{role} \rangle$ not marked **completed** then do:
  - If the record is **compromised**, or $\mathcal{P}$ or $\mathcal{P}'$ is corrupted, or $K^* = \bot$, then set $K := K^*$.
  - Else, if the record is **fresh** or **ready**, and $\exists$ a record $\langle sid, \mathcal{P}', \mathcal{P}, pw, \mathsf{role}' \rangle$ marked **ready** s.t. $\mathsf{role}' \neq \mathsf{role}$ then pick $K \leftarrow_{\mathrm{R}} \{0,1\}^\kappa$.
  - Else, if the record is **ready** and $\exists$ a **completed** record $\langle sid, \mathcal{P}', \mathcal{P}, pw, \mathsf{role}', K' \rangle$ with $\mathsf{role}' \neq \mathsf{role}$ that was **fresh** when $\mathcal{P}'$ output (sid, K'), then set $K := K'$.
  - In all other cases, set $K := \bot$.

  Finally, append K to record $\langle sid, \mathcal{P}, \mathcal{P}', pw, \mathsf{role} \rangle$, mark it **completed**, and output (sid, K) to $\mathcal{P}$.

Fig. 2. The $\mathcal{F}_{\mathsf{rPAKE\text{-}EA}}$ functionality for relaxed PAKE-EA. The original PAKE-EA of Groce and Katz [17] corresponds to the version with gray text omitted. The boxed text highlights the differences from $\mathcal{F}_{\mathsf{rPAKE}}$.

Katz required the attacker to make its password guess before the session key is generated, while we introduce a relaxed version of the PAKE-EA functionality, denoted $\mathcal{F}_{\mathsf{rPAKE\text{-}EA}}$ and shown in Fig. 2, that allows the attacker to delay its password guess until after the session has completed.[5] If the attacker's guess is correct, it is notified of that fact; our relaxation thus parallels that of $\mathcal{F}_{\mathsf{rPAKE}}$. Note that such late password guess can only be performed on aborted sessions, since the attacker must send a RegisterTest query before the session completes, which marks the session interrupted, and by the rule of explicit authentication, an interrupted session must result in aborting.

Besides the intuitive appeal of our relaxed definitions, we justify these relaxations by showing that it is easy to realize $\mathcal{F}_{\mathsf{rPAKE\text{-}EA}}$ in the $\mathcal{F}_{\mathsf{lePAKE}}$-hybrid world (Sect. 4), that any protocol realizing $\mathcal{F}_{\mathsf{rPAKE}}$ satisfies perfect forward secrecy (Sect. 5), and that any protocol realizing $\mathcal{F}_{\mathsf{lePAKE}}$ satisfies weak forward secrecy (Sect. 5.3).

Note on the relaxed PAKE functionality used in [18]. A preliminary version of the lazy-extraction PAKE functionality, referred as "relaxed PAKE" therein, appeared in an early version of [24] and was adopted by [18] as a model for the CPace protocol. This version was imprecise in several respects: First, it does not require the adversary to explicitly attack an online session via a RegisterTest query before issuing a LateTestPwd query on a completed session. This appears too weak, e.g. because it allows an adversary to issue LateTestPwd queries even on passively observed sessions. On the other hand, it restricts the adversary from making a LateTestPwd query upon completion of the matching counterpart's session (with a matching sid but not necessarily a matching password), which appears too strong, because a man-in-the-middle attacker can make $\mathcal{P}'$ complete with a random key or an abort, and this does not affect its capabilities regarding party $\mathcal{P}$. Our lazy-extraction PAKE functionality makes this notion more precise, and in Sect. 6 we show that TBPEKE [33] and SPEKE [22] realize the lePAKE fuctionality under (Gap) CDH and/or SDH assumptions. Since CPace [18,19] is a close variant of SPEKE, these results can be extended to cover CPace as well.[6]

---

[5] While relaxing the Groce-Katz functionality, we also make some minor changes to their original: (1) we make the parties symmetric, and do not require the server to generate a session key first, and (2) we allow the adversary to force a party to abort by sending a (NewKey, sid, $\mathcal{P}$, $\bot$) message. (This second modification is required, and its omission appears to be an oversight of Groce and Katz.).

[6] In CPace [18], the key derivation hash includes only the session ID and the Diffie-Hellman key, while our proof of TBPEKE security assumes that it also includes party IDs, the password-dependent base, and the transcript. The final version of CPace selected by the CFRG has been updated to include all these elements except the password. In the full version [2], we will analyze the security of this version of CPace.

3 Security of SPAKE2

We consider SPAKE2 as a motivating example for our work. SPAKE2 was proposed by Abdalla and Pointcheval [7] and shown secure in the game-based PAKE model [8] under the CDH assumption in the random-oracle model. SPAKE2 is, to the best of our knowledge, the most efficient PAKE protocol which does not assume ideal cipher over a group. Its costs are 2 fixed-base and 1 variable-base exponentiations per party, and it is round-minimal because it can be executed in a single simultaneous round of bi-directional communication.

We show that SPAKE2 realizes the lazy-extraction UC PAKE functionality under the *Gap* CDH assumption, and the result is tight in the sense that any environment which distinguishes between the real-world execution of SPAKE2 and the ideal-world interaction with a simulator and the lazy-extraction PAKE functionality, and does so in time T with advantage ϵ, implies an attack on Gap CDH which achieves roughly the same (T, ϵ) advantage, where "roughly" means that both T and ϵ are modified by only additive factors. This UC security proof complements the result that SPAKE2 meets the game-based PFS definition [1], which was not considered in [7]. Interestingly, the game-based PFS result of [1] is not tight: The proof relies on a special assumption introduced in [7] for which a reduction to Gap CDH is known, but it is not a tight reduction. Still, since we do not know that lazy-extraction UC PAKE security implies PFS security by itself, this result is the only one we currently know for PFS security of (raw) SPAKE2.[7]

We recall the two-flow, simultaneous round SPAKE2 protocol of [7] in Fig. 3, with some notational choices adjusted to the UC setting.

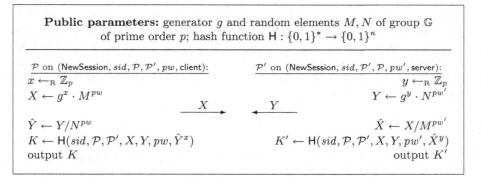

Fig. 3. SPAKE2 protocol of [7]

Theorem 1. SPAKE2 *realizes the Lazy-Extraction PAKE functionality* $\mathcal{F}_{\text{lePAKE}}$ *in the random-oracle model under the Gap-CDH assumption.*

---

[7] Note that the combined results of Sects. 3 to 5 show that SPAKE2 *followed by a key confirmation round* is PFS secure, with tight security with respect to Gap CDH.

Gap CDH and Gap DL assumptions. Recall that the Computational Diffie-Hellman (CDH) assumption states that, given generator g and two random elements $A = g^a$, and $B = g^b$ in a cyclic group of prime order, it is hard to find $C = \mathsf{DH}_g(A, B) = g^{ab}$, while the Discrete Logarithm (DL) assumption states that it is hard to find $a = \mathsf{DL}_g(A)$ given (g, A), for random A. In the gap version of either assumption, the respective problem must remain hard even if the adversary has access to a Decisional Diffie-Hellman oracle, which on any triple of group elements (A, B, C) returns 1 if $C = \mathsf{DH}_g(A, B)$ and 0 otherwise. The Gap DL assumption follows via a trivial (and tight) reduction from the Gap CDH assumption, but we introduce it to highlight the fact that certain forms of adversarial behavior in SPAKE2 imply solving the harder problem of Gap DL.

Simulator for SPAKE2. The UC simulator SIM for SPAKE2, given in full in Fig. 4, acts as the ideal adversary, with access to the ideal functionality $\mathcal{F}_{\mathsf{lePAKE}}$ (shortened to $\mathcal{F}$ in the subsequent discussion). The simulator's goal is to emulate, except for at most negligible probability, the real-world interaction between the environment $\mathcal{Z}$, a real-world adversary $\mathcal{A}$, and honest parties running the SPAKE2 protocol. Technically, SIM must simulate messages that appear to come from the real players, respond appropriately to adversarial messages, and answer random-oracle queries consistently, and to do so with access to the $\mathcal{F}$ interface, but not the secret inputs, i.e., the passwords, of the honest players.

We briefly describe how SIM simulates client $\mathcal{P}$'s interaction with an arbitrary environment $\mathcal{Z}$ and an adversary **Adv**. (The server case is similar since the protocol is symmetric.) SIM first embeds trapdoors into the CRS, i.e., it picks $m, n \leftarrow_{\mathrm{R}} \mathbb{Z}_p$ and sets $M = g^m$ and $N = g^n$. To simulate the protocol message X, SIM picks $z \leftarrow_{\mathrm{R}} \mathbb{Z}_p$ and sets $X = g^z$. Since X is also uniformly distributed in the real protocol, the environment cannot tell the difference. When $\mathcal{A}$ queries the random oracle $\mathsf{H}(sid, \mathcal{P}, \mathcal{P}', X, Y', pw, W)$, SIM decides whether it corresponds to a valid password guess: SIM first computes the exponent $\hat{x}$ such that $X = g^{\hat{x}} \cdot M^{pw}$, using the CRS trapdoor m, and then checks if $W = (Y'/N^{pw})^{\hat{x}}$. If so, then SIM stores (Y', pw). If $\mathcal{A}$ later sends a protocol message Y' aimed at $\mathcal{P}$, then this is an online attack: when $\mathcal{A}$ makes the RO query, SIM picks a random string K as the output, and stores K together with (Y', pw). Then, when $\mathcal{A}$ sends Y', SIM sends $(\mathsf{TestPwd}, sid, \mathcal{P}, pw)$ to $\mathcal{F}$, and if $\mathcal{F}$ replies "correct guess," then SIM sets $\mathcal{P}$'s key to K by sending $(\mathsf{NewKey}, sid, \mathcal{P}, K)$ to $\mathcal{F}$. (Otherwise, i.e., if $\mathcal{F}$ replies "wrong guess", SIM sends $(\mathsf{NewKey}, sid, \mathcal{P}, 0^\kappa)$ and $\mathcal{F}$ sets $\mathcal{P}$'s key to a random string). On the other hand, if $\mathcal{A}$ makes an above query to H *after* sending Y' to the client, then this is a postponed attack, so SIM sends $(\mathsf{RegisterTest}, sid, \mathcal{P})$ to $\mathcal{F}$ when $\mathcal{A}$ sends Y' for which no such query has been made yet, and later sends $(\mathsf{LateTestPwd}, sid, \mathcal{P}, pw)$ to $\mathcal{F}$ when $\mathcal{A}$ makes the above query to H. If $\mathcal{F}$ then replies with a key K (which is either correct or random, depending on whether pw is correct or not), SIM "programs" H output as K. An adversary could distinguish this emulation from a real interaction by querying H on $(sid, \mathcal{P}, \mathcal{P}', X, Y', pw_i, W_i)$ tuples for $W_i = (Y'/N^{pw_i})^{\hat{x}_i}$ and $\hat{x}_i = \mathsf{DL}(X/M^{pw_i})$ for *two* different passwords pw_i, but we show that this attack, as well as all others, can be reduced to Gap CDH.

Record keeping. For each party $\mathcal{P}$ and session *sid*, simulator SIM stores a state $\pi_{\mathcal{P}}^{sid} = (\mathsf{role}, \mathsf{exp}, \mathcal{C}, \mathcal{S}, X, Y, X^*, Y^*, \mathsf{pw}, \mathsf{guesses}, \mathsf{waiting})$ whose components are used as follows:

- Variable $\mathsf{role} \in \{\mathsf{client}, \mathsf{server}\}$ is the role of $\mathcal{P}$ in this session. (Note that in the protocol of Fig. 3 variable role is used only in the ordering of the identities in the hash H query).
- exp is the private exponent used in the network messages, x for $\mathcal{C}$ and y for $\mathcal{S}$. In the first few games, it has the same meaning as in the protocol, but for SIM it is the discrete log of the simulated network message.
- $\mathcal{C}, \mathcal{S}$ are the the party party identifiers for client and server respectively, X, Y are the simulated messages sent by resp. $\mathcal{C}$ and $\mathcal{S}$ (on sessions identified by *sid*), and X^*, Y^* are the messages the adversary sends to resp. $\mathcal{S}$ and $\mathcal{C}$. Simulator SIM stores messages X and Y^* for the client (copying Y from the server if it exists), and symmetrically it stores Y and X^* for the server (copying X from the client if it exists). Unknown values are set to $\perp$.
- pw is a password used by party $\mathcal{P}$ on session *sid*. It is used only in intermediate games, while simulator SIM always sets it to $\perp$.
- guesses is a table mapping group elements Z^* to pairs (pw, K^*), representing potential password guesses and corresponding keys, which the simulator constructs from adversary's queries to oracle H of the form $(sid, \mathcal{P}, \mathcal{P}', X, Z^*, \mathsf{pw}, \cdot)$ if $\mathcal{P}$ plays the client role, and $(sid, \mathcal{P}', \mathcal{P}, Y, Z^*, \mathsf{pw}, \cdot)$ if $\mathcal{P}$ plays the server role. If the adversary sends Z^* to party $\mathcal{P}$, the simulator looks up the corresponding password pw, which it sends to $\mathcal{F}$ as a tested password.
- waiting is a flag which is set to T for the session which has not received an adversarial message Z^*, and F otherwise. This flag is used to ensure that only the first message an adversary sends to a session is processed, and all others are ignored.

Let $\mathbf{Real}_{\mathcal{Z},\mathcal{A},\mathsf{SPAKE2}}$ be the probability of the event that environment $\mathcal{Z}$ with adversary $\mathcal{A}$ outputs 1 in the real world, and $\mathbf{Ideal}_{\mathcal{Z},\mathsf{SIM},\mathsf{SPAKE2}}$ be the corresponding probability in the ideal world. The goal is to show that $|\mathbf{Real}_{\mathcal{Z},\mathcal{A},\mathsf{SPAKE2}} - \mathbf{Ideal}_{\mathcal{Z},\mathsf{SIM},\mathsf{SPAKE2}}|$ is negligible. We use the well-known sequence-of-games proof strategy to show that we may move from the real game to the simulator in a manner indistinguishable to the environment, except for negligible probability. We begin with Game 0, the real game, and move through a series of steps, each of which we show to be indistinguishable from the previous, to the final simulator. Throughout the proof, **Gi** denotes the probability that $\mathcal{Z}$ outputs 1 while interacting with Game i.

Proof of Theorem 1.

GAME 0.   This is the real world, in which $\mathcal{A}$ interacts with real players, and may view, modify, and/or drop network messages.

$$\mathbf{Real}_{\mathcal{Z},\mathcal{A},\mathsf{SPAKE2}} = \Pr[\mathbf{G0}].$$

generate CRS
$\overline{M \leftarrow g^m; N \leftarrow g^n}$ for $(m, n) \leftarrow_R \mathbb{Z}_p$
return M, N

on (NewSession, $sid, \mathcal{P}, \mathcal{P}', role$) from $\mathcal{F}$
$\overline{\text{if } \pi_\mathcal{P}^{sid} \neq \bot : \text{return } \bot}$
$(X, Y) \leftarrow (\bot, \bot)$
if $role = $ client :
    $(\mathcal{C}, \mathcal{S}) \leftarrow (\mathcal{P}, \mathcal{P}')$
    $z \leftarrow_R \mathbb{Z}_p; X \leftarrow M^z; Z \leftarrow X$
    if $\pi_{\mathcal{P}'}^{sid} \neq \bot$ and $\pi_{\mathcal{P}'}^{sid}.role \neq$ client: $Y \leftarrow \pi_{\mathcal{P}'}^{sid}.Y; \pi_{\mathcal{P}'}^{sid}.X \leftarrow X$
else if $role = $ server :
    $(\mathcal{C}, \mathcal{S}) \leftarrow (\mathcal{P}', \mathcal{P})$
    $z \leftarrow_R \mathbb{Z}_p; Y \leftarrow N^z; Z \leftarrow Y$
    if $\pi_{\mathcal{P}'}^{sid} \neq \bot$ and $\pi_{\mathcal{P}'}^{sid}.role \neq$ server: $X \leftarrow \pi_{\mathcal{P}'}^{sid}.X; \pi_{\mathcal{P}'}^{sid}.Y \leftarrow Y$
$\pi_\mathcal{P}^{sid} \leftarrow (role, z, \mathcal{C}, \mathcal{S}, X, Y, \bot, \bot, \bot, \bot, \text{T})$
send Z from $\mathcal{P}$ to $\mathcal{A}$

on Z^* from $\mathcal{A}$ as msg to $(sid, \mathcal{P})$
$\overline{\text{if } \pi_\mathcal{P}^{sid} = \bot \text{ or } \pi_\mathcal{P}^{sid}.waiting = \text{F}: \text{return } \bot}$
$(role, \cdot, \mathcal{C}, \mathcal{S}, X, Y, \cdot, \cdot, \cdot, \text{guesses}, \cdot) \leftarrow \pi_\mathcal{P}^{sid}$
$K \leftarrow 0^\kappa$
if $role = $ client :
    $\pi_\mathcal{P}^{sid}.Y^* \leftarrow Z^*$
    if $Z^* = Y$: jump to end
else if $role = $ server :
    $\pi_\mathcal{P}^{sid}.X^* \leftarrow Z^*$
    if $Z^* = X$: jump to end
if $\pi_\mathcal{P}^{sid}.\text{guesses}[Z^*] = (pw, K^*)$:
    reply $\leftarrow$ (TestPwd, $sid, \mathcal{P}, pw$) to $\mathcal{F}$
    if reply = "correct": $K \leftarrow K^*$
else: send (RegisterTest, $sid, \mathcal{P}$) to $\mathcal{F}$
end: $\pi_\mathcal{P}^{sid}.waiting \leftarrow \text{F}$
    send (NewKey, $sid, \mathcal{P}, K$) to $\mathcal{F}$

on $\mathsf{H}(sid, \mathcal{C}, \mathcal{S}, X', Y', pw, W)$ from $\mathcal{A}$:
$\overline{\text{if } \mathsf{T}_\mathsf{H}[sid, \mathcal{C}, \mathcal{S}, X', Y', pw, W] = \bot}$:
    $K \leftarrow_R \{0, 1\}^\kappa; (\hat{x}, \hat{y}) \leftarrow (\bot, \bot)$
    if $\pi_\mathcal{C}^{sid} \neq \bot: \hat{x} \leftarrow m \cdot \pi_\mathcal{C}^{sid}.\exp - m \cdot pw$
    if $\pi_\mathcal{S}^{sid} \neq \bot: \hat{y} \leftarrow n \cdot \pi_\mathcal{S}^{sid}.\exp - n \cdot pw$
    if $\pi_\mathcal{C}^{sid}.X = X'$ and $\pi_\mathcal{S}^{sid}.Y = Y'$ and $W = g^{\hat{x}\hat{y}}$: abort
    else if $\pi_\mathcal{C}^{sid}.X = X'$ and $W = (Y'/N^{pw})^{\hat{x}}$:
        if $Y' = \pi_\mathcal{C}^{sid}.Y^*: \mathcal{P} \leftarrow \mathcal{C}$; jump to late_test_pw
        else: $\pi_\mathcal{C}^{sid}.\text{guesses}[Y'] \leftarrow (pw, K)$
    else if $\pi_\mathcal{S}^{sid}.Y = Y'$ and $W = (X'/M^{pw})^{\hat{y}}$:
        if $X' = \pi_\mathcal{S}^{sid}.X^*: \mathcal{P} \leftarrow \mathcal{S}$; jump to late_test_pw
        else: $\pi_\mathcal{S}^{sid}.\text{guesses}[X'] \leftarrow (pw, K)$
    jump to end
    late_test_pw: reply $\leftarrow$ (LateTestPwd, $sid, \mathcal{P}, pw$) to $\mathcal{F}$
                  $K \leftarrow$ reply; if no reply, abort
    end: $\mathsf{T}_\mathsf{H}[sid, \mathcal{C}, \mathcal{S}, X', Y', pw, W] \leftarrow K$
send $\mathsf{T}_\mathsf{H}[sid, \mathcal{C}, \mathcal{S}, X', Y', pw, W]$ to $\mathcal{A}$

Fig. 4. Simulator algorithm SIM for SPAKE2 security proof

GAME 1. (Simulate real world with trapdoors) We now simulate the behavior of the real players and the random oracle. The simulation is exactly as the real game, except for the inclusion of record keeping, and embedding of trapdoors in M and N, by setting $M = g^m$ and $N = g^n$ for known m and n. The embedding of trapdoors is not noticeable to the environment as M and N are still drawn from the same distribution as before, thus:

$$\Pr[\mathbf{G1}] = \Pr[\mathbf{G0}].$$

GAME 2. (Random key if adversary is passive) If the adversary passes a simulated Z message sent to $(sid, \mathcal{P})$ without modification, output a random key for $\mathcal{P}$ instead of the true random-oracle output. The environment notices this change only if $\mathcal{A}$ makes a hash query that would result in an inconsistency, namely $\mathsf{H}(sid, \mathcal{C}, \mathcal{S}, X', Y', pw, W = g^{xy})$, where $X' = g^x M^{pw}$ and $Y' = g^y N^{pw}$ are the simulated messages. We check for such queries, and abort if any occur.

We may reduce this event to Gap-CDH as follows. Let q_s be the maximum number of sessions invoked by the environment. Consider an adversary $\mathcal{B}_2$ against Gap-CDH. On generalized CDH challenge[8] $(A_1 = g^{a_1}, \cdots, A_{q_s} = g^{a_{q_s}}, B_1 = g^{b_1}, \cdots, B_{q_s} = g^{b_{q_s}})$, the reduction indexes sessions $(sid, \mathcal{P}, \mathcal{P}')$, and embeds $X_i = A_i \cdot M^{pw_i}$, $Y_i = B_i \cdot N^{pw_i}$ when generating the simulated messages for the ith session. The reduction can re-use the code of $\mathbf{G2}$, except for the cases where it requires the secret exponents a_i and b_i: (1) to generate $K \leftarrow \mathsf{H}(sid, \mathcal{C}, \mathcal{S}, X, Y, pw, \hat{Y}^{a_i}\{\text{or } \hat{X}^{b_i}\})$ and (2) to check for the "bad event" of an inconsistency in the hash response. To handle case (1), the reduction stores an additional value K for each session $(sid, \mathcal{C}, \mathcal{S})$ which is set randomly when either the reduction must handle case (1), or when $\mathcal{A}$ queries $\mathsf{H}(sid, \mathcal{C}, \mathcal{S}, X', Y', pw, W)$ such that the password is correct and $\mathsf{DDH}(X', Y', W)$ holds (checked via the DDH oracle): if either of these events happens again the same value of K is used. The check of case (2) can be done via the DDH oracle, i.e., by querying $\mathsf{DDH}(A_i, B_i, W)$: if the bad event occurs, $\mathcal{B}_2$ solves the CDH challenge with answer W. Thus:

$$|\Pr[\mathbf{G2}] - \Pr[\mathbf{G1}]| \leq \mathbf{Adv}_{\mathcal{B}_2}^{\mathsf{GCDH}}.$$

GAME 3. (Random simulated messages) On (NewSession, $sid, \mathcal{P}, \mathcal{P}'$, role), if this is the first NewSession for $(sid, \mathcal{P})$, set $Z \leftarrow g^z$ for $z \leftarrow_{\mathrm{R}} \mathbb{Z}_p$, and send Z to $\mathcal{A}$ as a message from $\mathcal{P}$ to $(\mathcal{P}', sid)$. Note that we may now compute the original exponents via: $\hat{x} = m \cdot \pi_{\mathcal{C}}^{sid}.\exp - m \cdot pw$ and $\hat{y} = n \cdot \pi_{\mathcal{S}}^{sid}.\exp - n \cdot pw$. This change is not observable to the environment, as it is merely a syntactic change in the calculation of the exponents:

$$\Pr[\mathbf{G3}] = \Pr[\mathbf{G2}].$$

GAME 4. (Random keys if adversary does not correctly guess password) We now detect when an adversarial hash query corresponds to a password guess. We can detect this event by inspecting the X', Y', pw and W values provided to the hash

---

[8] The generalized CDH problem is tightly equivalent to the CDH problem by random self-reducibility.

oracle. Let us assume the adversary is guessing the client's password (the server case is symmetric). To make a password guess against the client, the adversary must set $X' = \pi_{\mathcal{C}}^{sid}.X$, i.e., use the simulated message sent by the client. The adversary can use any choice of Y', but to correspond with a specific password guess, the following must hold: $W = (Y'/N^{pw})^{\hat{x}}$ (where $\hat{x}$ is the exponent such that $\pi_{\mathcal{C}}^{sid}.X = g^{\hat{x}}M^{pw}$). In other words, W must be the value that would be used by a real client if Y' were sent as the server's message. If such a password guess query is detected, we check if Y' was previously sent as an adversarial message on behalf of the server: if so, and if the password guess is correct, we program the random oracle to match the previously sent key. If Y' was not previously sent, we note the values Y', pw queried by the adversary and the random key K output by the RO. If Y' is later sent as the adversarial message, and the password is correct, we output the stored key K. If the password is incorrect, we output a random key independent of the RO table. If at any point a second password guess (correct or incorrect) is detected for the same sid and party, we abort the game.

This change is noticeable to the environment only in the abort case, i.e, the case where the adversary makes two password guesses with a single (X', Y') transcript, i.e.:

$$\mathsf{H}(sid, \mathcal{P}, \mathcal{P}', X', Y', pw, Z) \text{ and } \mathsf{H}(sid, \mathcal{P}, \mathcal{P}', X', Y', pw', Z'),$$

such that $pw \neq pw'$, and

$$\mathsf{CDH}(g^{mx}/M^{pw}, g^{ny}/N^{pw}) = Z \text{ and } \mathsf{CDH}(g^{mx}/M^{pw'}, g^{ny}/N^{pw'}) = Z'.$$

Call this event bad_4. It can be split into two cases: 1) for one of the passwords $pw^* \in \{pw, pw'\}$ it holds that $X' = M^{pw^*}$ or $Y' = N^{pw^*}$, i.e., there is a collision between the guessed password pw^* and the secret exponent x or y or 2) there is no such collision. Case 2, which we denote bad_4^1, can be reduced to Gap-CDH, as shown in Lemma 1. Case 1 can be reduced to Gap-DL as follows: Adversary $\mathcal{B}_{4.2}$ on Gap DL challenge $A = g^a$, sets simulated messages as: $X_i = A \cdot g^{\Delta_{i,x}}$ and $Y_i = A \cdot g^{\Delta_{i,y}}$, picking a fresh random $\Delta_{i,x}$ and $\Delta_{i,y}$ for each session $(sid, \mathcal{P}, \mathcal{P}')$. In the ith session (for every i), $\mathcal{B}_{4.2}$ uses the DDH oracle to check for bad_4. If true, $\mathcal{B}_{4.2}$ further checks if $Y' = N^{pw^*}$ or $X' = M^{pw^*}$ for one of the passwords: in the former case this means that $Y' = N^{pw} = A \cdot g^{\Delta_{i,y}}$, so $npw = a + \Delta_{i,y}$, and $\mathcal{B}_{4.2}$ can output the DL solution is $a = npw/\Delta_{i,y}$, and the latter case is symmetric. We have that

$$|\Pr[\mathbf{G4}] - \Pr[\mathbf{G3}]| \leq \mathbf{Adv}_{\mathcal{B}_{4.1}}^{\mathsf{GDL}} + \mathbf{Adv}_{\mathcal{B}_{4.2}}^{\mathsf{GCDH}}.$$

GAME 5. (Use $\mathcal{F}_{\mathsf{lePAKE}}$ interface) In the final game, we modify the challenger so that it uses the RegisterTest, TestPwd and LateTestPwd interfaces to check passwords, and the NewKey interface to set keys. This is an internal change that is not noticeable to the environment, thus

$$\Pr[\mathbf{G5}] = \Pr[\mathbf{G4}].$$

In addition, this simulator perfectly mimics the ideal world except for the cases where it aborts, which we have already shown to happen with negligible probability, so:

$$\mathbf{Ideal}_{\mathcal{Z},\mathsf{SIM},\mathsf{SPAKE2}} = \Pr[\mathbf{G5}].$$

Thus the distinguishing advantage of $\mathcal{Z}$ between the real world and the ideal world is:

$$|\mathbf{Ideal}_{\mathcal{Z},\mathsf{SIM},\mathsf{SPAKE2}} - \mathbf{Real}_{\mathcal{Z},\mathcal{A},\mathsf{SPAKE2}}| \leq \mathbf{Adv}_{\mathcal{B}_2}^{\mathsf{GCDH}} + \mathbf{Adv}_{\mathcal{B}_{4.1}}^{\mathsf{GDL}} + \mathbf{Adv}_{\mathcal{B}_{4.2}}^{\mathsf{GCDH}},$$

which is negligible if Gap-CDH is hard.

□

Lemma 1. *For every attacker $\mathcal{A}$, there exists an attacker $\mathcal{B}_{4.1}$ (whose running time is linear in the running time of $\mathcal{A}$) such that:*

$$\Pr[\mathbf{G4} \to bad_4^1] \leq \mathbf{Adv}_{\mathcal{B}_{4.1}}^{\mathsf{GCDH}}$$

Proof. Consider an attacker $\mathcal{B}_{4.1}$ against GCDH. It receives a challenge ($M = g^m, N = g^n$) and wants to find $\mathsf{CDH}(M, N) = g^{mn}$. The attacker emulates **G4**, except for setting the CRS values as M, N from the challenge instead of randomly. It uses the DDH oracle to carry out the three checks in the if/else if/else if structure of the hash response, and for detecting the bad event.

In particular, it detects the bad event bad_4^1 when it sees two hash queries (sid, X', Y', pw, Z) and (sid, X', Y', pw', Z') such that $pw \neq pw'$, and both of the following hold, where either x or y is known (i.e, chosen by the attacker as the exponent for a simulated message):

$$\mathsf{CDH}(g^{mx}/M^{pw}, g^{ny}/N^{pw}) = Z \tag{1}$$

$$\mathsf{CDH}(g^{mx}/M^{pw'}, g^{ny}/N^{pw'}) = Z' \tag{2}$$

The attacker can then solve for the CDH response, g^{nm}, as follows.

First, write $Z = g^z; Z' = g^{z'}$ for unknown $z, z' \in \mathbb{Z}_p$. Considering only the exponents in Eqs. (1) and (2), we have that:

$$m(x - pw) \cdot n(y - pw) = z \tag{3}$$

$$m(x - pw') \cdot n(y - pw') = z' \tag{4}$$

Assume that the attacker knows the exponent x (the other case is symmetric). Scaling Eqs. (3) and (4) by resp. $(x - pw')$ and $(x - pw)$, gives:

$$m(x - pw')(x - pw) \cdot n(y - pw) = z \cdot (x - pw') \tag{5}$$

$$m(x - pw)(x - pw') \cdot n(y - pw') = z' \cdot (x - pw) \tag{6}$$

Subtracting Eq. (6) from Eq. (5) allows us to remove the unknown y term:

$$mn(x - pw)(x - pw')(pw' - pw) = z \cdot (x - pw') - z' \cdot (x - pw) \tag{7}$$

Finally, we may solve for the desired CDH value:

$$g^{mn} = \left(Z^{(x-pw')} \cdot Z'^{(pw-x)} \right)^{1/(x-pw)(x-pw')(pw-pw')}$$

This is possible as long as we are not dividing by zero, i.e., if $pw \neq x$ and $pw' \neq x$, which is explicitly excluded in the definition of event bad_4^1 (see Case 1 of **G4** for handling of this case).   □

Remark on Gap CDH. The proof relies on the gap version of CDH, and it seems hard to prove security from the standard CDH assumption, because the Decision Diffie-Hellman oracle is used by CDH reductions to maintain consistency of answers to RO queries, and it is not clear how to ensure this consistency otherwise. This is also the case in the all the other PAKE protocols we consider in Sect. 6.

4   Adding Explicit Authentication

We will show that any protocol that securely realizes the lazy-extraction UC PAKE functionality $\mathcal{F}_{\mathsf{lePAKE}}$, followed by a key confirmation round, is a secure realization of the relaxed UC PAKE-EA functionality $\mathcal{F}_{\mathsf{rPAKE\text{-}EA}}$. (See Section 2 for the definition of these functionalities.) This protocol compiler construction is shown in Fig. 5.

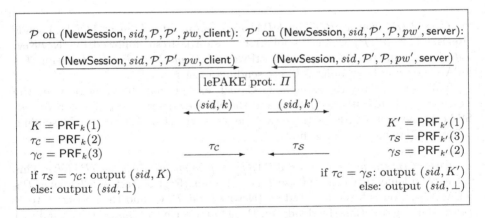

Fig. 5. Compiler from lePAKE protocol Π to rPAKE-EA protocol Π'.

Theorem 2. *Protocol Π' shown in Fig. 5 realizes the Relaxed PAKE-EA functionality $\mathcal{F}_{\mathsf{rPAKE\text{-}EA}}$ if Π realizes the Lazy-Extraction PAKE functionality $\mathcal{F}_{\mathsf{lePAKE}}$ and PRF is a secure PRF.*

Figure 6 shows the simulator used in the proof of Theorem 2. (For notational simplicity, we denote the functionality $\mathcal{F}_{\mathsf{rPAKE\text{-}EA}}$ as simply $\mathcal{F}$.) For the formal proof of this theorem we refer to the full version of this paper [2], but here we provide an informal overview.

The proof is essentially a case-by-case argument, where all possible scenarios are divided into several cases, according to whether $\mathcal{A}$ performs an online attack on party $\mathcal{P}$'s rPAKE session, and if so, whether it is an online attack or a postponed attack on $\mathcal{P}$'s lePAKE session.[9] Below we describe the cases, and how each case can be simulated:

Case 1 (online attack on lePAKE → online attack on rPAKE): $\mathcal{A}$ sends (TestPwd, $sid, \mathcal{P}, pw^*$) to $\mathcal{F}_{\mathsf{lePAKE}}$ when $\mathcal{P}$'s lePAKE session is fresh.

In this case SIM passes (TestPwd, $sid, \mathcal{P}, pw^*$) to $\mathcal{F}$. If $\mathcal{F}$ replies with "correct guess", i.e., $pw^* = pw$, then $\mathcal{P}$'s rPAKE session is compromised, so SIM can set its rPAKE output. Now on (NewKey, sid, k^*) from $\mathcal{A}$, SIM can compute (K, τ, γ) from $k = k^*$ as the real-world session would, and send τ to $\mathcal{A}$; on a tag τ^* from $\mathcal{A}$, SIM lets $\mathcal{P}$ output K if $\tau^* = \gamma$ and $\perp$ otherwise, matching the real-world execution.

On the other hand, if $\mathcal{F}$ replies with "wrong guess", i.e., $pw^* \neq pw$, then $\mathcal{P}$'s rPAKE session is interrupted, hence $\mathcal{P}$'s rPAKE output is $\perp$. SIM simply computes (K, τ, γ) from a random k and sends τ to $\mathcal{A}$. This again matches the real-world execution with overwhelming probability: $\mathcal{P}$'s rPAKE output is $\perp$ unless $\tau^* = \gamma$, which happens with negligible probability, and τ is computed in the exact same way.

Case 2 (postponed attack on lePAKE → online attack on rPAKE): $\mathcal{A}$ sends (RegisterTest, $sid, \mathcal{P}$) when $\mathcal{P}$'s lePAKE session is fresh, followed by (NewKey, $sid, \mathcal{P}, k^*$); and then sends (LateTestPwd, $sid, \mathcal{P}, pw^*$) to $\mathcal{F}_{\mathsf{lePAKE}}$ (causing $\mathcal{P}$'s lePAKE session to complete) *before* sending a tag τ^* to $\mathcal{P}$.

This is essentially the same as in Case 1, except that the order between the TestPwd (or LateTestPwd) queries and the NewKey query to $\mathcal{F}_{\mathsf{lePAKE}}$ is reversed. SIM can reverse the order of these two queries on the rPAKE level too, by sending a RegisterTest message to $\mathcal{F}$ first.

Case 3 (postponed attack on lePAKE → postponed attack on rPAKE): This is the complementary case of Case 2, i.e., $\mathcal{A}$ sends (RegisterTest, $sid, \mathcal{P}$) when $\mathcal{P}$'s lePAKE session is fresh, followed by (NewKey, $sid, \mathcal{P}, \star$); and then a tag τ^* to $\mathcal{P}$ *before* sending any (LateTestPwd, $sid, \mathcal{P}, pw^*$) message to $\mathcal{F}_{\mathsf{lePAKE}}$. (Eventually $\mathcal{A}$ may or may not send LateTestPwd.)

Again, in the real world $\mathcal{P}$'s rPAKE output is $\perp$ unless $\tau^* = \gamma$, which happens with negligible probability, so SIM can simply let $\mathcal{P}$ output $\perp$. However, if $pw^* =$

---

[9] Note that each rPAKE session runs a lePAKE session as a subprotocol, and these two sessions should not be confused. Similarly, each party has a lePAKE output (which is always a string) and an rPAKE output (which is either a string derived from its lePAKE output or $\perp$).

pw, $\mathcal{A}$ learns $\mathcal{P}$'s lePAKE output k (and thus can check if tag τ is the "correct" one, i.e., τ is derived from k using PRF). This can be simulated as follows: on NewKey from $\mathcal{A}$, SIM computes (K, τ, γ) from a random k and sends τ to $\mathcal{A}$; on τ^* from $\mathcal{A}$, SIM sends RegisterTest to $\mathcal{F}$; on (LateTestPwd, $sid, \mathcal{P}, pw^*$) from $\mathcal{A}$, SIM passes this message to $\mathcal{F}$, and if $\mathcal{F}$ replies with "correct guess", then SIM sends k to $\mathcal{A}$, making τ the "correct" tag. (If $\mathcal{F}$ replies with "wrong guess", then SIM sends a fresh random key to $\mathcal{A}$.)

Case 4 (no attack on lePAKE): $\mathcal{A}$ sends neither a (TestPwd, $sid, \mathcal{P}, \star$) nor a (RegisterTest, $sid, \mathcal{P}$) query to $\mathcal{F}_{\mathsf{lePAKE}}$ when $\mathcal{P}$'s lePAKE session is fresh (thus $\mathcal{P}$'s lePAKE session remains fresh until it becomes completed).

In this case, $\mathcal{A}$ never learns $\mathcal{P}$'s lePAKE output k, so SIM can send a random tag τ to $\mathcal{A}$. If $\mathcal{A}$ merely passes the tags between $\mathcal{P}$ and $\mathcal{P}'$, then SIM lets $\mathcal{P}$ complete its rPAKE session by sending (GetReady, $sid, \mathcal{P}$) and then (NewKey, $sid, \mathcal{P}, 0^\kappa$) to $\mathcal{F}$; if $\mathcal{P}$ and $\mathcal{P}'$'s passwords match, then $\mathcal{P}$ outputs a random K, otherwise $\mathcal{P}$ outputs $\perp$. On the other hand, if $\mathcal{A}$ modifies the tag from $\mathcal{P}'$ to $\mathcal{P}$, then it is not the "correct" tag of $\mathcal{P}$, so SIM lets $\mathcal{P}$ output $\perp$.

Compiler from PAKE to PAKE with entity authentication. If we replace the lazy-extraction PAKE functionality with the (standard) PAKE, then the same compiler construction realizes the (standard) PAKE with explicit authentication functionality. In other words, by dropping the "laziness" of the underlying PAKE protocol, we get a compiler from PAKE to PAKE with explicit authentication. While technically not a corollary of Theorem 2, it is clear that the proof of Theorem 2 can be slightly modified to prove this conclusion: In that proof, the simulator SIM sends a password test (i.e., send a LateTestPwd message to $\mathcal{F}_{\mathsf{rPAKE-EA}}$) only if $\mathcal{A}$ does so (i.e., sends LateTestPwd message aimed at $\mathcal{F}_{\mathsf{lePAKE}}$ played by SIM); therefore, if both SIM and $\mathcal{A}$ are not allowed to do a late password test, the simulation will still succeed.

While it is well known that PAKE plus "key confirmation" yields PAKE with explicit authentication, to the best of our knowledge, there has been no proof of this fact in the UC setting.

SPAKE2 with key confirmation. An immediate corollary of Theorems 2 and 1 is that SPAKE2 with key confirmation realizes the relaxed UC PAKE-EA functionality $\mathcal{F}_{\mathsf{rPAKE-EA}}$ under the Gap-CDH assumption in the random-oracle model.

5   PAKE Relaxations and PFS

In this section we prove that any protocol that realizes the Relaxed PAKE functionality satisfies the standard game-based notion of security for PAKE protocols offering perfect forward secrecy (PFS). This is an important sanity check for the definition, as it shows that the extra power given to the ideal-world adversary by the late test feature does not weaken the security guarantee for PAKE sessions that are completed before passwords are corrupted. We show that a similar

---

On (NewSession, $sid, \mathcal{P}, \mathcal{P}', \text{role}$) from $\mathcal{F}$

If there is no record $\langle sid, \mathcal{P}, \ldots \rangle$ then:

  Send (NewSession, $sid, \mathcal{P}, \mathcal{P}', \text{role}$) to $\mathcal{A}$ and store $\langle sid, \mathcal{P}, \mathcal{P}', \text{role} \rangle$ marked fresh.

On (TestPwd, $sid, \mathcal{P}, pw^*$) from $\mathcal{A}$

If there is a fresh record $\langle sid, \mathcal{P}, \ldots \rangle$ then:

  Send (TestPwd, $sid, \mathcal{P}, pw^*$) to $\mathcal{F}$;

  If $\mathcal{F}$ replies "correct guess" then pass it to $\mathcal{A}$ and mark this record compromised.

  If $\mathcal{F}$ replies "wrong guess" then pass it to $\mathcal{A}$ and mark this record interrupted.

On (RegisterTest, $sid, \mathcal{P}$) from $\mathcal{A}$

If there is a fresh record $\langle sid, \mathcal{P}, \ldots \rangle$ then:

  Mark this record interrupted and flag it tested.

On (NewKey, $sid, \mathcal{P}, k^*$) from $\mathcal{A}$

If there is a record $\langle sid, \mathcal{P}, \mathcal{P}', \text{role} \rangle$ not completed then:

  Define k as follows:

    If this record is compromised, or $\mathcal{P}$ or $\mathcal{P}'$ is corrupted, then set $k := k^*$.

    Else if this record is interrupted (tested or not), then set $k \leftarrow_R \{0,1\}^\kappa$.

    Else set $k := \bot$.

  If $k \neq \bot$ then:

    If role = client then set $\tau := \mathsf{PRF}_k(2)$ and $\gamma := \mathsf{PRF}_k(3)$;

    If role = server then set $\tau := \mathsf{PRF}_k(3)$ and $\gamma := \mathsf{PRF}_k(2)$;

  Else, i.e., if $k = \bot$, pick $\tau \leftarrow_R \{0,1\}^\kappa$, set $\gamma := \bot$, and send (GetReady, $sid, \mathcal{P}$) to $\mathcal{F}$;

  Mark record $\langle sid, \mathcal{P}, \mathcal{P}', \text{role} \rangle$ "completed with key k and tag γ";

  Send τ to $\mathcal{A}$ as the authenticator from $\mathcal{P}$ to $\mathcal{P}'$.

On delivery of an authenticator from $\mathcal{A}$

If record $\langle sid, \mathcal{P}, \mathcal{P}', \text{role} \rangle$ is marked "completed with key k and tag γ", and $\mathcal{A}$ sends a purported authenticator, denoted τ^*, to protocol instance $(sid, \mathcal{P})$ then:

  If $\langle sid, \mathcal{P}, \mathcal{P}', \text{role} \rangle$ is flagged tested:

    Send (RegisterTest, $sid, \mathcal{P}$) to $\mathcal{F}$.

  If $k \neq \bot$ then:

    If $\tau^* = \gamma$ then send (NewKey, $sid, \mathcal{P}, \mathsf{PRF}_k(1)$) to $\mathcal{F}$.

    If $\tau^* \neq \gamma$ then send (NewKey, $sid, \mathcal{P}, \bot$) to $\mathcal{F}$.

  If $k = \bot$ (i.e., the record was fresh right before it became completed) then:

    If there is a completed record $\langle sid, \mathcal{P}', \mathcal{P}, \text{role}' \rangle$ for role' $\neq$ role, which was marked fresh right before it became completed, and which sent out authenticator τ' s.t. $\tau^* = \tau'$, then send (NewKey, $sid, \mathcal{P}, 0^\kappa$) to $\mathcal{F}$.

    Else send (NewKey, $sid, \mathcal{P}, \bot$) to $\mathcal{F}$.

On (LateTestPwd, $sid, \mathcal{P}, pw^*$) from $\mathcal{A}$

If there is a record $\langle sid, \mathcal{P}, \ldots \rangle$ marked "completed with key k", and flagged tested:

  Remove the tested flag from this record;

  If $\mathcal{A}$ did not send an authenticator to protocol instance $(sid, \mathcal{P})$ then send (TestPwd, $sid, \mathcal{P}, pw^*$) to $\mathcal{F}$;

  Else send (LateTestPwd, $sid, \mathcal{P}, pw^*$) to $\mathcal{F}$;

  If $\mathcal{F}$ replies "correct guess" then send k to $\mathcal{A}$.

  If $\mathcal{F}$ replies "wrong guess" then send $k^\$ \leftarrow_R \{0,1\}^\kappa$ to $\mathcal{A}$.

Fig. 6. Simulation for relaxed PAKE-EA protocol in Fig. 5.

argument can be used to show that the weaker Lazy-Extraction PAKE definition implies a weak form of PFS, referred to as weak FS, where security in the presence of password leakage is only guaranteed with respect to passive attackers [27,30].

5.1 Defining PFS

We recall the standard game-based notion of security for PAKE protocols and which follows from a series of works [5,6] that refined the security notion proposed by Bellare, Pointcheval and Rogaway in [8]. Section 3 and [1] include the full details.

The definition is based on an experiment in which a challenger emulates a scenario where a set of parties $\mathcal{P}_1, \ldots, \mathcal{P}_n$, each running an arbitrary number of PAKE sessions, relies on a trusted setup procedure to establish pre-shared long-term (low-entropy) passwords for pairwise authentication. Passwords for each pair $(\mathcal{P}_i, \mathcal{P}_j)$ are sampled from a distribution over a dictionary $\mathcal{D}$; we assume here the case where $\mathcal{D}$ is any set of cardinality greater than one, and each password is sampled independently and uniformly at random from this set.[10] A ppt adversary $\mathcal{A}$ is challenged to distinguish established session keys from truly random ones with an advantage that is better than password guessing.

The security experiment goes as follows. The challenger first samples passwords for all pairs of parties, generates any global public parameters (CRS) that the protocol may rely on and samples a secret bit b. The challenger manages a set of instances π_i^j, each corresponding to the state of session instance j at party P_i, according to the protocol definition. The adversary is then executed with the CRS as input; it may interact with the following set of oracles, to which it may place multiple adaptive queries:

EXECUTE: Given a pair of party identities $(\mathcal{P}_i, \mathcal{P}_j)$ this oracle animates an honest execution of a new PAKE session established between the two parties and returns the communications trace to the attacker. This gives rise to two new session instances π_i^k and π_j^l, which for correct protocols will have derived the same established session key.

SEND: Given a party identity P_i, an instance j and a message m, this oracle processes m according to the state of instance π_i^j (or creates this state if the

---

[10] This assumption is standard for the corruption model captured by this game-based definition. If correlated passwords were allowed, then corrupting one password might reveal information that allows the attacker to trivially infer another one; preventing trivial attacks in this setting leads to a definition in the style of [8], where the corruption of a password must invalidate RoR queries associated with all correlated passwords; this means the whole dictionary if no restrictions are imposed on the distribution. The finer-grained definition of password corruption we adopt here does not easily extend to the case of arbitrary correlations between passwords. See [1] for a discussion. The UC definition covers arbitrary password sampling distributions and the results we prove in this section should extend to any reasonable game-based definition that deals with more complex password distributions. This is clearly the case for the concrete distributions discussed in [1] .

instance was not yet initialized) and returns any outgoing messages to the attacker.

CORRUPT: Given a pair of party identities $(\mathcal{P}_i, \mathcal{P}_j)$, this oracle returns the corresponding pre-shared password.

REVEAL: Given a party identity $\mathcal{P}_i$ and an instance j, this oracle checks π_i^j and, if this session instance has completed as defined by the protocol, the output of the session (usually either a secret key or an abort symbol) is returned to the attacker.

RoR: Given a party identity $\mathcal{P}_i$ and an instance j, this oracle checks π_i^j and, if this session instance has completed as defined by the protocol *and* this session instance is *fresh*, the adversary is challenged on guessing bit b: if $b = 0$ then the derived key is given to the attacker; otherwise a new random key is returned.[11]

Eventually the adversary terminates and outputs a guess bit b'. The definition of advantage excludes trivial attacks via the notion of session freshness used in the RoR oracle. Formal definitions are given in [1], here we give an informal description. Two session instances are *partnered* if their views match with respect to the identity of the peer, exchanged messages and derived secret keys—the first two are usually interpreted as a session identifier. A session is fresh if: a) the instance completed; b) the instance was not queried to RoR or REVEAL before; c) at least one of the following four conditions holds: i. the instance accepted during a query to EXECUTE; ii. there exists more than one partner instance; iii. no partner instance exists and the associated password was not corrupted prior to completion; iv. a unique fresh partner instance exists (implies not revealed).

A PAKE protocol is secure if, for any ppt attacker interacting with the above experiment and placing at most q_s queries to the SEND oracle, we have that

$$|\Pr[b' = b] - 1/2| \leq q_s/|\mathcal{D}| + \epsilon,$$

where ϵ is a negligible term.

The original definition proposed by Bellare, Pointcheval and Rogaway [8] allows for stronger corruption models—fixing the corrupt password maliciously and revealing the internal state of session instances—which we do not consider. We also do not deal with the asymmetry between client and server (also known as augmented PAKE).

Known results for UC PAKE. Canetti et al. [13] introduced the notion of UC-secure PAKE and proved that this definition implies game-based security of the protocol as defined in [8]. Our proof that Relaxed PAKE implies game-based PAKE with PFS follows along the same lines and relies on two auxiliary results from that original proof that we recover here; the first result concerns a generic mechanism for the handling of session identifiers called *SID-enhancement* and the second one is a general result for security against eavesdroppers.

---

[11] We use RoR (Real-or-Random) for this oracle rather than the standard TEST oracle designation to avoid confusion with the test and late test requests that are included in the UC PAKE ideal functionality definitions.

Given a two-party protocol Π, its SID-enhancement Π' is defined as the protocol that has the parties exchange nonces and then uses the concatenation of these nonces as SID. This transformation converts any protocol Π that assumes SIDs provided by an external environment as the means to define matching sessions, into another one that generates the SID on-the-fly as required by the syntax of the game-based security definition. Both the original proof and the one we give here show that the UC security of Π implies the game-based security of Π'. Intuitively, an environment simulating the PFS-game above can wait until the SID for the enhanced protocol is defined before calling NewSession to initiate the session of the parties in the UC setting.

For security against eavesdroppers, Canetti et al. show that no successful ideal world adversary can place TestPwd queries on sessions for which the environment $\mathcal{Z}$ instructed the adversary to pass messages between the players unmodified (i.e., to only eavesdrop on the session). We give here the intuition on why this is the case and refer the interested reader to [13] for a detailed proof.

The crucial observation is that, for eavesdropped sessions, the ideal-world adversary generates all the trace and hence has no side information on the password; this means that for every environment $\mathcal{Z}$ for which the ideal-world attacker might place such a query, there exists an environment $\mathcal{Z}'$ that can *catch* the simulator; $\mathcal{Z}'$ operates as $\mathcal{Z}$, but it uses a high-entropy password for the problematic session: in the real-world a session the two honest parties will end-up with matching keys with probability 1—one assumes perfect correctness here for simplicity—whereas an ideal-world adversary placing a TestPwd can never match the same behaviour. Indeed, querying a wrong password to TestPwd leads to mismatching keys with overwhelming probability in the ideal world and the ideal-world adversary cannot guess the password correctly except with small probability.

This argument extends trivially to LateTestPw queries, as these must be preceded by a RegisterTest query prior to session completion that also leads to mismatching keys with overwhelming probability. Furthermore, the above reasoning also applies when the ideal-world adversary may have the extra power of simulating an ideal object, i.e., the UC-secure PAKE protocol is defined in an $\mathcal{F}$-hybrid model. Indeed, whatever environment $\mathcal{Z}$ may have leaked to the ideal-world adversary via calls to $\mathcal{F}$, there exists an environment $\mathcal{Z}'$ that catches $\mathcal{S}$ as above.

5.2 Relaxed PAKE Implies PFS

Theorem 3. *Let $\mathcal{F}$ be an ideal object such as a random oracle or an ideal cipher. If Π securely realizes $\mathcal{F}_{rPAKE}$ without explicit authentication, in the $(\mathcal{F}_{CRS}, \mathcal{F})$-hybrid model, then its SID-enhanced version Π' is PFS-secure according to the game-based definition given above.*

We refer to the full version of this paper [2] for the proof of the above theorem, but this proof is quite similar to the proof of the corresponding theorem given in [13], which showed that the original notion of UC-secure PAKE implies game-based security (with PFS) of a PAKE protocol.

5.3   Lazy-Extraction PAKE Implies Weak FS

The proof of the above theorem can be adapted to show that any protocol that realizes the Lazy-Extraction UC PAKE functionality is secure under a weak form of game-based security: the attacker is not allowed to corrupt the passwords of sessions against which it launches an active attack. This notion of game-based security for PAKE is sometimes called weak FS.

Theorem 4. *Let $\mathcal{F}$ be an ideal object such as a random oracle or an ideal cipher. If Π securely realizes $\mathcal{F}_{\mathsf{lePAKE}}$ without explicit authentication, in the $(\mathcal{F}_{\mathsf{CRS}}, \mathcal{F})$-hybrid model, then its SID-enhanced version Π' is weak FS-secure.*

5.4   Practical Implications

Putting together the results in Sect. 3 and Sect. 4 we obtain positive results for rPAKE secure protocols in the Universal Composability framework, namely SPAKE2, TBPEKE, CPace and SPEKE, followed by a round of key confirmation (although we did not give a detailed proof for the latter). The result in this section shows that all such protocols are also PFS secure in the game-based setting. The caveat here is that this proof involves modifying the protocol to deal with session identifiers: The UC PAKE model requires a unique session identifier as an input of the protocol, while in practice agreeing on such identifier before the protocol starts can add extra communication rounds to the protocol. Nevertheless, a direct proof that SPAKE2 with key confirmation provides game-based PFS with a tight reduction to Gap CDH in the random-oracle model can be found in [1].

6   Security of TBPEKE, SPEKE, and Their Variants

In this section, we prove that the TBPEKE protocol proposed by Pointcheval and Wang [33] also realizes the lazy-extraction PAKE functionality under the same assumptions which were used to prove its game-based security. Moreover, since TBPEKE is a representative example of a class of protocols which includes SPEKE [20,22,31] and CPace [18,19], the same likely holds for these other protocols as well, or for their close variants. For example, it is straightforward to adapt our security proof for TBPEKE to show that lazy-extraction UC PAKE functionality is realized under the same assumptions also by SPEKE [20,22,31].[12] Due to its recent selection by the CFRG, we will analyze the specific case of CPace in the full version [2]. (See Footnote 6)

We now recall the two-flow, simultaneous round TBPEKE protocol [33] in Fig. 7, with some notational choices adjusted to the UC setting.

---

[12] For instance, in the case of SPEKE (in which $g = G(pw)$), one can adapt the proof for TBPEKE by simulating the random oracle G as $U \cdot V^{\mathsf{P}(pw)}$.

Public parameters: Random elements U, V of group $\mathbb{G}$ of prime order p;
hash function $\mathsf{H} : \{0,1\}^* \to \{0,1\}^\kappa$;
hash function $\mathsf{P} : \{0,1\}^* \to \mathbb{Z}_p$

$\mathcal{P}$ on $(\mathsf{NewSession}, sid, \mathcal{P}, \mathcal{P}', pw, \mathsf{client})$:

$g_{pw} \leftarrow U \cdot V^{\mathsf{P}(pw)}$

$x \leftarrow_{\mathrm{R}} \mathbb{Z}_p$

$X \leftarrow g_{pw}^x$

$\qquad\qquad \xrightarrow{\quad X \quad}$

$K \leftarrow \mathsf{H}(sid, \mathcal{P}, \mathcal{P}', g_{pw}, X, Y, Y^x)$

output K

$\mathcal{P}'$ on $(\mathsf{NewSession}, sid, \mathcal{P}', \mathcal{P}, pw', \mathsf{server})$:

$g_{pw'} \leftarrow U \cdot V^{\mathsf{P}(pw')}$

$y \leftarrow_{\mathrm{R}} \mathbb{Z}_p$

$Y \leftarrow g_{pw'}^y$

$\xleftarrow{\quad Y \quad}$

$K' \leftarrow \mathsf{H}(sid, \mathcal{P}, \mathcal{P}', g_{pw'}, X, Y, X^y)$

output K'

Fig. 7. TBPEKE protocol of [33], which uses an additional random oracle P for deriving the generator g_{pw}.

For the security proof of TBPEKE we require the following computational assumptions [33].

SDH and Gap SDH assumptions. The Simultaneous Diffie-Hellman (SDH) assumption states that, given three random elements X, $g = X^a$, and $h = X^b$ in a cyclic group of prime order, it is hard to find $Y \neq 1$ and R, S that simultaneously satisfy $R = \mathsf{CDH}_g(X, Y) = Y^{1/a}$ and $S = \mathsf{CDH}_h(X, Y) = Y^{1/b}$. In the gap version, the problem must remain hard even if the adversary has access to a Decisional Diffie-Hellman oracle.

Theorem 5. TBPEKE *realizes the Lazy-Extraction PAKE functionality* $\mathcal{F}_{\mathsf{lePAKE}}$ *in the random-oracle model under the Gap-CDH and Gap Simultaneous Diffie-Hellman (Gap-SDH) assumptions.*

For the formal proof of Theorem 5, we refer to the full version of this paper [2]. Here, we only present an informal overview of this proof and the simulator used in the proof, shown in Fig. 8.

The proof that TBPEKE is lazy-extraction UC PAKE secure is structurally similar to that of SPAKE2. In particular, the simulator adopts the same high-level strategy for dealing with passive and active attacks, while simulating the random oracle that is used for key derivation by taking advantage of knowing the CRS. The random oracle P is trivially simulated, excluding collisions to avoid ambiguity between passwords. The sequence of games that justifies the simulation also follows the same pattern.

The only significant difference between the proofs for TBPEKE and SPAKE2 lies in the step where one must exclude the possibility that the adversary places two random-oracle queries for two different passwords that are consistent with the same protocol trace, which would prevent the simulator from maintaining consistency. In TBPEKE, this bad event corresponds to the case in which the adversary queries the hash oracle H on inputs (g_{pw_1}, X, Y, W_1) and $(g_{pw_2}, X, Y,$

---

generate CRS
$\overline{U \leftarrow g^u; V \leftarrow g^v}$ for $(u, v) \leftarrow_R \mathbb{Z}_p$
return U, V

on (NewSession, $sid, \mathcal{P}, \mathcal{P}'$, role) from $\mathcal{P}$
$\overline{\text{if } \pi_{\mathcal{P}}^{sid} \neq \bot: \text{return } \bot}$
$(X, Y) \leftarrow (\bot, \bot)$
if role = client :
   $(\mathcal{C}, \mathcal{S}) \leftarrow (\mathcal{P}, \mathcal{P}')$
   $z \leftarrow_R \mathbb{Z}_p; X \leftarrow g^z; Z \leftarrow X$
   if $\pi_{\mathcal{P}'}^{sid} \neq \bot$ and $\pi_{\mathcal{P}'}^{sid}.\text{role} \neq \text{client}: Y \leftarrow \pi_{\mathcal{P}'}^{sid}.Y; \pi_{\mathcal{P}'}^{sid}.X \leftarrow X$
else if role = server :
   $(\mathcal{C}, \mathcal{S}) \leftarrow (\mathcal{P}', \mathcal{P})$
   $z \leftarrow_R \mathbb{Z}_p; Y \leftarrow g^z; Z \leftarrow Y$
   if $\pi_{\mathcal{P}'}^{sid} \neq \bot$ and $\pi_{\mathcal{P}'}^{sid}.\text{role} \neq \text{server}: X \leftarrow \pi_{\mathcal{P}'}^{sid}.X; \pi_{\mathcal{P}'}^{sid}.Y \leftarrow Y$
$\pi_{\mathcal{P}}^{sid} \leftarrow (\text{role}, z, \mathcal{C}, \mathcal{S}, X, Y, \bot, \bot, \bot, \bot, \mathtt{T})$
send Z from $\mathcal{P}$ to $\mathcal{A}$

on Z^* from $\mathcal{A}$ as msg to $(sid, \mathcal{P})$
$\overline{\text{if } \pi_{\mathcal{P}}^{sid} = \bot \text{ or } \pi_{\mathcal{P}}^{sid}.\text{waiting} = \mathtt{F}: \text{return } \bot}$
$(\text{role}, \cdot, \mathcal{C}, \mathcal{S}, X, Y, \cdot, \cdot, \cdot, \text{guesses}, \cdot) \leftarrow \pi_{\mathcal{P}}^{sid}$
$K \leftarrow 0^\kappa$
if role = client :
   $\pi_{\mathcal{P}}^{sid}.Y^* \leftarrow Z^*$
   if $Z^* = Y$: jump to end
else if role = server :
   $\pi_{\mathcal{P}}^{sid}.X^* \leftarrow Z^*$
   if $Z^* = X$: jump to end
if $\pi_{\mathcal{P}}^{sid}.\text{guesses}[Z^*] = (pw, K^*)$:
   reply $\leftarrow$ (TestPwd, $sid, \mathcal{P}, pw$) to $\mathcal{F}$
   if reply = "correct": $K \leftarrow K^*$
else: send (RegisterTest, $sid, \mathcal{P}$) to $\mathcal{F}$
end: $\pi_{\mathcal{P}}^{sid}.\text{waiting} \leftarrow \mathtt{F}$
   send (NewKey, $sid, \mathcal{P}, K$) to $\mathcal{F}$

on $H(sid, \mathcal{C}, \mathcal{S}, g_{pw}, X', Y', W)$ from $\mathcal{A}$:
$\overline{\text{if } T_H[sid, \mathcal{C}, \mathcal{S}, g_{pw}, X', Y', W] = \bot:}$
   $K \leftarrow_R \{0, 1\}^\kappa$
   find $pw \in T_\mathcal{P}$ s.t. $T_\mathcal{P}[pw] = g_{pw}$; if none found, jump to end
   $(\hat{x}, \hat{y}) \leftarrow (\bot, \bot)$
   if $\pi_{\mathcal{C}}^{sid} \neq \bot: \hat{x} \leftarrow \pi_{\mathcal{C}}^{sid}.\exp/(u + v \cdot pw)$
   if $\pi_{\mathcal{S}}^{sid} \neq \bot: \hat{y} \leftarrow \pi_{\mathcal{S}}^{sid}.\exp/(u + v \cdot pw)$
   if $\pi_{\mathcal{C}}^{sid}.X = X'$ and $\pi_{\mathcal{S}}^{sid}.Y = Y'$ and $W = g_{pw}^{\hat{x}\hat{y}}$: abort
   else if $\pi_{\mathcal{C}}^{sid}.X = X'$ and $W = (Y')^{\hat{x}}$:
      if $Y' = \pi_{\mathcal{C}}^{sid}.Y^*$: $\mathcal{P} \leftarrow \mathcal{C}$; jump to late_test_pw
      else: $\pi_{\mathcal{C}}^{sid}.\text{guesses}[Y'] \leftarrow (pw, K)$
   else if $\pi_{\mathcal{S}}^{sid}.Y = Y'$ and $W = (X')^{\hat{y}}$:
      if $X' = \pi_{\mathcal{S}}^{sid}.X^*$: $\mathcal{P} \leftarrow \mathcal{S}$; jump to late_test_pw
      else: $\pi_{\mathcal{S}}^{sid}.\text{guesses}[X'] \leftarrow (pw, K)$
   jump to end
   late_test_pw: reply $\leftarrow$ (LateTestPwd, $sid, \mathcal{P}, pw$) to $\mathcal{F}$
      $K \leftarrow$ reply; if no reply, abort
   end: $T_H[sid, \mathcal{C}, \mathcal{S}, g_{pw}, X', Y', W] \leftarrow K$
send $T_H[sid, \mathcal{C}, \mathcal{S}, g_{pw}, X', Y', W]$ to $\mathcal{A}$

on $P(pw)$ from $\mathcal{A}$:
$\overline{\text{if } T_\mathcal{P}[pw] = \bot:}$
   $\hat{p} \leftarrow_R \mathbb{Z}_p$; if $\hat{p} \in T_\mathcal{P}.\text{values}$: abort
   $T_\mathcal{P}[pw] \leftarrow \hat{p}$
send $T_\mathcal{P}[pw]$ to $\mathcal{A}$

Fig. 8. UC Simulator for TBPEKE.

W_2) such that at least one of the values X and Y is simulated and (X, Y, W_i) is a valid DDH tuple with respect to the generator g_{pw_i} for $i = 1, 2$. In the SPAKE2 proof, the corresponding event can be reduced to Gap CDH. For TBPEKE, the reduction to Gap CDH does not work and the stronger Gap SDH assumption (given above) is needed.

The strategy for embedding a Gap SDH instance in the reduction is the same as that adopted in [33]. More precisely, the reduction guesses the two queries to the oracle P that correspond to the passwords that are involved in the bad event and programs the random oracle output for these passwords with two random values p_1 and p_2 from $\mathbb{Z}_p$. Then, given a Gap SDH challenge (A, G_1, G_2), it sets $V \leftarrow (G_1/G_2)^{1/(p_1-p_2)}$ and $U \leftarrow G_1/V^{p_1}$ so that we have $U \cdot V^{p_i} = G_i$ for $i = 1, 2$. Next, it embeds the value of A in the client and server messages X and Y (randomizing them appropriately) whenever it needs to simulate these values. Finally, if the bad event happens and the guesses for pw_1 and pw_2 are correct, then we know that (X, Y, W_i) is a valid DDH tuple with respect to the generator G_i for $i = 1, 2$. If $X = A^\alpha$ is the simulated value (the case in which Y is simulated is similar) and α is the randomization factor, then it follows that $(Y, W_1^{1/\alpha}, W_2^{1/\alpha})$ is a valid solution to the Gap-SDH problem.

Acknowledgments. Michel Abdalla was supported in part by the ERC Project aSCEND (H2020 639554) and by the French ANR ALAMBIC Project (ANR-16-CE39-0006). Work of Manuel Barbosa was supported in part by the grant SFRH/BSAB/143018/2018 awarded by FCT, Portugal, and by the ERC Project aSCEND (H2020 639554). Stanisław Jarecki and Tatiana Bradley were supported by NSF SaTC award #1817143. Work of Jonathan Katz and Jiayu Xu was supported in part under financial assistance award 70NANB15H328 from the U.S. Department of Commerce, National Institute of Standards and Technology.

References

1. Abdalla, M., Barbosa, M.: Perfect forward security of SPAKE2. Cryptology ePrint Archive, Report 2019/1194 (2019). https://eprint.iacr.org/2019/1194
2. Abdalla, M., Barbosa, M., Bradley, T., Jarecki, S., Katz, J., Xu, J.: Universally composable relaxed password authenticated key exchange. IACR Cryptology ePrint Archive (2020). https://eprint.iacr.org/2020/320
3. Abdalla, M., Bellare, M., Rogaway, P.: The oracle Diffie-Hellman assumptions and an analysis of DHIES. In: Naccache, D. (ed.) CT-RSA 2001. LNCS, vol. 2020, pp. 143–158. Springer, Heidelberg (2001). https://doi.org/10.1007/3-540-45353-9_12
4. Abdalla, M., Catalano, D., Chevalier, C., Pointcheval, D.: Efficient two-party password-based key exchange protocols in the UC framework. In: Malkin, T. (ed.) CT-RSA 2008. LNCS, vol. 4964, pp. 335–351. Springer, Heidelberg (2008). https://doi.org/10.1007/978-3-540-79263-5_22
5. Abdalla, M., Fouque, P.-A., Pointcheval, D.: Password-based authenticated key exchange in the three-party setting. In: Vaudenay, S. (ed.) PKC 2005. LNCS, vol. 3386, pp. 65–84. Springer, Heidelberg (2005). https://doi.org/10.1007/978-3-540-30580-4_6

6. Abdalla, M., Fouque, P.A., Pointcheval, D.: Password-based authenticated key exchange in the three-party setting. IEE Proc. Inf. Secur. **153**(1), 27–39 (2006)
7. Abdalla, M., Pointcheval, D.: Simple password-based encrypted key exchange protocols. In: Menezes, A. (ed.) CT-RSA 2005. LNCS, vol. 3376, pp. 191–208. Springer, Heidelberg (2005). https://doi.org/10.1007/978-3-540-30574-3_14
8. Bellare, M., Pointcheval, D., Rogaway, P.: Authenticated key exchange secure against dictionary attacks. In: Preneel, B. (ed.) EUROCRYPT 2000. LNCS, vol. 1807, pp. 139–155. Springer, Heidelberg (2000). https://doi.org/10.1007/3-540-45539-6_11
9. Bellovin, S.M., Merritt, M.: Encrypted key exchange: password-based protocols secure against dictionary attacks. In: IEEE Symposium on Security and Privacy - S&P 1992, pp. 72–84. IEEE (1992)
10. Boyko, V., MacKenzie, P., Patel, S.: Provably secure password-authenticated key exchange using Diffie-Hellman. In: Preneel, B. (ed.) EUROCRYPT 2000. LNCS, vol. 1807, pp. 156–171. Springer, Heidelberg (2000). https://doi.org/10.1007/3-540-45539-6_12
11. Bradley, T., Camenisch, J., Jarecki, S., Lehmann, A., Neven, G., Xu, J.: Password-authenticated public-key encryption. In: Deng, R.H., Gauthier-Umaña, V., Ochoa, M., Yung, M. (eds.) ACNS 2019. LNCS, vol. 11464, pp. 442–462. Springer, Cham (2019). https://doi.org/10.1007/978-3-030-21568-2_22
12. Canetti, R.: Universally composable security: a new paradigm for cryptographic protocols. In: 42nd FOCS, pp. 136–145. IEEE Computer Society Press (2001)
13. Canetti, R., Halevi, S., Katz, J., Lindell, Y., MacKenzie, P.: Universally Composable password-based key exchange. In: Cramer, R. (ed.) EUROCRYPT 2005. LNCS, vol. 3494, pp. 404–421. Springer, Heidelberg (2005). https://doi.org/10.1007/11426639_24
14. Gennaro, R.: Faster and shorter password-authenticated key exchange. In: Canetti, R. (ed.) TCC 2008. LNCS, vol. 4948, pp. 589–606. Springer, Heidelberg (2008). https://doi.org/10.1007/978-3-540-78524-8_32
15. Gentry, C., MacKenzie, P., Ramzan, Z.: A method for making password-based key exchange resilient to server compromise. In: Dwork, C. (ed.) CRYPTO 2006. LNCS, vol. 4117, pp. 142–159. Springer, Heidelberg (2006). https://doi.org/10.1007/11818175_9
16. Goldreich, O., Lindell, Y.: Session-key generation using human passwords only. J. Cryptol. **19**(3), 241–340 (2006)
17. Groce, A., Katz, J.: A new framework for efficient password-based authenticated key exchange. In: Al-Shaer, E., Keromytis, A.D., Shmatikov, V. (eds.) ACM CCS 2010, pp. 516–525. ACM Press (2010)
18. Haase, B., Labrique, B.: AuCPace: efficient verifier-based PAKE protocol tailored for the IIoT. Cryptology ePrint Archive, Report 2018/286 (2018). https://eprint.iacr.org/2018/286
19. Haase, B., Labrique, B.: AuCPace: efficient verifier-based PAKE protocol tailored for the IIoT. IACR TCHES **2019**(2), 1–48 (2019). https://tches.iacr.org/index.php/TCHES/article/view/7384
20. Hao, F., Shahandashti, S.F.: The SPEKE protocol revisited. Cryptology ePrint Archive, Report 2014/585 (2014). http://eprint.iacr.org/2014/585
21. Hwang, J.Y., Jarecki, S., Kwon, T., Lee, J., Shin, J.S., Xu, J.: Round-reduced modular construction of asymmetric password-authenticated key exchange. In: Catalano, D., De Prisco, R. (eds.) SCN 2018. LNCS, vol. 11035, pp. 485–504. Springer, Cham (2018). https://doi.org/10.1007/978-3-319-98113-0_26

22. Jablon, D.P.: Extended password key exchange protocols immune to dictionary attacks. In: 6th IEEE International Workshops on Enabling Technologies: Infrastructure for Collaborative Enterprises (WETICE 1997), 18–20 June 1997, pp. 248–255. IEEE Computer Society, Cambridge (2007)

23. Jarecki, S., Krawczyk, H., Xu, J.: OPAQUE: An asymmetric PAKE protocol secure against pre-computation attacks. In: Nielsen, J.B., Rijmen, V. (eds.) EUROCRYPT 2018. LNCS, vol. 10822, pp. 456–486. Springer, Cham (2018). https://doi.org/10.1007/978-3-319-78372-7_15

24. Jarecki, S., Krawczyk, H., Xu, J.: OPAQUE: an asymmetric PAKE protocol secure against pre-computation attacks. Cryptology ePrint Archive, Report 2018/163 (2018). https://eprint.iacr.org/2018/163

25. Jutla, C.S., Roy, A.: Dual-system simulation-soundness with applications to UC-PAKE and more. In: Iwata, T., Cheon, J.H. (eds.) ASIACRYPT 2015. LNCS, vol. 9452, pp. 630–655. Springer, Heidelberg (2015). https://doi.org/10.1007/978-3-662-48797-6_26

26. Katz, J., Ostrovsky, R., Yung, M.: Efficient password-authenticated key exchange using human-memorable passwords. In: Pfitzmann, B. (ed.) EUROCRYPT 2001. LNCS, vol. 2045, pp. 475–494. Springer, Heidelberg (2001). https://doi.org/10.1007/3-540-44987-6_29

27. Katz, J., Ostrovsky, R., Yung, M.: Forward secrecy in password-only key exchange protocols. In: Cimato, S., Persiano, G., Galdi, C. (eds.) SCN 2002. LNCS, vol. 2576, pp. 29–44. Springer, Heidelberg (2003). https://doi.org/10.1007/3-540-36413-7_3

28. Katz, J., Vaikuntanathan, V.: Round-optimal password-based authenticated key exchange. In: Ishai, Y. (ed.) TCC 2011. LNCS, vol. 6597, pp. 293–310. Springer, Heidelberg (2011). https://doi.org/10.1007/978-3-642-19571-6_18

29. Krawczyk, H.: The OPAQUE asymmetric PAKE protocol (2019). https://www.ietf.org/id/draft-krawczyk-cfrg-opaque-03.txt

30. Krawczyk, H.: HMQV: a high-performance secure Diffie-Hellman protocol. In: Shoup, V. (ed.) CRYPTO 2005. LNCS, vol. 3621, pp. 546–566. Springer, Heidelberg (2005). https://doi.org/10.1007/11535218_33

31. MacKenzie, P.: On the security of the SPEKE password-authenticated key exchange protocol. Cryptology ePrint Archive, Report 2001/057 (2001). http://eprint.iacr.org/2001/057

32. Pedersen, T.P.: Non-interactive and information-theoretic secure verifiable secret sharing. In: Feigenbaum, J. (ed.) CRYPTO 1991. LNCS, vol. 576, pp. 129–140. Springer, Heidelberg (1992). https://doi.org/10.1007/3-540-46766-1_9

33. Pointcheval, D., Wang, G.: VTBPEKE: verifier-based two-basis password exponential key exchange. In: Karri, R., Sinanoglu, O., Sadeghi, A.R., Yi, X. (eds.) ASIACCS 17, pp. 301–312. ACM Press (2017)

34. Shoup, V.: Security analysis of spake2+. Cryptology ePrint Archive, Report 2020/313 (2020). https://eprint.iacr.org/2020/313

Anonymous Tokens with Private Metadata Bit

Ben Kreuter[1]($\boxtimes$), Tancrède Lepoint[1]($\boxtimes$), Michele Orrù[2,3,4]($\boxtimes$), and Mariana Raykova[1]($\boxtimes$)

[1] Google, New York, USA
benkreuter@google.com, tancrede@google.com, marianar@google.com
[2] École Normale Supérieure, CNRS, PSL University, Paris, France
michele.orru@ens.psl.eu
[3] Inria, Paris, France
[4] Recurse Center, New York, USA

Abstract. We present a cryptographic construction for anonymous tokens with private metadata bit, called PMBTokens. This primitive enables an issuer to provide a user with a lightweight, single-use anonymous trust token that can embed a single private bit, which is accessible only to the party who holds the secret authority key and is private with respect to anyone else. Our construction generalizes and extends the functionality of Privacy Pass (PETS'18) with this private metadata bit capability. It provides unforgeability, unlinkability, and privacy for the metadata bit properties based on the DDH and CTDH assumptions in the random oracle model. Both Privacy Pass and PMBTokens rely on non-interactive zero-knowledge proofs (NIZKs). We present new techniques to remove the need for NIZKs, while still achieving unlinkability. We implement our constructions and we report their efficiency costs.

1 Introduction

The need to propagate trust signals while protecting anonymity has motivated cryptographic constructions for anonymous credentials [Cha82, CL01]. While we have constructions that support complex statements, this comes with computation and communication costs. On the other hand, some practical uses require very simple functionality from the anonymous credential, while having very strict efficiency requirements. One such example is the setting of Privacy Pass [DGS+18]. Privacy Pass was designed as a tool for content delivery networks (CDNs), which need a way to distinguish honest from malicious content requests, so as to block illegitimate traffic that could drain network resources causing a denial of service (DoS). Previous solutions leveraged IP reputation to assess the reputation of users. While helpful in many cases, IP reputation may also lead to a high rate of false positives because of shared IP use. In particular, this is the case for users of privacy tools, such as Tor, VPNs, and I2P. Privacy Pass [DGS+18] proposes a solution for this problem using anonymous tokens as a mechanism to prove trustworthiness of the requests, without compromising the privacy of the user. Since CDNs need to potentially handle millions of requests per second, efficiency of the cryptographic construction is of extreme importance.

© International Association for Cryptologic Research 2020
D. Micciancio and T. Ristenpart (Eds.): CRYPTO 2020, LNCS 12170, pp. 308–336, 2020.
https://doi.org/10.1007/978-3-030-56784-2_11

In this paper, we consider anonymous tokens that can convey two trust signals, in such a way that the user cannot distinguish which of the two signals is embedded in her tokens. This extension is motivated by the fact that in a system relying on anonymous trust tokens, malicious users be identified as a threat if the issuer stops providing them with tokens. Since real-world attackers have means to corrupt honest users, finding out when they have been detected could serve as an incentive to corrupt more users or adversarial learning against spam detectors. Being able to pass on the information whether a user is on an allow or disallow list, and consume it in appropriate ways on the authentication side, mitigates such behavior. There has been recent interest in primitives that provide such functionality in standardization bodies such as the IETF and W3C. This includes a recent draft proposal for a *Trusted Token API* submitted by Google at the W3C, which calls for a secret metadata bit functionality.[1] Also an IETF working group[2] is discussing standardization of the core protocol of Privacy Pass used by Cloudflare[3] together with extensions including private metadata bit.

More concretely, we consider an anonymous token primitive that provides the following functionality: a user and an issuer interact and, as a result of this interaction, the user obtains a token with a private metadata bit (PMB) embedded in it. The private metadata bit can be read from a token using the secret key held by the issuer, at redemption time. Each token is one-time use, which enables the issuer to update the trust assigned to each user without requiring a complex revocation process, by just adjusting the number of tokens that can be issued at once and the frequency of serving new token requests. Anonymous token schemes offer the following security properties: unforgeability, unlinkability, and privacy of the metadata bit. *Unforgeability* guarantees that nobody but the issuer can generate new valid tokens. *Unlinkability* guarantees that the tokens that were issued with the same private metadata bit are indistinguishable to the issuer when redeemed. *Privacy of the metadata bit* states that no party that does not have the secret key can distinguish any two tokens, including tokens issued with different metadata bits.

Our goal is to construct a primitive which achieves the above properties, and has competitive efficiency introducing minimal overhead over Privacy Pass.

1.1   Our Contributions

Our work includes the following contributions. We formalize the security properties of the primitive of anonymous tokens with private metadata bit. We present a new construction for this primitive, called PMBToken, which extends Privacy Pass (PP) to support private metadata bit, while maintaining competitive efficiency. Further, we introduce new techniques that allow to remove the need for NIZK in the constructions of both Privacy Pass and PMBToken. This simplifies

---

[1] See https://github.com/WICG/trust-token-api#extension-metadata and https://web.dev/trust-tokens/.

[2] See https://datatracker.ietf.org/wg/privacypass/about/.

[3] See https://blog.cloudflare.com/cloudflare-supports-privacy-pass/.

and optimizes the constructions in which the NIZK proof computation is a major bottleneck. The resulting schemes satisfy a weaker unlinkability notion. Finally, we implement all the above candidate constructions in Rust, and we summarize the performance of our schemes.

A Failed Approach and Its Insight. The starting point of our study is Privacy Pass, which uses the verifiable oblivious PRF (VOPRF) primitive of Jarecki et al. [JKK14] $F_x(t) = x\mathsf{H}_t(t)$ (additively denoted). In the oblivious PRF evaluation mechanism, the user sends to the issuer $r\mathsf{H}_t(t)$ for a randomly selected value r, receives back $rx\mathsf{H}_t(t)$ from which she recovers the output $x\mathsf{H}_t(t)$.[4] Obliviousness is guaranteed by the blinding factor r, which makes the distribution of $r\mathsf{H}_t(t)$ uniform even when knowing t. The PRF output can be verified by the user providing her with a DLEQ proof, which guarantees that $\log_{\mathsf{H}_t(t)}(F_x(t)) = \log_G X$, where G is the base point and $X := xG$ is published by the issuer as a public parameter for the scheme.

There is a natural idea to upgrade the above functionality to support a private metadata bit, which is to have two secret keys and use each of these keys for one of the bits. However, this idea does not work directly; the reason for this stems from the fact that the underlying VOPRF is a deterministic primitive. In particular, this means that if we are using two different keys for tokens issued with different private metadata bit values, the VOPRF evaluations on the same input t will be the same if they are issued with the same key and will be different with high probability if used with different keys. Thus, if the user obtains multiple tokens using the same input value t (the issuer, by blindness, has no way of telling), she will be able to distinguish which ones were issued with the same bit.

New Randomized Tokens and Private Metadata. To resolve the above issue we introduce a construction which makes the token issuance a randomized functionality where the randomness is shared between the user and the issuer. We use the following function $F_{(x,y)}(t; S) = x\mathsf{H}_t(t) + yS$, where t is the value that will be input of the user and S is the randomness of the evaluation, which will be determined by the two parties, more specifically $S = r^{-1}\mathsf{H}_s(r\mathsf{H}_t(t); s)$ where r is the blinding factor chosen by the user and s is a random value chosen by the issuer. This functionality suffices to construct a new anonymized token where during the oblivious evaluation the user sends $T' = r\mathsf{H}_t(t)$, receives back from the issuer $s, W' = xT' + y\mathsf{H}_s(T'; s)$, unblinds the values $S = r^{-1}\mathsf{H}_s(T'; s)$ and $W = r^{-1}W'$, and outputs (S, W).

The token verification checks that $W = x\mathsf{H}_t(t) + yS$. In order to provide verifiability, the issuer provides an element of the form $X = xG + yH$ and sends a proof that $X = xG + yH$ and $W = x\mathsf{H}_t(t) + yS$ are computed using the same secret key (x, y). This is similar to Okamoto–Schnorr blind signatures [Oka92],

---

[4] In Privacy Pass the resulting value $x\mathsf{H}_t(t)$ is used for the derivation of a HMAC key in order to avoid credential hijacking. We cover token hijacking in the full version. Throughout this work, we assume that the communication channel between user and issuer is encrypted and authenticated.

with the key difference that we redefine this as a secret key primitive which enables us to have a round-optimal blind evaluation algorithm.

We apply the idea of using two different keys for each private metadata bit value to the above randomized construction; the resulting construction is called PMBTokens. The public parameters are now a pair $(X_0 := x_0 G + y_0 H, X_1 := x_1 G + y_1 H)$, a token issued with a private metadata bit b is of the form $W' = x_b \mathsf{H}_t(t) + y_b S$ and the DLEQ proof is replaced with a DLEQOR proof stating that either W' and X_0, or W' and X_1, are computed using the same secret key (x_0, y_0) or (x_1, y_1).

Removing the NIZK. Both Privacy Pass and PMBTokens employ zero-knowledge arguments of knowledge to achieve unlinkability. This approach guarantees that the user can verify that she has obtained a token issued under the same secret key as in the issuer's public parameters. Unlinkability follows from the fact that tokens issued under the same secret key are indistinguishable. We consider a slightly weaker unlinkability guarantee for the user during token issuance, which is that either the token she has received is issued under the public key or the token is indistinguishable from a random value, however, the user cannot distinguish these two cases. Now, a user will not be able to know in advance whether she has a token that will be valid at redemption. Another difference is that, if the issuer misbehaves, incorrectly issued tokens will be indistinguishable for the issuer from incorrectly formed tokens that a malicious user may try to use. Note that in any of the above constructions the issuer also distinguishes valid from invalid, however, the difference is that the she can check if the received tokens are valid.

We present modifications of both Privacy Pass and PMBTokens that satisfy this version of unlinkability, while removing the need for DLEQ or DLEQOR proofs and improving the computational cost for the issuer, which is the bottleneck in systems that need to support large number of users who perform many transactions and hence need to obtain tokens regularly.

Our approach for removing the DLEQ proof from Privacy Pass borrows ideas from the construction of a verifiable partially oblivious PRF of Jarecki et al. [JKR18], but simplifies their construction which has additional complexity in order to achieve user verifiability. We use the idea to use not only multiplicative but also additive blinding of the user's input in the form $T' = r(\mathsf{H}_t(t) - \rho G)$. Now, an honest evaluation of the issuer $W' = xr(\mathsf{H}_t(t) - \rho G)$ can be unblinded by the user by computing $r^{-1}W + \rho X = x\mathsf{H}_t(t) - \rho(xG) + \rho X = x\mathsf{H}_t(t)$, where $X = xG$ is the issuer's public key. On the other hand, any dishonestly computed W' which is of the form $W' = r^{-1}T' + P$ for some $P \neq 0$ when unblinded will contain a random additive factor $r^{-1}P$, thus the resulting value will be random. Similarly to Jarecki et al. [JKR18], we can recover verifiability by doing another oblivious evaluation on the same value t and comparing the outputs, which will be equal only if the issuer used the public key for both executions. We also observe that these checks can be batched for an arbitrary number of issued tokens by computing a random linear combination of the values $\mathsf{H}_t(t_i)$, obtaining a VOPRF evaluation on that value, and comparing with the same linear combination of the other tokens. Thus a user can verify n tokens by running one additional token request only. We note further that removing the zero knowledge argument significantly simplifies the issuer work, which now consist only of one multiplication.

Applying the above idea to the anonymous token construction with private metadata bit is more challenging since the user does not know which of the two public keys the issuer will use. However, the user can unblind the response from the issuer using each of the public keys and thus obtain one valid and one random token. This property turns out to be true if the issuer behaves honestly but if the issuer is malicious, he can create public keys and a response W' such that the two values obtained from the unblinding with each of the public keys are correlated and this correlation can be used for fingerprinting the user. Thus, in our construction the user computes two values $T'_d = r_d(\mathsf{H}_t(t) - \rho_d G)$, for $d = 0, 1$, and the issuer uses one of them to compute his response $W' = x_b T'_b + y_b S'_b$ with a private bit b. The user unblinds W' using both public keys and the scalars r_d, ρ_d for $d \in \{0, 1\}$ to obtain S_0, W_0, S_1, W_1, which she uses for the final token. The resulting token verifies with only one of the issuer's keys: the key corresponding to the private metadata value.

Verification Oracle. One last wrinkle in the security proof is whether the adversary for unforgeability and privacy of the metadata bit properties should have access to a verification oracle for tokens of his choice. This is not explicitly supported in the current Privacy Pass security proof [DGS+18]. We provide a new proof for unforgeability of Privacy Pass in the presence of a verification oracle based on a different hardness assumption, the *Chosen Target Gap Diffie–Hellman* assumption, which is a formalization of the Chosen Target Diffie–Hellman in a Gap DH group, which was defined by Boneh et al. [BLS01]. In the context of anonymous tokens with private metadata bit, we distinguish a VERIFY oracle which just simply checks validity of the token, and a READ oracle that returns the *value* of the private metadata bit (which could be 0, 1, or invalid, and in some applications, e.g. blocklisting, we can merge the states of value 0 and invalid bit). We present an anonymous token construction that provides unforgeability and privacy for the metadata bit even when the adversary has access to the VERIFY oracle, but we crucially require that the adversary *does not get an oracle access that reads the private metadata bit of a token.*

Efficiency of Our Constructions. We consider the most expensive computation operation in the above protocols (scalar multiplication) and the largest communication overhead (the number of group elements transferred). We report in Table 1 the efficiency of our constructions. Additionally, the variant of our constructions that supports a verification oracle in the PMB security game adds the overhead of Okamoto–Schnorr Privacy Pass to the overhead of PMBTokens. The modifications of the constructions that do not use DLEQ or DLEQOR proofs save work for the issuer with no or moderate increase in communication and increased user computation. This computation trade-off is beneficial for settings where the issuer handles orders of magnitude more token issuance requests than any particular user. We further implement our constructions in Rust, and

Table 1. Computation and communication costs of our constructions.

Construction	# Multiplications		Communication
	user	issuer	(# elements)
PP (Constr. 1), [DGS+18]	6	3	2
OSPP (Constr. 2)	9	6	2
PMBT (Constr. 3)	15	12	2
PPB (Constr. 4)	4	1	2
PMBTB (Constr. 5)	12	2	3

report their practicals costs in Sect. 8. Using a Ristretto group on Curve25519, PMBTokens issuance runs in 845 µs and redemption takes 235 µs, while Privacy Pass issuance runs in 303 µs and redemption takes 95 µs. Without the issuance NIZK, Construction 5 introduces a small overhead over Privacy Pass.

Paper Organization. We overview the hardness assumptions and the building block primitives we use in Sect. 2. Section 3 defines our new anonymous tokens primitive and its security notions. We recall the Privacy Pass construction in Sect. 4, and present a (randomized) Okamoto–Schnorr anonymous tokens construction in Sect. 5. Next, Sect. 6 presents our construction for anonymous tokens with private metadata bit, called PMBTokens. Section 7 proposes modifications of Privacy Pass and PMBTokens that avoid the need of zero-knowledge proofs. Finally, Sect. 8 reports on the efficiency costs of our implementation.

Due to space constraints, the security proofs are provided in the full version of this paper [KLOR20].

1.2 Related Work

Starting with the work of Chaum [Cha82], the concept of blind signatures has been widely used as a tool for building anonymous credentials. Blind Schnorr and Okamoto–Schnorr signatures, which have been studied and analyzed in the random oracle model [CP92, Oka92, PS00, Sch01, Sch06, FPS19], require three moves of interaction between the user and the issuer. Blind signatures constructions that achieve one round, which is the goal for our construction, rely on more expensive building blocks. Partially blind signatures, for which we also have round-optimal constructions [Fis06, SC12, BPV12], allow the issuer to embed some information in the signature, however, this information is *public*, unlike the private metadata bit that is the goal of our construction. The works of Boldyareva [Bol03] and Bellare et al. [BNPS03] achieve round optimal (one round) constructions in the random oracle model under interactive assumptions. These constructions use the same blinding idea as the VOPRF [JKK14] used by Privacy Pass, but are defined over groups where DDH is easy and CDH holds (or where the RSA assumptions hold), which enables public verifiability but requires larger group parameters. Other blind signature constructions have evolved from constructions that need a CRS [Fis06, SC12, BFPV11] to constructions in the standard model [GG14, FHS15, FHKS16], but they rely on bilinear groups. This adds complexity to the group instantiations for schemes and computational cost, which we aim to minimize.

Group signatures [CvH91, Cam97, BMW03] present functionality which allows all member of the group to sign messages, with the property that signatures from different signers are indistinguishable. At the same time there is a master secret key that belongs to a group manager, which can be used to identify the signer of a message. We can view different signer keys as signing keys for the private metadata bits, and the master secret key as a way to read that bit value. Group blind signatures [LR98], which provide also the oblivious evaluation for the signing algorithm we aim at, provide a solution for the anonymous token functionality with a private metadata bit. Existing blind group signatures constructions [LR98, Ram13, Gha13] require multiple rounds of interaction for the oblivious signing and communication of many group elements.

Abdalla et al. [ANN06] introduced a notion of blind message authentication codes (MACs), a secret key analog to blind signatures. They showed that this notion can exist only assuming a commitment of the private key, and showed how to instantiate that primitive with Chaum's blind signatures [Cha82]. Davidson et al. [DGS+18] construct a similar private key functionality for anonymous tokens using a VOPRF [JKK14]; it is called Privacy Pass and is the basis of this work.

Everspaugh et al. [ECS+15] introduce the primitive of a partially oblivious PRF, which analogously to blind signatures allows the party with the secret key to determine part of the input for the PRF evaluation. However, this input needs to be public for verifiability. The presented partially blind PRF uses bilinear groups and pairings. Jarecki et al. [JKR18] show how to obtain a threshold variant of the partially oblivious PRF.

The work of Tsang et al. [TAKS07] presents a construction for blacklistable anonymous credentials using bilinear maps, which enables the issuer to create a blacklist of identities and the user can only generate an authentication token if she is not blacklisted; hence the user does find out whether she has been blacklisted in this process.

In keyed-verification anonymous credentials [CMZ14], the issuer and verifier are the same party. They use an *algebraic* MAC in place of a signature scheme, where the message space is a n-tuple of elements in $\mathbb{Z}_p$ (or in $\mathbb{G}$). They can be used to provide an anonymous token primitive (at a slightly higher cost) but they're overall meant for multi-use credentials. We are not aware of any extension that allows for the embedding of a private metadata bit.

2   Preliminaries

Notation. When sampling the value x uniformly at random from the set S, we write $x \leftarrow_\$ S$. When sampling the value x from a probabilistic algorithm M, we write $x \leftarrow$ M. We use := to denote assignment. For an integer $n \in \mathbb{N}$, we denote

Game $\text{CTGDH}_{\text{GrGen},\text{A},\ell}(\lambda)$	Oracle $\text{TARGET}(t)$	Oracle $\text{HELP}(Y)$
$\Gamma := (\mathbb{G}, p, G) \leftarrow \text{GrGen}(1^\lambda)$	if $t \in \mathcal{Q}$ then	$q := q + 1$
$x \leftarrow_{\$} \mathbb{Z}_p;\ \ X := xG$	$\quad Y := \mathcal{Q}[t]$	return xY
$q := 0;\ \ \mathcal{Q} := [\,]$	else :	
$(t_i, Z_i)_{i \in [\ell+1]} \leftarrow \text{A}^{\text{TARGET},\text{HELP},\text{DDH}}(\Gamma, X)$	$\quad Y \leftarrow_{\$} \mathbb{G}$	Oracle $\text{DDH}(Y, Z)$
for $i \in [\ell + 1]$:	$\quad \mathcal{Q}[t] := Y$	return $(Z = x \cdot Y)$
$\quad$ if $t_i \notin \mathcal{Q}$ then return 0	return Y	
$\quad Y_i := \mathcal{Q}[t_i]$		
return $(q \leq \ell$ and		
$\quad\quad \forall i \neq j \in [\ell+1]\ \ t_i \neq t_j$ and		
$\quad\quad \forall i \in [\ell+1]\ \ xY_i = Z_i)$		

Fig. 1. The Chosen-target gap Diffie–Hellman security game.

with $[n]$ the interval $\{0, \ldots, n-1\}$. We denote vectors in bold. For a vector $\mathbf{a}$, we denote with a_i the i-th element of $\mathbf{a}$.

The output resulting form the interaction of two (interactive) PPT algorithms A, B is denoted as $[a, b] \leftarrow \langle \text{A}, \text{B} \rangle$. If only the first party receives a value at the end of the interaction, we write $a \leftarrow \langle \text{A}, \text{B} \rangle$ instead of $[a, \perp] \leftarrow \langle \text{A}, \text{B} \rangle$.

We assume the existence of a group generator algorithm $\text{GrGen}(1^\lambda)$ that, given as input the security parameter in unary form outputs the description $\Gamma = (\mathbb{G}, p, G, H)$ of a group $\mathbb{G}$ of prime order p; G and H are two nothing-up-my-sleeve (NUMS) generators of $\mathbb{G}$. For simplicity, we will assume that the prime p is of length λ.

2.1 Security Assumptions

We assume the reader to be familiar with the discrete logarithm (DLOG), decisional Diffie–Hellman (DDH), and computational Diffie–Hellman (CDH) assumptions. In this work, we will use the chosen-target gap Diffie–Hellman (CTGDH) assumption.

Chosen-Target Gap Diffie–Hellman. The chosen-target Diffie–Hellman (CTDH) assumption [Bol03, HL06] states that any PPT adversary A has negligible advantage in solving CDH on $\ell + 1$ *target* group elements, even when given access to a CDH helper oracle for ℓ instances. We formalize here its *gap* [OP01] flavor, in which the adversary has, in addition, access to a DDH oracle for arbitrary group elements. Note that the CTDH assumption was originally introduced by Boldyreva [Bol03] in gap DH groups [BLS01], that is, in groups where CDH is hard but DDH is assumed to be easy. In other words, the original definition of CTDH was *already* in groups where the adversary has access to a DDH oracle. Here, we introduce the *chosen-target gap Diffie–Hellman* assumption (CTGDH, that is, the gap version of CTDH) as a security experiment where the adversary is provided a challenge $X \in \mathbb{G}$, and has access to three oracles: the TARGET

Game $\text{KSND}_{\Pi,R,A,\text{Ext}}(\lambda)$	Game $\text{ZK}^{\beta}_{\Pi,R,A}(\lambda)$	Oracle $\text{PROVE}(\phi,w)$
$\Gamma \leftarrow \text{GrGen}(1^{\lambda})$	$\Gamma \leftarrow \text{GrGen}(1^{\lambda})$	if $R(\phi,w) = \textbf{false}$ then
$(\text{crs},\text{td}) \leftarrow \Pi.\text{Setup}(\Gamma)$	$(\text{crs},\tau) \leftarrow \Pi.\text{Setup}(\Gamma)$	return $\perp$
$r \leftarrow_{\$} \{0,1\}^{A.\text{rl}(\lambda)};\;\; (\phi,\pi) := A(\text{crs};r)$	$\beta' \leftarrow A^{\text{PROVE}}(\text{crs})$	$\pi_0 \leftarrow \Pi.\text{Prove}(\text{crs},\phi,w)$
$w \leftarrow \text{Ext}(\text{td},r)$	return β'	$\pi_1 \leftarrow \Pi.\text{Sim}(\text{crs},\tau,\phi)$
return $(\Pi.\text{Verify}(\text{crs},\phi,\pi)$ and $R(\phi,w) = \textbf{false})$		return π_{β}

Fig. 2. Games for knowledge soundness (KSND), and zero knowledge (ZK).

oracle, that given as input a string $t \in \{0,1\}^{*}$, outputs a random group element; the HELP oracle, that outputs the CDH of X with an arbitrary group element $Y \in \mathbb{G}$, and the DDH oracle, that given as input two group elements $(Y,Z) \in \mathbb{G}^{2}$ returns 1 if and only if (X,Y,Z) is a Diffie–Hellman tuple. We describe the TARGET oracle in this cumbersome way to ease readability of the security proofs later.

Formally, we say that CTGDH holds for the group generator GrGen if for any PPT adversary A, and any $\ell \geq 0$:

$$\text{Adv}^{\text{ctgdh}}_{\text{GrGen},A,\ell}(\lambda) := \Pr\left[\text{CTGDH}_{\text{GrGen},A,\ell}(\lambda) = 1\right] = \text{negl}(\lambda),$$

where $\text{CTGDH}_{\text{GrGen},A,\ell}(\lambda)$ is defined in Fig. 1. Note that for $\ell = 0$, the game $\text{CTGDH}_{\text{GrGen},A,0}(\lambda)$ is equivalent to gap CDH.

2.2 Non-interactive Arguments of Knowledge

A non-interactive proof system Π for relation R consists of the following three algorithms:

- $(\text{crs},\text{td}) \leftarrow \Pi.\text{Setup}(\Gamma)$, the setup algorithm that outputs a common reference string (CRS) crs together with some trapdoor information td.
- $\pi \leftarrow \Pi.\text{Prove}(\text{crs},\phi,w)$, a prover which takes as input some $(\phi,w) \in R$ and a CRS crs, and outputs a proof π.
- $bool \leftarrow \Pi.\text{Verify}(\text{crs},\phi,\pi)$ a verifier that, given as input a statement ϕ together with a proof π outputs **true** or **false**, indicating acceptance of the proof.

The proof system Π is a non-interactive zero-knowledge (NIZK) argument of knowledge if it satisfies the following properties:

Completeness. Π is complete if every correctly generated proof verifies. More formally, a proof system Π is *complete* if for any $\Gamma \in [\text{GrGen}(1^{\lambda})]$, $\text{crs} \in [\Pi.\text{Setup}(\Gamma)]$ and $(\phi,w) \in R$:

$$\Pr[\Pi.\text{Verify}(\text{crs},\phi,\Pi.\text{Prove}(\text{crs},\phi,w))] = 1 - \text{negl}(\lambda).$$

Knowledge Soundness. A proof system Π for relation R is *knowledge-sound* if for any PPT adversary A there exists a PPT extractor Ext such that:

$$\text{Adv}^{\text{ksnd}}_{\Pi,R,A,\text{Ext}}(\lambda) := \Pr\left[\text{KSND}_{\Pi,R,A,\text{Ext}}(\lambda)\right] = \text{negl}(\lambda),$$

where $\mathsf{KSND}_{\Pi,\mathsf{R},\mathsf{A},\mathsf{Ext}}(\lambda)$ is defined in Fig. 2 and $\mathsf{A}.\mathsf{rl}(\lambda)$ is the randomness length for the machine A. An *argument of knowledge* is a knowledge-sound proof system. In our proofs, for ease of notation, we will omit to specify explicitly that the extractor takes as input the coins of the adversary.

Zero Knowledge. A proof system Π for R is *zero-knowledge* if no information about the witness is leaked by the proof, besides membership in the relation. This is formalized by specifying an additional PPT algorithm $\Pi.\mathsf{Sim}$, that takes as input the trapdoor information td and a statement ϕ, and outputs a valid proof π indistinguishable from those generated via $\Pi.\mathsf{Prove}$. Formally, A proof system Π for relation R is zero-knowledge if for any PPT adversary A:

$$\mathsf{Adv}^{\mathsf{zk}}_{\Pi,\mathsf{R},\mathsf{A}}(\lambda) := \left| \Pr\left[\mathsf{ZK}^0_{\Pi,\mathsf{R},\mathsf{A}}(\lambda)\right] - \Pr\left[\mathsf{ZK}^1_{\Pi,\mathsf{R},\mathsf{A}}(\lambda)\right] \right| = \mathsf{negl}(\lambda),$$

where $\mathsf{ZK}^\beta_{\Pi,\mathsf{R},\mathsf{A}}(\lambda)$ is defined in Fig. 2.

Throughout this paper, we will assume the existence of the following proof systems, that we summarize here in Camenisch-Stadler notation [Cam97]:

$$\Pi_{\mathsf{DLOG}} := \mathrm{NIZK}\{(x) : X = xG\} \tag{1}$$

$$\Pi_{\mathsf{DLEQ}} := \mathrm{NIZK}\{(x) : X = xG \ \wedge \ W = xT\} \tag{2}$$

$$\Pi_{\mathsf{DLEQ2}} := \mathrm{NIZK}\{(x,y) : X = xG + yH \ \wedge \ W = xT + yS\} \tag{3}$$

$$\Pi_{\mathsf{DLOGAND2}} := \mathrm{NIZK}\{(\mathbf{x},\mathbf{y}) : \forall i \in \{0,1\}\ X_i = x_iG + y_iH\} \tag{4}$$

$$\Pi_{\mathsf{DLEQOR2}} := \mathrm{NIZK}\{(x,y) : \exists i \in \{0,1\}\ X_i = xG + yH \wedge W = xT + yS\} \tag{5}$$

Equation (1) and Eq. (4) are discrete logarithm proofs for one, respectively two generators. Equation (2) and Eq. (3) prove discrete logarithm equality under one, respectively two generators. Finally, Eq. (5) proves discrete logarithm equality for one out of two group elements (in the witness, the index is denoted as $i \in \{0,1\}$). In the full version [KLOR20], we provide a more formal description of the above relations, and efficient instantiations with techniques for batching proofs at issuance time.

3   Anonymous Tokens

We describe two flavors of anonymous tokens. The first flavor enables a *user* to obtain a *token* from an *issuer*; the user can later use this token as a trust signal, for one-time authentication. In the second flavor, the issuer has an additional input during the token issuance, a *private metadata bit*, that is hidden within the token. The private metadata bit can later be recovered by the issuer at redemption time. The following definition captures both functionalities; in shaded text, we refer only to the anonymous token with private metadata bit.

Anonymous Token. An *anonymous token scheme with private metadata bit* AT consists of the following algorithms:

- $(\mathsf{crs}, \mathsf{td}) \leftarrow \mathsf{AT}.\mathsf{Setup}(1^\lambda)$, the setup algorithm that takes as input the security parameter λ in unary form, and returns a CRS crs and a trapdoor td.
  All the remaining algorithms take crs as their first input, but for notational clarity, we usually omit it from their lists of arguments.

- $(\mathsf{pp}, \mathsf{sk}) \leftarrow \mathsf{AT.KeyGen}(\mathsf{crs})$, the key generation algorithm that generates a private key sk along with a set of public parameters pp;
- $\sigma \leftarrow \langle \mathsf{AT.User}(\mathsf{pp}, t), \mathsf{AT.Sign}(\mathsf{sk}, b) \rangle$, the token issuance protocol, that involves interactive algorithms $\mathsf{AT.User}$ (run by the user) with input a value $t \in \{0,1\}^\lambda$, and $\mathsf{AT.Sign}$ (run by the issuer) with input the private key sk and a bit b. At the end of the interaction, the issuer outputs nothing, while the user outputs σ, or $\perp$.
- $bool \leftarrow \mathsf{AT.Verify}(\mathsf{sk}, t, \sigma)$, the verification algorithm that takes as input the private key sk and a token (t, σ). It returns a boolean indicating if the token was valid or not.
- $\mathsf{ind} \leftarrow \mathsf{AT.ReadBit}(\mathsf{sk}, t, \sigma)$, the metadata extraction algorithm that takes as input the private key sk, and a token (t, σ). It returns an indicator $\mathsf{ind} \in \{\perp, 0, 1\}$, which is either the private metadata bit, or $\perp$.

Throughout the rest of this paper, we assume that AT has a one-round signing protocol initiated by the user. Thus, for simplicity, we split the signing algorithms ($\mathsf{AT.Sign}$ and $\mathsf{AT.User}$) into non-interactive algorithms that take as input a message, and the partial state (if any). They will return the next message together with the updated state st_i. Concretely, the signing protocol will be composed of the following (non-interactive) algorithms:

- $(\mathsf{usr\_msg}_0, \mathsf{st}_0) \leftarrow \mathsf{AT.User}_0(\mathsf{pp}, t)$;
- $\mathsf{srv\_msg}_1 \leftarrow \mathsf{AT.Sign}_0(\mathsf{sk}, b, \mathsf{usr\_msg}_0)$;
- $\sigma \leftarrow \mathsf{AT.User}_1(\mathsf{st}_0, \mathsf{srv\_msg}_1)$

We demand that anonymous token schemes satisfies correctness, unforgeability, unlinkability, and privacy of the metadata bit.

Correctness. An anonymous token scheme AT is *correct* if any honestly-generated token verifies and the correct private metadata bit is retrieved successfully. That is, for any $\mathsf{crs} \in [\mathsf{AT.Setup}(1^\lambda)]$, any $(\mathsf{pp}, \mathsf{sk}) \in [\mathsf{AT.KeyGen}(\mathsf{crs})]$, any $t \in \{0,1\}^\lambda$, and $b \in \{0,1\}$:

$$\Pr[\mathsf{AT.Verify}(\mathsf{sk}, t, \langle \mathsf{AT.User}(\mathsf{pp}, t), \mathsf{AT.Sign}(\mathsf{sk}, b) \rangle) = 1] = 1 - \mathsf{negl}(\lambda), \quad (6)$$

$$\Pr[\mathsf{AT.ReadBit}(\mathsf{sk}, t, \langle \mathsf{AT.User}(\mathsf{pp}, t), \mathsf{AT.Sign}(\mathsf{sk}, b) \rangle) = b] = 1 - \mathsf{negl}(\lambda) \quad (7)$$

Unforgeability. The first security property that we require from an anonymous token is unforgeability, which guarantees that no adversary can redeem more tokens than it is allowed. This is formalized with a standard one-more security game where the adversary can interact with the issuer at most ℓ times, and at the end must output $\ell + 1$ valid tokens. The adversary has also access to a verification oracle for tokens of its choice. In the private metadata bit variant, the adversary can interact with the issuer ℓ times for each private metadata bit, but should not be able to generate $\ell + 1$ valid tokens with the same private metadata.

Definition 1 (One-more unforgeability). *An anonymous token scheme* AT *is* one-more unforgeable *if for any* PPT *adversary* A, *and any* $\ell \geq 0$:

$$\mathsf{Adv}^{\mathrm{omuf}}_{\mathsf{AT}, A, \ell}(\lambda) := \Pr[\mathrm{OMUF}_{\mathsf{AT}, A, \ell}(\lambda) = 1] = \mathsf{negl}(\lambda),$$

Game $\text{OMUF}_{\text{AT},A,\ell}(\lambda)$	Oracle $\text{SIGN}(b, \text{msg})$
$(\text{crs}, \text{td}) \leftarrow \text{AT.Setup}(1^\lambda)$	$q_b := q_b + 1$
$(\text{pp}, \text{sk}) \leftarrow \text{AT.KeyGen}(\text{crs})$	**return** $\text{AT.Sign}_0(\text{sk}, b, \text{msg})$
for $b = 0, 1 : q_b := 0$	Oracle $\text{VERIFY}(t, \sigma)$
$(t_i, \sigma_i)_{i \in [\ell+1]} \leftarrow A^{\text{SIGN}, \text{VERIFY}, \text{READ}}(\text{crs}, \text{pp})$	
return $(\forall b = 0, 1 \ q_b \leq \ell$ **and**	**return** $\text{AT.Verify}(\text{sk}, t, \sigma)$
$\forall i \neq j \in [\ell+1] \ \ t_i \neq t_j$ **and**	Oracle $\text{READ}(t, \sigma)$
$\forall i \in [\ell+1] \ \ \text{AT.Verify}(\text{sk}, t_i, \sigma_i) = \textbf{true}$ **and**	
$\exists b \in \{0, 1\} : \ \forall i \in [\ell+1] \ \ \text{AT.ReadBit}(\text{sk}, t_i, \sigma_i) = b)$	**return** $\text{AT.ReadBit}(\text{sk}, t, \sigma)$

Fig. 3. One-more unforgeability game for the anonymous token scheme AT.

where $\text{OMUF}_{\text{AT},A,\ell}(\lambda)$ *is defined in Fig. 3.*

Unlinkability. This security property is concerned with user anonymity, and guarantees that a malicious issuer cannot link the redemption of a token with a particular execution of the token issuance protocol. More precisely, in κ-unlinkability, if m tokens were issued but not yet redeemed, the adversary cannot link the relative issuance session of a token with probability better than κ/m, even after seeing the remaining $m - 1$ tokens in a random order.

Definition 2 (Unlinkability). *An anonymous token scheme* AT *is* κ-unlinkable *if for any* PPT *adversary* A, *and any* $m > 0$:

$$\text{Adv}^{\text{unlink}}_{\text{AT},A,m}(\lambda) := \Pr\left[\text{UNLINK}_{\text{AT},A,m}(\lambda) = 1\right] \leq \frac{\kappa}{m} + \text{negl}(\lambda),$$

where $\text{UNLINK}_{\text{AT},A,m}(\lambda)$ *is defined in Fig. 4.*

Private Metadata Bit. The last security property protects the private metadata bit in the issued tokens.[5] It guarantees that the private metadata embedded in a token is entirely hidden from anyone who does not possess the private key including the user. More precisely, we require that, even if the adversary corrupts a large number of users, it cannot guess with probability non-negligibly bigger than $1/2$ if newly issued tokens have private metadata 0 or 1.

Formally, this is modeled as an indistinguishability game where the adversary has access to two signing oracles: one where it can provide both the message to be signed and the private metadata bit to be used, and one where the adversary chooses only the message (the metadata bit is fixed), and a verification oracle for the validity of the tokens. The adversary's goal is to guess the challenge private metadata bit used.

---

[5] Consider, e.g., the following practical scenario: the issuer is suspecting that it is targeted by a DoS attack, and decides to tag users that it believes are controlled by a bot using the private metadata bit. The private metadata bit property ensures it is difficult for anyone, but the issuer, to learn how malicious traffic is classified.

Game $\text{UNLINK}_{\text{AT},A,m}(\lambda)$	Oracle $\text{USER}_0()$
$(\text{crs},\text{td}) \leftarrow \text{AT.Setup}(1^\lambda)$	$q_0 := q_0 + 1$ // session id
$(\text{st},\text{pp}) \leftarrow A(\text{crs})$	$t_{q_0} \leftarrow_{\$} \{0,1\}^\lambda$
$q_0 := 0;\ q_1 := 0;\ \mathcal{Q} := \emptyset$	$(\text{msg}_{q_0}, \text{st}_{q_0}) \leftarrow \text{AT.User}_0(\text{pp}, t_{q_0})$
$(\text{st}, (\text{msg}_i)_{i\in\mathcal{Q}}) \leftarrow A^{\text{USER}_0,\text{USER}_1}(\text{st})$	$\mathcal{Q} := \mathcal{Q} \cup \{q_0\}$ // open sessions
if $\mathcal{Q} = \emptyset$ **then return** 0	**return** (q_0, msg_{q_0})
// compute a challenge token	
$j \leftarrow_{\$} \mathcal{Q};\ \mathcal{Q} := \mathcal{Q} \setminus \{j\}$	Oracle $\text{USER}_1(j, \text{msg})$
$\sigma_j \leftarrow \text{AT.User}_1(\text{st}_j, \text{msg}_j)$	**if** $j \notin \mathcal{Q}$ **then**
// compute and permute other tokens	**return** $\perp$
for $i \in \mathcal{Q} : \sigma_i \leftarrow \text{AT.User}_1(\text{st}_i, \text{msg}_i)$	$\sigma \leftarrow \text{AT.User}_1(\text{st}_j, \text{msg})$
$\phi \leftarrow_{\$} \mathcal{S}_{\mathcal{Q}}$	**if** $\sigma \neq\perp$ **then**
$j' \leftarrow A(\text{st}, (t_j, \sigma_j), (t_{\phi(i)}, \sigma_{\phi(i)})_{i\in\mathcal{Q}})$	$\mathcal{Q} := \mathcal{Q} \setminus \{j\}$
return $q_0 - q_1 \geq m$ **and** $j' = j$	$q_1 := q_1 + 1$
	return σ

Fig. 4. Unlinkability game for the anonymous token scheme AT. For a set X, $\mathcal{S}_X$ denotes the symmetric group of X.

Game $\text{PMB}^\beta_{\text{AT},A}(\lambda)$	Oracle $\text{SIGN}(\text{msg})$	Oracle $\text{VERIFY}(t,\sigma)$
$(\text{crs},\text{td}) \leftarrow \text{AT.Setup}(1^\lambda)$	**return** $\text{AT.Sign}_0(\text{sk}, \beta, \text{msg})$	**return** $\text{AT.Verify}(\text{sk}, t, \sigma)$
$(\text{pp},\text{sk}) \leftarrow \text{AT.KeyGen}(\text{crs})$		
$\beta' \leftarrow A^{\text{SIGN},\text{SIGN}',\text{VERIFY}}(\text{crs},\text{pp})$	Oracle $\text{SIGN}'(b, \text{msg})$	
return β'	**return** $\text{AT.Sign}_0(\text{sk}, b, \text{msg})$	

Fig. 5. Private metadata bit game for the anonymous token scheme AT.

Definition 3 (Private metadata bit). *An anonymous token scheme* AT *provides* private metadata bit *if for any* PPT *adversary* A:

$$\text{Adv}^{\text{pmb}}_{\text{AT},A}(\lambda) := \left| \Pr\left[\text{PMB}^0_{\text{AT},A}(\lambda)\right] - \Pr\left[\text{PMB}^1_{\text{AT},A}(\lambda)\right] \right| = \text{negl}(\lambda),$$

where $\text{PMB}^\beta_{\text{AT},A}(\lambda)$ *is defined in Fig. 5.*

Token Hijacking. In our formalization, we do not consider man-in-the-middle adversaries that can steal tokens from honest users. This attack vector, called *token hijacking*, can be mitigated with the use of message authentication codes (MACs). Roughly speaking, instead of sending the entire token (t, σ) over the wire, the user can derive a symmetric key $\text{k} := \text{H}(\sigma)$ to MAC a shared message (e.g., the resource or the URL she's trying to access). The resulting message authentication code is sent together with t to the issuer (and any supplementary randomness that the user needs to recompute σ). We discuss in detail such concerns in the full version of this paper [KLOR20].

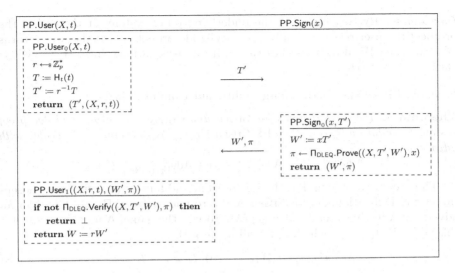

Fig. 6. Token issuance for PP (Construction 1).

4   Review: Privacy Pass

We start by recalling, using the notation from Sect. 3, the anonymous token scheme proposed in [DGS+18] (under the name Privacy Pass) and built on top of the verifiable oblivious PRF (VOPRF) "2HashDH-NIZK" [JKK14]. Privacy Pass uses a Schnorr proof in the issuance phase, that we generalize here to any NIZK. Differently from the initial proof of Goldberg et al. [DGS+18], our proof takes into account the presence of a verification oracle, and the knowledge error of the proof system.

Construction 1 (Privacy Pass). Let Π_{DLEQ} be a proof system for relation R_{DLEQ}; let H_t be a random oracle $\{0,1\}^* \to \mathbb{G}$. The anonymous token scheme PP [DGS+18] is composed of the following algorithms:

- $(\mathsf{crs}, \mathsf{td}) \leftarrow \mathsf{PP.Setup}(1^\lambda)$: invoke the group generator $\Gamma \leftarrow \mathsf{GrGen}(1^\lambda)$ and the CRS generation algorithm of the underlying proof system $(\mathsf{pcrs}, \mathsf{ptd}) \leftarrow \Pi_{\mathsf{DLEQ}}.\mathsf{Setup}(\Gamma)$. Return $\mathsf{crs} := (\Gamma, \mathsf{pcrs})$ and $\mathsf{td} := \mathsf{ptd}$.
- $(X, x) \leftarrow \mathsf{PP.KeyGen}(\mathsf{crs})$: sample a uniformly random element $x \leftarrow_\$ \mathbb{Z}_p^*$, that will constitute the secret key. Let $X := xG$ be the public parameter. Return (X, x).
- $W \leftarrow \langle \mathsf{PP.User}(X, t), \mathsf{PP.Sign}(x) \rangle$: illustrated in Fig. 6.
- $bool \leftarrow \mathsf{PP.Verify}(x, t, W)$: return **true** if $W = xH_t(t)$; else, return **false**.

Note that this anonymous token protocol is deterministic, i.e., there will exist a unique value $W \in \mathbb{G}$ corresponding to a string $t \in \{0,1\}^\lambda$ that verifies. This property will make difficult to directly extend the construction to support private metadata bit.

Correctness. By correctness of the underlying proof system, at the end of the protocol the user returns $\perp$ only with negligible probability. If the user returns $W \in \mathbb{G}$, then W always satisfies the verification equation, since: $W = rW' = r(xT') = xT = x\mathsf{H}_t(t)$.

Security. PP satisfies both unforgeability and 1-unlinkability.

Theorem 4. *If CTGDH holds for* GrGen *and* Π_{DLEQ} *is a zero-knowledge proof system for relation* R_{DLEQ}, *then* PP[GrGen, Π_{DLEQ}] *is one-more unforgeable with advantage:*

$$\mathsf{Adv}^{\mathrm{omuf}}_{\mathsf{PP},\ell}(\lambda) \le \mathsf{Adv}^{\mathrm{ctgdh}}_{\mathsf{GrGen},\ell}(\lambda) + \mathsf{Adv}^{\mathrm{zk}}_{\Pi_{\mathsf{DLEQ}},\mathsf{R}_{DLEQ}}(\lambda).$$

The proof can be found in the full version, and follows directly from chosen-target gap Diffie–Hellman for GrGen, and zero-knowledge of Π_{DLEQ}. Consider an adversary A in the game $\mathrm{OMUF}_{\mathsf{PP},\mathsf{A}}(\lambda)$. To win the game, A must return $\ell + 1$ tokens $(t_i, W_i)_{i \in [\ell+1]}$ such that, for all $i \in [\ell + 1]$:

$$\text{(a)} \quad x\mathsf{H}_t(t_i) = W_i, \qquad \text{(b)} \quad \forall j \ne i: \quad t_j \ne t_i \tag{8}$$

During its execution, the adversary A can query at most ℓ times the signing oracle, which given as input $T^* \in \mathbb{G}$ computes the Diffie–Hellman $W = xT^*$, and sends it together with a proof π that W was correctly computed; additionally, A can query the oracle $\mathrm{VERIFY}(t^*, W^*)$ that returns 1 if $W^* = x\mathsf{H}_t(t^*)$, that is, if $(X, \mathsf{H}_t(t^*), W^*)$ is a DH tuple. Since Π_{DLEQ} is zero-knowledge, it is possible to simulate the proof π. We are thus left with the game CTGDH (Fig. 1), where VERIFY can be replaced by the oracle DDH, H_t by TARGET, and SIGN by the oracle HELP (together with $\Pi_{\mathsf{DLEQ}}.\mathrm{Sim}$).

Theorem 5. *Let* GrGen *be a group generator algorithm. If* Π_{DLEQ} *is a knowledge-sound proof system for relation* R_{DLEQ}, *then* PP[GrGen, Π_{DLEQ}] *is 1-unlinkable.*

We remark that the i-th message sent by PP.User$_0$ is $T'_i = r^{-1}T_i$, for a uniformly random $r_i \in \mathbb{Z}_p^*$. Therefore, T'_i contains no information about T_i or t_i. Additionally, by knowledge soundness of Π_{DLEQ}, it is possible to extract the witness $x \in \mathbb{Z}_p$ used to compute the signatures. With it, the user can compute W_i herself, without ever using the responses from the issuer. It follows that the view of the adversary is limited to random group elements and PP is 1-unlinkable, as long as the proof system is knowledge-sound.

5   Okamoto–Schnorr Privacy Pass

In this section, we describe a novel anonymous token scheme that generalizes PP (Sect. 4) and allows for *randomized* tokens, which will be an important property when we extend the construction to support private metadata bit (Sect. 6). Roughly speaking, while in PP we issue tokens (and DLEQ proofs) using one generator G of $\mathbb{G}$, in this construction we will issue tokens under two generators (G, H), in a similar way to Okamoto–Schnorr [Oka92] signatures. Similarly to Okamoto–Schnorr, it is important here that the discrete logarithm of H base G is unknown. Fixing $y = 0$ in the protocol below, we obtain PP (cf. Sect. 4).

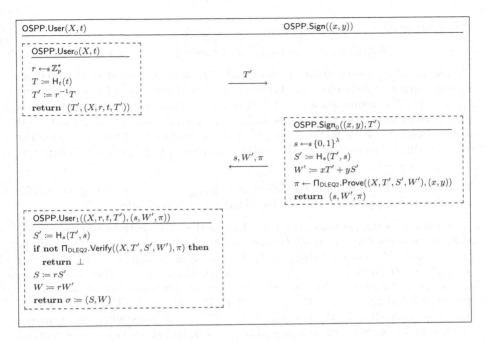

Fig. 7. Token issuance for OSPP (Construction 2).

Construction 2 (Okamoto–Schnorr Privacy Pass). Let GrGen be a group generator algorithm; let Π_{DLEQ2} be a proof system for relation $\mathsf{R}_{\mathsf{DLEQ2}}$; let $\mathsf{H}_t, \mathsf{H}_s$ be two random oracles $\{0,1\}^* \to \mathbb{G}$. We construct an anonymous token scheme OSPP defined by the following algorithms:

- $(\mathsf{crs}, \mathsf{td}) \leftarrow \mathsf{OSPP.Setup}(1^\lambda)$: invoke the group generator $\Gamma \leftarrow \mathsf{GrGen}(1^\lambda)$ and the CRS generation algorithm of the underlying proof system $(\mathsf{pcrs}, \mathsf{ptd}) \leftarrow \Pi_{\mathsf{DLEQ2}}.\mathsf{Setup}(\Gamma)$. Return $\mathsf{crs} := (\Gamma, \mathsf{pcrs})$ and $\mathsf{td} := \mathsf{ptd}$.
- $(X, (x,y)) \leftarrow \mathsf{OSPP.KeyGen}(\mathsf{crs})$: sample the secret key $(x,y) \leftarrow_\$ (\mathbb{Z}_p^*)^2$. Let $X := xG + yH$ be the public parameter. Return $(X, (x,y))$.
- $\sigma \leftarrow \langle \mathsf{OSPP.User}(X, t), \mathsf{OSPP.Sign}((x,y)) \rangle$: illustrated in Fig. 7.
- $bool \leftarrow \mathsf{OSPP.Verify}((x,y), t, \sigma)$: read $(S, W) := \sigma$. Return **true** if $W = x\mathsf{H}_t(t) + yS$; else, return **false**.

Correctness. By correctness of the underlying proof system, the protocol aborts only with negligible probability. If the user returns $\sigma := (S, W) \in \mathbb{G}^2$, then σ always satisfies the verification equation, since $W = rW' = r(xT' + yS') = xT + yS = x\mathsf{H}_t(t) + yS$.

Security. OSPP satisfies both unforgeability and 1-unlinkability.

Theorem 6. *If CTGDH holds for* GrGen, *and* Π_{DLEQ2} *is a zero-knowledge proof system for relation* $\mathsf{R}_{\mathsf{DLEQ2}}$, *then* $\mathsf{OSPP}[\mathsf{GrGen}, \Pi_{\mathsf{DLEQ2}}]$ *is one-more unforgeable* *with advantage:*

$$\mathsf{Adv}^{\mathrm{omuf}}_{\mathsf{OSPP},\ell}(\lambda) \leq \mathsf{Adv}^{\mathrm{ctgdh}}_{\mathsf{GrGen},\ell}(\lambda) + \mathsf{Adv}^{\mathrm{zk}}_{\Pi_{DLEQ2},R_{DLEQ2}}(\lambda).$$

The proof of unforgeability is essentially the same argument of the previous section, with a slightly more careful analysis to deal with the additional element $s \in \{0,1\}^{\lambda}$. The reduction for CTGDH receives a challenge $A \in \mathbb{G}$, that is now embedded in the public parameters as $X = A + yH$ for some $y \leftarrow_{\!\!\$} \mathbb{Z}_p$; the signing oracle computes $W' = \mathrm{HELP}(T') + yS'$, and the read oracle $\mathrm{DDH}(W - yS)$. The tokens returned by the adversary can be converted in CDH solutions computing $W_i - yS_i$, for all $i \in [\ell + 1]$.

Theorem 7. *If DDH holds for* GrGen *and* Π_{DLEQ2} *is an argument of knowledge for relation* R_{DLEQ2}, *then* OSPP[GrGen, Π_{DLEQ2}] *is 1-unlinkable.*

Similarly to the previous proof, we first notice that in the i-th message, T'_i contains no information about t; additionally, by knowledge soundness of the proof system, W_i must be computed with the same "witness" (x, y) satisfying $X = xG + yH$ (if there exists $(x', y') \neq (x, y)$, then it is possible to construct an adversary for discrete log for GrGen). The core difference now is that we use the same blinding factor r both on S' and W'. The proof hence proceeds in two steps: first, $W := rW'$ is computed as $W := xT + yS$ with the extracted witness, and next $S := rS'$ is replaced by $S \leftarrow_{\!\!\$} \mathbb{G}$. This last step can be reduced to DDH: if the adversary manages to distinguish $(T', T = rT', S', S = rS')$ from $(T', T = rT', S', U)$ for $U \leftarrow_{\!\!\$} \mathbb{G}$, then it is possible to construct an adversary B for game $\mathrm{DDH}^{\beta}_{\mathsf{GrGen},\mathsf{B}}(\lambda)$.

6   Private Metadata Bit Tokens

In this section, we present PMBTokens, an extension of the anonymous token construction from Sect. 5 that supports a private metadata bit. The high-level idea is that we use two different secret keys, one for each private metadata bit. In order to hide which bit is associated with the token, we will use OR proofs (i.e., $\Pi_{DLEQOR2}$ of Eq. (5)).

Construction 3 (PMBTokens). Let GrGen be a group generator algorithm; let $\Pi_{DLEQOR2}$ be a proof system for relation $R_{DLEQOR2}$; let H_t, H_s be two random oracles $\{0,1\}^* \to \mathbb{G}$. We construct an anonymous token scheme PMBT defined by the following algorithms:

- (crs, td) ← PMBT.Setup(1^{λ}): invoke the group generator $\Gamma \leftarrow$ GrGen(1^{λ}) and the CRS generation algorithm of the underlying proof system (pcrs, ptd) ← $\Pi_{DLEQOR2}$.Setup(Γ). Return crs := (Γ, pcrs) and td := ptd.
- (**X**, (**x**, **y**)) ← PMBT.KeyGen(crs): let (**x**, **y**) $\leftarrow_{\!\!\$}$ $(\mathbb{Z}_p^*)^2 \times (\mathbb{Z}_p^*)^2$ be the secret key. Define the public parameters as:

$$\mathbf{X} := \begin{bmatrix} X_0 \\ X_1 \end{bmatrix} := \begin{bmatrix} x_0 G + y_0 H \\ x_1 G + y_1 H \end{bmatrix};$$

restart if $X_0 = X_1$. Return (**X**, (**x**, **y**)).

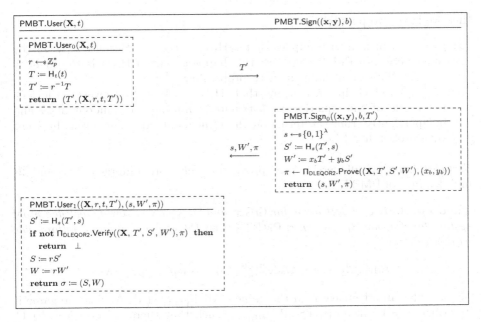

Fig. 8. Token issuance for PMBT (Construction 3).

- $\sigma \leftarrow \langle \mathsf{PMBT.User}(pp, t), \mathsf{PMBT.Sign}(sk, b) \rangle$: illustrated in Fig. 8.
- $bool \leftarrow \mathsf{PMBT.Verify}((\mathbf{x}, \mathbf{y}), t, \sigma)$: return **true**.
- $ind \leftarrow \mathsf{PMBT.ReadBit}((\mathbf{x}, \mathbf{y}), t, \sigma)$: read $(S, W) := \sigma$. Then:
  - (a) if $W = x_0 \mathsf{H}_t(t) + y_0 S$ and $W \neq x_1 \mathsf{H}_t(t) + y_1 S$, return 0;
  - (b) if $W \neq x_0 \mathsf{H}_t(t) + y_0 S$ and $W = x_1 \mathsf{H}_t(t) + y_1 S$, return 1;
  - (c) else, return $\bot$.

Our construction does *not* provide a (meaningful) implementation of Verify, but only a ReadBit functionality. We elaborate this point in Sect. 6.1; this construction can be combined with OSPP to provide an actual verification procedure (described in the full version).

Correctness. Validity of honestly-generated tokens (cf. Eq. (6)) holds perfectly because PMBT.Verify always returns **true**; we focus here on proving that the bit embedded is read correctly with overwhelming probability (Eq. (7)). By correctness of the underlying proof system, the protocol aborts only with negligible probability. If the user returns $(S, W) \in \mathbb{G}^2$, then there exists $b \in \{0, 1\}$ such that $W = rW' = r(x_b T' + y_b S') = x_b T + x_b S = x_b \mathsf{H}_t(t) + y_b S$. The probability that the above equation holds for both $b = 0$ and $b = 1$ (in which case, PMBT.ReadBit returns $\bot$), is statistically negligible. In fact, if:

$$W = x_0 \mathsf{H}_t(t) + y_0 S = x_1 \mathsf{H}_t(t) + y_1 S,$$

then we have two possibilities:

(a) $y_0 = y_1$, which in turn implies that $x_0 H_t(t) = x_1 H_t(t)$. Because $x_0 \neq x_1$ (by construction of PMBT.KeyGen), this happens only if $H_t(t)$ is the identity element. This event happens with probability $1/p$;

(b) $y_0 \neq y_1$, which in turn means that: $H_t(t) = \frac{x_0 - x_1}{y_0 - y_1} S$. However, the left-hand side of the equation is distributed uniformly at random in $\mathbb{G}$ and independently from the terms on the right-hand side. This event happens with probability $1/p$.

Security. In the full version, we prove the one-more unforgeability and **2-unlinkability** of PMBT.

Theorem 8. *If CTGDH holds for* GrGen *and* Π_{DLEQ2} *is a zero-knowledge proof system for relation* R_{DLEQ2}, *then* PMBT[GrGen, Π_{DLEQ2}] *is one-more unforgeable with advantage:*

$$\mathsf{Adv}^{\mathrm{omuf}}_{\mathsf{PMBT},\ell}(\lambda) \leq 2\mathsf{Adv}^{\mathrm{ctgdh}}_{\mathsf{GrGen},\ell}(\lambda) + \mathsf{Adv}^{\mathrm{zk}}_{\Pi_{\mathsf{DLEQ2}},R_{DLEQ}}(\lambda).$$

Consider an adversary A in the game $\mathrm{OMUF}_{\mathsf{PMBT},\mathsf{A}}(\lambda)$. A wins the game if it returns $\ell + 1$ tokens $(t_i, (S_i, W_i))_{i \in [\ell+1]}$ such that there exists a $b \in \{0,1\}$ satisfying:

$$(a) \ \forall i \in [\ell+1]: \ x_b H_t(t_i) + y_b S_i = W_i, \qquad (b) \ \forall j \neq i: \ t_j \neq t_i. \qquad (9)$$

During its execution, A can query $\ell + 1$ times the signing oracle for $b = 0$, *and* $\ell+1$ times for $b = 1$. We claim (in a similar way to Eq. (8)), that A can be used to construct an adversary B that solves CTGDH. We embed the CTGDH challenge $A \in \mathbb{G}$ in one of the two keys: we sample $b^* \leftarrow_\$ \{0,1\}$, and set $X_{b^*} := A + y_{b^*} H$, where $y_{b^*} \leftarrow_\$ \mathbb{Z}_p$. We construct X_{1-b^*} following the key generation algorithm. Queries by A to the oracle SIGN are responded in the following way: if the adversary demands issuance for hidden metadata b^*, we use the HELP oracle to return $W' = \mathrm{HELP}(t, T') + y_{b^*} S'$; otherwise B just follows the signing protocol and computes W' using (x_{1-b^*}, y_{1-b^*}). The zero-knowledge proof is simulated. Queries to the oracle READ can still be answered by B with the help of the oracle DDH available in the game $\mathrm{CTGDH}_{\mathsf{GrGen},\mathsf{B}}(\lambda)$. Queries to VERIFY are trivially dealt with, by answering **true**. If at the end of its execution A presents forgeries for the bit $b = b^*$, then by winning condition (a) (cf. Eq. (9)), for all $i \in [\ell + 1]$, $(W_i - y_{b^*} S_i)$ is the CDH of the challenge A with $H_t(t_i)$, which we replace with the CTGDH oracle TARGET thus presenting $\ell + 1$ CDH solutions for the challenge $A \in \mathbb{G}$. If the guess b^* was not correct, then B outputs $\bot$, and we consider the game lost. It follows that B wins the game $\mathrm{CTGDH}_{\mathsf{GrGen},\mathsf{B},\ell}(\lambda)$ half the time that A wins $\mathrm{OMUF}_{\mathsf{PMBT},\mathsf{A},\ell}(\lambda)$.

Theorem 9. *If DDH holds for* GrGen *and* Π_{DLEQOR2} *is a knowledge-sound proof system for relation* R_{DLEQOR2}, *then* PMBT[GrGen, Π_{DLEQOR2}] *is 2-unlinkable.*

The key idea is that adversary can now embed different private metadata bits at issuance time, at most halving the anonymity set. We use the knowledge extractor to partition the sessions in two buckets: U_0, those associated to the bit 0, and U_1, those with bit 1. We sample a biased $b \in \{0, 1\}$ (depending on the distribution of the private metadata bit in the tokens) and select two sessions coming from the same bucket U_b. The probability of success of the adversary will be upper bounded by $2/m + \mathsf{negl}(\lambda)$.

Theorem 10. *If DDH holds for the group generator* GrGen, *and* Π_{DLEQOR2} *is a zero-knowledge proof system for relation* $\mathsf{R}_{\mathsf{DLEQOR2}}$ *then* $\mathsf{PMBT}[\mathsf{GrGen}, \Pi_{\mathsf{DLEQOR2}}]$ *provides private metadata bit with advantage:*

$$\mathsf{Adv}^{\mathsf{pmb}}_{\mathsf{PMBT}}(\lambda) \leq \frac{O(q^2)}{2^\lambda} + 2\mathsf{Adv}^{\mathsf{ddh}}_{\mathsf{GrGen}}(\lambda) + 2\mathsf{Adv}^{\mathsf{zk}}_{\Pi_{\mathsf{DLEQOR2}}, \mathsf{R}_{\mathsf{DLEQOR2}}}(\lambda),$$

where q is the number of queries the adversary makes to H_s *or* SIGN.

The proof is done by means of a hybrid argument, where the first hybrid is $\mathsf{PMB}^0_{\mathsf{A},\mathsf{PMBT}}(\lambda)$ and the last hybrid is $\mathsf{PMB}^1_{\mathsf{A},\mathsf{PMBT}}(\lambda)$. In the first hybrid, instead of generating the proof using the prover $\Pi_{\mathsf{DLEQOR2}}.\mathsf{Prove}$ in the SIGN$'$ oracle, we use the zero-knowledge simulator $\Pi_{\mathsf{DLEQOR2}}.\mathsf{Sim}$. The advantage in distinguishing is trivially $\mathsf{Adv}^{\mathsf{zk}}_{\Pi_{\mathsf{DLEQOR2}}, \mathsf{R}_{\mathsf{DLEQOR2}}, \mathsf{B}}(\lambda)$. Then, instead of computing the signature as $W' = x_0 T' + y_0 S'$, it computes $W' := x_0 T' + y' S'$, for some $y' \leftarrow_{\$} \mathbb{Z}_p$ sampled after the key generation phase. This hybrid can be shown indistinguishable from the previous one under DDH assumption: $(X - x_0 G, S', W' - x_0 T') \in \mathbb{G}$ is in fact a DDH triple in the previous hybrid, and a random triple now. Using random self-reducibility of DDH we can answer all queries to SIGN$'$ using a single DDH challenge. At this point, we remark that W' is distributed uniformly at random (because $y'S'$ is so) and we can therefore swap x_0 with x_1. A final sequence of hybrids replaces y' with y_1 (again indistinguishable from DDH) and then the simulator with the honest prover. The full proof is available in the full version of this paper [KLOR20].

6.1   Enabling Token Verification

The anonymous token scheme PMBT (Construction 3) does not provide a meaningful verification algorithm, as it always output **true**. Indeed, we note that, given two tokens $(t_0, (S_0, W_0))$ and $(t_1, (S_1, W_1))$, if $t_0 = t_1$, then $(t^* = t_0 = t_1, (S^* = 2S_0 - S_1, W^* = 2W_0 - W_1))$ is a triple of random elements satisfying $W^* = x_b \mathsf{H}(t^*) + y_b S^*$ only if the same metadata bit b was used. Henceforth, having a verification oracle that checks for the above relation allows an adversary in the game $\mathsf{PMB}^\beta_{\mathsf{PMBT},\mathsf{A}}(\lambda)$ to check if two tokens corresponding to the same t were issued with the same private metadata bit.

Instead, we propose to enable such a functionality by combining the PMBT scheme with Okamoto–Schnorr Privacy Pass, into one token that has two parts: a token that has no private metadata and can be used for validity verification, and a second token, which provides a private metadata bit. It is important that these two parts could not be separated (they will depend on the same $H_t(t)$, S values) and used independently for the purpose of reading the metadata bit. We present in details the design combining Constrs. 2 and 3 in the full version [KLOR20].

Jumping ahead, we can also instantiate this design by combining Constrs. 4 and 5 that do not use NIZK during issuance. In the later case the unlinkability will degrade to 6-unlinkability since the issuer can cause each of the two token to be invalid independently.

7   Removing the NIZKs During Issuance

In this section, we present a general technique for removing the NIZK sent at issuance time in the previous schemes, and replace it with a proof of possession sent only once. We present a formal analysis of it for PP and PMBT (Constructions 1 and 3). We recall that the role of the NIZK is to provide unlinkability for the user, as they can check that the tokens received are consistent with the issuer's public parameters. In particular they prevent the issuer from fingerprinting users by using a unique key per user. In this section, we consider a weaker notion of unlinkability, which guarantees that the user either receives a valid token, or a completely random value (unpredictable by the issuer). This implies that the issuer *can* distinguish valid tokens from invalid tokens since the user cannot verify herself whether they have a valid token or not. In other words, the issuer can partition the users into two sets: one that receives valid tokens, and one that receives invalid tokens. The issuer will be able to identify which of these sets a user belongs to, at redemption time. For a more careful analysis on how this affect the success probability of the adversary in the unlinkability game, we refer the reader to the full version [KLOR20].

7.1   PP Without Issuance NIZK

We start with our new construction for the functionality of Privacy Pass. The change that we make is that the user blinds her token hash $H_t(t)$ using both multiplicative and additive blinding. The additive part can be removed during the unblinding if the issuer used the correct secret key. Otherwise, the generated token $(t, W) \in \{0,1\}^\lambda \times \mathbb{G}$ will be invalid and distributed uniformly at random.

Construction 4 (Privacy Pass without issuance NIZK). Let GrGen be a group generator algorithm; let Π_{DLOG} be a proof system for relation R_{DLOG}; let H_t be a random oracle $\{0,1\}^* \to \mathbb{G}$. We construct an anonymous token scheme PPB defined by the following algorithms:

- $(\mathsf{crs}, \mathsf{td}) \leftarrow \mathsf{PPB.Setup}(1^\lambda)$: invoke the group generator $\Gamma \leftarrow \mathsf{GrGen}(1^\lambda)$ and the CRS generation algorithm of the underlying proof system $(\mathsf{pcrs}, \mathsf{ptd}) \leftarrow \Pi_{\mathsf{DLOG}}.\mathsf{Setup}(\Gamma)$. Return $\mathsf{crs} := (\Gamma, \mathsf{pcrs})$ and $\mathsf{td} := \mathsf{ptd}$.
- $((X, \pi), x) \leftarrow \mathsf{PPB.KeyGen}(\mathsf{crs})$: sample the secret key $x \leftarrow_\$ \mathbb{Z}_p^*$. Define $\pi \leftarrow \Pi_{\mathsf{DLOG}}.\mathsf{Prove}(\mathsf{pcrs}, X, x)$. Return the public parameters (X, π), and the secret key x.

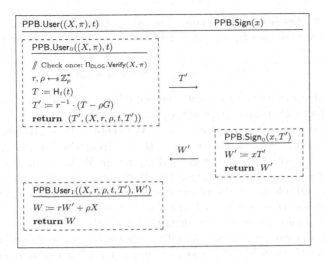

Fig. 9. Token issuance for PPB (Construction 4).

- $W \leftarrow \langle \mathsf{PPB.User}((X, \pi), t), \mathsf{PPB.Sign}(x) \rangle$: illustrated in Fig. 9.
- $bool \leftarrow \mathsf{PPB.Verify}(x, t, W)$: return **true** if $W = x\mathsf{H}_t(t)$; else, return **false**.

Correctness. By correctness of Π_{DLOG}, at the end of the protocol the user returns $\perp$ only with negligible probability. If the user returns $W \in \mathbb{G}$, then W always satisfies the verification equation, since: $W = rW' + \rho X = rxr^{-1}(T - \rho G) + \rho X = xT - \rho(xG) + \rho X = xT$.

Security. PPB satisfies unforgeability and 2-unlinkability.

Theorem 11. *If CTGDH holds for* GrGen, *and* Π_{DLEQ} *is a zero-knowledge proof system for relation* Π_{DLOG}, *then* PPB *is one-more unforgeable with advantage:*

$$\mathsf{Adv}^{\mathrm{omuf}}_{\mathsf{PPB}, \ell}(\lambda) \leq \mathsf{Adv}^{\mathrm{ctgdh}}_{\mathsf{GrGen}, \ell}(\lambda) + \mathsf{Adv}^{\mathrm{zk}}_{\Pi_{\mathsf{DLOG}}, \mathsf{R}_{\mathsf{DLOG}}}(\lambda).$$

The proof can be found in the full version. Intuitively, unforgeability must hold because the issuer is sending strictly less information than in PP. The adversary A in game $\mathrm{OMUF}_{\mathsf{PPB}, \mathsf{A}}(\lambda)$ takes as input the pair (X, π), where $X \in \mathbb{G}$ is the CTGDH challenge, and π is a DLOG proof. By zero-knowledge of Π_{DLOG}, the proof can be simulated; the adversary is now asked to return $\ell + 1$ pairs (t_i, W_i), all different, such that W_i is the CDH of $(X, \mathsf{H}_t(t_i))$. During its execution, the adversary has at disposal the random oracle H_t (which behaves exactly as the TARGET oracle), the VERIFY oracle, which given as input $(Y, W) \in \mathbb{G}^2$ returns 1 if (X, Y, W) is a DH tuple (just as the DDH oracle in the game for CTGDH), and the SIGN oracle, which computes at most ℓ times the CDH with an arbitrary group element (just as the HELP oracle in the game for CTGDH).

Theorem 12. *Let* GrGen *be a group generator. If* Π_{DLOG} *is a knowledge-sound proof system for relation* $\mathsf{R}_{\mathsf{DLOG}}$, *then* PPB *is 2-unlinkable with advantage:*

$$\mathsf{Adv}_{\mathsf{PPB},m}^{\mathsf{unlink}}(\lambda) \leq \frac{2}{m} + \mathsf{Adv}_{\Pi_{\mathsf{DLOG}},\mathsf{R}_{\mathsf{DLOG}}}^{\mathsf{ksnd}}(\lambda).$$

First of all, we note that by knowledge soundness of Π_{DLOG}, for any adversary A that produces th public parameters (X, π) with $X \in \mathbb{G}$, it is possible to extract a witness $x \in \mathbb{Z}_p$ such that $xG = X$, except with negligible probability $\mathsf{Adv}_{\Pi_{\mathsf{DLOG}},\mathsf{R}_{\mathsf{DLOG}},\mathsf{A}}^{\mathsf{ksnd}}(\lambda)$. We use this witness to partition the sessions in two sets, U_0 where W is correctly computed, and U_1 where W isn't. In the latter case, we remark that because the additive blinding $\rho \in \mathbb{Z}_p$ is sampled uniformly at random, in U_1 all tokens are distributed uniformly at random. In a similar way to Theorem 7, we select two sessions k and j from the same U_b (for a $b \in \{0, 1\}$ that sampled at random, following the distribution of the open sessions) and swap them. If k and j are in U_0, unlinkability follows the same reasoning used for proving unlinkability of PP. If k and j are in U_1, then both tokens are uniformly random elements in $\mathbb{G}$ independent from the elements used at issuance time.

User Verifiability. The protocol presented in the previous section does not enable the user to verify that she has received valid token at the end of an execution. We can enable such verifiability for any number of tokens at the cost of one additional issuance interaction between the user and the issuer. In particular, let $(t_i, W_i)_{i \in [m]}$ be m tokens that the user has been issued. She sends a token issuance request $T' = \sum_{i \in [m]} c_i \mathsf{H}_t(t_i)$ where $c_i \leftarrow_\$ \mathbb{Z}_p$ for $i \in [m]$. Let W be the issuer's response after unblinding, then the user checks that $W = \sum_{i \in [m]} c_i W_i$.

If the issuer was honest, then $W_i = x \mathsf{H}_t(t_i)$ and

$$W = x \left(\sum_{i \in [m]} c_i \mathsf{H}_t(t) \right) = \sum_{i \in [m]} c_i (x \mathsf{H}_t(t_i)) = \sum_{i \in [m]} c_i W_i.$$

Next, we argue that if $W = \sum_{i \in [m]} c_i W_i$, then the issuer could be cheating on any of the m token executions only with negligible probability. We will prove this by induction on m. Let $m = 1$, then we have $W = c_1 W_1$ and at the same time $W_1 \neq x \mathsf{H}_t(t_1)$. By the unlinkability argument above we know that W_1 and hence $c_1 W_1$ are uniformly distributed. Hence, the adversary has only negligible probability to guess the value W.

Now, let us assume that the statement holds for $m \leq k$ and we will be prove it for $m = k+1$. We have $W = \sum_{i \in [m]} c_i W_i$ and at the same time there exists an index j such that $W_j \neq x \mathsf{H}_t(t_j)$. If there is an index k such that $W_k = x \mathsf{H}_t(t_k)$, then $W - x \mathsf{H}_t(t_k) = \sum_{i \in [m] \setminus \{k\}} c_i W_i$ and $j \in [m] \setminus \{k\}$, which contradicts the induction assumption. Therefore, it must be the case that $W_i \neq x \mathsf{H}_t(t_i)$ for any $i \in [m]$. However, by the arguments in the unlinkability proof, we know that all W_i's, and hence $\sum_{i \in [m]} c_i W_i$, will be distributed uniformly at random. Hence, the adversary has only negligible probability in guessing the value of W, which concludes the inductive step.

7.2 PMBT Without Issuance NIZK

The challenge to generalizing the construction of the previous section to the setting of private metadata is that the user should not find out what metadata bit value the issuer used and hence which public key it should use when unblinding. Our solution will be to have the user run the unblinding with both keys where only one of the resulting values will be a valid token under the corresponding key for the bit value while the other unblinded value will be completely random. When we do this we need to be careful that the issuer who also generates the public keys should not be able to make the two unblinded values correlated, which would open an avenue for fingerprinting.

To guarantee that the unblinded value with the public key that does not correspond to the embedded private metadata bit is random and hence it is independent of the other unblinded value, even in the case when the issuer is misbehaving, we will need to have that the user generate two independent blinded values which it sends in its first message. The issuer will be using only one of the received blinded tokens to sign and embed his metadata bit, however, the user will be unblinding the message coming from the issuer using two independent sets of blinding parameters, which would thwart the issuer from embedding correlations.

Construction 5 (PMBTokens without issuance NIZK). Let GrGen be a group generator algorithm; let Π_{DLOGAND2} be a proof system for the relation R_{DLOGAND2}; let H_t, H_s be two random oracles $\{0,1\}^* \to \mathbb{G}$. We construct an anonymous token scheme PMBTB defined by the following algorithms:

- $(\mathsf{crs}, \mathsf{td}) \leftarrow \mathsf{PMBTB.Setup}(1^\lambda)$: invoke the group generator $\Gamma \leftarrow \mathsf{GrGen}(1^\lambda)$ and the CRS generation algorithm $(\mathsf{pcrs}, \mathsf{ptd}) \leftarrow \Pi_{\mathsf{DLOGAND2}}.\mathsf{Setup}(\Gamma)$. Return $\mathsf{crs} := (\Gamma, \mathsf{pcrs})$ and $\mathsf{td} := \mathsf{ptd}$.
- $((\mathbf{X}, \pi), (\mathbf{x}, \mathbf{y})) \leftarrow \mathsf{PMBTB.KeyGen}(1^\lambda)$: let $(\mathbf{x}, \mathbf{y}) \leftarrow_\$ (\mathbb{Z}_p^*)^2 \times (\mathbb{Z}_p^*)^2$ be the secret key. Define:

$$\mathbf{X} := \begin{bmatrix} X_0 \\ X_1 \end{bmatrix} := \begin{bmatrix} x_0 G + y_0 H \\ x_1 G + y_1 H \end{bmatrix},$$

  and let $\pi \leftarrow \Pi_{\mathsf{DLOGAND2}}.\mathsf{Prove}(\mathsf{pcrs}, \mathbf{X}, (\mathbf{x}, \mathbf{y}))$. The public parameters are $(\mathbf{X}, \pi)$. Return $((\mathbf{X}, \pi), (\mathbf{x}, \mathbf{y}))$.
- $\sigma \leftarrow \langle \mathsf{PMBTB.User}((\mathbf{X}, \pi), t), \mathsf{PMBTB.Sign}((\mathbf{x}, \mathbf{y})) \rangle$: illustrated in Fig. 10.
- $bool \leftarrow \mathsf{PMBTB.Verify}((\mathbf{x}, \mathbf{y}), t, \sigma)$: return **true**.
- $\mathsf{ind} \leftarrow \mathsf{PMBTB.ReadBit}((\mathbf{x}, \mathbf{y}), t, \sigma)$: read σ as $(S_0, S_1, W_0, W_1) \in \mathbb{G}^4$. Then,
  (a) if $W_0 = x_0 H_t(t) + y_0 S_0$ and $W_1 \neq x_1 H_t(t) + y_1 S_1$, return 0;
  (b) if $W_0 \neq x_0 H_t(t) + y_0 S_0$ and $W_1 = x_1 H_t(t) + y_1 S_1$, return 1;
  (c) else, return $\perp$.

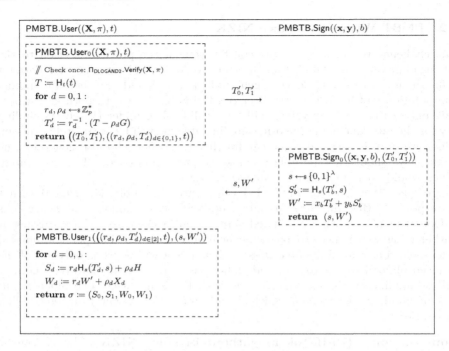

Fig. 10. Token issuance for PMBTB (Construction 5).

Correctness. Honestly-generated tokens are always valid, because the verification algorithm PMBTB.Verify always outputs **true**. We thus focus on Eq. (7). By correctness of the underlying proof system, the protocol aborts only with negligible probability. If the user returns a tuple $(S_0, S_1, W_0, W_1) \in \mathbb{G}^4$, then there exists $b \in \{0, 1\}$ such that:

$$W_b = r_b W' + \rho_b X_b = r_b(x_b T'_b + y_b S'_b) + \rho_b X_b$$
$$= r_b x_b (r_b^{-1}(T - \rho_b G)) + y_b r_b \mathsf{H}_s(T'_b, s) + \rho_b X_b$$
$$= x_b T + y_b(r_b \mathsf{H}_s(T'_b, s) + \rho_b H)$$
$$= x_b T + y_b S_b.$$

The probability that the above equation holds for both $b = 0$ and $b = 1$ (in which case, PMBTB.ReadBit returns $\bot$) is statistically negligible. In fact, if:

$$W_0 = x_0 \mathsf{H}_t(t) + y_0 S_0 = x_1 \mathsf{H}_t(t) + y_1 S_1 = W_1,$$

we have two possible cases:

(a) $x_0 = x_1$, which in turn implies that: $S_0 = y_1^{-1} y_0 S_1$. However, because S_0 is distributed uniformly at random in $\mathbb{G}$, this happens with probability $1/p$.
(b) $x_0 \neq x_1$, which in turn implies that $\mathsf{H}_t(t) = \frac{1}{x_1 - x_0}(y_0 S_0 - y_1 S_1)$, which happens with probability $1/p$.

Security. We provide the proofs for the security properties of the construction in the full version.

Theorem 13. *If CTGDH holds for the group generator algorithm* GrGen *and* Π_{DLOGAND2} *is a zero-knowledge proof system for* $\mathsf{R_{DLOGAND2}}$, *then* PMBTB[GrGen, $\Pi_{\mathsf{DLOGAND2}}]$ *is one-more unforgeable with advantage:*

$$\mathsf{Adv}^{\mathrm{omuf}}_{\mathsf{PMBTB},\ell}(\lambda) \leq 2\mathsf{Adv}^{\mathrm{ctgdh}}_{\mathsf{GrGen},\ell}(\lambda) + \mathsf{Adv}^{\mathrm{zk}}_{\Pi_{\mathsf{DLOGAND2}},\mathsf{R_{DLOGAND2}}}(\lambda).$$

Intuitively, unforgeability follows a similar reasoning of Theorem 8 (unforgeability of PMBT) except that here, at issuance time, we are sending strictly less information to the user, since we removed the NIZK at issuance time. The proof of knowledge of the discrete log, published at the beginning within the public parameters, can be simulated by zero knowledge.

Theorem 14. *If DDH holds for the group generator* GrGen *and* Π_{DLOGAND2} *is a knowledge-sound proof system for relation* $\mathsf{R_{DLOGAND2}}$, *then* PMBTB[GrGen, $\Pi_{\mathsf{DLOGAND2}}]$ *is 3-unlinkable.*

A PPT adversary in the game $\mathrm{UNLINK}_{\mathsf{PMBTB},\mathsf{A}}(\lambda)$ can now: compute W' using (x_0, y_0), using (x_1, y_1), or yet another key. Specifically in the latter case, the token σ will be distributed at random independently from W'. In the full version, we prove that now the adversary can partition the set of open sessions at most in 3, and that therefore the advantage in the game $\mathrm{UNLINK}_{\mathsf{PMBTB}}(\lambda) \leq 3/m + \mathsf{negl}(\lambda)$.

Theorem 15. *If DDH holds for the group generator* GrGen *and* Π_{DLOGAND2} *is a zero-knowledge proof system for relation* $\mathsf{R_{DLOGAND2}}$, *then* PMBTB[GrGen, $\Pi_{\mathsf{DLOGAND2}}]$ *provides private metadata bit with advantage:*

$$\mathsf{Adv}^{\mathrm{pmb}}_{\mathsf{PMBTB}}(\lambda) \leq \frac{O(q^2)}{2^\lambda} + 2\mathsf{Adv}^{\mathrm{ddh}}_{\mathsf{GrGen}}(\lambda) + 4\mathsf{Adv}^{\mathrm{zk}}_{\Pi_{\mathsf{DLOGAND2}},\mathsf{R_{DLOGAND2}}}(\lambda),$$

where q is the number of queries the adversary makes either to H_s *or* SIGN.

As for unforgeability, the proof follows a similar reasoning to the case of PMBT. We notice that now the issuer is sending strictly less information during signing, and that the zero-knowledge proof π can be simulated.

8   Implementation

We implemented our construction in pure Rust (stable, version 1.41.0), The second generator $H \in \mathbb{G}$ is chosen by hashing into the group the public generator G. Hashing into the group is done with a Elligator 2 map [Tib14] with SHA-512. Our implementation is not copyrighted and is released in the public domain.[6]

---

[6] https://www.di.ens.fr/~orru/anonymous-tokens.

Table 2. Benchmarks for our constructions.

Constructions	DLEQ/DLEQOR		User		Issuer		
	Prove	Verify	Token Gen.	Unblinding	Key Gen.	Signing	Redemption
PP [DGS+18]	212 μs	181 μs	111 μs	286 μs	84 μs	303 μs	95 μs
PMBT	576 μs	666 μs	135 μs	844 μs	234 μs	845 μs	235 μs
PPB	–	–	197 μs	164 μs	190 μs	87 μs	95 μs
PMBTB	–	–	368 μs	678 μs	512 μs	155 μs	247 μs

We benchmarked our own implementation on a single thread of an `Intel(R)` `Xeon(R)` `CPU E5-2650 v4 @ 2.20 GHz`, running Ubuntu 18.04.3 LTS (kernel version 4.15.0). They are summarized in Table 2. As expected, Constructions 4 and 5 feature very fast issuance time at a slight increase in the user computation. Our results are between ten and one thousand faster than the previous implementation proposed in [DGS+18] due to the different choice[7] of elliptic curve (NIST P-256) as well as the programming language used.

Acknowledgments. The authors thank Fabrice Benhamouda, Dan Boneh, Charlie Harrison, Michael Kleber, Hugo Krawczyk, Steven Valdez, and Moti Yung for helpful discussions. A part this work was completed while Michele Orrù was an intern at Google and at Web3 Foundation.

References

[ANN06] Abdalla, M., Namprempre, C., Neven, G.: On the (im)possibility of blind message authentication codes. In: Pointcheval, D. (ed.) CT-RSA 2006. LNCS, vol. 3860, pp. 262–279. Springer, Heidelberg (2006). https://doi.org/10.1007/11605805_17

[BFPV11] Blazy, O., Fuchsbauer, G., Pointcheval, D., Vergnaud, D.: Signatures on randomizable ciphertexts. In: Catalano, D., Fazio, N., Gennaro, R., Nicolosi, A. (eds.) PKC 2011. LNCS, vol. 6571, pp. 403–422. Springer, Heidelberg (2011). https://doi.org/10.1007/978-3-642-19379-8_25

[BLS01] Boneh, D., Lynn, B., Shacham, H.: Short signatures from the Weil pairing. In: Boyd, C. (ed.) ASIACRYPT 2001. LNCS, vol. 2248, pp. 514–532. Springer, Heidelberg (2001). https://doi.org/10.1007/3-540-45682-1_30

[BMW03] Bellare, M., Micciancio, D., Warinschi, B.: Foundations of group signatures: formal definitions, simplified requirements, and a construction based on general assumptions. In: Biham, E. (ed.) EUROCRYPT 2003. LNCS, vol. 2656, pp. 614–629. Springer, Heidelberg (2003). https://doi.org/10.1007/3-540-39200-9_38

[BNPS03] Bellare, M., Namprempre, C., Pointcheval, D., Semanko, M.: The one-more-RSA-inversion problems and the security of Chaum's blind signature scheme. J. Cryptol. **16**(3), 185–215 (2003)

---

[7] We comment on the choice of curve and its security in the full version of this paper [KLOR20].

[Bol03] Boldyreva, A.: Threshold signatures, multisignatures and blind signatures based on the Gap-Diffie-Hellman-Group signature scheme. In: Desmedt, Y.G. (ed.) PKC 2003. LNCS, vol. 2567, pp. 31–46. Springer, Heidelberg (2003). https://doi.org/10.1007/3-540-36288-6_3

[BPV12] Blazy, O., Pointcheval, D., Vergnaud, D.: Compact round-optimal partially-blind signatures. In: Visconti, I., De Prisco, R. (eds.) SCN 2012. LNCS, vol. 7485, pp. 95–112. Springer, Heidelberg (2012). https://doi.org/10.1007/978-3-642-32928-9_6

[Cam97] Camenisch, J.: Efficient and generalized group signatures. In: Fumy, W. (ed.) EUROCRYPT 1997. LNCS, vol. 1233, pp. 465–479. Springer, Heidelberg (1997). https://doi.org/10.1007/3-540-69053-0_32

[Cha82] Chaum, D.: Blind signatures for untraceable payments. In: CRYPTO, pp. 199–203. Plenum Press, New York (1982)

[CL01] Camenisch, J., Lysyanskaya, A.: An efficient system for non-transferable anonymous credentials with optional anonymity revocation. In: Pfitzmann, B. (ed.) EUROCRYPT 2001. LNCS, vol. 2045, pp. 93–118. Springer, Heidelberg (2001). https://doi.org/10.1007/3-540-44987-6_7

[CMZ14] Chase, M., Meiklejohn, S., Zaverucha, G.: Algebraic MACs and keyed-verification anonymous credentials, pp. 1205–1216 (2014)

[CP92] Chaum, D., Pedersen, T.P.: Wallet databases with observers. In: Brickell, E.F. (ed.) CRYPTO 1992. LNCS, vol. 740, pp. 89–105. Springer, Heidelberg (1993). https://doi.org/10.1007/3-540-48071-4_7

[CvH91] Chaum, D., van Heyst, E.: Group signatures. In: Davies, D.W. (ed.) EUROCRYPT 1991. LNCS, vol. 547, pp. 257–265. Springer, Heidelberg (1991). https://doi.org/10.1007/3-540-46416-6_22

[DGS+18] Davidson, A., Goldberg, I., Sullivan, N., Tankersley, G., Valsorda, F.: Privacy pass: bypassing internet challenges anonymously. PoPETs **2018**(3), 164–180 (2018)

[ECS+15] Everspaugh, A., Chatterjee, R., Scott, S., Juels, A., Ristenpart, T.: The Pythia PRF service. In: USENIX Security Symposium, pp. 547–562. USENIX Association (2015)

[FHKS16] Fuchsbauer, G., Hanser, C., Kamath, C., Slamanig, D.: Practical round-optimal blind signatures in the standard model from weaker assumptions. In: Zikas, V., De Prisco, R. (eds.) SCN 2016. LNCS, vol. 9841, pp. 391–408. Springer, Cham (2016). https://doi.org/10.1007/978-3-319-44618-9_21

[FHS15] Fuchsbauer, G., Hanser, C., Slamanig, D.: Practical round-optimal blind signatures in the standard model. In: Gennaro, R., Robshaw, M. (eds.) CRYPTO 2015. LNCS, vol. 9216, pp. 233–253. Springer, Heidelberg (2015). https://doi.org/10.1007/978-3-662-48000-7_12

[Fis06] Fischlin, M.: Round-optimal composable blind signatures in the common reference string model. In: Dwork, C. (ed.) CRYPTO 2006. LNCS, vol. 4117, pp. 60–77. Springer, Heidelberg (2006). https://doi.org/10.1007/11818175_4

[FPS19] Fuchsbauer, G., Plouviez, A., Seurin, Y.: Blind schnorr signatures in the algebraic group model. Cryptology ePrint Archive, Report 2019/877 (2019)

[GG14] Garg, S., Gupta, D.: Efficient round optimal blind signatures. In: Nguyen, P.Q., Oswald, E. (eds.) EUROCRYPT 2014. LNCS, vol. 8441, pp. 477–495. Springer, Heidelberg (2014). https://doi.org/10.1007/978-3-642-55220-5_27

[Gha13] Ghadafi, E.: Formalizing group blind signatures and practical constructions without random oracles. In: Boyd, C., Simpson, L. (eds.) ACISP 2013. LNCS, vol. 7959, pp. 330–346. Springer, Heidelberg (2013). https://doi. org/10.1007/978-3-642-39059-3_23

[HL06]   Herranz, J., Laguillaumie, F.: Blind ring signatures secure under the chosen-target-CDH assumption. In: Katsikas, S.K., López, J., Backes, M., Gritzalis, S., Preneel, B. (eds.) ISC 2006. LNCS, vol. 4176, pp. 117–130. Springer, Heidelberg (2006). https://doi.org/10.1007/11836810_9

[JKK14] Jarecki, S., Kiayias, A., Krawczyk, H.: Round-optimal password-protected secret sharing and T-PAKE in the password-only model. In: Sarkar, P., Iwata, T. (eds.) ASIACRYPT 2014. LNCS, vol. 8874, pp. 233–253. Springer, Heidelberg (2014). https://doi.org/10.1007/978-3-662-45608-8_13

[JKR18] Jarecki, S., Krawczyk, H., Resch, J.K.: Threshold partially-oblivious PRFs with applications to key management. IACR Cryptology ePrint Archive, 2018/733 (2018)

[KLOR20] Kreuter, B., Lepoint, T., Orru, M., Raykova, M.: Anonymous tokens with private metadata bit. Cryptology ePrint Archive, Report 2020/072 (2020). https://eprint.iacr.org/2020/072

[LR98]   Lysyanskaya, A., Ramzan, Z.: Group blind digital signatures: a scalable solution to electronic cash. In: Hirchfeld, R. (ed.) FC 1998. LNCS, vol. 1465, pp. 184–197. Springer, Heidelberg (1998). https://doi.org/10.1007/BFb0055483

[Oka92] Okamoto, T.: Provably secure and practical identification schemes and corresponding signature schemes. In: Brickell, E.F. (ed.) CRYPTO 1992. LNCS, vol. 740, pp. 31–53. Springer, Heidelberg (1993). https://doi.org/10.1007/3-540-48071-4_3

[OP01]   Okamoto, T., Pointcheval, D.: The gap-problems: a new class of problems for the security of cryptographic schemes. In: Kim, K. (ed.) PKC 2001. LNCS, vol. 1992, pp. 104–118. Springer, Heidelberg (2001). https://doi. org/10.1007/3-540-44586-2_8

[PS00]   Pointcheval, D., Stern, J.: Security arguments for digital signatures and blind signatures. J. Cryptol. **13**, 361–396 (2000)

[Ram13] Ramzan, Z.: Group blind digital signatures: theory and applications (2013). https://dspace.mit.edu/bitstream/handle/1721.1/80561/43557700-MIT.pdf?sequence=2&isAllowed=y

[SC12]   Seo, J.H., Cheon, J.H.: Beyond the limitation of prime-order bilinear groups, and round optimal blind signatures. In: Cramer, R. (ed.) TCC 2012. LNCS, vol. 7194, pp. 133–150. Springer, Heidelberg (2012). https://doi.org/10.1007/978-3-642-28914-9_8

[Sch01] Schnorr, C.P.: Security of blind discrete log signatures against interactive attacks. In: Qing, S., Okamoto, T., Zhou, J. (eds.) ICICS 2001. LNCS, vol. 2229, pp. 1–12. Springer, Heidelberg (2001). https://doi.org/10.1007/3-540-45600-7_1

[Sch06] Schnorr, C.P.: Enhancing the security of perfect blind DL-signatures. Inf. Sci. **176**(10), 1305–1320 (2006)

[TAKS07] Tsang, P.P., Au, M.H., Kapadia, A., Smith, S.W.: Blacklistable anonymous credentials: blocking misbehaving users without TTPs. In: ACM Conference on Computer and Communications Security, pp. 72–81. ACM (2007)

[Tib14] Tibouchi, M.: Elligator squared: uniform points on elliptic curves of prime order as uniform random strings. In: Christin, N., Safavi-Naini, R. (eds.) FC 2014. LNCS, vol. 8437, pp. 139–156. Springer, Heidelberg (2014). https://doi.org/10.1007/978-3-662-45472-5_10

Hardware Security and Leakage Resilience

Random Probing Security: Verification, Composition, Expansion and New Constructions

Sonia Belaïd[1]($\boxtimes$), Jean-Sébastien Coron[2]($\boxtimes$), Emmanuel Prouff[3]($\boxtimes$),
Matthieu Rivain[1]($\boxtimes$), and Abdul Rahman Taleb[1]($\boxtimes$)

[1] CryptoExperts, Paris, France
{sonia.belaid,matthieu.rivain,abdul.taleb}@cryptoexperts.com
[2] University of Luxembourg, Luxembourg, Luxembourg
jean-sebastien.coron@uni.lu
[3] ANSSI, Paris, France
emmanuel.prouff@ssi.gouv.fr

Abstract. The masking countermeasure is among the most powerful countermeasures to counteract side-channel attacks. Leakage models have been exhibited to theoretically reason on the security of such masked implementations. So far, the most widely used leakage model is the *probing model* defined by Ishai, Sahai, and Wagner at (CRYPTO 2003). While it is advantageously convenient for security proofs, it does not capture an adversary exploiting full leakage traces as, *e.g.*, in horizontal attacks. Those attacks target the multiple manipulations of the same share to reduce noise and recover the corresponding value. To capture a wider class of attacks another model was introduced and is referred to as the *random probing model*. From a leakage parameter p, each wire of the circuit leaks its value with probability p. While this model much better reflects the physical reality of side channels, it requires more complex security proofs and does not yet come with practical constructions.

In this paper, we define the first framework dedicated to the random probing model. We provide an automatic tool, called VRAPS, to quantify the random probing security of a circuit from its leakage probability. We also formalize a composition property for secure random probing gadgets and exhibit its relation to the *strong non-interference* (SNI) notion used in the context of probing security. We then revisit the expansion idea proposed by Ananth, Ishai, and Sahai (CRYPTO 2018) and introduce a compiler that builds a random probing secure circuit from small base gadgets achieving a *random probing expandability* property. We instantiate this compiler with small gadgets for which we verify the expected properties directly from our automatic tool. Our construction can tolerate a leakage probability up to 2^{-8}, against 2^{-25} for the previous construction, with a better asymptotic complexity.

Keywords: Compiler · Masking · Automated verification · Random probing model

© International Association for Cryptologic Research 2020
D. Micciancio and T. Ristenpart (Eds.): CRYPTO 2020, LNCS 12170, pp. 339–368, 2020.
https://doi.org/10.1007/978-3-030-56784-2_12

1   Introduction

Most cryptographic algorithms are assumed to be secure against *black-box* attacks where the adversary is limited to the knowledge of some inputs and outputs to recover the manipulated secrets. However, as revealed in the late nineties [19], when implemented on physical devices, they become vulnerable to the more powerful *side-channel attacks* which additionally exploit the physical emanations such as temperature, time, power consumption, electromagnetic radiations.

As such attacks may only require cheap equipment and can be easily mounted in a short time interval, the community had to adapt quickly by looking for efficient countermeasures. The most widely deployed approach to counteract side-channel attacks was simultaneously introduced in 1999 by Chari et al. [11] and by Goubin and Patarin [16] and is now called *masking*. Basically, the idea is to split each sensitive variable x of the implementation into n shares such that $n - 1$ of them are generated uniformly at random and the last one is computed as the combination of x and all the previous shares according to some group law $*$. When $*$ is the (bitwise) addition, we talk about *linear sharing* (aka Boolean masking). The adversary thus needs to get information on all the shares of x to recover information on the sensitive value. This countermeasure is really simple to implement for linear operations which are simply applied on each share separately. However, things are getting trickier for non-linear operations where it is impossible to compute the result without combining shares.

To reason about the security of masked implementations, the community introduced leakage models. One of the most broadly used is the *probing model*, introduced by Ishai, Sahai, and Wagner [18]. In a nutshell, a circuit is claimed to be t-probing secure if the exact values of any set of t intermediate variables do not reveal any information on the secrets. As leakage traces are assumed to reveal noisy functions of the manipulated data, this model is motivated by the difficulty to recover information from the combination of t variables from their noisy functions in masking schemes (as t grows). Nevertheless, the probing model fails to capture the huge amount of information resulting from the leakage of all manipulated data, and in particular from the repeated manipulation of identical values (see horizontal attacks in [7]). Therefore, after a long sequence of works building and analyzing masking schemes with respect to their security in the probing model [8,14,23], the community is now looking for security in more practical models.

The *noisy leakage model* was originally considered by Chari et al. in [11] and was later formalized by Prouff and Rivain in [22] as a specialization of the *only computation leaks* model [21] in order to better capture the reality of the physical leakage. Informally, a circuit is secure in the noisy leakage model if the adversary cannot recover the secrets from a noisy function of each intermediate variable of the implementation. While realistic, this model is not convenient for security proofs, and therefore masking schemes continued to be verified in the probing model relying on the *not tight* reduction that was formally established by Duc, Dziembowski, and Faust [15].

The latter reduction actually came with an intermediate leakage model, called *random probing model*, to which the security in the noisy leakage model reduces to. In the random probing model, each intermediate variable leaks with some constant leakage probability p. A circuit is secure in this model if there is a negligible probability that these leaking wires actually reveal information on the secrets. It is worth noting that this notion advantageously captures the horizontal attacks which exploit the repeated manipulations of variables throughout the implementation. Classical probing-secure schemes are also secure in the random probing model but the tolerated leakage probability (a.k.a. leakage rate) might not be constant which is not satisfactory from a practical viewpoint. Indeed, in practice the side-channel noise might not be customizable by the implementer.

Only a few constructions [1–3] tolerate a constant leakage probability. These three constructions are conceptually involved and their practical instantiation is not straightforward. The first one from Ajtai et al. and its extension [3] are based on expander graphs. The tolerated probability is not made explicit. The third work [2] is based on multi-party computation protocols and an expansion strategy; the tolerated probability is around 2^{-26} and for a circuit with $|C|$ gates, the complexity is $\mathcal{O}(|C| \cdot \mathsf{poly}(\kappa))$ for some parameter κ but the polynomial is not made explicit.

Following the long sequence of works relying on the probing security, formal tools have recently been built to supervise the development of masking implementations proven secure in the probing model. Namely, verification tools are now able to produce a security proof or identify potential attacks from the description of a masked implementation at up to some masking orders (i.e., <5) [4,10,13]. In the same vein, compilers have been built to automatically generate masked implementations at any order given the high level description of a primitive [5,9,10]. Nevertheless, no equivalent framework has yet been proposed to verify the security of implementations in the random probing model.

Our contributions. In this paper, we aim to fill this huge gap by providing a framework to verify, compose, and build random probing secure circuits from simple gadgets. Our contributions are three-fold.

Automatic verification tool. As a first contribution, we define a verification method that we instantiate in a tool to automatically exhibit the random probing security parameters of any small circuit defined with addition and multiplication gates whose wires leak with some probability p. In a nutshell, a circuit is (p, f)-random probing secure if it leaks information on the secret with probability $f(p)$, where $f(p)$ is the *failure probability function*. From these notations, our tool named VRAPS (for Verifier of Random Probing Security), based on top of a set of rules that were previously defined to verify the probing security of implementations [4], takes as input the description of a circuit and outputs an upper bound on the failure probability function. While it is limited to small circuits by complexity, the state-of-the-art shows that verifying those circuits can be particularly useful in practice (see e.g. the maskVerif tool [4]), for instance to verify gadgets and then deduce global security through composition properties and/or low-order masked implementations. The source code of VRAPS is publicly available.[1]

Composition and expanding compiler. We introduce a composition security property to make gadgets composable in a global random probing secure circuit. We exhibit the relation between this new *random probing composability* (RPC) notion and the *strong non-interference* (SNI) notion which is widely used in the context of probing security [5]. Then, we revisit the modular approach of Ananth, Ishai, and Sahai [2] which uses an expansion strategy to get random probing security from a multi-party computation protocol. We introduce the *expanding compiler* that builds random probing secure circuits from small base gadgets. We formalize the notion of *random probing expandability* (RPE) and show that a base gadget satisfying this notion can be securely used in the expanding compiler to achieve arbitrary/composable random probing security. As a complementary contribution, our verification tool, VRAPS, is extended to verify the newly introduced RPC and RPE properties.

Instantiation. We instantiate the expanding compiler with new constructions of simple base gadgets that fulfill the desired RPE property, which is verified by VRAPS. For a security level κ, our instantiation achieves a complexity of $\mathcal{O}(\kappa^{7.5})$ and tolerates a constant leakage probability $p \approx 0.0045 > 2^{-8}$. In comparison, and as a side contribution, we provide a precise analysis of the construction from [2] and show that it achieves an $\mathcal{O}(\kappa^{8.2})$ complexity for a much lower tolerated leakage probability ($p \approx 2^{-26}$). Finally, we note that our framework probably enables more efficient constructions based on different base gadgets; we leave such optimizations open for future works.

2   Preliminaries

Along the paper, $\mathbb{K}$ shall denote a finite field. For any $n \in \mathbb{N}$, we shall denote $[n]$ the integer set $[n] = [1, n] \cap \mathbb{Z}$. For any tuple $\boldsymbol{x} = (x_1, \ldots, x_n) \in \mathbb{K}^n$ and any set $I \subseteq [n]$, we shall denote $\boldsymbol{x}|_I = (x_i)_{i \in I}$. Any two probability distributions D_1 and D_2 are said ε-*close*, denoted $D_1 \approx_\varepsilon D_2$, if their statistical distance is upper bounded by ε, that is

$$\mathsf{SD}(D_1; D_2) := \frac{1}{2} \sum_x |p_{D_1}(x) - p_{D_2}(x)| \leq \varepsilon \,,$$

where $p_{D_1}(\cdot)$ and $p_{D_1}(\cdot)$ denote the probability mass functions of D_1 and D_2.

2.1   Circuit Compilers

In this paper, an *arithmetic circuit* over a field $\mathbb{K}$ is a labeled directed acyclic graph whose edges are *wires* and vertices are *arithmetic gates* processing operations over $\mathbb{K}$. We consider three types of arithmetic gate:

---

[1] See https://github.com/CryptoExperts/VRAPS.

- an addition gate, of fan-in 2 and fan-out 1, computes an addition over $\mathbb{K}$,
- a multiplication gate, of fan-in 2 and fan-out 1, computes a multiplication over $\mathbb{K}$,
- a copy gate, of fan-in 1 and fan-out 2, outputs two copies of its input.

A *randomized arithmetic circuit* is equipped with an additional type of gate:

- a random gate, of fan-in 0 and fan-out 1, outputs a fresh uniform random value of $\mathbb{K}$.

A (randomized) arithmetic circuit is further formally composed of input gates of fan-in 0 and fan-out 1 and output gates of fan-in 1 and fan-out 0. Evaluating an ℓ-input m-output circuit C consists in writing an input $\boldsymbol{x} \in \mathbb{K}^\ell$ in the input gates, processing the gates from input gates to output gates, then reading the output $\boldsymbol{y} \in \mathbb{K}^m$ from the output gates. This is denoted by $\boldsymbol{y} = C(\boldsymbol{x})$. During the evaluation process, each wire in the circuit is assigned with a value on $\mathbb{K}$. We call the tuple of all these wire values a *wire assignment* of C (on input $\boldsymbol{x}$).

Definition 1 (Circuit Compiler). *A circuit compiler is a triplet of algorithms* $(\mathsf{CC}, \mathsf{Enc}, \mathsf{Dec})$ *defined as follows:*

- CC *(circuit compilation) is a deterministic algorithm that takes as input an arithmetic circuit C and outputs a randomized arithmetic circuit $\widehat{C}$.*
- Enc *(input encoding) is a probabilistic algorithm that maps an input $\boldsymbol{x} \in \mathbb{K}^\ell$ to an encoded input $\widehat{\boldsymbol{x}} \in \mathbb{K}^{\ell'}$.*
- Dec *(output decoding) is a deterministic algorithm that maps an encoded output $\widehat{\boldsymbol{y}} \in \mathbb{K}^{m'}$ to a plain output $\boldsymbol{y} \in \mathbb{K}^m$.*

These three algorithms satisfy the following properties:

- **Correctness:** *For every arithmetic circuit C of input length ℓ, and for every $\boldsymbol{x} \in \mathbb{K}^\ell$, we have*

$$\Pr\left(\mathsf{Dec}(\widehat{C}(\widehat{\boldsymbol{x}})) = C(\boldsymbol{x}) \mid \widehat{\boldsymbol{x}} \leftarrow \mathsf{Enc}(\boldsymbol{x})\right) = 1 \ , \ \text{where } \widehat{C} = \mathsf{CC}(C).$$

- **Efficiency:** *For some security parameter $\lambda \in \mathbb{N}$, the running time of $\mathsf{CC}(C)$ is $\mathrm{poly}(\lambda, |C|)$, the running time of $\mathsf{Enc}(\boldsymbol{x})$ is $\mathrm{poly}(\lambda, |\boldsymbol{x}|)$ and the running time of $\mathsf{Dec}(\widehat{\boldsymbol{y}})$ is $\mathrm{poly}(\lambda, |\widehat{\boldsymbol{y}}|)$, where $\mathrm{poly}(\lambda, q) = O(\lambda^{k_1} q^{k_2})$ for some constants k_1, k_2.*

2.2 Linear Sharing and Gadgets

In the following, the *n-linear decoding* mapping, denoted LinDec, refers to the function $\bigcup_n \mathbb{K}^n \to \mathbb{K}$ defined as

$$\mathsf{LinDec} : (x_1, \ldots, x_n) \mapsto x_1 + \cdots + x_n \ ,$$

for every $n \in \mathbb{N}$ and $(x_1, \ldots, x_n) \in \mathbb{K}^n$. We shall further consider that, for every $n, \ell \in \mathbb{N}$, on input $(\widehat{x}_1, \ldots, \widehat{x}_\ell) \in (\mathbb{K}^n)^\ell$ the n-linear decoding mapping acts as

$$\mathsf{LinDec} : (\widehat{x}_1, \ldots, \widehat{x}_\ell) \mapsto (\mathsf{LinDec}(\widehat{x}_1), \ldots, \mathsf{LinDec}(\widehat{x}_\ell)) \ .$$

Let us recall that for some tuple $\widehat{x} = (x_1, \ldots, x_n) \in \mathbb{K}^n$ and for some set $I \subseteq [n]$, the tuple $(x_i)_{i \in I}$ is denoted $\widehat{x}|_I$.

Definition 2 (Linear Sharing). *Let* $n, \ell \in \mathbb{N}$. *For any* $x \in \mathbb{K}$, *an* n-*linear sharing of* x *is a random vector* $\widehat{x} \in \mathbb{K}^n$ *such that* $\mathsf{LinDec}(\widehat{x}) = x$. *It is said to be uniform if for any set* $I \subseteq [n]$ *with* $|I| < n$ *the tuple* $\widehat{x}|_I$ *is uniformly distributed over* $\mathbb{K}^{|I|}$. *A* n-*linear encoding is a probabilistic algorithm* LinEnc *which on input a tuple* $\boldsymbol{x} = (x_1, \ldots, x_\ell) \in \mathbb{K}^\ell$ *outputs a tuple* $\widehat{\boldsymbol{x}} = (\widehat{x}_1, \ldots, \widehat{x}_\ell) \in (\mathbb{K}^n)^\ell$ *such that* $\widehat{x}_i$ *is a uniform* n-*sharing of* x_i *for every* $i \in [\ell]$.

In the following, we shall call an (n-*share*, ℓ-*to-m*) *gadget*, a randomized arithmetic circuit that maps an input $\widehat{\boldsymbol{x}} \in (\mathbb{K}^n)^\ell$ to an output $\widehat{\boldsymbol{y}} \in (\mathbb{K}^n)^m$ such that $\boldsymbol{x} = \mathsf{LinDec}(\widehat{\boldsymbol{x}}) \in \mathbb{K}^\ell$ and $\boldsymbol{y} = \mathsf{LinDec}(\widehat{\boldsymbol{y}}) \in \mathbb{K}^m$ satisfy $\boldsymbol{y} = g(\boldsymbol{x})$ for some function g. In this paper, we shall consider gadgets for three types of functions (corresponding to the three types of gates): the addition $g : (x_1, x_2) \mapsto x_1 + x_2$, the multiplication $g : (x_1, x_2) \mapsto x_1 \cdot x_2$ and the copy $g : x \mapsto (x, x)$. We shall generally denote such gadgets G_{add}, G_{mult} and G_{copy} respectively.

Definition 3 (Standard Circuit Compiler). *Let* $\lambda \in \mathbb{N}$ *be some security parameter and let* $n = \mathrm{poly}(\lambda)$. *Let* G_{add}, G_{mult} *and* G_{copy} *be* n-*share gadgets respectively for the addition, multiplication and copy over* $\mathbb{K}$. *The standard circuit compiler with sharing order* n *and base gadgets* G_{add}, G_{mult}, G_{copy} *is the circuit compiler* $(\mathsf{CC}, \mathsf{Enc}, \mathsf{Dec})$ *satisfying the following:*

1. *The input encoding* Enc *is an* n-*linear encoding.*
2. *The output decoding* Dec *is the* n-*linear decoding mapping* LinDec.
3. *The circuit compilation* CC *consists in replacing each gate in the original circuit by an* n-*share gadget with corresponding functionality (either* G_{add}, G_{mult} *or* G_{copy}), *and each wire by a set of* n *wires carrying a* n-*linear sharing of the original wire. If the input circuit is a randomized arithmetic circuit, each of its random gates is replaced by* n *random gates, which duly produce a* n-*linear sharing of a random value.*

For such a circuit compiler, the correctness and efficiency directly holds from the correctness and efficiency of the gadgets G_{add}, G_{mult} *and* G_{copy}.

2.3   Random Probing Leakage

Let $p \in [0, 1]$ be some constant leakage probability parameter. This parameter is sometimes called *leakage rate* in the literature. Informally, the p-random probing model states that during the evaluation of a circuit C each wire leaks its value with probability p (and leaks nothing otherwise), where all the wire leakage events are mutually independent.

In order to formally define the random-probing leakage of a circuit, we shall consider two probabilistic algorithms:

- The *leaking-wires sampler* takes as input a randomized arithmetic circuit C and a probability $p \in [0, 1]$, and outputs a set $\mathcal{W}$, denoted as

$$\mathcal{W} \leftarrow \mathsf{LeakingWires}(C, p) ,$$

where $\mathcal{W}$ is constructed by including each wire label from the circuit C with probability p to $\mathcal{W}$ (where all the probabilities are mutually independent).

– The *assign-wires sampler* takes as input a randomized arithmetic circuit C, a set of wire labels $\mathcal{W}$ (subset of the wire labels of C), and an input $\boldsymbol{x}$, and it outputs a $|\mathcal{W}|$-tuple $\boldsymbol{w} \in (\mathbb{K} \cup \{\bot\})^{|\mathcal{W}|}$, denoted as

$$\boldsymbol{w} \leftarrow \mathsf{AssignWires}(C, \mathcal{W}, \boldsymbol{x}) \ ,$$

where $\boldsymbol{w}$ corresponds to the assignments of the wires of C with label in $\mathcal{W}$ for an evaluation on input $\boldsymbol{x}$.

We can now formally define the random probing leakage of a circuit.

Definition 4 (Random Probing Leakage). *The p-random probing leakage of a randomized arithmetic circuit C on input $\boldsymbol{x}$ is the distribution $\mathcal{L}_p(C, \boldsymbol{x})$ obtained by composing the leaking-wires and assign-wires samplers as*

$$\mathcal{L}_p(C, \boldsymbol{x}) \overset{id}{=} \mathsf{AssignWires}(C, \mathsf{LeakingWires}(C, p), \boldsymbol{x}) \ .$$

Remark 1. By convention the output wires of C (*i.e.* the wires incoming output gates) are excluded by the LeakingWires sampler whereas the input wires of C (*i.e.* the wires connecting input gates to subsequent gates) are included. Namely the output set $\mathcal{W}$ of $\mathsf{LeakingWires}(C, p)$ does not include any output wire label of C. This is because when composing several circuits (or gadgets), the output wires of a circuit are the input wires in a next circuit. This also relates to the widely admitted *only computation leaks* assumption [21]: the processing of a gate leaks information on its input values (and information on the output can be captured through information on the input).

Definition 5 (Random Probing Security). *A randomized arithmetic circuit C with $\ell \cdot n \in \mathbb{N}$ input gates is (p, ε)-random probing secure with respect to encoding Enc if there exists a simulator Sim such that for every $\boldsymbol{x} \in \mathbb{K}^\ell$:*

$$\mathsf{Sim}(C) \approx_\varepsilon \mathcal{L}_p(C, \mathsf{Enc}(\boldsymbol{x})) \ . \tag{1}$$

A circuit compiler $(\mathsf{CC}, \mathsf{Enc}, \mathsf{Dec})$ is (p, ε)-random probing secure if for every (randomized) arithmetic circuit C the compiled circuit $\widehat{C} = \mathsf{CC}(C)$ is $(p, |C| \cdot \varepsilon)$-random probing secure where $|C|$ is the size of original circuit.

As in [2] we shall consider a *simulation with abort*. In this approach, the simulator first calls the leaking-wires sampler to get a set $\mathcal{W}$ and then either aborts (or fails) with probability ε or outputs the exact distribution of the wire assignment corresponding to $\mathcal{W}$. Formally, for any leakage probability $p \in [0, 1]$, the simulator Sim is defined as

$$\mathsf{Sim}(\widehat{C}) = \mathsf{SimAW}(\widehat{C}, \mathsf{LeakingWires}(\widehat{C}, p)) \tag{2}$$

where SimAW, the *wire assignment simulator*, either returns $\bot$ (simulation failure) or a perfect simulation of the requested wires. Formally, the experiment

$$\mathcal{W} \leftarrow \mathsf{LeakingWires}(\widehat{C}, p)$$
$$out \leftarrow \mathsf{SimAW}(\widehat{C}, \mathcal{W})$$

leads to

$$\Pr[out = \bot] = \varepsilon \quad \text{and} \quad (out \mid out \neq \bot) \stackrel{\text{id}}{=} (\mathsf{AssignWires}(\widehat{C}, \mathcal{W}, \mathsf{Enc}(\boldsymbol{x})) \mid out \neq \bot) \ . \tag{3}$$

It is not hard to see that if we can construct such a simulator SimAW for a compiled circuit $\widehat{C}$, then this circuit is (p, ε)-random probing secure.

3   Formal Verification

In this section we show how to compute the simulation failure probability $f(p)$ as a function of the leakage probability p for the base gadgets. Since even for simple gadgets this tasks would be difficult to perform by hand, we use a formal verification tool to compute $f(p)$.

3.1   Simulation Failure Probability

We first derive an upper bound on the simulation failure probability as a function of the leakage probability p. We consider a compiled circuit $\widehat{C}$ composed of s wires labeled from 1 to s and a simulator SimAW as defined in previous section. For any sub-set $\mathcal{W} \subseteq [s]$ we denote by $\delta_{\mathcal{W}}$ the value defined as follows:

$$\delta_{\mathcal{W}} = \begin{cases} 1 & \text{if } \mathsf{SimAW}(\widehat{C}, \mathcal{W}) = \bot, \\ 0 & \text{otherwise.} \end{cases}$$

The simulation failure probability ε in (3) can then be explicitly expressed as a function of p. Namely, we have $\varepsilon = f(p)$ with f defined for every $p \in [0, 1]$ by:

$$f(p) = \sum_{\mathcal{W} \subseteq [s]} \delta_{\mathcal{W}} \cdot p^{|\mathcal{W}|} \cdot (1 - p)^{s - |\mathcal{W}|} \ . \tag{4}$$

Letting c_i be the number of sub-sets $\mathcal{W} \subseteq [s]$ of cardinality i for which $\delta_{\mathcal{W}} = 1$, namely for which the simulation fails, we have $c_i = \sum_{|\mathcal{W}| = i} \delta_{\mathcal{W}}$ and hence (4) simplifies to

$$f(p) = \sum_{i=1}^{s} c_i \cdot p^i \cdot (1 - p)^{s - i} \ . \tag{5}$$

For any circuit $\widehat{C}$ achieving t-probing security, the values $\delta_{\mathcal{W}}$ with $|\mathcal{W}| \leq t$ are equal to zero, and therefore the corresponding c_i's are zero, which implies the following simplification:

$$f(p) = \sum_{i=t+1}^{s} c_i \cdot p^i \cdot (1 - p)^{s - i} \ .$$

Moreover, by definition, the coefficients c_i satisfy:

$$c_i \leqslant \binom{s}{i} \tag{6}$$

which leads to the following upper-bound for $f(p)$:

$$f(p) \leqslant \sum_{i=t+1}^{s} \binom{s}{i} \cdot p^i \cdot (1-p)^{s-i} .$$

An example of the evaluation of $f(p)$ for the 2-share multiplication gadget from [18] is given in the full version of this paper.

3.2 Verification Method

For any compiled circuit $\widehat{C}$ and any simulator defined as in Sect. 2.3, the computation of the function $f(p)$ for any probability p essentially amounts to computing the values of the coefficients c_i's appearing in (5). If no assumption is made on the circuit, this task seems difficult to carry out by hand. Actually, it may be checked that an exhaustive testing of all the possible tuples of wires for a gadget with s wires has complexity lower bounded by 2^s, which gives 2^{21} for a simple gadget like the ISW multiplication gadget with two shares per input. Here, we introduce a verification tool, that we call VRAPS, enabling to automatically test the perfect simulation for any set of wires of size lower than or equal to some threshold β. The role of the latter threshold is simply to control the verification duration (which can be long if the circuit to test is complex). Our tool implicitly defines a simulator that may fail with a probability $\varepsilon = f(p)$ satisfying (5).

The verification tool takes as input the representation of a compiled circuit $\widehat{C}$ and a test parameter β, and outputs the list of coefficients $c_1, ..., c_\beta$. It is assumed that $\widehat{C}$ takes as input the n-linear encoding $\mathsf{Enc}(\boldsymbol{x})$ of vector $\boldsymbol{x} = (x_1, \ldots, x_\ell)$ defined in $\mathbb{K}^\ell$. It is moreover assumed that $\widehat{C}$ is composed of s wires respectively denoted by $w_1, ..., w_s$. In the following, we consider s-tuples in the form of $u = (u_1, \ldots, u_s) \in \{0,1\}^s$ together with the common rule $u' \subset u$ iff for every $i \in [s]$, $u'_i = 1 \Rightarrow u_i = 1$ (in this case u' will be said to be included in u). An s-tuple u for which there exists an assignment of the wires in $\mathcal{W} = \{w_i; i \in [s], u_i = 1\}$ such that the simulation fails shall be called a *failure tuple*. Such a tuple shall be said to be *incompressible* if no tuple $t' \subset t$ is a failure tuple. The main idea of the proposed verification tool is to test the simulation failure only on incompressible failure tuples whose Hamming weight ranges from 1 to β. The steps are described in Algorithm 1.

The function listTuples outputs the list of all s-tuples with Hamming weight h with $h \in [s]$. The function eliminateFromSmaller takes as input the list ℓ_h of current tuples of Hamming weight h and the list of incompressible failure tuples ℓ_p. It returns two lists:

- $\ell_h^{f_1}$: the elements of ℓ_h which are not incompressible (*i.e.* which include at least one element from ℓ_p)
- ℓ_h^p: the elements of ℓ_h which are incompressible (*i.e.* $\ell_h \backslash \ell_h^{f_1}$)

Algorithm 1. Verification tool

Input: a compiled circuit $\widehat{C}$ with s wires and a threshold $\beta \leqslant s$
Output: a list of β coefficients c_1, ..., c_β

1: $\ell_p \leftarrow []$ ▷ will be used to store a list of failure tuples
2: $c \leftarrow (0, \ldots, 0)$ ▷ will be used to store the output coefficients
3: **for** $h = 1$ to β **do**
4:      $\ell_h \leftarrow$ listTuples(s,h) ▷ list of s-tuples of Hamming weight h
5:      $(\ell_h^p, \ell_h^{f_1}) \leftarrow$ eliminateFromSmaller(ℓ_h, ℓ_p) ▷ select tuples including an
     incompressible failure tuple
6:      $\ell_h^{f_2} \leftarrow$ failureTest$(\widehat{C}, \ell_h^p)$ ▷ identify failure tuples in ℓ_h^p
7:      $\ell_p \leftarrow \ell_p \cup \ell_h^{f_2}$ ▷ update list of incompressible failure tuples
8:      $c \leftarrow$ updateCoeffs$(c, \ell_h^{f_1} \cup \ell_h^{f_2})$ ▷ update coefficients
9: **end for**
10: **return** c

The function failureTest takes as input the second list ℓ_h^p and checks if a perfect simulation can be achieved for each wire family $\mathcal{W}$ corresponding to a tuple in ℓ_h^p. Basically, for each wire family, a sequence of rules taken from maskVerif [4] is tested to determine whether $\mathcal{W}$ can be perfectly simulated. It outputs $\ell_h^{f_2}$, the list of incompressible failure s-tuples of Hamming weight h. In a nutshell, each wire w_i in $\mathcal{W}$ is considered together with the algebraic expression $\varphi_i(\cdot)$ describing its assignment by $\widehat{C}$ as a function of the circuit inputs and the random values returned by the random gates, then the three following rules are successively and repeatedly applied on all the wires families $\mathcal{W}$ (see [4] for further details):

rule 1: check whether all the expressions $\varphi_i(\cdot)$ corresponding to wires w_i in $\mathcal{W}$ contain all the shares of at least one of the coordinates of x;
rule 2: for every $\varphi_i(\cdot)$, check whether a random r (*i.e.* an output of a random gate) additively masks a sub-expression e (which does not involve r) and appears nowhere else in the other $\varphi_j(\cdot)$ with $j \neq i$; in this case replace the sum of the so-called sub-expression and r by r, namely $e + r \leftarrow r$;
rule 3: apply mathematical simplifications on the tuple.

Function updateCoeffs takes as input the current array of β coefficients c_i for $1 \leqslant i \leqslant \beta$ and the concatenation of both lists of potential failure tuples $\ell_h^{f_1}$ and $\ell_h^{f_2}$. For each failure tuple, these coefficients are updated.

Implementation. An implementation of Algorithm 1 has been developed in Python. This tool, named VRAPS, has been open sourced at:

https://github.com/CryptoExperts/VRAPS

Further details. The full version of this paper gives more details on the concrete link between VRAPS and maskVerif and provides two possible optimizations to improve the performances of the former. Three examples of multiplication gadgets are also displayed to illustrate the behavior of our verification tool.

4   Composition

This section aims to provide composition properties for random-probing secure gadgets. In a nutshell, we aim to show how to build random probing secure larger circuits from specific random probing secure building blocks.

4.1   Random Probing Composability

We introduce hereafter the *random probing composability* notion for a gadget. In the following definition, for an n-share, ℓ-to-m gadget, we denote by $\boldsymbol{I}$ a collection of sets $\boldsymbol{I} = (I_1, \ldots, I_\ell)$ with $I_1 \subseteq [n]$, ..., $I_\ell \subseteq [n]$ where $n \in \mathbb{N}$ refers to the number of shares. For some $\widehat{\boldsymbol{x}} = (\widehat{x}_1, \ldots, \widehat{x}_\ell) \in (\mathbb{K}^n)^\ell$, we then denote $\widehat{\boldsymbol{x}}|_{\boldsymbol{I}} = (\widehat{x}_1|_{I_1}, \ldots, \widehat{x}_\ell|_{I_\ell})$ where $\widehat{x}_i|_{I_i} \in \mathbb{K}^{|I_i|}$ is the tuple composed of the coordinates of the sharing $\widehat{x}_i$ of indexes included in I_i.

Definition 6 (Random Probing Composability). *Let $n, \ell, m \in \mathbb{N}$. An n-share gadget $G : (\mathbb{K}^n)^\ell \to (\mathbb{K}^n)^m$ is (t, p, ε)-random probing composable (RPC) for some $t \in \mathbb{N}$ and $p, \varepsilon \in [0,1]$ if there exists a deterministic algorithm Sim_1^G and a probabilistic algorithm Sim_2^G such that for every input $\widehat{\boldsymbol{x}} \in (\mathbb{K}^n)^\ell$ and for every set collection $J_1 \subseteq [n]$, ..., $J_m \subseteq [n]$ of cardinals $|J_1| \leq t$, ..., $|J_m| \leq t$, the random experiment*

$$\mathcal{W} \leftarrow \mathsf{LeakingWires}(G, p)$$

$$\boldsymbol{I} \leftarrow \mathsf{Sim}_1^G(\mathcal{W}, \boldsymbol{J})$$

$$out \leftarrow \mathsf{Sim}_2^G\left(\widehat{\boldsymbol{x}}|_{\boldsymbol{I}}\right)$$

yields

$$\Pr\left((|I_1| > t) \vee \ldots \vee (|I_\ell| > t)\right) \leq \varepsilon \tag{7}$$

and

$$out \overset{id}{=} \left(\mathsf{AssignWires}(G, \mathcal{W}, \widehat{\boldsymbol{x}}), \, \widehat{\boldsymbol{y}}|_{\boldsymbol{J}}\right)$$

where $\boldsymbol{J} = (J_1, \ldots, J_m)$ and $\widehat{\boldsymbol{y}} = G(\widehat{\boldsymbol{x}})$. Let $f : \mathbb{R} \to \mathbb{R}$. The gadget G is (t, f)-RPC if it is $(t, p, f(p))$-RPC for every $p \in [0, 1]$.

In the above definition, the first-pass simulator Sim_1^G determines the necessary input shares (through the returned collection of sets $\boldsymbol{I}$) for the second-pass simulator Sim_2^G to produce a perfect simulation of the leaking wires defined by the set $\mathcal{W}$ together with the output shares defined by the collection of sets $\boldsymbol{J}$. Note that there always exists such a collection of sets $\boldsymbol{I}$ since $\boldsymbol{I} = ([n], \ldots, [n])$ trivially allows a perfect simulation whatever $\mathcal{W}$ and $\boldsymbol{J}$. However, the goal of Sim_1^G is to return a collection of sets $\boldsymbol{I}$ with cardinals at most t. The idea behind this constraint is to keep the following composition invariant: for each gadget we can achieve a perfect simulation of the leaking wires plus t shares of each output sharing from t shares of each input sharing. We shall call *failure event* the event that at least one of the sets I_1, ..., I_ℓ output of Sim_1^G has cardinality greater than t. When (t, p, ε)-RPC is achieved, the failure event probability is upper bounded by ε according to (7). A failure event occurs whenever Sim_2^G requires more than t shares of one input sharing to be able to produce a perfect simulation of the leaking wires (*i.e.* the wires with label in $\mathcal{W}$) together with the output shares in $\widehat{\boldsymbol{y}}|_J$. Whenever such a failure occurs, the composition invariant is broken. In the absence of failure event, the RPC notion implies that a perfect simulation can be achieved for the full circuit composed of RPC gadgets. This is formally stated in the next theorem whose proof is given in the full version.

Theorem 1 (Composition). *Let $t \in \mathbb{N}$, $p, \varepsilon \in [0, 1]$, and CC be a standard circuit compiler with (t, p, ε)-RPC base gadgets. For every (randomized) arithmetic circuit C composed of $|C|$ gadgets, the compiled circuit $\mathsf{CC}(C)$ is $(p, |C| \cdot \varepsilon)$-random probing secure. Equivalently, the standard circuit compiler CC is (p, ε)-random probing secure.*

4.2   Relation with Standard Probing Composition Notions

We first reformulate the Strong Non-Interference notion introduced in [5] with the formalism used for our definition of the Random Probing Composability.

Definition 7 (Strong Non-Interference (SNI)). *Let n, ℓ and t be positive integers. An n-share gadget $G : (\mathbb{K}^n)^\ell \to \mathbb{K}^n$ is t-SNI if there exists a deterministic algorithm Sim_1^G and a probabilistic algorithm Sim_2^G such that for every set $J \subseteq [n]$ and subset $\mathcal{W}$ of wire labels from G satisfying $|\mathcal{W}| + |J| \leqslant t$, the following random experiment with any $\widehat{\boldsymbol{x}} \in (\mathbb{K}^n)^\ell$*

$$\boldsymbol{I} \leftarrow \mathsf{Sim}_1^G(\mathcal{W}, J)$$
$$out \leftarrow \mathsf{Sim}_2^G(\widehat{\boldsymbol{x}}|_{\boldsymbol{I}})$$

yields

$$|I_1| \leqslant |\mathcal{W}|, \ldots, |I_\ell| \leqslant |\mathcal{W}| \tag{8}$$

and

$$out \overset{id}{=} \left(\mathsf{AssignWires}(G, \mathcal{W}, \widehat{\boldsymbol{x}}), \, \widehat{\boldsymbol{y}}|_J\right) \tag{9}$$

where $\boldsymbol{I} = (I_1, \ldots, I_\ell)$ and $\widehat{\boldsymbol{y}} = G(\widehat{\boldsymbol{x}})$.

Then, we demonstrate that gadgets satisfying the t-SNI notion are also random probing composable for specific values that we explicit in the following proposition, whose proof is available in the full version of this paper.

Proposition 1. *Let n, ℓ and t be positive integers and let G be a gadget from $(\mathbb{K}^n)^\ell$ to $\mathbb{K}^n$. If G is t-SNI, then it is also $(t/2, p, \varepsilon)$-RPC for any probability p and ε satisfying:*

$$\varepsilon = \sum_{i=\lfloor \frac{t}{2}+1 \rfloor}^{s} \binom{s}{i} p^i (1-p)^{s-i}, \tag{10}$$

where s is the number of wires in G.

4.3   Verification of Gadget Composability

Our random probing verification tool (Algorithm 1) can be easily extended to define a simulator for the (t, p, ε)-random probing composability of a gadget for some t and some p. This essentially amounts to extend Algorithm 1 inputs with a multi-set $\mathcal{O}$ and to modify the failureTest procedure in order to test the simulation for each tuple in the input list ℓ_n^p augmented with the outputs coordinates with indices in $\mathcal{O}$. Then, our extended algorithm is called for every set $\mathcal{O}$ composed of at most t indices in each of the sets $J_1, \ldots, J_m$. The output for the call with input set $\mathcal{O}$ is denoted by $c_{\mathcal{O}} = (c_1^{\mathcal{O}}, \ldots, c_\beta^{\mathcal{O}})$. For our simulator construction, the probability ε satisfies

$$\varepsilon = \sum_{i=1}^{s} c_i \cdot p^i \cdot (1 - p)^{s-i},$$

where s denotes the number of wires in the tested gadget. Moreover, the c_i's satisfy $c_i = \max_{\mathcal{O}} c_i^{\mathcal{O}}$.

The full version of this paper provides an illustration of the proposition with the well deployed 3-share ISW multiplication gadget [18].

5   Expansion

Constructing random-probing-secure circuit compilers with a gadget expansion strategy has been proposed by Ananth, Ishai and Sahai in [2]. Such strategy was previously used in the field of multi-party computation (MPC) with different but close security goals [12,17]. Note that such approach is called *composition* in [2] since it roughly consists in composing a base circuit compiler several times. We prefer the terminology of *expansion* here to avoid any confusion with the notion of composition for gadgets as considered in Sect. 4 and usual in the literature – see for instance [5,8,10].

We recall hereafter the general principle of the gadget expansion strategy and provide an asymptotic analysis of the so-called *expanding circuit compiler*. Then we propose an implementation of this strategy which relies on the new notion of *gadget expandability*. In contrast, the construction of [2] relies on a t-out-n secure MPC protocol in the passive security model. The advantage of our notion is that it can be achieved and/or verified by simple atomic gadgets leading to simple and efficient constructions. After introducing the gadget expandability notion, we show that it allows to achieve random-probing security with the expansion strategy. We finally explain how to adapt the verification tool described in Sect. 3 to this expandability notion.

5.1   Expansion Strategy

The basic principle of the gadget expansion strategy is as follows. Assume we have three n-share gadgets G_{add}, G_{mult}, G_{copy} and denote CC the standard circuit compiler for these base gadgets. We can derive three new n^2-share gadgets by simply applying CC to each gadget: $G_{\text{add}}^{(2)} = \text{CC}(G_{\text{add}})$, $G_{\text{mult}}^{(2)} = \text{CC}(G_{\text{mult}})$ and $G_{\text{copy}}^{(2)} = \text{CC}(G_{\text{copy}})$. Let us recall that this process simply consists in replacing each addition gate in the original gadget by G_{add}, each multiplication gate by G_{mult} and each copy gate by G_{copy}, and by replacing each wire by n wires carrying a sharing of the original wire. Doing so, we obtain n^2-share gadgets for the addition, multiplication and copy on $\mathbb{K}$. This process can be iterated an arbitrary number of times, say k, to an input circuit C:

$$C \xrightarrow{\text{CC}} \widehat{C}_1 \xrightarrow{\text{CC}} \cdots \xrightarrow{\text{CC}} \widehat{C}_k \ .$$

The first output circuit $\widehat{C}_1$ is the original circuit in which each gate is replaced by a base gadget G_{add}, G_{mult} or G_{copy}. The second output circuit $\widehat{C}_2$ is the original circuit C in which each gate is replaced by an n^2-share gadget $G_{\text{add}}^{(2)}$, $G_{\text{mult}}^{(2)}$ or $G_{\text{copy}}^{(2)}$ as defined above. Equivalently, $\widehat{C}_2$ is the circuit $\widehat{C}_1$ in which each gate is replaced by a base gadget. In the end, the output circuit $\widehat{C}_k$ is hence the original circuit C in which each gate has been replaced by a k-expanded gadget and each wire as been replaced by n^k wires carrying an (n^k)-linear sharing of the original wire. The underlying compiler is called *expanding circuit compiler* which is formally defined hereafter.

Definition 8 (Expanding Circuit Compiler). *Let* CC *be the standard circuit compiler with sharing order n and base gadgets G_{add}, G_{mult}, G_{copy}. The* expanding circuit compiler *with* expansion level k *and* base compiler CC *is the circuit compiler* $(\text{CC}^{(k)}, \text{Enc}^{(k)}, \text{Dec}^{(k)})$ *satisfying the following:*

1. *The input encoding $\text{Enc}^{(k)}$ is an (n^k)-linear encoding.*
2. *The output decoding* Dec *is the (n^k)-linear decoding mapping.*
3. *The circuit compilation is defined as*

$$\text{CC}^{(k)}(\cdot) = \underbrace{\text{CC} \circ \text{CC} \circ \cdots \circ \text{CC}}_{k \ times}(\cdot)$$

The goal of the expansion strategy in the context of random probing security is to replace the leakage probability p of a wire in the original circuit by the failure event probability ε in the subsequent gadget simulation. If this simulation fails then one needs the full input sharing for the gadget simulation, which corresponds to leaking the corresponding wire value in the base case. The security is thus amplified by replacing the probability p in the base case by the probability ε (assuming that we have $\varepsilon < p$). If the failure event probability ε can be upper bounded by some function of the leakage probability: $\varepsilon < f(p)$ for every leakage probability $p \in [0, p_{\max}]$ for some $p_{\max} < 1$, then the expanding circuit compiler with expansion level k shall result in a security amplification as

$$p = \varepsilon_0 \xrightarrow{f} \varepsilon_1 \xrightarrow{f} \cdots \xrightarrow{f} \varepsilon_k = f^{(k)}(p) \ ,$$

which for an adequate function f (*e.g.* $f : p \mapsto p^2$) provides exponential security. In order to get such a security expansion, the gadgets must satisfy a stronger notion than the composability notion introduced in Sect. 4 which we call *random probing expandability*; see Sect. 5.3 below.

5.2   Asymptotic Analysis of the Expanding Compiler

In this section we show that the asymptotic complexity of a compiled circuit $\widehat{C} = \mathsf{CC}^{(k)}(C)$ is $|\widehat{C}| = \mathcal{O}(|C| \cdot \kappa^e)$ for security parameter κ, for some constant e that we make explicit.

Let us denote by $\boldsymbol{N} = (N_a, N_c, N_m, N_r)^{\mathsf{T}}$ the column vector of gate counts for some base gadget G, where N_a, N_c, N_m, N_r stands for the number of addition gates, copy gates, multiplication gates and random gates respectively. We have three different such vectors $\boldsymbol{N}_{\mathrm{add}} \doteq (N_{\mathrm{add},a}, N_{\mathrm{add},c}, N_{\mathrm{add},m}, N_{\mathrm{add},r})^{\mathsf{T}}$, $\boldsymbol{N}_{\mathrm{mult}} \doteq (N_{\mathrm{mult},a}, N_{\mathrm{mult},c}, N_{\mathrm{mult},m}, N_{\mathrm{mult},r})^{\mathsf{T}}$, $\boldsymbol{N}_{\mathrm{copy}} \doteq (N_{\mathrm{copy},a}, N_{\mathrm{copy},c}, N_{\mathrm{copy},m}, N_{\mathrm{copy},r})^{\mathsf{T}}$ for the gate counts respectively in the base addition gadget G_{add}, in the base multiplication gadget G_{mult} and in the base copy gadgets G_{copy}. Let us define the 4×4 square matrix $\boldsymbol{M}$ as

$$\boldsymbol{M} = (\boldsymbol{N}_{\mathrm{add}} \mid \boldsymbol{N}_{\mathrm{copy}} \mid \boldsymbol{N}_{\mathrm{mult}} \mid \boldsymbol{N}_{\mathrm{rand}}) \quad \text{with} \quad \boldsymbol{N}_{\mathrm{rand}} = (0, 0, 0, n)^{\mathsf{T}},$$

where the definition $\boldsymbol{N}_{\mathrm{rand}}$ holds from the fact that the standard circuit compiler replaces each random gate by n random gates.

It can be checked that applying the standard circuit compiler with base gadgets G_{add}, G_{mult} and G_{copy} to some circuit C with gate-count vector $\boldsymbol{N}_C$ gives a circuit $\widehat{C}$ with gate-count vector $\boldsymbol{N}_{\widehat{C}} = \boldsymbol{M} \cdot \boldsymbol{N}_C$. It follows that the kth power of the matrix $\boldsymbol{M}$ gives the gate counts for the level-k gadgets as:

$$\boldsymbol{M}^k = \underbrace{\boldsymbol{M} \cdot \boldsymbol{M} \cdots \boldsymbol{M}}_{k \text{ times}} = (\boldsymbol{N}_{\mathrm{add}}^{(k)} \mid \boldsymbol{N}_{\mathrm{copy}}^{(k)} \mid \boldsymbol{N}_{\mathrm{mult}}^{(k)} \mid \boldsymbol{N}_{\mathrm{rand}}^{(k)}) \quad \text{with} \quad \boldsymbol{N}_{\mathrm{rand}}^{(k)} = \begin{pmatrix} 0 \\ 0 \\ 0 \\ n^k \end{pmatrix}$$

where $\boldsymbol{N}_{\mathrm{add}}^{(k)}$, $\boldsymbol{N}_{\mathrm{mult}}^{(k)}$ and $\boldsymbol{N}_{\mathrm{copy}}^{(k)}$ are the gate-count vectors for the level-k gadgets $G_{\mathrm{add}}^{(k)}$, $G_{\mathrm{mult}}^{(k)}$ and $G_{\mathrm{copy}}^{(k)}$ respectively. Let us denote the eigen decomposition of $\boldsymbol{M}$ as $\boldsymbol{M} = \boldsymbol{Q} \cdot \boldsymbol{\Lambda} \cdot \boldsymbol{Q}^{-1}$, we get

$$\boldsymbol{M}^k = \boldsymbol{Q} \cdot \boldsymbol{\Lambda}^k \cdot \boldsymbol{Q}^{-1} \quad \text{with} \quad \boldsymbol{\Lambda}^k = \begin{pmatrix} \lambda_1^k & & & \\ & \lambda_2^k & & \\ & & \lambda_3^k & \\ & & & \lambda_4^k \end{pmatrix}$$

where λ_1, λ_2, λ_3, λ_4 are the eigenvalues of $\boldsymbol{M}$. We then obtain an asymptotic complexity of

$$|\widehat{C}| = \mathcal{O}(|C| \cdot (\lambda_1^k + \lambda_2^k + \lambda_3^k + \lambda_4^k)) = \mathcal{O}(|C| \cdot \max(\lambda_1, \lambda_2, \lambda_3, \lambda_4)^k)$$

for a compiled circuit $\widehat{C} = \mathsf{CC}^{(k)}(C)$ (where the constant in the $\mathcal{O}(\cdot)$ depends on $\boldsymbol{Q}$ and shall be fairly small).

Interestingly, if multiplication gates are solely used in the multiplication gadget (*i.e.* $N_{\mathrm{add},m} = N_{\mathrm{copy},m} = 0$) which is the case in the constructions we consider in this paper, it can be checked that (up to some permutation) the eigenvalues satisfy

$$(\lambda_1, \lambda_2) = \text{eigenvalues}(\boldsymbol{M}_{ac}), \quad \lambda_3 = N^k_{\text{mult},m} \quad \text{and} \quad \lambda_4 = n^k$$

where $\boldsymbol{M}_{ac}$ is the top left 2×2 block matrix of $\boldsymbol{M}$ i.e.

$$\boldsymbol{M}_{ac} = \begin{pmatrix} N_{\text{add},a} & N_{\text{copy},a} \\ N_{\text{add},c} & N_{\text{copy},c} \end{pmatrix} .$$

We finally get

$$|\widehat{C}| = \mathcal{O}\big(|C| \cdot N^k_{\max}\big) \quad \text{with} \quad N_{\max} = \max(\text{eigenvalues}(\boldsymbol{M}_{ac}), N_{\text{mult},m}) . \tag{11}$$

In order to reach some security level $\varepsilon = 2^{-\kappa}$ for some target security parameter κ and assuming that we have a security expansion $p \rightarrow f^{(k)}(p)$, the expansion level k must be chosen so that $f^{(k)}(p) \leq 2^{-\kappa}$. In practice, the function f is of the form

$$f : p \mapsto \sum_{i \geq d} c_i \, p^i \leq (c_d + \mathcal{O}(p)) \, p^d .$$

where $\mathcal{O}(p)$ is to be interpreted as p tends to 0. In the rest of this paper, we shall say that such a function has *amplification order* d.

The upper bound $f(p) \leq c'_d p^d$ with $c'_d = c_d + \mathcal{O}(p)$ implies $f^{(k)}(p) < (c'_d p)^{d^k}$. Hence, to satisfy the required security $f^{(k)}(p) \leq 2^{-\kappa}$ while assuming $c'_d \, p < 1$, the number k of expansions must satisfy:

$$k \geqslant \log_d(\kappa) - \log_d(-\log_2(c'_d \, p)) .$$

We can then rewrite (11) as

$$|\widehat{C}| = \mathcal{O}\big(|C| \cdot \kappa^e\big) \quad \text{with} \quad e = \frac{\log N_{\max}}{\log d} . \tag{12}$$

5.3 Random Probing Expandability

In the evaluation of random probing composability, let us recall that the failure event in the simulation of a gadget means that more that t shares from one of its inputs are necessary to complete a perfect simulation. For a gadget to be expandable we need slightly stronger notions than random probing composability. As first requirement, a two-input gadget should have a failure probability which is independent for each input. This is because in the base case, each wire as input of a gate leaks independently. On the other hand, in case of failure event in the child gadget, the overall simulator should be able to produce a perfect simulation of the full output (that is the full input for which the failure occurs). To do so, the overall simulator is given the clear output (which is obtained from the simulation of the base case) plus any set of $n - 1$ output shares. This means that whenever the set J is of cardinal greater than t, the gadget simulator can replace it by any set J' of cardinal $n - 1$.

Definition 9 (Random Probing Expandability). *Let* $f : \mathbb{R} \to \mathbb{R}$. *An n-share gadget* $G : \mathbb{K}^n \times \mathbb{K}^n \to \mathbb{K}^n$ *is* (t, f)*-random probing expandable (RPE) if there exists a deterministic algorithm* Sim_1^G *and a probabilistic algorithm* Sim_2^G *such that for every input* $(\widehat{x}, \widehat{y}) \in \mathbb{K}^n \times \mathbb{K}^n$, *for every set* $J \subseteq [n]$ *and for every* $p \in [0, 1]$, *the random experiment*

$$\mathcal{W} \leftarrow \mathsf{LeakingWires}(G, p)$$
$$(I_1, I_2, J') \leftarrow \mathsf{Sim}_1^G(\mathcal{W}, J)$$
$$out \leftarrow \mathsf{Sim}_2^G(\mathcal{W}, J', \widehat{x}|_{I_1}, \widehat{y}|_{I_2})$$

ensures that

1. *the failure events* $\mathcal{F}_1 \equiv \big(|I_1| > t\big)$ *and* $\mathcal{F}_2 \equiv \big(|I_2| > t\big)$ *verify*

$$\Pr(\mathcal{F}_1) = \Pr(\mathcal{F}_2) = \varepsilon \quad and \quad \Pr(\mathcal{F}_1 \wedge \mathcal{F}_2) = \varepsilon^2 \tag{13}$$

   with $\varepsilon = f(p)$ *(in particular* $\mathcal{F}_1$ *and* $\mathcal{F}_2$ *are mutually independent),*
2. J' *is such that* $J' = J$ *if* $|J| \leq t$ *and* $J' \subseteq [n]$ *with* $|J'| = n - 1$ *otherwise,*
3. *the output distribution satisfies*

$$out \stackrel{id}{=} \big(\mathsf{AssignWires}(G, \mathcal{W}, (\widehat{x}, \widehat{y})) , \widehat{z}|_{J'}\big) \tag{14}$$

where $\widehat{z} = G(\widehat{x}, \widehat{y})$.

The RPE notion can be simply extended to gadgets with 2 outputs: the Sim_1^G simulator takes two sets $J_1 \subseteq [n]$ and $J_2 \subseteq [n]$ as input and produces two sets J_1' and J_2' satisfying the same property as J' in the above definition (w.r.t. J_1 and J_2). The Sim_2^G simulator must then produce an output including $\widehat{z}_1|_{J_1'}$ and $\widehat{z}_2|_{J_1'}$ where $\widehat{z}_1$ and $\widehat{z}_2$ are the output sharings. The RPE notion can also be simply extended to gadgets with a single input: the Sim_1^G simulator produces a single set I so that the failure event $(|I| > t)$ occurs with probability lower than ε (and the Sim_2^G simulator is then simply given $\widehat{x}|_I$ where $\widehat{x}$ is the single input sharing). For the sake of completeness, and since we only focus in $2 \to 1$ and $1 \to 2$ gadgets in this paper, the RPE definition for the $1 \to 2$ case is given in the full version of this paper.

It is not hard to check that the above expandability notion is stronger that the composability notion introduced in Sect. 4. Formally, we have the following reduction:

Proposition 2. *Let* $f = \mathbb{R} \to \mathbb{R}$ *and* $n \in \mathbb{N}$. *Let* G *be an n-share gadget. If G is* (t, f)*-RPE then G is* (t, f')*-RPC, with* $f'(\cdot) = 2 \cdot f(\cdot)$.

Proof. We consider a (t, f)-RPE n-share gadget $G : \mathbb{K}^n \times \mathbb{K}^n \to \mathbb{K}^n$. The $(t, 2 \cdot f)$-random composability property is directly implied by the (t, f)-random probing expandability by making use of the exact same simulators and observing that

$$\Pr\big((|I_1| > t) \vee (|I_2| > t)\big) \leq \Pr(|I_1| > t) + \Pr(|I_2| > t) = 2 \cdot \varepsilon.$$

The case of $1 \to 2$ gadgets is even more direct. $\qquad\square$

5.4 Expansion Security

Definition 9 of random probing expandability is valid for base gadgets. For level-k gadgets $G^{(k)} = \mathsf{CC}^{(k-1)}(G)$ where $G \in \{G_{\mathrm{add}}, G_{\mathrm{mult}}, G_{\mathrm{copy}}\}$ is a base gadget, we provide a generalized definition of random probing expandability.

Adequate subsets of $[n^k]$. We first define the notion of "adequate" subsets of $[n^k]$, instead of only bounded subsets. For this we define recursively a family $S_k \in \mathcal{P}([n^k])$, where $\mathcal{P}([n^k])$ denotes the set of all subsets of $[n^k]$, as follows:

$$S_1 = \{I \in [n], \ |I| \leq t\}$$
$$S_k = \{(I_1, \ldots, I_n) \in (S_{k-1} \cup [n^{k-1}])^n, I_j \in S_{k-1} \ \forall \ j \in [1, n] \text{ except at most } t\}$$

In other words, a subset I belongs to S_k if among the n subset parts of I, at most t of them are full, while the other ones recursively belong to S_{k-1}; see the full version for an illustration with $n = 3$ and $t = 1$.

Generalized definition of random probing expandability. We generalize Definition 9 as follows. At level k the input sets I_1 and I_2 must belong to S_k, otherwise we have a failure event. As in Definition 9, the simulation is performed for an output subset J' with $J' = J$ if $J \in S_k$, otherwise $J' = [n^k] \setminus \{j^\star\}$ for some $j^\star \in [n^k]$.

Definition 10 (Random Probing Expandability with $\{S_k\}_{k \in \mathbb{N}}$). *Let $f : \mathbb{R} \to \mathbb{R}$ and $k \in \mathbb{N}$. An n^k-share gadget $G : \mathbb{K}^{n^k} \times \mathbb{K}^{n^k} \to \mathbb{K}^{n^k}$ is (S_k, f)-random probing expandable (RPE) if there exists a deterministic algorithm Sim_1^G and a probabilistic algorithm Sim_2^G such that for every input $(\widehat{x}, \widehat{y}) \in \mathbb{K}^{n^k} \times \mathbb{K}^{n^k}$, for every set $J \in S_k \cup [n^k]$ and for every $p \in [0, 1]$, the random experiment*

$$\mathcal{W} \leftarrow \mathsf{LeakingWires}(G, p)$$
$$(I_1, I_2, J') \leftarrow \mathsf{Sim}_1^G(\mathcal{W}, J)$$
$$out \leftarrow \mathsf{Sim}_2^G(\mathcal{W}, J', \widehat{x}|_{I_1}, \widehat{y}|_{I_2})$$

ensures that

1. *the failure events $\mathcal{F}_1 \equiv (I_1 \notin S_k)$ and $\mathcal{F}_2 \equiv (I_2 \notin S_k)$ verify*

$$\Pr(\mathcal{F}_1) = \Pr(\mathcal{F}_2) = \varepsilon \quad and \quad \Pr(\mathcal{F}_1 \wedge \mathcal{F}_2) = \varepsilon^2 \tag{15}$$

   with $\varepsilon = f(p)$ (in particular $\mathcal{F}_1$ and $\mathcal{F}_2$ are mutually independent),
2. *the set J' is such that $J' = J$ if $J \in S_k$, and $J' = [n^k] \setminus \{j^\star\}$ for some $j^\star \in [n^k]$ otherwise,*
3. *the output distribution satisfies*

$$out \stackrel{id}{=} \left(\mathsf{AssignWires}(G, \mathcal{W}, (\widehat{x}, \widehat{y})), \ \widehat{z}|_{J'}\right) \tag{16}$$

where $\widehat{z} = G(\widehat{x}, \widehat{y})$.

The notion of random probing expandability from Definition 10 naturally leads to the statement of our main theorem; the proof is given in the full version.

Theorem 2. *Let $n \in \mathbb{N}$ and $f : \mathbb{R} \to \mathbb{R}$. Let G_{add}, G_{mult}, G_{copy} be n-share gadgets for the addition, multiplication and copy on $\mathbb{K}$. Let CC be the standard circuit compiler with sharing order n and base gadgets G_{add}, G_{mult}, G_{copy}. Let $CC^{(k)}$ be the expanding circuit compiler with base compiler CC. If the base gadgets G_{add}, G_{mult} and G_{copy} are (t, f)-RPE then, $G_{add}^{(k)} = CC^{(k-1)}(G_{add})$, $G_{mult}^{(k)} = CC^{(k-1)}(G_{mult})$, $G_{copy}^{(k)} = CC^{(k-1)}(G_{copy})$ are $(S_k, f^{(k)})$-RPE, n^k-share gadgets for the addition, multiplication and copy on $\mathbb{K}$.*

The random probing security of the expanding circuit compiler can then be deduced as a corollary of the above theorem together with Proposition 2 (RPE $\Rightarrow$ RPC reduction) and Theorem 1 (composition theorem).

Corollary 1. *Let $n \in \mathbb{N}$ and $f : \mathbb{R} \to \mathbb{R}$. Let G_{add}, G_{mult}, G_{copy} be n-share gadgets for the addition, multiplication and copy on $\mathbb{K}$. Let CC be the standard circuit compiler with sharing order n and base gadgets G_{add}, G_{mult}, G_{copy}. Let $CC^{(k)}$ be the expanding circuit compiler with base compiler CC. If the base gadgets G_{add}, G_{mult} and G_{copy} are (t, f)-RPE then $CC^{(k)}$ is $(p, 2 \cdot f^{(k)}(p))$-random probing secure.*

5.5   Relaxing the Expandability Notion

The requirement of the RPE property that the failure events $\mathcal{F}_1$ and $\mathcal{F}_2$ are mutually independent might seem too strong. In practice it might be easier to show or verify that some gadgets satisfy a weaker notion. We say that a gadget is (t, f)-*weak random probing expandable* (wRPE) if the failure events verify $\Pr(\mathcal{F}_1) \leq \varepsilon$, $\Pr(\mathcal{F}_2) \leq \varepsilon$ and $\Pr(\mathcal{F}_1 \wedge \mathcal{F}_2) \leq \varepsilon^2$ instead of (13) in Definition 9. Although being easier to achieve and to verify this notion is actually not much weaker as the original RPE. We have the following reduction of RPE to wRPE; see the full version for the proof.

Proposition 3. *Let $f = \mathbb{R} \to [0, 0.14]$. Let $G : \mathbb{K}^n \times \mathbb{K}^n \to \mathbb{K}^n$ be an n-share gadget. If G is (t, f)-wRPE then G is (t, f')-RPE with $f'(\cdot) = f(\cdot) + \frac{3}{2}f(\cdot)^2$.*

Assume that we can show or verify that a gadget is wRPE with the following failure event probabilities

$$\Pr(\mathcal{F}_1) = f_1(p) , \quad \Pr(\mathcal{F}_2) = f_2(p) \quad \text{and} \quad \Pr(\mathcal{F}_1 \wedge \mathcal{F}_2) = f_{12}(p) ,$$

for every $p \in [0, 1]$. Then the above proposition implies that the gadget is (p, f)-RPE with

$$f : p \mapsto f_{\max}(p) + \frac{3}{2}f_{\max}(p)^2 \quad \text{with} \quad f_{\max} = \max(f_1, f_2, \sqrt{f_{12}}) .$$

We shall base our verification of the RPE property on the above equation as we describe hereafter.

5.6   Verification of Gadget Expandability

We can easily adapt our automatic tool to verify the weak random probing expandability for base gadgets (Definition 9). Basically, the verification is split into two steps that we first describe for the case of addition and multiplication gadgets with fan-in 2 and fan-out 1.

In a first step, our tool computes the function f to check the (t, f)-wRPE property for output sets of shares of cardinal at most t. For 2-input gadgets, this step leads to the computation of coefficients c_i corresponding to three failure events $\mathcal{F}_1$, $\mathcal{F}_2$, and $\mathcal{F}_1 \wedge \mathcal{F}_2$ as defined above but restricted to output sets of shares of cardinal less than t. The process is very similar to the verification of random probing composability but requires to separate the failure events counter into failure events for the first input ($|\mathcal{I}_1| > t$), for the second input ($|\mathcal{I}_2| > t$) or for both ($((|\mathcal{I}_1| > t) \wedge (|\mathcal{I}_2| > t))$). In the following, we denote the three functions formed from the corresponding coefficients as $f_1^{(1)}$, $f_2^{(1)}$, and $f_{12}^{(1)}$.

Then, in a second step, our tool verifies that there exists at least one set of $n-1$ shares for each output, such that the simulation failure is limited by $f(p)$ for some probability $p \in [0, 1]$. In that case, it still loops on the possible output sets of shares (of cardinal $n - 1$) but instead of computing the maximum coefficients, it determines whether the simulation succeeds for at least one of such sets. A failure event is recorded for a given tuple if no output sets of cardinal $n - 1$ can be simulated together with this tuple from at most t shares of each input. As for the first verification step, we record the resulting coefficients for the three failure events to obtain functions $f_1^{(2)}$, $f_2^{(2)}$, and $f_{12}^{(2)}$.

From these two steps, we can deduce f such that the gadget is (t, f)-wRPE:

$$\forall p \in [0, 1], f(p) = \max(f_1(p), f_2(p), \sqrt{f_{12}(p)})$$

with

$$f_\alpha(p) = \max(f_\alpha^{(1)}(p), f_\alpha^{(2)}(p)) \quad \text{for} \quad \alpha \in \{1, 2, 12\}$$

The computation of f for a gadget to satisfy (t, f)-weak random probing expandability is a bit trickier for copy gadgets which produce two outputs. Instead of two verification steps considering both possible ranges of cardinals for the output set of shares J, we need to consider four scenarios for the two possible features for output sets of shares J_1 and J_2. In a nutshell, the idea is to follow the first verification step described above when both J_1 and J_2 have cardinal equal or less than t and to follow the second verification step described above when both J_1 and J_2 have greater cardinals. This leads to functions $f^{(1)}$ and $f^{(2)}$. Then, two extra cases are to be considered, namely when ($|J_1| \leq t$) and ($|J_2| > t$) and the reverse when ($|J_1| > t$) and ($|J_2| \leq t$). To handle these scenarios, our tool loops over the output sets of shares of cardinal equal or less than t for the first output, and it determines whether there exists a set of $n - 1$ shares of the second output that a simulator can perfectly simulate with the leaking wires and the former set. This leads to function $f^{(12)}$ and reversely to function $f^{(21)}$. From these four verification steps, we can deduce f such that the copy gadget is (t, f)-wRPE:

$$\forall p \in [0, 1], f(p) = \max(f^{(1)}(p), f^{(2)}(p), f^{(12)}(p), f^{(21)}(p)).$$

Once gadgets have been proven (t, f)-weak RPE, they are also proven to be (t, f')-RPE from Proposition 3 with $f' : p \mapsto f(p) + \frac{3}{2}f(p)^2$. Examples of such computations for 3-share gadgets are provided in Sect. 6.

6   New Constructions

In this section, we exhibit and analyze $(1, f)$-wRPE gadgets for the addition, multiplication, and copy (on any base field $\mathbb{K}$) to instantiate the expanding circuit compiler. These gadgets are sound in the sense that their function f has amplification order strictly greater than one. As explained in previous sections, an amplification order strictly greater than one guarantees that there exists a probability $p_{max} \in [0, 1]$ such that $\forall p \leq p_{max}, f(p) \leq p$, which is necessary to benefit from the expansion. For 2-input gadgets, f is defined as the maximum between f_1, f_2, and $\sqrt{f_{12}}$. Therefore, the constraint on the amplification order also applies to the functions f_1, f_2, and $\sqrt{f_{12}}$. For the function f_{12}, this means that the amplification order should be strictly greater than two.

We start hereafter with an impossibility result, namely there are no (2-share, 2-to-1) $(1, f)$-RPE gadgets such that f has an amplification order greater than one. Then, we provide concrete instantiations of addition, multiplication, and copy gadgets based on 3 shares which successfully achieve $(1, f)$-RPE for amplification order greater than one and can be used in the expansion compiler.

6.1   About 2-Share Gadgets

Consider a gadget G with a 2-share single output $\boldsymbol{z} = (z_0, z_1)$ and two 2-share inputs $\boldsymbol{x} = (x_0, x_1)$ and $\boldsymbol{y} = (y_0, y_1)$. We reasonably assume that the latter are the outputs of gates with fan-in at most two (and not direct input shares). For G to be $(1, f)$-RPE with f of amplification order strictly greater than one, then f_{12} must be of amplification strictly greater than two. In other words, we should be able to exhibit a simulator such that one share of each input is enough to simulate anyone of the output shares and an arbitrary couple of leaking wires. But the output wire z_0 and both input gates of the second output share z_1 represent the full output and require the knowledge of both inputs to be simulated. Therefore, f_{12} has a non-zero coefficient in p and is thus not of amplification order strictly greater than two. We thus restrict our investigation to n-share gadgets, with $n \geq 3$ to instantiate our compiler.

In the upcoming gadget descriptions, notice that variables r_i are fresh random values, operations are processed with the usual priority rules, and the number of implicit copy gates can be deduced from the occurrences of each intermediate variable such that n occurrences require $n-1$ implicit copy gates. Also, the function expression below each gadget corresponds to the function obtained from our verification tool when verifying weak random probing expandability. It implies that the gadget is (t, f)-wRPE for t usually equal to one except when defined otherwise. A more complete description of each function (with more coefficients) is available in the full version of this paper.

6.2   Addition Gadgets

The most classical masked addition schemes are sharewise additions which satisfy the simpler probing security property. Basically, given two input n-sharings x and y, such an addition computes the output n-sharing z as $z_1 \leftarrow x_1 + y_1$, $z_2 \leftarrow x_2 + y_2, \ldots, z_n \leftarrow x_n + y_n$. Unfortunately, such elementary gadgets do not work in our setting. Namely consider an output set of shares J of cardinality t. Then, for any n, there exists sets $\mathcal{W}$ of leaking wires of cardinality one such that no set I of cardinality $\leq t$ can point to input shares that are enough to simulate both the leaking wire and the output shares of indexes in J. For instance, given a set $J = \{1, \ldots, t\}$, if $\mathcal{W}$ contains x_{t+1}, then no set I of cardinal $\leq t$ can define a set of input shares from which we can simulate both the leaking wire and $z_1, \ldots, z_t$. Indeed, each z_i for $1 \leq i \leq t$ requires both input shares x_i and y_i for its simulation. Thus, a simulation set I would contain at least $\{1, \ldots, t\}$ and $t + 1$ for the simulation of the leaking wire. I would thus be of cardinal $t + 1$ which represents a failure event in the random probing expandability definition. As a consequence, such a n-share addition gadget could only be (t, f)-RPE with f with a first coefficient c_1 as defined in Sect. 3 strictly positive. In other words, f would be of amplification order one such that $\forall p \in [0, 1], f(p) \geq p$.

In the following, we introduce two 3-share addition gadgets. From our automatic tool, both are $(1, f)$-wRPE with f of amplification order strictly greater than one. Basically, in our first addition gadget G^1_{add}, both inputs are first refreshed with a circular refreshing gadget as originally introduced in [6]:

$$G^1_{\mathrm{add}} : z_0 \leftarrow x_0 + r_0 + r_1 + y_0 + r_3 + r_4$$
$$z_1 \leftarrow x_1 + r_1 + r_2 + y_1 + r_4 + r_5 \qquad f_{max}(p) = \sqrt{10}p^{3/2} + \mathcal{O}(p^2)$$
$$z_2 \leftarrow x_2 + r_2 + r_0 + y_2 + r_5 + r_3$$

The second addition gadget G^2_{add} simply rearranges the order of the refreshing variables:

$$G^2_{\mathrm{add}} : z_0 \leftarrow x_0 + r_0 + r_4 + y_0 + r_1 + r_3$$
$$z_1 \leftarrow x_1 + r_1 + r_5 + y_1 + r_2 + r_4 \qquad f_{max}(p) = \sqrt{69}p^2 + \mathcal{O}(p^3)$$
$$z_2 \leftarrow x_2 + r_2 + r_3 + y_2 + r_0 + r_5$$

In each gadget, x and y are the input sharings and z the output sharing; f_{max} additionally reports the maximum of the first non zero coefficient (as defined in Sect. 3) of the three functions f_1, f_2, and f_{12}, as defined in the previous section, obtained for the random probing expandability automatic verifications. A further definition of these functions can be found in the full version of this paper. Note that both gadgets G^1_{add} and G^2_{add} are built with 15 addition gates and 6 implicit copy gates.

6.3   Multiplication Gadget

We start by proving an impossibility result: no 3-share multiplication gadget composed of direct products between input shares satisfies $(1, f)$-RPE with amplification order strictly greater than one. Consider such a gadget G with two 3-input sharings $\boldsymbol{x}$ and $\boldsymbol{y}$ whose shares are directly multiplied together. Let $(x_i \cdot y_j)$ and $(x_k \cdot y_\ell)$ be two such products such that $i, j, k, \ell \in [3]$ and $i \neq k$ and $j \neq \ell$. If both results are leaking, then the leakage can only be simulated using the four input shares. Namely, $\{i, k\} \subseteq I_1$ and $\{j, \ell\} \subseteq I_2$. This scenario represents a failure since cardinals of I_1 and I_2 are both strictly greater than one. As a consequence, function f_{12} which records the failures for both inputs is defined with a coefficient c_2 at least equal to one. Hence f_{12} is not of amplification greater than two and f cannot be of amplification order greater than one. Regular 3-share multiplication gadgets consequently cannot be used as base gadgets of our compiler.

To circumvent this issue, we build a 3-share multiplication gadget G^1_{mult} whose both inputs are first refreshed, before any multiplication is performed:

$$u_0 \leftarrow x_0 + r_5 + r_6; \qquad u_1 \leftarrow x_1 + r_6 + r_7; \qquad u_2 \leftarrow x_2 + r_7 + r_5$$
$$v_0 \leftarrow y_0 + r_8 + r_9; \qquad v_1 \leftarrow y_1 + r_9 + r_{10}; \qquad v_2 \leftarrow y_2 + r_{10} + r_8$$

$$z_0 \leftarrow \left(u_0 \cdot v_0 + r_0\right) + \left(u_0 \cdot v_1 + r_1\right) + \left(u_0 \cdot v_2 + r_2\right)$$
$$z_1 \leftarrow \left(u_1 \cdot v_0 + r_1\right) + \left(u_1 \cdot v_1 + r_4\right) + \left(u_1 \cdot v_2 + r_3\right)$$
$$z_2 \leftarrow \left(u_2 \cdot v_0 + r_2\right) + \left(u_2 \cdot v_1 + r_3\right) + \left(u_2 \cdot v_2 + r_0\right) + r_4$$
$$f_{max}(p) = \sqrt{83}p^{3/2} + \mathcal{O}(p^2)$$

6.4   Copy Gadget

We exhibit a 3-share $(1, f)$-wRPE copy gadget G^1_{copy} with f of amplification order strictly greater than one:

$$v_0 \leftarrow u_0 + r_0 + r_1; \ w_0 \leftarrow u_0 + r_3 + r_4$$
$$v_1 \leftarrow u_1 + r_1 + r_2; \ w_1 \leftarrow u_1 + r_4 + r_5 \qquad f_{max}(p) = 33p^2 + \mathcal{O}(p^3)$$
$$v_2 \leftarrow u_2 + r_2 + r_0; \ w_2 \leftarrow u_2 + r_5 + r_3$$

It simply relies on two calls of the circular refreshing from [6] on the input. This last gadget is made of 6 addition gates and 9 implicit copy gates.

6.5   Complexity and Tolerated Probability

Following the asymptotic analysis of Sect. 5.2, our construction yields the following instantiation of the matrix $\boldsymbol{M}$

$$\boldsymbol{M} = \begin{pmatrix} 15 & 12 & 28 & 0 \\ 6 & 9 & 23 & 0 \\ 0 & 0 & 9 & 0 \\ 6 & 6 & 11 & 3 \end{pmatrix} \tag{17}$$

with

$$M_{ac} = \begin{pmatrix} 15 & 12 \\ 6 & 9 \end{pmatrix} \quad \text{and} \quad N_{\text{mult},m} = 9 \ .$$

The eigenvalues of M_{ac} are 3 and 21, which gives $N_{\max} = 21$. We also have a random probing expandability with function f of amplification order $d = \frac{3}{2}$. Hence we get

$$e = \frac{\log N_{\max}}{\log d} = \frac{\log 21}{\log 1.5} \approx 7.5$$

which gives a complexity of $|\widehat{C}| = \mathcal{O}(|C| \cdot \kappa^{7.5})$. Finally, it can be checked from the coefficients of the RPE functions given in the full version of this paper that our construction tolerates a leakage probability up to

$$p_{\max} \approx 0.0045 > 2^{-8} \ .$$

This corresponds to the maximum value p for which we have $f(p) < p$ which is a necessary and sufficient condition for the expansion strategy to apply with (t, f)-RPE gadgets.

The full version of this paper displays the new gate count vectors for each of the compiled gadgets $G_{\text{add}}^{2(k)}, G_{\text{copy}}^{1(k)}, G_{\text{mult}}^{1(k)}$ by computing the matrix M^k and plots the values taken by the function f such that the base gadgets are (t, f)-RPE. For instance, for level $k = 9$ the number of gates in the compiled gadgets is around 10^{12} and assuming a leakage probability of $p = 0.0045$ (which is the maximum we can tolerate), we achieve a security of $\varepsilon \approx 2^{-76}$.

7   Comparison with Previous Constructions

In this section, we compare our scheme to previous constructions. Specifically, we first compare it to the well-known Ishai-Sahai-Wagner (ISW) construction and discuss the instantiation of our scheme from the ISW multiplication gadget. Then we exhibit the asymptotic complexity (and tolerated leakage probability) of the Ananth-Ishai-Sahai compiler and compare their results to our instantiation.

7.1   Comparison with ISW

The classical ISW construction [18] is secure in the t-probing model when the adversary can learn any set of t intermediate variables in the circuit, for $n = 2t + 1$ shares. This can be extended to t probes per gadget, where each gadget corresponds to a AND or XOR gate in the original circuit. Using Chernoff bound, security in the t-probing model per gadget implies security in the p-random probing model, where each wire leaks with probability p, with $p = \mathcal{O}(t/|G|)$, where $|G|$ is the gadget size. Since in ISW each gadget has complexity $\mathcal{O}(t^2)$, this gives $p = \mathcal{O}(1/t)$. Therefore, in the p-random probing model, the ISW construction is only secure against a leakage probability $p = \mathcal{O}(1/n)$, where the number of shares n must grow linearly with the security parameter κ in order to achieve security $2^{-\kappa}$. This means that ISW does not achieve security under a constant leakage probability p; this explains why ISW is actually vulnerable to horizontal attacks [7], in which the adversary can combine information from a constant fraction of the wires.

ISW-based instantiation of the expanding compiler. In our instantiation, we choose to construct a new 3-share multiplication gadget instead of using the ISW multiplication gadget from [18]. In fact, ISW first performs a direct product of the secret shares before adding some randomness, while we proved in Sect. 6 that no such 3-share multiplication gadget made of direct products could satisfy $(1, f)$-RPE with amplification order strictly greater than one. Therefore the ISW gadget is not adapted for our construction with 3 shares.

Table 1 displays the output of our tool when run on the ISW gadget for up to 7 shares with different values for t. It can be seen that an amplification order strictly greater than one is only achieved for $t > 1$, with 4 or more shares. And an order of $3/2$ is only achieved with a minimum of 4 shares for $t = 2$, whereas we already reached this order with our 3-share construction for $t = 1$. If we use the 4-share ISW gadget with appropriate 4-share addition and copy gadgets instead of our instantiation, the overall complexity of the compiler would be greater, while the amplification order would remain the same, and the tolerated leakage probability would be worse (recall that our instantiation tolerates a maximum leakage probability $p \approx 2^{-8}$, while 4-share ISW tolerates $p \approx 2^{-9.83}$). Clearly, the complexity of the 4-share ISW gadget $(N_a, N_c, N_m, N_r) = (24, 30, 16, 6)$ is higher than that of our 3-share multiplication gadget $(N_a, N_c, N_m, N_r) = (28, 23, 9, 11)$. In addition, using 3-share addition and copy gadgets (as in our case) provides better complexity than 4-share gadgets. Hence to reach an amplification order of $3/2$, a 4-share construction with the ISW gadget would be more complex and would offer a lower tolerated leakage probability.

For higher amplification orders, the ISW gadgets with more than 4 shares or other gadgets can be studied. This is a open construction problem as many gadgets can achieve different amplification orders and be globally compared.

7.2 Complexity of the Ananth-Ishai-Sahai Compiler

The work from [2] provides a construction of circuit compiler (the AIS compiler) based on the expansion strategy described in Sect. 5 with a (p, ε)-composable security property, analogous to our (t, f)-RPE property. To this purpose, the authors use an (m, c)-multi-party computation (MPC) protocol Π. Such a protocol allows to securely compute a functionality shared among m parties and tolerating at most c corruptions. In a nutshell, their composable circuit compiler consists of multiple layers: the bottom layer replaces each gate in the circuit by a circuit computing the (m, c)-MPC protocol for the corresponding functionality (either Boolean addition, Boolean multiplication, or copy). The next $k - 1$ above layers apply the same strategy recursively to each of the resulting gates. As this application can eventually have exponential complexity if applied to a whole circuit C directly, the top layer of compilation actually applies the k bottom layers

Table 1. Complexity, amplification order and maximum tolerated leakage probability of the ISW multiplication gadgets. Some leakage probabilities were not computed accurately by VRAPS for performances reasons. An interval on these probabilities is instead given by evaluating lower and upper bound functions f_{inf} and f_{sup} of $f(p)$.

# shares	Complexity (N_a, N_c, N_m, N_r)	t	Amplification order	$\log_2$ of maximum tolerated leakage probability
3	(12, 15, 9, 3)	1	1	−
4	(24, 30, 16, 6)	1	1	−
		2	3/2	−9.83
5	(40, 50, 25, 10)	1	1	−
		2	3/2	−11.00
		3	2	−8.05
6	(60, 75, 36, 15)	1	1	−
		2	3/2	−13.00
		3	2	[−9.83, −7.87]
		4	2	[−9.83, −5.92]
7	(84, 105, 49, 21)	1	1	−
		2	3/2	[−16.00, −14.00]
		3	2	[−12.00, −7.87]
		4	5/2	[−12.00, −2.27]
		5	2	[−12.00, −3.12]

to each of the gates of C independently and then stitches the inputs and outputs using the correctness of the XOR-encoding property. Hence the complexity is in

$$\mathcal{O}(|C| \cdot N_g^k) , \tag{18}$$

where $|C|$ is the number of gates in the original circuit and N_g is the number of gates in the circuit computing Π. The authors of [2] prove that such compiler satisfies (p, ε)-composition security property, where p is the tolerated leakage probability and ε is the simulation failure probability. Precisely:

$$\varepsilon = N_g^{c+1} \cdot p^{c+1} \tag{19}$$

Equations (18) and (19) can be directly plugged into our asymptotic analysis of Sect. 5.2, with N_g replacing our $N_{\max}$ and where $c+1$ stands for our amplification order d. The obtained asymptotic complexity for the AIS compiler is

$$\mathcal{O}(|C| \cdot \kappa^e) \quad \text{with} \quad e = \frac{\log N_g}{\log c + 1} . \tag{20}$$

This is to be compared to $e = \frac{\log N_{\max}}{\log d}$ in our scheme. Moreover, this compiler can tolerate a leakage probability

$$p = \frac{1}{N_g^2} .$$

The authors provide an instantiation of their construction using an existing MPC protocol due to Maurer [20]. From their analysis, this protocol can be implemented with a circuit of $N_{\mathrm{g}} = (4m - c) \cdot \left(\binom{m-1}{c}^2 + 2m\binom{m}{c}\right)$ gates. They instantiate their compiler with this protocol for parameters $m = 5$ parties and $c = 2$ corruptions, from which they get $N_{\mathrm{g}} = 5712$. From this number of gates, they claim to tolerate a leakage probability $p = \frac{1}{5712^2} \approx 2^{-25}$ and our asymptotic analysis gives a complexity of $\mathcal{O}(|C| \cdot \kappa^e)$ with $e \approx 7.87$ according to (20). In the full version of this paper, we give a detailed analysis of the Maurer protocol [20] in the context of the AIS compiler instantiation. From our analysis, we get the following number of gates for the associated circuit:

$$N_{\mathrm{g}} = (6m - 5) \cdot \left(\left(\frac{m-1}{c}\right)^2 + m(2k - 2) + 2k^2\right) \quad \text{where} \quad k = \binom{m}{c}.$$

Using the parameters $m = 5$ and $c = 2$ from the AIS compiler instantiation [2], we get $N_{\mathrm{g}} = 8150$. This yields a tolerated leakage probability of $p \approx 2^{-26}$ and an exponent $e = \log 8150 / \log 3 \approx 8.19$ in the asymptotic complexity $\mathcal{O}(|C| \cdot \kappa^e)$ of the AIS compiler.

These results are to be compared to the $p \approx 2^{-8}$ and $e \approx 7.5$ achieved by our construction. In either case ($N_{\mathrm{g}} = 5712$ as claimed in [2] or $N_{\mathrm{g}} = 8150$ according to our analysis), our construction achieves a slightly better complexity while tolerating a much higher leakage probability. We stress that further instantiations of the AIS scheme (based on different MPC protocols) or of our scheme (based on different gadgets) could lead to better asymptotic complexities and/or tolerated leakage probabilities. This is an interesting direction for further research.

8   Implementation Results

We developed an implementation in python of a compiler CC, that given three n-share gadgets G_{add}, G_{mult}, G_{copy} and an expansion level k, outputs the compiled gadgets $G_{\mathrm{add}}^{(k)}$, $G_{\mathrm{copy}}^{(k)}$, $G_{\mathrm{mult}}^{(k)}$, each as a C function. The source code (with an example of AES implementation) is publicly available at:

https://github.com/CryptoExperts/poc-expanding-compiler

The variables' type is given as a command line argument. Table 2 shows the complexity of the compiled gadgets from Sect. 6 using the compiler with several expansion levels k, as well as their execution time in milliseconds when run in C on randomly generated 8-bit integers. All implementations were run on a laptop computer (Intel(R) Core(TM) i7-8550U CPU, 1.80GHz with 4 cores) using Ubuntu operating system and various C, python and sage libraries. For the generation of random variables, we consider that an efficient external random number generator is available in practice, and so we simply use the values of an incremented counter variable to simulate random gates.

Table 2. Complexity and execution time (in ms, on an Intel i7-8550U CPU) for compiled gadgets $G_{\text{add}}^{2(k)}$, $G_{\text{copy}}^{1(k)}$, $G_{\text{mult}}^{1(k)}$ from Sect. 6 implemented in C.

k	# shares	Gadget	Complexity $(N_\text{a}, N_\text{c}, N_\text{m}, N_\text{r})$	Execution time
1	3	$G_{\text{add}}^{2(1)}$	(15, 6, 0, 6)	$1,69.10^{-4}$
		$G_{\text{copy}}^{1(1)}$	(12, 9, 0, 6)	$1,67.10^{-4}$
		$G_{\text{mult}}^{1(1)}$	(28, 23, 9, 11)	$5,67.10^{-4}$
2	9	$G_{\text{add}}^{2(2)}$	(297, 144, 0, 144)	$2,21.10^{-3}$
		$G_{\text{copy}}^{1(2)}$	(288, 153, 0, 144)	$2,07.10^{-3}$
		$G_{\text{mult}}^{1(2)}$	(948, 582, 81, 438)	$9,91.10^{-3}$
3	27	$G_{\text{add}}^{2(3)}$	(6183, 3078, 0, 3078)	$9,29.10^{-2}$
		$G_{\text{copy}}^{1(3)}$	(6156, 3105, 0, 3078)	$9,84.10^{-2}$
		$G_{\text{mult}}^{1(3)}$	(23472, 12789, 729, 11385)	$3,67.10^{-1}$

It can be observed that both the complexity and running time grow by almost the same factor with the expansion level, with multiplication gadgets being the slowest as expected. Base gadgets with $k = 1$ roughly take 10^{-4} ms, while these gadgets expanded 2 times ($k = 3$) take between 10^{-2} and 10^{-1} ms. The difference between the linear cost of addition and copy gadgets, and the quadratic cost of multiplication gadgets can also be observed through the gadgets' complexities.

References

1. Ajtai, M.: Secure computation with information leaking to an adversary. In: Fortnow, L., Vadhan, S.P. (eds.) 43rd Annual ACM Symposium on Theory of Computing, San Jose, CA, USA, 6–8 June 2011, pp. 715–724. ACM Press (2011)
2. Ananth, P., Ishai, Y., Sahai, A.: Private circuits: a modular approach. In: Shacham, H., Boldyreva, A. (eds.) CRYPTO 2018, Part III. LNCS, vol. 10993, pp. 427–455. Springer, Cham (2018). https://doi.org/10.1007/978-3-319-96878-0_15
3. Andrychowicz, M., Dziembowski, S., Faust, S.: Circuit compilers with $O(1/\log(n))$ leakage rate. In: Fischlin, M., Coron, J.-S. (eds.) EUROCRYPT 2016, Part II. LNCS, vol. 9666, pp. 586–615. Springer, Heidelberg (2016). https://doi.org/10.1007/978-3-662-49896-5_21
4. Barthe, G., Belaïd, S., Dupressoir, F., Fouque, P.-A., Grégoire, B., Strub, P.-Y.: Verified proofs of higher-order masking. In: Oswald, E., Fischlin, M. (eds.) EUROCRYPT 2015, Part I. LNCS, vol. 9056, pp. 457–485. Springer, Heidelberg (2015). https://doi.org/10.1007/978-3-662-46800-5_18
5. Barthe, G., et al.: Strong non-interference and type-directed higher-order masking. In: Weippl, E.R., Katzenbeisser, S., Kruegel, C., Myers, A.C., Halevi, S., (eds.) ACM CCS 2016: 23rd Conference on Computer and Communications Security, Vienna, Austria, 24–28 October 2016, pp. 116–129. ACM Press (2016)
6. Barthe, G., Dupressoir, F., Faust, S., Grégoire, B., Standaert, F.-X., Strub, P.-Y.: Parallel implementations of masking schemes and the bounded moment leakage model. In: Coron, J.-S., Nielsen, J.B. (eds.) EUROCRYPT 2017, Part I. LNCS, vol. 10210, pp. 535–566. Springer, Cham (2017). https://doi.org/10.1007/978-3-319-56620-7_19

7. Battistello, A., Coron, J.-S., Prouff, E., Zeitoun, R.: Horizontal side-channel attacks and countermeasures on the ISW masking scheme. In: Gierlichs, B., Poschmann, A.Y. (eds.) CHES 2016. LNCS, vol. 9813, pp. 23–39. Springer, Heidelberg (2016). https://doi.org/10.1007/978-3-662-53140-2_2

8. Belaïd, S., Benhamouda, F., Passelègue, A., Prouff, E., Thillard, A., Vergnaud, D.: Private multiplication over finite fields. In: Katz, J., Shacham, H. (eds.) CRYPTO 2017, Part III. LNCS, vol. 10403, pp. 397–426. Springer, Cham (2017). https://doi.org/10.1007/978-3-319-63697-9_14

9. Belaïd, S., Dagand, P.É., Mercadier, D., Rivain, M., Wintersdorff, R.: Tornado: automatic generation of probing-secure masked bitsliced implementations. In: Canteaut, A., Ishai, Y. (eds.) EUROCRYPT 2020, Part III. LNCS, vol. 12107, pp. 311–341. Springer, Cham (2020). https://doi.org/10.1007/978-3-030-45727-3_11

10. Belaïd, S., Goudarzi, D., Rivain, M.: Tight private circuits: achieving probing security with the least refreshing. In: Peyrin, T., Galbraith, S. (eds.) ASIACRYPT 2018, Part II. LNCS, vol. 11273, pp. 343–372. Springer, Cham (2018). https://doi.org/10.1007/978-3-030-03329-3_12

11. Chari, S., Jutla, C.S., Rao, J.R., Rohatgi, P.: Towards sound approaches to counteract power-analysis attacks. In: Wiener, M. (ed.) CRYPTO 1999. LNCS, vol. 1666, pp. 398–412. Springer, Heidelberg (1999). https://doi.org/10.1007/3-540-48405-1_26

12. Cohen, G., et al.: Efficient multiparty protocols via log-depth threshold formulae - (extended abstract). In: Canetti, R., Garay, J.A. (eds.) CRYPTO 2013, Part II. LNCS, vol. 8043, pp. 185–202. Springer, Heidelberg (2013). https://doi.org/10.1007/978-3-642-40084-1_11

13. Coron, J.-S.: Formal verification of side-channel countermeasures via elementary circuit transformations. In: Preneel, B., Vercauteren, F. (eds.) ACNS 2018. LNCS, vol. 10892, pp. 65–82. Springer, Cham (2018). https://doi.org/10.1007/978-3-319-93387-0_4

14. Coron, J.-S., Prouff, E., Rivain, M., Roche, T.: Higher-order side channel security and mask refreshing. In: Moriai, S. (ed.) FSE 2013. LNCS, vol. 8424, pp. 410–424. Springer, Heidelberg (2014). https://doi.org/10.1007/978-3-662-43933-3_21

15. Duc, A., Dziembowski, S., Faust, S.: Unifying leakage models: from probing attacks to noisy leakage. In: Nguyen, P.Q., Oswald, E. (eds.) EUROCRYPT 2014. LNCS, vol. 8441, pp. 423–440. Springer, Heidelberg (2014). https://doi.org/10.1007/978-3-642-55220-5_24

16. Goubin, L., Patarin, J.: DES and differential power analysis the "duplication" method. In: Koç, Ç.K., Paar, C. (eds.) CHES 1999. LNCS, vol. 1717, pp. 158–172. Springer, Heidelberg (1999). https://doi.org/10.1007/3-540-48059-5_15

17. Hirt, M., Maurer, U.M.: Player simulation and general adversary structures in perfect multiparty computation. J. Cryptol. 13(1), 31–60 (2000). https://doi.org/10.1007/s001459910003

18. Ishai, Y., Sahai, A., Wagner, D.: Private circuits: securing hardware against probing attacks. In: Boneh, D. (ed.) CRYPTO 2003. LNCS, vol. 2729, pp. 463–481. Springer, Heidelberg (2003). https://doi.org/10.1007/978-3-540-45146-4_27

19. Kocher, P., Jaffe, J., Jun, B.: Differential power analysis. In: Wiener, M. (ed.) CRYPTO 1999. LNCS, vol. 1666, pp. 388–397. Springer, Heidelberg (1999). https://doi.org/10.1007/3-540-48405-1_25

20. Maurer, U.: Secure multi-party computation made simple (invited talk). In: Cimato, S., Persiano, G., Galdi, C. (eds.) SCN 2002. LNCS, vol. 2576, pp. 14–28. Springer, Heidelberg (2003). https://doi.org/10.1007/3-540-36413-7_2

21. Micali, S., Reyzin, L.: Physically observable cryptography (extended abstract). In: Naor, M. (ed.) TCC 2004. LNCS, vol. 2951, pp. 278–296. Springer, Heidelberg (2004). https://doi.org/10.1007/978-3-540-24638-1_16

22. Prouff, E., Rivain, M.: Masking against side-channel attacks: a formal security proof. In: Johansson, T., Nguyen, P.Q. (eds.) EUROCRYPT 2013. LNCS, vol. 7881, pp. 142–159. Springer, Heidelberg (2013). https://doi.org/10.1007/978-3-642-38348-9_9

23. Rivain, M., Prouff, E.: Provably secure higher-order masking of AES. In: Mangard, S., Standaert, F.-X. (eds.) CHES 2010. LNCS, vol. 6225, pp. 413–427. Springer, Heidelberg (2010). https://doi.org/10.1007/978-3-642-15031-9_28

Mode-Level vs. Implementation-Level Physical Security in Symmetric Cryptography

A Practical Guide Through the Leakage-Resistance Jungle

Davide Bellizia[1], Olivier Bronchain[1], Gaëtan Cassiers[1], Vincent Grosso[2], Chun Guo[3], Charles Momin[1], Olivier Pereira[1], Thomas Peters[1], and François-Xavier Standaert[1(✉)]

[1] Crypto Group, ICTEAM Institute, UCLouvain, Louvain-la-Neuve, Belgium
{davide.bellizia,olivier.bronchain,gaetan.cassiers,charles.momin,
olivier.pereira,thomas.peters,fstandae}@uclouvain.be
[2] CNRS/Laboratoire Hubert Curien, Université de Lyon, Lyon, France
vincent.grosso@univ-st-etienne.fr
[3] School of Cyber Science and Technology and Key Laboratory of Cryptologic Technology and Information Security, Ministry of Education, Shandong University, Jinan, China
chun.guo.sc@gmail.com

Abstract. Triggered by the increasing deployment of embedded cryptographic devices (e.g., for the IoT), the design of authentication, encryption and authenticated encryption schemes enabling improved security against side-channel attacks has become an important research direction. Over the last decade, a number of modes of operation have been proposed and analyzed under different abstractions. In this paper, we investigate the practical consequences of these findings. For this purpose, we first translate the physical assumptions of leakage-resistance proofs into minimum security requirements for implementers. Thanks to this (heuristic) translation, we observe that (*i*) security against physical attacks can be viewed as a tradeoff between mode-level and implementation-level protection mechanisms, and (*ii*) security requirements to guarantee confidentiality and integrity in front of leakage can be concretely different for the different parts of an implementation. We illustrate the first point by analyzing several modes of operation with gradually increased leakage-resistance. We illustrate the second point by exhibiting leveled implementations, where different parts of the investigated schemes have different security requirements against leakage, leading to performance improvements when high physical security is needed. We finally initiate a comparative discussion of the different solutions to instantiate the components of a leakage-resistant authenticated encryption scheme.

1 Introduction

State-of-the-art. Since the introduction of side-channel attacks in the late nineties [55,57], securing cryptographic implementations against leakage has

© International Association for Cryptologic Research 2020
D. Micciancio and T. Ristenpart (Eds.): CRYPTO 2020, LNCS 12170, pp. 369–400, 2020.
https://doi.org/10.1007/978-3-030-56784-2_13

been a major research challenge. These attacks raise critical security concerns, as they enable recovering sensitive information such as long-term secret keys, and are virtually applicable to any type of implementation if no countermeasures are deployed [61]. As a result, various types of protection mechanisms have been introduced, working at different abstraction levels. Due to the physical nature of the leakage, the first countermeasures were typically proposed at low abstraction levels. For example, hardware countermeasures can target a reduction of the side-channel information by blurring the signal into noise in the time or amplitude domains [22,60], or by reducing this signal thanks to special (dual-rail) circuit technologies [81,82]. These hardware countermeasures can then be augmented by implementation-level randomization mechanisms aimed at amplifying the side-channel leakage reduction. Masking achieves this goal by exploiting data randomization (i.e., secret sharing) [20,40] and shuffling does it by randomizing the order of execution of the operations [48,85]. Steady progresses have been made in order to improve the understanding of these different countermeasures. For example, masking is supported by a strong theoretical background (see [5,31,32,49] to name a few). Yet, it remains that the secure implementation of low-level countermeasures (e.g., masking) is quite sensitive to physical defaults [3,23,62,66], and is expensive both in software and hardware contexts [42,43].

In view of the sensitive and expensive nature of hardware-level and implementation-level side-channel countermeasures, a complementary line of works initiated the investigation of cryptographic primitives with inherently improved security against physical leakage. In the case of symmetric cryptography, this trend started with heuristic proposals such as [37,56,63,69]. It was then formalized by Dziembowski and Pietrzak under the framework of leakage-resilient cryptography [33], which has been the inspiration of many follow up works and designs. Simple and efficient PRGs & stream ciphers were proposed in [70,78,86,87]. PRFs and PRPs can be found in [1,30,35,79]. Concretely, such leakage-resilient primitives typically require some type of bounded leakage assumption, which was found to be significantly easier to fulfill for PRGs and stream ciphers that are naturally amenable to key evolution schemes than for PRFs and PRPs for which each execution requires the manipulation of a long-term secret key [8].

The concept of leveled implementations introduced by Pereira et al. closely followed this finding: it aims at combining the minimum use of a PRF or PRP heavily protected against side-channel attacks thanks to (possibly expensive) hardware-level and implementation-level countermeasures with a mode of operation designed to cope with leakage, requiring much less protections (or even no protection at all) in order to process the bulk of the computation [68].

These seed results on basic cryptographic primitives (such as PRGs, PRFs and PRPs) next triggered analyzes of complete functionalities like encryption and authentication, and rapidly shifted the attention of designers to Authenticated Encryption (AE) schemes mixing both integrity and confidentiality guarantees. Following the seminal observation of Micali and Reyzin that indistinguish-ability-based notions are significantly harder to capture and ensure with leakage than unpredictability-based notions [64], strong integrity properties with leakage have then been investigated, first with leakage in encryption only [14], next with leakage in encryption and decryption [15]. It turns out they could indeed be satisfied with weak physical assumptions for the bulk of the computation. For example, ciphertext integrity can be achieved with full leakage of all the intermediate computations of an AE scheme and two manipulations of a long-term secret key with a strongly protected block cipher implementation. This is obviously insufficient for any type of confidentiality guarantee, as it would leak plaintexts immediately. This last conclusion motivated a systematic analysis of composite security definitions, enabling different physical requirements for integrity and confidentiality guarantees with leakage [46]. Eventually, various full-fledged AE schemes have been analyzed against leakage, based on Tweakable Block Ciphers (TBCs) [13], permutations [24,25,27] and combinations of both [47].

We note that our following investigations are restricted to symmetric cryptography, which is the most investigated target for practical side-channel attacks. Yet, security against leakage has also been considered for other important objects such as digital signatures schemes (e.g., [34,52,59]), public-key encryption schemes (e.g., [54,65]) and more advanced cryptographic functionalities like secure computation (e.g., [17,39]). We refer to [50] for a recent survey.

Contribution. The starting point of our investigations is the observation that the development of low-level side-channel countermeasures and the one of primitives and modes of operation to prevent leakage have for now followed quite independent paths. This can, in part, be explained by the very different abstractions used to analyze them. While low-level countermeasures are typically evaluated experimentally based on statistical metrics [77], proving the security of the aforementioned modes against leakage is rather based on cryptographic reductions leveraging some physical assumptions. In this respect, the quest for sound physical assumptions that are at the same time realistic (e.g., are falsifiable and can be quantified by evaluation laboratories) and sufficient for proofs has been and still is an important problem: see again [50]. To a large extent, the current situation therefore mimics the one of black box security proofs, with efficient schemes proven under idealized assumptions (e.g., the oracle-free leakages introduced in [87] and used for analyzing sponge constructions in [27,47]) and a quest for more standard analyses under weaker assumptions. Combined with the massive amount of definitions capturing all the possible combinations of security targets for confidentiality and integrity with leakage [46], the complexity of these theoretical investigations is therefore calling for a systematization effort towards the concrete interpretation of leakage security proofs, in order to determine how these results can help developers in the design of secure implementations.

Our main contributions in this direction are threefold:

1. We provide a simplifying framework that allows us (*a*) to identify a reduced number of relevant security targets (compared to the full zoo of definitions in [46]); and (*b*) to translate the physical assumptions used in leakage security proofs into practical implementation guidelines, stated in terms of security against Simple Power Analysis (SPA) and Differential Power Analysis (DPA),

as can be evaluated by evaluation laboratories with tools such as [21,76] and extensions thereof. Despite SPA and DPA requirements are only necessary conditions for the formal physical security assumptions to hold, this analysis allows us to pinpoint the minimum level of efforts that implementers must devote to protect different parts of an AE implementation in function of the security target.

2. We use this framework to illustrate that reasoning about security against leakage can be viewed as a tradeoff between mode-level and implementation-level (or hardware-level) protections. To give a simple example, a physical security property (e.g., the aforementioned ciphertext integrity with leakage) can theoretically be obtained from standard modes of operation like OCB [74], given that all the block cipher executions in the mode are strongly protected against DPA (which has high cost). Modes with better resistance against leakage can relax this DPA security requirement for certain parts of the implementations. Interestingly, we additionally observe that the literature already includes different modes of operation corresponding to different leakage security targets. This allows us to illustrate the physical security tradeoff based on actual algorithms, including candidates to the ongoing NIST standardization effort.[1] We will focus on OCB-Pyjamask [41], PHOTON-Beetle [4], Ascon [26], Spook [10], ISAP [25] and TEDT [13], but our analysis applies to many other similar ciphers.

3. Finally, we answer concrete questions that these analyzes suggest, namely:

   – We discuss the interest of leveled implementations compared to uniformly protected implementations based on a hardware implementation case study.
   – We compare the (masked) TBC-based and permutation-based initialization/finalization steps of two AE schemes (namely, Ascon [26] and Spook [10]) thanks to a software case study, and evaluate their respective advantages.
   – We compare a standard tag verification mechanism (that requires hardware-level or implementation-level DPA protections) with the inverse-based tag verification proposed in [15] that does not require DPA protections.
   – We evaluate the pros and cons of the two main solutions to implement a strongly protected component for AE, namely masking and fresh rekeying based on a leakage-resilient PRF [9], which is for example used in ISAP [25].

For completeness, and despite the practical focus of the paper, we additionally provide a high-level view of the formal security guarantees that the analyzed AE schemes offer. For this purpose, we leverage the existing literature and tailor some existing generic results to the investigated cases studies.

---

[1] https://csrc.nist.gov/projects/lightweight-cryptography.

Related work. In an independent line of work, Barwell et al. analyzed the security of AE schemes in a model where the leakage is excluded from the challenge encryption [6]. This model corresponds to a context of leakage-resilience, where security guarantees may vanish in the presence of leakage, but are restored once leakage is removed from the adversary's view. It enables strong composition results similar to the ones obtained without leakage, strong security against nonce misuse (i.e., misuse-resistance in the sense of Rogaway and Shrimpton [75]) and has been instantiated with uniformly protected implementations (e.g., the scheme in [6] is based on masking and pairings). Here, we rather focus on the composite definitions introduced by Guo et al. [46] which consider integrity and confidentiality properties separately, rely on the setting of leakage-resistance (i.e., aim to resist against leakage even during the challenge encryption) and can only be combined with a weaker guarantee of nonce misuse-resilience (introduced by Ashur et al. [2]) for the confidentiality guarantees in the presence of leakage.[2] The motivations for this choice are twofold. First, composite definitions enable the identification of meaningful security targets matching existing AE schemes that a single "all-in-one" definition as the one of Barwell et al. cannot capture. Second, the security gains of some design tweaks we aim to analyze (e.g., ephemeral key evolution) cannot be reflected in the leakage-resilience setting. We refer to Sect. 2.2 for more discussion about this definitional choice.

Cautionary notes. By focusing on the qualitative requirements that masking security proofs imply for implementers, our next analyzes and discussions naturally elude some additional important points that should also be considered in the evaluation of a leakage-resistant AE scheme, namely:
(i) We do not consider the quantitative aspects: for example, do the modes provide beyond-birthday and/or multi-user security against leakage attacks?
(ii) We ignore the impact of the primitives (e.g., the internals of the block ciphers and permutations) on the cost of low-level side-channel countermeasures. Yet, it is for example a well-known fact that minimizing the multiplicative complexity and depth of a block cipher is beneficial for masking [38,44,71].

The first point is an important scope for further research. A complete analysis would indeed require having quantitative (and ideally tight) bounds for all the investigated schemes. For the second one, we believe it should have limited impact since most current lightweight ciphers aimed at security against side-channel attacks (e.g., the NIST Lightweight Cryptography candidates) are based on small S-boxes with minimum AND complexity and depth.

2   Simplifying Framework

In this section, we present the simplifying framework that we will use in order to reason about leakage-resistant AE modes based on concrete (SPA and DPA)

---

[2] This limitation only holds in the presence of leakage, so nothing prevents to ask for black box misuse-resistance as an additional requirement of a mode, which we do not consider in this paper but could be investigated as future work.

attacks. For this purpose, we first propose an informal decomposition of the modes that we will consider, and then list the design tweaks that such modes can leverage in order to reach different leakage security guarantees.

2.1 Leakage-Resistant AE Modes Decomposition

We decompose the AE modes of operation under investigation into four informal parts, as illustrated in Fig. 1 for a simple Inner Keyed Sponge (IKS) design [16]. An optional Key Generation Function (KGF) is used to generate a fresh key K^* based on a long-term master key K and a nonce N. Next, the message processing part uses the (optionally fresh) key in order to encrypt the message blocks. A Tag Generation Function (TGF) finally uses the result of the message processing part and outputs a tag for message authentication. The tag is only verified (i.e., compared to the genuine tag) in case of decryption.

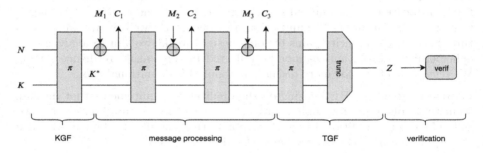

Fig. 1. Exemplary decomposition of an AE scheme.

We note that we make no claim regarding the generality of this decomposition. As will be clear next, it nicely matches a number of recent AE schemes with different levels of security against side-channel attacks, but other modes may not be directly adaptable to this simple framework. We believe this limitation is natural for a work aiming at specializing leakage-resistance analyzes to practical AE schemes. We note also that for simplicity, we ignore the associated data in our discussions, since it has limited impact on leakage analyzes.

2.2 Design Tweaks and Security Levels

The main design tweaks that enhance mode-based side-channel security are:

1. *Key evolution.* As formalized by Dziembowski and Pietrzak, updating the ephemeral keys of an implementation so that each of them is only used – and therefore leaks – minimally can improve confidentiality with leakage [33].
2. *Strengthened KGF and TGF.* As formalized by Berti et al., using key and tag generation functions so that, given their input (resp., output), it is not direct to compute their output (resp., input) can improve security with leakage [14, 15] – for example by preventing that recovering an ephemeral secret during message processing leads to the long-term master key.

3. *Two-pass designs.* As formalized by Guo et al. (resp., Barwell et al.) in the leakage-resistance setting [46] (resp., leakage-resilience setting [6]), two-pass modes can improve message confidentiality with decryption leakages, if the tag verification does not require the manipulation of sensitive plaintexts.

Based on these three main design tweaks, we select a number of practically-relevant security targets that reflect existing AE schemes from the leakage-resistance definition zoo of [46]. For this purpose, we first recall Guo et al.'s definitions of integrity and confidentiality with leakage in an abstracted way, which will be sufficient to guide our attack-based analysis in the next section. Their more formal introduction is additionally provided in the full paper [11].

Definition 1 (Ciphertext Integrity with Leakage [15], Informal.). *In the ciphertext integrity with leakage security game, the adversary can perform a number of queries to encryption and decryption oracles enhanced with leakage functions, that capture the implementation of an AE scheme. His goal is to produce a valid fresh ciphertext and the implementation is considered secure if the adversary cannot succeed with good probability. Variants that we will use next include: ciphertext integrity with (nonce-respecting adversary and) leakage in encryption only (CIL1) and ciphertext integrity with misuse-resistance (i.e., no constraint on nonces) and leakage in encryption and decryption (CIML2).*

Definition 2 (Confidentiality with Leakage [46], Informal.). *In the Chosen Ciphertext Attack (CCA) with leakage security game, the adversary can perform a number of queries to encryption and decryption oracles enhanced with leakage functions, that capture the implementation of an AE scheme. During a so-called "challenge query", he picks up two fresh messages X_0 and X_1 and receives a ciphertext Y_b encrypting X_b for $b \in \{0, 1\}$, with the corresponding leakage. His goal is to guess b and the implementation is considered secure if the adversary cannot succeed with good advantage. Variants that we will use next include: chosen ciphertext security with nonce-respecting adversary and leakage in encryption only (CCAL1), chosen ciphertext security with nonce misuse-resilience (i.e., fresh challenge nonce) and leakage in encryption only (CCAmL1) and chosen ciphertext security with nonce misuse-resilience and leakage in encryption and decryption, including decryption of the challenge Y_b (CCAmL2).*[3]

In our notations, small caps are for resilience to misuse or leakage and capital letters for resistance. For integrity guarantees, it is possible to ensure misuse-resistance and leakage-resistance jointly. As discussed in [46], such a combination is believed to be impossible under reasonable leakage models for confidentiality guarantees and one has to choose between Barwell et al.'s CCAMI2 security or Guo et al.'s CCAL1, CCAmL1 or CCAmL2 security (see also Sect. 3.1).

Based on these definitions, we list our security targets and their link with the aforementioned design tweaks. We insist that these links hold for the AE schemes

---

[3] We focus on the single-challenge definition for simplicity. Multi-challenge extensions are treated in the extended version of [46] – see also the full paper [11].

investigated in the next section. We do not claim they are necessary to reach the security targets and admit other design ideas could be leveraged. We further reckon a finer-grain analysis may be useful in order to analyze other modes.

- **Grade-1a.** CIL1 and CCAL1 security thanks to key evolution.
- **Grade-1b.** CIML2 security thanks to strengthened KGF and TGF (and only black box security guarantees for message confidentiality).
- **Grade-2.** CIML2 and CCAmL1 security thanks to a combination of key evolution (i.e., Grade-1a) and strengthened KGF and TGF (i.e., Grade-1b).
- **Grade-3.** CIML2 and CCAmL2 security thanks to a combination of key evolution and strengthened KGF and TGF with a two-pass design.

We also denote as **Grade-0** the AE schemes without leakage-resistant features.

Definitional framework motivation. The grades and design tweaks that we just described motivate our choice of definitions. On the one hand, the different grades exploit Micali and Reyzin's seminal observation that integrity requirements may be significantly easier to fulfill with leakage than confidentiality requirements. For example, Grade-2 designs achieve stronger integrity guarantees (with decryption leakage) than confidentiality guarantees (without decryption leakage). In Barwell et al.'s all-in-one definition, removing decryption leakage could only be done jointly for confidentiality and integrity guarantees. On the other hand, the security gains of some design tweaks cannot be reflected in the leakage-resilience setting. For example, excluding the challenge leakage implies that an implementation leaking challenge messages (and ephemeral keys) in full is deemed secure according to Barwell et al.'s definition. Hence, ephemeral key evolution has no impact in this case (and the construction in [6] is indeed based on CFB). We insist that this observation does not invalidate the interest of the leakage-resilience setting: whether (stronger) leakage-resistance or (weaker) leakage-resilience is needed depends on application constraints. In general, our only claim is that the definitional framework of Guo et al. enables a fine-grain analysis that can capture various designs and application constraints which are not apparent when using an all-in-one definition of leakage-resilience.

3   From Leakage-Resistance to Side-Channel Security

In this section, we first discuss how the physical assumptions used in leakage security proofs can be translated into minimum requirements for implementers. Next, we illustrate what are these minimum requirements for concrete instances of existing AE schemes. From the current literature, we identify Grade-0, Grade-1a, Grade 2 and Grade-3 AE schemes, which suggests the design of an efficient Grade-1b instance as an interesting scope for further investigations. We show that the minimum requirements suggested by security proofs are (qualitatively) tight and that failing to meet them leads to realistic SPA and DPA attacks.

3.1 Translating Physical Assumptions into Implementation Goals

Leakage security proofs for AE schemes rely on physical assumptions. As mentioned in introduction, the quest for sound and realistic assumptions is still a topic of ongoing research. In this section, we observe that the (sometimes strong) assumptions needed in proofs can be translated into minimum security requirements, expressed in terms of security against practical side-channel attacks.

Integrity with leakage requirements can be limited to the KGF, TGF (and optionally verification functions) for AE schemes with good leakage properties, and are extended to all the components of a mode of operation without such good properties (see Sect. 5 for the details). The simplest assumption is to consider the underlying blocks to be leak-free [68]. A recent relaxation introduces a weaker requirement of unpredictability with leakage [12]. In both cases, these assumptions need that implementations manipulating a long-term key limit the probability of success of key-recovery DPA attacks, which we express as:

$$\Pr\left[\mathcal{A}_{\mathsf{kr}}^{\mathsf{L}(.,.)}(X_1, \mathsf{L}(X_1, K), \dots, X_q, \mathsf{L}(X_q, K)) \rightarrow K | K \xleftarrow{\mathsf{u}} \{0,1\}^n\right] \approx 2^{-n+q\cdot\lambda(r)}, \tag{1}$$

where $\mathcal{A}_{\mathsf{kr}}^{\mathsf{L}(.,.)}$ is the key recovery adversary able to make offline calls to the (unkeyed) leakage function $\mathsf{L}(.,.)$, $X_1, \dots, X_q$ the different inputs for which the primitive is measured, K the long-term key of size n bits and $\lambda(r)$ the (informal) amount of information leakage obtained for a single input X_i measured r times (i.e., repeating the same measurement multiple times can be used to reduce the leakage noise). For security against DPA, it is required that this probability remains small even for large q values, since there is nothing that prevents the adversary to measure the target implementation for many different inputs. Such DPA attacks reduce the secrecy of the long-term key exponentially in q. Hence, preventing them requires a mechanism that counteracts this reduction. For example, masking can be used for this purpose and makes $\lambda(r)$ exponentially small in a security parameter (i.e., the number of masks or shares) [20,32].

Confidentiality with leakage requirements are significantly more challenging to nail down. For the KGF and TGF parts of the implementation, they at least require the same DPA security as required for integrity guarantees. For the message processing part, various solutions exist in the literature:

1. *Only computation leaks assumption and bounded leakage,* introduced by Dziembowski and Pietrzak [33]. By splitting a key in two parts and assuming that they leak independently, it allows maintaining some computational entropy in a key evolution scheme under a (strong) bounded leakage assumption.[4]

---

[4] Precisely, [33] assumes high min-entropy or high HILL pseudoentropy, which are quite high in the hierarchy of assumptions analyzed by Fuller and Hamlin [36]. Note also that for non-adaptive leakages, the "alternating structure" that splits the key in two parts can be replaced by alternating public randomness [35,86,87].

2. *Oracle-free and hard-to-invert leakage function,* introduced by Yu et al. [87]. The motivation for Dziembowski and Pietrzak's alternating structure is to limit the computational power of the leakage function, which can otherwise compute states of a leaking device before they are even produced in the physical world. A straightforward way to prevent such unrealistic attacks is to assume the underlying primitives of a symmetric construction to behave as random oracles and to prevent the leakage function to make oracle calls. This comes at the cost of an idealized assumption, but can be combined with a minimum requirement of hard-to-invert leakages.[5]

3. *Simulatability,* introduced by Standaert et al., is an attempt to enable standard security proofs with weak and falsifiable physical assumptions, without alternating structure [78]. It assumes the existence of a leakage simulator that can produce fake leakages that are hard to distinguish from the real ones, using the same hardware as used to produce the real leakages but without access to the secret key. The first instances of simulators were broken in [58]. It remains an open problem to propose new (stronger) ones.

Despite technical caveats, all these assumptions aim to capture the same intuition that an ephemeral key manipulated minimally also leaks in a limited manner, preserving some of its secrecy. As a result, they share the minimum requirement that the probability of success of a key-recovery SPA attack remains small. Such a probability of success has a similar expression to the one of Eq. 1, with as only (but paramount) difference that the number of inputs that can be measured is limited by design. Typically, $q = 2$ for leakage-resilient stream ciphers where one input is used to generate a new ephemeral key and the other to generate a key stream to be XORed with the plaintexts [70,78,86,87].

Note that because of these limited q values, the possibility to repeat measurements (by increasing the r of the leakage expression $\lambda(r)$) is an important asset for SPA adversaries. As will be detailed next, this creates some additional challenges when leakages can be obtained with nonce misuse or in decryption.

Besides the aforementioned requirements of security against key-recovery DPA and SPA, definitions of leakage-resistance provide the adversary with the leakage of the challenge query. In this setting, another path against the confidentiality of an AE scheme is to directly target the manipulation of the message blocks (e.g., in Fig. 1, this corresponds to the loading of the M_i blocks and their XOR with the rate of the sponge). Following [80], we express the probability of success of such Message Comparison (MC) attacks with:

$$\Pr\left[\mathcal{A}_{mc}^{L(\cdot,\cdot)}(X_0, X_1, L(X_b, K)) \to b | K \xleftarrow{u} \{0,1\}^n, b \xleftarrow{u} \{0,1\}\right]. \qquad (2)$$

In this case, the adversary has to find out whether the leakage $L(X_b, K)$ is produced with input X_0 or X_1. As discussed in [46], there are currently no

---

[5] The hard-to-invert leakage assumption was introduced beforehand [28,29], and is substantially weaker than entropic leakage requirements (see again [36]). For example, suppose $L(K)$ is the leakage, where K is secret and L is a one-way permutation. Then the leakage is non-invertible, but the conditional entropy of K could be 0.

mode-level solutions enabling to limit this probability of success to negligible values. So implementers have to deal with the goal to minimize the message leakage with lower-level countermeasures. Yet, as will be discussed next, even in this case it is possible to leverage mode-level protection mechanisms, by trying to minimize the manipulation of sensitive messages (e.g., in decryption).

Discussion. We note that combining leakage-resistance with misuse-resistance would require to resist attacks similar to the one of Eq. 2, but with a "State Comparison" (SC) adversary $\mathcal{A}_{\mathsf{sc}}^{\mathsf{L}(.,K)}$ able to make offline calls to a keyed leakage function. As discussed in [46,80], this allows the adversary to win the game by simply comparing $\mathsf{L}(X_0, K)$ and $\mathsf{L}(X_1, K)$ with $\mathsf{L}(X_b, K)$, which is believed to be hard to avoid (unless all parts of the implementations are assumed leak-free). As a result, we next consider a combination of misuse-resilience with leakage-resistance as our strongest target for confidentiality with leakage.

Summary. The heuristic security requirements for the different parts of an AE scheme with leakage (following the decomposition of Sect. 2.1) include:

- **For integrity guarantees:**
    - *For the KGF and TGF:* security against (long-term key) DPA.
    - *For the message processing part:* security against (ephemeral key) DPA or no requirements (i.e., full leakage of ephemeral device states).
    - *For tag verification:* security against DPA or no requirements.
- **For confidentiality guarantees:**
    - *For the KGF and TGF:* security against (long-term key) DPA.
    - *For the message processing part:* security against (ephemeral key) DPA or (ephemeral key) SPA and security against MC attacks.

As detailed next, for some parts of some (leakage-resistant) AE schemes, different levels of physical security are possible, hence enabling leveled implementations. For readability, we will illustrate our discussions with the following color code: blue for the parts of an AE scheme that require DPA security, light (resp., dark) green for the parts of an AE scheme that require SPA security without (resp., with) averaging, light (resp., dark) orange for the parts of an AE scheme that require security against MC attacks without (resp., with) averaging and white for the parts of an AE scheme that tolerate unbounded leakages.[6] We draw the tag verification in light grey when it is not computed (i.e., in encryption).

We note that precisely quantifying the implementation overheads associated with SPA and DPA security is highly implementation-dependent, and therefore beyond the scope of this paper. For example, the number of shares necessary to reach a given security level in software (with limited noise) may be significantly higher than in (noisier) hardware implementations [32]. Yet, in order to provide

---

[6] For the MC attacks, SPA without averaging is only possible in the single-challenge setting. In case multiple challenges are allowed, all MC-SPA attacks are with averaging. This change is not expected to create significant practical differences when the adversary can anyway use challenge messages with many identical blocks.

the reader with some heuristic rule-of-thumb, we typically assume that preventing SPA implies "small" overheads (i.e., factors from 1 to 5) [85] while preventing DPA implies "significant" overheads (i.e., factors from 5 to > 100) [42,43]. Some exemplary values will be given in our more concrete discussions of Sect. 4. We insist that the only requirement for the following reasoning to be practically-relevant is that enforcing SPA security is significantly cheaper than enforcing DPA security, which is widely supported by the side-channel literature.

In the rest of this section, we illustrate the taxonomy of Sect. 2.2 with existing modes of operation. For each grade, we first exhibit how leakage-resistance (formally analysed in Sect. 5) translates into leveled implementations; we then show that this analysis is qualitatively tight and describe attacks breaking the proposed implementations for stronger security targets than proven in Sect. 5; we finally discuss the results and their applicability to other ciphers.

3.2   Grade-0 Case Study: OCB-Pyjamask

Mode-level guarantees. The OCB mode of operation does not provide mode-level security against leakage. This is due to the use of the same long-term key in all the (T)BC invocations of the mode. As a result, all the (T)BC calls must be strongly protected against DPA. For completeness, a uniformly protected implementation of OCB-Pyjamask is illustrated in the full paper [11].

Proofs' (qualitative) tightness. Not applicable (no leakage-resistance proofs).

Discussion. As mentioned in introduction (cautionary notes) and will be further illustrated in Sect. 3.6, the absence of mode-level leakage-resistance does not prevent a mode of operation to be well protected against side-channel attacks: it only implies that the protections have to be at the primitive, implementation or hardware level. In this respect, the Pyjamask cipher is better suited to masking than (for example) the AES and should allow efficient masked implementations, thanks to its limited multiplicative complexity. A similar comment applies to the NIST lightweight candidates SKINNY-AEAD and SUNDAE-GIFT.

3.3   Grade-1a Case Study: PHOTON-Beetle

Mode-level guarantees. As detailed in Sect. 5.2, PHOTON-Beetle is CCAL1 and CIL1 under physical assumptions that, as discussed in Sect. 3.1, translate into SPA security requirements for its message processing part. Therefore, it can be implemented in a leveled fashion as illustrated in Fig. 2. Note that nonce repetition is prevented in the CCAL1 and CIL1 security games, which explains the light grey and orange color codes (for SPA security without averaging).

Proofs' qualitative tightness. As soon as nonce misuse or decryption leakages are granted to the adversary, the following DPA becomes possible against the message processing part of PHOTON-Beetle: fix the nonce and the ephemeral key K^*; generate several plaintext (or ciphertext) blocks M_1 (or C_1); recover

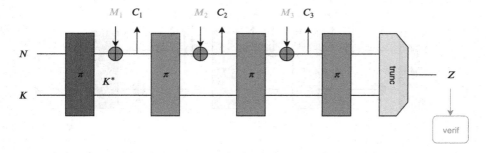

Fig. 2. PHOTON-Beetle, leveled implementation, CCAL1, CIL1.

the capacity part of the state including M_1 (or C_1) and finally inverse the permutation to recover the long-term key K. The number of plaintext/ciphertext blocks that can be measured in this way equals 2^r, where r (i.e., the rate of the sponge) equals 128 in the case of PHOTON-Beetle. This is (considerably) more than needed to perform a successful side-channel attack against a permutation without DPA protections [61]. Hence, we conclude that for any stronger security target than CCAL1 and CIL1, uniform protections are again needed.

Discussion. A similar analysis applies to many IKS designs in the literature, for example the NIST lightweight candidates Gimli and Oribatida and the CAESAR competition candidate Ketje. It formalizes the intuition that when encrypting without misuse, it is not necessary to protect the message processing part of IKS modes as strongly as their KGF. But this guarantee vanishes with nonce misuse or decryption leakage because it is then possible to control the ephemeral keys and the KGF is invertible. Hence, for stronger security targets, lower-level countermeasures have to be uniformly activated, the cost of which again depends on the structure (e.g., multiplicative complexity) of the underlying primitives.

3.4   Grade-2 Case Studies: Ascon and Spook

Mode-level guarantees. As detailed in Sect. 5.3, Ascon and Spook are CCAmL1 and CIML2 under different sets of physical assumptions for confidentiality and integrity guarantees. They represent interesting case studies where the composite nature of Guo et al.'s security definition enables different practical requirements for different parts of a mode and different security targets. We note that the previous requirement of DPA security for the KGF and TGF cannot be relaxed, so it will be maintained in this and the next subsection, without further discussion. By contrast, the security requirements for the message processing and tag verification parts can significantly vary, which we now discuss.

We start with Ascon's CCAmL1 requirements, illustrated in Fig. 3. They translate into SPA security (without averaging) for the message processing part even with nonce misuse.

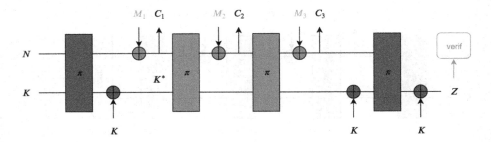

Fig. 3. Ascon, leveled implementation, CCAmL1.

This is because (*i*) in the misuse-resilience setting, the challenge query of Definition 2 comes with a fresh nonce (i.e., nonce misuse is only granted during non-challenge queries), and (*ii*) even a full permutation state leakage obtained for non-challenge queries (e.g., thanks to the same DPA as described against PHOTON-Beetle) does not lead to the long-term key K on which confidentiality relies (thanks to the strengthened KGF). A similar situation holds for Spook and is illustrated in the full paper [11].

We follow with Spook's CIML2 requirements, illustrated in Fig. 4. The main observation here is that integrity is proven in a weak (unbounded leakage) model where all the intermediate permutation states are given in full to the adversary. This is possible thanks to the strengthening of the KGF and TGF which prevents any of these ephemeral states to leak about long-term secrets and valid tags. In the case of Spook, even the tag verification can be implemented in such a leaky manner (thanks to the inverse-based verification trick analyzed in [15]). Optionally, a direct tag verification verif$_B$ can be used but requires DPA protections. A similar situation holds for the integrity of Ascon and is illustrated in the full paper [11], with as only difference that it can only be implemented with a direct DPA-secure tag verification. Note that without an inverse-based or DPA-secure verification, it is possible to forge valid messages without knowledge of the master key [15], which is for example critical for secure bootloading [67]. We will confirm the practical feasibility of such attacks in Sect. 4.3.

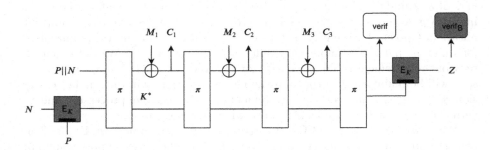

Fig. 4. Spook, leveled implementation, CIML2.

Proofs' qualitative tightness. From Fig. 3 (and 14 in the full paper [11]), it can be observed that as soon as decryption leakages are granted to the adversary, a DPA attack against the confidentiality of the messages becomes possible. The beginning of the attack is exactly the same as the one against PHOTON-Beetle: fix the nonce and the ephemeral key K^*; generate several plaintext (or ciphertext) blocks M_1 (or C_1) and recover the capacity part of the state including M_1 (or C_1). This time, the full state leakage cannot lead to the long-term key K but it still allows recovering all the decrypted messages in full. Note that this attack actually targets a weaker notion than CCAmL2 since it only exploits the decryption leakage, without access to the decryption oracle. Yet, as discussed in [15], it is a quite practical one in case of applications where IP protection matters (e.g., when a code or content can be decrypted and used but not copied).

Discussion. A similar analysis applies to other IKS designs with strengthened KGF and TGF, for example the NIST lightweight candidates ACE, WAGE and SPIX and the CAESAR competition candidate GIBBON. The TBC-based TET scheme also offers the same guarantees [13]. These designs reach the best integrity with leakage but due to their one-pass nature, cannot reach CCAmL2. The main concrete differences between Ascon and Spook are: (i) The KGF and TGF of Ascon are based on a permutation while Spook uses a TBC for this purpose, and (ii) the tag verification of Spook can be implemented in a leaky way with an inverse TBC call or in a DPA-protected way with a direct TBC call, while the tag verification of Ascon can only be implemented in the DPA-protected manner. The pros and cons of these options will be discussed in Sects. 4.2 and 4.3.

3.5   Grade-3 Case Studies: ISAP and TEDT

Mode-level guarantees. Leveled implementations of Ascon and Spook reach the highest security target for integrity with leakage (i.e., CIML2) but they are only CCAmL1 without uniform protections. ISAP and TEDT cross the last mile and their leveled implementations are proven CCAmL2 in Sect. 5.4, while also maintaining CIML2 security. The integrity guarantees of ISAP and TEDT follow the same principles as Ascon and Spook. Therefore, we only provide their CIML2 implementations in the full paper [11], Figures 16 and 17, and next focus on their practical requirements for confidentiality with decryption leakage.

We start with the ISAP design for which a leveled implementation is illustrated in Fig. 5. For now skipping the details of the re-keying function RK which aims at providing "out-of-the-box" DPA security without implementation-level countermeasures such as masking, the main observation is that ISAP is a two-pass design where the tag verification does not require manipulating plaintext blocks. Hence, as long as the KGF, TGF (instantiated with RK) and the default tag verification are secure against DPA, the only attack paths against the confidentiality of the message are a SPA against the message processing part and a MC attack against the manipulation of the plaintext blocks. In both cases, averaging is possible due to the deterministic nature of the decryption.

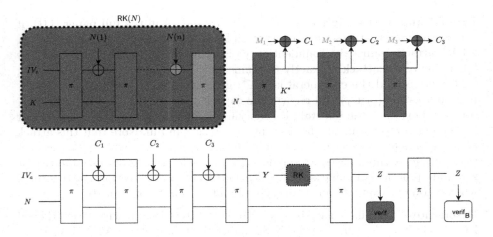

Fig. 5. ISAP, leveled implementation, CCAmL2.

The default tag verification of Fig. 5 must be secure against DPA. An exemplary attack path that becomes possible if this condition is not fulfilled is the following: given a challenge ciphertext (C, Z), flip some bits of C leading to related ciphertexts $C', C'', \ldots$ (which, due to the malleability of the encryption scheme, correspond to messages $M', M'', \ldots$ with single bits flipped compared to the target M); forge valid tags for these ciphertexts thanks to the leaking message comparison (as experimentally validated in Sect. 4.3) and finally perform a DPA against M thanks to the related messages' decryption leakage, which breaks the SPA requirements guaranteed by the proofs in Sect. 5.4 and leads to the same (practical) IP protection issue as mentioned for Ascon and Spook.

Alternatively, ISAP also comes with a tag verification that provides similar guarantees as Spook's inverse one at the cost of another permutation call.

TEDT's CCAmL2 requirements, illustrated in the full paper [11], Fig. 18, are mostly identical: the only difference is that the RK function is replaced by a TBC which must be secure against DPA thanks to masking or other low-level countermeasures, and optionally enables an inverse-based tag verification.

Discussion. TEDTSponge, a sponge-based variant of TEDT with similar guarantees, is proposed in [47]. Besides their DPA resistant tag verifications, the main difference between ISAP and TEDT is their KGF and TGF. The concrete pros and cons of both approaches will be discussed in Sect. 4.4. We also mention that TBC-based constructions allow proofs in the standard model (under the simulatability assumption), which is currently not possible with sponge-based constructions, for which idealized assumptions are frequently used even in black box security proofs. Whether this gap can be bridged (with the simulatability or a weaker physical assumption) is an interesting open problem.

3.6   Summary Table

The practical requirements that implementers must ensure for the different parts of the different modes of operation investigated in this section are summarized in Fig. 6, in function of the security target. It nicely supports the conclusion that security against side-channel attacks can be viewed as a tradeoff between mode-level and implementation-level (or hardware-level) protections.

In general, even the highest security targets (i.e., CCAmL2 and CIML2) can be reached by modes without any leakage-resistance features like OCB, but then require strong low-level countermeasures for all the implementation parts. As the security targets and the quantitative security levels needed by an application increase, it is expected that leveled implementations will lead to better performance figures, which will be further analyzed in the next section.

		CCAL1	CCAmL1	CCAmL2	CIL1	CIML1	CIML2
OCB-Pyjamask	KGF/TGF	DPA	DPA	DPA	DPA	DPA	DPA
	mess. proc	DPA	DPA	DPA	DPA	DPA	DPA
	verif.	NA	NA	unb.	NA	NA	DPA
	MC	SPA	SPA	SPA+avg	NA	NA	NA
PHOTON-Beetle	KGF/TGF	DPA	DPA	DPA	DPA	DPA	DPA
	mess. proc	SPA	DPA	DPA	SPA	DPA	DPA
	verif.	NA	NA	unb.	NA	NA	DPA
	MC.	SPA	SPA	SPA+avg	NA	NA	NA
Ascon	KGF/TGF	DPA	DPA	DPA	DPA	DPA	DPA
	mess. proc	SPA	SPA	DPA	unb.	unb.	unb.
	verif.	NA	NA	unb.	NA	NA	DPA
	MC.	SPA	SPA	SPA+avg	NA	NA	NA
Spook	KGF/TGF	DPA	DPA	DPA	DPA	DPA	DPA
	mess. proc	SPA	SPA	DPA	unb.	unb.	unb.
	verif.	NA	NA	unb.	NA	NA	unb.
	MC.	SPA	SPA	SPA+avg	NA	NA	NA
ISAP	KGF/TGF	DPA	DPA	DPA	DPA	DPA	DPA
	mess. proc	SPA	SPA	SPA+avg	unb.	unb.	unb.
	verif.	NA	NA	DPA	NA	NA	DPA
	MC.	SPA	SPA	SPA+avg	NA	NA	NA
TEDT	KGF/TGF	DPA	DPA	DPA	DPA	DPA	DPA
	mess. proc	SPA	SPA	SPA+avg	unb.	unb.	unb.
	verif.	NA	NA	DPA	NA	NA	unb.
	MC.	SPA	SPA	SPA+avg	NA	NA	NA

Fig. 6. Leveled implementations requirements (NA refers to attacks that cannot be mounted as they need access to leakage that is not available in the game).

4   Design Choices and Concrete Evaluations

The framework of Sect. 2 allowed us to put forward a range of AE schemes with various levels of leakage-resistance in Sect. 3. These modes of operation leverage a combination of design ideas in order to reach their security target. In this section, we analyze concrete questions related to these ideas and, when multiple options are possible, we discuss their pros and cons in order to clarify which one to use in which context. We insist that our goal is not to compare the performances of AE schemes but to better understand their designs. (For unprotected implementations, we refer to ongoing benchmarking initiatives for this purpose. For protected ones, this would require agreeing on security targets and evaluating the security levels that actual implementations provide).

4.1   Uniform vs. Leveled Implementations

Research question. One important pattern shared by several designs analyzed in the previous section is that they can enable leveled implementations where different parts of the designs have different levels of security against side-channel attacks. This raises the question whether and to what extent such leveled implementations can be beneficial. In software, it has already been shown in [13] that gains in cycles can be significant and increase with the level of security and message size. We next question whether the same observation holds in hardware, which is more tricky to analyze since enabling more speed vs. area tradeoffs. Precisely, we investigate whether leveled implementations can imply energy gains (which is in general a good metric to capture a design's efficiency [53]).

Experimental setting. In order to investigate the energy efficiency aspects of leveled implementations in presence of side-channel protections, we have designed FPGA and ASIC leveled implementations of Spook. We applied the masking countermeasure with $d = 2$ and $d = 4$ shares (with the HPC2 masking scheme [19]) to the Clyde 128-bit TBC (used as KGF and TGF in Spook), and no countermeasure to the Shadow 512-bit permutation. We used a 32-bit architecture for Clyde and a 128-bit architecture for Shadow. The FPGA implementations have been synthesized, tested and measured on a Sakura-G board, running on a Xilinx Spartan-6 FPGA at a clock frequency of 6 MHz. As a case study, we encrypted a message composed of one block of authentication data and six blocks of plaintext. ASIC implementations have been designed using *Cadence Genus 18* with a commercial 65 nm technology, and the power consumption has been estimated *post-synthesis*, running at a clock frequency of 333 MHz.

Experimental results. The power consumption versus time of the Spook FPGA implementation is shown in Fig. 7. Its main phases can be recognized: first, the Clyde KGF, then the Shadow executions and finally the Clyde TGF. We observe that a Shadow execution (48 clock cycles) is shorter than a masked Clyde execution (157 clock cycles). The power consumption of Shadow is independent of the masking order d, while the one of Clyde increases with d. The figure intuitively confirms the energy gains that leveled implementations enable. We note that larger architectures for Clyde would not change the picture: latency could be reduced down to 24 cycles (i.e., twice the AND depth of the algorithm) but this would cause significant area and dynamic power consumption increases.

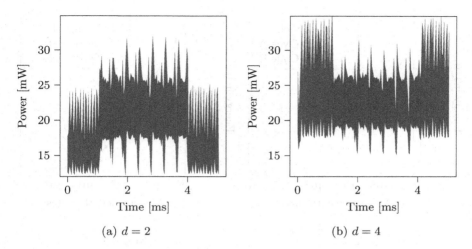

(a) $d = 2$ (b) $d = 4$

Fig. 7. Power consumption of a leveled implementation of Spook with a masked Clyde on a FPGA (Xilinx Spartan 6) at clock frequency $f_{CLK} = 6\,\text{MHz}$, for the encryption of one block of associated data and 5 blocks of message.

We confirm this intuitive figure with performance results for the ASIC implementations of Spook. For this purpose, we have extracted energy estimations for one execution of Clyde (about 3.4 nJ for $d = 2$ and 8.1 nJ for $d = 4$) and one execution of (unprotected) Shadow (about 1.2 nJ) independently, in order to easily study the contributions of the two primitives. Assuming that only the execution of the primitives consumes a significant amount of energy, we can then estimate the energy consumption per byte for both Spook (i.e., 2 Clyde executions and $n + 1$ Shadow executions where n is the number of 32-byte message blocks) and OCB-Clyde-A (resp., OCB-Clyde-B), assuming $n + 2$ (resp., $n + 1$) Clyde executions (where n is the number of 16-byte message blocks). The OCB mode was used as an example of Grade-0 mode, and we used the Clyde TBC in order to have a fairer comparison between the modes. The A (resp., B) variant models the case where the OCB initialization is not amortized (resp., amortized) over a larger number of encryptions. The estimated energy per byte encrypted on ASIC is shown in Fig. 8. For short messages (at most 16 bytes) and for both masking orders, OCB-Clyde-B consumes the least (with 2 Clyde executions), followed by Spook (2 Clyde and 2 Shadow executions), and OCB-Clyde-A is the most energy-intensive (with 3 Clyde executions). For long messages, both OCB-Clyde-A and -B converge to 1 Clyde execution per 16-byte block, while Spook converges to 1 Shadow execution per 32-byte block. In that scenario, a leveled implementation of Spook is therefore much more energy-efficient than OCB (e.g., 5 times more efficient for $d = 2$, and the difference increases with d).

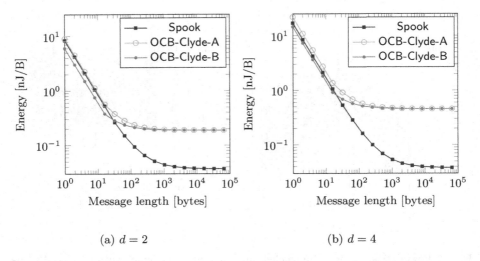

(a) $d = 2$ (b) $d = 4$

Fig. 8. Energy consumption of leveled Spook and uniform OCB-Clyde implementations on ASIC (65 nm technology), in function of the message length.

Discussion. Both the FPGA measurements and the ASIC synthesis results confirm that leveled implementations can lead to significant energy gains for long messages. This derives from the fact that the energy per byte of a protected primitive is larger than for a non-protected one. More interestingly, even for short messages our results show that leveled implementations can be beneficial. For example, Spook requires only two TBC executions. Hence, it is always more energy-efficient than OCB, excepted when the OCB initialization is perfectly amortized, and the message length is less than 16 bytes. Furthermore, even in this case, the Spook overhead is only 35% for $d = 2$ and 15% for $d = 4$.

These energy gains come at the cost of some area overheads since the leveled nature of the implementations limits the possibility to share resources between their strongly and weakly protected parts. In the case of Spook studied in this section, the total area requirements of a 2-share (resp., 4-share & 8-share) leveled implementation is worth 53,897 (resp., 90,311 & 191,214) μm^2. The Shadow-512 part of the implementation is only 22% of this total for the 2-share implementation and decreases to 13% (resp., 6%) with 4 shares (resp., 8 shares).[7]

4.2   TBC-Based vs. Sponge-Based KGF and TGF

Research question. The Grade-2 designs Ascon and Spook use strengthened KGF and TGF instantiated with a permutation and a TBC. This raises the question whether both approaches are equivalent or if one or the other solution is preferable in some application context. We next answer this question by

---

[7] All the results in this subsection include the cost of the PRNG used to generate the shares (we used a 128-bit LFSR) and the area costs include the interface.

leveraging recent results analyzing the (software) overheads that masked implementations of the Ascon permutation and Spook TBC imply.

Experimental setting. The Ascon permutation (used for the KGF and TGF) and Spook TBC have conveniently similar features: both are based on a quadratic S-box and both have 12 rounds. Hence, both have the same multiplicative depth and the different number of AND gates that these primitives have to mask (which usually dominates the overheads as soon as the number of shares increases) only depends on their respective sizes: 384 bits for the Ascon permutation and 128 bits for the Spook TBC. We next compare the cycle counts for masked implementations of these two primitives in an ARM Cortex-M4 device.

Experimental results. A work from Eurocrypt 2020 investigates the proposed setting. It uses a tool to automatically generate masked software implementations that are secure in the (conservative) register probing model [7]. The Ascon permutation and Spook TBC (denoted as Clyde) are among the analyzed primitives. As expected, the resulting cycle counts for the full primitive are roughly doubled for Ascon compared to Clyde (reflecting their state sizes). For example, with a fast RNG to generate the masks and $d = 3$ (resp., $d = 7$) shares, the Ascon permutation requires 42,000 (resp., 123,200) cycles and Clyde only 15,380 (resp., 56,480). When using a slower RNG, these figures become 53,600 (resp., 182,800) for the Ascon permutation and 30,080 (resp., 121,280) for Clyde.

Discussion. Assuming similar security against cryptanalysis, Spook's TBC allows reduced overheads for the KGF and TGF by an approximate factor two compared to Ascon's permutation. Since TBCs generally rely on smaller state sizes than the permutations used in sponge designs, we believe this conclusion generally holds qualitatively. That is, a DPA-protected KGF or TGF based on a TBC allows reduced multiplicative complexities compared to a (wider) permutation-based design. It implies performance gains, especially for small messages for which the execution of the KGF & TGF dominates the performance figures. This gain comes at the cost of two different primitives for Spook (which can be mitigated by re-using similar components for these two primitives). Based on the results of Sect. 4.1, we assume a similar conclusion holds in hardware. So overall, we conclude that the TBC-based KGF/TGF should lead to (mild) advantages when high security levels are required while the permutation-based design enjoys the simplicity of a single-primitive mode of operation which should lead to (mild) advantages in the unprotected (or weakly protected) cases.

4.3 Forward vs. Inverse Tag Verification

Research question. Another difference between Ascon and Spook is the possibility to exploit an inverse-based tag verification with unbounded leakage rather than a DPA-protected direct verification. We next question whether protecting the tag verification is needed and describe a DPA against an unprotected tag verification enabling forgeries for this purpose. We then estimate the cost of these two types of protections and discuss their benefits and disadvantages.

Experimental setting. We analyze a simple 32-bit tag verification algorithm implemented in a `Cortex-M0` device running at 48 [MHz], and measured the power side-channel at a sampling frequency of 500 [MSamples/s]. It computes the bitwise XNOR of both tags and the AND of all the resulting bits. The adversary uses multivariate Gaussian templates estimated with 100,000 profiling traces corresponding to random tag candidates and ciphertexts [21]. During the online phase, she performs a template attack on each byte of the tag individually. To do so, she records traces corresponding to known random tag candidates.

Experimental results. Figure 9 shows the guessing entropy of the correct tag according to the number of attack measurements. It decreases with the number of traces meaning that the attack converges to the correct tag. After the observation of 300 tag candidates, the guessing entropy is already reduced below 2^{32}. The correct tag can then be obtained by performing enumeration (e.g., with [72]).

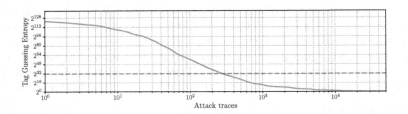

Fig. 9. Security of tag verification on ARM Cortex M0.

Discussion. The DPA of Fig. 9 is slightly more challenging than attacks targeting non-linear operations (e.g., S-box outputs) [73], but still succeeds in low number of traces unless countermeasures are implemented. As discussed in Sect. 3.4, two solutions can be considered to prevent it. First, protecting the tag verification against DPA with masking. Masking the XNOR operations is cheap since it is an affine operation. Masking the AND operations is more costly and implies performing 127 two-input secure AND gates (for a 128-bit tag), with a multiplicative depth of at least 7. The overall cost can be estimated as about 15% of a Clyde execution in cycle count/latency (in software and hardware), and corresponds to 20% in hardware area (for a 32-bit architecture similar to the one of Sect. 4.1). The second method is only applicable to TBC-based TGF. It computes the inverse of the TBC on the candidate tag, allowing a secure comparison with unbounded leakage. Being unprotected, the comparison is cheap but the inverse leads to overheads. For example, for the Clyde TBC, the inverse does not change the execution time, but increases the hardware area by 24% or the software code size by 23%.[8] We conclude that protecting the tag verification leads to limited overheads in front of other implementation costs, with a (mild) simplicity and performance advantage for the inverse-based solution.

---

[8] https://www.spook.dev/implementations.

We recall that ISAP also comes with a possibility to avoid the DPA-protected tag verification, at the cost of an additional call to its internal permutation. It implies an increase of the execution time (rather than area overheads).

4.4 Masked vs. Deterministic Initialization/Finalization

Research question. One important difference between ISAP and TEDT is the way they instantiate their KGF and TGF. TEDT relies on a TBC that has to resist DPA thanks to masking, for which we can rely on a wide literature. ISAP rather uses a re-keying mechanism which is aimed to provide out-of-the-box DPA security. In this case, the best attack is a SPA with averaging, which is a much less investigated context. We therefore question the security of ISAP against advanced Soft Analytical Side-Channel Attacks (SASCA) [84], and then discuss its pros and cons compared to a masked TBC as used in TEDT.

We insist that the following results do not contradict the security claims of ISAP since the investigated attacks are SPA, not DPA. Yet, they allow putting the strengths and weaknesses of ISAP and TEDT in perspective.

Experimental setting. In order to study the out-of-the-box side-channel security of ISAP, we target its reference implementation where the permutations of Fig. 5 are instantiated with the Keccak-400 permutation. We performed experiments against a Cortex-M0 device running at 48 [MHz], and measured the power side-channel at a sampling frequency of 500 [MSamples/s]. Even though this target has a 32-bit architecture, the compiler generates code processing 16-bit words at a time. This is a natural approach since it is the size of a lane in Keccak-400. Therefore, the intermediate variables exploited are 16-bit wide. We used 10,000 averaged traces corresponding to known (random) IV_e and K values for profiling. The profiling method is a linear regression with a 17-element basis corresponding to the 16 bits manipulated by the implementation and a constant [76]. We profiled models for all the intermediate variables produced when computing the permutation. During the attack phase the adversary is provided with a single (possibly averaged) leakage and optionally with IV_e (which is public in ISAP). She performs SASCA following the same (practical) steps as [45], but with 16-bit intermediate targets rather than 8-bit ones. For time & memory efficiency, she only exploits the first round of the full permutation.

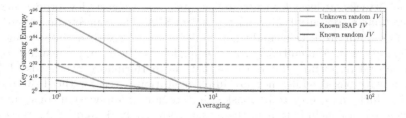

Fig. 10. Security of ISAP's re-keying in an ARM Cortex M0.

Experimental results. Figure 10 shows the guessing entropy of the 128-bit key K in function of the number of times the leakage is averaged. We note that the adversary can average her measurements for the permutations of ISAP's rekeying, since the first permutation has a fixed input and the next ones only integrate the nonce bit per bit (so for example, even without controlling the nonce, 50% of the second permutation calls are identical). Increased averaging allows reducing the noise and therefore reducing the key's guessing entropy.

Overall, if IV_e is known (as in the ISAP design) the guessing entropy of the key is already lower than 2^{32} without averaging. The correct key can then be retrieved by performing key enumeration. Interestingly, we observe that the value of IV_e has some impact on the attack success (i.e., the ISAP value, which has a lot of zeros, leads to slightly more challenging attacks than a random value). We further analyzed the unknown IV_e case and could successfully perform the same attack with a slight averaging (i.e., the attack trace measured ten times). The difference with the known IV_e case derives from the additional efforts that the adversary has to pay for dealing with more secret intermediate states.

Discussion. One important difference between the ISAP and TEDT approaches relates to the presence of a security parameter. While masking a TBC can use a number of shares as security parameter, there is no such security parameter for ISAP if used out-of-the-box. In this respect, the choice between one or the other approach can be viewed as a tradeoff between simplicity and expertise. On the one hand, implementations of ISAP deployed without specific countermeasures already enjoy security against a wide-class of (DPA) attacks; on the other hand, the deterministic nature of the (out-of-the-box implementation of the) re-keying function makes it susceptible to advanced (SPA) attacks that randomized countermeasures such as masking can prevent for TEDT implementations.

Admittedly, this conclusion is in part implementation-specific and the efficiency of SASCA generally degrades with the size of the implementation. In this respect, targeting 32-bit operations would be more challenging, which is an interesting scope for further investigations. Yet, we note that in case the size of the architecture makes power analysis attacks difficult, advanced measurement capabilities may be used [83], maintaining the intuition that for high-security levels, some algorithmic amplification of the noise is generally needed.

We mention that our results are in line with the recent investigations in [51] where similar attacks are reported. The authors conclude that "unprotected implementations should always be avoided in applications sensitive to side-channel attacks, at least for software targets", and suggest (low-order) masking and shuffling as potential solutions to prevent SPA. The concrete investigation of these minimum protections and their implementation cost is an interesting open problem given the difficulty to protect embedded software implementations [18].

A second important difference is that the performance overheads of ISAP are primitive-based while they are implementation-based for the TBC used in TEDT, which can therefore be masked in function of application constraints.

Overall, we conclude that in their basic settings, ISAP and TEDT target different goals: reduction from DPA security to SPA security with primitive-based performance oveaheads for ISAP and high-security against advanced adversaries with flexible overheads (e.g., if side-channel security is not needed) for TEDT.

5   Formal Qualitative Analysis

We conclude the paper with the security analysis of Beetle, Spook, Ascon, TEDT and ISAP, in the ideal permutation model. All the theorems below highlight that integrity requires weaker assumptions than confidentiality even in attack models where the adversary gets more leakage and nonce-misuse capabilities. The reader can find the formal definitions of the security notions in the full paper [11].

5.1   Background: Definitions and Assumptions

For leaking components, we follow [47] and enforce limitations on the leakages of the permutation calls as well as those of the XOR executions. Precisely:

- For the former, we define $(\mathsf{L}^{in}(U), \mathsf{L}^{out}(V))$ as the leakages of a permutation call $\pi(U) \rightarrow V$, where both L^{in} and L^{out} are probabilistic functions. Note that this means the leakage of a single permutation call is viewed as two independent "input" and "output" halves. And we assume the following non-invertibility: *given the leakages* $(\mathsf{L}^{out}(Y\|X), \mathsf{L}^{in}(Y'\|X))$ *of a secret c-bit value X and two adversarially chosen r-bit values Y, Y', the probability to guess X is negligible.* Note that this is a special case of Eq. (1).
- For the XOR executions, we define $\mathsf{L}_{\oplus}(Y, M)$ as the leakage of an XOR computation $Y \oplus M \rightarrow C$, where $\mathsf{L}_{\oplus}$ is also a probabilistic function. This time, we make an assumption on the following message distinguishing advantage: *given the leakages* $(\mathsf{L}^{out}(Y\|X), \mathsf{L}_{\oplus}(Y, M^b))$ *of a secret r-bit key Y and adversarially chosen r-bit values X, M^0, M^1, the probability to guess b is bounded to ε.* Note that this assumption is a special case of Eq. (2).

5.2   CCAL1 and CIL1 Security of PHOTON-Beetle

We first consider Grade-1a schemes and focus on PHOTON-Beetle. As mentioned in Sect. 3.3, the leakage properties of other IKS schemes are similar.

Theorem 1. *Assuming that a PHOTON-Beetle implementation satisfies (i) its KGF is leak-free, and (ii) the leakage of unprotected permutation calls are non-invertible as assumed in Sect. 5.1, the circuit ensure CIL1 integrity. Moreover, if this implementation also satisfies (iii) the leakages of XOR executions are bounded as assumed in Sect. 5.1, the circuit ensures CCAL1 confidentiality.*

The proof sketch is given in the full version of the paper [11].

5.3   CCAmL1 and CIML2 Security of Ascon/Spook

As the mode of Spook is analyzed in [47], we only focus on Ascon.

Theorem 2. *Assuming that an* Ascon *implementation satisfies (i) its KGF is leak-free, and (ii) the tag verification process is leak-free, the circuit ensures* CIML2 *integrity. Moreover, if the* Ascon *implementation also satisfies (iii) the leakages of unprotected permutation calls are non-invertible as assumed in Sect. 5.1, and (iv) the leakages of XOR executions are bounded as assumed in Sect. 5.1, then the* Ascon *implementation ensures* CCAmL1 *confidentiality.*

The proof sketch is given in the full version of the paper [11].

5.4   CCAmL2 and CIML2 Security of ISAP/TEDT

We finally consider 2-pass Encrypt-then-MAC designs. TEDT has been thoroughly analyzed in [13]. Hence we focus on (the 2.0 version of) ISAP.

Theorem 3. *Assuming that an* ISAP *implementation satisfies (i) its KGF is leak-free, and (ii) the tag verification process is leak-free, the circuit ensures* CIML2 *integrity. Moreover, if the* ISAP *implementation also satisfies (iii) the leakages of unprotected permutation calls are non-invertible as assumed in Sect. 5.1, and (iv) the leakages of XOR executions are bounded as assumed in Sect. 5.1, then the* ISAP *implementation ensures* CCAmL2 *confidentiality.*

The proof sketch is given in the full version of the paper [11].

6   Conclusion and Open Problems

The research in this work underlines that there is no single "right definition" of leakage-resistant AE. As the security targets (e.g., the grades of the designs we investigated) and the security levels required by an application increase, it becomes more interesting to exploit schemes that allow minimizing the implementation overheads of side-channel countermeasures. This observation suggests the connection of actual security targets with relevant application scenarios and the performance evaluation of different AE schemes to reach the same physical security levels as a natural next step of this study. Looking for security targets that are not captured by our taxonomy and improving existing designs to reach various targets more efficiency are other meaningful goals to investigate.

Acknowledgment. Gaëtan Cassiers, Thomas Peters and François-Xavier Standaert are respectively PhD student, postdoctoral researcher and senior research associate of the Belgian Fund for Scientific Research (F.R.S.-FNRS). Chun Guo was partly supported by the Program of Qilu Young Scholars (Grant Number 61580089963177) of Shandong University, the National Natural Science Foundation of China (Grant Number 61602276), and the Shandong Nature Science Foundation of China (Grant Number ZR2016FM22). This work has been funded in parts by the ERC project SWORD (Grant Number 724725), the Win2Wal project PIRATE and the UCLouvain ARC project NANOSEC.

References

1. Abdalla, M., Belaïd, S., Fouque, P.-A.: Leakage-resilient symmetric encryption via re-keying. In: Bertoni, G., Coron, J.-S. (eds.) CHES 2013. LNCS, vol. 8086, pp. 471–488. Springer, Heidelberg (2013). https://doi.org/10.1007/978-3-642-40349-1_27
2. Ashur, T., Dunkelman, O., Luykx, A.: Boosting authenticated encryption robustness with minimal modifications. In: Katz, J., Shacham, H. (eds.) CRYPTO 2017. LNCS, vol. 10403, pp. 3–33. Springer, Cham (2017). https://doi.org/10.1007/978-3-319-63697-9_1
3. Balasch, J., Gierlichs, B., Grosso, V., Reparaz, O., Standaert, F.-X.: On the cost of lazy engineering for masked software implementations. In: Joye, M., Moradi, A. (eds.) CARDIS 2014. LNCS, vol. 8968, pp. 64–81. Springer, Cham (2015). https://doi.org/10.1007/978-3-319-16763-3_5
4. Bao, Z., et al.: PHOTON-Beetle. Submission to the NIST Lightweight Cryptography Standardization Effort (2019)
5. Barthe, G., et al.: Strong non-interference and type-directed higher-order masking. In: ACM CCS, pp. 116–129. ACM (2016)
6. Barwell, G., Martin, D.P., Oswald, E., Stam, M.: Authenticated encryption in the face of protocol and side channel leakage. In: Takagi, T., Peyrin, T. (eds.) ASIACRYPT 2017. LNCS, vol. 10624, pp. 693–723. Springer, Cham (2017). https://doi.org/10.1007/978-3-319-70694-8_24
7. Belaïd, S., Dagand, P.É., Mercadier, D., Rivain, M., Wintersdorff, R.: Tornado: automatic generation of probing-secure masked bitsliced implementations. In: Canteaut, A., Ishai, Y. (eds.) EUROCRYPT 2020. LNCS, vol. 12107, pp. 311–341. Springer, Cham (2020). https://doi.org/10.1007/978-3-030-45727-3_11
8. Belaïd, S., Grosso, V., Standaert, F.-X.: Masking and leakage-resilient primitives: one, the other(s) or both? Crypt. Commun. 7(1), 163–184 (2014). https://doi.org/10.1007/s12095-014-0113-6
9. Belaïd, S., et al.: Towards fresh re-keying with leakage-resilient PRFs: cipher design principles and analysis. J. Cryptographic Eng. 4(3), 157–171 (2014). https://doi.org/10.1007/s13389-014-0079-5
10. Bellizia, D., et al.: Spook: sponge-based leakage-resistant authenticated encryption with a masked tweakable block cipher. Submission to the NIST Lightweight Cryptography Standardization Effort (2019)
11. Bellizia, D., et al.: Mode-Level vs. implementation-level physical security in symmetric cryptography: a practical guide through the leakage-resistance jungle. IACR Cryptol. ePrint Arch., 2020:211 (2020)
12. Berti, F., Guo, C., Pereira, O., Peters, T., Standaert, F.-X.: Strong authenticity with leakage under weak and falsifiable physical assumptions. In: Liu, Z., Yung, M. (eds.) Inscrypt 2019. LNCS, vol. 12020, pp. 517–532. Springer, Cham (2020). https://doi.org/10.1007/978-3-030-42921-8_31
13. Berti, F., Guo, C., Pereira, O., Peters, T., Standaert, F.: TEDT, a leakage-resist AEAD mode for high physical security applications. IACR Trans. Cryptogr. Hardw. Embed. Syst. 2020(1), 256–320 (2020)
14. Berti, F., Koeune, F., Pereira, O., Peters, T., Standaert, F.: Ciphertext integrity with misuse and leakage: definition and efficient constructions with symmetric primitives. In: AsiaCCS, pp. 37–50. ACM (2018)
15. Berti, F., Pereira, O., Peters, T., Standaert, F.: On leakage-resilient authenticated encryption with decryption leakages. IACR Trans. Symmetric Cryptol. 2017(3), 271–293 (2017)

16. Bertoni, G., Daemen, J., Peeters, M., Van Assche, G.: Duplexing the sponge: single-pass authenticated encryption and other applications. In: Miri, A., Vaudenay, S. (eds.) SAC 2011. LNCS, vol. 7118, pp. 320–337. Springer, Heidelberg (2012). https://doi.org/10.1007/978-3-642-28496-0_19

17. Boyle, E., Goldwasser, S., Jain, A., Kalai, Y.T.: Multiparty computation secure against continual memory leakage. In: STOC, pp. 1235–1254. ACM (2012)

18. Bronchain, O., Standaert, F.: Side-channel countermeasures' dissection and the limits of closed source security evaluations. IACR Trans. Cryptogr. Hardw. Embed. Syst. **2020**(2), 1–25 (2020)

19. Cassiers, G., Grégoire, B., Levi, I., Standaert, F.: Hardware Private Circuits: From Trivial Composition to Full Verification (aka Repairing Glitch-Resistant Higher-Order Masking). IACR ePrint Archive (2020)

20. Chari, S., Jutla, C.S., Rao, J.R., Rohatgi, P.: Towards sound approaches to counteract power-analysis attacks. In: Wiener, M. (ed.) CRYPTO 1999. LNCS, vol. 1666, pp. 398–412. Springer, Heidelberg (1999). https://doi.org/10.1007/3-540-48405-1_26

21. Chari, S., Rao, J.R., Rohatgi, P.: Template attacks. In: Kaliski, B.S., Koç, K., Paar, C. (eds.) CHES 2002. LNCS, vol. 2523, pp. 13–28. Springer, Heidelberg (2003). https://doi.org/10.1007/3-540-36400-5_3

22. Clavier, C., Coron, J.-S., Dabbous, N.: Differential power analysis in the presence of hardware countermeasures. In: Koç, Ç.K., Paar, C. (eds.) CHES 2000. LNCS, vol. 1965, pp. 252–263. Springer, Heidelberg (2000). https://doi.org/10.1007/3-540-44499-8_20

23. Coron, J.-S., Giraud, C., Prouff, E., Renner, S., Rivain, M., Vadnala, P.K.: Conversion of security proofs from one leakage model to another: a new issue. In: Schindler, W., Huss, S.A. (eds.) COSADE 2012. LNCS, vol. 7275, pp. 69–81. Springer, Heidelberg (2012). https://doi.org/10.1007/978-3-642-29912-4_6

24. Degabriele, J.P., Janson, C., Struck, P.: Sponges resist leakage: the case of authenticated encryption. In: Galbraith, S.D., Moriai, S. (eds.) ASIACRYPT 2019. LNCS, vol. 11922, pp. 209–240. Springer, Cham (2019). https://doi.org/10.1007/978-3-030-34621-8_8

25. Dobraunig, C., Eichlseder, M., Mangard, S., Mennink, F.M.B., Primas, R., Unterluggauer, T.: ISAP v2.0. Submission to the NIST Lightweight Cryptography Standardization Effort (2019)

26. Dobraunig, C., Eichlseder, M., Mendel, F., Schläffer, M.: Ascon v1.2. Submission to the NIST Lightweight Cryptography Standardization Effort (2019)

27. Dobraunig, C., Mennink, B.: Leakage resilience of the duplex construction. In: Galbraith, S.D., Moriai, S. (eds.) ASIACRYPT 2019. LNCS, vol. 11923, pp. 225–255. Springer, Cham (2019). https://doi.org/10.1007/978-3-030-34618-8_8

28. Dodis, Y., Goldwasser, S., Tauman Kalai, Y., Peikert, C., Vaikuntanathan, V.: Public-key encryption schemes with auxiliary inputs. In: Micciancio, D. (ed.) TCC 2010. LNCS, vol. 5978, pp. 361–381. Springer, Heidelberg (2010). https://doi.org/10.1007/978-3-642-11799-2_22

29. Dodis, Y., Kalai, Y.T., Lovett, S.: On cryptography with auxiliary input. In: STOC, pp. 621–630. ACM (2009)

30. Dodis, Y., Pietrzak, K.: Leakage-resilient pseudorandom functions and side-channel attacks on feistel networks. In: Rabin, T. (ed.) CRYPTO 2010. LNCS, vol. 6223, pp. 21–40. Springer, Heidelberg (2010). https://doi.org/10.1007/978-3-642-14623-7_2

31. Duc, A., Dziembowski, S., Faust, S.: Unifying leakage models: from probing attacks to noisy leakage. In: Nguyen, P.Q., Oswald, E. (eds.) EUROCRYPT 2014. LNCS, vol. 8441, pp. 423–440. Springer, Heidelberg (2014). https://doi.org/10.1007/978-3-642-55220-5_24

32. Duc, A., Faust, S., Standaert, F.-X.: Making masking security proofs concrete. In: Oswald, E., Fischlin, M. (eds.) EUROCRYPT 2015. LNCS, vol. 9056, pp. 401–429. Springer, Heidelberg (2015). https://doi.org/10.1007/978-3-662-46800-5_16

33. Dziembowski, S., Pietrzak, K.: Leakage-resilient cryptography. In: FOCS, pp. 293–302. IEEE Computer Society (2008)

34. Faust, S., Kiltz, E., Pietrzak, K., Rothblum, G.N.: Leakage-resilient signatures. In: Micciancio, D. (ed.) TCC 2010. LNCS, vol. 5978, pp. 343–360. Springer, Heidelberg (2010). https://doi.org/10.1007/978-3-642-11799-2_21

35. Faust, S., Pietrzak, K., Schipper, J.: Practical leakage-resilient symmetric cryptography. In: Prouff, E., Schaumont, P. (eds.) CHES 2012. LNCS, vol. 7428, pp. 213–232. Springer, Heidelberg (2012). https://doi.org/10.1007/978-3-642-33027-8_13

36. Fuller, B., Hamlin, A.: Unifying leakage classes: simulatable leakage and pseudoentropy. In: Lehmann, A., Wolf, S. (eds.) ICITS 2015. LNCS, vol. 9063, pp. 69–86. Springer, Cham (2015). https://doi.org/10.1007/978-3-319-17470-9_5

37. Gammel, B., Fischer, W., Mangard, S.: Generating a session key for authentication and secure data transfer. US Patent 8,861,722 (2014)

38. Gérard, B., Grosso, V., Naya-Plasencia, M., Standaert, F.-X.: Block ciphers that are easier to mask: how far can we go? In: Bertoni, G., Coron, J.-S. (eds.) CHES 2013. LNCS, vol. 8086, pp. 383–399. Springer, Heidelberg (2013). https://doi.org/10.1007/978-3-642-40349-1_22

39. Goldwasser, S., Rothblum, G.N.: Securing computation against continuous leakage. In: Rabin, T. (ed.) CRYPTO 2010. LNCS, vol. 6223, pp. 59–79. Springer, Heidelberg (2010). https://doi.org/10.1007/978-3-642-14623-7_4

40. Goubin, L., Patarin, J.: DES and differential power analysis the "Duplication" method. In: Koç, Ç.K., Paar, C. (eds.) CHES 1999. LNCS, vol. 1717, pp. 158–172. Springer, Heidelberg (1999). https://doi.org/10.1007/3-540-48059-5_15

41. Goudarzi, D. et al.: Pyjamask v1.0. Submission to the NIST Lightweight Cryptography Standardization Effort (2019)

42. Goudarzi, D., Rivain, M.: How fast can higher-order masking be in software? In: Coron, J.-S., Nielsen, J.B. (eds.) EUROCRYPT 2017. LNCS, vol. 10210, pp. 567–597. Springer, Cham (2017). https://doi.org/10.1007/978-3-319-56620-7_20

43. Gross, H., Mangard, S., Korak, T.: An efficient side-channel protected AES implementation with arbitrary protection order. In: Handschuh, H. (ed.) CT-RSA 2017. LNCS, vol. 10159, pp. 95–112. Springer, Cham (2017). https://doi.org/10.1007/978-3-319-52153-4_6

44. Grosso, V., Leurent, G., Standaert, F.-X., Varıcı, K.: LS-designs: bitslice encryption for efficient masked software implementations. In: Cid, C., Rechberger, C. (eds.) FSE 2014. LNCS, vol. 8540, pp. 18–37. Springer, Heidelberg (2015). https://doi.org/10.1007/978-3-662-46706-0_2

45. Grosso, V., Standaert, F.-X.: ASCA, SASCA and DPA with enumeration: which one beats the other and when? In: Iwata, T., Cheon, J.H. (eds.) ASIACRYPT 2015. LNCS, vol. 9453, pp. 291–312. Springer, Heidelberg (2015). https://doi.org/10.1007/978-3-662-48800-3_12

46. Guo, C., Pereira, O., Peters, T., Standaert, F.-X.: Authenticated encryption with nonce misuse and physical leakage: definitions, separation results and first construction. In: Schwabe, P., Thériault, N. (eds.) LATINCRYPT 2019. LNCS, vol. 11774, pp. 150–172. Springer, Cham (2019). https://doi.org/10.1007/978-3-030-30530-7_8

47. Guo, C., Pereira, O., Peters, T., Standaert, F.: Towards low-energy leakage-resistant authenticated encryption from the duplex sponge construction. IACR Trans. Symmetric Cryptol. **2020**(1), 6–42 (2020)

48. Herbst, C., Oswald, E., Mangard, S.: An AES smart card implementation resistant to power analysis attacks. In: Zhou, J., Yung, M., Bao, F. (eds.) ACNS 2006. LNCS, vol. 3989, pp. 239–252. Springer, Heidelberg (2006). https://doi.org/10.1007/11767480_16

49. Ishai, Y., Sahai, A., Wagner, D.: Private circuits: securing hardware against probing attacks. In: Boneh, D. (ed.) CRYPTO 2003. LNCS, vol. 2729, pp. 463–481. Springer, Heidelberg (2003). https://doi.org/10.1007/978-3-540-45146-4_27

50. Kalai, Y.T., Reyzin, L.: A survey of leakage-resilient cryptography. In: Providing Sound Foundations for Cryptography, pp. 727–794. ACM (2019)

51. Kannwischer, M.J., Pessl, P., Primas, R.: Single-trace attacks on Keccak. IACR Cryptol. ePrint Arch. 2020:371 (2020)

52. Katz, J., Vaikuntanathan, V.: Signature schemes with bounded leakage resilience. In: Matsui, M. (ed.) ASIACRYPT 2009. LNCS, vol. 5912, pp. 703–720. Springer, Heidelberg (2009). https://doi.org/10.1007/978-3-642-10366-7_41

53. Kerckhof, S., Durvaux, F., Hocquet, C., Bol, D., Standaert, F.-X.: Towards green cryptography: a comparison of lightweight ciphers from the energy viewpoint. In: Prouff, E., Schaumont, P. (eds.) CHES 2012. LNCS, vol. 7428, pp. 390–407. Springer, Heidelberg (2012). https://doi.org/10.1007/978-3-642-33027-8_23

54. Kiltz, E., Pietrzak, K.: Leakage resilient elgamal encryption. In: Abe, M. (ed.) ASIACRYPT 2010. LNCS, vol. 6477, pp. 595–612. Springer, Heidelberg (2010). https://doi.org/10.1007/978-3-642-17373-8_34

55. Kocher, P.C.: Timing attacks on implementations of Diffie-Hellman, RSA, DSS, and other systems. In: Koblitz, N. (ed.) CRYPTO 1996. LNCS, vol. 1109, pp. 104–113. Springer, Heidelberg (1996). https://doi.org/10.1007/3-540-68697-5_9

56. Kocher, P.C.: Leak-resistant cryptographic indexed key update. US Patent 6,539,092 (2003)

57. Kocher, P., Jaffe, J., Jun, B.: Differential power analysis. In: Wiener, M. (ed.) CRYPTO 1999. LNCS, vol. 1666, pp. 388–397. Springer, Heidelberg (1999). https://doi.org/10.1007/3-540-48405-1_25

58. Longo, J., Martin, D.P., Oswald, E., Page, D., Stam, M., Tunstall, M.J.: Simulatable leakage: analysis, pitfalls, and new constructions. In: Sarkar, P., Iwata, T. (eds.) ASIACRYPT 2014. LNCS, vol. 8873, pp. 223–242. Springer, Heidelberg (2014). https://doi.org/10.1007/978-3-662-45611-8_12

59. Malkin, T., Teranishi, I., Vahlis, Y., Yung, M.: Signatures resilient to continual leakage on memory and computation. In: Ishai, Y. (ed.) TCC 2011. LNCS, vol. 6597, pp. 89–106. Springer, Heidelberg (2011). https://doi.org/10.1007/978-3-642-19571-6_7

60. Mangard, S.: Hardware countermeasures against DPA – a statistical analysis of their effectiveness. In: Okamoto, T. (ed.) CT-RSA 2004. LNCS, vol. 2964, pp. 222–235. Springer, Heidelberg (2004). https://doi.org/10.1007/978-3-540-24660-2_18

61. Mangard, S., Oswald, E., Popp, T.: Power Analysis Attacks - Revealing the Secrets of Smart Cards. Springer, New York (2007). https://doi.org/10.1007/978-0-387-38162-6

62. Mangard, S., Popp, T., Gammel, B.M.: Side-channel leakage of masked CMOS gates. In: Menezes, A. (ed.) CT-RSA 2005. LNCS, vol. 3376, pp. 351–365. Springer, Heidelberg (2005). https://doi.org/10.1007/978-3-540-30574-3_24

63. Medwed, M., Standaert, F.-X., Großschädl, J., Regazzoni, F.: Fresh re-keying: security against side-channel and fault attacks for low-cost devices. In: Bernstein, D.J., Lange, T. (eds.) AFRICACRYPT 2010. LNCS, vol. 6055, pp. 279–296. Springer, Heidelberg (2010). https://doi.org/10.1007/978-3-642-12678-9_17

64. Micali, S., Reyzin, L.: Physically observable cryptography (extended abstract). In: Naor, M. (ed.) TCC 2004. LNCS, vol. 2951, pp. 278–296. Springer, Heidelberg (2004). https://doi.org/10.1007/978-3-540-24638-1_16

65. Naor, M., Segev, G.: Public-key cryptosystems resilient to key leakage. In: Halevi, S. (ed.) CRYPTO 2009. LNCS, vol. 5677, pp. 18–35. Springer, Heidelberg (2009). https://doi.org/10.1007/978-3-642-03356-8_2

66. Nikova, S., Rijmen, V., Schläffer, M.: Secure hardware implementation of nonlinear functions in the presence of glitches. J. Cryptol. **24**(2), 292–321 (2011)

67. O'Flynn, C., Chen, Z.D.: Side channel power analysis of an AES-256 bootloader. In: CCECE, pp. 750–755. IEEE (2015)

68. Pereira, O., Standaert, F., Vivek, S.: Leakage-resilient authentication and encryption from symmetric cryptographic primitives. In: ACM CCS, pp. 96–108. ACM (2015)

69. Petit, C., Standaert, F., Pereira, O., Malkin, T., Yung, M.: A block cipher based pseudo random number generator secure against side-channel key recovery. In: AsiaCCS, pp. 56–65. ACM (2008)

70. Pietrzak, K.: A leakage-resilient mode of operation. In: Joux, A. (ed.) EURO-CRYPT 2009. LNCS, vol. 5479, pp. 462–482. Springer, Heidelberg (2009). https://doi.org/10.1007/978-3-642-01001-9_27

71. Piret, G., Roche, T., Carlet, C.: PICARO – a block cipher allowing efficient higher-order side-channel resistance. In: Bao, F., Samarati, P., Zhou, J. (eds.) ACNS 2012. LNCS, vol. 7341, pp. 311–328. Springer, Heidelberg (2012). https://doi.org/10.1007/978-3-642-31284-7_19

72. Poussier, R., Standaert, F.-X., Grosso, V.: Simple key enumeration (and rank estimation) using histograms: an integrated approach. In: Gierlichs, B., Poschmann, A.Y. (eds.) CHES 2016. LNCS, vol. 9813, pp. 61–81. Springer, Heidelberg (2016). https://doi.org/10.1007/978-3-662-53140-2_4

73. Prouff, E.: DPA attacks and S-boxes. In: Gilbert, H., Handschuh, H. (eds.) FSE 2005. LNCS, vol. 3557, pp. 424–441. Springer, Heidelberg (2005). https://doi.org/10.1007/11502760_29

74. Rogaway, P., Bellare, M., Black, J.: OCB: a block cipher mode of operation for efficient authenticated encryption. ACM Trans. Inf. Syst. Secur. **6**(3), 365–403 (2003)

75. Rogaway, P., Shrimpton, T.: A provable-security treatment of the key-wrap problem. In: Vaudenay, S. (ed.) EUROCRYPT 2006. LNCS, vol. 4004, pp. 373–390. Springer, Heidelberg (2006). https://doi.org/10.1007/11761679_23

76. Schindler, W., Lemke, K., Paar, C.: A stochastic model for differential side channel cryptanalysis. In: Rao, J.R., Sunar, B. (eds.) CHES 2005. LNCS, vol. 3659, pp. 30–46. Springer, Heidelberg (2005). https://doi.org/10.1007/11545262_3

77. Standaert, F.-X.: Towards fair and efficient evaluations of leaking cryptographic devices - overview of the ERC project CRASH, Part I (invited talk). In: Carlet, C., Hasan, M.A., Saraswat, V. (eds.) SPACE 2016. LNCS, vol. 10076, pp. 353–362. Springer, Cham (2016). https://doi.org/10.1007/978-3-319-49445-6_20

78. Standaert, F.-X., Pereira, O., Yu, Yu.: Leakage-resilient symmetric cryptography under empirically verifiable assumptions. In: Canetti, R., Garay, J.A. (eds.) CRYPTO 2013. LNCS, vol. 8042, pp. 335–352. Springer, Heidelberg (2013). https://doi.org/10.1007/978-3-642-40041-4_19

79. Standaert, F.X., Pereira, O., Yu, Y., Quisquater, J.J., Yung, M., Oswald, E.: Leakage resilient cryptography in practice. In: Sadeghi, A.R., Naccache, D. (eds.) Towards Hardware-Intrinsic Security. Information Security and Cryptography. Springer, Heidelberg (2010). https://doi.org/10.1007/978-3-642-14452-3_5

80. Standaert, F.-X.: Towards and open approach to secure cryptographic implementations (invited talk). In: EUROCRYPT I. LNCS, vol. 11476, p. xv (2019). https://www.youtube.com/watch?v=KdhrsuJT1sE

81. Tiri, K., Verbauwhede, I.: Securing encryption algorithms against DPA at the logic level: next generation smart card technology. In: Walter, C.D., Koç, Ç.K., Paar, C. (eds.) CHES 2003. LNCS, vol. 2779, pp. 125–136. Springer, Heidelberg (2003). https://doi.org/10.1007/978-3-540-45238-6_11

82. Tiri, K., Verbauwhede, I.: A logic level design methodology for a secure DPA resistant ASIC or FPGA implementation. In: DATE, pp. 246–251. IEEE Computer Society (2004)

83. Unterstein, F., Heyszl, J., De Santis, F., Specht, R., Sigl, G.: High-resolution EM attacks against leakage-resilient PRFs explained. In: Smart, N.P. (ed.) CT-RSA 2018. LNCS, vol. 10808, pp. 413–434. Springer, Cham (2018). https://doi.org/10.1007/978-3-319-76953-0_22

84. Veyrat-Charvillon, N., Gérard, B., Standaert, F.-X.: Soft analytical side-channel attacks. In: Sarkar, P., Iwata, T. (eds.) ASIACRYPT 2014. LNCS, vol. 8873, pp. 282–296. Springer, Heidelberg (2014). https://doi.org/10.1007/978-3-662-45611-8_15

85. Veyrat-Charvillon, N., Medwed, M., Kerckhof, S., Standaert, F.-X.: Shuffling against side-channel attacks: a comprehensive study with cautionary note. In: Wang, X., Sako, K. (eds.) ASIACRYPT 2012. LNCS, vol. 7658, pp. 740–757. Springer, Heidelberg (2012). https://doi.org/10.1007/978-3-642-34961-4_44

86. Yu, Yu., Standaert, F.-X.: Practical leakage-resilient pseudorandom objects with minimum public randomness. In: Dawson, E. (ed.) CT-RSA 2013. LNCS, vol. 7779, pp. 223–238. Springer, Heidelberg (2013). https://doi.org/10.1007/978-3-642-36095-4_15

87. Yu, Y., Standaert, F., Pereira, O., Yung, M.: Practical leakage-resilient pseudorandom generators. In: ACM CCS, pp. 141–151. ACM (2010)

Leakage-Resilient Key Exchange and Two-Seed Extractors

Xin Li[1(✉)], Fermi Ma[2,3(✉)], Willy Quach[4(✉)], and Daniel Wichs[3,4(✉)]

[1] Johns Hopkins University, Baltimore, USA
lixints@cs.jhu.edu
[2] Princeton University, Princeton, USA
fermima@alum.mit.edu
[3] NTT Research, Palo Alto, USA
[4] Northeastern University, Boston, USA
quach.w@husky.neu.edu,wichs@ccs.neu.edu

Abstract. Can Alice and Bob agree on a uniformly random secret key without having any truly secret randomness to begin with? Here we consider a setting where Eve can get partial leakage on the internal state of both Alice and Bob individually before the protocol starts. They then run a protocol using their states without any additional randomness and need to agree on a shared key that looks uniform to Eve, even after observing the leakage and the protocol transcript. We focus on non-interactive (one round) key exchange (NIKE), where Alice and Bob send one message each without waiting for one another.

We first consider this problem in the symmetric-key setting, where the states of Alice and Bob include a shared secret as well as individual uniform randomness. However, since Eve gets leakage on these states, Alice and Bob need to perform *privacy amplification* to derive a fresh secret key from them. Prior solutions require Alice and Bob to sample fresh uniform randomness during the protocol, while in our setting all of their randomness was already part of their individual states a priori and was therefore subject to leakage. We show an information-theoretic solution to this problem using a novel primitive that we call a *two-seed extractor*, which we in turn construct by drawing a connection to communication-complexity lower-bounds in the number-on-forehead (NOF) model.

We then turn to studying this problem in the public-key setting, where the states of Alice and Bob consist of independent uniform randomness. Unfortunately, we give a black-box separation showing that leakage-resilient NIKE in this setting cannot be proven secure via a black-box reduction under any game-based assumption when the leakage is super-logarithmic. This includes virtually all assumptions used in cryptography, and even very strong assumptions such as indistinguishability obfuscation (*iO*). Nevertheless, we also provide positive results that get around the above separation:

- We show that every key exchange protocol (e.g., Diffie-Hellman) is secure when the leakage amount is logarithmic, or potentially even greater if we assume sub-exponential security without leakage.
- We notice that the black-box separation does not extend to schemes in the *common reference string* (CRS) model, or to schemes with

D. Micciancio and T. Ristenpart (Eds.): CRYPTO 2020, LNCS 12170, pp. 401–429, 2020.
https://doi.org/10.1007/978-3-030-56784-2_14

preprocessing, where Alice and Bob can individually pre-process their random coins to derive their secret state prior to leakage. We give a solution in the CRS model with preprocessing using bilinear maps. We also give solutions in just the CRS model alone (without preprocessing) *or* just with preprocessing (without a CRS), using $i\mathcal{O}$ and lossy functions.

1   Introduction

Leakage-resilient cryptography [1–3,17,20,23,28,30, ...] studies the security of cryptosystems when the adversary can get some partial information about the secret keys of honest users. However, in almost all cases, the schemes rely on some leak-free randomness to guarantee security. For example, leakage-resilient encryption [1,30] only guarantees security when the adversary gets leakage on the secret key, but requires the encryption randomness to be leak-free. In fact, leakage-resilience is closely related to cryptography with imperfect randomness (conditioned on the leakage, the randomness is no longer uniform) where it was shown that many cryptographic tasks are impossible with imperfect randomness [15].

In this work, we study the question of leakage-resilient key exchange, where Alice and Bob wish to agree on a nearly uniform secret key by communicating over a public channel whose contents are being observed by an adversary Eve. Before the protocol starts, Eve can additionally get partial leakage on the internal states of each of Alice and Bob individually. In particular, Eve can choose two functions f_A, f_B with ℓ-bit output, where ℓ is some *leakage bound*, and learn the output of these functions when applied on the states of Alice and Bob respectively. We assume that the state of each user includes all of the randomness that will be available to them during the protocol and they cannot sample any fresh randomness after the leakage occurs. Throughout this work, we focus on non-interactive key-exchange (NIKE) protocols (e.g., in the style of Diffie-Hellman key exchange) where Alice and Bob each non-adaptively send one message as a function of their state.

Symmetric-Key Setting. We first study leakage-resilient NIKE in the symmetric-key setting, where Alice and Bob share a uniformly random secret sk. Each of them has some additional independent randomness r_A, r_B and their states are $\mathsf{state}_A = (\mathsf{sk}, r_A)$ and $\mathsf{state}_B = (\mathsf{sk}, r_B)$ respectively. The adversary Eve can get ℓ bits of leakage on each of state_A and state_B, and therefore the secret key sk is no longer fully secure from her point of view. Alice and Bob wish to run a protocol to derive a fresh key k that looks (nearly) uniformly random to Eve. We study this problem in the information-theoretic setting.

The above problem is similar to that of *privacy amplification* [6–8,27], where Alice and Bob have a weakly random shared secret and want to agree on a (nearly) uniform key. The crucial difference is that privacy amplification allows Alice and Bob to sample fresh randomness, whereas our problem does not. In particular, the privacy amplification problem can be easily solved using a (strong) seeded randomness extractor Ext: Alice chooses a fresh random seed r_A that she sends to Bob, and then both Alice and Bob set their key to be $k = \text{Ext}(\text{sk}; r_A)$. However, this solution does not work in our setting if we think of r_A as a part of Alice's state, since the adversary can then get leakage on k via leakage on $\text{state}_A = (\text{sk}, r_A)$.

Instead, we introduce a new primitive called a (strong) two-seed extractor where two seeds r_A, r_B are used to extract randomness $k = \text{Ext}(\text{sk}; r_A, r_B)$. We require that the extracted randomness looks uniform even to an adversary that gets partial leakage on each of the tuples (sk, r_A) and (sk, r_b) together with the seeds r_A, r_B. Such extractors do not seem to follow easily from standard (strong) seeded extractors or even two-source extractors. Instead, we construct two-seed extractors by drawing a new connection to communication-complexity lower bounds in the number-on-forehead model [4]. Using two-seed extractors, we can easily solve our problem by having Alice and Bob exchange the messages r_A, r_B respectively and having them agree on the new key $k = \text{Ext}(\text{sk}; r_A, r_B)$.

As our final result in this setting, we show that if Alice and Bob have a shared secret of length n, we get a scheme where the randomness r_A, r_B is of length $O(n)$, we tolerate a leakage bound of $\ell = \Omega(n)$, the exchanged key k is of length $\Omega(n)$, and the statistical distance from uniform is $\epsilon = 2^{-\Omega(n)}$. It remains an interesting open problem to optimize the constants in the scheme.

Public-Key Setting: A Negative Result. We next turn to studying leakage-resilient NIKE in the public-key setting, where the states of Alice and Bob consist of independent uniform randomness $\text{state}_A = r_A$ and $\text{state}_B = r_B$ with no shared key.

We begin by giving a black-box separation showing that such schemes cannot be proven secure via a black-box reduction under any "(single-stage) game-based assumption," when the leakage bound ℓ is super-logarithmic in the security parameter. Game-based assumptions are ones that can be expressed via a game between a (potentially inefficient) challenger and a stateful adversary, where any polynomial-time adversary should have at most a negligible advantage. In particular, this includes essentially all assumptions used in cryptography such as DDH and LWE, and even very strong assumptions such as the existence of indistinguishability obfuscation ($i\mathcal{O}$). Our results rule out black-box reductions that treat the adversary as well as the leakage-functions as a black box, which is the case for all known positive results in leakage-resilient cryptography we are aware of. Our separation closely follows the framework of [35], which gave similar separations for other leakage-resilient primitives (e.g., leakage-resilient injective one-way functions).

Pinpointing the above barrier allows us to look for ways to overcome it. We identify three avenues toward getting around the negative result, and follow them to get positive results.

Public-Key Setting: Small Leakage. The first and most obvious avenue is to consider small leakage, where ℓ is only logarithmic in the security parameter. Interestingly, some types of cryptosystems (e.g., one-way functions, signatures, public-key encryption, weak pseudorandom functions) are known to be automatically secure with small leakage while others (pseudorandom generators/functions, semantically secure symmetric-key encryption) are known not to be [16,32]. Where does leakage-resilient NIKE fit in? The work of [16] gave a partial characterization of primitives that are automatically secure, but it does not appear to capture NIKE directly. Instead, we adapt the techniques of [16] for our purposes and show that any NIKE protocol is automatically secure when the leakage ℓ is logarithmic. The result also extends to allowing larger leakage ℓ by assuming stronger (sub-exponential) security of the underlying NIKE.

As an example, this shows that the Diffie-Hellman key agreement is secure with small leakage: even if an adversary gets small leakage on r_A and r_B individually and then sees g^{r_A}, g^{r_B}, the exchanged key $g^{r_A r_B}$ is indistinguishable from uniform.

Public-Key Setting: CRS or Preprocessing. The other two avenues for overcoming the negative result require us to add some flexibility to our setting to make the black-box separation fail. We can consider schemes in the *common reference string (CRS)* model, where the honest parties as well as the adversary get access to a CRS generated from some specified distribution. Note that, in this setting, the leakage functions can depend on the CRS. Alternately, we can consider schemes with *preprocessing*, where Alice and Bob can individually preprocess their random coins to derive their secret states prior to leakage. In particular, instead of having the two states r_A, r_B consist of uniformly random coins, we allow $r_A \leftarrow \mathsf{Gen}(\rho_A), r_B \leftarrow \mathsf{Gen}(\rho_B)$ to be sampled from some specified distribution using uniformly random coins ρ_A, ρ_B. We assume the adversary only gets leakage on the secret states r_A, r_B but not on the underlying random coins ρ_A, ρ_B used to sample them.

We construct a leakage-resilient NIKE using bilinear maps, which simultaneously requires a CRS *and* preprocessing. It can flexibly tolerate any polynomial leakage bound ℓ with states of size $|r_A|, |r_B| = O(\ell)$. We prove security under either the subgroup decision assumption in composite-order bilinear groups or the decision-linear (DLIN) assumption in prime order groups. Interestingly, we rely on two-seed extractors, which solved the problem in the symmetric setting, as a crucial tool to aid our construction in the public-key setting.

We also give an alternate construction of leakage-resilient NIKE using indistinguishability obfuscation (i$\mathcal{O}$) and lossy functions, which can be initialized with either just a CRS (without preprocessing) *or* just preprocessing (without a CRS). It can flexibly tolerate any polynomial leakage ℓ with states of size $(2 + o(1))\ell$.

Other Related Work. Prior works have proposed constructions of leakage-resilient NIKE, albeit under a leak-free hardware assumption, which, in particular, gives both parties access to some (limited) leak-free randomness during the protocol execution [11,12]. These results do not address the central goal of our work, which is for two parties to non-interactively agree on a shared key without relying on any fresh randomness after the leakage occurs.

Organization. In Sect. 4, we define and construct leakage-resilient symmetric-key NIKE and two-seed extractors. In Sect. 5, we define leakage-resilient NIKE in the public-key setting. In Sect. 6, we give a black-box separation of leakage-resilient NIKE from any single-stage assumption. In Sect. 7, we build a leakage-resilient NIKE in the CRS model with preprocessing from bilinear maps over composite-order groups.

2   Technical Overview

2.1   Symmetric-Key NIKE

We first consider the problem of leakage-resilient NIKE in the *symmetric-key* setting, where Alice and Bob start with a secret sk, and want to agree on a fresh uniform key k. We assume they each have internal randomness r_A and r_B, respectively. Here we want security to hold even given the protocol transcript together with leakages on the states of both Alice and Bob, $\mathsf{state}_A = (\mathsf{sk}, r_A)$ and $\mathsf{state}_B = (\mathsf{sk}, r_B)$, prior to the protocol execution. We study this problem in the information-theoretic setting.

We remark that the particular case when the messages sent by Alice and Bob consist of their entire randomness r_A and r_B corresponds to a natural notion of randomness extractors that we name (strong) *two-seed extractors*. Namely, a (strong) two-seed extractor $\mathsf{Ext}(x; r_A, r_B)$ uses two seeds r_A, r_B to extract randomness from a high-entropy source x in a setting where the distinguisher gets leakages on (x, r_A) and (x, r_B), as well as the entire seeds r_A and r_B. Given such an extractor, Alice and Bob, sharing a secret key $x = \mathsf{sk}$ can send their individual randomness r_A and r_B respectively to each other and compute $k = \mathsf{Ext}(x; r_A, r_B)$ as the exchanged key. Leakage resilience of this symmetric-key NIKE exactly follows from the security of the two-seed extractor described above.

We initially suspected that there should be simple solutions to the two-seed extractor problem via standard (strong) seeded extractors and/or two-source extractors. For example, we thought of applying a 2-source extractor on (r_A, r_B) to derive a seed $s = \mathsf{2SourceExt}(r_A, r_B)$ and then plugging it into a strong seeded extractor to extract $k = \mathsf{SeededExt}(x; s)$. Our intuition was that the leakage would not be able to predict s and therefore could not leak any information on x that depends on s. However, we were unable to prove security of this candidate (or other simple variants). The problem is that, although the leakage cannot predict s, it can cause x to be correlated with s once r_A, r_B are made public. We leave it as an open problem to explore the possibility of this construction or some variant and either show it secure via a more complex argument or find counter-examples.

Instead, we construct two-seed extractors by leveraging a connection with communication complexity lower bounds in the number-on-forehead (NOF) model [4]. Such lower bounds were also recently used in the context of leakage-resilient secret sharing in [24]. At a high level, the NOF communication complexity of a boolean function $f : (x_1, \cdots, x_N) \to \{0, 1\}$ is the minimal transcript size required to predict f with noticeable probability, over protocols where every party can exactly see all the others parties' inputs (but not their own; imagine it is on their forehead), and where parties speak one at a time. A NOF lower bound says that no such communication protocol of transcript length ℓ is sufficient to predict the output of f on uniformly random inputs.

To see the connection with two-seed extractors, consider the case where $N = 3$ and think of $x_1 = x, x_2 = r_A, x_3 = r_B$. Then an NOF lower bound implies that small leakage on each of the tuples $(x, r_A), (x, r_B), (r_A, r_B)$ does not allow one to predict $\mathsf{Ext}(x; r_A, r_B) \stackrel{\text{def}}{=} f(x_1, x_2, x_2)$. However, in the setting of (strong) two-seed extractors, the adversary does not just get leakage on (r_A, r_B) but rather gets the entire values r_A, r_B in full. We show that security is preserved in the latter setting. At a high level, if a distinguisher succeeds in the latter setting given r_A, r_B in full, then we could also run that distinguisher as the leakage on (r_A, r_B) to distinguish in the former setting. This is not entirely accurate, since the distinguisher in the latter setting also expects to get the challenge value z which is either $z = \mathsf{Ext}(x; r_A, r_B)$ or z uniform, while leakage on (r_A, r_B) in the former setting cannot depend on z. However, we can remedy this by guessing z ahead of time and taking a statistical security loss proportional to the length of the extracted output.

Combining the above with explicit constructions of efficiently computable boolean functions f with high NOF communication complexity [4,13], we get two-seed extractors with $|x| = |r_A| = |r_B| = n$ that tolerate $\ell = \Omega(n)$ leakage and have security $2^{-\Omega(n)}$, but only extract 1 bit of output. We show a simple generic method to get output length $m = \Omega(n)$ by choosing m independent seeds $r_A = (r_A^1, \ldots, r_A^m), r_B = (r_B^1, \ldots, r_B^m)$ and outputting $\mathsf{Ext}(x; r_A^i, r_B^i)_{i=1}^m$. However, this leads to seed length $\Omega(n^2)$. We also give an alternate construction using the techniques of [14] that relies on the linearity of the underlying 1-bit extractor and allows us to extract $\Omega(n)$ bits while preserving the seed length.

2.2   A Black-Box Separation

In the public-key setting, we show that it is impossible to construct leakage-resilient NIKE with perfect correctness, and prove security via a black-box reduction from any *single-stage game assumption* (also called *cryptographic games* in [21,35]). An assumption is a single-stage game assumption if it can be written in the format of an interactive game between a (potentially inefficient) challenger and a single stateful adversary, where the challenger decides whether or not the adversary succeeded at the end of the game. The assumption states that no polynomial time adversary can succeed with better than negligible probability. (This is a more general class than *falsifiable assumptions* [18,29], where the challenger is also required to be efficient.) Such single-stage game assumptions capture essentially all standard assumptions used in cryptography, such as the hardness of DDH, Factoring or LWE, as well as less standard assumptions such as the security of indistinguishability obfuscation $i\mathcal{O}$.

However, the security definition for leakage-resilient NIKE (and most other leakage-resilient primitives) is *not* a single-stage game. This is because the adversary consists three separate components—the two leakage functions and the distinguisher—that cannot fully communicate together or keep arbitrary state between invocations. In particular, the distinguisher does not get to see the inputs given to the leakage functions as this would make its task trivial. It was already observed in [35] that this potentially allows us to separate some cases of leakage-resilient security from all single-stage game assumptions. However, it was only shown to hold for a few very select cases. For example, a black-box separation was given for leakage-resilient one-way permutations with sufficiently large leakage, but *not* for one-way functions; the latter can be easily constructed from any standard one-way function. Where does leakage-resilient NIKE fit in?

In this work, we use the framework of [35] to separate leakage-resilient NIKE from all single-stage game assumptions. In fact, our separation even rules out "unpredictable NIKE" where the adversary has to predict the entire exchanged key, rather than just distinguish it from uniform. The proof follows the "simulatable attacker paradigm". We construct an inefficient attacker $\mathcal{A}$ that breaks the security of the primitive using brute force. However, by constructing $\mathcal{A}$ carefully, we show that there also exists an efficient simulator $\mathcal{S}$ such that no (even inefficient) distinguisher can distinguish between black-box access to $\mathcal{A}$ versus $\mathcal{S}$. The attacker $\mathcal{A} = (\mathcal{A}.f_A, \mathcal{A}.f_B, \mathcal{A}.\mathsf{Pred})$ is a multi-stage attacker consisting of three separate entities which do not communicate or keep state between invocations: the two leakage functions $\mathcal{A}.f_A, \mathcal{A}.f_B$ and the predictor $\mathcal{A}.\mathsf{Pred}$ who predicts the exchanged key given the leakage and the protocol transcript. However, the simulator $\mathcal{S} = (\mathcal{S}.f_A, \mathcal{S}.f_B, \mathcal{S}.\mathsf{Pred})$ is a single fully stateful entity and can remember any inputs given to $\mathcal{S}.f_A, \mathcal{S}.f_B$ and use them to answer calls to $\mathcal{S}.\mathsf{Pred}$. Therefore, $\mathcal{S}$ is not a valid attacker on leakage-resilient NIKE. Nevertheless, if we had a black-box reduction from any single-stage assumption, then the reduction would have to break the assumption given black-box oracle access to $\mathcal{A}$. However, since the reduction and the assumption challenger together cannot distinguish between black-box access to $\mathcal{A}$ versus $\mathcal{S}$, the reduction would also break the assumption given the latter. But this means that the reduction together with $\mathcal{S}$ give a fully efficient attack against the assumption and therefore the assumption must be insecure to begin with!

The high level idea of how to construct $\mathcal{A}$ and $\mathcal{S}$ is simple. The leakage function $\mathcal{A}.f_A$ gets as input Alice's randomness r_A, computes the protocol message p_A that Alice will send as a function of r_A, and outputs a random ℓ-bit hash $\sigma_A = H(p_A)$ as the leakage. The leakage function $\mathcal{A}.f_B$ works analogously. The predictor $\mathcal{A}.\mathsf{Pred}(p_A, p_B, \sigma_A, \sigma_B)$ gets the protocol messages p_A, p_B and the leakages σ_A, σ_B: it checks if $\sigma_A = H(p_A)$ and $\sigma_B = H(p_B)$ and if this does not hold it outputs $\bot$; otherwise, it performs a brute-force search on p_A, p_B to recover the exchanged key k and outputs it. We think of H as a completely random function, which is part of the description of the inefficient attacker $\mathcal{A}$. The simulator $\mathcal{S}$ simulates the leakage queries to $\mathcal{S}.f_A, \mathcal{S}.f_B$ by keeping a table of the inputs r_A and r_B that were queried so far and simulating H by choosing its outputs randomly on the fly for each new corresponding p_A or p_B. It simulates the predictor $\mathcal{S}.\mathsf{Pred}(p_A, p_B, \sigma_A, \sigma_B)$ by checking its table to see if it contains some values r_A, r_B that yield protocol messages p_A, p_B and on which the leakage functions outputted σ_A, σ_B respectively; if so, it uses these values to efficiently recover the exchanged key k and else it outputs $\bot$. If the key exchange has perfect correctness, then the only way to to distinguish between oracle access to $\mathcal{A}$ versus $\mathcal{S}$ is to "guess" some valid value $\sigma_A = H(p_A)$ or $\sigma_B = H(p_B)$ without querying the leakage functions, and the probability of this happening is $2^{-\ell}$. Therefore, if ℓ is super-logarithmic, then $\mathcal{A}$ and $\mathcal{S}$ are indistinguishable with polynomially many queries except with negligible probability.

2.3   Circumventing the Black-Box Separation

Unfortunately, we are not aware of any useful non-black-box techniques in the context of leakage-resilient cryptography. Therefore, to circumvent the black-box separation, we consider two options. First, we consider the case of small leakage, where ℓ is logarithmic in the security parameter. Second, we consider extensions of the basic NIKE setting that are not covered by the negative result.

The Small Leakage Setting. Our black-box impossibility result holds whenever the size of the leakage is super-logarithmic in the security parameter. It also only applies to poly/negligible single-stage assumptions that require polynomial-time attackers to have negligible success probability, but does not extend to assuming stronger levels of security. We demonstrate that this dependence on leakage size is in fact "tight." In particular, we show that any NIKE that is secure in a setting without leakage is also automatically leakage-resilient when the leakage bound ℓ is logarithmic in the security parameter. This can be extended to leakage bound $\ell = \omega(\log \lambda)$ if the original NIKE has $\mathrm{poly}(2^\ell)$-security without leakage.

Similar results were previously known to hold for all *unpredictability* primitives (e.g., one-way functions, message-authentication codes, signatures, etc.), where the goal of the attacker is to win some game with non-negligible probability. In such cases, it is always possible to guess the small leakage and get a 2^ℓ loss in security. It is also known that similar positive results hold for some but not all *indistinguishability* primitives, where the goal of the attacker is to win some game with probability that is non-negligibly larger than $1/2$. In particular, it holds for public-key encryption, CPA-secure symmetric-key encryption, and weak pseudorandom functions, but it does not hold for pseudorandom generators, pseudorandom functions, or one-time semantically secure symmetric-key encryption; in all of the latter cases even 1 bit of leakage can completely break security (see [16,32]). The aforementioned positive results can be proven using techniques due to [5,16] showing that any indistinguishability primitive satisfying a so-called "square friendliness" property is resilient to small leakage. However, it is not a priori clear if these techniques apply to leakage-resilient NIKE.

To illustrate the difficulty, we briefly recall what it means for a generic (indistinguishability) primitive to be "square-friendly" in the sense of [16]. Take an arbitrary partition of the challenger's random coins $\mathrm{rand}_{\mathcal{C}}$ into $\mathrm{rand}_{\mathcal{C}} = (\mathrm{rand}_{\mathcal{C}}^{\mathrm{fix}}, \mathrm{rand}_{\mathcal{C}}^{\mathrm{exp}})$ (e.g. for CPA-secure symmetric-key encryption, $\mathrm{rand}_{\mathcal{C}}^{\mathrm{fix}}$ could be the randomness of the secret key while $\mathrm{rand}_{\mathcal{C}}^{\mathrm{exp}}$ could be the challenge bit and the encryption randomness for chosen plaintext queries). The following "square-security" game is then defined with respect to this partition: an attacker (for the original primitive) is asked to play the standard security game twice, where in the first run the challenger samples both $\mathrm{rand}_{\mathcal{C}}^{\mathrm{fix}}$ and $\mathrm{rand}_{\mathcal{C}}^{\mathrm{exp}}$ at random as in the standard game, but in the second run, the challenger re-uses the same $\mathrm{rand}_{\mathcal{C}}^{\mathrm{fix}}$ coins and re-samples fresh $\mathrm{rand}_{\mathcal{C}}^{\mathrm{exp}}$ coins. The attacker wins the square-security game only if it obtains the same result in both runs (win-win or lose-lose); square-security holds if any efficient attacker's can only win the square-security game with probability negligibly greater than its chance of losing. [16] refer to a primitive as "square-friendly" if standard security implies square security. As previously mentioned, [16] prove that any square-friendly primitive with $\mathrm{poly}(2^{\ell})$-security can withstand ℓ bits of leakage on $\mathrm{rand}_{\mathcal{C}}^{\mathrm{fix}}$.

In the NIKE setting, we would like to argue security even given leakage on r_A and r_B, where r_A and r_B and Alice and Bob's secret values. A naive attempt to invoke the [16] lemma might set $\mathrm{rand}_{\mathcal{C}}^{\mathrm{fix}} = (r_A, r_B)$, but then leakage-resilience/square-friendliness cannot possibly hold since even 1 bit of leakage on $\mathrm{rand}_{\mathcal{C}}^{\mathrm{fix}}$ completely breaks security (simply leak the first bit of the shared key).

Instead, we take the following two-step approach. We first consider an alternate partitioning of the challenger's randomness where $\mathrm{rand}_{\mathcal{C}}^{\mathrm{fix}} = r_A$, and r_B is now viewed as part of the experiment randomness $\mathrm{rand}_{\mathcal{C}}^{\mathrm{exp}}$. Under this partitioning, the NIKE security experiment is square-friendly, but now the [16] lemma only implies security given leakage on r_A alone.

To handle independent leakage on r_A and r_B, we consider yet another partitioning of the challenger's randomness. However, we start from a syntactically different NIKE security game—parameterized by leakage function f_A—in which the attacker is given leakage $f_A(r_A)$ on Alice's random coins in addition to Alice and Bob's public values. By our previous argument, security of the original NIKE scheme implies security of this modified primitive provided f_A has bounded-length outputs. Since we want to handle leakage on Bob's coins r_B, we partition the challenger's random coins so that $\mathrm{rand}_{\mathcal{C}}^{\mathrm{fix}} = r_B$, and r_A is now part of $\mathrm{rand}_{\mathcal{C}}^{\mathrm{exp}}$. We prove that this is indeed square-friendly, so by [16], security holds with independent leakage on r_A and r_B.

Adding Setups: CRS or Preprocessing. On an intuitive level, our black-box separation result went through because, when everything can leak, there is no meaningful place for a reduction to embed its challenge. We consider two settings with some additional setup that allows us to overcome the black-box separation, precisely by creating a place for the reduction to meaningfully embed a challenge.

The first such setting considers a NIKE scheme with a *common reference string (CRS)*. We assume that the CRS is generated using some potentially secret, leak-free coins. The second setting considers NIKE where users *preprocess* their individual random coins to derive their secret state. In particular, instead of having the two secret states r_A, r_B consist of the uniformly random coins of Alice and Bob, we allow Alice and Bob to sample their internal secret states from some specified (secret coin) distribution by running $r_A \leftarrow \mathsf{Gen}(\rho_A)$, $r_B \leftarrow \mathsf{Gen}(\rho_B)$ on their secret random coins ρ_A, ρ_B respectively. The secret coins ρ_A, ρ_B are discarded afterwards, and Alice and Bob can run the NIKE protocol using only their preprocessed states r_A, r_B. We assume the adversary only gets leakage on the preprocessed states r_A, r_B but not on the underlying random coins ρ_A, ρ_B used to sample them. The above two settings give the reduction an opportunity to embed its challenge in either the CRS or in the states r_A, r_B without having to explain the underlying randomness.

Construction from Bilinear Maps. We first begin by constructing leakage-resilient NIKE in a model with *both* a CRS *and* preprocessing. We give two constructions. A simpler one under the subgroup decision assumption on composite-order groups with a bilinear map, and a slightly more complex one under the decision-linear assumption (DLIN) in prime-order groups with a bilinear map. We give a high-level overview of the first result.

The idea is inspired by "dual-system encryption" [25, 26, 34, ...]. In a nutshell, dual-system encryption allows us to switch regular ciphertexts and secret keys to so-called semi-functional counterparts, which individually look legitimate, but when "paired" together result in some randomness that is not dictated by the public key. In our case, we will switch the two states r_A, r_B to be semi-functional so that when Alice and Bob run the NIKE with these values, the exchanged key k has true entropy even given the corresponding protocol messages p_A, p_B. To convert such a key into a uniformly random one, we additionally apply a two-seed extractor on it, where Alice and Bob each supply one seed.

In more detail, our construction uses a source group G which is a cyclic of composite order $N = p_1 p_2$, so that it can be decomposed using the Chinese Remainder Theorem into $G \simeq G_{p_1} \times G_{p_2}$, where G_{p_1} and G_{p_2} are cyclic of prime order p_1 and p_2 respectively. In our construction, everything happens in the subgroup G_{p_1}. The CRS consists of two elements $g \leftarrow G_{p_1}, h = g^x \in G_{p_1}$ where $x \leftarrow \mathbb{Z}_N$. The secret states of Alice and Bob are pairs of group elements $r_A = (g^a, h^a), r_B = (g^b, h^b) \in G_{p_1}^2$ where $a, b \leftarrow \mathbb{Z}_N$. The key exchange protocol consists of Alice sending $p_A = g^a$ and Bob sending $p_B = g^b$. The exchanged key is set to $k = e(g, h)^{ab}$ which can be computed by Alice as $e(p_B, h^a)$ and by Bob as $e(p_A, h^b)$. Note that, both the CRS and secret states of Alice and Bob in the above construction, are sampled from some distributions using secret coins (namely the group G, and the exponents x, a and b) that we assume do not leak.

To argue leakage-resilience, we switch the secret states r_A, r_B to being sampled from the whole group G rather than the subgroup G_{p_1}. Namely, the whole execution of the NIKE is indistinguishable from sampling $x \leftarrow \mathbb{Z}_N$, $u \leftarrow G$, $v = u^x \in G$, and setting $r_A = (u^a, v^a)$ and $r_B = (u^b, v^b)$, while still keeping the CRS elements $g \leftarrow G_{p_1}$ and $h = g^x \in G_{p_1}$ in the subgroup. Indistinguishability follows from a standard subgroup decision assumption, even if the adversary gets to see the entire secret states r_A, r_B in full.

With the above change, even if an adversary sees the CRS $(g, h = g^x)$ and the protocol transcript $(p_A = u^a, p_B = u^b)$, the value of $x \bmod p_2$ is uniformly random since $h = g^x$ only reveals $x \bmod p_1$. Therefore the exchanged key $k = e(u^b, v^a) = e(u^a, v^b) = e(u, v)^{ab} = e(u, u)^{xab}$ also has $\log p_2$ bits of entropy conditioned on the above. This means that given ℓ bits of leakage on each of r_A, r_B, the exchanged key k has $\log p_2 - 2\ell$ bits of entropy. As mentioned previously, we can upgrade this to a scheme where the exchanged key is indistinguishable from uniform under leakage, by adding the two seeds of a two-seed extractor to the states of Alice and Bob respectively, and having them exchange these seeds during the protocol and use them to extract randomness from k as their final exchanged key.

To allow for a larger leakage bound ℓ, we can either choose a larger prime p_2, or we can execute many copies of this protocol in parallel. Overall, the scheme can flexibly tolerate any polynomial leakage bound ℓ while keeping the size of Alice's and Bob's secret states bounded by $O(\ell)$.

Constructions from Indistinguishability Obfuscation. We also give a construction from *indistinguishability obfuscation* ($i\mathcal{O}$) and lossy functions (which can be instantiated from either DDH or LWE [31]). This construction can be initialized with either just a CRS (without preprocessing) *or* just preprocessing (without a CRS). Let us start with the CRS version of the scheme. The idea starts with the construction of (multiparty) NIKE from $i\mathcal{O}$ due to Boneh and Zhandry [10]. Each party has randomness r and sets its protocol message to $p = G(r)$ where G is some function that we specify later. The CRS includes an obfuscated program that has a hard-coded PRF F: it takes as input two protocol messages p_A, p_B and r, and checks that either $p_A = G(r)$ or $p_B = G(r)$; if so it outputs an evaluation of the PRF $F(p_A, p_B)$ and else it outputs $\perp$. It is easy to see that this gives correctness.

To argue security, we will set G to be a function whose description is a part of the CRS and can be indistinguishably created in either lossy or injective mode. We puncture the PRF F on the point (p_A, p_B) and program a random output k. But instead of hard-coding k directly, we hard-code $k \oplus r_A$ and $k \oplus r_B$; i.e., two one-time pad encryptions of k under r_A and r_B respectively. This allows the obfuscated program to decrypt k given either r_A or r_B and so preserves correctness. But now we can switch G to lossy mode and argue that even given the obfuscated program with the hard-coded ciphertexts, the protocol transcript, and the leakages on r_A, r_B, the exchanged key k has high entropy. We can then convert this into a uniformly random exchanged key by additionally applying a two-seed extractor on top. (Our actual construction does something slightly more complicated to avoid two-seed extractors and gets better parameters via standard seeded extractors.)

The above can also be converted into a scheme with preprocessing and without a CRS. In this case, Alice creates the obfuscated program as part of the preprocessed state and sends it as her protocol message. Furthermore, instead of putting the description of G in the CRS, we will have each of Alice and Bob sample different functions G_1, G_2 that they send as part of their messages and are used as inputs to the obfuscated program; the obfuscated program also adds them to the input on which it evaluates the PRF $F(G_1, G_2, p_A, p_B)$.

3   Preliminaries

Basic Notation. For an integer N, we let $[N] := \{1, 2, \dots, N\}$. For a set S we let $x \leftarrow S$ denote sampling x uniformly at random from S. For a distribution $\mathcal{D}$ we let $x \leftarrow \mathcal{D}$ denote sampling x according to the distribution. We will denote the security parameter by λ. We say a function $f(\lambda)$ is negligible, denoted $f(\lambda) = \text{negl}(\lambda)$, if $f(\lambda) = O(\lambda^{-c})$ for every constant $c > 0$. A function is $f(\lambda)$ is polynomial, denoted $f(\lambda) = \text{poly}(\lambda)$, if $f(\lambda) = O(\lambda^c)$ for some constant $c > 0$.

Information Theory. For two random variables X, Y with support $\text{supp}(X)$ and $\text{supp}(Y)$ respectively, we define their statistical distance $\mathbf{SD}(X, Y)$ as

$$\mathbf{SD}(X, Y) := \sum_{u \in \text{supp}(X) \cup \text{supp}(Y)} \frac{1}{2} | \Pr[X = u] - \Pr[Y = u]|.$$

For two random variables X, Y with statistical distance $\mathbf{SD}(X, Y) \leq \epsilon$, we will sometimes use the shorthand $X \approx_\epsilon Y$.

Two ensembles of random variables $X = \{X_\lambda\}_\lambda, Y = \{Y_\lambda\}_\lambda$ are statistically close if $\mathbf{SD}(X_\lambda, Y_\lambda) = \text{negl}(\lambda)$. We will occasionally denote this as $X \approx_S Y$.

The min-entropy $\mathbf{H}_\infty(X)$ of a random variable X is defined as

$$\mathbf{H}_\infty(X) := -\log(\max_{x \in \text{supp}(X)} Pr[X = x]).$$

A random variable X with min-entropy k is referred to as a k-source. When X is supported over $\{0, 1\}^n$, we refer to it as an (n, k)-source. We denote the uniform distribution over $\{0, 1\}^n$ by U_n.

Definition 1 (Strong Seeded Extractors). *An efficient function* Ext $:$ $\{0, 1\}^n \times \{0, 1\}^d \to \{0, 1\}^\ell$ *is a strong (k, ϵ)-extractor if for every (n, k)-source X,*

$$\mathbf{SD}((U_d, \text{Ext}(X, U_d)), (U_d, U_m)) \leq \epsilon.$$

3.1   Background on Bilinear Maps

We review some definitions pertaining to bilinear maps, adapted from [26].

Composite-Order Bilinear Groups. Let $\mathcal{G}(1^\lambda)$ be a group generator, which outputs the description of a pairing-friendly group $\mathbb{G} = (G, G_T, N = p_1 p_2, e)$, where G and G_T are cyclic groups of order N, and p_1, p_2 are distinct primes of bit-size $\Omega(\lambda)$, and $e : G \times G \to G_T$ is an efficiently computable bilinear map, that satisfies:

1. (Bilinearity) $\forall g, h \in G$, $\forall a, b \in \mathbb{Z}_N$, we have:

$$e(g^a, h^b) = e(g, h)^{ab}.$$

2. (Non-degeneracy): There exists $g \in G$ such that $e(g, g) \in G_T$ has order N.

We will assume that the descriptions of G and G_T include respective generators. We also assume that the random coins of $\mathcal{G}$ reveal the factorization $N = p_1 p_2$.[1] We will denote by G_{p_1} and G_{p_2} the subgroups of G of order p_1 and p_2, respectively. Observe that any $g \in G_{p_1}$ and any $h \in G_{p_2}$ are "orthogonal" with respect to e, i.e. $e(g, h)$ is the identity element in G_T.

Assumption 1. Let $\mathcal{G}(1^\lambda)$ be a group generator. We define the following distributions:

$$\mathbb{G} = (G, G_T, N = p_1 p_2, e) \leftarrow \mathcal{G}, g \leftarrow G_{p_1}, T_1 \leftarrow G_{p_1}, T_{1,2} \leftarrow G.$$

We say that $\mathcal{G}$ satisfies Assumption 1 if for all PPT adversaries $\mathcal{A}$:

$$\big| \Pr[\mathcal{A}(\mathbb{G}, g, T_1) = 1] - \Pr[\mathcal{A}(\mathbb{G}, g, T_{1,2}) = 1] \big| \leq \mathsf{negl}(\lambda).$$

4   Leakage-Resilient NIKE in the Symmetric-Key Setting

4.1   Definitions

We first define leakage-resilient NIKE in the symmetric setting, where both parties share a common secret key with sufficiently high min-entropy.

Definition 2 (Symmetric-Key Leakage-Resilient NIKE). *A symmetric-key NIKE protocol* sk-NIKE *with secret key space* $\mathcal{SK}$, *private state space* $\mathcal{R}$, *public message space* $\mathcal{P}$ *and output key space* $\mathcal{K}$ *consists of the algorithms:*

- Publish(sk, r) *is a deterministic algorithm which takes as input a secret key* sk $\in \mathcal{SK}$, *a private state* $r \in \mathcal{R}$ *and outputs a public message* $p \in \mathcal{P}$.
- SharedKey(sk, r, p) *takes as input a secret key* sk $\in \mathcal{SK}$, *a private state* $r \in \mathcal{R}$ *and a public message* $p \in \mathcal{P}$, *and outputs a key* $K \in \mathcal{K}$.

We require sk-NIKE to satisfy the following properties.

---

[1] More generally, the ability to sample uniformly from G_{p_1} given the random coins of $\mathcal{G}$ would suffice for our purposes.

Perfect Correctness. An sk-NIKE = (Publish, SharedKey) protocol is perfectly correct if for all secret keys sk $\in \mathcal{SK}$ and all private states $r_A, r_B \in \mathcal{R}$:

$$\mathsf{SharedKey}(\mathsf{sk}, r_A, p_B) = \mathsf{SharedKey}(\mathsf{sk}, r_B, p_A),$$

where $p_A = \mathsf{Publish}(\mathsf{sk}, r_A)$ and $p_B = \mathsf{Publish}(\mathsf{sk}, r_B)$.

Information-Theoretic Leakage Resilience. We say that a symmetric-key NIKE protocol is (k, ℓ, ϵ)-secure if for any distribution $\mathcal{L}$ such that $H_\infty(\mathcal{L}) \geq k$ and all (potentially inefficiently computable) functions $f_A, f_B : \mathcal{SK} \times \mathcal{R} \to \{0,1\}^\ell$, we have:

$$(p_A, p_B, f_A(\mathsf{sk}, r_A), f_B(\mathsf{sk}, r_B), K_0) \approx_\epsilon (p_A, p_B, f_A(\mathsf{sk}, r_A), f_B(\mathsf{sk}, r_B), K_1),$$

where sk $\leftarrow \mathcal{L}$, $r_A, r_B \leftarrow \mathcal{R}$, $p_A = \mathsf{Publish}(\mathsf{sk}, r_A)$, $p_B = \mathsf{Publish}(\mathsf{sk}, r_B)$, $K_0 = \mathsf{SharedKey}(\mathsf{sk}, p_A, r_B)$, and $K_1 \leftarrow \mathcal{K}$.

Definition 3 (Leakage Rate). *For a (k, ℓ, ϵ)-secure symmetric-key NIKE, we define its leakage rate as*

$$\frac{\ell}{\max_{r \in \mathcal{R}} |r|}.$$

4.2   Two-Seed Extractors

We consider a new type of extractor called a *two-seed extractor* which suffices to construct leakage-resilient symmetric-key NIKE.

Definition 4 (Two-Seed Extractors). *A $(k, 2\ell)$-two-seed extractor* Ext $(X; R, S) : \{0,1\}^n \times \{0,1\}^{d_1} \times \{0,1\}^{d_2} \to \{0,1\}^m$ *with error ϵ is an efficient function such that for all (potentially inefficient) leakage functions $f : \{0,1\}^n \times \{0,1\}^{d_1} \to \{0,1\}^a$, $g : \{0,1\}^n \times \{0,1\}^{d_2} \to \{0,1\}^b$ with $a + b = 2\ell$, and any (n, k)-source X, we have:*

$$\big(\mathsf{Ext}(X; R, S), R, S, f(X, R), g(X, S)\big) \approx_\epsilon \big(U_m, R, S, f(X, R), g(X, S)\big),$$

where R, S are independent uniform random bits of length d_1 and d_2 respectively.

Remark 1. Our definition of a two-seed extractor corresponds to *strong* two-seed extractors in the sense that the output is close to uniform even given the two seeds R and S. For simplicity, when we say a two-seed extractor in this paper, we always mean a *strong* two-seed extractor. Without the "strong" condition, a two-seed extractor is implied by any two source extractor on R and S.

Remark 2. For all applications in this paper, we only need two-seed extractors for full entropy $k = n$. However such a construction also trivially implies a two-seed extractor for min-entropy k where the error becomes $2^{n-k}\epsilon$.

Claim 2. *Any $(k, 2\ell)$-two-seed extractor* Ext *with error ϵ induces a symmetric-key NIKE that is (k, ℓ, ϵ)-secure.*

Proof. Let Ext be a $(k, 2\ell)$-two-seed extractor Ext : $\{0,1\}^n \times \{0,1\}^{d_1} \times \{0,1\}^{d_2}$ $\rightarrow \{0,1\}^m$ with leakage size 2ℓ and error ϵ. We can construct an sk-NIKE as follows. Let the secret key space $\mathcal{SK}$ be $\{0,1\}^n$, let both the private state space $\mathcal{R}$ and the public message space $\mathcal{P}$ be $\{0,1\}^{\min(d_1,d_2)}$, and let the key space $\mathcal{K}$ be $\{0,1\}^m$. Suppose without loss of generality that $d_1 \geq d_2$. Define Publish$(\mathsf{sk}, r) = r \in \{0,1\}^{d_2}$ and SharedKey$(\mathsf{sk}, r, p) = \mathsf{Ext}(\mathsf{sk}, (r\|0^{d_1-d_2}), p)$. Then any (potentially unbounded) distinguisher for sk-NIKE is a distinguisher for Ext with the same advantage ϵ. $\qquad\square$

4.3   Construction

We show how to construct two-seed extractors from what we call BCP extractors, which are first studied implicitly in [4] and then explicitly defined in [24].[2] Looking ahead, we will build both two-seed extractors and symmetric-key NIKE that satisfy slightly stronger security definitions than standard leakage-resilience (Definition 6 and Definition 7).

We first recall the definition of a *bounded collusion protocol*, following [24].

Definition 5 (Bounded Collusion Protocol (BCP) [24]). *An (interactive, potentially randomized) communication protocol π among N parties is called a (p, N, μ)-bounded collusion protocol (BCP) if:*

- *the N parties start the protocol with input $X_1, \ldots, X_N$, and the transcript τ is empty at the beginning of the protocol;*
- *there is a function Next$(\tau) \rightarrow S$ takes as input a (partial) transcript τ, and outputs either a set $S \subset [N]$ with $|S| \leq p$ along with a function g, or $\perp$;*
- *at each round with current transcript τ, the protocol computes Next(τ). If Next$(\tau) = (S, f)$, the message $g(\{X_i\}_{i \in S})$ is appended to the current transcript τ; otherwise the protocol stops and outputs τ as the final transcript.*
- *the final transcript τ has size at most μ.*

We say that a (p, N, μ)-BCP π ϵ-computes a (deterministic) boolean function $f : (X_1, \ldots, X_N) \rightarrow b \in \{0,1\}$ if there exists a (potentially unbounded) predictor $\mathcal{P}$, given a BCP transcript τ of π, that computes b with probability $1/2 + \epsilon$ (over the randomness of $\{X_i\}_i, \pi$ and $\mathcal{P}$).

In this section, we will actually build a two-seed extractor with a stronger security property than Definition 4; namely, it remains secure against leakages computed as 3-party BCP transcripts over inputs X, R, S. This results in a symmetric-key NIKE that is secure against the same type of leakage, by directly adapting Claim 2.

Definition 6 (Two-Seed Extractors with BCP Leakage Resilience). *A $(k, 2\ell)$-two-seed extractor Ext$(X; R, S) : \{0,1\}^n \times \{0,1\}^{d_1} \times \{0,1\}^{d_2} \rightarrow \{0,1\}^m$ with error ϵ is an efficient function such that for all $(1, 2, 2\ell)$-BCP protocol π :*

---

[2] In [24], these are referred to as "extractors for cylinder-intersection sources".

$(\{0,1\}^n \times \{0,1\}^{d_1}) \times (\{0,1\}^n \times \{0,1\}^{d_2} \to \{0,1\}^{2\ell}$ and any (n,k)-source X, we have:

$$\left(\mathsf{Ext}(X;R,S), R, S, \pi((X,R),(X,S))\right) \approx_\epsilon \left(U_m, R, S, \pi((X,R),(X,S))\right),$$

where R, S are independent uniform random bits of length d_1 and d_2 respectively.

Definition 7 (Symmetric-Key NIKE with BCP Leakage Resilience).
We say that a symmetric-key NIKE sk-NIKE = (Publish, SharedKey) is (k, ℓ, ϵ)-secure against interactive leakages if for any distribution $\mathcal{L}$ such that $H_\infty(\mathcal{L}) \geq k$ all $(1, 2, 2\ell)$-BCP protocol $\pi((\mathsf{sk}, r_A), (\mathsf{sk}, r_B))$ (Definition 5), we have:

$$(p_A, p_B, \pi((\mathsf{sk}, r_A), (\mathsf{sk}, r_B)), K_0) \approx_\epsilon (p_A, p_B, \pi((\mathsf{sk}, r_A), (\mathsf{sk}, r_B)), K_1),$$

where $\mathsf{sk} \leftarrow \mathcal{L}$, $r_A, r_B \leftarrow \mathcal{R}$, $p_A = \mathsf{Publish}(\mathsf{sk}, r_A)$, $p_B = \mathsf{Publish}(\mathsf{sk}, r_B)$, $K_0 = \mathsf{SharedKey}(\mathsf{sk}, p_A, r_B)$, and $K_1 \leftarrow \mathcal{K}$.

Definition 8 (BCP Extractor). Let $X_1, \cdots, X_N$ be N independent (n,k)-sources. Let π be a (possibly randomized) (p, N, μ)-BCP and $\pi(X_1, \cdots, X_N)$ be the transcript. A deterministic function $\mathsf{Ext} : (\{0,1\}^n)^N \to \{0,1\}^m$ is an (n, k, p, N, μ)-BCP extractor with error ϵ if

$$(\mathsf{Ext}(X_1, \cdots, X_N), \pi(X_1, \cdots, X_N)) \approx_\epsilon (U_m, \pi(X_1, \cdots, X_N)).$$

Definition 9. The ϵ-distributional communication complexity of a Boolean function $f : (\{0,1\}^n)^N \to \{0,1\}$, $C_\epsilon(f)$ in a (p, N) bounded collusion model, is the minimum number μ of any (p, N, μ)-BCP that ϵ-computes f.

Using the standard argument that unpredictability is the same as indistinguishability for any 1-bit random variable, we have the following theorem.

Theorem 3. A Boolean function $f : (\{0,1\}^n)^N \to \{0,1\}$ with $C_\epsilon(f) \geq \mu + 1$ gives an (n, n, p, N, μ)-BCP extractor with error ϵ, and vice versa.

Next we show that any $(n, k, p, N, \mu + 1)$-BCP extractor with sufficiently small error must be strong in any subset of p sources if the transcript size is at most μ.

Theorem 4. Suppose $\mathsf{Ext} : (\{0,1\}^n)^N \to \{0,1\}^m$ is an $(n, k, p, N, \mu + 1)$-BCP extractor with error ϵ. Then for any (p, N, μ)-BCP transcript $\pi(X_1, \cdots, X_N)$ and any subset $S \subset [N]$ with $|S| = p$, we have

$$(\mathsf{Ext}(X_1, \cdots, X_N), \pi(X_1, \cdots, X_N), X_S) \approx_{2^m \cdot \epsilon} (U_m, \pi(X_1, \cdots, X_N), X_S),$$

where $X_S = \{X_i, i \in S\}$.

Proof. Assume that there exists a set $S \subset [N]$, a transcript $\pi(X_1, \cdots, X_N)$ of a (p, N, μ)-BCP, and a distinguisher D such that

$$\begin{aligned} \big| &\Pr[D(\mathsf{Ext}(X_1, \cdots, X_N), \pi(X_1, \cdots, X_N), X_S) = 1] \\ &- \Pr[D(U_m, \pi(X_1, \cdots, X_N), X_S) = 1] \big| = \epsilon'. \end{aligned}$$

Let V be a uniformly random m-bit string, and consider the following $(p, N, \mu + 1)$-BCP where the transcript is $(\pi(X_1, \cdots, X_N), D(V, \pi(X_1, \cdots, X_N), X_S))$. Now define another distinguisher T_V as follows. Given input

$$(W, \pi(X_1, \cdots, X_N), D(V, \pi(X_1, \cdots, X_N), X_S)),$$

T_V outputs $D(V, \pi(X_1, \cdots, X_N), X_S)$ if $W = V$ and outputs a uniformly random bit otherwise. We have

$$\big| \Pr[T_V(\mathsf{Ext}(X_1, \cdots, X_N), \pi(X_1, \cdots, X_N), D(V, \pi(X_1, \cdots, X_N), X_S)) = 1]$$
$$- \Pr[T_V(U_m, \pi(X_1, \cdots, X_N), D(V, \pi(X_1, \cdots, X_N), X_S)) = 1] \big|$$
$$= \big| 2^{-m} (\Pr[D(\mathsf{Ext}(X_1, \cdots, X_N), \pi(X_1, \cdots, X_N), X_s) = 1]$$
$$- \Pr[D(U_m, \pi(X_1, \cdots, X_N), X_S) = 1]) \big|$$
$$= 2^{-m} \epsilon'$$

However, note that the new protocol is a $(p, N, \mu + 1)$-BCP, thus we have $2^{-m} \epsilon' \leq \epsilon$. This means that $\epsilon' \leq 2^m \cdot \epsilon$. $\qquad\square$

In the case of $p = N-1$, BCP extractors with one bit of output are equivalent to hard functions in the number-on-forehead (NOF) communication model. The communication in the NOF model is exactly an $(N - 1, N, \mu)$-BCP, and thus we can use the results in [4] on hard functions in the NOF model. Specifically, [4] showed two explicit functions that are hard in the NOF model.

Generalized Inner Product (GIP): $\mathsf{GIP}_{N,n} : (\{0,1\}^n)^N \to \{0,1\}$ is defined as $\mathsf{GIP}_{N,n}(x_1, \cdots, x_N) = 1$ iff the number of positions where all the x_i's have 1 is odd.

Quadratic Residue (QR) $\mathsf{QR}_{N,n} : (\{0,1\}^n)^N \to \{0,1\}$ is defined as $\mathsf{QR}_{N,n}(x_1, \cdots, x_N) = 1$ iff $\sum_{i=1}^{N} x_i$ is a quadratic residue mod p.

Theorem 5. *In the NOF model with N parties, we have*

1. *[4] For any n-bit long prime number p, $C_\epsilon(\mathsf{QR}) = \Omega(\frac{n}{2^N} + \log \epsilon)$.*
2. *[13] $C_\epsilon(\mathsf{GIP}) = \Omega(\frac{n}{2^N} + \log \epsilon)$.*

Using this theorem together with Theorem 3, we obtain explicit, efficient BCP extractors, which are also two-seed extractors by Theorem 4 with $N = 3$:

Theorem 6. *There exist explicit constructions of (n, ℓ)-two-seed extractors $\mathsf{Ext} : \{0,1\}^n \times \{0,1\}^n \times \{0,1\}^n \to \{0,1\}$, with leakage size $\ell = \Omega(n)$ and error $\epsilon = 2^{-\Omega(n)}$.*

We would like to get more output bits. Below we show two different methods to achieve this. The first method is quite general and applies to any two-seed extractor, while the second method achieves better seed length but only applied to the GIP extractor.

Construction 1: Take any two-seed extractor Ext which outputs one bit, choose m independent copies of seeds $(R_1, \cdots R_m)$ and another independent copy of seed S. Compute $Z_i = \text{Ext}(X, R_i, S)$ for each i. The final output is $Z = (Z_1, \cdots, Z_m)$.

We have the following lemma.

Lemma 1. *If* Ext *is a $(k, \ell + m)$-two-seed extractor with error ϵ, then Construction 1 gives a (k, ℓ)-two-seed extractor with error $m\epsilon$.*

Proof. Let $R = (R_1, \cdots, R_m)$. Let the leakage be $L_1 = f(X, R)$ and $L_2 = g(X, S)$. Define $Z_{-i} = (Z_1, \cdots, Z_{i-1}, Z_{i+1}, \cdots, Z_m)$. We show that for any i,

$$(Z_i, Z_{-i}, L_1, L_2, R, S) \approx_\epsilon (U_1, Z_{-i}, L_1, L_2, R, S).$$

To see this, first fix all the R_j's except R_i. Note that after this fixing, (R_i, S) are still independent and uniform. Further note that conditioned on this fixing, L_1 becomes a deterministic function of X and R_i, while L_2 is a deterministic function of X and S. Now Z_{-i} can be viewed as an extra deterministic leakage from (X, S) with size $m - 1$ and therefore the total size of leakage is at most $m + \ell$.

Thus we have

$$(Z_i, Z_{-i}, L_1, L_2, R, S) \approx_\epsilon (U_1, Z_{-i}, L_1, L_2, R, S).$$

Now a standard hybrid argument implies that

$$(Z, L_1, L_2, R, S) \approx_{m\epsilon} (U_m, L_1, L_2, R, S). \qquad \square$$

This gives the following theorem.

Theorem 7. *There exist explicit constructions of (n, ℓ)-two-seed extractors* Ext $:$ $\{0,1\}^n \times \{0,1\}^{mn} \times \{0,1\}^n \to \{0,1\}^m$ *with leakage size $\ell = \Omega(n)$, error $\epsilon = 2^{-\Omega(n)}$ and output length $m = \Omega(n)$. One seed has length mn and the other has length n.*

Next we show a construction that uses smaller seed length. First we recall the following lemma from [14].

Lemma 2. *[14] For any number n, there exists an explicit construction of n matrices $A_1, \cdots, A_n$, where each A_i is an $n \times n$ matrix over $\mathbb{F}_2$, such that for any $S \subseteq [n]$ with $S \neq \emptyset$, we have that $\sum_{i \in S} A_i$ has full rank.*

We can now describe our second construction.

Construction 2: Let Ext be the two-seed extractor constructed from $\text{GIP}_{3,n}$. For some $m < n$, let $A_1, \cdots, A_m$ be the first m matrices from Lemma 2. Let the seed be $(R, S) \in \mathbb{F}_2^n$. For each $i \in [m]$ compute $Z_i = \text{Ext}(X, A_i R, S)$ and let $Z = (Z_1, \cdots, Z_m)$.

To analyze the lemma we will use a standard XOR lemma.

Lemma 3. *[19] For any m-bit random variable T, we have:*

$$\mathbf{SD}(T, U_m) \leq \sqrt{\sum_{0^m \neq a \in \{0,1\}^m} \mathbf{SD}(T \cdot a, U_1)^2},$$

where $T \cdot a$ denotes the inner product of T and a over $\mathbb{F}_2$.

We have the following lemma.

Lemma 4. *Construction 2 gives an (n, ℓ)-two-seed extractor with leakage size $\ell = \Omega(n)$ and error $\epsilon = 2^{m-\Omega(n)}$.*

Proof. Let the leakage be $L_1 = f(X, R)$ and $L_2 = g(X, S)$. For any $a \in \{0,1\}^m$ with $a \neq 0^m$, let $S_a \subseteq [m]$ denote the set of indices of a where the corresponding bit is 1. Then $S_a \neq \emptyset$. Observe that

$$Z \cdot a = \mathsf{GIP}(X, \sum_{i \in S_a} A_i R, S) = \mathsf{GIP}(X, (\sum_{i \in S_a} A_i)R, S).$$

Since $\sum_{i \in S_a} A_i$ has full rank, $(\sum_{i \in S_a} A_i)R$ is uniform in $\mathbb{F}_2^n$. Thus we have

$$(Z \cdot a, L_1, L_2, R, S) \approx_\epsilon (U_1, L_1, L_2, R, S),$$

where $\epsilon = 2^{-\Omega(n)}$. By Markov's inequality, with probability $1 - \sqrt{\epsilon}$ over the fixing of (L_1, L_2, R, S), we have that $Z \cdot a$ is $\sqrt{\epsilon}$-close to uniform. By a union bound, with probability $1 - 2^m \sqrt{\epsilon}$ over the fixing of (L_1, L_2, R, S), we have that for all $a \in \{0,1\}^m$ with $a \neq 0^m$, $Z \cdot a$ is $\sqrt{\epsilon}$-close to uniform. When this happens, by Lemma 3 we have that

$$|Z - U_m| \leq 2^{m/2}\sqrt{\epsilon}.$$

Thus overall we have that

$$(Z, L_1, L_2, R, S) \approx_{\epsilon'} (U_m, L_1, L_2, R, S),$$

where $\epsilon' \leq 2^m \sqrt{\epsilon} + 2^{m/2}\sqrt{\epsilon} = 2^{m-\Omega(n)}$. $\qquad\square$

This yields the following theorem.

Theorem 8. *There exist explicit constructions of (n, ℓ)-two-seed extractors $\mathsf{Ext} : \{0,1\}^n \times \{0,1\}^n \times \{0,1\}^n \to \{0,1\}^m$ with leakage size $\ell = \Omega(n)$, error $\epsilon = 2^{-\Omega(n)}$ and output length $m = \Omega(n)$. Each seed has length n.*

5 Definitions for Leakage-Resilient NIKE in the Public-Key Setting

We define NIKE in the public-key setting.

Definition 10 (Non-Interactive Key Exchange). *A Non-Interactive Key Exchange* NIKE *over parameter space* $\mathcal{C}$, *state space* $\mathcal{R}$, *public message space* $\mathcal{P}$ *and key space* $\mathcal{K}$ *consists of the following efficient algorithms:*

- Setup(1^λ) *is a randomized algorithm that takes as input the security parameter* 1^λ *and outputs public parameters* params $\in \mathcal{C}$.
- Gen(params) *is a randomized algorithm that takes as input public parameters* params $\in \mathcal{C}$ *and outputs a state* $r \in \mathcal{R}$.
- Publish(params, r) *is a deterministic algorithm that takes as input public parameters* params $\in \mathcal{C}$ *and a state* $r \in \mathcal{R}$ *and outputs a public message* $p \in \mathcal{P}$.
- SharedKey(params, r, p) *is a deterministic algorithm that takes as input public parameters* params $\in \mathcal{C}$, *a state* $r \in \mathcal{R}$ *and a public message* $p \in \mathcal{P}$, *and outputs a key* $K \in \mathcal{K}$.

For notational simplicity, we will omit the input params *from these algorithms in the rest of the paper.*

We require a NIKE *protocol to satisfy the two following properties:*

Perfect Correctness. We say that NIKE *is perfectly correct if, over the randomness of* Setup *and* Gen:

$$\Pr[\mathsf{SharedKey}(r_A, p_B) = \mathsf{SharedKey}(r_B, p_A)] = 1$$

where params $\leftarrow$ Setup(1^λ), $r_A \leftarrow$ Gen(params), $p_A =$ Publish(r_A), $r_B \leftarrow$ Gen(params), $p_B =$ Publish(r_B).

Security Against ℓ-bit Leakage. We say that a NIKE protocol is *secure against ℓ-bit leakage* if for all PPT distinguishers $\mathcal{D}$, and for all efficiently computable leakage functions $f_A, f_B : \mathcal{C} \times \mathcal{R} \to \{0, 1\}^\ell$, we have (where we omit also params as an input to the distinguisher $\mathcal{D}$ and the leakage functions f_A, f_B in the rest of the paper):

$$\big| \Pr\left[\mathcal{D}\left(p_A, p_B, f_A(r_A), f_B(r_B), K_0\right) = 1\right]$$
$$- \Pr\left[\mathcal{D}\left(p_A, p_B, f_A(r_A), f_B(r_B), K_1\right) = 1\right] \big| \leq \mathsf{negl}(\lambda),$$

where params $\leftarrow$ Setup(1^λ), $r_A \leftarrow$ Gen(params), $p_A =$ Publish(r_A), $r_B \leftarrow$ Gen(params), $p_B =$ Publish(r_B), $K_0 =$ SharedKey(r_A, p_B), and $K_1 \leftarrow \mathcal{K}$.

Default Definition versus Variants. We define several variants of NIKE depending on whether the Setup algorithm and the Gen algorithm just output uniformly random coins or sample from some more complex distribution. By default, we will only allow them to output uniformly random coins, which means that the leakage can depend on all of the random coins used by the scheme and there is no reliance on leak-free randomness. In particular, we say that a NIKE scheme is:

- a *plain NIKE* (default), if both Setup(1^λ) and Gen(params) just output (some specified number of) uniformly random bits. In particular Setup(1^λ; ρ_S) = ρ_S and Gen(params; ρ_G) = ρ_G. In this case, we will often exclude the algorithms Setup, Gen from the description of NIKE.
- a NIKE in the *common reference string model*, if the algorithm Setup(1^λ) can be arbitrary (sample from an arbitrary distribution). Note that this means that we rely on leak-free randomness to run the Setup algorithm.
- a NIKE in the *preprocessing model*, if the algorithm Gen(params) can be arbitrary (sample from an arbitrary distribution). Note that this means we rely on leak-free randomness to generate the states r_A, r_B of each party before the protocol starts (but we do not rely on any additional leak-free randomness during the protocol execution).
- a NIKE in the common reference string and preprocessinf model, if both the algorithms Setup, Gen can be arbitrary (sample from an arbitrary distribution).

6   A Black-Box Separation

In this section, we show a broad black-box separation result, which rules out any efficient black-box reduction from any *single-stage* assumption to the leakage-resilience of plain NIKE with sufficiently large leakage.

6.1   Single-Stage Assumptions

Roughly following [21, 35], we define single-stage (game-based) assumptions (also called *cryptographic games*). For comparison, single-stage assumptions differ from falsifiable assumptions [18, 29] as challengers can be potentially unbounded.

Definition 11 (Single-Stage Assumption). *A single-stage assumption consists of an interactive (potentially inefficient, stateful) challenger $\mathcal{C}$ and a constant $c \in [0, 1)$. On security parameter λ, the challenger $\mathcal{C}(1^\lambda)$ interacts with a (stateful) machine $\mathcal{A}(1^\lambda)$ called the adversary and may output a special symbol* win. *If this occurs, we say that $\mathcal{A}(1^\lambda)$ wins $\mathcal{C}(1^\lambda)$. The assumption associated with the tuple $(\mathcal{C}, c)$ states that for any PPT adversary $\mathcal{A}$, we have*

$$\Pr[\mathcal{A}(1^\lambda) \text{ wins } \mathcal{C}(1^\lambda)] \leq c + \mathrm{negl}(\lambda)$$

where the probability is over the random coins of $\mathcal{C}$ and $\mathcal{A}$.

Which assumptions are not single-stage? The definition above seems to cover all most common cryptographic assumptions, so one can naturally ask which assumptions our black-box impossibility does not cover. An example of a *multi-stage* assumption is the leakage resilience of NIKE itself (defined in Sect. 5)! In particular, one can equivalently define leakage-resilience as a two-stage game, where the adversary is split into two distinct entities: a *leaker* that produces the leakages $f_A(r_A), f_B(r_B)$, and a *distinguisher* that uses this leakage to distinguish the final key from uniform. Unlike the leaker, the distinguisher in that game does not see the secret states r_A, r_B, and the only state kept by the adversary between the two stages are the leakages $f_A(r_A)$ and $f_B(r_B)$.

6.2 Separating Leakage-Resilient NIKE from Single-Stage Assumptions

Next, we recall the notion of black-box reductions.

Definition 12 (Black-Box Reduction). *A black-box reduction showing the leakage-resilience (for ℓ-bit leakage) of* NIKE *based on a single-stage assumption* $(\mathcal{C}, c)$ *is an efficient oracle-access machine* $\mathcal{R}(\cdot)$ *such that, for every (possibly inefficient, non-uniform) distinguisher* $\mathcal{D}$ *to the NIKE with (possibily inefficient, non-uniform) leakage functions* $f_A, f_B : \mathcal{R} \to \{0,1\}^\ell$, *the machine* $\mathcal{R}^{\mathcal{D}, f_A, f_B}$ *breaks the assumption* $(\mathcal{C}, c)$.

We are ready to state our black-box impossibility result.

Theorem 9 (Black-Box Separation). *Let* $\ell = \omega(\log \lambda)$. *Let* NIKE = (Publish, SharedKey) *be a candidate plain NIKE satisfying perfect correctness. Then for any single-stage assumption* $(\mathcal{C}, c)$, *one of the following must hold:*

- $(\mathcal{C}, c)$ *is false.*
- *There is no black-box security reduction showing the leakage resilience of* NIKE *against* ℓ-bit leakages based on the assumption $(\mathcal{C}, c)$.

Proof. Our proof strategy closely follows the ideas of [35]. Looking ahead, our inefficient distinguisher against NIKE is a *simulatable attacker* in the sense of [35, Definition 4.1].

Let $(\mathcal{C}, c)$ be a single-stage assumption, and let $\mathcal{R}$ be a black-box reduction from the security of NIKE against ℓ-bit leakage to the assumption $(\mathcal{C}, c)$. In other words, for any (potentially inefficient, non-uniform) distinguisher $\mathcal{D}$ with non-negligible advantage along with (potentially inefficient, non-uniform) leakage functions $f_A, f_B : \mathcal{R} \to \{0,1\}^\ell$, the machine $\mathcal{R}^{\mathcal{D}, f_A, f_B}$ breaks $(\mathcal{C}, c)$ with non-negligible advantage.

Let $H : \mathcal{P} \to \{0,1\}^\ell$ be a random function. We first define a family of *inefficient* distinguishers $\overline{\mathcal{D}}^{(H)}$ along with (inefficient) leakage functions $\overline{f_A}^{(H)}, \overline{f_B}^{(H)}$ as follows.

- $\overline{f_A}^{(H)}$ takes as input a state $r_A \in \mathcal{R}$. It has the function H hard-coded (say as a truth table). It computes $p_A = \mathsf{Publish}(r_A)$ and outputs $\sigma_A = H(p_A)$.
- $\overline{f_B}^{(H)}$ takes as input a state $r_B \in \mathcal{R}$. It has the function H hard-coded (say as a truth table). It computes $p_B = \mathsf{Publish}(r_B)$ and outputs $\sigma_B = H(p_B)$.
- $\overline{\mathcal{D}}^{(H)}(p_A, p_B, \sigma_A, \sigma_B, K)$ takes as input public messages $p_A, p_B \in \mathcal{P}$, leakages $\sigma_A, \sigma_B \in \{0,1\}^\ell$ and a key $K \in \mathcal{K}$. It checks that $H(p_A) = \sigma_A$ and $H(p_B) = \sigma_B$.
  If this equality holds, brute-force search for any $r_A \in R$ such that $\mathsf{Publish}(r_A) = p_A$; output 1 if $K = \mathsf{SharedKey}(r_A, p_B)$ and 0 otherwise.
  Otherwise output a random bit $b \in \{0,1\}$.

Claim 10. *Assume* NIKE *is perfectly correct. Then* $\overline{\mathcal{D}}^{(H)}$ *along with* $\overline{f_A}^{(H)}, \overline{f_B}^{(H)}$ *is an (inefficient) distinguisher with leakage size ℓ and advantage* $1 - 1/|\mathcal{K}|$.

Proof. By perfect correctness of NIKE, for any p_B in the image of Publish and any r_A, r'_A such that $\mathsf{Publish}(r_A) = \mathsf{Publish}(r'_A)$, we have $\mathsf{SharedKey}(r_A, p_B) = \mathsf{SharedKey}(r'_A, p_B)$.

In particular, on input $\left(p_A, p_B, \overline{f_A}^{(H)}(r_A), \overline{f_B}^{(H)}(r_B), K_0\right)$ where $p_A = \mathsf{Publish}(r_A)$ and $K_0 = \mathsf{SharedKey}(r_A, p_B)$, the distinguisher $\overline{\mathcal{D}}^{(H)}$ always outputs 1.

Similarly, on input $\left(p_A, p_B, \overline{f_A}^{(H)}(r_A), \overline{f_B}^{(H)}(r_B), K_1\right)$ where $K_1 \leftarrow \mathcal{K}$, the distinguisher $\overline{\mathcal{D}}^{(H)}$ outputs 1 if and only if $K = \mathsf{SharedKey}(r_A, p_B)$ (for any r_A such that $p_A = \mathsf{Publish}(r_A)$), which happens with probability $1/|\mathcal{K}|$.   □

We now consider the following *efficient* algorithm $\mathcal{D}_{\mathsf{Sim}}$ along with efficient leakage functions f_A^*, f_B^*. These three algorithms share a look-up table T of entries in $\mathcal{R} \times \{0,1\}^\ell$ indexed by elements in $\mathcal{P}$; we will write $T[p \in \mathcal{P}] = (r, \sigma) \in \mathcal{R} \times \{0,1\}^\ell$. We stress that $\mathcal{D}_{\mathsf{Sim}}$ is *not* a distinguisher against NIKE because of this shared state T.

- $f_A^*(r)$ takes as input $r \in \mathcal{R}$. It computes $p = \mathsf{Publish}(r)$. If the entry of T indexed by p has not yet been assigned, it samples a uniform $\sigma \leftarrow \{0,1\}^\ell$, and define $T[p] = (r, \sigma)$. Otherwise it outputs the second element of $T[p]$.
- $f_B^*(r)$ takes as input $r \in \mathcal{R}$. It computes $p = \mathsf{Publish}(r)$. If the entry of T indexed by p has not yet been assigned, it samples a uniform $\sigma \leftarrow \{0,1\}^\ell$, and define $T[p] = (r, \sigma)$. Otherwise it outputs the second element of $T[p]$.
- $\mathcal{D}_{\mathsf{Sim}}$ takes as input public messages $p_A, p_B \in \mathcal{P}$, leakages $\sigma_A, \sigma_B \in \{0,1\}^\ell$ and a key $K \in \mathcal{K}$.
  It looks up in T whether both $T[p_A]$ and $T[p_B]$ are defined; if so it checks that the second elements of $T[p_A]$ and $T[p_B]$ equal σ_A and σ_B, respectively. If this is the case, let r_A be the first element of $T[p_A] \in \mathcal{R} \times \{0,1\}^\ell$. It outputs 1 if $\mathsf{SharedKey}(r_A, p_B) = K$, and 0 otherwise.
  Otherwise, it outputs a random bit b.

Claim 11. *Suppose* NIKE *is perfectly correct. Let $\mathcal{R}$ be an efficient oracle-access machine. Then the outputs of* $\mathcal{R}^{\overline{\mathcal{D}}^{(H)}, \overline{f_A}^{(H)}, \overline{f_B}^{(H)}}$ *and* $\mathcal{R}^{\mathcal{D}_{\mathsf{Sim}}, f_A^*, f_B^*}$ *are within statistical distance $Q/2^\ell$ over the randomness of $\mathcal{R}$ and H, where Q is the number of oracle queries of $\mathcal{R}$, and ℓ is the size of the leakages.*

Proof. Let $Q = \mathsf{poly}(\lambda)$ be the total number of oracle queries performed by $\mathcal{R}^{\mathcal{D}, f_A, f_B}$ to $\mathcal{D}, f_A, f_B$. It suffices to argue that the transcripts of the calls of $\mathcal{R}$ to $(\overline{\mathcal{D}}^{(H)}, \overline{f_A}^{(H)}, \overline{f_B}^{(H)})$ and to $(\mathcal{R}^{\mathcal{D}_{\mathsf{Sim}}, f_A^*, f_B^*})$ are within statistical distance $Q/2^\ell$.

We first note that the (transcripts of the) outputs of the calls to $\overline{f_A}^{(H)}, \overline{f_B}^{(H)}$ and f_A^*, f_B^* are identically distributed. We then distinguish two cases:

- $\mathcal{R}^{\mathcal{D}, f_A, f_B}$ calls $\mathcal{D}$ on input $p_A, p_B, \sigma_A, \sigma_B$ but has either not previously called f_A on any input r_A such that $\mathsf{Publish}(r_A) = p_A$, or has not previously called f_B on any input r_B such that $\mathsf{Publish}(r_B) = p_B$. Then $\mathcal{R}^{\mathcal{D}_{\mathsf{Sim}}, f_A^*, f_B^*}$ obtains a uniformly random output bit over such calls as either $T[p_A]$ or $T[p_B]$ has not been defined. Further, the probability that $\mathcal{R}^{\overline{\mathcal{D}}^{(H)}, \overline{f_A}^{(H)}, \overline{f_B}^{(H)}}$ does not get a random output bit over any such call to $\overline{\mathcal{D}}^{(H)}$ is at most $Q/2^\ell$ (over the randomness of $H(p_A)$ and $H(p_B)$).
- Otherwise for every call to $\mathcal{D}$ that does not result in a random output bit, $\mathcal{R}^{\mathcal{D}, f_A, f_B}$ has previously queried both f_A on r_A such that $\mathsf{Publish}(r_A) = p_A$ and f_B on r_B such that $\mathsf{Publish}(r_B) = p_B$. In particular p_B is in the image of $\mathsf{Publish}$, and by perfect correctness, both $\mathcal{D}_{\mathsf{Sim}}$ and $\overline{\mathcal{D}}^{(H)}$ compute the same value $\mathsf{SharedKey}(r_A, p_B)$. Therefore the two resulting distributions are identically distributed. $\qquad\square$

By Claim 11, we have in particular:

$$\Pr[\mathcal{R}^{\mathcal{D}_{\mathsf{Sim}}, f_A^*, f_B^*} \text{ wins } \mathcal{C}] \geq \Pr[\mathcal{R}^{\overline{\mathcal{D}}^{(H)}, \overline{f_A}^{(H)}, \overline{f_B}^{(H)}} \text{ wins } \mathcal{C}] - Q/2^\ell,$$

over the randomness of $\mathcal{R}$, $\mathcal{C}$ and H. Note that $\mathcal{R}^{\mathcal{D}_{\mathsf{Sim}}, f_A^*, f_B^*}$ is a PPT algorithm. Now by Claim 10, $\mathcal{R}^{\mathcal{D}_{\mathsf{Sim}}, f_A^*, f_B^*}$ is an efficient adversary that wins $(\mathcal{C}, c)$ with advantage at least $1 - 1/|\mathcal{K}| - Q/2^\ell$, which concludes the proof. $\qquad\square$

6.3 Circumventing the Impossibility Result

The black-box impossibility result of Theorem 9 suggests several natural avenues to avoid it. We mention below several such options, some of which lead to positive results in subsequent sections of the paper.

Small Leakage. Our impossibility result only covers *super-logarithmically-sized leakages*, and assumptions asserting security against PPT adversary with negligible advantage. One natural way around this is to restrict security to small leakages and/or to use stronger assumptions. In the full version, we show that any standard NIKE is actually directly secure against $\mathcal{O}(\log \lambda)$-bit leakages, and, more generally, that any ϵ-secure standard NIKE (where the advantage of any PPT distinguisher is at most ϵ) is $(\epsilon \cdot 2^{\mathcal{O}(\ell)})$-secure with ℓ-bit leakage.

Multi-Stage Assumptions and Non-Black-Box Reductions. Our impossibility result only covers *single-stage assumptions* under *black-box reductions*. All the constructions we are aware of for leakage resilience use black-box reductions, and essentially all standard cryptographic assumptions are phrased as single-stage game-based assumptions.

Imperfect Correctness. We crucially use in several steps of our proof that the NIKE is perfectly correct, to ensure that both $\overline{\mathcal{D}}^{(H)}$ is an (inefficient) distinguisher for NIKE, and that $\overline{\mathcal{D}}^{(H)}$ and $\mathcal{D}_{\mathsf{Sim}}$ compute the same shared key. However we do not see a way to leverage this gap alone to build a secure construction.

The Common Reference String Model. On a more constructive side, an interesting way to get around Theorem 9 is to further rely on trusted setup. A common setting is to assume the availability of a *common reference string* (CRS), where the randomness used to generate the CRS cannot leak. The reason our black-box impossibility result does not apply in that case is somewhat subtle: the reduction $\mathcal{R}$ can call $(\mathcal{D}, f_A, f_B)$ using a *malformed* CRS (not in the image of Setup), where perfect correctness might not hold. As a matter of fact, our black-box impossibility result does extend to the common *random* string model. In the full version, we build a leakage-resilient NIKE in the CRS model from $i\mathcal{O}$.

The Preprocessing Model. A very similar workaround is to consider what we call the *preprocessing* model, where parties generate their secret states r using some leak-free randomness. In the preprocessing model, our impossibility result does not apply for the same reason it does not apply in the CRS setting. This preprocessing could either be performed by the parties themselves during an earlier leak-free preprocessing stage, or it could be generated by a trusted third party. In Sect. 7, we build a leakage-resilient NIKE in the CRS model with preprocessing from bilinear maps; in the full version we build a leakage-resilient NIKE in the pure preprocessing model from $i\mathcal{O}$ and lossy functions.

7   Constructions from Bilinear Maps

In this section we leverage bilinear maps to build leakage-resilent NIKE in the CRS model with preprocessing. We first provide a construction using *composite-order* bilinear groups. In the full version, we give an alternate construction from the decisional linear assumption (DLIN) over prime order groups.

Construction 12. *Let* sk-NIKE $=$ (sk-NIKE.Publish, sk-NIKE.SharedKey) *be a leakage-resilient symmetric key NIKE (Definition 2) over secret key space* $\mathcal{SK}$, *internal randomness space* $\mathcal{R}$, *public message space* $\mathcal{P}$ *and output key space* $\mathcal{K}$. *We will assume that* sk-NIKE.Publish *does not take any secret key* sk *as input; all our constructions from two-seed extractors in Sect. 4 satisfy this property.*

Let $\mathcal{G}$ *be a group generator for a composite-order group (defined in Sect. 3.1). We will assume that there is a natural bijection* $G_T \simeq \mathcal{SK}$.

We construct NIKE $=$ (Setup, Gen, Publish, SharedKey) *as follows:*

- Setup(1^λ): *on input the security parameter, generate* $\mathbb{G} = (G, G_T, N = p_1 p_2, e) \leftarrow \mathcal{G}(1^\lambda)$ *of order* $N = p_1 p_2$ *where* p_1 *and* p_2 *are primes. Let* u *be a generator of* G.
  Sample $\alpha, x \leftarrow \mathbb{Z}_N$ *and use* p_2 *(given by the random coins used to run* $\mathcal{G}$) *to compute* $g = u^{\alpha \cdot p_2} \in G_{p_1}$ *and* $h = g^x \in G_{p_1}$.
  Output params $= (\mathbb{G}, g, h)$.
- Gen(params): *on input* params, *sample* $\rho \leftarrow \mathcal{R}$. *Sample* $a \leftarrow \mathbb{Z}_N$, *and output the state* $r = (\rho, (g^a, h^a)) \in \mathcal{R} \times G^2$.
- Publish(r): *on input a state* $r = (\rho, (X, Y)) \in \mathcal{R} \times G^2$, *output the public message* $p = (\text{sk-NIKE.Publish}(\rho), X)$.

- SharedKey(r, p): *on input a state* $r = (\rho, (X, Y)) \in \mathcal{R} \times G^2$ *and a public message* $p = (P, Z) \in \mathcal{P} \times G$, *compute:*

$$\mathsf{sk} = e(Y, Z),$$

that we identify as an element of $\mathcal{SK}$, *and output:*

$$K = \mathsf{sk}\text{-}\mathsf{NIKE}.\mathsf{SharedKey}(\mathsf{sk}, \rho, P).$$

Theorem 13 (Correctness). *Assuming* sk-NIKE *is perfectly correct, Construction 12 is perfectly correct.*

Proof. Let r_A, r_B be elements of $\mathcal{R} \times G^2$, $p_A = \mathsf{Publish}(r_A)$, $p_B = \mathsf{Publish}(r_B)$. By perfect correctness of sk-NIKE, it suffices to show that SharedKey(r_A, p_B) and SharedKey(r_B, p_A) compute the same intermediate secret key sk. But this follows as for all $Y, Z \in G^2$, $e(Y, Z) = e(Z, Y)$. $\qquad\square$

Theorem 14 (NIKE in the CRS model with Preprocessing). *Assume that Assumption 1 holds, and that* sk-NIKE *is leakage resilient. Then Construction 12 is leakage-resilient.*

Proof. Let $\mathcal{D}$ be an efficient algorithm which breaks the leakage resilience of NIKE with leakage functions f_A, f_B. We proceed via a sequence of hybrid games.

Hybrid 0. This is the real security experiment: $\mathcal{D}$ is given as input

$$(\mathsf{params}, p_A, p_B, f_A(r_A), f_B(r_B), K_b)$$

where b is the challenger's bit.

Hybrid 1. We change how we compute $\mathsf{params}, r_A, r_B$ given to the distinguisher. We now sample $g \leftarrow G_{p_1}$, $x, y \leftarrow \mathbb{Z}_N$, $v \leftarrow G_{p_1}$, and set:

$$h = g^x, \quad r_A = (\rho_A, v, v^x), \quad r_B = (\rho_A, v^y, v^{xy}).$$

The resulting input distributions to the distinguisher $\mathcal{D}$ in Hybrid 0 and Hybrid 1 are statistically close. Indeed, g is uniform in G_{p_1} in both cases, and for $a \leftarrow \mathbb{Z}_N$, g^a is uniform in G_{p_1}, except when $g = 1_G$ which happens with negligible probability $1/p_1$. If this is not the case, then h^a can be computed as $(g^a)^x$. Similarly, g^y is in this case uniformly distributed in G_{p_1}, and therefore follows the same distribution as $(g^a)^y$ where $y \leftarrow \mathbb{Z}_N$, except if $(g^a) = 1_G$, which happens with probability $1/p_1$ over the randomness of $a \leftarrow \mathbb{Z}_N$. Overall, the statistical distance between the distributions is at most $2/p_1$ which is negligible.

Hybrid 2. We change how we compute r_A, r_B given to the distinguisher. We now pick $x, y \leftarrow \mathbb{Z}_N$, $w \leftarrow G$, and set:

$$h = g^x, \quad r_A = (\rho_A, w, w^x), \quad r_B = (\rho_A, w^y, w^{xy}).$$

This change is undetectable to any efficient distinguisher, *even given* r_A, r_B:

Lemma 5. *Under Assumption 1, the following distributions are computationally indistinguishable:*

$$\left(\mathbb{G}, g, h = g^x, r_A = (\rho_A, (v, v^x)), r_B = (\rho_B, (v^y, v^{xy})), K_b\right)$$
$$\left(\mathbb{G}, g, h = g^x, r_A = (\rho_A, (w, w^x)), r_B = (\rho_B, (w^y, w^{xy})), K_b\right),$$

where $\mathbb{G} \leftarrow \mathcal{G}$, $g \leftarrow G_{p_1}$, $x, y \leftarrow \mathbb{Z}_N$, $v \leftarrow G_1$, $w \leftarrow G$; *and* $\rho_A, \rho_B \leftarrow \mathcal{R}$, $K_0 = \mathsf{SharedKey}(r_A, \mathsf{Publish}(r_B))$ *and* $K_1 \leftarrow \mathcal{K}$.

In particular since $\mathsf{Publish}$, f_A *and* f_B *are efficiently computable, the input distributions—and therefore the outputs of* $\mathcal{D}$ *in Hybrid 1 and Hybrid 2—are statistically indistinguishable.*

Proof. We define a reduction R to Assumption 1 that takes as input $\mathbb{G}, g, T$, where $\mathbb{G} \leftarrow \mathcal{G}$, $g \leftarrow G_{p_1}$ and T is either uniform in G_{p_1} or in G. R does the following:

- Samples $x \leftarrow \mathbb{Z}_N$ and sets $h = g^x$,
- Samples $\rho_A, \rho_B \leftarrow \mathcal{R}$, $y \leftarrow \mathbb{Z}_N$, and sets $r_A = (\rho_A, T, T^x)$ and $r_B = (\rho_B, T^y, T^{xy})$,
- Computes

$$K_0 = \mathsf{sk\text{-}NIKE.SharedKey}(e(T, T)^{xy}, \rho_A, \mathsf{sk\text{-}NIKE.Publish}(\rho_B)),$$

- Samples $K_1 \leftarrow \mathcal{K}$,
- Outputs

$$\left(\mathbb{G}, g, h, r_A, r_B, K_b\right).$$

If $T \leftarrow G_{p_1}$ then R produces the first distribution of Lemma 5, and if $T \leftarrow G$ then it produces the second distribution.   □

Hybrid 3. We again change how we compute r_A, r_B given to the distinguisher. In this experiment we sample $x \leftarrow \mathbb{Z}_N$. We now compute $h = g^x$, and generate the state as $r = (\rho, (u^a, u^{ax}))$ where $a \leftarrow \mathbb{Z}_N$.

The distributions induced by Hybrid 2 and Hybrid 3 are statistically indistinguishable. Indeed, they only differ when $w \in G_{p_1}$ or $w \in G_{p_2}$, which happens with probability $(p_1 + p_2 - 1)/(p_1 p_2) = \mathsf{negl}(\lambda)$.

Lemma 6. *Assume* $\mathsf{sk\text{-}NIKE}$ *is an* $(n, \ell + (\log p_1)/2, \epsilon)$-*secure symmetric key NIKE with error* $\epsilon = \mathsf{negl}(\lambda)$. *Then the advantage of any (even potentially unbounded) distinguisher in Hybrid 3 is negligible.*

Proof. In Hybrid 3, the secret key sk for $\mathsf{sk\text{-}NIKE}$ is computed as $\mathsf{sk} = e(u^a, u^{xy}) = e(u, u)^{axy}$. In particular, over the randomness of x alone (with high probability over a and y), sk is uniform in G_T conditioned on $h^x \in G_{p_1}$, $f_A(r_A)$ and $f_B(r_B)$. In particular, h^x can be computed given $x \bmod p_1$, and therefore the view of the distinguisher can be generated using $(f_A^*(r_A), f_B^*(r_B)) = (x \bmod p_1, f_A(r_A), f_B(r_B))$ which is of size $\log p_1 + 2\ell$.

By $(n, \ell + (\log p_1)/2, \epsilon)$-security of $\mathsf{sk\text{-}NIKE}$, the advantage of any (potentially unbounded) distinguisher is therefore at most $\epsilon = \mathsf{negl}(\lambda)$.   □

Overall we conclude that the advantage of $\mathcal{D}, f_A, f_B$ against Construction 12 is at most negligible.   □

The scheme above allows for a constant leakage rate. We refer to the full version for a short discussion on the parameters involved.

References

1. Akavia, A., Goldwasser, S., Vaikuntanathan, V.: Simultaneous hardcore bits and cryptography against memory attacks. In: Reingold [33], pp. 474–495 (2009)
2. Alwen, J., Dodis, Y., Naor, M., Segev, G., Walfish, S., Wichs, D.: Public-key encryption in the bounded-retrieval model. In: Gilbert, H. (ed.) EUROCRYPT 2010. LNCS, vol. 6110, pp. 113–134. Springer, Heidelberg (2010). https://doi.org/10.1007/978-3-642-13190-5_6
3. Alwen, J., Dodis, Y., Wichs, D.: Leakage-resilient public-key cryptography in the bounded-retrieval model. In: Halevi [22], pp. 36–54 (2009)
4. Babai, L., Nisan, N., Szegedy, M.: Multiparty protocols, pseudorandom generators for logspace, and time-space trade-offs. J. Comput. Syst. Sci. **45**(2), 204–232 (1992)
5. Barak, B., et al.: Leftover hash lemma, revisited. In: Rogaway, P. (ed.) CRYPTO 2011. LNCS, vol. 6841, pp. 1–20. Springer, Heidelberg (2011). https://doi.org/10.1007/978-3-642-22792-9_1
6. Bennett, C.H., Brassard, G.: Quantum cryptography: public key distribution and coin tossing. In: Proceedings of the IEEE International Conference on Computers, Systems and Signal Processing, pp. 175–179 (1984)
7. Bennett, C.H., Brassard, G., Crépeau, C., Maurer, U.M.: Generalized privacy amplification. IEEE Trans. Inf. Theory **41**(6), 1915–1923 (1995)
8. Bennett, C.H., Brassard, G., Robert, J.M.: Privacy amplification by public discussion. SIAM J. Comput. **17**(2), 210–229 (1988)
9. Boneh, Dan (ed.): CRYPTO 2003. LNCS, vol. 2729. Springer, Heidelberg (2003). https://doi.org/10.1007/b11817
10. Boneh, D., Zhandry, M.: Multiparty key exchange, efficient traitor tracing, and more from indistinguishability obfuscation. In: Garay, J.A., Gennaro, R. (eds.) CRYPTO 2014, Part I. LNCS, vol. 8616, pp. 480–499. Springer, Heidelberg (2014). https://doi.org/10.1007/978-3-662-44371-2_27
11. Chakraborty, S., Alawatugoda, J., Pandu Rangan, C.: Leakage-resilient non-interactive key exchange in the continuous-memory leakage setting. In: Okamoto, T., Yu, Y., Au, M.H., Li, Y. (eds.) ProvSec 2017. LNCS, vol. 10592, pp. 167–187. Springer, Cham (2017). https://doi.org/10.1007/978-3-319-68637-0_10
12. Chakraborty, S., Alawatugoda, J., Rangan, C.P.: New approach to practical leakage-resilient public-key cryptography. Cryptology ePrint Archive, Report 2017/441 (2017). http://eprint.iacr.org/2017/441
13. Chung, F.R.: Quasi-random classes of hypergraphs. Random Struct. Algorithms **1**(4), 363–382 (1990)
14. Dodis, Y., Elbaz, A., Oliveira, R., Raz, R.: Improved randomness extraction from two independent sources. In: Jansen, K., Khanna, S., Rolim, J.D.P., Ron, D. (eds.) APPROX/RANDOM -2004. LNCS, vol. 3122, pp. 334–344. Springer, Heidelberg (2004). https://doi.org/10.1007/978-3-540-27821-4_30
15. Dodis, Y., Ong, S.J., Prabhakaran, M., Sahai, A.: On the (im)possibility of cryptography with imperfect randomness. In: 45th FOCS, pp. 196–205. IEEE Computer Society Press, October 2004

16. Dodis, Y., Yu, Yu.: Overcoming weak expectations. In: Sahai, A. (ed.) TCC 2013. LNCS, vol. 7785, pp. 1–22. Springer, Heidelberg (2013). https://doi.org/10.1007/978-3-642-36594-2_1

17. Dziembowski, S., Pietrzak, K.: Leakage-resilient cryptography. In: 49th FOCS, pp. 293–302. IEEE Computer Society Press, October 2008

18. Gentry, C., Wichs, D.: Separating succinct non-interactive arguments from all falsifiable assumptions. In: Fortnow, L., Vadhan, S.P. (eds.) 43rd ACM STOC, pp. 99–108. ACM Press, June 2011

19. Goldreich, O.: Three XOR-lemmas—an exposition. In: Goldreich, O. (ed.) Studies in Complexity and Cryptography. Miscellanea on the Interplay Between Randomness and Computation. LNCS, vol. 6650, pp. 248–272. Springer, Heidelberg (2011). https://doi.org/10.1007/978-3-642-22670-0_22

20. Goldwasser, S., Rothblum, G.N.: How to compute in the presence of leakage. In: 53rd FOCS, pp. 31–40. IEEE Computer Society Press, October 2012

21. Haitner, I., Holenstein, T.: On the (im)possibility of key dependent encryption. In: Reingold [33], pp. 202–219 (2009)

22. Halevi, Shai (ed.): CRYPTO 2009. LNCS, vol. 5677. Springer, Heidelberg (2009). https://doi.org/10.1007/978-3-642-03356-8

23. Ishai, Y., Sahai, A., Wagner, D.: Private circuits: securing hardware against probing attacks. In: Boneh [9], pp. 463–481 (2003)

24. Kumar, A., Meka, R., Sahai, A.: Leakage-resilient secret sharing against colluding parties. In: Zuckerman, D. (ed.) 60th FOCS, pp. 636–660. IEEE Computer Society Press, November 2019

25. Lewko, A., Rouselakis, Y., Waters, B.: Achieving leakage resilience through dual system encryption. In: Ishai, Y. (ed.) TCC 2011. LNCS, vol. 6597, pp. 70–88. Springer, Heidelberg (2011). https://doi.org/10.1007/978-3-642-19571-6_6

26. Lewko, A., Waters, B.: New techniques for dual system encryption and fully secure HIBE with short ciphertexts. In: Micciancio, D. (ed.) TCC 2010. LNCS, vol. 5978, pp. 455–479. Springer, Heidelberg (2010). https://doi.org/10.1007/978-3-642-11799-2_27

27. Maurer, U.M.: Protocols for secret key agreement by public discussion based on common information. In: Brickell, E.F. (ed.) CRYPTO 1992. LNCS, vol. 740, pp. 461–470. Springer, Heidelberg (1993). https://doi.org/10.1007/3-540-48071-4_32

28. Micali, S., Reyzin, L.: Physically observable cryptography. In: Naor, M. (ed.) TCC 2004. LNCS, vol. 2951, pp. 278–296. Springer, Heidelberg (2004). https://doi.org/10.1007/978-3-540-24638-1_16

29. Naor, M.: On cryptographic assumptions and challenges. In: Boneh [9], pp. 96–109 (2003)

30. Naor, M., Segev, G.: Public-key cryptosystems resilient to key leakage. In: Halevi [22], pp. 18–35 (2009)

31. Peikert, C., Waters, B.: Lossy trapdoor functions and their applications. In: Ladner, R.E., Dwork, C. (eds.) 40th ACM STOC, pp. 187–196. ACM Press, May 2008

32. Pietrzak, K.: A leakage-resilient mode of operation. In: Joux, A. (ed.) EUROCRYPT 2009. LNCS, vol. 5479, pp. 462–482. Springer, Heidelberg (2009). https://doi.org/10.1007/978-3-642-01001-9_27

33. Reingold, O. (ed.): TCC 2009. LNCS, vol. 5444. Springer, Heidelberg (2009). https://doi.org/10.1007/978-3-642-00457-5

34. Waters, B.: Dual system encryption: realizing fully secure IBE and HIBE under simple assumptions. In: Halevi [22], pp. 619–636 (2009)

35. Wichs, D.: Barriers in cryptography with weak, correlated and leaky sources. In: Kleinberg, R.D. (ed.) ITCS 2013, pp. 111–126. ACM, January 2013

Outsourced Encryption

Lower Bounds for Encrypted Multi-Maps and Searchable Encryption in the Leakage Cell Probe Model

Sarvar Patel[1]([✉]), Giuseppe Persiano[1,2]([✉]), and Kevin Yeo[1]([✉])

[1] Google LLC, Mountain View, USA
sarvar@google.com, giuper@gmail.com, kwlyeo@google.com
[2] Università di Salerno, Salerno, Italy

Abstract. Encrypted multi-maps (EMMs) enable clients to outsource the storage of a multi-map to a potentially untrusted server while maintaining the ability to perform operations in a privacy-preserving manner. EMMs are an important primitive as they are an integral building block for many practical applications such as searchable encryption and encrypted databases. In this work, we formally examine the tradeoffs between privacy and efficiency for EMMs.

Currently, all known dynamic EMMs with constant overhead reveal if two operations are performed on the same key or not that we denote as the *global key-equality pattern*. In our main result, we present strong evidence that the leakage of the global key-equality pattern is inherent for any dynamic EMM construction with $O(1)$ efficiency. In particular, we consider the slightly smaller leakage of *decoupled key-equality pattern* where leakage of key-equality between update and query operations is decoupled and the adversary only learns whether two operations of the *same type* are performed on the same key or not. We show that any EMM with at most decoupled key-equality pattern leakage incurs $\Omega(\lg n)$ overhead in the *leakage cell probe model*. This is tight as there exist ORAM-based constructions of EMMs with logarithmic slowdown that leak no more than the decoupled key-equality pattern (and actually, much less). Furthermore, we present stronger lower bounds that encrypted multi-maps leaking at most the decoupled key-equality pattern but are able to perform one of either the update or query operations in the plaintext still require $\Omega(\lg n)$ overhead. Finally, we extend our lower bounds to show that dynamic, *response-hiding* searchable encryption schemes must also incur $\Omega(\lg n)$ overhead even when one of either the document updates or searches may be performed in the plaintext.

1 Introduction

In this work, we study *encrypted multi-maps* [18,37], which is an example of structured encryption (see Chase and Kamara [17]). Structured encryption considers the problem of a client that wishes to outsource the storage of an encrypted data structure to an untrusted server in a privacy-preserving manner. In addition, the structured encryption scheme must enable the client to perform

© International Association for Cryptologic Research 2020
D. Micciancio and T. Ristenpart (Eds.): CRYPTO 2020, LNCS 12170, pp. 433–463, 2020.
https://doi.org/10.1007/978-3-030-56784-2_15

operations over the encrypted, outsourced data structure in an efficient manner. For privacy, the goal is simply to reveal as little information as possible about the data structure as well as the performed operations.

Encrypted multi-maps (EMMs) are a specific structured encryption scheme for outsourcing *multi-maps*. For multi-maps, a client is able to update the tuple of values associated with a key as well as query for the value tuple associated with any key. In this paper, we focus on encrypted multi-maps due to its many important practical applications. Two examples of applications are searchable encryption and encrypted databases. The construction of private and efficient encrypted multi-maps is an important problem to enable the deployment of these privacy-preserving applications in the real-world.

Searchable encryption (also known as encrypted search) was first introduced by Song *et al.* [60] and has been a well studied topic in the past couple decades (see [2–4,7,9,11,14–16,18–20,35,37–39,49,54,61] as some examples). The representative scenario for searchable encryption considers a client that owns a large corpus of documents and an untrusted server with large amounts of available storage. The goal of searchable encryption is to enable the client to outsource the storage of the document corpus to the server. For functionality, the client wishes to maintain the ability to efficiently search over the corpus and retrieve the identifiers of all documents containing a specific keyword as well as update documents by inserting, deleting and/or modifying keywords. In terms of privacy, the client wishes to keep any information related to the contents of the document corpus and the queries hidden from the server. In many works, searchable encryption schemes utilize encrypted multi-maps as their main building block to map keywords to documents that contain the keyword. We note that various searchable encryption schemes have utilized encrypted multi-maps in other, more sophisticated, manners as well.

Another important application is encrypted databases. In this problem, the goal is to encrypt and outsource a database while enabling the database owner to privately perform database operations. Earlier works on encrypted databases [57] utilized property-preserving encryption schemes such as deterministic [4] and order-preserving encryption [5,6,8,48]. It has been shown that encrypted databases built from property-preserving encryption may have security vulnerabilities [50]. In the most recent work, a scheme for encrypting SQL databases was presented by Kamara and Moataz [36] utilizing encrypted multi-maps instead of property-preserving encryption.

Due to these applications, the problem of constructing both efficient and private encrypted multi-maps is very important. Unfortunately, the only way that is currently known to achieve very strong levels of privacy is using very expensive cryptographic primitives such as oblivious RAM [28,51] and/or fully homomorphic encryption [26]. These schemes only leak the size of inputs and outputs of operations, which can also be mitigated by using techniques from recent volume-hiding schemes [37,55]. However, the large performance overheads of these expensive cryptographic primitives preclude them from being used in practical applications. Instead, structured encryption schemes take a different approach by slightly relaxing privacy requirements with the hope of improving efficiency. In particular, the privacy of searchable encryption schemes is parameterized by a *leakage* function. The leakage function is an upper bound on the information revealed to the adversarial server when processing queries over a stored document corpus. Therefore, the design of encrypted multi-map schemes consists of minimizing the leakage function while ensuring the overhead is as small as possible. Using this relaxed variant of privacy, several dynamic encrypted multi-map schemes such as [18,39] with constant overhead have been presented. However, all these schemes have shown to have non-trivial leakage including the *global key-equality pattern* that enables the adversary to learn whether two multi-map operations are performed on the same key or not.

On the other hand, there has been a long line of work starting with the paper of Islam *et al.* [33] that evaluate the negative privacy consequences of various leakage profiles. Using various and continuously improving frequency analysis and statistical learning methods [13,50,58], it has been shown that the contents of documents and/or the queried keywords may be compromised by using *access pattern leakage* that shows whether a specific memory location is accessed by different queries or not. These ideas are further extended to present attacks on schemes that enable clients to perform range queries in [29,42]. In another line of work, Zhang *et al.* [64] consider the scenario where adversaries may inject files into encrypted search schemes. By carefully arranging keywords in the injected files, it is shown that viewing the identifiers of matching injected documents of any query enables the adversary to determine the queried keyword with perfect accuracy. Finally, a recent work by Kornaropoulos *et al.* [41] show new non-parameteric estimation techniques to utilize global key-equality pattern leakage to compromise privacy in certain settings.

Therefore, it is important to ensure that encrypted multi-map constructions are both efficient (to be deployable in practice) as well as only leak small amounts of information (to ensure privacy is not compromised). In this work, we explore and present formal tradeoffs of privacy and efficiency for encrypted multi-maps.

1.1 Our Results

In this section, we present our lower bounds in the *leakage cell probe model*. We start by focusing on encrypted multi-maps. Afterwards, we move onto dynamic searchable encryption schemes.

To start, we briefly describe how the efficiency of schemes in the leakage cell probe model is measured. Typically, data structures measure efficiency amortized over the number of operations. This approach cannot be used for data structures that may return outputs of varying sizes. As a concrete example, let us consider *multi-maps*. Roughly speaking, a multi-map is a data structure that maintains a sequence of pairs (key, vals), where key is taken from a *key universe* $\mathcal{K}$ and vals is a tuple of varying length of values from a *value universe* $\mathcal{V}$. A multi-map supports Get(key) operations, that return the tuple associated with key, and Add(key, val) operations, that add value val $\in \mathcal{V}$ to the tuple associated with key. So two Get operations might return tuples of values of vastly different sizes and thus cannot be expected to incur the same costs. So, we measure the *query efficiency* as the amount of server computation per *returned value*. The problem does not occur for Add updates operations as they operate on a single value and thus we can consider the *update efficiency* as the amount of server computation per Add operation. The efficiency of a dynamic scheme is the maximum of the update and query efficiency.

Encrypted multi-maps. We start by describing our results for encrypted multi-maps and we note our results also apply to encrypted arrays (which can be interpreted as oblivious RAMs with larger leakage). The efficiency of encrypted multi-maps crucially depends on the leakage one is willing to tolerate. If no security is sought and each operation may completely leak its inputs, the multi-map problem is identical to the classic dynamic dictionary problem (see [52] for a survey). One can obtain constructions of *plaintext* multi-maps with constant amortized efficiency by utilizing, for example, the optimal dynamic perfect hashing scheme in [21]. In this case, all operations are performed in the plaintext and the inputs and outputs of all operations are revealed.

At the other hand of the leakage spectrum, there exist folklore solutions of encrypted multi-maps with minimal leakage that can be obtained by using efficient ORAMs [1,53] while achieving logarithmic overhead for each updated value in update operations and for each returned value in query operations. In particular, these folklore solutions only leak the number of values (volume) associated with the queried key and nothing else. For completeness, we present a formal definition of this minimal leakage function as well as a description and a proof of the folklore solution in the full version.

In this work, we are interested in understanding the transition from constant to logarithmic amortized efficiency as a function of the leakage allowed. In particular, we attempt to identify the smallest leakage where $O(1)$ overhead solutions still exist. Furthermore, we want to find the largest leakage where constructions must incur asymptotically larger than constant overhead. Specifically, we start by observing that non-trivial leakage can be obtained with constant amortized efficiency by using a simple *hash-and-encrypt* approach. We start from the construction of plaintext multi-maps based on any dynamic perfect hashing scheme such as the one by Dietzfelbinger *et al.* [21]. During the initialization of the encrypted multi-map, the client randomly selects a key K_1 for a collision resistant hash function $\mathcal{H}$ and a random encryption key K_2 for an IND-CPA symmetric encryption scheme $(\mathcal{E}, \mathcal{D})$. For each Add(key, val) operation, the client executes the algorithm for the insertion operation for the dynamic perfect hashing scheme with the hashed value $\mathcal{H}(K_1, \text{key})$ as the key and an encryption $\mathcal{E}(K_2, \text{val})$ of the value being added. A query operation Get(key) is implemented by executing the query algorithm of the dynamic perfect hashing scheme using $\mathcal{H}(K_1, \text{key})$ as a key and then decrypting all the returned values with the IND-CPA key K_2. As a result, the client is successfully able to retrieve all plaintext values associated with the queried key. We note that the hash-and-encrypt method is not novel and implicitly appeared in many previous works such as [18,39].

The above implementation provides some privacy for the inserted and queried keys and values. In particular, the hash-and-encrypt version of dynamic perfect hashing does not leak the keys and values in the plaintext. However, the adversarial server learns the type of operation performed as well as the number of encrypted values returned by a Get operation. Additionally, the server learns whether two different operations are performed on the same key or not as the server learns the value $\mathcal{H}(K_1, \text{key})$ when either performing a Get or Add operation. We denote this leakage, $\mathcal{L}_{\text{glob}}$, as the *global key-equality pattern* that describes whether two operations are given the same key as input or not. We refer readers to the full version for a formal description and analysis of the hash-and-encrypt compiler when applied to dynamic perfect hashing.

The above simple hash-and-encrypt construction provides a baseline of what privacy may be efficiently implemented with $O(1)$ overhead. A natural next step is to try and improve the privacy of the above scheme without incurring significantly larger overhead. A slight improvement in privacy would be to consider the leakage function $\mathcal{L}_{\text{dec}}$ which allows the adversary to learn the equality pattern on keys but only for operations of the same type. In more detail, the adversary still learns whether two Get operations are on the same key or not as well as whether two Add operations are on the same key or not. However, the adversary cannot link an Add operation and a Get operation as operating on the same key. We denote this leakage $\mathcal{L}_{\text{dec}}$ as the *decoupled key-equality pattern* (see Sect. 3 for a formal definition) as it *decouples* the Add key-equality pattern from the Get key-equality pattern. From a quick glance, this small improvement in privacy seems insignificant. In the main result of our work, we show that any encrypted multi-map that leaks at most the decoupled key-equality pattern must incur logarithmic overhead.

Theorem 1 (Informal). *Let* **DS** *be a $\mathcal{L}_{\text{dec}}$-leakage encrypted multi-map that leaks at most the decoupled key-equality pattern. Then the amortized efficiency of* **DS** *must be $\Omega(\lg(n/c))$ per updated and/or returned value for any scheme storing n key-value pairs and using c bits of client storage.*

In other words, our results show that the global key-equality pattern is an inherent and seemingly necessary leakage for any $O(1)$ efficiency encrypted multi-map. By attempting to mitigate the global key-equality pattern even in an extremely small (seemingly meaningless) manner, the resulting encrypted multi-maps must incur logarithmically lower efficiency. As a result, one must either tolerate the leakage of the global key-equality pattern or at least logarithmic overhead when implementing encrypted multi-maps. Furthermore, if the mitigation of global key-equality pattern leakage is necessary or logarithmic overhead is tolerable, then the encrypted multi-map construction using oblivious RAMs may be used resulting in minimal leakage. We also note that the bound in Theorem 1 (with formal statement in Theorem 3) is tight in view of the upper bound provided by the ORAM-based construction (see the full version).

The proof of the lower bound for $\mathcal{L}_{\text{dec}}$ only relies on the fact that an adversary cannot link an Add and a Get operation as operating on the same key. Note that this property is guaranteed even if one of the two operations completely leaks the inputs on which it operates. For example, the leakage function $\mathcal{L}_{\mathsf{add}}$, that for any Add(key, val) operation leaks both key and val, can still be considered as decoupling the Get and Add key-equality patterns. We can strengthen the proof of our main result to show that encrypted multi-maps that only leak the decoupled key-equality pattern but are allowed to perform all Add operations in plaintext must also incur logarithmic overhead. The same holds also for leakage function $\mathcal{L}_{\mathsf{get}}$ in which Get operations are performed in the clear while keeping the key-equality patterns decoupled. These results further reinforce the difficulty of mitigating the global key-equality pattern leakage even when willing to sacrifice privacy in other areas. We refer the reader to the full version for more details.

Theorem 2 (Informal). *Let* **DS** *be a* $\{\mathcal{L}_{\mathsf{add}}, \mathcal{L}_{\mathsf{get}}\}$*-leakage encrypted multi-map that leaks at most the decoupled key-equality pattern but may perform one of either the* Add *or* Get *operations in the plaintext. Then the amortized efficiency of* **DS** *must be* $\Omega(\lg(n/c))$ *per updated and/or returned value for any scheme storing n key-value pairs and using c bits of client storage.*

Searchable encryption. We can further prove lower bounds for searchable encryption schemes. In particular, one can use a searchable encryption scheme to construct an encrypted multi-map. As a result, the lower bounds follow directly by interpreting the encrypted multi-map leakage functions as searchable encryption leakage functions.

First, we interpret the notion of decoupled key-equality pattern for searchable encryption scheme. The adversary may learn whether two distinct searches are performed for the same keyword or not. For two different document insertions, the adversary may learn the number of keywords that appear in the intersection of the two inserted documents (a generalization of key-equality for documents with multiple keywords). However, this keyword-equality knowledge is limited to operations of the same type. The adversary should not learn whether a queried keyword appears in an inserted document or not. As a result, we refer to these searchable encryption schemes as *response-hiding* where the adversary cannot learn the identity of documents matching a queried keyword.

For the static searchable encryption problem where documents are given during initialization and the documents are immutable, there exists response-hiding schemes with $O(1)$ overhead such as [18]. On the other hand, our lower bounds show that the dynamic version of response-hiding schemes require logarithmic overhead. Furthermore, our lower bounds still hold for searchable encryption schemes even when the construction may perform one of either document updates or searches in the plaintext. In more detail, plaintext updates mean the construction can reveal the entirety of the updated document in plaintext. Similarly, plaintext searches mean the scheme can reveal the queried keyword in plaintext. As a consequence, our results show that dynamic, response-hiding searchable encryption schemes must either leak the matching documents for any search or incur logarithmic efficiency. For more information, see the full version.

Comparison with [10]. In an independent work, Bost and Fouque [10] present lower bounds for searchable encryption in the "balls-and-bins" model (first used in [28] but formally introduced in [12]). Their work shows an $\Omega(\lg_c(n))$ lower bound for static searchable encryption schemes that mitigate key-equality leakage completely against unbounded adversaries. We note that Bost and Fouque [10] additionally present lower bounds for forward private leakage functions that is not considered in our work. We compare their key-equality leakage lower bounds with our key-equality leakage lower bounds.

First, for super-constant client storage, our lower bound of $\Omega(\lg(n/c))$ is higher than the lower bound proved in [10]. Our work rules out the use of large (but still sub-linear) client storage to speed up schemes. In contrast, the result of [10] gives the trivial bound of $\Omega(1)$ even for small client storage of, say, $c = \Theta(n^{0.1})$, for which our lower bound remains $\Omega(\lg n)$. Secondly, our results apply for computational adversaries while the results in [10] apply only for statistical adversaries. Our results are therefore more applicable to current techniques as, to our knowledge, all recent constructions use computationally-secure encryption and pseudorandom functions that circumvent the lower bound of [10]. Additionally, we prove our lower bounds in the leakage cell probe model where schemes may arbitrarily encode data before storage. The "balls-and-bins" model adopted by [10] only applies to scheme that store each key-value pair (ball) separately in memory locations (bins). Furthermore, the only permitted operations are moving key-value pairs between different memory locations. Therefore, our results rule out clever uses of FHE that might store the encrypted sum of two entries in a memory location for more efficient schemes that would, otherwise, have circumvented the lower bounds of [10]. Finally, our lower bounds only apply to dynamic schemes while [10] applies to both static and dynamic schemes. There is an inherent hardness in proving lower bounds in the leakage cell probe model for static data structures. Weiss and Wichs [62] have shown that proving non-trivial lower bounds for static ORAMs in the cell probe model would solve at least one of two major open problems in complexity. As encrypted multi-map and searchable encryption lower bounds imply ORAM lower bounds, non-trivial lower bounds for static searchable encryption seem out of reach for now.

Related works. Searchable encryption was introduced by Song *et al.* [60]. The notion of adaptive security was first presented by Curtmola *et al.* [18]. Chase and Kamara [17] present structured encryption that is a generalization of searchable encryption. Subsequent works study different variants such as dynamic schemes [14,39,61], cache locality [2,3,16,19,20,49], forward and backward security [9,11,22,27], expressive queries [15,17,23,35], public-key operations [7], multiple users [18,31,54] and using ORAMs or ORAM-like techniques [11,25,27,38]. Several works investigate the implications of leakage in searchable encryption by presenting leakage-abuse attacks [13,29,30,33,40,42,50,58,64].

Most data structure lower bounds are proven in the cell probe model [63]. The chronogram technique was first introduced by Fredman and Saks [24] to prove $\Omega(\lg n/\lg\lg n)$ bounds. Pǎtraşcu and Demaine [59] present the information transfer technique proving $\Omega(\lg n)$ bounds. Larsen [43] presented the first techniques that proved $\tilde{\Omega}(\lg^2 n)$ bound for dynamic, two-dimensional range counting, which is the highest lower bound proven for any data structure with $\Omega(\lg n)$ bit outputs. For dynamic data structures with boolean outputs, the highest lower bound is presented by Larsen et al. [47] of $\tilde{\Omega}(\lg^{1.5} n)$. Goldreich and Ostrovsky [28] first presented ORAM lower bounds in the "balls-and-bins" model [12]. The seminal work by Larsen and Nielsen [45] is the first to show the applicability of the cell probe model for privacy-preserving data structures by giving an $\Omega(\lg n)$ lower bound for ORAMs. Persiano and Yeo [56] extend the $\Omega(\lg n)$ lower bound for differentially private RAMs with weaker privacy. Hubáček et al. [32] extend the lower bounds to the case where the adversary is unaware when operations start and end. Larsen et al. [44] present $\tilde{\Omega}(\lg^2 n)$ lower bounds for oblivious near-neighbor search. Multi-server ORAM lower bounds are presented in [46].

1.2   Overview of Our Techniques

We present an overview of the techniques used to prove our lower bounds. Our lower bounds are proven in the cell probe model which only measures running time by the number of server memory accesses. We refer the reader to Sect. 2.1 for more details on the cell probe model. We will utilize the *information transfer* of Pătraşcu and Demaine [59], which Larsen and Nielsen [45] used to prove lower bounds for ORAMs. We review their proof which will be our starting point.

The information transfer technique starts by constructing the *information transfer tree* for a given sequence of n operations. The information transfer tree is a complete tree with one leaf node for each of the n operations. Operations are assigned to the leaves in chronological order: the first operation is assigned to the leftmost leaf node, the second operation is assigned to the second leftmost leaf node and so forth. Each cell probe is assigned to at most one node in the tree in the following manner. First, we determine the operation performing the probe and the associated leaf and then the most recent operation that overwrote the probed cell and its associated leaf. If this is the first probe for the cell then the probe is not assigned to any node; otherwise, the probe is assigned to the lowest common ancestor of the two leaves.

Having defined the information transfer tree, we move onto the hard distribution for the ORAM lower bounds in [45]. Fix any internal node v in the tree and consider the subtree rooted at v. The hard distribution for v consists of writing uniformly random strings to unique array indices in the leaves of the left subtree and, subsequently, querying for these array indices in the leaves of the right subtree. To answer the queries correctly, significant amounts of information must be transferred from the left subtree to the right subtree. For sufficiently large subtrees, it can be shown that the majority of this information must be transferred by query operations in the right subtree performing many probes to cells last overwritten by operations in the left subtree. As a result, these probes will be uniquely assigned to the root of the tree, v.

To complete the proof, Larsen and Nielsen [45] use the obliviousness requirements of ORAM. Suppose there exists another sequence of operations of the same length that assigns significantly less cell probes to the internal node v

compared to the hard distribution described above. Note, there exists polynomial time algorithms to compute the number of probes assigned to v. Therefore, a computationally bounded adversary can distinguish between the hard distribution for v and the sequence that does not assign enough probes to v. This contradicts obliviousness. Therefore, a large number of probes must be assigned to each node in the tree. As each probe is uniquely assigned to a node, adding the counts over all nodes gives the desired lower bound.

There are two major obstacles for using the information transfer technique to prove lower bounds for multi-maps. The first problem appears because the lower bounds for oblivious RAMs of [45], as well the one for differentially private RAMs of [56], assumes that the stored array entries are chosen as uniformly random strings. Recall that the crux of the information transfer argument shows that the large entropy of the random strings generated independently in the left subtree of a node v must be retrieved by the query operations in the right subtree of v. The natural extension for encrypted multi-maps would be to assume that all values are truly random strings. While this assumption might be appropriate for multi-maps, it is unreasonable for the application of searchable encryption as it would force either the keywords or the document identifiers to be truly random. It is well known in practice that the entropy of keywords is not too large. Similarly, there is no reason that document identifiers are required to be very random. For example, document identifiers could be titles of documents or just generated by a counter. Instead, our lower bounds will derive entropy from the random distribution of values into keys for multi-maps (or, the random distribution of keywords into documents for the searchable encryption application). As an example, consider an arbitrary set of values V and keys K. We view the distribution of the values V to keys K as a bipartite graph with K as the left partition and V as the right partition. An edge exists between a key $\in K$ and val $\in V$ if and only if val is associated with key in the multi-map. The edges are drawn randomly such that the resulting graph is l-left-regular so each key is associated with exactly l values. Consider the scenario where all values in V are inserted according to this randomly chosen bipartite graph. Suppose that queries are performed to all keys in K. The answers to these queries allows one to correctly retrieve the randomly chosen edges of the graph. In other words, the queries perfectly retrieve the entropy of the update operations. Furthermore, our lower bounds do not make assumptions that either the keys in K or values in V are random.

The other and more serious problem arises from the fact that we are attempting to prove lower bounds for encrypted multi-maps that leak significantly more information to the adversary compared to ORAMs. The ORAM lower bound proof of [45] critically uses the fact that the information transfer tree for any two sequences of the same length must be computationally indistinguishable. On the other hand, we will be proving lower bounds for encrypted multi-maps that leak at least the decoupled equality pattern as well as performing one of either the Add or Get operations in the plaintext. As a result, the overwhelming majority of pairs of sequences of encrypted multi-map operations of the same length will have different leakage and, thus, they will be computationally distinguishable to the adversary.

Therefore, we must choose the hard distributions for each node v such that the decoupled equality pattern leakage is the same for the hard distribution of all nodes in the tree. To do this, we will carefully coordinate Get operations and Add performed on the same key. Recall that $\mathcal{L}_{\mathsf{dec}}$ leaks whether two Add operations are performed on the same key as well as whether two Get operations are performed on the same key. To ensure that leakage incurred by Get operations are identical, we choose our hard distribution such that all Get operations are performed on unique keys. As a result, we are able to swap any two Get operations without changing the leakage as long as the number of values returned by both operations are identical. We will arrange Add operations such that each queried key is always associated with exactly $l \geq 1$ values where l is a parameter (one can achieve encrypted arrays by setting $l = 1$). Using the above properties, we construct our hard distribution for each node v. We assign each leaf node in the information transfer tree with two disjoint equal-sized set of keys K_v^{a} and K_v^{g} and a set of values K_v. Furthermore, all assigned key and value sets are pairwise node disjoint. Each leaf node will be associated with $|K_v^{\mathsf{a}}| \cdot l$ Add operations where each key in K_v^{a} is associated with l uniformly random chosen values from V_v. Recall that we can model these random assignments of values to keys as picking a random l-left-regular bipartite graph with K_v^{a} and V_v acting as the left and right partition respectively. Additionally, each leaf node will perform $|K_v^{\mathsf{g}}|$ Get operations for each key in K_v^{g}. We will use this distribution of sequences as our baseline to construct hard distributions for each internal node v in the information transfer tree. Each of these node-specific hard distributions will have the same leakage with respect to the decoupled leakage function $\mathcal{L}_{\mathsf{dec}}$.

Recall that the goal of a hard distribution for node v is to ensure that a large number of cell probes are assigned to v in the information transfer tree. To do this, we should pick a hard distribution that requires queries in the right subtree of v to retrieve large amounts of entropy generated in the left subtree of v. To start, we denote $K^{\mathsf{a}}, K^{\mathsf{g}}$ and V as the union of the sets $K_{v'}^{\mathsf{a}}, K_{v'}^{\mathsf{g}}, V_{v'}$ that are assigned to leaf nodes v' that appear in the left subtree of v. We keep the identical Add and Get operations that appear in the left subtree of v. We modify the Get operations that appear in the right subtree to query keys in K^{a}, which are all the keys updated in the left subtree of v. As a result, the answers to Get operations in the right subtree of v are able to retrieve the random l-left-regular bipartite graph generated in the left subtree of v forcing a large number of cell probes to be assigned to v. Furthermore, our hard distribution for v only swapped the key parameters of Get operations maintaining the same leakage as the baseline hard distribution. By privacy, it must be that a large number of cell probes are assigned to many nodes of the information transfer tree. As a result, we are able to prove lower bounds for the leakage $\mathcal{L}_{\mathsf{dec}}$ that is significantly larger compared to ORAM leakage. Similar ideas can be used to prove lower bounds for the leakage functions $\mathcal{L}_{\mathsf{add}}$ and $\mathcal{L}_{\mathsf{get}}$ which enable schemes to perform one of either the Add or Get operations in the plaintext. We refer the reader to Sect. 4 for full details on the lower bound.

2 Definitions and Models

In this section, we formalize the notion of a *leakage function* and the *leakage cell probe model*, which is a generalization of the oblivious cell probe model of Larsen and Nielsen [45] and it can be used to derive lower bounds on the efficiency of general data structures with respect to a leakage function. We will then describe the *dynamic encrypted multi-map* problem for which we will derive lower bounds. We also consider the dynamic searchable encryption problem whose formal definition can be found in the full version.

2.1 Cell Probe Model

The cell probe model was introduced by Yao [63] and has widely been used to prove lower bounds for data structures (see [24,43,47,59] as examples). The goal of the cell probe model is to abstract the interactions of CPUs and word-RAM architectures. Memory in the cell probe model is an array of *cells* where each cell consists of exactly w bits. The operations of a data structure consist of *cell probes* where each probe may read the contents of a cell and/or update the cell's content. The *cost* or *running time* of an operation is measured by the number of cell probes. A data structure in the cell probe model may perform unlimited computation based on the contents of cells that were probed. Note, lower bounds in the cell probe model immediately imply results to more realistic models that measure costs using both memory accesses and computation.

In the context of privacy-preserving data structure, the cell probe model is adapted to a two-party setting: the *client* and the *server*. The client outsources the storage of data to the server and uses the data structure algorithms to perform operations that read and/or update the data stored on the server. For privacy, the client wishes to hide the content of outsourced data and/or the operations performed from the adversarial server. The adversarial server's view consists of the content of all cells on the server and the probes performed by operations. The adversary does not view the content of the client's storage nor the probes performed to the client's storage. In the first work relating the cell probe model to privacy-preserving data structures, Larsen and Nielsen [45] introduced the *oblivious cell probe model* in which any two sequences of operations of the same length are required to induce indistinguishable server's views. This model has been used to prove a lower bound for oblivious RAMs [45] and for other data structures, like stacks and queue [34]. Subsequently, Persiano and Yeo [56] introduced the *differentially private cell probe model*, a generalization of the oblivious cell probe model in which the adversary's view must abide to the standard differential privacy definition for neighboring sequences.

In this work, we define the *leakage cell probe model* which considers data structures with more complex leakage. For a *leakage function* $\mathcal{L}$, we denote the

$\mathcal{L}$-*leakage cell probe model* such that the adversary's view when processing two sequences of operations O and O' must be indistinguishable if $\mathcal{L}(O)$ and $\mathcal{L}(O')$ are equal. The leakage cell probe model is a generalization of the oblivious cell probe model as obliviousness can be viewed as privacy with respect to a leakage function that only leaks the number of operations performed. We note that the client-server interaction in the leakage cell probe model is identical to both the oblivious cell probe model [45] and the differentially private cell probe model [56]. The only difference is in the privacy notion.

We next describe the notion of a *data structure problem* in the cell probe model as consisting of a set $\mathbb{U}$ of update operations and a set $\mathbb{Q}$ of queries that return values in the domain $\mathbb{O}$. The response to a query $q \in \mathbb{Q}$ is determined by a function $\mathbb{R} : \mathbb{U}^* \times \mathbb{Q} \to \mathbb{O}$ based on the choice of the query $q \in \mathbb{Q}$ and the sequence of updates $(u_1, \ldots, u_l) \in \mathbb{U}^*$ that have been executed before the query q. For any **DS** solving a data structure problem in the cell probe model, the server's memory is assumed to consist of w-bit cells. The client's storage consists of c bits. There exists a random string $\mathcal{R}$ accessible by the operations of **DS**. We will assume that $\mathcal{R}$ is finite, but may be arbitrarily large. For cryptographic purposes, $\mathcal{R}$ may act as a private random function or a random oracle. An operation of **DS** is allowed to perform probes to cells in server memory, access bits in the client storage and access bits in $\mathcal{R}$. The data structure is only charged for probes to server cells. Accessing bits in client storage or $\mathcal{R}$ are free. The sequence of cell probes chosen by an operation of **DS** are a deterministic function of the client storage, random string $\mathcal{R}$ and the contents of cells that were previously probed in the current operation. Note, this deterministic function need not be efficiently computable as the cell probe model does not charge for computation. We denote the *failure probability* as the maximum probability that **DS** outputs the incorrect answer over all query operations and preceding sequence of operations. Note that the probability is strictly over the random choice of $\mathcal{R}$. Additionally, we note that the cell probe model assumes that **DS** processes operations in an *online* manner. **DS** must finish processing an operation before receiving the next operation. As a result, each cell probe performed by **DS** may be uniquely associated to an operation. The assumption of online operations is realistic as the majority of practical scenarios consider online operations.

The assumption that $\mathcal{R}$ is finite does not preclude the applicability of our result to algorithms with vanishing failure probabilities that may run infinitely. We show they can be converted into data structures with finite running time but non-zero failure probabilities by a standard reduction. The data structure is run for an arbitrary number of cell probes until the failure probability is sufficiently small. At this point, the data structure must return an answer. Our lower bounds will consider data structures with any constant failure probability strictly less than $1/2$. As a result, our lower bounds also apply to data structures whose failure probabilities decrease as the running time increases but have no termination guarantees.

2.2   Leakage Cell Probe Model

In this section, we formalize the privacy notion for data structures in the *leakage cell probe model*. Roughly speaking, we give an upper bound on the maximum amount of information viewed by the adversary when processing a sequence of operations by specifying a *leakage function* $\mathcal{L}$. Concretely, a leakage function $\mathcal{L}$ takes as input any valid sequence of operations, O, of **DS**. For online **DS** and for any sequence $O = (\mathsf{op}_1, \ldots, \mathsf{op}_\ell)$, we can rewrite the leakage $\mathcal{L}(O)$ as:

$$\mathcal{L}(O) = \mathcal{L}(\mathsf{op}_1), \mathcal{L}(\mathsf{op}_1, \mathsf{op}_2), \ldots, \mathcal{L}(\mathsf{op}_1, \ldots, \mathsf{op}_\ell) = \mathcal{L}(O_1), \mathcal{L}(O_2), \ldots, \mathcal{L}(O_\ell),$$

where O_i denotes the prefix $O_i = (\mathsf{op}_1, \ldots, \mathsf{op}_i)$ consisting of all operations up to and including the i-th operation. We formalize the notion that **DS** leaks at most $\mathcal{L}$ by means of an *indistinguishability-based* definition in which we require that, for any two sequences O and O' such that $\mathcal{L}(O) = \mathcal{L}(O')$, no efficient adversary $\mathcal{A}$ can distinguish a sequence of cell probes executed by **DS** while performing O from one executed while performing sequence O'. For two sequences O and O', we say that $\mathcal{L}(O) = \mathcal{L}(O')$ if and only if $\mathcal{L}(O_i) = \mathcal{L}(O_i')$ for every $i = 1, \ldots, \ell$.

Let us now proceed more formally. For any sequence of operations $O = (\mathsf{op}_1, \ldots, \mathsf{op}_\ell)$, the *adversary's view* $\mathcal{V}_{\mathbf{DS}}(O)$ of **DS** processing O consists of the sequence of probes performed by **DS** while processing sequence O. The randomness of $\mathcal{V}_{\mathbf{DS}}(O)$ is over the choice of the random string $\mathcal{R}$. For online **DS**, each cell probe is uniquely assigned to an operation. So, we can rewrite $\mathcal{V}_{\mathbf{DS}}(O) = (\mathcal{V}_{\mathbf{DS}}(O_1), \ldots, \mathcal{V}_{\mathbf{DS}}(O_\ell))$.

The formal definition of *non-adaptively $\mathcal{L}$-IND* is given below.

Definition 1 (Non-adaptively $\mathcal{L}$-IND). **DS** *is ν-non-adaptively $\mathcal{L}$-IND if for every pair of sequences O and O' such that $\mathcal{L}(O) = \mathcal{L}(O')$ and any deterministic polynomial time algorithm $\mathcal{A}$, then*

$$| \Pr[\mathcal{A}(\mathcal{V}_{\mathbf{DS}}(O)) = 1] - \Pr[\mathcal{A}(\mathcal{V}_{\mathbf{DS}}(O')) = 1]| \le \nu$$

The acute reader might notice several differences between the above security notion and previous definitions (for example, see [14,17,18,39]). First, our definition uses the weaker indistinguishability notion as opposed to the stronger simulation paradigm. Secondly, many previous works consider *adaptive* security where the adversary is allowed to view the leakage by **DS** on previous operations before picking the next operation. Our definition does not allow the operations to be picked depending on the adversary's view. Both differences result in a weaker security notion. However, a lower bound for a scheme satisfying this weaker security notion also implies a lower bound for the normal, stronger security notion. In other words, by assuming a weaker security notion, we improve the strength and applicability of our lower bound. We also note that our definition considers deterministic, polynomial time adversaries.

Finally, we formally define a *$\mathcal{L}$-leakage cell probe model data structure*.

Definition 2. *A **DS** is a $\mathcal{L}$-leakage cell probe model data structure if **DS** has failure probability strictly less than $1/2$ and is $1/4$-non-adaptively $\mathcal{L}$-IND.*

Note that, the distinguishing probability only has to be at most $1/4$ as opposed to $\mathsf{negl}(\lambda)$ where λ is the security parameter. Once again, we stress that this results in a weaker security notion and a lower bound for any **DS** that is $1/4$-non-adaptively $\mathcal{L}$-IND applies for any **DS** satisfying a stronger security notion. Overall, our lower bounds for $\mathcal{L}$-*leakage cell probe model data structure* imply lower bounds to the standard simulation-based, adaptive security notions against PPT adversaries with $\mathsf{negl}(\lambda)$ advantage.

In practice, the assumption of failure probability close to $1/2$ is unacceptably large. Once again, this is to improve the strength of our lower bound as it immediately implies results for **DS** with small or zero failure probability.

We also note that leakage cell probe model is a generalization of the oblivious cell probe model [45]. Consider the leakage function, $\mathcal{L}(\mathsf{op}_1, \ldots, \mathsf{op}_i) = i$, that only leaks the number of operations. In the $\mathcal{L}$-leakage cell probe model, all sequences of the same length must be indistinguishable which is identical to the oblivious cell probe model [45].

Comparing leakage functions. In general, leakage functions are not numerical as they encapsulate all the information learned by the adversary and for this reason it is hard to linearly order leakage functions. We can nonetheless define the following partial order on leakage functions.

Definition 3. *Leakage function* $\mathcal{L}_1$ *is at least as secure as leakage function* $\mathcal{L}_2$ *(in symbols* $\mathcal{L}_1 \leq \mathcal{L}_2$*) if any* **DS** *that is* $\mathcal{L}_1$*-IND is also* $\mathcal{L}_2$*-IND.*

We note the we use $\mathcal{L}_1 \leq \mathcal{L}_2$ as the leakage of $\mathcal{L}_1$ is smaller than the leakage of $\mathcal{L}_2$ and that a lower bound for a **DS** with leakage $\mathcal{L}_2$, also applies to any **DS**$'$ with leakage $\mathcal{L}_1 \leq \mathcal{L}_2$. The following lemma gives a sufficient condition for $\mathcal{L}_1 \leq \mathcal{L}_2$.

Lemma 1. *If there exists an efficient function* F *such that for all sequences* O *of operations it holds that* $\mathcal{L}_1(O) = F(\mathcal{L}_2(O))$*, then* $\mathcal{L}_1 \leq \mathcal{L}_2$*.*

2.3   Encrypted Multi-Maps

In this section, we present the *dynamic multi-map problem* where we consider the *multi-map* data structure that maintains m pairs $\mathsf{MM} = \{(\mathsf{key}_i, \mathsf{vals}_i)\}_{i \in [m]}$ where each key_i is from the *key universe* $\mathcal{K}$ and vals_i is a tuple of values from the *value universe* $\mathcal{V}$. We assume that all keys are unique (that is, $\mathsf{key}_i \neq \mathsf{key}_j$ for all $i \neq j$). This assumption is without loss of generality as any multi-map with duplicate keys can merge the associated tuples of values. For any key_i, we denote the number of values associated with key_i by $\ell(\mathsf{key}_i)$ (that is, $\ell(\mathsf{key}_i) := |\mathsf{vals}_i|$). Note, different keys can be associated with tuples of different length. We denote the total number of values by $n := \sum_{i \in [m]} \ell(\mathsf{key}_i) = \sum_{i \in [m]} |\mathsf{vals}_i|$. Additionally, we introduce the following notation for convenience. For any key, $\mathsf{vals}(\mathsf{MM}, \mathsf{key})$ is the tuple of values associated with key. Whenever the multi-map MM is clear from the context, we will omit MM and write $\mathsf{vals}(\mathsf{key})$ instead of $\mathsf{vals}(\mathsf{MM}, \mathsf{key})$.

We consider dynamic multi-maps with Create, Get and Add operations.

1. Create returns an empty MM $:= \emptyset$.
2. Get(key) takes as input key $\in \mathcal{K}$ and outputs vals(key), the tuple of values associated with key.
3. Add(key, val) adds value val to the tuple associated with key.

Note that we only allow a very simple type of insertions in which only one value is added for each operation. By proving a lower bound on a multi-map with only a simple insertion operation, our lower bound will also apply to more general multi-maps with more complex insertions and update operations.

Definition 4. *The* dynamic encrypted multi-map *problem is parameterized by* $\mathcal{K}$, *the* key universe, *and by* $\mathcal{V}$, *the* value universe. *The problem is defined by the tuple* $(\mathbb{U}, \mathbb{Q}, \mathbb{R})$ *where*

- $\mathbb{U} = \{\mathsf{Add}(\mathsf{key}, \mathsf{val}) \mid \mathsf{key} \in \mathcal{K}, \mathsf{val} \in \mathcal{V}\} \cup \{\mathsf{Create}\}$;
- $\mathbb{Q} = \{\mathsf{Get}(\mathsf{key}) \mid \mathsf{key} \in \mathcal{K}\}$;

and for any sequence $O = (\mathsf{Create}, \mathsf{Add}(\mathsf{key}_1, \mathsf{val}_1), \ldots, \mathsf{Add}(\mathsf{key}_m, \mathsf{val}_m))$,

$$\mathbb{R}(O, \mathsf{Get}(\mathsf{key})) = \{\mathsf{val} \mid \exists 1 \leq i \leq m \text{ s.t. } \mathsf{key}_i = \mathsf{key} \text{ and } \mathsf{val}_i = \mathsf{val}\}.$$

In other words, Get(key) *returns* vals(MM, key), *where* MM *is the instance obtained by executing the sequence* O *of update operations.*

Efficiency measure. For a data structure **DS** solving the dynamic encrypted multi-map problem, we denote $\mathsf{Cost}_{\mathbf{DS}}(O)$ as the expected number of cell probes needed by **DS** to perform the sequence of operations O where the expectation is taken over the random coin tosses of **DS**. We note that, unlike ORAMs, $\mathsf{Cost}_{\mathbf{DS}}$ is not a good measure of the efficiency of the data structure **DS**. For example, some Get operations might return an extremely long tuple while others only a few values and it would be unreasonable to expect these vastly different operations to perform the same number of cell probes. We thus define the *amortized efficiency* $\mathsf{Eff}_{\mathbf{DS}}$ of a data structure **DS** solving the dynamic encrypted multi-map problem with respect to a sequence of operations $O = (\mathsf{op}_1, \ldots, \mathsf{op}_\ell)$ as the expected value of the total number of cell probes executed by **DS** divided by the total number of values returned by Get or taken as inputs by Add. More precisely, the add op $=$ Add(key, v) operation will receive a single value tuple as input as in our setting only one value can be added to a key. Therefore, $\mathsf{Eff}_{\mathbf{DS}}(\mathsf{op}) := \mathsf{Cost}_{\mathbf{DS}}(\mathsf{op})$. For each get op $=$ Get(key), we consider the length of the returned tuple vals(key) as the length of the output and thus $\mathsf{Eff}_{\mathbf{DS}}(\mathsf{op}) := \mathsf{Cost}_{\mathbf{DS}}(\mathsf{op})/|\mathsf{vals}(\mathsf{key})|$.

In this paper, we prove lower bounds on $\mathsf{Eff}_{\mathbf{DS}}(n)$ for all probabilistic **DS** where $\mathsf{Eff}_{\mathbf{DS}}(n)$ is defined to be the maximum over all possible sequences O of n operations of the total expected amortized efficiency of all n operations where the expectation is taken over the random coin tosses of **DS**.

3   Leakage Profiles

In this section, we formally define the leakage profile $\mathcal{L}_{\mathsf{dec}}$ for which we prove our main result. As stated before, the efficiency of encrypted multi-maps crucially depends on its leakage. For strong privacy, there exist several solutions of encrypted multi-maps with minimal leakage using efficient oblivious RAMs [1,53] while achieving logarithmic efficiency. Minimal leakage $\mathcal{L}_{min}$ refers to the adversary learning only the size of inputs and outputs of operations and nothing else. We formally define $\mathcal{L}_{min}$ and present a simplified version of a folklore construction in the full version.

To understand the transition from constant to logarithmic efficiency as a function of the leakage allowed, we consider the smallest leakage achieved by constant efficiency encrypted multi-maps. In particular, these schemes leak the *global key-equality pattern*, $\mathcal{L}_{glob}$, where adversaries learn whether two operations use the same key as input or not. We formally define $\mathcal{L}_{glob}$ and present the simple *hash-and-encrypt* compiler that achieves $\mathcal{L}_{glob}$ leakage in the full version.

The next step up in security would be to still allow the adversary to learn which operations are on the same key but to limit this ability to operations of the same type. That is, the adversary still learns whether two Get operations are on the same key or not and whether two Add operations are on the same key but it cannot link an Add and a Get that receive the same key as input. This is captured by the following leakage function.

Definition 5 (Decoupled Key-Equality Leakage $\mathcal{L}_{dec}$). *For sequence $O = (\text{op}_0 = \text{Create}, \text{op}_1, \ldots, \text{op}_\ell)$ of operations where $\text{key}_1, \ldots, \text{key}_\ell$ are the input keys to each non-create operation, then the* decoupled key-equality leakage *$\mathcal{L}_{dec}(O)$ associated with O consists of $\mathcal{L}_{dec}(O) = (\mathcal{L}_{dec}(O_0), \ldots, \mathcal{L}_{dec}(O_\ell))$ where $O_i = (\text{op}_0, \ldots, \text{op}_i)$ and MM^{O_i} is the multi-map resulting from the first i operations. Then, $\mathcal{L}_{dec}(O_i)$ is defined as:*

1. *if $\text{op}_i = \text{Create}$ then $\mathcal{L}_{dec}(O_i) = (\text{Create})$;*
2. *if $\text{op}_i = \text{Add}(\text{key}_i, \text{val}_i)$ then $\mathcal{L}_{dec}(O_i) = (\text{Add}, \text{ep}^{dec}_i)$;*
3. *if $\text{op}_i = \text{Get}(\text{key}_i)$ then $\mathcal{L}_{dec}(O_i) = (\text{Get}, |\text{vals}(\text{MM}^{O_{i-1}}, \text{key}_i)|, \text{ep}^{dec}_i)$.*

The decoupled key-equality pattern *$\text{ep}^{dec}_i := (\text{ep}^{dec}_{i,1}, \ldots, \text{ep}^{dec}_{i,i-1})$ is:*

$$
\text{ep}^{dec}_{i,j} = \begin{cases} \bot, & \text{if } \text{op}_i \text{ and } \text{op}_j \text{ are not of the same type.} \\ 0, & \text{if } \text{op}_i \text{ and } \text{op}_j \text{ are of the same type and } \text{key}_i \neq \text{key}_j. \\ 1, & \text{if } \text{op}_i \text{ and } \text{op}_j \text{ are of the same type and } \text{key}_i = \text{key}_j. \end{cases}
$$

We note that the above leakage still leaks the number of returned values for each Get operation. Using Add key-equality leakage, the adversary can observe the number of values added for a pseudonymous representation of a key. If the number of values added is unique for any key, then the adversary will learn the global key-equality pattern about this specific key that leaks whether specific Add and Get operations operate on this key with a unique number of associated values. In particular, $\mathcal{L}_{dec}$ hides key-equality patterns between Add and Get operations when there exist multiple keys with the same number of associated values when Get is executed. In other words, $\mathcal{L}_{dec}$ is a very minimal increase in privacy over $\mathcal{L}_{glob}$. The main result of this paper is that $\mathcal{L}_{dec}$-IND security for encrypted multi-maps (and arrays) incurs $\Omega(\lg n)$ overhead even though it is minimally more secure than $\mathcal{L}_{glob}$-IND schemes.

We can further extend our lower bounds to **DS** with even larger leakage functions. We define leakage functions $\mathcal{L}_{add}$ and $\mathcal{L}_{get}$, which leak the decoupled key-equality pattern like $\mathcal{L}_{dec}$. Additionally, $\mathcal{L}_{add}$ leaks the keys and values that are input to all Add operations while $\mathcal{L}_{get}$ leaks the keys that are input to all Get operations. In other words, $\mathcal{L}_{add}$ enables the multi-map to perform Add operations in the plaintext while $\mathcal{L}_{get}$ enables the multi-map to perform Get operations in the plaintext. It turns out our lower bounds still apply as long as the encrypted multi-map performs at most one of either Get or Add operations are performed in the plaintext. We formally define $\mathcal{L}_{add}$ and $\mathcal{L}_{get}$ in the full version. The counterparts of $\mathcal{L}_{add}$ and $\mathcal{L}_{glob}$ for dynamic searchable encryption may also be found in the full version.

4   Lower Bounds for Decoupled Key-Equality Leakage

In this section, we present our main result that any encrypted multi-map with leakage at most $\mathcal{L}_{dec}$ must incur logarithmic overhead.

Theorem 3. *Let* **DS** *be a* $\mathcal{L}_{dec}$*-leakage cell probe model dynamic encrypted multi-map implemented over w-bit cells and a client with c bits of storage. Then*

$$\mathsf{Eff}_{\mathbf{DS}}(n) = \Omega\left(\lg\left(\frac{n}{c}\right) \cdot \frac{\lg(n)}{w}\right).$$

In the natural setting that $c = O(n^\alpha)$, for some constant $0 \le \alpha < 1$, and cell sizes of $w = \Theta(\lg n)$ bits, the above bound simplifies to $\Omega(\lg n)$.

This result will be proven using the information transfer technique [59]. Throughout the proof, we will assume that **DS** has error probability at most $1/128$ (instead of strictly smaller than $1/2$) and this is without loss of generality as we can apply a standard reduction of executing a constant number of independent copies and returning the majority answer without affecting the asymptotic efficiency.

4.1   Hard Distribution

We start by formalizing the hard distribution and the random variables used in our proof. Fix positive integers n and l and constant $0 < \epsilon < 1$ such that $l < n^\epsilon$. Set $p := n^{1-\epsilon}$. The hard distribution will use the following $p + 1$ disjoint sets of values:

1. V_0 consisting of l values;
2. $V_1, \ldots, V_p$ each consisting of n^ϵ values;

Additionally, we define the following $2p$ pairwise disjoint sets of keys:

1. Sets K_j^{a}, for $j = 1, \ldots, p$, each of size n^ϵ;
2. Sets K_j^{g}, for $j = 1, \ldots, p$, each of size n^ϵ.

Table 1. Generation of hard distribution.

$\mathsf{Hard}_{n,l,\epsilon}(V_0, V_1, \ldots, V_p, K_1^{\mathsf{a}}, \ldots, K_p^{\mathsf{a}}, K_1^{\mathsf{g}}, \ldots, K_p^{\mathsf{g}})$

- Phase 0:
  Execute SubPhase Init$_i$ for each $i \in \{1, \ldots, p\}$:
    For each **key** $\in K_i^{\mathsf{g}}$:
      For each **val** $\in V_0$:
        output: Add(**key**, **val**).
- Phase j for each $j \in \{1, \ldots, p\}$:
  Execute SubPhase A$_j$ of add operations and SubPhase G$_j$ of get operations.
  1. SubPhase A$_j$
     For each **key** $\in K_j^{\mathsf{a}}$:
       Select subset $V_{\mathsf{key}} \subset V_j$ of l values uniformly at random.
       For each **val** $\in V_{\mathsf{key}}$:
         output: Add(**key**, **val**).
  2. SubPhase G$_j$
     For each **key** $\in K_j^{\mathsf{g}}$:
       output: Get(**key**).

We describe the probabilistic process that generates our hard distribution of sequences of encrypted multi-map operations in Table 1. We denote the resulting distribution by $\mathsf{Hard}(V_0, V_1, \ldots, V_p, K_1^{\mathsf{a}}, \ldots, K_p^{\mathsf{a}}, K_1^{\mathsf{g}}, \ldots, K_p^{\mathsf{g}})$. For convenience, we will assume that all of n, l, ϵ as well as the sets $V_0, V_1, \ldots, V_p, K_1^{\mathsf{a}}, \ldots, K_p^{\mathsf{a}}, K_1^{\mathsf{g}}, \ldots, K_p^{\mathsf{g}}$ are fixed going forward and denote our hard distribution by Hard.

As described in Table 1, a sequence in the support of our hard distribution consists of $p + 1$ phases. In phase 0, each of the l values of V_0 is added to the tuple of each key in K_i^{g}, for all $i \in \{1, \ldots, p\}$. Phase j, for $j = 1, \ldots, p$, consists of two sub-phases: sub-phase A_j that consists of $l \cdot n^\epsilon$ Add operations, directly followed by sub-phase G_j that consists of n^ϵ Get operations. The Add operations of phase j add a subset of l values chosen uniformly at random from the set V_j to each key in K_j^{a}. This naturally defines a bipartite graph $B_j = (K_j^{\mathsf{a}}, V_j, E_j)$ where the set of key K_j^{a} appear in the left partition, the set of values V_j appear in the right partition, and E_j represents the edge set. An edge (**key**, **val**) appears in E_j if and only if **val** is added to the tuple of values associated with **key**; that is, **val** $\in$ vals(**key**). We note that our choice of adding l randomly chosen values to each **key** $\in K_j^{\mathsf{a}}$ is equivalent to choosing B_j uniformly at random from the set of all left l-regular bipartite graphs. Furthermore, bipartite graph B_j uniquely identifies the Add operations that appear in phase j. Note that a sequence of operations in the support of Hard builds an encrypted multi-map that contains $2n$ different keys.

Leakage of the hard sequence. We now describe the leakage $\mathcal{L}_{\mathsf{dec}}(H)$ associated with a sequence H in the support of our hard distribution.

We observe that each Get operation returns the l values in V_0 and, as the K_i^{g}s are pairwise disjoint by definition, each Get operates on a different key. Thus, all Get operations in H will have identical leakage; specifically, the adversary learns that the size of the tuple associated with each query key is l and that the queried keys are distinct.

For the leakage incurred by Add operations, we observe that the $2p$ sets $\{K_i^g\}_{i \in \{1,...,p\}}$ and $\{K_i^a\}_{i \in \{1,...,p\}}$ are pairwise disjoint by definition. H will perform exactly l consecutive Add operations to each of the n^ϵ keys of K_i^g, for $i = 1, \ldots, p$ during phase 0. In phase j, H will perform exactly l consecutive Add operations to each of the n^ϵ keys in K_j^a. Therefore, the Add key-equality leakage pattern will reveal to the adversary that Add operations to the same key always occurs in consecutive blocks of l operations.

From the above, it is not hard to see that $\mathcal{L}_{dec}$ is the same on any two pair of sequences H_1 and H_2 in the support of the hard distribution. Indeed, the leakage for the Get operations depends only on the choice of l and, similarly, the leakage for the Add operations depends only on the choice of l and n^ϵ. As both l and n^ϵ are fixed, the leakages $\mathcal{L}_{dec}(H_1)$ and $\mathcal{L}_{dec}(H_2)$ for any H_1 and H_2 in the support of the hard sequence is identical.

Information transfer tree. Next, we define an abstract model of data flow called the information transfer tree, which will be integral in our lower bound proofs. For each sequence H in the support of the hard distribution, we will denote the information transfer tree of H by $\mathcal{T}(H)$. $\mathcal{T}(H)$ is a binary tree whose nodes contain the cell probes performed by **DS** when executing H. Without loss of generality, we assume that p is a power of 2 and construct a complete binary tree with p leaves. For all $j \in \{1, \ldots, p\}$, we assign phase j, consisting of subphases A_j and G_j, to the j-th leftmost leaf. Phase 0 is ignored in the construction of the information transfer tree.

Next, we proceed by uniquely assigning cell probes to nodes of the information transfer tree. Consider a probe to cell address x that occurs as part of an operation of the phase j. If this is the first probe to cell address x, then the probe is not assigned to any node. Otherwise, pick the most recent phase i that precedes phase j ($i \leq j$) such that an operation in phase i overwrote the contents at cell address x. The probe is then assigned to the least common ancestor of the leaf nodes associated with phase j and phase i. Note that the assignment of probes to nodes is probabilistic and depends on the random coin tosses $\mathcal{R}$ of **DS**. So, $\mathcal{T}(H)$ is also a random variable over $\mathcal{R}$. For each node v, we define $\mathcal{C}_v(H)$ as the set of probes assigned to v when executing H over the choice of $\mathcal{R}$. We denote $\mathcal{T}(\mathsf{Hard})$ and $\mathcal{C}_v(\mathsf{Hard})$ as probability distributions over the random choices of both Hard and $\mathcal{R}$.

4.2 Bounding Probes Assigned to Internal Nodes

To prove our lower bound, we will show that for many nodes v, the expected size of $\mathcal{C}_v(\mathsf{Hard})$ must be large. Since each probe is assigned to at most one node, the sum of the number of probes assigned over all the nodes v will result in a lower bound on the expected number of cell probes needed to process a random sequence generated by Hard.

Denote depth(v) as the distance of v from the root. As there are $p = n^{1-\epsilon}$ leaf nodes, the leaf nodes have depth $\lg(p) = (1-\epsilon)\lg(n)$ where all logarithms are base 2. We will prove the following lemma which states that a large number of cells must be assigned to nodes in expectations for all nodes that are not too close to either the root node or the leaf nodes.

Lemma 2. *Let* **DS** *be a $\mathcal{L}_{\text{dec}}$-leakage cell probe model dynamic encrypted multi-map scheme that errs with probability at most $1/128$. For any $1 \leq l \leq n^{\epsilon/2}$, there exists a constant $\gamma_1 > 0$ such that for every node v of depth $8 \leq d \leq \frac{1-\epsilon}{2}\lg(\frac{n}{c})$, it must be that*

$$\mathsf{E}\left[|\mathcal{C}_v(\mathsf{Hard})|\right] \geq \gamma_1 \cdot \frac{n}{2^d} \cdot \frac{l\lg n}{w}.$$

We now show that Lemma 2 would complete the proof of Theorem 3.

Proof of Theorem 3. Recall that each probe is assigned to a most one node of the tree. So, counting the cell probes assigned to a subset of nodes gives a lower bound on the number of cell probes. A complete binary tree has 2^d nodes at depth d. By Lemma 2, all nodes v such that $8 \leq \text{depth}(v) \leq \frac{1-\epsilon}{2}\lg(\frac{n}{c})$ have $\Omega(\frac{n}{2^d}\frac{l\lg n}{w})$ assigned cell probes in expectation. Therefore, each level in this range contributes $\Omega(n \cdot \frac{l\lg n}{w})$ cell probes in expectation and by multiplying by the number of levels for which Lemma 2 holds we obtain $\Omega(n\lg(\frac{n}{c})\frac{l\lg n}{w})$ cell probes. Recall that we are considering both the Get and Add operations and the efficiency is measured as running time per response of a query and per value added. Note, a hard sequence performs $\Theta(n)$ queries with exactly l responses each and performs $\Theta(n \cdot l)$ Add each of exactly one value. So, we get the expected amortized running time is $\Omega(\lg(\frac{n}{c}) \cdot \frac{\lg n}{w})$. $\qquad\square$

4.3   Using the Privacy Guarantees

Therefore, it remains to prove Lemma 2 to finish the proof of our main result. To do this, we will prove a weaker lemma which shows that for a large number of nodes v there exists a probability distribution Hard_v (specifically built for node v) that forces the number of probes assigned to v, $\mathcal{C}_v(\mathsf{Hard}_v)$, to be large in expectation. This lemma is significantly weaker than Lemma 2 which states that there exists a *single* distribution, Hard, that simultaneously assigns many probes to the sets $\mathcal{C}_v(\mathcal{H})$ for a large number of nodes v. We note that our proof must critically use the privacy guarantees of **DS** as there exist constructions with $O(1)$ efficiency that do not provide any privacy such as the dynamic perfect hashing solutions [21]. By leveraging the privacy guarantees of **DS**, we can show the two statements are equivalent. First, we formally state our weaker lemma.

Lemma 3. *Fix integers n and l and $0 \leq \epsilon \leq 1$ such that $1 \leq l \leq n^{\epsilon/2}$. Let* **DS** *be a $\mathcal{L}_{\text{dec}}$-leakage cell probe model dynamic encrypted multi-map scheme that errs with probability at most $1/128$. Then, there exists a constant $\gamma_2 > 0$ such that, for every node v with $8 \leq \text{depth}(v) \leq \frac{1-\epsilon}{2}\lg\frac{n}{c}$, there exists a probability distribution Hard_v such that $\mathcal{L}_{\text{dec}}(\mathsf{Hard}) = \mathcal{L}_{\text{dec}}(\mathsf{Hard}_v)$ and*

$$\Pr\left[|\mathcal{C}_v(\mathsf{Hard}_v)| \geq \gamma_2 \cdot \frac{n}{2^d} \cdot \frac{l\lg n}{w}\right] \geq \frac{1}{2}.$$

By combining Lemma 3 with the privacy guarantees of **DS**, we show that we can prove Lemma 2. By Lemma 3, there exists a distribution Hard_v that forces any **DS** with at most $1/128$ failure probability to assign many cell probes to $\mathcal{C}_v(\mathsf{Hard}_v)$ in expectation. Furthermore, Hard_v and Hard have the same leakage with respect to leakage function $\mathcal{L}_{\mathsf{dec}}$. Since the size of $\mathcal{C}_v(O)$ can be computed by a deterministic, polynomial time algorithm for any sequence O, it must be that the expected sizes of $\mathcal{C}_v(\mathsf{Hard})$ and $\mathcal{C}_v(\mathsf{Hard}_v)$ cannot differ significantly. Otherwise, a deterministic, polynomial time adversary will be able to distinguish whether **DS** is executing a sequence randomly drawn from Hard or Hard_v. As a result, it can be shown that the size of $\mathcal{C}_v(\mathsf{Hard})$ for all nodes v must be large in expectation. We proceed to formalize these ideas.

Proof of Lemma 2. Pick $\gamma_1 < \gamma_2/4$ and suppose, for the sake of contradiction, that there exists a node v of depth $8 \leq \mathrm{depth}(v) \leq \frac{1-\epsilon}{2} \lg \frac{n}{c}$, such that $\mathsf{E}[|\mathcal{C}_v(\mathsf{Hard})|] < \frac{\gamma_2}{4} \frac{n}{2^d} \cdot \frac{l \lg n}{w}$. By Markov's inequality, we have that

$$\Pr\left[|\mathcal{C}_v(\mathsf{Hard})| \geq \gamma_2 \cdot \frac{n}{2^d} \cdot \frac{l \lg n}{w}\right] < 1/4.$$

On the other hand, by Lemma 3 we know that

$$\Pr\left[|\mathcal{C}_v(\mathsf{Hard}_v)| \geq \gamma_2 \cdot \frac{n}{2^d} \cdot \frac{l \lg n}{w}\right] \geq 1/2.$$

Therefore a deterministic, polynomial time adversary that computes the number of probes assigned to v and outputs 1 if and only if the number of cell probes assigned to v is less than $\gamma_2 \cdot \frac{n}{2^d} \cdot \frac{l \lg n}{w}$. This adversary successfully distinguishes whether **DS** is processing Hard or Hard_v. Thus, this contradicts that **DS** is non-adaptively $\mathcal{L}_{\mathsf{dec}}$-IND.   □

4.4   An Encoding Argument

Finally, we present the proof of Lemma 3 that requires finding a distribution Hard_v with the properties that $\mathcal{C}_v(\mathsf{Hard}_v)$ is large in expectation and that Hard_v has the same leakage as Hard with respect to $\mathcal{L}_{\mathsf{dec}}$. We start by describing simple modifications to Hard that are used to construct Hard_v while keeping $\mathcal{L}_{\mathsf{dec}}$ unchanged.

$\mathcal{L}_{\mathsf{dec}}$-*invariant swaps.* Let us start with a simple example and consider distribution $\mathsf{Hard}^{(s,s')}$ defined as follows for indices $1 \leq s \leq s' \leq p$. Recall that in our definition of Hard, phase $1 \leq j \leq p$ consists of subphase A_j where Add operations are performed on the keys in K_j^{a} and subphase G_j where Get operations are performed on the keys in K_j^{g}. In distribution $\mathsf{Hard}^{(s,s')}$ where $s \leq s'$, subphase $\mathsf{A}_{s'}$ still consists of Add operations performed on the keys in $K_{s'}^{\mathsf{a}}$ but the Get operations of subphase $\mathsf{G}_{s'}$ are performed on the keys in K_s^{a} instead of $K_{s'}^{\mathsf{g}}$. We show that this swap does not change the leakage with respect to $\mathcal{L}_{\mathsf{dec}}$.

Lemma 4. *For any* $1 \leq s \leq s' \leq p$, $\mathcal{L}_{\mathsf{dec}}(\mathsf{Hard}) = \mathcal{L}_{\mathsf{dec}}\left(\mathsf{Hard}^{(s,s')}\right)$.

Proof. Since no Add operation is affected by the swap, the leakage generated by the Add operations remains the same. For the Get operations, observe that the Get operations in $\mathsf{Hard}^{(s,s')}$ are always performed on distinct keys, just as in Hard and thus the key-equality pattern does not change. Moreover, since $s \leq s'$, when the keys in K_s^{a} are queried in phase s', l values have already been added to them. Therefore the Get operations of $\mathsf{Hard}^{(s,s')}$ return l values just as in Hard and thus the volume pattern does not change either.   □

The same argument applies to any set $S = \{(s_1, s_1'), \ldots, (s_t, s_t')\}$ of swaps provided that $s_i \leq s_i'$, for $i = 1, \ldots, t$, and that each index is involved in at most one swap. We call such a set S of swaps a *legal* set of swaps and we denote by Hard^S the distribution resulting from first sampling according to Hard and then performing the swaps in S. The following lemma follows by considering the swaps one at a time and by invoking Lemma 4 for each swap.

Lemma 5. *For any legal set* $S = \{(s_1, s_1'), \ldots, (s_t, s_t')\}$, *it holds that* $\mathcal{L}_{\mathsf{dec}}(\mathsf{Hard}) = \mathcal{L}_{\mathsf{dec}}(\mathsf{Hard}^S)$.

Defining Hard_v. Distribution Hard_v is designed to make the set of cell probes assigned to v, $\mathcal{C}_v(\mathsf{Hard}_v)$ large in expectation for any **DS** with a bounded failure probability while ensuring the leakages of Hard and Hard_v remain identical according to $\mathcal{L}_{\mathsf{dec}}$. Recall that $\mathcal{C}_v(\mathsf{Hard}_v)$ contains only probes that occur in the right subtree of v to a cell last overwritten in the left subtree of v. Suppose we design Hard_v so that the Add operations in the left subtree of v insert a large amount of random information that is independent from all other operations and that this information must be extracted by Get operations in the right subtree of v. For **DS** to answer the queries with low failure probability, a lot of the information inserted in the left subtree of v must be transferred to the answers of the queries in the right subtree of v. We show that there are only two ways to transfer information between the left and right subtree. First, the client can store information in the c bits of client storage. The other option is that queries in the right subtree of v must probe cells that were last overwritten in the left subtree of v. If the information required to transfer is much larger than the c bits of client storage, it must be the number of probes performed by queries in the right subtree of v to cells that were last overwritten by operations in left subtree of v must be sufficiently large. All these probes will be assigned to $\mathcal{C}_v(\mathsf{Hard}_v)$.

Let us be more precise. Fix any node v of depth d and denote by 2ℓ the number of leaves in the tree rooted at v so that each of the left and right subtree has exactly $\ell := p/2^{d+1}$. Let i be the index of the leftmost leaf of the subtree rooted at v. Then, the Add operations performed in the left subtree of v add values to keys in $K_i^{\mathsf{a}}, \ldots, K_{i+\ell-1}^{\mathsf{a}}$ according to the bipartite graphs $B_i, \ldots, B_{i+\ell-1}$. Recall that each of the bipartite graphs B_j where $j \in \{i, \ldots, i+\ell-1\}$ arrange the keys K_j^{a} in the left subtree and the values V_j in the right subtree. An edge occurs between a key $\mathtt{key} \in K_j^{\mathsf{a}}$ and value $\mathtt{val} \in V_j$ if and only if $\mathtt{val}$ is added to the tuple of values associated with $\mathtt{key}$. In other words, the operation $\mathsf{Add}(\mathtt{key}, \mathtt{val})$ was executed in the left subtree of v. The Get operations performed in the right subtree of v are for keys in $K_{i+\ell}^{\mathsf{g}}, \ldots, K_{i+2\ell-1}^{\mathsf{g}}$. Each of these keys has been associated with the l values of V_0 by the Add operations of phase 0. We construct Hard_v by modifying the Get operations in the right subtree of v to query the keys that were used as inputs by the Add operations of the left subtree of v. Specifically, the leaves in the right subtree of v will contain Get operations to the keys in $K_i^a, \ldots, K_{i+\ell-1}^a$. This corresponds to the set of swaps $\mathsf{swap}_v = \{(i, i+\ell), \ldots, (i+\ell-1, i+2\ell-1)\}$ which is easily seen to be legal. By invoking Lemma 5, we get the following lemma.

Lemma 6. *Leakage distributions $\mathcal{L}_{\mathsf{dec}}(\mathsf{Hard}_v)$ and $\mathcal{L}_{\mathsf{dec}}(\mathsf{Hard})$ are identical.*

We remind the reader that in phase j, each keyword of K_j^a is assigned a random subset of exactly l values from the set of values V_j. These chosen values are uniquely defined by a left l-regular bipartite graph B_j that is chosen uniformly at random. The entropy of the left subtree of v in Hard_v originates from the chosen bipartite graphs B_j that are chosen uniformly and independently at random for all $j \in \{i, \ldots, i+\ell-1\}$. For each key that appears in the left partition of B_j, there are $\binom{|V_j|}{l} = \binom{n^\epsilon}{l}$ possible choices for the l edges (corresponding to the l values that will be associated with the key). Therefore, the choice of the l edges adjacent to each key in the left partition of B_j has entropy $\lg \binom{n^\epsilon}{l}$. By picking $l \in \{1, \ldots, n^{\epsilon/2}\}$, the choice of the edges adjacent to each key in the left partition of B_j generates $\Omega(l \lg n)$ bits of entropy by applying Stirling's approximation. We note our lower bound do not assume any entropy for the actual values as done in previous lower bound results [45,56].

As the right subtree of v will query for all keys that were input to Add operations in the left subtree and **DS** has low failure probability, most of this entropy must be retrieved by **DS** from the left subtree of v. Note, there are a total of $\Theta(\frac{n}{2^d})$ queries performed in the right subtree of v. As a result, $\Omega(\frac{n}{2^d} \cdot l \lg n)$ bits of entropy must be transferred from the left subtree. Each cell probe can transfer at most w bits of entropy and, intuitively, this implies that $\Omega(\frac{n}{2^d} \cdot \frac{l \lg n}{w})$ cell probes must be assigned to v. We now formalize these arguments.

Lemma 7. *Fix integers n and l and $0 \leq \epsilon \leq 1$ such that $1 \leq l \leq n^{\epsilon/2}$. Let **DS** be a $\mathcal{L}_{\mathsf{dec}}$-leakage cell probe model dynamic encrypted multi-map that errs with probability at most $1/128$. For every node v of depth $8 \leq d \leq \frac{1-\epsilon}{2} \lg \frac{n}{c}$,*

$$\Pr\left[|\mathcal{C}_v(\mathsf{Hard}_v)| \geq \frac{1}{100} \cdot \frac{n}{2^d} \cdot \frac{l \lg n}{w} \right] \geq \frac{1}{2}.$$

Proof. Fix any vertex v with depth $8 \leq d \leq \frac{1-\epsilon}{2} \lg \frac{n}{c}$. We consider the one-way communication problem between Alice and Bob in which a sequence O of operations is sampled according to Hard_v. The entirety of O is given to Alice whereas Bob receives all of O except the operations performed in the left subtree of O. That is, the operations of phases $i, \ldots, i+\ell-1$ in O are only given to Alice and not to Bob for some i where $\ell = \frac{n}{2^{d+1}}$. Both Alice and Bob receive common randomness $\mathcal{R}$ used by **DS**. Furthermore, they have agreed on an arbitrary, but fixed ordering for each of the value and key sets. The goal of the one-way communication is for Alice to allow Bob to reconstruct the missing operations which are uniquely defined by the bipartite graphs $B_i, \ldots, B_{i+\ell-1}$. We observe that the entropy of the missing bipartite graphs is $\ell \cdot \lg \binom{n^\epsilon}{l} = \Theta((n/2^d) \cdot \lg \binom{n^\epsilon}{l})$ even when conditioned on Bob's input as all the graphs are chosen independently of $\mathcal{R}$ and all other operations that appear in O. By Shannon's source coding theorem, the expected length of Alice's message must be at least as large as the entropy of the graphs.

Towards a contradiction, we will assume that there exists $\mathbf{DS}$ with error probability at most $1/128$ such that $\Pr[|\mathcal{C}_v(\mathsf{Hard}_v)| \geq \frac{1}{100} \cdot \frac{1}{w} \cdot \frac{n}{2^{d+1}} \cdot \lg \binom{n^\epsilon}{l}] < \frac{1}{2}$. We will use $\mathbf{DS}$ to construct an impossible encoding contradicting Shannon's source coding theorem. Note this assumption contradicts the statement of Lemma 7 for any $1 \leq l \leq n^{\epsilon/2}$ as by Stirling's approximation it implies that $\lg \binom{n^\epsilon}{l} = \Omega(l \lg(n))$.

Alice's encoding. Alice receives the sequence O sampled according to Hard_v and $\mathcal{R}$ as input and produces the following encoding:

1. Alice executes $\mathbf{DS}$ using $\mathcal{R}$ as the randomness and performs all operations in sequence O up to, but not including, phase $i + \ell$. Note that phase $i + \ell$ is the first phase in O that belongs to the right subtree of v. At this point, Alice takes a snapshot of the contents of all memory cells on the server as well as the contents of client storage.

2. Alice executes the remaining operations in v's right subtree. That is, all operations of phases $i+\ell, \ldots, i+2\ell-1$ in O. Alice collects the set F of all query operations in v's right subtree where $\mathbf{DS}$ fails to return the correct answer. Additionally, Alice collects the set $C_v(O)$ of the cell probes that are assigned to v along with the addresses of the probed cells.

3. If either $|F| \geq \frac{1}{32} \cdot \frac{n}{2^{d+1}}$ or $|C_v(O)| \geq \frac{1}{100} \cdot \frac{n}{2^{d+1}} \cdot \lg \binom{n^\epsilon}{l}/w$, then Alice's encoding will start with a 0 followed by the response to each of the queries in the right subtree of v. Specifically, for $j \in \{i, \ldots, i+\ell-1\}$, Alice iterates through all $\mathsf{key} \in K_j^\mathsf{a}$ in the order agreed upon with Bob and encodes the subset of l values V_j associated with each key using $\lg \binom{n^\epsilon}{l}$ bits. This completes Alice's encoding for this case.

4. Suppose instead that $|F| < \frac{1}{32} \cdot \frac{n}{2^{d+1}}$ and $|C_v(O)| < \frac{1}{100} \cdot \frac{n}{2^{d+1}} \cdot \lg \binom{n^\epsilon}{l}/w$. In this case, Alice's encoding will start with a 1-bit and continues by encoding the following information:
   (a) The c bits of client storage recorded in snapshot.
   (b) The number $|F|$ of failed query using $\Theta(\lg n)$ bits as $|F| \leq n$.
   (c) The index and the answer of the $|F|$ keys in $K_i^\mathsf{a} \cup \ldots \cup K_{i+\ell-1}^\mathsf{a}$ for which $\mathbf{DS}$ fails to return the correct answer. The indices are encoded using $\lg \binom{n/2^{d+1}}{|F|}$ bits and the answer to each of the failing queries are encoded using $\lg \binom{n^\epsilon}{l}$.
   (d) The number $|C_v(O)|$ of the probes assigned to v using $\Theta(\lg n)$ bits.
   (e) The address and content of each cell probe in $C_v(O)$ where w bits are used to encode the address and another w bits to encode the contents.

Bob's decoding. Bob receives Alice's encoding, the sequence of operations O except for the operations of that occur phases $i, \ldots, i+\ell-1$ and the random string $\mathcal{R}$. Bob decodes in the following manner:

1. If Alice's encoding starts with a 0-bit then the answers to all Get queries of Phases $i + \ell, \ldots, i + 2\ell - 1$ are explicitly encoded in Alice's message and thus Bob proceeds as follows. For $j \in \{i, \ldots, i + \ell - 1\}$ and for each key $\in K_j^a$ in the agreed upon order, Bob reads the $\lg \binom{n^e}{l}$ bits that encode which l values of V_j have been assigned to key. This directly provides the l edges of the vertex in B_j corresponding to key. Repeating this process for all keywords allows Bob to completely retrieve B_j completing the decoding when Alice's message starts with a 0-bit.

2. From now on, we suppose Alice's encoding starts with a 1-bit.

   (a) Bob simulates **DS** using $\mathcal{R}$ for phases $0, \ldots, i - 1$. That is, all operations up to, but not including, the first operation of v's left subtree. The result of this execution is identical to Alice's execution as they both use the same random string $\mathcal{R}$. Bob will record the contents of all cells in snapshot$'$.

   (b) Bob skips phases $i, \ldots, i + \ell - 1$ that are the left subtree operations of v.

   (c) Bob retrieves the following information from Alice's encoding:

      i. The contents of client storage in snapshot where snapshot is the state of **DS** just before any operations in the right subtree of v.

      ii. The set F of keywords for which **DS** will fail to return the correct answer. For each of these failed keywords, Bob will also retrieve the correct answer from Alice's encoding using the same algorithm as the one where Alice's encoding started with a 0-bit described above.

      iii. The address and content of each of the cells in $C_v(O)$.

   (d) Bob simulates **DS** on the operations in the right subtree of v. That is, all phases $j \in \{i + \ell, \ldots, i + 2\ell - 1\}$ using $\mathcal{R}$. Specifically, for each cell probe performed by **DS**, Bob checks if the probed cell was last overwritten by any of the preceding operations in the right subtree of v. If so, Bob will use the most recent contents of the cell. Otherwise, checks if the cell belongs to $C_v(O)$ in which case Bob will use the contents of the cell that were encoded by Alice. Finally if the cell was last overwritten before any operations in the left subtree of v, Bob will use the cell content as reported by snapshot$'$. After Bob completes the simulation, Bob successfully decodes the answer for all queries where **DS** returns the correct answer. As a result, Bob successfully decodes all bipartite graphs $B_i, \ldots, B_{i+\ell-1}$.

We now argue that Bob's simulation of **DS** for operations in the right subtree of v (phases $j \in \{i + \ell, \ldots, i + 2\ell - 1\}$) is identical to Alice's execution. Consider the first time any cell is probed during Bob's execution of operations in v's right subtree. Either the cell is read from Alice's encoding of $C_v(O)$ or the cell is read from snapshot$'$. Bob's execution will be different from Alice if and only if Bob uses the incorrect contents of a cell when first probed. This only happens if Bob uses the contents of a cell from snapshot$'$ yet that cell was overwritten by an operation in the left subtree of v (phases $j \in \{i, \ldots, i + \ell - 1\}$). If this were the case, this cell probe is assigned to v and, thus, the cell contents would have been encoded by Alice in $C_v(O)$. As a result, we know both executions by Alice and Bob are identical and Bob successfully decodes all answers in v's right subtree.

Analysis. We now analyze the expected length of the encoding and show that the expected size of Alice's encoding is smaller than the entropy of the bipartite graphs decoded by Bob contradicting Shannon's source coding theorem.

We distinguish two cases. In the case that Alice's encoding starts with a 0-bit, the length is exactly $1 + \frac{n}{2^{d+1}} \cdot \lg \binom{n^\epsilon}{l}$ bits. Let us upper bound probability that Alice produces an encoding that starts with 0. There are two cases in which this happens. In the first case, it is because F is large and thus **DS** made too many errors. Since **DS** has error probability at most $1/128$, we know that $E[\|F(\mathsf{Hard}_v)\|] \leq (1/128)n/2^{d+1}$ by linearity of expectation. By Markov's inequality, it follows that $\Pr[\|F(\mathsf{Hard}_v)\| \geq (1/32)n/2^{d+1}] \leq 1/4$. In the second case, $C_v(O)$ is too large and, by our assumption towards a contradiction, this happens with probability at most $1/2$. Therefore, Alice's encoding starts with a 0-bit with probability at most $3/4$. Let us now analyze the expected length of an encoding that starts with a 1-bit.

(a) Client storage is encoded using c bits. Recall that we chose $8 \leq d \leq (1/2)(1 - \epsilon)\lg(n/c)$. As a result, we know that

$$c \leq \frac{n}{2^{2d}} \leq \frac{1}{2^{d-1}} \cdot \frac{nl}{2^{d+1}} \leq \frac{1}{128} \cdot \frac{n}{2^{d+1}} \cdot \lg \binom{n^\epsilon}{l}.$$

(b) $|F| \leq n$ and thus $\Theta(\lg n)$ bits are needed;
(c) The indices and the answers for the failed queries are encoded using

$$\Theta(\lg n) + \lg \binom{\frac{n}{2^{d+1}}}{|F|} + |F| \lg \binom{n^\epsilon}{l}$$

bits. The above encoding size increases as a function of $|F|$. The largest encoding occurs when $|F| = (1/32)n/2^{d+1}$. By substituting and adding the $\Theta(\lg n)$ bits from above items, we obtain

$$\Theta(\lg n) + \frac{1}{32} \cdot \frac{n}{2^{d+1}} \left(\lg(32e) + \lg \binom{n^\epsilon}{l} \right) \leq \frac{1}{16} \cdot \frac{n}{2^{d+1}} \cdot \lg \binom{n^\epsilon}{l}.$$

(d) $|C_v(O)| = O(\frac{n}{2^{d+1}} \lg \binom{n^\epsilon}{l}/w)$ and thus $\Theta(\lg n)$ bits are needed;
(e) By our contradiction assumption, the expected length of the encoding of $C_v(O)$ requires at most $(1/100) \cdot \frac{n}{2^{d+1}} \cdot \lg \binom{n^\epsilon}{l}$ bits. If we sum the $\Theta(\lg n)$ bits from (d) we obtain a total of

$$\frac{1}{100} \cdot \frac{n}{2^{d+1}} \cdot \lg \binom{n^\epsilon}{l}.$$

Altogether, the expected length of the encoding starting with a 1-bit is at most

$$\left(\frac{1}{128} + \frac{1}{16} + \frac{1}{50} \right) \cdot \frac{n}{2^{d+1}} \cdot \lg \binom{n^\epsilon}{l} < \frac{1}{8} \cdot \frac{n}{2^{d+1}} \cdot \lg \binom{n^\epsilon}{l}.$$

By putting the two cases together, we can conclude that the expected length of the encoding is at most $1 + (3/4 + 1/8) \cdot \frac{n}{2^{d+1}} \cdot \lg \binom{n^\epsilon}{l} < \frac{n}{2^{d+1}} \cdot \lg \binom{n^\epsilon}{l}$ which contradicts Shannon's source coding theorem thus completing the proof. □

We note the proof of Lemma 3 follows directly from Lemma 6 and Lemma 7. Thus, the proof of Theorem 3 is complete. We refer readers to the full version for extensions to larger leakage functions and searchable encryption.

Discussion 1. Previous works in the ORAM literature consider *passive* servers that act exclusively as storage that may only retrieve or update server memory. In this model, a cell probe corresponds to one cell of bandwidth. As a result, the above lower bounds can be interpreted as bandwidth lower bounds for passive servers. For servers with general computation (like we assumed in our work), cell probe lower bounds apply to server computation.

Discussion 2. As noted above, our lower bounds can be applied to the encrypted array primitive that is much closer to the ORAM primitive. One can interpret our leakage cell probe model with respect to the $\Omega(\lg n)$ ORAM lower bounds that appear in [45,56]. In particular, our lower bounds show that the $\Omega(\lg n)$ overhead necessarily incurred by ORAMs is caused by mitigating the global key-equality pattern leakage. After mitigating global key-equality pattern leakage, other leakage mitigation by ORAMs do not cost additional asymptotic overhead.

Discussion 3. We note that the efficiency of some previous schemes are evaluated for specific scenarios. For example, the schemes in [38] are evaluated assuming queries are drawn according to the Zipf's distribution. We note that our lower bounds do not apply to any scenario where our hard distribution is not a valid input. Our lower bounds can be interpreted as if one wishes to leak at most $\mathcal{L}_{\mathsf{dec}}$, then one must either incur $\Omega(\lg n)$ overhead or only accept specific input distributions. We leave it as an interesting and important open question to study the efficiency schemes assuming specific distributions.

5   Conclusions

To summarize, our work presents the first lower bounds for encrypted multi-maps as well as searchable encryption schemes in the natural setting of computational adversaries without any limitations of the data encoding used by the constructions. In particular, we show that mitigating the global key-equality pattern leakage (even in a very small manner) fundamentally incurs an $\Omega(\lg n)$ overhead. We show our lower bounds hold even when the encrypted multi-map is able to perform one of the Add or Get operations in plaintext. These results may be applied to the setting of searchable encryption where we show that dynamic schemes that are response-hiding also must use $\Omega(\lg n)$ overhead even when one of the document updates or searches may be performed in the plaintext.

In terms of techniques, our paper introduces several new ideas that may be widely applicable. First, we introduce the notion of the leakage cell probe model that allows proving lower bounds for structured encryption with arbitrary leakage profiles. Next, our lower bounds apply to the setting where the data structure contents do not necessarily have to be random such as the keywords that appear in documents. Finally, we present new methods to construct hard distributions even when considering much larger leakage profiles than previous results. We believe these techniques may be helpful in analyzing the efficiency and privacy tradeoffs for many other primitives.

References

1. Asharov, G., Komargodski, I., Lin, W.-K., Nayak, K., Peserico, E., Shi, E.: OptORAMa: optimal oblivious RAM. Cryptology ePrint Archive, Report 2018/892
2. Asharov, G., Naor, M., Segev, G., Shahaf, I.: Searchable symmetric encryption: optimal locality in linear space via two-dimensional balanced allocations. In: STOC 2016 (2016)
3. Asharov, G., Segev, G., Shahaf, I.: Tight tradeoffs in searchable symmetric encryption. In: Shacham, H., Boldyreva, A. (eds.) CRYPTO 2018. LNCS, vol. 10991, pp. 407–436. Springer, Cham (2018). https://doi.org/10.1007/978-3-319-96884-1_14
4. Bellare, M., Boldyreva, A., O'Neill, A.: Deterministic and efficiently searchable encryption. In: Menezes, A. (ed.) CRYPTO 2007. LNCS, vol. 4622, pp. 535–552. Springer, Heidelberg (2007). https://doi.org/10.1007/978-3-540-74143-5_30
5. Boldyreva, A., Chenette, N., Lee, Y., O'Neill, A.: Order-preserving symmetric encryption. In: Joux, A. (ed.) EUROCRYPT 2009. LNCS, vol. 5479, pp. 224–241. Springer, Heidelberg (2009). https://doi.org/10.1007/978-3-642-01001-9_13
6. Boldyreva, A., Chenette, N., O'Neill, A.: Order-preserving encryption revisited: improved security analysis and alternative solutions. In: Rogaway, P. (ed.) CRYPTO 2011. LNCS, vol. 6841, pp. 578–595. Springer, Heidelberg (2011). https://doi.org/10.1007/978-3-642-22792-9_33
7. Boneh, D., Di Crescenzo, G., Ostrovsky, R., Persiano, G.: Public key encryption with keyword search. In: Cachin, C., Camenisch, J.L. (eds.) EUROCRYPT 2004. LNCS, vol. 3027, pp. 506–522. Springer, Heidelberg (2004). https://doi.org/10. 1007/978-3-540-24676-3_30
8. Boneh, D., Lewi, K., Raykova, M., Sahai, A., Zhandry, M., Zimmerman, J.: Semantically secure order-revealing encryption: multi-input functional encryption without obfuscation. In: Oswald, E., Fischlin, M. (eds.) EUROCRYPT 2015. LNCS, vol. 9057, pp. 563–594. Springer, Heidelberg (2015). https://doi.org/10.1007/978-3-662-46803-6_19
9. Bost, R.: Sophos: forward secure searchable encryption. In: CCS 2016 (2016)
10. Bost, R., Fouque, P.-A.: Security-efficiency tradeoffs in searchable encryption. In: PoPETS (2019)
11. Bost, R., Minaud, B., Ohrimenko, O.: Forward and backward private searchable encryption from constrained cryptographic primitives. In: CCS 2017 (2017)
12. Boyle, E., Naor, M.: Is there an oblivious RAM lower bound? In: Proceedings of the 2016 ACM Conference on Innovations in Theoretical Computer Science (2016)
13. Cash, D., Grubbs, P., Perry, J., Ristenpart, T.: Leakage-abuse attacks against searchable encryption. In: CCS 2015 (2015)
14. Cash, D., et al.: Dynamic searchable encryption in very-large databases: data structures and implementation. In: NDSS, vol. 14, pp. 23–26 (2014)
15. Cash, D., Jarecki, S., Jutla, C., Krawczyk, H., Roşu, M.-C., Steiner, M.: Highly-scalable searchable symmetric encryption with support for boolean queries. In: Canetti, R., Garay, J.A. (eds.) CRYPTO 2013. LNCS, vol. 8042, pp. 353–373. Springer, Heidelberg (2013). https://doi.org/10.1007/978-3-642-40041-4_20
16. Cash, D., Tessaro, S.: The locality of searchable symmetric encryption. In: Nguyen, P.Q., Oswald, E. (eds.) EUROCRYPT 2014. LNCS, vol. 8441, pp. 351–368. Springer, Heidelberg (2014). https://doi.org/10.1007/978-3-642-55220-5_20

17. Chase, M., Kamara, S.: Structured encryption and controlled disclosure. In: Abe, M. (ed.) ASIACRYPT 2010. LNCS, vol. 6477, pp. 577–594. Springer, Heidelberg (2010). https://doi.org/10.1007/978-3-642-17373-8_33

18. Curtmola, R., Garay, J., Kamara, S., Ostrovsky, R.: Searchable symmetric encryption: improved definitions and efficient constructions. J. Comput. Secur. **19**(5), 895–934 (2011)

19. Demertzis, I., Papadopoulos, D., Papamanthou, C.: Searchable encryption with optimal locality: achieving sublogarithmic read efficiency. In: Shacham, H., Boldyreva, A. (eds.) CRYPTO 2018. LNCS, vol. 10991, pp. 371–406. Springer, Cham (2018). https://doi.org/10.1007/978-3-319-96884-1_13

20. Demertzis, I., Papamanthou, C.: Fast searchable encryption with tunable locality. In: SIGMOD 2017 (2017)

21. Dietzfelbinger, M., Karlin, A., Mehlhorn, K., Meyer auf der Heide, F., Rohnert, H., Tarjan, R.E.: Dynamic perfect hashing: upper and lower bounds. SIAM J. Comput. **23**(4), 738–761 (1994)

22. Etemad, M., Küpçü, A., Papamanthou, C., Evans, D.: Efficient dynamic searchable encryption with forward privacy. In: PETS 2018 (2018)

23. Fisch, B.A., et al.: Malicious-client security in blind seer: a scalable private DBMS. In: 2015 IEEE Symposium on Security and Privacy (SP) (2015)

24. Fredman, M., Saks, M.: The cell probe complexity of dynamic data structures. In: Proceedings of the 21st Annual ACM Symposium on Theory of Computing (1989)

25. Garg, S., Mohassel, P., Papamanthou, C.: **TWORAM**: efficient oblivious RAM in two rounds with applications to searchable encryption. In: Robshaw, M., Katz, J. (eds.) CRYPTO 2016. LNCS, vol. 9816, pp. 563–592. Springer, Heidelberg (2016). https://doi.org/10.1007/978-3-662-53015-3_20

26. Gentry, C.: Fully homomorphic encryption using ideal lattices. In: STOC 2009 (2009)

27. Ghareh Chamani, J., Papadopoulos, D., Papamanthou, C., Jalili, R.: New constructions for forward and backward private symmetric searchable encryption. In: CCS 2018 (2018)

28. Goldreich, O., Ostrovsky, R.: Software protection and simulation on oblivious RAMs. J. ACM (JACM) **43**(3), 431–473 (1996)

29. Grubbs, P., Lacharité, M.-S., Minaud, B., Paterson, K.G.: Learning to reconstruct: statistical learning theory and encrypted database attacks. Cryptology ePrint Archive, Report 2019/011

30. Grubbs, P., Ristenpart, T., Shmatikov, V.: Why your encrypted database is not secure. In: HotOS 2017 (2017)

31. Hamlin, A., Shelat, A., Weiss, M., Wichs, D.: Multi-key searchable encryption, revisited. In: Abdalla, M., Dahab, R. (eds.) PKC 2018. LNCS, vol. 10769, pp. 95–124. Springer, Cham (2018). https://doi.org/10.1007/978-3-319-76578-5_4

32. Hubáček, P., Koucký, M., Král, K., Slívová, V.: Stronger lower bounds for online ORAM. CoRR, abs/1903.03385 (2019)

33. Islam, M.S., Kuzu, M., Kantarcioglu, M.: Access pattern disclosure on searchable encryption: ramification, attack and mitigation. In: NDSS (2012)

34. Jacob, R., Larsen, K.G., Nielsen, J.B.: Lower bounds for oblivious data structures. In: SODA 2019 (2019)

35. Kamara, S., Moataz, T.: Boolean searchable symmetric encryption with worst-case sub-linear complexity. In: Coron, J.-S., Nielsen, J.B. (eds.) EUROCRYPT 2017. LNCS, vol. 10212, pp. 94–124. Springer, Cham (2017). https://doi.org/10.1007/978-3-319-56617-7_4

36. Kamara, S., Moataz, T.: SQL on structurally-encrypted databases. In: Peyrin, T., Galbraith, S. (eds.) ASIACRYPT 2018. LNCS, vol. 11272, pp. 149–180. Springer, Cham (2018). https://doi.org/10.1007/978-3-030-03326-2_6

37. Kamara, S., Moataz, T.: Computationally volume-hiding structured encryption. In: Ishai, Y., Rijmen, V. (eds.) EUROCRYPT 2019. LNCS, vol. 11477, pp. 183–213. Springer, Cham (2019). https://doi.org/10.1007/978-3-030-17656-3_7

38. Kamara, S., Moataz, T., Ohrimenko, O.: Structured encryption and leakage suppression. In: Shacham, H., Boldyreva, A. (eds.) CRYPTO 2018. LNCS, vol. 10991, pp. 339–370. Springer, Cham (2018). https://doi.org/10.1007/978-3-319-96884-1_12

39. Kamara, S., Papamanthou, C., Roeder, T.: Dynamic searchable symmetric encryption. In: CCS 2012 (2012)

40. Kellaris, G., Kollios, G., Nissim, K., O'Neill, A.: Generic attacks on secure outsourced databases. In: CCS 2016 (2016)

41. Kornaropoulos, E.M., Papamanthou, C., Tamassia, R.: The state of the uniform: attacks on encrypted databases beyond the uniform query distribution. Cryptology ePrint Archive, Report 2019/441 (2019)

42. Lacharité, M.-S., Minaud, B., Paterson, K.G.: Improved reconstruction attacks on encrypted data using range query leakage. In: IEEE S&P 2018 (2018)

43. Larsen, K.G.: The cell probe complexity of dynamic range counting. In: Proceedings of the Forty-Fourth Annual ACM Symposium on Theory of Computing (2012)

44. Larsen, K.G., Malkin, T., Weinstein, O., Yeo, K.: Lower bounds for oblivious nearneighbor search. arXiv preprint arXiv:1904.04828 (2019)

45. Larsen, K.G., Nielsen, J.B.: Yes, there is an oblivious RAM lower bound!. In: Shacham, H., Boldyreva, A. (eds.) CRYPTO 2018. LNCS, vol. 10992, pp. 523–542. Springer, Cham (2018). https://doi.org/10.1007/978-3-319-96881-0_18

46. Larsen, K.G., Simkin, M., Yeo, K.: Lower bounds for multi-server oblivious rams. Cryptology ePrint Archive, Report 2019/1108 (2019). https://eprint.iacr.org/2019/1108

47. Larsen, K.G., Weinstein, O., Yu, H.: Crossing the logarithmic barrier for dynamic Boolean data structure lower bounds. In: STOC 2018 (2018)

48. Lewi, K., Wu, D.J.: Order-revealing encryption: new constructions, applications, and lower bounds. In: CCS 2016 (2016)

49. Miers, I., Mohassel, P.: IO-DSSE: scaling dynamic searchable encryption to millions of indexes by improving locality. IACR Cryptology ePrint Archive (2016)

50. Naveed, M., Kamara, S., Wright, C.V.: Inference attacks on property-preserving encrypted databases. In: CCS 2015 (2015)

51. Ostrovsky, R.: Efficient computation on oblivious RAMs. In: STOC 1990 (1990)

52. Pagh, R.: Hashing, Randomness and Dictionaries. BRICS (2002)

53. Patel, S., Persiano, G., Raykova, M., Yeo, K.: PanORAMa: oblivious RAM with logarithmic overhead. In: FOCS 2018 (2018)

54. Patel, S., Persiano, G., Yeo, K.: Symmetric searchable encryption with sharing and unsharing. In: Lopez, J., Zhou, J., Soriano, M. (eds.) ESORICS 2018. LNCS, vol. 11099, pp. 207–227. Springer, Cham (2018). https://doi.org/10.1007/978-3-319-98989-1_11

55. Patel, S., Persiano, G., Yeo, K., Yung, M.: Mitigating leakage in secure cloud-hosted data structures: volume-hiding for multi-maps via hashing. In: CCS (2019)

56. Persiano, G., Yeo, K.: Lower bounds for differentially private RAMs. In: Ishai, Y., Rijmen, V. (eds.) EUROCRYPT 2019. LNCS, vol. 11476, pp. 404–434. Springer, Cham (2019). https://doi.org/10.1007/978-3-030-17653-2_14

57. Popa, R.A., Redfield, C., Zeldovich, N., Balakrishnan, H.: CryptDB: protecting confidentiality with encrypted query processing. In: SOSP 2011 (2011)
58. Pouliot, D., Wright, C.V.: The shadow nemesis: inference attacks on efficiently deployable, efficiently searchable encryption. In: CCS 2016 (2016)
59. Pătraşcu, M., Demaine, E.D.: Logarithmic lower bounds in the cell-probe model. SIAM J. Comput. **35**(4), 932–963 (2006)
60. Song, D., Wagner, D., Perrig, A.: Practical techniques for searches on encrypted data. In: Proceedings of IEEE Symposium on Security and Privacy (2000)
61. Stefanov, E., Papamanthou, C., Shi, E.: Practical dynamic searchable encryption with small leakage. In: NDSS, vol. 71, pp. 72–75 (2014)
62. Weiss, M., Wichs, D.: Is there an oblivious RAM lower bound for online reads? Cryptology ePrint Archive, Report 2018/619 (2018)
63. Yao, A.C.-C.: Should tables be sorted? J. ACM **28**(3), 615–628 (1981)
64. Zhang, Y., Katz, J., Papamanthou, C.: All your queries are belong to us: the power of file-injection attacks on searchable encryption. In: USENIX Security Symposium, pp. 707–720 (2016)

Fast and Secure Updatable Encryption

Colin Boyd[1], Gareth T. Davies[2(✉)] (iD), Kristian Gjøsteen[1(✉)],
and Yao Jiang[1(✉)]

[1] Norwegian University of Science and Technology, NTNU, Trondheim, Norway
{kristian.gjosteen,yao.jiang}@ntnu.no
[2] Bergische Universität Wuppertal, Wuppertal, Germany
davies@uni-wuppertal.de

Abstract. Updatable encryption allows a client to outsource cipher-texts to some untrusted server and periodically rotate the encryption key. The server can update ciphertexts from an old key to a new key with the help of an update token, received from the client, which should not reveal anything about plaintexts to an adversary.

We provide a new and highly efficient suite of updatable encryption schemes that we collectively call SHINE. In the variant designed for short messages, ciphertext generation consists of applying one permutation and one exponentiation (per message block), while updating ciphertexts requires just one exponentiation. Variants for longer messages provide much stronger security guarantees than prior work that has comparable efficiency. We present a new confidentiality notion for updatable encryption schemes that implies prior notions. We prove that SHINE is secure under our new confidentiality definition while also providing ciphertext integrity.

1 Introduction

The past decades have demonstrated clearly that key compromise is a real threat for deployed systems. The standard technique for mitigating key compromise is to regularly *rotate* the encryption keys – generate new ones and switch the ciphertexts to encryption under the new keys. Key rotation is a well-established technique in applications such as payment cards [9] and cloud storage [16].

For a local drive or server, key rotation is feasible by decrypting and re-encrypting with a new key, since symmetric encryption operations are fast and parallelizable and bandwidth is often plentiful. When ciphertext storage has been outsourced to some (untrusted) cloud storage provider, bandwidth is often considerably more expensive than computation, and even for small volumes of data it may be prohibitively expensive to download, re-encrypt and upload the entire database even once. This means that key rotation by downloading, decrypting, re-encrypting and reuploading is practically infeasible.

An alternative approach to solving this problem is to use *updatable encryption* (UE), first defined by Boneh et al. [3] (henceforth BLMR). The user computes a *token* and sends it to the storage server. The token allows the server to update

© International Association for Cryptologic Research 2020
D. Micciancio and T. Ristenpart (Eds.): CRYPTO 2020, LNCS 12170, pp. 464–493, 2020.
https://doi.org/10.1007/978-3-030-56784-2_16

the ciphertexts so that they become encryptions under some new key. Although the token clearly depends on both the old and new encryption keys, knowledge of the token alone should not allow the server to obtain either key. In a typical usage of UE, the cloud storage provider will receive a new token on a periodic basis, and the provider then updates every stored ciphertext. The time period for which a given key is valid for is called an *epoch*.

In the past few years there has been considerable interest in extending the understanding of UE. A series of prominent papers [3,12,17,21] have provided both new (typically stronger) security definitions and concrete or generic constructions to meet their definitions. (We make a detailed comparison of related work in Sect. 1.1 next.) An important distinction between earlier schemes is whether or not the token (and in particular its size) depends on the ciphertexts to be updated (and in particular the number of ciphertexts). Schemes for which a token is assigned to each ciphertext are *ciphertext-dependent* and were studied by Everspaugh et al. [12] (henceforth EPRS). If the token is independent of the ciphertexts to be updated, such as in BLMR [4], we have a *ciphertext-independent*[1] scheme. A clear and important goal is to limit the bandwidth required and so, in general, one should prefer ciphertext-independent schemes. Thus, as with the most recent work [17,21], we focus on such schemes in this paper. The ciphertext update procedure, performed by the server, may be *deterministic* or *randomized* – note that in the latter case the server is burdened with producing (good) randomness and using it correctly.

Despite the considerable advances of the past few years, there remain some important open questions regarding basic properties of UE. In terms of security, various features have been added to protect against stronger adversaries. Yet it is not obvious what are the realistic and optimal security goals of UE and whether they have been achieved. In terms of efficiency, we only have a few concrete schemes to compare. As may be expected, schemes with stronger security are generally more expensive but it remains unclear whether this cost is necessary. In this paper we make contributions to both of these fundamental questions by defining **new and stronger security properties** and showing that these can be achieved with **more efficient concrete UE schemes**.

Security. The main security properties that one would expect from updatable encryption are by now well studied; however the breadth of information that is possible to protect in this context is more subtle than at first glance. Consider, for example, a journalist who stores a contact list with a cloud storage provider. At some point, the storage is compromised and an adversary recovers the ciphertexts. At this point, it may be important that the cryptography does not reveal which of the contacts are recent, and which are old. That is, it must be hard to decide if some ciphertext was recently created, or if it has been updated from a ciphertext stored in an earlier epoch.

---

[1] Note that Boneh et al. [[4], § Definition 7.6] use ciphertext-independence to mean that the updated ciphertext should have the same distribution as a fresh ciphertext (i.e. independent of the ciphertext in the previous epoch) – we follow the nomenclature of Lehmann and Tackmann [21].

So how do we define realistic adversaries in this environment? A natural first step for security in updatable encryption is *confidentiality* of ciphertexts – given a single ciphertext, the adversarial server should not be able to determine anything about the underlying plaintext. The security model here must take into account that this adversary could be in possession of a number of prior keys or update tokens, and snapshot access to the storage database in different epochs. The next step is to consider *unlinkability* between different epochs arising from the ciphertext update procedure: given a ciphertext for the current epoch, the adversary should not be able to tell which ciphertext (that existed in the previous epoch) a current ciphertext was updated from. Both of these properties can be naturally extended to chosen-ciphertext (CCA) security via provision of a decryption oracle.

These steps have been taken by prior work, but unfortunately even a combination of these properties is not enough to defend against our motivating example. Previous security definitions cannot guarantee that the adversary is unable to distinguish between a ciphertext new in the current epoch and an updated ciphertext from an earlier epoch. We give a single new security property that captures this requirement and implies the notions given in prior work. Therefore we believe that this definition is *the natural confidentiality property* that is required for updatable encryption.

An additional factor to consider is integrity: the user should be confident that their ciphertexts have not been modified by the adversarial server. While prior work has shown how to define and achieve integrity in the context of updatable encryption, a composition result of the style given by Bellare and Namprempre for symmetric encryption [2] – the combination of CPA security and integrity of ciphertexts gives CCA security – has been missing. We close this gap.

Efficiency and Functionality. Although UE is by definition a form of symmetric key cryptography, techniques from asymmetric cryptography appear to be needed to achieve the required functionality in a sensible fashion. All of the previous known schemes with security proofs use exponentiation in both the encryption and update functions, even for those with limited security properties. Since a modern database may contain large numbers of files, efficiency is critical both for clients who will have to encrypt plaintexts initially and for servers who will have to update ciphertexts for all of their users.

To bridge the gap between the academic literature and deployments of encrypted outsourced storage, *it is crucial to design fast schemes*. We present three novel UE schemes that not only satisfy our strong security definitions (CCA and ciphertext integrity), but in the vast majority of application scenarios are also at least twice as fast (in terms of computation each message block) as any previous scheme with comparable security level.

The *ciphertext expansion* of a scheme says how much the size of a ciphertext grows compared to the size of the message. For a cloud server that stores vast numbers of files, it is naturally crucial to minimize the ciphertext expansion rate. It is also desirable to construct UE schemes that can encrypt *arbitrarily large files*, since a client might want to upload media files such as images or videos.

Prior schemes that have achieved these two properties have only been secure in comparatively weak models. Our construction suitable for long messages – enabling encryption of arbitrarily large files with almost no ciphertext expansion – is secure in our strong sense and is thus the first to bridge this gap.

1.1 Related Work

Security Models for UE. We regard the sequential, epoch-based corruption model of Lehmann and Tackmann [21] (LT18) as the most suitable execution environment to capture the threats in updatable encryption. In this model, the adversary advances to the next epoch via an oracle query. It can choose to submit its (single) challenge when it pleases, and it can later update the challenge ciphertext to the 'current' epoch. Further, the adversary is allowed to adaptively corrupt epoch (i.e. file encryption) keys and update tokens at any point in the game: only at the end of the adversary's execution does the challenger determine whether a trivial win has been made possible by some combination of the corruption queries and the challenge.

LT18 introduced two notions: IND-ENC asks the adversary to submit two plaintexts and distinguish the resulting ciphertext, while possibly having corrupted tokens (but of course not keys) linking this challenge ciphertext to prior or later epochs. Further, they introduced IND-UPD: the adversary provides two ciphertexts that it received via regular encryption-oracle queries in the previous epoch, and has to work out which one has been updated. They observed that plaintext information can be leaked not only through the encryption procedure, but also via updates. For schemes with deterministic updates, the adversary would trivially win if it could acquire the update token that takes the adversarially-provided ciphertexts into the challenge epoch, hence the definition for this setting, named detIND-UPD, is different from that for the randomized setting, named randIND-UPD.

LT18's IND-UPD definition was not the first approach to formalizing the desirable property of *unlinkability* of ciphertexts, which attempts to specify that given two already-updated ciphertexts, the adversary cannot tell if the plaintext is the same. Indeed EPRS (UP-REENC) and later KLR19 (UP-REENC-CCA) also considered this problem, in the ciphertext-dependent update and CCA-secure setting respectively. KLR19 [[17], § Appendix A] stated that "an even stronger notion [than IND-UPD] might be desirable: namely that fresh and re-encrypted ciphertexts are indistinguishable... which is not guaranteed by UP-REENC" – we will answer this open question later on in our paper.

In the full version of their work [4], BLMR introduced a security definition for UE denoted update – an extension of a model of symmetric proxy re-encryption. This non-sequential definition is considerably less adaptive than the later work of LT18, since the adversary's key/token corruption queries and ciphertext update queries are very limited. Further, they only considered schemes with deterministic update algorithms.

EPRS [12] provided (non-sequential) definitions for updatable authenticated encryption, in the ciphertext-dependent setting. Their work (inherently) covered

CCA security and ciphertext integrity (CTXT). These definitions were ambiguous regarding adaptivity: these issues have since been fixed in the full version [13].

KLR19 attempted to provide stronger security guarantees for ciphertext-independent UE than LT18, concentrating on chosen-ciphertext security (and the weaker replayable CCA) in addition to integrity of plaintexts and ciphertexts. We revisit these definitions later on, and show how a small modification to their INT-CTXT game gives rise to natural composition results.

In practice, LT18's randIND-UPD definition insists that the ciphertext update procedure Upd requires the server to generate randomness for updating each ciphertext. Further, a scheme meeting both IND-ENC and IND-UPD can still leak the epoch in which the file was uploaded (the 'age' of the ciphertext). While it is arguable that metadata is inherent in outsourced storage, the use of updatable encryption is for high-security applications, and it would not be infeasible to design a system that does not reveal meta-data, which is clearly impossible if the underlying cryptosystem reveals the meta-data.

Recent work by Jarecki et al. [15] considers the key wrapping entity as a separate entity from the data owner or the storage server. While this approach seems promising, their security model is considerably weaker than those considered in our work or the papers already mentioned in this section: the adversary must choose whether to corrupt the key management server (and get the epoch key) or the storage server (and get the update token) for each epoch, and thus it cannot dynamically corrupt earlier keys or tokens at a later stage.

Constructions of Ciphertext-Independent UE. The initial description of updatable encryption by Boneh et al. [3] was motivated by providing a symmetric-key version of proxy re-encryption (see below). BLMR imagined doing this in a symmetric manner, where each epoch is simply one period in which re-encryption (rotation) has occurred. Their resulting scheme, denoted BLMR, deploys a key-homomorphic PRF, yet the nonce attached to a ciphertext ensures that IND-UPD cannot be met (the scheme pre-dates the IND-UPD notion).

The symmetric-Elgamal-based scheme of LT18, named RISE, uses a randomized update algorithm and is proven to meet IND-ENC and randIND-UPD under DDH. These proofs entail a seemingly unavoidable loss – a cubic term in the total number of epochs – our results also have this factor. LT18 also presented an extended version of the scheme by BLMR, denoted BLMR+, where the nonce is encrypted: they showed that this scheme meets a weak version of IND-UPD.

The aim of KLR19 was to achieve stronger security than BLMR, EPRS and LT18 in the ciphertext-independent setting: in particular CCA security and integrity protection. They observed that the structure of RISE ensures that ciphertext integrity cannot be achieved: access to just one update token allows the storage provider to construct ciphertexts of messages of its choice. Their generic constructions, based on encrypt-and-MAC and the Naor-Yung paradigm, are strictly less efficient than RISE. We show how to achieve CCA security and integrity protections with novel schemes that are comparably efficient with RISE.

Related Primitives. *Proxy re-encryption* (PRE) allows a ciphertext that is decryptable by some secret key to be re-encrypted such that it can be decrypted by some other key. Security models for PRE are closer to those for encryption than the strictly sequential outsourced-storage-centric models for UE, and as observed by Lehmann and Tackmann [21] the concepts of allowable corruptions and trivial wins for UE need considerable care when translating to the (more general) PRE setting. Unlinkability is not necessarily desired in PRE – updating the entire ciphertext may not be essential for a PRE scheme to be deemed secure – thus even after conversion to the symmetric setting, prior schemes [1,7] cannot meet the indistinguishability requirements that we ask of UE schemes. Recent works by Lee [20] and Davidson et al. [10] have highlighted the links between the work of BLMR and EPRS and PRE, and in particular the second work gives a public-key variant of the (sequential) IND-UPD definition of LT18. Myers and Shull [22] presented security models for hybrid proxy re-encryption, and gave a single-challenge version of the UP-IND notion of EPRS. While the models are subtly different, the techniques for achieving secure UE and PRE are often similar: in particular rotating keys via exponentiation to some simple function of old and new key. Further, the symmetric-key PRE scheme of Sakurai et al. [25] is at a high level similar to SHINE (their all-or-nothing-transform as an inner layer essentially serves the same purpose as the ideal cipher in SHINE), but in a security model that does not allow dynamic corruptions.

Tokenization schemes aim to protect short secrets, such as credit card numbers, using deterministic encryption and deterministic updates: this line of work reflects the PCI DSS standard [9] for the payment card industry. Provable security of such schemes was initially explored by Diaz-Santiago et al. [11] and extended to the updatable setting by Cachin et al. [6]. While much of the formalism in the model of Cachin et al. has been used in recent works on UE (in particular the epoch-based corruption model), the requirements on ciphertext indistinguishability are stronger in the UE setting, where we expect probabilistic encryption of (potentially large) files.

1.2 Contributions

Our first major contribution is defining the xxIND-UE-atk security notion, for $(xx, atk) \in \{(det, CPA), (rand, CPA), (det, CCA)\}$, and comprehensively analyzing its relation to other, existing[2] security notions (xxIND-ENC-atk, xxIND-UPD-atk). Our single definition requires that ciphertexts output by the encryption algorithm are indistinguishable from ciphertexts output by the update algorithm. We show that our new notion is strictly stronger even than combinations of prior notions, both in the randomized- and deterministic-update settings under

---

[2] The notions IND-ENC, randIND-UPD and detIND-UPD (which we denote as IND-ENC-CPA, randIND-UPD-CPA and detIND-UPD-CPA, resp.) are from LT18. The notions UP-IND-CCA and UP-REENC-CCA (detIND-ENC-CCA and detIND-UPD-CCA, resp.) are from KLR19. LT18 and KLR19 both build upon the definitions given by EPRS.

	IND	INT	$|M|$	$|C|$	Enc (Upd)
BLMR [3]	(det, ENC, CPA)	✗	$l|\mathbb{G}|$	$(l+1)|\mathbb{G}|$	$l\mathbf{E}$
BLMR+ [3,21]	(weak, ENC, CPA) (weak, UPD, CPA)	✗	$l|\mathbb{G}|$	$(l+1)|\mathbb{G}|$	$l\mathbf{E}$
RISE [21]	(rand, UE, CPA)	✗	$1|\mathbb{G}|$	$2|\mathbb{G}|$	$2\mathbf{E}$
SHINE0[CPA] § 5.1	(det, UE, CPA)	✗	$(1-\gamma)|\mathbb{G}|$	$1|\mathbb{G}|$	$1\mathbf{E}$
NYUE [17]	(rand, ENC, RCCA) (rand, UPD, RCCA)	✗	$1|\mathbb{G}_1|$	$(34|\mathbb{G}_1|, 34|\mathbb{G}_2|)$	$(60\mathbf{E}, 70\mathbf{E})$
NYUAE [17]	(rand, ENC, RCCA) (rand, UPD, RCCA)	PTXT	$1|\mathbb{G}_1|$	$(58|\mathbb{G}_1|, 44|\mathbb{G}_2|)$	$(110\mathbf{E}, 90\mathbf{E})$
E&M [17]	(det, ENC, CCA) (det, UPD, CCA)	CTXT	$1|\mathbb{G}|$	$3|\mathbb{G}|$	$3\mathbf{E}$
SHINE0 § 5.1	(det, UE, CCA)	CTXT	$(1-2\gamma)|\mathbb{G}|$	$1|\mathbb{G}|$	$1\mathbf{E}$
MirrorSHINE [5]	(det, UE, CCA)	CTXT	$(1-\gamma)|\mathbb{G}|$	$2|\mathbb{G}|$	$2\mathbf{E}$
OCBSHINE § 5.1	(det, UE, CCA)	CTXT	$l|\mathbb{G}|$	$(l+2)|\mathbb{G}|$	$(l+2)\mathbf{E}$

Fig. 1. Comparison of security, ciphertext expansion and efficiency for updatable encryption schemes. $(\mathsf{xx}, \mathsf{yy}, \mathsf{atk})$ represents the best possible xxIND-yy-atk notion that each scheme can achieve. $\mathbf{E}$ represents the cost of an exponentiation, for encryption Enc and ciphertext update Upd. γ represents the bit-size of the used nonce as a proportion of the group element bit-size. For NYUE and NYUAE, size/cost is in pairing groups $\mathbb{G}_1, \mathbb{G}_2$. SHINE0[CPA] is SHINE0 with a zero-length integrity tag. BLMR, BLMR+ and OCBSHINE support encryption of arbitrary size messages (of l blocks), with $|M| \approx l|\mathbb{G}|$.

chosen-plaintext attack and chosen-ciphertext attack. This not only gives us the unlinkability desired by prior works, but also answers the open question posed by KLR19 mentioned on page 4. Figure 13 describes the relationship between our new notion xxIND-UE-atk and prior notions.

We slightly tweak KLR19's definition of CTXT and CCA for UE and prove that detIND-yy-CPA + INT-CTXT $\Rightarrow$ detIND-yy-CCA for $\mathsf{yy} \in \{\mathsf{UE}, \mathsf{ENC}, \mathsf{UPD}\}$. Combining this result with the relations from detIND-UE-atk above, we thus show that the combination of detIND-UE-CPA and INT-CTXT yields detIND-yy-CCA *for all* $\mathsf{yy} \in \{\mathsf{UE}, \mathsf{ENC}, \mathsf{UPD}\}$.

Our second major contribution is in designing a new, fast updatable encryption scheme SHINE. Our scheme is based on a random-looking permutation combined with the exponentiation map in a cyclic group, and comes in a number of variants: SHINE0, MirrorSHINE (in our full version [5]) and OCBSHINE, for small messages, medium-sized messages and arbitrarily large messages respectively. In Fig. 1, we provide a comparison of security, ciphertext expansion and efficiency between our new schemes and those from prior literature. We also further the understanding of schemes with deterministic update mechanisms. In particular, we identify the properties that are necessary of such schemes to meet a generalized version of our detIND-UE-atk notion. Another important contribution is that we further improve on the existing epoch insulation techniques that have been used to create proofs of security in the strong corruption environment we pursue. These have been shown to be very useful for studying updatable encryption schemes, and we expect our new techniques to be useful in the future.

1.3 Further Discussion

We have had to make a number of practical design decisions for our new UE scheme SHINE. The main idea is to permute the (combination of nonce and) message and then exponentiate the resulting value, with different mechanisms for enforcing ciphertext integrity depending on the flavor that is being used (which is in turn defined by the desired message length). In this subsection we give some motivation for why we believe that these choices are reasonable.

Deterministic Updates. Since we will require indistinguishability of ciphertexts, we know that the UE encryption algorithm should be randomized. The update algorithm may or may not be randomized, however. All known schemes indicate that randomized updates are more expensive than deterministic updates, but there is a small, well-understood security loss in moving to deterministic updates: an adversary with an update token in an appropriate epoch can trivially distinguish between an update of a known ciphertext and other ciphertexts in the next epoch. As a result, in the detIND-UE-CPA case the adversary is only forbidden from obtaining one token compared to randIND-UE-CPA. Furthermore, UE schemes with randomized updates cannot achieve CTXT and CCA security, which is possible for the deterministic-update setting. We believe that the minor CPA security loss is a small price to pay for stronger security (CTXT and CCA) and efficiency gain, in particular to reduce computations in the UE encryption and update algorithms and also improve ciphertext expansion.

Limited Number of Epochs. In many applications that we would like to consider, the user of the storage service will control when updates occur (perhaps when an employee with access to key material leaves the organisation, or if an employee loses a key-holding device): this indicates that the total number of key rotations in the lifetime of a storage system might be numbered in the thousands, and in particular could be considerably smaller than the number of outsourced files.

2 Preliminaries

Pseudocode **return** $b' \stackrel{?}{=} b$ is used as shorthand for **if** $b' = b$ **then return** 1 // **else return** 0, with an output of 1 indicating adversarial success. We use the concrete security framework, defining adversarial advantage as probability of success in the security game, and avoid statements of security with respect to security notions. In the cases where we wish to indicate that notion A implies notion B (for some fixed primitive), i.e. an adversary's advantage against B carries over to an advantage against A, we show this by bounding these probabilities.

We follow the syntax of prior work [17], defining an Updatable Encryption (UE) scheme as a tuple of algorithms {UE.KG, UE.TG, UE.Enc, UE.Dec, UE.Upd}

Algorithm		Rand/Det	Input	Output	Syntax
UE.KG	Key Gen	Rand	λ	k_e	$k_e \xleftarrow{\$} \mathsf{UE.KG}(\lambda)$
UE.TG	Token Gen	Det	k_e, k_{e+1}	Δ_{e+1}	$\Delta_{e+1} \leftarrow \mathsf{UE.TG}(k_e, k_{e+1})$
UE.Enc	Encryption	Rand	M, k_e	C_e	$C_e \xleftarrow{\$} \mathsf{UE.Enc}(k_e, M)$
UE.Dec	Decryption	Det	C_e, k_e	M' or $\perp$	$\{M' / \perp\} \leftarrow \mathsf{UE.Dec}(k_e, C_e)$
UE.Upd	Update Ctxt	Rand/det	C_e, Δ_{e+1}	C_{e+1}	$C_{e+1} \xleftarrow{\$} \mathsf{UE.Upd}(\Delta_{e+1}, C_e)$

Fig. 2. Syntax of algorithms defining an Updatable Encryption scheme UE.

that operate in epochs, these algorithms are described in Fig. 2. A scheme is defined over some plaintext space $\mathcal{MS}$, ciphertext space $\mathcal{CS}$, key space $\mathcal{KS}$ and token space $\mathcal{TS}$. We specify integer $n + 1$ as the (total) number of epochs over which a UE scheme can operate, though this is only for proof purposes. Correctness [17] is defined as expected: fresh encryptions and updated ciphertexts should decrypt to the correct message under the appropriate epoch key.

In addition to enabling ciphertext updates, in many schemes the token allows ciphertexts to be 'downgraded': performing some analog of the UE.Upd operation on a ciphertext C created in (or updated to) epoch e yields a valid ciphertext in epoch e-1. Such a scheme is said to have *bi-directional ciphertext updates*. Furthermore, for many constructions, the token additionally enables key derivation, given one adjacent key. If this can be done in both directions – i.e. knowledge of k_e and Δ_{e+1} allows derivation of k_{e+1} AND knowledge of k_{e+1} and Δ_{e+1} allows derivation of k_e – then such schemes are referred to by LT18 as having *bi-directional key updates*. If such derivation is only possible in one 'direction' then the scheme is said to have *uni-directional key updates*. Much of the prior literature on updatable encryption has distinguished these notions: we stress that <u>all schemes and definitions</u> of security considered in this paper have <u>bi-directional key</u> updates and <u>bi-directional ciphertext updates</u>.

3   Security Models for Updatable Encryption

We consider a number of indistinguishability-based confidentiality games and integrity games for assessing security of updatable encryption schemes. The environment provided by the challenger attempts to give as much power as possible to adversary $\mathcal{A}$. The adversary may call for a number of oracles, and after $\mathcal{A}$ has finished running the challenger computes whether or not any of the actions enabled a trivial win. The available oracles are described in Fig. 3. An overview of the oracles $\mathcal{A}$ has access to in each security game is provided in Fig. 4.

Confidentiality. A generic representation of all confidentiality games described in this paper is detailed in Fig. 5. The current epoch is advanced by an adversarial call to $\mathcal{O}.\mathsf{Next}$ – simulating UE.KG and UE.TG – and keys and tokens (for the current or any prior epoch) can be corrupted via $\mathcal{O}.\mathsf{Corr}$. The adversary can

Setup(λ)
$k_0 \leftarrow$ UE.KG(λ)
$\Delta_0 \leftarrow \perp$; e, c $\leftarrow$ 0; phase, twf $\leftarrow$ 0
$\mathcal{L}, \tilde{\mathcal{L}}, \mathcal{C}, \mathcal{K}, \mathcal{T} \leftarrow \emptyset$

$\mathcal{O}$.Enc(M) :
$C \leftarrow$ UE.Enc(k_e, M)
c $\leftarrow$ c + 1; $\mathcal{L} \leftarrow \mathcal{L} \cup \{(c, C, e)\}$
return C

$\mathcal{O}$.Dec(C) :
  if phase = 1 **and** $C \in \tilde{\mathcal{L}}^*$ **then**
    twf $\leftarrow$ 1
  M' or $\perp \leftarrow$ UE.Dec(k_e, C)
  return M' or $\perp$

$\mathcal{O}$.Next() :
e $\leftarrow$ e + 1
$k_e \xleftarrow{\$}$ UE.KG(λ); $\Delta_e \xleftarrow{\$}$ UE.TG(k_{e-1}, k_e)
if phase = 1 **then**
  $\tilde{C}_e \leftarrow$ UE.Upd($\Delta_e, \tilde{C}_{e-1}$)

$\mathcal{O}$.Upd(C_{e-1}) :
if $(j, C_{e-1}, e - 1) \notin \mathcal{L}$ **then**
  return $\perp$
$C_e \leftarrow$ UE.Upd(Δ_e, C_{e-1})
$\mathcal{L} \leftarrow \mathcal{L} \cup \{(j, C_e, e)\}$
return C_e

$\mathcal{O}$.Corr(inp, ê) :
  if ê > e **then**
    return $\perp$
  if inp = key **then**
    $\mathcal{K} \leftarrow \mathcal{K} \cup \{$ê$\}$
    return $k_{\hat{e}}$
  if inp = token **then**
    $\mathcal{T} \leftarrow \mathcal{T} \cup \{$ê$\}$
    return $\Delta_{\hat{e}}$

$\mathcal{O}$.Upd$\tilde{C}$:
$\mathcal{C} \leftarrow \mathcal{C} \cup \{e\}$
$\tilde{\mathcal{L}} \leftarrow \tilde{\mathcal{L}} \cup \{(\tilde{C}_e, e)\}$
return $\tilde{C}_e$

$\mathcal{O}$.Try($\tilde{C}$) :
  if phase = 1 **then**
    return $\perp$
  phase $\leftarrow$ 1
  twf $\leftarrow$ 1 if :
    $e \in \mathcal{K}^*$ **or** $\tilde{C} \in \mathcal{L}^*$
  M' or $\perp \leftarrow$ UE.Dec($k_e, \tilde{C}$)
  if M' $\neq \perp$**then**
    win $\leftarrow$ 1

Fig. 3. Oracles in security games for updatable encryption. The shaded statement in $\mathcal{O}$.Try only applies to INT-CTXT^s: in this game the adversary is allowed to query the $\mathcal{O}$.Try oracle only once. Computing $\tilde{\mathcal{L}}^*$ is discussed in Sect. 3.2.

encrypt arbitrary messages via $\mathcal{O}$.Enc, and update these 'non-challenge' ciphertexts via $\mathcal{O}$.Upd. In CCA games, the adversary can additionally call decryption oracle $\mathcal{O}$.Dec (with some natural restrictions to prevent trivial wins). At some point $\mathcal{A}$ makes its challenge by providing two inputs, and receives the challenge ciphertext – and in later epochs can receive an updated version by calling $\mathcal{O}$.Upd$\tilde{C}$ (computing this value is actually done by $\mathcal{O}$.Next, a call to $\mathcal{O}$.Upd$\tilde{C}$ returns it). $\mathcal{A}$ can then interact with its other oracles again, and eventually outputs its guess bit. The flag phase tracks whether or not $\mathcal{A}$ has made its challenge, and we always give the epoch in which the challenge happens a special identifier ẽ. If $\mathcal{A}$ makes any action that would lead to a trivial win, the flag twf is set as 1 and $\mathcal{A}$'s output is discarded and replaced by a random bit. We follow the bookkeeping techniques of LT18 and KLR19, using the following sets to track ciphertexts and their updates that can be known to the adversary.

- $\mathcal{L}$: List of non-challenge ciphertexts (from $\mathcal{O}$.Enc or $\mathcal{O}$.Upd) with entries of form $(\mathsf{c}, \mathsf{C}, \mathsf{e})$, where query identifier c is a counter incremented with each new $\mathcal{O}$.Enc query.
- $\tilde{\mathcal{L}}$: List of updated versions of challenge ciphertext (created via $\mathcal{O}$.Next, received by adversary via $\mathcal{O}$.Upd$\tilde{\mathsf{C}}$), with entries of form $(\tilde{\mathsf{C}}, \mathsf{e})$.

Further, we use the following lists that track epochs only.

- $\mathcal{C}$: List of epochs in which adversary learned updated version of challenge ciphertext (via CHALL or $\mathcal{O}$.Upd$\tilde{\mathsf{C}}$).
- $\mathcal{K}$: List of epochs in which the adversary corrupted the encryption key.
- $\mathcal{T}$: List of epochs in which the adversary corrupted the update token.

All experiments necessarily maintain some state, but we omit this for readability reasons. The challenger's state is $\mathbf{S} \leftarrow \{\mathcal{L}, \tilde{\mathcal{L}}, \mathcal{C}, \mathcal{K}, \mathcal{T}\}$, and the system state in the current epoch is given by $\mathsf{st} \leftarrow (\mathsf{k_e}, \Delta_\mathsf{e}, \mathbf{S}, \mathsf{e})$.

An at-a-glance overview of CHALL for various security definitions is given in Fig. 7. For security games such as LT18's IND-UPD notion, where the adversary must submit as its challenge two ciphertexts (that it received from $\mathcal{O}$.Enc) and one is updated, the game must also track in which epochs the adversary has updates of these ciphertexts. We will later specify a version of our new xxIND-UE-atk notion that allows the adversary to submit a ciphertext that existed in any epoch prior to the challenge epoch, not just the one immediately before: this introduces some additional bookkeeping (discussed further in Sect. 3.2).

A note on nomenclature: the adversary can make its challenge query to receive *the challenge ciphertext*, and then acquire *updates of the challenge ciphertext* via calls to $\mathcal{O}$.Upd$\tilde{\mathsf{C}}$, and additionally it can calculate *challenge-equal ciphertexts* via applying tokens it gets via $\mathcal{O}$.Corr queries.

When appropriate, we will restrict our experiments to provide definitions of security that are more suitable for assessing schemes with deterministic update mechanisms. For such schemes, access to the update token for the challenge epoch $(\Delta_{\tilde{\mathsf{e}}})$ allows the adversary to trivially win detIND-UPD-atk and detIND-UE-atk for atk $\in \{\mathsf{CPA}, \mathsf{CCA}\}$. Note however that the definitions are not restricted to schemes with deterministic updates: such schemes are simply insecure in terms of randIND-UPD-CPA and randIND-UE-CPA.

Notion	$\mathcal{O}$.Enc	$\mathcal{O}$.Dec	$\mathcal{O}$.Next	$\mathcal{O}$.Upd	$\mathcal{O}$.Corr	$\mathcal{O}$.Upd$\tilde{\mathsf{C}}$	$\mathcal{O}$.Try
detIND-yy-CPA	✓	✗	✓	✓	✓	✓	✗
randIND-yy-CPA	✓	✗	✓	✓	✓	✓	✗
detIND-yy-CCA	✓	✓	✓	✓	✓	✓	✗
INT-CTXT	✓	✗	✓	✓	✓	✗	✓

Fig. 4. Oracles the adversary is allowed to query in different security games, where yy $\in \{\mathsf{ENC}, \mathsf{UPD}, \mathsf{UE}\}$. ✓ indicates the adversary has access to the corresponding oracle.

$\mathbf{Exp}_{UE,\,\mathcal{A}}^{\text{xxIND-yy-atk-b}}$

do Setup
CHALL $\leftarrow \mathcal{A}^{\mathcal{O}.\text{Enc},(\mathcal{O}.\text{Dec}),\mathcal{O}.\text{Next},\mathcal{O}.\text{Upd},\mathcal{O}.\text{Corr}}(\lambda)$
phase $\leftarrow 1; \tilde{e} \leftarrow e$
Create $\tilde{C}$ with CHALL; $\tilde{\mathcal{L}} \leftarrow \tilde{\mathcal{L}} \cup \{(\tilde{C}_e, e)\}$
b$' \leftarrow \mathcal{A}^{\mathcal{O}.\text{Enc},(\mathcal{O}.\text{Dec}),\mathcal{O}.\text{Next},\mathcal{O}.\text{Upd},\mathcal{O}.\text{Corr},\mathcal{O}.\text{Upd}\tilde{C}}(\tilde{C})$
$\underline{\text{twf} \leftarrow 1 \text{ if}}$:
   $\mathcal{K}^* \cap \mathcal{C}^* \neq \emptyset$ **or**
   xx $=$ **det and** $\mathcal{I}^* \cap \mathcal{C}^* \neq \emptyset$
if twf $= 1$ **then**
   b$' \xleftarrow{\$} \{0,1\}$
return b$'$

$\mathbf{Exp}_{UE,\,\mathcal{A}}^{\text{INT-CTXT}}$

do Setup; win $\leftarrow 0$
$\mathcal{A}^{\mathcal{O}.\text{Enc},\mathcal{O}.\text{Next},\mathcal{O}.\text{Upd},\mathcal{O}.\text{Corr},\mathcal{O}.\text{Try}}(\lambda)$
if twf $= 1$ **then**
   win $\leftarrow 0$
return win

Fig. 5. Generic description of confidentiality experiment $\mathbf{Exp}_{UE,\,\mathcal{A}}^{\text{xxIND-yy-atk-b}}$ for scheme UE, for xx $\in \{\text{det, rand}\}$, yy $\in \{\text{ENC, UPD, UE}\}$ and atk $\in \{\text{CPA, CCA}\}$. We do not consider (and thus do not formally define) randIND-yy-CCA; only in detIND-yy-CCA games does $\mathcal{A}$ have access to $\mathcal{O}.\text{Dec}$.

Fig. 6. INT-CTXT security notion for updatable encryption scheme UE. Deciding twf and computing $\mathcal{L}^*$ are discussed in Sect. 3.2.

Ciphertext Integrity. In ciphertext integrity (CTXT) game, the adversary is allowed to make calls to oracles $\mathcal{O}.\text{Enc}$, $\mathcal{O}.\text{Next}$, $\mathcal{O}.\text{Upd}$ and $\mathcal{O}.\text{Corr}$. At some point $\mathcal{A}$ attempts to provide a forgery via $\mathcal{O}.\text{Try}$; as part of this query the challenger will assess if it is valid. We distinguish between the single-$\mathcal{O}.\text{Try}$ case (INT-CTXT^s) and the multi-$\mathcal{O}.\text{Try}$ case (INT-CTXT). Here, "valid" means decryption outputs a message (i.e. not $\perp$). In the single-$\mathcal{O}.\text{Try}$ case, $\mathcal{A}$ can continue making oracle queries after its $\mathcal{O}.\text{Try}$ query, however this is of no benefit since it has already won or lost. In the multi-$\mathcal{O}.\text{Try}$ case, $\mathcal{A}$ can make any number of $\mathcal{O}.\text{Try}$ queries: as long as it wins once, it wins the ciphertext integrity game. Formally, the definition of ciphertext integrity is given in Definition 1.

Definition 1. *Let* UE $= \{$UE.KG, UE.TG, UE.Enc, UE.Dec, UE.Upd$\}$ *be an updatable encryption scheme. Then the* INT-CTXT *advantage of an adversary* $\mathcal{A}$ *against* UE *is defined as*

	CHALL	Output of " Create $\tilde{C}$ with CHALL"(in $\tilde{e}$)
xxIND-ENC-atk	$\bar{M}_0, \bar{M}_1$	UE.Enc$_{k_{\tilde{e}}}(\bar{M}_0)$ **or** UE.Enc$_{k_{\tilde{e}}}(\bar{M}_1)$
xxIND-UPD-atk	$\bar{C}_0, \bar{C}_1$	UE.Upd$_{\Delta_{\tilde{e}}}(\bar{C}_0)$ **or** UE.Upd$_{\Delta_{\tilde{e}}}(\bar{C}_1)$
xxIND-UE-atk	$\bar{M}, \bar{C}$	UE.Enc$_{k_{\tilde{e}}}(\bar{M})$ **or** UE.Upd$_{\Delta_{\tilde{e}}}(\bar{C})$

Fig. 7. Intuitive description of challenge inputs and outputs in confidentiality games for updatable encryption schemes, for (xx, atk) $\in \{(\text{det, CPA}), (\text{rand, CPA}), (\text{det, CCA})\}$.

$$\mathbf{Adv}_{\mathsf{UE},\,\mathcal{A}}^{\mathsf{INT\text{-}CTXT}}(\lambda) = \Pr[\mathbf{Exp}_{\mathsf{UE},\,\mathcal{A}}^{\mathsf{INT\text{-}CTXT}} = 1]$$

where the experiment $\mathbf{Exp}_{\mathsf{UE},\,\mathcal{A}}^{\mathsf{INT\text{-}CTXT}}$ *is given in Fig. 3 and Fig. 6. Particularly, if* $\mathcal{A}$ *is allowed to ask only one* $\mathcal{O}.\mathsf{Try}$ *query, denote such notion as* INT-CTXT^s.

Note that INT-CTXT trivially implies INT-CTXT^s. In the full version [5] we prove that INT-CTXT^s implies INT-CTXT too, with loss upper-bounded by the number of $\mathcal{O}.\mathsf{Try}$ queries. KLR19 define ciphertext integrity with one $\mathcal{O}.\mathsf{Try}$ query plus access to $\mathcal{O}.\mathsf{Dec}$, and the game ends when the $\mathcal{O}.\mathsf{Try}$ query happens. It is hard to prove the generic relation among CPA, CTXT and CCA using this formulation. Notice that decryption oracles give the adversary power to win the CTXT game even it only has one $\mathcal{O}.\mathsf{Try}$ query. The adversary can send its forgery to the decryption oracle to test if it is valid (if $\mathcal{O}.\mathsf{Dec}$ outputs a message and not $\perp$) – thus $\mathcal{A}$ can continue to send forgeries to $\mathcal{O}.\mathsf{Dec}$ until a valid one is found, and then send this as a $\mathcal{O}.\mathsf{Try}$ query (and win the game). So intuitively, a decryption oracle is equivalent to multiple $\mathcal{O}.\mathsf{Try}$ queries. Proving that all these variants of CTXT definitions are equivalent to each other is straightforward, with the loss upper-bounded by the sum of $\mathcal{O}.\mathsf{Try}$ queries and decryption queries.

Remark 1. The definition of INT-CTXT is more natural for defining ciphertext integrity, however, it is easier to use INT-CTXT^s notion to prove ciphertext integrity for specific UE schemes. As INT-CTXT $\iff$ INT-CTXT^s, we use both definitions in this paper.

3.1   Existing Definitions of Confidentiality

Here we describe existing confidentiality notions given by LT18 and KLR19, including formal definitions for their IND-yy-CPA and IND-yy-CCA notions, respectively. (Note that KLR19 used UP-REENC to refer to the the unlinkability notion that we and LT18 call IND-UPD). We will define our new security notion in Sect. 4.1 and compare the relationship between all notions in Sect. 4.2.

Definition 2. *Let* UE $= \{\mathsf{UE.KG}, \mathsf{UE.TG}, \mathsf{UE.Enc}, \mathsf{UE.Dec}, \mathsf{UE.Upd}\}$ *be an updatable encryption scheme. Then the* xxIND-ENC-atk *advantage, for* $(\mathsf{xx}, \mathsf{atk}) \in \{(\mathsf{det}, \mathsf{CPA}), (\mathsf{rand}, \mathsf{CPA}), (\mathsf{det}, \mathsf{CCA})\}$, *of an adversary* $\mathcal{A}$ *against* UE *is defined as*

$$\mathbf{Adv}_{\mathsf{UE},\,\mathcal{A}}^{\mathsf{xxIND\text{-}ENC\text{-}atk}}(\lambda) = \left| \Pr[\mathbf{Exp}_{\mathsf{UE},\,\mathcal{A}}^{\mathsf{xxIND\text{-}ENC\text{-}atk\text{-}1}} = 1] - \Pr[\mathbf{Exp}_{\mathsf{UE},\,\mathcal{A}}^{\mathsf{xxIND\text{-}ENC\text{-}atk\text{-}0}} = 1] \right|,$$

where the experiment $\mathbf{Exp}_{\mathsf{UE},\,\mathcal{A}}^{\mathsf{xxIND\text{-}ENC\text{-}atk\text{-}b}}$ *is given in Fig. 3, Fig. 5 and Fig. 8.*

Definition 3. *Let* UE $= \{\mathsf{UE.KG}, \mathsf{UE.TG}, \mathsf{UE.Enc}, \mathsf{UE.Dec}, \mathsf{UE.Upd}\}$ *be an updatable encryption scheme. Then the* xxIND-UPD-atk *advantage, for* $(\mathsf{xx}, \mathsf{atk}) \in \{(\mathsf{det}, \mathsf{CPA}), (\mathsf{rand}, \mathsf{CPA}), (\mathsf{det}, \mathsf{CCA})\}$, *of an adversary* $\mathcal{A}$ *against* UE *is defined as*

$$\mathbf{Adv}_{\mathsf{UE},\,\mathcal{A}}^{\mathsf{xxIND\text{-}UPD\text{-}atk}}(\lambda) = \left| \Pr[\mathbf{Exp}_{\mathsf{UE},\,\mathcal{A}}^{\mathsf{xxIND\text{-}UPD\text{-}atk\text{-}1}} = 1] - \Pr[\mathbf{Exp}_{\mathsf{UE},\,\mathcal{A}}^{\mathsf{xxIND\text{-}UPD\text{-}atk\text{-}0}} = 1] \right|,$$

where the experiments $\mathbf{Exp}_{\mathsf{UE},\,\mathcal{A}}^{\mathsf{xxIND\text{-}UPD\text{-}atk\text{-}b}}$ *are given in Fig. 3, Fig. 5 and Fig. 9.*

$$\underline{\mathbf{Exp}_{\mathsf{UE},\,\mathcal{A}}^{\mathsf{xxIND\text{-}ENC\text{-}atk\text{-}b}}(\lambda) :}$$

$(\bar{\mathrm{M}}_0, \bar{\mathrm{M}}_1) \leftarrow \mathcal{A}$

Create $\tilde{\mathrm{C}}$ with $(\bar{\mathrm{M}}_0, \bar{\mathrm{M}}_1)$:

  if $|\bar{\mathrm{M}}_0| \neq |\bar{\mathrm{M}}_1|$ **then**

    return $\bot$

  $\tilde{\mathrm{C}} \xleftarrow{\$} \mathsf{UE.Enc}(\mathrm{k}_{\tilde{\mathrm{e}}}, \bar{\mathrm{M}}_b)$

  return $\tilde{\mathrm{C}}$

$$\underline{\mathbf{Exp}_{\mathsf{UE},\,\mathcal{A}}^{\mathsf{xxIND\text{-}UPD\text{-}atk\text{-}b}}(\lambda) :}$$

$(\bar{\mathrm{C}}_0, \bar{\mathrm{C}}_1) \leftarrow \mathcal{A}$

Create $\tilde{\mathrm{C}}$ with $(\bar{\mathrm{C}}_0, \bar{\mathrm{C}}_1)$:

  if $|\bar{\mathrm{C}}_0| \neq |\bar{\mathrm{C}}_1|$ **or** $(\bar{\mathrm{C}}_0, \tilde{\mathrm{e}}\text{-}1) \notin \mathcal{L}$

  or $(\bar{\mathrm{C}}_1, \tilde{\mathrm{e}}\text{-}1) \notin \mathcal{L}$ **then**

    return $\bot$

  $\tilde{\mathrm{C}} \xleftarrow{\$} \mathsf{UE.Upd}(\Delta_{\tilde{\mathrm{e}}}, \bar{\mathrm{C}}_b)$

  return $\tilde{\mathrm{C}}$

Fig. 8. Challenge call definition for xxIND-ENC-atk security experiment; the full experiment is given in combination with Fig. 3 and Fig. 5.

Fig. 9. Challenge call definition for xxIND-UPD-atk security experiment; the full experiment is given in combination with Fig. 3 and Fig. 5.

We do not define randIND-ENC-CCA or randIND-UPD-CCA – these notions were formalized by KLR19. Note that trivial win via direct update (see Sect. 3.2) is never triggered in the detIND-ENC-CPA game. Thus, randIND-ENC-CPA is equivalent to detIND-ENC-CPA. For simplicity, we will often denote the notion xxIND-ENC-CPA as IND-ENC-CPA.

Remark 2. LT18 defined weakIND-ENC-CPA and weakIND-UPD-CPA for analyzing BLMR+, a modification of BLMR's scheme where the nonce is encrypted using symmetric encryption. In this notion, the adversary trivially loses if it obtains an update token linking the challenge epoch to the epoch before or after.

3.2 Trivial Win Conditions

Trivial Win Conditions in Confidentiality Games

Trivial Wins via Keys and Ciphertexts. The following is for analyzing all confidentiality games. We again follow LT18 in defining the epoch identification sets $\mathcal{C}^*$, $\mathcal{K}^*$ and $\mathcal{T}^*$ as the extended sets of $\mathcal{C}$, $\mathcal{K}$ and $\mathcal{T}$ in which the adversary has learned or inferred information via its acquired tokens. These extended sets are used to exclude cases in which the adversary trivially wins, i.e. if $\mathcal{C}^* \cap \mathcal{K}^* \neq \emptyset$, then there exists an epoch in which the adversary knows the epoch key and a valid update of the challenge ciphertext. Note that the challenger computes these sets once the adversary has finished running. We employ the following algorithms of LT18 (for bi-directional updates):

$\mathcal{K}^* \leftarrow \{e \in \{0,\ldots,n\}|\mathsf{CorrK}(e) = \mathrm{true}\}$

  $\mathrm{true} \leftarrow \mathsf{CorrK}(e) \iff (e \in \mathcal{K}) \vee (\mathsf{CorrK}(e\text{-}1) \wedge e \in \mathcal{T}) \vee (\mathsf{CorrK}(e\text{+}1) \wedge e\text{+}1 \in \mathcal{T})$

$\mathcal{T}^* \leftarrow \{e \in \{0,\ldots,n\}|(e \in \mathcal{T}) \vee (e \in \mathcal{K}^* \wedge e\text{-}1 \in \mathcal{K}^*)\}$

$\mathcal{C}^* \leftarrow \{e \in \{0,\ldots,n\}|\mathsf{ChallEq}(e) = \mathrm{true}\}$

  $\mathrm{true} \leftarrow \mathsf{ChallEq}(e) \iff$

    $(e = \tilde{e}) \vee (e \in \mathcal{C}) \vee (\mathsf{ChallEq}(e\text{-}1) \wedge e \in \mathcal{T}^*) \vee (\mathsf{ChallEq}(e\text{+}1) \wedge e\text{+}1 \in \mathcal{T}^*)$

Trivial Wins via Direct Updates. The following is for analyzing detIND-yy-atk security notions, for yy $\in \{\mathsf{UE}, \mathsf{UPD}\}$ and atk $\in \{\mathsf{CPA}, \mathsf{CCA}\}$, where the adversary provides as its challenge one or two ciphertexts that it received from $\mathcal{O}.\mathsf{Enc}$. The challenger needs to use $\mathcal{L}$ to track the information the adversary has about these challenge input values.

Define a new list $\mathcal{I}$ as the list of epochs in which the adversary learned an updated version of the ciphertext(s) given as a challenge input. Furthermore, define $\mathcal{I}^*$ to be the extended set in which the adversary has learned or inferred information via token corruption. We will use this set to exclude cases which the adversary trivially wins, i.e. if $\mathcal{I}^* \cap \mathcal{C}^* \neq \emptyset$, then there exists an epoch in which the adversary knows the updated ciphertext of $\bar{C}$ and a valid challenge-equal ciphertext. For deterministic updates, the adversary can simply compare these ciphertexts to win the game. In particular, if $\bar{C}$ is restricted to come from $\tilde{e} - 1$ (recall the challenge epoch is $\tilde{e}$), then the condition $\mathcal{I}^* \cap \mathcal{C}^* \neq \emptyset$ is equivalent to the win condition that LT18 used for IND-UPD: $\Delta_{\tilde{e}} \in \mathcal{T}^*$ or $\mathcal{A}$ did $\mathcal{O}.\mathsf{Upd}(\bar{C})$ in $\tilde{e}$. Our generalization is necessary for a variant of xxIND-UE-atk that we define later in which the challenge ciphertext input can come from any prior epoch, and not just the epoch immediately before the one in which the challenge is made.

To compute $\mathcal{I}$, find an entry in $\mathcal{L}$ that contains challenge input $\bar{C}$. Then for that entry, note the query identifier c, scan $\mathcal{L}$ for other entries with this identifier, and add into list $\mathcal{I}$ all found indices: $\mathcal{I} \leftarrow \{e \in \{0,\ldots,n\}|(c,\cdot,e) \in \mathcal{L}\}$. Then compute $\mathcal{I}^*$ as follows:

$\mathcal{I}^* \leftarrow \{e \in \{0,\ldots,n\}|\mathsf{ChallinputEq}(e) = \mathrm{true}\}$

  $\mathrm{true} \leftarrow \mathsf{ChallinputEq}(e) \iff$

    $(e \in \mathcal{I}) \vee (\mathsf{ChallinputEq}(e\text{-}1) \wedge e \in \mathcal{T}^*) \vee (\mathsf{ChallinputEq}(e\text{+}1) \wedge e\text{+}1 \in \mathcal{T}^*)$

Additionally, if the adversary submits two ciphertexts $\bar{C}_0, \bar{C}_1$ as challenge (as in xxIND-UPD-atk), we compute $\mathcal{I}_i, \mathcal{I}_i^*, i \in \{0,1\}$ first and then use $\mathcal{I}^* = \mathcal{I}_0^* \cup \mathcal{I}_1^*$ to check the trivial win condition. An example of trivial win conditions $\mathcal{K}^* \cap \mathcal{C}^* \neq \emptyset$ and $\mathcal{I}^* \cap \mathcal{C}^* \neq \emptyset$ is provided in the full version [5].

We do not consider this trivial win condition for the ENC notion, as there is no ciphertext in the challenge input value, i.e. $\mathcal{I}^* = \emptyset$. Thus, the assessment $\mathcal{I}^* \cap \mathcal{C}^* \neq \emptyset$ in experiment $\mathbf{Exp}_{\mathsf{UE},\,\mathcal{A}}^{\mathsf{detIND}\text{-}\mathsf{ENC}\text{-}\mathsf{atk}\text{-}b}$ (see Fig. 5) will never be true.

Trivial Wins via Decryptions. The following is for analyzing detIND-yy-CCA notions, for yy $\in$ {UE, ENC, UPD}, where the adversary has access to $\mathcal{O}$.Dec. We follow the trivial win analysis in KLR19: suppose the adversary knows a challenge ciphertext $(\tilde{C}, e_0) \in \tilde{\mathcal{L}}$ and tokens from epoch $e_0 + 1$ to epoch e, then the adversary can update the challenge ciphertext from epoch e_0 to epoch e. If $\mathcal{A}$ sends the updated ciphertext to $\mathcal{O}$.Dec this will reveal the underlying message, and $\mathcal{A}$ trivially wins the game: we shall exclude this type of attack.

Define $\tilde{\mathcal{L}}^*$ to be the extended set of $\tilde{\mathcal{L}}$ in which the adversary has learned or inferred information via token corruption. Whenever $\mathcal{O}$.Dec receives a ciphertext located in $\tilde{\mathcal{L}}^*$, the challenger will set the trivial win flag twf to be 1. The list $\tilde{\mathcal{L}}^*$ is updated while the security game is running. After the challenge query happens, the challenger updates $\tilde{\mathcal{L}}^*$ whenever an element is added to list $\tilde{\mathcal{L}}$ or a token is corrupted. In Fig. 10 we show how list $\tilde{\mathcal{L}}^*$ is updated.

Trivial Win Conditions in Ciphertext Integrity Games. We again follow the trivial win analysis in KLR19. In ciphertext integrity games for updatable encryption, we do not consider the randomized update setting as the adversary can update an old ciphertext via a corrupted token to provide any number of new valid forgeries to the Try query to trivially win this game.

Trivial Wins via Keys. If an epoch key is corrupted, then the adversary can use this key to forge ciphertexts in this epoch. We exclude this trivial win: if the adversary provides a forgery in an epoch in list $\mathcal{K}^*$, the challenger sets twf to 1.

Trivial Wins via Ciphertexts. Suppose the adversary knows a ciphertext $(C, e_0) \in \mathcal{L}$ and tokens from epoch $e_0 + 1$ to epoch e, then the adversary can provide a forgery by updating C to epoch e. We shall exclude this type of forgeries.

Define $\mathcal{L}^*$ to be the extended set of $\mathcal{L}$ in which the adversary has learned or inferred information via token corruption. If $\mathcal{O}$.Try receives a ciphertext located in $\mathcal{L}^*$, the challenger will set twf to 1. The list $\mathcal{L}^*$ is updated while the security game is running. Ciphertexts output by $\mathcal{O}$.Enc and $\mathcal{O}$.Upd are known to the adversary. Furthermore, whenever a token is corrupted, the challenger may update list $\mathcal{L}^*$ as well. In Fig. 11 we show how list $\mathcal{L}^*$ is updated.

if challenge query or $\mathcal{O}$.Upd$\tilde{C}$ happens then
    $\tilde{\mathcal{L}}^* \leftarrow \tilde{\mathcal{L}}^* \cup \{(\tilde{C}, \cdot)\}$
if phase = 1 and $\mathcal{O}$.Corr(token, $\cdot$) happens then
    for $i \in \mathcal{T}^*$ and $(\tilde{C}_{i-1}, i-1) \in \tilde{\mathcal{L}}^*$ do
        $\tilde{\mathcal{L}}^* \leftarrow \tilde{\mathcal{L}}^* \cup \{(\tilde{C}_i, i)\}$

Fig. 10. Updating list $\tilde{\mathcal{L}}^*$.

if $\mathcal{O}$.Enc or $\mathcal{O}$.Upd happens then
    $\mathcal{L}^* \leftarrow \mathcal{L}^* \cup \{(\cdot, C, \cdot)\}$
if $\mathcal{O}$.Corr(token, $\cdot$) happens then
    for $i \in \mathcal{T}^*$ do
        for $(j, C_{i-1}, i-1) \in \mathcal{L}^*$ do
            $C_i \leftarrow$ UE.Upd(Δ_i, C_{i-1})
            $\mathcal{L}^* \leftarrow \mathcal{L}^* \cup \{(j, C_i, i)\}$

Fig. 11. Updating list $\mathcal{L}^*$.

3.3   Firewall Technique

In order to prove security for updatable encryption in the epoch-based model with strong corruption capabilities, cryptographic separation is required between the epochs in which the adversary knows key material, and those in which it knows challenge-equal ciphertexts (acquired/calculated via queries to $\mathcal{O}.\mathsf{Upd}\tilde{\mathsf{C}}$ and $\mathcal{O}.\mathsf{Corr}(\Delta)$). To ensure this, we follow prior work in explicitly defining the 'safe' or *insulated* regions, as we explain below. These regions insulate epoch keys, tokens and ciphertexts: outside of an insulated region a reduction in a security proof can generate keys and tokens itself, but within these regions it must embed its challenge while still providing the underlying adversary with access to the appropriate oracles. A thorough discussion of how we leverage these insulated regions in proofs is given in Sect. 5.3.

To understand the idea of firewalls, consider any security game (for bi-directional schemes) in which the trivial win conditions are *not* triggered. If the adversary $\mathcal{A}$ corrupts all tokens then either it never corrupts any keys or it never asks for a challenge ciphertext. Suppose that $\mathcal{A}$ does ask for a challenge ciphertext in epoch $\tilde{e}^3$. Then there exists an (unique) epoch continuum around $\tilde{e}$ such that no keys in this epoch continuum, and no tokens in the boundaries of this epoch continuum are corrupted. Moreover, we can assume that all tokens within this epoch continuum are corrupted, because once the adversary has finished corrupting keys, it can corrupt any remaining tokens that do not 'touch' those corrupted keys. This observation is first used in the IND-UPD proof of RISE provided by Lehmann and Tackmann [21], and Klooß et al. [17] provided an extended description of this 'key insulation' technique. We name these epoch ranges *insulated regions* and their boundaries to be *firewalls*.

Definition 4. *An* insulated region *with* firewalls fwl *and* fwr *is a consecutive sequence of epochs* (fwl, . . . , fwr) *for which:*

- *no key in the sequence of epochs* (fwl, . . . , fwr) *is corrupted;*
- *the tokens* Δ_{fwl} *and* $\Delta_{\mathsf{fwr}+1}$ *are not corrupted (if they exist);*
- *all tokens* $(\Delta_{\mathsf{fwl}+1}, . . . , \Delta_{\mathsf{fwr}})$ *are corrupted (if any exist).*

We denote the firewalls bordering the special insulated region that contains $\tilde{e}$ as $\hat{\mathsf{fwl}}$ and $\hat{\mathsf{fwr}}$ – though note that there could be (many, distinct) insulated regions elsewhere in the epoch continuum. Specifically, when the adversary asks for updated versions of the challenge ciphertext, the epoch in which this query occurs must also fall within (what the challenger later calculates as) an insulated region. In the full version [5] we give an algorithm for computing firewall locations. The list $\mathcal{FW}$ tracks, and appends a label to, each insulated region and its firewalls. Observe that if an epoch is a left firewall, then neither the key nor the token for that epoch are corrupted. From the left firewall, since we assume that all tokens are corrupted, track to the right until either a token is not corrupted or a key is.

---

[3] In the situation that the adversary does not corrupt any keys to the left or the right (or both) of the challenge epoch, the insulated region thus extends to the boundary (or boundaries) of the epoch continuum.

4   On the Security of Updates

In this section we present a new notion of security for updatable encryption schemes, which we denote xxIND-UE-atk. This notion captures both security of fresh encryptions (i.e. implies xxIND-ENC-atk) and unlinkability (i.e. implies xxIND-UPD-atk). We first explain the new notion and then describe its relation to previous notions. Then, we prove a generic relationship among CPA, CTXT and CCA to complete the picture for security notions for UE schemes.

4.1   A New Definition of Confidentiality

In the security game for xxIND-UE-atk, the adversary submits one message and a ciphertext from an earlier epoch that the adversary received via a call to $\mathcal{O}$.Enc. The challenger responds with either an encryption of that message or an update of that earlier ciphertext, in the challenge (current) epoch $\tilde{e}$.

Definition 5 (xxIND-UE-atk). *Let* UE $= \{$UE.KG, UE.TG, UE.Enc, UE.Dec, UE.Upd$\}$ *be an updatable encryption scheme. Then the* xxIND-UE-atk *advantage, for* $(xx, atk) \in \{(det, CPA), (rand, CPA), (det, CCA)\}$, *of an adversary* $\mathcal{A}$ *against* UE *is defined as*

$$\mathbf{Adv}_{UE,\, \mathcal{A}}^{xxIND-UE-atk}(\lambda) = \left| \Pr[\mathbf{Exp}_{UE,\, \mathcal{A}}^{xxIND-UE-atk-1} = 1] - \Pr[\mathbf{Exp}_{UE,\, \mathcal{A}}^{xxIND-UE-atk-0} = 1] \right|$$

where the experiment $\mathbf{Exp}_{UE,\, \mathcal{A}}^{xxIND-UE-atk-b}$ *is given in Fig. 3, Fig. 5 and Fig. 12.*

Note that randIND-UE-CPA is strictly stronger than detIND-UE-CPA, since the adversary has strictly more capabilities. A generalized version of xxIND-UE-atk, denoted xxIND-UE*-atk, is also given in Fig. 12. In this game the input challenge ciphertext can come from (i.e. be known to $\mathcal{A}$ in) any prior epoch, not just the epoch immediately before $\tilde{e}$. Note that xxIND-UE-atk is a special case of xxIND-UE*-atk. Under some fairly weak requirements (that all schemes discussed in this paper satisfy) we can prove that xxIND-UE-atk implies xxIND-UE*-atk – this analysis is given in the full version [5].

$\mathbf{Exp}_{UE,\, \mathcal{A}}^{xxIND-UE-atk-b}(\lambda):$	$\mathbf{Exp}_{UE,\, \mathcal{A}}^{xxIND-UE^{*}-atk-b}(\lambda):$
$(\bar{M}, \bar{C}) \leftarrow \mathcal{A}$	$(\bar{M}, (\bar{C}, e')) \leftarrow \mathcal{A}$
Create $\tilde{C}$ with $(\bar{M}, \bar{C})$:	Create $\tilde{C}$ with $(\bar{M}, (\bar{C}, e'))$:
if $(\bar{C}, \tilde{e} - 1) \notin \mathcal{L}$ then	if $(\bar{C}, e') \notin \mathcal{L}$ then
return $\perp$	return $\perp$
if $b = 0$ then	if $b = 0$ then
$\tilde{C} \leftarrow$ UE.Enc$(k_{\tilde{e}}, \bar{M})$	$\tilde{C}_{\tilde{e}} \leftarrow$ UE.Enc$(k_{\tilde{e}}, \bar{M})$
else	else
$\tilde{C} \leftarrow$ UE.Upd$(\Delta_{\tilde{e}}, \bar{C})$	$\tilde{C}_{e'} \leftarrow \bar{C}$
return $\tilde{C}$	for $j \in \{e'+1, ..., \tilde{e}\}$ do
	$\tilde{C}_j \leftarrow$ UE.Upd$(\Delta_j, \tilde{C}_{j-1})$
	return $\tilde{C}_{\tilde{e}}$

Fig. 12. Challenge call definition for xxIND-UE-atk and xxIND-UE*-atk security experiments, the full experiment is defined in Fig. 3, Fig. 5.

Remark 3. The definition of xxIND-UE-atk is more concise and intuitively easier to understand than xxIND-UE*-atk, however in the full version [5] we show that xxIND-UE-atk $\iff$ xxIND-UE*-atk. This result and our generic proof techniques mean that all results in this paper that hold for xxIND-UE-atk, also hold for xxIND-UE*-atk, and vice versa.

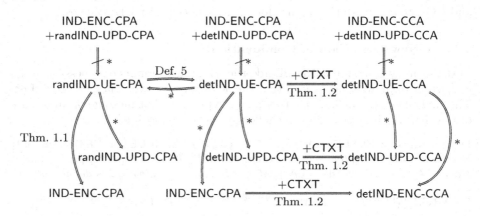

Fig. 13. Relations among confidentiality notions xxIND-yy-atk for xx ∈ {det, rand}, yy ∈ {UE, ENC, UPD}, atk ∈ {CPA, CCA}, and ciphertext integrity (INT-CTXT). Results that are given only in the full version [5] are marked with *.

Remark 4. In the full version [5] we show that the RISE scheme presented by LT18 is randIND-UE-CPA secure under DDH. While this result is perhaps unsurprising, the proof techniques we use are novel. We give an Oracle-DDH-like game that inherits the epoch-based nature of the updatable encryption security model, and then use this as a bridge to prove security.

4.2   Relations Among Security Notions

In Fig. 13 we show the relationship between the new and existing UE security notions. Note that our new notion is strictly stronger than the xxIND-ENC-atk and xxIND-UPD-atk notions presented in prior work, and is in fact stronger than the combination of the prior notions. Further, we show that the generic relation among CPA, CTXT and CCA, that CPA security coupled with ciphertext integrity implies CCA security, also holds for updatable encryption schemes.

Theorem 1 (Informal Theorem). *The relationship among the security notions* xxIND-UE-atk, xxIND-ENC-atk *and* xxIND-UPD-atk *are as in Fig. 13. The relationship is proven via Theorems in the full version [5] and due to space constraints we show Theorems 1.1 and Theorem 1.2 only.*

Theorem 1.1 *Let* $\mathsf{UE} = \{\mathsf{UE.KG}, \mathsf{UE.TG}, \mathsf{UE.Enc}, \mathsf{UE.Dec}, \mathsf{UE.Upd}\}$ *be an updatable encryption scheme. For any* $\mathsf{IND\text{-}ENC\text{-}CPA}$ *adversary* $\mathcal{A}$ *against* UE, *there exists an* $\mathsf{randIND\text{-}UE\text{-}CPA}$ *adversary* $\mathcal{B}_{1.1}$ *against* UE *such that*

$$\mathbf{Adv}_{\mathsf{UE},\,\mathcal{A}}^{\mathsf{IND\text{-}ENC\text{-}CPA}}(\lambda) \leq 2 \cdot \mathbf{Adv}_{\mathsf{UE},\,\mathcal{B}_{1.1}}^{\mathsf{randIND\text{-}UE\text{-}CPA}}(\lambda).$$

Proof. We construct a reduction $\mathcal{B}_{1.1}$ running the $\mathsf{randIND\text{-}UE\text{-}CPA}$ experiment which will simulate the responses of queries made by the $\mathsf{IND\text{-}ENC\text{-}CPA}$ adversary $\mathcal{A}$. To provide a valid non-challenge ciphertext to its own challenger, $\mathcal{B}_{1.1}$ must run $\mathcal{A}$ out of step with its own game, so epoch 0 as far as $\mathcal{A}$ is concerned is actually epoch 1 for $\mathcal{B}_{1.1}$, and so on.

1. $\mathcal{B}_{1.1}$ chooses $b \overset{\$}{\leftarrow} \{0,1\}$.
2. $\mathcal{B}_{1.1}$ receives the setup parameters from its $\mathsf{randIND\text{-}UE\text{-}CPA}$ challenger, chooses $\mathrm{M} \overset{\$}{\leftarrow} \mathcal{MS}$ and calls $\mathcal{O}.\mathsf{Enc}(\mathrm{M})$ which returns some C^0. Then $\mathcal{B}_{1.1}$ calls $\mathcal{O}.\mathsf{Next}$ once and sends the setup parameters to $\mathcal{A}$.
3. (a) Whenever $\mathcal{B}_{1.1}$ receives the queries $\mathcal{O}.\mathsf{Enc}, \mathcal{O}.\mathsf{Upd}, \mathcal{O}.\mathsf{Corr}$ from $\mathcal{A}$, $\mathcal{B}_{1.1}$ sends these queries to its $\mathsf{randIND\text{-}UE\text{-}CPA}$ challenger, and forwards the responses to $\mathcal{A}$.
   (b) Whenever $\mathcal{O}.\mathsf{Next}$ is called by $\mathcal{A}$, $\mathcal{B}_{1.1}$ randomly chooses a message $\mathrm{M} \overset{\$}{\leftarrow} \mathcal{MS}$ and calls $\mathcal{O}.\mathsf{Enc}(\mathrm{M})$ to receive some C^e, and then calls $\mathcal{O}.\mathsf{Next}$.
4. At some point, in epoch $\tilde{e}$ (for its game), $\mathcal{B}_{1.1}$ receives the challenge query $(\bar{\mathrm{M}}_0, \bar{\mathrm{M}}_1)$ from $\mathcal{A}$. Then $\mathcal{B}_{1.1}$ sends the pair $(\bar{\mathrm{M}}_b, \mathrm{C}^{\tilde{e}-1})$ as challenge to its own $\mathsf{randIND\text{-}UE\text{-}CPA}$ challenger. After receiving the challenge ciphertext, $\tilde{\mathrm{C}}_{\tilde{e}}$, from its challenger, $\mathcal{B}_{1.1}$ sends $\tilde{\mathrm{C}}_{\tilde{e}}$ to $\mathcal{A}$.
5. $\mathcal{B}_{1.1}$ continues to answer $\mathcal{A}$'s queries using its own oracles, now including the challenge ciphertext update oracle $\mathcal{O}.\mathsf{Upd}\tilde{\mathrm{C}}$.
6. Finally $\mathcal{B}_{1.1}$ receives the output bit b' from $\mathcal{A}$. If $b = b'$ then $\mathcal{B}_{1.1}$ returns 0. Otherwise $\mathcal{B}_{1.1}$ returns 1.

We now bound the advantage of $\mathcal{B}_{1.1}$. The point is that whenever $\mathcal{B}_{1.1}$ returns a random encryption to $\mathcal{A}$, $\mathcal{B}_{1.1}$'s probability of winning is exactly $1/2$ because the bit b' from $\mathcal{A}$ is independent of its choice of b. This happens with probability $1/2$. However, when $\mathcal{B}_{1.1}$ returns a "correct" value to $\mathcal{A}$ (an encryption of $\bar{\mathrm{M}}_0$ or $\bar{\mathrm{M}}_1$), then $\mathcal{B}_{1.1}$'s probability of winning is the same as the probability that $\mathcal{A}$ wins. First note that, as usual,

$$\mathbf{Adv}_{\mathsf{UE},\mathcal{B}_{1.1}}^{\mathsf{randIND\text{-}UE\text{-}CPA}} = |\mathbf{Pr}[\mathbf{Exp}_{\mathsf{UE},\,\mathcal{B}_{1.1}}^{\mathsf{randIND\text{-}UE\text{-}CPA\text{-}1}} = 1] - \mathbf{Pr}[\mathbf{Exp}_{\mathsf{UE},\,\mathcal{B}_{1.1}}^{\mathsf{randIND\text{-}UE\text{-}CPA\text{-}0}} = 1]|.$$

We claim that $\mathbf{Pr}[\mathbf{Exp}_{\mathsf{UE},\,\mathcal{B}_{1.1}}^{\mathsf{randIND\text{-}UE\text{-}CPA\text{-}1}} = 1] = 1/2$ because in this case $\tilde{\mathrm{C}}_{\tilde{e}}$ is independent of b and so b' must also be independent of b. Then we have:

$$\mathbf{Adv}_{\mathsf{UE},\mathcal{B}_{1.1}}^{\mathsf{randIND\text{-}UE\text{-}CPA}} = \left| \frac{1}{2} - \mathbf{Pr}[\mathbf{Exp}_{\mathsf{UE},\,\mathcal{B}_{1.1}}^{\mathsf{randIND\text{-}UE\text{-}CPA\text{-}0}} = 1] \right|$$

$$= \left| \frac{1}{2} - \left(\frac{1}{2} \cdot \mathbf{Pr}[\mathbf{Exp}_{\mathsf{UE},\,\mathcal{A}}^{\mathsf{IND\text{-}ENC\text{-}CPA\text{-}0}} = 1] + \frac{1}{2} \cdot \mathbf{Pr}[\mathbf{Exp}_{\mathsf{UE},\,\mathcal{A}}^{\mathsf{IND\text{-}ENC\text{-}CPA\text{-}1}} = 0] \right) \right|$$

$$= \frac{1}{2} \cdot \mathbf{Adv}_{\mathsf{UE},\,\mathcal{A}}^{\mathsf{IND\text{-}ENC\text{-}CPA}}. \qquad \square$$

The three separation arrows at the top of Fig. 13 are all demonstrated in the same manner. Begin with a scheme UE that meets both of the two notions at the very top of the figure. All algorithms for UE′ are the same as for UE, except UE′.Enc is defined by modifying UE.Enc to append the epoch number in which the ciphertext was initially created (and UE′.Dec ignores this appended value). This does not affect an adversary's ability to win the IND-ENC-atk or xxIND-UPD-atk games but trivially breaks xxIND-UE-atk security.

Generic Composition. The following theorem tells the relation among CPA, CTXT and CCA security. The full proof is given in the full version [5].

Theorem 1.2 *Let* UE = {UE.KG, UE.TG, UE.Enc, UE.Dec, UE.Upd} *be an updatable encryption scheme. For any* detIND-yy-CCA *adversary* $\mathcal{A}$ *against* UE, *there exists an* INT-CTXT *adversary* $\mathcal{B}_{1.2a}$ *and an* detIND-yy-CPA *adversary* $\mathcal{B}_{1.2b}$ *against* UE *such that*

$$\mathbf{Adv}_{\mathsf{UE},\,\mathcal{A}}^{\mathsf{detIND\text{-}yy\text{-}CCA}}(\lambda) \leq 2\mathbf{Adv}_{\mathsf{UE},\,\mathcal{B}_{1.2a}}^{\mathsf{INT\text{-}CTXT}}(\lambda) + \mathbf{Adv}_{\mathsf{UE},\,\mathcal{B}_{1.2b}}^{\mathsf{detIND\text{-}yy\text{-}CPA}}(\lambda)$$

where yy ∈ {UE, ENC, UPD}.

Proof sketch. The proof is adapted from the proof of Theorem 3.2 of Bellare and Namprempre [2]. We modify the detIND-yy-CCA game such that in the new game the decryption oracle will answer ⊥ if the input is a fresh ciphertext.

In more detail, suppose $\mathcal{A}$ is an adversary playing the new game, then we can then construct a reduction playing detIND-yy-CPA game and simulating the responses to $\mathcal{A}$. To answer decryption oracle queries made by $\mathcal{A}$, the reduction performs bookkeeping for ciphertexts and messages to successfully respond to the decryption of already-existing ciphertexts, or simply replying ⊥ for the decryption of fresh ciphertexts. So the advantage of winning the new game is upper-bounded by the detIND-yy-CPA advantage.

Furthermore, notice that two games are identical until a valid fresh ciphertext is sent to the decryption oracle. Which means the probability of an adversary these games is upper-bounded by the probability that a valid fresh forgery is produced: this successful adversary can win the INT-CTXT game. Therefore, the difference between the new game and the original detIND-yy-CCA game can be upper-bounded by the INT-CTXT advantage. □

5 The SHINE Schemes

We now describe our new UE scheme SHINE (Secure Homomorphic Ideal-cipher Nonce-based Encryption). The encryption algorithm uses a permutation to obfuscate the input to the exponentiation function. Updating a ciphertext simply requires exponentiation once by the update token, which itself is the quotient of the current epoch key and the previous epoch key. The scheme comes in three flavors: SHINE0 is presented in Fig. 14 and takes in short messages and only uses a single permutation. The second flavor, MirrorSHINE, is provided in the

SHINE0.KG(λ) :

$\quad$ k $\xleftarrow{\$}$ $\mathbb{Z}_q^*$

$\quad$ **return** k

SHINE0.TG(k_e, k_{e+1}) :

$\quad$ $\Delta_{e+1} \leftarrow \frac{k_{e+1}}{k_e}$

$\quad$ **return** Δ_{e+1}

SHINE0.Enc(k_e, M) :

$\quad$ N $\xleftarrow{\$}$ $\mathcal{N}$

$\quad$ $C_e \leftarrow (\pi(N\|M\|0^t))^{k_e}$

$\quad$ **return** C_e

SHINE0.Dec(k_e, C_e) :

$\quad$ $a \leftarrow \pi^{-1}(C_e^{1/k_e})$

$\quad$ parse† a as $N'\|M'\|Z$

$\quad$ **if** $Z = 0^t$ **then**

$\quad\quad$ **return** M'

$\quad$ **else**

$\quad\quad$ **return** $\perp$

SHINE0.Upd(Δ_{e+1}, C_e) :

$\quad$ $C_{e+1} \leftarrow (C_e)^{\Delta_{e+1}}$

$\quad$ **return** C_{e+1}

Fig. 14. Updatable encryption scheme SHINE0. $\dagger$: $\|N'\| = v$, $\|M'\| = m$, $\|Z\| = t$. Note that there may be an additional embedding step after the permutation π, as discussed in Sect. 5.6.

full version [5] and runs two different permutations with the same input. The third flavor OCBSHINE is given in Fig. 16 and is for applications with arbitrarily long messages, using a family of permutations.

We discuss implementation details of the SHINE schemes in Sect. 5.6. In particular, for each scheme in the SHINE suite, it is necessary to embed the output of the permutation (a regular block cipher) into an appropriate DDH-hard group.

Our proofs of security, given as Theorem 2 (Theorem 3), bound an adversary's detIND-UE-CPA (INT-CTXT^s) advantage by DDH (CDH), and are provided in the ideal cipher model. Furthermore, combining the results of Theorem 1.2, Theorem 2 and Theorem 3, we have that the suite of SHINE schemes (i.e. SHINE0, MirrorSHINE and OCBSHINE) are detIND-UE-CCA secure.

5.1 Construction of SHINE Schemes

SHINE via Zero Block: SHINE0. Suppose a message space of $\mathcal{MS} = \{0,1\}^m$ and random nonce space $\mathcal{N} = \{0,1\}^v$. The encryption algorithm feeds as input to the permutation a nonce, the message, and a zero string. The decryption algorithm will return $\perp$ if the decrypted value does not end with 0^t. The SHINE0 scheme is defined in Fig. 14. If ciphertext integrity is not required (or file/ciphertext integrity is performed in some other manner), then SHINE0 without the zero block results in a scheme (denoted SHINE0[CPA]) that is still detIND-UE-CPA secure.

SHINE for Long Messages via Checksum: OCBSHINE. The schemes SHINE0 and MirrorSHINE both require that the message space be smaller than the size of an element of the exponentiation group. This ciphertext expansion is undesirable in many practical scenarios, and so we wish to construct a SHINE scheme which gives us (almost) no ciphertext expansion and can be applied to arbitrarily long messages. We build a new SHINE scheme, OCBSHINE, with these properties.

The construction of OCBSHINE is inspired by the authenticated encryption scheme OCB [24]. Different from OCB mode, the nonce is encrypted inside the ciphertext instead of sending it along with the ciphertext. In order to determine the length of the last message block, the encryption algorithm of OCB mode removes some bits of the last ciphertext block to reveal this information. However in our setting, the output of the permutations are (mapped to) the input of the exponentiation function: thus all bits of permutation outputs must be included. Therefore, OCBSHINE includes the length of the last message block in the first ciphertext component. If ciphertext integrity is not required, then OCBSHINE can be improved by removing the last ciphertext block.

OCBSHINE is formally defined in Fig. 16 and the encryption process is pictorially represented in Fig. 15; we give an intuitive description here. Suppose the blocksize is m, and assume the encryption algorithm OCBSHINE.Enc has input message M. By "partition M into $M_1, \ldots, M_l$" we mean setting $l \leftarrow \max\{\lceil |M|/m \rceil, 1\}$ and dividing M into l blocks, i.e. $M_1, \ldots, M_l$, where $|M_1| = \cdots = |M_{l-1}| = m$. The last message block M_l is padded with zeros to make it length m before computing the permutation output and the checksum, i.e $M_l \| 0^*$ with $|M_l \| 0^*| = m$. Let $a = \lceil \log(m) \rceil$, so the length of M_l ($|M_l| \leq m$) can be written as an a-bit representation.

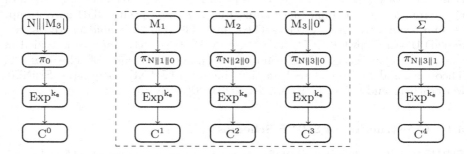

Fig. 15. Diagram describing how the OCBSHINE encryption algorithm works on message $M = (M_1, M_2, M_3)$. $\Sigma = M_1 \oplus M_2 \oplus M_3 \| 0^*$. There may be an additional embedding step after the permutations, as discussed in Sect. 5.6.

Let Perm(m) be the set of all permutations on $\{0,1\}^m$. Randomly choose $\pi_0 \xleftarrow{\$} \text{Perm}(m)$, and use this permutation to randomize the concatenation of the nonce N and an a-bit representation of the last message block length. Then, index the (random) permutations used to encrypt message blocks by the nonce and a counter. Let Perm(S, m) be the set of all mappings from S to permutations on $\{0,1\}^m$. Suppose the nonce space is $\mathcal{N} = \{0,1\}^{m-a}$, $S = \mathcal{N} \times \mathbb{N}^* \times \{0,1\}$, for each (N $\in \mathcal{N}, i \in \mathbb{N}^*, b \in \{0,1\}$), set $\pi_{N\|i\|b} \xleftarrow{\$} \text{Perm}(\mathcal{N} \times \mathbb{N}^* \times \{0,1\}, m)$, which

OCBSHINE.KG(m) :

$k \xleftarrow{\$} \mathbb{Z}_q^*$
return k

OCBSHINE.TG(k_e, k_{e+1}) :

$\Delta_{e+1} \leftarrow \frac{k_{e+1}}{k_e}$
return Δ_{e+1}

OCBSHINE.Enc(k_e, M) :

partition M into $M_1, ..., M_l$
$\Sigma \leftarrow \oplus_{i=1}^{l-1} M_i \oplus M_l \| 0^*$
$N \xleftarrow{\$} \mathcal{N}$
$C^0 \leftarrow \left(\pi_0(N \| \| M_l |) \right)^{k_e}$
$C^{l+1} \leftarrow \left(\pi_{N\|l\|1}(\Sigma) \right)^{k_e}$
for $i = 1, ..., l\text{-}1$ **do**
$\quad C^i \leftarrow \left(\pi_{N\|i\|0}(M_i) \right)^{k_e}$
$C^l \leftarrow \left(\pi_{N\|l\|0}(M_l \| 0^*) \right)^{k_e}$
$C_e \leftarrow (C^0, ..., C^l, C^{l+1})$
return C_e

OCBSHINE.Dec(k_e, C_e) :

parse $C_e = (C^0, ..., C^l, C^{l+1})$
$N' \| A' \leftarrow \pi_0^{-1}((C^0)^{1/k_e})$
$\Sigma' \leftarrow \pi_{N'\|l\|1}^{-1}((C^{l+1})^{1/k_e})$
for $i = 1, ..., l$ **do**
$\quad M_i' \leftarrow \pi_{N'\|i\|0}^{-1}((C^i)^{1/k_e})$
if $\Sigma' = \oplus_{i=1}^l M_i'$ **then**
$\quad M' \leftarrow (M_1', ..., M_l'[\text{first } A'\text{-bit}])$
$\quad$ **return** M'
else
$\quad$ **return** $\perp$

OCBSHINE.Upd(Δ_{e+1}, C_e) :

parse $C_e = (C^0, ..., C^l, C^{l+1})$
for $i = 0, ..., l+1$ **do**
$\quad C_{e+1}^i \leftarrow (C_e^i)^{\Delta_{e+1}}$
return C_{e+1}

Fig. 16. Updatable encryption scheme OCBSHINE. Note that there may be an additional embedding step after the permutations, as discussed in Sect. 5.6.

form a random permutation family: we use these permutations to randomize message blocks and the checksum.

5.2 Security - SHINE is detIND-UE-CPA, INT-CTXT, detIND-UE-CCA Secure

All three SHINE schemes, i.e. SHINE0, MirrorSHINE and OCBSHINE, have the same security properties, and the proofs are very similar for each flavor. We refer to SHINE to mean the family containing all these three schemes. In Theorem 2, we show that SHINE is detIND-UE-CPA in the ideal cipher model, if DDH holds. In Theorem 3, we show that SHINE is INT-CTXT^s, and therefore INT-CTXT (INT-CTXT and INT-CTXT^s are equivalent, recall Sect. 3), in the ideal cipher model, if CDH holds. The loss incurred by this proof is the normal $(n+1)^3$ (or $(n+1)^2$ for INT-CTXT) and also the number of encryption queries the adversary makes before it makes its challenge: to avoid the issues described in Sect. 5.3 we not only need to guess the locations of the challenge firewalls but also the ciphertext that the adversary will submit as its challenge.

The ideal cipher model, a version of which was initially given by Shannon [26] and shown to be equivalent to the random oracle model by Coron et al. [8], gives all parties access to a permutation chosen randomly from all possible key-permutation possibilities of appropriate length. The SHINE schemes exponentiate the output of the permutation by the epoch key to encrypt, so our reduction can 'program' the transformation from permutation outputs to group elements.

In the following two Theorems we detail the security properties met by SHINE, i.e. detIND-UE-CPA, INT-CTXT and thus detIND-UE-CCA. Note that this is the strongest known security property for updatable encryption schemes with deterministic updates. In Sect. 5.3 we discuss the challenges that arise in the proofs of these two theorems, and in Sect. 5.4 and Sect. 5.5 we describe the novel techniques and methods used in the proofs. Full proofs are provided in the full version [5].

Theorem 2 (SHINE is detIND-UE-CPA). *Let* SHINE $\in$ {SHINE0, MirrorSHINE, OCBSHINE} *be the UE scheme described above. For any ideal cipher model adversary* $\mathcal{A}$ *(that makes max* Q_E *encryption queries before its challenge), there exists an adversary* $\mathcal{B}_2$ *such that*

$$\mathbf{Adv}_{\mathsf{SHINE},\ \mathcal{A}}^{\mathsf{detIND\text{-}UE\text{-}CPA}}(\lambda) \leq O(1)(n+1)^3 \cdot Q_E \cdot \mathbf{Adv}_{\mathbb{G},\ \mathcal{B}_2}^{\mathsf{DDH}}(\lambda).$$

Theorem 3 (SHINE is INT-CTXT^s). *Let* SHINE $\in$ {SHINE0, MirrorSHINE, OCBSHINE} *be the UE scheme described above. For any ideal cipher model adversary* $\mathcal{A}$ *(that makes max* Q_E *encryption queries before calling* $\mathcal{O}.\mathsf{Try}$*), there exists an adversary* $\mathcal{B}_3$ *such that*

$$\mathbf{Adv}_{\mathsf{SHINE},\ \mathcal{A}}^{\mathsf{INT\text{-}CTXT}^s}(\lambda) \leq O(1)(n+1)^2 \cdot Q_E \cdot \mathbf{Adv}_{\mathcal{B}_3}^{\mathsf{CDH}} + negligible\ terms$$

Remark 5. Combining the results of Theorem 1.2, Theorem 2 and Theorem 3, we have that SHINE is detIND-UE-CCA.

5.3 Proof Challenges in Schemes with Deterministic Updates

In each variant of SHINE all ciphertext components are raised to the epoch key, so the update mechanism transforms a ciphertext for epoch e to one for e + 1 by raising this value to $\frac{k_{e+1}}{k_e}$. We now highlight the difficulties in creating security proofs for such 'single-component' updatable encryption schemes. Randomness is used in creation of the initial ciphertext (via N) but updates are completely deterministic, and thus in any reduction it is necessary to provide consistent ciphertexts to the adversary (i.e. the N value must be consistent). The (cryptographic) separation gained by using the firewall technique (see Sect. 3.3 for discussion and definition) assists with producing (updates of) non-challenge ciphertexts, but embedding any challenge value while also providing answers to the $\mathcal{O}.\mathsf{Corr}$ queries of the underlying adversary is very challenging.

The regular key insulation technique as introduced by LT18 – where the reduction constructs one hybrid for each epoch – does not work. Specifically, in any reduction to a DDH-like assumption, it is not possible to provide a challenge ciphertext in a left or right sense (to the left of this challenge ciphertext are of some form, and to the right of this challenge ciphertext are of some other form) if the underlying adversary asks for tokens around the challenge epoch:

deterministic updates mean that tokens will make these ciphertexts of the same form and this gap will be easily distinguishable.

We counteract this problem by constructing a *hybrid argument across insulated regions*. This means that in each hybrid, we can embed at one firewall of the insulated region, and simulate all tokens within that insulated region to enable answering queries to both $\mathcal{O}.\mathsf{Upd}$ and $\mathcal{O}.\mathsf{Upd\tilde{C}}$. The reduction's distinguishing task is thus ensured to be at the boundaries of the insulated regions, the firewalls, so any (non-trivial) win for the underlying adversary is ensured to carry through directly to the reduction.

5.4   Proof Method for Confidentiality: Constructing a Hybrid Argument Across Insulated Regions

The confidentiality proof of SHINE0 is extendable to MirrorSHINE and OCBSHINE, so we only show proof method of SHINE0. We now explain how we bound the advantage of any adversary playing the detIND-UE-CPA game for SHINE0 by the advantage of a reduction playing DDH.

We apply the firewall technique to set up hybrid games such that in hybrid i, we embed within the i-th insulated region: this means that to the left of the i-th insulated region the game responds with the b = 1 case of the detIND-UE-CPA experiment, and to the right of the i-th insulated region it gives an encryption of the challenge input message as output, i.e. b = 0. This means we have one hybrid for each insulated region, moving left-to-right across the epoch space.

We construct a reduction $\mathcal{B}$ playing the DDH experiment in hybrid i. Initially, $\mathcal{B}$ guesses the location of the i-th insulated region. If the underlying adversary has performed a corrupt query within this insulated region that would lead to the reduction failing, the reduction aborts the game. In the full version [5] we detail a dedicated algorithm for checking this event.

In particular, within the insulated region, the reduction can simulate challenge ciphertexts and non-challenge ciphertexts using its DDH tuple. Furthermore, ciphertexts can be moved around within the insulated region by tokens.

Remark 6. We note that the problem of challenge insulation in schemes with deterministic updates was also observed independently by Klooß et al. [[18] § B.2]. Their solution (though in the different context of CCA security of UE with certain properties) is to form a hybrid argument with a hybrid for each epoch, and essentially guess an epoch r which is the first token 'after' the hybrid index that the adversary has not corrupted, and use the inherent 'gap' in the adversary's knowledge continuum to replace challenge updates across this gap with encryptions of just one of the challenge messages. It is not clear if this approach would work for showing detIND-UE-CPA (or IND-ENC-CPA) of SHINE0. We conjecture that even if it were possible to construct a reduction in this vein, our approach enables a more direct proof: in particular we do not need to assume specific additional properties of the UE scheme in question for it to work.

5.5   Proof Method for Integrity

The integrity proof of SHINE0 is extendable to MirrorSHINE and OCBSHINE, so we only show proof method of SHINE0.In the INT-CTXT^s game, the challenger will keep a list of consistent values for ciphertexts (i.e. the underlying permutation output $\pi(N\|M\|0^l)$). Suppose $\tilde{C}$ is a forgery attempt sent to the $\mathcal{O}$.Try query in epoch $\tilde{e}$. Let $\tilde{c} = (\tilde{C})^{1/k_{\tilde{e}}}$ be the underlying permutation output. We claim that if $\tilde{c}$ is a new value, then the adversary wins the game with negligible probability; if $\tilde{c}$ is a value that existed before, then the probability that the adversary wins the game can be bounded by the CDH advantage.

If $\tilde{c}$ is a new value, since π is a random permutation, then the INT-CTXT^s challenger simulates the preimage of $\tilde{c}$ under π to be a random string. So the probability that this random string ends with a (fixed length) zero block is negligible, and this carries over to the probability that the adversary wins the INT-CTXT^s game. If $\tilde{c}$ is an already-existing value, and suppose this event happens with probability p. We construct a reduction playing the CDH game such that it wins CDH game with probability $p \cdot \frac{1}{Q_E(n+1)^2}$. Similar to the proof method of confidentiality, we construct a reduction playing the CDH experiment by guessing the location of the firewalls around the challenge epoch. The reduction embeds the CDH value and simulates the INT-CTXT^s game, using any successfully-forged ciphertext to compute the CDH output to its CDH challenger.

5.6   Implementing the SHINE Schemes

In the proofs of Theorem 2 and Theorem 3, we require that π is a random (unkeyed) permutation which must be followed by a mapping to an appropriate group for exponentiation by the epoch key. For the permutation we do not need any specific and strong properties that are provided by modern constructions of block ciphers and sponges. As far as the proof goes, and in practice, the property that we want from this permutation is that given a ciphertext and the inverse of the epoch key k_e, the only way to extract useful information about the message is to apply the inverse permutation π^{-1}. The random permutation model (or ideal cipher model) is thus the tool we need here to create a simple interface for this aspect of our proof.

The different members of the SHINE family are suited to different application scenarios. The variants SHINE0 and MirrorSHINE are best suited to cases where messages are of small, fixed size, such as customer credentials (or phone contact details, to return to the motivating example in the Introduction). For applications with longer messages (i.e. larger than the size of the exponentiation group), OCBSHINE is considerably faster and we will assume that these choices are made in our implementation suggestions. This removes any need for larger groups in order to encrypt longer messages. Using larger groups would not only carry a significant performance penalty, but also force us to construct custom large blocklength block ciphers. Although this can be done (and has been for RSA groups [14], where our approach would not work), the analysis is tricky.

Instantiating the Ideal Permutation. The message block in SHINE0, MirrorSHINE and the final message block in OCBSHINE must be appropriately padded to allow application of the permutation. The permutation could be deployed using a variable-output-length sponge construction, a block cipher or an authenticated encryption scheme with a fixed key and suitably large nonce space. In practice, we suggest to instantiate the random permutation with a block cipher of a suitable block length. AES has only 128-bit blocks which does not match the minimum required size of the group, so we instead suggest block ciphers such as Threefish, or original Rijndael, allowing block lengths of 256 or 512 bits.

Mapping to Elliptic Curve Group. We would like to instantiate our groups using elliptic curves. Using modern techniques it is always possible to find a suitable curve over a field with a size matching the block length of the ideal permutation, but using standard curves like NIST P-256 or P-521 seems desirable. A standard approach [19] is to embed bit strings in the X-coordinate of a point as follows. Note that close to half the field elements are X-coordinates of points. Given a field of size q, we consider a t-bit block as an integer x_0 and find a small integer u such that $u2^t + x_0$ is the X-coordinate of a curve point. If $\log q - t$ is between 8 and 9, this will fail to terminate with probability around 2^{-256} under reasonable assumptions.

With this approach we could use Threefish with 512-bit blocks together with NIST P-521 curve. If we want to use 256-bit blocks from Threefish, or original Rijndael, together with NIST P-256 curve, we can use a standard block cipher iteration trick [23] to reduce the block length from 256 bits, so that embedding in the X-coordinate still works, as follows. With block length $t + \tau$, concatenate a t-bit block with τ leading zeros and apply the block cipher until the τ leading bits of the result are all zeros. Discard these zeros to get a t-bit block. This is fairly cheap as for our purposes 8 or 9 bits will do.

Note that we have constructed an injective embedding of a block into an elliptic curve, not a bijection as assumed in our proofs. When we sample group elements in our proof, we must take care to sample points in the image of our embedding, but this can be done cheaply.

Acknowledgements. This research was funded by the Research Council of Norway under Project No. 248166. The second author is supported by the European Research Council (ERC) under the European Union's Horizon 2020 research and innovation programme, grant agreement 802823. We would like to thank Frederik Armknecht, Håvard Raddum and Mohsen Toorani for fruitful discussions in the initial stages of this project, and anonymous reviewers for a number of useful suggestions for improvement.

References

1. Ateniese, G., Fu, K., Green, M., Hohenberger, S.: Improved proxy re-encryption schemes with applications to secure distributed storage. In: Proceedings of NDSS 2005. The Internet Society (2005). https://doi.org/10.1145/1127345.1127346

2. Bellare, M., Namprempre, C.: Authenticated encryption: relations among notions and analysis of the generic composition paradigm. J. Cryptol. **21**(4), 469–491 (2008). https://doi.org/10.1007/s00145-008-9026-x

3. Boneh, D., Lewi, K., Montgomery, H., Raghunathan, A.: Key homomorphic PRFs and their applications. In: Canetti, R., Garay, J.A. (eds.) CRYPTO 2013, Part I. LNCS, vol. 8042, pp. 410–428. Springer, Heidelberg (2013). https://doi.org/10.1007/978-3-642-40041-4_23

4. Boneh, D., Lewi, K., Montgomery, H.W., Raghunathan, A.: Key homomorphic PRFs and their applications. IACR Cryptology ePrint Archive, Report 2015/220 (2015). http://eprint.iacr.org/2015/220

5. Boyd, C., Davies, G.T., Gjøsteen, K., Jiang, Y.: Fast and secure updatable encryption. IACR Cryptology ePrint Archive, Report 2019/1457 (2019). https://eprint.iacr.org/2019/1457

6. Cachin, C., Camenisch, J., Freire-Stögbuchner, E., Lehmann, A.: Updatable tokenization: formal definitions and provably secure constructions. In: Kiayias, A. (ed.) FC 2017. LNCS, vol. 10322, pp. 59–75. Springer, Cham (2017). https://doi.org/10.1007/978-3-319-70972-7_4

7. Canetti, R., Hohenberger, S.: Chosen-ciphertext secure proxy re-encryption. In: Ning, P., di Vimercati, S.D.C., Syverson, P.F. (eds.) Proceedings of ACM CCS 2007, pp. 185–194. ACM (2007). https://doi.org/10.1145/1315245.1315269

8. Coron, J.-S., Patarin, J., Seurin, Y.: The random oracle model and the ideal cipher model are equivalent. In: Wagner, D. (ed.) CRYPTO 2008. LNCS, vol. 5157, pp. 1–20. Springer, Heidelberg (2008). https://doi.org/10.1007/978-3-540-85174-5_1

9. Council, P.S.S.: Data security standard (PCI DSS v3.2.1) (2018). https://www.pcisecuritystandards.org/

10. Davidson, A., Deo, A., Lee, E., Martin, K.: Strong post-compromise secure proxy re-encryption. In: Jang-Jaccard, J., Guo, F. (eds.) ACISP 2019. LNCS, vol. 11547, pp. 58–77. Springer, Cham (2019). https://doi.org/10.1007/978-3-030-21548-4_4

11. Diaz-Santiago, S., Rodríguez-Henríquez, L.M., Chakraborty, D.: A cryptographic study of tokenization systems. In: Obaidat, M.S., Holzinger, A., Samarati, P. (eds.) Proceedings of SECRYPT 2014, pp. 393–398. SciTePress (2014). https://doi.org/10.5220/0005062803930398

12. Everspaugh, A., Paterson, K., Ristenpart, T., Scott, S.: Key rotation for authenticated encryption. In: Katz, J., Shacham, H. (eds.) CRYPTO 2017, Part III. LNCS, vol. 10403, pp. 98–129. Springer, Cham (2017). https://doi.org/10.1007/978-3-319-63697-9_4

13. Everspaugh, A., Paterson, K.G., Ristenpart, T., Scott, S.: Key rotation for authenticated encryption. IACR Cryptology ePrint Archive, Report 2017/527 (2017). http://eprint.iacr.org/2017/527

14. Gentry, C., O'Neill, A., Reyzin, L.: A unified framework for trapdoor-permutation-based sequential aggregate signatures. In: Abdalla, M., Dahab, R. (eds.) PKC 2018. LNCS, vol. 10770, pp. 34–57. Springer, Cham (2018). https://doi.org/10.1007/978-3-319-76581-5_2

15. Jarecki, S., Krawczyk, H., Resch, J.K.: Updatable oblivious key management for storage systems. In: Cavallaro, L., Kinder, J., Wang, X., Katz, J. (eds.) Proceedings of ACM CCS 2019, pp. 379–393. ACM (2019). https://doi.org/10.1145/3319535.3363196

16. Kallahalla, M., Riedel, E., Swaminathan, R., Wang, Q., Fu, K.: Plutus: scalable secure file sharing on untrusted storage. In: Chase, J. (ed.) Proceedings of FAST 2003. USENIX (2003). https://doi.org/10.5555/1090694.1090698

17. Klooß, M., Lehmann, A., Rupp, A.: (R)CCA secure updatable encryption with integrity protection. In: Ishai, Y., Rijmen, V. (eds.) EUROCRYPT 2019, Part I. LNCS, vol. 11476, pp. 68–99. Springer, Cham (2019). https://doi.org/10.1007/978-3-030-17653-2_3

18. Klooß, M., Lehmann, A., Rupp, A.: (R)CCA secure updatable encryption with integrity protection. IACR Cryptology ePrint Archive, Report 2019/222 (2019). https://eprint.iacr.org/2019/222

19. Koblitz, N.: Elliptic curve cryptosystems. Math. Comput. **48**(177), 203–209 (1987)

20. Lee, E.: Improved security notions for proxy re-encryption to enforce access control. In: Lange, T., Dunkelman, O. (eds.) LATINCRYPT 2017. LNCS, vol. 11368, pp. 66–85. Springer, Cham (2019). https://doi.org/10.1007/978-3-030-25283-0_4

21. Lehmann, A., Tackmann, B.: Updatable encryption with post-compromise security. In: Nielsen, J.B., Rijmen, V. (eds.) EUROCRYPT 2018, Part III. LNCS, vol. 10822, pp. 685–716. Springer, Cham (2018). https://doi.org/10.1007/978-3-319-78372-7_22

22. Myers, S., Shull, A.: Practical revocation and key rotation. In: Smart, N.P. (ed.) CT-RSA 2018. LNCS, vol. 10808, pp. 157–178. Springer, Cham (2018). https://doi.org/10.1007/978-3-319-76953-0_9

23. Rivest, R.L., Shamir, A., Adleman, L.M.: A method for obtaining digital signatures and public-key cryptosystems. Commun. ACM **21**, 120–126 (1978)

24. Rogaway, P., Bellare, M., Black, J., Krovetz, T.: OCB: a block-cipher mode of operation for efficient authenticated encryption. In: Reiter, M.K., Samarati, P. (eds.) Proceedings of ACM CCS 2001, pp. 196–205. ACM (2001). https://doi.org/10.1145/501983.502011

25. Sakurai, K., Nishide, T., Syalim, A.: Improved proxy re-encryption scheme for symmetric key cryptography. In: Proceedings of IWBIS 2017, pp. 105–111. IEEE (2017). https://doi.org/10.1109/IWBIS.2017.8275110

26. Shannon, C.E.: Communication theory of secrecy systems. Bell Syst. Tech. J. **28**(4), 656–715 (1949)

Incompressible Encodings

Tal Moran[1]([⊠]) and Daniel Wichs[2,3]([⊠])

[1] IDC Herzliya, Herzliya, Israel
talm@idc.ac.il
[2] Northeastern University, Boston, USA
wichs@ccs.neu.edu
[3] NTT Research Inc., Palo Alto, USA

Abstract. An *incompressible encoding* can probabilistically encode some data m into a codeword c, which is not much larger. Anyone can decode the codeword c to recover the original data m. However, the codeword c cannot be efficiently compressed, even if the original data m is given to the decompression procedure on the side. In other words, c is an efficiently decodable representation of m, yet is computationally incompressible even given m. An incompressible encoding is *composable* if many encodings cannot be simultaneously compressed.

The recent work of Damgård, Ganesh and Orlandi (CRYPTO '19) defined a variant of incompressible encodings as a building block for "proofs of replicated storage". They constructed incompressible encodings in an ideal permutation model, but it was left open if they can be constructed under standard assumptions, or even in the more basic random-oracle model. In this work, we undertake the comprehensive study of incompressible encodings as a primitive of independent interest and give new constructions, negative results and applications:

- We construct incompressible encodings in the *common random string (CRS)* model under either Decisional Composite Residuosity (DCR) or Learning with Errors (LWE). However, the construction has several drawbacks: (1) it is not composable, (2) it only achieves selective security, and (3) the CRS is as long as the data m.
- We leverage the above construction to also get a scheme in the random-oracle model, under the same assumptions, that avoids all of the above drawbacks. Furthermore, it is significantly more efficient than the prior ideal-model construction.
- We give black-box separations, showing that incompressible encodings in the plain model cannot be proven secure under any standard hardness assumption, and incompressible encodings in the CRS model must inherently suffer from all of the drawbacks above.
- We give a new application to "big-key cryptography in the bounded-retrieval model", where secret keys are made intentionally huge to make them hard to exfiltrate. Using incompressible encodings, we can get all the security benefits of a big key without wasting storage space, by having the key to encode useful data.

D. Wichs—Research supported by NSF grants CNS-1314722, CNS-1413964, CNS-1750795 and the Alfred P. Sloan Research Fellowship.

D. Micciancio and T. Ristenpart (Eds.): CRYPTO 2020, LNCS 12170, pp. 494–523, 2020.
https://doi.org/10.1007/978-3-030-56784-2_17

1   Introduction

The entire contents of Wikipedia can be downloaded as a compressed (gzip) file that is several gigabytes in size. Can it be compressed further? This is an interesting question, and there is much work on optimizing compression for various types of data. But there is also an uninteresting answer – the Wikipedia contents can be easily compressed via the link "www.wikipedia.org", which allows anyone on the Internet to recover the data! We consider the compression problem in exactly the above scenario, where the data is readily available publicly. However, our goal is to make such data incompressible. That is, we want to come up with an *incompressible encoding* scheme that takes some such data (e.g., Wikipedia content) and probabilistically represents it in a way that is guaranteed to be incompressible, even when the decompression procedure is given the original data on the side for free (e.g., can access Wikipedia over the Internet). We now elaborate on what this primitive is and why it is useful.

Incompressible Encodings. An incompressible encoding scheme consists of a pair of efficient and key-less encoding and decoding procedures (Enc, Dec), such that $c \leftarrow \mathsf{Enc}(m)$ probabilistically encodes some data m into a codeword c that anybody can efficiency decode to recover $m = \mathsf{Dec}(c)$. The size of the codeword c should not be "much larger" than that of the underlying data m. Even though the codeword c is an efficiently decodable representation of the data m, and cannot contain much additional information since its size is not much larger, we want c to be incompressible even given m. In particular, we consider the following *incompressibility* security game:

1. An adversary chooses some arbitrary data m, which is encoded to get a codeword $c \leftarrow \mathsf{Enc}(m)$.
2. The codeword c is given to an adversarial compression algorithm that outputs some compressed value w.
3. The compressed value w along with underlying data m are given to an adversarial decompressor, who wins if it outputs the codeword c.

We require that no efficient adversary can win the above game with better than negligible probability, unless w is "almost as large" as the entire codeword.

Good vs. Trivial Encodings. The definition of incompressible encodings has two parameters: for data $m \in \{0,1\}^k$, we let $\alpha(k)$ denote the *codeword size*, and $\beta(k)$ denote the *incompressibility parameter*, which bounds size of the value w output by the compressor in the security game.

For a "good" incompressible encoding, we want the codeword size to be essentially the same as the size of the underlying data $\alpha(k) = (1 + o(1))k$ and we want the encoded data to be incompressible below the size of essentially the entire data/codeword $\beta(k) = (1 - o(1))k = (1 - o(1))\alpha(k)$.[1]

---

[1] Throughout the introduction, we will ignore additive polynomial terms in the security parameter, which means that the above bounds only hold when the data size k is sufficiently large.

On the other hand, there is a "trivial" incompressible encoding, which just appends some randomness r to the data and sets the codeword to $c = (m, r)$. Since r cannot be compressed, the encoding also cannot be compressed below the length of r. This ensures that $\alpha(k) = k + |r|$ and $\beta(k) = |r|$. Therefore a scheme with $\alpha(k) \geq k + \beta(k)$ is "trivial" and we say that an incompressible encoding is "non-trivial" if it beats this bound.

It is easy to see that non-trivial incompressible encodings cannot be constructed information theoretically. This is because, there are at most $2^{\alpha(k)-k}$ possible codewords per message on average, and therefore also certainly for the worst-case message m. A pair of inefficient compression/decompression procedures can enumerate the list of all such codewords (e.g., in lexiographic order) and compress/decompress any codeword in the list just by writing down its index using $\beta(k) = \alpha(k) - k$ bits. Therefore, we will need to rely on computational assumptions to construct non-trivial incompressible encodings.

Local Decoding. We will also want our incompressible encodings to be *locally decodable*, so that any bit of the message can be recovered by only reading a few bits of the codeword. While our constructions have this property, most of the challenges are already present even without this requirement.

Composability. We say that an incompressible encoding scheme, with some incompressibility parameter β, is *composable* if any n independently generated encodings of various messages cannot be compressed below $\sum_{i \in [n]} \beta(k_i)$ bits, where k_i denotes the length of the i'th message. Moreover, the probability of the adversarial compression algorithm outputting less than $\sum_{i \in \mathcal{I}} \beta(k_i)$ bits and the decompression procedure reconstructing all of the codewords $c_i : i \in \mathcal{I}$ for some set $\mathcal{I} \subseteq [n]$ should be negligible. As we will discuss later, we do not know whether all incompressible encodings are inherently composable (we conjecture otherwise) and therefore we define it as a separate security property of interest.

Keyed vs. Key-less Schemes. We mention that any semantically secure encryption scheme would give an incompressible encoding where the decoding procedure needs a secret key. This is because the encryption of some arbitrary data m is indistinguishable from an encryption of random data, which is inherently incompressible even given m. The main difficulty of our problem is that we require the encoding and decoding procedures to be public and key-less; anybody should be able to decode the codeword to recover the data.

1.1   Prior and Concurrent Work

Proofs of Replicated Storage. The work of Damgård, Ganesh and Orlandi [17] studied a primitive called "Proofs of Replicated Storage", which considers a setting where we want to store some data m with a cloud storage provider, who promises to store n replicated copies of the data at different locations ("replicas") to increase fault tolerance. We want to be able to check that the provider is indeed storing n copies of the data. To solve this problem they defined a novel building block called a "replica encoding", which corresponds to our notion of an incompressible encodings that is also *bounded self-composable*; i.e., it is composable when the same message is encoded n times for some a-priori bound n. Using such encodings, they construct "proofs of replicated storage" by encoding the data n separate times and having each replica store a different codeword. This is combined with "Proof of Retreivability" [22,35,51], which are used to periodically audit each replica and check that it is storing its codeword. The cloud provider cannot meaningfully save on storage while maintaining the ability to pass the audit with non-negligible probability. "Proofs of Replicated Storage" also have applications to the *Filecoin* cryptocurrency [37,38], where replicated storage of user data is a resource for mining coins; see [17] for details. We note that some prior notions of "proofs of replicated storage" and "incompressible/replica encodings" were also previously considered by [9,13,24] in settings where the adversary is computationally more constrained than the encoding/decoding procedures and does not have the ability to run these procedures; here we focus on the setting where the adversary can run in arbitrary polynomial time.

Construction of Incompressible Encodings of [17]. In the above context, the work of Damgård, Ganesh and Orlandi [17] (building on an idea from an earlier work of [52]) proposed a construction of incompressible (replica) encodings based on a family of trapdoor permutations (TDPs) denoted by f_{pk} and an ideal invertible public random permutation P, P^{-1}. To encode a message m, the encoder samples a random TDP public key and trapdoor $(\mathsf{pk}, \mathsf{td})$ and outputs a codeword $c = (\mathsf{pk}, (f_{\mathsf{pk}}^{-1} \circ P)^r(m))$ by applying the function $g(x) = f_{\mathsf{pk}}^{-1}(P(x))$ iteratively for r rounds starting with the message m, where r is some parameter. The codeword is efficiently decodable by computing f_{pk} in the forward direction and making calls to P^{-1}. While the above requires using a TDP whose domain is as large as the entire file, it is also possible to apply the TDP on smaller blocks of the file separately. Unfortunately, the construction has several big deficiencies:

- We discovered that the security proof in the published version of [17] is fundamentally flawed. In fact, we identified some heuristic counter-examples to suggest that their scheme is unlikely to be secure in general with the number of rounds r claimed. However, we conjectured (and it has since been confirmed by a concurrent work, see below) that the scheme can be proved secure when the number of rounds r is made very large: $r = \Omega(kn)$ where k is the file-size (in bits), n is the number of compositions and λ is the security parameter. Since each round takes $\Omega(k)$ time, this means that the scheme has complexity $\Omega(k^2 n)$ and, in particular, runs in time quadratic in the file size, which we envision to be large. Moreover, the scheme needs to perform essentially that many public key operations (RSA exponentiations), which makes the scheme highly impractical. Furthermore, the scheme only achieves bounded-composability where the number of compositions n needs to be known ahead of time and affects the complexity of the scheme.
- The construction works in the "ideal invertible random permutation" model. Furthermore, the domain/range of the ideal permutation has to match that

of the TDP. For example, if we use the RSA TDP, then the domain/range of P needs to be $\mathbb{Z}_N^*$ where N is the RSA modulus. It remained as an open problem to give a construction in the standard model, or even in the random oracle model, or even using an ideal permutations where the domain/range is just $\{0,1\}^s$ for some parameter s. (While it is possible to construct indifferentiable [41] ideal permutations from a random oracle [16], they will not have the required structured domain/range. Furthermore, the indifferentiability framework is insufficient to guarantee security for multi-stage games [49], which includes the security game for incompressible encodings.)

Concurrent Work of [26]. A concurrent and independent work of Garg, Lu and Waters [26] independently discovered the flaw in the proof of [17]. They managed to patch the result by providing a completely new (and highly involved) proof of security for their scheme, when the number of rounds r is made sufficiently large $r = \Omega(kn)$ as discussed above. They also managed to remove the reliance on an "ideal invertible random permutation" with a structured domain and showed how to instantiate the scheme using the random oracle model alone.

1.2   Our Results

Our work initiates the study of incompressible encodings as a primitive of independent interest. We give new positive and negative results as well as a new application of this primitive as follows.

Constructions in the CRS and RO Model. We give a new construction of incompressible encodings in the *common random string (CRS)* model under either the *Decisional Composite Residuosity (DCR)* or the *Learning with Errors (LWE)* assumptions. Our construction relies on certain types of *lossy trapdoor functions* (LTFs) [47] that are also permutations/surjective, and our constructions of these may be of independent interest. The encodings have good parameters with codeword size $\alpha(k) = (1 + o(1))k$ and incompressibility parameter $\beta(k) = (1 - o(1))k = (1 - o(1))\alpha(k)$. Furhtermore, the encoding/decoding runtime only scales linearly in the data-size. The scheme is also locally decodable. However, it suffers from three drawbacks:

1. It is *not composable* if all the encodings use the same CRS (but is composable if each encoding gets a fresh CRS).
2. It only achieves *selective security*, where the message being encoded cannot be chosen adaptively depending on the CRS.
3. It has a *long CRS*, linear in the length of the data m.

We also leverage our construction in the CRS model to get a construction in the *random-oracle (RO) model* under the same assumptions that avoids all of the above drawbacks. Namely, it is fully composable without any a priori bound on the number of compositions n, and achieves adaptive security, where the adversary can choose the message after making random-oracle queries.

Our schemes represent a significant improvement over the construction and analysis of [17,26] since:

- We get the first constructions in the CRS model without relying on an ideal object (ideal permutation or random oracle), albeit with the above-mentioned drawbacks.
- Our schemes in both the CRS and RO models are significantly more efficient and our encoding/decoding run time is $O(k)$ rather than $O(k^2)$, where k is the data size. Since we generally envision encoding large data where k is several gigabytes or terabytes, the difference between linear and quadratic run-time is highly significant. (We omit factors in the security parameter in the above bounds).
- Our RO scheme is fully composable and we do not need to bound the number of compositions n ahead of time nor does the efficiency of the scheme degrade with n.
- We can plausibly achieve post-quantum security via our LWE-based construction whereas [17,26] seemed to inherently require trapdoor permutations for which we have no good candidates with post-quantum security.
- Our proof of security is in many ways significantly simpler than that of [26].

Black-Box Separations. We give black-box separations, showing that non-trivial incompressible encodings in the plain model cannot be proven secure via a black-box reduction from any standard hardness assumption, including strong assumptions such as the existence of indistinguishability obfuscation. Moreover, we show that similar black-box separations apply to good incompressible encodings in the CRS model, unless they suffer from all 3 of the above drawbacks: they cannot be fully composable with a single CRS, they cannot achieve adaptive security, and the CRS needs to be essentially as long as the data m. This shows that our results are in some sense optimal.

Application to Big-Key Crypto. We give a new application of incompressible encodings to "big-key cryptography in the bounded-retrieval model" [2,3,8,12, 19,23, ...]. Big-key cryptosystems are designed with intentionally huge secret keys in order to make them hard to exfiltrate. They guarantee security even if the adversary can get large amounts of arbitrary "leakage" on the secret key.

Using incompressible encodings, we can get all the security benefits of a big key without wasting storage space, by allowing the key to encode useful data. We do not need to assume that the data has any entropy from the point of view of the adversary; for example the user's secret key could encode the contents of Wikipedia, or the user's movie collection, or other data that a user may want to store offline but is also publicly available on the Internet and may be fully known to the adversary.

In particular, we show how to construct public-key encryption in this model, where the secret key is an incompressible encoding of the user's arbitrary data. Security is maintained even if the adversary can exfiltrate arbitrary information about the secret key, as long as the size of such leakage is bounded by some $(1 - o(1))$ fraction of the secret key size. The public key size, ciphertext size and the encryption/decryption run time are all small and only poly-logarithmic in the data size. In particular, each decryption operation only accesses some small subset of the secret key bits.

1.3   Our Techniques

We now delve into each of the results above and the relevant techniques in turn.

Incompressible Encodings in the CRS Model. We construct incompressible encodings in the CRS model. In this model, the honest encoding/decoding algorithms as well as the adversarial compression/decompression algorithms have access to a public uniformly random string. Our construction relies on certain types of *lossy tradpor functions* (LTFs) [47]. An LTF consists of a family of function f_{pk} indexed by a public key pk. The public key can be sampled in one of two indistinguishable modes: in *injective mode* the function f_{pk} is injective and we can sample pk along with a trapdoor td that allows us to efficiently invert it, and in *lossy mode* the function f_{pk} has a very small image, meaning that $f_{pk}(x)$ reveals very little information about the input x.

As a starting point, to illustrate the main ideas, let's assume that we have an LTF family $f_{pk} : \{0,1\}^d \to \{0,1\}^d$ where both the domain and range are equal to $\{0,1\}^d$ for some polynomial d. This means that f_{pk} is a permutation over $\{0,1\}^d$ in injective mode. Let's also assume that the LTF is highly lossy, meaning that the output $f_{pk}(x)$ in lossy mode only reveals $o(d)$ bits of information about x. To encode some data $m \in \{0,1\}^k$ we think of $m = (m_1, \ldots, m_{k'})$ as consisting of $k' = k/d$ blocks of length d each. We also rely on a common random string $crs = (u_1, \ldots, u_{k'})$ consisting of k' random blocks of length d each. The encoding procedure $\mathsf{Enc}_{crs}(m)$ samples a random pk in injective mode, together with a trapdoor td and sets the codeword to be $c = (pk, f_{pk}^{-1}(m_1 \oplus u_1), \ldots, f_{pk}^{-1}(m_{k'} \oplus u_{k'}))$. The decoding procedure $\mathsf{Dec}_{crs}(c)$ recovers m by applying f_{pk} in the forward direction and xor'ing out the u_i components. Moreover, it's easy to see that individual locations of the data can be decoded locally. The codeword is of size $k + |pk| = (1 + o(1))k$.

We prove incompressible security of the above scheme in the selective setting, where the choice of the message m is worst-case but cannot depend on the CRS. We first observe that the joint distribution of $crs = (u_1, \ldots, u_{k'}), c = (pk, x_1, \ldots, x_{k'})$ sampled as above with $u_i \leftarrow \{0,1\}^d$ and $x_i = f_{pk}^{-1}(m_i \oplus u_i)$ is identical to the distribution where we choose $x_i \leftarrow \{0,1\}^d$ uniformly at random and set $u_i = f_{pk}(x_i) \oplus m_i$. The latter distribution can be sampled without a trapdoor. Therefore, we can indistinguishably switch pk to lossy mode. Now the codeword c has $(1 - o(1))k$ bits of true entropy even conditioned on crs and m, since each of the values $u_i = f_{pk}(x_i) \oplus m_i$ reveals only $o(d)$ bits of information about each x_i. Therefore, we can argue that in this case the codeword c is (even information-theoretically) incompressible below $(1 - o(1))k$ bits, even given crs and m. But since this case is computationally indistinguishable from the real distribution of crs, c, the same must hold computationally there as well.

To give some more intuition on the above idea, note that in reality the codeword c has very little actual entropy given crs, m. This is inherent since we want to c to be almost the same size as m and it has to decode to m so there is no space left to inject actual entropy. But in the security proof, we indistinguishably move the information about the message m into the crs and allow the codeword to have a high amount of real entropy even given crs, m while preserving the condition that it decodes to m. Therefore, we can argue incompressibility.

Surjective Lossy Functions. There are many constructions of lossy trapdoor functions (LTFs) in the literature (e.g.,) [6,25,36,47,55]. However, the vast majority of them are not *surjective* and hence are unusable for our scheme where we need to compute inverses $f_{\mathsf{pk}}^{-1}(m_1 \oplus u_1)$ on arbitrary values that we cannot force to be in the image. Fortunately, the work of [25] gives a construction of a surjective LTF (permutation) based on Paillier's Decisional Composite Residuosity (DCR) assumption [44] using the ideas behind the Damgård-Jurik cryptosystem [18]. Furthermore, this LTF can be made highly lossy to ensure that the output only reveals an $o(1)$ fraction of the information in the input. There is still some subtlety in that the domain and range of the LTF are not bit-strings $\{0,1\}^d$ but rather the group $\mathbb{Z}_{N^{s+1}}^*$ for some RSA modulus N and some parameter s. It turns out that we can nevertheless use it in our construction with minor modifications, while maintaining a uniformly random CRS. This is because we can use truly random bits in the CRS to obliviously sample random elements in the group $\mathbb{Z}_{N^{s+1}}^*$.

Since surjective LTFs are also trapdoor permutations (TDPs), all good candidates rely on assuming the hardness of factoring and it is a long-standing open problem to get constructions from other assumptions, such as DDH or LWE. However, we notice that we don't need our functions to be *injective*. Instead we define a relaxation of surjective LTFs that we call *Surjective Lossy Functions (SLFs)*. SLFs have two modes: a surjective (but not necessarily injective) mode and a lossy mode. In surjective mode, the image of the function f_{pk} is the entire range while in lossy mode the image is much smaller. Furthermore, in surjective mode we require a trapdoor that allows us to sample a random preimage of any value in the range. If the function is surjective but not injective, the input-length must be larger than the output-length, and we will require that it is at most $(1 + o(1))$ times larger to ensure that our encodings have small α. We show that such SLFs suffice in our construction of incompressible encodings. We then proceed to construct such SLFs under the learning with errors (LWE) assumption [48]. Our starting point is the surjective trapdoor function of [1,27,42] defined as $f_{\mathbf{A}}(\mathbf{x}) = \mathbf{A}\mathbf{x}$ where $\mathbf{A} \in \mathbb{Z}_q^{n \times m}$ and $\mathbf{x} \in \mathbb{Z}_q^m$ has "small" entries. Unfortunately, in the best known instantiations [42], the input length (in bits) is at least twice as large as the output length, while we only want a $(1 + o(1))$ increase. We show a new technique to get around this. The high level idea is somewhat similar to a recent work of [14], and we rely on "approximate trapdoors" where, given $\mathbf{y}$, we can sample $\mathbf{x}$ such that $\mathbf{A}\mathbf{x}$ is close but not identical to $\mathbf{y}$. We modify the function to $f_{\mathbf{A}}(\mathbf{x}) = \lceil \mathbf{A}\mathbf{x} \rfloor_p$ by applying some rounding to the output to get rid of this difference. This allows us to optimize the ratio of input-size to output-size and get an improvements over exact trapdoors. To ensure a $(1 + o(1))$ overhead, our instantiation of this idea is somewhat different and arguably simpler than that of [14]. Furthermore, we also show that this function has a lossy mode where the output only reveals an $o(1)$ fraction of the information in the input, using the techniques of [4,29]. Overall, we believe that this construction may be of independent interest.

Composability and HILL vs Yao Entropies. We cannot prove our construction of incompressible encodings in the CRS model to be composable if the same CRS is used to generate all the encodings. However, we show that it is composable if each encoding is given a fresh CRS. But first, let us discuss why composability is generally difficult.

One may be tempted to conjecture that *all* incompressible encodings are inherently composable. For example, it seems intuitive that if the adversary needs to store $\beta(k)$ bits to compress one codeword, she would need $2\beta(k)$ bits to compress two codewords of two length k messages (potentially the same message). Surprisingly, this intuition does not naturally translate into a proof—how would one design a reduction which leverages a compression algorithm that takes two codewords and compressed them below 2β bits to compress a single codeword below β bits? The situation is highly reminiscent of the "leakage amplification" problem in leakage-resilient cryptography: if some cryptosystem is secure even given β bits of leakage on its secret key, does that mean that two copies of the cryptosystem cannot be simultaneously broken even given 2β bits of leakage on the two keys? Surprisingly this is not the case and it was possible to construct clever counter-examples showing that the above does not generically hold in some cases [20,34,40]. We conjecture that counter-examples may also exist for incompressible encodings, at least under strong enough assumptions, and leave it as an open problem to come up with one.

Given that it is unknown (and perhaps unlikely) that all incompressible encodings are composable, we leverage a special property of our construction to show composability. In particular, the definition of incompressible encodings essentially says that c has high "Yao incompressibility entropy" [7,33,54] even given crs. However, for our construction, we showed that c even has a high HILL entropy [32] given crs, since the distribution of (crs, c) is computationally indistinguishable from one, where c has true (statistical) entropy given crs. Having HILL entropy is a stronger property than having incompressibility entropy and we leverage this to prove composition. In particular, while we do not know if the "Yao incompressibility entropy" of independent samples adds up, we do know that this is the case for HILL entropy: i.e., the HILL entropy of independent samples (crs$_i$, c_i) for $i \in [n]$ is the sum of the individual HILL entropies. This property implies composability for our encodings.

Construction in the Random Oracle Model. Our CRS model construction needed a long CRS, and a fresh CRS for each encoding if we wanted to argue composition. Furthermore, it only achieved selective security. We show how to resolve all of these drawbacks in the random oracle model. In this model all honest and adversarial algorithms have access to a truly random (fixed-length) function RO : $\{0,1\}^\lambda \times \{0,1\}^\lambda \to \{0,1\}^\lambda$, where λ is the security parameter. The idea behind our construction is simple: the encoding procedure chooses fresh short randomness $r \leftarrow \{0,1\}^\lambda$ on each execution and then calls $\mathsf{RO}(r,1), \mathsf{RO}(r,2), \ldots$ to expand it into an arbitrarily long crs as needed; it then uses the incompressible encoding scheme in the CRS model with the above crs to encode the data and appends r to the codeword. This essentially corresponds to using a fresh CRS for each encoding. Note that, in the random oracle model, we allow the adversary to choose the message adaptively after making random oracle queries. However, we only need to rely on selective security in the CRS model since the adversary cannot predict r ahead of time and hence the crs used in each encoding is essentially freshly chosen after the adversary selects the message.

Black-Box Separations. We give black-box separations, showing that incompressible encodings in the plain model cannot be proven secure under any standard hardness assumption, and incompressible encodings in the CRS model must inherently suffer from all of the drawbacks that ours has. Our black-box separations have a similar flavor to those of [53] and we first explain their framework tailored to our setting.

They define the class of "single-stage game" assumptions, which are modeled via a game between a (potentially inefficient) challenger and a single stateful adversary; the assumption states that any polynomial-time adversary should have at most a negligible advantage in winning the game. This captures essentially all standard assumptions used in cryptography, from the hardness of factoring to indistinguishability obfuscation (iO).[2] We observe that the security definition of incompressible encodings is *not* a single-stage game since it involves two separate entities (the compressor and the decompressor) who cannot fully share state or communicate with each other—the compressor is limited in the number of bits it can pass to the decompressor. This makes it possible to separate the security of incompressible encodings from all single-stage game assumptions.

The separation works by constructing a "simulatable attacker". This is an *inefficient* (exponential size) attacker $\mathcal{A} = (\mathcal{A}.\mathsf{Compress}, \mathcal{A}.\mathsf{Expand})$ that breaks incompressible-encoding security. However we also design an efficient simulator $\mathcal{A}'$, such that one cannot (statistically) distinguish between black-box access to $\mathcal{A}$ versus $\mathcal{A}'$. Unlike the attackers $\mathcal{A}$, the simulator $\mathcal{A}'$ is a single fully stateful entity that can fully remember any inputs for invocations of $\mathcal{A}'.\mathsf{Compress}$ and use them to answer future invocations of $\mathcal{A}'.\mathsf{Expand}$. Therefore $\mathcal{A}'$ is not a legal attacker against the incompressible encoding. However, if some reduction can break a single-stage game assumption given black-box access to the legal (but inefficient) $\mathcal{A}$ then it would also be able to do so given access to the efficient (but illegal) $\mathcal{A}'$ which means that the assumption is false.

On a very high level, our adversary $\mathcal{A}$ uses "brute-force" to find the index i of the codeword in the lexicographic ordering of all codewords that decode to m and applies a random permutation on i to get the compressed value w. The decompressor inverts the permutation on w to recover i and uses that to

---

[2] This is a larger class than falsifiable assumptions [28,43], where the challenger is also required to be efficient.

recover the codeword. The efficient simulator $\mathcal{A}'$ just chooses a fresh random w to compress each codeword but keeps a table of codewords it has seen with the corresponding w values it gave. To decompress given w, it just finds the corresponding codeword in the table.

In the above, we need to argue that the brute-force approach always works and that the number of codewords that decode to m is small so that the index i does not require too many bits to transmit. This holds in the plain model, when we choose the worst case message, or even in the CRS model when the message m can be chosen randomly but after the CRS if fixed. However, it fails in the selective-security setting in the CRS model – as it should, since we have a construction! This is because $\mathcal{A}$ may be given a CRS for which there are too many codewords that decode to the message m and hence it cannot write down the index i. If $\mathcal{A}$ failed in these cases but succeeded otherwise, we could use it to distinguish between such a CRS and a truly random one, which is something that cannot be efficiently simulated and indeed allows for a security reduction under standard assumptions.

Application to Big-Key Crypto. We give a new application of incompressible encodings to "big-key cryptography in the bounded-retrieval model" [2,3,8,12, 19,23], where secret keys are intentionally huge to make them hard to exfiltrate. In particular, these works envision cryptosystems where the keys are many giga-bytes or terabytes in size. Even if an adversary hacks into the system storing the secret key and manages to leak out large amounts of arbitrary data (but sufficiently less than the key size), we want the security of the cryptosystem to be maintained. For example, in the case of encryption, this should not enable the adversary to break semantic security of any ciphertexts sent in the future (unfor-tunately, the adversary can always perform decryption on past ciphertexts on the compromised device and leak out some plaintext bits so we cannot guaran-tee security of past ciphertexts). In such schemes, we want to maintain efficiency of honest users even as the key grows, and therefore the cryptosystem cannot even read the entire key to perform basic operations such as encryption and decryption. Prior work focused on constructing various primitives in this setting including symmetric-key encryption, public-key encryption and authenticated key agreement.

One big disadvantage of big-key cryptography is that it forces honest users to "waste" space by storing a huge random key of the cryptosystem. In this work, we propose to get rid of this waste by converting useful data that the user would store anyway into a cryptographic key. For example, the user can take their local movie/music collection (or an offline copy of Wikipedia etc.) and turn it into a cryptographic key for a "big-key" cryptosystem. We do not assume that the underlying data has any entropy from the point of view of the attacker; for example, the movie/music collection may be easily compressible into a very short list of titles that are available for download on the Internet. In general, we allow the attacker to choose the data in a worst-case fashion. This seems to make such data unusable as a cryptographic key, since it may be completely known to the adversary! However, this is where incompressible encodings come in.

We ask the user to store an encoded version of the data and use the codeword as the key. The user can still access the data since it can be efficiently (locally) decoded. However, an adversary cannot easily exfiltrate the key by compressing it, even if the underlying data is completely known.

Turning the above high-level idea into workable big-key cryptosystems presents two challenges:

- We need to rely on big-key cryptosystems where the secret key can be an arbitrary string, rather than cryptosystems that choose a carefully structured secret key. This is especially a challenge for public-key encryption (PKE) schemes, where keys tend to have a lot of structure.
- We need to rely on a big-key cryptosystem that is secure with leakage, as long as the secret key is incompressible, even if it is not uniformly random. In particular, any attack against the leakage resilience of the encryption scheme should translate into a compression/decompression procedure on the secret key.

We call such cryptosystems *encoding-friendly*, and it is easy to see that they remain secure if we set their key to be an incompressible encoding of some arbitrary data.

We construct an *encoding-friendly* big-key PKE in the bounded-retrieval model, where the secret key can be arbitrarily large but the public key, ciphertexts, and encryption/decryption complexity are all small, only poly-logarithmic in the key size. Our work departs significantly from the prior construction of big-key PKE in the bounded-retrieval model of [2], which was not encoding friendly (the secret key in that scheme consisted of many "identity secret keys" in a special identity-based encryption scheme and hence required a large amount of structure). Instead, our construction relies on *laconic oblivious transfer (LOT)* [15], which can in turn be constructed under a wide range of assumptions such as CDH, LWE, and Factoring [11]. In an LOT scheme, one can take a long string $x \in \{0,1\}^k$ and hash it down into a short digest which acts as a public-key $\mathsf{pk} = h(x)$. One can then encrypt some arbitrary data μ under the public key pk with respect to a tuple $(i, b) \in [k] \times \{0, 1\}$ such that the resulting ciphertext $\mathsf{ct} \leftarrow \mathsf{Enc}_{\mathsf{pk}}(\mu, (i, b))$ can be decrypted correctly using x if the i'th bit of x is $x[i] = b$. On the other hand, if $x[i] = 1 - b$ then the encryption is semantically secure even given x.

In our construction of an encoding-friendly big-key PKE, we can take an arbitrary (big) value x as the secret key and define the corresponding (short) public key as $\mathsf{pk} = h(x)$. To encrypt a message μ, we apply a secret sharing to derive random shares $\mu_1, \ldots, \mu_\lambda$ that sum up to μ, where λ is the security parameter. We then choose λ random indices $i_1, \ldots, i_\lambda$ and create 2λ LOT ciphertexts $\mathsf{ct}_{j,0} \leftarrow \mathsf{Enc}_{\mathsf{pk}}(\mu_j, (i_j, 0))$ and $\mathsf{ct}_{j,1} \leftarrow \mathsf{Enc}_{\mathsf{pk}}(\mu_j, (i_j, 1))$ where $\mathsf{ct}_{j,0}$ can be decrypted if $x[i_j] = 0$ and $\mathsf{ct}_{j,1}$ can be decrypted if $x[i_j] = 1$ respectively. We send all the ciphertexts along with the indices i_j. The decryption algorithms runs the LOT decryption on the ciphertexts $\mathsf{ct}_{j,x[i_j]}$ using the secret key x.

To prove security, we argue that we can extract (almost all of) x from any successful distinguisher given the leakage. We do this by choosing random ciphertexts and for each j testing if the distinguisher's advantage goes down noticeably when we replace the component $ct_{j,0}$ by an encryption of random junk: if it does then we learn $x[i_j] = 0$ (since otherwise he could not notice this change) and otherwise we know $x[i_j] = 1$ (since if his advantage remains high, he must be decrypting $ct_{j,1}$). By doing this for sufficiently many random ciphertexts we can recover a $(1 - o(1))$ fraction of the bits of x. This gives us a way to compresss x, by writing down the leakage together with a few additional bits that we can't recover from the distinguisher, and decompress it by running the distinguisher.

Organization. Due to lack of space, our black-box separation results, the application to big-key cryptography, and some proofs are deferred to the full version.

2   Preliminaries

Throughout, we let λ denote the security parameter. By default, all our statements hold in the non-uniform model of computation and we define PPT algorithms as circuits of size polynomial in their input and the security parameter. For $n \in \mathbb{Z}$ we let $[n]$ denote the set $[n] = \{1, \ldots, n\}$. When X is a distribution, or a random variable following this distribution, we let $x \leftarrow X$ denote the process of sampling x according to the distribution X. If $\mathcal{X}$ is a set, we let $x \leftarrow \mathcal{X}$ denote sampling x uniformly at random from $\mathcal{X}$.

Let X, Y be random variables, potentially parameterized by the security parameter. We define their *statistical difference* as $\mathsf{SD}(X, Y) = \frac{1}{2} \sum_u |\Pr[X = u] - \Pr[Y = u]|$. We write $X \overset{s}{\approx} Y$ if the statistical distance is negligible in the security parameter. We write $X \overset{c}{\approx} Y$ if they are computationally indistinguishable: for all PPT distinguishers D we have $|\Pr[D(X) = 1] - Pr[D(Y) = 1]| \leq \mathrm{negl}(\lambda)$.

The *min-entropy* of a random variable X is $H_\infty(X) = -\log(\max_x \Pr[X = x])$. Following Dodis et al. [21], we define the (average) conditional min-entropy of X given Y as: $H_\infty(X|Y) = -\log \left(\mathbb{E}_{y \leftarrow Y} \left[2^{-H_\infty(X|Y=y)} \right] \right)$. Note that $H_\infty(X|Y) = k$ iff the optimal strategy for guessing X given Y succeeds with probability 2^{-k}.

Lemma 1. *For any random variables X, Y where Y is supported over a set of size T we have $H_\infty(X|Y) \leq H_\infty(X) - \log T$.*

3   Defining Incompressible Encodings

We begin by giving a definition of incompressible encodings. Our first definition does not require composability and can be thought of as a simplified version of the replica encoding definition of [17].

Definition 1. *An (α, β)-incompressible encoding scheme consists of PPT algorithms* (Enc, Dec). *We require the following properties:*

Correctness: *There is some negligible μ such that for all $\lambda \in \mathbb{N}$ and all $m \in \{0,1\}^*$ we have $\Pr[\mathsf{Dec}(\mathsf{Enc}(1^\lambda, m)) = m] = 1 - \mu(\lambda)$.*

α-**Expansion:** *For all* $\lambda, k \in \mathbb{N}$ *and all* $m \in \{0,1\}^k$ *we have* $\Pr[|\mathsf{Enc}(1^\lambda, m)| \leq \alpha(\lambda, k)] = 1$.

β-**Incompressibility:**   *Consider   the   following   "compression   experiment"* $\mathsf{CompExp}_\mathcal{A}(1^\lambda)$ *with an adversary* $\mathcal{A} = (\mathcal{A}.\mathsf{Select}, \mathcal{A}.\mathsf{Compress}, \mathcal{A}.\mathsf{Expand})$:
 - $(m, \mathsf{aux}) \leftarrow \mathcal{A}.\mathsf{Select}(1^\lambda)$.
 - $c \leftarrow \mathsf{Enc}(1^\lambda, m)$.
 - $w \leftarrow \mathcal{A}.\mathsf{Compress}(\mathsf{aux}, c)$.
 - $c' \leftarrow \mathcal{A}.\mathsf{Expand}(\mathsf{aux}, w)$.
 - *Output 1 if* $c = c'$ *and* $|w| \leq \beta(\lambda, |m|)$.

We require that for all PPT $\mathcal{A}$ *we have* $\Pr[\mathsf{CompExp}_\mathcal{A}(1^\lambda) = 1] = \mathsf{negl}(\lambda)$.

We also refer to a "good" incompressible encoding, without specifying parameters (α, β) to refer to an (α, β)-incompressible encoding where $\alpha(\lambda, k) = k(1 + o(1)) + \mathsf{poly}(\lambda)$ and $\beta(\lambda, k) = k(1 - o(1)) - \mathsf{poly}(\lambda) = \alpha(\lambda, \mathrm{k})(1 - o(1)) - \mathsf{poly}(\lambda)$.

Composability. We also define a stronger notion of *composable* incompressible encodings. This can be thought of as a generalization of the replica encoding definition of [17], which only required "self-composition" when the same message was encoded many times.

Definition 2. *An* (α, β)*-incompressible encoding is* composable *if the following holds. Consider the following "composable compression experiment"* $\mathsf{CCExp}_\mathcal{A}(1^\lambda)$ *with an adversary* $\mathcal{A} = (\mathcal{A}.\mathsf{Select}, \mathcal{A}.\mathsf{Compress}, \mathcal{A}.\mathsf{Expand})$:

 - $(\{m_i\}_{i=1}^n, \mathsf{aux}) \leftarrow \mathcal{A}.\mathsf{Select}(1^\lambda)$.
 - *For* $i = 1 \ldots, n$: $c_i \leftarrow \mathsf{Enc}(1^\lambda, m_i)$.
 - $w \leftarrow \mathcal{A}.\mathsf{Compress}(\mathsf{aux}, \{c_i\}_{i=1}^n)$.
 - $\{c_i'\}_{i=1}^n \leftarrow \mathcal{A}.\mathsf{Expand}(\mathsf{aux}, w)$.
 - *Let* $\mathcal{I} = \{i \ : \ c_i' = c_i\}$. *Output 1 if* $\mathcal{I} \neq \emptyset$ *and* $|w| \leq \sum_{i \in \mathcal{I}} \beta(\lambda, |m_i|)$.

We require that for all PPT $\mathcal{A}$ *we have* $\Pr[\mathsf{CCExp}_\mathcal{A}(1^\lambda) = 1] = \mathsf{negl}(\lambda)$.

CRS Model. We can generalize the above definitions to the *common random string* (CRS) model, where the encoding/decoding algorithms as well as the adversary $\mathcal{A}$ are given a random string $\mathsf{crs} \leftarrow \{0,1\}^{t(\lambda,k)}$ as an input. The length $t(\lambda, k)$ of the crs may depend on the message length k. In the CRS model, we distinguish between *selective security* and *adaptive security*. For selective security, the crs is not given to $\mathcal{A}.\mathsf{Select}$ but is given to $\mathcal{A}.\mathsf{Compress}, \mathcal{A}.\mathsf{Expand}$, meaning that the adversary's choice of the data m cannot depend on the crs. For adaptive security, $\mathcal{A}.\mathsf{Select}$ is also given the crs, and therefore the choice of m can depend on the crs. We say a scheme is selectively (resp. adaptively) β-incompressible in the CRS model.

Random Oracle Model. We can also generalize the above definitions to the *random-oracle model*, where the encoding/decoding algorithms as well as the adversarial algorithms $\mathcal{A}.\mathsf{Select}, \mathcal{A}.\mathsf{Compress}, \mathcal{A}.\mathsf{Expand}$ are given oracle access to a truly random function $\mathsf{RO} \ : \ \{0,1\}^\lambda \times \{0,1\}^\lambda \to \{0,1\}^\lambda$. Note that, in the random oracle model, we automatically require adaptive security, where the adversary's choice of the message m can adaptively depend on its random-oracle queries.

Locally Decodable. An incompressible encoding scheme (Enc, Dec) is locally decodable if there is some additional local decoding procedure that can recover any bit of the encoded message in time that is only poly-logarithmic in the message length k. In particular, we require that there is an algorithm $\mathsf{LocalDec}^c(1^\lambda, k, i)$ that gets RAM access to the input c and runs in time $\mathrm{poly}(\lambda, \log k)$ such that the following holds. There is a negligible μ such that for any $\lambda, k \in \mathbb{N}$, any $m = (m_1, \ldots, m_k) \in \{0, 1\}^k$ and any $i \in [k]$ we have $\Pr[\mathsf{LocalDec}^c(1^\lambda, k, i) = m_i \ : \ c \leftarrow \mathsf{Enc}(1^\lambda, m)] = 1 - \mu(\lambda)$.

Note on (Im)Perfect Correctness. While it will be convenient to allow imperfect correctness (with negligible failure probability) in our definition, we note that we can take any scheme with imperfect correctness and convert it into one with perfect correctness at a slight loss of security. The idea is to modify the encoding algorithm to also tests whether decoding succeeds: if so it outputs the codeword with a 0 appended to it and otherwise it outputs the message in the clear with a 1 appended to it. The decoding checks the appended bit and either applies the original decoding if it is a 0 or just outputs the rest of the codeword if the bit is a 1. If correctness of the original scheme holds with overwhelming probability than the above transformation cannot harm security.

Note on Message Selection. In the above, we allow an adversary $\mathcal{A}.\mathsf{Select}$ to choose the message m along with some auxiliary information aux (which can without loss of generality include the message m). For non-uniform adversaries, we can assume that $\mathcal{A}.\mathsf{Select}$ is deterministic (by hard-coding the worst-case choice of its random coins). For incompressibility in the plain model or with selective security in the CRS model, this means that we can get rid of $\mathcal{A}.\mathsf{Select}$ from the definition and simply quantify over all worst-case choices of the message m and think of the corresponding aux as being hard-coded in the algorithms $\mathcal{A}.\mathsf{Compress}, \mathcal{A}.\mathsf{Expand}$. However, for adaptive security in the CRS model or security in the random oracle model, we must allow m to be chosen adaptively depending on the CRS or the random oracle queries.

4   HILL-Entropic Encodings and Composition

HILL-Entropic Encodings. We can think of the definition of incompressible encodings as roughly requiring that c has high "Yao incompressibility entropy" [7,33,54]. In other words, one cannot efficiently compress c below β bits. We could have defined a stronger variant of "HILL-Entropic Encodings" that would require c to have high HILL entropy [32]. In other words, for any fixed message m, if we consider the random variable C denoting the output of $\mathsf{Enc}(1^\lambda, m)$ then it is computationally indistinguishable from some C' such that the conditional min-entropy $H_\infty(C') \geq \beta$.

Impossibility in the Plain Model. Unfortunately, the notion of "HILL-Entropic Encodings" is simply unachievable in the plain model for any non-trivial $\beta \geq$

$\alpha - k$. In particular, consider the message $m^* = \operatorname{argmin}_m |\mathcal{C}_m|$ that minimizes the size of the set $\mathcal{C}_m = \{c : \mathsf{Dec}(c) = m\}$ of codewords that decode to m. Since $\sum_m |\mathcal{C}_m| \leq 2^\alpha$ we know that $|\mathcal{C}_{m^*}| \leq 2^{\alpha-k}$. Consider a PPT distinguisher $\mathcal{D}$ that gets m^* as non-uniform advice such that $\mathcal{D}(c) = 1$ if $\mathsf{Dec}(c) = m^*$. Then $\Pr[\mathcal{D}(C) = 1] = 1$ for $C \equiv \mathsf{Enc}(1^\lambda, m^*)$ but for any random variable C' such that $H_\infty(C') \geq \alpha - k + 1$ we have

$$\Pr[\mathcal{D}(C') = 1] = \Pr[C' \in \mathcal{C}_{m^*}] = \sum_{c \in \mathcal{C}_{m^*}} \Pr[C' = c] \leq 2^{\alpha-k} 2^{-(\alpha-k+1)} \leq \frac{1}{2}.$$

HILL-Entropic Encodings in the CRS Model. On the other, the above impossibility fails in the CRS model and we will construct (selectively-secure) "HILL-Entropic Encodings" in the CRS model. We define these precisely as follows.

Definition 3 (HILL-Entropic Encoding). *An (α, β)-HILL-Entropic encoding scheme with selective security in the CRS model consists of PPT algorithms* $(\mathsf{Enc}, \mathsf{Dec})$ *with the same syntax, correctness, and expansion requirements as incompressible encodings. We also require that there is a (potentially inefficient) algorithm* SimEnc. *For any polynomial $k = k(\lambda)$ and any ensemble of messages $m = \{m_\lambda\}$ of length $|m_\lambda| = k(\lambda)$, consider the following "real" experiment:*

- $\mathsf{crs} \leftarrow \{0,1\}^{t(\lambda, k)}$
- $c \leftarrow \mathsf{Enc}_{\mathsf{crs}}(1^\lambda, m_\lambda)$

and let CRS, C *denote the random variables for the corresponding values in the "real" experiment. Also consider the following "simulated" experiment:*

- $(\mathsf{crs}', c') \leftarrow \mathsf{SimEnc}(1^\lambda, m_\lambda)$

and let CRS', C' *denote the random variables for the corresponding values in the "simulated" experiment. We require that* $(\mathsf{CRS}, C) \overset{c}{\approx} (\mathsf{CRS}', C')$ *and* $H_\infty(C' \mid \mathsf{CRS}') \geq \beta(\lambda, k)$.

Theorem 1. *Any (α, β)-HILL-Entropic encoding with selective security in the CRS model is also a (α, β')-incompressible encoding scheme with selective security in the CRS model, where $\beta' = \beta - \lambda$.*

For lack of space, we defer the proof of the above theorem to the full version.

Composable Encodings in the RO Model. We now show how to convert any selectively HILL-entropic encoding in the CRS model into a composable incompressible encoding scheme in the random oracle model. We rely on a "fixed length" random oracle $\mathsf{RO} : \{0,1\}^\lambda \times \{0,1\}^\lambda \to \{0,1\}^\lambda$. Note that, although we start with a selectively secure scheme in the CRS model where the adversary must choose the message before seeing the CRS, our resulting scheme in the random-oracle model allows the adversary to choose the message after making random-oracle queries.

Our construction proceeds as follows. Assume $(\mathsf{Enc}', \mathsf{Dec}')$ is an encoding in the CRS model with a CRS of length $t(\lambda, k)$. We define:

- $\mathsf{Enc}^{\mathsf{RO}}(1^\lambda, m)$: Choose $r \leftarrow \{0,1\}^\lambda$. Compute $\mathsf{crs} = (\mathsf{RO}(r,1), \ldots, \mathsf{RO}(r,t')) \in \{0,1\}^{t(\lambda,|m|)}$ where $t' = t(\lambda, k)/\lambda$. Let $\hat{c} \leftarrow \mathsf{Enc}'_{\mathsf{crs}}(1^\lambda, m)$. Output $c = (r, \hat{c})$.
- $\mathsf{Dec}^{\mathsf{RO}}(c = (r, \hat{c}))$: Compute $\mathsf{crs} = (\mathsf{RO}(r,1), \ldots, \mathsf{RO}(r,t')) \in \{0,1\}^{t(\lambda,|m|)}$ where $t' = t(\lambda, k)/\lambda$. Output $\mathsf{Dec}'_{\mathsf{crs}}(\hat{c})$.

Theorem 2. *If* $(\mathsf{Enc}', \mathsf{Dec}')$ *is an* (α', β')-*HILL-entropy encoding with selective security in the CRS model, then* $(\mathsf{Enc}, \mathsf{Dec})$ *is a composable* (α, β)-*incompressible encoding in the Random Oracle model where* $\alpha = \alpha' + \lambda$ *and* $\beta = \beta' - \lambda$.

For lack of space, we defer the proof of the above theorem to the full version.

Composability in the Multi-CRS Model. We observe that the above result in the RO model also implies that our CRS model construction is composable in a setting where each encoding is performed with a fresh CRS. In particular, if there were an attack against composable security in the latter setting, it would immediately translate into an attack on the composable security of the former setting.

5   Surjective Lossy Trapdoor Functions

We now introduce our main building block, which we call surjective lossy functions (SLFs). This can be thought of as a relaxation of lossy trapdoor functions [47] that are also *permutations*. In particular, while we insist on the functions being surjective, we relax the requirement that they are injective. Instead, we require a surjective mode and a lossy mode. In surjective mode, we also have an inversion trapdoor. There is some domain distribution D such that, when we sample a random value in the range and invert it using the trapdoor, we get (statistically close to) a random sample from D. In lossy mode, there is some small set of size $\le 2^\ell$ such that the output of the function almost always ends up in that set - we call ℓ the leakage and want to make it as small as possible.

Definition 4. *A family of* ℓ-*surjective lossy trapdoor functions* (ℓ-*SLFs*) *consists of a polynomial-time computable family of functions* $f_{\mathsf{pk}} : \mathcal{D}_{\mathsf{pk}} \to \mathcal{R}_{\mathsf{pk}}$ *along with the following PPT algorithms:*

- $\mathsf{pk} \leftarrow \mathsf{LossyGen}(1^\lambda)$: *generates a public-key in lossy mode.*
- $(\mathsf{pk}, \mathsf{td}) \leftarrow \mathsf{SurGen}(1^\lambda)$: *generates a public-key in surjective mode, along with a trapdoor.*
- $x \leftarrow D(\mathsf{pk})$: *samples a value* $x \in \mathcal{D}_{\mathsf{pk}}$.
- $x \leftarrow \mathsf{Inv}_{\mathsf{td}}(y)$: *samples a pre-image* x *of* $\in \mathcal{R}_{\mathsf{pk}}$.

We require the following properties.

Surjective Mode: *The following distributions over* (pk, x, y) *are statistically indistinguishable:*

- *Sample* $(\mathsf{pk}, \mathsf{td}) \leftarrow \mathsf{SurGen}(1^\lambda)$, $x \leftarrow D(\mathsf{pk}), y = f_{\mathsf{pk}}(x)$ *and output* (pk, x, y)

– *Sample* (pk, td) $\leftarrow$ SurGen(1^λ), $y \leftarrow \mathcal{R}_{\mathsf{pk}}, x \leftarrow \mathsf{Inv}_{\mathsf{td}}(y)$ *and output*
(pk, x, y).

The above implies that, in particular, we invert correctly:

$$\Pr[f_{\mathsf{pk}}(\mathsf{Inv}_{\mathsf{td}}(y)) = y \; : \; (\mathsf{pk}, \mathsf{td}) \leftarrow \mathsf{SurGen}(1^\lambda), y \leftarrow \mathcal{R}_{\mathsf{pk}}] \geq 1 - \mathrm{negl}(\lambda).$$

Lossy Mode: *For any* pk *in the support of* LossyGen(1^λ) *there exists a set* $\mathcal{L}_{\mathsf{pk}}$ *of size* $|\mathcal{L}_{\mathsf{pk}}| \leq 2^{\ell(\lambda)}$ *such that* $\Pr[f_{\mathsf{pk}}(x) \in \mathcal{L}_{\mathsf{pk}} \; : \; \mathsf{pk} \leftarrow \mathsf{LossyGen}(1^\lambda), x \leftarrow D(\mathsf{pk})] = 1 - \mathrm{negl}(\lambda)$.

Indistinguishability: *The following distributions are computationally indistinguishable:*

$$\{\mathsf{pk} : \mathsf{pk} \leftarrow \mathsf{LossyGen}(1^\lambda)\} \overset{c}{\approx} \{\mathsf{pk} \; : \; (\mathsf{pk}, \mathsf{td}) \leftarrow \mathsf{SurGen}(1^\lambda)\}.$$

The above definition captures the main properties of an SLF. However, in the application, we also need some additional properties on the domain, range and the domain distribution. All of the properties would be satisfied ideally if we had a permutation where the domain and range were just $\mathcal{D}_{\mathsf{pk}} = \mathcal{R}_{\mathsf{pk}} = \{0,1\}^{d(\lambda)}$ and the domain distribution $D(\mathsf{pk})$ was just uniform. However, we will need to be more flexible subject to satisfying the following properties.

Definition 5 (SLF*: Enhanced SLF). *We say that an ℓ-SLF is an (r, r', d, e, ℓ)-enhanced SLF, denoted by SLF*, if the domain $\mathcal{D}_{\mathsf{pk}}$, the range $\mathcal{R}_{\mathsf{pk}}$ and the domain distribution $D(\mathsf{pk})$ satisfy the following properties:*

– *Elements of $\mathcal{D}_{\mathsf{pk}}$ can be represented using (at most) $d(\lambda)$ bits.*
– *For any fixed* pk, *the min-entropy of the distribution $D(\mathsf{pk})$ is at least $H_\infty(D(\mathsf{pk})) \geq e(\lambda)$.*
– *The range $\mathcal{R}_{\mathsf{pk}}$ is a group. (We will denote the group operation by addition.)*
– *We can efficiently embed bit-string of length $r(\lambda)$ as elements of $\mathcal{R}_{\mathsf{pk}}$. In particular, there are efficiently computable functions* $\mathsf{embed}_{\mathsf{pk}} : \{0,1\}^{r(\lambda)} \to \mathcal{R}_{\mathsf{pk}}$ *and* $\mathsf{unembed}_{\mathsf{pk}} : \mathcal{R}_{\mathsf{pk}} \to \{0,1\}^{r(\lambda)}$ *such that for all $m \in \{0,1\}^{r(\lambda)}$ we have*

$$\Pr[\mathsf{unembed}_{\mathsf{pk}}(\mathsf{embed}_{\mathsf{pk}}(m)) = m \; : \; (\mathsf{pk}, \mathsf{td}) \leftarrow \mathsf{SurGen}(1^\lambda)] = 1 - \mathrm{negl}(\lambda).$$

– *We can obliviously sample uniformly random elements of $\mathcal{R}_{\mathsf{pk}}$. In particular, there exists some PPT algorithm $y \leftarrow \mathsf{sam}(\mathsf{pk})$ that uses $r'(\lambda)$ random bits to sample a uniformly random values $y \in \mathcal{R}_{\mathsf{pk}}$ along with a PPT algorithm* $\mathsf{explain}_{\mathsf{pk}}(y)$ *such that $(u, y) \overset{s}{\approx} (u', y')$, where $u \leftarrow \{0,1\}^{r'(\lambda)}$, $y = \mathsf{sam}(\mathsf{pk}; u)$, $y' \leftarrow \mathcal{R}_{\mathsf{pk}}, u' \leftarrow \mathsf{explain}_{\mathsf{pk}}(y)$.*

We say that a scheme is a "good" SLF*, without specifying parameters, if it is an (r, r', d, e, ℓ)-SLF* for some $r = r(\lambda)$ with $d = (1 + o(1))r$, $r' = (1 + o(1))r$, $e = (1 - o(1))r$, and $\ell = o(r)$.

5.1   SLFs from Decision Composite Residuosity

We describe a construction of a good SLF* under the Decision Composite Residuosity (DCR) assumption of Paillier [44]. The construction is identical to that of [25] and is based on the Damgård-Jurik Cryptosystem [18]. We provide it here for completeness.

The Damgård-Jurik Cryptosystem. Let $N = PQ$ where P, Q are odd primes such that $\gcd(N, \varphi(N)) = 1$. We call such N admissible. When P and Q are sufficiently large and randomly chosen, $N = PQ$ is admissible with all but negligible probability. The following theorem gives the structure of the group $\mathbb{Z}_{N^{s+1}}^*$.

Theorem 3 ([18]). *For any admissible $N = PQ$ and $s < \min\{P, Q\}$ the map $\psi_{N,s} : \mathbb{Z}_{N^s} \times \mathbb{Z}_N^* \to \mathbb{Z}_{N^{s+1}}^*$ given by $\psi_{N,s}(m, r) = (1 + N)^m r^{N^s} \bmod N^{s+1}$ is an isomprphism satisfying*

$$\psi_{N,s}(m_1 + m_2 \bmod N, r_1 r_2 \bmod N^s) = \psi_{N,s}(m_1, r_1) \cdot \psi_{N,s}(m_2, r_2) \bmod N^{s+1}.$$

Moreover, $\psi_{N,s}$ can be inverted in polynomial time given P, Q.

In the Damgård-Jurik [18] cryptosystem, the public key is N and the secret key is P, Q. The encryption of a message $m \in \mathbb{Z}_{N^s}$ is $\psi_{N,s}(m, r)$ for a random $r \in \mathbb{Z}_N^*$ and the decryption inverts $\psi_{N,s}$ using the secret key. The cryptosystem is proven secure under the decision composite residuosity (DCR) assumption stated below.

Definition 6 ([44]). *The decision composite residuosity (DCR) assumption states that for randomly chosen primes P, Q in the range $[2^{\lambda-1}, 2^\lambda]$ and $N = PQ$ the distributions (N, x) and (N, y) are computatinally indistinguishable where $x \leftarrow \mathbb{Z}_{N^2}^*$ is uniformly random and $y \leftarrow \{z^N \bmod N^2 : z \in \mathbb{Z}_N^*\}$ is a random N-residue over $\mathbb{Z}_{N^2}^*$.*

Intuitively the DCR assumption states that for $s = 1$, one cannot distinguish between $\psi_{N,s}(m, r)$ versus $\psi_{N,s}(0, r)$ for a uniformly random m, r. It's easy to see that this implies that for any fixed m, m' one cannot distinguish between $\psi_{N,s}(m, r)$ versus $\psi_{N,s}(m', r)$. Moreover, it turns out that the DRC assumption, which is stated for $s = 1$, automatically implies security for arbitrary polynomial s. The following theorem essentially states the that the Damgård-Jurik cryptosystem is semantically secure under the DCR assumption.

Theorem 4 ([18]). *For any polynomial $s = \mathrm{poly}(\lambda)$, and for randomly chosen primes P, Q in the range $[2^{\lambda-1}, 2^\lambda]$ with $N = PQ$ and for any values $m, m' \in \mathbb{Z}_{N^s}$, the distributions $(N, \psi_{N,s}(m, r))$ and $(N, \psi_{N,s}(m', r))$ over $r \leftarrow \mathbb{Z}_N^*$ are computationally indistinguishable under the DCR assumption.*

Constructing SLFs from DCR. Since $\psi_{N,s}$ is a permutation with cryptographic properties, we could think of setting $\psi_{N,s}$ as the SLF. Unfortunately, it's not clear how to make it lossy directly. Instead, in addition to the modulus N, we add a "ciphertext" $c \in \mathbb{Z}_{N^{s+1}}^*$ to the public key and define

$$f_{\mathsf{pk}} : \mathbb{Z}_{N^s} \times \mathbb{Z}_N^* \to \mathbb{Z}_{N^{s+1}}^* \quad \text{given by} \quad f_{\mathsf{pk}}(x = (m, r)) = c^m \psi_{N,s}(0, r)$$

In surjective (bijective) mode, we set $c = \psi_{N,s}(1, \hat{r})$ to be an encryption of the message 1, and we also add the randomness $\hat{r}$ to the secret key. In that case, $f_{pk}(m,r) = c^m \psi_{N,s}(0,r) = \psi_{N,s}(m, \hat{r}^m \cdot r)$. We can invert f_{pk} on any value $y \in \mathbb{Z}_{N^{s+1}}^*$ using the secret key, by computing $\psi_{N,s}^{-1}(y) = (m, r')$ and outputting $x = (m, r)$ were $r = r'/\hat{r}^m$. In lossy mode, we set $c = \psi_{N,s}(0, \hat{r})$ to be a random encryption of 0. In that case, the image of the function f_{pk} is the set $\mathcal{L}_{pk} = \{\psi_{N,s}(0, r') : r' \in \mathbb{Z}_N^*\}$. In other words, in lossy mode, $f_{pk}(x)$ only contains $\approx \log(N)$ bits of information about the $\approx (s+1)\log N$ bit value x.

We describe the construction in detail below. Let $s = s(\lambda)$ be a parameter.

- $(pk, td) \leftarrow \mathsf{SurGen}(1^\lambda)$: Generate random λ-bit primes P, Q such that $N = PQ$ is admissible. Let $\hat{r} \leftarrow \mathbb{Z}_N^*$ and set $c = \psi_{N,s}(1, \hat{r})$. Output $pk = (N, c), sk = (P, Q, \hat{r})$.
- $\mathsf{LossyGen}(1^\lambda)$: Generate random λ-bit primes P, Q such that $N = PQ$ is admissible. Let $\hat{r} \leftarrow \mathbb{Z}_N^*$ and set $c = \psi_{N,s}(0, \hat{r})$. Output $pk = (N, c)$.
- $y = f_{pk}(x)$: The function $f_{pk} : \mathcal{D}_{pk} \to \mathcal{R}_{pk}$ has domain $\mathcal{D}_{pk} = \mathbb{Z}_{N^s} \times \mathbb{Z}_N^*$ and range $\mathcal{R}_{pk} = \mathbb{Z}_{N^{s+1}}^*$. It is defined by $f_{pk}(x) = c^m \psi_{N,s}(0,r) \bmod N^{s+1}$, where $x = (m, r) \in \mathbb{Z}_{N^s} \times \mathbb{Z}_N^*$.
- $x = (m, r) \leftarrow D(pk)$: samples a uniformly random value $x \leftarrow \mathcal{D}_{pk}$.
- $x \leftarrow \mathsf{Inv}_{td}(y)$: use the secret key P, Q to computr $\psi_{N,s}^{-1}(y) = (m, r')$ and output $x = (m, r)$ were $r = r'/\hat{r}^m$.

Theorem 5. *For any polynomial $s = s(\lambda)$ the above construction is an (r, r', d, e, ℓ)-SLF* where:*

$$r = (s+1)2(\lambda - 1), \quad r' = (s+1)2\lambda + \lambda, \quad d = (s+1)2\lambda, \quad e = (s+1)2(\lambda - 1) - 1, \quad \ell = 2\lambda$$

In particular, when $s = \omega(1)$ then the above construction is a good SLF.*

Proof. We begin by showing each of the SLF properties:

- Surjective Mode: When $(pk, td) \leftarrow \mathsf{SurGen}(1^\lambda)$ is sampled in surjective mode, the function f_{pk} is a bijection over $\mathcal{D}_{pk} \cong \mathcal{R}_{pk}$ and Inv_{td} is the inverse of f_{pk}. In particular, the distribution of (pk, x, y) for $x \leftarrow D(pk)$, $y = f_{pk}(x)$ is identical to sampling $y \leftarrow \mathcal{R}_{pk}$ and $x = \mathsf{Inv}_{td}(y)$.
- Lossy Mode: When $pk \leftarrow \mathsf{LossyGen}(1^\lambda)$ is sampled in lossy mode, we have

$$\mathcal{L}_{pk} = \{f_{pk}(x) : x \in \mathcal{D}_{pk}\} = \{\psi_{N,s}(0, r') : r' \in \mathbb{Z}_N^*\}$$

and therefore $|\mathcal{L}_{pk}| \leq \log N \leq 2\lambda$.
- Indistinguishability: This follows immediately from Theorem 4 with $m = 0$ and $m' = 1$.

Next we discuss the augmented properties to show that the above SLF is also an SLF*.

- Elements of $\mathcal{D}_{pk} = \mathbb{Z}_{N^s} \times \mathbb{Z}_N^*$ can be represented using $d(\lambda) = (s+1)2\lambda$ bits.
- The min-entropy of the distribution $D(pk)$, which is uniform over $\mathcal{D}_{pk}$ is $\log|\mathcal{D}_{pk}| \geq (s+1)2(\lambda - 1) - 1$. This is because $N \geq 2^{2(\lambda-1)}$.
- The range $\mathcal{R}_{pk} = \mathbb{Z}_{N^{s+1}}^*$ is a group under multiplication.

– We can efficiently embed bit-string of length $r(\lambda) = (s + 1)2(\lambda - 1) - 1$ as elements of $\mathcal{R}_{\mathsf{pk}}$. We do so, by simply taking the string and interpreting it as an integer $y < N^{s+1}$ in binary. The probability of $y \notin \mathbb{Z}^*_{N^{s+1}}$ is negligible over the random choice of $N = PQ$.
– We can obliviously sample from $\mathcal{R}_{\mathsf{pk}} = \mathbb{Z}^*_{N^{s+1}}$ using $r'(\lambda) = ((s + 1)2\lambda + \lambda)$-bits. We do so by defining $\mathsf{sam}(\mathsf{pk})$ to choose a random $r'(\lambda)$-bit integer z and outputting $y = z \bmod N^{s+1}$. This is $2^{-\lambda}$ statistically close to sampling $y \leftarrow \mathbb{Z}^{s+1}_N$ which is statistically close to sampling $y \leftarrow \mathbb{Z}^*_{N^{s+1}}$. The $\mathsf{explain}_{\mathsf{pk}}(y)$ algorithm outputs a random $r'(\lambda)$-bit value z such that $z = y \bmod N^{s+1}$; it does so by setting $t = \lfloor 2^{r'}/N^{s+1} \rfloor$ and outputting $z = y + v \cdot N^{s+1}$ where $v \leftarrow \{0, \ldots, t\}$. For any y, $z = \mathsf{explain}(y)$ is uniformly random over all z such that $\mathsf{sam}(\mathsf{pk}; z) = y$.

5.2 SLFs from Learning with Errors

Lattice Preliminaries. For any integer $q \geq 2$, we let $\mathbb{Z}_q$ denote the ring of integers modulo q. For a vector $\mathbf{e} \in \mathbb{Z}^n$ we write $||\mathbf{e}||_\infty \leq \beta$ if each entry e_i in $\mathbf{e}$ satisfies $|e_i| \leq \beta$. Similarly, for a matrix $\mathbf{E} \in \mathbb{Z}_q^{n \times m}$ we write $||\mathbf{E}||_\infty \leq \beta$ if each entry $e_{i,j}$ in $\mathbf{E}$ satisfies $|e_{i,j}| \leq \beta$. We say that a distribution χ over $\mathbb{Z}$ is β-bounded if $\Pr[|x| \leq \beta : x \leftarrow \chi] \leq \mathsf{negl}(\lambda)$. By default, all vectors are assumed to be *column* vectors. For integers $q \geq p \geq 2$ we define the rounding function

$$\lceil \cdot \rceil_p \ : \ \mathbb{Z}_q \to \mathbb{Z}_p \ : \ x \mapsto \lfloor (p/q) \cdot x \rceil$$

If p divides q then the rounding function divides $\mathbb{Z}_q$ into p intervals of size q/p each. If $q = 2^k$ and $p = 2^{k'}$ then $\lceil x \rceil_p$ corresponds to outputting the k' most significant bits of the k-bit integer x. If $\mathbf{x}$ is a vector we let $\lceil \mathbf{x} \rceil_p$ denote the component-wise rounding operation.

Learning with Errors (LWE). The learning with errors (LWE) assumption was introduced by Regev in [48].

Definition 7 ([48]). *Let n, q be integers and χ a probability distribution over $\mathbb{Z}_q$, all parameterized by the security parameter λ. The (n, q, χ)-LWE assumption says that for all polynomial m the following distributions are computationally indistinguishable*

$$(\mathbf{A}, \mathbf{As} + \mathbf{e}) \stackrel{c}{\approx} (\mathbf{A}, \mathbf{u}^t) \quad : \mathbf{A} \leftarrow \mathbb{Z}_q^{m \times n}, \mathbf{s} \leftarrow \mathbb{Z}_q^n, \mathbf{e} \leftarrow \chi^m, \mathbf{u} \leftarrow \mathbb{Z}_q^m.$$

The work of [5] showed that the (n, q, χ)-LWE assumption above also implies security when the secret is chosen from the error distribution χ:

$$(\mathbf{A}, \mathbf{As} + \mathbf{e}) \stackrel{c}{\approx} (\mathbf{A}, \mathbf{u}) \quad : \mathbf{A} \leftarrow \mathbb{Z}_q^{m \times n}, \mathbf{s} \leftarrow \chi^n, \mathbf{e} \leftarrow \chi^m, \mathbf{u} \leftarrow \mathbb{Z}_q^m.$$

The works of [10, 45, 48] show that the LWE assumption is as hard as (quantum) solving GapSVP and SIVP under various parameter regimes. In particular, we will assume that for every $q = 2^{\mathsf{poly}(\lambda)}$ there exists some polynomial

$n = \text{poly}(\lambda)$ and $\beta = \text{poly}(\lambda)$ along with β-bounded distribution χ such that the $\text{LWE}_{n,q,\chi}$ assumption holds. We refer to the above as the LWE assumption when we don't specify parameters. This is known to be as hard as solving GapSVP and (quantum) SIVP with sub-exponential approximation factors, which is believed to be hard.

The Gadget Matrix and Preimage Sampling. Let $q = B^\gamma$ be a modulus. We define the base-B gadget matrix of dimension n as the matrix $\mathbf{G} \in \mathbb{Z}_q^{n \times \gamma n}$ given by

$$\mathbf{G} = \mathbf{I}_n \times \mathbf{g} = \begin{bmatrix} \cdots \mathbf{g}^t \cdots & & & \\ & \cdots \mathbf{g}^t \cdots & & \\ & & \ddots & \\ & & & \cdots \mathbf{g}^t \cdots \end{bmatrix}$$

where $\mathbf{g} = [1, B, B^2, \ldots, B^{\gamma-1}]$.

Lemma 2 (Preimage Sampling [27,42]). *Let $q = B^\gamma$ and n, n' be some parameters such that $n, n', \log q$ are polynomial in the security parameter λ and $n \geq \lambda$. There exist PPT algorithms $\mathsf{SamPre}, \mathsf{Sam}$ such that the following holds. Let $\mathbf{G} \in \mathbb{Z}_q^{n \times \gamma n}$ be the base-B gadget matrix of dimension n. Let $\overline{\mathbf{A}} \in \mathbb{Z}_q^{n \times n'}$ and let $\mathbf{A} = [\overline{\mathbf{A}} \mid \overline{\mathbf{A}}\mathbf{R} + \mathbf{G}] \in \mathbb{Z}_q^{n \times m}$ where $m = n' + \gamma n$ and $\mathbf{R} \in \mathbb{Z}_q^{n' \times \gamma n}$ with $||\mathbf{R}||_\infty \leq \beta$. Then:*

- *$\mathbf{u} \leftarrow \mathsf{Sam}(1^\lambda)$ samples $\mathbf{u} \in \mathbb{Z}_q^m$ such that $||\mathbf{u}||_\infty \leq m^{2.5}\beta B$,*
- *$\mathbf{u} \leftarrow \mathsf{SamPre}_{\mathbf{A},\mathbf{R}}(\mathbf{v})$ samples $\mathbf{u} \in \mathbb{Z}_q^m$ such that $\mathbf{A}\mathbf{u} = \mathbf{v}$ and $||\mathbf{u}||_\infty \leq m^{2.5}\beta B$,*

where the distribution of $(\mathbf{u}, \mathbf{v})$ is statistically close to $(\mathbf{u}', \mathbf{v}')$ with $\mathbf{u} \leftarrow \mathsf{Sam}(1^\lambda), \mathbf{v} = \mathbf{A}\mathbf{u}, \mathbf{v}' \leftarrow \mathbb{Z}_q^n, \mathbf{u}' \leftarrow \mathsf{SamPre}_{\mathbf{A},\mathbf{R}}(\mathbf{v}')$. Furthermore, the distribution of $\mathsf{Sam}(1^\lambda)$ has min-entropy $H_\infty(\mathsf{Sam}(1^\lambda)) \geq m \log B$.

The above lemma follows from the works of [27,42]. Firstly, [42] shows that the lattice $\Lambda^\perp(\mathbf{G})$ has a public basis $\mathbf{S} \in \mathbb{Z}^{m' \times m'}$ with $||\mathbf{S}||_\infty \leq B$ where $m' = \gamma n$. Furthermore, this can be efficiently extended to a basis $\mathbf{T} \in \mathbb{Z}^{m \times m}$ for the lattice $\Lambda^\perp(\mathbf{A})$ using knowledge of $\mathbf{A}, \mathbf{R}$, where $||\mathbf{T}||_\infty \leq m'\beta B$. This also shows that the smoothing parameter of $\eta_\varepsilon(\Lambda^\perp(\mathbf{A})) \leq ||\mathbf{T}|| \leq m^{1.5}\beta B$. We define $\mathsf{Sam}(1^\lambda)$ to sample from the Discrete Gaussian $D_{\mathbb{Z}^m,s}$ with parameter $s = m^2\beta B$. Following [27], the algorithm $\mathsf{SamPre}_{\mathbf{A},\mathbf{R}}(\mathbf{v})$ uses $\mathbf{A}, \mathbf{R}$ to find the basis $\mathbf{T}$ and uses that to sample from the Discrete Gaussaian $\mathbf{t} + D_{\Lambda^\perp(\mathbf{A}),s,-\mathbf{t}}$ where $\mathbf{t}$ is any solution to $\mathbf{A}\mathbf{t} = \mathbf{v}$ (which is guaranteed to exist and can be found efficiently). For $\mathbf{u} \leftarrow \mathsf{Sam}(1^\lambda)$ the value $\mathbf{A}\mathbf{u}$ is then statistically close to uniform over $\mathbb{Z}_q^n$ and for any $\mathbf{v}$, the distribution of $\mathbf{u}' \leftarrow \mathsf{SamPre}_{\mathbf{A},\mathbf{R}}(\mathbf{v})$ is exactly the conditional distribution of $\mathbf{u} \leftarrow \mathsf{Sam}(1^\lambda)$ subject to $\mathbf{A}\mathbf{u} = \mathbf{v}$. The probability that $\mathbf{u} \leftarrow \mathsf{Sam}(1^\lambda)$ or $\mathbf{u}' \leftarrow \mathsf{SamPre}_{\mathbf{A},\mathbf{R}}(\mathbf{v})$ have norm greater than $s\sqrt{m} = m^{2.5}\beta B$ is negligible and, for simplicity, we will modify the algorithms to never output such values. Lastly, we rely on Lemma 2.11 in [46] and the fact that the min-entropy of the discrete Gaussian $D_{\mathbb{Z}^m,s}$ is greater than $(s/(2\eta_\varepsilon(\mathbb{Z}^m)))^m \geq (s/\log m)^m \geq B^m$ for the min-entropy claim.

Constructing of SLFs from LWE. Let $n > n'$ and $B, q = B^\gamma, C, p$ be parameters depending on the security parameter λ and assume that p divides q. Let χ be some β-bounded error distribution. Define $m' = \gamma n$ and $m = n' + m'$. Let $\mathbf{G}$ be the base-B gadget matrix of dimension n over $\mathbb{Z}_q$.

For a public key $\mathsf{pk} = \mathbf{A} \in \mathbb{Z}_q^{n \times m}$ define the function $f_{\mathsf{pk}} : \{-C, \dots, C\}^m \to \mathbb{Z}_p^n$ via

$$f_{\mathsf{pk}}(\mathbf{x}) = \lceil \mathbf{A}\mathbf{x} \rfloor_p .$$

The domain is $\mathcal{D} = \{-C, \dots, C\}^m$ and the range is $\mathcal{R} = \mathbb{Z}_p^n$. We define all of the algorithms of the SLF as follows

- $(\mathsf{pk}, \mathsf{td}) \leftarrow \mathsf{SurGen}(1^\lambda)$: Choose a random $\overline{\mathbf{A}} \leftarrow \mathbb{Z}_q^{n \times n'}$, $\mathbf{R} \leftarrow \chi^{n' \times m'}, \mathbf{E} \leftarrow \chi^{n \times m'}$ and set

$$\mathsf{pk} = \mathbf{A} = [\overline{\mathbf{A}} \mid \overline{\mathbf{A}}\mathbf{R} + \mathbf{G} + \mathbf{E}]$$
$$\mathsf{td} = (\mathbf{A}, \mathbf{R}, \mathbf{E})$$

- $\mathsf{pk} \leftarrow \mathsf{LossyGen}(1^\lambda)$: Choose a random $\overline{\mathbf{A}} \leftarrow \mathbb{Z}_q^{n \times n'}$, $\mathbf{S} \leftarrow \mathbb{Z}_q^{n' \times m}$, $\mathbf{E} \leftarrow \chi^{n \times m}$ and set

$$\mathbf{A} = \overline{\mathbf{A}} \cdot \mathbf{S} + \mathbf{E}$$

- $\mathbf{x} \leftarrow D(\mathsf{pk})$: samples a uniformly random value $\mathbf{x} \leftarrow \mathsf{Sam}(1^\lambda)$.
- $\mathbf{x} \leftarrow \mathsf{Inv}_{\mathsf{td}}(\mathbf{y})$: Choose $\mathbf{v} \in \mathbb{Z}_q^n$ uniformly at random subject to $\lceil \mathbf{v} \rfloor_p = \mathbf{y}$ by choosing each coordinate uniformly from the appropriate interval. Let $\mathbf{A}' = \mathbf{A} - [\mathbf{0}|\mathbf{E}] = [\overline{\mathbf{A}} \mid \overline{\mathbf{A}}\mathbf{R} + \mathbf{G}]$ and output $\mathbf{x} \leftarrow \mathsf{SamPre}_{\mathbf{A}', \mathbf{R}}(\mathbf{v})$.

For concreteness, we set $B = 2^\lambda$, we set $\gamma = \lambda$ so that $q = B^\gamma = 2^{\lambda^2}$ and $p = 2^{\lambda^2 - 2\lambda}$. By the LWE assumption, there are some polynomials $n' = \mathrm{poly}(\lambda), \beta = \mathrm{poly}(\lambda)$ and a β-bounded distribution χ so that the $\mathsf{LWE}_{n', q, \chi}$ assumption hold. We set $n = n' \cdot \lambda$. Lastly, we choose $C = \lceil m^{2.5} \beta B \rceil$. This ensures that $\mathbf{x} \leftarrow \mathsf{Sam}(1^\lambda)$ outputs $\mathbf{x}$ such that $\|\mathbf{x}\|_\infty \leq C$.

Theorem 6. *The above construction is an (r, r', d, e, ℓ)-SLF* under the LWE assumption where*

$$r = r' = n \log p = n(\lambda^2 - 2\lambda) = \lambda^2 n(1 - o(1))$$
$$d = \lceil m \log(2C + 1) \rceil = (n + \gamma n)(b + O(\log m + \log \beta)) = \lambda^2 n(1 + o(1)) = (1 + o(1))r$$
$$e = m \log B = (n + \gamma n)\lambda \geq \lambda^2 n \geq r$$
$$\ell = n' \log q \leq (n/\lambda)\lambda^2 = o(r)$$

In particular, it is a good SLF*.

Proof. We show each property of SLFs in turn below:

- Surjective Mode: Let $(\mathsf{pk} = \mathbf{A}, \mathsf{td}) \leftarrow \mathsf{SurGen}(1^\lambda)$ be some key pair sampled in surjective mode with $\mathbf{A} = [\overline{\mathbf{A}} \mid \overline{\mathbf{A}}\mathbf{R} + \mathbf{G} + \mathbf{E}]$ and let $\mathbf{A}' = \mathbf{A} - [\,\mathbf{0} \mid \mathbf{E}\,] = [\overline{\mathbf{A}} \mid \overline{\mathbf{A}}\mathbf{R} + \mathbf{G}]$. By Lemma 2, we have

$$(\mathbf{x}, \mathbf{A}'\mathbf{x}) \overset{s}{\approx} (\mathbf{x}', \mathbf{v})$$

where $\mathbf{x} \leftarrow \mathsf{Sam}(1^\lambda)$, $\mathbf{v} \leftarrow \mathbb{Z}_q^n$ and $\mathbf{x}' \leftarrow \mathsf{SamPre}_{\mathbf{A}',\mathbf{R}}(\mathbf{v})$. This implies that

$$(\mathbf{x}, \lceil \mathbf{A}\mathbf{x} \rfloor_p) \equiv (\mathbf{x}, \lceil \mathbf{A}'\mathbf{x} + [\, \mathbf{0} \mid \mathbf{E}\,]\mathbf{x} \rfloor_p) \stackrel{s}{\approx} (\mathbf{x}', \lceil \mathbf{v} + [\, \mathbf{0} \mid \mathbf{E}\,]\mathbf{x}' \rfloor_p) \stackrel{s}{\approx} (\mathbf{x}', \lceil \mathbf{v} \rfloor_p) \equiv (\mathbf{x}', \mathbf{y})$$

where $\mathbf{y} \leftarrow \mathbb{Z}_p^n$. Here we use the fact that $\Pr[\lceil \mathbf{v} \rfloor_p \neq \lceil \mathbf{v} + \mathbf{e} \rfloor_p] = \mathsf{negl}(\lambda)$ where $\mathbf{e} = [\, \mathbf{0} \mid \mathbf{E}\,]\mathbf{x}'$. This is because $\mathbf{v}$ is uniform over $\mathbb{Z}_q$ and $\mathbf{e}$ has norm $\tau = \|\mathbf{e}\|_\infty \leq Cm'\beta = 2^{\lambda + O(\log \lambda)}$. Therefore the only way that $\lceil \mathbf{v} + \mathbf{e} \rfloor_p \neq \lceil \mathbf{v} \rfloor_p$ is if some coordinate of $\mathbf{v}$ lies within distance τ of the boundary of an interval of size q/p that gets rounded to the same value, but for any coordinate this happens with probability $(2\tau + 1)/(q/p) = 2^{\lambda + O(\log \lambda)}/2^{2\lambda} = \mathsf{negl}(\lambda)$.

– Lossy Mode: For $(\mathsf{pk} = \mathbf{A}) \leftarrow \mathsf{LossyGen}(1^\lambda)$ we have $\mathbf{A} = \overline{\mathbf{A}}\mathbf{S} + \mathbf{E}$. We define

$$\mathcal{L}_{\mathsf{pk}} = \left\{ \lceil \overline{\mathbf{A}}\mathbf{S}\mathbf{x} \rfloor_p \; : \; \mathbf{x} \in \{-C, \ldots, C\}^m \right\} \subseteq \left\{ \lceil \overline{\mathbf{A}}\mathbf{y} \rfloor_p \; : \; \mathbf{y} \in \mathbb{Z}_q^{n'} \right\}$$

which is of size $|\mathcal{L}_{\mathsf{pk}}| \leq q^{n'} \leq 2^\ell$. For any $\mathbf{x} \in \{-C, \ldots, C\}^m = \mathcal{D}_{\mathsf{pk}}$ and a random $\mathbf{A} \leftarrow \mathsf{LossyGen}(1^\lambda)$ we have

$$\Pr\left[\lceil \mathbf{A}\mathbf{x} \rfloor_p \notin \mathcal{L}_{\mathsf{pk}} \right] \leq \Pr\left[\lceil \overline{\mathbf{A}}\mathbf{S}\mathbf{x} + \mathbf{E}\mathbf{x} \rfloor_p \neq \lceil \overline{\mathbf{A}}\mathbf{S}\mathbf{x} \rfloor_p \right] \leq \mathsf{negl}(\lambda)$$

Here, we rely on the fact that $\tau = \|\mathbf{E}\mathbf{x}\|_\infty \leq Cm\beta = 2^{\lambda + O(\log \lambda)}$. If $\mathbf{S}\mathbf{x} = \mathbf{0}$ then the above can never happen. Otherwise $\overline{\mathbf{A}}\mathbf{S}\mathbf{x}$ is uniformly random over the choice of $\overline{\mathbf{A}}$ and the above can only happen if some some coordinate of $\overline{\mathbf{A}}\mathbf{S}\mathbf{x}$ lies within distance τ of the boundary of an interval of size q/p that gets rounded to the same value, but for any coordinate this happens with probability $(2\tau + 1)/(q/p) = 2^{\lambda + O(\log \lambda)}/2^{2\lambda} = \mathsf{negl}(\lambda)$.

– Indistinguishability: We claim that the distributions of pk sampled from either $\mathsf{LossyGen}(1^\lambda)$ or $\mathsf{SurGen}(1^\lambda)$ are both computationally indistinguishable from the uniform distribution over $\mathbb{Z}_q^{n \times m}$, and therefore also indistinguishable from each other.

Firstly for $(\mathsf{pk}, \mathsf{td}) \leftarrow \mathsf{SurGen}(1^\lambda)$ we have $\mathsf{pk} = [\overline{\mathbf{A}} \mid \overline{\mathbf{A}}\mathbf{R} + \mathbf{G} + \mathbf{E}]$. By thinking of the columns of $\mathbf{R}$ as LWE secrets that come from the error distribution and $\overline{\mathbf{A}}$ as the LWE coefficients, we get that $[\overline{\mathbf{A}}, \overline{\mathbf{A}}\mathbf{R} + \mathbf{E}]$ is computationally indistinguishable from uniform, which also shows that $\mathsf{pk} = [\overline{\mathbf{A}}, \overline{\mathbf{A}}\mathbf{R} + \mathbf{E}] + [\mathbf{0} \mid \mathbf{G}]$ is indistinguishable from uniform.

Second for $\mathsf{pk} \leftarrow \mathsf{LossyGen}(1^\lambda)$ we have $\mathsf{pk} = [\overline{\mathbf{A}}\mathbf{S} + \mathbf{E}]$. By thinking of the columns of $\mathbf{S}$ as LWE secrets and $\overline{\mathbf{A}}$ as the LWE coefficients, it is immediate that pk is computationally indistinguishable from uniform.

Next, we prove that the domain and range satisfy the enhanced properties that make it an SLF*.

– Elements of $\mathcal{D}_{\mathsf{pk}} = \{-C, \ldots, C\}^m$ can be represented using $d = \lceil m \log(2C + 1) \rceil$ bits.
– By Lemma 2, the min-entropy of the distribution $D(\mathsf{pk}) = \mathsf{Sam}(1^\lambda)$ is at least $m \log B$.
– The range $\mathcal{R}_{\mathsf{pk}} = \mathbb{Z}_p^n$ is a group under addition (or we can interpret $\mathcal{R}_{\mathsf{pk}} = \{0,1\}^{n(\lambda^2 - 2\lambda)}$ as a group under XOR).

- We can efficiently embed bit-string of length $r = n \log p = n(\lambda^2 - 2\lambda)$ as elements of $\mathcal{R}_{\mathsf{pk}} = \mathbb{Z}_p^n$.
- We can obliviously sample from $\mathcal{R}_{\mathsf{pk}} = \mathbb{Z}_p^n$ using r' random bits by equating elements of $\mathbb{Z}_p^n$ with bit-strings of length $r' = n \log p$.

6   Incompressible Encodings from SLFs

We now construct incompressible encodings in the CRS model. We will show that these encodings satisfy the stronger notion of HILL-entropic security (Definition 3 from Sect. 4), which implies incompressibility by Theorem 1. Furthermore, this means that we can also use this construction to get a composable incompressible encoding in the random oracle model using Theorem 2.

Construction. Given an (r, r', d, e, ℓ)-SLF*, we define the incompressible encoding scheme in the CRS model as follows:

- $\mathsf{crs} = (u_1, \ldots, u_{k'}) \leftarrow \{0, 1\}^{r'(\lambda) \cdot k'}$, where $r'(\lambda)$ is the number of random bits needed to obliviously sample from the range of the SLF and $k' = \lceil r/r(\lambda) \rceil$.
- $\mathsf{Enc}_{\mathsf{crs}}(1^\lambda, m)$: Choose $(\mathsf{pk}, \mathsf{td}) \leftarrow \mathsf{SurGen}(1^\lambda)$. Interpret $m = (m_1, \ldots, m_{k'}) \in \{0, 1\}^{r(\lambda) \cdot k'}$. For $i \in [k']$, let $\hat{m}_i = \mathsf{embed}_{\mathsf{pk}}(m_i) \in \mathcal{R}_{\mathsf{pk}}$, $y_i := \mathsf{sam}(\mathsf{pk}; u_i) \in \mathcal{R}_{\mathsf{pk}}$ and $c_i \leftarrow \mathsf{Inv}_{\mathsf{td}}(y_i + \hat{m}_i)$. Output $c = (\mathsf{pk}, c_1, \ldots, c_{k'})$.
- $\mathsf{Dec}_{\mathsf{crs}}(\, c = (\mathsf{pk}, c_1, \ldots, c_{k'}))$: For $i \in [k']$, let $y_i := \mathsf{sam}(\mathsf{pk}; u_i)$, $\hat{m}_i := f_{\mathsf{pk}}(c_i) - y_i$, $m_i := \mathsf{embed}_{\mathsf{pk}}^{-1}(\hat{m}_i)$. Output $(m_1, \ldots, m_{k'})$.

Theorem 7. *Assuming the existence of an (r, r', d, e, ℓ)-SLF*, the above construction yields an (α, β)-HILL-Entropic encoding scheme with selective security in the CRS model, where $\alpha(\lambda, k) = k'(\lambda)d(\lambda) + \mathrm{poly}(\lambda)$, $\beta(\lambda, k) = k'(\lambda)(e(\lambda) - \ell(\lambda))$ and the crs is of length $t(\lambda, k) = k'(\lambda) \cdot r'(\lambda)$ for $k'(\lambda) = \lceil \frac{k}{r(\lambda)} \rceil$. Furthermore, the encoding is locally decodable.*

In particular, any good SLF* yields a good incompressible encoding that is locally decodable and achieves either:

1. *Selective security in the CRS model, where the CRS is of length $t(\lambda, k) = k(1 + o(1)) + \mathrm{poly}(\lambda)$.*
2. *Composable security in the Random Oracle model.*

Proof. We only prove the first part of the theorem and the second part ("in particular...") follows from Theorems 1 and 2.

The correctness of the scheme and the parameter α (length of encoding), t (length of CRS) are clear from the construction. To show β-HILL-Entropic security, define the procedure $(\mathsf{crs}, c) \leftarrow \mathsf{SimEnc}(1^\lambda, m)$ that, on input $m = (m_1, \ldots, m_{k'}) \in \{0, 1\}^{r(\lambda) \cdot k'}$, samples $\mathsf{crs} = (u_1, \ldots, u_{k'})$ and $c = (\mathsf{pk}, c_1, \ldots, c_{k'})$ as follows:

- Choose $\mathsf{pk} \leftarrow \mathsf{LossyGen}(1^\lambda)$.
- For $i \in [k']$, choose $c_i \leftarrow D(\mathsf{pk})$.

- For $i \in [k']$, let $\hat{m}_i = \mathsf{embed}_{\mathsf{pk}}(m_i) \in \mathcal{R}_{\mathsf{pk}}$. Let $y_i = f_{\mathsf{pk}}(c_i) - \hat{m}_i$ if $f_{\mathsf{pk}}(c_i) \in \mathcal{L}_{\mathsf{pk}}$ or else set $y_i = L - \hat{m}_i$ where L is some arbitrary element of $\mathcal{L}_{\mathsf{pk}}$. Let $u_i \leftarrow \mathsf{explain}_{\mathsf{pk}}(y_i)$.

First we show that SimEnc satisfies the entropy requirements. For any fixed m, pk, let $\mathsf{CRS} = (U_1, \ldots, U_{k'})$, $C = (\mathsf{pk}, C_1, \ldots, C_{k'})$ be random variables for the output $(\mathsf{crs}, c) \leftarrow \mathsf{SimEnc}(1^\lambda, m)$. Then

$$H_\infty(C|\mathsf{CRS}) \geq \sum_{i \in [k']} H_\infty(C_i|U_i) \geq k'(\lambda)(e(\lambda) - \ell(\lambda))$$

where the first inequality follows from the fact that (C_i, U_i) are k' independent random variables, and the second inequality follows since $U_i \in \mathcal{L}_{\mathsf{pk}} - \hat{m}_i$ is supported over a set of size $2^{\ell(\lambda)}$. This shows that the SimEnc satisfies the entropy requirement.

Let $m = \{m_\lambda\}$ be any ensemble of messages of length $|m_\lambda| = k(\lambda)$. We show that the two distributions of (crs, c) are indistinguishable for $\mathsf{crs} \leftarrow \{0,1\}^{t(\lambda,k)}, c \leftarrow \mathsf{Enc}_{\mathsf{crs}}(1^\lambda, m)$ versus $(\mathsf{crs}, c) \leftarrow \mathsf{SimEnc}(1^\lambda, m)$. We do so via a sequence of hybrids.

Hybrid 0: This is the distribution of $\mathsf{crs} \leftarrow \{0,1\}^{t(\lambda,k)}, c \leftarrow \mathsf{Enc}_{\mathsf{crs}}(1^\lambda, m)$ where $m = (m_1, \ldots, m_{k'}) \in \{0,1\}^{r(\lambda) \cdot k'}$. The values are sampled as follows:
- For $i \in [k']$, choose $u_i \leftarrow \{0,1\}^{r'(\lambda)}$.
- Choose $(\mathsf{pk}, \mathsf{td}) \leftarrow \mathsf{SurGen}(1^\lambda)$.
- For $i \in [k']$, let $\hat{m}_i = \mathsf{embed}_{\mathsf{pk}}(m_i) \in \mathcal{R}_{\mathsf{pk}}$, $y_i := \mathsf{sam}(\mathsf{pk}; u_i) \in \mathcal{R}_{\mathsf{pk}}$ and $c_i \leftarrow \mathsf{Inv}_{\mathsf{td}}(y_i + \hat{m}_i)$.
- Output $(\mathsf{crs} = (u_1, \ldots, u_{k'}), c = (\mathsf{pk}, c_1, \ldots, c_{k'}))$.

Hybrid 1: Instead of choosing $u_i \leftarrow \{0,1\}^{r'(\lambda)}$ and setting $y_i := \mathsf{sam}(\mathsf{pk}; u_i) \in \mathcal{R}_{\mathsf{pk}}$, we now choose $y_i \leftarrow \mathcal{R}_{\mathsf{pk}}$ and set $u_i \leftarrow \mathsf{explain}_{\mathsf{pk}}(y_i)$. That is, hybrid 1 is defined as follows:
- Choose $(\mathsf{pk}, \mathsf{td}) \leftarrow \mathsf{SurGen}(1^\lambda)$.
- For $i \in [k']$, choose $y_i \leftarrow \mathcal{R}_{\mathsf{pk}}$ and $u_i \leftarrow \mathsf{explain}_{\mathsf{pk}}(y_i)$.
- For $i \in [k']$, let $\hat{m}_i = \mathsf{embed}_{\mathsf{pk}}(m_i) \in \mathcal{R}_{\mathsf{pk}}$, $y_i := \mathsf{sam}(\mathsf{pk}; u_i) \in \mathcal{R}_{\mathsf{pk}}$ and $c_i \leftarrow \mathsf{Inv}_{\mathsf{td}}(y_i + \hat{m}_i)$.
- Output $(\mathsf{crs} = (u_1, \ldots, u_{k'}), c = (\mathsf{pk}, c_1, \ldots, c_{k'}))$.

Hybrids 0 and 1 are statistically indistinguishable by the "oblivious sampling" property of the range $\mathcal{R}_{\mathsf{pk}}$ of the SLF*.

Hybrid 2: In hybrid 2, instead of choosing $y_i \leftarrow \mathcal{R}_{\mathsf{pk}}$ and setting $c_i \leftarrow \mathsf{Inv}_{\mathsf{td}}(y_i + \hat{m}_i)$, we choose $c_i \leftarrow D(\mathsf{pk})$ at random and set $y_i = f_{\mathsf{pk}}(c_i) - \hat{m}_i$. That is, hybrid 2 is defines as follows:
- Choose $(\mathsf{pk}, \mathsf{td}) \leftarrow \mathsf{SurGen}(1^\lambda)$.
- For $i \in [k']$, choose $c_i \leftarrow D(\mathsf{pk})$.
- For $i \in [k']$, let $\hat{m}_i = \mathsf{embed}_{\mathsf{pk}}(m_i) \in \mathcal{R}_{\mathsf{pk}}$, $y_i = f_{\mathsf{pk}}(c_i) - \hat{m}_i$ and $u_i \leftarrow \mathsf{explain}_{\mathsf{pk}}(y_i)$.
- Output $(\mathsf{crs} = (u_1, \ldots, u_{k'}), c = (\mathsf{pk}, c_1, \ldots, c_{k'}))$.

Hybrids 1 and 2 are statistically indistinguishable by the requirement on the surjective mode of the SLF*, which ensures that the two distributions on (y_i, c_i) in hybrids 1 and 2 are indistinguishable.

Hybrid 3: In hybrid 3, instead of choosing $(\mathsf{pk}, \mathsf{td}) \leftarrow \mathsf{SurGen}(1^\lambda)$ we choose $\mathsf{pk} \leftarrow \mathsf{LossyGen}(1^\lambda)$. Note that td is never used hybrid 2. That is, hybrid 3 is defined as follows.

- Choose $\mathsf{pk} \leftarrow \mathsf{LossyGen}(1^\lambda)$.
- For $i \in [k']$, choose $c_i \leftarrow D(\mathsf{pk})$.
- For $i \in [k']$, let $\hat{m}_i = \mathsf{embed}_{\mathsf{pk}}(m_i) \in \mathcal{R}_{\mathsf{pk}}$, $y_i = f_{\mathsf{pk}}(c_i) - \hat{m}_i$ and $u_i \leftarrow \mathsf{explain}_{\mathsf{pk}}(y_i)$.
- Output $(\mathsf{crs} = (u_1, \ldots, u_{k'}), c = (\mathsf{pk}, c_1, \ldots, c_{k'})$.

Hybrids 2 and 3 are computationally indistinguishable by the indistinguishability requirement on the SLF.

Hybrid 4: In hybrid 4, if $f_{\mathsf{pk}}(c_i) \notin \mathcal{L}_{\mathsf{pk}}$ we set $y_i = L - \hat{m}_i$ where L is some arbitrary fixed element of $\mathcal{L}_{\mathsf{pk}}$. That is, hybrid 4 is defined as follows:

- Choose $\mathsf{pk} \leftarrow \mathsf{LossyGen}(1^\lambda)$.
- For $i \in [k']$, choose $c_i \leftarrow D(\mathsf{pk})$.
- For $i \in [k']$, let $\hat{m}_i = \mathsf{embed}_{\mathsf{pk}}(m_i) \in \mathcal{R}_{\mathsf{pk}}$. Let $y_i = f_{\mathsf{pk}}(c_i) - \hat{m}_i$ if $f_{\mathsf{pk}}(c_i) \in \mathcal{L}_{\mathsf{pk}}$ or else set $y_i = L - \hat{m}_i$ where L is some arbitrary element of $\mathcal{L}_{\mathsf{pk}}$. Let $u_i \leftarrow \mathsf{explain}_{\mathsf{pk}}(y_i)$.
- For $i \in [k']$, let $\hat{m}_i = \mathsf{embed}_{\mathsf{pk}}(m_i) \in \mathcal{R}_{\mathsf{pk}}$, $y_i = f_{\mathsf{pk}}(c_i) - \hat{m}_i$ and $u_i \leftarrow \mathsf{explain}_{\mathsf{pk}}(y_i)$.
- Output $(\mathsf{crs} = (u_1, \ldots, u_{k'}), c = (\mathsf{pk}, c_1, \ldots, c_{k'})$.

Hybrids 3,4 are indistinguishable by the lossy mode property of the SLF*. In particular, for a random $\mathsf{pk} \leftarrow \mathsf{LossyGen}(1^\lambda)$ and $c_i \leftarrow D(\mathsf{pk})$, the probability that $f_{\mathsf{pk}}(c_i) \notin \mathcal{L}_{\mathsf{pk}}$ is negligible.

Hybrid 4 is exactly the distribution of $(\mathsf{crs}, c) \leftarrow \mathsf{SimEnc}(1^\lambda, m)$. Therefore, we have shown that the two target distributions in Hybrid 0 and Hybrid 4 are indeed indistinguishable, which concludes the proof.

Corollary 1. *Under either the DCR or LWE assumptions, there exist good incompressible encodings that are locally decodable and achieve either:*

1. *Selective security in the CRS model, with a CRS of length $t(\lambda, k) = k(1 + o(1))$.*
2. *Composable security in the Random Oracle model.*

Furthermore the complexity of encoding/decoding is $k \cdot \mathrm{poly}(\lambda)$.

References

1. Ajtai, M.: Generating hard instances of lattice problems (extended abstract). In: 28th ACM STOC, pp. 99–108. ACM Press (1996)
2. Alwen, J., Dodis, Y., Naor, M., Segev, G., Walfish, S., Wichs, D.: Public-key encryption in the bounded-retrieval model. In: Gilbert, H. (ed.) EUROCRYPT 2010. LNCS, vol. 6110, pp. 113–134. Springer, Heidelberg (2010). https://doi.org/10.1007/978-3-642-13190-5_6
3. Alwen, J., Dodis, Y., Wichs, D.: Leakage-resilient public-key cryptography in the bounded-retrieval model. In: Halevi [30], pp. 36–54 (2009)

4. Alwen, J., Krenn, S., Pietrzak, K., Wichs, D.: Learning with rounding, revisited. In: Canetti, R., Garay, J.A. (eds.) CRYPTO 2013. LNCS, vol. 8042, pp. 57–74. Springer, Heidelberg (2013). https://doi.org/10.1007/978-3-642-40041-4_4

5. Applebaum, B., Cash, D., Peikert, C., Sahai, A.: Fast cryptographic primitives and circular-secure encryption based on hard learning problems. In: Halevi [30], pp. 595–618 (2009)

6. Auerbach, B., Kiltz, E., Poettering, B., Schoenen, S.: Lossy trapdoor permutations with improved lossiness. In: Matsui, M. (ed.) CT-RSA 2019. LNCS, vol. 11405, pp. 230–250. Springer, Cham (2019). https://doi.org/10.1007/978-3-030-12612-4_12

7. Barak, B., Shaltiel, R., Wigderson, A.: Computational analogues of entropy. In: Arora, S., Jansen, K., Rolim, J.D.P., Sahai, A. (eds.) APPROX/RANDOM -2003. LNCS, vol. 2764, pp. 200–215. Springer, Heidelberg (2003). https://doi.org/10.1007/978-3-540-45198-3_18

8. Bellare, M., Kane, D., Rogaway, P.: Big-key symmetric encryption: resisting key exfiltration. In: Robshaw and Katz [50], pp. 373–402 (2016)

9. Boneh, D., Bonneau, J., Bünz, B., Fisch, B.: Verifiable delay functions. In: Shacham, H., Boldyreva, A. (eds.) CRYPTO 2018, Part I. LNCS, vol. 10991, pp. 757–788. Springer, Cham (2018). https://doi.org/10.1007/978-3-319-96884-1_25

10. Brakerski, Z., Langlois, A., Peikert, C., Regev, O., Stehlé, D.: Classical hardness of learning with errors. In: Boneh, D., Roughgarden, T., Feigenbaum, J. (eds.) 45th ACM STOC, pp. 575–584. ACM Press (2013)

11. Brakerski, Z., Lombardi, A., Segev, G., Vaikuntanathan, V.: Anonymous IBE, leakage resilience and circular security from new assumptions. In: Nielsen, J.B., Rijmen, V. (eds.) EUROCRYPT 2018, Part I. LNCS, vol. 10820, pp. 535–564. Springer, Cham (2018). https://doi.org/10.1007/978-3-319-78381-9_20

12. Cash, D., Ding, Y.Z., Dodis, Y., Lee, W., Lipton, R., Walfish, S.: Intrusion-resilient key exchange in the bounded retrieval model. In: Vadhan, S.P. (ed.) TCC 2007. LNCS, vol. 4392, pp. 479–498. Springer, Heidelberg (2007). https://doi.org/10.1007/978-3-540-70936-7_26

13. Cecchetti, E., Fisch, B., Miers, I., Juels, A.: PIEs: public incompressible encodings for decentralized storage. In: Cavallaro, L., Kinder, J., Wang, X., Katz, J. (eds.) ACM CCS 2019, pp. 1351–1367. ACM Press, Nov. (2019)

14. Chen, Y., Genise, N., Mukherjee, P.: Approximate trapdoors for lattices and smaller hash-and-sign signatures. In: Galbraith, S.D., Moriai, S. (eds.) ASIACRYPT 2019, Part III. LNCS, vol. 11923, pp. 3–32. Springer, Cham (2019). https://doi.org/10.1007/978-3-030-34618-8_1

15. Cho, C., Döttling, N., Garg, S., Gupta, D., Miao, P., Polychroniadou, A.: Laconic oblivious transfer and its applications. In: Katz, J., Shacham, H. (eds.) CRYPTO 2017, Part II. LNCS, vol. 10402, pp. 33–65. Springer, Cham (2017). https://doi.org/10.1007/978-3-319-63715-0_2

16. Coron, J.-S., Holenstein, T., Künzler, R., Patarin, J., Seurin, Y., Tessaro, S.: How to build an ideal cipher: the indifferentiability of the Feistel construction. J. Cryptol. **29**(1), 61–114 (2016). https://doi.org/10.1007/s00145-014-9189-6

17. Damgård, I., Ganesh, C., Orlandi, C.: Proofs of replicated storage without timing assumptions. In: Boldyreva, A., Micciancio, D. (eds.) CRYPTO 2019, Part I. LNCS, vol. 11692, pp. 355–380. Springer, Cham (2019). https://doi.org/10.1007/978-3-030-26948-7_13

18. Damgård, I., Jurik, M.: A generalisation, a simplification and some applications of Paillier's probabilistic public-key system. In: Kim, K. (ed.) PKC 2001. LNCS, vol. 1992, pp. 119–136. Springer, Heidelberg (2001). https://doi.org/10.1007/3-540-44586-2_9

19. Di Crescenzo, G., Lipton, R.J., Walfish, S.: Perfectly secure password protocols in the bounded retrieval model. In: Halevi and Rabin [31], pp. 225–244 (2006)
20. Dodis, Y., Jain, A., Moran, T., Wichs, D.: Counterexamples to hardness amplification beyond negligible. In: Cramer, R. (ed.) TCC 2012. LNCS, vol. 7194, pp. 476–493. Springer, Heidelberg (2012). https://doi.org/10.1007/978-3-642-28914-9_27
21. Dodis, Y., Ostrovsky, R., Reyzin, L., Smith, A.D.: Fuzzy extractors: How to generate strong keys from biometrics and other noisy data. SIAM J. Comput. **38**(1), 97–139 (2008)
22. Dodis, Y., Vadhan, S., Wichs, D.: Proofs of retrievability via hardness amplification. In: Reingold, O. (ed.) TCC 2009. LNCS, vol. 5444, pp. 109–127. Springer, Heidelberg (2009). https://doi.org/10.1007/978-3-642-00457-5_8
23. Dziembowski, S.: Intrusion-resilience via the bounded-storage model. In: Halevi and Rabin [31], pp. 207–224 (2006)
24. Fisch, B.: Tight proofs of space and replication. Cryptology ePrint Archive, Report 2018/702 (2018). https://eprint.iacr.org/2018/702
25. Freeman, D.M., Goldreich, O., Kiltz, E., Rosen, A., Segev, G.: More constructions of lossy and correlation-secure trapdoor functions. J. Cryptol. **26**(1), 39–74 (2013). https://doi.org/10.1007/s00145-011-9112-3
26. Garg, R., Lu, G., Waters, B.: New techniques in replica encodings with client setup. Cryptology ePrint Archive, Report 2020/617 (2020). https://eprint.iacr.org/2020/617
27. Gentry, C., Peikert, C., Vaikuntanathan, V.: Trapdoors for hard lattices and new cryptographic constructions. In: Ladner and Dwork [39], pp. 197–206 (2008)
28. Gentry, C., Wichs, D.: Separating succinct non-interactive arguments from all falsifiable assumptions. In: Fortnow, L., Vadhan, S.P. (eds.) 43rd ACM STOC, pp. 99–108. ACM Press (2011)
29. Goldwasser, S., Kalai, Y.T., Peikert, C., Vaikuntanathan, V.: Robustness of the learning with errors assumption. In: Yao, A.C.-C. (ed.) ICS 2010, pp. 230–240. Tsinghua University Press, Beijing (2010)
30. Halevi, S. (ed.): CRYPTO 2009. LNCS, vol. 5677. Springer, Heidelberg (2009). https://doi.org/10.1007/978-3-642-03356-8
31. Halevi, S., Rabin, T. (eds.): TCC 2006. LNCS, vol. 3876. Springer, Heidelberg (2006). https://doi.org/10.1007/11681878
32. Håstad, J., Impagliazzo, R., Levin, L.A., Luby, M.: A pseudorandom generator from any one-way function. SIAM J. Comput. **28**(4), 1364–1396 (1999)
33. Hsiao, C.-Y., Lu, C.-J., Reyzin, L.: Conditional computational entropy, or toward separating pseudoentropy from compressibility. In: Naor, M. (ed.) EUROCRYPT 2007. LNCS, vol. 4515, pp. 169–186. Springer, Heidelberg (2007). https://doi.org/10.1007/978-3-540-72540-4_10
34. Jain, A., Pietrzak, K.: Parallel repetition for leakage resilience amplification revisited. In: Ishai, Y. (ed.) TCC 2011. LNCS, vol. 6597, pp. 58–69. Springer, Heidelberg (2011). https://doi.org/10.1007/978-3-642-19571-6_5
35. Juels, A., Kaliski Jr., B.S.: Pors: proofs of retrievability for large files. In: Ning, P., De Capitani, S., di Vimercati, Syverson, P.F. (eds.) ACM CCS 2007, pp. 584–597. ACM Press (2007)
36. Kiltz, E., O'Neill, A., Smith, A.: Instantiability of RSA-OAEP under chosen-plaintext attack. In: Rabin, T. (ed.) CRYPTO 2010. LNCS, vol. 6223, pp. 295–313. Springer, Heidelberg (2010). https://doi.org/10.1007/978-3-642-14623-7_16
37. Labs, P.:Filecoin: A decentralized storage network (2017)

38. Labs, P.: Proof of replication (2017)
39. Ladner, R.E., Dwork, C. (eds.) 40th ACM STOC. ACM Press (2008)
40. Lewko, A.B., Waters, B.: On the insecurity of parallel repetition for leakage resilience. In: 51st FOCS, pp. 521–530. IEEE Computer Society Press (2010)
41. Maurer, U., Renner, R., Holenstein, C.: Indifferentiability, impossibility results on reductions, and applications to the random oracle methodology. In: Naor, M. (ed.) TCC 2004. LNCS, vol. 2951, pp. 21–39. Springer, Heidelberg (2004). https://doi. org/10.1007/978-3-540-24638-1_2
42. Micciancio, D., Peikert, C.: Trapdoors for lattices: simpler, tighter, faster, smaller. In: Pointcheval, D., Johansson, T. (eds.) EUROCRYPT 2012. LNCS, vol. 7237, pp. 700–718. Springer, Heidelberg (2012). https://doi.org/10.1007/978-3-642-29011-4_41
43. Naor, M.: On cryptographic assumptions and challenges. In: Boneh, D. (ed.) CRYPTO 2003. LNCS, vol. 2729, pp. 96–109. Springer, Heidelberg (2003). https:// doi.org/10.1007/978-3-540-45146-4_6
44. Paillier, P.: Public-key cryptosystems based on composite degree residuosity classes. In: Stern, J. (ed.) EUROCRYPT 1999. LNCS, vol. 1592, pp. 223–238. Springer, Heidelberg (1999). https://doi.org/10.1007/3-540-48910-X_16
45. Peikert, C.: Public-key cryptosystems from the worst-case shortest vector problem: extended abstract. In: Mitzenmacher, M. (ed.) 41st ACM STOC, pp. 333–342. ACM Press (2009)
46. Peikert, C., Rosen, A.: Efficient collision-resistant hashing from worst-case assumptions on cyclic lattices. In: Halevi and Rabin [31], pp. 145–166 (2006)
47. Peikert, C., Waters, B.: Lossy trapdoor functions and their applications. In: Ladner and Dwork [39], pp. 187–196 (2011)
48. Regev, O.: On lattices, learning with errors, random linear codes, and cryptography. In: Gabow, H.N., Fagin, R. (eds.) 37th ACM STOC, pp. 84–93. ACM Press (2005)
49. Ristenpart, T., Shacham, H., Shrimpton, T.: Careful with composition: limitations of the indifferentiability framework. In: Paterson, K.G. (ed.) EUROCRYPT 2011. LNCS, vol. 6632, pp. 487–506. Springer, Heidelberg (2011). https://doi.org/10. 1007/978-3-642-20465-4_27
50. Robshaw, M., Katz, J. (eds.): CRYPTO 2016, Part I. LNCS, vol. 9814. Springer, Heidelberg (2016). https://doi.org/10.1007/978-3-662-53018-4
51. Shacham, H., Waters, B.: Compact proofs of retrievability. In: Pieprzyk, J. (ed.) ASIACRYPT 2008. LNCS, vol. 5350, pp. 90–107. Springer, Heidelberg (2008). https://doi.org/10.1007/978-3-540-89255-7_7
52. van Dijk, M., Juels, A., Oprea, A., Rivest, R.L., Stefanov, E., Triandopoulos, N.: Hourglass schemes: how to prove that cloud files are encrypted. In: Yu, T., Danezis, G., Gligor, V.D. (eds.) ACM CCS 2012, pp. 265–280. ACM Press (2012)
53. Wichs, D.: Barriers in cryptography with weak, correlated and leaky sources. In: Kleinberg, R.D. (ed.) ITCS 2013, pp. 111–126. ACM (2013)
54. Yao, A.C.-C.: Theory and applications of trapdoor functions (extended abstract). In: 23rd FOCS, pp. 80–91. IEEE Computer Society Press (1982)
55. Zhandry, M.: The magic of ELFs. In: Robshaw and Katz [50], pp. 479–508 (2016)

Constructions

New Constructions of Hinting PRGs, OWFs with Encryption, and More

Rishab Goyal[1]($\boxtimes$), Satyanarayana Vusirikala[2]($\boxtimes$), and Brent Waters[2,3]($\boxtimes$)

[1] MIT, Cambridge, USA
goyal@utexas.edu
[2] University of Texas at Austin, Austin, USA
{satya,bwaters}@cs.utexas.edu
[3] NTT Research, Palo Alto, USA

Abstract. Over the last few years, there has been a surge of new cryptographic results, including laconic oblivious transfer [13,16], (anonymous/ hierarchical) identity-based encryption [9], trapdoor functions [19,20], chosen-ciphertext security transformations [32,33], designated-verifier zero-knowledge proofs [30,34,37], due to a beautiful framework recently introduced in the works of Cho et al. [13], and Döttling and Garg [14]. The primitive of one-way function with encryption (OWFE) [19,20] and its relatives (chameleon encryption, one-time signatures with encryption, hinting PRGs, trapdoor hash encryption, batch encryption) [9,14,16,17, 33] have been a centerpiece in all these results.

While there exist multiple realizations of OWFE (and its relatives) from a variety of assumptions such as CDH, Factoring, and LWE, all such constructions fall under the same general "missing block" framework [13,14]. Although this framework has been instrumental in opening up a new pathway towards various cryptographic functionalities via the abstraction of OWFE (and its relatives), it has been accompanied by undesirable inefficiencies that might inhibit a much wider adoption in many practical scenarios. Motivated by the surging importance of the OWFE abstraction (and its relatives), a natural question to ask is whether the existing approaches can be diversified to not only obtain more constructions from different assumptions, but also in developing newer frameworks. We believe answering this question will eventually lead to important and previously unexplored performance trade-offs in the overarching applications of this novel cryptographic paradigm.

In this work, we propose a new *accumulation-style* framework for building a new class of OWFE as well as hinting PRG constructions with a special focus on achieving shorter ciphertext size and shorter public parameter size (respectively). Such performance improvements parlay into shorter parameters in their corresponding applications. Briefly, we explore the following performance trade-offs—(1) for OWFE, our constructions outperform in terms of ciphertext size as well as encryption time, but this comes at the cost of larger evaluation and setup times, (2) for hinting PRGs, our constructions provide a rather dramatic trade-off between evaluation time versus parameter size, with our construction leading to significantly shorter public parameter size. The trade-off

© International Association for Cryptologic Research 2020
D. Micciancio and T. Ristenpart (Eds.): CRYPTO 2020, LNCS 12170, pp. 527–558, 2020.
https://doi.org/10.1007/978-3-030-56784-2_18

enabled by our hinting PRG construction also leads to interesting implications in the CPA-to-CCA transformation provided in [33]. We also provide concrete performance measurements for our constructions and compare them with existing approaches. We believe highlighting such trade-offs will lead to a wider adoption of these abstractions in a practical sense.

1   Introduction

A major goal in cryptography is to study cryptographic primitives that could be used for securely implementing useful functionalities as well as lead to interesting applications. Significant effort in cryptographic research is geared towards diversifying existing frameworks and constructions for realizing such primitives to improve efficiency as well as obtain more constructions from a wider set of well-studied assumptions. Over the last few years there has been a surge of new constructions [1,2,9,14–17,19–22,24–26,30,32–34,37] due to a beautiful framework recently introduced in the works of Cho et al. [13], and Döttling and Garg [14]. This new wave of cryptographic results, including laconic oblivious transfer [13,16], (anonymous/hierarchical) identity-based encryption [9], trapdoor functions [19,20], chosen-ciphertext security transformations [32,33], designated-verifier zero-knowledge proofs [30,34,37], registration-based encryption [21,22] has been propelled by the primitive of one-way function with encryption (OWFE) [19,20] and its relatives (chameleon encryption, one-time signatures with encryption, hinting PRGs, trapdoor hash encryption, batch encryption) [9,14,16,17,33] .

A one-way function with encryption scheme extends the notion of one-way functions to allow a special form of encryption. During setup one samples public parameters pp that fixes an underlying one-way function $f = f_{\mathsf{pp}}$. In an OWFE scheme, the encryption procedure is abstracted out into two components— algorithms E_1, E_2 which work as follows. Both E_1 and E_2 share the same random coins ρ, and take as inputs a value y (that lies in the image space of f), an index-bit pair (i, b), and parameters pp. Algorithm E_1 is used to compute the "ciphertext" ct, whereas E_2 computes the encrypted KEM key k. The decryption algorithm D on input a ciphertext ct, pre-image string x, and parameters pp, outputs a decrypted KEM key k'. For correctness it is important that if the string x is such that $y = f_{\mathsf{pp}}(x)$ and $x_i = b$, then the KEM keys should match, i.e., $k' = k$. While for security, other than the unpredictability of the OWF f, it is required that the ciphertext does not leak the KEM key trivially. That is, given an input x, parameters pp, and a ciphertext ct, the associated KEM key k must be indistinguishable from random as long as the encryption is performed for some value $y = f_{\mathsf{pp}}(x)$ and any index-bit pair of the form $(i, 1 - x_i)$.

Intuitively, an OWFE scheme is simply a one-way function f equipped with matching encryption-decryption procedures such that encryption allows to encrypt messages with respect to an OWF output string y and a pre-image bit (i, b), while decryption requires a pre-image x such that $f(x) = y$ and $x_i = b$.

The "Missing Block" Framework. While there exist multiple realizations of OWFE (and its relatives) from a variety of assumptions such as CDH, Factoring, and LWE, all such constructions fall under the same general "missing block" framework [13,14]. To illustrate the aforementioned framework we sketch a DDH-based variant of the OWFE construction provided by Garg and Hajiabadi [20]. The public parameters consists of $2n$ randomly sampled group generators $\{g_{i,b}\}_{(i,b)\in[n]\times\{0,1\}}$, where n is the input length of the OWF. The function output is computed by performing subset-product on the public parameters, where the subset selection is done as per the input bits. Concretely, on an input $x \in \{0,1\}^n$, the output is $f(x) = \prod_i g_{i,x_i}$. The ciphertext structurally looks like the public parameters, that is it also consists of $2n$ group elements $\{c_{i,b}\}_{i,b}$. Here to encrypt to pre-image bit (i^*, b^*) under randomness ρ, the encryption algorithm E_1 simply sets $c_{i,b} = g_{i,b}^\rho$ for all $(i,b) \neq (i^*, 1-b^*)$, with the $(i^*, 1-b^*)^{th}$ term not being set (i.e., $c_{i^*,1-b^*} = \perp$). Pictorially, this can be represented as follows (where $i^* = 2$ and $b^* = 0$):

$$\mathsf{pp} = \begin{array}{|c|c|c|c|c|} \hline g_{1,0} & g_{2,0} & g_{3,0} & \cdots & g_{n,0} \\ \hline g_{1,1} & g_{2,1} & g_{3,1} & \cdots & g_{n,1} \\ \hline \end{array} \quad \xrightarrow[E_1(\mathsf{pp},(2,0);\rho)]{\text{Encryption}} \quad \mathsf{ct} = \begin{array}{|c|c|c|c|c|} \hline g_{1,0}^\rho & g_{2,0}^\rho & g_{3,0}^\rho & \cdots & g_{n,0}^\rho \\ \hline g_{1,1}^\rho & \times & g_{3,1}^\rho & \cdots & g_{n,1}^\rho \\ \hline \end{array}$$

The KEM key is simply computed by the encryptor as y^ρ, where y is the output of the OWF. The decryptor on the other hand does not know the randomness ρ, thus given the ciphertext ct and a valid pre-image x, it computes the subset-product on ct (followed by applying the hardcore predicate), where the subset selection is done as per x. That is, decryptor computes the key as $\prod_i c_{i,x_i}$.

This notion of not setting up the $(i^*, 1-b^*)^{th}$ term in the ciphertext is what we refer to as adding a "missing block". The intuition behind this is that the ciphertext should only be decryptable using pre-images x such that $x_{i^*} = b^*$, thus the ciphertext component corresponding to the pre-image bit $(i^*, 1-b^*)$ can be omitted. Here the omission of the $(i^*, 1-b^*)^{th}$ block is very crucial in proving the security of encryption.

Limitations of the Framework. Although the "missing block" framework has been instrumental in opening up a new pathway towards various cryptographic functionalities via the abstraction of OWFE (and its relatives), it has been accompanied with undesirable inefficiencies that have led to large system parameters in most of the applications. In particular, the OWFE described above in this framework leads to large "ciphertexts" where the size grows linearly with the input length n of the OWF. Now this inefficiency gets amplified differently in each of its applications. For instance, large OWFE ciphertexts lead to large public parameters of a trapdoor function (/deterministic encryption) [19,20], since the public parameters as per those transformations consist of a polynomial number of OWFE ciphertexts which themselves grow linearly with n. Similar situations arise when we look at a related primitive called Hinting PRG (introduced by Koppula and Waters [33]), where the existing constructions via the "missing block" framework leads to much worse public parameters, and the performance overhead gets significantly amplified if we look at its application to chosen-ciphertext security transformations [33].[1]

Motivated by the surging importance of the abstraction of one-way function with encryption and its relatives, a natural question to ask is whether the existing approaches can be diversified to not only obtain more constructions from different assumptions, but also in developing newer frameworks. We believe answering this question will eventually lead to important and previously unexplored performance trade-offs in the overarching applications of this novel cryptographic paradigm.

1.1 Our Approach

In this work, we develop a new framework for building a new class of one-way function with encryption (as well as hinting PRG) constructions with a special focus on achieving shorter ciphertext size (and shorter public parameter size, respectively), which will parlay into shorter parameters in their corresponding applications.[2]

Concretely, we explore the following performance trade-offs. For OWFE, our constructions based on this new framework outperform the existing ones in terms of ciphertext size as well as encryption time, but this comes at the cost of larger evaluation and setup times. In terms of applications of OWFE to deterministic encryption, this trade-off translates to a scheme with much smaller public parameters and setup time, but larger encryption/decryption times. For hinting PRGs, our constructions provide a rather dramatic trade-off between evaluation time versus parameter size compared to prior schemes, with our construction leading to significantly shorter public parameter size. In terms of applications of hinting PRG to chosen-ciphertext security transformations, the trade-off between public parameter size and evaluation time in the hinting PRG constructions carries forward to a trade-off between encryption key/ciphertext sizes and encryption/decryption times in the resultant CCA-secure construction. Next, we describe the main ideas behind our constructions, and later we give some concrete performance metrics.

OWF with Encryption from Φ-Hiding Assumption. We begin by sketching our Φ-Hiding based construction and security proof. Recall that the the Φ-Hiding assumption states that given an RSA modulus N and a prime e, no polynomial time adversary can distinguish whether e divides $\phi(N)$ or not. Our construction is summarized as follows:

---

[1] Roughly speaking, a hinting PRG is same as a regular PRG, except that it has a stronger pseudorandomness property in the sense that the adversary must not break pseudorandomness even when given a hint about the preimage of the challenge string.

[2] We call our framework "accumulator style" due to a similarities in our algebraic structure to earlier number-theoretic works on cryptographic accumulators [3,4,6, 10–12,27,36,38]. However, neither the definition nor concept of the accumulator will be used in this work.

- The public parameters pp of our OWFE scheme consist of an RSA modulus N, n pairs of λ-bit primes $\{e_{i,b}\}_{(i,b)\in[n]\times\{0,1\}}$, and a generator $g \in \mathbb{Z}_N^*$. (Here n is the input length.)
- For any input $x \in \{0,1\}^n$, the one-way function $f_{\mathsf{pp}}(x)$ is computed as $g^{H(x)\cdot\prod_i e_{i,x_i}}(\bmod\ N)$, where H is a pairwise independent hash function sampled during setup.
- The encryption algorithm E_1 on input a pre-image bit (i^*, b^*) and randomness ρ, outputs ciphertext as $\mathsf{ct} = g^{\rho\cdot e_{i^*,b^*}}(\bmod\ N)$.[3] The corresponding KEM key is set as $k = y^\rho(\bmod\ N)$, where y is the output of the OWF.
- Lastly, the decryption procedure given a ciphertext ct and a pre-image x such that $f_{\mathsf{pp}}(x) = y$ and $x_{i^*} = b^*$, computes the key as $k' = \mathsf{ct}^{\prod_{i\neq i^*} e_{i,x_i}}(\bmod\ N)$. Next, we briefly sketch the main arguments behind the security of this construction.

For security, we will need to show (1) that the function is one way, (2) that encryption security holds and (3) that an additional smoothness property holds. We will sketch the arguments for the first two here. The final smoothness property is only needed for some applications. This involves a more nuanced number theory to prove which we defer to the main body.

The one-wayness argument proceeds as follows—suppose an adversary finds a collision $x \neq x'$, i.e. $f_{\mathsf{pp}}(x) = f_{\mathsf{pp}}(x')$, then a reduction algorithm can sample the λ-bit primes in such a way that, as long as n is larger than $\log N + \lambda$, it can break RSA assumption for one of the primes sampled as part of the public parameters.

For proving security of encryption we need to slightly modify the construction wherein we need to apply an extractor on the KEM key to prove it looks indistinguishable from random, that is $k = \mathsf{Ext}(\mathfrak{s}, y^\rho)$ where Ext is a strong seeded extractor and seed $\mathfrak{s}$ is sampled during setup. Recall that security of encryption requires that for any index-bit pair (i^*, b^*) and input x such that $x_{i^*} \neq b^*$, given a ciphertext $\mathsf{ct} = E_1(\mathsf{pp}, (i^*, b^*); \rho)$ the associated KEM key $k = E_2(\mathsf{pp}, f_{\mathsf{pp}}(x), (i^*, b^*); \rho)$ must be indistinguishable from random.

The idea behind proving the same for the above construction is the following—a ciphertext looks like $\mathsf{ct} = g^{\rho\cdot e_{i^*,b^*}}$ whereas the key is computed as $k = \mathsf{Ext}(\mathfrak{s}, g^{\rho\cdot\prod_i e_{i,x_i}})$. Since $b^* \neq x_{i^*}$, thus the key can be re-written as $k = \mathsf{Ext}(\mathfrak{s}, (\mathsf{ct}^{\prod_i e_{i,x_i}})^{e_{i^*,b^*}^{-1}})$. Now under the Φ-hiding assumption, we can argue that an adversary can not distinguish between the cases where e_{i^*,b^*} is co-prime with respect to $\phi(N)$, and when e_{i^*,b^*} divides $\phi(N)$. Note that in the latter case, there are e_{i^*,b^*} many distinct e_{i^*,b^*}^{th} roots of $\mathsf{ct}^{\prod_i e_{i,x_i}}$. Thus, by strong extractor guarantee we can conclude that key k looks uniformly random to the adversary as the underlying source has large (λ bits of) min-entropy.

Comparing with DDH-Based Constructions. Comparing the asymptotic efficiency of our Φ-Hiding based OWFE construction with the existing DDH-based constructions, we observe the following: (1) the size of the public parameters

---

[3] Technically, the ciphertext should also include the index i^* but we drop it for ease of exposition.

grows linearly with the input length n in both constructions, (2) both OWF evaluation and decryption operations require $O(n)$ group operations and $O(n)$ exponentiations (with λ-bit exponents) respectively, (3) for the Φ-hiding based construction, both E_1 and E_2 algorithms perform single exponentiation, and outputs a ciphertext and key containing just one group element; whereas for DDH-based construction, the E_1 algorithm performs $O(n)$ exponentiations and outputs a ciphertext containing $O(n)$ group elements.

We implemented the above construction and observed that, at 128-bit security level, our Φ-hiding based construction has $\sim$80x shorter ciphertext size over the existing DDH-based construction [20]. Also, the E_1 algorithm of our Φ-hiding based construction is $\sim$14x faster than the DDH baseline. A detailed efficiency comparison for other security levels is discussed in Sect. 6.1.

Hinting PRGs from Φ-Hiding Assumption. We also provide a hinting PRG [33] construction based on Φ-hiding that leads to similar performance trade-offs. Let us briefly recall the notion of hinting PRGs. It consists of two algorithms—Setup and Eval, where the setup algorithm generates the public parameters pp, and the PRG evaluation algorithm takes as input the parameters pp, a seed $s \in \{0,1\}^n$ and a block index $i \in \{0, 1, \ldots, n\}$. The Hinting PRG security requirement is that for a randomly choosen seed $s \in \{0,1\}^n$, the following two distributions over $\{r_{i,b}\}_{(i,b) \in [n] \times \{0,1\}}$ are indistinguishable: in the first distribution, $r_{i,s_i} =$ Eval(pp, s, i) and $r_{i,1-s_i}$ is sampled uniformly at random for every i; whereas in the second distribution, all $r_{i,b}$ terms are sampled uniformly at random.

Our hinting PRG construction is based on our OWFE construction, where the setup algorithm is identical, that is the public parameters pp consist of an RSA modulus N, n pairs of λ-bit primes $\{e_{i,b}\}_{(i,b) \in [n] \times \{0,1\}}$, a generator $g \in \mathbb{Z}_N^*$, and a pairwise independent hash H. And, the evaluation algorithm also bears strong resemblance with the one-way function f described previously. Concretely, the i^{*th} block of the PRG output, i.e. Eval(pp, s, i^*), is computed as $g^{H(s) \cdot \prod_{i \neq i^*} e_{i,s_i}} (\text{mod } N)$. Proving security of this construction follows in a similar line to our OWFE construction. More details on this are provided later in full version of the paper.

Comparing with DDH-Based Constructions. Comparing the asymptotic efficiency of our Φ-Hiding based hinting PRG construction with the existing DDH-based constructions, we observe the following: (1) the public parameters consists of $2n$ (λ-bit) prime exponents along with the RSA modulus, extractor seed, group generator, and a hash key; whereas in the DDH-based constructions, it contains $O(n^2)$ group elements, (2) for evaluating a single hinting PRG block, the evaluator needs to perform $O(n)$ exponentiations in our new construction; whereas in the DDH case it performs $O(n)$ group operations. Additionally, using an elegant Dynamic Programming style algorithm, we can reduce the number of exponentiation operations needed per block to grow only logarithmically in n. The intuition behind such an improvement is that we show how to re-use various intermediate exponentiations obtained during a single hinting PRG block evaluation for accelerating the PRG evaluation for other blocks.

We implemented the above construction and observed that, at 128-bit security level, our Φ-hiding based construction has $\sim$80x shorter ciphertext size over the existing DDH-based construction [20]. Also, the E_1 algorithm of our Φ-hiding based construction is $\sim$14x faster than the DDH baseline. A detailed efficiency comparison for other security levels is discussed in full version of the paper.

Limitations of Φ-Hiding Based Constructions. A quick glance shows that these new constructions lead to much shorter ciphertext size (in the case of OWFE) and public parameters (in the case of hinting PRGs), therefore they will lead to better parameters in their corresponding applications such as deterministic encryption [19] and chosen-ciphertext security transformations [33]. However, looking more closely we observe that our Φ-hiding based construction has an undesirable consequence which is the hinting PRG seed length (or equivalently input length for OWF) n is much larger for our Φ-hiding based scheme when compared with its DDH counterpart. This is due to the fact because of number field sieve attacks, the recommended RSA modulus length (and thereby the input/seed length n) increases super linearly with target security level for the Φ-based construction. While the recommended field size (and thereby the input/seed length n) will increase only linearly for the elliptic curve DDH-based constructions.

Fortunately, the notion of accumulators has been well studied in prime order group setting [3, 10, 12, 36] as well, thus this gives us a different type of number theoretic accumulator. Pivoting to such accumulators, we show how to achieve performance improvements similar to that in the Φ-hiding setting while keeping the input/seed length n close to that in their existing counterparts. Next, we provide our OWFE construction which uses bilinear maps in the prime order group setting.

OWF with Encryption from DBDHI. Let us start by recalling the Decisional Bilinear Diffie-Hellman Inversion (DBDHI) assumption [7]. The strength of the assumption is characterized by a parameter ℓ, and it states that given a sequence of group elements as follows—$(g, g^\alpha, g^{\alpha^2}, \ldots, g^{\alpha^\ell})$, where g is a random group generator and α is a randomly chosen non-zero exponent, no PPT adversary should be able to distinguish $e(g, g)^{1/\alpha}$ from a random element in the target group. Below we describe our OWFE construction in which we directly include the sequence of elements as described above as part of the public parameters.

Concretely, the public parameters pp consist of $n + 1$ group elements $(g, g^\alpha, \ldots, g^{\alpha^n})$ for a random exponent α and group generator g, and a pairwise independent hash H. (Here n is the input length.) Given an input $x \in \{0, 1\}^n$, the one-way function $f_{\mathsf{pp}}(x)$ is computed in two stages. First, the evaluator symbolically evaluates (i.e. simplifies) the polynomial $p(z) = H(x) \cdot \prod_i (z + 2i + x_i)$. Let $p(z) = \sum_{j=0}^n c_j z^j$ be the evaluated polynomial. Next, the evaluator sets the output of the OWF as $\prod_j (g^{\alpha^j})^{c_j}$. The encryption algorithm E_1 on input a pre-image bit (i^*, b^*) and randomness ρ, outputs ciphertext as $\mathsf{ct} = (g^{\alpha + 2i^* + b^*})^{\rho}$.[4] The corresponding KEM key is set as $k = e(g^{\rho}, y)$, where y is the output of the OWF. Lastly, the decryption procedure given a ciphertext ct and a pre-image x such that $f_{\mathsf{pp}}(x) = y$ and $x_{i^*} = b^*$, also takes a two step approach where first it symbolically evaluates the polynomial $p'(z) = H(x) \cdot \prod_{i \neq i^*}(z + 2i + x_i)$. Let $p'(z) = \sum_{j=0}^{n-1} c'_j z^j$ be the evaluated polynomial. Lastly, the decryptor computes the key as $k' = e(\mathsf{ct}, \prod_j (g^{\alpha^j})^{c'_j})$.

The proof of one-wayness is similar to that in the case of Φ-hiding where if an adversary finds a collision $x \neq x'$, i.e. $f_{\mathsf{pp}}(x) = f_{\mathsf{pp}}(x')$, then a reduction algorithm can set the public parameters appropriately such that, as long as n is large enough, it can be used to not only distinguish the DBDHI challenge but also directly compute the DBDHI challenge. The proof of encryption security is also quite similar, where the main idea can be described as follows: the ciphertext looks like $\mathsf{ct} = (g^{\alpha + 2i^* + b^*})^{\rho}$ whereas the key is computed as $k = e(g^{\rho}, \prod_j (g^{\alpha^j})^{c_j})$. Whenever $b^* \neq x_{i^*}$, then the key can be re-written such that it is of the form $k = e(g, g)^{c'/\beta} \cdot e(g, \prod_j (g^{\beta^j})^{c'_j})$ for some constants $c', c'_1, \ldots, c'_{n-1}$, and where β linearly depends on α. By careful analysis, we can reduce this to the DBDHI assumption. Lastly, the proof of smoothness for this construction is significantly simpler than that of its Φ-hiding based counterpart. This is primarily because in this case, we can directly prove that the function $H(x) \cdot \prod_i (\alpha + 2i + x_i) \pmod{p}$, where p is the order of the group is an (almost) 2-universal hash function, therefore by applying LHL, we can argue smoothness of the OWF. More details are provided later in Sect. 5.

We implemented the above construction and observed that, at 128-bit security level, our DBDHI-based construction has $\sim$340x shorter ciphertext size over the existing DDH-based construction [20] and $\sim$4x over our Φ-hiding based construction. Also, the E_1 algorithm of our DBDHI-based construction is $\sim$300x faster than the DDH baseline and $\sim$22x faster than our Φ-hiding construction. Note that even though Φ-hiding and DBDHI-based constructions have nearly identical asymptotic complexity, DBDHI-based construction still performs better as the recommended group size for the elliptic curve groups is smaller than that for RSA.

Hinting PRGs from DDHI and OWFE Without Bilinear Maps. Again to emphasize the general applicability of our *accumulation-style* framework, we provide a hinting PRG construction based on the DDHI assumption as well. The translation from OWFE to hinting PRG is done analogous to that for Φ-hiding based constructions, except in our hinting PRG construction we do not require the bilinear map functionality. Briefly, this is because (unlike OWFE schemes) hinting PRGs do not provide any decryption-like functionality, and for evaluating the hinting PRG, standard group operations are sufficient. Our construction is described in detail later in full version of the paper. We also point out that in full version of the paper we provide an OWFE construction in the prime order

---

[4] Technically, the ciphertext should also include the index i^* but we drop it for ease of exposition.

group setting without using bilinear maps, but the caveat is that it does not lead to better performance when compared with existing DDH-based constructions.

We implemented the above schemes and observed that, at 128-bit security level, the setup algorithm of our Φ-hiding and DDHI-based HPRGs are $\sim$1.35x and $\sim$200x respectively faster than the DDH baseline [33]. Our constructions also have $\sim$105x and $\sim$2100x shorter public parameters respectively than DDH baseline. However, our schemes have less efficient Eval algorithm, and thereby offer a noticeable trade-off between efficiency of Setup and Enc algorithm when used in chosen-ciphertext security transformation of [33]. More details are provided later in full version of the paper.

Recent Work in Trapdoor Functions. One of the applications of our result is in constructing trapdoor functions (TDFs) with smaller parameter sizes. Building on the work of [20], Garg, Gay, and Hajiabadi [19] show how OWF with encryption gives trapdoor functions with image size linear in the input size. However, their construction requires a quadratic number of group elements. Plugging in either our bilinear map or ϕ-hiding constructions will reduce the public parameter size to $O(n)$ group elements. (Since our OWFE schemes also satisfy the smoothness criteria, thus the resulting TDF also leads to a construction of deterministic encryption.)

In a concurrent work, Garg, Hajiabadi, and Ostrovsky [23] using different techniques give new constructions for "trapdoor hash functions" [16] with small public key size. Among other applications, this also gives an injective trapdoor function whose public key contains $O(n)$ group elements. They prove security from the q-power DDH assumption and use other ideas to also reduce the evaluation time. From bilinear maps, however, the work of Boyen and Waters [8] provides TDF constructions secure under the Decisional Bilinear Diffie-Hellman (DBDH) assumption in which the public keys also have only $O(n)$ group elements. Later, [16] presented a TDF construction with $O(\sqrt{n})$ group elements in the public key using SXDH assumption on bilinear maps.

One interpretation is that the primitive of OWF with encryption can perhaps serve a broader range of applications, but to squeeze out better performance for a particular, more narrow set of applications a more specialized abstraction such as trapdoor hash functions might be more useful. This mirrors our experience with hinting PRGs, where our direct constructions had efficiency benefits. Finally, we emphasize that part of our contribution is to provide concrete experimental performance measurements of our constructions.

Roadmap. We recall the notions of Hinting PRG and OWFE in Sect. 2. We then present number-theoretic techniques introduced in this work in Sect. 3. We then present our OWFE constructions based on Φ-hiding, DBDHI assumptions in Sects. 4 and 5. Finally, we implement our schemes and analyze their performance in Sect. 6. In full version of the paper, we present our OWFE from DDHI assumption, our HPRG constructions based on Φ-hiding and DDHI assumptions, and also describe how to construct Hinting PRG generically from OWFE.

2   Preliminaries

Notations. Let PPT denote probabilistic polynomial-time. We denote the set of all positive integers up to n as $[n] := \{1, \ldots, n\}$. Throughout this paper, unless specified, all polynomials we consider are positive polynomials. For any finite set S, $x \leftarrow S$ denotes a uniformly random element x from the set S. Similarly, for any distribution $\mathcal{D}$, $x \leftarrow \mathcal{D}$ denotes an element x drawn from distribution $\mathcal{D}$. The distribution $\mathcal{D}^n$ is used to represent a distribution over vectors of n components, where each component is drawn independently from the distribution $\mathcal{D}$. We call any distribution on n-length bit strings with minimum entropy k as a (k, n) source.

2.1   One Way Function with Encryption

Here we recall the definition of recyclable one-way function with encryption from [19,20]. We adapt the definition to a setting where the KEM key is an ℓ-bit string instead of just a single bit. A recyclable (k, n, ℓ)-OWFE scheme consists of the PPT algorithms K, f, E_1, E_2 and D with the following syntax.

$K(1^\lambda) \rightarrow$ pp: Takes the security parameter 1^λ and outputs public parameters pp.

$f(\mathsf{pp}, x) \rightarrow y$: Takes a public parameter pp and a preimage $x \in \{0,1\}^n$, and deterministically outputs y.

$E_1(\mathsf{pp}, (i, b); \rho) \rightarrow$ ct: Takes public parameters pp, an index $i \in [n]$, a bit $b \in \{0,1\}$ and randomness ρ, and outputs a ciphertext ct.

$E_2(\mathsf{pp}, y, (i, b); \rho) \rightarrow k$: Takes a public parameter pp, a value y, an index $i \in [n]$, a bit $b \in \{0,1\}$ and randomness $\rho \in \{0,1\}^r$, and outputs a key $k \in \{0,1\}^\ell$. Notice that unlike E_1, which does not take y as input, the algorithm E_2 does take y as input.

$D(\mathsf{pp}, \mathsf{ct}, x) \rightarrow k$: Takes a public parameter pp, a ciphertext ct, a preimage $x \in \{0,1\}^n$, and deterministically outputs a key $k \in \{0,1\}^\ell$.

We require the following properties.

Correctness. For security parameter λ, for any choice of $\mathsf{pp} \in K(1^\lambda)$, any index $i \in [n]$, any preimage $x \in \{0,1\}^n$ and any randomness value ρ, the following holds: letting $y := f(\mathsf{pp}, x)$, and $\mathsf{ct} := E_1(\mathsf{pp}, (i, x_i); \rho)$, we have $E_2(\mathsf{pp}, y, (i, x_i); \rho) = D(\mathsf{pp}, \mathsf{ct}, x)$.

Definition 1 ((k, n)-One-wayness.). *For any PPT adversary $\mathcal{A}$, there exists a negligible function $negl(\cdot)$ such that for all $\lambda \in \mathbb{N}$, we have*

$$\Pr\left[f(\mathsf{pp}, \mathcal{A}(\mathsf{pp}, y)) = y \; : \; S \leftarrow \mathcal{A}(1^\lambda), \mathsf{pp} \rightarrow K(1^\lambda); x \leftarrow S; y = f(\mathsf{pp}, x) \right] \le negl(\lambda).$$

Here, the adversary is constrained to output only a (k, n)-source.

Definition 2 (Security for encryption.). *For any PPT adversary $\mathcal{A}$, there exists a negligible function $negl(\cdot)$ such that for all $\lambda \in \mathbb{N}$, we have*

$$\Pr\left[\mathcal{A}(\mathsf{pp}, x, \mathsf{ct}, k_b) = b \; : \; \begin{array}{c} (x, i) \leftarrow \mathcal{A}(1^\lambda); \mathsf{pp} \leftarrow K(1^\lambda); \\ b \leftarrow \{0,1\}; \rho \leftarrow \{0,1\}^r; k_1 \leftarrow \{0,1\}^\ell \\ \mathsf{ct} \leftarrow E_1(\mathsf{pp}, (i, 1 - x_i); \rho); \\ k_0 \leftarrow E_2(\mathsf{pp}, f(\mathsf{pp}, x), (i, 1 - x_i); \rho); \end{array} \right] \le 1/2 + negl(\lambda).$$

Definition 3 ((k, n)-Smoothness.). *We say that (K, f, E_1, E_2, D) is (k, n)-smooth if for any PPT adversary $\mathcal{A}$, there exists a negligible function $\mathsf{negl}(\cdot)$, such that for all $\lambda \in \mathbb{N}$, we have*

$$\Pr\left[\mathcal{A}(\mathsf{pp}, y) = b \ : \ \begin{array}{l} (S_0, S_1) \leftarrow \mathcal{A}(1^\lambda); \mathsf{pp} \leftarrow K(1^\lambda); \\ b \leftarrow \{0, 1\}; x_0 \leftarrow S_0; x_1 \leftarrow S_1; y = f(\mathsf{pp}, x_b) \end{array}\right] \leq 1/2 + \mathsf{negl}(\lambda).$$

where the distributions S_0 and S_1 output by the adversary $\mathcal{A}$ are constrained to be (k, n)-sources.

2.2 Hinting PRG

Next, we review the definition of Hinting PRG proposed in [33]. Let $n(\cdot)$ and $\ell(\cdot)$ be some polynomials. An (n, ℓ)-hinting PRG scheme consists of two PPT algorithms Setup, Eval with the following syntax.

Setup(1^λ) $\rightarrow$ (pp, n): The setup algorithm takes as input the security parameter λ, and length parameter ℓ, and outputs public parameters pp and input length $n = n(\lambda)$.

Eval(pp, $s \in \{0, 1\}^n, i \in [n] \cup \{0\}$) $\rightarrow y \in \{0, 1\}^\ell$: The evaluation algorithm takes as input the public parameters pp, an n-bit string s, an index $i \in [n] \cup \{0\}$ and outputs an ℓ bit string y.

Definition 4. *An (n, ℓ)-hinting PRG scheme (Setup, Eval) is said to be secure if for any PPT adversary $\mathcal{A}$, there exists a negligible function $\mathsf{negl}(\cdot)$ such that for all $\lambda \in \mathbb{N}$, the following holds:*

$$\Pr\left[\mathcal{A}\left(\mathsf{pp}, y_0^\beta, \{y_{i,b}^\beta\}_{i \in [n], b \in \{0,1\}}\right) = \beta \ : \ \begin{array}{l} (\mathsf{pp}, n) \leftarrow \mathsf{Setup}(1^\lambda); s \leftarrow \{0, 1\}^n; \\ \beta \leftarrow \{0, 1\}; y_0^0 = \mathsf{Eval}(\mathsf{pp}, s, 0); \\ y_0^1 \leftarrow \{0, 1\}^\ell; y_{i, s_i}^0 = \mathsf{Eval}(\mathsf{pp}, s, i); \\ y_{i, \overline{s_i}}^0 \leftarrow \{0, 1\}^\ell \ \forall i \in [n] \\ y_{i, b}^1 \leftarrow \{0, 1\}^\ell \ \forall i \in [n], b \in \{0, 1\}; \end{array}\right] \leq 1/2 + \mathsf{negl}(\lambda)$$

3 Hashing and Randomness Extraction Under Φ-Hiding

In this section, we will prove two useful lemmas about universal hashing and randomness extraction under the Φ-hiding assumption. Here we consider special groups defined w.r.t. an RSA modulus N. These lemmas will be crucial in proving the security of our Φ-hiding based constructions later in Sect. 4.

3.1   A New Hashing Lemma

Consider an RSA modulus $N = pq$ for $\kappa/2$-bit primes p, q, and let $g \in \mathbb{Z}_N^*$ be a random element in the multiplicative group $\mathbb{Z}_N^*$. Consider the following family of hash functions which hash an n-bit string x ($x \in \mathcal{X} = \{0,1\}^n$) to an element in $\mathbb{Z}_N$:

$$\mathcal{K} = \left\{ (a, b, \{e_{i,c}\}_{i \in [n], b \in \{0,1\}}) \in \mathbb{Z}_N^{2n+2} \; : \; a, b \in \mathbb{Z}_N; \forall \, i \in [n], b \in \{0,1\}, \; e_{i,c} \in \mathrm{PRIMES}(\lambda) \right\},$$

$$H \; : \; \mathcal{K} \times \mathcal{X} \to \mathbb{Z}_N, \qquad H\left((a, b, \{e_{i,c}\}_{i,c}), x\right) = g^{(ax+b) \prod_i e_{i,x_i}} \pmod{N}.$$

Here x is intepreted as an integer for arithmetic operations, and x_i denotes the ith bit of x when intepreted as a binary string. Whenever it is clear from context, we will drop the hash key as an explicit input to the function and write either $H(x)$ or $H_K(x)$ instead of $H(K, x)$ for some hash key $K = (a, b, \{e_{i,c}\}_{i,c})$. Also, throughout we assume that n is sufficiently large, i.e. $n > \kappa + 2\lambda$.

Consider any integer T, and let $T = \prod_{i=1}^t r_i^{k_i}$ be its prime factorization i.e., $k_i \geq 1$ and r_i's are the distinct prime factors arranged in an increasing order. For any integer $y \in \mathbb{Z}_T$, we define its chinese remainder theorem (CRT) representation to be the vector $(y^{(1)}, y^{(2)}, \cdots, y^{(t)})$, where for each $i \in [t]$, $y^{(i)} = y \bmod r_i^{k_i}$. Note that each integer $y \in \mathbb{Z}_T$ has distinct CRT representation.

Looking ahead to our HPRG and OWFE constructions based on Φ-hiding assumption, we use the hash function described above. For security, we require that (for a randomly chosen key K and input $x \leftarrow \mathcal{X}$) the output distribution of the hash function $H(K, x)$ to be indistinguishable from a distribution with large enough min-entropy while looking independent of the input x. A natural idea would be to use a variant of Leftover Hash Lemma (LHL) to prove such a statement, but since $e_{i,c}$'s are randomly sampled primes (and not random exponents), thus the distribution of the exponent $(ax + b) \prod_i e_{i,x_i} \bmod \Phi(N)$ is not well understood. Due to this, we could not rely only on LHL to prove pseudorandomness of the desired distribution, but instead, show that hash function satisfies the following weaker property which is sufficient for our applications. The technical difficulty here lies in proving that the hash function satisfies this weaker property and utilizing this to prove the security of our HPRG and OWFE constructions.

Theorem 1. *Let p_i denote the ith prime, i.e. $p_1 = 2, p_2 = 3, \ldots,$ and $\widetilde{e}_i = \lceil \log_{p_i} N \rceil$. And, let f_i denote $p_i^{\widetilde{e}_i}$ for all i.*

Assuming the Φ-hiding assumption holds, for every PPT adversary $\mathcal{A}$, nonnegligible function $\epsilon(\cdot)$, polynomial $v(\cdot)$, for all $\lambda, \kappa \in \mathbb{N}$, satisfying $\kappa \geq 5\lambda$ and $\epsilon = \epsilon(\lambda) > 1/v(\lambda)$, the following holds:

$$\Pr[\mathsf{Expt\text{-}Hashing}_{\mathcal{A},\epsilon}(0) = 1] - \Pr[\mathsf{Expt\text{-}Hashing}_{\mathcal{A},\epsilon}(1) = 1] \leq \epsilon(\lambda)/2,$$

where the experiment Expt-Hashing *is described in Fig. 1.*

Proof. Let the prime factorization of $\phi(N)$ be $\phi(N) = \prod_i r_i^{k_i}$ for $i = 1$ to ℓ_N, where $k_i \geq 1$, ℓ_N denotes number of distinct prime factors of $\phi(N)$, and r_i's are

---

Expt-Hashing$_{\mathcal{A},\epsilon}(\beta)$

The challenger samples RSA modulus $N \leftarrow \mathsf{RSA}(\kappa)$, 2 group elements $a, b \leftarrow \mathbb{Z}_N$ and $2n$ λ-bit primes $e_{i,c} \leftarrow \mathsf{PRIMES}(\lambda)$ for $i \in [n], c \in \{0,1\}$. The challenger sets $K = (a, b, \{e_{i,c}\}_{i,c})$.

The challenger now samples (g, y) depending on bit β in the following way.

— If $\beta = 0$, the challenger samples a generator $g \leftarrow \mathbb{Z}_N^*$ and a bit string $x \leftarrow \mathcal{X}$ and computes $y = H_K(x)^{f_1 \cdot f_2}$.

— If $\beta = 1$, the challenger samples generators $\widetilde{g}, h \leftarrow \mathbb{Z}_N^*$. It then sets j_ϵ to be the smallest index such that $p_{j_\epsilon} > (2\sqrt{2} \log N/\epsilon)^3$ and computes $g = \widetilde{g}^{\prod_{i=3}^{j_\epsilon} f_i}$ and $y = h^{\prod_{i=1}^{j_\epsilon} f_i}$.

The challenger sends (N, g, K, y) to the adversary. The adversary then outputs a bit β', and the output of the experiment is set to be the same bit β'.

Fig. 1. Security experiment for Hashing Lemma

the distinct prime factors arranged in an increasing order. The proof is divided into two parts. First, we argue that $(ax + b) \prod_i e_{i,x_i} \bmod r_j^{k_j}$ is statistically close to random over $\mathbb{Z}_{r_j^{k_j}}$ for all prime factors of $\phi(N)$ greater than p_{j_ϵ}. In the second part of the proof, we show using Φ-hiding that the hash function H could be made lossy on all prime factors of $\phi(N)$ less than or equal to p_{j_ϵ}. Thus, the theorem follows. For proving the first part, we employ a tight Leftover Hash Lemma proof. And for the second part, we rely on Φ-hiding to introduce lossiness.

Notation. Here and throughout, for any n-bit string x, we use $\mathbf{e}_x$ to denote the following product $\prod_{i \in [n]} e_{i,x_i}$.

Part 1. The statistical argument. Here we show that if we look at the congruent CRT representation of the exponent $(ax + b) \cdot \mathbf{e}_x$ corresponding to prime factors greater p_{j_ϵ}, then (for a randomly chosen hash key K and input x) they are at most $\epsilon/3$-statistically far from an integer that is chosen at random with the constraint that its congruent CRT representation corresponding to prime factors less than or equal to p_{j_ϵ} is same as for $(ax + b) \cdot \mathbf{e}_x$. Concretely, we show that following:

Lemma 1. *Let p_i denote the ith prime, i.e. $p_1 = 2, p_2 = 3, \ldots$, and $\widetilde{e}_i = \lceil \log_{p_i} N \rceil$.*

For every (possibly unbounded) adversary $\mathcal{A}$, non-negligible function $\epsilon(\cdot)$, polynomial $v(\cdot)$, for all $\lambda, \kappa \in \mathbb{N}$, satisfying $\kappa \geq 5\lambda$ and $\epsilon = \epsilon(\lambda) > 1/v(\lambda)$, the following holds:

$$\Pr[\mathsf{Expt\text{-}NewLHL}_{\mathcal{A},\epsilon}(0) = 1] - \Pr[\mathsf{Expt\text{-}NewLHL}_{\mathcal{A},\epsilon}(1) = 1] \leq \epsilon(\lambda)/3,$$

where the experiment $\mathsf{Expt\text{-}NewLHL}_{\mathcal{A},\epsilon}$ is described in Fig. 2.

Proof. Due to space constraints, we postpone the proof to full version of the paper.

Expt-NewLHL$_{\mathcal{A},\epsilon}(\beta)$

The challenger samples RSA modulus $N \leftarrow \mathsf{RSA}(\kappa)$, 2 group elements $a, b \leftarrow \mathbb{Z}_N$ and $2n$ λ-bit primes $e_{i,c} \leftarrow \mathsf{PRIMES}(\lambda)$ for $i \in [n], c \in \{0, 1\}$. It then samples a bit string $x \leftarrow \mathcal{X}$, sets $K = (a, b, \{e_{i,c}\}_{i,c})$.

The challenger now computes y depending on challenge bit β in the following way.

- If $\beta = 0$, the challenger sets $y = (ax + b) \cdot \mathbf{e}_x \pmod{\phi(N)}$.
- If $\beta = 1$,
    - Let the prime factorization of $\phi(N)$ be $\phi(N) = \prod r_i^{k_i}$, where $k_i \geq 1$, and r_i's are the distinct prime factors arranged in an increasing order. Let ℓ_N denotes number of distinct prime factors of $\phi(N)$.
    - It then sets $\widetilde{y} = (ax + b) \cdot \mathbf{e}_x \pmod{\phi(N)}$ and computes its CRT representation $\widetilde{y} = (\widetilde{y}^{(1)}, \ldots, \widetilde{y}^{(\ell_N)})$, where $\widetilde{y}^{(i)} = \widetilde{y} \pmod{r_i^{k_i}}$.
    - The challenger then sets j_ϵ to be the smallest index such that $p_{j_\epsilon} > (2\sqrt{2}\log N/\epsilon)^3$. For each for $i \in [\ell_N]$ such that $r_i \leq p_{j_\epsilon}$, the challenger sets $y^{(i)} = \widetilde{y}^{(i)}$. For each $i \in [\ell_N]$ such that $r_i > p_{j_\epsilon}$, it samples $y^{(i)} \leftarrow \mathbb{Z}_{r_i^{k_i}}$.
    - The challenger then computes y which has CRT representation $(y^{(1)}, \ldots, y^{(\ell_N)})$.

The challenger sends (N, K, y) to the adversary. The adversary then outputs a bit $\beta' \in \{0, 1\}$, and the output of the experiment is set to be the same bit β'.

Fig. 2. Security Game for Lemma 1

Part 2. The computational argument. Here we show that, using Φ-hiding, the generator g instead of sampling uniformly at random could be sampled as $g^{\prod_{i=1}^{j_\epsilon} f_i}$, where j_ϵ is the smallest index such that $p_{j_\epsilon} > (2\sqrt{2}\log N/\epsilon)3$. This removes information about the input x completely. Concretely, we show that following:

Lemma 2. *Let p_i denote the ith prime, i.e. $p_1 = 2, p_2 = 3, \ldots$, and $\widetilde{e}_i = \lceil \log_{p_i} N \rceil$ and let f_i denote $p_i^{\widetilde{e}_i}$ for all i. Assuming the Φ-hiding assumption holds, for every PPT adversary $\mathcal{A}$, non-negligible function $\epsilon(\cdot)$, polynomial $v(\cdot)$, for all $\lambda, \kappa \in \mathbb{N}$, satisfying $\kappa \geq 5\lambda$ and $\epsilon = \epsilon(\lambda) > 1/v(\lambda)$, there exists a negligible function $negl(\cdot)$ such that the following holds,*

$$\Pr[\mathsf{Expt\text{-}Comp}_{\mathcal{A},\epsilon}(0) = 1] - \Pr[\mathsf{Expt\text{-}Comp}_{\mathcal{A},\epsilon}(1) = 1] \leq negl(\lambda),$$

where the experiment $\mathsf{Expt\text{-}Comp}_{\mathcal{A},\epsilon}$ is described in Fig. 3.

Proof. Due to space constraints, we postpone the proof to full version of the paper. □

Lastly, by combining Lemmas 1 and 2, we obtain the proof of Theorem 1.

$$\mathsf{Expt\text{-}Comp}_{\mathcal{A},\epsilon}(\beta)$$

The challenger samples RSA modulus $N \leftarrow \mathsf{RSA}(\kappa)$, 2 group elements $a, b \leftarrow \mathbb{Z}_N$ and $2n$ λ-bit primes $e_{i,c} \leftarrow \mathsf{PRIMES}(\lambda)$ for $i \in [n], c \in \{0,1\}$, and sets $K = (a, b, \{e_{i,c}\}_{i,c})$. It then samples a bit string $x \leftarrow \mathcal{X}$.

The challenger then sets j_ϵ to be the smallest index such that $p_{j_\epsilon} > (2\sqrt{2}\log N/\epsilon)^3$.

The challenger now computes (g, h) depending on challenge bit β in the following way.

- If $\beta = 0$,
  - Let the prime factorization of $\phi(N)$ be $\phi(N) = \prod r_i^{k_i}$, where $k_i \geq 1$, and r_i's are the distinct prime factors arranged in an increasing order. Let ℓ_N denotes number of distinct prime factors of $\phi(N)$.
  - It then sets $\widetilde{y} = (ax + b) \cdot \mathbf{e}_x \pmod{\phi(N)}$.
  - For each for $i \in [\ell_N]$ such that $r_i \leq p_{j_\epsilon}$, the challenger sets $y^{(i)} = \widetilde{y} \pmod{r_i^{k_i}}$. For each $i \in [\ell_N]$ such that $r_i > p_{j_\epsilon}$, it samples $y^{(i)} \leftarrow \mathbb{Z}_{r_i^{k_i}}$. The challenger then computes y which has CRT representation $(y^{(1)}, \ldots, y^{(\ell_N)})$.
  - It then samples a generator $g \leftarrow \mathbb{Z}_N^*$ and sets $h = g^{y \cdot f_1 \cdot f_2}$.
- If $\beta = 1$, the challenger samples generators $\tilde{g}, \tilde{h} \leftarrow \mathbb{Z}_N^*$ and sets $g = \tilde{g}^{\prod_{i=3}^{j_\epsilon} f_i}$, $h = \tilde{h}^{\prod_{i=1}^{j_\epsilon} f_i}$.

The challenger sends (N, g, K, h) to the adversary. The adversary then outputs a bit $\beta' \in \{0,1\}$, and the output of the experiment is set to be the same bit β'.

Fig. 3. Security Game for Lemma 2

Strengthening the Hash Lemma. In this section, we briefly provide a slight strengthening of the Theorem 1 where we argue that the indistinguishability holds even if the input $x \in \mathcal{X}$, instead of being sampled uniformly at random, is sampled from any arbitrary distribution with certain min-entropy. Formally, we prove the following.

Theorem 2. *Let p_i denote the ith prime, i.e. $p_1 = 2, p_2 = 3, \ldots$, and $\tilde{e}_i = \lceil \log_{p_i} N \rceil$. And, let f_i denote $p_i^{\tilde{e}_i}$ for all i.*

Assuming the Φ-hiding assumption holds, for every PPT adversary $\mathcal{A}$, nonnegligible function $\epsilon(\cdot)$, polynomial $v(\cdot)$, for all $\lambda, \kappa \in \mathbb{N}$, satisfying $\kappa \geq 5\lambda$ and $\epsilon = \epsilon(\lambda) > 1/v(\lambda)$, and every (m, n)-source $\mathcal{S}$ over $\mathcal{X}$ such that $n - m = O(\log \lambda)$, the following holds,

$$\Pr[\mathsf{Expt\text{-}Hashing\text{-}Smooth}_{\mathcal{A},\mathcal{S},\epsilon}(0) = 1] - \Pr[\mathsf{Expt\text{-}Hashing\text{-}Smooth}_{\mathcal{A},\mathcal{S},\epsilon}(1) = 1] \leq \epsilon(\lambda)/2,$$

where the experiment $\mathsf{Expt\text{-}Hashing\text{-}Smooth}$ is described in Fig. 4.

Proof. Due to space constraints, we postpone the proof to full version of the paper.

$$\text{Expt-Hashing-Smooth}_{\mathcal{A},\mathcal{S},\epsilon}(\beta)$$

The challenger samples RSA modulus $N \leftarrow \mathsf{RSA}(\kappa)$, 2 group elements $a, b \leftarrow \mathbb{Z}_N$ and $2n$ λ-bit primes $e_{i,c} \leftarrow \mathsf{PRIMES}(\lambda)$ for $i \in [n], c \in \{0, 1\}$. The challenger sets $K = (a, b, \{e_{i,c}\}_{i,c})$.

The challenger now samples (g, y) depending on bit β in the following way.

— If $\beta = 0$, the challenger samples a generator $g \leftarrow \mathbb{Z}_N^*$ and a bit string $x \leftarrow \mathcal{S}$ and computes $y = H_K(x)^{f_1 \cdot f_2}$.

— If $\beta = 1$, the challenger samples generators $\widetilde{g}, h \leftarrow \mathbb{Z}_N^*$. It then sets j_ϵ to be the smallest index such that $p_{j_\epsilon} > (2^{n-m+2} \log N/\epsilon)^3$ and computes $g = \widetilde{g}^{\prod_{i=3}^{j_\epsilon} f_i}$ and $y = h^{\prod_{i=1}^{j_\epsilon} f_i}$.

The challenger sends (N, g, K, y) to the adversary. The adversary then outputs a bit β', and the output of the experiment is set to be the same bit β'.

Fig. 4. Security experiment for Smooth Hashing Lemma (Theorem 2)

3.2 Φ-Hiding Based Extractor Lemma

In this section, we prove a useful lemma that will aid in proving the security of our Φ-hiding based constructions later. This has appeared (and implicitly used) in most existing Φ-hiding based works. Here we abstract it out for ease of exposition.

Let $\mathsf{Ext} : \mathbb{Z}_N \times \mathcal{S} \to \mathcal{Y}$ be a $(\lambda - 1, \epsilon)$ strong extractor, where ϵ is negligible in the parameter λ. Informally, the lemmas states that, for every λ-bit prime e, applying extractor on an eth root of a generator $g \in \mathbb{Z}_N^*$ is indistinguishable from random. Formally, we claim the following:

Lemma 3. *Assuming the Φ-hiding assumption holds, then for every admissible stateful PPT adversary $\mathcal{A}$, there exists a negligible function $negl(\cdot)$ such that for all $\lambda, \kappa \in \mathbb{N}$, such that $\kappa \geq 5\lambda$, the following hold,*

$$\Pr\left[\mathcal{A}(y_b) = b \ : \ \begin{array}{c} N \leftarrow \mathsf{RSA}(\kappa); \ \mathfrak{s} \leftarrow \mathbb{S} \\ e \leftarrow \mathsf{PRIMES}(\lambda); \ g \leftarrow \mathbb{Z}_N^* \\ F \leftarrow \mathcal{A}(N, \mathfrak{s}, e, g); \ b \leftarrow \{0, 1\} \\ y_0 = \mathsf{Ext}(g^{F/e}, \mathfrak{s}); \ y_1 \leftarrow \mathcal{Y} \end{array}\right] \leq negl(\lambda),$$

where $\mathcal{A}$ is an admissible adversary as long as $e \nmid F$.

Proof. Due to space constraints, we postpone the proof to full version of the paper.

4 One-Way Function with Encryption from Φ-Hiding Assumption

In this section, we construct (k, n, ℓ)-recyclable One-Way Function with Encryption (OWFE) from Phi-Hiding assumption. The construction assumes $k \geq 7\lambda$

and $n - k \leq \alpha \log n$ for any fixed constant α. For any parameters λ, ℓ, let $\mathsf{Ext}_{\lambda, \ell} : \{0,1\}^\lambda \times \mathcal{S} \rightarrow \{0,1\}^\ell$ be a $(\lambda - 1, \epsilon_{\mathsf{Ext}})$ strong seeded extractor, where ϵ_{Ext} is negligible in λ.[5] Let p_i denote the ith (smallest) prime, i.e. $p_1 = 2, p_2 = 3, \ldots$, and $\widetilde{e}_i = \lceil \log_{p_i} N \rceil$ for all i. And, let f_i denote $p_i^{\widetilde{e}_i}$ for all i. The construction proceeds as follows.

$K(1^\lambda)$: On input security parameter λ and length ℓ, set RSA modulus length $\kappa = 5\lambda$, and sample RSA modulus $N \leftarrow \mathsf{RSA}(\kappa)$. Next, sample a generator $g \leftarrow \mathbb{Z}_N^*$, $2n$ (λ-bit) primes $e_{i,b} \leftarrow \mathsf{PRIMES}(\lambda)$ for $(i,b) \in [n] \times \{0,1\}$ and elements $d_0, d_1 \leftarrow \mathbb{Z}_N$. Then, sample a seed $\mathfrak{s} \leftarrow \mathcal{S}$ of extractor $\mathsf{Ext}_{\lambda, \ell}$ and output public parameters $\mathsf{pp} = (N, \mathfrak{s}, g, \{e_{i,b}\}_{i,b}, d_0, d_1)$.
   $f(\mathsf{pp}, x)$: Let $\mathsf{pp} = (N, \mathfrak{s}, g, \{e_{i,b}\}_{i,b}, d_0, d_1)$. Output $y = g^{f_1 \cdot f_2 \cdot (d_0 x + d_1)} \prod_i e_{i,x_i} \bmod N$.
   $E_1(\mathsf{pp}, (i,b); \rho)$: Parse pp as $\mathsf{pp} = (N, \mathfrak{s}, g, \{e_{i,b}\}_{i,b}, d_0, d_1)$. Output ciphertext $\mathsf{ct} = (g^{\rho \cdot e_{i,b}} \bmod N, i, b)$.
   $E_2(\mathsf{pp}, (y, i, b); \rho)$: Let pp be $\mathsf{pp} = (N, \mathfrak{s}, g, \{e_{i,b}\}_{i,b}, d_0, d_1)$. Compute $h = y^\rho \bmod N$ and output $z = \mathsf{Ext}(h, \mathfrak{s})$.
   $D(\mathsf{pp}, \mathsf{ct}, x)$: Let $\mathsf{pp} = (N, \mathfrak{s}, g, \{e_{i,b}\}_{i,b}, d_0, d_1)$. Parse ct as (t, i, b). If $b = x_i$, compute $h = t^{f_1 \cdot f_2 \cdot (d_0 x + d_1)} \prod_{j \neq i} e_{j,x_j} \bmod N$ and output $\mathsf{Ext}(h, \mathfrak{s})$. Otherwise, output $\perp$.

Correctness. For any public parameters $\mathsf{pp} = (N, \mathfrak{s}, g, \{e_{i,b}\}_{i,b}, d_0, d_1)$, any string $x \in \{0,1\}^n$, any index $i \in [n]$, any randomness ρ, we have $D(\mathsf{pp}, E_1(\mathsf{pp}, (i, x_i); \rho), x) = g^{\rho f_1 \cdot f_2 \cdot (d_0 x + d_1)} \prod_j e_{j,x_j} = f(\mathsf{pp}, x)^\rho = E_2(\mathsf{pp}, (f(\mathsf{pp}, x), i, x_i); \rho)$.

4.1   Security

We now prove the one-wayness, encryption security and smoothness properties of the above scheme.

One-Wayness. We now prove that the above construction satisifes (k, n)-one-wayness property when $k \geq 7\lambda$ and $n - k \leq \alpha \log n$ for any fixed constant α.

Theorem 3. *Assuming the Φ-hiding assumption holds, the above construction satisfies (k, n, ℓ)-one-wayness property as per Definition 1.*

Proof. We first prove that no PPT adversary can win the following game with non-negligible advantage assuming the Φ-hiding assumption. We then prove how a PPT adversary breaking one-wayness property of the above scheme can be used to break the following game.

Game G: The challenger chooses RSA modulus $\kappa = 5\lambda$, samples $N \leftarrow \mathsf{RSA}(\kappa)$, prime $e \leftarrow \mathsf{PRIMES}(\lambda)$ and a value $z \leftarrow \mathbb{Z}_N^*$. The challenger sends (N, e, z) to the adversary, which then outputs w. The adversary wins if $w^e = z \bmod N$.

---

[5] Note that such an extractor exists for $\ell = c \cdot \lambda$ for some constant $c < 1$. The construction can be extended for any $\ell \geq \lambda$ with the help of PRGs.

We now argue that no PPT adversary can win the above game with non-negligible probability.

Lemma 4. *Assuming the Φ-hiding assumption holds, for every PPT adversary $\mathcal{A}$, there exists a negligible function $negl(\cdot)$ such that for every $\lambda \in \mathbb{N}$, the probability that $\mathcal{A}$ wins in Game G is at most $negl(\lambda)$.*

Proof. We prove the lemma using the following intermediate Game H.

Game H: The challenger chooses RSA modulus $\kappa = 5\lambda$, samples prime $e \leftarrow$ PRIMES(λ) and $N \leftarrow$ RSA(κ) s.t. $e|\phi(N)$. It then samples an element $z \leftarrow \mathbb{Z}_N^*$. The challenger sends (N, e, z) to the adversary, which then outputs w. The adversary wins if $w^e = z \bmod N$.

Let the advantage of any adversary $\mathcal{A}$ in Game G be $\mathsf{Adv}_G^{\mathcal{A}}$ and in Game H be $\mathsf{Adv}_H^{\mathcal{A}}$.

Claim 1. *For every adversary $\mathcal{A}$, there exists a negligible function $negl(\cdot)$ such that for every $\lambda \in \mathbb{N}$, $\mathsf{Adv}_H^{\mathcal{A}} \leq negl(\lambda)$.*

Proof. As $e|\phi(N)$, only a negligible fraction of $z \in \mathbb{Z}_N^*$ have a w s.t. $w^e = z \bmod N$. Therefore, no PPT adversary can find a w s.t. $w^e = z \bmod N$ with non-negligible probability.

Claim 2. *Assuming the Φ-hiding assumption holds, for every PPT adversary $\mathcal{A}$, there exists a negligible function $negl(\cdot)$ such that for every $\lambda \in \mathbb{N}$, $|\mathsf{Adv}_G^{\mathcal{A}} - \mathsf{Adv}_H^{\mathcal{A}}| \leq negl(\lambda)$.*

Proof. Suppose there exists a PPT adversary $\mathcal{A}$ such that $|\mathsf{Adv}_G^{\mathcal{A}} - \mathsf{Adv}_H^{\mathcal{A}}|$ is non-negligible. We construct a reduction algorithm that breaks Φ-hiding assumption. $\mathcal{B}$ samples $e \leftarrow$ PRIMES(λ) and plays Φ-hiding game for e. The challenger sends RSA modulus N to $\mathcal{B}$, which samples $z \leftarrow \mathbb{Z}_N^*$ and sends (N, e, z) to $\mathcal{A}$. If $\mathcal{A}$ outputs w s.t. $w^e = z \bmod N$, then $\mathcal{B}$ guesses that $\phi(N)$ is uniformly sampled from RSA(κ). Otherwise, it guesses that $e|\phi(N)$.

By the above 2 claims and triangle inequality, no PPT adversary can win Game G with non-negligible advantage.

Lemma 5. *Assuming the Φ-hiding assumption holds, for every PPT adversary $\mathcal{A}$, there exists a negligible function $negl(\cdot)$ such that for every $\lambda \in \mathbb{N}$, the advantage of $\mathcal{A}$ in (k, n)-one-wayness game is at most $negl(\lambda)$.*

Proof. Suppose there exist a PPT adversary $\mathcal{A}$ that breaks (k, n)-one-wayness property of the encryption scheme with non-negligible probability ϵ. We construct a reduction algorithm $\mathcal{B}$ that wins against Game G challenger $\mathcal{C}$.

The adversary first sends a (k, n) source S to $\mathcal{B}$. The challenger $\mathcal{C}$ then sends (N, e, z) to $\mathcal{B}$. The reduction algorithm samples a bit string $x \leftarrow S$, an index $j \leftarrow [n]$, extractor seed $\mathfrak{s} \leftarrow S$, exponents $d_0, d_1 \leftarrow \mathbb{Z}_p$ primes $e_{i,b'} \leftarrow$ PRIMES(λ) for $(i, b') \neq (j, 1 - x_j)$. It then sets generator $g = z$ and prime $e_{j,1-x_j} = e$.

$\mathcal{B}$ then sends public parameters $\mathsf{pp} = (N, \mathfrak{s}, g, \{e_{i,b'}\}_{i,b'}, d_0, d_1)$ and challenge $y = z^{\prod_i e_{i,x_i}} \bmod N$ to the adversary. The adversary outputs x'. If $f(\mathsf{pp}, x') \neq f(\mathsf{pp}, x)$ or $x_j = x'_j$, then $\mathcal{B}$ aborts. Otherwise, we have $h^e = z^F \bmod N$, where $F = f_1 \cdot f_2 \cdot (d_0 x + d_1) \prod_i e_{i,x_i}$ and $h = z^{f_1 \cdot f_2 \cdot (d_0 x' + d_1) \prod_{i \neq j} e_{i,x'_i}} \bmod N$. As e is a randomly sampled λ-bit prime, $e \nmid F$ with overwhelming probability. $\mathcal{B}$ computes $z^{1/e} \bmod N$ using Shamir's trick [39]. Concretely, $\mathcal{B}$ first computes integers a, b s.t. $a \cdot e + b \cdot F = 1$ and outputs $w = h^b \cdot z^a \bmod N$.

We now analyze the advantage of $\mathcal{B}$ in Game G. By our assumption, $f(\mathsf{pp}, x') = f(\mathsf{pp}, x)$ with non-negligible probability ϵ. We prove that $x' \neq x$ with non-negligible probability. As $k \geq \kappa + 2\lambda$, we know that for any pp, $\Pr_{x \leftarrow S}[\exists t \in \{0,1\}^n \text{ s.t. } x \neq t \wedge f(\mathsf{pp}, x) = f(\mathsf{pp}, t)] \geq 1 - \mathsf{negl}(\lambda)$. Therefore, $\Pr[x' \neq x \wedge f(\mathsf{pp}, x) = f(\mathsf{pp}, x')] \geq \epsilon/2 - \mathsf{negl}(\lambda)$ and $\Pr[x'_j \neq x_j \wedge f(\mathsf{pp}, x) = f(\mathsf{pp}, x')] \geq \epsilon/2n - \mathsf{negl}(\lambda)$ as j is sampled uniformly from $[n]$. Note that if $\mathcal{B}$ does not abort, it outputs w s.t. $w^e = z \bmod N$ with overwhelming probability. Therefore, $\mathcal{B}$ breaks Game G security with non-negligible probability $\epsilon/2n - \mathsf{negl}(\lambda)$.

Security of Encryption. We now prove that the above construction satisifes encryption security property.

Theorem 4. *Assuming the Φ-hiding assumption holds, the above construction satisfies encryption security property as per Definition 2.*

Proof. We prove the above theorem via a sequence of following hybrids.

Hybrid H_0: This is same as original OWFE security of encryption game when the challenger chooses $\beta = 0$.
1. The adversary sends bit string $x \leftarrow \{0,1\}^n$ and index $j \in [n]$ to the challenger.
2. The challenger sets modulus length $\kappa = 5\lambda$ and samples $N \leftarrow \mathsf{RSA}(\kappa)$, generator $g \leftarrow \mathbb{Z}_N^*$, extractor seed $\mathfrak{s} \leftarrow \mathcal{S}$ and primes $e_{i,b} \leftarrow \mathsf{PRIMES}(\lambda)$ for $(i, b) \in [n] \times \{0, 1\}$.
3. The challenger samples $\rho \leftarrow \mathbb{Z}_N$, computes $\mathsf{ct} = g^{\rho \cdot e_{j,1-x_j}}$, $z = \mathsf{Ext}(g^{\rho f_1 \cdot f_2 \cdot (d_0 x + d_1) \cdot \prod_i e_{i,x_i}} \bmod N, \mathfrak{s})$.
4. The challenger sends $\mathsf{pp} = (N, \mathfrak{s}, g, \{e_{i,b}\}_{i,b}), \mathsf{ct}, z$ to the adversary $\mathcal{A}$, which outputs a bit α.
Hybrid H_1: This hybrid is similar to previous hybrid except for the following changes.
3. The challenger samples $\tilde{g} \leftarrow \mathbb{Z}_N^*$, computes $\mathsf{ct} = \tilde{g}$,
$$z = \mathsf{Ext}(\tilde{g}^{f_1 \cdot f_2 \cdot (d_0 x + d_1) \prod_i e_{i,x_i} \cdot e_{j,1-x_j}^{-1}} \bmod N, \mathfrak{s}).$$
Hybrid H_2: This hybrid is same as previous game except that the challenger samples z uniformly at random.
3. The challenger samples $\tilde{g} \leftarrow \mathbb{Z}_N^*$, computes $\mathsf{ct} = \tilde{g}, z \leftarrow \{0,1\}^\ell$.
Hybrid H_3: This is same as original OWFE security of encryption game when the challenger chooses $\beta = 1$.
3. The challenger samples $\rho \leftarrow \mathbb{Z}_N$, computes $\mathsf{ct} = g^{\rho \cdot e_{j,1-x_j}}, z \leftarrow \{0,1\}^\ell$.

For any PPT adversary $\mathcal{A}$, let the probability that $\mathcal{A}$ outputs 1 in Hybrid H_s be $p_s^{\mathcal{A}}$. We prove that Hybrids H_0 and H_3 are computationally indstinguishable via the sequence of following lemmas.

Lemma 6. *For any adversary $\mathcal{A}$, there exists a negligible function $negl(\cdot)$ such that for every security parameter $\lambda \in \mathbb{N}$, we have $|p_0^{\mathcal{A}} - p_1^{\mathcal{A}}| \leq negl(\lambda)$.*

Proof. We first observe that for any N, prime $e \nmid \phi(N)$ and generator $g \in \mathbb{Z}_N^*$, the distribution of $g^{\rho \cdot e} \bmod N$ for a randomly sampled $\rho \leftarrow \mathbb{Z}_{\phi(N)}$ is identical to the distribution $\tilde{g} \leftarrow \mathbb{Z}_N^*$. This follows from the fact that g and g^e are generators of $\mathbb{Z}_N^*$. For a randomly sampled λ bit prime e, we know that $e \nmid \phi(N)$ with overwhelming probability. Similarly, for a randomly sampled $\rho \leftarrow \mathbb{Z}_N$, we know that $\rho \in \mathbb{Z}_{\phi(N)}$ with overwhelming probability. As a result, $\{\tilde{g} : \tilde{g} \leftarrow \mathbb{Z}_N^*\}$ is statistically indistinguishable from $\{g^{\rho \cdot e} : g \leftarrow \mathbb{Z}_N^*, \rho \leftarrow \mathbb{Z}_N, e \leftarrow \text{PRIMES}(\lambda)\}$. By a similar argument, for any F, the distribution $\{(g^{\rho \cdot e} \bmod N, g^{\rho \cdot F} \bmod N) : g \leftarrow \mathbb{Z}_N^*, \rho \leftarrow \mathbb{Z}_N, e \leftarrow \text{PRIMES}(\lambda)\}$ is statistically indistinguishable from the distribution $\{(\tilde{g}, \tilde{g}^{F \cdot e^{-1}} \bmod N) : \tilde{g} \leftarrow \mathbb{Z}_N^*, e \leftarrow \text{PRIMES}(\lambda)\}$. Therefore, for every adversary $\mathcal{A}$, $|p_0^{\mathcal{A}} - p_1^{\mathcal{A}}| \leq negl(\lambda)$.

Lemma 7. *Assuming the Φ-hiding assumption holds, for any PPT adversary $\mathcal{A}$, there exists a negligible function $negl(\cdot)$ such that for every security parameter $\lambda \in \mathbb{N}$, we have $|p_1^{\mathcal{A}} - p_2^{\mathcal{A}}| \leq negl(\lambda)$.*

Proof. The above lemma follows from ϕ-based Extractor lemma (Lemma 3). Suppose there exists a PPT adversary $\mathcal{A}$ such that $|p_1^{\mathcal{A}} - p_2^{\mathcal{A}}|$ is non-negligible. We construct a reduction algorithm $\mathcal{B}$ that violates ϕ-based extractor lemma.

The extractor lemma challenger first samples $N \leftarrow \text{RSA}(\kappa)$, $\mathfrak{s} \leftarrow \mathcal{S}$, $e \leftarrow \text{PRIMES}(\lambda)$, $\tilde{g} \leftarrow \mathbb{Z}_N^*$ and sends $(N, \mathfrak{s}, e, \tilde{g})$ to reduction algorithm $\mathcal{B}$. The adversary $\mathcal{A}$ then sends a string $x \in \{0,1\}^n$ and index $j \in [n]$ to $\mathcal{B}$. $\mathcal{B}$ samples generator g, values $d_0, d_1 \leftarrow \mathbb{Z}_N$, and primes $e_{i,b} \leftarrow \text{PRIMES}(\lambda)$ for $(i,b) \neq (j, 1 - x_j)$. $\mathcal{B}$ then sets $e_{j,1-x_j} = e$ and computes $F = f_1 \cdot f_2 \cdot (d_0 x + d_1) \prod_i e_{i,x_i}$. If $e|F$, the reduction algorithm aborts and guesses randomly. As e is a λ-bit prime, this happens with negligible probability. If $e \nmid F$, then $\mathcal{B}$ sends F to the challenger, which samples a bit $\gamma \leftarrow \{0,1\}$. If $\gamma = 0$, $\mathcal{C}$ computes $\tilde{z} \leftarrow \text{Ext}(\tilde{g}^{F/e}, \mathfrak{s})$. If $\gamma = 1$, $\mathcal{C}$ samples $\tilde{z} \leftarrow \{0,1\}^\ell$. The challenger sends $\tilde{z}$ to $\mathcal{B}$. The reduction algorithm sets $\text{ct} = \tilde{g}, z = \tilde{z}$ and sends $\text{pp} = (N, \mathfrak{s}, g, \{e_{i,b}\}_{i,b}, d_0, d_1), \text{ct}, z$ to $\mathcal{A}$. The adversary outputs a bit α. $\mathcal{B}$ outputs α as its guess in extractor lemma game.

Note that if $\gamma = 0$, then the distribution of pp, ct, z sent by $\mathcal{B}$ is statistically indistinguishable from that of Hybrid H_1 challenger. If $\gamma = 1$, then the distribution of pp, ct, z sent by $\mathcal{B}$ is statistically indistinguishable from that of H_2 challenger. Consequently if $\mathcal{B}$ does not abort, the advantage $|\Pr[\alpha = 1|\gamma - 0] - \Pr[\alpha = 1|\gamma = 1]| \geq |p_1^{\mathcal{A}} - p_2^{\mathcal{A}}| - negl(\lambda)$ is non-negligible. As $\mathcal{B}$ aborts with only negligible probability, it wins the extractor lemma game with non-negligible probability.

Lemma 8. *For any PPT adversary $\mathcal{A}$, there exists a negligible function $negl(\cdot)$ such that for every security parameter $\lambda \in \mathbb{N}$, we have $|p_2^{\mathcal{A}} - p_3^{\mathcal{A}}| \leq negl(\lambda)$.*

Proof. The distribution $\{\tilde{g} : \tilde{g} \leftarrow \mathbb{Z}_N^*\}$ is statistically indistinguishable from $\{g^{\rho \cdot e} : g \leftarrow \mathbb{Z}_N^*, \rho \leftarrow \mathbb{Z}_N, e \leftarrow \mathrm{PRIMES}(\lambda)\}$ as mentioned in proof of Claim 6.

By the above lemmas and triangle theorem, no PPT adversary can distinguish between Hybrids H_0 and H_3 with non-negligible probability assuming the Φ-hiding assumption.

Smoothness. We now prove that the above construction satisifes (k, n)-smoothness property when $k \geq 7\lambda$ and $n - k \leq \alpha \log n$ for any fixed constant α.

Theorem 5. *Assuming the Φ-hiding assumption holds, the above construction satisfies (k, n)-smoothness security property as per Definition 3.*

Proof. First, we introduce a useful notation. For any constant $\epsilon > 0$, let j_ϵ be the smallest index such that $p_{j_\epsilon} > (2^{n-k+2} \log N/\epsilon)^3$. Note that $(2^{n-k+2} \log N/\epsilon)^3$ is polynomial in λ for the given setting of parameters. The proof of security follows via a sequence of hybrids. Below we first describe the sequence of hybrids and later argue indistinguishability to complete the proof. At a very high level, the proof structure is somewhat similar to that used in [40], where for proving security one first assumes (for the sake of contradiction) that the adversary wins with some non-negligible probability δ and then depending upon δ, one could describe a sequence of hybrids such that no PPT adversary can win with probability more than $2\delta/3$. This acts as a contradiction, thereby completing the proof.

For any PPT adversary $\mathcal{A}$, let $p_s^{\mathcal{A}}$ be the probability that $\mathcal{A}$ outputs 1 in Hybrid H_s. For the sake of contradiction, we assume that $\mathcal{A}$ breaks (k, n)-smoothness property with non-negligible advantage $\delta(\lambda)$ i.e., there exists a polynomial $v(\cdot)$ s.t. $|p_0^{\mathcal{A}} - p_2^{\mathcal{A}}| = \delta(\lambda) > \frac{1}{v(\lambda)}$ for infinitely often $\lambda \in \mathbb{N}$. Let $\epsilon = \frac{1}{2v(\lambda)}$. We provide a non-uniform reduction where the description of hybrids and the reduction algorithm depends on ϵ.

Hybrid H_0: This is same as the original smoothness security game, except that the challenger always chooses source S_0.
1. The adversary first sends two (k, n) sources S_0, S_1 to the challenger. The challenger sets modulus length $\kappa = 5\lambda$ and samples $N \leftarrow \mathrm{RSA}(\kappa)$, extractor seed $\mathfrak{s} \leftarrow \mathcal{S}$, elements $d_0, d_1 \leftarrow \mathbb{Z}_N$ and primes $e_{i,b} \leftarrow \mathrm{PRIMES}(\lambda)$ for $(i, b) \in [n] \times \{0, 1\}$.
2. The challenger then samples a generator $g \leftarrow \mathbb{Z}_N^*$ and sets public parameters $\mathsf{pp} = (N, \mathfrak{s}, g, \{e_{i,b}\}_{i,b}, d_0, d_1)$.
3. The challenger samples $x \leftarrow S_0$ and sends $\mathsf{pp}, y = g^{f_1 \cdot f_2 \cdot (d_0 x + d_1) \prod_{i=1}^{n} e_{i,x_i}} \bmod N$ to the adversary.
4. The adversary outputs a bit b'.

Hybrid H_1: In this hybrid, the challenger does not sample x and picks the challenge y from a uniform distribution.
2. The challenger then samples a generator $\tilde{g} \leftarrow \mathbb{Z}_N^*$, sets $g = \tilde{g}^{\prod_{i=3}^{j_\epsilon} f_i}$ and sets public parameters $\mathsf{pp} = (N, \mathfrak{s}, g, \{e_{i,b}\}_{i,b}, d_0, d_1)$.

3. The challenger samples $z \leftarrow \mathbb{Z}_N^*$ and sends $\mathsf{pp}, y = z^{\prod_{i=1}^{j_\epsilon} f_i} \bmod N$ to the adversary.

Hybrid H_2: This is same as the original smoothness security game, except that the challenger always chooses source S_1.

2. The challenger then samples a generator $g \leftarrow \mathbb{Z}_N^*$ and sets public parameters $\mathsf{pp} = (N, \mathfrak{s}, g, \{e_{i,b}\}_{i,b}, d_0, d_1)$.

3. The challenger samples $x \leftarrow S_1$ and sends $\mathsf{pp}, y = g^{f_1 \cdot f_2 \cdot (d_0 x + d_1)} \prod_{i=1}^n e_{i,x_i} \bmod N$ to the adversary.

Lemma 9. *Assuming the Φ-hiding assumption holds, for any PPT adversary $\mathcal{A}$, there exists a negligible function $negl(\cdot)$ such that for all $\lambda \in \mathbb{N}$ satisfying $\delta(\lambda) \geq 2\epsilon = 1/v(\lambda)$, we have $|p_0^{\mathcal{A}} - p_1^{\mathcal{A}}| \leq \epsilon/2 + negl(\lambda)$.*

Proof. Suppose there exists a PPT adversary $\mathcal{A}$ that has a non-negligible advantage $\delta(\lambda)$ in smoothness game, and can distinguish between Hybrids H_0 and H_1 with probability $\epsilon/2 + \gamma$ for some non-negligible value γ. We construct a reduction algorithm $\mathcal{B}$ that breaks our strengthened hashing lemma (Theorem 2) and thereby breaking Φ-hiding assumption.

The adversary $\mathcal{A}$ sends two (k, n)-sources S_0, S_1 to the reduction algoritm $\mathcal{B}$. $\mathcal{B}$ plays hashing lemma game for source S_0 with the challenger $\mathcal{C}$. The hashing lemma challenger $\mathcal{C}$ sends $(N, g, a, b, \{e_{i,b}\}_{i,b}, y)$ to the reduction algorithm $\mathcal{B}$. The reduction algorithm samples a seed $\mathfrak{s} \leftarrow S$, sets $d_0 = a, d_1 = b$ and sends public parameters $\mathsf{pp} = (N, \mathfrak{s}, g, \{e_{i,b}\}_{i,b}, d_0, d_1)$, challenge y to the adverary $\mathcal{A}$. The adversary outputs a bit b'. $\mathcal{B}$ outputs b' as its guess in hashing lemma game.

Let us analyze advantage of $\mathcal{B}$ in hashing lemma game. If the challenger samples $g \leftarrow \mathbb{Z}_N^*, x \leftarrow S_0, y = g^{f_1 \cdot f_2 \cdot (ax+b)} \prod_{i=1}^n e_{i,x_i} \bmod N$, then $\mathcal{B}$ emulates Hybrid H_0 challenger to $\mathcal{A}$. If the challenger samples $\tilde{g} \leftarrow \mathbb{Z}_N^*, z \leftarrow \mathbb{Z}_N^*$ and sets $g = \tilde{g}^{\prod_{i=3}^{j_\epsilon} f_i}, y = z^{\prod_{i=1}^{j_\epsilon} f_i}$, then $\mathcal{B}$ emulates Hybrid H_1 challenger to $\mathcal{A}$. Therefore, $\mathcal{B}$ breaks hashing lemma game with advantage $|p_1^{\mathcal{A}} - p_2^{\mathcal{A}}| \geq \epsilon/2 + \gamma$.

Lemma 10. *Assuming the Φ-hiding assumption holds, for any PPT adversary $\mathcal{A}$, there exists a negligible function $negl(\cdot)$ such that for all $\lambda \in \mathbb{N}$ satisfying $\delta(\lambda) \geq 2\epsilon = 1/v(\lambda)$, we have $|p_1^{\mathcal{A}} - p_2^{\mathcal{A}}| \leq \epsilon/2 + negl(\lambda)$.*

Proof. This proof is similar to the proof of Lemma 9.

By the above 2 lemmas and triangle inequality, $\mathcal{A}$ can distinguish between Hybrids H_0 and H_2 with probability at most $\epsilon + negl(\lambda) < 2\delta/3$. This contradicts the assumption that $\mathcal{A}$ has an advantage of δ.[6] Therefore, no PPT adversary can break (k, n)-smoothness property of the above construction with non-negligible probability.

---

[6] Note that the contradiction does not happen when δ is negligible. If δ is negligible, then j_ϵ is superpolynomial and the reduction algorithm takes superpolynomial time to execute.

5   One-Way Function with Encryption from q-DBDHI Assumption

We now construct (k, n, ℓ)-OWFE from any n-DBDHI hard group generator GGen. Suppose $\mathsf{GGen}(1^\lambda)$ generates a group of size $\theta(2^m)$, the below construction requires $k \geq m + 2\lambda$ and $n \leq k + m - 2\lambda$. For the sake of simplicity, we construct a OWFE scheme where the encryption algorithm outputs elements in a group. The construction can be extended to output ℓ-length bit strings by using PRGs and randomness extractors. We present a variant of this construction with longer ciphertext from n-DDHI assumption (without pairings) in the full version of the paper.

$K(1^\lambda)$: Sample a group $\mathcal{G} = (\mathbb{G}_1, \mathbb{G}_T, e, p) \leftarrow \mathsf{GGen}(1^\lambda)$. Sample a generator $g \leftarrow \mathbb{G}_1$ and random values $\alpha, d_0, d_1 \leftarrow \mathbb{Z}_p$. Output the public parameters $(\mathcal{G}, g, g^\alpha, g^{\alpha^2}, \cdots, g^{\alpha^n}, d_0, d_1)$.

$f(\mathsf{pp}, x)$: Parse public parameters pp as $\mathsf{pp} = (\mathcal{G}, g, g^\alpha, g^{\alpha^2}, \cdots, g^{\alpha^n}, d_0, d_1)$. Let the polynomial $(d_0 x + d_1) \cdot \prod_{j=1}^n (\alpha + 2j + x_j) = \sum_{i=0}^n c_i \alpha^i$, where c_i is a function of d_0, d_1, x. Output $\prod_{i=0}^n \left(g^{\alpha^i} \right)^{c_i}$.

$E_1(\mathsf{pp}, (i, b); h)$: Compute and output $(h^{(\alpha + 2i + b)}, i)$.

$E_2(\mathsf{pp}, (y, i, b); h)$: Compute and output $e(h, y)$.

$D(\mathsf{pp}, \mathsf{ct}, x)$: Let $\mathsf{ct} = (\mathsf{ct}', i)$. Consider the polynomial $(d_0 x + d_1) \cdot \prod_{j \neq i} (\alpha + 2j + x_j) = \sum_{j=0}^{n-1} c_j \alpha^j$, where c_j is a function of d_0, d_1, x. Compute and output $e \left(\mathsf{ct}', \prod_{j=0}^{n-1} \left(g^{\alpha^j} \right)^{c_j} \right)$.

Correctness. For any set of public parameters $\mathsf{pp} = (\mathcal{G}, g, g^\alpha, g^{\alpha^2}, \cdots, g^{\alpha^n}, d_0, d_1)$, string $x \in \{0, 1\}^n$, index $j \in [n]$ and randomness h, we have $\mathsf{ct} = E_1(\mathsf{pp}, (j, x_j); h) = (h^{(\alpha + 2j + x_j)}, j)$ and $D(\mathsf{pp}, \mathsf{ct}, x) = e(g, h)^{(d_0 x + d_1) \prod_i (\alpha + 2i + x_i)} = e(h, f(\mathsf{pp}, x)) = E_2(\mathsf{pp}, (f(\mathsf{pp}, x), j, x_j); h)$.

5.1   Security

We now prove that the above construction satisfies one-wayness, encryption security, and smoothness properties.

One-Wayness. We now prove that the above construction satisfies (k, n)-one-wayness property for any $k \geq m + 2\lambda$ and $n \leq k + m - 2\lambda$.

Lemma 11. *Assuming n-DBDHI assumption holds, the above construction satisfies (k, n)-one-wayness property for any (k, n) s.t. $k \geq m + 2\lambda$ and $n \leq k + m - 2\lambda$ as per Definition 1.*

Proof. Suppose there exists a PPT adversary $\mathcal{A}$ that breaks one-wayness property of the above construction with non-negligible probability. We construct a reduction algorithm $\mathcal{B}$ that wins n-DBDHI game with non-negligible probability.

The adversary $\mathcal{A}$ first sends a (k, n)-source S to the reduction algorithm $\mathcal{B}$. The challenger then sends $(\mathcal{G}, h, h^\alpha, h^{\alpha^2}, \cdots, h^{\alpha^n}, T)$ to the reduction algorithm

$\mathcal{B}$. The reduction algorithm samples a string $x \leftarrow S$, $d_0, d_1 \leftarrow \mathbb{Z}_p$, computes public parameters $\mathsf{pp} = (\mathcal{G}, h, h^\alpha, h^{\alpha^2}, \cdots h^{\alpha^n}, d_0, d_1)$ and sends $\mathsf{pp}, y = f(\mathsf{pp}, x)$ to the adversary $\mathcal{A}$. The adversary outputs a string x'. If $x' = x$ or $f(\mathsf{pp}, x) \neq f(\mathsf{pp}, x')$, the reduction algorithm aborts and outputs a random bit. Otherwise, $\mathcal{B}$ computes α s.t. $(d_0 x + d_1) \cdot \prod_{i=1}^n (\alpha + 2i + x_i) = (d_0 x' + d_1) \cdot \prod_{i=1}^n (\alpha + 2i + x'_i) \bmod p$. The reduction algorithm then checks if $T = e(g, g)^{1/\alpha}$. If $T = e(g, g)^{1/\alpha}$, it outpus 1. Otherwise, it outputs 0.

We now analyze the advantage of $\mathcal{B}$ in n-DBDHI game. By our assumption, $f(\mathsf{pp}, x') = f(\mathsf{pp}, x)$ with non-negligible probability ϵ. We prove that the reduction algorithm does not abort with non-negligible probability. As $k \geq m + 2\lambda$, we know that for any pp, $\Pr_{x \leftarrow S}[\exists t \in \{0,1\}^n \text{ s.t. } x \neq t \wedge f(\mathsf{pp}, x) = f(\mathsf{pp}, t)] \geq 1 - \mathsf{negl}(\lambda)$. Therefore, $\Pr[x' \neq x \wedge f(\mathsf{pp}, x) = f(\mathsf{pp}, x')] \geq \epsilon/2 - \mathsf{negl}(\lambda)$. Note that if $\mathcal{B}$ does not abort, it breaks the n-DBDHI game with advantage $1/2$. Therefore, the overall advantage of $\mathcal{B}$ in breaking n-DBDHI game is $\epsilon/4 - \mathsf{negl}(\lambda)$.

Security of Encryption. We now prove that the above construction satisfies encryption security property.

Lemma 12. *Assuming n-DBDHI assumption holds, the above construction satisfies encryption security property as per Definition 2.*

Proof. Suppose there exists a PPT adversary $\mathcal{A}$ that breaks encryption security of the above construction with non-negligible probability. We construct a reduction algorithm $\mathcal{B}$ that wins n-DBDHI game with non-negligible probability.

The challenger $\mathcal{C}$ first samples a group structure $\mathcal{G} = (\mathbb{G}_1, \mathbb{G}_T, e, p) \leftarrow \mathsf{GGen}(1^\lambda)$, a generator $h \leftarrow \mathbb{G}_1$, a value $\beta \leftarrow \mathbb{Z}_p^*$ and a bit $\gamma \leftarrow \{0,1\}$. If $\gamma = 0$, it sets $T = e(h, h)^{1/\beta}$. Otherwise, it samples $T \leftarrow \mathbb{G}_T$. The challenger then sends $(\mathcal{G}, h, h^\beta, h^{\beta^2}, \cdots, h^{\beta^n}, T)$ to the reduction algorithm $\mathcal{B}$. The adversary sends a string $x \in \{0,1\}^n$ and an index j to $\mathcal{B}$. $\mathcal{B}$ samples $d_0, d_1 \leftarrow \mathbb{Z}_p$ and implicitly sets $\alpha = \beta - 2j - 1 + x_j$. It then computes public parameters $\mathsf{pp} = (\mathcal{G}, h, h^\alpha, h^{\alpha^2}, \cdots, h^{\alpha^n}, d_0, d_1)$, samples $\rho \leftarrow \mathbb{Z}_p$ and implicitly uses $h^{\rho/(\alpha + 2j + 1 - x_j)}$ as randomness for encryption. It computes $\mathsf{ct}^* = (h^\rho, j)$. Consider the polynomial

$$\frac{\rho \cdot (d_0 x + d_1) \cdot \prod_{i=1}^n (\alpha + 2i + x_i)}{\alpha + 2j + 1 - x_j} = \frac{c}{\beta} + \sum_{i=0}^{n-1} c_i \beta^i$$

where $c, \{c_i\}_i$ are dependent only on ρ, x, d_0, d_1. The reduction algorithm computes $k^* = T^c \cdot e\left(h, \prod_{i=0}^{n-1} \left(h^{\beta^i}\right)^{c_i}\right)$ and sends $\mathsf{pp}, \mathsf{ct}^*, k^*$ to the adversary. The adversary outputs a bit γ'. $\mathcal{B}$ outputs γ' as its guess in n-DBDHI game.

We now analyze the advantage of $\mathcal{B}$ in n-DBDHI game. As β is sampled uniformly, α is also uniformly distributed. As $\beta \neq 0 \bmod p$ and ρ is uniformly distributed, $h^{\rho/\beta}$ is also uniformly distributed in $\mathbb{G}_1$. If $\gamma = 0$, then $(\mathsf{pp}, \mathsf{ct}^*, k^*)$ is same as $\left(\mathsf{pp}, E_1(\mathsf{pp}, (j, 1 - x_j); \rho'), E_2(\mathsf{pp}, (f(\mathsf{pp}, x), j, 1 - x_j); \rho')\right)$. If $\gamma = 1$, then k^* is uniformly random. As $\mathcal{A}$ distinguishes these 2 distributions with non-negligible probability, $|\Pr[\gamma' = 1|\gamma = 0] - \Pr[\gamma' = 1|\gamma = 1]|$ is non-negligible. Therefore, $\mathcal{B}$ breaks n-DBDHI assumption.

Smoothness. We now prove that the above construction satisfies (k, n)-smoothness property for any $k \geq m + 2\lambda$ and $n \leq k + m - 2\lambda$.

Lemma 13. *The above construction satisfies (k, n)-smoothness property for any $k \geq m + 2\lambda$ and $n \leq k + m - 2\lambda$ as per Definition 3.*

Proof. We prove the theorem via a sequence of following hybrids.

Hybrid H_0: This is same as the original smoothness security game.
1. The adversary sends two (k, n)-sources S_0 and S_1 to the challenger. The challenger samples a group $\mathcal{G} = (\mathbb{G}_1, \mathbb{G}_T, e, p) \leftarrow \mathsf{Setup}(1^\lambda)$, a generator $g \leftarrow \mathbb{G}_1$ and exponents $d_0, d_1 \leftarrow \mathbb{Z}_p$.
2. It then samples exponent $\alpha \leftarrow \mathbb{Z}_p^*$ and computes $\mathsf{pp} = (\mathcal{G}, g, g^\alpha, \cdots, g^{\alpha^n}, d_0, d_1)$.
3. The challenger samples a bit $b \leftarrow \{0, 1\}$, a string $x \leftarrow S_b$ and sends $\mathsf{pp}, y = g^{(d_0 x + d_1) \cdot \prod_{j=1}^n (\alpha + 2j + x_j)}$ to the adversary.
4. The adversary outputs a bit b'.

Hybrid H_1: In this hybrid, the challenger samples α in public parameters from $[1, p - 2n - 2]$ instead of $\mathbb{Z}_p^*$
2. It then samples exponent $\alpha \leftarrow [1, p - 2n - 2]$ and computes $\mathsf{pp} = (\mathcal{G}, g, g^\alpha, \cdots, g^{\alpha^n}, d_0, d_1)$.

Hybrid H_2: In this hybrid, the challenger samples the challenge y uniformly at random.
3. The challenger samples $y \leftarrow \mathbb{G}_1$ and sends pp, y to the adversary.

For any adversary $\mathcal{A}$, let the probability that $b' = b$ in Hybrid H_s be $p_s^\mathcal{A}$. We know that, $p_2^\mathcal{A} = 1/2$ as y is independent of b. We prove that for every PPT adversary $\mathcal{A}$, $|p_0^\mathcal{A} - p_2^\mathcal{A}|$ is negligible.

Claim 3. *For every adversary $\mathcal{A}$, there exists a negligible function $\mathsf{negl}(\cdot)$ such that for every $\lambda \in \mathbb{N}$, $|p_0^\mathcal{A} - p_1^\mathcal{A}| \leq \mathsf{negl}(\lambda)$.*

Proof. The distribution of challenger's output is same in Hybrids H_0 and H_1, except when $\alpha \in [p-1, p-2n-1]$. This event happens with probability $(2n+1)/p$. Assuming p is super-polynomial in λ, the event $\alpha \in [p - 1, p - 2n - 1]$ happens with negligible probability.

Claim 4. *For every adversary $\mathcal{A}$, there exists a negligible function $\mathsf{negl}(\cdot)$ such that for every $\lambda \in \mathbb{N}$, $|p_1^\mathcal{A} - p_2^\mathcal{A}| \leq \mathsf{negl}(\lambda)$.*

Proof. As the minimum entropy of the distribution $\{x : b \leftarrow \{0, 1\}, x \leftarrow S_b\}$ is $k \geq \log p + 2\lambda$ and as α is sampled from $[1, p - 2n - 2]$, $(d_0 x + d_1) \cdot \prod_{j=1}^n (\alpha + 2j + x_j)$ for $x \leftarrow S_b$ is indistinguishable from uniform distribution on $\mathbb{Z}_p$. We present more details in the full version of the paper.

By the above claims and triangle inequality, the advantage of any adversary in the original smoothness game H_0 is negligible.

6   Performance Evaluation

In this section, we discuss how our HPRG and OWFE constructions based on Φ-Hiding and D(B)DHI assumptions compare with the constructions based on DDH provided in [20,33]. In the full version of the paper, we present our performance evaluation for Hinting PRG constructions.

6.1   OWF with Encryption: Comparing with [20]

We now discuss the efficiency of our OWFE constructions and compare it with existing constructions. First, we provide an asymptotic comparison and then give a more concrete performance evaluation.

An Asymptotic Comparison. In the [20] construction, the public parameters consist of $O(n)$ group elements, where n is at least $\log p + 2\lambda$, and p is the group size. The function evaluation and decryption algorithm performs $O(n)$ group operations. The E_1 algorithm performs $O(n)$ exponentiations and outputs a ciphertext containing $O(n)$ group elements. The E_2 algorithm performs one exponentiation and outputs a key containing one group element.

Comparing that to our Φ-Hiding based OWFE construction described in Sect. 4, the public parameters consist of $2n$ (λ-bit) prime exponents along with the RSA modulus N, extractor seed, group generator, and a hash key. The function evaluation and decryption algorithm performs $O(n)$ exponentiations with λ-bit exponents, where n is at least $\log N + 2\lambda$. Both E_1 and E_2 algorithms perform single exponentiation and output a ciphertext and key containing just one group element, respectively.

In our DDHI based construction described in the full version of the paper, the setup phase performs $O(n)$ exponentiations and outputs public parameters containing n group elements, where n is at least $\log p + 2\lambda$, and p is the group size. The function evaluation and decryption algorithms evaluate a degree-n polynomial symbolically and later on performs n exponentiation operations and n group operations. The E_1 algorithm performs $O(n)$ exponentiations and outputs a ciphertext containing $O(n)$ group elements. The E_2 algorithm performs one exponentiation and outputs a key containing 1 group element. We also provide a more efficient OWFE construction Sect. 5 by relying on bilinear maps and prove it secure under DBDHI. It is similar to the DDHI based OWFE, except that E_1 algorithm only performs $O(1)$ exponentiations, E_2 and decryption algorithms additionally perform a pairing operation, and ciphertext contains only one group element.

Concrete Performance Evaluation. The evaluations were performed on a 2015 Macbook Pro with Dual Core 2.7 GHz Intel Core i5 CPU and 8 GB DDR3 RAM. We evaluated the performance of DDH and DDHI based constructions using MCL Library [29] (written in C++) on NIST standardized elliptic curves P-192, P-224, P-256, P-384 and P-521 providing 96, 112, 128, 192 and 260-bit security respectively. We evaluated our Φ-Hiding based construction using Flint

Libary [28] written in C++ on 1024, 2048, 3072, 7680 and 15360 bit RSA modulus providing 80, 112, 128, 192 and 256-bit security respectively.[7] We evaluated the performance of DBDHI based OWFE using MCL Library [29] on BN-254, BN-381, BN-462 pairing-friendly elliptic curves [5] (providing 100, 128, 140-bit security after the recent tower number field sieve attacks [18,31,35]).

It turns out that the baseline DDH based OWFE offers the shortest setup, evaluation, and decryption times. Whereas the Φ-hiding based OWFE outperforms in terms of E_1 time and ciphertext size. And, due to smaller group size (and thereby smaller n), DBDHI based OWFE leads to shortest E_1 time and ciphertext size. Lastly, for the shortest E_2 time and key size, both the DDH and DDHI based constructions are equally useful. The concrete performance numbers are provided in Table 1.

Note that even though both DDHI and DBDHI based OWFE schemes have the same one-way function, DDHI based scheme has faster evaluation time. In fact, the DDHI based construction is more efficient than DBDHI construction in all aspects other than E_1 time and ciphertext size. This is because the recommended group size of pairing-based elliptic curves grows super linearly in the security parameter due to the number field sieve attacks. And, the function evaluation and decryption procedures of Φ-hiding based scheme performs $O(n)$ exponentiations, when compared to $O(n)$ group operations performed by other schemes. As a result, Φ-hiding based scheme has the slowest function evaluation and decryption procedures.

Deterministic Encryption from OWFE. A very interesting application of OWFE is of deterministic encryption as shown by [19]. In the deterministic encryption scheme of [19], the setup phase invokes the OWFE setup phase once and E_1 algorithm $O(\ell)$ times, where ℓ is proportional to the length of message being encrypted. The encryption key includes OWFE public parameters and $O(\ell)$ OWFE ciphertexts. The encryption algorithm invokes OWFE f algorithm once and OWFE D algorithm $O(\ell)$ times. The decryption algorithm invokes OWFE E_2 algorithm $O(\ell)$ times. Consequently, our DBDHI based OWFE leads to a deterministic encryption scheme with much smaller public parameters and setup time. Concretely, at 128-bit security, the setup phase and public parameters of our DBDHI based deterministic encryption scheme for 128-bit messages is more than 200x faster and 240x shorter respectively than the baseline DDH based deterministic encryption described in [19].

---

[7] Note that we proved the security of our schemes in an asymptotic sense. However, for experiments, we use NIST recommended RSA modulus for the sake of simplicity. The RSA modulus derived from applying a concrete analysis is slightly higher. However as we mention in proof of Sect. 3.1 (full version of the paper), the analysis could be improved further by using a tighter bound for $\Pi(r^i)$, which is $O(1/r^i)$.

Table 1. Concrete performance evaluation of various OWFE constructions

Metric	Security	DDH [20]	Φ-Hiding (§4)	DDHI	DBDHI (§5)
pp Size	80/96/BN254	18.4 KB	71.8 KB	9.2 KB	14.4 KB
	112	25.1 KB	192.4 KB	12.6 KB	–
	128/BN381	32.7 KB	321.8 KB	16.4 KB	30.4 KB
	140/BN462	–	–	–	42.85 KB
	192	73.7 KB	1167 KB	36.9 KB	–
	256	131.1 KB	3059 KB	65.7 KB	–
ct Size	80/96/BN254	18.4 KB	128 Bytes	9.2 KB	64 Bytes
	112	25 KB	256 Bytes	12.4 KB	–
	128/BN381	32.7 KB	384 Bytes	16.3 KB	96 Bytes
	140/BN462	–	–	–	116 Bytes
	192	73.68 KB	960 Bytes	36.9 KB	–
	256	131 KB	1920 Bytes	65.5 KB	–
Key Size	80/96/BN254	24 Bytes	128 Bytes	24 Bytes	381 Bytes
	112	28 Bytes	256 Bytes	28 Bytes	–
	128/BN381	32 Bytes	384 Bytes	32 Bytes	573 Bytes
	140/BN462	–	–	–	593 Bytes
	192	48 Bytes	960 Bytes	48 Bytes	–
	256	64 Bytes	1920 Bytes	64 Bytes	–
Time (Setup)	80/96/BN254	0.0096 s	1.40 s	0.026 s	0.0435 s
	112	0.093 s	6.69 s	0.052 s	–
	128/BN381	0.016 s	12.43 s	0.070 s	0.158 s
	140/BN462	–	–	–	0.493 s
	192	0.065 s	101.38 s	0.307 s	–
	256	0.203 s	475.55 s	1.326 s	–
Time (f)	80/96/BN254	0.0001 s	0.11 s	0.037 s	0.059 s
	112	0.0002 s	1.06 s	0.068 s	–
	128/BN381	0.0002 s	3.67 s	0.090 s	0.19 s
	140/BN462	–	–	–	0.54 s
	192	0.0006 s	59.14 s	0.353 s	–
	256	0.0020 s	473.36 s	1.41 s	–
Time (E_1)	80/96/BN254	49.1 ms	0.69 ms	29.44 ms	0.188 ms
	112	100.87 ms	3.10 ms	56.80 ms	–
	128/BN381	134.90 ms	9.40 ms	76.40 ms	0.45 ms
	140/BN462	–	–	–	1.435 ms
	192	600.84 ms	106.57 ms	326.49 ms	–
	256	2590.14 ms	601.5 ms	1357.93 ms	–
Time (E_2)	80/96/BN254	0.067 ms	0.40 ms	0.066 ms	0.68 ms
	112	0.12 ms	2.80 ms	0.11 ms	–
	128/BN381	0.14 ms	8.38 ms	0.136 ms	1.79 ms
	140/BN462	–	–	–	4.52 ms
	192	0.40 ms	99.50 ms	0.40 ms	–
	256	1.26 ms	600.03 ms	1.29 ms	–
Time (D)	80/96/BN254	0.0001 s	0.109 s	0.036 s	0.059 s
	112	0.0003 s	1.09 s	0.067 s	–
	128/BN381	0.0003 s	3.57 s	0.090 s	0.19 s
	140/BN462	–	–	–	0.54 s
	192	0.00083 s	58.96 s	0.355 s	–
	256	0.00286 s	466.84 s	1.41 s	–

Acknowledgements. We thank anonymous reviewers for useful feedback. The work is done in part while the first author was at UT Austin (supported by IBM PhD Fellowship), and at the Simons Institute for the Theory of Computing (supported by Simons-Berkeley research fellowship). The second author is supported by Packard Fellowship, NSF CNS-1908611, CNS-1414082, DARPA SafeWare and Packard Foundation Fellowship. The third author is supported by NSF CNS-1908611, CNS-1414082, DARPA SafeWare and Packard Foundation Fellowship.

References

1. Alamati, N., Montgomery, H., Patranabis, S.: Symmetric primitives with structured secrets. In: Boldyreva, A., Micciancio, D. (eds.) CRYPTO 2019. LNCS, vol. 11692, pp. 650–679. Springer, Cham (2019). https://doi.org/10.1007/978-3-030-26948-7_23

2. Alamati, N., Montgomery, H., Patranabis, S., Roy, A.: Minicrypt primitives with algebraic structure and applications. In: Ishai, Y., Rijmen, V. (eds.) EUROCRYPT 2019. LNCS, vol. 11477, pp. 55–82. Springer, Cham (2019). https://doi.org/10.1007/978-3-030-17656-3_3

3. Au, M.H., Tsang, P.P., Susilo, W., Mu, Y.: Dynamic universal accumulators for DDH groups and their application to attribute-based anonymous credential systems. In: Fischlin, M. (ed.) CT-RSA 2009. LNCS, vol. 5473, pp. 295–308. Springer, Heidelberg (2009). https://doi.org/10.1007/978-3-642-00862-7_20

4. Barić, N., Pfitzmann, B.: Collision-free accumulators and fail-stop signature schemes without trees. In: Fumy, W. (ed.) EUROCRYPT 1997. LNCS, vol. 1233, pp. 480–494. Springer, Heidelberg (1997). https://doi.org/10.1007/3-540-69053-0_33

5. Barreto, P.S.L.M., Naehrig, M.: Pairing-friendly elliptic curves of prime order. In: Preneel, B., Tavares, S. (eds.) SAC 2005. LNCS, vol. 3897, pp. 319–331. Springer, Heidelberg (2006). https://doi.org/10.1007/11693383_22

6. Benaloh, J., de Mare, M.: One-way accumulators: a decentralized alternative to digital signatures. In: Helleseth, T. (ed.) EUROCRYPT 1993. LNCS, vol. 765, pp. 274–285. Springer, Heidelberg (1994). https://doi.org/10.1007/3-540-48285-7_24

7. Boneh, D., Boyen, X.: Efficient selective-id secure identity-based encryption without random oracles. In: Cachin, C., Camenisch, J.L. (eds.) EUROCRYPT 2004. LNCS, vol. 3027, pp. 223–238. Springer, Heidelberg (2004). https://doi.org/10.1007/978-3-540-24676-3_14

8. Boyen, X., Waters, B.: Shrinking the keys of discrete-log-type lossy trapdoor functions. In: Zhou, J., Yung, M. (eds.) ACNS 2010. LNCS, vol. 6123, pp. 35–52. Springer, Heidelberg (2010). https://doi.org/10.1007/978-3-642-13708-2_3

9. Brakerski, Z., Lombardi, A., Segev, G., Vaikuntanathan, V.: Anonymous IBE, leakage resilience and circular security from new assumptions. Cryptology ePrint Archive, Report 2017/967 (2017). http://eprint.iacr.org/2017/967

10. Camenisch, J., Kohlweiss, M., Soriente, C.: An accumulator based on bilinear maps and efficient revocation for anonymous credentials. In: Jarecki, S., Tsudik, G. (eds.) PKC 2009. LNCS, vol. 5443, pp. 481–500. Springer, Heidelberg (2009). https://doi.org/10.1007/978-3-642-00468-1_27

11. Camenisch, J., Lysyanskaya, A.: Dynamic accumulators and application to efficient revocation of anonymous credentials. In: Yung, M. (ed.) CRYPTO 2002. LNCS, vol. 2442, pp. 61–76. Springer, Heidelberg (2002). https://doi.org/10.1007/3-540-45708-9_5

12. Catalano, D., Fiore, D.: Vector commitments and their applications. In: Kurosawa, K., Hanaoka, G. (eds.) PKC 2013. LNCS, vol. 7778, pp. 55–72. Springer, Heidelberg (2013). https://doi.org/10.1007/978-3-642-36362-7_5

13. Cho, C., Döttling, N., Garg, S., Gupta, D., Miao, P., Polychroniadou, A.: Laconic oblivious transfer and its applications. In: Katz, J., Shacham, H. (eds.) CRYPTO 2017. LNCS, vol. 10402, pp. 33–65. Springer, Cham (2017). https://doi.org/10.1007/978-3-319-63715-0_2

14. Döttling, N., Garg, S.: Identity-based encryption from the Diffie-Hellman assumption. In: Katz, J., Shacham, H. (eds.) CRYPTO 2017. LNCS, vol. 10401, pp. 537–569. Springer, Cham (2017). https://doi.org/10.1007/978-3-319-63688-7_18

15. Döttling, N., Garg, S., Hajiabadi, M., Masny, D.: New constructions of identity-based and key-dependent message secure encryption schemes. In: Abdalla, M., Dahab, R. (eds.) PKC 2018. LNCS, vol. 10769, pp. 3–31. Springer, Cham (2018). https://doi.org/10.1007/978-3-319-76578-5_1

16. Döttling, N., Garg, S., Ishai, Y., Malavolta, G., Mour, T., Ostrovsky, R.: Trapdoor hash functions and their applications. In: Boldyreva, A., Micciancio, D. (eds.) CRYPTO 2019. LNCS, vol. 11694, pp. 3–32. Springer, Cham (2019). https://doi.org/10.1007/978-3-030-26954-8_1

17. Döttling, N., Garg, S.: From selective IBE to full IBE and selective HIBE. In: Kalai, Y., Reyzin, L. (eds.) TCC 2017. LNCS, vol. 10677, pp. 372–408. Springer, Cham (2017). https://doi.org/10.1007/978-3-319-70500-2_13

18. Fotiadis, G., Konstantinou, E.: TNFS resistant families of pairing-friendly elliptic curves. IACR Cryptology ePrint Archive (2018). https://eprint.iacr.org/2018/1017

19. Garg, S., Gay, R., Hajiabadi, M.: New techniques for efficient trapdoor functions and applications. In: Ishai, Y., Rijmen, V. (eds.) EUROCRYPT 2019. LNCS, vol. 11478, pp. 33–63. Springer, Cham (2019). https://doi.org/10.1007/978-3-030-17659-4_2

20. Garg, S., Hajiabadi, M.: Trapdoor functions from the computational Diffie-Hellman assumption. In: Shacham, H., Boldyreva, A. (eds.) CRYPTO 2018. LNCS, vol. 10992, pp. 362–391. Springer, Cham (2018). https://doi.org/10.1007/978-3-319-96881-0_13

21. Garg, S., Hajiabadi, M., Mahmoody, M., Rahimi, A.: Registration-based encryption: removing private-key generator from IBE. In: Beimel, A., Dziembowski, S. (eds.) TCC 2018. LNCS, vol. 11239, pp. 689–718. Springer, Cham (2018). https://doi.org/10.1007/978-3-030-03807-6_25

22. Garg, S., Hajiabadi, M., Mahmoody, M., Rahimi, A., Sekar, S.: Registration-based encryption from standard assumptions. In: Lin, D., Sako, K. (eds.) PKC 2019. LNCS, vol. 11443, pp. 63–93. Springer, Cham (2019). https://doi.org/10.1007/978-3-030-17259-6_3

23. Garg, S., Hajiabadi, M., Ostrovsky, R.: Efficient range-trapdoor functions and applications: Rate-1 OT and more. Cryptology ePrint Archive, Report 2019/990 (2019). https://eprint.iacr.org/2019/990

24. Garg, S., Ostrovsky, R., Srinivasan, A.: Adaptive garbled RAM from laconic oblivious transfer. In: Shacham, H., Boldyreva, A. (eds.) CRYPTO 2018. LNCS, vol. 10993, pp. 515–544. Springer, Cham (2018). https://doi.org/10.1007/978-3-319-96878-0_18

25. Garg, S., Srinivasan, A.: Garbled protocols and two-round MPC from bilinear maps. In: FOCS 2017 (2017)

26. Garg, S., Srinivasan, A.: Adaptively secure garbling with near optimal online complexity. In: Nielsen, J.B., Rijmen, V. (eds.) EUROCRYPT 2018. LNCS, vol. 10821, pp. 535–565. Springer, Cham (2018). https://doi.org/10.1007/978-3-319-78375-8_18

27. Gentry, C., Ramzan, Z.: RSA accumulator based broadcast encryption. In: Zhang, K., Zheng, Y. (eds.) ISC 2004. LNCS, vol. 3225, pp. 73–86. Springer, Heidelberg (2004). https://doi.org/10.1007/978-3-540-30144-8_7

28. Hart, W.B.: Fast library for number theory: an introduction. In: Fukuda, K., Hoeven, J., Joswig, M., Takayama, N. (eds.) ICMS 2010. LNCS, vol. 6327, pp. 88–91. Springer, Heidelberg (2010). https://doi.org/10.1007/978-3-642-15582-6_18, http://flintlib.org

29. Herumi: A portable and fast pairing-based cryptography library (2019). https://github.com/herumi/mcl

30. Katsumata, S., Nishimaki, R., Yamada, S., Yamakawa, T.: Designated verifier/prover and preprocessing NIZKs from Diffie-Hellman assumptions. In: Ishai, Y., Rijmen, V. (eds.) EUROCRYPT 2019. LNCS, vol. 11477, pp. 622–651. Springer, Cham (2019). https://doi.org/10.1007/978-3-030-17656-3_22

31. Kim, T., Barbulescu, R.: Extended tower number field sieve: a new complexity for the medium prime case. In: Robshaw, M., Katz, J. (eds.) CRYPTO 2016. LNCS, vol. 9814, pp. 543–571. Springer, Heidelberg (2016). https://doi.org/10.1007/978-3-662-53018-4_20

32. Kitagawa, F., Matsuda, T., Tanaka, K.: CCA security and trapdoor functions via key-dependent-message security. In: Boldyreva, A., Micciancio, D. (eds.) CRYPTO 2019. LNCS, vol. 11694, pp. 33–64. Springer, Cham (2019). https://doi.org/10.1007/978-3-030-26954-8_2

33. Koppula, V., Waters, B.: Realizing chosen ciphertext security generically in attribute-based encryption and predicate encryption. In: Boldyreva, A., Micciancio, D. (eds.) CRYPTO 2019. LNCS, vol. 11693, pp. 671–700. Springer, Cham (2019). https://doi.org/10.1007/978-3-030-26951-7_23

34. Lombardi, A., Quach, W., Rothblum, R.D., Wichs, D., Wu, D.J.: New constructions of reusable designated-verifier NIZKs. In: Boldyreva, A., Micciancio, D. (eds.) CRYPTO 2019. LNCS, vol. 11694, pp. 670–700. Springer, Cham (2019). https://doi.org/10.1007/978-3-030-26954-8_22

35. Menezes, A., Sarkar, P., Singh, S.: Challenges with assessing the impact of NFS advances on the security of pairing-based cryptography. In: Phan, R.C.-W., Yung, M. (eds.) Mycrypt 2016. LNCS, vol. 10311, pp. 83–108. Springer, Cham (2017). https://doi.org/10.1007/978-3-319-61273-7_5

36. Nguyen, L.: Accumulators from bilinear pairings and applications. In: Menezes, A. (ed.) CT-RSA 2005. LNCS, vol. 3376, pp. 275–292. Springer, Heidelberg (2005). https://doi.org/10.1007/978-3-540-30574-3_19

37. Quach, W., Rothblum, R.D., Wichs, D.: Reusable designated-verifier NIZKs for all NP from CDH. In: Ishai, Y., Rijmen, V. (eds.) EUROCRYPT 2019. LNCS, vol. 11477, pp. 593–621. Springer, Cham (2019). https://doi.org/10.1007/978-3-030-17656-3_21

38. Sander, T., Ta-Shma, A., Yung, M.: Blind, auditable membership proofs. In: Frankel, Y. (ed.) FC 2000. LNCS, vol. 1962, pp. 53–71. Springer, Heidelberg (2001). https://doi.org/10.1007/3-540-45472-1_5
39. Shamir, A.: On the generation of cryptographically strong pseudorandom sequences. ACM Trans. Comput. Syst. 1(1), 38–44 (1983)
40. Zhandry, M.: The magic of ELFs. In: Robshaw, M., Katz, J. (eds.) CRYPTO 2016. LNCS, vol. 9814, pp. 479–508. Springer, Heidelberg (2016). https://doi.org/10.1007/978-3-662-53018-4_18

Adaptively Secure Constrained Pseudorandom Functions in the Standard Model

Alex Davidson[1,4]([⊠]), Shuichi Katsumata[2]([⊠]), Ryo Nishimaki[3]([⊠]),
Shota Yamada[2]([⊠]), and Takashi Yamakawa[3]([⊠])

[1] Cloudflare, Lisbon, Portugal
alex.davidson92@gmail.com
[2] AIST, Tokyo, Japan
{shuichi.katsumata,yamada-shota}@aist.go.jp
[3] NTT Secure Platform Laboratories, Tokyo, Japan
{ryo.nishimaki.zk,takashi.yamakawa.ga}@hco.ntt.co.jp
[4] ISG, Royal Holloway University of London, London, UK

Abstract. Constrained pseudorandom functions (CPRFs) allow learning "constrained" PRF keys that can evaluate the PRF on a subset of the input space, or based on some predicate. First introduced by Boneh and Waters [AC'13], Kiayias et al. [CCS'13] and Boyle et al. [PKC'14], they have shown to be a useful cryptographic primitive with many applications. These applications often require CPRFs to be adaptively secure, which allows the adversary to learn PRF values and constrained keys in an arbitrary order. However, there is no known construction of adaptively secure CPRFs based on a standard assumption in the standard model for any non-trivial class of predicates. Moreover, even if we rely on strong tools such as indistinguishability obfuscation (IO), the state-of-the-art construction of adaptively secure CPRFs in the standard model only supports the limited class of $\mathbf{NC}^1$ predicates.

In this work, we develop new adaptively secure CPRFs for various predicates from different types of assumptions in the standard model. Our results are summarized below.

– We construct adaptively secure and $O(1)$-collision-resistant CPRFs for t-conjunctive normal form (t-CNF) predicates from one-way functions (OWFs) where t is a constant. Here, $O(1)$-collision-resistance means that we can allow the adversary to obtain a constant number of constrained keys. Note that t-CNF includes bit-fixing predicates as a special case.

A. Davidson—Part of this work was completed while the author undertook a research internship at NTT when he was a PhD student at Royal Holloway. The author was also supported by the EPSRC and the UK Government as part of the Centre for Doctoral Training in Cyber Security at Royal Holloway, University of London (EP/K035584/1).
S. Katsumata, S. Yamada—The authors were supported by JST CREST Grant Number JPMJCR19F6. The forth author was also supported by JSPS KAKENHI Grant Number 19H01109.

D. Micciancio and T. Ristenpart (Eds.): CRYPTO 2020, LNCS 12170, pp. 559–589, 2020.
https://doi.org/10.1007/978-3-030-56784-2_19

- We construct adaptively secure and single-key CPRFs for inner-product predicates from the learning with errors (LWE) assumption. Here, single-key security means that we only allow the adversary to learn one constrained key. Note that inner-product predicates include t-CNF predicates for a constant t as a special case. Thus, this construction supports more expressive class of predicates than that supported by the first construction though it loses the collusion-resistance and relies on a stronger assumption.
- We construct adaptively secure and $O(1)$-collusion-resistant CPRFs for all circuits from the LWE assumption and indistinguishability obfuscation (IO).

The first and second constructions are the first CPRFs for any non-trivial predicates to achieve adaptive security outside of the random oracle model or relying on strong cryptographic assumptions. Moreover, the first construction is also the first to achieve any notion of collusion-resistance in this setting. Besides, we prove that the first and second constructions satisfy weak 1-key privacy, which roughly means that a constrained key does not reveal the corresponding constraint. The third construction is an improvement over previous adaptively secure CPRFs for less expressive predicates based on IO in the standard model.

1   Introduction

Pseudorandom functions (PRFs) provide the basis of a huge swathe of cryptography. Intuitively, such functions take a secret key and some binary string x as input, and output (deterministically) some value y. The pseudorandomness requirement dictates that y is indistinguishable from the output of a uniformly sampled function operating solely on x. PRFs provide useful sources of randomness in cryptographic constructions that take adversarially-chosen inputs. Many constructions of PRFs from standard assumptions are known, e.g., [7,25,37,38].

There have been numerous expansions of the definitional framework surrounding PRFs. In this work, we focus on a strand of PRFs that are known as *constrained* PRFs or CPRFs. CPRFs were first introduced by Boneh and Waters [15] alongside the concurrent works of Kiayias et al. [33] and Boyle et al. [17]. They differ from standard PRFs in that they allow users to learn *constrained* keys to evaluate the PRF only on a subset of the input space defined by a predicate. Let K be a master key used to compute the base PRF value and let K_C be the constrained key with respect to a predicate C. Then, the output computed using the master key $y = \mathsf{CPRF.Eval}(K, x)$ can be evaluated using a constrained key K_C if the input x satisfies the constraint, i.e., $C(x) = 1$. However, if $C(x) = 0$, then the output y will remain pseudorandom from a holder of K_C. The expressiveness of a CPRF is based on the class of constraints $\mathcal{C}$ it supports, where the most expressive class is considered to be P/poly.

Similarly to the security notion of standard PRFs, we require CPRFs to satisfy the notion of *pseudorandomness on constrained points*. Formally, the adversary is permitted to make queries for learning PRF evaluations on arbitrary points as with standard PRFs. The adversary is also permitted to learn constrained keys for any predicates $C_i \in \mathcal{C}$ where $i \in [Q]$ for $Q = \mathsf{poly}$.[1] The security requirement dictates that the CPRF remains pseudorandom on a target input x^* that has not been queried so far, where $C_i(x^*) = 0$ for all i. There have been several flavors of this security requirement that have been considered in previous works: when the adversary can query the constrained keys arbitrarily, then we say the CPRF is *adaptively* secure on constrained points; otherwise, if all the constrained keys must be queried at the outset of the game it is *selectively* secure.[2] When $Q > 1$, then we say the CPRF is Q-*collusion-resistant*. In case $Q = \mathsf{poly}$, we write poly-collusion-resistant and when $Q = 1$, we say it is a *single-key* CPRF. These two notions capture the requirements of CPRFs and satisfying both requirements (adaptively-secure, poly-collusion-resistant) is necessary for many applications of CPRFs [15]. For instance, in one of the most appealing applications of CPRFs such as length-optimal broadcast encryption schemes and non-interactive policy-based key exchanges, we require an adaptive and poly-collusion-resistant CPRF for an expressive class of predicates.

We focus on known constructions of CPRFs in the standard model from standard assumptions, that is, CPRFs that do not rely on the random oracle model (ROM) and non-standard assumptions such as indistinguishability obfuscation (IO) or multilinear maps. We notice that there exists no construction of adaptively secure CPRFs for any class of predicates in this standard setting. For instance, even if we consider the most basic puncturable or prefix-fixing predicates, we require the power of IO or the ROM to achieve adaptive security. (For an explanation on different types of predicates, we refer to the full version). Notably, even though we now have many CPRFs for various predicate classes from different types of standard assumptions such as the learning with errors (LWE) and Diffie-Hellman (DH) type assumptions [3,5,18–20,22,39], all constructions only achieve the weaker notion of selective security. In addition, other than selectively-secure CPRFs for the very restricted class of prefix-fixing predicates [5], all the above constructions of CPRFs provide no notion of Q-collusion-resistance for any $Q > 1$. Indeed, most constructions admit trivial collapses in security once more than one constrained key is exposed. A natural open question arises:

> *(Q1). Can we construct adaptively secure constrained PRFs for any class of predicates based on standard assumptions in the standard model; preferably with collusion-resistance?*

Next, we focus on CPRFs based on any models and assumptions. So far the best CPRF we can hope for—an optimal CPRF—(i.e., it supports the constraint class of P/poly, it is adaptively secure, and it is poly-collusion resistant) is only

---

[1] Throughout the introduction, poly will denote an arbitrary polynomial in the security parameter.

[2] In general, we can upgrade selective security to adaptive security by complexity leveraging. However, we want to avoid this since complexity leveraging needs subexponentially hard assumptions.

known based on IO in the ROM [28]. The moment we restrict ourselves to the standard model without relying on the ROM, we can only achieve a weaker notion of CPRF regardless of still being able to use strong tools such as IO. Namely, the following three incomparable state-of-the-art CPRFs (based on IO in the standard model) do not instantiate one of the requirements of the optimal CPRF: [29] only supports the very limited class of puncturing predicates; [14] only achieves selective security; and [4] only achieves single-key security for the limited class of $\mathbf{NC}^1$ predicates. Therefore, a second open question that we are interested in is:

> *(Q2). Can we construct an adaptively secure and Q-collusion resistant (for any $Q > 1$) constrained PRFs for the widest class of P/poly predicates in the standard model?*

Note that solving the above question for *all* $Q > 1$ will result in an optimal CPRF, which we currently only know how to construct in the ROM.

1.1   Our Contribution

In this study, we provide concrete solutions to the questions $(Q1)$ and $(Q2)$ posed above. We develop new *adaptively* secure CPRF constructions for various expressive predicates from a variety of assumptions *in the standard model*. We summarize our results below. The first two results are answers to $(Q1)$, and the last result is an answer to $(Q2)$.

1. We construct an adaptively secure and $O(1)$-collusion-resistant CPRF for t-conjunctive normal form (t-CNF) predicates from one-way functions (OWFs), where t is any constant. Here, $O(1)$-collusion-resistance means that it is secure against adversaries who learn a constant number of constrained keys. This is the first construction to satisfy *adaptive* security or *collusion-resistance* from any standard assumption and in the standard model regardless of the predicate class it supports. Our CPRF is based solely on the existence of OWFs. In particular, it is a much weaker assumption required than all other CPRF constructions for the bit-fixing predicate (which is a special case of t-CNF predicates) [3,14,15,20]. Previous works rely on either the LWE assumption, the decisional DH assumption, or multilinear maps.
2. We construct an adaptively secure and single-key CPRF for inner-product predicates from the LWE assumption. Although our second CPRF does not admit any collusion-resistance, inner-product predicates are a strictly wider class of predicates compared to the t-CNF predicates considered above. (See the full version.) All other lattice-based CPRFs supporting beyond inner-product predicates ($\mathbf{NC}^1$ or P/poly) [18–20,22,39] achieve only selective security and admits no collusion-resistance.
3. We construct an adaptively secure and $O(1)$-collusion-resistant CPRF for P/poly from IO and the LWE assumption. More specifically, we use IO and shift-hiding shiftable functions [39], where the latter can be instantiated from the LWE assumption. This is the first adaptively secure CPRF for the class

of P/poly in the standard model (it further enjoys any notion of collusion-resistance). As stated above, current constructions of CPRFs in the standard model either: only support the limited class of puncturing predicates [29]; achieves only selective security [14]; or only achieves single-key security for the limited class of $\mathbf{NC}^1$ predicates [4].

We also note that our first two constructions satisfy (weak) 1-key privacy, previously coined by Boneh et al. [14] (see the full version for more details on the definition of key privacy).

Applications. As one interesting application, our CPRF for bit-fixing predicates can be used as a building block to realize adaptively-secure t-CNF attribute-based-encryption (ABE) based on lattices, as recently shown by Tsabary [41]. Other than identity-based encryption [1,21] and non-zero inner product encryption [32], this is the first lattice-based ABE satisfying adaptive-security for a non-trivial class of policies. The ABE scheme by Tsabary shows that other than their conventional use-cases, CPRFs may be a useful tool to achieve higher security of more advanced cryptographic primitives.

An attentive reader may wonder whether our CPRFs have any other applications. For instance, as Boneh and Waters proved [15], one can construct length-optimal broadcast encryption schemes from CPRFs for bit-fixing predicates. However, unfortunately, for these types of applications, we require Q-collusion-resistance where Q is an a-priori bounded polynomial. Therefore, we cannot plug in our construction for these types of applications. We leave it as an interesting open problem to progress our CPRF constructions to achieve Q-collusion-resistance for larger Q; achieving $Q = \omega(1)$ would already seem to require a new set of ideas.

Relation to the Lower Bound by Fuchsbauer et al. [24]. One may wonder how our adaptively secure CPRF relates to the lower bound of adaptively secure CPRFs proven by Fuchsbauer et al. [24]. They proved that we could not avoid exponential security loss to prove adaptive pseudorandomness of *the specific CPRF for bit-fixing predicates by Boneh and Waters based on multilinear maps* [15]. Fortunately, their proofs rely heavily on the checkability of valid constrained keys by using multilinear maps. Therefore, their lower bounds do not apply to our setting since none of our constructions have checkability.

Comparison with Existing Constructions. There are several dimensions to consider when we compare CPRF constructions. In this section, we focus on *adaptively* secure CPRFs as it is one of our main contributions. Along with related works, a more extensive comparison is provided in the full version. The following Table 1 lists all the adaptively secure CPRFs known thus far. One clear advantage of our first two CPRFs is that they are the first CPRF to achieve adaptive security without relying on IO or the ROM. However, it can be seen that this comes at the cost of supporting a weaker predicate class, or achieving single-key or $O(1)$-collusion-resistance. Regarding our third CPRF, the main advantage is that it achieves adaptive security and supports the broadest predicate class

Table 1. Comparison among adaptively secure CPRFs. In column "Predicate", LR, BF, t-CNF, and IP stand for left-right-fixing, bit-fixing, t-conjunctive normal form, and inner-product predicates, respectively. In column "Assumption", BDDH, LWE, SGH, and L-DDHI stand for bilinear decisional Diffie-Hellman, multilinear decisional Diffie-Hellman, learning with errors, subgroup hiding assumption, and L-decisional Diffie-Hellman inversion assumptions, respectively. Regarding key privacy, ‡ means that this satisfies *weak* key privacy.

	Adaptive	Collusion-resistance	Privacy	Predicate	Assumption
BW [15]	✓	poly	poly	LR	BDDH & ROM
HKKW [28]	✓	poly	0	P/poly	IO & ROM
HKW [29]	✓	poly	0	Puncturing	SGH & IO
AMNYY [3]	✓	1	1	BF	ROM
	✓	1	0	NC^1	L-DDHI & ROM
AMNYY [4]	✓	1	0	NC^1	SGH & IO
Sec. 4	✓	$O(1)$	1‡	t-CNF ($\supseteq$ BF)	OWF
Sec. 5	✓	1	1‡	IP	LWE
Sec. 4	✓	$O(1)$	0	P/poly	LWE & IO

P/poly without resorting to the ROM. Compared to the recent CPRF by Attra-padung et al. [4], we provide a strict improvement since our first construction supports $O(1)$-collusion-resistance.

Historical Note on Our First Contribution. In the initial version of this paper, we gave a construction of adaptively secure and $O(1)$-collusion-resistant CPRFs for bit-fixing predicates. After the initial version, Tsabary [41] observed that essentially the same idea could be used to construct adaptively single-key secure CPRFs for t-CNF predicates for a constant t. We further extend her construction to construct adaptively secure and $O(1)$-collusion-resistant CPRFs for t-CNF predicates for a constant t in the current version. We stress that (the initial version of) this paper is the first to give adaptively secure or collusion-resistant CPRFs under a standard assumption and in the standard model, for any non-trivial class of predicates.

2   Technical Overview

In this section, we explain the approach we took for achieving each of our CPRFs. For CPRFs for bit-fixing (and t-CNF) predicates, we take a combinatorial approach. For CPRFs for inner-product predicates, we take an algebraic approach based on lattices incorporating the so-called lossy mode. For CPRFs for P/poly, we use shift-hiding shiftable functions [39] and IO as main building blocks. In the subsequent subsections, we explain these approaches in more detail.

2.1   CPRF for Bit-Fixing/t-CNF

We achieve CPRFs for t-CNF predicates. However, we consider our CPRF for bit-fixing predicates in the technical overview rather than the more general CPRF for t-CNF predicates for ease of presentation. The high-level idea is very similar and generalizes naturally. Here, a bit-fixing predicate is defined by a string $v \in \{0, 1, *\}^\ell$ where $*$ is called the "wildcard". A bit-fixing predicate v on input $x \in \{0, 1\}$ is said to be satisfied if and only if $(v_i = x_i) \vee (v_i = *)$ for all $i \in [\ell]$.

We first focus on how to achieve collusion-resistance because the structure for achieving collusion-resistance naturally induces adaptive security.

Combinatorial Techniques for CPRFs for Bit-Fixing Predicates. We start with a simpler case of *single-key* CPRF for bit-fixing predicates as our starting point. We use 2ℓ keys of standard PRFs to construct an ℓ-bit input CPRF for bit-fixing predicates. Let $\mathsf{PRF.Eval} : \{0,1\}^\kappa \times \{0,1\}^\ell \mapsto \{0,1\}^n$ be the evaluation algorithm of a PRF. We uniformly sample keys $\mathsf{K}_{i,b} \in \{0,1\}^\kappa$ for $i \in [\ell]$ and $b \in \{0,1\}$. The master key of the CPRF is $\mathsf{K} = \{\mathsf{K}_{i,b}\}_{i \in [\ell], b \in \{0,1\}}$ and evaluation on some $x \in \{0,1\}^\ell$ is computed as the output of:

$$\mathsf{CPRF.Eval}(\mathsf{K}, x) = \bigoplus_{i=1}^{\ell} \mathsf{PRF.Eval}(\mathsf{K}_{i,x_i}, x).$$

Figure 1 depicts the construction.

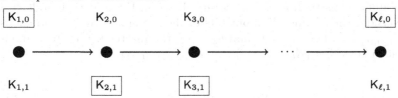

Fig. 1. Length-ℓ directed line representation where each nodes are labeled with two PRF keys. In the figure, the choices of PRF keys correspond to some input $x = 011 \cdots 0$.

The constrained key for a bit-fixing predicate $v \in \{0, 1, *\}^\ell$ constitutes a single PRF key K_{i,v_i} (where $v_i \in \{0, 1\}$), and a pair of PRF keys $(\mathsf{K}_{i,0}, \mathsf{K}_{i,1})$ (where $v_i = *$). Constrained evaluation is clearly possible for any input x that satisfies the bit-fixing predicate v since we have keys K_{i,v_i} for non-wildcard parts and both keys $(\mathsf{K}_{i,0}, \mathsf{K}_{i,1})$ for wildcard parts.

The (selective) security of the scheme rests upon the fact that for a single constrained key, with respect to v, there must exist a $j \in [\ell]$ such that $(x_j^* \neq v_j) \wedge (v_j \neq *)$ for the challenge input x^*. This is due to the fact that the bit-fixing predicate v does not satisfy x^*. Then, pseudorandomness of $y \leftarrow \mathsf{CPRF.Eval}(\mathsf{K}, x^*)$ is achieved because

$$y \leftarrow \bigoplus_{i=1}^{\ell} \mathsf{PRF.Eval}(\mathsf{K}_{i,x_i^*}, x^*) = \mathsf{PRF.Eval}(\mathsf{K}_{j,x_j^*}, x^*) \oplus \left(\bigoplus_{i \neq j} \mathsf{PRF.Eval}(\mathsf{K}_{i,x_i^*}, x^*) \right)$$

where $\mathsf{PRF.Eval}(\mathsf{K}_{j,x_j^*}, x^*)$ is evaluated using the key that is unknown to the adversary. Thus, this evaluation can be replaced with a uniformly sampled $y_j \in \{0,1\}^n$ by the pseudorandomness of PRF for key K_{j,x_j^*}. In turn, this results in a uniformly distributed CPRF output y and so pseudorandomness is ensured. We can instantiate pseudorandom functions using only one-way functions [25,27], and therefore, so can the above single-key CPRF for the bit-fixing predicate.

Allowing >1 Constrained Key Query. If we allow for more than two constrained key queries in the above construction, the scheme is trivially broken. Consider an adversary that queries the two bit-fixing predicates $v = 0 * * \ldots * *0$ and $\bar{v} = 1 * * \ldots * *1$ as an example. Notice that any binary string x of the form $x = 0 \ldots 1$ or $x = 1 \ldots 0$ will not satisfy either of the predicates. Therefore, we would like the evaluation value y on such input x by the master key to remain pseudorandom to the adversary. However, the adversary will be able to collect all PRF keys $\{\mathsf{K}_{i,b}\}_{i \in [\ell], b \in \{0,1\}}$ by querying v and $\bar{v}$, and recover the master key itself in our construction above. Therefore, the adversary will be able to compute on any input x regardless of its constraints.

Collusion-Resistance for Two Constrained Key Queries. At a high level, the reason why our construction could not permit more than one constrained key query is because we examined each of the input bits individually when choosing the underlying PRF keys. Now, consider a scheme that considered two input bits instead of considering one input bit at each node in Fig. 1. Figure 2 illustrates this modified construction. In the set-up shown in Fig. 2 at each node (i,j), we now consider the ith and j^{th} input bits of the string $x \in \{0,1\}^\ell$ and choose the key $\mathsf{K}_{(i,j),(b_1,b_2)}$ where $b_1 = x_i$ and $b_2 = x_j$; the master key is the combination of all such keys $\mathsf{K} = \{\mathsf{K}_{(i,j),(b_1,b_2)}\}_{(i,j) \in [\ell]^2, (b_1,b_2) \in \{0,1\}^2}$.

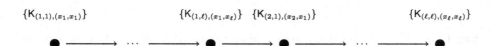

$$\{\mathsf{K}_{(1,1),(x_1,x_1)}\} \qquad\qquad \{\mathsf{K}_{(1,\ell),(x_1,x_\ell)}\} \quad \{\mathsf{K}_{(2,1),(x_2,x_1)}\} \qquad\qquad\qquad \{\mathsf{K}_{(\ell,\ell),(x_\ell,x_\ell)}\}$$

Fig. 2. Length-ℓ^2 directed line representation where each nodes consider two input bits, where $(x_i, x_j) \in \{0,1\} \times \{0,1\}$ for all $i,j \in [\ell]$.

Evaluation is then carried out by adding the PRF values along the directed line illustrated in Fig. 2:

$$\mathsf{CPRF.Eval}(\mathsf{K}, x) = \bigoplus_{(i,j) \in [\ell] \times [\ell]} \mathsf{PRF.Eval}(\mathsf{K}_{(i,j),(x_i,x_j)}, x),$$

and constrained keys for $v \in \{0, 1, *\}^\ell$ contain the key $\mathsf{K}_{(i,j),(b_1,b_2)}$, for all $b_1, b_2 \in \{0,1\}$ such that

$$\Big((v_i = b_1) \vee (v_i = *)\Big) \bigwedge \Big((v_j = b_2) \vee (v_j = *)\Big),$$

is satisfied.

To see how this combinatorial change in the construction has an impact on the collusion-resistance of the scheme, consider a pair of constrained key queries for bit-fixing predicates $v, \bar{v} \in \{0, 1, *\}^\ell$. Let x^* be the challenge input that is constrained with respect to both $v, \bar{v}$. Then there exists an $i' \in [\ell]$ where $(x^*_{i'} \neq v_{i'}) \wedge (v_{i'} \neq *)$ and likewise $(x^*_{j'} \neq \bar{v}_{j'}) \wedge (\bar{v}_{j'} \neq *)$ for some $j' \in [\ell]$. Equivalently, we must have $x^*_{i'} = 1 - v_{i'}$ and $x^*_{j'} = 1 - \bar{v}_{j'}$ for some $i', j' \in [\ell]$. As a result, for these constrained key queries we observe that the underlying PRF key $\mathsf{K}_{(i',j'),(1-v_{i'},1-\bar{v}_{j'})}$ will never be revealed to the adversary.

Using this fact, we can prove that our new CPRF construction achieves collusion-resistance for two constrained key queries using essentially the same aforementioned proof technique. We rewrite the CPRF evaluation on x^* as:

$$\mathsf{CPRF.Eval}(\mathsf{K}, x^*) = \bigoplus_{(i,j) \in [\ell] \times [\ell]} \mathsf{PRF.Eval}(\mathsf{K}_{(i,j),(x^*_i, x^*_j)}, x^*)$$

$$= \mathsf{PRF.Eval}(\mathsf{K}_{(i',j'),(x^*_{i'}, x^*_{j'})}, x^*) \oplus \left(\bigoplus_{(i,j) \neq (i',j')} \mathsf{PRF.Eval}(\mathsf{K}_{(i,j),(x^*_i, x^*_j)}, x^*) \right).$$

Notice that, since $\mathsf{K}_{(i',j'),(x^*_{i'}, x^*_{j'})}$ is never revealed to the adversary, this evaluation is indistinguishable from a uniformly sampled value y^*. In a simulation where y^* replaces the underlying PRF evaluation, the entire CPRF evaluation on x^* is distributed uniformly and pseudorandomness follows accordingly.

Expanding to $O(1)$-Collusion-Resistance. The technique that we demonstrate in this work is a generalisation of the technique that we used for two-key collusion-resistance. Instead of considering two input bits at a time, we consider Q input bits at a time and index each node in the evaluation by the vector $(i_1, \ldots, i_Q) \in [\ell]^Q$. Then we evaluate the CPRF on $x \in \{0, 1\}^\ell$ as the output of:

$$\mathsf{CPRF.Eval}(\mathsf{K}, x) = \bigoplus_{(i_1, \ldots, i_Q) \in [\ell]^Q} \mathsf{PRF.Eval}(\mathsf{K}_{(i_1, \ldots, i_Q),(x_{i_1}, \ldots, x_{i_Q})}, x).$$

The constraining algorithm works for a bit-fixing predicate defined by $v \in \{0, 1, *\}^\ell$ by providing all keys $\mathsf{K}_{(i_1, \ldots, i_Q),(b_1, \ldots, b_Q)}$ such that

$$\bigwedge_{j \in [Q]} (b_j = v_{i_j}) \vee (v_{i_j} = *)$$

is satisfied. Constrained evaluation is then possible for any input x satisfying the bit-fixing predicate defined by v.

For any set of Q constrained key queries associated with strings $v^{(1)}, \ldots, v^{(Q)}$ and any constrained input x^*, there must exist a vector $(i'_1, \ldots, i'_Q)$ such that $(x^*_{i'_j} \neq v^{(j)}_{i'_j}) \wedge (v^{(j)}_{i'_j} \neq *)$ for all $j \in [Q]$. Therefore, the key $\mathsf{K}_{(i'_1, \ldots, i'_Q),(x^*_{i'_1}, \ldots, x^*_{i'_Q})}$ is never revealed to the adversary. Finally, we can prove the selective pseudorandomness of the CPRF on input x^* using exactly the same technique as mentioned in the case when $Q = 2$. The proof of security is given in the proof of Theorem 4.1.

Importantly, we cannot achieve collusion-resistance for unbounded Q because there is an exponential dependency on Q associated with the size of the CPRF. For instance, for the node indexed by the vector $(i_1, \ldots, i_Q)$, there are 2^Q underlying PRF keys associated with this node; moreover, there are ℓ^Q such nodes. Therefore the total size of K is $(2\ell)^Q$. As a result, we are only able to afford $Q = O(1)$ since ℓ is the input length of PRF, which is a polynomial in the security parameter. This bound is inherent in the directed line paradigm because our technique is purely combinatorial.

Finally, we assess the security properties achieved by our CPRF for bit-fixing predicates. Although we have been showing selective security of our CPRF, we observe that our construction satisfies adaptive security when the underlying pseudorandom functions satisfy adaptive pseudorandomness.

Achieving Adaptive Security. Our construction arrives at adaptive security essentially *for free*. Previous constructions for bit-fixing predicates (or as a matter of fact, any non-trivial predicates) incur sub-exponential security loss during the reduction from adaptive to selective security, or relies on the random oracle model or IO; see the full version for an overview. The sub-exponential security loss is incurred as previous constructions achieve adaptive security by letting the reduction guess the challenge input x^* that the adversary chooses.

We can achieve adaptive security with a polynomial security loss (e.g. $1/\mathsf{poly}(\kappa)$): by instead guessing the key (not the challenge input) that is implicitly used by the adversary (i.e. K_{T^*, x_T^*} for $T^* \subset [\ell], |T^*| = Q$). For example in the 2-key setting explained above, this amounts to correctly guessing the values (i, j) and (x_i^*, x_j^*) of the PRF key $\mathsf{K}_{(i,j),(x_i^*, x_j^*)}$, which happens with probability at most $(1/2\ell)^2$. If this key is not eventually used by the challenge ciphertext, or it is revealed via a constrained key query, then the reduction algorithm aborts. This is because *the entire proof hinges on the choice of this key*, rather than the input itself. Since there are only polynomially many keys (for $Q = O(1)$), we can achieve adaptive security with only a $1/\mathsf{poly}(\kappa)$ probability of aborting.

Finally, we note that there is a subtle technical issue we must resolve due to the non-trivial abort condition. Similar problems were identified by Waters [42] who introduced the "artificial abort step".

2.2 CPRF for Inner-Product

We construct CPRF for the class of inner-product predicates (over the integers) based on lattices.

The starting point of our CPRF is the lattice-based PRF of [6,13]. At a very high level, the secret key K of these PRFs is a vector $\mathbf{s} \in \mathbb{Z}_q^n$ and the public parameters is some matrices $(\mathbf{A}_i \in \mathbb{Z}_q^{n \times m})_{i \in [k]}$. To evaluate on an input $\mathbf{x}$, one first generates a (publicly computable) matrix $\mathbf{A}_\mathbf{x} \in \mathbb{Z}_q^{n \times m}$ related to input $\mathbf{x}$ and simply outputs the value $\lfloor \mathbf{s}^\top \mathbf{A}_\mathbf{x} \rfloor_p \in \mathbb{Z}_p^m$, where $\lfloor a \rfloor_p$ denotes rounding of an element $a \in \mathbb{Z}_q$ to $\mathbb{Z}_p$ by multiplying it by (p/q) and rounding the result. Roughly, the values $\mathbf{s}^\top \mathbf{A_x} + \mathsf{noise}$ are jointly indistinguishable from uniform for different inputs $\mathbf{x}$ since $\mathbf{A_x}$ acts as an LWE matrix. Therefore, if the noise term is sufficiently small, then $\lfloor \mathbf{s}^\top \mathbf{A_x} \rfloor_p = \lfloor \mathbf{s}^\top \mathbf{A_x} + \mathsf{noise} \rfloor_p$, and hence, pseudorandomness follows.

Pioneered by the lattice-based CPRF of Brakerski and Vaikuntanathan [19], many constructions of CPRF [12,18] have built on top of the PRF of [6,13]. The high-level methodology is as follows: the constrained key for a constraint C would be a set of LWE ciphertexts of the form $\mathsf{K}_C := (\mathsf{ct}_i = \mathbf{s}^\top(\mathbf{A}_i - C_i \cdot \mathbf{G}) + \mathsf{noise})_{i \in [k]}$, where C_i is the ith bit of the description of the constraint C and $\mathbf{G}$ is the so-called gadget matrix [36]. To evaluate on input $\mathbf{x}$ using the constrained key K_C, one evaluates the ciphertexts $(\mathsf{ct}_i)_{i \in [k]}$ to $\mathsf{ct_x} = \mathbf{s}^\top(\mathbf{A_x} - (1 - C(\mathbf{x})) \cdot \mathbf{G}) + \mathsf{noise}$, using the by now standard homomorphic computation technique of [11] originally developed for attribute-based encryption (ABE) schemes. Here, $\mathbf{A_x}$ is independent of the constraint C, that is, $\mathbf{A_x}$ can be computed without the knowledge of C. Then, the final output of the CPRF evaluation with the constrained key will be $\lfloor \mathsf{ct_x} \rfloor_p$. Now, if the constraint is satisfied, i.e., $C(\mathbf{x}) = 1$, then computing with the constrained key K_C will result in the same output as the master key K since we would have $\mathsf{ct_x} = \mathbf{s}^\top \mathbf{A_x} + \mathsf{noise}$.

Unfortunately, all works which follow this general methodology only achieves *selective* security. There is a noted resemblance between this construction with the above types of CPRF and the ABE scheme of [11]. As a consequence, achieving an adaptively secure CPRF following the above methodology would likely shed some light onto the construction of an adaptively secure lattice-based ABE. Considering that adaptively secure ABEs are known to be one of the major open problems in lattice-based cryptography, it does not seem to be an easy task to achieve an adaptively secure CPRF following this approach.

We take a different approach by taking advantage of the fact that our constraint is a simple linear function in this work due to the technical hurdle above. Specifically, we only embed the constraint in the master key $\mathbf{s}$ instead of embedding the constraint in the master key $\mathbf{s}$ *and* the public matrices $(\mathbf{A}_i)_{i \in [k]}$ as $(\mathbf{s}^\top(\mathbf{A}_i - C_i \cdot \mathbf{G}))_{i \in [k]}$. To explain this idea, we need some preparation. Let $\mathbf{y} \in \mathbb{Z}^\ell$ be the vector associated with the inner-product constraint $C_{\mathbf{y}}$, that is, the constrained key $\mathsf{K}_{C_{\mathbf{y}}}$ can evaluate on input $\mathbf{x} \in \mathbb{Z}^\ell$ if and only if $\langle \mathbf{x}, \mathbf{y} \rangle = 0$ (over the integers). We also slightly modify the PRF of [6,13] so that we use a matrix $\mathbf{S} \in \mathbb{Z}_q^{n \times \ell}$ instead of a vector $\mathbf{s} \in \mathbb{Z}_q^n$ as the secret key. To evaluate on input $\mathbf{x} \in \mathbb{Z}^\ell$ with the secret key $\mathbf{S}$, we will first compute the vector $\mathbf{s_x} = \mathbf{Sx} \in \mathbb{Z}^n$ and then run the PRF of [6,13], viewing $\mathbf{s_x}$ as the secret key. That is, the output of the PRF is now $\lfloor \mathbf{s_x}^\top \mathbf{A_x} \rfloor_p$.

The construction of our CPRF is a slight extension of this. The master key and evaluation with the master key is the same as the modified PRF. Namely, the master key is defined as $\mathsf{K} := \mathbf{S}$ and the output of the evaluation is $\lfloor \mathbf{s_x}^\top \mathbf{A_x} \rfloor_p$. Our constrained key for the constraint $C_{\mathbf{y}}$ is then defined as $\mathsf{K}_{C_{\mathbf{y}}} := \mathbf{S_y} = \mathbf{S} + \mathbf{d} \otimes \mathbf{y}^\top \in \mathbb{Z}_q^{n \times \ell}$ where $\mathbf{d}$ is a uniformly random vector sampled over $\mathbb{Z}_q^n$. Evaluation with the constrained key $\mathsf{K}_{C_{\mathbf{y}}} = \mathbf{S_y}$ is done exactly the same as with the master key $\mathsf{K} = \mathbf{S}$; it first computes $\mathbf{s}_{\mathbf{y},\mathbf{x}} = \mathbf{S}_{\mathbf{y}}\mathbf{x}$ and outputs $\lfloor \mathbf{s}_{\mathbf{y},\mathbf{x}}^{\top}\mathbf{A}_{\mathbf{x}} \rfloor_p$. It is easy to check that if $\langle \mathbf{x},\mathbf{y} \rangle = 0$ (i.e., $C_{\mathbf{y}}(\mathbf{x}) = 1$), then $\mathbf{S}_{\mathbf{y}}\mathbf{x} = (\mathbf{S}+\mathbf{d}\otimes\mathbf{y}^{\top})\mathbf{x} = \mathbf{s}_{\mathbf{x}}$. Hence, the constrained key computes the same output as the master key for the inputs for which the constraint is satisfied. The construction is very simple, but the proof for adaptive security requires a bit of work.

As a warm-up, let us consider the easy case of selective security and see why it does not generalize to adaptive security. When the adversary $\mathcal{A}$ submits $C_{\mathbf{y}}$ as the challenge constraint at the beginning of the selective security game, the simulator samples $\hat{\mathbf{S}} \xleftarrow{\$} \mathbb{Z}_q^{n \times \ell}$ and $\mathbf{d} \xleftarrow{\$} \mathbb{Z}_q^n$; sets the master key as $\mathsf{K} = \hat{\mathbf{S}} - \mathbf{d} \otimes \mathbf{y}^{\top}$ and the constrained key as $\mathsf{K}_{C_{\mathbf{y}}} = \hat{\mathbf{S}}$; and returns $\mathsf{K}_{C_{\mathbf{y}}}$ to $\mathcal{A}$. Since the distribution of K and $\mathsf{K}_{C_{\mathbf{y}}}$ is exactly the same as in the real world, the simulator perfectly simulates the keys to $\mathcal{A}$. Now, notice that evaluation on input $\mathbf{x}$ with the master key K results as

$$
\begin{aligned}
\mathbf{z} &= \left\lfloor \left((\hat{\mathbf{S}} - \mathbf{d} \otimes \mathbf{y}^{\top})\mathbf{x} \right)^{\top} \mathbf{A}_{\mathbf{x}} \right\rfloor_p \\
&\approx \lfloor (\hat{\mathbf{S}}\mathbf{x})^{\top}\mathbf{A}_{\mathbf{x}} \rfloor_p - \langle \mathbf{x},\mathbf{y} \rangle \cdot \lfloor \mathbf{d}^{\top}\mathbf{A}_{\mathbf{x}} \rfloor_p = \mathsf{CPRF}_{\mathsf{K}_{C_{\mathbf{y}}}}(\mathbf{x}) - \langle \mathbf{x},\mathbf{y} \rangle \cdot \mathsf{PRF}_{\mathbf{d}}(\mathbf{x}),
\end{aligned}
$$

where $\mathsf{CPRF}_{\mathsf{K}_{C_{\mathbf{y}}}}(\mathbf{x})$ is the CPRF evaluation with constrained key $\mathsf{K}_{C_{\mathbf{y}}}$ and $\mathsf{PRF}_{\mathbf{d}}(\mathbf{x})$ is the PRF evaluation of [6,13] with secret key $\mathbf{d} \in \mathbb{Z}_q^n$.[3] In particular, the simulator can simply reply to the evaluation query $\mathbf{x}$ made by $\mathcal{A}$ by first evaluating $\mathbf{x}$ with the constrained key $\mathsf{K}_{C_{\mathbf{y}}}$ and then shifting it by $\langle \mathbf{x},\mathbf{y} \rangle \cdot \mathsf{PRF}_{\mathbf{d}}(\mathbf{x})$. With this observation, selective security readily follows from the security of the underlying PRF. Specifically, $\mathcal{A}$ will obtain many output values $\mathsf{PRF}_{\mathbf{d}}(\mathbf{x})$ for any $\mathbf{x}$ of its choice in the course of receiving $\mathbf{z}$ back on an evaluation query on input $\mathbf{x}$. However, $\mathsf{PRF}_{\mathbf{d}}(\mathbf{x}^*)$ will remain pseudorandom for a non-queried input $\mathbf{x}^*$ due to the security of the PRF. Hence, the challenge output $\mathbf{z}^*$ will remain pseudorandom from the view of $\mathcal{A}$.

Unfortunately, the above approach breaks down if we want to show adaptive security. This is because the simulator will no longer be able to simulate the "shift" $\langle \mathbf{x},\mathbf{y} \rangle \cdot \mathsf{PRF}_{\mathbf{d}}(\mathbf{x})$ if it does not know the vector $\mathbf{y}$ associated with the challenge constraint $C_{\mathbf{y}}$. In particular, it seems the simulator is bound to honestly compute the master key $\mathsf{K} = \mathbf{S}$ and to use K to answer the evaluation query made before the challenge constraint query. Therefore, to cope with this apparent issue, we deviate from the above approach used to show selective security.

Our high-level approach for adaptive security will be to argue that $\mathbf{d}$ retains sufficient min-entropy conditioned on the view of $\mathcal{A}$, where $\mathcal{A}$ obtains a constrained key $\mathsf{K}_{C_{\mathbf{y}}} = \mathbf{S}_{\mathbf{y}}$ and honest evaluation on inputs $(\mathbf{x}_j)_{j \in [Q]}$ where Q is an arbitrary polynomial. Intuitively, if $\mathbf{d} \in \mathbb{Z}_q^n$ retains enough min-entropy, then it will mask part of the master key $\mathbf{S}$ conditioned on $\mathcal{A}$'s knowledge on $\mathbf{S}_{\mathbf{y}} = \mathbf{S}+\mathbf{d}\otimes\mathbf{y}^{\top}$, and hence, we would be able to argue that the output evaluated using the master key $\mathbf{S}$ is pseudorandom using some randomness extractor-type argument.

---

[3] Note that *a lot* of subtlety on parameter selections and technicalities regarding rounding are swept under the rug. However, we believe the rough details are enough to convey the intuition.

The proof for adaptive security is roughly as follows: Let $\mathsf{K} = \mathbf{S}$. The simulator will basically run identically to the challenger in the real world. It will honestly answer to $\mathcal{A}$'s evaluation query on input $\mathbf{x}$ by returning $\lfloor (\mathbf{Sx})^\top \mathbf{A_x} \rceil_p$ computed via the master key. When $\mathcal{A}$ queries for a constrained key on constraint $C_\mathbf{y}$, the simulator honestly responds by returning $\mathsf{K}_{C_\mathbf{y}} = \mathbf{S_y}$. Evaluation queries after the constrained key query will also be answered using the master key. Then, similarly to the above equation, the output $\mathbf{z}$ returned to $\mathcal{A}$ as an evaluation query on input $\mathbf{x}$ can be written as

$$\mathbf{z} = \lfloor (\mathbf{Sx})^\top \mathbf{A_x} \rceil_p$$
$$\approx \lfloor (\mathbf{S_y x})^\top \mathbf{A_x} \rceil_p - \langle \mathbf{x}, \mathbf{y} \rangle \cdot \lfloor \mathbf{d}^\top \mathbf{A_x} \rceil_p = \mathsf{CPRF}_{\mathsf{K}_{C_\mathbf{y}}}(\mathbf{x}) - \langle \mathbf{x}, \mathbf{y} \rangle \cdot \lfloor \mathbf{d}^\top \mathbf{A_x} \rceil_p.$$

Therefore, conditioned on $\mathcal{A}$'s view, each query will leak information of $\mathbf{d}$ through the term $\lfloor \mathbf{d}^\top \mathbf{A_x} \rceil_p$. Moreover, if we run the standard homomorphic computation of [11], $\mathbf{A_x}$ will be a full-rank matrix with overwhelming probability, and hence, $\lfloor \mathbf{d}^\top \mathbf{A_x} \rceil_p$ may uniquely define $\mathbf{d}$. Notably, information theoretically, everything about $\mathbf{d}$ may completely leak through a *single* evaluation query. Therefore, the question to be solved is: how can we restrict the information of $\mathbf{d}$ leaked through the evaluation query?

The main idea to overcome this problem is to use the *lossy mode* of the LWE problem [2,8,26,34]. The lossy LWE mode is a very powerful tool which states that if we sample $\mathbf{A} \in \mathbb{Z}_q^{n \times m}$ from a special distribution which is computationally indistinguishable from random (assuming the hardness of LWE), then $(\mathbf{A}, \mathbf{d}^\top \mathbf{A} + \mathsf{noise})$ leaks almost no information on $\mathbf{d}$. We call such a matrix $\mathbf{A}$ as "lossy". Our idea draws inspiration from the recent work of Libert, Stehlé, and Titiu [35] that shows that this lossy LWE mode can be combined with homomorphic computation of [11] to obtain adaptively secure distributed lattice-based PRFs. We will setup the public matrices $(\mathbf{A}_i)_{i \in [k]}$ in a special way during the simulation. Concretely, the special setup induces a lossy matrix on all the evaluation queries and a non-lossy matrix (i.e., $(\mathbf{A_x}, \mathbf{d}^\top \mathbf{A_x} + \mathsf{noise})$ uniquely defines $\mathbf{d}$) on the challenge query with non-negligible probability when we homomorphically compute $\mathbf{A_x}$. For the knowledgeable readers, this programming of $\mathbf{A_x}$ is accomplished by using admissible hash functions [10]. With this idea in hand, we will be able to argue that each evaluation query will always leak the same information on $\mathbf{d}$. Then, we will be able to argue that $\mathbf{z}^* = \lfloor \mathbf{d}^\top \mathbf{A_x^*} \rceil_p$ will have high min-entropy conditioned on $\mathcal{A}$'s view since $\mathbf{A_x^*}$ will be a non-lossy matrix on the challenge input $\mathbf{x}^*$. Finally, we will use a deterministic randomness extractor to extract statistically uniform bits from $\mathbf{z}^*$.

We end this part by noting that $\mathsf{K} = \mathbf{S}$ and $\mathbf{d}$ will be taken from a more specific domain and there will be many subtle technical issues regarding the rounding operation in our actual construction. Moreover, similarly to [35], there are subtle issues on why we have to resort to *deterministic* randomness extractors and not any randomness extractors. For more detail, see Sect. 5.

2.3   CPRF for P/poly

Our CPRF for P/poly is constructed based on IO and shift-hiding shiftable functions (SHSF) [39].

First, we briefly recall SHSF. An SHSF consists of the following algorithms: a key generation algorithm SHSF.KeyGen, which generates a master key msk; an evaluation algorithm SHSF.Eval, which takes msk and $x \in \mathcal{X}$ as input and outputs $y \in \mathcal{Y}$; a shifting algorithm SHSF.Shift, which takes msk and a function $C : \mathcal{X} \rightarrow \mathcal{Y}$ as input and outputs a shifted secret key sk_C; and a shifted evaluation algorithm SHSF.SEval, which takes a shifted evaluation key sk_C and $x \in \mathcal{X}$ as input and outputs $y \in \mathcal{Y}$. As correctness, we require that SHSF.SEval$(\mathsf{sk}_C, x) \approx$ SHSF.Eval$(\mathsf{msk}, x) + C(x)$ holds where $+$ denotes an appropriately defined addition in $\mathcal{Y}$ and $\approx$ hides a small error. In this overview, we neglect the error and assume that this equation exactly holds for simplicity. The security of SHSF roughly says that sk_C does not reveal the shifting function C. More precisely, we require that there exists a simulator SHSF.Sim that simulates sk_C without knowing C so that it is computationally indistinguishable from an honestly generated one.

Before going into detail on our CPRF, we make one observation, which simplifies our security proof. Specifically, we can assume that an adversary does not make an evaluation query without loss of generality when we consider a (constant) collusion-resistant CPRF for P/poly. This is because we can replace polynomial number of evaluation queries with one extra constrained key query on a "partitioning function" by the standard partitioning technique. (See Lemma 6.2 and its proof in the full version for the detail.) Thus, we assume that an adversary does not make any evaluation query at all, and only makes constrained key queries and a challenge query in the following.

We describe our construction of CPRF. A master key K of the CPRF is a secret key $\mathsf{sk}^{\mathsf{sim}}$ of SHSF generated by SHSF.Sim, and the evaluation algorithm of the CPRF with the master key $\mathsf{K} = \mathsf{sk}^{\mathsf{sim}}$ is just defined as SHSF.SEval$(\mathsf{sk}^{\mathsf{sim}}, \cdot)$. A constrained key K_C for a circuit C is defined to be an obfuscated program in which $\mathsf{sk}^{\mathsf{sim}}$ and C are hardwired and that computes SHSF.SEval$(\mathsf{sk}^{\mathsf{sim}}, x)$ if $C(x) = 1$ and returns $\bot$ otherwise. This construction clearly satisfies the correctness of CPRF.

In the following, we show that this CPRF is adaptively secure against adversaries that make $O(1)$ constrained key queries and no evaluation query, which is sufficient to obtain $O(1)$ collusion-resistant adaptive CPRF that tolerates polynomial number of evaluation queries as explained above. First, we remark that constrained key queries made after the challenge query are easy to deal with. Namely, we can replace the master key hardwired into the constrained keys with a "punctured key" that can evaluate the CPRF on all inputs except for the challenge input by using the security of IO and the shift-hiding property of SHSF. Then, we can argue that the challenge output is still pseudorandom even given these constrained keys. We omit the details since this is a simple adaptation of the standard puncturing technique [16,40]. In the following, we assume that all constrained key queries are made before the challenge query so that we can focus on the most non-trivial part.

We begin by considering the single-key security, and later explain how to extend the proof to the $O(1)$-collusion-resistant case. In the single-key security game, an adversary only makes one constrained key query C and a challenge query x^* in this order. Recall that we are assuming that an adversary does not make any evaluation query and does not make any constrained key query after a challenge query is made without loss of generality. The main observation is that the simulator can generate the master key K *with knowledge of the constraint C* associated to the constrained key query since it can postpone generation of K until a constrained key query is made. For proving the security in this setting, we consider the following game hops.

In the first, we replace the master key $\mathsf{K} = \mathsf{sk}^{\mathsf{sim}}$ with a shifted secret key sk_1 generated by $\mathsf{SHSF.Shift}(\mathsf{msk}_1, \overline{C}(\cdot) \cdot r)$. Here, $\mathsf{msk}_1 \xleftarrow{\$} \mathsf{SHSF.KeyGen}$, $\overline{C}$ denotes a negated circuit of C, and $r \xleftarrow{\$} \mathcal{Y}$. This change will go unnoticed due to the shift-hiding property of SHSF. Now, by the correctness of SHSF, we have $\mathsf{SHSF.SEval}(\mathsf{sk}_1, x) = \mathsf{SHSF.Eval}(\mathsf{msk}_1, x) + \overline{C}(x) \cdot r$ for all x. In particular, the challenge output can be written as $\mathsf{SHSF.Eval}(\mathsf{msk}_1, x^*) + r$ since we must have $C(x^*) = 0$. On the other hand, for all inputs x such that $C(x) = 1$, we have $\mathsf{SHSF.SEval}(\mathsf{sk}_1, x) = \mathsf{SHSF.Eval}(\mathsf{msk}_1, x)$. Since the constrained key K_C is an obfuscated program that computes $\mathsf{SHSF.SEval}(\mathsf{sk}_1, x)$ for x such that $C(x) = 1$ and $\perp$ otherwise, the same functionality can be computed by using msk_1 instead of sk_1.

Thus, as a next game hop, we use the security of IO to hardwire msk_1 instead of sk_1 into the constrained key K_C. At this point, the constrained key K_C leaks no information of r since the distribution of msk_1 and r are independent. Thus, we can use the randomness of r to argue that the challenge output is independently uniform from the view of the adversary, which completes the security proof.

Next, we explain how to extend the above proof to the case of $O(1)$-collusion-resistance. A rough idea is to propagate a "masking term" (which was r in the single-key case) through a "chain" of secret keys of SHSF so that the masking term only appears in the challenge output and not used at all for generating constrained keys. We let C_j denote the j-th constrained key query. Then we consider the following game hops.

The first game hop is similar to the single-key case except for the choice of the shifting function. Specifically, we replace the master key $\mathsf{K} = \mathsf{sk}^{\mathsf{sim}}$ with a shifted secret key sk_1 that is generated by $\mathsf{SHSF.Shift}(\mathsf{msk}_1, \overline{C}_1(\cdot) \cdot \mathsf{SHSF.SEval}(\mathsf{sk}_2^{\mathsf{sim}}, \cdot))$ where msk_1 is a master key generated by $\mathsf{SHSF.KeyGen}$ and $\mathsf{sk}_2^{\mathsf{sim}}$ is another secret key generated by $\mathsf{SHSF.Sim}$. Similarly to the case of the single-key security, the way of generating K can be made dependent on the first constrained key query C_1 since K is needed for the first time when responding to the first constrained key query.[4] By the correctness of SHSF, we have $\mathsf{SHSF.SEval}(\mathsf{sk}_1, x) = \mathsf{SHSF.Eval}(\mathsf{msk}_1, x) + \overline{C}_1(x) \cdot \mathsf{SHSF.SEval}(\mathsf{sk}_2^{\mathsf{sim}}, x)$ for all x. Especially, for all

---

[4] Recall that we assume that an adversary does not make an evaluation query and that the challenge query is made at the end of the game.

inputs x such that $C_1(x) = 1$, we have $\mathsf{SHSF.SEval}(\mathsf{sk}_1, x) = \mathsf{SHSF.Eval}(\mathsf{msk}_1, x)$. Therefore, by using the security of IO, we can hardwire (msk_1, C_1) instead of $(\mathsf{K} = \mathsf{sk}_1, C_1)$ into the first constrained key K_{C_1} since it only evaluates the CPRF on x such that $C_1(x) = 1$. Here, note that we do *not* need to hard-wire the value $\mathsf{sk}_2^{\mathsf{sim}}$ in the first constrained key K_{C_1} since $\mathsf{SHSF.SEval}(\mathsf{sk}_2^{\mathsf{sim}}, x)$ part is canceled when $C_1(x) = 1$.

Similarly, for the j-th constrained key for $j \geq 2$, we hardwire $(\mathsf{msk}_1, \mathsf{sk}_2^{\mathsf{sim}}, C_1, C_j)$ instead of $(\mathsf{K} = \mathsf{sk}_1, C_j)$. We note that we have to hardwire $\mathsf{sk}_2^{\mathsf{sim}}$ and C_1 into these constrained keys since they may need to evaluate the CPRF on x such that $C_1(x) = 0$. At this point, the challenge value is $\mathsf{SHSF.SEval}(\mathsf{sk}_1, x^*) = \mathsf{SHSF.Eval}(\mathsf{msk}_1, x^*) + \mathsf{SHSF.SEval}(\mathsf{sk}_2^{\mathsf{sim}}, x^*)$ where x^* denotes the challenge query since we must have $C_1(x^*) = 0$. Next, we apply similar game hops for the next secret key $\mathsf{sk}_2^{\mathsf{sim}}$. Specifically, we replace $\mathsf{sk}_2^{\mathsf{sim}}$ with sk_2 generated by $\mathsf{SHSF.Shift}(\mathsf{msk}_2, \overline{C}_2(\cdot) \cdot \mathsf{SHSF.SEval}(\mathsf{sk}_3^{\mathsf{sim}}, \cdot))$ where msk_2 is another master key generated by $\mathsf{SHSF.KeyGen}$ and $\mathsf{sk}_3^{\mathsf{sim}}$ is another secret key generated by $\mathsf{SHSF.Sim}$. Again, we remark that the way of generating sk_2 can be made dependent on C_2 since it is needed for the first time when responding to the second constrained key query. At this point, we only have to hardwire (msk_1, C_1) into the first constrained key, $(\mathsf{msk}_1, \mathsf{msk}_2, C_1, C_2)$ into the second constrained key, and $(\mathsf{msk}_1, \mathsf{msk}_2, \mathsf{sk}_3^{\mathsf{sim}}, C_1, C_2, C_j)$ into the j-th constrained key for $j \geq 3$, and the challenge output is $\mathsf{SHSF.Eval}(\mathsf{msk}_1, x^*) + \mathsf{SHSF.Eval}(\mathsf{msk}_2, x^*) + \mathsf{SHSF.SEval}(\mathsf{sk}_3^{\mathsf{sim}}, x^*)$. Repeating similar game hops Q times where Q is the number of constrained key queries, we eventually reach the game where

- for each $j \in [Q]$, $\{(\mathsf{msk}_i, C_i)\}_{i \in [j]}$ is hardwired into the j-th constrained key, and
- the challenge output is $\sum_{i \in [Q]} \mathsf{SHSF.Eval}(\mathsf{msk}_i, x^*) + \mathsf{SHSF.SEval}(\mathsf{sk}_{Q+1}^{\mathsf{sim}}, x^*)$.

Especially, in this game, $\mathsf{sk}_{Q+1}^{\mathsf{sim}}$ is only used for generating the challenge output and independent of all constrained keys. Thus, we can conclude that the challenge output is random relying on the randomness of $\mathsf{sk}_{Q+1}^{\mathsf{sim}}$.[5] This completes the proof of the $O(1)$-collusion-resistant adaptive security of our CPRF.

At first glance, the above security proof may work even if an adversary makes (bounded) polynomial number of constrained keys since we only have to hardwire polynomial number of keys and circuits into constrained keys. However, the problem is that the size of the master key msk depends on the maximal size of the shifting function in the LWE-based construction of SHSF given in [39]. In our construction of CPRF, the corresponding shifting function for msk_i depends on sk_{i+1}, and thus msk_i must be polynomially larger than sk_{i+1}, which itself is larger than msk_{i+1}. Thus, the size of msk_i grows polynomially in each layer of the nest. This is the reason why our proof is limited to the $O(1)$-collusion-resistant case.

---

[5] We can show that $\mathsf{SHSF.SEval}(\mathsf{sk}^{\mathsf{sim}}, x)$ is uniformly distributed in $\mathcal{Y}$ over the choice of $\mathsf{sk}^{\mathsf{sim}}$ for any fixed x.

We leave it open to construct an SHSF whose master key size does not depend on the maximal size of the shifting function, which would result in a bounded polynomial collusion-resistant adaptively secure CPRF for P/poly.

3   Preliminaries

Notations. For a distribution or random variable X, we write $x \xleftarrow{\$} X$ to denote the operation of sampling a random x according to X. For a set S, we write $s \xleftarrow{\$} S$ to denote the operation of sampling a random s from the uniform distribution over S. Let $U(S)$ denote the uniform distribution over the set S. For a prime q, we represent the elements in $\mathbb{Z}_q$ by integers in the range $[-(q-1)/2, (q-1)/2]$. For $2 \le p < q$ and $x \in \mathbb{Z}_q$ (or $\mathbb{Z}$), we define $\lfloor x \rceil_p := \lfloor (p/q) \cdot x \rceil \in \mathbb{Z}_p$. We will represent vectors by bold-face letters, and matrices by bold-face capital letters. Unless stated otherwise, we will assume that all vectors are column vectors.

Gadget Matrix. Let $n, q \in \mathbb{Z}$ and $m \ge n\lceil \log q \rceil$. A gadget matrix $\mathbf{G}$ is defined as $\mathbf{I}_n \otimes (1, 2, ..., 2^{\lceil \log q \rceil - 1})$ padded with $m - n\lceil \log q \rceil$ zero columns. For any t, there exists an efficient deterministic algorithm $\mathbf{G}^{-1} : \mathbb{Z}_q^{n \times t} \to \{0, 1\}^{m \times t}$ that takes $\mathbf{U} \in \mathbb{Z}_q^{n \times t}$ as input and outputs $\mathbf{V} \in \{0, 1\}^{m \times t}$ such that $\mathbf{GV} = \mathbf{U}$.

3.1   Admissible Hash Functions and Matrix Embeddings

We prepare the definition of (balanced) admissible hash functions.

Definition 3.1. *Let $\ell := \ell(\kappa)$ and $n := n(\kappa)$ be integer valued polynomials. For $K \in \{0, 1, \bot\}^\ell$, we define the* partitioning function $P_K : \{0, 1\}^\ell \to \{0, 1\}$ *as*

$$P_K(z) = \begin{cases} 0, & \text{if } (K_i = \bot) \vee (K_i = z_i) \\ 1, & \text{otherwise} \end{cases}$$

where K_i and z_i denote the ith bit of K and z, respectively. We say that an efficiently computable function $\mathsf{H}_{\mathsf{adm}} : \{0, 1\}^n \to \{0, 1\}^\ell$ is a balanced admissible hash function, *if there exists a PPT algorithm $\mathsf{PrtSmp}(1^\kappa, Q(\kappa), \delta(\kappa))$, which takes as input a polynomially bounded function $Q := Q(\kappa)$ where $Q : \mathbb{N} \to \mathbb{N}$ and a noticeable function $\delta := \delta(\kappa)$ where $\delta : \mathbb{N} \to (0, 1]$, and outputs $K \in \{0, 1, \bot\}^\ell$ such that:*

1. *There exists $\kappa_0 \in \mathbb{N}$ such that*

$$\Pr\left[K \xleftarrow{\$} \mathsf{PrtSmp}(1^\kappa, Q(\kappa), \delta(\kappa)) : K \in \{0, 1, \bot\}^\ell \right] = 1$$

   for all $\kappa > \kappa_0$. Here κ_0 may depend on the functions Q and δ.
2. *For $\kappa > \kappa_0$, there exists functions $\gamma_{\max}(\kappa)$ and $\gamma_{\min}(\kappa)$ that depend on functions Q and δ such that for all $x_1, \cdots, x_{Q(\kappa)}, x^* \in \{0, 1\}^n$ with $x^* \notin \{x_1, \cdots, x_{Q(\kappa)}\}$,*

$$\gamma_{\min}(\kappa) \le \Pr\left[P_K(\mathsf{H}_{\mathsf{adm}}(x_1)) = \cdots = P_K(\mathsf{H}_{\mathsf{adm}}(x_{Q(\kappa)})) = 1 \wedge P_K(\mathsf{H}_{\mathsf{adm}}(x^*)) = 0 \right] \le \gamma_{\max}(\kappa)$$

holds and the function $\tau(\kappa)$ defined as

$$\tau(\kappa) := \gamma_{\min}(\kappa) \cdot \delta(\kappa) - \frac{\gamma_{\max}(\kappa) - \gamma_{\min}(\kappa)}{2}$$

is noticeable. The probability is taken over the choice of $K \xleftarrow{\$} \mathsf{PrtSmp}(1^\kappa, Q(\kappa), \delta(\kappa))$.

Theorem 3.1 ([30], Theorem 1). *Let $n = \Theta(\kappa)$ and $\ell = \Theta(\kappa)$. If $\mathsf{H}_{\mathsf{adm}} : \{0,1\}^n \to \{0,1\}^\ell$ is a code with minimal distance $c \cdot \ell$ for a constant $c \in (0, 1/2]$, then $\mathsf{H}_{\mathsf{adm}}$ is a balanced admissible hash function. Specifically, there exists a PPT algorithm $\mathsf{PrtSmp}(1^\kappa, Q, \delta)$ which takes as input $Q \in \mathbb{N}$ and $\delta \in (0, 1]$ and outputs $K \in \{0, 1, \bot\}^\ell$ with η' components not equal to $\bot$, where*

$$\eta' = \left\lfloor \frac{\log(2Q + Q/\delta)}{-\log(1 - c)} \right\rfloor \quad and \quad \gamma(\kappa) = 2^{-\eta'-1} \cdot \delta.$$

In particular, when $Q = \mathsf{poly}(\kappa)$ and $\delta = 1/\mathsf{poly}(\kappa)$, then $\eta' = O(\log \kappa)$ and $\gamma(\kappa) = 1/\mathsf{poly}(\kappa)$.

The following is taken from [11] and [43].

Lemma 3.1 (Compatible Algorithms with Partitioning Functions).
Let $P_K : \{0,1\}^\ell \to \{0,1\}$ be a partitioning function where $K \in \{0, 1, \bot\}^\ell$ and assume that K has at most $O(\log \kappa)$ entries in $\{0,1\}$. Then, there exist deterministic PPT algorithms (Encode, PubEval, TrapEval) with the following properties:

- Encode(K) : *on input K, it outputs $\mu \in \{0,1\}^u$ where $u = O(\log^2 \kappa)$,*
- PubEval$(x, \mathbf{A})$: *on input $x \in \{0,1\}^\ell$ and $\mathbf{A} \in \mathbb{Z}_q^{n \times mu}$, it outputs $\mathbf{A}_x \in \mathbb{Z}_q^{n \times m}$,*
- TrapEval$(\mu, x, \mathbf{A}_0, \mathbf{R})$: *on input $\mu \in \{0,1\}^u$, $x \in \{0,1\}^\ell$, $\mathbf{A}_0 \in \mathbb{Z}_q^{n \times m}$, and $\mathbf{R} \in \{-1, 0, 1\}^{m \times mu}$, it outputs $\mathbf{R}_x \in \mathbb{Z}^{m \times m}$,*
- *If $\mathbf{A} := \mathbf{A}_0 \mathbf{R} + \mu \otimes \mathbf{G}$ and $\mathbf{R} \in \{0,1\}^{m \times mu}$ where μ is viewed as a row vector in $\{0,1\}^u$, then for $\mathbf{A}_x = \mathsf{PubEval}(x, \mathbf{A})$ and $\mathbf{R}_x = \mathsf{TrapEval}(\mu, x, \mathbf{A}, \mathbf{R})$, we have $\mathbf{A}_x = \mathbf{A}_0 \mathbf{R}_x + (1 - P_K(x)) \cdot \mathbf{G}$ and $\|\mathbf{R}_x\|_\infty \leq m^3 u \ell$.*
- *Moreover, $\mathbf{R}_x$ can be expressed as $\mathbf{R}_x = \mathbf{R}_0 + \mathbf{R}'_x$ where $\mathbf{R}_0$ is the first m columns of $\mathbf{R}$ and is distributed independently from $\mathbf{R}'_x$.*

Remark 3.1. The last item is non-standard, however, we note that it is without loss of generality. This is because we can always satisfy the last condition by constructing a new PubEval$'$ which simply samples one extra random matrix $\bar{\mathbf{R}}$ and adds $\mathbf{A}_0 \bar{\mathbf{R}}$ to $\mathbf{A}_x = \mathsf{PubEval}(x, \mathbf{A})$. This requirement is only required in our security proof of our CPRF for inner product predicates. More details can be found in [35], Section 4.3.

The following lemma is taken from [31], and is implicit in [9,30,43].

Lemma 3.2 ([31], Lemma 8). *Let us consider a random variable* $\mathsf{coin} \xleftarrow{\$} \{0, 1\}$ *and a distribution* $\mathcal{D}$ *that takes as input a bit* $b \in \{0, 1\}$ *and outputs* $(x, \widehat{\mathsf{coin}})$ *such that* $x \in \mathcal{X}$ *and* $\widehat{\mathsf{coin}} \in \{0, 1\}$, *where* $\mathcal{X}$ *is some domain. For* $\mathcal{D}$, *define* ϵ *as*

$$\epsilon := \left| \Pr\left[\mathsf{coin} \xleftarrow{\$} \{0, 1\}, (x, \widehat{\mathsf{coin}}) \xleftarrow{\$} \mathcal{D}(\mathsf{coin}) : \mathsf{coin} = \widehat{\mathsf{coin}} \right] - \frac{1}{2} \right|.$$

Let γ *be a map that maps an element in* $\mathcal{X}$ *to a value in* $[0, 1]$. *Let us further consider a modified distribution* $\mathcal{D}'$ *that takes as input a bit* $b \in \{0, 1\}$ *and outputs* $(x, \widehat{\mathsf{coin}})$. *To sample from* $\mathcal{D}'$, *we first sample* $(x, \widehat{\mathsf{coin}}) \xleftarrow{\$} \mathcal{D}(b)$, *and then with probability* $1 - \gamma(x)$, *we re-sample* $\widehat{\mathsf{coin}}$ *as* $\widehat{\mathsf{coin}} \xleftarrow{\$} \{0, 1\}$. *Finally,* $\mathcal{D}'$ *outputs* $(x, \widehat{\mathsf{coin}})$. *Then, the following holds.*

$$\left| \Pr\left[\mathsf{coin} \xleftarrow{\$} \{0, 1\}, (x, \widehat{\mathsf{coin}}) \xleftarrow{\$} \mathcal{D}'(\mathsf{coin}) : \mathsf{coin} = \widehat{\mathsf{coin}} \right] - \frac{1}{2} \right| \geq \gamma_{\min} \cdot \epsilon - \frac{\gamma_{\max} - \gamma_{\min}}{2}$$

where $\gamma_{\min}$ *(resp.* $\gamma_{\max}$*) is the maximum (resp. minimum) of* $\gamma(x)$ *taken over all possible* $x \in \mathcal{X}$.

4 CPRFs for Bit-Fixing Predicates from Standard PRFs

In this section, we provide a construction of an adaptively pseudorandom on constrained points, Q-collusion resistant CPRFs for the bit-fixing predicate from any PRF, where Q can be set to be any constant independent of the security parameter. In particular, the result implies the existence of such CPRFs from one-way functions [25, 27]. Recall that no other CPRFs are known to be adaptive and/or to achieve Q-collusion resistance for any $Q > 1$ both from the standard assumptions and in the standard model, excluding the CPRF for the trivial singleton sets $F = \{\{x\} \mid x \in \{0, 1\}^n\}$ [15] or the selectively-secure and collusion-resistant CPRF for prefix-fixing predicates by [5].

Note that it is easy to extend our CPRF for the bit-fixing predicate to a CPRF for the t-CNF predicate where t is a constant. See the full version for the detail.

4.1 Preparation: Bit-Fixing Predicates

Here, we provide the constraint class we will be considering: bit-fixing predicates.

Definition 4.1 (Bit-Fixing Predicate). *For a vector* $v \in \{0, 1, *\}^\ell$, *define the circuit* $C_v^{\mathsf{BF}} : \{0, 1\}^\ell \to \{0, 1\}$ *associated with* v *as*

$$C_v^{\mathsf{BF}}(x) = \bigwedge_{i=1}^{\ell} \left(\left(v_i \stackrel{?}{=} x_i\right) \bigvee \left(v_i \stackrel{?}{=} *\right) \right),$$

where v_i *and* x_i *denote the* i^{th} *bit of the string* v *and* x, *respectively. Then, the family of bit-fixing predicates (with input length* ℓ*) is defined as*

$$\mathcal{C}_\ell^{\mathsf{BF}} := \{C_v^{\mathsf{BF}} \mid v \in \{0, 1, *\}^\ell\}.$$

Since we can consider a canonical representation of the circuit C_v^{BF} given the string $v \in \{0, 1, *\}^{\ell}$, with an abuse of notation, we may occasionally write $v \in C_{\ell}^{\mathsf{BF}}$ and view v as C_v^{BF} when the meaning is clear.

We also define a helper function $G_{\mathsf{auth}}^{\mathsf{BF}}$ which, informally, outputs a set of all the authorized inputs corresponding to a bit-fixing predicate. For any $v \in \{0, 1, *\}^{\ell}$ and $T = (t_1, \cdots, t_Q) \in [\ell]^Q$ such that $Q \le \ell$, let us define $v_T \in \{0, 1, *\}^Q$ as the string $v_{t_1} v_{t_2} \cdots v_{t_Q}$, where v_i is the ith bit of v. Then we define the function $G_{\mathsf{auth}}^{\mathsf{BF}}$ as follows.

$$G_{\mathsf{auth}}^{\mathsf{BF}}(v_T) = \{w \in \{0, 1\}^Q \mid C_{v_T}^{\mathsf{BF}}(w) = 1\}.$$

In words, it is the set of all points with the same length as v_T that equals to v_T on the non-wild card entries. For example, if $\ell = 8, Q = 5$, $v = 011 * 01 * 1$, and $T = (4, 1, 2, 6, 1)$, then $v_T = *0110$ and the authorized set of points would be $G_{\mathsf{auth}}^{\mathsf{BF}}(v_T) = \{00110, 10110\}$. Here, with an abuse of notation, we define the function $G_{\mathsf{auth}}^{\mathsf{BF}}$ for all input lengths.

4.2   Construction

Let $n = n(\kappa)$, and $k = k(\kappa)$ be integer-valued positive polynomials of the security parameter κ and Q be any constant positive integer smaller than n. Let $\mathcal{C}^{\mathsf{BF}} := \{\mathcal{C}_{\kappa}\}_{\kappa \in \mathbb{N}} := \{\mathcal{C}_{n(\kappa)}^{\mathsf{BF}}\}_{\kappa \in \mathbb{N}}$ be a set of family of circuits representing the class of constraints. Let $\Pi_{\mathsf{PRF}} = (\mathsf{PRF.Gen}, \mathsf{PRF.Eval})$ be any PRF with input length n and output length k.

Our Q-collusion resistance CPRF Π_{CPRF} for the constrained class $\mathcal{C}^{\mathsf{BF}}$ is provided as follows:

$\mathsf{CPRF.Gen}(1^{\kappa})$: On input the security parameter 1^{κ}, it runs $\mathsf{K}_{T,w} \xleftarrow{\$} \mathsf{PRF.Gen}(1^{\kappa})$ and $\widehat{\mathsf{K}}_{T,w} \xleftarrow{\$} \mathsf{PRF.Gen}(1^{\kappa})$ for all $T \in [n]^Q$ and $w \in \{0, 1\}^Q$. Then it outputs the master key as

$$\mathsf{K} = \left((\mathsf{K}_{T,w}), (\widehat{\mathsf{K}}_{T,w})\right)_{T \in [n]^Q, w \in \{0,1\}^Q}.$$

$\mathsf{CPRF.Eval}(\mathsf{K}, x)$: On input the master key K and input $x \in \{0, 1\}^n$, it first parses

$$\left((\mathsf{K}_{T,w}), (\widehat{\mathsf{K}}_{T,w})\right)_{T \in [n]^Q, w \in \{0,1\}^Q} \leftarrow \mathsf{K}.$$

It then computes

$$y = \bigoplus_{T \in [n]^Q} \mathsf{PRF.Eval}(\mathsf{K}_{T,x_T}, x),$$

where recall $x_T \in \{0, 1\}^Q$ is defined as the string $x_{t_1} x_{t_2} \cdots x_{t_Q}$ and $T = (t_1, \cdots, t_Q)$. Finally, it outputs $y \in \{0, 1\}^k$.

CPRF.Constrain($\mathsf{K}, C_v^{\mathsf{BF}}$): On input the master key K and a circuit $C_v^{\mathsf{BF}} \in \mathcal{C}_n^{\mathsf{BF}}$, it first parses K into $((\mathsf{K}_{T,w}), (\widehat{\mathsf{K}}_{T,w}))_{T \in [n]^Q, w \in \{0,1\}^Q} \leftarrow \mathsf{K}$ and sets $v \in \{0, 1, *\}^n$ as the representation of C_v^{BF}. Then it outputs the constrained key

$$\mathsf{K}_v = \left(\widetilde{\mathsf{K}}_{T,w} \right)_{T \in [n]^Q, w \in \{0,1\}^Q},$$

where $\widetilde{\mathsf{K}}_{T,w} = \mathsf{K}_{T,w}$ if $w \in G_{\mathsf{auth}}^{\mathsf{BF}}(v_T)$, and $\widetilde{\mathsf{K}}_{T,w} = \widehat{\mathsf{K}}_{T,w}$ otherwise. Recall that $G_{\mathsf{auth}}^{\mathsf{BF}}(v_T) = \{w \in \{0,1\}^Q \mid C_{v_T}^{\mathsf{BF}}(w) = 1\}$.

CPRF.ConstrainEval(K_v, x): On input the constrained key K_v and an input $x \in \{0,1\}^n$, it first parses $(\widetilde{\mathsf{K}}_{T,w})_{T \in [n]^Q, w \in \{0,1\}^Q} \leftarrow \mathsf{K}_v$. It then uses the PRF keys included in the constrained key and computes

$$y = \bigoplus_{T \in [n]^Q} \mathsf{PRF.Eval}(\widetilde{\mathsf{K}}_{T,x_T}, x).$$

Finally, it outputs $y \in \{0,1\}^k$.

Theorem 4.1. *If the underlying PRF Π_{PRF} is adaptively pseudorandom, then our above CPRF Π_{CPRF} for the bit-fixing predicate $\mathcal{C}^{\mathsf{BF}}$ is adaptively pseudorandom on constrained points and Q-collusion resistant for any $Q = O(1)$.*

We omit the proofs of correctness and security due the space limit. See the full version for omitted proofs.

5 CPRF for Inner Products

5.1 Construction

In this section, we construct CPRFs for inner products over the integer. Fix a security parameter κ and define the following quantities:

- Let $\mathcal{D} := [-B, B]^\ell \subset \mathbb{Z}^\ell$ where inner products between two vectors $\mathbf{v}, \mathbf{w} \in \mathcal{D}$ are defined in the natural way over the integers. Let $\mathcal{C}^{\mathsf{IP}} := \{C_{\mathbf{v}}\}_{\mathbf{v} \in \mathcal{D}}$ be the set of circuits where each $C_{\mathbf{v}} : \mathcal{D} \to \mathbb{Z}$ is defined as $C_{\mathbf{v}}(\mathbf{w}) = (\langle \mathbf{v}, \mathbf{w} \rangle \overset{?}{=} 0)$, that is, if the inner product is zero then it outputs 1, and otherwise 0.
- Let $\mathsf{bin} : \mathcal{D} \to \{0,1\}^{\hat{\ell}}$ be a one-to-one map which provides a binary representation of elements in $\mathcal{D}$ where $\hat{\ell} := \ell \cdot \lceil \log(2B+1) \rceil$.
- Let $\mathsf{H}_{\mathsf{adm}} : \{0,1\}^{\hat{\ell}} \to \{0,1\}^L$ be a balanced admissible hash function where $L = \Theta(\kappa)$ by Theorem 3.1.
- Let $\mathcal{H}_{\mathsf{wise}} = \{\mathsf{H}_{\mathsf{wise}} : \mathbb{Z}_p^m \to \mathbb{Z}_p^k\}$ be a family of ζ-wise independent hash functions.
- Let $n, m, u, q, p, \beta, \bar{\beta}$ be additional parameters used within the CPRF scheme and let $h, \alpha_{\mathsf{LWE}}, \alpha_1, \alpha_2$ be parameters used within the security proof, where h, α_{LWE} are LWE-related. The details on the parameters setting is provide after our construction below.

Our CPRF Π_{CPRF} for the constrained class of inner products over the integer $\mathcal{C}^{\mathsf{IP}}$ is provided below. Here, the domain, range, and key space of our CPRF are $\mathcal{D}$, $\mathbb{Z}_p^k$, and $\mathbb{Z}^{n \times \ell}$, respectively.

CPRF.Setup(1^κ): On input the security parameter 1^κ, it first samples random matrix $\mathbf{A} \xleftarrow{\$} \mathbb{Z}_q^{n \times mu}$. It also samples a ζ-wise independent hash function $\mathsf{H}_{\mathsf{wise}} : \mathbb{Z}_p^m \to \mathbb{Z}_p^k$.

$$\mathsf{pp} = \left(\mathbf{A}, \mathsf{H}_{\mathsf{wise}}\right).$$

CPRF.Gen(pp): On input the public parameter pp, it samples a matrix $\mathbf{S} \xleftarrow{\$} [-\bar{\beta}, \bar{\beta}]^{n \times \ell} \subset \mathbb{Z}^{n \times \ell}$ and sets the master key as $\mathsf{K} = \mathbf{S}$.

CPRF.Eval(pp, K, x): On input the public parameter pp, master key $\mathsf{K} = \mathbf{S} \in \mathbb{Z}^{n \times \ell}$ and input $\mathbf{x} \in \mathcal{D}$, it first computes $\mathbf{s} = \mathbf{S}\mathbf{x} \in \mathbb{Z}^n$ and $x = \mathsf{H}_{\mathsf{adm}}(\mathsf{bin}(\mathbf{x})) \in \{0,1\}^L$. It then computes

$$\mathbf{z} = \left\lfloor \mathbf{s}^\top \mathbf{A}_x \right\rfloor_p \in \mathbb{Z}_p^m,$$

where $\mathbf{A}_x = \mathsf{PubEval}(x, \mathbf{A})$. Finally, it outputs $\mathbf{v} = \mathsf{H}_{\mathsf{wise}}(\mathbf{z}) \in \mathbb{Z}_p^k$.

CPRF.Constrain($\mathsf{K}, C_\mathbf{y}$): On input the master key $\mathsf{K} = \mathbf{S}$ and constraint $C_\mathbf{y} \in \mathcal{C}^{\mathsf{IP}}$, it first samples a random vector $\mathbf{d} \xleftarrow{\$} [-\beta, \beta]^n$. It then outputs constrained key $\mathsf{K}_\mathbf{y} \in \mathbb{Z}^{n \times \ell}$ defined as

$$\mathsf{K}_\mathbf{y} = \mathbf{S} + \mathbf{d} \otimes \mathbf{y}^\top.$$

CPRF.ConstrainEval(pp, $\mathsf{K}_\mathbf{y}, x$): On input the public parameter pp, constrained key $\mathsf{K}_\mathbf{y} = \mathbf{S}_\mathbf{y} \in \mathbb{Z}^{n \times \ell}$ and input $\mathbf{x} \in \mathcal{D}$, it first computes $\mathbf{s}_\mathbf{y} = \mathbf{S}_\mathbf{y}\mathbf{x} \in \mathbb{Z}^n$ and $x = \mathsf{H}_{\mathsf{adm}}(\mathsf{bin}(\mathbf{x})) \in \{0,1\}^L$. It then computes

$$\mathbf{z}_\mathbf{y} = \left\lfloor \mathbf{s}_\mathbf{y}^\top \mathbf{A}_x \right\rfloor_p \in \mathbb{Z}_p^m,$$

where $\mathbf{A}_x = \mathsf{PubEval}(x, \mathbf{A})$. Finally, it outputs $\mathbf{v} = \mathsf{H}_{\mathsf{wise}}(\mathbf{z}_\mathbf{y}) \in \mathbb{Z}_p^k$.

5.2   Correctness and Parameter Selection

Correctness. We check correctness of our CPRF. Let $C_\mathbf{y}$ be any inner-product predicate in $\mathcal{C}^{\mathsf{IP}}$. By construction when we evaluate with a constrained key $\mathsf{K}_\mathbf{y}$ on input $\mathbf{x}$ we have

$$\mathbf{z}_\mathbf{y} = \left\lfloor \mathbf{s}_\mathbf{y}^\top \mathbf{A}_x \right\rfloor_p = \left\lfloor \left((\mathbf{S} + \mathbf{d} \otimes \mathbf{y}^\top)\mathbf{x}\right)^\top \mathbf{A}_x \right\rfloor_p = \left\lfloor \mathbf{s}^\top \mathbf{A}_x + \langle \mathbf{x}, \mathbf{y} \rangle \cdot \mathbf{d}^\top \mathbf{A}_x \right\rfloor_p,$$

where $\mathbf{s} = \mathbf{S}\mathbf{x}$. Therefore, if $\langle \mathbf{x}, \mathbf{y} \rangle = 0$ over $\mathbb{Z}$, i.e., the input $\mathbf{x}$ satisfies the constraint $C_\mathbf{y}$, then the right hand side will equal to $\lfloor \mathbf{s}^\top \mathbf{A}_x \rfloor_p$, which is exactly what is computed by algorithm CPRF.Eval using the master key K. Hence, the output value $\mathbf{v} = \mathsf{H}_{\mathsf{wise}}(\mathbf{z})$ is the same for both values computed by the master key K and constrained key $\mathsf{K}_\mathbf{y}$.

Parameter Selection. We summarize the relation which our parameters must satisfy below. Note that some parameters only show up during the security proof. See the full version for the reasons of these parameter choices.

- $m > (n+1)\log q + \omega(\log n)$
- $\alpha_{\mathsf{LWE}} q > 2\sqrt{h}$
- $\|\mathbf{x}^\top \mathbf{S}^\top \mathbf{ER}_x\|_\infty \leq \alpha_1$ for all $\mathbf{x} \in \mathcal{D}$
- $\|\ell B \mathbf{d}^\top \mathbf{ER}_x\|_\infty \leq \alpha_2$ for all $\mathbf{x} \in \mathcal{D}$
- $q = 2mpB^\ell \cdot (\alpha_1 + \alpha_2) \cdot \kappa^{\omega(1)}$ for all $\mathbf{x} \in \mathcal{D}$
- $\bar{\beta} \geq \beta B$ and $\bar{\beta} = n\ell\beta B \cdot \kappa^{\omega(1)}$
- $\bar{n} := n \cdot \log(2\beta+1) - h \cdot \log q = \Omega(\kappa)$

Fix $\ell = \ell(\kappa)$, $B = B(\kappa)$, $h = h(\kappa)$, and $u = O(\log^2 \kappa)$, where ℓ and B defines the constraint space (i.e., the set of vectors $\mathcal{D}$), $h(\geq \kappa)$ defines the lattice dimension for the underlying LWE problem, and u is the parameter for the admissible hash (see Sect. 3.1). We assume without loss of generality that ℓ and h are polynomial in κ. Then, one way to set the parameters would be as follows:

$$
\begin{array}{lll}
n = \ell h^{1.1}, & m = \ell^2 h^{1.2}, & q = 2^\ell \ell^{14} h^{7.6} B^{\ell+2} \kappa^{3\log\kappa}, \\
p = 10, & \alpha_{\mathsf{LWE}} = 2\sqrt{h} \cdot q^{-1}, & \zeta = \bar{n} + \ell \cdot \log B, \\
\alpha_1 = \alpha_2 = \ell^{12} h^{6.4} B^2 \kappa^{2\log\kappa}, & \beta = 1, & \bar{\beta} = \ell^2 h^{1.1} B \kappa^{\log\kappa},
\end{array}
$$

where we set q to be the next largest prime. Above we use the simplifying argument that for any positive constant c, we have $\kappa^{0.1} = \omega(\log^c \kappa)$ and $\log \kappa = \omega(1)$ for sufficiently large $\kappa \in \mathbb{N}$ and set ζ according to the deterministic randomness extractor lemma by Dodis [23] (see the full version for the detail) The output space of our CPRF is $\{0,1\}^{\bar{n}} = \{0,1\}^{\Theta(\kappa)}$.

5.3   Security Proof

Theorem 5.1. *The above CPRF Π_{CPRF} for the inner product predicate $\mathcal{C}^{\mathsf{IP}}$ is adaptively single-key pseudorandom on constrained points against adversaries that make exactly one constrained key query, assuming hardness of the* $\mathsf{LWE}_{n,m,q,D_{\mathbb{Z},\alpha_{\mathsf{LWE}}q}}$ *problem.*

Remark 5.1. We note that we can assume the adversary makes *exactly* one constrained key query without loss of generality. This is a useful condition to assume to handle adversaries that make no constrained key query but queries $\mathbf{x}^* = 0$ as the target input at the challenge phase. The above assumption holds because we can generically add security against adversaries that make no evaluation query by simply xoring an evaluated value of a (standard) PRF. The details are as follows. We add the same (standard) PRF key k both in the master secret key and constrained key. When evaluating on input $\mathbf{x}$, we will also xor the value $\mathsf{PRF}(k, \mathbf{x})$. Therefore, in case no constraint queries are made, pseudorandomness of $\mathsf{PRF}(k, \mathbf{x})$ can be used instead since k is not revealed.

We omitted the proofs due to the space limit. See the full version for the proofs.

6   CPRF for **P/poly**

6.1   Shift-Hiding Shiftable Function

Here, we review the notion of shift-hiding shiftable function (SHSF) introduced by Peikert and Shiehian [39]. We note that our definition of correctness is slightly different from theirs. Specifically, we need a statistical notion of correctness whereas they only considered a computational notion of correctness. Nonetheless, a simple variant of their SHSF also satisfies our definition of correctness as seen in Lemma 6.1.

A SHSF with input space $\{0,1\}^\ell$ and output space $\mathbb{Z}_q^m$ with a rounding modulus $p < q$ consists of a tuple of PPT algorithms $\Pi_{\mathsf{SHSF}} = (\mathsf{SHSF.KeyGen}, \mathsf{SHSF.Eval}, \mathsf{SHSF.Shift}, \mathsf{SHSF.SEval}, \mathsf{SHSF.Sim})^6$ where:

$\mathsf{SHSF.KeyGen}(1^\kappa, 1^\sigma) \to \mathsf{msk}$: The key generation algorithm takes as input the security parameter 1^κ and the circuit size parameter 1^σ, and outputs a master key msk.

$\mathsf{SHSF.Eval}(\mathsf{msk}, x) \to \mathbf{y}$: The evaluation algorithm takes as input a master key msk and an input $x \in \{0,1\}^\ell$, and outputs $\mathbf{y} \in \mathbb{Z}_q^m$.

$\mathsf{SHSF.Shift}(\mathsf{msk}, C) \to \mathsf{sk}_C$: The shift algorithm takes as input a master key msk and a circuit C that computes a shift function, and outputs a shifted secret key sk_C.

$\mathsf{SHSF.SEval}(\mathsf{sk}_C, x) \to \mathbf{y}$: The shifted evaluation algorithm takes as input a secret key sk_C and an input $x \in \{0,1\}^\ell$, and outputs $\mathbf{y} \in \mathbb{Z}_q^m$.

$\mathsf{SHSF.Sim}(1^\kappa, 1^\sigma) \to \mathsf{sk}$: The key simulation algorithm takes as input the security parameter 1^κ and the circuit size parameter 1^σ, and outputs a simulated secret key sk.

We require Π_{SHSF} to satisfy the following properties.

p-**Rounded** ϵ-**Correctness.**

For all $x \in \{0,1\}^\ell$, circuit $C : \{0,1\}^\ell \to \mathbb{Z}_q^m$ whose description size is at most σ, and $\mathbf{v} \in \mathbb{Z}_q^m$, we have

$$\Pr[\lfloor \mathsf{SHSF.SEval}(\mathsf{sk}_C, x) + \mathbf{v} \rfloor_p \neq \lfloor \mathsf{SHSF.Eval}(\mathsf{msk}, x) + C(x) + \mathbf{v} \rfloor_p] \leq \epsilon$$

where $\mathsf{msk} \xleftarrow{\$} \mathsf{SHSF.KeyGen}(1^\kappa, 1^\sigma)$ and $\mathsf{sk}_C \xleftarrow{\$} \mathsf{SHSF.Shift}(\mathsf{msk}, C)$.

Shift Hiding. We define the notion of *shift hiding* for SHSFs. Informally, we require that a shifted secret key sk_C does not reveal the corresponding shifting circuit C.

Formally, this security notion is defined by the following game between an adversary $\mathcal{A}$ and a challenger:

Key Query: At the beginning of the game, the adversary is given the security parameter 1^κ, the circuit size parameter 1^σ, and returns a circuit $C : \{0,1\}^\ell \to \mathbb{Z}_q^m$ whose description size is at most σ.

---

[6] In the original definition of [39], there is an additional setup algorithm that generates a public parameter. We omit this algorithm since in general we can always include the public parameter in the secret key.

Key Generation: The challenger chooses a random bit coin $\xleftarrow{\$} \{0,1\}$. Then it generates sk as follows:

- If coin $= 0$, it generates msk $\xleftarrow{\$}$ SHSF.KeyGen$(1^\kappa, 1^\sigma)$ and sk $\xleftarrow{\$}$ SHSF.Shift(msk, C).
- If coin $= 1$, it generates sk $\xleftarrow{\$}$ SHSF.Sim$(1^\kappa, 1^\sigma)$.

It returns sk to $\mathcal{A}$.

Guess: Eventually, $\mathcal{A}$ outputs $\widehat{\text{coin}}$ as a guess for coin.

We say the adversary $\mathcal{A}$ wins the game if $\widehat{\text{coin}} = \text{coin}$.

Definition 6.1. *An SHSF Π_{SHSF} is said to be shift hiding if for all $\sigma = \mathsf{poly}(\kappa)$ and PPT adversary $\mathcal{A}$, $|\Pr[\mathcal{A} \text{ wins}] - 1/2| = \mathsf{negl}(\kappa)$ holds.*

Lemma 6.1 ([39]). *If $\mathsf{LWE}_{n,m,q,D_{\mathbb{Z},\alpha}}$ is hard for $q = 2^{\mathsf{poly}(\kappa,\sigma)} \cdot \epsilon^{-1}$, $m = n\lfloor \log q \rfloor$ and $\alpha = \mathsf{poly}(n)$, then for any $\ell = \mathsf{poly}(\kappa)$, there exists an SHSF from $\{0,1\}^\ell$ to $\mathbb{Z}_q^m$ that is shift hiding and satisfies p-rounded ϵ-correctness for some divisor p of q such that $p < \epsilon q$.*

Proof. Shiehian and Peikert [39] proved that if $\mathsf{LWE}_{n,m,q,D_{\mathbb{Z},\alpha}}$ is hard for $q = 2^{\mathsf{poly}(\kappa,\sigma)}$, $m = n\lfloor \log q \rfloor$ and $\alpha = \mathsf{poly}(n)$, then there exists an SHSF that is shift hiding and satisfies "approximated correctness", where the latter states that

$$\left| \left(\mathsf{SHSF.SEval}(\mathsf{sk}_C, x) - (\mathsf{SHSF.Eval}(\mathsf{msk}, x) + C(x)) \right)_i \right| \le B = \kappa^{\mathsf{poly}(\kappa)}$$

for all $i \in [m]$, where $(\mathbf{z})_i$ for any $\mathbf{z} \in \mathbb{Z}^m$ denotes the i-th entry of $\mathbf{z}$. This implies that for any $\mathbf{v} \in \mathbb{Z}_q^m$ and p that divides q, we have

$$\lfloor \mathsf{SHSF.SEval}(\mathsf{sk}_C, x) + \mathbf{v} \rfloor_p = \lfloor \mathsf{SHSF.Eval}(\mathsf{msk}, x) + C(x) + \mathbf{v} \rfloor_p$$

as long as we have, for all $i \in [m]$,

$$(\mathsf{SHSF.SEval}(\mathsf{sk}_C, x) + \mathbf{v})_i \notin \frac{q}{p}\mathbb{Z} + [-B, B]. \tag{1}$$

Let us now consider a slight modification of their SHSF where an additional random vector $\mathbf{r} \xleftarrow{\$} \mathbb{Z}_q^m$ is included in both msk and sk_C.[7] The modified SHSF.Eval and SHSF.SEval will now add $\mathbf{r}$ to the original outputs, e.g., run SHSF.Eval of [39] and add $\mathbf{r}$ to the output. It is clear that this modification does not harm the shift hiding property. With this slightly modified variant, for any fixed $x \in \{0,1\}^\ell$ and C, $\mathsf{SHSF.SEval}(\mathsf{sk}_C, x)$ is uniformly distributed over $\mathbb{Z}_q^m$ where the randomness is taken over the choice of msk $\xleftarrow{\$}$ SHSF.KeyGen$(1^\kappa, 1^\sigma)$ and $\mathsf{sk}_C \xleftarrow{\$}$ SHSF.Shift(msk, C). Then, the probability that Eq. 1 does not hold is at most $\frac{2pB}{q}$ for each $i \in [m]$. By taking the union bound, the probability that there exists $i \in [m]$ such that Eq. 1 does not hold is at most $\frac{2pBm}{q}$. By taking the parameters so that $\frac{2pBm}{q} \le \epsilon$, the slightly modified SHSF satisfies p-rounded ϵ-correctness. $\qquad \square$

---

[7] Note that the vector $\mathbf{r}$ is sampled in the key generation, and not relevant to the vector $\mathbf{v}$ that appeared above.

6.2   Construction of CPRF

Here, we give a construction of an adaptively secure CPRF for all polynomial-size circuits (i.e., P/poly) from SHSF and IO.

Preparation. Before describing our construction, we prove a general lemma that enables us to focus on adversaries that do not make any evaluation queries. Namely, if we call constrained key queries made before (resp. after) the challenge query *pre-challenge (resp. post-challenge) constrained key queries*, then we have the following lemma.

Lemma 6.2. *If there exists a CPRF for* P/poly *that is adaptively secure against adversaries that make at most Q_1 pre-challenge constrained key queries, Q_2 post-challenge constrained key queries, and no evaluation query, then the CPRF is adaptively secure against all adversaries that make at most $Q_1 - 1$ pre-challenge constrained key queries, Q_2 post-challenge constrained key queries, and* poly(κ) *evaluation queries.*

Roughly speaking, the lemma follows by considering a no-evaluation query adversary $\mathcal{A}$ which queries its challenger for a constrained key for the "partitioning function" [30,43]. Then, $\mathcal{A}$ can simulate the view to the standard CPRF adversary $\mathcal{B}$ by simulating all evaluation queries made by $\mathcal{B}$ with this constrained key. In particular, with non-negligible probability, the partitioning function will output 1 for all evaluation queries and will output 0 for the challenge query. Therefore, $\mathcal{A}$ will be able to answer the evaluation queries made by $\mathcal{B}$ using its constrained key while it will not be able to answer the challenge query. Hence, with one extra constrained key query on the partitioning function, all evaluation queries can be simulated, which eliminates the necessity of evaluation queries. The full proof can be found in the full version.

Construction. Here, we construct an adaptively secure CPRF that tolerates $Q_1 = O(1)$ pre-challenge constrained key queries and $Q_2 = $ poly(κ) post-challenge constrained key queries. By Lemma 6.2, we can assume that $\mathcal{A}$ does not make an evaluation query without loss of generality. Let z be the maximum description size of the circuit that is supported by our CPRF. Let $\Pi_{\mathsf{SHSF}} = (\mathsf{SHSF.KeyGen}, \mathsf{SHSF.Eval}, \mathsf{SHSF.Shift}, \mathsf{SHSF.SEval}, \mathsf{SHSF.Sim})$ be an SHSF with input space $\{0,1\}^\ell$ and output space $\mathbb{Z}_q^m$ that is shift hiding with a rounding modulus $p < $ negl(κ) $\cdot q$ that satisfies p-rounded ϵ-correctness where $\epsilon := 2^{-\ell}$negl(κ). We define parameters $\sigma_{Q_1+1}, ..., \sigma_1$ in the following recursive way.[8]

1. Set σ_{Q_1+1} as the maximum size of the circuit in the set $\{C_{\mathsf{eq}}[x^*, \mathbf{r}] \mid x^* \in \{0,1\}^\ell, \mathbf{r} \in \mathbb{Z}_q^m\}$, where $C_{\mathsf{eq}}[x^*, \mathbf{r}](\cdot)$ is a circuit which outputs $\mathbf{r}$ on input $x = x^*$, and 0 otherwise.[9]

---

[8] In the actual scheme, only σ_1 will appear and $\sigma_2, ..., \sigma_{Q_1+1}$ are only used in the security proof.

[9] Although there may be many ways to describe the circuit $C_{\mathsf{eq}}[x^*, \mathbf{r}]$, we consider the most obvious and standard one.

```
ConstrainedKey[sk_1, C]
Input: x ∈ {0, 1}^ℓ
Constants:sk_1, C
If C(x) = 1
    Output ⌊SHSF.SEval(sk_1, x)⌋_p
Else
    Output ⊥
```

Fig. 3. Description of program ConstrainedKey[sk_1, C]

2. For $i = Q_1, ..., 1$, set σ_i as the maximum size of the circuit that computes $\overline{C}(\cdot) \cdot \mathsf{SHSF.SEval}(sk_{i+1}, \cdot)$, where the max is taken over all $sk_{i+1} \xleftarrow{\$} \mathsf{SHSF.Sim}(1^\kappa, 1^{\sigma_{i+1}})$ and circuit $C : \{0, 1\}^\ell \rightarrow \{0, 1\}$ with description size at most z. Here, $\overline{C}$ denotes a circuit such that $\overline{C}(x) := (1 - C(x))$ for all $x \in \{0, 1\}^\ell$ and $\overline{C}(\cdot) \cdot \mathsf{SHSF.SEval}(sk_{i+1}, \cdot)$ denotes the circuit that takes $x \in \{0, 1\}^\ell$ as input and returns $\overline{C}(x) \cdot \mathsf{SHSF.SEval}(sk_{i+1}, x)$.

Note that the size of parameters satisfy $\sigma_1 > \sigma_2 > \cdots > \sigma_{Q_1+1}$.

Whenever we use IO, the circuit to be obfuscated is supposed to be padded so that they are as large as any circuit that replaces the circuit in the security proof. Then our CPRF is described as follows:[10]

CPRF.Gen(1^κ): On input the security parameter 1^κ, it generates $sk_1 \xleftarrow{\$} \mathsf{SHSF.Sim}(1^\kappa, 1^{\sigma_1})$, and outputs $K := sk_1$.

CPRF.Eval(K, x): On input the master key $K = sk_1$ and input $x \in \{0, 1\}^\ell$, it computes $\mathbf{y} := \mathsf{SHSF.SEval}(sk_1, x)$ and outputs $\lfloor \mathbf{y} \rfloor_p$.

CPRF.Constrain(K, C): On input the master key $K = sk_1$ and constraint C, it returns $K_C := \mathsf{iO}(\mathsf{ConstrainedKey}[sk_1, C])$ where ConstrainedKey[sk_1, C] is a program described in Figure 3 (with an appropriate padding).

CPRF.ConstrainEval(pp, K, x): On input the public parameter pp, constrained key K_C and input $x \in \{0, 1\}^\ell$, it outputs $K_C(x)$.

The following theorem addresses security of the above CPRF.

Theorem 6.1. *If* iO *is a secure indistinguishability obfuscator and* Π_{SHSF} *satisfies p-rounded ϵ-correctness and the shift hiding, then the above CPRF is adaptively secure against adversaries that make at most* $Q_1 = O(1)$ *pre-challenge constrained key queries,* $Q_2 = \mathsf{poly}(\kappa)$ *post-challenge constrained key queries, and no evaluation query.*

Combining this theorem with Lemmata 6.1 and 6.2 we obtain the following theorem.

Theorem 6.2. *If* $\mathsf{LWE}_{n,m,q,D_{\mathbb{Z},\alpha}}$ *is hard for* $n = \mathsf{poly}(\kappa)$, $q = 2^{\mathsf{poly}(\kappa,z)+\ell}$, $m = n\lfloor \log q \rfloor$, *and* $\alpha = \mathsf{poly}(n)$, *then there exists a CPRF for* $\mathsf{P/poly}$ *that is adaptively*

---

[10] In our scheme, a public parameter is just the security parameter. So we omit the setup algorithm CPRF.Setup.

secure against adversaries that make at most $O(1)$ pre-challenge constrained key queries, poly(κ) post-challenge constrained key queries, and poly(κ) evaluation queries. Especially, under the same assumption, there exists an $O(1)$-collusion-resistant adaptively secure CPRF for P/poly.

We omit the proof of Theorem 6.1 due to the space limit. See the full version for the proof.

References

1. Agrawal, S., Boneh, D., Boyen, X.: Efficient lattice (H)IBE in the standard model. In: Gilbert, H. (ed.) EUROCRYPT 2010. LNCS, vol. 6110, pp. 553–572. Springer, Heidelberg (2010). https://doi.org/10.1007/978-3-642-13190-5_28
2. Alwen, J., Krenn, S., Pietrzak, K., Wichs, D.: Learning with rounding, revisited. In: Canetti, R., Garay, J.A. (eds.) CRYPTO 2013, Part I. LNCS, vol. 8042, pp. 57–74. Springer, Heidelberg (2013). https://doi.org/10.1007/978-3-642-40041-4_4
3. Attrapadung, N., Matsuda, T., Nishimaki, R., Yamada, S., Yamakawa, T.: Constrained PRFs for NC^1 in traditional groups. In: Shacham, H., Boldyreva, A. (eds.) CRYPTO 2018, Part II. LNCS, vol. 10992, pp. 543–574. Springer, Cham (2018). https://doi.org/10.1007/978-3-319-96881-0_19
4. Attrapadung, N., Matsuda, T., Nishimaki, R., Yamada, S., Yamakawa, T.: Adaptively single-key secure constrained PRFs for NC^1. In: Lin, D., Sako, K. (eds.) PKC 2019, Part II. LNCS, vol. 11443, pp. 223–253. Springer, Cham (2019). https://doi.org/10.1007/978-3-030-17259-6_8
5. Banerjee, A., Fuchsbauer, G., Peikert, C., Pietrzak, K., Stevens, S.: Key-homomorphic constrained pseudorandom functions. In: Dodis, Y., Nielsen, J.B. (eds.) TCC 2015, Part II. LNCS, vol. 9015, pp. 31–60. Springer, Heidelberg (2015). https://doi.org/10.1007/978-3-662-46497-7_2
6. Banerjee, A., Peikert, C.: New and improved key-homomorphic pseudorandom functions. In: Garay, J.A., Gennaro, R. (eds.) CRYPTO 2014, Part I. LNCS, vol. 8616, pp. 353–370. Springer, Heidelberg (2014). https://doi.org/10.1007/978-3-662-44371-2_20
7. Banerjee, A., Peikert, C., Rosen, A.: Pseudorandom functions and lattices. In: Pointcheval, D., Johansson, T. (eds.) EUROCRYPT 2012. LNCS, vol. 7237, pp. 719–737. Springer, Heidelberg (2012). https://doi.org/10.1007/978-3-642-29011-4_42
8. Bellare, M., Kiltz, E., Peikert, C., Waters, B.: Identity-based (lossy) trapdoor functions and applications. In: Pointcheval, D., Johansson, T. (eds.) EUROCRYPT 2012. LNCS, vol. 7237, pp. 228–245. Springer, Heidelberg (2012). https://doi.org/10.1007/978-3-642-29011-4_15
9. Bellare, M., Ristenpart, T.: Simulation without the artificial abort: simplified proof and improved concrete security for Waters' IBE scheme. In: Joux, A. (ed.) EUROCRYPT 2009. LNCS, vol. 5479, pp. 407–424. Springer, Heidelberg (2009). https://doi.org/10.1007/978-3-642-01001-9_24
10. Boneh, D., Boyen, X.: Secure identity based encryption without random oracles. In: Franklin, M. (ed.) CRYPTO 2004. LNCS, vol. 3152, pp. 443–459. Springer, Heidelberg (2004). https://doi.org/10.1007/978-3-540-28628-8_27

11. Boneh, D., et al.: Fully key-homomorphic encryption, arithmetic circuit ABE and compact garbled circuits. In: Nguyen, P.Q., Oswald, E. (eds.) EUROCRYPT 2014. LNCS, vol. 8441, pp. 533–556. Springer, Heidelberg (2014). https://doi.org/10.1007/978-3-642-55220-5_30

12. Boneh, D., Kim, S., Montgomery, H.: Private puncturable PRFs from standard lattice assumptions. In: Coron, J.-S., Nielsen, J.B. (eds.) EUROCRYPT 2017, Part I. LNCS, vol. 10210, pp. 415–445. Springer, Cham (2017). https://doi.org/10.1007/978-3-319-56620-7_15

13. Boneh, D., Lewi, K., Montgomery, H., Raghunathan, A.: Key homomorphic PRFs and their applications. In: Canetti, R., Garay, J.A. (eds.) CRYPTO 2013, Part I. LNCS, vol. 8042, pp. 410–428. Springer, Heidelberg (2013). https://doi.org/10.1007/978-3-642-40041-4_23

14. Boneh, D., Lewi, K., Wu, D.J.: Constraining pseudorandom functions privately. In: Fehr, S. (ed.) PKC 2017, Part II. LNCS, vol. 10175, pp. 494–524. Springer, Heidelberg (2017). https://doi.org/10.1007/978-3-662-54388-7_17

15. Boneh, D., Waters, B.: Constrained pseudorandom functions and their applications. In: Sako, K., Sarkar, P. (eds.) ASIACRYPT 2013, Part II. LNCS, vol. 8270, pp. 280–300. Springer, Heidelberg (2013). https://doi.org/10.1007/978-3-642-42045-0_15

16. Boneh, D., Zhandry, M.: Multiparty key exchange, efficient traitor tracing, and more from indistinguishability obfuscation. In: Garay, J.A., Gennaro, R. (eds.) CRYPTO 2014, Part I. LNCS, vol. 8616, pp. 480–499. Springer, Heidelberg (2014). https://doi.org/10.1007/978-3-662-44371-2_27

17. Boyle, E., Goldwasser, S., Ivan, I.: Functional signatures and pseudorandom functions. In: Krawczyk, H. (ed.) PKC 2014. LNCS, vol. 8383, pp. 501–519. Springer, Heidelberg (2014). https://doi.org/10.1007/978-3-642-54631-0_29

18. Brakerski, Z., Tsabary, R., Vaikuntanathan, V., Wee, H.: Private constrained PRFs (and More) from LWE. In: Kalai, Y., Reyzin, L. (eds.) TCC 2017, Part I. LNCS, vol. 10677, pp. 264–302. Springer, Cham (2017). https://doi.org/10.1007/978-3-319-70500-2_10

19. Brakerski, Z., Vaikuntanathan, V.: Constrained key-homomorphic PRFs from standard lattice assumptions. In: Dodis, Y., Nielsen, J.B. (eds.) TCC 2015, Part II. LNCS, vol. 9015, pp. 1–30. Springer, Heidelberg (2015). https://doi.org/10.1007/978-3-662-46497-7_1

20. Canetti, R., Chen, Y.: Constraint-hiding constrained PRFs for NC^1 from LWE. In: Coron, J.-S., Nielsen, J.B. (eds.) EUROCRYPT 2017, Part I. LNCS, vol. 10210, pp. 446–476. Springer, Cham (2017). https://doi.org/10.1007/978-3-319-56620-7_16

21. Cash, D., Hofheinz, D., Kiltz, E., Peikert, C.: Bonsai trees, or how to delegate a lattice basis. In: Gilbert, H. (ed.) EUROCRYPT 2010. LNCS, vol. 6110, pp. 523–552. Springer, Heidelberg (2010). https://doi.org/10.1007/978-3-642-13190-5_27

22. Chen, Y., Vaikuntanathan, V., Wee, H.: GGH15 beyond permutation branching programs: proofs, attacks, and candidates. In: Shacham, H., Boldyreva, A. (eds.) CRYPTO 2018, Part II. LNCS, vol. 10992, pp. 577–607. Springer, Cham (2018). https://doi.org/10.1007/978-3-319-96881-0_20

23. Dodis, Y.: Exposure-resilient cryptography. Ph.D. thesis, Massachusetts Institute of Technology, Cambridge, MA, USA (2000)

24. Fuchsbauer, G., Konstantinov, M., Pietrzak, K., Rao, V.: Adaptive security of constrained PRFs. In: Sarkar, P., Iwata, T. (eds.) ASIACRYPT 2014, Part II. LNCS, vol. 8874, pp. 82–101. Springer, Heidelberg (2014). https://doi.org/10.1007/978-3-662-45608-8_5

25. Goldreich, O., Goldwasser, S., Micali, S.: How to construct random functions. J. ACM **33**(4), 792–807 (1986)
26. Goldwasser, S., Kalai, Y., Peikert, C., Vaikuntanathan, V.: Robustness of the learning with errors assumption. In: ICS, pp. 230–240 (2010)
27. Håstad, J., Impagliazzo, R., Levin, L.A., Luby, M.: A pseudorandom generator from any one-way function. SIAM J. Comput. **28**(4), 1364–1396 (1999)
28. Hofheinz, D., Kamath, A., Koppula, V., Waters, B.: Adaptively secure constrained pseudorandom functions. In: Goldberg, I., Moore, T. (eds.) FC 2019. LNCS, vol. 11598, pp. 357–376. Springer, Cham (2019). https://doi.org/10.1007/978-3-030-32101-7_22
29. Hohenberger, S., Koppula, V., Waters, B.: Adaptively secure puncturable pseudorandom functions in the standard model. In: Iwata, T., Cheon, J.H. (eds.) ASIACRYPT 2015, Part I. LNCS, vol. 9452, pp. 79–102. Springer, Heidelberg (2015). https://doi.org/10.1007/978-3-662-48797-6_4
30. Jager, T.: Verifiable random functions from weaker assumptions. In: Dodis, Y., Nielsen, J.B. (eds.) TCC 2015, Part II. LNCS, vol. 9015, pp. 121–143. Springer, Heidelberg (2015). https://doi.org/10.1007/978-3-662-46497-7_5
31. Katsumata, S., Yamada, S.: Partitioning via non-linear polynomial functions: more compact IBEs from ideal lattices and bilinear maps. In: Cheon, J.H., Takagi, T. (eds.) ASIACRYPT 2016, Part II. LNCS, vol. 10032, pp. 682–712. Springer, Heidelberg (2016). https://doi.org/10.1007/978-3-662-53890-6_23
32. Katsumata, S., Yamada, S.: Non-zero inner product encryption schemes from various assumptions: LWE, DDH and DCR. In: Lin, D., Sako, K. (eds.) PKC 2019, Part II. LNCS, vol. 11443, pp. 158–188. Springer, Cham (2019). https://doi.org/10.1007/978-3-030-17259-6_6
33. Kiayias, A., Papadopoulos, S., Triandopoulos, N., Zacharias, T.: Delegatable pseudorandom functions and applications. In: Sadeghi, A.-R., Gligor, V.D., Yung, M. (eds.) ACM CCS 2013, pp. 669–684. ACM Press, New York (2013)
34. Libert, B., Sakzad, A., Stehlé, D., Steinfeld, R.: All-but-many lossy trapdoor functions and selective opening chosen-ciphertext security from LWE. In: Katz, J., Shacham, H. (eds.) CRYPTO 2017, Part III. LNCS, vol. 10403, pp. 332–364. Springer, Cham (2017). https://doi.org/10.1007/978-3-319-63697-9_12
35. Libert, B., Stehlé, D., Titiu, R.: Adaptively secure distributed PRFs from LWE. In: Beimel, A., Dziembowski, S. (eds.) TCC 2018, Part II. LNCS, vol. 11240, pp. 391–421. Springer, Cham (2018). https://doi.org/10.1007/978-3-030-03810-6_15
36. Micciancio, D., Peikert, C.: Trapdoors for lattices: simpler, tighter, faster, smaller. In: Pointcheval, D., Johansson, T. (eds.) EUROCRYPT 2012. LNCS, vol. 7237, pp. 700–718. Springer, Heidelberg (2012). https://doi.org/10.1007/978-3-642-29011-4_41
37. Naor, M., Reingold, O.: Number-theoretic constructions of efficient pseudo-random functions. J. ACM **51**(2), 231–262 (2004)
38. Naor, M., Reingold, O., Rosen, A.: Pseudorandom functions and factoring. SIAM J. Comput. **31**(5), 1383–1404 (2002)
39. Peikert, C., Shiehian, S.: Privately constraining and programming PRFs, the LWE way. In: Abdalla, M., Dahab, R. (eds.) PKC 2018, Part II. LNCS, vol. 10770, pp. 675–701. Springer, Cham (2018). https://doi.org/10.1007/978-3-319-76581-5_23
40. Sahai, A., Waters, B.: How to use indistinguishability obfuscation: deniable encryption, and more. In: Shmoys, D.B. (ed.) 46th ACM STOC, pp. 475–484. ACM Press, May/June 2014

41. Tsabary, R.: Fully secure attribute-based encryption for t-CNF from LWE. In: Boldyreva, A., Micciancio, D. (eds.) CRYPTO 2019, Part I. LNCS, vol. 11692, pp. 62–85. Springer, Cham (2019). https://doi.org/10.1007/978-3-030-26948-7_3

42. Waters, B.: Efficient identity-based encryption without random oracles. In: Cramer, R. (ed.) EUROCRYPT 2005. LNCS, vol. 3494, pp. 114–127. Springer, Heidelberg (2005). https://doi.org/10.1007/11426639_7

43. Yamada, S.: Asymptotically compact adaptively secure lattice IBEs and verifiable random functions via generalized partitioning techniques. In: Katz, J., Shacham, H. (eds.) CRYPTO 2017, Part III. LNCS, vol. 10403, pp. 161–193. Springer, Cham (2017). https://doi.org/10.1007/978-3-319-63697-9_6

Collusion Resistant Watermarkable PRFs from Standard Assumptions

Rupeng Yang[1(✉)], Man Ho Au[1(✉)], Zuoxia Yu[1], and Qiuliang Xu[2]

[1] Department of Computer Science, The University of Hong Kong, Hong Kong, China
orbbyrp@gmail.com, allenau@cs.hku.hk, zuoxia.yu@gmail.com
[2] School of Software, Shandong University, Jinan 250101, China
xql@sdu.edu.cn

Abstract. A software watermarking scheme can embed a message into a program without significantly changing its functionality. Moreover, any attempt to remove the embedded message in a marked program will substantially change the functionality of the program. Prior constructions of watermarking schemes focus on watermarking cryptographic functions, such as pseudorandom function (PRF), public key encryption, etc.

A natural security requirement for watermarking schemes is collusion resistance, where the adversary's goal is to remove the embedded messages given multiple marked versions of the same program. Currently, this strong security guarantee has been achieved by watermarking schemes for public key cryptographic primitives from standard assumptions (Goyal et al., CRYPTO 2019) and by watermarking schemes for PRFs from indistinguishability obfuscation (Yang et al., ASIACRYPT 2019). However, no collusion resistant watermarking scheme for PRF from standard assumption is known.

In this work, we solve this problem by presenting a generic construction that upgrades a watermarkable PRF without collusion resistance to a collusion resistant one. One appealing feature of our construction is that it can preserve the security properties of the original scheme. For example, if the original scheme has security with extraction queries, the new scheme is also secure with extraction queries. Besides, the new scheme can achieve unforgeability even if the original scheme does not provide this security property. Instantiating our construction with existing watermarking schemes for PRF, we obtain collusion resistant watermarkable PRFs from standard assumptions, offering various security properties.

1 Introduction

A watermarking scheme allows one to embed some information into a program while preserving its functionality. Moreover, it should be difficult for an adversary to remove the embedded information without destroying the marked program. Watermarking schemes are widely employed in many applications, including ownership protection, traitor tracing, etc.

R. Yang and Z. Yu—Part of the work was done while the author was with the Department of Computing, The Hong Kong Polytechnic University.

D. Micciancio and T. Ristenpart (Eds.): CRYPTO 2020, LNCS 12170, pp. 590–620, 2020.
https://doi.org/10.1007/978-3-030-56784-2_20

The theoretical study of watermarking schemes was initiated by Barak et al. [BGI+01] and Hopper et al. [HMW07]. However, no concrete construction is provided in both works. It is extremely difficult to construct provably secure watermarking schemes and early works in this area [NSS99, YF11, Nis13] only consider restricted adversaries, which are not allowed to change the format of the watermarked object.

The first watermarking scheme with provable security against arbitrary removal strategies is presented by Cohen et al. in [CHN+16]. Specifically, they construct a watermarkable pseudorandom function (PRF) from indistinguishability obfuscation. In subsequent works [BLW17, KW17, QWZ18, YAL+18, KW19, YAL+19], watermarkable PRFs are constructed from either indistinguishability obfuscation or standard (lattice) assumptions. However, there is still a significant gap in security between the schemes constructed from indistinguishability obfuscation and those from standard assumptions.

In [CHN+16], Cohen et al. also construct watermarking schemes for public key encryption (PKE) and signature from their watermarkable PRFs. Subsequently, (stateful) watermarking schemes for PKE are constructed from any PKE scheme [BKS17]. Recently, in [GKM+19], Goyal et al. construct watermarking schemes for various public key cryptographic primitives with nearly all desired security properties from simple assumptions, such as the existence of one-way function, standard lattice assumptions, etc. This is achieved by a slight relaxation on the correctness of the watermarking scheme. More precisely, in their definition, a marked program is not required to approximately preserve the input/output behaviors of the original program, and instead, it is only required to preserve the "functionality" of the original program.[1] Unfortunately, such relaxation is not applicable to watermarkable PRF, whose functionality is exactly specified by its input/output behaviors.

Watermarking PRFs. A watermarking scheme for a PRF family F consists of two main algorithms, namely, the marking algorithm and the extraction algorithm. The marking algorithm takes as input the mark key, a message, and a PRF key k, and outputs a watermarked circuit, which evaluates $F_k(\cdot)$ correctly on almost all inputs. The extraction algorithm takes as input the extraction key and a circuit, and outputs either a message or a symbol $\perp$, which indicates that the circuit is unmarked.

The main security property of a watermarking scheme is *unremovability*, which requires that given a marked circuit C^* for a random PRF key (namely, the challenge key), the adversary is not able to remove or modify the embedded message[2] without altering the outputs of C^* on a significant fraction of inputs. An additional security property is *unforgeability*, which prevents anyone without the mark key from generating a new watermarked circuit. Besides, for watermarkable PRF, it is usually required to have *pseudorandomness against the watermarking*

---

[1] For example, to mark a signing algorithm, it is sufficient that the marked program can still output valid signatures.

[2] That is, the extraction algorithm should still output the original message when extracting a circuit created by the adversary.

authority, i.e., the pseudorandomness holds against an adversary who possesses the mark key and the extraction key.

When defining security (either unremovability or unforgeability) for watermarking schemes, adversaries with different capabilities are considered. For example, if the adversary is allowed to access more than one marked circuit of the challenge key, the scheme is *collusion resistant*. Moreover, we say that the scheme has security with *marking (oracle) queries* if the security is defined against an adversary who can obtain marked circuits of its generated keys and we say that the scheme has security with *public marking* if the adversary can obtain the mark key. Besides, we say that the scheme has security with *extraction (oracle) queries* if the security is defined against an adversary who can obtain extraction results of its generated circuits and we say that the scheme has security with *public extraction* if the adversary can obtain the extraction key.

Prior works on watermarkable PRFs. Watermarkable PRF is first constructed by Cohen et al. in [CHN+16]. The scheme is constructed from indistinguishability obfuscation and has unremovability with public extraction. Later, in [YAL+19], Yang et al. improve Cohen et al.'s scheme to achieve collusion resistance. Both constructions rely on the full power of indistinguishability obfuscation and it seems infeasible to instantiate them from standard assumptions.

Towards constructing watermarkable PRF from standard assumptions, Boneh et al. [BLW17] propose a new approach that builds watermarkable PRF from variants of constrained PRFs [BW13, KPTZ13, BGI14]. The schemes provided in [BLW17] still rely on the existence of indistinguishability obfuscation. Then, building on Boneh et al.'s framework, watermarkable PRFs from standard assumptions are developed. In [KW17], Kim and Wu present the first watermarkable PRF from standard assumptions. The scheme only achieves security with marking queries. Subsequently, in [QWZ18, KW19], watermarkable PRFs that have security with public marking and extraction queries are constructed. However, all of these constructions (from standard assumptions) fail to provide desirable security properties such as security with public extraction and collusion resistance.

The goal of this work is to narrow the gap in security between indistinguishability obfuscation based watermarkable PRFs and standard assumptions based ones. We note that security with extraction queries, which is a natural stepping stone towards security with public extraction, is already achieved by previous watermarkable PRFs from standard assumptions [QWZ18, KW19]. In contrast, no positive result on collusion resistant watermarkable PRF from standard assumptions is known. Therefore, our main objective is to design *collusion resistant* watermarkable PRF that can be instantiated from *standard assumptions*.

1.1 Our Results

In this work, we explore the possibility to build collusion resistant watermarkable PRF from standard assumption and show that:

Table 1. Security properties achieved by watermarkable PRFs from standard assumption. The default setting for unremovability, which is achieved by all constructions, is unremovability with marking queries. We use unremovability with PM to denote unremovability with public marking and use unremovability with EO to denote unremovability with extraction (oracle) queries. The default setting for unforgeability is unforgeability with marking queries. We use unforgeability with EO to denote unforgeability with extraction (oracle) queries and use unforgeability with PE to denote unforgeability with public extraction. We refer the reader to Sect. 4.1 for a more detailed discussion on different levels of unremovability and unforgeability.

	Collusion	Unremovability with		Unforgeability	Unforgeability with		Pseudorandomness against
	Resistance	PM	EO		EO	PE	Authority
[KW17]	✗	✗	✗	✓	✗	✗	fully
[QWZ18]	✗	✓	✓	✗	–	–	✗
[KW19]	✗	✗	✓	✓	✓	✗	weak[†]
	✗	✓	✓	✗	–	–	weak[†]
Ours + [KW17]	✓	✗	✗	✓	✓	✓	fully
Ours + [QWZ18]	✓	✓	✓*	✓	✓	✓	✗
Ours + [KW19]	✓	✓	✓*	✓	✓	✓	weak[†]

*: The adversary can only query the extraction oracle for a prior bounded number of times.

†: Actually, a stronger T-restricted pseudorandomness (see [KW19]) can be achieved.

Theorem 1.1 (Informal). *Assuming the existence of secure watermarkable PRF, there exist collusion resistant watermarkable PRFs. Especially, collusion resistant watermarkable PRFs exist assuming the worst-case hardness of appropriately parameterized GapSVP problems.*

We prove Theorem 1.1 by presenting a generic transformation from watermarkable PRF without collusion resistance to collusion resistant watermarkable PRF. Our transformation can approximately preserve the security of the original scheme. For example, if the original scheme has security with public marking, then so does the new scheme. Besides, by using our transformation, the new scheme has very strong unforgeability even if the original scheme is not unforgeable. This is achieved by a novel technique that adds unforgeability to a large class of watermarkable PRFs, which may be of independent interest.

By applying our transformation to existing watermarkable PRFs from standard assumptions [KW17, QWZ18, KW19], we obtain lattice based collusion resistant watermarkable PRFs with various features. The results are summarized in Table 1.

The key component of our transformation is a fingerprinting code with enhanced security, where the adversary can query an extraction oracle that outputs the decoding of its submitted word. Surprisingly, this natural security requirement has not been considered in previous works. In this work, we change this situation by defining and constructing fingerprinting code that has security with extraction queries. The new primitive is also potentially useful for copyright protection in practical applications.

One caveat is that our constructions of fingerprinting code (and thus collusion resistant watermarking schemes) are only secure against an adversary that can make at most q queries to the extraction oracle, where q is a priori bounded polynomial. Also, the message spaces of our fingerprinting code and watermarkable PRFs are of polynomial-size.[3] It is an interesting open problem to design fingerprinting codes and standard assumption based collusion resistant watermarkable PRFs without these restrictions.

1.2 Technical Overview

In this section, we provide an overview of our techniques. We first recall current approach for constructing (single key secure) watermarkable PRF from standard assumption and identify the difficulty for achieving collusion resistance via this approach. Then we show our ideas to overcome the difficulty.

The difficulty. Existing constructions of watermarkable PRF from standard assumptions [KW17, QWZ18, KW19] are all built on (variants of) constrained PRFs, following the blueprint proposed by Boneh et al. in [BLW17]. A constrained PRF F is a family of PRF that allows one to derive a constrained key ck from a PRF key k, where $\mathsf{F}_{ck}(\cdot)$ and $\mathsf{F}_k(\cdot)$ evaluate identically on almost all inputs except at some "punctured" points[4]. Its security requires that given the constrained key ck, $\mathsf{F}_k(x)$ is still pseudorandom if x is a punctured point. A constrained PRF is constraint-hiding if the constrained key does not reveal the punctured points. A (constraint-hiding) constrained PRF is collusion resistant if the security remains even if the adversary can obtain multiple constrained keys derived from a PRF key. Next, we briefly review how to watermark a constrained PRF family F.

To watermark a PRF key k of F, the marking algorithm first generates an input x^* and produces a constrained key ck that is punctured on x^* (i.e., $\mathsf{F}_{ck}(x^*) \neq \mathsf{F}_k(x^*)$ and $\mathsf{F}_{ck}(x) = \mathsf{F}_k(x)$ for all $x \neq x^*$). The marked version of k is just a circuit that evaluates $\mathsf{F}_{ck}(\cdot)$. To test if a circuit C is marked, the extraction algorithm recovers x^* by using the extraction key and checks if C is a constrained key punctured on x^*. This is accomplished via either checking if $\mathsf{C}(x^*)$ is in a specific set [KW17] or checking if $\mathsf{C}(x^*) \neq \mathsf{F}_k(x^*)$ [QWZ18, KW19]. The variants of constrained PRF used in these works support such checks. Security of the watermarking schemes relies on the fact that the punctured point x^* (or the output $\mathsf{F}_k(x^*)$) is hidden from the adversary. Based on this, to embed a message $msg \in \{0,1\}^l$ (instead of a mark) into a PRF key, the marking algorithm will encode the message into the punctured points. One simple method is to generate $2l$ inputs $(x^*_{1,0}, x^*_{1,1}, \ldots, x^*_{l,0}, x^*_{l,1})$ and puncture the PRF key on $\{x^*_{i,msg[i]}\}_{i \in [l]}$. Then, the extraction algorithm can recover the i-th bit of the embedded message via checking if the circuit is punctured on $x^*_{i,0}$ or if it is punctured on $x^*_{i,1}$.

---

[3] In contrast, existing watermarkable PRFs without collusion resistance have exponential message spaces.

[4] The punctured points may be selected by a general constraint, e.g. a circuit.

The main obstacle to achieving collusion resistance via the above approach is that the underlying (variants of) constrained PRFs are not collusion resistant. Specifically, for the instantiations provided in [KW17,KW19], one can recover the PRF key k and thus compromise security of the watermarking scheme if it is given two different constrained keys derived from k. For the scheme constructed in [QWZ18], it can be instantiated from any constraint-hiding constrained PRF for general constraint. However, to the best of our knowledge, no constraint-hiding constrained PRF from standard assumption [BKM17,CC17,BTVW17,PS18,CVW18,AMN+18,DKN+20] is known to achieve collusion resistance. Moreover, as proved in [CC17], collusion resistant constraint-hiding constrained PRF for general constraint implies indistinguishability obfuscation.

Our solution. To get around this obstacle, our key idea is to encode bits of a message into different "keys" instead of encoding them into different inputs. Next, we first illustrate how the idea works with a *failed* attempt, then we show how to correct it. We also discuss some barriers to achieving other desirable security properties and explain how to solve them.

The first attempt. The watermarking object of our initial attempt is a new PRF family $\tilde{F}$ that is a "repetition" of l constrained PRFs, i.e., $\tilde{F}_{k_1,\ldots,k_l}(x) = (F_{k_1}(x), \ldots, F_{k_l}(x))$. To embed a message $msg \in \{0,1\}^l$ into a key $\boldsymbol{k} = (k_1,\ldots,k_l)$ of $\tilde{F}$, the marking algorithm first generates $2l$ inputs $(x_{1,0}^*, x_{1,1}^*, \ldots, x_{l,0}^*, x_{l,1}^*)$, then it punctures k_i on $x_{i,msg[i]}^*$ to obtain a constrained key ck_i. The marked version of $\boldsymbol{k}$ is a circuit that computes $(F_{ck_1}(\cdot),\ldots,F_{ck_l}(\cdot))$. Then, on input a circuit, the extraction algorithm can recover the i-th bit of the embedded message via checking if the i-th part of the circuit is punctured on $x_{i,0}^*$ or if it is punctured on $x_{i,1}^*$.

Now, we examine what is guaranteed from this construction. For simplicity, we consider the simplified case that $l = 3$ and that the adversary only obtains two marked circuits $C^{(1)} = (F_{ck_1^{(1)}}(\cdot), F_{ck_2^{(1)}}(\cdot), F_{ck_3^{(1)}}(\cdot))$ and $C^{(2)} = (F_{ck_1^{(2)}}(\cdot), F_{ck_2^{(2)}}(\cdot), F_{ck_3^{(2)}}(\cdot))$ of $\boldsymbol{k} = (k_1, k_2, k_3)$, embedded with messages

$$msg^{(1)} = 101 \quad \text{and} \quad msg^{(2)} = 110$$

respectively. First, we have $ck_1^{(1)} = ck_1^{(2)}$ since both of them are generated by puncturing k_1 on $x_{1,1}^*$ (we derive the randomness for the puncturing algorithm from $\boldsymbol{k}$). Thus, by the *single key* security of the underlying (constraint-hiding) constrained PRF, the adversary is not able to modify the mark 1 in k_1. However, as $ck_2^{(1)}$ and $ck_2^{(2)}$ (also, $ck_3^{(1)}$ and $ck_3^{(2)}$) are generated by puncturing k_2 (resp. k_3) on different points, we have $ck_2^{(1)} \neq ck_2^{(2)}$ (resp. $ck_3^{(1)} \neq ck_3^{(2)}$). So, the adversary is able to obtain different constrained versions of k_2 and k_3, and thus it has the capability to remove or modify the marks in them. As a result, when extracting a circuit produced by the adversary, the extraction algorithm may obtain a message in $\{1\} \times \{?, 0, 1\} \times \{?, 0, 1\}$,[5] which contains new messages

---

[5] We use ? to denote that no mark is detected for this position.

such as 111 and 100. That is, the adversary still has the ability to modify the embedded messages even if it fails at some position.

A secure solution using fingerprinting code. To solve this problem, we employ a fingerprinting code to amplify the robustness of our initial construction, from extracting some bits of the embedded messages to extracting one of the embedded messages, when dealing with adversarially-generated circuits. A fingerprinting code scheme consists of two algorithms, namely, the generation algorithm and the decoding algorithm. The generation algorithm generates a codebook and a trapdoor, where the codebook assigns a unique codeword to each message and the trapdoor is used for decoding. The decoding algorithm decodes a word (not necessarily in the codebook) using the trapdoor. Its security ensures that given a few codewords for messages in a specific set C, no one could produce a word that is decoded to a message outside C. This security is defined assuming the "marking assumption", where the adversary is not allowed to modify the bit at a position if all given codewords agree at this position. For example, if the given codewords are 101 and 110, then a word w such that $w[1] = 0$ is invalid.

Now, we integrate the fingerprinting code into our construction. More precisely, the marking algorithm first gets the codeword for the given message from the codebook. Then it embeds the codeword into the PRF keys via invoking the marking algorithm provided in our initial construction. Then, on input a circuit, the extraction algorithm first invokes the extraction algorithm of our initial construction. It replaces all "?" in the returned string with "0", and decodes the string using the decoding algorithm of the fingerprinting code. The marking assumption is guaranteed by security of our initial construction and thus the new extraction algorithm can succeed in extracting one of the embedded messages.

It is worth noting that our construction does not rely on concrete properties of the underlying constrained PRF, thus it is safe to replace it with any secure watermarkable PRF. In other words, our idea can be seen as a compiler that compiles a single key secure watermarkable PRF into a collusion resistant one.

Achieving security with marking queries/public marking. We have shown how to achieve collusion resistant watermarkable PRF in a setting that the adversary is only allowed to obtain some "challenge circuits", which are produced by embedding messages in a set C into a random PRF key. However, in previous works, the adversary is always allowed to further learn marked circuits for its selected keys. The above solution is not secure with such marking queries. This is because the marking query will provide codewords of messages outside C, which can help the adversary to alter the embedded messages in the challenge circuits.

We fix this issue by forcing the marking algorithm to use different codebooks for different keys. In particular, the marking algorithm will first generate a codebook and the associated trapdoor (using randomness derived from the input PRF key), and then produce the marked circuit with this fresh codebook. As the codewords acquired from the marking queries are from different codebooks, they will not help the adversary in modifying the embedded messages in the challenge circuits.

The next issue is how to send the trapdoor to the extraction algorithm. Here we need to guarantee that the extraction algorithm can always receive the correct trapdoor and that the trapdoor is hidden to the adversary[6]. Note that, however, the only communication channel between the marking algorithm and the extraction algorithm is the watermarked circuits, which can be arbitrarily modified by the adversary.

We complete this task by embedding an encryption of the trapdoor into a new watermarkable PRF. More precisely, the watermarking object now is $l + 1$ single key secure watermarkable PRF, where each of the first l parts is embedded with one bit of the codeword and the last part is embedded with the ciphertext. For the same PRF key, we use the same randomness to generate the trapdoor and its encryption, thus single key security of a watermarkable PRF is sufficient to guarantee a reliable transmission of the trapdoor. Also, confidentiality of the trapdoor is guaranteed by security of the encryption scheme.

By applying above tweaks, security with marking queries of the new construction can be based on the security with marking queries of the underlying (single key secure) watermarkable PRF. Besides, we can also show that if the underlying watermarkable PRF is secure with public marking (i.e., the mark key is public), the new scheme also supports public marking.

Achieving security with extraction queries. Another desirable security property for watermarking schemes is security with extraction queries, which allows the adversary to learn what can be extracted from its generated circuits. Note that the extraction algorithm of our scheme consists of three steps. First, it extracts a word and a ciphertext from the marked circuit; then it decrypts the ciphertext to get the trapdoor; finally, it uses the trapdoor to retrieve the message from the word. Therefore, security with extraction queries of our scheme can be guaranteed if the underlying watermarkable PRF has security with extraction queries (achieved in [QWZ18,KW19]), the underlying encryption scheme has security with decryption queries (i.e., CCA-security, which is achieved by numerous previous works), and the underlying fingerprinting code has security with extraction queries. However, no fingerprinting code that is provable secure with extraction queries is known. To solve this problem, in this work, we construct the first fingerprinting code that is secure with extraction queries. We provide an overview of this construction later in this section.

Achieving unforgeability. One drawback of the current construction is that it cannot achieve unforgeability even if the underlying watermarking scheme is unforgeable. To see this, recall that given a marked circuit, which is a combination of $l + 1$ marked circuits, the extraction algorithm will extract one bit from each of the first l circuits. The bit is set to be 1 if it gets 1 from the circuit and the bit is set to be 0 either if it gets 0 from the circuit or if it gets an unmarked symbol $\perp$. That is to say, the extraction algorithm could still output some message even if part of the circuit is unmarked. Thus, an adversary may break the unforgeability of our construction by replacing part of a marked

---

[6] This is because current fingerprinting code is not secure if the trapdoor is revealed.

circuit with a random circuit. The new circuit and the original marked circuit should behave differently on nearly all inputs, yet the extraction algorithm will probably extract some message from it.

We solve this problem by presenting a general approach to adding strong unforgeability to watermarkable PRFs.[7] Let G be a secure watermarkable PRF (without unforgeability). We show how to construct a secure watermarkable PRF with unforgeability from G. The construction employs a signature scheme and an encryption scheme. In more detail, the revised marking algorithm first signs on the PRF key and encrypts the PRF key and the signature. Then, it embeds the ciphertext as well as the message into the PRF key using the original marking algorithm of G. The new extraction algorithm will first extract the ciphertext and the message from the circuit. Then, it decrypts the ciphertext to obtain the PRF key k and the signature. Next, the extraction algorithm checks if the signature is valid and if the circuit behaves almost identically to G_k. It outputs the message only if both checks are passed, and it outputs $\perp$ otherwise.

Unforgeability of the watermarking scheme comes from unforgeability of the signature scheme. In particular, due to the unforgeability of the signature scheme, the adversary is not able to generate valid signatures for a new PRF key. Therefore, if the adversary wishes to create a circuit that can pass the extraction algorithm, the circuit must be close to one of previously marked PRF keys, which is exactly what the unforgeability requires. We stress that the claim holds even if the extraction key of the scheme is revealed. Thus, we provide the first watermarkable PRF achieving unforgeability with public extraction from standard assumption (yet, it does not have unremovability with public extraction).

Next, we argue why the new construction still has unremovability. There are two main concerns. Firstly, the original PRF key is included in the marked circuit, but as only an encryption of the key is embedded, this will not leak additional information to the adversary.[8] Secondly, an additional check is performed in the extraction algorithm to test if the circuit preserves the functionality of the original key. Since the adversary (for unremovability) is not allowed to significantly change the functionality of the challenge circuit(s), its submitted circuit should pass the check.

Putting it all together. Piecing together all ideas and techniques proposed above, we obtain a generic construction of collusion resistant watermarkable PRF from any single key secure watermarkable PRF. The construction preserves the security with marking queries/public marking/extraction queries of the underlying single key secure watermarking scheme. Also, it achieves unforgeability for free. We provide a detailed description of the construction in Sect. 4.

---

[7] The technique only works for watermarkable PRFs with exponential message space, which is not achieved by our collusion resistant watermarkable PRF (due to the polynomially sized message space of the underlying fingerprinting code). Nonetheless, we can still apply it in our construction specifically since the underlying single key secure schemes do support exponential message space.

[8] This only holds when the decryption key of the encryption scheme is kept private, so, the upgrading does not preserve the unremovability in the public extraction setting.

Fingerprinting code secure with extraction queries. It remains to show how to construct a fingerprinting code that is secure with extraction queries. We start by briefly reviewing the well-known Boneh-Shaw code [BS95], which is widely used in cryptography.

Let N be the size of the message space and let L be a polynomial in security parameter and N. The code generation algorithm first samples N disjoint subsets $\mathcal{P}_1, \ldots, \mathcal{P}_N$ of $[NL]$, where $|\mathcal{P}_i| = L$, and sets them as the trapdoor. Then it sets the codeword for a message $\mathbf{m} \in [N]$ to be an NL-bit binary string $\bar{w}_{\mathbf{m}}$, where $\bar{w}_{\mathbf{m}}[j] = 1$ iff $j \in \mathcal{P}_i$ for some $i \leq \mathbf{m}$. To decode a word w, the decoding algorithm sets $A_0 = 1$ and $A_{N+1} = 0$, then it computes $A_i = (\sum_{j \in \mathcal{P}_i} w[j])/L$ and outputs the first i s.t. $A_i - A_{i+1}$ is large.

To see security of the Boneh-Shaw code, considering a simple example where $N = 4$ and the adversary is given two codewords $\bar{w}_1$ and $\bar{w}_3$, let w be the word output by the adversary. Then, the decoding algorithm will not output a message outside $\{1, 3\}$ on input w, because:

1. For any $j \in \mathcal{P}_1$, $\bar{w}_1[j] = \bar{w}_3[j] = 1$ and for any $j \in \mathcal{P}_4$, $\bar{w}_1[j] = \bar{w}_3[j] = 0$, then from the marking assumption, the adversary is not allowed to modify the bit at a position in $\mathcal{P}_1$ and $\mathcal{P}_4$. Thus, we still have $A_1 = 1$ and $A_4 = 0$. Therefore, the decoding algorithm will not output 0 or 4.
2. For bits at positions in $\mathcal{P}_2$ and $\mathcal{P}_3$, the adversary can modify them arbitrarily. But, since the trapdoor is kept *hidden* to the adversary, it cannot distinguish positions in $\mathcal{P}_2$ and that in $\mathcal{P}_3$. So, the adversary cannot make $A_2 - A_3$ large and thus the decoding algorithm will not output 2.

However, if the adversary is allowed to make queries to an extraction oracle, it can learn some information about the trapdoor from each query. Thus, the second claim above will be invalidated in this case.[9]

We deal with this issue by using *part* of the trapdoor in each invocation of the decoding algorithm. In particular, the decoding algorithm randomly picks a fixed size subset $\mathcal{S}_i \subseteq \mathcal{P}_i$ for $i \in [N]$. Then it computes $A_i' = (\sum_{j \in \mathcal{S}_i} w[j])/|\mathcal{S}_i|$ and finds the large gap between A_i' and A_{i+1}'. The fraction A_i' can be viewed as an estimation of A_i and the two numbers are close, so the modification here will not compromise security of the Boneh-Shaw code.

To see why the revised decoding algorithm can provide security with extraction queries, let $\mathcal{S}_1^*, \ldots, \mathcal{S}_N^*$ be the partial trapdoor used when decoding a word w from the adversary, who has seen codewords for messages in a set $\mathcal{C}$. Due to the security of the original Boneh-Shaw code, the decoding algorithm should output a message in $\mathcal{C}$, if all $\mathcal{S}_i$ used in previous extraction queries are sampled from $\mathcal{P}_i - \mathcal{S}_i^*$. Thus, it is sufficient to show that the output of the extraction oracle will not change (significantly) if the decoding algorithm uses a random subset of $\mathcal{P}_i - \mathcal{S}_i^*$ instead of a random subset of $\mathcal{P}_i$. Unfortunately, it seems that there is a non-negligible gap between the oracle outputs in these two cases and the conventional statistical distance is not applicable here to bound the adversary's

---

[9] In fact, the adversary could find positions in $\mathcal{P}_2$ via altering bits of $\bar{w}_3$ one by one and observe when the extraction oracle outputs 1 instead of 3.

advantage. To overcome this hurdle, we use the Rényi divergence to measure the distribution closeness and limit the number of extraction queries from the adversary. See Sect. 3 for a more detailed description of our construction.

1.3 Related Works

The notion of fingerprinting code is first studied in [Wag83, BMP85]. Considering the adversary's ability in altering the codewords, many different models for fingerprinting code are studied. In this work, we consider the model presented in [BS98]. Boneh and Shaw [BS98] construct the first fingerprinting code that is secure in this model. Then, in [Tar03], Tardos presents a shorter code and shows that the code length is optimal in the asymptotic sense. Some subsequent works (see e.g., [NFH+09, AT09, LdW14] and references therein) aim at improving the concrete efficiency of the scheme. However, to the best of our knowledge, no work has considered an adversary that can ask for the decoding of its created words.

One important application of fingerprinting code is to build traitor tracing schemes [CFN94], which aims at tracing secret key leakers in a broadcast encryption setting. The notion of traitor tracing is somewhat similar to the notion of collusion resistant watermarking. But our construction has several differences from previous fingerprinting code based traitor tracing schemes [BN08]. First, we embed each bit of the codeword into the underlying single key watermarkable PRF directly, while in [BN08], codewords are used to select secret keys for users. Besides, we need to additionally send the trapdoor from the marking algorithm to the extraction algorithm. In addition, we require a stronger fingerprinting code that has adaptive security with extraction queries, and provide an instantiation.

2   Notations

Let s be a string, we use $|s|$ to denote the length of s. For integers $a \leq |s|$, we use $s[a]$ to denote the i-th character of s and for integers $a \leq b \leq |s|$, we use $s[a : b]$ to denote the substring $(s[a], s[a + 1], \ldots, s[b])$. Let $\mathcal{S}$ be a finite set, we use $|\mathcal{S}|$ to denote the size of $\mathcal{S}$, and use $s \xleftarrow{\$} \mathcal{S}$ to denote sampling an element s uniformly from set $\mathcal{S}$. Let $\mathcal{D}$ be a distribution, we use $d \leftarrow \mathcal{D}$ to denote sampling d according to $\mathcal{D}$ and use $Supp(\mathcal{D})$ to denote the support of $\mathcal{D}$.

We write $negl(\cdot)$ to denote a negligible function, and write $poly(\cdot)$ to denote a polynomial. For integers $a \leq b$, we write $[a, b]$ to denote all integers from a to b and use $[b]$ to denote all integers from 1 to b. For natural numbers $a \leq b$, we use $\binom{b}{a}$ to denote the binomial coefficient, i.e., $\binom{b}{a} = \frac{b \cdot (b-1) \cdot \ldots \cdot (b-a+1)}{a \cdot (a-1) \cdot \ldots \cdot 1}$.

For more background knowledge and definitions of cryptographic primitives employed, we refer the readers to the full version of this paper.

3   Fingerprinting Code with Enhanced Security

3.1   The Definition

In this section, we provide the definition of fingerprinting code. Compared to previous definitions [BS95, Tar03, BN08], we require a stronger security, where the adversary is allowed to 1) make queries to an extraction oracle that outputs the decoding of a given word and 2) make challenge oracle queries adaptively.

Definition 3.1 (Fingerprinting Code). *A fingerprinting code* FC = (Gen, Dec) *with message space* $[1, N]$ *and code length* l *consists of the following algorithms:*

- Gen$(1^\lambda) \rightarrow (td, \Gamma = (\bar{w}_\mathtt{m})_{\mathtt{m} \in [N]})$: *On input the security parameter* λ, *the code generation algorithm outputs the trapdoor* td *and* N *codewords* $\bar{w}_1, \ldots \bar{w}_N$ *(for messages* $1, \ldots, N$ *respectively) in* $\{0, 1\}^l$.
- Dec$(td, w) \rightarrow \mathtt{m}$: *On input the trapdoor* td *and a word* $w \in \{0, 1\}^l$ *(w is not necessarily in* Γ*), the decoding algorithm outputs a message* $\mathtt{m} \in [1, N] \cup \{\perp\}$.

The correctness property requires that the the decoding algorithm will decode codewords in Γ correctly.

Definition 3.2 (Correctness). *Let* $(td, (\bar{w}_\mathtt{m})_{\mathtt{m} \in [N]}) \leftarrow$ Gen(1^λ), *then for any* $\mathtt{m}$, *we have:*

$$\Pr[\mathsf{Dec}(td, \bar{w}_\mathtt{m}) \neq \mathtt{m}] = 0$$

The security property requires that given a few codewords $\{\bar{w}_\mathtt{m}\}_{\mathtt{m} \in \mathcal{C}^*} \subseteq \Gamma$ for messages in a set $\mathcal{C}^*$, no adversary can generate a "feasible" word that decodes to a new message outside $\mathcal{C}^*$. Here, we say that a word w is **feasible** if

$$\forall j \in [l], \exists \mathtt{m} \in \mathcal{C}^*, \bar{w}_\mathtt{m}[j] = w[j]$$

In this work, we consider a strong security, where the adversary is allowed to learn the decoding of q feasible words for an a priori bounded q. Also, we allow the adversary to make challenge oracle queries adaptively, i.e., it can request codewords for its selected messages after viewing some codewords and the decoding of some words.

Definition 3.3 (Security with q Extraction Queries). *A fingerprinting code is secure with* q *extraction queries if for all polynomial-time (PPT) adversaries* $\mathcal{A}$, *we have* $\Pr[\mathsf{Expt}_{\mathcal{A},q}(\lambda) = 1] \leq negl(\lambda)$, *where we define the experiment* **Expt** *as follows:*

1. *The challenger samples* $(td, (\bar{w}_\mathtt{m})_{\mathtt{m} \in [N]}) \leftarrow$ Gen(1^λ) *and initializes the set* $\mathcal{C}^* = \emptyset$.
2. *Then, the adversary is allowed to make a priori unbounded number of queries to the challenge oracle and make up to* q *queries to the extraction oracle, which are defined as follows:*
   - **Challenge Oracle.** *On input a message* $\mathtt{m} \in [1, N]$, *the challenger returns* $\bar{w}_\mathtt{m}$ *to the adversary and sets* $\mathcal{C}^* = \mathcal{C}^* \cup \{\mathtt{m}\}$.
   - **Extraction Oracle.** *On input a word* w, *the challenger does not return anything to* $\mathcal{A}$ *if* w *is not feasible (according to current* $\mathcal{C}^*$*). Otherwise, it computes* $\mathtt{m} \leftarrow$ Dec(td, w). *The challenger returns* $\mathtt{m}$ *to* $\mathcal{A}$ *if* $\mathtt{m} \in \mathcal{C}^*$. *Otherwise, the experiment aborts and outputs 1.*
3. *The experiment outputs 0 if it does not abort in Step 2.*

3.2   The Construction

In this section, we present our construction of fingerprinting code that has adaptive security with extraction queries.

Let λ be the security parameter. Let N, L, l, q be positive integers that are polynomial in λ and satisfy $l = 8\lambda(N+1)^2$, $L = 8l - 4 + 4l^2 Nq$. Let $\theta = 1/(2(N+1))$. Let $\mathfrak{S} = \{\mathcal{S} \subseteq [1, L] : |\mathcal{S}| = l\}$ be the set of all subsets of $[1, L]$ that contain l elements.

We construct the fingerprinting code $\mathsf{FC} = (\mathsf{Gen}, \mathsf{Dec})$ with message space $[1, N]$ and code length NL as follows:

- **Gen.** On input a security parameter λ, the code generation algorithm first samples a random permutation P over $[NL]$. Then for $\mathtt{m} \in [1, N]$, and $h \in [NL]$, it sets

$$\bar{w}_\mathtt{m}[h] = \begin{cases} 1 & \text{if } \lceil \mathsf{P}(h)/L \rceil \leq \mathtt{m} \\ 0 & \text{otherwise} \end{cases}$$

  Finally, it outputs the trapdoor $td = \mathsf{P}$ and the codewords $(\bar{w}_\mathtt{m})_{\mathtt{m} \in [N]}$.
- **Dec.** On input the trapdoor $td = \mathsf{P}$ and a word $w \in \{0,1\}^{NL}$, the decoding algorithm proceeds as follows:
  1. For $i \in [N]$:
     (a) Sample $\mathcal{S}_i \xleftarrow{\$} \mathfrak{S}$
     (b) $A_i = 0$
     (c) For $j \in \mathcal{S}_i$:
         i. $A_i = A_i + w[\mathsf{P}^{-1}((i-1)L + j)]$
     (d) If $\frac{A_i}{l} \leq \frac{3}{4} - i\theta$:
         i. If $i = 1$: Output $\bot$
         ii. Output $i - 1$
  2. Output N

Theorem 3.1. FC *is a secure fingerprinting code that has correctness and adaptive security with q extraction queries.*

We give proof of Theorem 3.1 in the full version.

4   Collusion Resistant Watermarkable PRF

4.1   The Definition

In this section, we provide the definition of watermarkable PRF, which is adapted and generalized from definitions in previous works [CHN+16, BLW17, KW17, QWZ18, KW19, YAL+19].

Definition 4.1 (Watermarkable PRFs). *A watermarkable PRF* WPRF $=$ (Setup, KeyGen, Eval, Mark, Extract) *with key space $\mathcal{K}$, input space $\{0,1\}^n$, output space $\{0,1\}^m$, and message space $\mathcal{M}$ consists of the following algorithms:*

- Setup(1^λ) → (PP, MK, EK) : *On input the security parameter λ, the setup algorithm outputs the public parameter PP, the mark key MK and the extraction key EK.*
- KeyGen(PP) → k : *On input the public parameter PP, the key generation algorithm outputs a PRF key $k \in \mathcal{K}$.*
- Eval(PP, k, x) → y : *On input the public parameter PP, a PRF key $k \in \mathcal{K}$, and an input $x \in \{0,1\}^n$, the evaluation algorithm outputs an output $y \in \{0,1\}^m$.*
- Mark(PP, MK, k, msg) → C : *On input the public parameter PP, the mark key MK, a PRF key $k \in \mathcal{K}$, and a message $msg \in \mathcal{M}$, the marking algorithm outputs a marked circuit C : $\{0,1\}^n \to \{0,1\}^m$.*
- Extract(PP, EK, C) → msg : *On input the public parameter PP, the extraction key EK, and a circuit C, the extraction algorithm outputs a message $m \in \mathcal{M} \cup \{\bot\}$, where $\bot$ denotes that the circuit is unmarked.*

Correctness. The correctness of a watermarking scheme includes three properties. The functionality preserving property requires that the watermarked key can roughly preserve the functionality of the original key.

Definition 4.2 (Functionality Preserving). *For any $msg \in \mathcal{M}$, let $(PP, MK, EK) \leftarrow$ Setup(1^λ), $k \leftarrow$ KeyGen(PP), C $\leftarrow$ Mark(PP, MK, k, msg), $x \xleftarrow{\$} \{0,1\}^n$, then we have $\Pr[C(x) \neq$ Eval(PP, k, x)$] \leq negl(\lambda)$.*

The extraction correctness requires that the extraction algorithm can extract the correct message from an honestly-watermarked key.

Definition 4.3 (Extraction Correctness). *For any $msg \in \mathcal{M}$, let $(PP, MK, EK) \leftarrow$ Setup(1^λ), $k \leftarrow$ KeyGen(PP), C $\leftarrow$ Mark(PP, MK, k, msg), then we have $\Pr[$Extract(PP, EK, C)$\neq msg] \leq negl(\lambda)$.*

The meaningfulness property requires that most circuits are unmarked, which rules out the trivial construction that regards all circuits as marked.

Definition 4.4 (Watermarking Meaningfulness). *For any circuit C : $\{0,1\}^n \to \{0,1\}^m$, let $(PP, MK, EK) \leftarrow$ Setup(1^λ), then we have:*

$$\Pr[\text{Extract}(PP, EK, C) \neq \bot] \leq negl(\lambda)$$

Remark 4.1. In Definition 4.2 and Definition 4.3, correctness properties are defined for honestly-generated PRF keys only. A stronger notion of correctness consider adversarially-chosen keys, where k is chosen by the adversary. See [KW17,KW19] for more detailed discussions on different notions of correctness.

Pseudorandomness. The pseudorandomness property of a watermarkable PRF is twofold. First, it requires that the watermarkable PRF should be pseudorandom against an external adversary.

Definition 4.5 (Pseudorandomness). *Let* $(PP, MK, EK) \leftarrow \mathtt{Setup}(1^\lambda)$, $k \leftarrow \mathtt{KeyGen}(PP)$, *and* f *be a random function from* $\{0,1\}^n$ *to* $\{0,1\}^m$. *Also, let* $\mathcal{O}_1(\cdot)$ *be an oracle that takes as input a string* $x \in \{0,1\}^n$ *and returns* $\mathtt{Eval}(PP, k, x)$, *and let* $\mathcal{O}_2(\cdot)$ *be an oracle that takes as input a string* $x \in \{0,1\}^n$ *and returns* $f(x)$. *Then for all PPT adversary* $\mathcal{A}$, *we have:*

$$| \Pr[\mathcal{A}^{\mathcal{O}_1(\cdot)}(PP) = 1] - \Pr[\mathcal{A}^{\mathcal{O}_2(\cdot)}(PP) = 1] | \leq negl(\lambda)$$

Moreover, the watermarkable PRF should be (weak) pseudorandom against the watermarking authority, who holds the mark key and the extraction key.

Definition 4.6 (Pseudorandomness against the Watermarking Authority). *Let* $(PP, MK, EK) \leftarrow \mathtt{Setup}(1^\lambda)$, $k \leftarrow \mathtt{KeyGen}(PP)$, *and* f *be a random function from* $\{0,1\}^n$ *to* $\{0,1\}^m$. *Also, let* $\mathcal{O}_1(\cdot)$ *be an oracle that takes as input a string* $x \in \{0,1\}^n$ *and returns* $\mathtt{Eval}(PP, k, x)$, *and let* $\mathcal{O}_2(\cdot)$ *be an oracle that takes as input a string* $x \in \{0,1\}^n$ *and returns* $f(x)$. *Then for all PPT adversary* $\mathcal{A}$, *we have:*

$$| \Pr[\mathcal{A}^{\mathcal{O}_1(\cdot)}(PP, MK, EK) = 1] - \Pr[\mathcal{A}^{\mathcal{O}_2(\cdot)}(PP, MK, EK) = 1] | \leq negl(\lambda)$$

Definition 4.7 (Weak Pseudorandomness against the Watermarking Authority). *Let* $(PP, MK, EK) \leftarrow \mathtt{Setup}(1^\lambda)$, $k \leftarrow \mathtt{KeyGen}(PP)$, *and* f *be a random function from* $\{0,1\}^n$ *to* $\{0,1\}^m$. *Also, let* $\mathcal{O}_1$ *be an oracle that samples* $x \xleftarrow{\$} \{0,1\}^n$ *and returns* $(x, \mathtt{Eval}(PP, k, x))$ *on each query, and let* $\mathcal{O}_2$ *be an oracle that samples* $x \xleftarrow{\$} \{0,1\}^n$ *and returns* $(x, f(x))$ *on each query. Then for all PPT adversary* $\mathcal{A}$, *we have:*

$$| \Pr[\mathcal{A}^{\mathcal{O}_1}(PP, MK, EK) = 1] - \Pr[\mathcal{A}^{\mathcal{O}_2}(PP, MK, EK) = 1] | \leq negl(\lambda)$$

Unremovability. This is the main security requirement for a watermarking scheme. Roughly, it requires that the adversary is not able to remove or modify the messages embedded in a random PRF key without significantly changing the functionality.

Definition 4.8 (ϵ-Unremovability). *A watermarkable PRF is* ϵ-*unremovable if for all PPT and* ϵ-*unremoving-admissible adversaries* $\mathcal{A}$, *we have* $\Pr[\mathtt{ExptUR}_{\mathcal{A}}(\lambda) = 1] \leq negl(\lambda)$, *where we define the experiment* $\mathtt{ExptUR}$ *as follows:*

1. *The challenger samples* $(PP, MK, EK) \leftarrow \mathtt{Setup}(1^\lambda)$ *and returns* PP *to* $\mathcal{A}$. *Also, it samples a challenge key* $k^* \leftarrow \mathtt{KeyGen}(PP)$, *which is used in answering the adversary's challenge oracle queries.*
2. *Then,* $\mathcal{A}$ *is given access to the following oracles (but it may be restricted in querying them as discussed below):*
   - ***Mark Key Oracle.*** *The mark key oracle returns* MK *to the adversary.*
   - ***Extraction Key Oracle.*** *The extraction key oracle returns* EK *to the adversary.*

- **Marking Oracle.** On input a PRF key $k \in \mathcal{K}$ and a message $msg \in \mathcal{M}$, the marking oracle returns a circuit $C \leftarrow \text{Mark}(PP, MK, k, msg)$.
- **Extraction Oracle.** On input a circuit C, the extraction oracle returns a message $msg \leftarrow \text{Extract}(PP, EK, C)$.
- **Challenge Oracle.** On input a message msg, the challenge oracle returns a circuit $C^* \leftarrow \text{Mark}(PP, MK, k^*, msg)$ to the adversary.

3. Finally, $\mathcal{A}$ submits a circuit $\tilde{C}$ and the experiment outputs 1 iff $\text{Extract}(PP, EK, \tilde{C}) \notin \mathsf{M}^*$. Here, we use M^* to denote all messages submitted to the challenge oracle and use C^* to denote all circuits returned by the challenge oracle.

We say that an adversary $\mathcal{A}$ is ϵ-unremoving-admissible if there exists circuit $C^* \in \mathsf{C}^*$ that $|\{x \in \{0,1\}^n : C^*(x) \neq \tilde{C}(x)\}| \leq \epsilon \cdot 2^n$.

We can get different levels of unremovability by restricting the adversary's ability in querying oracles. In a nutshell, we write unremovability as $\mathcal{C}$-$(\mathcal{M}, \mathcal{E})$-$\epsilon$-unremovability, where $\mathcal{C} \in \{$single key, bounded collusion resistant, fully collusion resistant$\}$, $\mathcal{M} \in \{-, \text{MO}, \text{PM}\}$, and $\mathcal{E} \in \{-, \text{bounded EO}, \text{EO}, \text{PE}\}$. In more detail, the security notions are organized along the following three dimensions:

- **Ability to Query the Challenge Oracle.** The unremovability can be defined against an adversary that can:
  - make only one query to the challenge oracle (single key).
  - make queries to the challenge oracle for a priori bounded number of times (bounded collusion resistant).
  - make queries to the challenge oracle for a priori unbounded number of times (fully collusion resistant).
- **Ability in Obtaining Information about MK.** The unremovability can be defined against an adversary that can:
  - make query to neither the mark key oracle nor the marking oracle $(-)$.
  - make a priori unbounded number of queries to the marking oracle but make no query to the mark key oracle (MO).
  - make query to the mark key oracle (PM).
- **Ability in Obtaining Information about EK.** The unremovability can be defined against an adversary that can:
  - make query to neither the extraction key oracle nor the extraction oracle $(-)$.
  - make at most q queries to the extraction oracle but make no query to the extraction key oracle, where q is a priori bounded (bounded EO or q-EO).
  - make a priori unbounded number of queries to the extraction oracle but make no query to the extraction key oracle (EO).
  - make query to the extraction key oracle (PE).

Remark 4.2. In our definition of collusion resistant unremovability, the adversary is allowed to make challenge oracle queries adaptively. Such adaptive security is not defined (and achieved) in previous works about collusion resistant watermarkable PRF [YAL+19].

Unforgeability. This property is dual to the unremovability. Roughly, it prevents one from embedding messages to PRF keys without the mark key.

Definition 4.9 (δ-Unforgeability). *A watermarkable PRF is δ-unforgeable if for all PPT and δ-unforging-admissible adversaries $\mathcal{A}$, we have $\Pr[\mathtt{ExptUF}_{\mathcal{A}}(\lambda) = 1] \leq negl(\lambda)$, where we define the experiment $\mathtt{ExptUF}$ as follows:*

1. *The challenger samples $(PP, MK, EK) \leftarrow \mathtt{Setup}(1^\lambda)$ and returns PP to $\mathcal{A}$.*
2. *Then, $\mathcal{A}$ is given access to the following oracles (but it may be restricted in querying them as discussed below):*
   - *Extraction Key Oracle. The extraction key oracle returns EK to the adversary.*
   - *Marking Oracle. On input a PRF key $k \in \mathcal{K}$ and a message $msg \in \mathcal{M}$, the marking oracle returns a circuit $\mathtt{C} \leftarrow \mathtt{Mark}(PP, MK, k, msg)$.*
   - *Extraction Oracle. On input a circuit $\mathtt{C}$, the extraction oracle returns a message $msg \leftarrow \mathtt{Extract}(PP, EK, \mathtt{C})$.*
3. *Finally, $\mathcal{A}$ submits a circuit $\tilde{\mathtt{C}}$ and the experiment outputs 1 iff $\mathtt{Extract}(PP, EK, \tilde{\mathtt{C}}) \neq \perp$.*

Here, an adversary $\mathcal{A}$ is δ-unforging-admissible if for every circuit $\mathtt{C}_i$ returned by the marking oracle, $|\{x \in \{0,1\}^n : \mathtt{C}_i(x) \neq \tilde{\mathtt{C}}(x)\}| \geq \delta \cdot 2^n$.[10]

We can get different levels of unforgeability by restricting the adversary's ability in querying oracles. In a nutshell, we write unforgeability as $(\mathcal{M}, \mathcal{E})$-$\delta$-unforgeability, where $\mathcal{M} \in \{-, \mathrm{MO}\}$, and $\mathcal{E} \in \{-, \mathrm{EO}, \mathrm{PE}\}$. In more detail, the security notions are organized along the following two dimensions:

- **Ability in Obtaining Information about MK.** The unforgeability can be defined against an adversary that can:
  - make no query to the marking oracle $(-)$.
  - make a priori unbounded number of queries to the marking oracle (MO).
- **Ability in Obtaining Information about EK.** The unforgeability can be defined against an adversary that can:
  - make query to neither the extraction key oracle nor the extraction oracle $(-)$.
  - make a priori unbounded number of queries to the extraction oracle but make no query to the extraction key oracle (EO).
  - make query to the extraction key oracle (PE).

4.2   The Construction

In this section, we show our main construction, which upgrades single key secure watermarkable PRF families into fully collusion resistant ones.

Let λ be the security parameter. Let n, m, N, l, s, κ, q be positive integers that are polynomial in λ. Let $\epsilon, \epsilon', \bar{\epsilon}$ be positive real values s.t. $1/\bar{\epsilon}$ is polynomial in λ, $\bar{\epsilon} = (1 + 1/\lambda) \cdot \epsilon$, $\epsilon' = (1 + 2/\lambda) \cdot \epsilon$. Also, let $t = \lambda^3/\epsilon$.

Our construction is built on the following building blocks:

---

[10] An alternative definition of δ-unforging-admissibility, which is used in [KW17], additionally requires that for every PRF key k_i submitted to the marking oracle, $|\{x \in \{0, 1\}^n : \mathtt{C}_i(x) \neq \mathtt{Eval}(PP, k_i, x)\}| \geq \delta \cdot 2^n$.

- A watermarkable PRF family $\mathsf{WPRF_0} = (\mathsf{WPRF_0.Setup}, \mathsf{WPRF_0.KeyGen},$ $\mathsf{WPRF_0.Eval}, \mathsf{WPRF_0.Mark}, \mathsf{WPRF_0.Extract})$ with input space $\{0,1\}^n$, output space $\{0,1\}^m$, and message space $\{0,1\}^\kappa$. Also, we use $\mathcal{R}_0$ and $\mathcal{R}'_0$ to denote the randomness space for the algorithm $\mathsf{WPRF_0.KeyGen}$ and the algorithm $\mathsf{WPRF_0.Mark}$ respectively.
- A fingerprinting code $\mathsf{FC} = (\mathsf{FC.Gen}, \mathsf{FC.Dec})$ with message space $[1, N]$ and code length l. Also, we use $\mathcal{T}$ and $\mathcal{R}_{\mathsf{FC}}$ to denote the key space (i.e., the set of all trapdoors for FC) and the randomness space for the algorithm $\mathsf{FC.Gen}$ respectively.
- A signature scheme $\mathsf{SIG} = (\mathsf{SIG.KeyGen}, \mathsf{SIG.Sign}, \mathsf{SIG.Verify})$ with message space $\{0,1\}^\lambda$, signature space $\{0,1\}^s$ and signing randomness space $\mathcal{R}_{\mathsf{SIG}}$.
- A PKE scheme $\mathsf{PKE} = (\mathsf{PKE.KeyGen}, \mathsf{PKE.Enc}, \mathsf{PKE.Dec})$ with message space $\mathcal{T} \times \{0,1\}^\lambda \times \{0,1\}^s$, ciphertext space $\{0,1\}^\kappa$, and encryption randomness space $\mathcal{R}_{\mathsf{PKE}}$.
- Pseudorandom generators:

$$\mathsf{G} : \{0,1\}^\lambda \rightarrow \{0,1\}^\lambda \times \{0,1\}^\lambda \times \mathcal{R}_{\mathsf{FC}} \times \mathcal{R}_{\mathsf{SIG}} \times \mathcal{R}_{\mathsf{PKE}}$$
$$\mathsf{G}' : \{0,1\}^\lambda \rightarrow \mathcal{R}_0^{l+1} \qquad \mathsf{G}'' : \{0,1\}^\lambda \rightarrow \mathcal{R}_0'^{2l+1}$$

- A pseudorandom function family $\mathsf{F} = (\mathsf{F.KeyGen}, \mathsf{F.Eval})$ with input space $\mathcal{R}_0'^{2l+1}$ and output space $\mathcal{R}_0'^{2l+1}$.

We construct $\mathsf{WPRF} = (\mathsf{Setup}, \mathsf{KeyGen}, \mathsf{Eval}, \mathsf{Mark}, \mathsf{Extract})$, which has input space $\{0,1\}^n$, output space $\{0,1\}^{(l+1)m}$, and message space $[1, N]$, as follows:

- **Setup.** On input a security parameter λ, the setup algorithm first generates $(PP_0, MK_0, EK_0) \leftarrow \mathsf{WPRF_0.Setup}(1^\lambda)$, $(VK, SK) \leftarrow \mathsf{SIG.KeyGen}(1^\lambda)$, $(PK, DK) \leftarrow \mathsf{PKE.KeyGen}(1^\lambda)$, and $K \leftarrow \mathsf{F.KeyGen}(1^\lambda)$. Then, it outputs the public parameter $PP = (PP_0, VK, PK)$, the mark key $MK = (MK_0, SK, K)$, and the extraction key $EK = (EK_0, DK)$.
- **KeyGen.** On input the public parameter PP, the key generation algorithm outputs the PRF key $s \xleftarrow{\$} \{0,1\}^\lambda$.
- **Eval.** On input the public parameter $PP = (PP_0, VK, PK)$, a PRF key $s \in \{0,1\}^\lambda$ and an input $x \in \{0,1\}^n$, the evaluation algorithm proceeds as follows:
  1. $(\check{r}, \hat{r}, R_{\mathsf{FC}}, R_{\mathsf{SIG}}, R_{\mathsf{PKE}}) = \mathsf{G}(s)$.
  2. $(r_0, r_1, \ldots, r_l) = \mathsf{G}'(\check{r})$.
  3. For $i \in [0, l]$, $k_i = \mathsf{WPRF_0.KeyGen}(PP_0; r_i)$.
  4. Output $(\mathsf{WPRF_0.Eval}(PP_0, k_i, x))_{i \in [0,l]}$.
- **Mark.** On input the public parameter $PP = (PP_0, VK, PK)$, the mark key $MK = (MK_0, SK, K)$, a PRF key $s \in \{0,1\}^\lambda$ and a message $msg \in [1, N]$, the marking algorithm proceeds as follows:
  1. $(\check{r}, \hat{r}, R_{\mathsf{FC}}, R_{\mathsf{SIG}}, R_{\mathsf{PKE}}) = \mathsf{G}(s)$.
  2. $(r_0, r_1, \ldots, r_l) = \mathsf{G}'(\check{r})$.
  3. For $i \in [0, l]$, $k_i = \mathsf{WPRF_0.KeyGen}(PP_0; r_i)$.

4. $(td, (\bar{w}_i)_{i \in [N]}) = \mathsf{FC.Gen}(1^\lambda; R_{\mathsf{FC}})$.
5. $\sigma = \mathsf{SIG.Sign}(SK, \check{r}; R_{\mathsf{SIG}})$.
6. $ct = \mathsf{PKE.Enc}(PK, td\|\check{r}\|\sigma; R_{\mathsf{PKE}})$.
7. $(r'_0, (r'_{i,\iota})_{i \in [l], \iota \in \{0,1\}}) = \mathsf{F.Eval}(K, \mathsf{G}''(\hat{r}))$.
8. $\mathsf{W}_0 = \mathsf{WPRF}_0.\mathsf{Mark}(PP_0, MK_0, k_0, ct; r'_0)$.
9. For $i \in [l]$:
   (a) $b_i = \bar{w}_{msg}[i]$.
   (b) $\mathsf{W}_i = \mathsf{WPRF}_0.\mathsf{Mark}(PP_0, MK_0, k_i, b_i; r'_{i,b_i})$.
10. Outputs a circuit $\mathsf{C} : \{0,1\}^n \to \{0,1\}^{(l+1)m}$ s.t. $\mathsf{C}(x) = (\mathsf{W}_i(x))_{i \in [0,l]}$.

- **Extract.** On input the public parameter $PP = (PP_0, VK, PK)$, the extraction key $EK = (EK_0, DK)$, and a circuit C, the extraction algorithm proceeds as follows:
  1. Set the circuit $\mathsf{W}_0 : \{0,1\}^n \to \{0,1\}^m$ as $\mathsf{W}_0(x) = \mathsf{C}(x)[1 : m]$.
  2. $ct = \mathsf{WPRF}_0.\mathsf{Extract}(PP_0, EK_0, \mathsf{W}_0)$.
  3. If $ct = \perp$, **output** $\perp$.
  4. $(td\|\check{r}\|\sigma) = \mathsf{PKE.Dec}(DK, ct)$.
  5. If $(td\|\check{r}\|\sigma) = \perp$, **output** $\perp$.
  6. If $\mathsf{SIG.Verify}(VK, \check{r}, \sigma) = 0$, **output** $\perp$.
  7. $(r_0, r_1, \ldots, r_l) = \mathsf{G}'(\check{r})$.
  8. For $i \in [0,l]$, $k_i = \mathsf{WPRF}_0.\mathsf{KeyGen}(PP_0; r_i)$.
  9. $A = 0$.
  10. For $j \in [t]$:
      (a) Sample $x \xleftarrow{\$} \{0,1\}^n$.
      (b) If $\mathsf{C}(x) \neq (\mathsf{WPRF}_0.\mathsf{Eval}(PP_0, k_i, x))_{i \in [0,l]}$, $A = A + 1$.
  11. If $A > t \cdot \bar{\epsilon}$, **output** $\perp$.
  12. For $i \in [l]$:
      (a) $a = im + 1$, $b = (i+1)m$.
      (b) Set the circuit $\mathsf{W}_i : \{0,1\}^n \to \{0,1\}^m$ as $\mathsf{W}_i(x) = \mathsf{C}(x)[a : b]$.
      (c) $w[i] = \mathsf{WPRF}_0.\mathsf{Extract}(PP_0, EK_0, \mathsf{W}_i)$.
      (d) If $w[i] \notin [0,1]$, $w[i] = 0$.
  13. $msg \leftarrow \mathsf{FC.Dec}(td, w)$.
  14. **Output** msg.

Theorem 4.1. *If* WPRF_0 *is a single key secure watermarkable PRF family,* FC *is a secure fingerprinting code that is adaptively secure with* $q + 1$ *extraction queries as defined in Sect. 3,* PKE *is a CCA secure PKE scheme,* SIG *is a secure signature scheme,* $\mathsf{G}, \mathsf{G}', \mathsf{G}''$ *are secure pseudorandom generators, and* F *is secure pseudorandom function, then* WPRF *is a secure watermarkable PRF family with collusion resistant security. In particular:*

- *If* WPRF_0 *has (weak) pseudorandomness against the watermarking authority, then* WPRF *also has (weak) pseudorandomness against the watermarking authority.*
- *If* WPRF_0 *is single key-*$(\mathcal{M}, \mathcal{E})$-$\epsilon'$-*unremovable, then* WPRF *is fully collusion resistant-*$(\mathcal{M}, \mathcal{E})$-$\epsilon$-*unremovable, where* $\mathcal{M} \in \{MO, PM\}$, *and* $\mathcal{E} \in \{-, bounded\ EO\}$. *In more detail, if* WPRF_0 *is single key-*$(\mathcal{M}, (l + 1)q\text{-}EO)$-$\epsilon'$-*unremovable, then* WPRF *is fully collusion resistant-*$(\mathcal{M}, q\text{-}EO)$-$\epsilon$-*unremovable.*

- WPRF *is* (MO, PE)-ϵ'-*unforgeable.*

We present proof of Theorem 4.1 later in this section, which includes proof of the correctness and pseudorandomness (Sect. 4.4), the unremoveability (Sect. 4.5), and the unforgeability (Sect. 4.6) of WPRF.

4.3   The Instantiations

In this section, we show how to instantiate our construction via employing existing watermarkable PRFs from standard assumptions [KW17, QWZ18, KW19]. Note that, all of them can be instantiated from some standard lattice assumptions, which can be further reduced to the worst-case hardness of appropriately parameterized GapSVP problem. Therefore, the watermarking schemes provided in this work also rely on the worst-case hardness of the GapSVP problem.

Instantiating from [KW17]. The scheme in [KW17] can achieve a single key-$(MO, -)$-ϵ'-unremovability and a $(MO, -)$-δ'-unforgeability, where ϵ' is negligible in λ and $\delta' = 1/poly(\lambda)$. Besides, the scheme has pseudorandomness against the watermarking authority.

Unfortunately, the scheme can not be used in our general construction directly. This is because in our construction, ϵ' is required to be significantly larger than $\bar{\epsilon}$, where $1/\bar{\epsilon} = poly(\lambda)$. Nonetheless, the requirement (i.e., $\epsilon' - \bar{\epsilon}$ is large) is only desired when proving unremovability against an adversary that can query the extraction oracle. Since the scheme in [KW17] does not achieve security with extraction queries, we do not need to argue it during the upgrading. So, we can still instantiate $\mathsf{WPRF_0}$ with the scheme. Formally, we have:

Corollary 4.1. *Assuming the worst-case hardness of appropriately parameterized GapSVP problem, there exist watermarkable PRF families with fully collusion resistant-$(MO, -)$-ϵ-unremovability, (MO, PE)-δ-unforgeability, and pseudorandomness against the watermarking authority, where $\epsilon = negl(\lambda)$ and $\delta = 1/poly(\lambda)$.*

Instantiating from [QWZ18]. The scheme in [QWZ18] can achieve a single key-(PM, EO)-ϵ'-unremovability, where $\epsilon' = 1/2 - 1/poly(\lambda)$. When instantiating our construction with this scheme, we have:

Corollary 4.2. *Assuming the worst-case hardness of appropriately parameterized GapSVP problem, there exist watermarkable PRF families with fully collusion resistant-$(PM, bounded\ EO)$-ϵ-unremovability and (MO, PE)-δ-unforgeability, where $\epsilon = \delta - 1/poly(\lambda)$ and $\delta = 1/2 - 1/poly(\lambda)$.*

Instantiating from [KW19]. The scheme provided in [KW19] has single key-(PM, EO)-ϵ'-unremovability and weak pseudorandomness against the watermarking authority[11], where $\epsilon' = 1/2 - 1/poly(\lambda)$. When instantiating our construction with this scheme, we have

---

[11] In fact, the scheme can achieve a T-restricted pseudorandomness against the watermarking authority, which guarantees security as long as the authority does not query the PRF on some pre-defined T inputs.

Corollary 4.3. *Assuming the worst-case hardness of appropriately parameterized GapSVP problem, there exist watermarkable PRF families with fully collusion resistant-(PM, bounded EO)-ϵ-unremovability, (MO, PE)-δ-unforgeability, and weak pseudorandomness against the watermarking authority, where $\epsilon = \delta - 1/poly(\lambda)$ and $\delta = 1/2 - 1/poly(\lambda)$.*

4.4   Correctness and Pseudorandomness of WPRF

Functionality Preserving. The functionality preserving property comes from the functionality preserving property of WPRF_0 and the pseudorandomness of $\mathsf{G}, \mathsf{G}', \mathsf{G}'', \mathsf{F}$ directly.

Note that if WPRF_0 has functionality preserving against adversarially-chosen keys (achieved in [QWZ18, KW19]), WPRF also has this stronger correctness property. Besides, even if WPRF_0 does not satisfy it, WPRF can still achieve functionality preserving against adversarially-chosen keys if the outputs of G are "random" enough (e.g., if G is modeled as a random oracle).

Extraction Correctness. The extraction correctness comes from the extraction correctness of WPRF_0, the correctness of PKE, the correctness of SIG, the functionality preserving property of WPRF_0, the correctness of FC, and the pseudorandomness of $\mathsf{G}, \mathsf{G}', \mathsf{G}'', \mathsf{F}$ directly.

Watermarking Meaningfulness. The watermarking meaningfulness comes from the watermarking meaningfulness of WPRF_0 directly.

Pseudorandomness. The pseudorandomness comes from the pseudorandomness of WPRF_0 and the pseudorandomness of G, G' by a direct reduction.

(Weak) Pseudorandomness Against the Watermarking Authority. The (weak) pseudorandomness against the watermarking authority comes from the (weak) pseudorandomness against the watermarking authority of WPRF_0 and the pseudorandomness of G, G' by a direct reduction.

4.5   Unremovability of WPRF

In this section, we prove the fully collusion resistant-$(\mathcal{M}, \mathcal{E})$-$\epsilon$-unremovability of WPRF, assuming that WPRF_0 is single key-$(\mathcal{M}, \mathcal{E})$-$\epsilon'$-unremovable, where $\mathcal{M} \in \{\mathrm{MO}, \mathrm{PM}\}$ and $\mathcal{E} \in \{-, \text{bounded EO}\}$. For simplicity, here we only provide the detailed proof for $\mathcal{M} = \mathrm{PM}$ and $\mathcal{E} = \text{bounded EO}$. The proofs are similar in cases that $\mathcal{M} \in \{\mathrm{PM}\}$ and $\mathcal{E} \in \{-, \text{bounded EO}\}$, and at the end of this section, we also discuss how to deal with a few subtle issues in the proofs when $\mathcal{M} = \mathrm{MO}$.

First, we define the following games between a challenger and a PPT ϵ-unremoving-admissible adversary $\mathcal{A}$:

- **Game 0.** This is the real experiment ExptUR with some purely conceptual changes. More precisely, the challenger proceeds as follows.

I. First, the challenger generates $(PP_0, MK_0, EK_0) \leftarrow \mathsf{WPRF}_0.\mathsf{Setup}(1^\lambda)$, $(VK, SK) \leftarrow \mathsf{SIG}.\mathsf{KeyGen}(1^\lambda)$, $(PK, DK) \leftarrow \mathsf{PKE}.\mathsf{KeyGen}(1^\lambda)$, and $K \leftarrow \mathsf{F}.\mathsf{KeyGen}(1^\lambda)$. Then, it returns the public parameter $PP = (PP_0, VK, PK)$ and the mark key $MK = (MK_0, SK, K)$ to $\mathcal{A}$.

II. Then the challenger samples the challenge key $s^* \xleftarrow{\$} \{0,1\}^\lambda$ and generates some variables (determined by s^*), which are used in answering the challenge oracle:

    1. $(\tilde{r}^*, \hat{r}^*, R^*_{\mathsf{FC}}, R^*_{\mathsf{SIG}}, R^*_{\mathsf{PKE}}) = \mathsf{G}(s^*)$.

    2. $(r_0^*, r_1^*, \ldots, r_l^*) = \mathsf{G}'(\tilde{r}^*)$.

    3. For $i \in [0,l]$, $k_i^* = \mathsf{WPRF}_0.\mathsf{KeyGen}(PP_0; r_i^*)$.

    4. $(td^*, (\bar{w}_i^*)_{i \in [N]}) = \mathsf{FC}.\mathsf{Gen}(1^\lambda; R^*_{\mathsf{FC}})$.

    5. $\sigma^* = \mathsf{SIG}.\mathsf{Sign}(SK, \tilde{r}^*; R^*_{\mathsf{SIG}})$.

    6. $ct^* = \mathsf{PKE}.\mathsf{Enc}(PK, td^* \| \tilde{r}^* \| \sigma^*; R^*_{\mathsf{PKE}})$.

    7. $(r_0'^*, (r_{i,\iota}'^*)_{i \in [l], \iota \in \{0,1\}}) = \mathsf{F}.\mathsf{Eval}(K, \mathsf{G}''(\hat{r}^*))$.

III. Next the challenger answers $\mathcal{A}$'s oracle queries, including the extraction oracle queries and the challenge oracle queries. Once $\mathcal{A}$ submits a circuit C to the extraction oracle, the challenger proceeds as follows:

    1. Set the circuit $\mathsf{W}_0 : \{0,1\}^n \to \{0,1\}^m$ as $\mathsf{W}_0(x) = \mathsf{C}(x)[1:m]$.

    2. $ct = \mathsf{WPRF}_0.\mathsf{Extract}(PP_0, EK_0, \mathsf{W}_0)$.

    3. If $ct = \perp$, **return** $\perp$ to $\mathcal{A}$.

    4. $(td \| \tilde{r} \| \sigma) = \mathsf{PKE}.\mathsf{Dec}(DK, ct)$.

    5. If $(td \| \tilde{r} \| \sigma) = \perp$, **return** $\perp$ to $\mathcal{A}$.

    6. If $\mathsf{SIG}.\mathsf{Verify}(VK, \tilde{r}, \sigma) = 0$, **return** $\perp$ to $\mathcal{A}$.

    7. $(r_0, r_1, \ldots, r_l) = \mathsf{G}'(\tilde{r})$.

    8. For $i \in [0,l]$, $k_i = \mathsf{WPRF}_0.\mathsf{KeyGen}(PP_0; r_i)$.

    9. $A = 0$.

    10. For $j \in [t]$:

        (a) Sample $x \xleftarrow{\$} \{0,1\}^n$.

        (b) If $\mathsf{C}(x) \neq (\mathsf{WPRF}_0.\mathsf{Eval}(PP_0, k_i, x))_{i \in [0,l]}$, $A = A + 1$.

    11. If $A > t \cdot \bar{\epsilon}$, **return** $\perp$ to $\mathcal{A}$.

    12. For $i \in [l]$:

        (a) $a = im + 1$, $b = (i+1)m$.

        (b) Set the circuit $\mathsf{W}_i : \{0,1\}^n \to \{0,1\}^m$ as $\mathsf{W}_i(x) = \mathsf{C}(x)[a:b]$.

        (c) $w[i] = \mathsf{WPRF}_0.\mathsf{Extract}(PP_0, EK_0, \mathsf{W}_i)$.

        (d) If $w[i] \notin [0,1]$, $w[i] = 0$.

    13. $msg \leftarrow \mathsf{FC}.\mathsf{Dec}(td, w)$.

    14. **Return** msg to $\mathcal{A}$.

    Also, for the h-th challenge oracle query with message msg_h^*, the challenger generates the circuit C_h^* as follows and returns it back to the adversary.

    1. $\mathsf{W}_{h,0}^* = \mathsf{WPRF}_0.\mathsf{Mark}(PP_0, MK_0, k_0^*, ct^*; r_0'^*)$.

    2. For $i \in [l]$:

        (a) $b_{h,i}^* = \bar{w}_{msg_h^*}^*[i]$.

        (b) $\mathsf{W}_{h,i}^* = \mathsf{WPRF}_0.\mathsf{Mark}(PP_0, MK_0, k_i^*, b_{h,i}^*; r_{i,b_i}'^*)$.

    3. Set the circuit C_h^* as $\mathsf{C}_h^*(x) = (\mathsf{W}_{h,i}^*(x))_{i \in [0,l]}$.

IV. Finally, $\mathcal{A}$ submits a circuit $\tilde{C}$ to the challenge oracle and the challenger checks if $\mathcal{A}$ succeeds in attacking the unremovability of WPRF as follows. Here, we use M to denote the set of all messages submitted to the challenge oracle.

1. Set the circuit $W_0 : \{0,1\}^n \to \{0,1\}^m$ as $W_0(x) = \tilde{C}(x)[1:m]$.
2. $ct = \text{WPRF}_0.\text{Extract}(PP_0, EK_0, W_0)$.
3. If $ct = \perp$, **output** 1.
4. $(td\|\check{r}\|\sigma) = \text{PKE.Dec}(DK, ct)$.
5. If $(td\|\check{r}\|\sigma) = \perp$, **output** 1.
6. If $\text{SIG.Verify}(VK, \check{r}, \sigma) = 0$, **output** 1.
7. $(r_0, r_1, \ldots, r_l) = G'(\check{r})$.
8. For $i \in [0, l]$, $k_i = \text{WPRF}_0.\text{KeyGen}(PP_0; r_i)$.
9. $A = 0$.
10. For $j \in [t]$:
    (a) Sample $x \xleftarrow{\$} \{0,1\}^n$.
    (b) If $\tilde{C}(x) \neq (\text{WPRF}_0.\text{Eval}(PP_0, k_i, x))_{i \in [0,l]}$, $A = A + 1$.
11. If $A > t \cdot \bar{\epsilon}$, **output** 1.
12. For $i \in [l]$:
    (a) $a = im + 1$, $b = (i+1)m$.
    (b) Set the circuit $W_i : \{0,1\}^n \to \{0,1\}^m$ as $W_i(x) = \tilde{C}(x)[a:b]$.
    (c) $w[i] = \text{WPRF}_0.\text{Extract}(PP_0, EK_0, W_i)$.
    (d) If $w[i] \notin [0,1]$, $w[i] = 0$.
13. $msg \leftarrow \text{FC.Dec}(td, w)$.
14. If $msg \notin M$, **output** 1.
15. **Output** 0.

- **Game 1.** This is identical to Game 0 except that in Step II, the challenger samples $(\check{r}^*, R_{FC}^*, R_{SIG}^*, R_{PKE}^*, r_0'^*, (r_{i,\iota}'^*)_{i \in [l], \iota \in \{0,1\}})$ uniformly at random instead of computing them using pseudorandom generators and pseudorandom functions.

- **Game 2.** This is identical to Game 1 except that the challenger changes the way to answer extraction oracle queries. In particular, after receiving a circuit C and extracting the ciphertext ct from the first part of C, the challenger works as follows (instead of continuing the extraction procedure defined above) if $ct = ct^*$:
  1. $A = 0$.
  2. For $j \in [t]$:
     (a) Sample $x \xleftarrow{\$} \{0,1\}^n$.
     (b) If $C(x) \neq C_1^*(x)$, $A = A + 1$.
  3. If $A > t \cdot \bar{\epsilon}$, **return** $\perp$ to $\mathcal{A}$.
  4. For $i \in [l]$:
     (a) $a = im + 1$, $b = (i+1)m$.
     (b) Set the circuit $W_i : \{0,1\}^n \to \{0,1\}^m$ as $W_i(x) = C(x)[a:b]$.
     (c) $w[i] = \text{WPRF}_0.\text{Extract}(PP_0, EK_0, W_i)$.
     (d) If $w[i] \notin [0,1]$, $w[i] = 0$.
  5. $msg \leftarrow \text{FC.Dec}(td^*, w)$.

6. **Return** msg to $\mathcal{A}$.
- **Game 3.** This is identical to Game 2 except that in Step IV, after extracting the ciphertext ct, it works as follows (instead of continuing the extraction procedure defined above) if $ct = ct^*$:
  1. For $i \in [l]$:
     (a) $a = im + 1$, $b = (i + 1)m$.
     (b) Set the circuit $W_i : \{0, 1\}^n \to \{0, 1\}^m$ as $W_i(x) = \tilde{C}(x)[a : b]$.
     (c) $w[i] = \mathsf{WPRF}_0.\mathsf{Extract}(PP_0, EK_0, W_i)$.
     (d) If $w[i] \notin [0, 1]$, $w[i] = 0$.
  2. $msg \leftarrow \mathsf{FC.Dec}(td^*, w)$.
  3. If $msg \notin \mathsf{M}$, **output** 1.
  4. **Output** 0.
- **Game 4.** This is identical to Game 3 except that the challenger changes the way to generate ct^*. In particular, it computes $ct^* \leftarrow \mathsf{PKE.Enc}(PK, 0)$.
- **Game 5.** This is identical to Game 4 except that the challenger samples $(r_0^*, r_1^*, \ldots, r_l^*)$ uniformly at random instead of setting them as $(r_0^*, r_1^*, \ldots, r_l^*) = \mathsf{G}'(\tilde{r}^*)$. Note that in Game 5, each C_h^* is set as

$$\mathsf{C}_h^*(x) = \mathsf{W}_0^*(x) \| (\mathsf{W}_{i, \bar{w}_{msg_h^*}^*[i]}^*(x))_{i \in [1, l]}$$

where $\mathsf{W}_0^*, \{\mathsf{W}_{i,j}^*\}_{i \in [l], j \in \{0,1\}}$ are generated as follows in Step II:
  1. For $i \in [0, l]$, $k_i^* \leftarrow \mathsf{WPRF}_0.\mathsf{KeyGen}(PP_0)$.
  2. $(td^*, (\bar{w}_i^*)_{i \in [N]}) \leftarrow \mathsf{FC.Gen}(1^\lambda)$.
  3. $ct^* \leftarrow \mathsf{PKE.Enc}(PK, 0)$.
  4. $\mathsf{W}_0^* \leftarrow \mathsf{WPRF}_0.\mathsf{Mark}(PP_0, MK_0, k_0^*, ct^*)$.
  5. For $i \in [l]$:
     (a) $\mathsf{W}_{i,0}^* \leftarrow \mathsf{WPRF}_0.\mathsf{Mark}(PP_0, MK_0, k_i^*, 0)$.
     (b) $\mathsf{W}_{i,1}^* \leftarrow \mathsf{WPRF}_0.\mathsf{Mark}(PP_0, MK_0, k_i^*, 1)$.
- **Game 6.** This is identical to Game 5 except that in Step IV, after extracting the ciphertext ct, the challenger aborts the experiment and outputs 2 if $ct \neq ct^*$.
- **Game 7.** This is identical to Game 6 except that when
  - answering an extraction oracle query with extracted ciphertext $ct = ct^*$,
  - performing the final check in Step IV,
  the challenger aborts and outputs 2 if the extracted word w satisfies

$$\exists i \in [l], b \in \{0, 1\} : w[i] \neq b \wedge \forall msg \in \mathsf{M}, \bar{w}_{msg}^*[i] = b$$

We call this event as *Bad*. Here, we abuse the notion M as the set of all messages submitted to the challenge oracle before the event occurs.

Next, we prove the indistinguishability of each consecutive pair of games defined above and show that the adversary $\mathcal{A}$ will win in the final game (Game 7) with a negligible probability. For simplicity of notation, we use $\mathcal{E}_i$ to denote the output of Game i.

Lemma 4.1. $|\Pr[\mathcal{E}_0 = 1] - \Pr[\mathcal{E}_1 = 1]| \leq negl(\lambda)$.

Proof. In Game 1, some random variables are sampled uniformly instead of being set as output of pseudorandom generators. As the PRG seed $s^*, \hat{r}^*$ does not appear in the view of $\mathcal{A}$ directly, indistinguishability between Game 0 and Game 1 comes from the pseudorandomness of G, G''.   □

Lemma 4.2. $|\Pr[\mathcal{E}_1 = 1] - \Pr[\mathcal{E}_2 = 1]| \leq negl(\lambda)$.

Proof. Game 1 and Game 2 are identical as long as

1. $(td^* \| \check{r}^* \| \sigma^*) = \mathsf{PKE.Dec}(DK, ct^*)$.
2. $\mathsf{SIG.Verify}(VK, \check{r}^*, \sigma^*) = 1$.
3. For all tested input x, $\mathsf{C}_1^*(x) = (\mathsf{WPRF}_0.\mathsf{Eval}(PP_0, k_i^*, x))_{i \in [0,l]}$.

The first two conditions are satisfied (with all but negligible probability) due to the correctness of PKE and the correctness of SIG respectively. The last condition comes from the functionality preserving property (against an honest key) of WPRF, which guarantees that the probability that $\mathsf{C}_1^*(x) \neq (\mathsf{WPRF}_0.\mathsf{Eval}(PP_0, k_i^*, x))_{i \in [0,l]}$ is negligible for a uniform x.   □

Lemma 4.3. $|\Pr[\mathcal{E}_2 = 1] - \Pr[\mathcal{E}_3 = 1]| \leq negl(\lambda)$.

Proof. Proof of Lemma 4.3 is similar to the proof of Lemma 4.2. Note that as $\mathcal{A}$ is ϵ-unremoving-admissible, there exists $\tilde{i} \in [Q]$ s.t.

$$|\{x \in \{0,1\}^n : \mathsf{C}_{\tilde{i}}^*(x) \neq \tilde{\mathsf{C}}(x)\}| \leq \epsilon \cdot 2^n$$

Also, by the functionality preserving property (against an honest key) of WPRF,

$$|\{x \in \{0,1\}^n : \mathsf{C}_{\tilde{i}}^*(x) \neq (\mathsf{WPRF}_0.\mathsf{Eval}(PP_0, k_i^*, x))_{i \in [0,l]}\}| \leq negl(\lambda) \cdot 2^n$$

So, we have

$$|\{x \in \{0,1\}^n : \tilde{\mathsf{C}}(x) \neq (\mathsf{WPRF}_0.\mathsf{Eval}(PP_0, k_i^*, x))_{i \in [0,l]}\}| \leq (\epsilon + negl(\lambda)) \cdot 2^n$$

By the Chernoff bounds,

$$\Pr[A \geq t \cdot \bar{\epsilon}] \leq e^{-\frac{\lambda}{60}}$$

Therefore, it will not affect the output even if the challenger does not check whether $\tilde{\mathsf{C}}$ is close to $(\mathsf{WPRF}_0.\mathsf{Eval}(PP_0, k_i^*, x))_{i \in [0,l]}$.   □

Lemma 4.4. $|\Pr[\mathcal{E}_3 = 1] - \Pr[\mathcal{E}_4 = 1]| \leq negl(\lambda)$.

Proof. Indistinguishability between Game 3 and Game 4 comes from the CCA-security of PKE by a direct reduction. Note that the reduction can answer the extraction oracle queries and perform the check in Step IV by querying its decryption oracle, and in both cases it is not required to decrypt the challenge ciphertext ct^*.   □

Lemma 4.5. $|\Pr[\mathcal{E}_4 = 1] - \Pr[\mathcal{E}_5 = 1]| \leq negl(\lambda)$.

Proof. As the PRG seed $\tilde{r}^*$ is not used in any other part of the experiment, indistinguishability between Game 4 and Game 5 comes from the pseudorandomness of G' directly.   □

Lemma 4.6. $|\Pr[\mathcal{E}_5 = 1] - \Pr[\mathcal{E}_6 = 1]| \leq negl(\lambda)$.

Proof. Indistinguishability between Game 5 and Game 6 comes from the single key-(PM, $(l + 1)q$-EO)-ϵ'-unremovability of WPRF_0.

More precisely, if the adversary is able to generate a circuit $\tilde{C}$ such that $\mathsf{W}_0(\cdot) = \tilde{C}[1 : m]$ is marked with a message not equal to ct^* (with a non-negligible probability), then we can construct an adversary $\mathcal{B}$ that breaks the single key-(PM, $(l + 1)q$-EO)-ϵ'-unremovability of WPRF_0.

In particular, the adversary $\mathcal{B}$ sets the circuit W_0^* as its challenge, which is obtained by submitting ct^* to its challenge oracle. Moreover, $\mathcal{B}$ can answer extraction oracle queries via querying its own extraction oracle. Also, using the mark key returned from its mark key oracle, it can answer the mark key oracle query from $\mathcal{A}$ and to generate $\{\mathsf{W}_{i,b}^*\}_{i \in [l], j \in \{0,1\}}$ when answering the challenge oracle. Finally, $\mathcal{B}$ submits $\mathsf{W}_0(\cdot) = \tilde{C}[1 : m]$ to its challenger. Note that, $\mathcal{B}$ is ϵ'-unremoving-admissible since $\mathcal{A}$ is ϵ-unremoving-admissible, which ensures that $|\{x \in \{0,1\}^n : \mathsf{W}_0(x) \neq \mathsf{W}_0^*(x)\}| \leq \epsilon \cdot 2^n$.   □

Lemma 4.7. $|\Pr[\mathcal{E}_6 = 1] - \Pr[\mathcal{E}_7 = 1]| \leq negl(\lambda)$.

Proof. Indistinguishability between Game 6 and Game 7 comes from the single key-(PM, $(l + 1)q$-EO)-ϵ'-unremovability of WPRF_0 by a hybrid argument and the reductions are similar to the reduction provided in the proof of Lemma 4.6.

Note that for $i \in [l]$, if $\bar{w}_{msg_1^*}^*[i] = \bar{w}_{msg_2^*}^*[i]$ for all $msg_1^*, msg_2^* \in \mathsf{M}$, then the adversary $\mathcal{A}$ can only obtain one marked circuit for k_i^*, thus, single key security for WPRF_0 is enough. Also, for $i \in [l]$,

- If *Bad* occurs at Step IV: Let $\mathsf{W}_i(\cdot) = \tilde{C}(\cdot)[il + 1, (i+1)l]$. Then $|\{x \in \{0,1\}^n : \mathsf{W}_i(x) \neq \mathsf{W}_i^*(x)\}| \leq \epsilon \cdot 2^n$ due to the fact that $\mathcal{A}$ is ϵ-unremoving-admissible.
- If *Bad* occurs at an extraction oracle query: Let $\mathsf{W}_i(\cdot) = \mathsf{C}(\cdot)[il + 1, (i+1)l]$, where C is the circuit submitted to the extraction oracle. Assuming that $|\{x \in \{0,1\}^n : \mathsf{W}_i(x) \neq \mathsf{W}_i^*(x)\}| \geq \epsilon' \cdot 2^n$, then by the chernoff bound, the probability that C can pass the check in Step 3 (in the new extraction procedure defined in Game 2) is negligible, i.e., the challenger is not able to recover a word w in this case.

Thus, the adversary $\mathcal{B}$ is ϵ'-unremoving-admissible.

□

Lemma 4.8. $\Pr[\mathcal{E}_7 = 1] \leq negl(\lambda)$.

Proof. Lemma 4.8 comes from adaptive security with $(q + 1)$ extraction queries of FC by a direction reduction.   □

Combining Lemma 4.1 to Lemma 4.8, we have $\Pr[\mathcal{E}_0 = 1] \leq negl(\lambda)$, i.e., the probability that $\mathcal{A}$ wins in the real experiment ExptUR is negligible. This completes the proof of unremovability.

The Proofs in Cases That $\mathcal{M} = \mathbf{MO}$. The above proof strategies (almost) work perfectly in cases that $\mathcal{M} = \mathbf{MO}$. One subtle issue is that in the proof of Lemma 4.6 and that of Lemma 4.7, the adversary $\mathcal{B}$ for single key security of WPRF_0 needs to simulate the marking oracle for $\mathcal{A}$ via its own marking oracle. However, as the seed (WPRF's PRF key) is chosen by $\mathcal{A}$, security of pseudorandom generator is not enough to ensure that the simulated marking oracle (which runs $\mathsf{WPRF}_0.\mathsf{Mark}$ on fresh randomness) is indistinguishable from an honest marking oracle (which runs $\mathsf{WPRF}_0.\mathsf{Mark}$ on randomness output by some pseudorandomness generation component). To solve this subtle issue, we employ a pseudorandom function F to generate the randomness for $\mathsf{WPRF}_0.\mathsf{Mark}$. Since the secret key K of F is put in the mark key, which is not given to $\mathcal{A}$ in this case, we can argue the indistinguishability of these two modes for answering marking oracle queries.

4.6   Unforgeability of WPRF

Next, we prove the unforgeability of WPRF. First, we define the following games between a challenger and a PPT ϵ'-unforging-admissible adversary $\mathcal{A}$:

- **Game 0.** This is the real experiment ExptUF. More precisely, the challenger proceeds as follows.
  I. First, the challenger generates $(PP_0, MK_0, EK_0) \leftarrow \mathsf{WPRF}_0.\mathsf{Setup}(1^\lambda)$, $(VK, SK) \leftarrow \mathsf{SIG}.\mathsf{KeyGen}(1^\lambda)$, $(PK, DK) \leftarrow \mathsf{PKE}.\mathsf{KeyGen}(1^\lambda)$, and $K \leftarrow \mathsf{F}.\mathsf{KeyGen}(1^\lambda)$. Then, it returns the public parameter $PP = (PP_0, VK, PK)$ to $\mathcal{A}$.
  II. Next, it answers $\mathcal{A}$'s oracle queries:
     - If $\mathcal{A}$ submits a query to the extraction key oracle, the challenger returns $EK = (EK_0, DK)$ to $\mathcal{A}$.
     - If $\mathcal{A}$ submits the h-th marking oracle query $(s^h, msg^h) \in \{0,1\}^\lambda \times [N]$, the challenger returns $\mathsf{C}^h \leftarrow \mathsf{Mark}(PP, MK, s^h, msg^h)$ to $\mathcal{A}$.
  III. Finally, $\mathcal{A}$ submits a circuit $\tilde{\mathsf{C}}$ and the challenger proceeds as follows:
     1. Set the circuit $\mathsf{W}_0 : \{0,1\}^n \to \{0,1\}^m$ as $\mathsf{W}_0(x) = \tilde{\mathsf{C}}(x)[1 : m]$.
     2. $ct = \mathsf{WPRF}_0.\mathsf{Extract}(PP_0, EK_0, \mathsf{W}_0)$.
     3. If $ct = \perp$, **output 0**.
     4. $(td\|\tilde{r}\|\sigma) = \mathsf{PKE}.\mathsf{Dec}(DK, ct)$.
     5. If $(td\|\tilde{r}\|\sigma) = \perp$, **output 0**.
     6. If $\mathsf{SIG}.\mathsf{Verify}(VK, \tilde{r}, \sigma) = 0$, **output 0**.
     7. $(r_0, r_1, \ldots, r_l) = \mathsf{G}'(\tilde{r})$.
     8. For $i \in [0, l]$, $k_i = \mathsf{WPRF}_0.\mathsf{KeyGen}(PP_0; r_i)$.
     9. $A = 0$.
     10. For $j \in [t]$:
        (a) Sample $x \xleftarrow{\$} \{0,1\}^n$.

(b) If $\tilde{\mathsf{C}}(x) \neq (\mathsf{WPRF}_0.\mathsf{Eval}(PP_0, k_i, x))_{i \in [0,l]}$, $A = A + 1$.

11. If $A > t \cdot \bar{\epsilon}$, **output 0**.
12. For $i \in [l]$:
    (a) $a = im + 1$, $b = (i + 1)m$.
    (b) Set the circuit $\mathsf{W}_i : \{0,1\}^n \to \{0,1\}^m$ as $\mathsf{W}_i(x) = \tilde{\mathsf{C}}(x)[a : b]$.
    (c) $w[i] = \mathsf{WPRF}_0.\mathsf{Extract}(PP_0, EK_0, \mathsf{W}_i)$.
    (d) If $w[i] \notin [0,1]$, $w[i] = 0$.
13. $msg \leftarrow \mathsf{FC.Dec}(td, w)$.
14. If $msg = \perp$, **output 0**.
15. **Output 1**.

- **Game 1.** This is identical to Game 0 except that in Step III.6, after checking if σ is a valid signature for $\check{r}$, the challenger further checks if $\check{r}$ has appeared. In particular, let Q be the number of marking oracle queries the adversary made and for $h \in [Q]$, let $(\check{r}^h, \hat{r}^h, R_{\mathsf{FC}}^h, R_{\mathsf{SIG}}^h, R_{\mathsf{PKE}}^h) = \mathsf{G}(s^h)$, then the challenger outputs 0 if $\forall h \in [Q], \check{r} \neq \check{r}^h$.

Game 0 and Game 1 are identical unless $\mathsf{SIG.Verify}(VK, \check{r}, \sigma) = 1$ but $\forall h \in [Q], \check{r} \neq \check{r}^h$, i.e., the adversary generates a valid signature σ for a new message $\check{r}$ after viewing signatures for messages $\check{r}^1, \ldots, \check{r}^Q$. This occurs with only a negligible probability due to the existentially unforgeable of SIG. Thus, the probability that $\mathcal{A}$ succeeds in Game 0 and that in Game 1 are close.

Next, we argue that Game 1 outputs 1 with only a negligible probability. First, due to the new checking rule in Game 1, $\check{r} = \check{r}^h$ for some $h \in [Q]$ (otherwise, the experiment outputs 0 directly). Then, by the functionality preserving property (against adversarially-chosen PRF keys) of WPRF, with all but negligible probability,

$$|\{x \in \{0,1\}^n : (\mathsf{WPRF}_0.\mathsf{Eval}(PP_0, k_i, x))_{i \in [0,l]} \neq \mathsf{C}^h(x)\}| \leq negl(\lambda) \cdot 2^n$$

Since $\mathcal{A}$ is ϵ'-unforging-admissible,

$$|\{x \in \{0,1\}^n : \tilde{\mathsf{C}}(x) \neq \mathsf{C}^h(x)\}| \geq \epsilon' \cdot 2^n$$

So, we have[12]

$$|\{x \in \{0,1\}^n : \tilde{\mathsf{C}}(x) \neq (\mathsf{WPRF}_0.\mathsf{Eval}(PP_0, k_i, x))_{i \in [0,l]}\}| \geq (\epsilon' - negl(\lambda)) \cdot 2^n \quad (1)$$

Finally, by the Chernoff bounds,

$$\Pr[A \leq t \cdot \bar{\epsilon}] \leq e^{-\frac{\lambda - 2}{8}}$$

i.e., $\tilde{\mathsf{C}}$ can pass the check in Step III.11 with only negligible probability. This completes the proof of unforgeability.

---

[12] If we use the alternative definition of unforging-admissibility (see Footnote 10), then ϵ'-unforging-admissibility implies Eq. (1) directly and we do not need functionality preserving against adversarially-chosen PRF keys for WPRF.

Acknowledgement. We appreciate the anonymous reviewers for their valuable comments and especially to one reviewer for suggesting defining collusion resistant unremovability against adversaries that can adaptively make challenge queries. Part of this work was supported by the National Natural Science Foundation of China (Grant No. 61972332, U1636205, 61572294, 61632020), and the Research Grant Council of Hong Kong (Grant No. 25206317).

References

[AMN+18] Attrapadung, N., Matsuda, T., Nishimaki, R., Yamada, S., Yamakawa, T.: Constrained PRFs for NC^1 in traditional groups. In: Shacham, H., Boldyreva, A. (eds.) CRYPTO 2018. LNCS, vol. 10992, pp. 543–574. Springer, Cham (2018). https://doi.org/10.1007/978-3-319-96881-0_19

[AT09] Amiri, E., Tardos, G.: High rate fingerprinting codes and the fingerprinting capacity. In: SODA, pp. 336–345. SIAM (2009)

[BGI+01] Barak, B., et al.: On the (im)possibility of obfuscating programs. In: Kilian, J. (ed.) CRYPTO 2001. LNCS, vol. 2139, pp. 1–18. Springer, Heidelberg (2001). https://doi.org/10.1007/3-540-44647-8_1

[BGI14] Boyle, E., Goldwasser, S., Ivan, I.: Functional signatures and pseudorandom functions. In: Krawczyk, H. (ed.) PKC 2014. LNCS, vol. 8383, pp. 501–519. Springer, Heidelberg (2014). https://doi.org/10.1007/978-3-642-54631-0_29

[BKM17] Boneh, D., Kim, S., Montgomery, H.: Private puncturable PRFs from standard lattice assumptions. In: Coron, J.-S., Nielsen, J.B. (eds.) EUROCRYPT 2017. LNCS, vol. 10210, pp. 415–445. Springer, Cham (2017). https://doi.org/10.1007/978-3-319-56620-7_15

[BKS17] Baldimtsi, F., Kiayias, A., Samari, K.: Watermarking public-key cryptographic functionalities and implementations. In: Nguyen, P., Zhou, J. (eds.) ISC 2017. LNCS, vol. 10599, pp. 173–191. Springer, Cham (2017). https://doi.org/10.1007/978-3-319-69659-1_10

[BLW17] Boneh, D., Lewi, K., Wu, D.J.: Constraining pseudorandom functions privately. In: Fehr, S. (ed.) PKC 2017. LNCS, vol. 10175, pp. 494–524. Springer, Heidelberg (2017). https://doi.org/10.1007/978-3-662-54388-7_17

[BMP85] Blakley, G.R., Meadows, C., Purdy, G.B.: Fingerprinting long forgiving messages. In: Williams, H.C. (ed.) CRYPTO 1985. LNCS, vol. 218, pp. 180–189. Springer, Heidelberg (1986). https://doi.org/10.1007/3-540-39799-X_15

[BN08] Boneh, D., Naor, M.: Traitor tracing with constant size ciphertext. In: CCS, pp. 501–510. ACM (2008)

[BS95] Boneh, D., Shaw, J.: Collusion-secure fingerprinting for digital data. In: Coppersmith, D. (ed.) CRYPTO 1995. LNCS, vol. 963, pp. 452–465. Springer, Heidelberg (1995). https://doi.org/10.1007/3-540-44750-4_36

[BS98] Boneh, D., Shaw, J.: Collusion-secure fingerprinting for digital data. IEEE Trans. Inf. Theory **44**(5), 1897–1905 (1998)

[BTVW17] Brakerski, Z., Tsabary, R., Vaikuntanathan, V., Wee, H.: Private constrained PRFs (and more) from LWE. In: Kalai, Y., Reyzin, L. (eds.) TCC 2017. LNCS, vol. 10677, pp. 264–302. Springer, Cham (2017). https://doi.org/10.1007/978-3-319-70500-2_10

[BW13] Boneh, D., Waters, B.: Constrained pseudorandom functions and their applications. In: Sako, K., Sarkar, P. (eds.) ASIACRYPT 2013. LNCS, vol. 8270, pp. 280–300. Springer, Heidelberg (2013). https://doi.org/10.1007/978-3-642-42045-0_15

[CC17] Canetti, R., Chen, Y.: Constraint-hiding constrained PRFs for NC^1 from LWE. In: Coron, J.-S., Nielsen, J.B. (eds.) EUROCRYPT 2017. LNCS, vol. 10210, pp. 446–476. Springer, Cham (2017). https://doi.org/10.1007/978-3-319-56620-7_16

[CFN94] Chor, B., Fiat, A., Naor, M.: Tracing traitors. In: Desmedt, Y.G. (ed.) CRYPTO 1994. LNCS, vol. 839, pp. 257–270. Springer, Heidelberg (1994). https://doi.org/10.1007/3-540-48658-5_25

[CHN+16] Cohen, A., Holmgren, J., Nishimaki, R., Vaikuntanathan, V., Wichs, D.: Watermarking cryptographic capabilities. In: STOC, pp. 1115–1127 (2016)

[CVW18] Chen, Y., Vaikuntanathan, V., Wee, H.: GGH15 beyond permutation branching programs: proofs, attacks, and candidates. In: Shacham, H., Boldyreva, A. (eds.) CRYPTO 2018. LNCS, vol. 10992, pp. 577–607. Springer, Cham (2018). https://doi.org/10.1007/978-3-319-96881-0_20

[DKN+20] Davidson, A., Katsumata, S., Nishimaki, R., Yamada, S., Yamakawa, T.: Adaptively secure constrained pseudorandom functions in the standard model. Cryptology ePrint Archive, Report 2020/111 (2020). https://eprint.iacr.org/2020/111

[GKM+19] Goyal, R., Kim, S., Manohar, N., Waters, B., Wu, D.J.: Watermarking public-key cryptographic primitives. In: Boldyreva, A., Micciancio, D. (eds.) CRYPTO 2019. LNCS, vol. 11694, pp. 367–398. Springer, Cham (2019). https://doi.org/10.1007/978-3-030-26954-8_12

[HMW07] Hopper, N., Molnar, D., Wagner, D.: From weak to strong watermarking. In: Vadhan, S.P. (ed.) TCC 2007. LNCS, vol. 4392, pp. 362–382. Springer, Heidelberg (2007). https://doi.org/10.1007/978-3-540-70936-7_20

[KPTZ13] Kiayias, A., Papadopoulos, S., Triandopoulos, N., Zacharias, T.: Delegatable pseudorandom functions and applications. In: CCS, pp. 669–684. ACM (2013)

[KW17] Kim, S., Wu, D.J.: Watermarking cryptographic functionalities from standard lattice assumptions. In: Katz, J., Shacham, H. (eds.) CRYPTO 2017. LNCS, vol. 10401, pp. 503–536. Springer, Cham (2017). https://doi.org/10.1007/978-3-319-63688-7_17

[KW19] Kim, S., Wu, D.J.: Watermarking PRFs from lattices: stronger security via extractable PRFs. In: Boldyreva, A., Micciancio, D. (eds.) CRYPTO 2019. LNCS, vol. 11694, pp. 335–366. Springer, Cham (2019). https://doi.org/10.1007/978-3-030-26954-8_11

[LdW14] Laarhoven, T., de Weger, B.: Optimal symmetric tardos traitor tracing schemes. Des. Codes Crypt. **71**(1), 83–103 (2014)

[NFH+09] Nuida, K., et al.: An improvement of discrete tardos fingerprinting codes. Des. Codes Crypt. **52**(3), 339–362 (2009)

[Nis13] Nishimaki, R.: How to watermark cryptographic functions. In: Johansson, T., Nguyen, P.Q. (eds.) EUROCRYPT 2013. LNCS, vol. 7881, pp. 111–125. Springer, Heidelberg (2013). https://doi.org/10.1007/978-3-642-38348-9_7

[NSS99] Naccache, D., Shamir, A., Stern, J.P.: How to copyright a function? In: Imai, H., Zheng, Y. (eds.) PKC 1999. LNCS, vol. 1560, pp. 188–196. Springer, Heidelberg (1999). https://doi.org/10.1007/3-540-49162-7_14

[PS18] Peikert, C., Shiehian, S.: Privately constraining and programming PRFs, the LWE way. In: Abdalla, M., Dahab, R. (eds.) PKC 2018. LNCS, vol. 10770, pp. 675–701. Springer, Cham (2018). https://doi.org/10.1007/978-3-319-76581-5_23

[QWZ18] Quach, W., Wichs, D., Zirdelis, G.: Watermarking PRFs under standard assumptions: public marking and security with extraction queries. In: Beimel, A., Dziembowski, S. (eds.) TCC 2018. LNCS, vol. 11240, pp. 669–698. Springer, Cham (2018). https://doi.org/10.1007/978-3-030-03810-6_24

[Tar03] Tardos, G.: Optimal probabilistic fingerprint codes. In: STOC, pp. 116–125. ACM (2003)

[Wag83] Wagner, N.R.: Fingerprinting. In: S & P, pp. 18–18. IEEE (1983)

[YAL+18] Yang, R., Au, M.H., Lai, J., Xu, Q., Yu, Z.: Unforgeable watermarking schemes with public extraction. In: Catalano, D., De Prisco, R. (eds.) SCN 2018. LNCS, vol. 11035, pp. 63–80. Springer, Cham (2018). https://doi.org/10.1007/978-3-319-98113-0_4

[YAL+19] Yang, R., Au, M.H., Lai, J., Xu, Q., Yu, Z.: Collusion resistant watermarking schemes for cryptographic functionalities. In: Galbraith, S.D., Moriai, S. (eds.) ASIACRYPT 2019. LNCS, vol. 11921, pp. 371–398. Springer, Cham (2019). https://doi.org/10.1007/978-3-030-34578-5_14

[YF11] Yoshida, M., Toru, F.: Toward digital watermarking for cryptographic data. IEICE Trans. Fundam. Electron. Commun. Comput. Sci. 94(1), 270–272 (2011)

Verifiable Registration-Based Encryption

Rishab Goyal[1]([✉]) and Satyanarayana Vusirikala[2]([✉])

[1] MIT, Cambridge, USA
goyal@utexas.edu
[2] UT Austin, Austin, USA
satya@cs.utexas.edu

Abstract. In recent work, Garg, Hajiabadi, Mahmoody, and Rahimi [18] introduced a new encryption framework, which they referred to as Registration-Based Encryption (RBE). The central motivation behind RBE was to provide a novel methodology for solving the well-known *key-escrow* problem in Identity-Based Encryption (IBE) systems [33]. Informally, in an RBE system, there is no private-key generator unlike IBE systems, but instead, it is replaced with a public *key accumulator*. Every user in an RBE system samples its own public-secret key pair and sends the public key to the accumulator for registration. The key accumulator has no secret state and is only responsible for compressing all the registered user identity-key pairs into a short public commitment. Here the encryptor only requires the compressed parameters along with the target identity, whereas a decryptor requires supplementary key material along with the secret key associated with the registered public key.

The initial construction in [18] based on standard assumptions only provided weak efficiency properties. In a follow-up work by Garg, Hajiabadi, Mahmoody, Rahimi, and Sekar [19], they gave an efficient RBE construction from standard assumptions. However, both these works considered the key accumulator to be honest which might be too strong an assumption in real-world scenarios. In this work, we initiate a formal study of RBE systems with *malicious* key accumulators. To that end, we introduce a strengthening of the RBE framework which we call *Verifiable RBE* (VRBE). A VRBE system additionally gives the users an extra capability to obtain *short* proofs from the key accumulator proving correct (and unique) registration for every registered user as well as proving non-registration for any yet unregistered identity.

We construct VRBE systems that provide succinct proofs of registration and non-registration from standard assumptions (such as CDH, Factoring, LWE). Our proof systems also naturally allow a much more efficient audit process which can be performed by any non-participating third party as well. A by-product of our approach is that we provide a more efficient RBE construction than that provided in the prior work of Garg et al. [19]. And lastly, we initiate a study on the extension of VRBE to a wider range of access and trust structures.

© International Association for Cryptologic Research 2020
D. Micciancio and T. Ristenpart (Eds.): CRYPTO 2020, LNCS 12170, pp. 621–651, 2020.
https://doi.org/10.1007/978-3-030-56784-2_21

1   Introduction

Public-key encryption (PKE) [13, 21, 30] has remained a cornerstone in modern-day cryptography and has been one of the most widely used and studied crypto-graphic primitive. Traditionally, a public-key encryption system enables a one-to-one private communication channel between any two users over a public broad-cast network as long as it is possible to disambiguate any user's public key information honestly. Over the last few decades, significant research effort has been made by the cryptographic community in re-envisioning the original goals of public-key encryption, in turn pushing towards more expressiveness from such systems. This effort has lead to introduction of encryption systems with better functionalities such as Identity-Based Encryption (IBE) [5, 12, 33], Attribute-Based Encryption (ABE) [23, 32], and most notably Functional Encryption (FE) [6] which is meant to encapsulate both IBE and ABE functionalities.

Very briefly, in FE systems there is a trusted authority which sets up the system by sampling public parameters pp along with a master secret key msk. The public parameters pp can be used by any party to encrypt a message m of its choice, while the master key msk enables the generation of certain pri-vate decryption keys sk_f for any function f in the associated function class. The most useful aspect of such systems is that decryption now leads to users either conditionally learning the full message (as in IBE/ABE where the condi-tion is specified at encryption time) or learning some partial information about the message such as $f(m)$ (as in general FE). The security of all such systems guarantees that no computationally bounded adversary should be able to learn anything other than what can be uncovered using the private decryption keys in its possession.

Notably, in all such highly expressive systems it is crucial that the master key msk is never compromised as given the master key any adversary can arbitrarily sample private decryption keys to learn desired messages. Thus, an unfortunate consequence of adding such powerful functionalities to public-key cryptosystems is the introduction of a central trusted authority (or key generator) which is responsible for sampling the public parameters, distributing the private decryp-tion keys to authorized users, and most importantly securely storing the master secret key. Now, this could be very worrisome for many applications, since the authority must be fully trustworthy, otherwise, it would turn out to be a single point of failure. While it would be quite reasonable to put some trust in the cen-tral authority, it so happens that even an honest-but-curious key generator can cause great havoc in such an environment. Specifically, any honest-but-curious key generator can arbitrarily decrypt ciphertexts that are intended for specific recipients since it has the master key. And, it could perform such an attack in an undetectable way. This problem is widely regarded as the "key-escrow" problem.

While many previous works ([1, 5, 8, 9, 11, 22, 25, 29] to name a few) have sug-gested different approaches to solving the key-escrow problem, none of these solutions were able to resolve the key-escrow problem completely. Very recently, in a beautiful work by Garg, Hajiabadi, Mahmoody, and Rahimi [18], a novel approach for handling key-escrow was proposed. The central motivation of that work was to remove the requirement of private key generators completely from IBE systems, and to that end, they introduced the notion of Registration-Based Encryption (RBE). In an RBE system, each user samples its own public-secret key pair, and the private key generator is replaced with a public key accumulator. Every user registers their public key and identity information with the key accumulator, and the job of a key accumulator is to compress all these user identity-key pairs into a short public commitment with efficiently computable openings. Here the commitment is set as the public parameters of the RBE system, and the user-specific openings are used as supplementary key information during decryption. Now ideally one would expect the registration process to be time-unrestricted, that is users must be allowed to register at arbitrary time intervals. However, this would imply that public parameters will get updated after every registration, which could possibly lead to every registered user requesting fresh supplementary key information after another user registers. Thus, to make the notion more attractive, [18] required the following efficiency properties from an RBE system—(1) public parameters must be short, i.e. $|\mathsf{pp}| = \mathsf{poly}(\lambda, \log n)$ where λ is the security parameter and n is the number of users registered so far, (2) the registration process as well as the supplementary key generation process must be efficient, i.e. must run in time $\mathsf{poly}(\lambda, \log n)$, (3) number of times any user needs to request a fresh supplementary key from the accumulator (over the lifetime of the system) is also $\mathsf{poly}(\lambda, \log n)$. In short, an RBE system is meant to be a public key accumulation service which provides efficient and adaptive user registration while avoiding the problems associated with a private key generator.

In a sequence of two works [18,19], efficient construction of RBE systems were provided from a wide variety of assumptions (such as CDH, Factoring, LWE, iO). Specifically, [18] gave an efficient construction from indistinguishability obfuscation (iO) [2,17], and a weakly efficient construction from hash garbling scheme [18]. In a follow-up work by Garg et al. [19], a fully efficient RBE construction from hash garbling was provided. At first glance, it seems like efficient constructions for RBE systems fill the gap between regular PKE systems (which do not suffer from key-escrow but also do not provide any extra functionality) and IBE systems (which permit a simpler identity-based encryption paradigm but suffers from key-escrow). However, it turns out there is still a significant gap due to which even RBE systems potentially could be surprisingly compromised due to a corrupt key accumulator. To better understand the gap, let us look back at the excerpt from Rogaway's essay [31] which was one of the prompts behind the initial work on RBE in [18]:

> "[...] But this convenience is enabled by a radical change in the trust model: Bob's secret key is no longer self-selected. It is issued by a trusted authority. That authority knows everyone's secret key in the system. IBE embeds key-escrow indeed a form of key-escrow where a single entity implicitly holds all secret keys even ones that haven't yet been issued. [...]"

Now an RBE system solves the problem of self-selection of Bob's (or any user's) secret key faced in IBE systems, that is during honest registration every user samples its own public-secret key pair. However, the *embedding key-escrow problem* is still not directly prevented by the RBE abstraction. This is because a dishonest key accumulator could potentially add either certain trapdoors, or secretly register multiple keys for already registered users, or register any key for currently unregistered users. There could be many such scenarios in which malicious behavior of a key accumulator permits decryptability of ciphertexts intended towards arbitrary users by the key accumulator depending upon its adversarial strategy. Although such attack scenarios were not explicitly studied in the prior works [18,19], an extremely useful by-product of the approaches taken in those works was that the user registration process (and all the computations performed by the key accumulator) was completely deterministic. It thus leads to an extremely simple and elegant methodology for avoiding the embedding key-escrow problem by providing full public auditability. Basically, any user (or even a non-participating third party) could audit key accumulator and verify honest behavior by rebuilding the RBE public parameters and comparing that with the accumulated public parameters. As honestly generated public parameters do not have any trapdoors or faulty keys embedded by construction, thus public auditability solves the embedding key-escrow problem.

Although the above deterministic reconstructability feature of the RBE systems serves as a possible solution to embedding key-escrow problem, this is not at all efficient. Concretely, if any new (or even already registered) user wants to verify that the key accumulation has been done honestly, then that particular user needs to obtain a $O(n)$ (linear-sized) proof as well as spend $O(n)$ (linear amount of) time for verification, where n is the number of users registered until that point. In this work, we study the question of whether we can build RBE systems in which such verifications could be sped up. Specifically, we ask the following:

> *Do there exist efficient Registration-Based Encryption schemes in which any user can obtain short proofs of unique registration as well as short proofs of non-registration? Can such proof mechanisms be useful for speeding up the auditability process? Is it even possible to provide all such guarantees with only a* $\mathsf{poly}(\lambda, \log n)$ *cost incurred in the size of proof and running time of provers/verifiers?*

We answer the above questions in affirmative by introducing a notion of efficient verifiability for RBE systems and providing an instantiation from hash garbling schemes [18] thereby giving constructions based on standard assumptions (such as CDH, Factoring, LWE). Concretely, our contributions are described below.

Our Results. In this work, we introduce a new notion for key accumulation which we call Verifiable Registration-Based Encryption (VRBE). Briefly, a VRBE system is simply a standard RBE system in which the key accumulator can also provide proofs of correct (and unique) registration for every registered user as well as proofs of non-registration for any yet unregistered identity. We give new constructions for VRBE from hash garbling schemes which provide succinct proofs of registration and non-registration, where the key accumulator can efficiently carry out the registration and proof generation processes. Our proof systems also naturally allow a much more efficient audit process which can be performed by any non-participating third party as well. A by-product of our approach is that we provide a more efficient RBE construction than that provided in the most recent work of Garg et al. [19], wherein the size of ciphertexts in our construction is significantly smaller.[1] And, lastly we briefly discuss how the notion of VRBE can also be naturally extended to a wider range of access and trust structures, wherein the keys accumulated are no more associated with a PKE system, but for even more expressive encryption systems. Such systems might be practically more interesting in the future.

Next, we provide a detailed overview of our approach and describe the technical ideas. Later on, we discuss some related works.

1.1 Technical Overview

We start by recalling the notion of RBE as it appears in prior works. We then discuss our proposed notions of efficient verifiability for such systems. Since the starting point of our construction is the RBE scheme proposed in [19], thus we first recall the main ideas and high-level structure of their approach. And, later we describe our construction and show how to provide succinct proofs of registration and non-registration for any user identity, thereby adding verifiability to the system.

The RBE Abstraction. In an RBE system, there is a dedicated party which we call the key accumulator. A key accumulator runs the registration procedure indefinitely[2], where any user could make one of two types of queries—(1) registration query, where a new user sends in its identity and public key pair $(\mathsf{id}, \mathsf{pk})$ for registration, (2) update query, where an already registered user requests for supplementary key material u which is used for decryption. (The supplementary key material is usually referred to as the update information.) The key accumulator maintains the public parameters pp along with some auxiliary information aux throughout its execution. After each registration query of the form $(\mathsf{id}, \mathsf{pk})$, it updates the parameters to pp' and aux' to reflect addition and sends back the associated key material u to the corresponding user. For each update query made by a user with identity id, the accumulator extracts an update u from the auxiliary information aux and sends it over to the user. The encryption and decryption procedures are defined analogous to the IBE counterparts, except

---

[1] Looking ahead, our efficiency gain is due to the fact that our construction takes a one-shot (single-step) approach whereas [19] takes a two-step approach. Here the outcome of a two-step approach is that the ciphertext consists of two layers of cascaded garbled circuits, while our solution consists of a single sequence of garbled circuits.

[2] It could run it sporadically as well, where it simply records all new registrations made in a certain time window, and later registers them all at once. For simplicity, here we consider the key accumulator is always online.

during decryption a user needs a piece of appropriate update information u to complete the operation.

At a high level, the correctness requirement states that any honestly registered user with identity id and key pair (pk, sk) must be able to decrypt a ciphertext encrypted for identity id under public parameters pp (which could have been updated after id was registered) using its own secret key sk as long as it also gets an update information u corresponding to pp from the accumulator. For efficiency, it is important that the size of public parameters pp, size of update information u, and the number of updates required by any user throughout its lifetime grow at most poly-logarithmically with the number of registered users n. Additionally, the registration process and update generation should run in time poly$(\lambda, \log n)$. Lastly, for security, it is essential that a ciphertext encrypting a message m for identity id under parameters pp should hide the message as long as either id was not registered by the time pp was computed, or the key pair registered with identity id was honestly sampled and the corresponding secret key is unknown to an attacker.

Inadequacies of RBE and Workarounds. Now as we discussed before, the above abstraction still suffers from the embedding key-escrow problem. Specifically, the RBE system does not provide any abstraction for efficiently verifying whether a dishonest key accumulator—(1) secretly registers a public-secret key pair for any yet unregistered identity, (2) or while registering any new user (or even at any later point in time), also introduces a trapdoor (or register multiple keys for the same identity) that enables unauthorized decryption. For this specific reason, we study the possibility of efficient verifiability for RBE systems. Concretely, we consider two orthogonal notions of verifiability for an RBE scheme—*pre-registration* and *post-registration* proofs. Intuitively, the goal of pre-registration verifiability is to provide a short proof π validating that a given id has not yet been registered as per public parameters pp and any ciphertext ct encrypted towards such an identity id will completely hide the plaintext even if all other secret keys are leaked. Similarly, the intuition behind post-registration verifiability is to provide a short proof π of *unique* accumulation, where the proof π guarantees that the key accumulator must not have added a trapdoor (or doubly registered) during a possibly dishonest registration which allows decryption of ciphertexts intended for that particular user. (Looking ahead, our formal definitions of pre/post-registration verifiability are stated in a much stronger way where we allow an adversary to completely control the key accumulator and still require the soundness/message-hiding property to hold.)

Defining Verifiable RBE. Formally, a verifiable RBE system is just like a regular RBE system with four additional (deterministic) algorithms—PreProve, PostProve, PreVerify, and PostVerify. The pre-registration prover takes as input a common reference string crs, public parameters pp, and a target identity id for which a proof π of pre-registration is provided. The post-registration prover on the other hand also takes a target public key pk as input. Both these provers are given random-access to the auxiliary information for time-efficient computation.

Informally, the completeness of these proof systems states that the pre/post-registration verifier should always accept honestly generated proofs. And for soundness, the requirement is that if the pre-registration verifier accepts a proof π for an identity id w.r.t. parameters pp, then ciphertexts encrypted towards id must hide the message completely from a malicious key accumulator which computes the parameters pp and proof π. Similarly, for post-registration soundness, the property states that if the verifier accepts a proof π for identity-key pair (id, pk) w.r.t. parameters pp, then ciphertexts encrypted towards id must hide the message completely from a malicious key accumulator as long as the accumulator does not possess the secret key sk associated with the public key pk.

Stronger Correctness Guarantees. In addition to above-stated properties, we also define a very strong form of extractable correctness property for our post-registration proof. Concretely, the extractable correctness property states that there exists a deterministic update extraction algorithm such that if there exists an accepting post-registration proof π for identity-key pair (id, pk) w.r.t. parameters pp, then the extraction algorithm computes update information u from the proof π itself such that using update u, anybody could decrypt ciphertexts encrypted for identity id. Intuitively, extractable correctness states that completeness would still hold even for maliciously generated proofs. Our definitions are formally introduced later in Sect. 3.

A Simple Paradigm for Efficient Auditability. Looking back at our verifiability properties, one could interpret them as follows. The pre/post-registration proofs together help in ensuring that a key accumulator is behaving honestly at least *locally*. The idea behind a more global verification process is to perform the pre/post-registration verification on a randomly chosen (small) subset of users similar to what is done in probabilistically-checkable proof (PCP) literature. Specifically, suppose that a party claims that it has accumulated public parameters pp with the list of registered users R and non-registered users S. Any third party can efficiently audit the registration process by proceeding as follows—it samples a random subset of users in R and S, it requests post-registration and pre-registration proofs for users in those subsets respectively. If all the proofs are valid, then the auditor approves declaring that registration was done honestly. Note that depending upon the desired soundness threshold, the auditor can appropriately set the size of the subsets it samples. Thus, such randomized auditing would be more efficient than rebuilding the entire registration logs for most parameter regimes.

Reviewing Prior RBE Systems [18,19]. Before outlining our approach, we quickly recall the high-level structure used in prior works [18,19] since our construction uses similar building blocks. Let us first look at the weakly efficient RBE construction provided in [18] since it lays major groundwork for the follow-up works (including ours). At a high level, the ideas behind their construction can be summarized as follows. The key accumulator stores all the registered identity-key pairs $\{(\mathsf{id}_i, \mathsf{pk}_i)\}_{i \in [n]}$ using a shortlist of Merkle tree $\mathsf{Tree}_1, \mathsf{Tree}_2, \ldots, \mathsf{Tree}_k$, where every tree Tree_i is at least twice as large as Tree_{i+1}. Here the leaves of each tree encode one of the registered identity-key pairs (id, pk), while the internal nodes are like standard Merkle tree nodes (which is that they encode the hash of its children) except each node also stores the largest identity registered in its left sub-tree as well. In words, each tree Tree_i is binary search Merkle tree, with all the leaves are lexicographically sorted as per the identities. Consequently, the public key of any registered identity can be obtained efficiently via a binary search, and the root values of each Merkle tree serve as a short commitment to the entire registry tree. To encrypt a message m to identity id, encryptor needs to search the Merkle trees to obtain id's public key pk. However, the public parameters only contain the root node, not the entire tree. To overcome this issue, the [18] construction uses the ideas developed in a long line of works [7,10,14–16] of deferring the binary search to the decryption side by sending a set of garbled circuits as part of the ciphertext. Basically, for decryption, a user needs to obtain an opening (i.e., path of nodes from root to leaf) in one of the merkle trees to its registered key, and this corresponds to the supplementary key material. Now, what makes the registration process only weakly efficient is that in order to register an identity-key pair (id, pk), the key accumulator creates a new tree consisting of only node (id, pk), and then merges all merkle trees of equal size. This helps in keeping the size of the public parameters short, but since the leaves of the merkle trees have to be sorted, thus tree merging process is quite inefficient which results in only a weakly efficient system.

In the follow-up work [19], the authors observed that the weakly efficient RBE construction described above is fully efficient if the identities being registered are already coming in sorted order. They call RBE schemes with these restrictions as Timed-RBE (T-RBE). Starting with this observation, they suggest a powerful two-step approach for building an efficient RBE system without this restriction, i.e. they provide a nice bootstrapping construction from T-RBE to general (non-timed) RBE with full efficiency. In their construction, the key accumulator associates every identity id with a timestamp t_{id} as well, where t_{id} is an internal counter incrementally maintained by the accumulator. The idea is that since timestamps t_{id} will be accumulated in a sorted order, thus for storing the association between the timestamp t_{id} and public key $\mathsf{pk}_{\mathsf{id}}$ one could simply use T-RBE scheme. And, for storing the association between identity id and timestamp t_{id}, the accumulator maintains a *balanced* merkle tree $\mathsf{TimeTree}$. The leaves of $\mathsf{TimeTree}$ encode the identity-timestamp pairs (id, t_{id}) for all registered users, and are sorted as per the identities. The most crucial aspect of $\mathsf{TimeTree}$ is that it is balanced (for instance, they use a red-black tree). Let us look into more details about how such an additional balanced merkle tree is useful in improving efficiency.

The key accumulator stores all the registered identity-timestamp pairs $\{(\mathsf{id}_i, i)\}_{i \in [n]}$ using a balanced merkle $\mathsf{TimeTree}$, and stores the timestamp-key association using a short list of (standard) merkle trees $\{\mathsf{Tree}_j\}_j$ as in [18]. The public parameters consists of multiple versions of the root node of the $\mathsf{TimeTree}$ along with the root nodes for $\{\mathsf{Tree}_j\}_j$. (Specifically, the public parameters store the root node and depth information of $\mathsf{TimeTree}$ for all timestamps whenever the underlying T-RBE merkle tree was updated.) To register an $(\mathsf{id}, \mathsf{pk})$ pair, the key accumulator inserts the identity-timestamp pair $(\mathsf{id}, t_{\mathsf{id}})$ into TimeTree, and timestamp-key $(t_{\mathsf{id}}, \mathsf{pk}_{\mathsf{id}})$ to the sequence of T-RBE trees. The most important aspect of the construction is that if the T-RBE trees storing timestamp-key associations are merged, then the versions of root nodes being stored in the public parameters are updated as well. Next, let us look at how encryption and decryption are performed since the efficiency of registration follows almost immediately.

While encrypting message m for identity id, the encryptor now provides two levels of garbled circuit sequences, where the first level of garbled circuit sequence is used to find the timestamp t_{id} associated with id, and in next level one simply uses the T-RBE garbled circuit sequence to encrypt m under the corresponding public key pk. For building both levels of garbled circuit sequences, they employ the same approach of deferring binary search to decryption. The supplementary key material (or update) consists of two distinct paths, where the first path is w.r.t. the TimeTree and the second path is as per the T-RBE system which is w.r.t. one of the merkle trees in $\{\mathsf{Tree}_j\}_j$. The most important component of this extended construction is that in order to tightly bound the number of updates (for any user identity id), the first portion of key material/update u (required for evaluating the first level of garbled circuits) are only issued whenever the first T-RBE merkle tree in which identity id was registered gets merged. It turns out that executing the above idea formally leads to an efficient RBE scheme.

Our Verifiable RBE Solution. The starting point of our construction is the [19] RBE scheme described above. As a first step, we start by simplifying their construction and present a one-shot (single-step) approach to building efficient RBE systems. Later we describe how the simplified system can be made verifiable, both in pre-registration and post-registration settings, without making any additional assumptions. Lastly, we provide some comparisons and discuss potential generic methods for making existing RBE schemes verifiable.

Although the basic principles behind our simplified construction and the one provided in [19] are quite similar, there are significant structural differences in both the approaches. Therefore, we provide a direct outline of our construction instead of going through the [19] construction and explaining the differences. Later on, we briefly compare our construction with theirs. Below we sketch the main ideas behind our construction. The actual construction is a little more complicated but follows quite naturally from the following outline. A detailed description appears later in Sect. 4.

In our construction, the key accumulator maintains a single *balanced* merkle tree which directly stores the mapping between identities and their respective public keys. Concretely, the key accumulator stores a balanced merkle tree which we call EncTree and it consists of two types of nodes—leaf and intermediate. Similar to existing works, a leaf node stores an identity-key pair $(\mathsf{id}, \mathsf{pk})$ for every registered identity, whereas an intermediate node stores a tuple of the form $(h_{\mathsf{left}}, \mathsf{id}, h_{\mathsf{right}})$, where h_{left} and h_{right} are hash values of its left and right child (respectively) and id is the largest identity in its left sub-tree. Since EncTree is balanced and the nodes are ordered as per the registered identities, therefore given an identity id the key accumulator could both efficiently search its associated public key (if id has been registered) and efficiently insert a new identity-key pair. The key accumulator stores EncTree as auxiliary information aux, and publishes root value rt and depth d of the tree as part of public parameters pp. The registration algorithm inserts given identity-key pair (id, pk) as a leaf in the EncTree, balances the tree, and updates the hash values stored in all the ancestors of the newly inserted leaf. The registration algorithm then updates the public parameters pp to store the root value and depth of the updated EncTree.

Encryption and Decryption. The encryption and decryption procedures follow the aforementioned 'deferred binary search' approach in which the ciphertext for identity id contains a sequence of d garbled circuits which work as follows. Given a path (a sequence of nodes from root to a leaf) in EncTree as input, the sequence of garbled circuits jointly check that the path is well-formed, and the leaf node encodes the identity id, and outputs a PKE ciphertext under the public key encoded in the leaf node. Individually, the ith garbled circuit performs the local well-formedness check on the path and outputs the garbled input for $(i + 1)^{th}$ garbled circuit. For decryption, the decryptor needs to obtain a valid path u from the accumulator which can be efficiently generated by the accumulator by performing a binary search on the EncTree. Given a well-formed path, the decryptor can sequentially evaluate the garbled circuits and eventually obtain a PKE ciphertext which it decrypts using its secret key.

How To Get the Desired Efficiency? The Snapshotting Trick. The above scheme is highly inefficient since updates must be issued each time a new user joins. At a very high level, we visualize our approach to improve efficiency as that of storing multiple *'snapshots'* of the registration process, where an older snapshot is deleted only after new user registration leads to a new snapshot that is used by as many number of users as those using the older snapshot.[3] The intuition is to split the registered user space into disjoint groups of sizes—$1, 2, 4, \ldots, 2^\lambda$. For each group size, the public parameters will consist of *at most* one snapshot which consists of root node and depth information of (a possibly older version of) the balanced merkle tree EncTree.

Concretely, the public parameters look like $\{(j_1, \mathsf{snapshot}_{j_1}), \ldots, (j_\ell, \mathsf{snapshot}_{j_\ell})\}$ where every $j_i \in \{1, 2, \ldots, 2^\lambda\}$, and $j_i > j_{i+1}$, and $\mathsf{snapshot}_{j_i}$ consists of a root node and tree depth. These public parameters are interpreted as follows:

(1) the first j_1 users who registered refer to the EncTree corresponding to $\mathsf{snapshot}_{j_1}$ for decryption/obtaining update information;

---

[3] The snapshotting trick was implicitly used in [19] for similar reasons which is to build an *efficient* RBE scheme, but their construction instead highlighted the notion of explicitly mapping identities to corresponding timestamps as the more important aspect. Here we instead choose to focus mostly on the snapshotting principle since it is the major contributor in improving efficiency.

(2) next j_2 users who registered refer to the EncTree corresponding to snapshot$_{j_2}$;

$\vdots$

(ℓ) and similarly the last j_ℓ users to register refer to the EncTree corresponding to snapshot$_{j_\ell}$.

Basically, the key accumulator still adds new users to the single balanced merkle tree EncTree defined before, but now it also stores older snapshots of the EncTree (thereby older snapshots of the registration process). When a new user is added then a tuple (1, snapshot) is added to list of parameters, where snapshot is the latest description of EncTree. Now older snapshots get replaced with latest snapshots, after new user registration, if there exist two different snapshots but for same group size. By careful analysis and non-trivial execution of the above idea, we were able to show that the resulting RBE scheme is efficient. (Hereby non-trivial execution we mean that a straightforward implementation/generic usage of balanced merkle trees lead to an RBE system which is only efficient in the amortized sense, but if the balanced merkle tree are *lazily* created then we obtain a fully efficient RBE scheme as desired. More details are provided in the main body.)

Making RBE Verifiable. It turns out that our simplified RBE construction is already very well suited for providing succinct proofs of pre/post-registration. This is due to the fact that the underlying technology being used is a merkle tree for which we know how to provide succinct proofs of membership, and since the merkle trees we are building are balanced and sorted, thus we also can provide succinct proofs of non-membership. Looking ahead, the proofs of pre-registration will consist of proofs of non-membership, and proofs of post-registration would be a combination of proofs of membership and non-membership.

Pre-registration Proofs. For ease of exposition, consider that the public parameters contain exactly one root node and depth value (rt, d). The idea behind pre-registration proof readily extends to the general case when the public parameters contain more than one root node and depth value pairs. Recall that for soundness of pre-registration verifiability we need to argue that if the adversary produces an accepting pre-registration proof π for an identity id and parameters pp, then any ciphertext ct encrypted towards id under parameters pp must hide the plaintext. Now we know that in our construction, in order to decrypt such a ciphertext ct the adversary must be able to generate a *well-formed* path in the encryption tree EncTree such that the leaf node contains the identity id.

Here well-formedness of a path (a sequence of nodes from root to a leaf) is formally defined as follows. Let the path under consideration be path $= (\mathsf{node}_1, \ldots, \mathsf{node}_d)$ where $\mathsf{node}_i = (h_{i,\mathsf{left}}, \mathsf{id}_i, h_{i,\mathsf{right}})$ for all i. We say path is well-formed if the following conditions are satisfied:

1. All the adjacent nodes obey the merkle tree hash constraints, i.e. either $h_{i,\mathsf{left}} = \mathsf{Hash}(\mathsf{hk}, \mathsf{node}_{i+1})$ or $h_{i,\mathsf{right}} = \mathsf{Hash}(\mathsf{hk}, \mathsf{node}_{i+1})$ for all i,
   (this also tells whether node_{i+1} is a left child or a right child of node_i)

2. If node_{i+1} is the left child of node_i, then it must be that $\mathsf{id}_j \leq \mathsf{id}_i$; otherwise $\mathsf{id}_j > \mathsf{id}_i$, (for all $j > i$)
3. Root rt is same as node_1.

Similarly, we define the notion of adjacent paths. For $b \in \{0, 1\}$, consider two paths $\mathsf{path}^{(b)} = (\mathsf{node}_1^{(b)}, \ldots, \mathsf{node}_d^{(b)})$ where $\mathsf{node}_i^{(b)} = (h_{i,\mathsf{left}}^{(b)}, \mathsf{id}_i^{(b)}, h_{i,\mathsf{right}}^{(b)})$. For two distinct paths $\mathsf{path}^{(0)}$ and $\mathsf{path}^{(1)}$, we say they are adjacent if the following conditions are satisfied:

1. Paths $\mathsf{path}^{(0)}$ and $\mathsf{path}^{(1)}$ are well-formed,
2. Nodes $\mathsf{node}_{k+1}^{(0)}$ and $\mathsf{node}_{k+1}^{(1)}$ are left and right child (respectively) of nodes $\mathsf{node}_k^{(0)}$ and $\mathsf{node}_k^{(1)}$
   (where k is the largest index such that first k nodes in paths $\mathsf{path}^{(0)}$ and $\mathsf{path}^{(1)}$ are identical)
3. For all $j > k + 1$, nodes $\mathsf{node}_j^{(0)}$ and $\mathsf{node}_j^{(1)}$ are right and left child of their respective parent nodes
   (where k is as defined above).

At this point, the pre-registration proofs follow from a natural observation which is that—if some identity id has not yet been registered as per the encryption tree EncTree (maintained by the key accumulator), then there must exist two identities $\mathsf{id}_{\mathsf{lwr}}$ and $\mathsf{id}_{\mathsf{upr}}$ such that $\mathsf{id}_{\mathsf{lwr}} < \mathsf{id} < \mathsf{id}_{\mathsf{upr}}$ and paths from the root node to leaf nodes containing $\mathsf{id}_{\mathsf{lwr}}$ and $\mathsf{id}_{\mathsf{upr}}$ are adjacent. That is, a pre-registration proof consists of two adjacent paths $\mathsf{path}_{\mathsf{lwr}}$ and $\mathsf{path}_{\mathsf{upr}}$ with identity relations as described above.[4] Now such proofs can be very efficiently computed by performing an extended binary search for id, where the extension corresponds to finding the closest registered identities both larger and smaller than id. Note that a verifier can perform the adjacency-check along with the check that the identities are arranged as $\mathsf{id}_{\mathsf{lwr}} < \mathsf{id} < \mathsf{id}_{\mathsf{upr}}$ for verifying the pre-registration proof.

In summary, the idea is that proof of pre-registration for an identity id can be provided using *structured* proofs of membership for two identities $\mathsf{id}_{\mathsf{lwr}}$ and $\mathsf{id}_{\mathsf{upr}}$, where the structure is formalized by the concept of adjacency as described above. The proof of soundness and correctness builds upon the aforementioned intuition and is provided in detail later in the main body.

Post-registration Proofs. As in the case for pre-registration proofs, let us focus on the case where the public parameters contain a single root node and depth pair. Recall that an accepting post-registration proof π for identity-key pair (id, pk) w.r.t parameters pp must guarantee that a key accumulator uniquely added the identity-key pair (id, pk) to accumulated list of registered users. The post-registration proofs in our construction can also be visualized similar to the pre-registration proofs.

---

[4] In case id is either smaller or larger than all registered identities, then the proof will consist of exactly one path instead of two. Here we ignore that for simplicity.

Specifically, observe that if some identity id has been registered as per the encryption tree EncTree (maintained by the key accumulator), then there must exist two identities id_{lwr} and id_{upr} such that $id_{lwr} < id < id_{upr}$ and paths from the root node to leaf nodes containing id_{lwr} and id, and id and id_{upr} are adjacent. In other words, if identity id was uniquely registered, then there must exist three disjoint paths $path_{lwr}$, $path_{mid}$ and $path_{upr}$ such that $path_{lwr}$, $path_{mid}$ are adjacent as well as $path_{mid}$, $path_{upr}$ with the identities in their respective leaf nodes are related as described above.[5] As for pre-registration proofs, the aforementioned post-registration proof can be computed analogously in an efficient manner. The verification procedure can also be naturally extended from pre-registration proof.

There is however one important distinction in the case of post-registration proofs. Note that a pre-registration proof w.r.t. public parameters that contain multiple root node and depth pairs simply consist of independently computed pre-registration proofs for each root node and depth pair. This is because each sub-proof would guarantee that id was not registered as per that corresponding encryption tree snapshot. Thus, together all these sub-proof would guarantee that id was not registered as per any existing encryption tree snapshot. On the other hand, a post-registration proof w.r.t. public parameters with multiple root node and depth pairs will *not* consist of independently computed post-registration proofs for each root node and depth pair. This is because it is possible that the identity-key pair (id, pk) is registered as per only one root node and depth pair (say the latest snapshot), whereas it is not registered as per remaining (older) snapshots. Therefore, a post-registration proof, in this case, will consist of a mixture of post-registration and pre-registration proofs depending upon whether (id, pk) was registered as per that encryption tree snapshot.

A Generic Approach to Verifiability? A natural question a reader might ask is whether it would be possible to provide proofs of pre/post-registration verifiability generically for any RBE scheme by using a succinct non-interactive proof system such as SNARGs/SNARKs [4,20,24,26,27] for instance. One possible approach along these lines could be to maintain an external sorted hash tree of registered identities, and for providing a pre/post-registration proof the accumulator would generate (non-)membership proofs for the hash tree along with a SNARK for proving the consistency of the external tree w.r.t. the RBE public parameters. Such a generic approach seems possible, but would require maintaining additional data structures for consistency checks. More importantly, this approach necessitates making additional assumptions as for most succinct non-interactive proof systems we either need to make certain non-falsifiable assumptions [20,28], or work in the Random Oracle model [3,27]. Our construction and the proofs of verifiability do not rely on any extra assumptions other than what is already required in existing RBE systems [18,19] themselves, thus our results show that verifiability comes for free.

---

[5] As before, in case id is either the smallest or largest registered identity, then the proof will consist of exactly two paths instead of three. Here we ignore that for simplicity.

Also, note that SNARKs are usually defined for a family of circuits, thus the running time of prover is always as large as the size of the circuit, whereas in this case our provers already have random-access over the auxiliary information and we were able to provide highly efficient provers in which the running time of prover grows only poly-logarithmically with the number of users. Therefore, our non-generic approach is more interesting both theoretically as well as practically, since we do not make any non-standard assumptions, nor do we incur an additional overhead in the efficiency.

Related Work and Future Directions. Due to space constraints, we postpone this to full version of the paper.

2   Hash Garbling

We now review the notion of hash garbling scheme introduced in [18].

$\mathsf{Setup}(1^\lambda, 1^\ell) \to \mathsf{hk}$. The setup algorithm takes as input the security parameter λ, an input length parameter ℓ, and outputs a hash key hk.

$\mathsf{Hash}(\mathsf{hk}, x) \to y$. This is a deterministic algorithm that takes as input a hash key hk and a value $x \in \{0,1\}^\ell$ and outputs a value $y \in \{0,1\}^\lambda$.

$\mathsf{GarbleCkt}(\mathsf{hk}, C, \mathsf{state}) \to \tilde{C}$. It takes as input hash key hk, a circuit C, a secret state $\mathsf{state} \in \{0,1\}^\lambda$ and outputs a garbled circuit $\tilde{C}$.

$\mathsf{GarbleInp}(\mathsf{hk}, y, \mathsf{state}) \to \tilde{y}$. It takes as input hash key hk, a value $y \in \{0,1\}^\lambda$, a secret state $\mathsf{state} \in \{0,1\}^\lambda$ and outputs a garbled value $\tilde{y}$.

$\mathsf{Eval}(\tilde{C}, \tilde{y}, x) \to z$. This takes as input a garbled circuit $\tilde{C}$, a garbled value $\tilde{y}$, a value $x \in \{0,1\}^\ell$ and outputs a value z.

Definition 1 (Correctness). *A hash garbling scheme is said to be correct if for all $\lambda \in \mathbb{N}$, $\ell \in \mathbb{N}$, hash key $\mathsf{hk} \leftarrow \mathsf{Setup}(1^\lambda, 1^\ell)$, circuit C, input $x \in \{0,1\}^\ell$, state $\in \{0,1\}^\lambda$, garbled circuit $\tilde{C} \leftarrow \mathsf{GarbleCkt}(\mathsf{hk}, C, \mathsf{state})$ and a garbled value $\tilde{y} \leftarrow \mathsf{GarbleInp}(\mathsf{hk}, \mathsf{Hash}(\mathsf{hk}, x), \mathsf{state})$, we have $\mathsf{Eval}(\tilde{C}, \tilde{y}, x) = C(x)$.*

Definition 2 (Security). *A hash garbling scheme is said to be secure if there exists a PPT simulator Sim such that for every stateful PPT adversary $\mathcal{A}$, there exists a negligible function $\mathrm{negl}(\cdot)$ such that for every $\lambda, \ell \in \mathbb{N}$, we have*

$$\Pr\left[\mathcal{A}(\tilde{C}_b, \tilde{y}_b) = b \; : \; \begin{array}{c} \mathsf{hk} \leftarrow \mathsf{Setup}(1^\lambda, 1^\ell); (C, x) \leftarrow \mathcal{A}(\mathsf{hk}); \mathsf{state} \leftarrow \{0,1\}^\lambda \\ \tilde{C}_0 \leftarrow \mathsf{GarbleCkt}(\mathsf{hk}, C, \mathsf{state}); \\ \tilde{y}_0 \leftarrow \mathsf{GarbleInp}(\mathsf{hk}, \mathsf{Hash}(\mathsf{hk}, x), \mathsf{state}); \\ (\tilde{C}_1, \tilde{y}_1) \leftarrow \mathsf{Sim}(\mathsf{hk}, x, 1^{|C|}, C(x)); b \leftarrow \{0,1\} \end{array} \right] \leq \frac{1}{2} + \mathrm{negl}(\lambda).$$

3   Verifiable Registration Based Encryption

In this section, we define the notion of Verifiable Registration Based Encryption (VRBE). First, we recall the definition of Registration Based Encryption (RBE) as introduced in [18]. For message space $\mathcal{M} = \{\mathcal{M}_\lambda\}_\lambda$ and identity space $\mathcal{ID} = \{\mathcal{ID}_\lambda\}_\lambda$, an RBE system consists of the following algorithms—

CRSGen(1^λ) → crs. The CRS generation algorithm takes as input the security parameter λ, and outputs a common reference string crs.

Gen(1^λ) → (pk, sk). The key generation algorithm takes as input the security parameter 1^λ, and outputs a public-secret key pair (pk, sk). (Note that these are only public and secret keys, not the encryption/decryption keys.)

Reg$^{[\text{aux}]}$(crs, pp, id, pk) → pp′. The registration algorithm is a deterministic algorithm, that takes as input the common reference string crs, current public parameter pp, an identity id to be registered, and a corresponding public key pk. It maintains auxiliary information aux, and outputs the updated parameters pp′. The registration algorithm is modelled as a RAM program where it can read/write to arbitrary locations of the auxiliary information aux. (The system is initialized with pp and aux set to ϵ.)

Enc(crs, pp, id, m) → ct. The encryption algorithm takes as input the common reference string crs, public parameters pp, a recipient identity id, and a plaintext message m. It outputs a ciphertext ct.

Upd^{aux}(pp, id) → u. The key update algorithm is a deterministic algorithm, that takes as input the public parameters pp and an identity id. Given the auxiliary information aux, it generates the key update $u \in \{0, 1\}^*$. Similar to the registration algorithm, this is also modelled as a RAM program, but it is only given read access to arbitrary locations of the auxiliary information aux.

Dec(sk, u, ct) → m/GetUpd/ $\perp$. The decryption algorithm takes as input a secret key sk, a key update u, and a ciphertext ct, and it outputs either a message $m \in \mathcal{M}$, or a special symbol in $\{\perp, \text{GetUpd}\}$. (Here GetUpd indicates that a key update might be needed for decryption.)

Next, we introduce the notion of verifiability for an RBE system. Here we consider the notions of pre-registration as well as post-registration verifiability. Intuitively, the goal of pre-registration verifiability is to provide a short proof validating that a given id has not yet been registered and any ciphertext encrypted towards such an identity will completely hide the message even if all other secret keys are leaked. Similarly, the intuition behind post-registration verifiability is to provide a short proof of unique addition, where the proof guarantees that the key accumulator (i.e., the party responsible for registration) must not have added a trapdoor during a possibly dishonest registration which allows decryption of ciphertexts intended for that particular user. Formally, we introduce four new algorithms—PreProve, PreVerify, PostProve, PostVerify with the following syntax:

PreProve^{aux}(crs, pp, id) → π. The pre-registration prover algorithm is a deterministic algorithm, that takes as input the common reference string crs, public parameters pp, and an identity id. Given the auxiliary information aux, it outputs a pre-registration proof π. Similar to the registration algorithm, this is also modeled as a RAM program, but it is only given read access to arbitrary locations of the auxiliary information aux.

PreVerify(crs, pp, id, π) → 0/1. The pre-registration verifier algorithm takes as input the common reference string crs, public parameter pp, an identity id, and a proof π. It outputs a single bit $0/1$ denoting whether the proof is accepted or not.

PostProve^{aux}(crs, pp, id, pk) $\rightarrow$ π. The post-registration prover algorithm is a deterministic algorithm, that takes as input the common reference string crs, public parameters pp, an identity id, and a public key pk. Given the auxiliary information aux, it outputs a post-registration proof π. Similar to the registration algorithm, this is also modeled as a RAM program, but it is only given read access to arbitrary locations of the auxiliary information aux.

PostVerify(crs, pp, id, pk, π) $\rightarrow$ $0/1$. The post-registration verifier algorithm takes as input the common reference string crs, public parameter pp, an identity id, a public key pk, and a proof π. It outputs a single bit $0/1$ denoting whether the proof is accepted or not.

Note that if one does not impose any succinctness requirements on the pre/post-registration proofs, then the above algorithms are directly implied by the fact that the registration process is deterministic. This is because the proofs themselves can set to be the auxiliary information aux, and one could perform verification by simply rebuilding the public parameters given in aux. This is quite inefficient, thus we impose succinctness restrictions along with completeness and soundness restrictions on the pre/post-registration.

3.1 Correctness

The definition of completeness, compactness, and efficiency for RBE system is studied in [18, 19]. For completeness, we review the definition in full version of the paper. Next, we introduce the completeness, compactness, and efficiency conditions we require from the pre/post-registration procedures of a Verifiable RBE system. Briefly, the completeness of (PreProve, PreVerify) algorithms states that for any identity id* that has not yet been registered, the key accumulator should be able to compute a proof π (by running the PreProve algorithm) such that proof π guarantees id* has not yet been registered. Similarly for the post-registration verification, the completeness of (PostProve, PostVerify) algorithms states that for any identity id* that has been (honestly) registered, the key accumulator should be able to compute a proof π (by running the PostProve algorithm) such that proof π guarantees id* has been registered.

In addition to the above natural completeness definition for the post-registration verification, we also define a stronger completeness property that provides certain extractability guarantee. Informally, it states that if there exists a post-registration proof π for identity-key pair (id*, pk*) that is accepted by the PostVerify algorithm, then every honestly generated ciphertext intended towards id* can be decrypted by the corresponding secret key sk* and some update u. Here the update u is (publicly, efficiently and deterministically) computable from the proof π itself, instead of the auxiliary information aux. Due to space constraints, we postpone the formal definitions to full version of the paper.

3.2   Security

Below we first recall the definition of security for RBE systems as studied previously. After that, we introduce the definitions for soundness of the pre/post-registration proofs.

Definition 3 (Message Hiding Security). *For any (stateful) interactive PPT adversary $\mathcal{A}$, consider the following game $\mathsf{Sec}_{\mathcal{A}}^{\mathsf{RBE}}(\lambda)$.*

1. *(Initialization) The challenger initializes parameters as $(\mathsf{pp}, \mathsf{aux}, u, S_{\mathsf{ID}}, \mathsf{id}^*) = (\epsilon, \epsilon, \epsilon, \emptyset, \bot)$, samples $\mathsf{crs} \leftarrow \mathsf{CRSGen}(1^\lambda)$, and sends the crs to $\mathcal{A}$.*
2. *(Query Phase) $\mathcal{A}$ makes polynomially many queries of the following form:*
   (a) **Registering new (non-target) identity.** *On a query of the form $(\mathsf{regnew}, \mathsf{id}, \mathsf{pk})$, the challenger checks that $\mathsf{id} \notin S_{\mathsf{ID}}$, and registers $(\mathsf{id}, \mathsf{pk})$ by running the registration procedure as $\mathsf{pp} := \mathsf{Reg}^{[\mathsf{aux}]}(\mathsf{crs}, \mathsf{pp}, \mathsf{id}, \mathsf{pk})$. It adds id to the set as $S_{\mathsf{ID}} := S_{\mathsf{ID}} \cup \{\mathsf{id}\}$.*
   (b) **Registering target identity.** *On a query of the form $(\mathsf{regtgt}, \mathsf{id})$, the challenger first checks that $\mathsf{id}^* = \bot$. If the check fails, it aborts. Else, it sets $\mathsf{id}^* := \mathsf{id}$, samples challenge key pair $(\mathsf{pk}^*, \mathsf{sk}^*) \leftarrow \mathsf{Gen}(1^\lambda)$, updates public parameters as $\mathsf{pp} := \mathsf{Reg}^{[\mathsf{aux}]}(\mathsf{crs}, \mathsf{pp}, \mathsf{id}^*, \mathsf{pk}^*)$, and sets $S_{\mathsf{ID}} := S_{\mathsf{ID}} \cup \{\mathsf{id}^*\}$. Finally, it sends the challenge public key pk^* to $\mathcal{A}$.*
3. *(Challenge Phase) On a query of the form $(\mathsf{chal}, \mathsf{id}, m_0, m_1)$, then the challenger checks if $\mathsf{id} \notin S_{\mathsf{ID}} \setminus \{\mathsf{id}^*\}$. It aborts if the check fails. Otherwise, it samples a bit $b \leftarrow \{0,1\}$ and computes challenge ciphertext $\mathsf{ct} \leftarrow \mathsf{Enc}(\mathsf{crs}, \mathsf{pp}, \mathsf{id}, m_b)$.*
4. *(Output Phase) The adversary $\mathcal{A}$ outputs a bit b' and wins the game if $b' = b$.*

We say that an RBE scheme is message-hiding secure if for every (stateful) interactive PPT adversary $\mathcal{A}$, there exists a negligible function $\mathsf{negl}(\cdot)$ such that for every $\lambda \in \mathbb{N}$, $\Pr[\mathcal{A} \text{ wins in } \mathsf{Sec}_{\mathcal{A}}^{\mathsf{RBE}}(\lambda)] \leq \frac{1}{2} + \mathsf{negl}(\lambda)$.

Finally, we define the soundness requirements for our pre/post-registration proof systems. Informally, the pre-registration soundness states that any adversarial key accumulator must not be able to simultaneously—1) provide a valid (acceptable) proof of pre-registration for some identity id, 2) able to break semantic security for (honestly generated) ciphertexts intended towards identity id. Intuitively, this says that even a corrupt key accumulator must not be able to decrypt ciphertexts intended for unregistered users while being able to provide an accepting pre-registration proof. Thus, any new user can ask for a pre-registration proof to verify that the key accumulator has not inserted any trapdoor that enables the accumulator to decrypt ciphertexts encrypted for that user.

In a similar vein, the post-registration soundness informally states that any adversarial key accumulator must not be able to simultaneously—1) provide a valid (acceptable) proof of post-registration for some identity-key pair $(\mathsf{id}, \mathsf{pk})$ (where pk has honestly generated and the associated secret key was not revealed), 2) able to break semantic security for (honestly generated) ciphertexts intended towards identity id. Intuitively, this says that even a corrupt key accumulator must not be able to decrypt ciphertexts intended for registered users while being able to provide an accepting post-registration proof. Thus, any registered user can ask for a post-registration proof to verify that the key accumulator has not inserted any trapdoor that enables the accumulator to decrypt ciphertexts encrypted for that user. Now we give the formal definitions.

Definition 4 (Soundness of Pre-Registration Verifiability). *A VRBE scheme satisfies soundness of pre-registration verifiability if for every stateful admissible PPT adversary $\mathcal{A}$, there exists a negligible function negl($\cdot$) such that for every $\lambda \in \mathbb{N}$, the following holds*

$$\Pr\left[\mathcal{A}(\mathsf{ct}) = b : \begin{array}{c} \mathsf{crs} \leftarrow \mathsf{CRSGen}(1^\lambda) \\ (\mathsf{pp}, \mathsf{id}, \pi, m_0, m_1) \leftarrow \mathcal{A}(\mathsf{crs}) \\ b \leftarrow \{0,1\}; \ \mathsf{ct} \leftarrow \mathsf{Enc}(\mathsf{crs}, \mathsf{pp}, \mathsf{id}, m_b) \end{array}\right] \leq \frac{1}{2} + negl(\lambda),$$

where $\mathcal{A}$ is admissible if and only if π is a valid pre-registration proof, i.e. $\mathsf{PreVerify}(\mathsf{crs}, \mathsf{pp}, \mathsf{id}, \pi) = 1$.

Definition 5 (Soundness of Post-Registration Verifiability). *A VRBE scheme satisfies soundness of post-registration verifiability if for every stateful admissible PPT adversary $\mathcal{A}$, there exists a negligible function negl($\cdot$) such that for every $\lambda \in \mathbb{N}$, the following holds*

$$\Pr\left[\mathcal{A}(\mathsf{ct}) = b : \begin{array}{c} \mathsf{crs} \leftarrow \mathsf{CRSGen}(1^\lambda); \ (\mathsf{pk}, \mathsf{sk}) \leftarrow \mathsf{Gen}(1^\lambda) \\ (\mathsf{pp}, \mathsf{id}, \pi, m_0, m_1) \leftarrow \mathcal{A}(\mathsf{crs}, \mathsf{pk}) \\ b \leftarrow \{0,1\}; \ \mathsf{ct} \leftarrow \mathsf{Enc}(\mathsf{crs}, \mathsf{pp}, \mathsf{id}, m_b) \end{array}\right] \leq \frac{1}{2} + negl(\lambda),$$

where $\mathcal{A}$ is admissible if and only if π is a valid post-registration proof, i.e. $\mathsf{PostVerify}(\mathsf{crs}, \mathsf{pp}, \mathsf{id}, \mathsf{pk}, \pi) = 1$.

4 Verifiable RBE from Standard Assumptions

In this section, we present our VRBE construction. Our construction relies on two primitives—a regular PKE scheme PKE = (PKE.Setup, PKE.Enc, PKE.Dec), and a hash garbling scheme HG = (HG.Setup, HG.Hash, HG.GarbleCkt, HG.GarbleInp, HG.Eval). Below we provide a detailed outline of our construction.

4.1 Construction

For ease of exposition, we assume that the length of identities supported, length of public keys generated by Gen algorithm, the output length of the hash is λ-bits, and the input length of the hash function is $(3\lambda + 1)$-bits. Note that this can be avoided by simply selecting parameters accordingly. Below we define some useful notation that we will reuse throughout the sequel. Additionally, we describe how to interpret the auxiliary information and the public parameters in our construction.

Abstractions, Trees, and Notations. In our construction, the key accumulator maintains two types of balanced binary trees. The first tree which we refer to as the IDTree is a balanced binary tree in which each node has a label of the form $(\mathsf{id}, t) \in \{0,1\}^{2\lambda}$, and the nodes are basically being sorted as per the first tuple entry which is id. (Concretely, $(\mathsf{id}_1, t_1) \prec (\mathsf{id}_2, t_2)$ iff $\mathsf{id}_1 < \mathsf{id}_2$, where $\prec$ denotes the node ordering.) This tree is simply used as an internal storage object (which provides fast node insertion/lookup) by the key accumulator. Here id denotes the registered identity and t denotes the timestamp (i.e., number of users already registered $+1$).

The second family of trees which we refer to are the *encryption* trees $\{\mathsf{EncTree}_i\}_{i \in [\ell_n]}$ for some $\ell_n > 0$. Each such tree consists of two-types of nodes— (1) leaf nodes which store a registered identity-key pair, (2) non-leaf nodes which store the hash values of its children and largest registered identity in its left sub-tree. Concretely, each node in the tree has a label of the form $(\mathsf{flag}||a||\mathsf{id}||b) \in \{0,1\}^{3\lambda+1}$. For a leaf node $\mathsf{flag} = 1$, $a = 0^\lambda$, $b = \mathsf{pk}$ and $(\mathsf{id}, \mathsf{pk})$ is identity-key pair of the corresponding registered user. For a non-leaf node, $\mathsf{flag} = 0$, and id denotes the largest registered identity in its left sub-tree, a and b are the hash value of its left and right child's label (respectively). The leaf nodes are inserted as per their registered identity (i.e., the nodes are ordered with an increasing ordering amongst the identities). Concretely, a new leaf node $(1||0^\lambda||\mathsf{id}||\mathsf{pk})$ is added as follows—

1. Perform a binary search, by using the 'largest registered identity in the left sub-tree' information stored in the label of each intermediate node, to find the leaf node with the smallest identity $\widetilde{\mathsf{id}}$ such that $\widetilde{\mathsf{id}} > \mathsf{id}$. (Let $\widetilde{\mathsf{pk}}$ be the key associated with $\widetilde{\mathsf{id}}$.)
2. Delete the leaf node associated with $\widetilde{\mathsf{id}}$, and replace it with a new intermediate node such that $(1||0^\lambda||\mathsf{id}||\mathsf{pk})$ and $(1||0^\lambda||\widetilde{\mathsf{id}}||\widetilde{\mathsf{pk}})$ are its left and right children (respectively).
3. Perform the *re-balance* operation on the binary tree.[6]
4. Re-compute the labels for all intermediate nodes which have been re-balanced (i.e., moved around). This involves updating the largest registered identity in the left sub-tree information as well as re-computing the corresponding hash values.

Looking ahead, here the first $\ell_n - 1$ encryption trees $\mathsf{EncTree}_1, \ldots, \mathsf{EncTree}_{\ell_n-1}$ represent the older snapshots of the registration process, whereas $\mathsf{EncTree}_{\ell_n}$ represents the latest encryption tree which contains all the identities registered so far. Also, the above tree insertion operation is efficient ($O(\log n)$ updates and running time) as long as the underlying tree abstraction provides efficient lookup

---

[6] Note that the tree re-balancing operation has to be carefully performed as in our abstraction (as well as the [19] abstraction) the leaf nodes and intermediate nodes are not exchangeable. Thus, the leaf-nodes must always stay the leaf nodes. Roughly one might consider that the re-balancing operation is only performed on the tree obtained by removing all leaf-nodes. This is not completely accurate but captures the underlying intuition.

and insertion. Since we use a balanced tree as the underlying abstraction, thus efficiency follows.

A very useful piece of notation in our scheme is the notion of *'paths'* from the root node to a leaf node in some encryption tree EncTree. Concretely, throughout this section, we will define a *path* w.r.t. a tree EncTree (with root rt and depth d) as a sequence of (at most) d nodes where the first node is the root node of the tree and last node is a leaf node with certain specific properties. Concretely, any path path will look like path $= (\mathsf{node}_1, \ldots, \mathsf{node}_{d-1}, \mathsf{node}_d)$, where for $i < d$, $\mathsf{node}_i = (0||a_i||\mathsf{id}_i||b_i)$ for some hash values a_i, b_i and identity id_i. Similarly, $\mathsf{node}_d = (1||0^\lambda||\mathsf{id}_d||\mathsf{pk})$ for some identity-key pair $\mathsf{id}_d, \mathsf{pk}$, and the remaining intermediate nodes are such that for every i, $a_i = \mathsf{HG.Hash}(\mathsf{hk}, \mathsf{node}_{i+1})$ if node_{i+1} is left child of node_i, else $b_i = \mathsf{HG.Hash}(\mathsf{hk}, \mathsf{node}_{i+1})$. Also, if node_{i+1} is left child of node_i then $\mathsf{id}_i \geq \mathsf{id}_{i+1}$, else $\mathsf{id}_i < \mathsf{id}_{i+1}$. Now note that such a path can be efficiently computed for every identity id, which has been added to encryption tree EncTree, by simply performing an extended binary search. We will be re-using this fact many times throughout the sequel.

Lastly, we define a notion which we refer to as *'adjacent'* paths. This is extremely useful for verifiability of our scheme. Note that if during binary search in any balanced search tree, if the node/label that is being searched does not exist, then one could prove that efficiently by giving two paths to nodes with labels that are just bigger than and smaller than the label as per the ordering defined in the tree. More formally, for any two paths path_1 and path_2 in an encryption tree, we can perform an adjacency check efficiently as follows. Let $\mathsf{path}_j = (\mathsf{node}_{1,j}, \ldots, \mathsf{node}_{d-1,j}, \mathsf{node}_{d,j})$ for $j \in [2]$ where $\mathsf{node}_{i,j} = (0||a_{i,j}||\mathsf{id}_{i,j}||b_{i,j})$ for $j < d$ and $\mathsf{node}_{d,j} = (1||0^\lambda||\mathsf{id}_{d,j}||\mathsf{pk}_{d,j})$: (1) First, check that both paths are valid. Note that path validity is checked as that either $\mathsf{HG.Hash}(\mathsf{hk}, \mathsf{node}_{i+1,j})$ is equal to $a_{i,j}$ or $b_{i,j}$.[7] (2) Next, the verifier first computes the largest common prefix of nodes in paths path_1 and path_2. That is, let k be the largest index such that $\mathsf{node}_{i,1} = \mathsf{node}_{i,2}$ for all $i \leq k$. Now if $\mathsf{id}_{d,1} < \mathsf{id}_{d,2}$, then check that $\mathsf{node}_{k+1,1}$ and $\mathsf{node}_{k+1,2}$ are left and right children of $\mathsf{node}_{k,1} = \mathsf{node}_{k,2}$. Next, it must check that, for all $i > k+1$, $\mathsf{node}_{i,1}$ is always the right child of its parent and $\mathsf{node}_{i,2}$ is always the left child of its parent. Basically, this is done to make sure that these two paths are adjacent and there does not exist any intermediate registered identity between these.

Construction. The key accumulator initializes the public parameters pp and auxiliary information aux as empty strings ϵ. And, afterwards at any point, the auxiliary information will contain the IDTree and (at most a λ number of) encryption trees $\mathsf{EncTree}_i$ along with a number n_i.[8] And, the public parameters pp consists of root value and depth pairs (rt_i, d_i) for each encryption tree $\mathsf{EncTree}_i$ present in auxiliary information aux. Here rt_i is the root node and d_i is the depth of $\mathsf{EncTree}_i$. We now formally describe our construction.

---

[7] Note that this also tells whether $\mathsf{node}_{i+1,j}$ is a left child of $\mathsf{node}_{i,j}$, or right child.

[8] Looking ahead, the number n_i signifies the number of users who will refer to the tree $\mathsf{EncTree}_i$ for decryption. The significance of n_i will become clear in the construction.

$\mathsf{CRSGen}(1^\lambda) \to \mathsf{crs}$. The CRS generation algorithm samples a hash key for the hash garbling scheme as $\mathsf{hk} \leftarrow \mathsf{HG.Setup}(1^\lambda, 1^{3\lambda+1})$, and outputs $\mathsf{crs} = \mathsf{hk}$.

$\mathsf{Reg}^{[\mathsf{aux}]}(\mathsf{crs}, \mathsf{pp}, \mathsf{id}, \mathsf{pk}) \to \mathsf{pp}'$. Let $\mathsf{pp} = \{(\mathsf{rt}_i, d_i)\}_{i \in [\ell_n]}$ and $\mathsf{aux} = \Big(\mathsf{IDTree},$ $\{(\mathsf{EncTree}_i, n_i)\}_{i \in [\ell_n]}\Big)$. Also, let $n = \sum_i n_i + 1$. The key accumulator performs the following operations:

1. It creates a leaf node with the label $(1||0^\lambda||\mathsf{id}||\mathsf{pk})$, and update the current (latest) encryption tree $\mathsf{EncTree}_{\ell_n}$ by inserting the new leaf node. (Note that the insertion is performed as described above, and it involves balancing the tree and updating the hash values accordingly.)

2. Let $\mathsf{NewTree}$ be the new encryption tree. It continues by adding (id, n) to the IDTree, and the tuple $(\mathsf{EncTree}_{\ell_n+1}, 1) := (\mathsf{NewTree}, 1)$ to current auxiliary information aux. (This new tuple should be interpreted as signifying that only one user (which is the current, i.e. n^{th}, user with identity id) would refer to the latest encryption tree $\mathsf{NewTree}$ during decryption.)

3. Next it modifies the list of encryption trees as follows. Let $\mathsf{aux} = \Big(\mathsf{IDTree},$ $\{(\mathsf{EncTree}_i, n_i)\}_{i \in [\ell_n]}\Big)$, and

$$\delta = \max\left(\{0\} \cup \left\{i \in [\ell_n - 1] \; : \; \forall\, j \in [i],\; n_{\ell_n+1-j} = 2^{j-1}\right\}\right).$$

It modifies the auxilliary information as $\mathsf{aux} = \Big(\mathsf{IDTree},$ $\{(\mathsf{EncTree}'_i, n'_i)\}_{i \in [\ell_n+1-\delta]}\Big)$, where

$$(\mathsf{EncTree}'_i, n'_i) := \begin{cases} (\mathsf{EncTree}_i, n_i) & \text{if } i < \ell_n + 1 - \delta, \\ (\mathsf{NewTree}, 2 \cdot n_i) & \text{otherwise.} \end{cases}$$

In words, the accumulator removes all the old versions of the encryption trees as long as it could replace all of them with the latest tree until the number of users which would then refer to the latest tree stays a power of 2. To illustrate this operation, we give a detailed running example of the Reg algorithm in Fig. 1.

4. Lastly, the accumulator modifies the public parameters to $\mathsf{pp}' = \{(\mathsf{rt}'_i, d'_i)\}_{i \in [\ell_n+1-\delta]}$, where rt'_i, d'_i are root node and depth of the encryption tree $\mathsf{EncTree}'_i$ (respectively).

   Note. At a high level, the accumulator maintains the invariant that the ith encryption tree $\mathsf{EncTree}'_i$ is an accumulation of the identity-key pairs for exactly the first $\sum_{j \leq i} n'_j$, and this tree is intended to be precisely used during decryption by those n'_i users who registered just after the first $\sum_{j \leq i-1} n'_i$ users. Additionally, the n_i values for the last and the second last encryption trees are more than a factor of 2 apart. (The last point is quite crucial in ensuring that number of updates grows only logarithmically.)

$\mathsf{Enc}(\mathsf{crs}, \mathsf{pp}, \mathsf{id}, m) \to \mathsf{ct}$. Let $\mathsf{pp} = \{(\mathsf{rt}_i, d_i)\}_{i \in [\ell_n]}$ and $\mathsf{crs} = \mathsf{hk}$. The encryptor proceeds as follows:

Sample Execution of Reg Algorithm

Consider the scenario where 7 users ($\mathsf{id}_1, \mathsf{id}_2, \mathsf{id}_3, \mathsf{id}_4, \mathsf{id}_5, \mathsf{id}_6, \mathsf{id}_7$) are registered into the system. The auxilliary information aux now stores IDTree and 3 versions of EncTree. IDTree consists of all the identites along with their timestamps. $\mathsf{EncTree}_1, \mathsf{EncTree}_2$ are the versions of EncTree when only 4 users and 6 users were registered respectively. $\mathsf{EncTree}_3$ is the latest version of the EncTree when all 7 users are registered in the system. More precisely, the list of identities present in each $\mathsf{EncTree}_i$ is as follows.

$$\mathsf{aux} = \{\mathsf{IDTree}, (\mathsf{EncTree}_1, 4) : [\mathsf{id}_1, \dots, \mathsf{id}_4], \ (\mathsf{EncTree}_2, 2) : [\mathsf{id}_1, \dots, \mathsf{id}_6],$$
$$(\mathsf{EncTree}_3, 1) : [\mathsf{id}_1, \dots, \mathsf{id}_7]\}$$

Let us now look at when we register a new identity id_8. The key accumulator sets $n = 8$, inserts id_8 into IDTree, creates NewTree by inserting id_8 into $\mathsf{EncTree}_3$, and sets $(\mathsf{EncTree}_4, 1) = (\mathsf{NewTree}, 1)$. To compute δ, the key accumulator observes that $n_{\ell_n + 1 - j} = n_{4-j} = 2^{j-1}$ for all $j \in [3]$, and sets $\delta = 3$. The key accumulator now deletes $\mathsf{EncTree}_i$ for each $i \geq \ell_n + 1 - \delta = 1$, and sets $(\mathsf{EncTree}_1', n_1') = (\mathsf{NewTree}, 2 \cdot n_1 = 8)$. So, now the updated auxilliary information is $\mathsf{aux} = \{\mathsf{IDTree}, (\mathsf{EncTree}_1', 8) : [\mathsf{id}_1, \dots, \mathsf{id}_8]\}$.

Fig. 1. An example demonstrating aux being updated during registration

1. First, it samples $\mathsf{state}_{i,j} \leftarrow \{0,1\}^\lambda$ and $r_{i,j} \leftarrow \{0,1\}^\lambda$ for each $i \in [\ell_n]$, and $j \in [d_i + 1]$.
2. Next, for each encryption tree $\mathsf{EncTree}_i$, it computes a sequence of d_i hash-garbled circuits as follows:
   For $i \in [\ell_n]$:
   - For $j \in [d_i]$: It constructs a step-circuit $\mathsf{Enc\text{-}Step}_{i,j}$ as defined in Fig. 2 with $\mathsf{hk}, \mathsf{id}, m, \mathsf{state}_{i,j+1}, r_{i,j+1}$ hardwired. It then garbles the circuit as $\widetilde{\mathsf{Enc\text{-}Step}}_{i,j} \leftarrow \mathsf{HG.GarbleCkt}(\mathsf{hk}, \mathsf{Enc\text{-}Step}_{i,j}, \mathsf{state}_{i,j})$.
   - It computes the hash value of root node as $h_i = \mathsf{HG.Hash}(\mathsf{hk}, \mathsf{rt}_i)$, and computes the input garbling as $\widetilde{y}_{i,1} = \mathsf{HG.GarbleInp}(\mathsf{hk}, h_i, \mathsf{state}_{i,1}; r_{i,1})$.
3. Finally, it outputs the ciphertext ct as $\mathsf{ct} = \left(\{(\mathsf{rt}_i, d_i)\}_i, \left\{ \widetilde{\mathsf{Enc\text{-}Step}}_{i,j} \right\}_{i,j}, \{\widetilde{y}_{i,1}\}_i \right)$.

$\mathsf{Upd}^{\mathsf{aux}}(\mathsf{pp}, \mathsf{id}) \rightarrow u$. Let $\mathsf{pp} = \{(\mathsf{rt}_i, d_i)\}_{i \in [\ell_n]}$ and $\mathsf{aux} = \left(\mathsf{IDTree}, \{(\mathsf{EncTree}_i, n_i)\}_{i \in [\ell_n]} \right)$. The update computation is a two-step approach. In the first step, the algorithm performs a binary search over the IDTree to obtain the timestamp associated with the identity id. As IDTree is a balanced binary search tree, thus this can done efficiently. Let t be the timestamp associated with id that the binary search outputs. (It aborts if no such timestamp exists.) In the second phase, the update generator computes the index $i^* \in [\ell_n]$ such that $\sum_{j \in [i^*-1]} n_j < t \leq \sum_{j \in [i^*]} n_j$. Index i^* corresponds to the smallest index of the encryption tree in which id has been registered.

Circuit Enc-Step$_{i,j}$

Constants: hk, id, m, state$_{i,j+1}$, $r_{i,j+1}$.
Input: flag$||a||$id$^*||b \in \{0,1\}^{3\lambda+1}$.

1. If flag $= 1$ and id$^* =$ id, output $1||$PKE.Enc$(b, m; r_{i,j+1})$.
2. If flag $= 1$ and id$^* \neq$ id, output $1||\bot$.
3. If id $>$ id*, output $0||$HG.GarbleInp(hk, b, state$_{i,j+1}; r_{i,j+1}$)
   Else, output $0||$HG.GarbleInp(hk, a, state$_{i,j+1}; r_{i,j+1}$).

Fig. 2. Description of the step-circuit Enc-Step$_{i,j}$

Now the algorithm performs a binary search for identity id in the encryption tree EncTree$_{i^*}$. It stores the path of nodes traversed from root rt$_{i^*}$ to leaf node containing identity id. Let path be the searched path in tree EncTree$_{i^*}$. Finally, it outputs the update u as $u =$ path. (Again, it aborts if no such index or a path to a leaf node containing identity id exists.)

Dec(sk, u, ct) $\rightarrow m/\bot/$GetUpd. The decryption algorithm first parses the inputs as: ct $= \left(\{(\mathsf{rt}_i, d_i)\}_i, \left\{\widetilde{\mathsf{Enc\text{-}Step}}_{i,j}\right\}_{i,j}, \{\widetilde{y}_{i,1}\}_i\right)$ and $u =$ path $=$ (node$_1, \ldots,$ node$_{d-1}$, node$_d$). It then proceeds as follows:

1. Let i be the smallest index $i \in [\ell_n]$ such that node$_1 =$ rt$_i$. If such an i does not exist, then it outputs GetUpd. Otherwise, it continues.
2. Now the decryptor iteratively runs the hash garbling evaluation algorithms as follows.
   For $j \in [d_i]$:
   - It evaluates the jth step-circuit as (flag$||\widetilde{y}_{i,j+1}) \leftarrow$ HG.Eval($\widetilde{\mathsf{Enc\text{-}Step}}_{i,j}$, $\widetilde{y}_{i,j}$, node$_i$).
   - If flag $= 1$ and $\widetilde{y}_{i,j+1} = \bot$, the algorithm outputs $\bot$.
   - Otherwise, if flag $= 1$ and $\widetilde{y}_{i,j+1} \neq \bot$, then interpret $\widetilde{y}_{i,j+1}$ as a PKE ciphertext, and decrypt it as $\widetilde{y}_{i,j+1}$ using key sk to obtain the message as $m \leftarrow$ PKE.Dec(sk, $\widetilde{y}_{i,j+1}$). And, it outputs the message m.
3. If the algorithm did not terminate, then it outputs $\bot$.

PreProve^{aux}(pp, id) $\rightarrow \pi$. Let pp $= \{(\mathsf{rt}_i, d_i)\}_{i \in [\ell_n]}$ and aux $= \Big($IDTree, $\{(\mathsf{EncTree}_i, n_i)\}_{i \in [\ell_n]}\Big)$. The pre-registration proof consists of ℓ_n sub-proofs π_i for $i \in [\ell_n]$, where each sub-proof π_i consist of two[9] adjacent paths in the ith encryption tree EncTree$_i$. Concretely, the algorithm proceeds as follows: For $i \in [\ell_n]$:
- It runs a binary search on tree EncTree$_i$ to find identity id. If id is contained in EncTree$_i$, then it outputs $\bot$. Otherwise, it continues.
- It runs an extended binary search on tree EncTree$_i$ to find two adjacent paths path$_{i,\mathsf{lwr}}$ and path$_{i,\mathsf{upr}}$ for identities id$_{i,\mathsf{lwr}}$ and id$_{i,\mathsf{upr}}$, respectively.

---

[9] Sometimes one of the paths might just be an empty path.

(Here $\mathsf{id}_{i,\mathsf{lwr}}$ is the largest identity in $\mathsf{EncTree}_i$ such that $\mathsf{id}_{i,\mathsf{lwr}} < \mathsf{id}$ and similarly $\mathsf{id}_{i,\mathsf{upr}}$ is the smallest identity in $\mathsf{EncTree}_i$ such that $\mathsf{id}_{i,\mathsf{upr}} > \mathsf{id}$.) If $\mathsf{id}_{i,\mathsf{lwr}}$ is the largest identity registered in the tree $\mathsf{EncTree}_i$, that is no such $\mathsf{id}_{i,\mathsf{upr}}$ exists, then path $\mathsf{path}_{i,\mathsf{upr}}$ is set as $\mathsf{path}_{i,\mathsf{upr}} = \epsilon$. Similarly, if $\mathsf{id}_{i,\mathsf{upr}}$ is the smallest identity, that is no such $\mathsf{id}_{i,\mathsf{lwr}}$ exists, then path $\mathsf{path}_{i,\mathsf{lwr}}$ is set as $\mathsf{path}_{i,\mathsf{lwr}} = \epsilon$.

- It sets sub-proof π_i as $\pi_i = (\mathsf{path}_{i,\mathsf{lwr}}, \mathsf{path}_{i,\mathsf{upr}})$.

Finally, it outputs the pre-registration proof as $\pi = (\pi_1, \ldots, \pi_{\ell_n})$.

$\mathsf{PreVerify}(\mathsf{crs}, \mathsf{pp}, \mathsf{id}, \pi) \rightarrow 0/1$. Let $\mathsf{crs} = \mathsf{hk}$, $\mathsf{pp} = \{(\mathsf{rt}_i, d_i)\}_{i \in [\ell_n]}$, $\pi = (\pi_i)_{i \in [\ell_n]}$.[10] Also, let each sub-proof be $\pi_i = (\mathsf{path}_{i,\mathsf{lwr}}, \mathsf{path}_{i,\mathsf{upr}})$ for $i \in [\ell_n]$. The pre-registration proof verification procedure proceeds as follows. For every $i \in [\ell_n]$, it runs the pre-registration sub-proof verification procedure which is described in Fig. 3.

If the pre-registration sub-proof verification procedure rejects for any index $i \in [\ell_n]$, then the main verification algorithm also rejects and outputs 0. Otherwise, if all sub-proof verification routines accept, then the main verification algorithm also accepts and outputs 1.

$\mathsf{PostProve}^{\mathsf{aux}}(\mathsf{pp}, \mathsf{id}, \mathsf{pk}) \rightarrow \pi$. Let $\mathsf{pp} = \{(\mathsf{rt}_i, d_i)\}_{i \in [\ell_n]}$ and $\mathsf{aux} = \Big(\mathsf{IDTree},$ $\{(\mathsf{EncTree}_i, n_i)\}_{i \in [\ell_n]}\Big)$. The post-registration proof consists of ℓ_n sub-proofs π_i for $i \in [\ell_n]$, where each sub-proof π_i consist of either two or *three* adjacent paths in the ith encryption tree $\mathsf{EncTree}_i$.[11] (Very briefly, having 3 adjacent paths w.r.t. an encryption tree will correspond to the proof of uniqueness of decryptability by the registered user's secret key; whereas 2 adjacent paths will mostly correspond to a proof of non-decryptability.) Concretely, the algorithm proceeds as follows:

Initialize $\ell = \bot$, where ℓ will eventually denote the index of the first encryption tree $\mathsf{EncTree}_\ell$ in which identity id was registered. For $i \in [\ell_n]$:

- It runs a binary search on tree $\mathsf{EncTree}_i$ to find identity id. If the tree contains a leaf node of the form $1||0^\lambda||\mathsf{id}||\mathsf{pk}'$ for some key $\mathsf{pk}' \neq \mathsf{pk}$, then the algorithm simply outputs $\bot$. Otherwise, it continues as follows.
- If id is *not* contained in $\mathsf{EncTree}_i$, then it first checks that $\ell = \bot$. If the check fails, it aborts. Otherwise, it proceeds as for the pre-registration sub-proof which is to run an extended binary search on tree $\mathsf{EncTree}_i$ to find two adjacent paths $\mathsf{path}_{i,\mathsf{lwr}}, \mathsf{path}_{i,\mathsf{upr}}$ for identities $\mathsf{id}_{i,\mathsf{lwr}}, \mathsf{id}_{i,\mathsf{upr}}$ (respectively). Here $\mathsf{id}_{i,\mathsf{lwr}}$ is the largest identity in $\mathsf{EncTree}_i$ such that $\mathsf{id}_{i,\mathsf{lwr}} < \mathsf{id}$ and similarly $\mathsf{id}_{i,\mathsf{upr}}$ is the smallest identity in $\mathsf{EncTree}_i$ such that $\mathsf{id}_{i,\mathsf{upr}} > \mathsf{id}$. And, it sets sub-proof π_i as $\pi_i = (\mathsf{path}_{i,\mathsf{lwr}}, \mathsf{path}_{i,\mathsf{upr}})$. (Recall that one of these paths might be empty.)
- If id is contained in $\mathsf{EncTree}_i$, then it proceeds as follows:

---

[10] If the number of sub-proofs and number of encryption trees are distinct, then the verifier rejects. Here we simply consider that while parsing the inputs, the verifier verifies that the crs and pp are consistent which simply corresponds to checking that the number of trees and their depths are consistent.

[11] See footnote 9.

Verification procedure for pre-registration sub-proof

For simplicity of exposition, suppose that none of paths $\mathsf{path}_{i,\mathsf{lwr}}$, $\mathsf{path}_{i,\mathsf{upr}}$ are empty. At the end, we explain how to handle if either of these paths is ϵ.

Non-empty paths. It interprets every path $\mathsf{path}_{i,\mathsf{tag}}$ as $(\mathsf{node}_{i,1,\mathsf{tag}}, \ldots, \mathsf{node}_{i,d_i,\mathsf{tag}})$ for $i \in [\ell_n]$ and $\mathsf{tag} \in \{\mathsf{lwr}, \mathsf{upr}\}$. And every node $\mathsf{node}_{i,j,\mathsf{tag}}$, is interpreted as $(\mathsf{flag}_{i,j,\mathsf{tag}} || a_{i,j,\mathsf{tag}} || \mathsf{id}_{i,j,\mathsf{tag}} || b_{i,j,\mathsf{tag}})$.

1. First, it checks that both paths $\mathsf{path}_{i,\mathsf{lwr}}$ and $\mathsf{path}_{i,\mathsf{upr}}$ are well-formed. That is, $\mathsf{node}_{i,1,\mathsf{tag}} = \mathsf{rt}_i$ for both $\mathsf{tag} \in \{\mathsf{lwr}, \mathsf{upr}\}$. Also, it checks that $\mathsf{node}_{i,j+1,\mathsf{tag}}$ is either left child of $\mathsf{node}_{i,j,\mathsf{tag}}$ (i.e., $a_{i,j,\mathsf{tag}} = \mathsf{HG.Hash}(\mathsf{hk}, \mathsf{node}_{i,j+1,\mathsf{tag}})$ and $\mathsf{id}_{i,j,\mathsf{tag}} \geq \mathsf{id}_{i,j+1,\mathsf{tag}}$), or right child of $\mathsf{node}_{i,j,\mathsf{tag}}$ (i.e., $b_{i,j,\mathsf{tag}} = \mathsf{HG.Hash}(\mathsf{hk}, \mathsf{node}_{i,j+1,\mathsf{tag}})$ and $\mathsf{id}_{i,j,\mathsf{tag}} < \mathsf{id}_{i,j+1,\mathsf{tag}}$). If $\mathsf{node}_{i,j+1,\mathsf{tag}}$ is left child of $\mathsf{node}_{i,j,\mathsf{tag}}$, then it checks that $\mathsf{id}_{i,k,\mathsf{tag}} \leq \mathsf{id}_{i,j,\mathsf{tag}}$ for each $k > j$. Similarly, If $\mathsf{node}_{i,j+1,\mathsf{tag}}$ is right child of $\mathsf{node}_{i,j,\mathsf{tag}}$, then it checks that $\mathsf{id}_{i,k,\mathsf{tag}} > \mathsf{id}_{i,j,\mathsf{tag}}$ for each $k > j$. And, it checks that $\mathsf{flag}_{i,j,\mathsf{tag}} = 0$ for $j < d_i$, and $\mathsf{flag}_{i,d_i,\mathsf{tag}} = 1$, $a_{i,d_i,\mathsf{tag}} = 0^\lambda$. (Note that during this validity check, the verifier also stores whether that node is left child or right child.).
2. Next, it checks that $\mathsf{id}_{i,d_i,\mathsf{lwr}} < \mathsf{id} < \mathsf{id}_{i,d_i,\mathsf{upr}}$, that is the identity in the *lower* path is less than that in the *upper* path, and the identity id whose non-registration is being proven lies between both these identities.
3. It then computes the largest common prefix of nodes in paths $\mathsf{path}_{i,\mathsf{lwr}}$ and $\mathsf{path}_{i,\mathsf{upr}}$. That is, let k be the largest index such that $\mathsf{node}_{i,j,\mathsf{lwr}} = \mathsf{node}_{i,j,\mathsf{upr}}$ for all $j \leq k$. It checks that $\mathsf{id}_{i,k,\mathsf{lwr}} = \mathsf{id}_{i,d_i,\mathsf{lwr}}$. Also, it checks:
   (a) It checks that $\mathsf{node}_{i,k+1,\mathsf{lwr}}$ and $\mathsf{node}_{i,k+1,\mathsf{upr}}$ are *left* and *right* children of $\mathsf{node}_{i,k,\mathsf{lwr}} = \mathsf{node}_{i,k,\mathsf{upr}}$. That is, $a_{i,k,\mathsf{lwr}} = \mathsf{HG.Hash}(\mathsf{hk}, \mathsf{node}_{i,k+1,\mathsf{lwr}})$ and $b_{i,k,\mathsf{upr}} = \mathsf{HG.Hash}(\mathsf{hk}, \mathsf{node}_{i,k+1,\mathsf{upr}})$.
   (b) For every index $j > k$, $\mathsf{node}_{i,j+1,\mathsf{lwr}}$ and $\mathsf{node}_{i,j+1,\mathsf{upr}}$ are *right* and *left* children of $\mathsf{node}_{i,j,\mathsf{lwr}}$ and $\mathsf{node}_{i,j,\mathsf{upr}}$, respectively. That is, $b_{i,j,\mathsf{lwr}} = \mathsf{HG.Hash}(\mathsf{hk}, \mathsf{node}_{i,j+1,\mathsf{lwr}})$ and $a_{i,j,\mathsf{upr}} = \mathsf{HG.Hash}(\mathsf{hk}, \mathsf{node}_{i,j+1,\mathsf{upr}})$.

It rejects, i.e. outputs 0, if any of these checks fails. Otherwise, it accepts and outputs 1.

One empty path. Suppose $\mathsf{path}_{i,\mathsf{lwr}} = \epsilon$. The verifier checks first well-formedness of $\mathsf{path}_{i,\mathsf{upr}}$ as in Step 1 (above). Next, it checks that $\mathsf{id} < \mathsf{id}_{i,d_i,\mathsf{upr}}$, and lastly verifies that $\mathsf{id}_{i,d_i,\mathsf{upr}}$ is the smallest registered node in $\mathsf{EncTree}_i$. For the last check, the verifier check that for every index j, $\mathsf{node}_{i,j+1,\mathsf{upr}}$ is the *left* child of $\mathsf{node}_{i,j,\mathsf{upr}}$. It rejects, i.e. outputs 0, if any of these checks fails. Otherwise, it accepts and outputs 1.

Similarly, if $\mathsf{path}_{i,\mathsf{upr}} = \epsilon$, then it proceeds as above, except it checks that $\mathsf{id}_{i,d_i,\mathsf{lwr}}$ is the largest identity in $\mathsf{EncTree}_i$ instead.

Fig. 3. Conditions for verifying a proof $\pi_i = (\mathsf{path}_{i,\mathsf{lwr}}, \mathsf{path}_{i,\mathsf{upr}})$ that id is NOT registered as per $\mathsf{EncTree}_i$

– If $\ell = \perp$, then it sets $\ell = i$ (i.e., sets ℓ as the first tree where id was found).

– It runs an extended binary search on tree $\mathsf{EncTree}_i$ to find three adjacent paths $\mathsf{path}_{i,\mathsf{lwr}}$, $\mathsf{path}_{i,\mathsf{mid}}$, $\mathsf{path}_{i,\mathsf{upr}}$ for identities $\mathsf{id}_{i,\mathsf{lwr}}$, id, $\mathsf{id}_{i,\mathsf{upr}}$ (respectively). Here $\mathsf{id}_{i,\mathsf{lwr}}$ is the largest identity in $\mathsf{EncTree}_i$ such that $\mathsf{id}_{i,\mathsf{lwr}} < \mathsf{id}$ and similarly $\mathsf{id}_{i,\mathsf{upr}}$ is the smallest identity in $\mathsf{EncTree}_i$ such that $\mathsf{id}_{i,\mathsf{upr}} > \mathsf{id}$.

If id is the largest identity registered in the tree $\mathsf{EncTree}_i$, that is no such $\mathsf{id}_{i,\mathsf{upr}}$ exists, then path $\mathsf{path}_{i,\mathsf{upr}}$ is set as $\mathsf{path}_{i,\mathsf{upr}} = \epsilon$. Similarly, if id is the smallest identity, that is no such $\mathsf{id}_{i,\mathsf{lwr}}$ exists, then path $\mathsf{path}_{i,\mathsf{lwr}}$ is set as $\mathsf{path}_{i,\mathsf{lwr}} = \epsilon$.

– It sets sub-proof π_i as $\pi_i = (\mathsf{path}_{i,\mathsf{lwr}}, \mathsf{path}_{i,\mathsf{mid}}, \mathsf{path}_{i,\mathsf{upr}})$.

Finally, it outputs the post-registration proof as $\pi = (\pi_1, \ldots, \pi_{\ell_n}, \ell)$. (Note that the cut-off index ℓ in included as part of the proof.)

$\mathsf{PostVerify}(\mathsf{crs}, \mathsf{pp}, \mathsf{id}, \mathsf{pk}, \pi) \to 0/1$. Let $\mathsf{crs} = \mathsf{hk}$, $\mathsf{pp} = \{(\mathsf{rt}_i, d_i)\}_{i \in [\ell_n]}$, $\pi = (\pi_1, \ldots, \pi_{\ell_n}, \ell)$.[12] Now each sub-proof either is interpreted as 3 adjacent paths $\pi_i = (\mathsf{path}_{i,\mathsf{lwr}}, \mathsf{path}_{i,\mathsf{mid}}, \mathsf{path}_{i,\mathsf{upr}})$, or as 2 adjacent paths $\pi_i = (\mathsf{path}_{i,\mathsf{lwr}}, \mathsf{path}_{i,\mathsf{upr}})$ for every i.

The post-registration proof verification procedure proceeds as follows. For every $i \in [\ell]$, it runs the *pre-registration* sub-proof verification procedure which is described in Fig. 3. Now, for every $i \in \{\ell, \ell+1, \ldots, \ell_n\}$, it runs the *post-registration* sub-proof verification procedure which is described in Fig. 4. If any of the pre-registration or post-registration sub-proof verification procedure rejects for any index $i \in [\ell_n]$, then the main verification algorithm also rejects and outputs 0. Otherwise, if all sub-proof verification routines accept, then the main verification algorithm also accepts and outputs 1.

Remark 1. In the above construction, we make the key accumulator maintain a special balanced tree IDTree privately. It turns out this is not necessary, and one could easily remove it from our construction, thereby only leaving the list of encryption trees $\{\mathsf{EncTree}_i\}_i$ as part of the auxiliary information. However, for ease of exposition, we include IDTree explicitly as part of the description.

4.2   Efficiency and Completeness

The above VRBE construction is efficient in the sense that if n is the number of registered users, then (1) The time complexity of Reg algorithm is $O(\log^2 n)$, (2) The size of the public parameters is $O(\log n)$, (3) The time complexity of Upd algorithm is $O(\log n)$, (4) The size of an update is $O(\log n)$, (5) The number of updates to any user is $O(\log n)$, (6) The time complexity of PreProve, PostProve algorithms is $O(\log^2 n)$, and (7) The size of pre/post-registration

---

[12] If the number of sub-proofs and number of encryption trees are distinct, then the verifier rejects. Here we simply consider that while parsing the inputs, the verifier verifies that the crs and pp are consistent which simply corresponds to checking that the number of trees and their depths are consistent.

Verification procedure for post-registration sub-proof

For simplicity of exposition, suppose that none of paths $\mathsf{path}_{i,\mathsf{lwr}}$, $\mathsf{path}_{i,\mathsf{upr}}$ are empty. At the end, we explain how to handle if either of these paths are ϵ.

Non-empty paths. It interprets every path $\mathsf{path}_{i,\mathsf{tag}}$ as $(\mathsf{node}_{i,1\mathsf{tag}}, \ldots, \mathsf{node}_{i,d_i\mathsf{tag}})$ for $i \in [\ell_n]$ and $\mathsf{tag} \in \{\mathsf{lwr}, \mathsf{mid}, \mathsf{upr}\}$. And every node $\mathsf{node}_{i,j,\mathsf{tag}}$, is interpreted as $(\mathsf{flag}_{i,j,\mathsf{tag}} || a_{i,j,\mathsf{tag}} || \mathsf{id}_{i,j,\mathsf{tag}} || b_{i,j,\mathsf{tag}})$.

1. First, it checks that both paths $\mathsf{path}_{i,\mathsf{lwr}}$, $\mathsf{path}_{i,\mathsf{mid}}$ and $\mathsf{path}_{i,\mathsf{upr}}$ are well-formed. That is, $\mathsf{node}_{i,1,\mathsf{tag}} = \mathsf{rt}_i$ for both $\mathsf{tag} \in \{\mathsf{lwr}, \mathsf{mid}, \mathsf{upr}\}$. Also, it checks that $\mathsf{node}_{i,j+1,\mathsf{tag}}$ is either a left child of $\mathsf{node}_{i,j,\mathsf{tag}}$ (i.e., $a_{i,j,\mathsf{tag}} = \mathsf{HG.Hash}(\mathsf{hk}, \mathsf{node}_{i,j+1,\mathsf{tag}})$ and $\mathsf{id}_{i,j,\mathsf{tag}} \geq \mathsf{id}_{i,j+1,\mathsf{tag}}$), or is a right child of $\mathsf{node}_{i,j,\mathsf{tag}}$ (i.e., $b_{i,j,\mathsf{tag}} = \mathsf{HG.Hash}(\mathsf{hk}, \mathsf{node}_{i,j+1,\mathsf{tag}})$ and $\mathsf{id}_{i,j,\mathsf{tag}} < \mathsf{id}_{i,j+1,\mathsf{tag}}$). If $\mathsf{node}_{i,j+1,\mathsf{tag}}$ is left child of $\mathsf{node}_{i,j,\mathsf{tag}}$, then it checks that $\mathsf{id}_{i,k,\mathsf{tag}} \leq \mathsf{id}_{i,j,\mathsf{tag}}$ for each $k > j$. Similarly, If $\mathsf{node}_{i,j+1,\mathsf{tag}}$ is right child of $\mathsf{node}_{i,j,\mathsf{tag}}$, then it checks that $\mathsf{id}_{i,k,\mathsf{tag}} > \mathsf{id}_{i,j,\mathsf{tag}}$ for each $k > j$. And, it checks that $\mathsf{flag}_{i,j,\mathsf{tag}} = 0$ for $j < d_i$, and $\mathsf{flag}_{i,d_i,\mathsf{tag}} = 1$, $a_{i,d_i,\mathsf{tag}} = 0^\lambda$. (Note that during this validity check, the verifier also stores whether that node is left child or right child.)

2. Next, it checks that $\mathsf{id}_{i,d_i,\mathsf{lwr}} < \mathsf{id} = \mathsf{id}_{i,d_i,\mathsf{mid}} < \mathsf{id}_{i,d_i,\mathsf{upr}}$, that is the identity in the *lower* path is less than that in the *upper* path, and the identity id whose non-registration is being proven is equal to the identity in the *middle* path and lies between the other two identities. It also checks that $b_{i,d_i,\mathsf{mid}} = \mathsf{pk}$.

3. For both tag pairs $(\mathsf{tag}_1, \mathsf{tag}_2) \in \{(\mathsf{lwr}, \mathsf{mid}), (\mathsf{mid}, \mathsf{upr})\}$, it proceeds as follows:
   It computes the largest common prefix of nodes in paths $\mathsf{path}_{i,\mathsf{tag}_1}$ and $\mathsf{path}_{i,\mathsf{tag}_2}$. That is, let k be the largest index such that $\mathsf{node}_{i,j,\mathsf{tag}_1} = \mathsf{node}_{i,j,\mathsf{tag}_2}$ for all $j \leq k$. It checks that $\mathsf{id}_{i,k,\mathsf{tag}_1} = \mathsf{id}_{i,d_i,\mathsf{tag}_1}$. Also, it checks:
   (a) It checks that $\mathsf{node}_{i,k+1,\mathsf{tag}_1}$ and $\mathsf{node}_{i,k+1,\mathsf{tag}_2}$ are *left* and *right* children of $\mathsf{node}_{i,k,\mathsf{tag}_1} = \mathsf{node}_{i,k,\mathsf{tag}_2}$. That is, $a_{i,k,\mathsf{tag}_1} = \mathsf{HG.Hash}(\mathsf{hk}, \mathsf{node}_{i,k+1,\mathsf{tag}_1})$ and $b_{i,k,\mathsf{tag}_2} = \mathsf{HG.Hash}(\mathsf{hk}, \mathsf{node}_{i,k+1,\mathsf{tag}_2})$.
   (b) For every index $j > k$, $\mathsf{node}_{i,j+1,\mathsf{tag}_1}$ and $\mathsf{node}_{i,j+1,\mathsf{tag}_2}$ are *right* and *left* children of $\mathsf{node}_{i,j,\mathsf{tag}_1}$ and $\mathsf{node}_{i,j,\mathsf{tag}_2}$, respectively. That is, $b_{i,j,\mathsf{tag}_1} = \mathsf{HG.Hash}(\mathsf{hk}, \mathsf{node}_{i,j+1,\mathsf{tag}_1})$ and $a_{i,j,\mathsf{tag}_2} = \mathsf{HG.Hash}(\mathsf{hk}, \mathsf{node}_{i,j+1,\mathsf{tag}_2})$.

It rejects, i.e. outputs 0, if any of these checks fails. Otherwise, it accepts and outputs 1.

One empty path. Suppose $\mathsf{path}_{i,\mathsf{lwr}} = \epsilon$. The verifier checks first well-formedness of $\mathsf{path}_{i,\mathsf{mid}}, \mathsf{path}_{i,\mathsf{upr}}$ as in Step 1 (above). Next, it checks that $\mathsf{id} = \mathsf{id}_{i,d_i,\mathsf{mid}} < \mathsf{id}_{i,d_i,\mathsf{upr}}$ as in Step 2 (above). And lastly, it performs the Step 3 verification checks as described above only for the tag pair $(\mathsf{tag}_1, \mathsf{tag}_2) = (\mathsf{mid}, \mathsf{upr})$. Lastly verifies that $\mathsf{node}_{i,d_i,\mathsf{mid}}$ is the smallest registered node in $\mathsf{EncTree}_i$ i.e., the verifier checks that for every index j, $\mathsf{node}_{i,j+1,\mathsf{mid}}$ is the *left* child of $\mathsf{node}_{i,j,\mathsf{mid}}$. It rejects, i.e. outputs 0, if any of these checks fail. Otherwise, it accepts and outputs 1.

The case when $\mathsf{path}_{i,\mathsf{upr}} = \epsilon$ is handled analogously.

Fig. 4. Conditions for verifying a proof $\pi_i = (\mathsf{path}_{i,\mathsf{lwr}}, \mathsf{path}_{i,\mathsf{mid}}, \mathsf{path}_{i,\mathsf{upr}})$ that id is registered as per $\mathsf{EncTree}_i$

proofs is $O(\log^2 n)$. Due to space constraints, we provide the full efficiency analysis of the above construction in full version of the paper.

The above scheme satisfies the correctness property as the decryptor internally performs a binary search on id in the EncTree and always obtains a PKE encryption of the message m using his public key $\mathsf{pk}_{\mathsf{id}}$. The above scheme satisfies the completeness of pre/post-registration as any proof obtained by PreProve/PostProve algorithms satisfy the conditions in Figs. 3 and 4. Due to space constraints, we postpone full proofs to the full version of the paper.

4.3 Security

In this section, we prove that the above scheme satisfies soundness of pre/post-Registration Verifiability and Message Hiding properties as defined in Definitions 3 to 5. We now provide a brief overview of the proofs.

Recall that soundness of pre-registration verifiability property ensures that if a PPT adversary $\mathcal{A}$ can create valid public parameters pp along with a pre-registration proof π that an identity id is not registered, then he will not be able to decrypt any ciphertext ct encrypted for id with non-negligible probability. To provide the proof's intuition, consider the scenario where a cheating accumulator/adversary creates public parameters by inserting (id, pk) at a wrong leaf location by violating property that the EncTree is to be sorted as per identities. Such an adversary could provide a valid pre-registration proof that the identity is not registered. However, it cannot decrypt the ciphertexts encrypted for the identity. For example, the EncTree generated by adversary has 3 registered identities $\mathsf{id}_1 < \mathsf{id}_2 < \mathsf{id}_3$, has root value $\mathsf{rt} = h_1 \| \mathsf{id}_3 \| h_2$ with left subtree containing $\mathsf{id}_1, \mathsf{id}_3$ and right subtree containing id_2. Clearly, the paths to the leaves containing $\mathsf{id}_1, \mathsf{id}_3$ form a valid pre-registration proof. A ciphertext contains 3 garbled circuits $\{\mathsf{Enc\text{-}Step}_i\}_i$ and garbling of $\mathsf{Hash}(\mathsf{rt})$. When the garbled circuit $\mathsf{Enc\text{-}Step}_1$ is run with input as the root value rt, it identifies that id_2 is in left subtree (as $\mathsf{id}_2 < \mathsf{id}_3$) and outputs garbling of h_1. Now, $\mathsf{Enc\text{-}Step}_2$ can only be run on the left child value of the root node. The garbling values output the garbled circuits would follow the path that is present as part of pre-registration proof, and as a result the final garbled circuit outputs $\bot$ and the adversary cannot decrypt the ciphertext. We formally prove that the scheme satisfies the property, by arguing that when the adversary is forced to generate public parameters along with a pre-registration proof, it cannot distinguish between a real ciphertext and a simulated ciphertext that is generated without using the message.

Soundness of post-registration verifiability property guarantees that if an adversary can create valid public parameters pp along with a post-registration proof π that an identity-key pair (id, pk) is registered (for an honestly generated pk such that corresponding secret key sk is not revealed to the adversary), then he will not be able decrypt any ciphertext ct encrypted for id. The proof is similar to the proof of pre-registration verifiability, except that the simulated ciphertext is now generated using only PKE encryptions of the message with the identity's public key (the corresponding secret key is unknown to the adversary).

Message Hiding properties guarantees that if the public parameters pp are honestly generated, then a PPT adversary cannot decrypt ciphertexts of unregistered identities, and cannot decrypt ciphertexts of registered identities without the knowledge of their secret keys. We argue that if any RBE scheme satisfies soundness of pre/post-registration verifiability properties along with completeness property, it also satisfies message hiding property. If an (id, pk) pair is registered as part of pp, then one could also create a valid post-registration proof as per the completeness property. Therefore, as per soundness of post-registration verifiability the ciphertexts meant for id cannot be decrypted with non-negligible probability when secret key corresponding to pk is unknown. If an id is not registered as part of pp, then one could create a valid pre-registration proof as per the completeness property. Therefore, as per soundness of pre-registration verifiability, the ciphertexts meant for id cannot be decrypted with non-negligible probability.

Due to space constraints, we postpone the full proofs to full version of the paper.

Acknowledgements.. We thank anonymous reviewers for useful feedback, especially for pointing out a possible black-box approach for achieving verifiability. The work is done in part while the first author was at UT Austin (supported by IBM PhD Fellowship), and at the Simons Institute for the Theory of Computing (supported by Simons-Berkeley research fellowship). The second author is supported by Packard Fellowship, NSF CNS-1908611, CNS-1414082, DARPA SafeWare and Packard Foundation Fellowship.

References

1. Al-Riyami, S.S., Paterson, K.G.: Certificateless public key cryptography. In: Laih, C.-S. (ed.) ASIACRYPT 2003. LNCS, vol. 2894, pp. 452–473. Springer, Heidelberg (2003). https://doi.org/10.1007/978-3-540-40061-5_29
2. Barak, B., et al.: On the (Im)possibility of obfuscating programs. In: Kilian, J. (ed.) CRYPTO 2001. LNCS, vol. 2139, pp. 1–18. Springer, Heidelberg (2001). https://doi.org/10.1007/3-540-44647-8_1
3. Bellare, M., Rogaway, P.: Random oracles are practical: a paradigm for designing efficient protocols. In: CCS (1993)
4. Bitansky, N., Chiesa, A.: Succinct arguments from multi-prover interactive proofs and their efficiency benefits. In: Safavi-Naini, R., Canetti, R. (eds.) CRYPTO 2012. LNCS, vol. 7417, pp. 255–272. Springer, Heidelberg (2012). https://doi.org/10.1007/978-3-642-32009-5_16
5. Boneh, D., Franklin, M.: Identity-based encryption from the Weil Pairing. In: Kilian, J. (ed.) CRYPTO 2001. LNCS, vol. 2139, pp. 213–229. Springer, Heidelberg (2001). https://doi.org/10.1007/3-540-44647-8_13
6. Boneh, D., Sahai, A., Waters, B.: Functional encryption: definitions and challenges. In: Ishai, Y. (ed.) TCC 2011. LNCS, vol. 6597, pp. 253–273. Springer, Heidelberg (2011). https://doi.org/10.1007/978-3-642-19571-6_16

7. Brakerski, Z., Lombardi, A., Segev, G., Vaikuntanathan, V.: Anonymous IBE, leakage resilience and circular security from new assumptions. In: Nielsen, J.B., Rijmen, V. (eds.) EUROCRYPT 2018. LNCS, vol. 10820, pp. 535–564. Springer, Cham (2018). https://doi.org/10.1007/978-3-319-78381-9_20

8. Chen, L., Harrison, K., Soldera, D., Smart, N.P.: Applications of multiple trust authorities in pairing based cryptosystems. In: Davida, G., Frankel, Y., Rees, O. (eds.) InfraSec 2002. LNCS, vol. 2437, pp. 260–275. Springer, Heidelberg (2002). https://doi.org/10.1007/3-540-45831-X_18

9. Cheng, Z., Comley, R., Vasiu, L.: Remove key escrow from the identity-based encryption system. In: Levy, J.-J., Mayr, E.W., Mitchell, J.C. (eds.) TCS 2004. IIFIP, vol. 155, pp. 37–50. Springer, Boston, MA (2004). https://doi.org/10.1007/1-4020-8141-3_6

10. Cho, C., Döttling, N., Garg, S., Gupta, D., Miao, P., Polychroniadou, A.: Laconic oblivious transfer and its applications. In: Katz, J., Shacham, H. (eds.) CRYPTO 2017. LNCS, vol. 10402, pp. 33–65. Springer, Cham (2017). https://doi.org/10.1007/978-3-319-63715-0_2

11. Chow, S.S.: Removing escrow from identity-based encryption. In: PKC (2009)

12. Cocks, C.: An identity based encryption scheme based on quadratic residues. In: Honary, B. (ed.) Cryptography and Coding 2001. LNCS, vol. 2260, pp. 360–363. Springer, Heidelberg (2001). https://doi.org/10.1007/3-540-45325-3_32

13. Diffie, W., Hellman, M.E.: New directions in cryptography (1976)

14. Döttling, N., Garg, S.: Identity-based encryption from the Diffie-Hellman assumption. In: Katz, J., Shacham, H. (eds.) CRYPTO 2017. LNCS, vol. 10401, pp. 537–569. Springer, Cham (2017). https://doi.org/10.1007/978-3-319-63688-7_18

15. Döttling, N., Garg, S., Hajiabadi, M., Masny, D.: New constructions of identity-based and key-dependent message secure encryption schemes. In: Abdalla, M., Dahab, R. (eds.) PKC 2018. LNCS, vol. 10769, pp. 3–31. Springer, Cham (2018). https://doi.org/10.1007/978-3-319-76578-5_1

16. Döttling, N., Garg, S.: From selective IBE to full IBE and selective HIBE. In: Kalai, Y., Reyzin, L. (eds.) TCC 2017. LNCS, vol. 10677, pp. 372–408. Springer, Cham (2017). https://doi.org/10.1007/978-3-319-70500-2_13

17. Garg, S., Gentry, C., Halevi, S., Raykova, M., Sahai, A., Waters, B.: Candidate indistinguishability obfuscation and functional encryption for all circuits. In: FOCS (2013)

18. Garg, S., Hajiabadi, M., Mahmoody, M., Rahimi, A.: Registration-based encryption: removing private-key generator from IBE. In: Beimel, A., Dziembowski, S. (eds.) TCC 2018. LNCS, vol. 11239, pp. 689–718. Springer, Cham (2018). https://doi.org/10.1007/978-3-030-03807-6_25

19. Garg, S., Hajiabadi, M., Mahmoody, M., Rahimi, A., Sekar, S.: Registration-based encryption from standard assumptions. In: Lin, D., Sako, K. (eds.) PKC 2019. LNCS, vol. 11443, pp. 63–93. Springer, Cham (2019). https://doi.org/10.1007/978-3-030-17259-6_3

20. Gentry, C., Wichs, D.: Separating succinct non-interactive arguments from all falsifiable assumptions. In: STOC 2011 (2011)

21. Goldwasser, S., Micali, S.: Probabilistic encryption. J. Comput. Syst. Sci. **28**, 270–299 (1984)

22. Goyal, V.: Reducing trust in the PKG in identity based cryptosystems. In: Menezes, A. (ed.) CRYPTO 2007. LNCS, vol. 4622, pp. 430–447. Springer, Heidelberg (2007). https://doi.org/10.1007/978-3-540-74143-5_24

23. Goyal, V., Pandey, O., Sahai, A., Waters, B.: Attribute-based encryption for fine-grained access control of encrypted data. In: CCS 2006 (2006)

24. Groth, J.: Short pairing-based non-interactive zero-knowledge arguments. In: Abe, M. (ed.) ASIACRYPT 2010. LNCS, vol. 6477, pp. 321–340. Springer, Heidelberg (2010). https://doi.org/10.1007/978-3-642-17373-8_19

25. Kate, A., Goldberg, I.: Distributed private-key generators for identity-based cryptography. In: Garay, J.A., De Prisco, R. (eds.) SCN 2010. LNCS, vol. 6280, pp. 436–453. Springer, Heidelberg (2010). https://doi.org/10.1007/978-3-642-15317-4_27

26. Lipmaa, H.: Progression-free sets and sublinear pairing-based non-interactive zero-knowledge arguments. In: Cramer, R. (ed.) TCC 2012. LNCS, vol. 7194, pp. 169–189. Springer, Heidelberg (2012). https://doi.org/10.1007/978-3-642-28914-9_10

27. Micali, S.: CS proofs (extended abstracts). In: FOCS (1994)

28. Naor, M.: On cryptographic assumptions and challenges. In: Boneh, D. (ed.) CRYPTO 2003. LNCS, vol. 2729, pp. 96–109. Springer, Heidelberg (2003). https://doi.org/10.1007/978-3-540-45146-4_6

29. Paterson, K.G., Srinivasan, S.: Security and anonymity of identity-based encryption with multiple trusted authorities. In: Galbraith, S.D., Paterson, K.G. (eds.) Pairing 2008. LNCS, vol. 5209, pp. 354–375. Springer, Heidelberg (2008). https://doi.org/10.1007/978-3-540-85538-5_23

30. Rivest, R.L., Shamir, A., Adleman, L.M.: A method for obtaining digital signatures and public-key cryptosystems. Commun. ACM **21**(2), 120–126 (1978)

31. Rogaway, P.: The moral character of cryptographic work. Cryptology ePrint Archive, Report 2015/1162. https://eprint.iacr.org/2015/1162

32. Sahai, A., Waters, B.: Fuzzy identity-based encryption. In: Cramer, R. (ed.) EUROCRYPT 2005. LNCS, vol. 3494, pp. 457–473. Springer, Heidelberg (2005). https://doi.org/10.1007/11426639_27

33. Shamir, A.: Identity-based cryptosystems and signature schemes. In: Blakley, G.R., Chaum, D. (eds.) CRYPTO 1985. LNCS, vol. 196. Springer, Heidelberg (1985). https://doi.org/10.1007/3-540-39568-7_5

New Techniques for Traitor Tracing: Size $N^{1/3}$ and More from Pairings

Mark Zhandry[1,2($\boxtimes$)]

[1] Princeton University, Princeton, USA
mzhandry@gmail.com
[2] NTT Research, Palo Alto, USA

Abstract. The best existing pairing-based traitor tracing schemes have $O(\sqrt{N})$-sized parameters, which has stood since 2006. This intuitively seems to be consistent with the fact that pairings allow for degree-2 computations, yielding a quadratic compression.

In this work, we show that this intuition is false by building a traitor tracing scheme from pairings with $O(\sqrt[3]{N})$-sized parameters. We additionally give schemes with a variety of parameter size trade-offs, including a scheme with constant-size ciphertexts and public keys (but linear-sized secret keys). We obtain our schemes by developing a number of new traitor tracing techniques, giving the first significant parameter improvements in pairings-based traitor tracing in over a decade.

1 Introduction

Traitor tracing [CFN94] allows a content distributor to trace the source of a pirate decoder. Every user is given a unique secret key that allows for decrypting ciphertexts. A "traitor" might distribute their key to un-authorized users, or even hide their key inside a pirate decoder capable of decrypting. A tracing algorithm can be run on the decoder that will identify the traitor. In a collusion-resistant scheme, even if several traitors collude, the tracing algorithm will be able to identify at least one of them[1], without ever falsely identifying an honest user. Much of the traitor tracing literature considers *fully collusion-resistant* schemes, where the coalition of traitors can be arbitrarily large. In this work, we will only consider fully collusion-resistant schemes.

The main goal of traitor tracing is to build schemes with short parameters, in particular short ciphertexts that depend minimally on the number N of users. Boneh, Sahai, and Waters [BSW06] demonstrated the first collusion-resistant scheme with $O(\sqrt{N})$-sized parameters using pairings[2]. Shortly after their work, Boneh and Waters [BW06] augmented the construction with a broadcast functionality, achieving a so-called broadcast and trace scheme also with

---

[1] A traitor could be completely passive, so it is impossible to identify *all* traitors.
[2] Following convention, the Big-Oh notation throughout this paper will hide constants that depend on the security parameter, and focus on the dependence on N.

© International Association for Cryptologic Research 2020
D. Micciancio and T. Ristenpart (Eds.): CRYPTO 2020, LNCS 12170, pp. 652–682, 2020.
https://doi.org/10.1007/978-3-030-56784-2_22

$O(\sqrt{N})$-sized parameters. These works remain the state-of-the-art in pairings-based collusion-resistant traitor tracing. Using other tools such as obfuscation or LWE, better parameters are possible [GGH+13, BZ14, GKW18].

1.1 Some Existing Approaches to Traitor Tracing

Fingerprinting Codes. One of the earliest approaches to collusion-resistant tracing was shown by Boneh and Naor [BN08][3], who construct traitor tracing using an object called *fingerprinting codes* [BS95]. Their scheme is combinatorial, relying simply on generic public key encryption, and ciphertexts have optimal $O(1)$ size.

The Boneh-Naor scheme, however, is generally not considered to resolve the traitor tracing problem. Curiously, different authors seem to have different interpretations of why. Some works (e.g. [BZ14, GKSW10, TZ17]) note that Boneh-Naor requires very large secret keys—namely quadratic in the number of users—which is inherent to fingerprinting codes [Tar03]. The main limitation according to these works appears to be simultaneously achieving small ciphertext *and* small secret/public keys. Other works more or less ignore the secret key size limitation (e.g. [GKW18, KW19, GQWW19][4]), suggesting the main limitation of Boneh-Naor is that it is a *threshold* scheme: it can only trace decoders whose decryption probability exceeds some a priori threshold. These works appear to consider it an open problem, for example, to construct *non-threshold* traitor tracing with constant-sized ciphertexts (and any secret or public key size) from anything implied by pairings.

Private Linear Broadcast Encryption (PLBE). A Private Linear Broadcast Encryption (PLBE) scheme is a limited type of functional encryption that allows for encrypting to ranges of user identities, and is known to imply traitor tracing [BSW06]. Algebraic constructions of PLBE achieve simultaneously smaller parameters, and are not subject to the threshold restriction. PLBE is by far the most popular approach to traitor tracing today, being taken by the current best pairings-based constructions [BSW06, BW06], as well as the obfuscation and LWE-based constructions [GGH+13, BZ14, GKW18]. In fact, in the last five years (2014–2019) of traitor tracing papers, we could identify ten papers appearing at EUROCRYPT, CRYPTO, ASIACRYPT, TCC, STOC, and FOCS giving positive results for traitor tracing. With perhaps one exception (discussed below) *every single one* can be seen as following the PLBE or closely related approaches [BZ14, LPSS14, NWZ16, KMUZ16, GKRW18, KMUW18, CVW+18, GKW18, GQWW19, GKW19].

---

[3] The work originated from 2002, but was not published until 2008.
[4] Example: Goyal, Koppula, and Waters [GKW18] make the central claim of achieving a "secure traitor tracing with [constant]-sized ciphertexts from standard assumptions," without discussing the secret key size of their construction at all.

Risky Traitor Tracing. Recently, Goyal et al. [GKRW18] define a relaxed notion of "risky traitor tracing" where the pirate decoder is only guaranteed to be traced with some non-zero probability, say α for some $\alpha \ll 1$. Their approach follows the PLBE framework, but actually *strengthens* PLBE. Essentially, their scheme constructs PLBE for αN users, but then since $\alpha < 1$, it must assign multiple users to the same identity. In order to get tracing to work, however, it must be that users cannot tell what identity they were assigned to. This requires strengthening PLBE, as in standard PLBE every user knows their identity.

1.2   This Work: New Techniques for Traitor Tracing

In this work, we explore the use of different structures to build traitor tracing, giving rich set of traitor tracing techniques beyond the usual approaches. We then use these techniques to build several new schemes from pairings and weaker primitives that offer new trade-offs that were not possible before. Below we describe our results, with a summary given in Table 1.

In the following, we will say a traitor tracing system has size (P, K, C) if its public key, secret keys, and ciphertexts have sizes at most $O(P), O(K)$, and $O(C)$, respectively, where constants hidden in the Big Oh notation are allowed to depend on the security parameter[5]. We abbreviate size (A, A, A) as simply A.

- The first scheme of size $(N^2, N^2, 1)$ *without the threshold limitation* from the minimal assumption of general public key encryption[6]. Thus, we remove the threshold limitation of fingerprinting code-based tracing schemes. The main limitation of these schemes is then the large public and secret key sizes. We note that we easily can compress the public keys to get a scheme of size $(1, N^2, 1)$, relying on the stronger assumption of identity-based encryption.
- The first pairings-based scheme of size $(1, N, 1)$, or generally $(1, N^{1-a}, N^a)$ for any constant $a \in [0, 1]$. For all constants $a < 1$, this gives a new parameter trade-off that was not possible before from pairings.
- An (N^{1-a}, N^{1-a}, N^a)-sized scheme from pairings, attaining the stronger notion of broadcast and trace [BW06], which augments traitor tracing with a broadcast functionality. For $a = 0$, this gives the first broadcast and trace scheme with constant-size ciphertexts from pairings. This improves on the recent work of [GQWW19] which attained arbitrarily-small polynomial ciphertext size, while also requiring lattices in addition to pairings.
- A new model for traitor tracing, which we call the *shared randomness model* (SRM), where encryption, decryption, and the decoder have access to a large source of randomness that is not included in the communication costs. While we define the model as a stepping stone toward a full tracing algorithm in the plain model, our shared randomness model may be useful in its own right.

---

[5] We will also suppress $\log N$ terms. This is without loss of generality since it is always the case that $\log N < \lambda$, and the Big-Oh already hides $\mathsf{poly}(\lambda)$ terms.

[6] Our definition of traitor tracing has public encryption, which in particular implies public key encryption.

For example, the shared randomness could be derived from some publicly available data, such as stock market fluctuations or blockchains.

- A broadcast and trace scheme of size $(N, 1, 1)$, or more generally $(N^{1-a}, 1, N^a)$ for any constant $a \in [N]$, in the shared randomness model from pairings. The size of the shared randomness is N^{1-a}; thus, for $a \geq 1/2$, the shared randomness can simply be included in the ciphertext, in which case we get a scheme in the plain model. We note that for $a = 1/2$, we get the first broadcast and trace scheme of size $(N^{1/2}, 1, N^{1/2})$ from pairings, improving on the $(N^{1/2}, N^{1/2}, N^{1/2})$-sized scheme of [BW06].
- Putting it all together: a traitor tracing (non-broadcast) scheme of size $\sqrt[3]{N}$.

Our results are obtained by a number of new techniques that may have applications beyond the immediate scope of this work:

- A generic procedure to increase the number of users by expanding the ciphertext size, but in many cases keeping the other parameters fixed (Theorem 1).
- A generic procedure to convert any threshold scheme into a non-threshold scheme without affecting the dependence on N (Theorem 2).
- A generic procedure to convert a risky scheme into a non-risky scheme, without asymptotically affecting ciphertext size (Theorem 3).
- A conversion from a certain broadcast functionality into a traitor tracing scheme, with shared randomness (Theorem 4).
- New instantiations of broadcast encryption from pairings (Theorem 5).

Table 1. Comparing parameters sizes of our schemes to some existing protocols. This table only includes schemes based on pairings or weaker assumptions implied by pairings. N is the number of users. All sizes hide multiplicative constants dependent on the security parameter (but not N). $a \in [0, 1]$ is any constant.

Scheme	$|pk|$	$|sk|$	$|ct|$	Broadcast & Trace?	Tool	Limitations
Trivial	N	1	N	✓	PKE	
	1	1	N		IBE	
[BN08]	N^2	N^2	1	✗	PKE	Threshold
	1	N^2	1		IBE	
[BSW06]	$\sqrt{N}$	1	$\sqrt{N}$	✗	Pairing	
[BW06]	$\sqrt{N}$	$\sqrt{N}$	$\sqrt{N}$	✓		
Cor 1	N^{2-a}	N^{2-2a}	N^a	✗	PKE	
	1	N^{2-2a}	N^a		IBE	
Cor 2	1	N^{1-a}	N^a		Pairing	
Cor 3	N^{1-a}	N^{1-a}	N^a	✓		
Cor 4	$N^{1/2-a/2}$	1	$N^{1/2+a/2}$			
Cor 5	$\sqrt[3]{N}$	$\sqrt[3]{N}$	$\sqrt[3]{N}$	✗		

2   Technical Overview

In order to abstract and modularize the discussion, the central object we will consider is a generalization of a traitor tracing system, which we call a "multi-scheme," which can roughly be seen as a scaled-down version of "identity-based traitor tracing" as defined in [ADM+07]. Intuitively, a multi-scheme is M essentially independent tracing systems running in parallel, each with distinct secret keys and ciphertexts. All N users within a single instance can decrypt ciphertexts to that instance, but not to other instances. Tracing also works within an instance: any pirate decoder that decrypts for an instance can be traced to traitors within that instance. A plain traitor tracing scheme implies a multi-scheme by simply setting up M separate instances of the scheme. The point of a multi-scheme, however, is that the M schemes are allowed share a common public key, which may be smaller than M copies of a single public key. See Definition 1.

We will also consider broadcast and trace schemes [BW06], which augment plain traitor tracing with a broadcast functionality. That is, the encrypter can specify a subset $S \subseteq [N]$, and only users in S should be able to decrypt the ciphertext. S is also incorporated into the tracing definition. See Sect. 4.1.

We will say that a scheme Π has size (P, K, C) for functions $P = P(N, M)$, $K = K(N, M)$, and $C = C(N, M)$, if there is a polynomial $\mathsf{poly}(\lambda)$ such that, for all polynomials $N = N(\lambda)$ and $M = M(\lambda)$, we have $|\mathsf{pk}| \leq P(N, M) \times \mathsf{poly}(\lambda)$, $|\mathsf{sk}_{j,i}| \leq K(N, M) \times \mathsf{poly}(\lambda)$, and $|c| \leq C(N, M) \times \mathsf{poly}(\lambda)$. For example, if $|\mathsf{pk}| = |\mathsf{sk}_{j,i}| = |c| = 2N^{1/2}M\lambda^2 + \lambda^5$, we could set $\mathsf{poly}(\lambda) = 2\lambda^5$, which shows that the protocol has size $(N^{1/2}M, N^{1/2}M, N^{1/2}M)$.

2.1   User Expansion Compiler

Our first result shows how to expand the number of users by grouping different instances together. That is, we compile a scheme with N/T users and MT instances into a scheme with N users and M instances. Essentially, we just partition the MT instances into M sets of size T. Within each set, there are now N users (N/T for each instance, T instances). We then encrypt the message separately to each of the T instances within the set, ensuring that all N users in the set can decrypt. This conversion blows up the ciphertext size by a factor of T, but hopefully results in smaller public/secret keys. Concretely, we prove:

Theorem 1 (User Expansion). *Let* $P = P(N, M), K = K(N, M), C = C(N, M), T = T(N, M)$ *be polynomials such that* $T(N, M) \leq N$. *Suppose there exists a secure multi-scheme* Π_0 *with size* (P, K, C). *Then there exists a secure multi-scheme* Π *with size* $(\ P(N/T, MT)\ ,\ K(N/T, MT)\ ,\ T \times C(N/T, MT)\ )$. *If* Π_0 *is a broadcast and trace scheme, then so is* Π.

Our compiler can be seen as a generalization of the most basic traitor tracing scheme, which simply gives each user a different secret key for a public key encryption scheme and encrypts to each user separately. Abstracting the ideas behind this scheme will lead to useful results later in this paper.

The tracing algorithm in our compiler essentially views the construction as an instance of *private linear broadcast encryption* (PLBE), and then uses a tracing algorithm analogous to [BSW06]. Given a decoder D for the compiled scheme, we test the decoder on invalid ciphertexts where the first t components have been modified to encrypt gibberish, and see if the decoder still decrypts. For a good decoder, a simple hybrid argument shows that there will be some t where the decoder decrypts $t-1$ with probability noticeably higher than it decrypts t. This will allow us to construct from the original decoder D a new decoder D_t for Π_0, targeting the t'th instance. We then run Π_0's tracing algorithm on D_t, which will accuse a set $A \subseteq [N/T]$. For each $i \in A$, we then accuse the user who was assigned index i within instance t. See Sect. 5 for details.

2.2 Threshold Elimination Compiler

Our next compiler converts a *threshold* scheme—which can only trace decoders that have *constant* decryption probability—into a full tracing scheme which can trace decoders arbitrary-small inverse-polynomial decryption probability.

Theorem 2 (Threshold Elimination). *Let P, K, C be polynomials in N, M. If there exists a threshold secure multi-scheme Π_{Thresh} with size (P, K, C), then there exists a (non-threshold) secure multi-scheme Π with size (P, K, C). If Π_{Thresh} is a broadcast and trace scheme, then so is Π.*

As an application, the Boneh-Naor traitor tracing scheme [BN08], when instantiated with "robust" Tardos fingerprinting codes [Tar03,BKM10], yields a threshold scheme of size $(N^2, N^2, 1)$, or a multi-scheme of size $(MN^2, N^2, 1)$. Applying Theorem 2 gives a non-threshold scheme with the same size. We can also eliminate the public key size by using identity-based encryption (IBE) instead of public key encryption. Finally, applying Theorem 1 with $T = N^a$ gives:

Corollary 1. *Assuming public key encryption, there exists a (non-threshold) secure multi-scheme of size $(MN^{2-a}, N^{2-2a}, N^a)$. Assuming IBE, there exists a secure (non-threshold) multi-scheme of size $(1, N^{2-2a}, N^a)$.*

Setting $a = 2/3$ and using IBE from the computational Diffie-Hellman (CDH) assumption in plain groups [DG17] gives a (non-threshold) scheme of size $(1, N^{2/3}, N^{2/3})$ from CDH, the first such scheme with sublinear size.

Proving Theorem 2. Our goal is to design Π such that any decoder D for the scheme—even one with small but noticeable decryption probability—can be converted into a decoder D' that decrypts with high probability, for the original scheme Π_{Thresh}. Importantly, we cannot asymptotically expand the parameters.

To encrypt a message m, our basic idea is to choose random $m_1, \ldots, m_n$ such that $m_1 \oplus m_2 \oplus \cdots \oplus m_n = m$. We encrypt each of the m_i separately using Π_{Thresh}, the final ciphertext for Π being the n encryptions of the m_i. To decrypt, simply decrypt each component to recover m_i, and then reconstruct m.

Since the m_i are an n-out-of-n secret sharing of m, a decoder needs to, in some sense, be able to recover *all* of the m_i in order to compute m. Supposing the "decryptability" of the n individual ciphertexts were independent events, then the decryptability of the individual ciphertexts must very high in order to have noticeable chance at decrypting all n ciphertexts simultaneously.

To turn this intuition into a proof, we show how to extract the m_i whenever the individual ciphertext is decryptable, in order to build a decoder D' for Π_0 with high-enough decryption probability so that it can be traced using Π_0. On input a ciphertext c, D' chooses a random $i \in [n]$ and sets $c_i = c$. It then fills in a ciphertext tuple $(c_1, \ldots, c_n)$ where the $c_j, j \neq i$ are encryptions of random messages m_j. When D gives a guess m' for m, D' can compute a guess m'_i for m_i using m' and the $m_j, j \neq i$. D' decrypts with the same probability as D, and by repeating the process many times on the same ciphertext c, the hope is to amplify the decryption probability.

Unfortunately, there are a few issues. For a fixed ciphertext c, the various trials share a common ciphertext, and therefore their success probabilities are not independent. Also, there is no obvious way to tell which of the trials produced the correct message. Finally, recent traitor tracing definitions [NWZ16, GKRW18, GKW18] actually require tracing to hold in the stronger indistinguishability setting, which means roughly that D does not have to actually produce the message, but only needs to distinguish it from, say, a random message.

We resolve these issues in a couple steps. We use Goldreich-Levin [GL89] to convert an indistinguishability decoder into a predicting decoder. We analyze the decoder's decryption probability on the correlated instances, and show that the success probability over multiple trials amplifies as necessary, when $n = \mathsf{poly}(\lambda)$. Finally, we leverage the indistinguishability security of Π_{Thresh}—meaning D' only needs to distinguish the correct message from random—which allows D' to tell when a trial produces the correct output. Details are given in Sect. 6.

Putting everything together, if D distinguishes with non-negligible probability, D' will distinguish with probability $1 - o(1)$. Our compiler leaves public and secret keys intact, and blows up the ciphertext by a factor independent of the number of users N, as desired. See Sect. 6 for additional details.

2.3   Risk Mitigation Compiler

Next, we give a compiler that eliminates risk from risky traitor tracing schemes:

Theorem 3 (Risk Mitigation). *Let $P = P(N, M), K = K(N, M), C = C(N, M)$ be polynomials. Let $\alpha = \alpha(N)$ be a polynomial. If there exists an α-risky multi-scheme Π_{Risky} with size (P, K, C), then there exists a secure (non-risky) multi-scheme Π with size $\left(P(N, M\alpha^{-1}), \alpha^{-1} \times K(N, M\alpha^{-1}), C(N, M\alpha^{-1}) \right)$. If Π_{Risky} is a broadcast and trace scheme, then so is Π.*

Thus, by multiplying M by $O(\alpha^{-1})$ and increasing the secret key size by a factor of $O(\alpha^{-1})$, one can eliminate α-riskiness. In Sect. 7.2, we extend the risky scheme from [GKRW18] into a $1/N$-risky multi-scheme of size $(1, 1, 1)$. Theorem 3 plus Theorem 1 with $T = N^a$ gives:

Corollary 2. *For any $a \in [0,1]$, if Assumptions 1 and 2 from [GKRW18] hold, there exists a secure multi-scheme of size $(1, N^{1-a}, N^a)$.*

Note that the computational assumptions are the same as in [GKRW18]. Also, for any $a < 1$, such parameters were not known before from pairings.

We also demonstrate how to add a broadcast functionality to the risky scheme of [GKRW18], at the cost of increasing the public key size and relying on the generic group model for security. Running through our compilers gives:

Corollary 3. *For any $a \in [0,1]$, there exists a broadcast and trace multi-scheme of size (N^{1-a}, N^{1-a}, N^a) from pairings, with security in the generic group model.*

For $a = 0$, this gives the first broadcast and trace scheme with constant-sized ciphertexts from standard tools, and improves on [GQWW19], which attained N^ϵ ciphertext size for any $\epsilon > 0$, while also requiring lattices in addition to pairings[7].

Proving Theorem 3. Let Π_{Risky} be an α-risky multi-scheme. Consider a new protocol Π which runs Π_{Risky} with $T = \omega(\log \lambda)/\alpha$ instances. The secret key for a user consists of the all the secret keys for that user across the T instances. To encrypt, encrypt to a *single* random instance from Π_{Risky}. The overall ciphertext is simply the label of the instance (a number in $[T]$), and a ciphertext from Π_{Risky}. Since each user has a secret key from each instance, each user can decrypt.

Thus, we expand the secret key by a factor of $O(1/\alpha)$, and add $\log T = \log \lambda + \log(1/\alpha) = O(\log \lambda)$ bits to the ciphertext. We can easily extend the above to yield a riskless *multi*-scheme for M instances, by increasing the number of instances of Π_{Risky} to $M \times T$ and grouping them into sets of size T.

Analysis. Suppose a pirate decoder D for Π decrypts with *certainty*. Then it must decrypt, no matter which instance of Π_{Risky} is chosen during encryption. Thus, a perfect decoder for Π actually yields a decoder for each of the T instances of Π_{Risky}. α-riskiness means that each of the T decoders has an α chance of being traced to a traitor, and intuitively the probabilities should be independent. Over all T instances, we expect the tracing probability to be $1 - (1 - \alpha)^T = 1 - \mathsf{negl}(\lambda)$.

Toward tracing imperfect decoders, suppose D instead only decrypts for a single instance of Π_0; D has non-negligible decryption probability $1/T$, but will only be traced with probability α. Thus, we cannot trace arbitrary decoders[8]. We will instead aim for a threshold scheme; we can then apply Theorem 2 to get a full tracing scheme.

Even in the threshold setting, however, difficulties arise. The decoder may only decrypt, say, half of the instances, which we will call "good" instances. The good instances are chosen adaptively, *after* the adversary interacts with

---

[7] The size of the broadcast and secret keys are never explicitly calculated in [GQWW19]. From personal communication with the authors of [GQWW19], we understand that the public key has size $\Omega(N)$ and the secret keys have size $\Omega(N^2)$. Thus, our scheme also improves on the secret key size from their work.

[8] This is similar to the reason behind why Boneh-Naor [BN08] is a threshold scheme.

the many instances of the scheme. This means that the tracing probabilities for the various good instances will not be independent. Nevertheless, we show by a careful argument that, for the right definition of security for a multi-scheme, the tracing probabilities cannot be too correlated, which is sufficient to get our proof to go through. More details are given in Sect. 7.

2.4 Traitor Tracing from Threshold Broadcast Encryption

We next turn to constructing traitor tracing from a certain type of attribute-based encryption which we call threshold broadcast encryption (this notion of "threshold" not to be confused with the notion of "threshold" for traitor tracing). A (plain) broadcast encryption scheme allows for broadcasting a ciphertext to arbitrary subsets of users with a single constant-sized ciphertext. Broadcast encryption with constant sized secret keys and ciphertexts (but linear-sized public keys) is possible using pairings, as first shown by Boneh, Gentry, and Waters [BGW05].

Describing an arbitrary subset of recipients takes linear space; therefore, broadcast schemes obtain sub-linear ciphertexts by assuming S is *public* and not counted in the ciphertext. On the other hand, traitor tracing typically requires a "private" broadcast, where the recipient set is at least partially hidden. For example, private linear broadcast encryption (PLBE) [BSW06] allows for encrypting to sets $[i]$, and only user i can distinguish between $[i-1]$ and $[i]$.

Our goal is to show how to use broadcast functionalities—with *public* recipient sets—to enable a *private* broadcast structure that allows for tracing.

Our Idea. To trace N users, we will instantiate a broadcast scheme with NT users, for some parameter T. We will think of the NT identities as being pairs $(i, x) \in [N] \times [T]$. For each user $i \in [N]$, we will choose a random $x_i \in [T]$, and give that user the secret key for broadcast identity (i, x_i). Only user i knows x_i. To encrypt, we will simply broadcast to a random subset $S \subseteq [N] \times [T]$.

For tracing, consider choosing S uniformly at random conditioned on $(i, x_i) \notin S$; doing so "turns off" user i, preventing them from decrypting. If i is honest, the adversary does not know x_i and hopefully cannot distinguish between this distribution and a truly uniform S. If turning off a user causes a change in decryption probability, we then accuse that user.

The description so far has several issues. First, in regular execution of the above scheme, any (i, x_i) will only be in the recipient set with probability $1/2$, meaning honest users can only decrypt half the time. Second, an attacker may guess x_i with non-negligible probability $1/T$, and create a decoder that fails if $(i, x_i) \notin S$, thus fooling the tracing algorithm into accusing an honest user with non-negligible probability. Finally, encoding an arbitrary subset S takes NT bits, meaning we have (at least) linear-sized ciphertexts.

Threshold Broadcast. To rectify the first two issues, we will rely on a stronger version of broadcast encryption, which we call *threshold* broadcast encryption[9]. Here, every secret key is associated with a set U; this key can decrypt a ciphertext to set S if and only if $|U \cap S| \geq t$ for some threshold t.

We now give users the secret key for disjoint sets U of identities. The size of $S \cap U$ for a random set S will concentrate around $|U|/2$; by setting t slightly smaller than $|U|/2$, users will be able to decrypt with overwhelming probability. For tracing, the attacker can only guess a small fraction of an honest user's identities. We turn off the identities the attacker *does not* guess, which will drop $|S \cap U|$ below t, thereby turning off the user while keeping the decoder on.

In slightly more detail, we set $T = 2\lambda$. We interpret the $N \times 2\lambda$ identities as triples $(i, j, b) \in [N] \times [\lambda] \times [2]$. For each user, we will choose a random vector $x^i \in \{0,1\}^\lambda$, and give the user the secret key for set $U_i = \{(i, j, x^i_j)\}_{j \in [\lambda]}$. When we trace, for each user i, we will iterate over all $j \in [\lambda]$, trying to turn off identity (i, j, x^i_j) by removing that element from S. If removing that element causes too-large a decrease in the decoder's decryption probability, we keep it in S; otherwise we remove it. We demonstrate that, if the user is outside the adversary's control (meaning in particular the adversary does not know x^i), that with high probability we can remove enough of the elements to completely turn off that user. A diagram illustrating our idea is given in Fig. 1.

Interestingly, our tracing algorithm makes *adaptive* queries to the decoder: which elements are in the set S depends on the results of previous queries to the decoder. This is unlike the vast majority of tracing techniques (including both fingerprinting codes and PLBE), where all queries can be made in parallel.

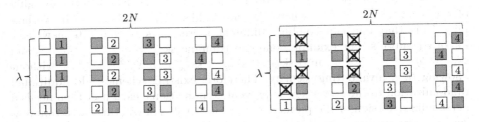

Fig. 1. An illustration in the case $\lambda = 5$, $N = 4$, $t = 2$. Here, the ith pair of columns corresponds to the identities (i, j, b), $j \in [\lambda]$, $b \in \{0,1\}$. U_i is the set of boxes with the number i in them. Gray boxes are those contained in S. Left: Normal usage. In this case, if $t = 2$, all users would be able to decrypt. Right: An example tracing attempt. An "X" represents an element that has been explicitly removed from S. Here, removing $(1, 2, 1)$ (1st pair of columns, 2nd row) failed, and so $(1, 2, 1)$ was left in S. Tracing succeeds in fully turning off users 1 and 2.

---

[9] The prior literature on this topic such as [AHL+12] uses the terminology of "threshold attribute based encryption".

The Shared Randomness Model. For now, we side-step the need to communicate S by considering a new model for traitor tracing, which we call the *shared randomness model*. Here, every ciphertext is encrypted using a large public source of randomness (in addition to private random coins). This public randomness is also available for decryption, but we will not count it as part of the ciphertext. In this model, we simply have S be derived from the shared randomness.

We update our size notation, to include a fourth term R which bounds the size of the shared randomness; C now only bounds the ciphertext component excluding the shared randomness. For example, a scheme of size $(P, K, C, R) = (N, N, 1, N)$ would have linear-sized public and secret keys, constant-sized ciphertexts, and linear-sized shared randomness. We prove the following in Sect. 8:

Theorem 4 (Informal). *If there exists a secure threshold broadcast scheme of size (P, K, C), then there exists a secure broadcast and trace scheme of size (P, K, C, N) in the shared randomness model.*

Instantiation. We now turn to constructing a threshold broadcast scheme. Existing pairing-based constructions such as [AHL+12] have size $(N, N, 1)$, allowing us to match Corollary 3 with entirely different techniques, but in the weaker shared randomness model. We observe, however, that we do not need a full threshold broadcast scheme. Prior works required security to hold, even if multiple users had overlapping sets U_i. In our case, all users have disjoint U_i. This turns out to let us strip away much of the secret key material, arriving at smaller secret keys.

In slightly more detail, the secret key for a set U consists of terms roughly of the form $g^{\beta \prod_{i \in U}(\gamma - i)^{-1}}$ where β, γ are hidden. The problem with overlapping U is that one can combine different secret keys to generate new keys for other subsets. For example, one can combine $\mathsf{sk}_{12} = g^{\beta(\gamma-1)^{-1}(\gamma-2)^{-1}}$ and $\mathsf{sk}_{13} = g^{\beta(\gamma-1)^{-1}(\gamma-3)^{-1}}$ into $\mathsf{sk}_{23} = \mathsf{sk}_{12}^{-1} \times \mathsf{sk}_{13}^2 = g^{\beta(\gamma-2)^{-1}(\gamma-3)^{-1}}$ without knowing β, γ, invalidating security. Therefore, existing schemes add additional randomization to the secret key to prevent combinations; each user then needs a personalized version of the public key in order to strip away this extra randomization during decryption. This expands the secret keys to size $O(N)$.

Our main observation is that no such randomization is necessary if the U's are disjoint; we describe our scheme in Sect. 8. We justify the security of our scheme (for disjoint U) in the generic group model for pairings:

Theorem 5 (Informal). *There exists a threshold broadcast scheme with size $(N, 1, 1)$ from pairings with security for disjoint U in the generic group model.*

User Expansion in the Shared Randomness Model. Interestingly, in the shared randomness model, user expansion (Theorem 1) increases the ciphertext size, but *not* shared randomness size. Concretely, Theorem 1 becomes:

Theorem 1. *Let $P = P(N, M), K = K(N, M), C = C(N, M), R = R(N, M)$ and $T = T(N, M)$ be polynomials such that $T(N, M) \leq N$. If* there exists a secure multi-scheme Π_0 with size (P, K, C, R) in the shared randomness model, then there exists a secure multi-scheme Π with size $(P(N/T, MT),\ K(N/T, MT),\ T \times C(N/T, MT),\ R(N/T, MT))$ in the shared randomness model. If Π_0 is a broadcast and trace scheme, then so is Π.

Next, note that if $R \leq C$, we can include the shared randomness in the ciphertext, giving a scheme with the same ciphertext size without shared randomness. Combining Theorems 4 and 5, and then applying our updated Theorem 1 gives:

Corollary 4. *For any constant $a \in [0, 1]$, there exists a broadcast and trace scheme of size $(N^{1-a}, 1, N^a, N^{1-a})$ from pairings in the shared randomness model, whose security is justified in the generic group model. For $a \in [1/2, 1]$, the scheme has size $(N^{1-a}, 1, N^a)$ in the plain model.*

Setting $a = 1/2$ gives the first pairing-based broadcast and trace scheme with size $(N^{1/2}, 1, N^{1/2})$, improving on $(N^{1/2}, N^{1/2}, N^{1/2})$ from [BW06].

2.5 Putting it All Together: Our $\sqrt[3]{N}$ Construction

Finally, we combine all of the ideas above to yield a traitor tracing scheme where all parameters have size $\sqrt[3]{N}$. At a high level, we take our shared randomness scheme of size $(N, 1, 1, N)$ for N users, augment the construction with ideas from [GKRW18] to expand it to N^2 users while hopefully keeping the size $(N, 1, 1, N)$, at the expense of only achieving $1/N$-riskiness. If this worked, scaling down $N^2 \mapsto N$ would give $1/\sqrt{N}$-risky scheme of size $(\sqrt{N}, 1, 1, \sqrt{N})$ for N users. Then we apply Theorem 3 to eliminate the risk, then Theorem 1 with $T = \sqrt[3]{N}$ to balance the number of users, and finally including the shared randomness in the ciphertext, achieving size $\sqrt[3]{N}$ in the plain model.

We follow the above idea, but unfortunately there are some subtle issues with the above approach which make the combination non-trivial. Concretely, when adding riskiness to our shared randomness scheme, we multiply the number of users by N. However, we cannot expand the set of recipients for the threshold broadcast scheme, since doing so would require expanding the public key. Since the recipient set is limited, the sets U_i for the various users will actually need to overlap. As discussed above, overlapping U_i requires expanding the secret key size, preventing us from achieving our goal.

While we are unable to achieve a $1/\sqrt{N}$-risky scheme of size $(\sqrt{N}, 1, 1, \sqrt{N})$, we build a scheme with large but redundant secret keys, so that the secret keys resulting from Theorem 3 can then be compressed by eliminating the redundancy. The result is the following, proved in Sect. 9:

Theorem 6. *There exists a secure multi-scheme with size $(\sqrt{N}, \sqrt{N}, 1, \sqrt{N})$ in the shared randomness model from pairings with security proved in the generic group model.*

Then, we apply the shared randomness version of Theorem 1 to obtain:

Corollary 5. *There exists a secure multi-scheme with size $\sqrt[3]{N}$ from pairings with security proved in the generic group model.*

3   Discussion, Other Related Work, and Open Problems

3.1   Takeaways

Beyond PLBE and Fingerprinting Codes. PLBE has been the stalwart abstraction in traitor tracing literature for some time, and PLBE and fingerprinting codes make up the vast majority of the fully collusion-resistant tracing literature. Our work demonstrates other useful approaches, and in doing so we hope motivate the further study of alternative approaches to traitor tracing.

Mind Your Public and Secret Key Sizes. As a result of our work, the threshold limitation of fingerprinting code-based traitor tracing is eliminated. The only remaining limitation is the size of the other parameters. What is important for traitor tracing, therefore, is the *trade-off* between the various parameter sizes, rather than any one parameter on its own.

   With this view in mind, perhaps a sub-quadratic scheme from pairings could have been anticipated. After all, the $\sqrt{N}$ scheme of Boneh, Sahai, and Waters [BSW06] has some "slack", in the sense that its secret keys are constant sized. On the other hand, Boneh and Naor [BN08] show that ciphertexts can potentially be compressed by expanding the secret key size. However, prior to our work there was no clear way to actually leverage this slack to get a $\sqrt[3]{N}$ scheme.

$|pk| \times |sk| \times |ct| = N$ *for Pairings?:* Our pairing-based traitor tracing schemes, as well as [BSW06], all have size (N^a, N^b, N^c) where $a + b + c = 1$. We conjecture that *any* setting of $a, b, c \geq 0$ such that $a + b + c = 1$ should be possible from pairings. While me make progress towards this conjecture, there are still a number of gaps: for example, is a $(\sqrt{N}, \sqrt{N}, 1)$ scheme possible?

   For broadcast and trace, we conjecture that any setting where $a + c \geq 1$ is satisfiable, matching what is known for plain broadcast from pairings. We achieve this in the shared randomness model, and for $c \geq 1/2$ in the plain model.

3.2   Limitations

Generic Groups. Some of our constructions, including our $\sqrt[3]{N}$-size scheme, have security proofs in the generic group model, as opposed to concrete assumptions on pairings. We believe the results are nevertheless meaningful. Our schemes are based on new attribute-based encryption-style primitives, and generic groups have been used in many such cases [BSW07, AY20]. We hope that further work will demonstrate a $\sqrt[3]{N}$ scheme based on concrete assumptions.

Concrete Efficiency. While our schemes improve the dependence on N, they may be worse in terms of the dependence on the security parameter. We therefore view our schemes more as a proof-of-concept that improved asymptotics are possible, and leave as an important open question achieving better concrete efficiency. The same can be said of the prior LWE and obfuscation-based constructions, which incur enormous overhead (much worse than ours) due to non-black box techniques and other inefficiencies.

Private Tracing. Our schemes all achieve only private traceability, meaning the tracing key must be kept secret. Most schemes from the literature, including the recent LWE schemes, also have private tracing. On the other hand, some schemes have public tracing, allowing the tracing key to be public [BW06, GGH+13, BZ14].

3.3 Other Related Work

$(1,1,1)$ *Traitor Tracing.* Recent developments have given the first traitor tracing schemes where *all* parameters are independent of the number of users. These schemes, however, require tools other than pairings, namely LWE [GKW18, CVW+18] or obfuscation-related objects [GGH+13, BZ14, GVW19].

Embedded Identities. Some tracing schemes [NWZ16, KW19, GKW19] allow for information beyond an index to be embedded into an identity and extracted during tracing. It is not obvious how to extend our scheme to handle embedded identities, and we leave this as an open question.

Bounded Collusions. In this work, we only consider the unbounded collusion setting, where all users may conspire to build a pirate decoder that defeats tracing. It is also possible to consider bounded collisions, which often result in more efficient schemes [CFN94, BF99, KY02, ADM+07, LPSS14, ABP+17].

4 Traitor Tracing Definitions

In this section, we define traitor tracing, as well as some variants. The central object we will study is actually a slight generalization of traitor tracing, which we call a a "multi-scheme." Here, there are many separate instances of the traitor tracing scheme being run, but the public keys of the different instances are aggregated into a single common public key. Yet, despite this aggregation, the separate instances must behave as essentially independent traitor tracing schemes. Multi-schemes similar to *identity-based* traitor tracing [ADM+07], except that identity-based traitor tracing has an exponential number of instances.

In this work, we consider a key encapsulation variant of traitor tracing. A traitor tracing multi-scheme is a tuple $\Pi = (\mathsf{Gen}, \mathsf{Enc}, \mathsf{Dec}, \mathsf{Trace})$ of PPT algorithms with the following syntax:

- $\mathsf{Gen}(1^N, 1^M, 1^\lambda)$ takes as input a security parameter, a number of users N, and a number of instances M. It outputs a public key pk, a (secret) tracing key tk, and $N \times M$ user secret keys $\{\mathsf{sk}_{j,i}\}_{i \in [N], j \in [M]}$.
- $\mathsf{Enc}(\mathsf{pk}, j)$ takes as input the public key bk and an instance number j, and outputs a ciphertext c together with a key k.
- $\mathsf{Dec}(\mathsf{pk}, \mathsf{sk}_{j,i}, c)$ takes as input the public key pk, the secret key $\mathsf{sk}_{j,i}$ for user i in instance j, and a ciphertext c; it outputs a message k.
- $\mathsf{Trace}^D(\mathsf{tk}, j, \epsilon)$ takes as input the tracing key tk, and instance j, and an advantage ϵ. It then makes queries to a decoder D. Finally, it outputs a set $A \subseteq [N]$. We require that the running time of Trace, when counting queries as unit cost, is $\mathsf{poly}(\lambda, N, M, 1/\epsilon)$.

We require that Dec recovers k: for any polynomials $N = N(\lambda), M = M(\lambda)$, there exists a negligible function negl such that for all $i \in [N], j \in [M], \lambda > 0$:

$$\Pr\left[\mathsf{Dec}(\mathsf{pk},\mathsf{sk}_{j,i},c) = k : {}^{(\mathsf{pk},\mathsf{tk},(\mathsf{sk}_{j',i'})_{i' \in [N], j' \in [M]}) \leftarrow \mathsf{Gen}(1^N,1^M,1^\lambda)}_{(c,k) \leftarrow \mathsf{Enc}(\mathsf{pk},j)}\right] \geq 1 - \mathsf{negl}(\lambda)$$

For security, we generalize [GKRW18] to the case of multi-schemes. Let $\mathcal{A}$ be an adversary, and ϵ an inverse polynomial. Consider the following experiment:

- $\mathcal{A}$ receives the security parameter λ, written in unary.
- $\mathcal{A}$ sends numbers N, M (in unary) and commits to an instance $j^* \in [M]$. Run $(\mathsf{pk}, \mathsf{tk}, \{\mathsf{sk}_{j,i}\}_{i \in [N], j \in [M]}) \leftarrow \mathsf{Gen}(1^N, 1^M, 1^\lambda)$ and send pk to $\mathcal{A}$.
- $\mathcal{A}$ then makes two kinds of queries, in an arbitrary order.
  - Secret key queries, on pairs $(j, i) \in [M] \times [N]$. In response, it receives $\mathsf{sk}_{j,i}$. For $j \in [M]$, let $C_j \subseteq [N]$ be the set of queries (j, i) of this type.
  - Tracing queries, on pairs (j, D); D is a poly-sized circuit and $j \in [M] \backslash \{j^*\}$. All tracing queries must be on distinct j. Return $A_j \leftarrow \mathsf{Trace}^D(\mathsf{tk}, j, \epsilon)$.
- $\mathcal{A}$ produces a decoder D, and the challenger outputs $A_{j^*} \leftarrow \mathsf{Trace}^D(\mathsf{tk}, j^*, \epsilon)$.

We define the following events. BadTr is the event $A_{j^*} \nsubseteq C_{j^*}$. Let $\mathsf{GoodDec}$ be the event that $\Pr[D(c, k^b) = b] \geq 1/2 + \epsilon(\lambda)$, where $(c, k^0) \leftarrow \mathsf{Enc}(\mathsf{pk}, j^*)$, k^1 is chosen uniformly at random from the key space, and $b \leftarrow \{0, 1\}$. In this case, we call D a "good" decoder. Finally, let GoodTr be the event that $|A_{j^*}| > 0$.

Definition 1. *A traitor tracing multi-scheme Π is secure if, for all PPT adversaries $\mathcal{A}$ and all inverse-polynomials ϵ, there exists a negligible function negl such that $\Pr[\mathsf{BadTr}] \leq \mathsf{negl}(\lambda)$ and $\Pr[\mathsf{GoodTr}] \geq \Pr[\mathsf{GoodDec}] - \mathsf{negl}(\lambda)$.*[10]

4.1   Variations, Special Cases, and Extensions

Standard Traitor Tracing. A standard tracing scheme is obtained by setting $M = 1$ in the multi-scheme definition. By a straightforward hybrid argument, a standard traitor tracing scheme also gives a multi-scheme by running independent instances for each $j \in [M]$. The result is that, if there exists a standard tracing scheme of size (P, K, C), then there exists a secure multi-scheme of size $(M \times P, K, C)$.

Threshold Schemes. A threshold scheme [NP98] is one where a malicious user is accused only for very good decoders that succeed a constant fraction of the time.

Definition 2. *A multi-scheme Π is threshold secure if there exists a constant $\epsilon \in (0, 1/2)$ such that, for all PPT adversaries $\mathcal{A}$, there exists a negligible function negl such that $\Pr[\mathsf{BadTr}] \leq \mathsf{negl}(\lambda)$ and $\Pr[\mathsf{GoodTr}] \geq \Pr[\mathsf{GoodDec}] - \mathsf{negl}(\lambda)$.*

In the case of threshold secure schemes, the constant ϵ is hard-coded into the algorithm Trace, and we omit ϵ as an input to Trace.

---

[10] The definition given in [GKRW18] additionally introduces an inverse polynomial p, but relaxes ϵ to be *non-negligible*, with a more complicated condition for security. The simpler definition we use is readily shown to be equivalent to their definition.

Risky Schemes. In a risky scheme [GKRW18], a traitor is only accused with some small but noticeable probability. Let $\alpha = \alpha(N, M, \lambda)$ be a polynomial.

Definition 3. *A traitor tracing multi-scheme Π is α-risky if, for all PPT adversaries $\mathcal{A}$ and all inverse-polynomials ϵ, there exists a negligible function* negl *such that* $\Pr[\mathsf{BadTr}] \leq \mathsf{negl}(\lambda)$ *and* $\Pr[\mathsf{GoodTr}] \geq \alpha \Pr[\mathsf{GoodDec}] - \mathsf{negl}(\lambda)$.

Broadcast and Trace. A broadcast and trace multi-scheme [BW06] is a multi-scheme augmented with a broadcast functionality. $\mathsf{Enc}, \mathsf{Dec}, \mathsf{Trace}$ and the decoder all take as input a subset $S \subseteq [N]$. $\mathcal{A}$ additionally produces a set S at the beginning (when it produces N, M, j^*). $\mathsf{BadTr}, \mathsf{GoodDec}, \mathsf{GoodTr}$ are all defined relative to S, where BadTr happens when $A_{j^*} \not\subseteq S \cap C_{j^*}$. The ciphertext size does *not* include the description of S.

4.2   New Notion: The Shared Randomness Model

We now give a new model for traitor tracing, which we call the *shared randomness model*. In the shared randomness model, encryption has the form $(c = (r, c'), k) \leftarrow \mathsf{Enc}(\mathsf{bk}, j \; ; \; r, s)$. That is, some of the random coins for Enc are *public*, and included in the output of Enc. In this model, we will consider the "ciphertext length" to exclude the public random coins, and just be the length of c'.

The shared randomness model captures a setting where the sender and receiver have access to a common source of randomness, for example randomness beacons, stock market fluctuations, etc. The sender can use this randomness as r during encryption, but then does not actually need to send r to the receiver. Thus, communication costs depend only on c', rather than the entire length of (r, c').

For our parameter size notation, we will explicitly consider the size of c' and r separately. That is, for a traitor tracing multi-scheme in the shared randomness model, we say the scheme has parameter size (P, S, C, R) for functions P, K, C, R, where $C \times \mathsf{poly}(\lambda)$ is a bound on the size of c' and $R \times \mathsf{poly}(\lambda)$ is a bound on the size of r. We note that any multi-scheme with parameter size (P, K, C, R) in the shared randomness model is also a scheme with parameter size $(P, K, C + R)$ in the plain model, by having the encrypter choose r and send it as part of the ciphertext. We also note that any plain-model scheme with parameter size (P, K, C) is also a shared-randomness scheme with parameter size $(P, K, C, 0)$.

5   User Expansion Compiler

We now prove Theorem 1, which offers a trade-off between ciphertext size and number of users. For full generality, we give describe our compiler in the shared randomness model. By setting the shared randomness to be empty, our compiler immediately extends to the plain model.

Let $\Pi_0 = (\mathsf{Gen}_0, \mathsf{Enc}_0, \mathsf{Dec}_0, \mathsf{Trace}_0)$ be a traitor tracing multi-scheme in the shared randomness model. We will assume without loss of generality that the encapsulated key has length at most the size of the ciphertext.

Construction 1 (User Expansion Compiler) *Let $T = T(N, M)$ be a polynomial. Let $\Pi = (\mathsf{Gen}, \mathsf{Enc}, \mathsf{Dec}, \mathsf{Trace})$ be the tuple of PPT algorithms:*

- $\mathsf{Gen}(1^N, 1^M, 1^\lambda)$*: Run* $(\mathsf{pk}', \mathsf{tk}', (\mathsf{sk}'_{j',i'})_{i' \in [N'], j' \in [M']}) \leftarrow \mathsf{Gen}_0(1^{N'}, 1^{M'}, 1^\lambda)$ *where $N' = N/T$ and $M' = M \times T$. Set $\mathsf{pk} = \mathsf{pk}', \mathsf{tk} = \mathsf{tk}'$. Interpret $[M']$ as $[M] \times [T]$ and $[N]$ as $[N'] \times [T]$. Then set $\mathsf{sk}_{j,(i,t)} = \mathsf{sk}'_{(j,t),i}$*
- $\mathsf{Enc}(\mathsf{pk}, j, r)$*: Here, r is the shared randomness, which is taken from the same space of shared randomness as in Π_0. For each $t \in [T]$, run $(c_t, k_t) \leftarrow \mathsf{Enc}_0(\mathsf{pk}, (j,t), r)$, again using our interpretation of $[M']$ as $[M] \times [T]$. Choose a random key k from the key space. Output $c = ((c_t)_{t \in [T]}, (k_t \oplus k)_{t \in [T]})$ as the ciphertext and k as the key.*
- $\mathsf{Dec}(\mathsf{pk}, \mathsf{sk}_{j,i}, c, r)$*: Write i as (i', t) and $c = ((c_t)_{t \in [T]}, (u_t)_{t \in [T]})$. Compute $k'_t \leftarrow \mathsf{Dec}_0(\mathsf{pk}, \mathsf{sk}_{j,i}, c_t, r)$. Output $k' = u_t \oplus k'_t$.*
- $\mathsf{Trace}^D(\mathsf{tk}, j, \epsilon)$*: For each $t \in [T]$ run $A_t \leftarrow \mathsf{Trace}_0^{D_t}(\mathsf{tk}, (j,t), \epsilon/4T)$, and output $A = \cup_{t \in [T]}\{(i, t) : i \in A_t\}$. Here, D_t be the following decoder for instance (j,t) of Π_0: on input $(c, r), u$, do the following:*
  - *For $t' \neq t$, compute $(c_{t'}, k_{t'}) \leftarrow \mathsf{Enc}_0(\mathsf{pk}, (j, t'), r)$. Set $c_t = c$.*
  - *Choose a random bit $b \leftarrow \{0,1\}$, and random keys k^0, k^1.*
  - *For $t' < t$, choose random $u_{t'}$. For $t' > t$, $u_{t'} = k_{t'} \oplus k^0$. Set $u_t = u \oplus k^0$.*
  - *Set $c' = ((c_{t'})_{t' \in [T]}, (u_{t'})_{t' \in [T]})$. Output $b \oplus D((c', r), k^b)$. (Note that XORing with b turns a distinguisher into a predictor)*

By the correctness of Π_0, we will have that $k'_t = k_t$, and therefore $k' = u_t \oplus k'_t = u_t \oplus k_t = k$, so Π is correct. Since the encapsulated key in Π_0 is at most the size of the ciphertext, we see that the desired sizes hold.

5.1 Security of Our Compiler

Theorem 7. *If Π_0 is a secure multi-scheme, then so is Π.*

Proof. Due to lack of space, we only sketch the proof, see the full version [Zha20] for a complete proof. Fix an adversary $\mathcal{A}$ for Π and inverse-polynomial ϵ. Let $\mathsf{GoodTr}, \mathsf{BadTr}, \mathsf{GoodDec}$ be the events as in Definition 1.

$\Pr[\mathsf{BadTr}] \leq \mathsf{negl}$ follows by a straightforward argument, using the fact that Trace_0 only accuses honest users with negligible probability. We now sketch why $\Pr[\mathsf{GoodTr}] \geq \Pr[\mathsf{GoodDec}] - \mathsf{negl}$. Our goal is to show that at least one of the decoders D_t will be traced. We set up a sequence of hybrid distributions by gradually replacing the u_t by independent random strings. Before any changes, a good decoder is correct with probability at least $1/2 + \epsilon$; after all the changes, the view of the decoder is statistically independent of b, and therefore it is correct with probability exactly $1/2$. Therefore, there is some t where changing u_t to random causes the decoder's success probability to drop by at least ϵ/T. This corresponds to the decoder D_t being a "good" decoder; by the security of Π_0, tracing this D_t will result in A_t being non-empty, as desired. $\square$

6   Threshold Elimination Compiler

We now prove Theorem 2, generically removing thresholds from tracing schemes. For simplicity, we give our compiler for plain-model traitor tracing. Let $\Pi_{\mathsf{Thresh}} = (\mathsf{Gen}_{\mathsf{Thresh}}, \mathsf{Enc}_{\mathsf{Thresh}}, \mathsf{Dec}_{\mathsf{Thresh}}, \mathsf{Trace}_{\mathsf{Thresh}})$ be a multi-scheme.

Construction 2 (Threshold Elimination Compiler)   *Assume the encapsulated key space of* Π_{Thresh} *is* $\mathcal{K} = \{0, 1\}^\ell$. *Let* $t = t(\lambda)$ *be any polynomial. Let* $\Pi = (\mathsf{Gen}, \mathsf{Enc}, \mathsf{Dec}, \mathsf{Trace})$ *be the tuple of the following PPT algorithms:*

- $\mathsf{Gen}(1^N, 1^M, 1^\lambda) = \mathsf{Gen}_{\mathsf{Thresh}}(1^N, 1^M, 1^\lambda)$
- $\mathsf{Enc}(\mathsf{pk}, j)$: *Let* $n = \omega(\log \lambda)$. *For each* $u \in [n], v \in [t]$, *run* $(c_{u,v}, k_{u,v}) \leftarrow \mathsf{Enc}_{\mathsf{Thresh}}(\mathsf{pk}, j)$. *Choose a random* $s \leftarrow \mathcal{K}$. *For each* $v \in [t]$, *let* $k_v = k_{1,v} \oplus \cdots \oplus k_{n,v}$ *and let* $b_v = s \cdot k_v \bmod 2$ *be the bit-wise inner product of* s *and* k_v. *Let* $k = k_1 k_2 \cdots k_t$. *Let* $c = (s, (c_{u,v})_{u \in [n], v \in [t]})$. *Output* (c, k).
- $\mathsf{Dec}(\mathsf{pk}, \mathsf{sk}_{j,i}, c)$: *Write* $c = (s, (c_{u,v})_{u \in [n], v \in [t]})$. *For each* $u \in [n], v \in [t]$, *run* $k'_{u,v} \leftarrow \mathsf{Dec}_{\mathsf{Thresh}}(\mathsf{pk}, \mathsf{sk}_i, c_{u,v})$. *For each* $v \in [t]$, *compute* $k'_v = k'_{1,v} \oplus \cdots \oplus k'_{n,v}$ *and* $b'_v = r \cdots k'_v \bmod 2$. *Output* $k' = b'_1 b'_2 \cdots b'_t$.
- *The algorithm* $\mathsf{Trace}^D(\mathsf{tk}, \epsilon)$ *will be described below.*

By the correctness of Π_{Thresh}, we have with overwhelming probability that $k'_{u,v} = k_{u,v}$ for all $u \in [n], v \in [t]$. This implies $k'_v = k_v$ and hence $b'_v = b_v$ for all $v \in [t]$, meaning $k' = k$. Thus Π is correct. We also see that Π has the desired parameter size: only the ciphertext is increased by a factor of $n \times t \leq \mathsf{poly}(\lambda)$. We now give our algorithm $\mathsf{Trace}^D(\mathsf{tk}, j, \epsilon)$, which proceeds in several stages:

Target Single Bit: First, we define a decoder $D_1(s, (c_u)_{u \in [n]})$, where $s \in \{0, 1\}^\ell$, c_u are ciphertexts from Π_{Thresh}. The goal of D_1 is to predict the bit $s \cdot k$ where k is the XOR of all the keys encapsulated in the c_u. It does so by embedding its challenge into a random position of an input for D:

- Choose a random $v \in [t]$.
- Let $c_{u,v} = c_u$ and choose $(c_{u,v'}, k_{u,v'}) \leftarrow \mathsf{Enc}_{\mathsf{Thresh}}(\mathsf{pk}, j)$ for $u \in [n]$ and $v' \in [t] \setminus \{v\}$. Let $c = (s, (c_{u,v})_{u \in [n], v \in [t]})$.
- For each $v' \in [t] \setminus \{v\}$, compute $k_{v'} = k_{1,v'} \oplus \cdots \oplus k_{n,v'}$. For $v' \leq v$, choose random $b_{v'} \leftarrow \{0, 1\}$, and for $v' > v$, set $b_{v'} = r \cdot k'_{u,v'} \bmod 2$. Set $k = b_1 \cdots b_t$.
- Output $b_v \oplus D(c, k)$ (XORing with b_v turns a distinguisher into a predictor)

Apply Goldreich-Levin. Next, we will need the following theorem:

Theorem 8 ([GL89]). *There exists a constant* Γ *and oracle algorithm* $\mathsf{GL}^D(\ell, \epsilon')$ *running in time* $\mathsf{poly}(\ell, \log(1/\epsilon'))$ *and making* $\mathsf{poly}(\ell, \log(1/\epsilon'))$ *queries to* D, *such that the following holds. If there exists an* $x \in \{0, 1\}^\ell$ *such that* $\Pr[D(r) = x \cdot r \bmod 2 : r \leftarrow \{0, 1\}^\ell] \geq 1/2 + \epsilon'$, *then* $\Pr[\mathsf{GL}^D(\ell, \epsilon') = x] \geq \Gamma \times (\epsilon')^2$.

Trace will define $D_2((c_u)_{u \in [n]}) := \mathsf{GL}^{D_1(\cdot, (c_u)_{u \in [n]})}(\ell, \epsilon' = \epsilon/t)$; D_2 is given $(c_u)_{u \in [n]}$ that encrypt $k_1, \ldots, k_n$, and its goal is to compute $k_1 \oplus \cdots \oplus k_n$.

Generate List of Potential Decryptions: Let $D_3(c, k)$ be the following, where c is a ciphertext for Π_{Thresh} and $k \in \{0, 1\}^\ell$. For $z = 1, \ldots, \xi = (2nt^3/\Gamma\epsilon^3) \times \omega(\log \lambda)$:

- Choose a random $u \in [n]$, and set $c_u = c$.
- Then for each $u' \in [n] \setminus \{u\}$, run $(c_{u'}, k_{u'}) \leftarrow \text{Enc}_{\text{Thresh}}(\text{bk}, j)$.
- Run $k' \leftarrow D'_{v,b}((c_u)_{u \in [n]})$, and set $k^{(z)} = k' \oplus k_1 \oplus \cdots \oplus k_{u-1} \oplus k_{u+1} \cdots \oplus k_n$.

Next, if $k = k^{(z)}$ for any $z \in [\xi]$, output 1. Otherwise, output 0.

Trace. Finally, run and output $A \leftarrow \text{Trace}_{\text{Thresh}}{}^{D_3}(\text{tk}, j)$

6.1 Security of Our Compiler

Theorem 9. *Set* $n = \omega(\log \lambda), \epsilon' = \epsilon/t, \xi = (2nt^3/\Gamma\epsilon^3) \times \omega(\log \lambda)$. *Suppose* $\ell = \omega(\log \lambda)$. *If* Π_{Thresh} *is a secure threshold multi-cheme, then* Π *is a secure (non-threshold) multi-scheme.*

Proof. Due to lack of space, we only sketch the proof, see the full version [Zha20] for a complete proof. Fix an adversary $\mathcal{A}$ for Π and inverse-polynomial ϵ. Let $\text{GoodTr}, \text{BadTr}, \text{GoodDec}$ be the events as in Definition 1. That $\Pr[\text{BadTr}]$ is negligible follows readily from an analogous argument to the proof of Theorem 7.

To show that $\Pr[\text{GoodTr}] \geq \Pr[\text{GoodDec}] - \text{negl}$, we assume GoodTr happens (D guesses b with probability $\geq 1/2 + \epsilon$) and analyze the decoders D_1, D_2, D_3. If D is such a decoder, we can perform an analogous hybrid step as in Theorem 7; for a *randomly* selected position, we obtain that D can distinguish the bit of the key in that position from a random bit. Then, by a routine calculation, we can convert D into a *predictor* for said bit; the result is exactly the predictor D_1.

Claim. If GoodDec happens, then $\Pr[D_1(s, (c_u)_{u \in [n]}) = s \cdot k \mod 2] \geq 1/2 + 2\epsilon/t$, where $s \leftarrow \{0, 1\}^\ell, (c_u, k_u) \leftarrow \text{Enc}_{\text{Thresh}}(\text{bk}, j)$ for $u \in [n]$, and $k = k_1 \oplus \cdots \oplus k_n$.

This claim is proved in the full version [Zha20]. Next, the following claim shows that D_2 actually guesses k, which follows from Goldreich-Levin (Theorem 8):

Claim. If GoodDec happens, then $\Pr[D_2((d_u, r_u)_{u \in [n]}) = k] \geq \Gamma \times (\epsilon')^3$, where $(c_u, k_u) \leftarrow \text{Enc}_{\text{Thresh}}(\text{bk}, j, r_u)$, r_u is uniformly random, and $k = k_1 \oplus \cdots \oplus k_n$.

Next, we need to show that D_3 can decrypt with high probability. Let $\gamma > 0$. Very roughly, we define S_γ to be the set of "good" ciphertexts, defined as: if we choose a random $u \in [n]$, a random c_u from S_γ, and choose the remaining ciphertexts from $\text{Enc}_{\text{Thresh}}(\text{pk}, j)$, then D_2 outputs the correct key with probability at least γ.

Claim. Let η be the fraction of $c \in S_\gamma$. Then $\Gamma \times (\epsilon')^3 \leq \eta^n + n(1 - \eta)\gamma$.

The claim is proved in the full version [Zha20]; the intuition is that either (1) all n of the ciphertexts were in S_γ, or (2) at least one of the ciphertexts is not in S_γ. Case (1) happens with probability γ^n. For case (2), there are n possible positions for the "bad" ciphertext; for each position, the probability of being bad is $(1 - \eta)$, and conditioned on being bad, the decryption probability is at most γ.

We choose $\gamma = \Gamma \times (\epsilon')^3/2n$, giving $\eta^n \geq \Gamma \times (\epsilon')^3/2$. Taking the nth root of both sides and using $n = \omega(\log \lambda)$ gives $\eta \geq 1 - o(1)$, meaning most ciphertexts are good. We then set the number of trials D_3 runs to be high enough so that, on a good ciphertext, with overwhelming probability at least one of the trials will be correct. Thus, if D_3 is given the correct key, it will find the key amongst its trials with probably $1 - o(1)$. If D_3 is given a random key as input, it will almost certainly not find the given key among its trials. Thus, D_3 is a good decoder for Π_{Thresh}. By the security of Π_{Thresh}, a user will be accused, as desired. $\square$

7 Risk Mitigation Compiler

We now prove Theorem 3 by giving our risk mitigation compiler, converting any risky scheme into one that is not. For notational simplicity, we give our compiler for plain-model traitor tracing; our compiler is readily adapted to work in the shared randomness model as well. Let Π_{Risky} be an $\alpha(N)$-risky multi-scheme. For full generality, we will only assume that Π_{Risky} is a *threshold* scheme.

Construction 3 (Risk Mitigation Compiler) *Let* Π_{Thresh} *be a tuple of PPT algorithms* $(\mathsf{Gen}_{\mathsf{Thresh}}, \mathsf{Enc}_{\mathsf{Thresh}}, \mathsf{Dec}_{\mathsf{Thresh}}, \mathsf{Trace}_{\mathsf{Thresh}})$ *where:*

- $\mathsf{Gen}_{\mathsf{Thresh}}(1^N, 1^M, 1^\lambda)$: *set* $T = (1/\alpha) \times \omega(\log \lambda)$, $M' = M \times T$. *Interpret* $[M']$ *as* $[M] \times [T]$. *Run* $(\mathsf{pk}, \mathsf{tk}, \{\mathsf{sk}_{(j,t),i}\}_{i \in [N], j \in [M], t \in [T]}) \leftarrow \mathsf{Gen}_{\mathsf{Risky}}(1^N, 1^{M'}, 1^\lambda)$. *Output* $(\mathsf{pk}, \mathsf{tk}, (\mathsf{sk}_{j,i})_{i \in [N], j \in [M]})$, *where* $\mathsf{sk}_{j,i} = (\mathsf{sk}_{(j,t),i})_{t \in [T]}$.
- $\mathsf{Enc}_{\mathsf{Thresh}}(\mathsf{pk}, j)$: *Run* $(c, k) \leftarrow \mathsf{Enc}_{\mathsf{Risky}}(\mathsf{pk}, (j,t), r)$ *for a random choice of* $t \in [T]$. *Output the ciphertext* (t, c) *and encapsulated key* k.
- $\mathsf{Dec}_{\mathsf{Thresh}}(\mathsf{pk}, \mathsf{sk}_{j,i}, (j,c), r)$: *Run and output* $k' \leftarrow \mathsf{Dec}_{\mathsf{Risky}}(\mathsf{pk}, \mathsf{sk}_{(j,t),i}, c)$.
- $\mathsf{Trace}_{\mathsf{Thresh}}{}^D(\mathsf{tk}, j)$: *Let* D_t *be the decoder* $D_t(c, k) = D((t,c), k)$. *For* $t \in [T]$, *run* $A_t \leftarrow \mathsf{Trace}_{\mathsf{Risky}}{}^{D_t}(\mathsf{tk}, (j,t))$. *Output* $A = \cup_t A_t$.

Correctness follows readily from the correctness of Π_{Risky}. We also see that the desired parameter sizes hold.

7.1 Security of Our Compiler

Theorem 10. *Assume* $T = (1/\alpha) \times \omega(\log \lambda)$. *If* Π_{Risky} *is an* α-*risky threshold multi-scheme, then* Π_{Thresh} *is a secure* threshold *tracing scheme.*

Note that Theorem 10 only gives a threshold scheme; applying Theorem 2 then gives a non-threshold scheme of the same parameters, thus proving Theorem 3.

Proof. We say that $t \in [T]$ is "good" if D_t has a high chance of decrypting ciphertexts for instance (j,t) of Π_{Risky}. D can only decrypt ciphertexts for t where D_t is good; thus $\mathsf{GoodDec}_{\mathsf{Thresh}}$ implies that the fraction of good t is large. Since each t represents a different instance of the risky scheme, each of the decoders D_t should have a $1/\alpha$ chance of being traced to some user. As long as the number of good t is larger than $\omega(\log \lambda)/\alpha$, then we would expect that, with overwhelming probability, at least one of the D_t traces. One challenge is that the attacker can choose adaptively which of the t will good and hence traceable, so the tracing probabilities are not independent events. Nonetheless, we show a careful security proof—and also show that $\Pr[\mathsf{BadTr_{Thresh}}]$ is negligible—in the full version [Zha20] which demonstrates that the intuition indeed holds.   □

7.2   Instantiation

Our goal now is to prove the following, which suffices to prove Corollary 2:

Theorem 11. *If Assumptions 1 and 2 of [GKRW18] on pairings hold, there exists a $1/N$-risky multi-scheme of size $(1, 1, 1)$.*

Due to lack of space, we only sketch the proof; see the full version [Zha20] for details. As a starting point, [GKRW18] build a $1/N$-risky traitor tracing tracing scheme of size $(1, 1, 1)$, based on pairing assumptions that they call Assumption 1 and 2. Their scheme is not a multi-scheme, but trivially gives a multi-scheme of size $(M, 1, 1)$ by running M instances in parallel. We show how to tweak the construction to obtain a $1/N$-risky *multi*-scheme of size $(1, 1, 1)$.

In more detail, [GKRW18] build a primitive called mixed Bit Matching Encryption (MBME). Here, ciphertexts and secret keys are associated to attribute vectors in $\{0, 1\}^n$. A secret key with attribute $\mathbf{x}$ can decrypt a ciphertext with attribute $\mathbf{y}$ if and only if $\mathbf{x} \cdot \mathbf{y} = 0$ (the inner product taken over the *integers*). For security, a message encrypted to attribute $\mathbf{x}$ stays hidden to all secret keys $\mathbf{y}$ that satisfy $\mathbf{x} \cdot \mathbf{y} > 0$. Moreover, given a secret key $\mathbf{x}$ and ciphertext $\mathbf{y}$, the attacker learns whether or not $\mathbf{x} \cdot \mathbf{y} = 0$, but learns nothing else about $\mathbf{x}, \mathbf{y}$.

[GKRW18] instantiate their scheme with $n = 2$. A random index $i^* \in [N]$ is chosen. Users $i < i^*, i = i^*$, and $i > i^*$ are given a secret key with attributes $(0, 0), (1, 0)$, and $(1, 1)$, respectively. A normal ciphertext is encrypted with attribute $\mathbf{y} = (0, 0)$ so that all users can decrypt. To trace a decoder D, D is tested on ciphertexts to attributes $(0, 1)$, and $(1, 1)$ to see whether it can distinguish. If so, accuse user i^*; otherwise accuse no one. MBME security implies that only user i^* can distinguish between encryptions to $(0, 1)$ and $(1, 1)$, so we only accuse i^* if they are indeed a traitor. A careful hybrid argument then shows that i^* is indeed accused with probability negligibly-close to $1/N$.

Adding Identities. Our idea is to add "identities" to get a multi-scheme, where each instance of the multi-scheme is an "independent" copy of the above. We set $n = 2\kappa + 2$, where κ is the bit-length of integers in $[M]$. Each $j \in [M]$ will give rise to a separate instance, which we distinguish using the first 2κ positions. The remaining 2 positions will be used as above to construct the risky scheme.

In slightly more detail, we group the first 2κ bit positions into κ pairs. For each $j \in [M]$, write j as a bit-vector $\mathbf{v} \in \{0, 1\}^\kappa$. Let $\mathbf{v}^0 \in \{0, 1\}^{2\kappa}$ be vector where the tth pair of positions is $(1 - v_t, v_t)$. Let $\mathbf{v}^1 \in \{0, 1\}^{2\kappa}$ be the opposite, setting the tth pair to $(v_t, 1 - v_t)$. Notice that $\mathbf{v}^0 \cdot \mathbf{v}^1 = 0$, while for $\mathbf{v} \neq \mathbf{w}$, $\mathbf{v}^0 \cdot \mathbf{w}^1 > 0$. For each $j \in [M]$, we set up the risky scheme as above, choosing a random i_j^*. To encrypt to the jth instance, we set the first 2κ positions of $\mathbf{y}$ to be $\mathbf{v}^0$, and for a secret key, we set the first 2κ positions to be $\mathbf{v}^1$. This ensures that only secret keys for the jth scheme can decrypt ciphertexts for the jth scheme, thus fully separating the j instances. We then set the last two positions analogous to the sketch above. By using essentially the same analysis as in [GKRW18], we can show that each separate scheme is $1/N$-risky, regardless of what secret keys and ciphertexts the adversary possesses for the various other schemes. This suffices to establish the $1/N$-riskiness of the entire multi-scheme. Theorem 11 follows from the fact that n is bounded by $O(\log M)$, which can be absorbed into $\mathsf{poly}(\lambda)$ terms. Then, applying Theorem 3 and then Theorem 1 gives Corollary 2.

7.3 A Broadcast and Trace Scheme

Our next result is the following, which suffices to prove Corollary 3:

Theorem 12. *There exists a $1/N$-risky broadcast and trace multi-scheme of size $(N, 1, 1)$ from pairings, with security proved in the generic group model.*

We sketch the construction; see the full version [Zha20] for additional details. The high-level idea is to add a mixed Bit Matching Encryption (MBME) functionality on top of a broadcast scheme of size $(N, 1, 1)$ (in particular, we use [Del07]), and then use the MBME functionality to create a $1/N$-risky tracing scheme.

The Delerablée Broadcast Scheme. We briefly recall Delerablée's scheme [Del07]. Let $\mathbb{G}_1, \mathbb{G}_2, \mathbb{G}'$ be groups of prime order p with pairing operation $e : \mathbb{G}_1 \times \mathbb{G}_2 \to \mathbb{G}'$. Let g_1, g_2 be generators of $\mathbb{G}_1, \mathbb{G}_2$, respectively. The set of possible user identities is $\mathbb{Z}_p \setminus \{0\}$. The public and secret keys are

$$\mathsf{pk} = (e(g_1, g_2)^\beta, g_1^{\beta\gamma}, (g_2^{\gamma^i})_{j \in [0,N]}) \qquad \mathsf{sk}_i = g_1^{\beta/(1-\gamma/i)}$$

for random secrets $\beta, \gamma \in \mathbb{Z}_p$. The public key allows for computing $J(P) := g_2^{P(\gamma)}$, for any polynomial P of degree at $\leq N$. The ciphertext to a set S is:

$$c_1 = g_1^{\alpha\beta\gamma} , \quad c_2 = J \left(\prod_{i \in S} (1 - \gamma/i) \right)^\alpha = g_2^{\alpha \prod_{i \in S} (1 - \gamma/i)}$$

where $\alpha \in \mathbb{Z}_p$ is random. The encapsulated key is $k = e(g_1, g_2)^{\alpha\beta}$. Notice that any user in $\mathbb{Z}_p \setminus \{0\}$ (which has exponential size) can be a recipient, as long as the number of recipients is at most N.

To decrypt, let $Q(\gamma) = \prod_{j \in S \setminus \{i\}} (1 - \gamma/j)$ and $P(\gamma) = (1 - Q(\gamma))/\gamma$. Notice that $1 - Q(0) = 0$, meaning $1 - Q(\gamma)$ is a polynomial of degree $\leq N - 1$ with a 0 constant term; thus $P(\gamma)$ is also a polynomial. Therefore, compute

$$e(c_1, J(P)) \cdot e(\mathsf{sk}_i, c_2) = e(g_1, g_2)^{\alpha\beta\gamma P(\gamma) + \alpha\beta Q(\gamma)} = e(g_1, g_2)^{\alpha\beta} = k$$

The intuition for security is that, for any $i \notin S$, pairing sk_i with c_2 will leave a pole in γ, which cannot be canceled; thus users outside of S cannot decrypt.

Our Construction. We now briefly explain how to augment Delerablée's scheme with a mixed Bit Matching functionality, in order to create a risky scheme. For a (row) vector $\mathbf{v} \in \mathbb{Z}_p^n$, we use the notation $g^{\mathbf{v}} = (g^{v_1}, \ldots, g^{v_n})$.

Let $[\![\cdot]\!]$ be an arbitrary efficient injection from $[M] \times [N]$ into $\mathbb{Z}_p \setminus \{0\}$, which we use to embed instance/identity pairs into $\mathbb{Z}_p \setminus \{0\}$. We choose a random $R \in \mathbb{Z}_q^{4 \times 4}$ in addition to α, β. Our public key is:

$$\mathsf{pk} = \left(e(g_1, g_2)^{\beta}, g_1^{(\beta\gamma\,,\,0\,,\,0\,,\,0) \cdot R^{-1}}, \left(g_2^{(\gamma^i\,,\,0\,,\,0\,,\,0) \cdot R^T} \right)_{j \in [0, N]} \right)$$

The secret key for user i in instance j, with attribute (x_0, x_1), is computed as

$$\mathsf{sk}_{j,i} = g_1^{(\beta(1 - \gamma/[\![j,i]\!])^{-1}\,,\,x_1 u_1\,,\,x_2 u_2\,,\,u_3) \cdot R^{-1}}$$

Here, u_1, u_2, u_3 are freshly chosen at random in $\mathbb{Z}_p$ for each secret key. A ciphertext to set S in instance j, with attribute (y_0, y_1) is set to

$$c_1 = g_1^{(\alpha\beta\gamma\,,\,0\,,\,0\,,\,0) \cdot R^{-1}}\,,\qquad c_2 = g_2^{(\alpha \prod_{i \in S}(1 - \gamma/[\![j,i]\!])\,,\,y_1 v_1\,,\,y_2 v_2\,,\,0) \cdot R^T}$$

where α, v_1, v_2 are freshly chosen at random in $\mathbb{Z}_p$ for each ciphertext. The encapsulated key is $e(g_1, g_2)^{\alpha\beta}$. Let $J(P) := g_2^{(P(\gamma)\,,\,0\,,\,0\,,\,0) \cdot R^T}$, which can be computed from pk for any polynomial P of degree at most N. Notice if $(y_1, y_2) = (0, 0)$, then the ciphertext can thus be computed from pk. To decrypt, output $e(c_1, J(P)) \cdot e(\mathsf{sk}_{j,i}, c_2)$ as in Delerablée, where we use the notation $e(\mathbf{g}, \mathbf{h}) = \prod_i e(g_i, h_i)$, so that $e(g_1^{\mathbf{v}}, g_2^{\mathbf{w}}) = e(g_1, g_2)^{\mathbf{v} \cdot \mathbf{w}^T}$. Correctness follows by essentially the same calculation as in Delerablée, but working with vectors of group elements.

Notice that the construction has the desired size parameters, and readily gives a tracing scheme analogous to Sect. 7.2. We prove security in the full version [Zha20]. The rough intuition is that in the generic group model, we can prove that the MBME functionality combines correctly with the broadcast functionality, which allows us to trace as in [GKRW18].

8   Traitor Tracing from Threshold Broadcast

Here, we prove Corollary 4 by formalizing Theorems 4 and 5, showing how to construct traitor tracing from threshold broadcast, and then giving a new instantiation of threshold broadcast from pairings. A threshold broadcast scheme is a tuple $\Pi = (\mathsf{Gen}, \mathsf{Enc}, \mathsf{Extract}, \mathsf{Dec})$ of PPT algorithms where:

- $\mathsf{Gen}(1^u, 1^v, 1^t, 1^\lambda)$ takes as input a security parameter, bounds $u, v \leq 2^\lambda$, and a threshold $t \leq u, v$. It outputs a public key pk and a master secret key msk.
- $\mathsf{Enc}(\mathsf{pk}, S)$ takes as input the public key pk and a set of users $S \subseteq [2^\lambda]$ of size at most v. It outputs a ciphertext c and key k.
- $\mathsf{Extract}(\mathsf{msk}, U)$ takes as input the master secret key and a subset $U \subseteq [2^\lambda]$ of size at most u. It outputs a secret key sk_U.

- Dec(pk, sk$_U$, S, c) takes as input the public key pk, the secret key sk$_U$ for set U, and a ciphertext c; it outputs a key k.

For correctness, we require that Dec correctly recovers k, provided $|U \cap S| \geq t$: for any polynomials $v = v(\lambda), u = u(\lambda)$, there exists a negligible function negl such that for all $t \leq u, v$ and all $S, U \subseteq [2^\lambda]$ where $|U| \leq u, |S| \leq v$ and $|U \cap S| \geq t$:

$$\Pr\left[\text{Dec}(\text{pk}, \text{sk}_U, c) = k : \begin{array}{l} (\text{pk,msk}) \leftarrow \text{Gen}(1^u, 1^v, 1^t, 1^\lambda) \\ \text{sk}_U \leftarrow \text{Extract}(\text{msk}, U), (c, k) \leftarrow \text{Enc}(\text{pk}, S) \end{array} \right] \geq 1 - \text{negl}(\lambda)$$

We also use the same size notation as for traitor tracing schemes, except that the size parameters depend on u, v instead of M, N. For security, let $\mathcal{A}$ be an adversary, and consider the following experiment:

- $\mathcal{A}$ receives the security parameter λ, written in unary.
- $\mathcal{A}$ chooses numbers u, v, t, written in unary. It also chooses a set $S \subseteq [2^\lambda], |S| \leq v$, and a number of *disjoint* sets $U_i \subseteq [2^\lambda], |U_i| \leq u$ such that $|U_i \cap S| < t$. Send $u, v, t, (U_i)_{i \in [N]}, S$ to the challenger.
- The challenger runs (pk, msk) $\leftarrow$ Gen($1^u, 1^v, 1^t, 1^\lambda$), and for each i runs sk$_{U_i} \leftarrow$ Extract(msk, U_i). It chooses a random bit b, samples random k^1, runs $(c, k^0) \leftarrow$ Enc(pk, S), and sends the adversary ((sk$_{U_i}$)$_{i \in [N]}$, c , k^b).
- Finally, the adversary produces a guess b' for b.

Definition 4. *A threshold broadcast scheme is secure if, for all PPT adversaries $\mathcal{A}$, there exists a negligible* negl *such that* $\Pr[b' = b] \leq 1/2 + \text{negl}(\lambda)$.

8.1   From Threshold Broadcast to Traitor Tracing

Here, we formalize and prove Theorem 4:

Theorem 4 (Formal Version). *Suppose there exists a secure threshold broadcast scheme which, for $u = \lambda$ has size $(P = P(v), S = S(v), C = C(v))$. Then there exists a secure broadcast and trace multi-scheme in the shared randomness model with size $(P(N), S(N), C(N), N)$.*

To prove the theorem, let $\Pi_0 = (\text{Gen}_0, \text{Enc}_0, \text{Extract}_0, \text{Dec}_0)$ be a threshold broadcast scheme satisfying the given size requirement.

Construction 4. *Let $\Pi = (\text{Gen}, \text{Enc}, \text{Dec}, \text{Trace})$ be the tuple of the following PPT algorithms:*

- *Gen($1^N, 1^M, 1^\lambda$): run (pk, msk) $\leftarrow$ Gen$_0$($1^u, 1^v, 1^t, 1^\lambda$), where $u = \omega(\log \lambda)$, $v = Nu$, and $t = (2/5)u$. Let $[\![\cdot]\!]$ be an arbitrary efficient injection from $[M] \times [N] \times [u] \times \{0, 1\}$ into the identity space $[2^\lambda]$. For each $i \in [N], j \in [M]$, choose a random $x_{j,i} \in \{0, 1\}^u$. Set $U_{j,i} = \{[\![j, i, \ell, x_{i,j,\ell}]\!]\}_{\ell \in [u]} \subseteq [2^\lambda]$ and run sk$_{j,i} \leftarrow$ Extract$_0$(msk, $U_{j,i}$). Output pk as the public key, tk $= (x_{j,i})_{i \in [N], j \in [M]}$ as the tracing key, and (sk$_{j,i}$)$_{i \in [N], j \in [M]}$ as the secret keys.*
- *Enc(pk, j, S, r): here, $r \in \{0, 1\}^{N \times u}$ is the public randomness, which will be interpreted as the list $r = (r_{i,\ell})_{i \in [N], \ell \in [u]}$, $r_{i\ell} \in \{0, 1\}$. Let $T_{j,S,r} = \{[\![j, i, \ell, r_{i,\ell}]\!]\}_{i \in S, \ell \in [u]}$. Run and output $(c, k) \leftarrow$ Enc$_0$(pk, $T_{j,S,r}$).*

- $\mathsf{Dec}(\mathsf{pk}, \mathsf{sk}_{j,i}, S, r, c)$: *Output* $k' \leftarrow \mathsf{Dec}_0(\mathsf{pk}, \mathsf{sk}_{j,i}, T_{j,S,r}, c)$ *for* $T_{j,S,r}$ *as above.*
- $\mathsf{Trace}^D(\mathsf{tk}, j, \epsilon)$ *will be described below.*

Notice that $|U_{j,i}| = u$ and $|T_{j,r}| = Nu$ to that $|T_{j,S,r}| \leq Nu = v$. Also, notice that if we set $u \leq \lambda$, Π will have the desired size parameter, since the factor of $u \leq \lambda$ can be absorbed into the terms hidden by the notation. Next, notice that, by the correctness of Π_0, we must have that $k' = k$, so Π is correct.

Trace. We now explain how to trace. Due to lack of space, we sketch the tracing algorithm, assuming the ability to *perfectly* estimate the decoder's success probability on distributions of ciphertexts. In reality, such probabilities will need to be estimated; it is straightforward but tedious to handle such estimates.

1. We will initialize a probability distribution Z over $\{0,1\}^{Nu}$, which is initially uniform. Let $p_Z = \Pr[D(c, r, k^b) = b : r \leftarrow Z, (c, k^0) \leftarrow \mathsf{Enc}_0(\mathsf{pk}, T_{j,S,r}), k^1 \leftarrow \mathcal{K}, b \leftarrow \{0,1\}]$ be the probability that D correctly distinguishes a random ciphertext using the set $T_{j,S,r}$ for $r \leftarrow Z$. Let p^* be the initial value of p_Z, the probability the decoder correctly guesses b uniform r.
2. Initialize an empty set A. Then, for each $i \in S$ do the following:
   (a) Initialize a counter $\mathsf{ctr}_i = 0$.
   (b) For $\ell = 1, \ldots, u$ do the following:
      i. Let Z_b be the current Z, but conditioned on $r_{i,\ell} = b$. Compute probabilities $p_0 := p_{Z_0}, p_1 := p_{Z_1}$.
      ii. If $p_{1-x_{j,i,\ell}} \geq p^*$, update Z to $Z_{1-x_{j,i,\ell}}$ and set $\mathsf{ctr}_i = \mathsf{ctr}_i + 1$. Otherwise do not update Z.
   (c) If $\mathsf{ctr}_i/u \leq 2/5$, add user i to A.
3. Output A.

The following theorem then establishes Theorem 4:

Theorem 13. *Assuming Π_0 is a secure threshold broadcast scheme and $u = \omega(\log \lambda)$, Construction 4 is a secure broadcast and trace multi-scheme.*

Proof. Due to lack of space, we only sketch the proof. Trace always maintains the invariant that $p_Z \geq p^*$. In Step 2(b)i, we thus have $(p_0 + p_1)/2 \geq p^*$, meaning at least one of p_0 or p_1 are at least p^*. If user i of instance j is honest, $x_{j,i,\ell}$ is independent of the attacker's view and therefore $p_{1-x_{j,i,\ell}} \geq p^*$ with probability $\geq 1/2$. For honest users, ctr_i will therefore concentrate around $u/2$, and be larger than $(2/5)u$ with overwhelming probability. Thus honest users are not accused.

On the other hand, consider a user i of instance j that is *not* accused. Consider the set $T_{j,S,r} \cap \{[\![j,i,\ell,b]\!]\}_{\ell \in [u], b \in \{0,1\}}$. Once we have finished processing user i, the distribution Z fixes at least $(2/5)u$ of the entries within this set to be *outside* of $U_{j,i}$, and the remaining $\leq (3/5)u$ of the entries are randomly chosen to be either in the set or outside. Therefore, the size of the overlap with $U_{j,i}$ will concentrate around $(3/10)u \leq (2/5)u$. Thus, any user that is not accused will, with overwhelming probability, be unable to decrypt by the end. Since by the end we know that some user can still decrypt (due to our invariant $\geq p^*$), this means *some* user must be accused. $\square$

8.2 Construction of Threshold Broadcast Encryption

We prove the following, which combined with Theorem 13 gives Corollary 4:

Theorem 5 (Formal Version). *There exists a threshold broadcast scheme from pairings which, for $u = \lambda$ has size $(v, 1, 1)$, with security proved in the generic group model.*

Proof. Here, we only sketch the construction; the proof in the generic group model is given in the full version [Zha20]. The scheme is based on ideas from [Del07] (see Sect. 7.3) and from [AHL+12]. For an upper bound v on $|S|$, the public key is identical to Delerablée's scheme:

$$\mathsf{pk} = (e(g_1, g_2)^\beta, g_1^{\beta\gamma}, (g_2^{\gamma^j})_{j \in [0,v]})$$

Recalling $J(P) = g_2^{P(\gamma)}$, the ciphertext is also identical to Delerablée:

$$c_1 = g_1^{\alpha\beta\gamma} \quad, \quad c_2 = J\left(\prod_{i \in S}(1 - \gamma/i)\right)^\alpha = g_2^{\alpha \prod_{i \in S}(1 - \gamma/i)}$$

with encapsulated key $k = e(g_1, g_2)^{\alpha\beta}$. The secret key for a set U is

$$\mathsf{sk}_U = \left(g_1^{\beta\gamma^j / \prod_{i \in U}(1 - \gamma/i)}\right)_{j=0,\ldots,|U|-t}$$

where t is the threshold. Notice the size of the secret key is $O(|U|)$; in particular for $|U| = \lambda$ it is independent of v. Notice that, from sk_U, one can compute $g_1^{\beta Q(\gamma)/\prod_{i \in U}(1 - \gamma/i)}$ for any polynomial Q of degree at most $|U| - t$.

To decrypt, notice that, since $U \cap S$ has size at least t, $\prod_{i \in U \setminus S}(1 - \gamma/i)$ is a polynomial of degree at most $|U| - t$. Therefore, using sk_U, compute

$$g_1^{\beta \prod_{i \in U \setminus S}(1 - \gamma/i)/\prod_{i \in U}(1 - \gamma/i)} = g_1^{\beta/\prod_{i \in U \cap S}(1 - \gamma/i)} \quad ,$$

canceling out all poles in sk_U that are not in S. From here, decryption proceeds analogously to Delerablée. Security—in the generic group model—follows a similar argument as in Delerablée, see the full version [Zha20] for details. $\square$

9 Our $\sqrt[3]{N}$ Scheme

We now briefly explain how to prove Theorem 6, establishing a pairing-based multi-scheme of size $(\sqrt{N}, \sqrt{N}, 1, \sqrt{N})$ in the shared randomness model, with security proved in the generic group model. Combined with Theorem 1 setting $T = N^{1/3}$ gives our $\sqrt[3]{N}$-sized scheme.

Set $u = \omega(\log \lambda)$ and $t = (2/5)u$. We interpret the user identity space $[N]$ as $[\sqrt{N}] \times [\sqrt{N}]$; we will alternatively treat each identity i as either a number in

$[N]$ or a pair $(i_0, i_1) \in [\sqrt{N}]^2$. Our public key is identical to our risky version of Delerablée (Sect. 7.3), just for $\sqrt{N}$ users:

$$\mathsf{pk} = \left(e(g_1, g_2)^\beta, g_1^{(\beta\gamma\,,\,0\,,\,0\,,\,0)\cdot R^{-1}}, \left(g_2^{(\gamma^i\,,\,0\,,\,0\,,\,0)\cdot R^T}\right)_{j\in[0,\sqrt{N}]} \right)$$

Let $[\![\cdot]\!]$ be an arbitrarily efficient injection from $[M] \times [\sqrt{N}] \times [u] \times \{0,1\}$ into $\mathbb{Z}_p \setminus \{0\}$. Let $\mathcal{X}$ be a polynomial-sized set and $f : [M] \times [N] \to \mathcal{X}$ be a function to be specified later.

For each instance j, choose a random $i_j^* \in [\sqrt{N}]$, and assign identity $i = (i_0, i_1)$ the attribute $(x_0, x_1) = (0,0), (1,0)$, and $(1,1)$, for $i_0 < i_j^*, i_0 = i_j^*$, and $i_0 > i_j^*$ respectively. Additionally, for each $\theta \in \mathcal{X}$, choose a random scalar $\tau_\theta \in \mathbb{Z}_p$.

To generate secret key for user i of instance j, let $\theta = f(j, i)$. Let $i = (i_0, i_1)$. Choose a random $x_{j,i} \in \{0,1\}^u$, and let $U_{j,i} = \{[\![j, i_1, \ell, x_{i,j,\ell}]\!]\}_{\ell \in [u]} \subseteq \mathbb{Z}_p \setminus \{0\}$. The secret key is very similar to our risky broadcast scheme, but modified to use τ_θ instead of β:

$$\mathsf{sk}_{j,i} = \left(g_1^{\left(\tau_\theta \gamma^\ell / \prod_{s\in U_{j,i}}(1-\gamma/s)\,,\,x_1 v_{1,\ell}\,,\,x_2 v_{2,\ell}\,,\,v_{3,\ell}\right)\cdot R^{-1}} \right)_{\ell=0,\dots,u-t}$$

where the $v_{x,\ell}$ are chosen freshly for each secret key. Additionally, user i of instance j is given a "helper key":

$$\mathsf{hk}_\theta = \left(h_\theta := g_2^{\left(\frac{\beta-\tau_\theta}{\beta\gamma}\,,\,0\,,\,0\,,\,0\right)\cdot R^T}, \left(g_2^{(\tau_\theta \gamma^i\,,\,0\,,\,0\,,\,0)\cdot R^T}\right)_{j\in[0,\sqrt{N}]} \right)$$

The ciphertext for attribute (y_1, y_2) is

$$c_1 = g_1^{(\alpha\beta\gamma\,,\,0\,,\,0\,,\,0)\cdot R^{-1}} \quad,\quad c_2 = g_2^{\left(\alpha\prod_{s\in T_{j,r}}(1-\gamma/s)\,,\,y_1 v_1\,,\,y_2 v_2\,,\,0\right)\cdot R^T}$$

where $r \in \{0,1\}^{u\sqrt{N}}$ is the $u\sqrt{N} = O(\sqrt{N})$ bits of shared randomness, and $T_{j,r} = \{[\![j, i_1, \ell, r_{i_1,\ell}]\!]\}_{i_1 \in [\sqrt{N}], \ell\in[u]}$. The encapsulated key is $e(g_1, g_2)^{\alpha\beta}$. A valid ciphertext has attribute $(0,0)$, and can be computed from the public key.

Decryption starts off analogously to our threshold broadcast scheme, allowing a user who is authorized to decrypt to compute $H = e(g_1, g_2)^{\alpha\tau_\theta}$, using the components of hk_θ in place of the public key. It remains to convert this into $e(g_1, g_2)^{\alpha\beta}$. This is accomplished by multiplying H by $e(c_1, h_\theta) = e(g_1, g_2)^{\alpha(\beta-\tau_\theta)}$.

(Risky) tracing works roughly as follows: first we perform a risky tracing, analogous to [GKRW18], and then we trace using our threshold broadcast technique from Sect. 8. In more detail, we first test a decoder on ciphertexts with attributes $(0,1), (1,1)$. If the decoder *cannot* distinguish $(0,1)$ from $(1,1)$, we abort and accuse no one. If the decoder *can* distinguish, then we accuse the "half identity" $i_0 = i_j^*$. We are not done, since we need to fill in the second half identity

i_1. Here, we trace as in Sect. 8, gradually attempting to "turn off" all the users (i_j^*, i_1) for $i_1 = 1, \ldots, \sqrt{N}$ by trying to remove elements in $U_{j,(i_j^*, i_1)}$ from $T_{j,r}$. We accuse any user (i_j^*, i_1) where turning off that user fails.

Note that two users with the same i_1 and j will have overlapping sets U. Turning off both users would thus place incompatible constraints on the set $T_{j,r}$, and hence both cannot be simultaneously turned off. Therefore, we can only freely turn off users for distinct i_1. This is why we trace i_0 first, and then i_1. Also note that, when tracing i_1, turning off an honest user (i_0, i_1) will succeed even if the adversary controls a different user with the same i_1 (but different i_0), since turning off users only required that the set $U_{j,i}$ was unknown to the adversary. This "independence" is crucial for this layered tracing approach to work[11].

Choosing f. There are two requirements we need from f. First, for security, we need that no two secret keys with overlapping U get mapped to the same θ, for reasons similar to why our threshold broadcast scheme is insecure for overlapping U. Therefore, we need that $f(j, (i_0, i_1)) \neq f(j, (i_0', i_1))$ for any j, i_1 and $i_0 \neq i_0'$. Once this requirement is met, the following is proved in the full version [Zha20]:

Lemma 1. *The scheme above is $1/\sqrt{N}$-risky in the generic group model.*

Second, excluding the helper keys hk_θ (which have size $O(\sqrt{N})$), the secret keys are constant-sized. Applying Theorem 3/Construction 3, the secret key will now contain the secret keys and helper keys from $O(\sqrt{N})$ different instances. In order to ensure that the overall secret key remains $O(\sqrt{N})$, we require all of the constituent instances to have the same helper key. Thus, we need $f(j_0, i) = f(j_1, i)$, for all j_0, j_1 that get mapped to the same secret key when applying Construction 3. Recall that Construction 3 interpreted $[M]$ as $[M'] \times [T]$, and instance $j = (j', t)$ gets mapped to j'. Thus, setting $\mathcal{X}$ to be the set $[M'] \times [N]$ and $f((j', t), i) = (j', i)$ will satisfy both conditions, giving Theorem 6.

10   Running Times

Here, we briefly discuss the running times of our constructions; see the full version [Zha20] for a more in-depth discussion.

We will say that a traitor tracing scheme Π is *asymptotically efficient* if each of Gen, Enc, and Dec have running times bounded by $(|\mathsf{input}| + |\mathsf{output}|) \times \mathsf{poly}(\lambda)$.

---

[11] A natural question is whether a similar layer of risky tracing can be added on top of [BSW06], potentially giving a simpler path toward $\sqrt[3]{N}$. Unfortunately, [BSW06] in a sense "uses up" the pairing, preventing any risky layer from being independent of the underlying PLBE-based tracing. Concretely, the obvious approach would yield a scheme where it was *not* possible to turn off an honest user if the adversary controlled a different user with the same i_1. Our construction gets around this issue by having the second layer tracing happen "outside" the pairing, in the shared randomness.

We note that all of our algebraic instantiations are asymptotically efficient, and that our threshold elimination and risk mitigation compilers (Theorems 2 and 3) preserve asymptotic efficiency. However, if the running time of Enc is longer than the ciphertext size (which is in particular possible when public keys are larger than ciphertexts), our user expansion compiler (Theorem 7) does *not* preserve asymptotic efficiency: the running time and ciphertext size get multiplied by a factor of T, but the input to Enc (namely, the public key) stays the same.

This issue affects our $(N^{1-a}, 1, N^a, N^{1-a})$ threshold broadcast-based construction, as well as our $\sqrt[3]{N}$ scheme. For our other schemes, the public key is smaller than the ciphertext, and hence this is not an issue.

In the full version, we explain how to remove the inefficiency from these two constructions; thus all of our constructions can be made asymptotically efficient. We carefully choose how the user identities are embedded in $\mathbb{Z}_p$. The result is that generating the multiple ciphertext components for Theorem 7 reduces to evaluating a polynomial at multiple points, except that the coefficients of the polynomial and the resulting evaluations are *in the exponent* of the pairing. Thus, we carry out fast multi-point polynomial evaluation methods "in the exponent"; this incurs a $\mathsf{polylog}(N)$ overhead, which can be absorbed into the $\mathsf{poly}(\lambda)$ term.

References

[ABP+17] Agrawal, S., Bhattacherjee, S., Phan, D.H., Stehlé, D., Yamada, S.: Efficient public trace and revoke from standard assumptions: extended abstract. In: Thuraisingham, B.M., Evans, D., Malkin, T., Xu, D. (eds.) ACM CCS 2017, pp. 2277–2293. ACM Press (2017)

[ADM+07] Abdalla, M., Dent, A.W., Malone-Lee, J., Neven, G., Phan, D.H., Smart, N.P.: Identity-based traitor tracing. In: Okamoto, T., Wang, X. (eds.) PKC 2007. LNCS, vol. 4450, pp. 361–376. Springer, Heidelberg (2007). https://doi.org/10.1007/978-3-540-71677-8_24

[AHL+12] Attrapadung, N., Herranz, J., Laguillaumie, F., Libert, B., de Panafieu, E., Ràfols, C.: Attribute-based encryption schemes with constant-size ciphertexts. Theor. Comput. Sci. **422**, 15–38 (2012)

[AY20] Agrawal, S., Yamada, S.: Optimal broadcast encryption from pairings and LWE. In: Canteaut, A., Ishai, Y. (eds.) EUROCRYPT 2020. LNCS, vol. 12105, pp. 13–43. Springer, Cham (2020). https://doi.org/10.1007/978-3-030-45721-1_2

[BF99] Boneh, D., Franklin, M.: An efficient public key traitor tracing scheme. In: Wiener, M. (ed.) CRYPTO 1999. LNCS, vol. 1666, pp. 338–353. Springer, Heidelberg (1999). https://doi.org/10.1007/3-540-48405-1_22

[BGW05] Boneh, D., Gentry, C., Waters, B.: Collusion resistant broadcast encryption with short ciphertexts and private keys. In: Shoup, V. (ed.) CRYPTO 2005. LNCS, vol. 3621, pp. 258–275. Springer, Heidelberg (2005). https://doi.org/10.1007/11535218_16

[BKM10] Boneh, D., Kiayias, A., Montgomery, H.W.: Robust fingerprinting codes: a near optimal construction. In: Proceedings of the Tenth Annual ACM Workshop on Digital Rights Management, DRM 2010, pp. 3–12. Association for Computing Machinery (2010)

[BN08]   Boneh, D., Naor, M.: Traitor tracing with constant size ciphertext. In: Ning, P., Syverson, P.F., Jha, S. (eds.) ACM CCS 2008, pp. 501–510. ACM Press (2008)

[BS95]   Boneh, D., Shaw, J.: Collusion-secure fingerprinting for digital data. In: Coppersmith, D. (ed.) CRYPTO 1995. LNCS, vol. 963, pp. 452–465. Springer, Heidelberg (1995). https://doi.org/10.1007/3-540-44750-4_36

[BSW06] Boneh, D., Sahai, A., Waters, B.: Fully collusion resistant traitor tracing with short ciphertexts and private keys. In: Vaudenay, S. (ed.) EURO-CRYPT 2006. LNCS, vol. 4004, pp. 573–592. Springer, Heidelberg (2006). https://doi.org/10.1007/11761679_34

[BSW07] Bethencourt, J., Sahai, A., Waters, B.: Ciphertext-policy attribute-based encryption. In: 2007 IEEE Symposium on Security and Privacy, pp. 321–334. IEEE Computer Society Press (2007)

[BW06]   Boneh, D., Waters, B.: A fully collusion resistant broadcast, trace, and revoke system. In: Juels, A., Wright, R.N., De Capitani di Vimercati, S. (eds.) ACM CCS 2006, pp. 211–220. ACM Press (2006)

[BZ14]   Boneh, D., Zhandry, M.: Multiparty key exchange, efficient traitor tracing, and more from indistinguishability obfuscation. In: Garay, J.A., Gennaro, R. (eds.) CRYPTO 2014. LNCS, vol. 8616, pp. 480–499. Springer, Heidelberg (2014). https://doi.org/10.1007/978-3-662-44371-2_27

[CFN94] Chor, B., Fiat, A., Naor, M.: Tracing traitors. In: Desmedt, Y.G. (ed.) CRYPTO 1994. LNCS, vol. 839, pp. 257–270. Springer, Heidelberg (1994). https://doi.org/10.1007/3-540-48658-5_25

[CVW+18] Chen, Y., Vaikuntanathan, V., Waters, B., Wee, H., Wichs, D.: Traitor-tracing from LWE made simple and attribute-based. In: Beimel, A., Dziembowski, S. (eds.) TCC 2018, Part II. LNCS, vol. 11240, pp. 341–369. Springer, Cham (2018). https://doi.org/10.1007/978-3-030-03810-6_13

[Del07] Delerablée, C.: Identity-based broadcast encryption with constant size ciphertexts and private keys. In: Kurosawa, K. (ed.) ASIACRYPT 2007. LNCS, vol. 4833, pp. 200–215. Springer, Heidelberg (2007). https://doi.org/10.1007/978-3-540-76900-2_12

[DG17]   Döttling, N., Garg, S.: Identity-based encryption from the Diffie-Hellman assumption. In: Katz, J., Shacham, H. (eds.) CRYPTO 2017, Part I. LNCS, vol. 10401, pp. 537–569. Springer, Cham (2017). https://doi.org/10.1007/978-3-319-63688-7_18

[GGH+13] Garg, S., Gentry, C., Halevi, S., Raykova, M., Sahai, A., Waters, B.: Candidate indistinguishability obfuscation and functional encryption for all circuits. In: 54th FOCS, pp. 40–49. IEEE Computer Society Press (2013)

[GKRW18] Goyal, R., Koppula, V., Russell, A., Waters, B.: Risky traitor tracing and new differential privacy negative results. In: Shacham, H., Boldyreva, A. (eds.) CRYPTO 2018, Part I. LNCS, vol. 10991, pp. 467–497. Springer, Cham (2018). https://doi.org/10.1007/978-3-319-96884-1_16

[GKSW10] Garg, S., Kumarasubramanian, A., Sahai, A., Waters, B.: Building efficient fully collusion-resilient traitor tracing and revocation schemes. In: Al-Shaer, E., Keromytis, A.D., Shmatikov, V. (eds.) ACM CCS 2010, pp. 121–130. ACM Press (2010)

[GKW18] Goyal, R., Koppula, V., Waters, B.: Collusion resistant traitor tracing from learning with errors. In: Diakonikolas, I., Kempe, D., Henzinger, M. (eds.) 50th ACM STOC, pp. 660–670. ACM Press (2018)

[GKW19] Goyal, R., Koppula, V., Waters, B.: New approaches to traitor tracing with embedded identities. In: Hofheinz, D., Rosen, A. (eds.) TCC 2019, Part II. LNCS, vol. 11892, pp. 149–179. Springer, Cham (2019). https://doi.org/10.1007/978-3-030-36033-7_6

[GL89] Goldreich, O., Levin, L.A.: A hard-core predicate for all one-way functions. In: 21st ACM STOC, pp. 25–32. ACM Press (1989)

[GQWW19] Goyal, R., Quach, W., Waters, B., Wichs, D.: Broadcast and trace with N^ε ciphertext size from standard assumptions. In: Boldyreva, A., Micciancio, D. (eds.) CRYPTO 2019, Part II. LNCS, vol. 11694, pp. 826–855. Springer, Cham (2019). https://doi.org/10.1007/978-3-030-26954-8_27

[GVW19] Goyal, R., Vusirikala, S., Waters, B.: Collusion resistant broadcast and trace from positional witness encryption. In: Lin, D., Sako, K. (eds.) PKC 2019, Part I. LNCS, vol. 11443, pp. 3–33. Springer, Cham (2019). https://doi.org/10.1007/978-3-030-17259-6_1

[KMUW18] Kowalczyk, L., Malkin, T., Ullman, J., Wichs, D.: Hardness of non-interactive differential privacy from one-way functions. In: Shacham, H., Boldyreva, A. (eds.) CRYPTO 2018, Part I. LNCS, vol. 10991, pp. 437–466. Springer, Cham (2018). https://doi.org/10.1007/978-3-319-96884-1_15

[KMUZ16] Kowalczyk, L., Malkin, T., Ullman, J., Zhandry, M.: Strong hardness of privacy from weak traitor tracing. In: Hirt, M., Smith, A. (eds.) TCC 2016, Part I. LNCS, vol. 9985, pp. 659–689. Springer, Heidelberg (2016). https://doi.org/10.1007/978-3-662-53641-4_25

[KW19] Kim, S., Wu, D.J.: Collusion resistant trace-and-revoke for arbitrary identities from standard assumptions. Cryptology ePrint Archive, Report 2019/984 (2019). https://eprint.iacr.org/2019/984

[KY02] Kiayias, A., Yung, M.: Self-tallying elections and perfect ballot secrecy. In: Naccache, D., Paillier, P. (eds.) PKC 2002. LNCS, vol. 2274, pp. 141–158. Springer, Heidelberg (2002). https://doi.org/10.1007/3-540-45664-3_10

[LPSS14] Ling, S., Phan, D.H., Stehlé, D., Steinfeld, R.: Hardness of k-LWE and applications in traitor tracing. In: Garay, J.A., Gennaro, R. (eds.) CRYPTO 2014, Part I. LNCS, vol. 8616, pp. 315–334. Springer, Heidelberg (2014). https://doi.org/10.1007/978-3-662-44371-2_18

[NP98] Naor, M., Pinkas, B.: Threshold traitor tracing. In: Krawczyk, H. (ed.) CRYPTO 1998. LNCS, vol. 1462, pp. 502–517. Springer, Heidelberg (1998). https://doi.org/10.1007/BFb0055750

[NWZ16] Nishimaki, R., Wichs, D., Zhandry, M.: Anonymous traitor tracing: how to embed arbitrary information in a key. In: Fischlin, M., Coron, J.-S. (eds.) EUROCRYPT 2016, Part II. LNCS, vol. 9666, pp. 388–419. Springer, Heidelberg (2016). https://doi.org/10.1007/978-3-662-49896-5_14

[Tar03] Tardos, G.: Optimal probabilistic fingerprint codes. In: 35th ACM STOC, pp. 116–125. ACM Press (2003)

[TZ17] Tang, B., Zhang, J.: Barriers to black-box constructions of traitor tracing systems. In: Kalai, Y., Reyzin, L. (eds.) TCC 2017, Part I. LNCS, vol. 10677, pp. 3–30. Springer, Cham (2017). https://doi.org/10.1007/978-3-319-70500-2_1

[Zha20] Zhandry, M.: New techniques for traitor tracing (2020). Full Version

Public Key Cryptography

Functional Encryption for
Attribute-Weighted Sums from k-Lin

Michel Abdalla[1] , Junqing Gong[2]([⊠]), and Hoeteck Wee[1,3]

[1] CNRS, ENS and PSL, Paris, France
michel.abdalla@ens.fr, wee@di.ens.fr
[2] East China Normal University, Shanghai, China
jqgong@sei.ecnu.edu.cn
[3] NTT Research, Palo Alto, CA, USA

Abstract. We present functional encryption schemes for attribute-weighted sums, where encryption takes as input N attribute-value pairs (x_i, z_i) where x_i is public and z_i is private; secret keys are associated with arithmetic branching programs f, and decryption returns the weighted sum $\sum_{i=1}^{N} f(x_i)z_i$ while leaking no additional information about the z_i's. Our main construction achieves

(1) compact public parameters and key sizes that are independent of N and the secret key can decrypt a ciphertext for any a-priori unbounded N;

(2) short ciphertexts that grow with N and the size of z_i but not x_i;

(3) simulation-based security against unbounded collusions;

(4) relies on the standard k-linear assumption in prime-order bilinear groups.

1 Introduction

In this work, we consider the problem of computing aggregate statistics on encrypted databases. Consider a database of N attribute-value pairs $(x_i, z_i)_{i=1,\ldots,N}$, where x_i is a public attribute of user i (e.g. demographic data), and z_i is private sensitive data associated with user i (e.g. salary, medical condition, loans, college admissions outcome). Given a function f, we want to privately compute weighted sums over the z_i's corresponding to

$$\sum_{i=1}^{N} f(x_i)z_i$$

We refer to this quantity as an *attribute-weighted sum*. An important special case is when f is a boolean predicate, so that the attribute-weighted sum

$$\sum_{i=1}^{N} f(x_i)z_i = \sum_{i:f(x_i)=1} z_i \tag{1}$$

M. Abdalla—Supported by ERC Project aSCEND (H2020 639554) and the French FUI project ANBLIC.

J. Gong—Supported by NSFC-ISF Joint Scientific Research Program (61961146004) and the ERC Project aSCEND (H2020 639554). Part of this work was done while at ENS, Paris.

H. Wee—Supported in part by ERC Project aSCEND (H2020 639554).

© International Association for Cryptologic Research 2020
D. Micciancio and T. Ristenpart (Eds.): CRYPTO 2020, LNCS 12170, pp. 685–716, 2020.
https://doi.org/10.1007/978-3-030-56784-2_23

corresponds to the average z_i over all users whose attribute x_i satisfies the predicate f. Concrete examples include average salaries of minority groups holding a particular job title (z_i = salary) and approval ratings of an election candidate amongst specific demographic groups in a particular state (z_i = rating). Similarly, if z_i is boolean, then the attribute-weighted sum becomes $\sum_{i:z_i=1} f(x_i)$. This could capture for instance the number of and average age of smokers with lung cancer (z_i = lung cancer).

This work. We study functional encryption (FE) schemes for attribute-weighted sums [13,24,26,36], for a more general setting where the attribute-value pairs and the output of f are vectors. That is, we would like to encrypt N attribute-value pairs $(\mathbf{x}_i, \mathbf{z}_i)_{i=1,\dots,N}$ to produce a ciphertext ct, and generate secret keys sk_f so that decrypting ct with sk_f returns the attribute-weighted sum $\sum_i f(\mathbf{x}_i)^\top \mathbf{z}_i$ while leaking no additional information about the individual $\mathbf{z}_i$'s. We want to support rich and expressive functions f, such as boolean formula and simple arithmetic computation. In addition, we want simulation-based security against collusions, so that an adversary holding secret keys for different functions learns nothing about the $\mathbf{z}_i$'s beyond the attribute-weighted sums for all of these functions.

In many databases, it is often the case that the size of each attribute-value pair $(\mathbf{x}_i, \mathbf{z}_i)$ is small and a-priori bounded, whereas the number of *slots* N is large and a-priori *unbounded*. This motivates the notion of an *unbounded-slot* FE scheme for attribute-weighted sums, where a secret key sk_f can decrypt encrypted databases with an arbitrary number of slots. Indeed, handling arbitrary-sized inputs is also the motivation behind studying ABE and FE schemes for DFA and NFA [7,38]. In an unbounded-slot FE, key generation and the size of sk_f depends only on f and not N. This provides stronger flexibility than standard ABE and FE (even in the so-called unbounded setting [14,19,25,32]), where each sk_f only works for a fixed N. In practice, this means that we can reuse the same set-up and secret keys across multiple databases without an a-priori upper bound on the database size N.

1.1   Our Results

We present an *unbounded-slot* functional encryption scheme for attribute-weighted sums for the class of functions f captured by arithmetic branching programs (ABP), a powerful model of computation that captures both boolean formula and branching programs with only a linear blow-up in size. Our construction achieves:

(1) compact public parameters and key sizes that are independent of N;
(2) short ciphertexts that grow with N and the size of $\mathbf{z}_i$ but not $\mathbf{x}_i$;
(3) selective[1], simulation-based security against unbounded collusions;
(4) relies on the standard k-linear assumption in prime-order bilinear groups.

---

[1] We actually achieve semi-adaptive security [16], a slight strengthening of selective security.

As with all prior FE schemes that rely on DDH and bilinear groups [1,3,6,10, 17,28,29,33], efficient decryption requires that the output of the computation $\sum_{i=1}^{N} f(\mathbf{x}_i)^\top \mathbf{z}_i$ lies in a polynomial-size domain. We also show how to extend our unbounded-slot scheme to a setting where the database is distributed across multiple clients that do not completely trust one another [18,21], assuming some simple non-interactive MPC set-up amongst the clients that does not depend on the database and does not require interaction with the key authority.

Prior works. While we regard the unbounded-slot setting as the key conceptual and technical novelty of this work, we note that FE for attribute-weighted sums for $N = 1$ already captures many functionalities considered in the literature, e.g.

  (i) FE for inner product [1,6] where f outputs a fixed vector,
 (ii) attribute-based encryption (ABE) by taking z to be the payload,
(iii) attribute-based inner-product FE [2,17], where ciphertexts are associated with a public $\mathbf{x}$ and a private $\mathbf{z}$, and keys with a boolean formula g and a vector $\mathbf{y}$, and decryption returns $\mathbf{z}^\top \mathbf{y}$ iff $g(\mathbf{x}) = 1$, by taking $f(\mathbf{x}) := \mathbf{y} \cdot g(\mathbf{x})$, which can be computed using an ABP.

On the other hand, none of these three classes captures the special case of attribute-weighted sums in (1). We show a comparison in Fig. 1. The more recent works in [28,29] do capture a larger class supporting quadratic instead of linear functions over $\mathbf{z}$,[2] but in a weaker secret-key setting with indistinguishability-based security, which is nonetheless sufficient for the application to obfuscation. As articulated [13], simulation-based security is the right notion for functional encryption applied to real-world data. Finally, none of these works consider the unbounded-slot setting.

1.2 Our Construction

We present a high-level overview of our unbounded-slot FE scheme for attribute-weighted sums. We start with a one-slot scheme that only handles $N = 1$, and then "bootstrap" to the unbounded-slot setting. The main technical novelty of this work lies in the bootstrapping, which is what we would focus on in this section.

A one-slot scheme. In a one-slot FE scheme, we want to encrypt $(\mathbf{x}, \mathbf{z})$ and generate secret keys sk_f for computing $f(\mathbf{x})^\top \mathbf{z}$, while leaking no additional information about $\mathbf{z}$. We adopt the framework of Wee's [40] (which in turn builds on [27,30,37,39]) that builds a FE scheme for a closely related functionality $f(\mathbf{x})^\top \mathbf{z} \stackrel{?}{=} 0$; the construction also achieves selective, simulation-based security under the k-Lin assumption in prime-order bilinear groups. We achieve a smaller

---

[2] Note that we can also capture the same class with a quadratic blow-up in ciphertext size.

ciphertext, and an algebraically more concise and precise description. Our simulator also embeds the output of the ideal functionality $f(\mathbf{x})^\top \mathbf{z}$ into the simulated sk_f. This is in some sense inherent for two reasons: (i) the ciphertext has a fixed size and cannot accommodate an a-priori unbounded number of key queries [4], (ii) in the selective setting, we do not know f or $f(\mathbf{x})^\top \mathbf{z}$ while simulating the ciphertext.

The unbounded-slot scheme. A very natural approach is to use the one-slot scheme to compute

$$f(\mathbf{x}_i)^\top \mathbf{z}_i, i = 1, 2, \ldots, N \tag{2}$$

by providing N independent encryptions $\mathsf{ct}_{\mathbf{x}_i, \mathbf{z}_i}$ of $(\mathbf{x}_i, \mathbf{z}_i)$. The secret key is exactly that for the one-slot scheme and therefore independent of N, and decryption proceeds by decrypting each of the N one-slot ciphertexts, and then computing their sum. The only problem with this approach is that it is insecure since decryption leaks the intermediate summands.

First idea. To avoid this leakage, we would computationally mask the summands using DDH tuples, by using the one-slot scheme to compute

$$[f(\mathbf{x}_i)^\top \mathbf{z}_i + w_i r], \ i = 1, 2, \ldots, N \tag{3}$$

where

- the w_i's are sampled during encryption subject to the constraint $\sum_{i=1}^N w_i = 0$;
- r is fresh per secret key; and
- $[\cdot]$ denotes "in the exponent" of a bilinear group.

Multiplying the partial decryptions yields $[\sum_i f(\mathbf{x}_i)^\top \mathbf{z}_i]$, and we need to perform a brute-force discrete log to recover the answer. Indeed, we can modify the one-slot scheme to support the functionality in (3), where the one-slot encryption takes as input $(\mathbf{x}_i, \mathbf{z}_i \| w_i)$ (where w_i is also private) to produce a ciphertext $\mathsf{ct}_{\mathbf{x}_i, \mathbf{z}_i \| w_i}$, and with secret keys $\mathsf{sk}_{f,r}$ associated with (f, r). Henceforth, we describe the proof strategy for a single secret key query for simplicity, but everything we describe extends quite readily to an unbounded number of key queries.

The intuition is that the partial decryptions now yield

$$
\begin{aligned}
&(\ \mathsf{Dec}(\mathsf{sk}_{f,r}, \mathsf{ct}_{\mathbf{x}_1, \mathbf{z}_1 \| w_1}), \ \mathsf{Dec}(\mathsf{sk}_{f,r}, \mathsf{ct}_{\mathbf{x}_2, \mathbf{z}_2 \| w_2}), \ \ldots, \ \mathsf{Dec}(\mathsf{sk}_{f,r}, \mathsf{ct}_{\mathbf{x}_N, \mathbf{z}_N \| w_N}) \ ) \\
=\ &(\ [f(\mathbf{x}_1)^\top \mathbf{z}_1 + w_1 r], \quad [f(\mathbf{x}_2)^\top \mathbf{z}_2 + w_2 r], \quad \ldots, [f(\mathbf{x}_N)^\top \mathbf{z}_N + w_N r] \quad), \\
\overset{\text{DDH}}{\approx_c}\ &(\ [f(\mathbf{x}_1)^\top \mathbf{z}_1 + w_1'], \quad [f(\mathbf{x}_2)^\top \mathbf{z}_2 + w_2'], \quad \ldots, [f(\mathbf{x}_N)^\top \mathbf{z}_N + w_N'] \quad), \ \sum w_i' = 0 \\
\approx_s\ &(\ [\textstyle\sum_i f(\mathbf{x}_i)^\top \mathbf{z}_i + w_1'], \quad [w_2'], \qquad\qquad \ldots, [w_N'] \qquad\qquad),
\end{aligned}
$$

As with the one-slot scheme, we need to embed these N partial descriptions into $\mathsf{sk}_{f,r}$ in the proof of security. Translating this intuition into a proof would then require embedding $\approx N$ units of statistical entropy into the simulated $\mathsf{sk}_{f,r}$ in the final game; this means that the size of $\mathsf{sk}_{f,r}$ would grow with N, which we want to avoid!

Second idea. Instead, we will do a hybrid argument over the N slots, collecting "partial sums" $\sum_{i \leq \eta} f(\mathbf{x}_i)^\top \mathbf{z}_i$ (with $1 \leq \eta \leq N$) as we go along, which we then embed into the simulated $\mathsf{sk}_{f,r}$. This proof strategy is in fact inspired by proof techniques introduced in the recent ABE for DFA from k-Lin [22], notably the idea of propagating entropy along the execution path of a DFA.

In particular, for $N = 3$, partial decryption now yields

$$
\begin{array}{llll}
& (\ \mathsf{Dec}(\mathsf{sk}_{f,r}, \mathsf{ct}_{\mathbf{x}_1, \mathbf{z}_1 \| w_1}), & \mathsf{Dec}(\mathsf{sk}_{f,r}, \mathsf{ct}_{\mathbf{x}_2, \mathbf{z}_2 \| w_2}), & \mathsf{Dec}(\mathsf{sk}_{f,r}, \mathsf{ct}_{\mathbf{x}_3, \mathbf{z}_3 \| w_3}) \ ) \\
= & (\ [f(\mathbf{x}_1)^\top \mathbf{z}_1 + w_1 r], & [f(\mathbf{x}_2)^\top \mathbf{z}_2 + w_2 r], & [f(\mathbf{x}_3)^\top \mathbf{z}_3 + w_3 r] \ ) \\
\overset{\mathsf{DDH}}{\approx_c} & (\ [f(\mathbf{x}_1)^\top \mathbf{z}_1 + f(\mathbf{x}_2)^\top \mathbf{z}_2 + w_1 r], & [w_2 r], & [f(\mathbf{x}_3)^\top \mathbf{z}_3 + w_3 r] \ ) \\
\overset{\mathsf{DDH}}{\approx_c} & (\ [f(\mathbf{x}_1)^\top \mathbf{z}_1 + f(\mathbf{x}_2)^\top \mathbf{z}_2 + f(\mathbf{x}_3)^\top \mathbf{z}_3 + w_1 r], & [w_2 r], & [w_3 r] \ )
\end{array} \tag{4}
$$

where the first $\overset{\mathsf{DDH}}{\approx_c}$ uses pseudorandomness of $([w_2 r], [r])$ and the second uses that of $([w_3 r], [r])$.

Next, we need to design the ciphertext and key distributions for the unbounded-slot scheme so that partial decryption yields the quantities in (4). We begin by defining the final simulated ciphertext-key pair as follows:

$$
(\mathsf{ct}^*_{\mathbf{x}_1}, \mathsf{ct}_{\mathbf{x}_2, 0 \| w_2}, \ldots, \mathsf{ct}_{\mathbf{x}_N, 0 \| w_N}), \quad \mathsf{sk}^*_{f,r} \tag{5}
$$

where

- $(\mathsf{ct}^*_{\mathbf{x}_1}, \mathsf{sk}^*_{f,r})$ are obtained using the simulator for the one-slot scheme so that

$$
\mathsf{Dec}(\mathsf{sk}^*_{f,r}, \mathsf{ct}^*_{\mathbf{x}_1}) = [w_1 r + \sum_i f(\mathbf{x}_i)^\top \mathbf{z}_i]
$$

That is, we embed $[w_1 r + \sum_i f(\mathbf{x}_i)^\top \mathbf{z}_i]$ into the simulated $\mathsf{sk}^*_{f,r}$;
- $\mathsf{ct}_{\mathbf{x}_i, 0 \| w_i}, i > 1$ are generated as normal encryptions of $(\mathbf{x}_i, 0 \| w_i)$ (instead of normal encryptions of $(\mathbf{x}_i, \mathbf{z}_i \| w_i)$) so that

$$
\mathsf{Dec}(\mathsf{sk}^*_{f,r}, \mathsf{ct}_{\mathbf{x}_i, 0 \| w_i}) = \mathsf{Dec}(\mathsf{sk}_{f,r}, \mathsf{ct}_{\mathbf{x}_i, 0 \| w_i}) = [w_i r], i > 1
$$

Here, we use fact that simulated secret keys behave like normal secret keys when used to decrypt normal ciphertexts.

This distribution can be computed given just $\sum_i f(\mathbf{x}_i)^\top \mathbf{z}_i$ and matches exactly what we need in the final game in (4).

Third idea. Now, consider the following attempt to interpolate between the normal distributions and the simulated distributions for the case $N = 2$:

$$
\begin{array}{llll}
& (\ \mathsf{ct}_{\mathbf{x}_1, \mathbf{z}_1 \| w_1}, & \mathsf{ct}_{\mathbf{x}_2, \mathbf{z}_2 \| w_2}, & \mathsf{sk}_{f,r} \ ) \\
\approx_c & (\ \mathsf{ct}^*_{\mathbf{x}_1}, & \mathsf{ct}_{\mathbf{x}_2, \mathbf{z}_2 \| w_2}, & \mathsf{sk}^*_{f,r} \ ), & \mathsf{Dec}(\mathsf{sk}^*_{f,r}, \mathsf{ct}^*_{\mathbf{x}_1}) = [f(\mathbf{x}_1)^\top \mathbf{z}_1 + w_1 r] \\
\approx_c & (\ \mathsf{ct}^*_{\mathbf{x}_1}, & ???, & \mathsf{sk}^*_{f,r} \ ), \\
\approx_c & (\ \mathsf{ct}^*_{\mathbf{x}_1}, & \mathsf{ct}_{\mathbf{x}_2, 0 \| w_2}, & \mathsf{sk}^*_{f,r} \ ), & \mathsf{Dec}(\mathsf{sk}^*_{f,r}, \mathsf{ct}^*_{\mathbf{x}_1}) = [f(\mathbf{x}_1)^\top \mathbf{z}_1 + f(\mathbf{x}_2)^\top \mathbf{z}_2 + w_1 r]
\end{array}
$$

where the first row is the real distribution, the last row is the simulated distribution in (5), and the first $\approx_c$ follows from simulation-based security of the one-slot scheme. A natural idea is to replace "???" with a simulated ciphertext $\mathsf{ct}^*_{\mathbf{x}_2}$ but this is problematic for two reasons: first, we cannot switch between a normal and simulated ciphertext in the presence of a simulated key, and second, the simulator can only generate a single simulated ciphertext.

Luckily, we can overcome both difficulties by modifying the unbounded-slot FE scheme to use *two* independent copies of the one-slot scheme as follows:

- setup generates two one-slot master public-secret key pairs $(\mathsf{mpk}_1, \mathsf{msk}_1)$, $(\mathsf{mpk}_2, \mathsf{msk}_2)$;
- to encrypt $(\mathbf{x}_i, \mathbf{z}_i)_{i=1,\ldots,N}$, we generate $\mathsf{ct}_{\mathbf{x}_1, \mathbf{z}_1 \| w_1}$ w.r.t mpk_1 and the remaining $\mathsf{ct}_{\mathbf{x}_i, \mathbf{z}_i \| w_i}, i = 2, \ldots, N$ w.r.t. mpk_2;
- the secret key contains two one-slot secret keys $\mathsf{sk}_{f,r,1}, \mathsf{sk}_{f,r,2}$ generated for (f, r) but using $\mathsf{msk}_1, \mathsf{msk}_2$ respectively.

That would in fact be our final construction, where the asymmetry of encryption with respect to the first slot reflects the asymmetry of the simulated ciphertext in (5). Note that the first issue goes away because we can switch between a normal and simulated ciphertext w.r.t. mpk_2 in the presence of a simulated secret key w.r.t. mpk_1; the second goes away because the two simulated ciphertext correspond to mpk_1 and mpk_2 respectively. We defer the remaining details to the technical overview in Sect. 2 and the formal scheme in Sect. 7.

Scheme	Enc	KeyGen	Function	Security	$|\mathsf{ct}|$
OT12, KSW08 [30,34,35]	$\mathbf{z}$	$\mathbf{y}$	$\mathbf{z}^\top \mathbf{y} \overset{?}{=} 0$	AD-IND	$O(|\mathbf{z}|)$
ALS16, ABDP15 [1,6]	$\mathbf{z}$	$\mathbf{y}$	$\mathbf{z}^\top \mathbf{y}$	AD-IND	$O(|\mathbf{z}|)$
W17 [40]	$\mathbf{x}, \mathbf{z}$	f ABP	$\mathbf{z}^\top f(\mathbf{x}) \overset{?}{=} 0$	SA-SIM	$O(|\mathbf{x}| + |\mathbf{z}|)$
DOT18 [19]	$\mathbf{x}, \mathbf{z}$	f ABP	$\mathbf{z}^\top f(\mathbf{x}) \overset{?}{=} 0$	AD-SIM	$O(|\mathbf{x}| + |\mathbf{z}|)$
ACGU20, CZY19 [2,17]	$\mathbf{x}, \mathbf{z}$	$\mathbf{y}, f$ NC1	$f(\mathbf{x}) \cdot \mathbf{z}^\top \mathbf{y}$	AD-IND	$O(|\mathbf{x}| + |\mathbf{z}|)$
ACGU20 [2]	$\mathbf{z}_1, \mathbf{z}_2$	$\mathbf{y}_1, \mathbf{y}_2$	$\mathbf{z}_1^\top \mathbf{y}_1$ if $\mathbf{z}_2^\top \mathbf{y}_2 = 0$	AD-IND	$O(|\mathbf{z}_1| + |\mathbf{z}_2|)$
This work (§5)	$\mathbf{x}, \mathbf{z}$	f ABP	$\mathbf{z}^\top f(\mathbf{x})$	SA-SIM	$O(|\mathbf{z}|)$

Fig. 1. Comparison of prior public-key schemes with our construction for $N = 1$. Throughout, $\mathbf{x}$ is public and $\mathbf{z}, \mathbf{z}_1, \mathbf{z}_2$ are private, and $|\mathsf{ct}|$ omits the contribution from $\mathbf{x}$.

The multi-client setting. Now, consider a setting where the database $(\mathbf{x}_i, \mathbf{z}_i)_{i=1,\ldots,N}$ are distributed across multiple clients that do not completely trust one another [18,21]; in practice, the clients could correspond to hospitals holding medical records for different patients, or colleges holding admissions data. It suffices to just consider the setting with N clients where client i holds $(\mathbf{x}_i, \mathbf{z}_i)$. Note that to produce the ciphertext in our unbounded-slot FE scheme, it suffices for the N clients to each hold a random private w_i (per database) subject to the constraint $\sum w_i = 0$, which is simple to generate via a non-interactive MPC protocol where each client sends out additive shares of 0 [11]. Moreover, generating the w_i's can take place in an offline, pre-processing phase before knowing the database, and does not require interacting with the key generation authority. Moreover, our unbounded-slot FE scheme also achieves a meaningful notion of security, namely that if some subset S of clients collude and additionally learn some sk_f, they will not learn anything about the remaining $\mathbf{z}_i$'s apart from $\sum_{i \notin S} f(\mathbf{x}_i)^\top \mathbf{z}_i$ (that is, the attribute-weighted sum as applied to the honest clients' inputs); security is simulation-based and also extends to the many-key setting. In order to achieve this, we require a slight modification to the scheme to break the asymmetry with respect to the first slot: to encrypt $(\mathbf{x}_i, \mathbf{z}_i)$, client i samples random $\mathbf{z}_i', w_i'$ and publishes a one-slot encryption of $(\mathbf{x}_i, \mathbf{z}_i' \| w_i')$ under mpk_1 and another of $(\mathbf{x}_i, \mathbf{z} - \mathbf{z}_i' \| w_i - w_i')$ under mpk_2. This readily gives us a multi-client unbounded-slot FE for attribute-weighted sums; we refer the reader to full paper for more details of the definition, construction and proof.

1.3 Discussion

Additional related works. As noted earlier in the introduction, our unbounded-slot notion is closely related to uniform models of computation with unbounded input lengths, such as ABE and FE for DFA and NFA [7,8,22,38]. At a very high level, our construction may be viewed as following the paradigm in [7,8] for building ABE/FE for uniform models of computation by "stitching" together ABE/FE for the smaller step functions; in our setting, the linear relation between the step functions and the overall computation makes "stitching" much simpler. The way we use two copies of the one-slot scheme is also analogous to the "two-slot, interweaving dual system encryption" argument used in the previous ABE for DFA from k-Lin in [22], except our implementation is simpler and more modular.

On selective vs adaptive security. We believe that selective, simulation-based security already constitutes a meaningful notion of security for many of the applications we have in mind. For instance, in medical studies, medical records and patient conditions (the $\mathbf{x}_i, \mathbf{z}_i$'s) will not depend –not in the short run, at least– adaptively on the correlations (the functions f's) that researchers would like to investigate. Nonetheless, we do agree that extending our results to achieve adaptive security is an important research direction. Concretely,

- Can we show that the one-slot scheme achieves simulation-based, adaptive security in the generic group model, as has been shown for a large class of selectively secure ABEs [9]?
- Can we construct an adaptively secure unbounded-slot FE for arithmetic branching programs with compact ciphertexts without the one-use restriction from k-Lin? We conjecture that our transformation from one-slot to unbounded-slot preserves adaptive security. Solving the one-slot problem would require first adapting the techniques for adaptive simulation-based security in [5,19], and more recent advances in [31] to avoid the one-use restriction.

Open problems. We conclude with two other open problems. One is whether we can construct (one-slot) FE for attribute-weighted sums from LWE, simultaneously generalizing prior ABE and IPFE schemes from LWE [6,12,23]; an affirmative solution would likely also avoid the polynomial-size domain limitation. Another is to achieve stronger notions of security for the multi-client setting where the w_i's could be reused across multiple databases.

Organization. We provide a more detailed technical overview in Sect. 2. We present preliminaries, definitions and tools in Sects. 3 and 4. We present our one-slot scheme and an extension in Sects. 5 and 6, and the unbounded-slot scheme in Sect. 7.

2   Technical Overview

We proceed with a more technical overview of our construction, building on the overview given in Sect. 1.2, and giving more details on the one-slot scheme. We summarize the parameters of the one-slot and unbounded-slot scheme in Fig. 2.

2.1   One-Slot Scheme

Notation. We will make extensive use of tensor products. For instance, we will write the linear function $x_1 \mathbf{U}_1 + x_2 \mathbf{U}_2$ as

$$(\mathbf{U}_1 \| \mathbf{U}_2) \begin{pmatrix} x_1 \mathbf{I} \\ x_2 \mathbf{I} \end{pmatrix} = (\mathbf{U}_1 \| \mathbf{U}_2) \left(\begin{pmatrix} x_1 \\ x_2 \end{pmatrix} \otimes \mathbf{I} \right)$$

Scheme	$\|\text{ct}\|$	$\|\text{sk}\|$	Assumption
Π_{one} (§ 5)	$n' + 2k + 1$	$(k+1)nm + (2k+1)m + (k+1)n'$	k-Lin
	$n' + 3$	$2nm + 3m + 2n'$	SXDH
Π_{ubd} (§ 7)	$n'N + (3k+1)N$	$(2k+2)nm + (4k+2)m + (2k+2)n' + k$	k-Lin
	$n'N + 4N$	$4nm + 6m + 4n' + 1$	SXDH

Fig. 2. Summary of ciphertext and key sizes of our one-slot scheme Π_{one} and unbounded-slot scheme Π_{ubd}. Recall that $n = |\mathbf{x}| = |\mathbf{x}_i|$, $n' = |\mathbf{z}| = |\mathbf{z}_i|$, m is proportional to the size of f and N is the number of slots. In the table, we count the number of group elements in $\mathbb{G}_1$ (resp. $\mathbb{G}_2$) in the column $|\text{ct}|$ (resp. column $|\text{sk}|$). Note that SXDH = 1−Lin.

This allows us to concisely and precisely capture "compilers" where we substitute scalars with matrices, as well as the underlying linear relations, which may refer to left or right multiplication, and act on scalars or matrices.

Partial garbling. Recall the starting point for ABE for ABP as an "arithmetic secret-sharing scheme" that on input an ABP $f : \mathbb{Z}_p^n \to \mathbb{Z}_p$ and a secret $z \in \mathbb{Z}_p$, outputs m affine functions $\ell_1, \ldots, \ell_m : \mathbb{Z}_p^n \to \mathbb{Z}_p$ such that for all $\mathbf{x} \in \mathbb{Z}_p^n$:

- (correctness) given $\ell_1(\mathbf{x}), \ldots, \ell_m(\mathbf{x})$ along with $f, \mathbf{x}$, we can recover z if $f(\mathbf{x}) \neq 0$.
- (privacy) given $\ell_1(\mathbf{x}), \ldots, \ell_m(\mathbf{x})$ along with $f, \mathbf{x}$, we learn nothing about z if $f(\mathbf{x}) = 0$.

In particular, the coefficients of the functions $\ell_1, \ldots, \ell_m$ depends linearly on the randomness used in secret sharing.

Partial garbling generalizes the above as follows: on input an ABP $f : \mathbb{Z}_p^n \to \mathbb{Z}_p^{n'}$, outputs $m+1$ affine functions $\ell_0, \ell_1, \ldots, \ell_m$ such that for all $\mathbf{x} \in \mathbb{Z}_p^n, \mathbf{z} \in \mathbb{Z}_p^{n'}$:

- (correctness) given $\ell_0(\mathbf{z}), \ell_1(\mathbf{x}), \ldots, \ell_m(\mathbf{x})$ along with $f, \mathbf{x}$, we can recover $f(\mathbf{x})^\top \mathbf{z}$.
- (privacy) given $\ell_0(\mathbf{z}), \ell_1(\mathbf{x}), \ldots, \ell_m(\mathbf{x})$ along with $f, \mathbf{x}$, we learn nothing about $\mathbf{z}$ apart from $f(\mathbf{x})^\top \mathbf{z}$.

Henceforth, we will use $\mathbf{t}^\top (\mathbf{L}_1(\mathbf{x} \otimes \mathbf{I}_m) + \mathbf{L}_0) \in \mathbb{Z}_p^m$ to denote the m linear functions $\ell_1(\mathbf{x}), \ldots, \ell_m(\mathbf{x})$,[3] where $\mathbf{t} \leftarrow \mathbb{Z}_p^{m+n'-1}$ corresponds to the randomness used in the secret sharing; $\mathbf{L}_1 \in \mathbb{Z}_p^{(m+n'-1) \times mn}, \mathbf{L}_0 \in \mathbb{Z}_p^{(m+n'-1) \times m}$ depends only on the function f, and m is linear in the size of the ABP f.

Basic scheme. We rely on an asymmetric bilinear group $(\mathbb{G}_1, \mathbb{G}_2, \mathbb{G}_T, e)$ of prime order p where $e : \mathbb{G}_1 \times \mathbb{G}_2 \to \mathbb{G}_T$. We use $[\cdot]_1, [\cdot]_2, [\cdot]_T$ to denote component-wise exponentiations in respective groups $\mathbb{G}_1, \mathbb{G}_2, \mathbb{G}_T$ [20]. Our starting point is the following scheme[4]:

$$\mathsf{mpk} = \big([\mathbf{w}]_1, [\mathbf{u}]_1, [v]_1 \big) \quad \text{and} \quad \mathsf{msk} = \big(\mathbf{w}, \mathbf{u}, v \big) \tag{6}$$

$$\mathsf{ct}_{\mathbf{x},\mathbf{z}} = \big([s]_1, [\mathbf{z} + s\mathbf{w}]_1, [s(\mathbf{u}^\top \mathbf{x} + v)]_1 \big) \in \mathbb{G}_1^{n'+2}$$

$$\mathsf{sk}_f = \big([\underline{\mathbf{t}} + \mathbf{w}]_2, [\mathbf{t}^\top \mathbf{L}_1 + \mathbf{u}^\top (\mathbf{I}_n \otimes \mathbf{r}^\top)]_2, [\mathbf{t}^\top \mathbf{L}_0 + v\mathbf{r}^\top]_2, [\mathbf{r}]_2 \big)$$

where

$$\mathbf{w} \leftarrow \mathbb{Z}_p^{n'}, \mathbf{u} \leftarrow \mathbb{Z}_p^n, v \leftarrow \mathbb{Z}_p, \mathbf{t} \leftarrow \mathbb{Z}_p^{m+n'-1}, \mathbf{r} \leftarrow \mathbb{Z}_p^m$$

---

[3] As an example with $n = 2, m = 3$, we have

$$\big(a_{11}x_1 + a_{12}x_2 + b_1, \ a_{21}x_1 + a_{22}x_2 + b_2, \ a_{31}x_1 + a_{32}x_2 + b_3 \big)$$

$$= (a_{11}, a_{21}, a_{31}, a_{12}, a_{22}, a_{32}) \left(\begin{pmatrix} x_1 \\ x_2 \end{pmatrix} \otimes \mathbf{I}_3 \right) + (b_1, b_2, b_3).$$

[4] The scheme in [40] has a larger ciphertext of the form: $\mathsf{ct}_{\mathbf{x},\mathbf{z}} = \big([s]_1, [\mathbf{z}+s\mathbf{w}]_1, [s(\mathbf{u}+v\mathbf{x})]_1 \big) \in \mathbb{G}_1^{n+n'+1}$.

Decryption uses the fact that

$$\mathbf{t}^\top(\mathbf{L}_1(\mathbf{x} \otimes \mathbf{I}_m) + \mathbf{L}_0) =$$
$$(\mathbf{t}^\top\mathbf{L}_1 + \mathbf{u}^\top(\mathbf{I}_n \otimes \mathbf{r}^\top)) \cdot (\mathbf{x} \otimes \mathbf{I}_m) + (\mathbf{t}^\top\mathbf{L}_0 + v\mathbf{r}^\top) - (\mathbf{u}^\top\mathbf{x} + v) \cdot \mathbf{r}^\top \quad (7)$$

which in turn uses $(\mathbf{I}_n \otimes \mathbf{r}^\top) \cdot (\mathbf{x} \otimes \mathbf{I}_m) = \mathbf{x} \cdot \mathbf{r}^\top$. Using the pairing and the above relation, we can recover

$$[\mathbf{z} - s\underline{\mathbf{t}}]_T, [s\mathbf{t}^\top(\mathbf{L}_1(\mathbf{x} \otimes \mathbf{I}_m) + \mathbf{L}_0)]_T$$

We can then apply reconstruction "in the exponent" to recover $[f(\mathbf{x})^\top\mathbf{z}]_T$ and thus $f(\mathbf{x})^\top\mathbf{z}$ via brute-force DLOG.

Security in the secret-key setting. The scheme as written already achieves simulation-based selective security in the secret-key, many-key setting (that is, against an adversary that does not see mpk); this holds under the DDH assumption in $\mathbb{G}_2$. We sketch how we can simulate $(\mathsf{ct}_{\mathbf{x},\mathbf{z}}, \mathsf{sk}_f)$ given $\mathbf{x}, f, f(\mathbf{x})^\top\mathbf{z}$; the proof extends readily to the many-key setting. The idea is to program

$$\tilde{\mathbf{w}} = \mathbf{z} + s\mathbf{w}, \quad \tilde{v} = s(\mathbf{u}^\top\mathbf{x} + v)$$

In addition, using (7), we can rewrite $(\mathsf{ct}_{\mathbf{x},\mathbf{z}}, \mathsf{sk}_f)$ as

$$\mathsf{ct}_{\mathbf{x},\mathbf{z}} = ([s]_1, [\tilde{\mathbf{w}}]_1, [\tilde{v}]_1) \in \mathbb{G}_1^{n'+2}$$
$$\mathsf{sk}_f = ([\underline{\mathbf{t}} + s^{-1}(\tilde{\mathbf{w}} - \mathbf{z})]_2, [\hat{\mathbf{u}}^\top]_2, [\mathbf{t}^\top(\mathbf{L}_1(\mathbf{x} \otimes \mathbf{I}_m) + \mathbf{L}_0) - \hat{\mathbf{u}}^\top \cdot (\mathbf{x} \otimes \mathbf{I}_m) + s^{-1}\tilde{v}\mathbf{r}^\top]_2, [\mathbf{r}]_2)$$

where $\hat{\mathbf{u}}^\top := \mathbf{t}^\top\mathbf{L}_1 + \mathbf{u}^\top(\mathbf{I}_n \otimes \mathbf{r}^\top)$. Under the DDH assumption in $\mathbb{G}_2$, we know that[5]

$$[\mathbf{u}^\top(\mathbf{I}_n \otimes \mathbf{r}^\top)]_2, [\mathbf{r}^\top]_2, \mathbf{u} \leftarrow \mathbb{Z}_p^n, \mathbf{r} \leftarrow \mathbb{Z}_p^m$$

is pseudorandom, which means that $[\hat{\mathbf{u}}^\top]_2, [\mathbf{r}^\top]_2$ is pseudorandom.

We can therefore simulate $(\mathsf{ct}_{\mathbf{x},\mathbf{z}}, \mathsf{sk}_f)$ as follows: on input $\mu = f(\mathbf{x})^\top\mathbf{z}$,

1. run the simulator for partial garbling on input $f, \mathbf{x}, \mu$ to obtain $(\mathbf{p}_1^\top, \mathbf{p}_2^\top)$;
2. sample $s \leftarrow \mathbb{Z}_p, \tilde{\mathbf{w}} \leftarrow \mathbb{Z}_p^{n'}, \tilde{v} \leftarrow \mathbb{Z}_p, \hat{\mathbf{u}} \leftarrow \mathbb{Z}_p^{mn}$;
3. output

$$\mathsf{ct}_{\mathbf{x},\mathbf{z}} = ([s]_1, [\tilde{\mathbf{w}}]_1, [\tilde{v}]_1) \in \mathbb{G}_1^{n'+2}$$
$$\mathsf{sk}_f = ([-\mathbf{p}_1 + s^{-1}\tilde{\mathbf{w}}]_2, [\hat{\mathbf{u}}^\top]_2, [\mathbf{p}_2^\top - \hat{\mathbf{u}}^\top \cdot (\mathbf{x} \otimes \mathbf{I}_m) + s^{-1}\tilde{v}\mathbf{r}^\top]_2, [\mathbf{r}]_2)$$

Looking ahead, we note that the above analysis extends to the k-Lin assumption, at the cost of blowing up the width of $\mathbf{u}, v, \mathbf{r}^\top$ by a factor of k. In the analysis, we use the fact that under k-Lin over $\mathbb{G}_2$, $([\mathbf{u}^\top(\mathbf{I}_n \otimes \mathbf{R})]_2, [\mathbf{R}]_2)$ is pseudorandom where $\mathbf{u} \leftarrow \mathbb{Z}_p^{kn}, \mathbf{R} \leftarrow \mathbb{Z}_p^{k \times m}$.

---

[5] Recall that if we write $\mathbf{u} = (u_1, \ldots, u_n)$, then $\mathbf{u}^\top(\mathbf{I}_n \otimes \mathbf{r}^\top) = (u_1\mathbf{r}^\top, \ldots, u_n\mathbf{r}^\top)$.

The compiler. To obtain a public-key scheme secure under the k-Lin assumption, we perform the following substitutions to (6), following [15, 40]:

$$s \mapsto \mathbf{s}^\top \mathbf{A}^\top \in \mathbb{Z}_p^{1 \times (k+1)}, \; \mathbf{r}^\top \mapsto \mathbf{R} \in \mathbb{Z}_p^{k \times m}, \; \mathbf{t}^\top \mapsto \mathbf{T} \in \mathbb{Z}_p^{(k+1) \times (m+n'-1)}$$

$$\mathbf{w}^\top \mapsto \mathbf{W} \in \mathbb{Z}_p^{(k+1) \times n'}, \; \mathbf{u}^\top \mapsto \mathbf{U} \in \mathbb{Z}_p^{(k+1) \times kn}, \; v \mapsto \mathbf{V} \in \mathbb{Z}_p^{(k+1) \times k}$$

That is, we blow up the height of $\mathbf{w}^\top, \mathbf{u}^\top, v, \mathbf{t}^\top$ by a factor of $k+1$, and the width of $\mathbf{u}^\top, v, \mathbf{r}$ by a factor of k. The proof of security follows the high-level strategy in [40]:

- We first switch $[\mathbf{s}^\top \mathbf{A}^\top]_1$ in the ciphertext with a random $[\mathbf{c}^\top]_1$.
- We decompose sk_f into two parts, $\mathbf{A}^\top \mathsf{sk}_f, \mathbf{c}^\top \mathsf{sk}_f$, corresponding to componentwise multiplication by $\mathbf{A}^\top, \mathbf{c}^\top$ respectively, using the fact that $(\mathbf{A}|\mathbf{c})$ forms a full-rank basis.
- We simulate $\mathbf{A}^\top \mathsf{sk}_f$ using (mpk, f), and simulate the ciphertext and $\mathbf{c}^\top \mathsf{sk}_f$ as in the secret-key setting we just described.

We refer the reader to Sect. 6 to see how the construction can be extended to handle the "extended" functionality in (3); an overview is given at the beginning of that section.

2.2 Unbounded-Slot Scheme

We refer the reader to Sect. 1.2 for a high-level overview of the unbounded-slot scheme, and proceed directly to describe the construction and the security proof.

The construction. We run two copies of the one-slot scheme, which we denote by $(\mathsf{Enc}_b, \mathsf{KeyGen}_b) = (\mathsf{Enc}(\mathsf{mpk}_b, \cdot), \mathsf{KeyGen}(\mathsf{msk}_b, \cdot))$ for $b = 1, 2$. We denote the corresponding simulators by $(\mathsf{Enc}_b^*, \mathsf{KeyGen}_b^*)$. Informally, we have

$$(\mathsf{Enc}_b(\mathbf{x}, \mathbf{z}\|w), \mathsf{KeyGen}_b(f, [r]_2)) \approx_c (\mathsf{Enc}_b^*(\mathbf{x}), \mathsf{KeyGen}_b^*((f, [r]_2), [f(\mathbf{x})^\top \mathbf{z} + wr]_2))$$

Then, $\mathsf{Enc}, \mathsf{KeyGen}$ in the unbounded-slot scheme are given by

$$\mathsf{Enc}((\mathbf{x}_i, \mathbf{z}_i)_i) = \mathsf{Enc}_1(\mathbf{x}_1, \mathbf{z}_1 \| - \textstyle\sum_{i \in [2,N]} w_i), \mathsf{Enc}_2(\mathbf{x}_2, \mathbf{z}_2 \| w_2), \cdots, \mathsf{Enc}_2(\mathbf{x}_N, \mathbf{z}_N \| w_N)$$
$$\mathsf{KeyGen}(f) = \mathsf{KeyGen}_1(f, [r]_2), \mathsf{KeyGen}_2(f, [r]_2), [r]_2$$

$\mathsf{Enc}_1(\mathbf{x}_1, \mathbf{z}_1 \| -w_2 - w_3)$, $\mathsf{Enc}_2(\mathbf{x}_2, \mathbf{z}_2 \| w_2)$, $\mathsf{Enc}_2(\mathbf{x}_3, \mathbf{z}_3 \| w_3)$

$\mathsf{KeyGen}_1(f, [r]_2), \mathsf{KeyGen}_2(f, [r]_2)$

$\overset{\text{SIM-1}}{\approx_c}$ $\boxed{\mathsf{Enc}_1^*(\mathbf{x}_1)}$, $\mathsf{Enc}_2(\mathbf{x}_2, \mathbf{z}_2 \| w_2)$, $\mathsf{Enc}_2(\mathbf{x}_3, \mathbf{z}_3 \| w_3)$

$\boxed{\mathsf{KeyGen}_1^*((f, [r]_2), [f(\mathbf{x}_1)^\top \mathbf{z}_1 - w_2 r - w_3 r]_2)}$, $\mathsf{KeyGen}_2(f, [r]_2)$

$\overset{\text{SIM-2}}{\approx_c} \mathsf{Enc}_1^*(\mathbf{x}_1)$, $\boxed{\mathsf{Enc}_2^*(\mathbf{x}_2)}$, $\mathsf{Enc}_2(\mathbf{x}_3, \mathbf{z}_3 \| w_3)$

$\mathsf{KeyGen}_1^*((f, [r]_2), [f(\mathbf{x}_1)^\top \mathbf{z}_1 - w_2 r - w_3 r]_2)$, $\boxed{\mathsf{KeyGen}_2^*((f, [r]_2), [f(\mathbf{x}_2)^\top \mathbf{z}_2 + w_2 r]_2)}$

$\overset{\text{DDH}}{\approx_c} \mathsf{Enc}_1^*(\mathbf{x}_1)$, $\mathsf{Enc}_2^*(\mathbf{x}_2)$, $\mathsf{Enc}_2(\mathbf{x}_3, \mathbf{z}_3 \| w_3)$

$\mathsf{KeyGen}_1^*((f, [r]_2), [f(\mathbf{x}_1)^\top \mathbf{z}_1 + f(\mathbf{x}_2)^\top \mathbf{z}_2 - w_2 r - w_3 r]_2)$, $\mathsf{KeyGen}_2^*((f, [r]_2), [\boxed{w_2 r}]_2)$

$\overset{\text{SIM-2}}{\approx_c} \mathsf{Enc}_1^*(\mathbf{x}_1)$, $\boxed{\mathsf{Enc}_2(\mathbf{x}_2, \mathbf{0} \| w_2)}$, $\mathsf{Enc}_2(\mathbf{x}_3, \mathbf{z}_3 \| w_3)$

$\mathsf{KeyGen}_1^*((f, [r]_2), [f(\mathbf{x}_1)^\top \mathbf{z}_1 + f(\mathbf{x}_2)^\top \mathbf{z}_2 - w_2 r - w_3 r]_2)$, $\boxed{\mathsf{KeyGen}_2(f, [r]_2)}$

$\overset{\text{SIM-2}}{\approx_c} \mathsf{Enc}_1^*(\mathbf{x}_1)$, $\mathsf{Enc}_2(\mathbf{x}_2, \mathbf{0} \| w_2)$, $\boxed{\mathsf{Enc}_2^*(\mathbf{x}_3)}$

$\mathsf{KeyGen}_1^*((f, [r]_2), [f(\mathbf{x}_1)^\top \mathbf{z}_1 + f(\mathbf{x}_2)^\top \mathbf{z}_2 - w_2 r - w_3 r]_2)$, $\boxed{\mathsf{KeyGen}_2^*((f, [r]_2), [f(\mathbf{x}_3)^\top \mathbf{z}_3 + w_3 r]_2)}$

$\overset{\text{DDH}}{\approx_c} \mathsf{Enc}_1^*(\mathbf{x}_1)$, $\mathsf{Enc}_2(\mathbf{x}_2, \mathbf{0} \| w_2)$, $\mathsf{Enc}_2^*(\mathbf{x}_3)$

$\mathsf{KeyGen}_1^*((f, [r]_2), [f(\mathbf{x}_1)^\top \mathbf{z}_1 + f(\mathbf{x}_2)^\top \mathbf{z}_2 + \boxed{f(\mathbf{x}_3)^\top \mathbf{z}_3} - w_2 r - w_3 r]_2)$, $\mathsf{KeyGen}_2^*((f, [r]_2), [\boxed{w_3 r}]_2)$

$\overset{\text{SIM-2}}{\approx_c} \mathsf{Enc}_1^*(\mathbf{x}_1)$, $\mathsf{Enc}_2(\mathbf{x}_2, \mathbf{0} \| w_2)$, $\boxed{\mathsf{Enc}_2(\mathbf{x}_3, \mathbf{0} \| w_3)}$

$\mathsf{KeyGen}_1^*((f, [r]_2), [f(\mathbf{x}_1)^\top \mathbf{z}_1 + f(\mathbf{x}_2)^\top \mathbf{z}_2 + f(\mathbf{x}_3)^\top \mathbf{z}_3 - w_2 r - w_3 r]_2)$, $\boxed{\mathsf{KeyGen}_2(f, [r]_2)}$

Fig. 3. Summary of game sequence for $N = 3$. In the figure, $\overset{\text{SIM-}b}{\approx_c}$ indicates that this step uses the simulate-based semi-adaptive security of $(\mathsf{Enc}_b, \mathsf{KeyGen}_b)$.

The final simulator is given by:

$$\mathsf{Enc}^*((\mathbf{x}_i)_i) = \mathsf{Enc}_1^*(\mathbf{x}_1), \mathsf{Enc}_2(\mathbf{x}_2, \mathbf{0} \| w_2), \cdots, \mathsf{Enc}_2(\mathbf{x}_N, \mathbf{0} \| w_N)$$
$$\mathsf{KeyGen}^*(f, \mu) = \mathsf{KeyGen}_1^*((f, [r]_2), [\mu - \textstyle\sum_{i \in [2,N]} w_i r]_2), \mathsf{KeyGen}_2(f, [r]_2)$$

As a sanity check, observe that decrypting $\mathsf{Enc}^*((\mathbf{x}_i)_i)$ using $\mathsf{KeyGen}^*(f, \sum_i f(\mathbf{x}_i)^\top \mathbf{z}_i)$ returns $\sum_i f(\mathbf{x}_i)^\top \mathbf{z}_i$.

Proof overview. For simplicity, we focus on the setting $N = 3$ with one secret key query in Fig. 3 where in $\overset{\text{DDH}}{\approx_c}$, we use pseudorandomness of $([w_1 r]_2, [r]_2)$ and $([w_2 r]_2, [r]_2)$ respectively; in $\overset{\text{SIM-1}}{\approx_c}$ and $\overset{\text{SIM-2}}{\approx_c}$, we use simulation-based semi-adaptive security of $(\mathsf{Enc}_1, \mathsf{KeyGen}_1)$ and $(\mathsf{Enc}_2, \mathsf{KeyGen}_2)$, respectively.

In the setting for general N and Q secret key queries,

- we will invoke simulation-based security of $(\mathsf{Enc}_1, \mathsf{KeyGen}_1)$ once, and that of $(\mathsf{Enc}_2, \mathsf{KeyGen}_2)$ for $2(N-1)$ times, while using the fact that both of these schemes are also secure against Q secret key queries;
- in $\overset{\text{DDH}}{\approx_c}$, we will rely on pseudorandomness of $\{[w_i r_j]_2, [r_j]_2)\}_{j \in [Q]}$ for $i \in [2, N]$.

3   Preliminaries

Notations. We denote by $s \leftarrow S$ the fact that s is picked uniformly at random from a finite set S. We use $\approx_s$ to denote two distributions being statistically indistinguishable, and $\approx_c$ to denote two distributions being computationally indistinguishable. We use lower case boldface to denote *column* vectors and upper case boldcase to denote matrices. We use $\mathbf{e}_i$ to denote the i'th elementary column vector (with 1 at the i'th position and 0 elsewhere, and the total length of the vector specified by the context). For any positive integer N, we use $[N]$ to denote $\{1, 2, \ldots, N\}$ and $[2, N]$ to denote $\{2, \ldots, N\}$.

The tensor product (Kronecker product) for matrices $\mathbf{A} = (a_{i,j}) \in \mathbb{Z}^{\ell \times m}$, $\mathbf{B} \in \mathbb{Z}^{n \times p}$ is defined as

$$\mathbf{A} \otimes \mathbf{B} = \begin{bmatrix} a_{1,1}\mathbf{B}, & \ldots, & a_{1,m}\mathbf{B} \\ \ldots, & \ldots, & \ldots \\ a_{\ell,1}\mathbf{B}, & \ldots, & a_{\ell,m}\mathbf{B} \end{bmatrix} \in \mathbb{Z}^{\ell n \times mp}. \tag{8}$$

Arithmetic Branching Programs. A branching program is defined by a directed acyclic graph (V, E), two special vertices $v_0, v_1 \in V$ and a labeling function ϕ. An arithmetic branching program (ABP), where p is a prime, computes a function $f : \mathbb{Z}_p^n \to \mathbb{Z}_p$. Here, ϕ assigns to each edge in E an affine function in some input variable or a constant, and $f(x)$ is the sum over all $v_0 - v_1$ paths of the product of all the values along the path. We refer to $|V| + |E|$ as the size of f. The definition extends in a coordinate-wise manner to functions $f : \mathbb{Z}_p^n \to \mathbb{Z}_p^{n'}$. Henceforth, we use $\mathcal{F}_{\mathsf{ABP},n,n'}$ to denote the class of ABP $f : \mathbb{Z}_p^n \to \mathbb{Z}_p^{n'}$.

We note that there is a linear-time algorithm that converts any boolean formula, boolean branching program or arithmetic formula to an arithmetic branching program with a constant blow-up in the representation size. Thus, ABPs can be viewed as a stronger computational model than all of the above. Recall also that branching programs and boolean formulas correspond to the complexity classes **LOGSPACE** and **NC1** respectively.

3.1 Prime-Order Bilinear Groups

A generator $\mathcal{G}$ takes as input a security parameter 1^λ and outputs a description $\mathbb{G} := (p, \mathbb{G}_1, \mathbb{G}_2, \mathbb{G}_T, e)$, where p is a prime of $\Theta(\lambda)$ bits, $\mathbb{G}_1$, $\mathbb{G}_2$ and $\mathbb{G}_T$ are cyclic groups of order p, and $e : \mathbb{G}_1 \times \mathbb{G}_2 \to \mathbb{G}_T$ is a non-degenerate bilinear map. We require that the group operations in $\mathbb{G}_1$, $\mathbb{G}_2$, $\mathbb{G}_T$ and the bilinear map e are computable in deterministic polynomial time in λ. Let $g_1 \in \mathbb{G}_1$, $g_2 \in \mathbb{G}_2$ and $g_T = e(g_1, g_2) \in \mathbb{G}_T$ be the respective generators. We employ the *implicit representation* of group elements: for a matrix $\mathbf{M}$ over $\mathbb{Z}_p$, we define $[\mathbf{M}]_1 := g_1^{\mathbf{M}}, [\mathbf{M}]_2 := g_2^{\mathbf{M}}, [\mathbf{M}]_T := g_T^{\mathbf{M}}$, where exponentiation is carried out component-wise. Also, given $[\mathbf{A}]_1, [\mathbf{B}]_2$, we let $e([\mathbf{A}]_1, [\mathbf{B}]_2) = [\mathbf{AB}]_T$. We recall the matrix Diffie-Hellman (MDDH) assumption on $\mathbb{G}_1$ [20]:

Assumption 1 (MDDH$_{k,\ell}^d$ **Assumption**). *Let $k, \ell, d \in \mathbb{N}$. We say that the MDDH$_{k,\ell}^d$ assumption holds if for all PPT adversaries $\mathcal{A}$, the following advantage function is negligible in λ.*

$$\mathsf{Adv}_{\mathcal{A}}^{\mathrm{MDDH}_{k,\ell}^d}(\lambda) := \big| \Pr[\mathcal{A}(\mathbb{G}, [\mathbf{M}]_1, \boxed{[\mathbf{MS}]_1}) = 1] - \Pr[\mathcal{A}(\mathbb{G}, [\mathbf{M}]_1, \boxed{[\mathbf{U}]_1}) = 1] \big|$$

where $\mathbb{G} := (p, \mathbb{G}_1, \mathbb{G}_2, \mathbb{G}_T, e) \leftarrow \mathcal{G}(1^\lambda)$, $\mathbf{M} \leftarrow \mathbb{Z}_p^{\ell \times k}$, $\mathbf{S} \leftarrow \mathbb{Z}_p^{k \times d}$ and $\mathbf{U} \leftarrow \mathbb{Z}_p^{\ell \times d}$.

The MDDH assumption on $\mathbb{G}_2$ can be defined in an analogous way. Escala *et al.* [20] showed that

$$k\text{-Lin} \Rightarrow \text{MDDH}^1_{k,k+1} \Rightarrow \text{MDDH}^d_{k,\ell} \ \forall \ k, d \geq 1, \ell > k$$

with a tight security reduction. (In the setting where $\ell \leq k$, the $\text{MDDH}^d_{k,\ell}$ assumption holds unconditionally.)

We state the following lemma implied by $\text{MDDH}^1_{k,Q}$ without proof.

Lemma 1. *For all $Q \in \mathbb{N}$ and $\mu_1, \ldots, \mu_Q \in \mathbb{Z}_p$, we have*

$$\begin{aligned} &\left\{ \quad [-\mathbf{w}^\top \mathbf{r}_j]_2, \ \boxed{[\mu_j]} + \mathbf{w}^\top \mathbf{r}_j]_2, \ [\mathbf{r}_j]_2 \right\}_{j \in [Q]} \\ \approx_c &\left\{ \boxed{[\mu_j]} - \mathbf{w}^\top \mathbf{r}_j]_2, \qquad [\mathbf{w}^\top \mathbf{r}_j]_2, \ [\mathbf{r}_j]_2 \right\}_{j \in [Q]} \end{aligned}$$

where $\mathbf{w}, \mathbf{r}_j \leftarrow \mathbb{Z}_p^k$ for all $j \in [Q]$. Concretely, the distinguishing advantage is bounded by $2 \cdot \text{Adv}_{\mathcal{B}}^{\text{MDDH}^1_{k,Q}}(\lambda)$.

4   Definitions and Tools

In this section, we formalize functional encryption for attribute-weighted sums, using the framework of partially-hiding functional encryption [13,24,40].

4.1   FE for Attribute-Weighted Sums

Syntax. An *unbounded-slot FE for attribute-weighted sums* consists of four algorithms:

Setup$(1^\lambda, 1^n, 1^{n'})$: The setup algorithm gets as input the security parameter 1^λ and function parameters $1^n, 1^{n'}$. It outputs the master public key mpk and the master secret key msk.

Enc$(\text{mpk}, (\mathbf{x}_i, \mathbf{z}_i)_{i \in [N]})$: The encryption algorithm gets as input mpk and message $(\mathbf{x}_i, \mathbf{z}_i)_{i \in [N]} \in (\mathbb{Z}_p^n \times \mathbb{Z}_p^{n'})^\star$. It outputs a ciphertext $\text{ct}_{(\mathbf{x}_i, \mathbf{z}_i)}$ with $(\mathbf{x}_i)$ being public.

KeyGen(msk, f) : The key generation algorithm gets as input msk and a function $f \in \mathcal{F}_{\text{ABP},n,n'}$. It outputs a secret key sk_f with f being public.

Dec$((\text{sk}_f, f), (\text{ct}_{(\mathbf{x}_i, \mathbf{z}_i)}, (\mathbf{x}_i)_{i \in [N]}))$: The decryption algorithm gets as input sk_f and $\text{ct}_{(\mathbf{x}_i, \mathbf{z}_i)}$ along with f and $(\mathbf{x}_i)_{i \in [N]}$. It outputs a value in $\mathbb{Z}_p$.

Correctness. For all $(\mathbf{x}_i, \mathbf{z}_i)_{i \in [N]} \in (\mathbb{Z}_p^n \times \mathbb{Z}_p^{n'})^\star$ and $f \in \mathcal{F}_{\text{ABP},n,n'}$, we require

$$\Pr[\text{Dec}((\text{ct}_{(\mathbf{x}_i, \mathbf{z}_i)}, (\mathbf{x}_i)_{i \in [N]}), (\text{sk}_f, f)) = \sum_{i \in [N]} f(\mathbf{x}_i)^\top \mathbf{z}_i] = 1$$

where $(\text{mpk}, \text{msk}) \leftarrow \text{Setup}(1^\lambda, 1^n, 1^{n'})$, $\text{sk}_f \leftarrow \text{KeyGen}(\text{msk}, f)$ and $\text{ct}_{(\mathbf{x}_i, \mathbf{z}_i)} \leftarrow \text{Enc}(\text{mpk}, (\mathbf{x}_i, \mathbf{z}_i)_{i \in [N]})$.

Remark 1 (Relaxation of correctness.). Our scheme only achieves a relaxation of correctness where the decryption algorithm takes an additional bound 1^B (and runs in time polynomial in B) and outputs $\sum_{i \in [N]} f(\mathbf{x}_i)^\top \mathbf{z}_i$ if the value is bounded by B. This limitation is also present in prior works on (IP)FE from DDH and bilinear groups [1,3,6,10,33], due to the reliance on brute-force discrete log to recover the answer "from the exponent". We stress that the relaxation only refers to functionality and does not affect security.

Security definition. We consider semi-adaptive [16] (strengthening of selective), simulation-based security, which stipulates that there exists a randomized simulator (Setup*, Enc*, KeyGen*) such that for every efficient stateful adversary $\mathcal{A}$,

$$
\begin{bmatrix}
1^N \leftarrow \mathcal{A}(1^\lambda); \\
(\mathsf{mpk}, \mathsf{msk}) \leftarrow \mathsf{Setup}(1^\lambda, 1^n, 1^{n'}); \\
(\mathbf{x}_i^*, \mathbf{z}_i^*)_{i \in [N]} \leftarrow \mathcal{A}(\mathsf{mpk}); \\
\mathsf{ct}^* \leftarrow \mathsf{Enc}(\mathsf{mpk}, (\mathbf{x}_i^*, \mathbf{z}_i^*)_{i \in [N]}); \\
\text{output } \mathcal{A}^{\mathsf{KeyGen}(\mathsf{msk}, \cdot)}(\mathsf{mpk}, \mathsf{ct}^*)
\end{bmatrix}
\approx_c
\begin{bmatrix}
1^N \leftarrow \mathcal{A}(1^\lambda); \\
(\mathsf{mpk}, \mathsf{msk}^*) \leftarrow \mathsf{Setup}^*(1^\lambda, 1^n, 1^{n'}, 1^N); \\
(\mathbf{x}_i^*, \mathbf{z}_i^*)_{i \in [N]} \leftarrow \mathcal{A}(\mathsf{mpk}); \\
\mathsf{ct}^* \leftarrow \mathsf{Enc}^*(\mathsf{msk}^*, (\mathbf{x}_i^*)_{i \in [N]}); \\
\text{output } \mathcal{A}^{\mathsf{KeyGen}^*(\mathsf{msk}^*, (\mathbf{x}_i^*)_{i \in [N]}, \cdot, \cdot)}(\mathsf{mpk}, \mathsf{ct}^*)
\end{bmatrix}
$$

such that whenever $\mathcal{A}$ makes a query f to KeyGen, the simulator KeyGen* gets f along with $\sum_{i \in [N]} f(\mathbf{x}_i^*)^\top \mathbf{z}_i^*$. We use $\mathsf{Adv}_{\mathcal{A}}^{\mathsf{FE}}(\lambda)$ to denote the advantage in distinguishing the real and ideal games.

One-slot scheme. A *one-slot* scheme is the same thing, except we always have $N = 1$ for both correctness and security.

4.2   Partial Garbling Scheme

The partial garbling scheme [27,40] for $f(\mathbf{x})^\top \mathbf{z}$ with $f \in \mathcal{F}_{\mathsf{ABP},n,n'}$ is a randomized algorithm that on input f outputs an affine function in $\mathbf{x}, \mathbf{z}$ of the form:

$$
\mathbf{p}_{f,\mathbf{x},\mathbf{z}}^\top = \left(\mathbf{z}^\top - \underline{\mathbf{t}}^\top, \mathbf{t}^\top (\mathbf{L}_1 (\mathbf{x} \otimes \mathbf{I}_m) + \mathbf{L}_0) \right)
$$

where $\mathbf{L}_0 \in \mathbb{Z}_p^{(m+n'-1) \times mn}, \mathbf{L}_1 \in \mathbb{Z}_p^{(m+n'-1) \times m}$ depends only on f; $\mathbf{t} \leftarrow \mathbb{Z}_p^{m+n'-1}$ is the random coin and $\underline{\mathbf{t}}$ consists of the last n' entries in $\mathbf{t}$, such that given $(\mathbf{p}_{f,\mathbf{x},\mathbf{z}}^\top, f, \mathbf{x})$, we can recover $f(\mathbf{x})^\top \mathbf{z}$, while learning nothing else about $\mathbf{z}$.

Lemma 2 (partial garbling [27,40]). *There exists four efficient algorithms* (lgen, pgb, rec, pgb*) *with the following properties:*

- *syntax: on input* $f \in \mathcal{F}_{\mathsf{ABP},n,n'}$, $\mathsf{lgen}(f)$ *outputs* $\mathbf{L}_0 \in \mathbb{Z}_p^{(m+n'-1) \times mn}, \mathbf{L}_1 \in \mathbb{Z}_p^{(m+n'-1) \times m}$, *and*

$$
\begin{aligned}
\mathsf{pgb}(f, \mathbf{x}, \mathbf{z}; \mathbf{t}) &= \left(\mathbf{z}^\top - \underline{\mathbf{t}}^\top, \mathbf{t}^\top (\mathbf{L}_1 (\mathbf{x} \otimes \mathbf{I}_m) + \mathbf{L}_0) \right) \\
\mathsf{pgb}^*(f, \mathbf{x}, \mu; \mathbf{t}) &= \left(\quad -\underline{\mathbf{t}}^\top, \mathbf{t}^\top (\mathbf{L}_1 (\mathbf{x} \otimes \mathbf{I}_m) + \mathbf{L}_0) + \mu \cdot \mathbf{e}_1^\top \right)
\end{aligned}
$$

where $\mathbf{t} \in \mathbb{Z}_p^{m+n'-1}$ *and* $\underline{\mathbf{t}}$ *consists of the last* n' *entries in* $\mathbf{t}$ *and* m *are linear in the size of* f.

- *reconstruction*: $\mathsf{rec}(f, \mathbf{x})$ outputs $\mathbf{d}_{f,\mathbf{x}} \in \mathbb{Z}_p^{n'+m}$ *such that for all* $f, \mathbf{x}, \mathbf{z}, \mathbf{t}$, *we have* $\mathbf{p}_{f,\mathbf{x},\mathbf{z}}^{\top} \mathbf{d}_{f,\mathbf{x}} = f(\mathbf{x})^{\top} \mathbf{z}$ *where* $\mathbf{p}_{f,\mathbf{x},\mathbf{z}}^{\top} = \mathsf{pgb}(f, \mathbf{x}, \mathbf{z}; \mathbf{t})$.
- *privacy: for all* $f, \mathbf{x}, \mathbf{z}$, $\mathsf{pgb}(f, \mathbf{x}, \mathbf{z}; \mathbf{t}) \approx_s \mathsf{pgb}^*(f, \mathbf{x}, f(\mathbf{x})^{\top} \mathbf{z}; \mathbf{t})$ *where the randomness is over* $\mathbf{t} \leftarrow \mathbb{Z}_p^{m+n'-1}$.

Extension. We will also rely on an extra property of the above construction to handle shifts by $\delta \in \mathbb{Z}_p$, namely that, given

$$\mathbf{p}_{f,\mathbf{x},\mathbf{z}, \boxed{\delta}}^{\top} = \left(\mathbf{z}^{\top} - \underline{\mathbf{t}}^{\top}, \mathbf{t}^{\top}(\mathbf{L}_1(\mathbf{x} \otimes \mathbf{I}_m) + \mathbf{L}_0) + \boxed{\delta \cdot \mathbf{e}_1^{\top}} \right)$$

together with $(f, \mathbf{x})$, we can recover $f(\mathbf{x})^{\top} \mathbf{z} + \delta$, while learning nothing else about $\mathbf{z}, \delta$. That is, for all $f, \mathbf{x}, \mathbf{z}$ and $\delta \in \mathbb{Z}_p$:

- reconstruction: $(\mathsf{pgb}(f, \mathbf{x}, \mathbf{z}; \mathbf{t}) + (\mathbf{0}, \boxed{\delta} \cdot \mathbf{e}_1^{\top})) \mathbf{d}_{f,\mathbf{x}} = f(\mathbf{x})^{\top} \mathbf{z} + \boxed{\delta}$;
- privacy: $\mathsf{pgb}(f, \mathbf{x}, \mathbf{z}; \mathbf{t}) + (\mathbf{0}, \boxed{\delta} \cdot \mathbf{e}_1^{\top}) \approx_s \mathsf{pgb}^*(f, \mathbf{x}, f(\mathbf{x})^{\top} \mathbf{z} + \boxed{\delta}; \mathbf{t})$ where the randomness is over $\mathbf{t} \leftarrow \mathbb{Z}_p^{m+n'-1}$.

See the full paper for more detail about Lemma 2 and the extension.

5 Π_{one}: One-Slot Scheme

In this section, we present our one-slot FE scheme for attribute-weighted sums. This scheme achieves simulation-based semi-adaptive security under k-Linear assumptions.

5.1   Construction

Our one-slot FE scheme Π_{one} in prime-order bilinear group is described as follows.

- $\mathsf{Setup}(1^\lambda, 1^n, 1^{n'})$: Run $\mathbb{G} = (p, \mathbb{G}_1, \mathbb{G}_2, \mathbb{G}_T, e) \leftarrow \mathcal{G}(1^\lambda)$. Sample

$$\mathbf{A} \leftarrow \mathbb{Z}_p^{(k+1)\times k} \quad \text{and} \quad \mathbf{W} \leftarrow \mathbb{Z}_p^{(k+1)\times n'}, \mathbf{U} \leftarrow \mathbb{Z}_p^{(k+1)\times kn}, \mathbf{V} \leftarrow \mathbb{Z}_p^{(k+1)\times k}$$

and output

$$\mathsf{mpk} = \left(\mathbb{G}, [\mathbf{A}^{\top}]_1, [\mathbf{A}^{\top}\mathbf{W}]_1, [\mathbf{A}^{\top}\mathbf{U}]_1, [\mathbf{A}^{\top}\mathbf{V}]_1 \right) \quad \text{and} \quad \mathsf{msk} = \left(\mathbf{W}, \mathbf{U}, \mathbf{V} \right).$$

- $\mathsf{Enc}(\mathsf{mpk}, (\mathbf{x}, \mathbf{z}))$: Sample $\mathbf{s} \leftarrow \mathbb{Z}_p^k$ and output

$$\mathsf{ct}_{\mathbf{x},\mathbf{z}} = \left([\mathbf{s}^{\top}\mathbf{A}^{\top}]_1, [\mathbf{z}^{\top} + \mathbf{s}^{\top}\mathbf{A}^{\top}\mathbf{W}]_1, [\mathbf{s}^{\top}\mathbf{A}^{\top}\mathbf{U}(\mathbf{x} \otimes \mathbf{I}_k) + \mathbf{s}^{\top}\mathbf{A}^{\top}\mathbf{V}]_1 \right) \quad \text{and} \quad \mathbf{x}.$$

- $\mathsf{KeyGen}(\mathsf{msk}, f)$: Run $(\mathbf{L}_1, \mathbf{L}_0) \leftarrow \mathsf{lgen}(f)$ where $\mathbf{L}_1 \in \mathbb{Z}_p^{(m+n'-1)\times mn}, \mathbf{L}_0 \in \mathbb{Z}_p^{(m+n'-1)\times m}$ (cf. Sect. 4.2). Sample $\mathbf{T} \leftarrow \mathbb{Z}_p^{(k+1)\times(m+n'-1)}$ and $\mathbf{R} \leftarrow \mathbb{Z}_p^{k\times m}$ and output

$$\mathsf{sk}_f = \left([\underline{\mathbf{T}} + \mathbf{W}]_2, [\mathbf{T}\mathbf{L}_1 + \mathbf{U}(\mathbf{I}_n \otimes \mathbf{R})]_2, [\mathbf{T}\mathbf{L}_0 + \mathbf{V}\mathbf{R}]_2, [\mathbf{R}]_2 \right) \quad \text{and} \quad f$$

where $\underline{\mathbf{T}}$ refers to the matrix composed of the right most n' columns of $\mathbf{T}$.

– $\mathsf{Dec}((\mathsf{sk}_f, f), (\mathsf{ct}_{\mathbf{x},\mathbf{z}}, \mathbf{x}))$: On input key:

$$\mathsf{sk}_f = \big([\mathbf{K}_1]_2, [\mathbf{K}_2]_2, [\mathbf{K}_3]_2, [\mathbf{R}]_2\big) \quad \text{and} \quad f$$

and ciphertext:

$$\mathsf{ct}_{\mathbf{x},\mathbf{z}} = \big([\mathbf{c}_0^\top]_1, [\mathbf{c}_1^\top]_1, [\mathbf{c}_2^\top]_1\big) \quad \text{and} \quad \mathbf{x}$$

the decryption works as follows:
1. compute

$$[\mathbf{p}_1^\top]_T = e([\mathbf{c}_1^\top]_1, [\mathbf{I}_{n'}]_2) \cdot e([\mathbf{c}_0^\top]_1, [-\mathbf{K}_1]_2) \tag{9}$$

2. compute

$$[\mathbf{p}_2^\top]_T = e([\mathbf{c}_0^\top]_1, [\mathbf{K}_2(\mathbf{x} \otimes \mathbf{I}_m) + \mathbf{K}_3]_2) \cdot e([-\mathbf{c}_2^\top]_1, [\mathbf{R}]_2) \tag{10}$$

3. run $\mathbf{d}_{f,\mathbf{x}} \leftarrow \mathsf{rec}(f, \mathbf{x})$ (cf. Sect. 4.2), compute

$$[D]_T = [(\mathbf{p}_1^\top, \mathbf{p}_2^\top)\mathbf{d}_{f,\mathbf{x}}]_T \tag{11}$$

and use brute-force discrete log to recover D as the output.

Correctness. For $\mathsf{ct}_{\mathbf{x},\mathbf{z}}$ and sk_f, we have

$$\mathbf{p}_1^\top = \mathbf{z}^\top - \mathbf{s}^\top \mathbf{A}^\top \underline{\mathbf{T}} \tag{12}$$
$$\mathbf{p}_2^\top = \mathbf{s}^\top \mathbf{A}^\top \mathbf{T} \mathbf{L}_1(\mathbf{x} \otimes \mathbf{I}_m) + \mathbf{s}^\top \mathbf{A}^\top \mathbf{T} \mathbf{L}_0 \tag{13}$$
$$(\mathbf{p}_1^\top, \mathbf{p}_2^\top)\mathbf{d}_{f,\mathbf{x}} = f(\mathbf{x})^\top \mathbf{z} \tag{14}$$

Here (14) follows from the fact that

$$(\mathbf{p}_1^\top, \mathbf{p}_2^\top) = \mathsf{pgb}(f, \mathbf{x}, \mathbf{z}; (\mathbf{s}^\top \mathbf{A}^\top \mathbf{T})^\top) \quad \text{and} \quad \mathbf{d}_{f,\mathbf{x}} = \mathsf{rec}(f, \mathbf{x})$$

and reconstruction of the partial garbling in (9); the remaining two equalities
follow from:

(12) $\quad \mathbf{z}^\top - \mathbf{s}^\top \mathbf{A}^\top \underline{\mathbf{T}} = (\mathbf{z}^\top + \mathbf{s}^\top \mathbf{A}^\top \mathbf{W}) \cdot \mathbf{I}_{n'} - \mathbf{s}^\top \mathbf{A}^\top \cdot (\underline{\mathbf{T}} + \mathbf{W})$

(13) $\mathbf{s}^\top \mathbf{A}^\top \mathbf{T} \mathbf{L}_1(\mathbf{x} \otimes \mathbf{I}_m) + \mathbf{s}^\top \mathbf{A}^\top \mathbf{T} \mathbf{L}_0 = \mathbf{s}^\top \mathbf{A}^\top \cdot ((\mathbf{T} \mathbf{L}_1 + \mathbf{U}(\mathbf{I}_n \otimes \mathbf{R}))(\mathbf{x} \otimes \mathbf{I}_m) + (\mathbf{T} \mathbf{L}_0 + \mathbf{V} \mathbf{R}))$
$\qquad\qquad\qquad\qquad\qquad\qquad\qquad\qquad\qquad\qquad - (\mathbf{s}^\top \mathbf{A}^\top \mathbf{U}(\mathbf{x} \otimes \mathbf{I}_k) + \mathbf{s}^\top \mathbf{A}^\top \mathbf{V}) \cdot \mathbf{R}$

in which we use the equality $(\mathbf{I}_n \otimes \mathbf{R})(\mathbf{x} \otimes \mathbf{I}_m) = (\mathbf{x} \otimes \mathbf{I}_k)\mathbf{R}$. This readily proves
the correctness.

Remark 2 (Comparison with W17 [40]). The ciphertext in [40] contains a term
of the form

$$[\mathbf{x}^\top \otimes \mathbf{s}^\top \mathbf{A}^\top \mathbf{V} + \mathbf{s}^\top \mathbf{A}^\top \mathbf{U}]_1 \in \mathbb{G}_1^{kn} \quad \text{in the place of} \quad [\mathbf{s}^\top \mathbf{A}^\top \mathbf{U}(\mathbf{x} \otimes \mathbf{I}_k) + \mathbf{s}^\top \mathbf{A}^\top \mathbf{V}]_1 \in \mathbb{G}_1^{k}$$

where $\mathbf{U} \leftarrow \mathbb{Z}_p^{(k+1) \times kn}, \mathbf{V} \leftarrow \mathbb{Z}_p^{(k+1) \times k}$. The secret key sizes in both our schemes
and that in [40] are $O(mn + n')$. In our scheme, the multiplicative factor of n
comes at the cost of a smaller ciphertext. In [40], the multiplicative factor of n
comes from a locality requirement that each column of $\mathbf{L}_1(\mathbf{x} \otimes \mathbf{I}_m) + \mathbf{L}_0$ depends
on a single entry of $\mathbf{x}$, which can be achieved generically at the cost of a blow-up
of n. We remove the locality requirement in our scheme.

Security. We have the following theorem with the proof shown in the subsequent subsection.

Theorem 1. *Our one-slot scheme Π_{one} for attribute-weighted sums described in this section achieves simulation-based semi-adaptive security under the MDDH assumption in $\mathbb{G}_1$ and in $\mathbb{G}_2$.*

5.2 Simulator

We start by describing the simulator.

- Setup$^*(1^\lambda, 1^n, 1^{n'})$: Run $\mathbb{G} = (p, \mathbb{G}_1, \mathbb{G}_2, \mathbb{G}_T, e) \leftarrow \mathcal{G}(1^\lambda)$. Sample

$$
\begin{array}{lll}
\mathbf{A} \leftarrow \mathbb{Z}_p^{(k+1)\times k} & \text{and} & \mathbf{W} \leftarrow \mathbb{Z}_p^{(k+1)\times n'}, \mathbf{U} \leftarrow \mathbb{Z}_p^{(k+1)\times kn}, \mathbf{V} \leftarrow \mathbb{Z}_p^{(k+1)\times k} \\
\mathbf{c} \leftarrow \mathbb{Z}_p^{k+1} & & \widetilde{\mathbf{w}} \leftarrow \mathbb{Z}_p^{n'}, \qquad\qquad\qquad\qquad\qquad\qquad \widetilde{\mathbf{v}} \leftarrow \mathbb{Z}_p^{k}
\end{array}
$$

and output

$$
\begin{aligned}
\mathsf{mpk} &= \big(\mathbb{G}, [\mathbf{A}^\top]_1, [\mathbf{A}^\top\mathbf{W}]_1, [\mathbf{A}^\top\mathbf{U}]_1, [\mathbf{A}^\top\mathbf{V}]_1 \big) \\
\mathsf{msk}^* &= \big(\mathbf{W}, \mathbf{U}, \mathbf{V}, \widetilde{\mathbf{w}}, \widetilde{\mathbf{v}}, \mathbf{c}, \mathbf{C}^\perp, \mathbf{A}, \mathbf{a}^\perp \big)
\end{aligned}
$$

where $(\mathbf{A}|\mathbf{c})^\top(\mathbf{C}^\perp|\mathbf{a}^\perp) = \mathbf{I}_{k+1}$. Here we assume that $(\mathbf{A}|\mathbf{c})$ has full rank, which happens with probability $1 - 1/p$.
- Enc$^*(\mathsf{msk}^*, \mathbf{x}^*)$: Output

$$
\mathsf{ct}^* = \big([\mathbf{c}^\top]_1, [\widetilde{\mathbf{w}}^\top]_1, [\widetilde{\mathbf{v}}^\top]_1 \big) \quad \text{and} \quad \mathbf{x}^*.
$$

- KeyGen$^*(\mathsf{msk}^*, \mathbf{x}^*, f, \mu \in \mathbb{Z}_p)$: Run

$$
(\mathbf{L}_1, \mathbf{L}_0) \leftarrow \mathsf{lgen}(f) \quad \text{and} \quad ((\mathbf{p}_1^*)^\top, (\mathbf{p}_2^*)^\top) \leftarrow \mathsf{pgb}^*(f, \mathbf{x}^*, \mu).
$$

Sample $\hat{\mathbf{u}} \leftarrow \mathbb{Z}_p^{nm}$, $\mathbf{T} \leftarrow \mathbb{Z}_p^{(k+1)\times(m+n'-1)}$ and $\mathbf{R} \leftarrow \mathbb{Z}_p^{k\times m}$ and output

$$
\mathsf{sk}_f^* = \big(\mathbf{C}^\perp \cdot \mathsf{sk}_f^*[1] + \mathbf{a}^\perp \cdot \mathsf{sk}_f^*[2], [\mathbf{R}]_2 \big) \quad \text{and} \quad f \tag{15}
$$

where

$$
\begin{aligned}
\mathsf{sk}_f^*[1] &= \big([\mathbf{A}^\top\underline{\mathbf{T}} + \mathbf{A}^\top\mathbf{W}]_2, [\mathbf{A}^\top\mathbf{T}\mathbf{L}_1 + \mathbf{A}^\top\mathbf{U}(\mathbf{I}_n \otimes \mathbf{R})]_2, [\mathbf{A}^\top\mathbf{T}\mathbf{L}_0 + \mathbf{A}^\top\mathbf{V}\mathbf{R}]_2 \big) \\
\mathsf{sk}_f^*[2] &= \big([-(\mathbf{p}_1^*)^\top + \widetilde{\mathbf{w}}^\top]_2, [\hat{\mathbf{u}}^\top]_2, [(\mathbf{p}_2^*)^\top - \hat{\mathbf{u}}^\top(\mathbf{x}^* \otimes \mathbf{I}_m) + \widetilde{\mathbf{v}}^\top\mathbf{R}]_2 \big)
\end{aligned}
$$

Here $\underline{\mathbf{T}}$ refers to the matrix composed of the right most n' columns of $\mathbf{T}$. That is,

$$
\mathsf{sk}_f^* = \left(\begin{array}{ll}
[\mathbf{C}^\perp(\mathbf{A}^\top\underline{\mathbf{T}} + \mathbf{A}^\top\mathbf{W}) & +\mathbf{a}^\perp(-(\mathbf{p}_1^*)^\top + \widetilde{\mathbf{w}}^\top)]_2, \\
[\mathbf{C}^\perp(\mathbf{A}^\top\mathbf{T}\mathbf{L}_1 + \mathbf{A}^\top\mathbf{U}(\mathbf{I}_n \otimes \mathbf{R})) & +\mathbf{a}^\perp(\hat{\mathbf{u}}^\top)]_2 \\
[\mathbf{C}^\perp(\mathbf{A}^\top\mathbf{T}\mathbf{L}_0 + \mathbf{A}^\top\mathbf{V}\mathbf{R}) & +\mathbf{a}^\perp((\mathbf{p}_2^*)^\top - \hat{\mathbf{u}}^\top(\mathbf{x}^* \otimes \mathbf{I}_m) + \widetilde{\mathbf{v}}^\top\mathbf{R})]_2
\end{array} , [\mathbf{R}]_2 \right)
$$

Remark 3 (decryption checks). As a sanity check, we check that an adversary cannot use the decryption algorithm to distinguish between the real and simulated output.

Observe that when we decrypt the simulated ciphertext $\mathsf{ct}^*_{\mathbf{x}^*} \leftarrow \mathsf{Enc}^*(\mathsf{msk}^*, \mathbf{x}^*)$ with the simulated secret key $\mathsf{sk}^*_f \leftarrow \mathsf{KeyGen}^*(\mathsf{msk}^*, \mathbf{x}^*, f, f(\mathbf{x}^*)^\top \mathbf{z}^*)$, the $\mathsf{sk}^*_f[1]$ part cancels out and leaves just the $\mathsf{sk}^*_f[2]$ part since $\mathbf{c}^\top \mathbf{C}^\perp = \mathbf{0}, \mathbf{c}^\top \mathbf{a}^\perp = 1$ and we end up with $((\mathbf{p}^*_1)^\top, (\mathbf{p}^*_2)^\top)\mathbf{d}_{f,\mathbf{x}^*} = f(\mathbf{x}^*)^\top \mathbf{z}^*$ where $((\mathbf{p}^*_1)^\top, (\mathbf{p}^*_2)^\top) \leftarrow \mathsf{pgb}^*(f, \mathbf{x}^*, f(\mathbf{x}^*)^\top \mathbf{z}^*)$.

Similarly, when we decrypt a normal ciphertext $\mathsf{ct}_{\mathbf{x},\mathbf{z}} \leftarrow \mathsf{Enc}(\mathsf{mpk}, (\mathbf{x}, \mathbf{z}))$ corresponding to any $(\mathbf{x}, \mathbf{z})$ with a simulated secret key, the $\mathsf{sk}^*_f[2]$ part cancels out and leaves just the $\mathsf{sk}^*_f[1]$ part since $\mathbf{A}^\top \mathbf{C}^\perp = \mathbf{I}, \mathbf{A}^\top \mathbf{a}^\perp = \mathbf{0}$. We end up with $(\mathbf{p}^\top_1, \mathbf{p}^\top_2)\mathbf{d}_{f,\mathbf{x}} = f(\mathbf{x})^\top \mathbf{z}$ where $(\mathbf{p}^\top_1, \mathbf{p}^\top_2) = \mathsf{pgb}(f, \mathbf{x}, \mathbf{z}; (\mathbf{s}^\top \mathbf{A}^\top \mathbf{T})^\top)$ as in the real Dec algorithm.

5.3 Proof

With our simulator, we prove the following theorem which implies Theorem 1.

Theorem 2. *For all* $\mathcal{A}$, *there exist* $\mathcal{B}_1$ *and* $\mathcal{B}_2$ *with* $\mathsf{Time}(\mathcal{B}_1), \mathsf{Time}(\mathcal{B}_2) \approx \mathsf{Time}(\mathcal{A})$ *such that*

$$\mathsf{Adv}^{\Pi_{\mathsf{one}}}_{\mathcal{A}}(\lambda) \leq \mathsf{Adv}^{\mathrm{MDDH}^1_{k,k+1}}_{\mathcal{B}_1}(\lambda) + \mathsf{Adv}^{\mathrm{MDDH}^n_{k,mQ}}_{\mathcal{B}_2}(\lambda) + 1/p$$

where n *is length of public input* $\mathbf{x}^*$ *in the challenge,* m *is the parameter depending on size of function* f *and* Q *is the number of key queries.*

Note that this yields a tight security reduction to the k-Lin assumption. Before we proceed to describe the game sequence and proof, we state the following lemma we will use.

Lemma 3 (statistical lemma). *For any full-rank* $(\mathbf{A}|\mathbf{c}) \in \mathbb{Z}^{(k+1) \times k}_p \times \mathbb{Z}^{k+1}_p$, *we have*

$$\left\{ \mathbf{A}^\top \mathbf{W}, \boxed{\mathbf{c}^\top \mathbf{W}} : \mathbf{W} \leftarrow \mathbb{Z}^{(k+1) \times k}_p \right\} \equiv \left\{ \mathbf{A}^\top \mathbf{W}, \boxed{\tilde{\mathbf{w}}^\top} : \mathbf{W} \leftarrow \mathbb{Z}^{(k+1) \times k}_p, \boxed{\tilde{\mathbf{w}} \leftarrow \mathbb{Z}^k_p} \right\}.$$

Game sequence. We use $(\mathbf{x}^*, \mathbf{z}^*)$ to denote the semi-adaptive challenge and for notational simplicity, assume that all key queries f_j share the same parameter m. We prove Theorem 2 via a series of games.

$\underline{\mathsf{Game}_0}$: Real game.

$\underline{\mathsf{Game}_1}$: Identical to Game_0 except that ct^* for $(\mathbf{x}^*, \mathbf{z}^*)$ is given by

$$\mathsf{ct}^* = \left([\boxed{\mathbf{c}^\top}]_1, [(\mathbf{z}^*)^\top + \boxed{\mathbf{c}^\top}\mathbf{W}]_1, [\boxed{\mathbf{c}^\top}\mathbf{U}(\mathbf{x}^* \otimes \mathbf{I}_k) + \boxed{\mathbf{c}^\top}\mathbf{V}]_1 \right)$$

where $\mathbf{c} \leftarrow \mathbb{Z}^{k+1}_p$. We claim that $\mathsf{Game}_0 \approx_c \mathsf{Game}_1$. This follows from $\mathrm{MDDH}^1_{k,k+1}$ assumption:

$$[\mathbf{A}^\top]_1, [\mathbf{s}^\top \mathbf{A}^\top]_1 \approx_c [\mathbf{A}^\top]_1, \boxed{[\mathbf{c}^\top]_1}.$$

In the reduction, we sample $\mathbf{W}, \mathbf{U}, \mathbf{V}$ honestly and use them to simulate mpk and KeyGen(msk, $\cdot$) along with $[\mathbf{A}^\top]_1$; the challenge ciphertext ct* is generated using the challenge term given above.

Game$_2$: Identical to Game$_1$ except that the j-th query f_j to KeyGen KeyGen(msk, $\cdot$) is answered by

$$\mathsf{sk}_{f_j} = \big(\mathbf{C}^\perp \cdot \mathsf{sk}_{f_j}[1] + \mathbf{a}^\perp \cdot \mathsf{sk}_{f_j}[2], \; [\mathbf{R}_j]_2 \big)$$

with

$$\mathsf{sk}_{f_j}[1] = \big([\mathbf{A}^\top \mathbf{T}_j + \mathbf{A}^\top \mathbf{W}]_2, \; [\mathbf{A}^\top \mathbf{T}_j \mathbf{L}_{1,j} + \mathbf{A}^\top \mathbf{U}(\mathbf{I}_n \otimes \mathbf{R}_j)]_2, \; [\mathbf{A}^\top \mathbf{T}_j \mathbf{L}_{0,j} + \mathbf{A}^\top \mathbf{V} \mathbf{R}_j]_2 \big)$$
$$\mathsf{sk}_{f_j}[2] = \big([\mathbf{c}^\top \mathbf{T}_j + \mathbf{c}^\top \mathbf{W}]_2, \; [\mathbf{c}^\top \mathbf{T}_j \mathbf{L}_{1,j} + \mathbf{c}^\top \mathbf{U}(\mathbf{I}_n \otimes \mathbf{R}_j)]_2, \; [\mathbf{c}^\top \mathbf{T}_j \mathbf{L}_{0,j} + \mathbf{c}^\top \mathbf{V} \mathbf{R}_j]_2 \big)$$

where $(\mathbf{L}_{1,j}, \mathbf{L}_{0,j}) \leftarrow \mathsf{lgen}(f_j)$, $\mathbf{T}_j \leftarrow \mathbb{Z}_p^{(k+1)\times(m+n'-1)}$, $\mathbf{R}_j \leftarrow \mathbb{Z}_p^{k\times m}$, $\mathbf{c}$ is the randomness in ct* and $\mathbf{C}^\perp, \mathbf{a}^\perp$ are defined such that $(\mathbf{A}|\mathbf{c})^\top(\mathbf{C}^\perp|\mathbf{a}^\perp) = \mathbf{I}_{k+1}$ (cf. Setup* in Sect. 5.2). By basic linear algebra, we have Game$_1$ = Game$_2$.

Game$_3$: Identical to Game$_2$ except that we replace Setup, Enc with Setup*, Enc* where ct* is given by

$$\mathsf{ct}^* = \big([\mathbf{c}^\top]_1, \; \boxed{[\widetilde{\mathbf{w}}^\top]_1, \; [\widetilde{\mathbf{v}}^\top]_1} \big)$$

and replace KeyGen(msk, $\cdot$) with KeyGen$_3^*$(msk*, $\cdot$), which works as KeyGen(msk, $\cdot$) in Game$_2$ except that, for the j-th query f_j, we compute

$$\mathsf{sk}_{f_j}[2] = \left(\frac{\boxed{[\widetilde{\mathbf{t}}_j^\top - (\mathbf{z}^*)^\top + \widetilde{\mathbf{w}}^\top]_2}, \; [\boxed{\widetilde{\mathbf{t}}_j^\top}\mathbf{L}_{1,j} + \boxed{\widetilde{\mathbf{u}}^\top}(\mathbf{I}_n \otimes \mathbf{R}_j)]_2,}{[\boxed{\widetilde{\mathbf{t}}_j^\top}\mathbf{L}_{0,j}\boxed{-\widetilde{\mathbf{u}}^\top(\mathbf{I}_n \otimes \mathbf{R}_j)(\mathbf{x}^* \otimes \mathbf{I}_m)} + \widetilde{\mathbf{v}}^\top \mathbf{R}_j]_2} \right)$$

where $\widetilde{\mathbf{w}}, \widetilde{\mathbf{v}}$ are given in msk* (output by Setup*) and $\widetilde{\mathbf{u}} \leftarrow \mathbb{Z}_p^{kn}$, $\mathbf{t}_j \leftarrow \mathbb{Z}_p^{m+n'-1}$, $\mathbf{R}_j \leftarrow \mathbb{Z}_p^{k\times m}$. We claim that Game$_2 \approx_s$ Game$_3$. This follows from the following statement: for any full-rank $(\mathbf{A}|\mathbf{c})$, we have

$$(\mathbf{A}^\top \mathbf{U}, \mathbf{c}^\top \mathbf{U}, \mathbf{A}^\top \mathbf{W}, \mathbf{c}^\top \mathbf{W}, \qquad \mathbf{A}^\top \mathbf{V}, \mathbf{c}^\top \mathbf{V}, \qquad\qquad \mathbf{A}^\top \mathbf{T}_j, \mathbf{c}^\top \mathbf{T}_j)$$
$$\equiv (\mathbf{A}^\top \mathbf{U}, \boxed{\widetilde{\mathbf{u}}^\top}, \mathbf{A}^\top \mathbf{W}, \boxed{\widetilde{\mathbf{w}}^\top - (\mathbf{z}^*)^\top}, \mathbf{A}^\top \mathbf{V}, \boxed{\widetilde{\mathbf{v}}^\top - \widetilde{\mathbf{u}}^\top(\mathbf{x}^* \otimes \mathbf{I}_k)}, \mathbf{A}^\top \mathbf{T}_j, \boxed{\widetilde{\mathbf{t}}_j^\top})$$

which is implied by Lemma 3.

Game$_4$: Identical to Game$_3$ except that we replace KeyGen$_3^*$ with KeyGen$_4^*$ which works as KeyGen$_3^*$ except that, for the j-th query f_j, we compute

$$\mathsf{sk}_{f_j}[2] = \big([\widetilde{\mathbf{t}}_j^\top - (\mathbf{z}^*)^\top + \widetilde{\mathbf{w}}^\top]_2, \; [\widetilde{\mathbf{t}}_j^\top \mathbf{L}_{1,j} + \boxed{\widehat{\mathbf{u}}_j^\top}]_2, \; [\widetilde{\mathbf{t}}_j^\top \mathbf{L}_{0,j} - \boxed{\widehat{\mathbf{u}}_j^\top}(\mathbf{x}^* \otimes \mathbf{I}_m) + \widetilde{\mathbf{v}}^\top \mathbf{R}_j]_2 \big)$$

where $\widehat{\mathbf{u}}_j \leftarrow \mathbb{Z}_p^{nm}$ and $\mathbf{R}_j \leftarrow \mathbb{Z}_p^{k\times m}$. We claim that Game$_3 \approx_c$ Game$_4$. This follows from $\widehat{\mathrm{MDDH}}_{k,mQ}^n$ assumption which tells us that

$$\big\{ [\widetilde{\mathbf{u}}^\top(\mathbf{I}_n \otimes \mathbf{R}_j)]_2, \; [\mathbf{R}_j]_2 \big\}_{j\in[Q]} \approx_c \big\{ \boxed{[\widehat{\mathbf{u}}_j^\top]_2}, \; [\mathbf{R}_j]_2 \big\}_{j\in[Q]}$$

where Q is the number of key queries.

Game$_5$: Identical to Game$_4$ except that we replace KeyGen$_4^*$ with KeyGen*; this is the ideal game. We claim that Game$_4 \approx_s$ Game$_5$. This follows from the privacy of partial garbling scheme in Sect. 4.2.

We prove the indistinguishability of adjacent games listed above in the full paper.

6 Π_{ext}: Extending Π_{one}

In this section, we extend our one-slot FE scheme Π_{one} in Sect. 5 to handle the randomization offsets $\mathbf{w}^{\top}\mathbf{r}$. The scheme achieves simulation-based semi-adaptive security under k-Linear assumption.

Extension. The extended scheme is the same as a one-slot FE for attribute-weighted sums, except we replace functionality $((\mathbf{x}, \mathbf{z}), f) \mapsto f(\mathbf{x})^{\top}\mathbf{z}$ with

$$((\mathbf{x}, \mathbf{z}\|\mathbf{w}), (f, [\mathbf{r}]_2)) \mapsto [f(\mathbf{x})^{\top}\mathbf{z} + \mathbf{w}^{\top}\mathbf{r}]_T$$

where $\mathbf{w}, \mathbf{r} \in \mathbb{Z}_p^k$. That is, we make the following modifications:

- Enc takes $\mathbf{z}\|\mathbf{w}$ instead of $\mathbf{z}$ as the second input;
- KeyGen, KeyGen* takes $(f, [\mathbf{r}]_2)$ instead of f as input;
- in correctness, decryption computes $[f(\mathbf{x})^{\top}\mathbf{z} + \mathbf{w}^{\top}\mathbf{r}]_T$ instead of $f(\mathbf{x})^{\top}\mathbf{z}$;
- in the security definition, $\mathcal{A}$ produces $(\mathbf{x}^*, \mathbf{z}^*\|\mathbf{w}^*)$ instead of $(\mathbf{x}^*, \mathbf{z}^*)$, and KeyGen* gets $[f(\mathbf{x}^*)^{\top}\mathbf{z}^* + (\mathbf{w}^*)^{\top}\mathbf{r}]_2$ instead of $f(\mathbf{x}^*)^{\top}\mathbf{z}^*$.

In particular, correctness states that:

$$\mathsf{Dec}(\mathsf{Enc}(\mathsf{mpk}, (\mathbf{x}, \mathbf{z}\|\mathbf{w})), \mathsf{KeyGen}(\mathsf{msk}, (f, [\mathbf{r}]_2))) = [f(\mathbf{x})^{\top}\mathbf{z} + \mathbf{w}^{\top}\mathbf{r}]_T$$

Construction overview. To obtain a scheme with the extension, the idea — following the IPFE in [6]— is to augment the previous construction Π_{one} with $[\mathbf{A}^{\top}\mathbf{W}_0]_1$ in mpk, $[\mathbf{w}^{\top} + \mathbf{s}^{\top}\mathbf{A}^{\top}\mathbf{W}_0]_1$ in the ciphertext, and $[\mathbf{W}_0\mathbf{r}]_2$ in the secret key. During decryption, we will additionally compute

$$e([\mathbf{w}^{\top} + \mathbf{s}^{\top}\mathbf{A}^{\top}\mathbf{W}_0]_1, [\mathbf{r}]_2) \cdot e([\mathbf{s}^{\top}\mathbf{A}^{\top}]_1, [\mathbf{W}_0\mathbf{r}]_2)^{-1} = [\mathbf{w}^{\top}\mathbf{r}]_T$$

This works for correctness, but violates security since the decryptor learns both $[f(\mathbf{x})^{\top}\mathbf{z}]_T$ and $[\mathbf{w}^{\top}\mathbf{r}]_T$ instead of just the sum. To avoid this leakage while preserving correctness, we will carefully embed $\mathbf{W}_0\mathbf{r}$ into the secret key for Π_{one}, while relying on the extension of the garbling scheme for handling shifts to argue both correctness and security, cf. Sect. 4.2. We will describe the scheme and simulator but defer the details for the proof to full paper.

6.1 Our Scheme

Scheme. Our extended one-slot FE scheme Π_{ext} in prime-order bilinear group is described as follows. The boxes indicate the changes from the scheme in Sect. 5.1.

- Setup($1^\lambda, 1^n, 1^{n'}$): Run $\mathbb{G} = (p, \mathbb{G}_1, \mathbb{G}_2, \mathbb{G}_T, e) \leftarrow \mathcal{G}(1^\lambda)$. Sample $\mathbf{A} \leftarrow \mathbb{Z}_p^{(k+1)\times k}$ and

$$\mathbf{W} \leftarrow \mathbb{Z}_p^{(k+1)\times n'}, \boxed{\mathbf{W}_0 \leftarrow \mathbb{Z}_p^{(k+1)\times k}}, \mathbf{U} \leftarrow \mathbb{Z}_p^{(k+1)\times kn}, \mathbf{V} \leftarrow \mathbb{Z}_p^{(k+1)\times k}$$

and output

$$\mathsf{mpk} = \big(\, \mathbb{G},\, [\mathbf{A}^\top]_1,\, [\mathbf{A}^\top\mathbf{W}]_1,\, [\mathbf{A}^\top\mathbf{U}]_1,\, [\mathbf{A}^\top\mathbf{V}]_1,\, \boxed{[\mathbf{A}^\top\mathbf{W}_0]_1}\,\big)$$

$$\mathsf{msk} = \big(\, \mathbf{W},\, \mathbf{U},\, \mathbf{V},\, \boxed{\mathbf{W}_0}\,\big).$$

- Enc($\mathsf{mpk}, (\mathbf{x}, \mathbf{z}\|\mathbf{w})$): Sample $\mathbf{s} \leftarrow \mathbb{Z}_p^k$ and output

$$\mathsf{ct}_{\mathbf{x},\mathbf{z}\|\mathbf{w}} = \left(\begin{array}{c} [\mathbf{s}^\top\mathbf{A}^\top]_1,\, [\mathbf{z}^\top + \mathbf{s}^\top\mathbf{A}^\top\mathbf{W}]_1,\, [\mathbf{s}^\top\mathbf{A}^\top\mathbf{U}(\mathbf{x}\otimes\mathbf{I}_k) + \mathbf{s}^\top\mathbf{A}^\top\mathbf{V}]_1, \\ \boxed{[\mathbf{w}^\top + \mathbf{s}^\top\mathbf{A}^\top\mathbf{W}_0]_1} \end{array}\right),\, \mathbf{x}.$$

- KeyGen($\mathsf{msk}, (f, [\mathbf{r}]_2)$): Run $(\mathbf{L}_1, \mathbf{L}_0) \leftarrow \mathsf{lgen}(f)$ where $\mathbf{L}_1 \in \mathbb{Z}_p^{(m+n'-1)\times mn}$, $\mathbf{L}_0 \in \mathbb{Z}_p^{(m+n'-1)\times m}$ (cf. Sect. 4.2). Sample $\mathbf{T} \leftarrow \mathbb{Z}_p^{(k+1)\times(m+n'-1)}$ and $\mathbf{R} \leftarrow \mathbb{Z}_p^{k\times m}$ and output[6]

$$\mathsf{sk}_{f,\mathbf{r}} = \big(\, [\underline{\mathbf{T}} + \mathbf{W}]_2,\, [\mathbf{T}\mathbf{L}_1 + \mathbf{U}(\mathbf{I}_n\otimes\mathbf{R})]_2,\, [\mathbf{T}\mathbf{L}_0 - \boxed{\mathbf{W}_0\mathbf{r}\cdot\mathbf{e}_1^\top} + \mathbf{V}\mathbf{R}]_2,\, [\mathbf{R}]_2\,),\, (f, \boxed{[\mathbf{r}]_2}\,)$$

where $\underline{\mathbf{T}}$ refers to the matrix composed of the right most n' columns of $\mathbf{T}$.

- Dec($(\mathsf{sk}_{f,\mathbf{r}}, (f, \boxed{[\mathbf{r}]_2}\,)), (\mathsf{ct}_{\mathbf{x},\mathbf{z}\|\mathbf{w}}, \mathbf{x})$): On input key:

$$\mathsf{sk}_{f,\mathbf{r}} = \big(\, [\mathbf{K}_1]_2,\, [\mathbf{K}_2]_2,\, [\mathbf{K}_3]_2,\, [\mathbf{R}]_2\,\big) \quad\text{and}\quad (f, [\mathbf{r}]_2)$$

and ciphertext:

$$\mathsf{ct}_{\mathbf{x},\mathbf{z}\|\mathbf{w}} = \big(\, [\mathbf{c}_0^\top]_1,\, [\mathbf{c}_1^\top]_1,\, [\mathbf{c}_2^\top]_1,\, [\mathbf{c}_3^\top]_1\,\big) \quad\text{and}\quad \mathbf{x}$$

the decryption works as follows:
1. compute

$$[\mathbf{p}_1^\top]_T = e([\mathbf{c}_1^\top]_1, [\mathbf{I}_{n'}]_2) \cdot e([\mathbf{c}_0^\top]_1, [-\mathbf{K}_1]_2) \tag{16}$$

2. compute

$$[\mathbf{p}_2^\top]_T = e([\mathbf{c}_0^\top]_1, [\mathbf{K}_2(\mathbf{x}\otimes\mathbf{I}_m) + \mathbf{K}_3]_2) \cdot e([-\mathbf{c}_2^\top]_1, [\mathbf{R}]_2) \cdot \boxed{e([\mathbf{c}_3^\top]_1, [\mathbf{r}\cdot\mathbf{e}_1^\top]_2)} \tag{17}$$

3. run $\mathbf{d}_{f,\mathbf{x}} \leftarrow \mathsf{rec}(f, \mathbf{x})$ (see Sect. 4.2), output

$$[D]_T = [(\mathbf{p}_1^\top, \mathbf{p}_2^\top)\mathbf{d}_{f,\mathbf{x}}]_T \tag{18}$$

---

[6] We use $\mathbf{r}$ instead of $[\mathbf{r}]_2$ in the subscript here and note that the function is described by $(f, [\mathbf{r}]_2)$ rather than $(f, \mathbf{r})$.

Simulator. The simulator for Π_{ext} is as follows. The boxes indicate the changes from the simulator for Π_{one} in Sect. 5.2.

– Setup*$(1^\lambda, 1^n, 1^{n'})$: Run $\mathbb{G} = (p, \mathbb{G}_1, \mathbb{G}_2, \mathbb{G}_T, e) \leftarrow \mathcal{G}(1^\lambda)$. Sample

$$\mathbf{A} \leftarrow \mathbb{Z}_p^{(k+1)\times k} \quad \text{and} \quad \mathbf{c} \leftarrow \mathbb{Z}_p^{k+1} \quad \text{and}$$

$$\mathbf{W} \leftarrow \mathbb{Z}_p^{(k+1)\times n'}, \quad \boxed{\mathbf{W}_0 \leftarrow \mathbb{Z}_p^{(k+1)\times k}}, \quad \mathbf{U} \leftarrow \mathbb{Z}_p^{(k+1)\times kn}, \quad \mathbf{V} \leftarrow \mathbb{Z}_p^{(k+1)\times k}$$

$$\widetilde{\mathbf{w}} \leftarrow \mathbb{Z}_p^{n'}, \quad \boxed{\widetilde{\mathbf{w}}_0 \leftarrow \mathbb{Z}_p^{k}}, \quad\quad\quad\quad\quad\quad \widetilde{\mathbf{v}} \leftarrow \mathbb{Z}_p^{k}$$

and output

$$\mathsf{mpk} = \left(\mathbb{G}, [\mathbf{A}^\top]_1, [\mathbf{A}^\top\mathbf{W}]_1, \boxed{[\mathbf{A}^\top\mathbf{W}_0]_1}, [\mathbf{A}^\top\mathbf{U}]_1, [\mathbf{A}^\top\mathbf{V}]_1 \right)$$

$$\mathsf{msk}^* = \left(\mathbf{W}, \boxed{\mathbf{W}_0}, \mathbf{U}, \mathbf{V}, \widetilde{\mathbf{w}}, \boxed{\widetilde{\mathbf{w}}_0}, \widetilde{\mathbf{v}}, \mathbf{c}, \mathbf{C}^\perp, \mathbf{A}, \mathbf{a}^\perp \right)$$

where $(\mathbf{A}|\mathbf{c})^\top (\mathbf{C}^\perp|\mathbf{a}^\perp) = \mathbf{I}_{k+1}$. Here we assume that $(\mathbf{A}|\mathbf{c})$ has full rank, which happens with probability $1 - 1/p$.

– Enc*$(\mathsf{msk}^*, \mathbf{x}^*)$: Output

$$\mathsf{ct}^* = \left([\mathbf{c}^\top]_1, [\widetilde{\mathbf{w}}^\top]_1, [\widetilde{\mathbf{v}}^\top]_1, \boxed{[\widetilde{\mathbf{w}}_0^\top]_1} \right) \quad \text{and} \quad \mathbf{x}^*.$$

– KeyGen*$(\mathsf{msk}^*, \mathbf{x}^*, (f, [\mathbf{r}]_2), [\mu]_2)$: Run

$$(\mathbf{L}_1, \mathbf{L}_0) \leftarrow \mathsf{lgen}(f) \quad \text{and} \quad ([(\mathbf{p}_1^*)^\top]_2, [(\mathbf{p}_2^*)^\top]_2) \leftarrow \mathsf{pgb}^*(f, \mathbf{x}^*, \boxed{[\mu]_2}).$$

Here, we use the fact that $\mathsf{pgb}^*(f, \mathbf{x}^*, \cdot)$ is an affine function. Sample $\hat{\mathbf{u}} \leftarrow \mathbb{Z}_p^{nm}$, $\mathbf{T} \leftarrow \mathbb{Z}_p^{(k+1)\times(m+n'-1)}$ and $\mathbf{R} \leftarrow \mathbb{Z}_p^{k\times m}$ and output

$$\mathsf{sk}_{f,\mathbf{r}}^* = \left(\mathbf{C}^\perp \cdot \mathsf{sk}_{f,\mathbf{r}}^*[1] + \mathbf{a}^\perp \cdot \mathsf{sk}_{f,\mathbf{r}}^*[2], [\mathbf{R}]_2 \right) \quad \text{and} \quad (f, [\mathbf{r}]_2) \tag{19}$$

where

$$\mathsf{sk}_{f,\mathbf{r}}^*[1] = \left([\mathbf{A}^\top\underline{\mathbf{T}} + \mathbf{A}^\top\mathbf{W}]_2, [\mathbf{A}^\top\mathbf{T}\mathbf{L}_1 + \mathbf{A}^\top\mathbf{U}(\mathbf{I}_n \otimes \mathbf{R})]_2, \right.$$
$$\left. [\mathbf{A}^\top\mathbf{T}\mathbf{L}_0 - \boxed{\mathbf{A}^\top\mathbf{W}_0\mathbf{r}\cdot\mathbf{e}_1^\top} + \mathbf{A}^\top\mathbf{V}\mathbf{R}]_2 \right)$$

$$\mathsf{sk}_{f,\mathbf{r}}^*[2] = \left([-(\mathbf{p}_1^*)^\top + \widetilde{\mathbf{w}}^\top]_2, [\hat{\mathbf{u}}^\top]_2, [(\mathbf{p}_2^*)^\top - \hat{\mathbf{u}}^\top(\mathbf{x}^* \otimes \mathbf{I}_m) - \boxed{\widetilde{\mathbf{w}}_0^\top\mathbf{r}\cdot\mathbf{e}_1^\top} + \widetilde{\mathbf{v}}^\top\mathbf{R}]_2 \right)$$

Here $\underline{\mathbf{T}}$ refers to the matrix composed of the right most n' columns of $\mathbf{T}$. That is,

$$\mathsf{sk}_{f,\mathbf{r}}^* = \begin{pmatrix} [\mathbf{C}^\perp(\mathbf{A}^\top\underline{\mathbf{T}} + \mathbf{A}^\top\mathbf{W}) & +\mathbf{a}^\perp(-(\mathbf{p}_1^*)^\top + \widetilde{\mathbf{w}}^\top)]_2, \\ [\mathbf{C}^\perp(\mathbf{A}^\top\mathbf{T}\mathbf{L}_1 + \mathbf{A}^\top\mathbf{U}(\mathbf{I}_n \otimes \mathbf{R})) & +\mathbf{a}^\perp(\hat{\mathbf{u}}^\top)]_2 \\ [\mathbf{C}^\perp(\mathbf{A}^\top\mathbf{T}\mathbf{L}_0 - \boxed{\mathbf{A}^\top\mathbf{W}_0\mathbf{r}\cdot\mathbf{e}_1^\top} + \mathbf{A}^\top\mathbf{V}\mathbf{R}) & +\mathbf{a}^\perp((\mathbf{p}_2^*)^\top - \hat{\mathbf{u}}^\top(\mathbf{x}^* \otimes \mathbf{I}_m) - \boxed{\widetilde{\mathbf{w}}_0^\top\mathbf{r}\cdot\mathbf{e}_1^\top} + \widetilde{\mathbf{v}}^\top\mathbf{R})]_2 \end{pmatrix}, [\mathbf{R}]_2$$

7 Π_{ubd}: Unbounded-Slot Scheme

In this section, we describe our unbounded-slot FE scheme. We give a generic transformation from scheme Π_{ext} in Sect. 6 and present a self-contained description of the scheme in the full paper.

7.1   Scheme

Let $\Pi_{\mathsf{ext}} = (\mathsf{Setup}_{\mathsf{ext}}, \mathsf{Enc}_{\mathsf{ext}}, \mathsf{KeyGen}_{\mathsf{ext}}, \mathsf{Dec}_{\mathsf{ext}})$ be the extended one-slot FE scheme in Sect. 6. Our unbounded-slot FE scheme Π_{ubd} is as follows:

– $\mathsf{Setup}(1^\lambda, 1^n, 1^{n'})$: Run

$$(\mathsf{mpk}_1, \mathsf{msk}_1) \leftarrow \mathsf{Setup}_{\mathsf{ext}}(1^\lambda, 1^n, 1^{n'}); \quad (\mathsf{mpk}_2, \mathsf{msk}_2) \leftarrow \mathsf{Setup}_{\mathsf{ext}}(1^\lambda, 1^n, 1^{n'})$$

and output

$$\mathsf{mpk} = (\mathsf{mpk}_1, \mathsf{mpk}_2) \quad \text{and} \quad \mathsf{msk} = (\mathsf{msk}_1, \mathsf{msk}_2).$$

– $\mathsf{Enc}(\mathsf{mpk}, (\mathbf{x}_i, \mathbf{z}_i)_{i \in [N]})$: Sample $\mathbf{w}_2, \dots, \mathbf{w}_N \leftarrow \mathbb{Z}_p^k$, compute

$$\mathsf{ct}_1 \leftarrow \mathsf{Enc}_{\mathsf{ext}}(\mathsf{mpk}_1, (\mathbf{x}_1, \mathbf{z}_1 \| - \textstyle\sum_{i \in [2, N]} \mathbf{w}_i))$$
$$\mathsf{ct}_i \leftarrow \mathsf{Enc}_{\mathsf{ext}}(\mathsf{mpk}_2, (\mathbf{x}_i, \mathbf{z}_i \| \mathbf{w}_i)), \quad \forall i \in [2, N]$$

and output

$$\mathsf{ct}_{(\mathbf{x}_i, \mathbf{z}_i)} = (\mathsf{ct}_1, \dots, \mathsf{ct}_N) \quad \text{and} \quad (\mathbf{x}_i)_{i \in [N]}.$$

– $\mathsf{KeyGen}(\mathsf{msk}, f)$: Pick $\mathbf{r} \leftarrow \mathbb{Z}_p^k$, compute

$$\mathsf{sk}_{f,1} \leftarrow \mathsf{KeyGen}_{\mathsf{ext}}(\mathsf{msk}_1, (f, [\mathbf{r}]_2)); \quad \mathsf{sk}_{f,2} \leftarrow \mathsf{KeyGen}_{\mathsf{ext}}(\mathsf{msk}_2, (f, [\mathbf{r}]_2))$$

and output

$$\mathsf{sk}_f = (\mathsf{sk}_{f,1}, \mathsf{sk}_{f,2}, [\mathbf{r}]_2) \quad \text{and} \quad f.$$

– $\mathsf{Dec}((\mathsf{sk}_f, f), (\mathsf{ct}_{(\mathbf{x}_i, \mathbf{z}_i)}, (\mathbf{x}_i)_{i \in [N]}))$: Parse ciphertext and key as

$$\mathsf{sk}_f = (\mathsf{sk}_{f,1}, \mathsf{sk}_{f,2}, [\mathbf{r}]_2) \quad \text{and} \quad \mathsf{ct}_{(\mathbf{x}_i, \mathbf{z}_i)} = (\mathsf{ct}_1, \dots, \mathsf{ct}_N).$$

We proceed as follows:

1. Compute
$$[D_1]_T \leftarrow \mathsf{Dec}_{\mathsf{ext}}((\mathsf{sk}_{f,1}, (f, [\mathbf{r}]_2)), (\mathsf{ct}_1, \mathbf{x}_1)); \tag{20}$$

2. For all $i \in [2, N]$, compute
$$[D_i]_T \leftarrow \mathsf{Dec}_{\mathsf{ext}}((\mathsf{sk}_{f,2}, (f, [\mathbf{r}]_2)), (\mathsf{ct}_i, \mathbf{x}_i)); \tag{21}$$

3. Compute
$$[D]_T = [D_1]_T \cdots [D_N]_T \tag{22}$$

and output D via brute-force discrete log.

Correctness. For $\mathsf{ct}_{(\mathbf{x}_i, \mathbf{z}_i)}$ with randomness $\mathbf{w}_2, \ldots, \mathbf{w}_N$ and sk_f with randomness $\mathbf{r}$, we have

$$D_1 = f(\mathbf{x}_1)^\top \mathbf{z}_1 - \sum_{i \in [2,N]} \mathbf{w}_i^\top \mathbf{r} \tag{23}$$

$$D_i = f(\mathbf{x}_i)^\top \mathbf{z}_i + \mathbf{w}_i^\top \mathbf{r}, \qquad\qquad \forall i \in [2, N] \tag{24}$$

$$D = \sum_{i \in [N]} f(\mathbf{x}_i)^\top \mathbf{z}_i \tag{25}$$

Here (23) and (24) follow from the correctness of Π_{ext} and the last (25) is implied by (23) and (24). This readily proves the correctness.

Security. We have the following theorem with the proof shown in the subsequent subsection.

Theorem 3. *Assume that extended one-slot scheme Π_{ext} achieves simulation-based semi-adaptive security, our unbounded-slot FE scheme Π_{ubd} described in this section achieves simulation-based semi-adaptive security under the k-Linear assumption in $\mathbb{G}_2$.*

7.2   Simulator

Let $(\mathsf{Setup}_{\mathsf{ext}}^*, \mathsf{Enc}_{\mathsf{ext}}^*, \mathsf{KeyGen}_{\mathsf{ext}}^*)$ be the simulator for Π_{ext}, we start by describing the simulator for Π_{ubd}. As written, the adversary needs to commit to the length N in advance; this is merely an artifact of our formalization of simulation-based security, and can be avoided by having Enc^* pass auxiliary information to KeyGen^*.

- $\mathsf{Setup}^*(1^\lambda, 1^n, 1^{n'}, 1^N)$: Sample $\mathbf{w}_2, \ldots, \mathbf{w}_N \leftarrow \mathbb{Z}_p^k$, run

$$(\mathsf{mpk}_1, \mathsf{msk}_1^*) \leftarrow \mathsf{Setup}_{\mathsf{ext}}^*(1^\lambda, 1^n, 1^{n'}); \quad (\mathsf{mpk}_2, \mathsf{msk}_2) \leftarrow \mathsf{Setup}_{\mathsf{ext}}(1^\lambda, 1^n, 1^{n'})$$

and output

$$\mathsf{mpk} = (\mathsf{mpk}_1, \mathsf{mpk}_2) \quad \text{and} \quad \mathsf{msk}^* = (\mathsf{msk}_1^*, \mathsf{msk}_2, \mathbf{w}_2, \ldots, \mathbf{w}_N).$$

- $\mathsf{Enc}^*(\mathsf{msk}^*, (\mathbf{x}_i^*)_{i \in [N]})$: Compute

$$\mathsf{ct}_1^* \leftarrow \mathsf{Enc}_{\mathsf{ext}}^*(\mathsf{msk}_1^*, \mathbf{x}_1^*) \quad \text{and} \quad \mathsf{ct}_i \leftarrow \mathsf{Enc}_{\mathsf{ext}}(\mathsf{mpk}_2, (\mathbf{x}_i^*, \mathbf{0} \| \mathbf{w}_i)), \forall i \in [2, N]$$

and output

$$\mathsf{ct}^* = (\mathsf{ct}_1^*, \mathsf{ct}_2, \ldots, \mathsf{ct}_N) \quad \text{and} \quad (\mathbf{x}_i^*)_{i \in [N]}.$$

- $\mathsf{KeyGen}^*(\mathsf{msk}^*, (\mathbf{x}_i^*)_{i \in [N]}, f, \mu \in \mathbb{Z}_p)$: Pick $\mathbf{r} \leftarrow \mathbb{Z}_p^k$, compute

$$\mathsf{sk}_{f,1}^* \leftarrow \mathsf{KeyGen}_{\mathsf{ext}}^*(\mathsf{msk}_1^*, \mathbf{x}_1^*, (f, [\mathbf{r}]_2), [\mu - \textstyle\sum_{i \in [2,N]} \mathbf{w}_i^\top \mathbf{r}]_2)$$

$$\mathsf{sk}_{f,2} \leftarrow \mathsf{KeyGen}_{\mathsf{ext}}(\mathsf{msk}_2, (f, [\mathbf{r}]_2))$$

and output

$$\mathsf{sk}_f^* = (\mathsf{sk}_{f,1}^*, \mathsf{sk}_{f,2}, [\mathbf{r}]_2) \quad \text{and} \quad f.$$

7.3 Proof

With our simulator, we prove the following theorem which implies Theorem 3.

Theorem 4. *For all $\mathcal{A}$, there exist $\mathcal{B}_1$ and $\mathcal{B}_2$ with $\mathsf{Time}(\mathcal{B}_1), \mathsf{Time}(\mathcal{B}_2) \approx \mathsf{Time}(\mathcal{A})$ such that*

$$\mathsf{Adv}_{\mathcal{A}}^{\Pi_{\mathsf{ubd}}}(\lambda) \leq (2N-1) \cdot \mathsf{Adv}_{\mathcal{B}_1}^{\Pi_{\mathsf{ext}}}(\lambda) + (N-1) \cdot \mathsf{Adv}_{\mathcal{B}_2}^{\mathsf{MDDH}_{k,Q}^1}(\lambda)$$

where Q is the number of key queries and N is number of slots.

Game sequence. We use $(\mathbf{x}_1^*, \mathbf{z}_1^*, \ldots, \mathbf{x}_N^*, \mathbf{z}_N^*)$ to denote the semi-adaptive challenge and prove Theorem 4 via the following game sequence summarized in Fig. 4, where

$$\mathsf{Game}_0 \approx_c \mathsf{Game}_1 = \mathsf{Game}_{2.0} \approx_c \mathsf{Game}_{2.1} \approx_c \mathsf{Game}_{2.2} \approx_c \mathsf{Game}_{2.3}$$
$$\cdots$$
$$= \mathsf{Game}_{N.0} \approx_c \mathsf{Game}_{N.1} \approx_c \mathsf{Game}_{N.2} \approx_c \mathsf{Game}_{N.3}$$

<u>Game_0</u>: Real game.

<u>Game_1</u>: Identical to Game_0 except for the boxed terms below:

- we generate $\mathsf{mpk} = (\mathsf{mpk}_1, \mathsf{mpk}_2)$ and $\mathsf{msk} = (\boxed{\mathsf{msk}_1^*}, \mathsf{msk}_2)$ where

$$\boxed{(\mathsf{mpk}_1, \mathsf{msk}_1^*) \leftarrow \mathsf{Setup}_{\mathsf{ext}}^*(1^\lambda, 1^n, 1^{n'})}; \quad (\mathsf{mpk}_2, \mathsf{msk}_2) \leftarrow \mathsf{Setup}_{\mathsf{ext}}(1^\lambda, 1^n, 1^{n'})$$

- the challenge ciphertext for $(\mathbf{x}_1^*, \mathbf{z}_1^*, \ldots, \mathbf{x}_N^*, \mathbf{z}_N^*)$ is $\mathsf{ct}^* = (\boxed{\mathsf{ct}_1^*}, \mathsf{ct}_2, \ldots, \mathsf{ct}_N)$ where

$$\boxed{\mathsf{ct}_1^* \leftarrow \mathsf{Enc}_{\mathsf{ext}}^*(\mathsf{msk}_1^*, \mathbf{x}_1^*)}; \quad \mathsf{ct}_i \leftarrow \mathsf{Enc}_{\mathsf{ext}}(\mathsf{mpk}_2, (\mathbf{x}_i^*, \mathbf{z}_i^* \| \mathbf{w}_i)), \forall i \in [2, N]$$

- the key for the j-th query f_j is $\mathsf{sk}_{f_j} = (\boxed{\mathsf{sk}_{f_j,1}^*}, \mathsf{sk}_{f_j,2}, [\mathbf{r}_j]_2)$ where

$$\boxed{\mathsf{sk}_{f_j,1}^* \leftarrow \mathsf{KeyGen}_{\mathsf{ext}}^*\big(\mathsf{msk}_1^*, \mathbf{x}_1^*, (f_j, [\mathbf{r}_j]_2), [f_j(\mathbf{x}_1^*)^\top \mathbf{z}_1^* - \textstyle\sum_{i \in [2,N]} \mathbf{w}_i^\top \mathbf{r}_j]_2)\big)}$$

$$\mathsf{sk}_{f_j,2} \leftarrow \mathsf{KeyGen}_{\mathsf{ext}}(\mathsf{msk}_2, (f_j, [\mathbf{r}_j]_2));$$

where $\mathbf{w}_2, \ldots, \mathbf{w}_N \leftarrow \mathbb{Z}_p^k$ and $\mathbf{r}_j \leftarrow \mathbb{Z}_p^k$ for all $j \in [Q]$. We claim that $\mathsf{Game}_0 \approx_c \mathsf{Game}_1$. This follows from the simulation-based semi-adaptive security of Π_{ext}.

<u>$\mathsf{Game}_{\eta.0}$</u> for $\eta \in [2, N]$: Identical to Game_1 except for the boxed terms below:

- the challenge ciphertext for $(\mathbf{x}_1^*, \mathbf{z}_1^*, \ldots, \mathbf{x}_N^*, \mathbf{z}_N^*)$ is $\mathsf{ct}^* = (\mathsf{ct}_1^*, \mathsf{ct}_2, \ldots, \mathsf{ct}_N)$ where

$$\mathsf{ct}_1^* \leftarrow \mathsf{Enc}_{\mathsf{ext}}^*(\mathsf{msk}_1^*, \mathbf{x}_1^*); \quad \mathsf{ct}_i \leftarrow \begin{cases} \mathsf{Enc}_{\mathsf{ext}}(\mathsf{mpk}_2, (\mathbf{x}_i^*, \boxed{\mathbf{0}} \| \mathbf{w}_i)) & i \in [2, \eta - 1] \\ \mathsf{Enc}_{\mathsf{ext}}(\mathsf{mpk}_2, (\mathbf{x}_i^*, \mathbf{z}_i^* \| \mathbf{w}_i)) & i \in [\eta, N] \end{cases}$$

- the key for the j-th query f_j is $\mathsf{sk}_{f_j} = (\mathsf{sk}^*_{f_j,1}, \mathsf{sk}_{f_j,2}, [\mathbf{r}_j]_2)$ where

$$\mathsf{sk}^*_{f_j,1} \leftarrow \mathsf{KeyGen}^*_{\mathsf{ext}}\left(\mathsf{msk}^*_1, \mathbf{x}^*_1, (f_j, [\mathbf{r}_j]_2), \left[\boxed{\Sigma_{i \in [\eta-1]} f_j(\mathbf{x}^*_i)^\top \mathbf{z}^*_i} - \Sigma_{i \in [2,N]} \mathbf{w}^\top_i \mathbf{r}_j]_2\right)\right.$$

$$\mathsf{sk}_{f_j,2} \leftarrow \mathsf{KeyGen}_{\mathsf{ext}}(\mathsf{msk}_2, (f_j, [\mathbf{r}_j]_2));$$

where $\mathbf{w}_2, \ldots, \mathbf{w}_N \leftarrow \mathbb{Z}^k_p$ and $\mathbf{r}_j \leftarrow \mathbb{Z}^k_p$ for all $j \in [Q]$.

$\underline{\mathsf{Game}_{\eta.1}}$ for $\eta \in [2, N]$: Identical to $\mathsf{Game}_{\eta.0}$ except for the boxed terms below:
- we generate $\mathsf{mpk} = (\mathsf{mpk}_1, \mathsf{mpk}_2)$ and $\mathsf{msk} = (\mathsf{msk}^*_1, \boxed{\mathsf{msk}^*_2})$ where

$$(\mathsf{mpk}_1, \mathsf{msk}^*_1) \leftarrow \mathsf{Setup}^*_{\mathsf{ext}}(1^\lambda, 1^n, 1^{n'}); \quad \boxed{(\mathsf{mpk}_2, \mathsf{msk}^*_2) \leftarrow \mathsf{Setup}^*_{\mathsf{ext}}(1^\lambda, 1^n, 1^{n'})}$$

- the challenge ciphertext for $(\mathbf{x}^*_1, \mathbf{z}^*_1, \ldots, \mathbf{x}^*_N, \mathbf{z}^*_N)$ is $\mathsf{ct}^* = (\mathsf{ct}^*_1, \mathsf{ct}_2, \ldots, \mathsf{ct}_{\eta-1}, \boxed{\mathsf{ct}^*_\eta}, \mathsf{ct}_{\eta+1}, \ldots, \mathsf{ct}_N)$ where

$$\mathsf{ct}^*_1 \leftarrow \mathsf{Enc}^*_{\mathsf{ext}}(\mathsf{msk}^*_1, \mathbf{x}^*_1), \begin{cases} \mathsf{ct}_i \leftarrow \mathsf{Enc}_{\mathsf{ext}}(\mathsf{mpk}_2, (\mathbf{x}^*_i, \mathbf{0} \| \mathbf{w}_i)) & i \in [2, \eta-1] \\ \boxed{\mathsf{ct}^*_\eta \leftarrow \mathsf{Enc}^*_{\mathsf{ext}}(\mathsf{msk}^*_2, \mathbf{x}^*_\eta)} & i = \eta \\ \mathsf{ct}_i \leftarrow \mathsf{Enc}_{\mathsf{ext}}(\mathsf{mpk}_2, (\mathbf{x}^*_i, \mathbf{z}^*_i \| \mathbf{w}_i)) & i \in [\eta+1, N] \end{cases}$$

- the key for the j-th query f_j is $\mathsf{sk}_{f_j} = (\mathsf{sk}^*_{f_j,1}, \boxed{\mathsf{sk}^*_{f_j,2}}, [\mathbf{r}_j]_2)$ where

$$\mathsf{sk}^*_{f_j,1} \leftarrow \mathsf{KeyGen}^*_{\mathsf{ext}}\left(\mathsf{msk}^*_1, \mathbf{x}^*_1, (f_j, [\mathbf{r}_j]_2), [\Sigma_{i \in [\eta-1]} f_j(\mathbf{x}^*_i)^\top \mathbf{z}^*_i - \Sigma_{i \in [2,N]} \mathbf{w}^\top_i \mathbf{r}_j]_2\right)$$

$$\boxed{\mathsf{sk}^*_{f_j,2} \leftarrow \mathsf{KeyGen}^*_{\mathsf{ext}}(\mathsf{msk}^*_2, \mathbf{x}^*_\eta, (f_j, [\mathbf{r}_j]_2), [f_j(\mathbf{x}^*_\eta)^\top \mathbf{z}^*_\eta + \mathbf{w}^\top_\eta \mathbf{r}_j]_2)}$$

where $\mathbf{w}_2, \ldots, \mathbf{w}_N \leftarrow \mathbb{Z}^k_p$ and $\mathbf{r}_j \leftarrow \mathbb{Z}^k_p$ for all $j \in [Q]$. We claim that $\mathsf{Game}_{\eta.0} \approx_c \mathsf{Game}_{\eta.1}$. This follows from the simulation-based semi-adaptive security of Π_{ext}.

$\underline{\mathsf{Game}_{\eta.2}}$ for $\eta \in [2, N]$: Identical to $\mathsf{Game}_{\eta.1}$ except for the boxed terms below:
- the key for the j-th query f_j is $\mathsf{sk}_{f_j} = (\mathsf{sk}^*_{f_j,1}, \mathsf{sk}^*_{f_j,2}, [\mathbf{r}_j]_2)$ where

$$\mathsf{sk}^*_{f_j,1} \leftarrow \mathsf{KeyGen}^*_{\mathsf{ext}}\left(\mathsf{msk}^*_1, \mathbf{x}^*_1, (f_j, [\mathbf{r}_j]_2), \left[\boxed{\Sigma_{i \in [\eta]} f_j(\mathbf{x}^*_i)^\top \mathbf{z}^*_i} - \Sigma_{i \in [2,N]} \mathbf{w}^\top_i \mathbf{r}_j]_2\right)\right.$$

$$\mathsf{sk}^*_{f_j,2} \leftarrow \mathsf{KeyGen}^*_{\mathsf{ext}}(\mathsf{msk}^*_2, \mathbf{x}^*_\eta, (f_j, [\mathbf{r}_j]_2), [\boxed{\mathbf{w}^\top_\eta \mathbf{r}_j}]_2)$$

where $\mathbf{w}_2, \ldots, \mathbf{w}_N \leftarrow \mathbb{Z}^k_p$ and $\mathbf{r}_j \leftarrow \mathbb{Z}^k_p$ for all $j \in [Q]$. We claim that $\mathsf{Game}_{\eta.1} \approx_c \mathsf{Game}_{\eta.2}$. This follows from Lemma 1 w.r.t. $\mathbf{w}_\eta$ and $f_j(\mathbf{x}^*_\eta)^\top \mathbf{z}^*_\eta$ which is implied by $\mathsf{MDDH}^1_{k,Q}$ assumption: for all $f_j, \mathbf{x}^*_\eta, \mathbf{z}^*_\eta$,

$$\left\{ \overbrace{[-\mathbf{w}^\top_\eta \mathbf{r}_j]_2,}^{\mathsf{sk}^*_{f_j,1}} \overbrace{\boxed{f_j(\mathbf{x}^*_\eta)^\top \mathbf{z}^*_\eta} + \mathbf{w}^\top_\eta \mathbf{r}_j]_2, [\mathbf{r}_j]_2}^{\mathsf{sk}^*_{f_j,2}} \right\}_{j \in [Q]} \quad (26)$$
$$\approx_c \left\{ \boxed{f_j(\mathbf{x}^*_\eta)^\top \mathbf{z}^*_\eta} - \mathbf{w}^\top_\eta \mathbf{r}_j]_2, \quad [\mathbf{w}^\top_\eta \mathbf{r}_j]_2, [\mathbf{r}_j]_2 \right\}_{j \in [Q]}$$

where $\mathbf{w}_\eta, \mathbf{r}_j \leftarrow \mathbb{Z}^k_p$ for all $j \in [Q]$.

Game	ct*				sk$_f$		Remark
	ct$_1$	ct$_i$, $1 < i < \eta$	ct$_\eta$	ct$_i$, $\eta < i \leq N$	sk$_{f,1}$	sk$_{f,2}$	
0	real: $\mathbf{x}_1^*, \mathbf{z}_1^* \| -\sum\mathbf{w}_i$	real: $\mathbf{x}_i^*, \mathbf{z}_i^* \| \mathbf{w}_i$	real: $\mathbf{x}_\eta^*, \mathbf{z}_\eta^* \| \mathbf{w}_i$	real: $\mathbf{x}_i^*, \mathbf{z}_i^* \| \mathbf{w}_i$	real:	real:	Real game
1	sim: $\mathbf{x}_1^*$	real: $\mathbf{x}_i^*, \mathbf{z}_i^* \| \mathbf{w}_i$	real: $\mathbf{x}_i^*, \mathbf{z}_i^* \| \mathbf{w}_i$	real: $\mathbf{x}_i^*, \mathbf{z}_i^* \| \mathbf{w}_i$	sim: $[f(\mathbf{x}_1^*)^\top\mathbf{z}_1 - \sum\mathbf{w}_i^\top\mathbf{r}_i]_2$	real:	Π_{ext}
$\eta.0$	sim: $\mathbf{x}_1^*$	real: $\mathbf{x}_i$; $\mathbf{0}\|\mathbf{w}_i$	real: $\mathbf{x}_\eta^*, \mathbf{z}_\eta^* \| \mathbf{w}_\eta$	real: $\mathbf{x}_i^*, \mathbf{z}_i^* \| \mathbf{w}_i$	real: $\sum_{i<\eta} f(\mathbf{x}_i^*)^\top\mathbf{z}_i - \sum\mathbf{w}_i^\top\mathbf{r}_i]_2$	real:	Π_{ext}
$\eta.1$	sim: $\mathbf{x}_1^*$	real: $\mathbf{x}_i$; $\mathbf{0}\|\mathbf{w}_i$	sim: $\mathbf{x}_\eta$	real: $\mathbf{x}_i^*, \mathbf{z}_i^* \| \mathbf{w}_i$	sim: $\sum_{i<\eta} f(\mathbf{x}_i^*)^\top\mathbf{z}_i - \sum\mathbf{w}_i^\top\mathbf{r}_i]_2$	sim: $[f(\mathbf{x}_\eta^*)^\top\mathbf{z}_\eta^* + \mathbf{w}_\eta^\top\mathbf{r}]_2$	MDDH
$\eta.2$	sim: $\mathbf{x}_1^*$	real: $\mathbf{x}_i$; $\mathbf{0}\|\mathbf{w}_i$	sim: $\mathbf{x}_\eta^*$	real: $\mathbf{x}_i^*, \mathbf{z}_i^* \| \mathbf{w}_i$	sim: $\sum_{i\leq\eta} f(\mathbf{x}_i^*)^\top\mathbf{z}_i^* - \sum\mathbf{w}_i^\top\mathbf{r}_i]_2$	sim: $[\mathbf{w}_\eta^\top\mathbf{r}]_2$	Π_{ext}
$\eta.3$	sim: $\mathbf{x}_1^*$	real: $\mathbf{x}_i$; $\mathbf{0}\|\mathbf{w}_i$	real: $\mathbf{x}_\eta$, $\mathbf{0}\|\mathbf{w}_\eta$	real: $\mathbf{x}_i^*, \mathbf{z}_i^* \| \mathbf{w}_i$	sim: $\sum_{i<\eta} f(\mathbf{x}_i^*)^\top\mathbf{z}_i^* - \sum\mathbf{w}_i^\top\mathbf{r}_i]_2$	real:	
$N.3$	sim: $\mathbf{x}_1^*$	real: $\mathbf{x}_i^*$, $\mathbf{0}\|\mathbf{w}_i$			sim: $\sum_{i\in[N]} f(\mathbf{x}_i^*)^\top\mathbf{z}_i^* - \sum\mathbf{w}_i^\top\mathbf{r}_i]_2$	real:	Simulator

Fig. 4. Game sequence for Π_{ubd} with $\eta \in [2, N]$, where $\text{Game}_{2.0} = \text{Game}_1$, $\text{Game}_{3.0} = \text{Game}_{2.3}, \ldots, \text{Game}_{N.0} = \text{Game}_{N-1.3}$. Each cell is in the format "xxx:yyy" where $xxx \in \{\text{real}, \text{sim}\}$ indicates whether the ciphertext/key component is generated using real algorithm or simulator and yyy gives out the information fed to algorithm/simulator. Throughout, the first input to $\text{KeyGen}_{\text{ext}}/\text{KeyGen}_{\text{ext}}^*$ for generating $\text{sk}_{f,1}$ is $(f, [\mathbf{r}]_2)$; the same applies to $\text{sk}_{f,2}$. The sum of $\mathbf{w}_i^\top\mathbf{r}$ is always over $i \in [2, N]$.

$\underline{\mathsf{Game}_{\eta.3}}$ for $\eta \in [2, N]$: Identical to $\mathsf{Game}_{\eta.2}$ except for the boxed terms below:

- we generate $\mathsf{mpk} = (\mathsf{mpk}_1, \mathsf{mpk}_2)$ and $\mathsf{msk} = (\mathsf{msk}_1^*, \boxed{\mathsf{msk}_2})$ where

$$(\mathsf{mpk}_1, \mathsf{msk}_1^*) \leftarrow \mathsf{Setup}_{\mathsf{ext}}^*(1^\lambda, 1^n, 1^{n'}), \quad \boxed{(\mathsf{mpk}_2, \mathsf{msk}_2) \leftarrow \mathsf{Setup}_{\mathsf{ext}}(1^\lambda, 1^n, 1^{n'})}$$

- the challenge ciphertext for $(\mathbf{x}_1^*, \mathbf{z}_1^*, \dots, \mathbf{x}_N^*, \mathbf{z}_N^*)$ is $\mathsf{ct}^* = (\mathsf{ct}_1^*, \mathsf{ct}_2, \dots, \mathsf{ct}_{\eta-1}, \boxed{\mathsf{ct}_\eta}, \mathsf{ct}_{\eta+1}, \dots, \mathsf{ct}_N)$ where

$$\mathsf{ct}_1^* \leftarrow \mathsf{Enc}_{\mathsf{ext}}^*(\mathsf{msk}_1^*, \mathbf{x}_1^*), \quad \begin{cases} \mathsf{ct}_i \leftarrow \mathsf{Enc}_{\mathsf{ext}}(\mathsf{mpk}_2, (\mathbf{x}_i^*, \mathbf{0}\|\mathbf{w}_i)) & i \in [2, \eta-1] \\ \boxed{\mathsf{ct}_i \leftarrow \mathsf{Enc}_{\mathsf{ext}}(\mathsf{mpk}_2, (\mathbf{x}_\eta^*, \mathbf{0}\|\mathbf{w}_\eta))} & i = \eta \\ \mathsf{ct}_i \leftarrow \mathsf{Enc}_{\mathsf{ext}}(\mathsf{mpk}_2, (\mathbf{x}_i^*, \mathbf{z}_i^*\|\mathbf{w}_i)) & i \in [\eta+1, N] \end{cases}$$

- the key for the j-th query f_j is $\mathsf{sk}_{f_j} = (\mathsf{sk}_{f_j,1}^*, \boxed{\mathsf{sk}_{f_j,2}}, [\mathbf{r}_j]_2)$ where

$$\mathsf{sk}_{f_j,1}^* \leftarrow \mathsf{KeyGen}_{\mathsf{ext}}^*(\mathsf{msk}_1^*, \mathbf{x}_1^*, (f_j, [\mathbf{r}_j]_2), [\textstyle\sum_{i \in [\eta]} f_j(\mathbf{x}_i^*)^\top \mathbf{z}_i^* - \sum_{i \in [2,N]} \mathbf{w}_i^\top \mathbf{r}_j]_2)$$

$$\boxed{\mathsf{sk}_{f_j,2} \leftarrow \mathsf{KeyGen}_{\mathsf{ext}}(\mathsf{msk}_2, (f_j, [\mathbf{r}_j]_2))}$$

where $\mathbf{w}_2, \dots, \mathbf{w}_N \leftarrow \mathbb{Z}_p^k$ and $\mathbf{r}_j \leftarrow \mathbb{Z}_p^k$ for all $j \in [Q]$. We claim that $\mathsf{Game}_{\eta.2} \approx_c \mathsf{Game}_{\eta.3}$. This follows from the simulation-based semi-adaptive security of Π_{ext} with the fact $f_j(\mathbf{x}_\eta^*)^\top \mathbf{0} + \mathbf{w}_\eta^\top \mathbf{r} = \mathbf{w}_\eta^\top \mathbf{r}$.

Here we have $\mathsf{Game}_{2.0} = \mathsf{Game}_1$ and $\mathsf{Game}_{\eta.0} = \mathsf{Game}_{\eta-1.3}$ for all $\eta \in [3, N]$. Note that $\mathsf{Game}_{N.3}$ corresponds to the output of the simulator in the ideal game. We summarize the game sequence in Fig. 4. We prove the indistinguishability of adjacent games listed above in the full paper.

References

1. Abdalla, M., Bourse, F., De Caro, A., Pointcheval, D.: Simple functional encryption schemes for inner products. In: Katz, J. (ed.) PKC 2015. LNCS, vol. 9020, pp. 733–751. Springer, Heidelberg (2015). https://doi.org/10.1007/978-3-662-46447-2_33

2. Abdalla, M., Catalano, D., Gay, R., Ursu, B.: Inner-product functional encryption with fine-grained access control. Cryptology ePrint Archive, Report 2020/577 (2020)

3. Abdalla, M., Gay, R., Raykova, M., Wee, H.: Multi-input inner-product functional encryption from pairings. In: Coron, J.-S., Nielsen, J.B. (eds.) EUROCRYPT 2017, Part I. LNCS, vol. 10210, pp. 601–626. Springer, Cham (2017). https://doi.org/10.1007/978-3-319-56620-7_21

4. Agrawal, S., Gorbunov, S., Vaikuntanathan, V., Wee, H.: Functional encryption: new perspectives and lower bounds. In: Canetti, R., Garay, J.A. (eds.) CRYPTO 2013, Part II. LNCS, vol. 8043, pp. 500–518. Springer, Heidelberg (2013). https://doi.org/10.1007/978-3-642-40084-1_28

5. Agrawal, S., Libert, B., Maitra, M., Titiu, R.: Adaptive simulation security for inner product functional encryption. In: Kiayias, A., Kohlweiss, M., Wallden, P., Zikas, V. (eds.) PKC 2020, Part I. LNCS, vol. 12110, pp. 34–64. Springer, Cham (2020). https://doi.org/10.1007/978-3-030-45374-9_2

6. Agrawal, S., Libert, B., Stehlé, D.: Fully secure functional encryption for inner products, from standard assumptions. In: Robshaw, M., Katz, J. (eds.) CRYPTO 2016, Part III. LNCS, vol. 9816, pp. 333–362. Springer, Heidelberg (2016). https://doi.org/10.1007/978-3-662-53015-3_12

7. Agrawal, S., Maitra, M., Yamada, S.: Attribute based encryption (and more) for nondeterministic finite automata from LWE. In: Boldyreva, A., Micciancio, D. (eds.) CRYPTO 2019, Part II. LNCS, vol. 11693, pp. 765–797. Springer, Cham (2019). https://doi.org/10.1007/978-3-030-26951-7_26

8. Agrawal, S., Maitra, M., Yamada, S.: Attribute based encryption for deterministic finite automata from DLIN. In: Hofheinz, D., Rosen, A. (eds.) TCC 2019, Part II. LNCS, vol. 11892, pp. 91–117. Springer, Cham (2019). https://doi.org/10.1007/978-3-030-36033-7_4

9. Ambrona, M., Barthe, G., Gay, R., Wee, H.: Attribute-based encryption in the generic group model: automated proofs and new constructions. In: Thuraisingham, B.M., Evans, D., Malkin, T., Xu, D. (eds.) ACM CCS 2017, pp. 647–664. ACM Press, October/November 2017

10. Baltico, C.E.Z., Catalano, D., Fiore, D., Gay, R.: Practical functional encryption for quadratic functions with applications to predicate encryption. In: Katz, J., Shacham, H. (eds.) CRYPTO 2017, Part I. LNCS, vol. 10401, pp. 67–98. Springer, Cham (2017). https://doi.org/10.1007/978-3-319-63688-7_3

11. Ben-Or, M., Goldwasser, S., Wigderson, A.: Completeness theorems for non-cryptographic fault-tolerant distributed computation (extended abstract). In: 20th ACM STOC, pp. 1–10. ACM Press, May 1988

12. Boneh, D., Gentry, C., Gorbunov, S., Halevi, S., Nikolaenko, V., Segev, G., Vaikuntanathan, V., Vinayagamurthy, D.: Fully key-homomorphic encryption, arithmetic circuit ABE and Compact Garbled Circuits. In: Nguyen, P.Q., Oswald, E. (eds.) EUROCRYPT 2014. LNCS, vol. 8441, pp. 533–556. Springer, Heidelberg (2014). https://doi.org/10.1007/978-3-642-55220-5_30

13. Boneh, D., Sahai, A., Waters, B.: Functional encryption: definitions and challenges. In: Ishai, Y. (ed.) TCC 2011. LNCS, vol. 6597, pp. 253–273. Springer, Heidelberg (2011). https://doi.org/10.1007/978-3-642-19571-6_16

14. Brakerski, Z., Vaikuntanathan, V.: Circuit-ABE from LWE: unbounded attributes and semi-adaptive security. In: Robshaw, M., Katz, J. (eds.) CRYPTO 2016, Part III. LNCS, vol. 9816, pp. 363–384. Springer, Heidelberg (2016). https://doi.org/10.1007/978-3-662-53015-3_13

15. Chen, J., Gay, R., Wee, H.: Improved dual system ABE in prime-order groups via predicate encodings. In: Oswald, E., Fischlin, M. (eds.) EUROCRYPT 2015, Part II. LNCS, vol. 9057, pp. 595–624. Springer, Heidelberg (2015). https://doi.org/10.1007/978-3-662-46803-6_20

16. Chen, J., Wee, H.: Semi-adaptive attribute-based encryption and improved delegation for Boolean formula. In: Abdalla, M., De Prisco, R. (eds.) SCN 2014. LNCS, vol. 8642, pp. 277–297. Springer, Cham (2014). https://doi.org/10.1007/978-3-319-10879-7_16

17. Chen, Y., Zhang, L., Yiu, S.-M.: Practical attribute based inner product functional encryption from simple assumptions. Cryptology ePrint Archive, Report 2019/846 (2019)

18. Chotard, J., Dufour Sans, E., Gay, R., Phan, D.H., Pointcheval, D.: Decentralized multi-client functional encryption for inner product. In: Peyrin, T., Galbraith, S. (eds.) ASIACRYPT 2018, Part II. LNCS, vol. 11273, pp. 703–732. Springer, Cham (2018). https://doi.org/10.1007/978-3-030-03329-3_24

19. Datta, P., Okamoto, T., Takashima, K.: Adaptively simulation-secure attribute-hiding predicate encryption. In: Peyrin, T., Galbraith, S. (eds.) ASIACRYPT 2018, Part II. LNCS, vol. 11273, pp. 640–672. Springer, Cham (2018). https://doi.org/10.1007/978-3-030-03329-3_22

20. Escala, A., Herold, G., Kiltz, E., Ràfols, C., Villar, J.: An algebraic framework for Diffie-Hellman assumptions. In: Canetti, R., Garay, J.A. (eds.) CRYPTO 2013, Part II. LNCS, vol. 8043, pp. 129–147. Springer, Heidelberg (2013). https://doi.org/10.1007/978-3-642-40084-1_8

21. Goldwasser, S., Gordon, S.D., Goyal, V., Jain, A., Katz, J., Liu, F.-H., Sahai, A., Shi, E., Zhou, H.-S.: Multi-input functional encryption. In: Nguyen, P.Q., Oswald, E. (eds.) EUROCRYPT 2014. LNCS, vol. 8441, pp. 578–602. Springer, Heidelberg (2014). https://doi.org/10.1007/978-3-642-55220-5_32

22. Gong, J., Waters, B., Wee, H.: ABE for DFA from k-Lin. In: Boldyreva, A., Micciancio, D. (eds.) CRYPTO 2019. LNCS, vol. 11693, pp. 732–764. Springer, Cham (2019). https://doi.org/10.1007/978-3-030-26951-7_25

23. Gorbunov, S., Vaikuntanathan, V., Wee, H.: Attribute-based encryption for circuits. In: Boneh, D., Roughgarden, T., Feigenbaum, J. (eds.) 45th ACM STOC, pp. 545–554. ACM Press, June 2013

24. Gorbunov, S., Vaikuntanathan, V., Wee, H.: Predicate encryption for circuits from LWE. In: Gennaro, R., Robshaw, M. (eds.) CRYPTO 2015, Part II. LNCS, vol. 9216, pp. 503–523. Springer, Heidelberg (2015). https://doi.org/10.1007/978-3-662-48000-7_25

25. Goyal, R., Koppula, V., Waters, B.: Semi-adaptive security and bundling functionalities made generic and easy. In: Hirt, M., Smith, A. (eds.) TCC 2016, Part II. LNCS, vol. 9986, pp. 361–388. Springer, Heidelberg (2016). https://doi.org/10.1007/978-3-662-53644-5_14

26. Goyal, V., Pandey, O., Sahai, A., Waters, B.: Attribute-based encryption for fine-grained access control of encrypted data. In: Juels, A., Wright, R.N., De Capitani di Vimercati, S. (eds.) ACM CCS 2006, pp. 89–98. ACM Press, October/November 2006. Available as Cryptology ePrint Archive Report 2006/309

27. Ishai, Y., Wee, H.: Partial garbling schemes and their applications. In: Esparza, J., Fraigniaud, P., Husfeldt, T., Koutsoupias, E. (eds.) ICALP 2014, Part I. LNCS, vol. 8572, pp. 650–662. Springer, Heidelberg (2014). https://doi.org/10.1007/978-3-662-43948-7_54

28. Jain, A., Lin, H., Matt, C., Sahai, A.: How to leverage hardness of constant-degree expanding polynomials over $\mathbb{R}$ to build $i\mathcal{O}$. In: Ishai, Y., Rijmen, V. (eds.) EUROCRYPT 2019, Part I. LNCS, vol. 11476, pp. 251–281. Springer, Cham (2019). https://doi.org/10.1007/978-3-030-17653-2_9

29. Jain, A., Lin, H., Sahai, A.: Simplifying constructions and assumptions for $i\mathcal{O}$. IACR Cryptology ePrint Archive, 2019:1252 (2019)

30. Katz, J., Sahai, A., Waters, B.: Predicate encryption supporting disjunctions, polynomial equations, and inner products. In: Smart, N. (ed.) EUROCRYPT 2008. LNCS, vol. 4965, pp. 146–162. Springer, Heidelberg (2008). https://doi.org/10.1007/978-3-540-78967-3_9

31. Kowalczyk, L., Wee, H.: Compact adaptively secure ABE for NC^1 from k-Lin. In: Ishai, Y., Rijmen, V. (eds.) EUROCRYPT 2019, Part I. LNCS, vol. 11476, pp. 3–33. Springer, Cham (2019). https://doi.org/10.1007/978-3-030-17653-2_1

32. Lewko, A., Waters, B.: Unbounded HIBE and attribute-based encryption. In: Paterson, K.G. (ed.) EUROCRYPT 2011. LNCS, vol. 6632, pp. 547–567. Springer, Heidelberg (2011). https://doi.org/10.1007/978-3-642-20465-4_30

33. Lin, H.: Indistinguishability obfuscation from SXDH on 5-linear maps and locality-5 PRGs. In: Katz, J., Shacham, H. (eds.) CRYPTO 2017, Part I. LNCS, vol. 10401, pp. 599–629. Springer, Cham (2017). https://doi.org/10.1007/978-3-319-63688-7_20

34. Okamoto, T., Takashima, K.: Adaptively attribute-hiding (hierarchical) inner product encryption. In: Pointcheval, D., Johansson, T. (eds.) EUROCRYPT 2012. LNCS, vol. 7237, pp. 591–608. Springer, Heidelberg (2012). https://doi.org/10.1007/978-3-642-29011-4_35

35. Okamoto, T., Takashima, K.: Efficient (hierarchical) inner-product encryption tightly reduced from the decisional linear assumption. IEICE Trans. Fundam. Electron. Commun. Comput. Sci. **96–A**(1), 42–52 (2013)

36. Sahai, A., Waters, B.: Fuzzy identity-based encryption. In: Cramer, R. (ed.) EUROCRYPT 2005. LNCS, vol. 3494, pp. 457–473. Springer, Heidelberg (2005). https://doi.org/10.1007/11426639_27

37. Waters, B.: Dual system encryption: realizing fully secure IBE and HIBE under simple assumptions. In: Halevi, S. (ed.) CRYPTO 2009. LNCS, vol. 5677, pp. 619–636. Springer, Heidelberg (2009). https://doi.org/10.1007/978-3-642-03356-8_36

38. Waters, B.: Functional encryption for regular languages. In: Safavi-Naini, R., Canetti, R. (eds.) CRYPTO 2012. LNCS, vol. 7417, pp. 218–235. Springer, Heidelberg (2012). https://doi.org/10.1007/978-3-642-32009-5_14

39. Wee, H.: Dual system encryption via predicate encodings. In: Lindell, Y. (ed.) TCC 2014. LNCS, vol. 8349, pp. 616–637. Springer, Heidelberg (2014). https://doi.org/10.1007/978-3-642-54242-8_26

40. Wee, H.: Attribute-hiding predicate encryption in bilinear groups, revisited. In: Kalai, Y., Reyzin, L. (eds.) TCC 2017, Part I. LNCS, vol. 10677, pp. 206–233. Springer, Cham (2017). https://doi.org/10.1007/978-3-319-70500-2_8

Amplifying the Security of Functional Encryption, Unconditionally

Aayush Jain[(✉)], Alexis Korb[(✉)], Nathan Manohar[(✉)], and Amit Sahai[(✉)]

UCLA, Los Angeles, CA, USA
{aayushjain,alexiskorb,nmanohar,sahai}@cs.ucla.edu

Abstract. Security amplification is a fundamental problem in cryptography. In this work, we study security amplification for functional encryption (FE). We show two main results:

- For any constant $\epsilon \in (0,1)$, we can amplify any FE scheme for P/poly which is ϵ-secure against all polynomial sized adversaries to a fully secure FE scheme for P/poly, unconditionally.
- For any constant $\epsilon \in (0,1)$, we can amplify any FE scheme for P/poly which is ϵ-secure against subexponential sized adversaries to a fully subexponentially secure FE scheme for P/poly, unconditionally.

Furthermore, both of our amplification results preserve compactness of the underlying FE scheme. Previously, amplification results for FE were only known assuming subexponentially secure LWE.

Along the way, we introduce a new form of homomorphic secret sharing called set homomorphic secret sharing that may be of independent interest. Additionally, we introduce a new technique, which allows one to argue security amplification of nested primitives, and prove a general theorem that can be used to analyze the security amplification of parallel repetitions.

1 Introduction

Security amplification is a fundamental problem in which one takes a weakly secure cryptographic primitive and transforms it into a fully secure primitive. For instance, suppose (G, E, D) is a public-key encryption (PKE) scheme satisfying standard correctness, but which only satisfies the weak security guarantee that there exists a constant $\epsilon \in (0,1)$ such that for all messages $m_0, m_1 \in \{0,1\}^\lambda$ and for all polynomial-time adversaries $\mathcal{A}$, we have

$$| \Pr[\mathcal{A}(\mathsf{pk}, E(\mathsf{pk}, m_0)) = 1 \mid (\mathsf{pk}, \mathsf{sk}) \leftarrow G(1^\lambda)]$$
$$- \Pr[\mathcal{A}(\mathsf{pk}, E(\mathsf{pk}, m_1)) = 1 \mid (\mathsf{pk}, \mathsf{sk}) \leftarrow G(1^\lambda)]| \leq \epsilon.$$

Then, the relevant security amplification goal for such an ϵ-secure public-key encryption would be to construct a new PKE (G', E', D') that satisfies standard security, where the constant ϵ above would be replaced with a negligible function in λ. It has long been known [22,37] that the security of ϵ-secure PKE can be amplified to achieve fully secure PKE unconditionally. (Remarkably, however,

D. Micciancio and T. Ristenpart (Eds.): CRYPTO 2020, LNCS 12170, pp. 717–746, 2020.
https://doi.org/10.1007/978-3-030-56784-2_24

there are still natural questions about security amplification for ϵ-secure PKE that remain open – see below.)

Aside from being a fundamental question in its own right, security amplification also opens the door to building cryptographic primitives from new intractability assumptions. For instance, in the future, we may discover natural sources of hardness that yield cryptographic primitives with only a weak level of security. Using security amplification, such novel sources of hardness would still yield fully secure cryptographic primitives. This motivation is especially important for cryptographic primitives for which only a few assumptions are known to yield that primitive.

There have been numerous works throughout the years on security amplification for various cryptographic primitives (for example, [5,8,13,19–21,31–33,35–38,41,47,50–52,54,59,62,63]). As with all cryptographic primitives, minimizing assumptions is a major goal in security amplification research. Indeed, unlike many results in cryptography, security amplification results can be *unconditional* (e.g. [13,19,21,33,35–38,47,51,52,54,59,62,63]).

Security Amplification for Functional Encryption. The focus of this paper is to study security amplification in the context of functional encryption. Functional encryption (FE), introduced by [56] and first formalized by [18,53], is one of the core primitives in the area of computing on encrypted data. This notion allows an authority to generate and distribute keys associated with functions $f_1, \ldots, f_q$, called *functional keys*, which can be used to learn the values $f_1(x), \ldots, f_q(x)$ given an encryption of x. Intuitively, the security notion states that the functional keys associated with $f_1, \ldots, f_q$ and an encryption of x reveal nothing beyond the values $f_1(x), \ldots, f_q(x)$.

Functional encryption has been the subject of intense study [1,3,5,8–10,16,17,24–29,39,45,46,48,49,55,56] and has opened the floodgates to important cryptographic applications that have long remained elusive. These applications include, but are not limited to, multi-party non-interactive key exchange [27], universal samplers [27], reusable garbled circuits [28], verifiable random functions [11,14,30], and adaptive garbling [34]. FE has also helped improve our understanding of important theoretical questions, such as the hardness of Nash equilibrium [26,27]. One of the most important applications of FE is its implication to indistinguishability obfuscation (iO for short) [9,16]. There have also been several recent works on functional encryption combiners [2,7,40] and the related problem of iO combiners [6,23]. While amplifiers allow one to transform a weakly secure candidate into a fully secure one, combiners allow one to take many candidates of which at least one is fully secure (and the others are potentially completely insecure) and transform them into a fully secure scheme.

Our Results. Remarkably, although functional encryption was introduced 15 years ago in [56], security amplification for ϵ-secure FE, defined analogously to ϵ-secure PKE above, was first studied only recently in [5,8], which achieved amplification assuming *subexponentially secure LWE*. In fact, no security amplification results for FE are known under any other assumptions. In this paper, we show that one can obtain amplification for FE *unconditionally*. In particular, we obtain the following:

Theorem 1 (Informal). *Assuming an ϵ-secure FE scheme for* P/poly *secure against all polynomial sized adversaries for some constant $\epsilon \in (0,1)$, there exists a fully secure FE scheme secure against all polynomial sized adversaries. Furthermore, the transformation preserves compactness.*

Additionally, our amplification result can be generalized to hold against larger adversaries, in particular, adversaries of subexponential size.

Theorem 2 (Informal). *Assuming an ϵ-secure FE scheme for* P/poly *secure against subexponential sized adversaries for some constant $\epsilon \in (0,1)$, there exists a subexponentially secure FE scheme. Furthermore, the transformation preserves compactness.*

As a consequence of the above theorem and the FE to iO transformations of [9,15,16,42,44], we observe that we can construct iO from an ϵ-secure FE scheme secure against subexponential sized adversaries without the need for any additional assumptions.

Techniques and additional results. To achieve our results, we introduce and construct a new form of homomorphic secret sharing called set homomorphic secret sharing (SetHSS), informally defined below in our Technical Overview. This generalizes a recent notion of combiner friendly homomorphic secret sharing introduced in [40] to a probabilistic scenario tailored for security amplification.

Our work also involves an intertwined use of hardcore measures [12,38,43, 51,61] and efficient leakage simulation [20,41,57,58,60]. First, we improve upon and simplify a technique introduced in [5,8] and then used in [31] that allows one to argue that some fraction of many parallel repetitions of a weakly secure primitive are likely to be secure. The original technique critically uses the leakage simulation theorems [20,41] in conjunction with a hardcore measure theorem [51], which allows one to escape the computational overhead of sampling from hardcore measures. We simplify their technique by using a different leakage simulation theorem [57] which allows for more direct simulation of the applicable leakage. Moreover, we introduce a new "fine-grained" analysis that is crucial to achieving the parameters we need for unconditional amplification. Finally, we isolate the core of their technique and derive a general and applicable theorem (which we call the probabilistic replacement theorem). This theorem is not specific to any cryptographic primitive and, thus, we believe that it might be useful for future efforts in cryptographic amplification beyond FE.

Our second technique is a new technique which allows one to argue security amplification of nested encryptions. In particular, using this technique, we are able to prove the following:

Theorem 3 (Informal). *For any constant $\epsilon \in (0,1)$ and ϵ-secure FE scheme* FE, *the FE scheme* FE* *obtained by composing* FE *with itself is $\epsilon^2 + $ negl(λ) -secure.*

We remark that this technique can also be generalized to argue similar security for public-key encryption (PKE). As such, we also show the following:

Theorem 4 (Informal). *For any constant $\epsilon \in (0,1)$ and ϵ-secure PKE scheme PKE, the PKE scheme PKE* obtained by composing PKE with itself is $\epsilon^2 + \mathsf{negl}(\lambda)$ -secure.*

Prior to our paper, to the best of our knowledge, it was not known how to prove that a simple nesting provided this amplification even for public-key encryption.

Lastly, we remark that this amplification by nesting technique also critically relies on a combination of leakage simulation and hardcore measures. We believe our results exemplify how potent this combination can be for security amplification of cryptographic primitives.

2 Technical Overview

To establish our results, we proceed in two phases:

1. First, we construct an amplifier that converts an ϵ-secure FE scheme for any constant $\epsilon \in (0,1)$ to an ϵ'-secure FE scheme for any arbitrarily small constant $\epsilon' < \epsilon$.
2. Second, we construct an amplifier that converts an ϵ-secure FE scheme for any sufficiently small constant $\epsilon < \frac{1}{6}$ to a fully secure FE scheme.

The above template also works to give an amplifier that is subexponentially secure (Theorem 2). By composing the amplifiers of these two stages, we arrive at our results. We will begin by focusing on the second stage of our amplification procedure, namely, how we amplify an FE scheme that is ϵ-secure for a constant $\epsilon < \frac{1}{6}$ to one that is fully secure.

2.1 Amplification via Secret Sharing and Parallel Repetition

Typically, in order to amplify a weakly secure primitive to a fully secure one, one proceeds by constructing a scheme that uses many copies of the weakly secure primitive and is secure if a fraction of these copies are secure. Intuitively, we expect that if these copies of the weakly secure primitive are independent, then at least some fraction should be secure, and the resulting construction will also be secure. This idea of parallel repetitions of the weakly secure primitive is utilized typically in tandem with a secret sharing scheme. For example, the canonical public-key encryption amplifier works by secret sharing the message and then encrypting each of these shares independently in parallel using the weakly-secure public-key encryption scheme [47]. This paradigm has also been used to amplify other primitives such as non-interactive zero-knowledge [31], by constructing a suitable secret sharing scheme.

In order to amplify functional encryption (FE), a natural approach to utilize this framework is via function secret sharing (FSS). Function secret sharing allows one to split a function f into shares $f_1, \ldots, f_n$ such that for any input

x, we can also split x into shares $x_1, \ldots, x_n$ such that learning the evaluations $f_1(x_1), \ldots, f_n(x_n)$ allows one to recover $f(x)$. Informally, the security property associated with a function secret sharing scheme is that given all but one of the input shares, the input should remain hidden (beyond what is revealed by $f(x)$) even if one is given all the function shares and their evaluations on the input shares. If we had such a function secret sharing scheme, we could simply encrypt each input share x_i under an instantiation FE_i of our weakly secure FE scheme to obtain ct_i. A ciphertext in our scheme would be $(\mathsf{ct}_i)_{i \in [n]}$. Similarly, key generation could use FE_i to generate a key sk_i for the function f_i. The function key in our scheme would then be $(\mathsf{sk}_i)_{i \in [n]}$. From these ciphertexts and function keys, one could learn $(f_i(x_i))_{i \in [n]}$ and recover $f(x)$. For security, one would expect that if the FE scheme is weakly secure, then at least one out of the n instantiations would be secure, in which case, the overall scheme's security would follow by the security of the function secret sharing scheme. This general approach was used in [5,8] to amplify FE assuming subexponentially secure LWE.

In this work, our goal is to amplify FE *unconditionally*. We first observe that we can assume secure one-way functions and still achieve unconditional amplification since a weakly-secure FE implies a weakly-secure one-way function, which can subsequently be amplified using the result of [38]. Unfortunately, we do not know how to construct function secret sharing schemes of the above form assuming only secure one-way functions. However, we note that the above function secret sharing scheme allows up to $n-1$ of the shares to be corrupted while maintaining security. Yet, if we take many copies of an ϵ-secure FE scheme, we would expect roughly a $(1-\epsilon)$ fraction of copies to be secure, not just one! Thus, the above function secret sharing scheme has a stronger security property than the one we would intuitively expect to require for amplification. All we actually need is a secret sharing scheme that is secure against *typical* corruption patterns (that is, one that is secure with high probability if each share is corrupted independently with some probability p). To capitalize on this intuition, we introduce and construct a new type of homomorphic secret sharing scheme, called a *set homomorphic secret sharing scheme*.

Set Homomorphic Secret Sharing Scheme. In a set homomorphic secret sharing (SetHSS) scheme, function shares are associated with sets $(T_i)_{i \in [m]}$, where each set $T_i \subset \{1, 2, \ldots, n\}$. The input x is split into n shares $x_1, \ldots, x_n$. A function f_i associated with the set T_i takes as input all x_j's such that $j \in T_i$. Thus, we can think of the T_i's as sets of the indices of the input shares that the function takes as input. The security guarantee is that if the adversary corrupts some of the T_i's and learns all the input shares corresponding to these sets, security still holds provided there is at least one input share x_{i^*} that the adversary does not learn.

Using a SetHSS scheme, it is possible to build (what we expect to be) an FE amplifier. We follow the same approach detailed above for a function secret sharing scheme to build FE, except we instead use SetHSS with respect to sets $(T_i)_{i \in [m]}$. That is, we run m copies of the FE setup algorithm to obtain m

master secret keys $(\mathsf{msk}_i)_{i \in [m]}$. To encrypt a message x, we n-out-of-n secret share x into shares $x_1, \ldots, x_n$. For each $i \in [m]$, we encrypt $(x_j)_{j \in T_i}$ under msk_i to obtain ct_i and set the ciphertext ct as $(\mathsf{ct}_i)_{i \in [m]}$. To generate function keys, we use the SetHSS scheme to obtain function shares $f_1, \ldots, f_m$ and then set $\mathsf{sk}_f = (\mathsf{sk}_i)_{i \in [m]}$, where sk_i is the function key for f_i generated using msk_i. Observe that by the correctness of the SetHSS scheme and the FE scheme, the above is a correct FE construction. Since the FE scheme is only weakly-secure, if we assume that each encryption becomes corrupted with some probability p (this corresponds to a set T_i becoming corrupted in the SetHSS scheme), we can calculate the probability that the SetHSS scheme remains secure when the corresponding input shares are leaked.

The question that naturally follows is how do we construct such a SetHSS scheme? The first step towards this was taken in the recent work of [40], which introduced a specialized form of function secret sharing, called *combiner-friendly homomorphic secret sharing* (CFHSS), which was constructed assuming only one-way functions. Essentially, a CFHSS is a SetHSS where $m = \binom{n}{3}$, and the sets T_i are all possible size 3 subsets of $\{1, 2, \ldots, n\}$. We observe that unfortunately, such a SetHSS scheme will not suffice for our purposes, because if any constant fraction of the sets T_i are corrupted, then almost certainly every input share x_j would be corrupted.

Instead, for some parameters n and m, we generate sets $(T_i)_{i \in [m]}$ by including each element in $[n]$ in each T_i independently at random with some probability q. We can then calculate two probabilities: First, we can ensure that the probability that at least one share x_j is not corrupted, is sufficiently high – this should intuitively guarantee security. Second, we can ensure that all sets of size 3 are covered by at least one of the sets T_i – this will allow us to ensure correctness by setting the function share f_i in our SetHSS scheme to be the concatenation of the CFHSS function shares corresponding to each size 3 subset contained in T_i.

It turns out that setting the parameters n, m, and q above to achieve both properties simultaneously is nontrivial, and, in fact, we iterate this process twice. The first SetHSS scheme lets us amplify from $\epsilon < \frac{1}{6}$ security to $1/\mathsf{poly}(\lambda)$ security. The second SetHSS scheme lets us amplify from $1/\mathsf{poly}(\lambda)$ security to negligible (or sub-exponential) security.

However, our security calculations only give us a sense of what we expect the resulting security level to be. How do we actually prove that the scheme attains this level of security?

2.2 Proving Security: Probabilistic Replacement Theorem

Consider the following situation: There are $n \in \mathbb{N}$ independent copies of some primitive that is known to be only weakly secure (over the randomness of the primitive) for some notion of security. Then, one wants to claim that if n is large enough, with high probability, at least one of these n instantiations will be secure. Or as a stronger notion, one might want some fraction of the n instantiations to be secure. This is useful when security of some larger primitive holds provided that some fraction of these n instantiations are secure. For example, if one were to additively secret share a message and then independently encrypt each share, the message remains hidden as long as at least one of the encryptions cannot be broken.

Proofs Using Hardcore Lemmas: Typical proofs of this sort rely on hardcore lemmas that define hardcore measures. First, we review the notion of a hardcore measure. Suppose that a primitive is secure with some low probability over its randomness. Then, Impagliazzo's hardcore lemma [38] states that there exists some "hard core" of the primitive's randomness such that the primitive is secure with high probability (against a somewhat smaller class of adversaries) when its randomness is restricted to this "hard core". In other words, though the primitive may be weakly secure over uniform randomness, there is some "hard core" portion of the randomness on which the primitive is strongly secure. This "hard core" may be defined as a measure over the randomness (which we call a hardcore measure) or as a subset of the randomness (which we call a hardcore set). A more precise specification of the relationship between the security gain and the density of the hardcore measure can be found in various hardcore lemmas (refer to Sect. 3).

Then, typical security amplification proofs proceed as follows: In the scenario above, each of the n instances of the primitive independently samples its randomness from a uniform distribution. However, this is equivalent to having each primitive sample its randomness from its hardcore measure with probability proportional to the density of the hardcore measure and sample from the complement of the hardcore measure with probability proportional to the density of the complement. When considered this way, if the density of the hardcore measure is large enough, with high probability, some of the instances of the primitive will sample randomness from their hardcore measures. Therefore, those primitives are secure by the definition of the hardcore measure.

Dealing with the Time Complexity of Sampling Hardcore Measures: Now, this proof technique works whenever it is the final step in a larger proof of security. But what happens when this is not the case? For instance, suppose we independently encrypt secret shares of a message m, and then after claiming some fraction of the encryptions are secure, suppose we want to move to an experiment where the secure shares are replaced with shares corresponding to the message 0. A natural idea would be to replace the shares known to be secure (those where the randomness of the encryption was sampled from the hardcore measures) with simulated shares via a reduction to some notion of indistinguishability between the real and simulated shares when the real shares are hidden.

We note that the reduction in this case, upon receiving either the simulated or real shares, would need to encrypt these challenge shares using the secure encryption instances. This means the reduction needs to sample randomness from the hardcore measures of the encryption. This can be problematic because there is no bound on the efficiency of sampling from these hardcore measures. Therefore, there is no bound on the efficiency of the reduction. This would be fine if the secret sharing satisfied a *statistical* notion of security. Unfortunately, this will not work if the underlying secret sharing scheme achieves only computational security, such as is the case with our SetHSS scheme. In general, the same issue can occur whenever computational assumptions need to be used in the remainder of the proof of security, after applying an appropriate hardcore lemma.

In essence, the issue is that once one uses the fact that one is sampling from the hardcore measures to prove that an instance is secure, then later reductions may also have to sample from the hardcore measures. But this sampling may not be efficient, so the reduction may also be inefficient. To address this problem, we build upon a technique introduced in [5,8]. We first observe that hardcore measures of sufficiently high density also have high min-entropy. Then, we use a leakage simulation theorem from [57] which allows one to simulate sampling from measures with high min-entropy in a manner that is more efficient; by careful choice of parameters, we show that this simulation can be made efficient enough to allow us to perform cryptographic reductions. This allows one to continue performing reductions even after one has invoked the hardcore measures (instead of sampling from the hardcore measure, we can instead run the simulator for the measure). Furthermore, we can ensure that the simulator is independent of some of its inputs through the appropriate use of commitments. We note that instead of using [57] for leakage simulation, [5,8] uses a different leakage simulation lemma [20] that deals with low output length leakage instead of high min-entropy leakage and, therefore, requires the leakage to be first transformed into an appropriate form. Our proof is thus simpler and more direct. Additionally, by considering the output of the simulator as a single joint distribution, we can also get slightly better and more fine-grained parameters, which allows us to get polynomial time simulators for all of the appropriate parameter regimes we use in this paper. We then present the core of this technique in a more abstract and modular way so that it can be applied to other situations and proofs. We note that our abstracted theorem does not refer to hardcore measures at all, but instead refers to the more natural problem of claiming that some fraction of n primitives is secure.

The Probabilistic Replacement Theorem: More specifically, suppose there are two randomized functions E and F that are weakly indistinguishable over their randomness. Then, our theorem shows indistinguishability between the following two experiments: In one experiment, the adversary gets n independent evaluations of E on n inputs. In the other experiment, we probabilistically replace some of the instances of E with F. Then, we give the adversary evaluations of these instances of E and F using randomness generated by some bounded-time function h. Essentially, we show that one can replace some of the instances of E with instances of F, while still maintaining overall efficiency. Please refer to Sect. 7 for more details.

Relating this back to the notion of security, we could let F be a "secure" variant of some primitive E. For instance, F could be an encryption of 0 and E an encryption of the message m. If E is weakly secure in the sense that E is weakly indistinguishable from F, then if one has enough independent instances of E, we show that at least some fraction of them will be secure (in the sense that one can replace these instances of E with the secure variant F). For more details, please refer to the proof overview in Sect. 7.

Applying the Probabilistic Replacement Theorem: Having shown the probabilistic replacement theorem (Sect. 7), it is now possible to prove the security of our FE amplifier described above fairly easily. Roughly, we will use the probabilistic replacement theorem to replace FE encryptions of SetHSS shares with simulated FE encryptions. Once this has been done, we can use the security of the underlying SetHSS scheme to argue security of our FE amplifier.

Setting the Parameters: By appropriately setting the parameters n (number of input shares), m (number of sets in the SetHSS scheme), and q (the probability of an element in $[n]$ being included in any set), we are able to show that our construction indeed amplifies security. We will have to apply the construction twice. First, we are able to amplify from a constant $\epsilon < \frac{1}{6}$ secure FE scheme to one that is $1/\mathsf{poly}(\lambda)$ secure. Then, we are able to amplify a $1/\mathsf{poly}(\lambda)$ scheme to one that is fully secure. An astute reader may have noticed that at each invocation of our amplifier, we also lose some correctness. However, in between applications of our amplifier, we can easily amplify correctness by parallel repetition. This is because we only need one of our repetitions to be correct. This approach does lose a factor of security proportional to the number of repetitions, but the parameters can be set so that overall we gain in security while preserving correctness. Please refer to Sect. 8 for more details.

2.3   Amplifying Security via Nesting

The above FE amplifier was already sufficient to amplify an ϵ-secure FE scheme with $\epsilon < \frac{1}{6}$ to a fully secure one. However, we would like to be able to amplify an ϵ-secure FE scheme for any constant $\epsilon \in (0, 1)$. Here, we show how to amplify an ϵ-secure FE scheme for any $\epsilon \in (0, 1)$ to an ϵ'-secure FE scheme for any $\epsilon' \in (0, 1)$. To do this, we first show how to amplify an ϵ-secure FE scheme to a (roughly) ϵ^2-secure one. By repeatedly applying this transformation a constant number of times, we can amplify to any smaller constant. The construction itself is to simply nest two independent copies of the underlying ϵ-secure FE scheme. Namely, first encrypt the message under FE_1 to compute ct_1 and then encrypt ct_1 under FE_2 to obtain the final ciphertext ct, with appropriate functional secret keys. Intuitively, since there are two layers of encryption, where each layer is secure with probability $(1 - \epsilon)$, we would expect the double encryption to be secure with probability $(1 - \epsilon^2)$. However, proving this requires some care. Indeed, to the best of our knowledge, such a security amplification result, even for nested public-key encryption, was not previously known.

Proof Overview: As noted above, we expect our nested scheme to be secure if one of the encryption layers is secure. Now, if we could prove that each layer is *independently* insecure with probability at most ϵ, then we could show that the amplified FE* scheme is only insecure with probability at most ϵ^2. Unfortunately, the security of the two layers is not independent; in general the hard core sets of randomness which lead to secure encryptions could depend on the message being encrypted. Instead, we will achieve similar amplification by in some sense "simulating" the security of the outer FE in a way that is independent of the security of the inner FE.

First, we quantify the security of the outer FE using hardcore measures. If we have an ϵ-secure FE, then for any fixed output of the inner FE, the outer FE is secure with probability at least $1 - \epsilon$. Therefore, by [51], there exist hardcore measures (of density $1 - \epsilon$) of the randomness of the outer FE such that the outer FE is strongly secure when its randomness is sampled from these hardcore measures. So, with probability at least $1 - \epsilon$, we sample randomness from the hardcore measures of the outer FE and achieve security via these hardcore measures. But with probability ϵ, we have no guarantee that the outer FE is secure, so we must rely on the security of the inner FE.

Now, we want to show that conditioned on the outer FE being potentially insecure (i.e. when we do not sample from these hardcore measures), then the inner FE is still only insecure with probability close to ϵ. In other words, we want to show that the security of the inner and outer FE schemes are close to independent. To do so, we need to perform a reduction to the ϵ-security of the inner FE. At this point, we run into two issues. First, in order to perform our reduction to the security of the inner FE, we will need to sample from the complement hardcore measures of the outer FE. (Recall that we first conditioned on the outer FE being potentially insecure.) However, this is problematic because we have no bound on the efficiency of computing or sampling from these hardcore measures. Secondly, the hardcore measures of the outer FE depend implicitly on the randomness used by the inner FE. Or, in other words, the security of the outer FE, as quantified by these measures, is not independent of the security of the inner FE.

To resolve these issues, we need to find a way to give an efficient reduction to the security of the inner FE, despite the inefficiencies and dependencies outlined above. Intuitively, we proceed as follows: Our reduction takes as input the ciphertext produced by the inner FE. The reduction then uses the fact that the complement of the hard core measure of the outer FE has density ϵ to efficiently simulate randomness that is indistinguishable from hardcore randomness; this simulation uses the leakage simulation theorem of [57]. This allows our reduction to create the outer FE ciphertext that the adversary expects. Please refer to Sect. 9 for more details.

2.4   Organization

In Sect. 3, we recall necessary preliminaries. In Sect. 4, we define functional encryption notions with partial security. In Sects. 5 and 6, we define and instantiate set homomorphic secret sharing schemes and analyze their correctness and security when the underlying sets are sampled in a probabilistic manner. In Sect. 7, we state and prove the Probabilistic Replacement Theorem. In Sect. 8, we show our parallel repetition amplification theorem. In Sect. 9, we show our nesting amplification theorem. In Sect. 10, we show that nesting amplifies the security of public-key encryption. Finally, in Sect. 11, we combine our nesting and parallel repetition amplification results.

3   Preliminaries

Notation. Let $\lambda \in \mathbb{N}$ be the security parameter. Throughout, we define various size and advantage parameters as functions of λ. We say that a function $f(\lambda)$ is negligible, denoted $f(\lambda) = \mathsf{negl}(\lambda)$, if $f(\lambda) = \lambda^{-\omega(1)}$. We say that a function $f(\lambda)$ is polynomial, denoted $f(\lambda) = \mathsf{poly}(\lambda)$, if $f(\lambda) = p(\lambda)$ for some fixed polynomial p. Throughout, when we write inequalities in terms of functions of λ, we mean that these inequalities hold for sufficiently large λ. For $n \in \mathbb{N}$, let $[n]$ denote the set $\{1, \ldots, n\}$. For a set S, let $x \leftarrow S$ denote the process of sampling x from the uniform distribution over S. For a distribution $\mathcal{D}$, let $x \leftarrow \mathcal{D}$ denote the process of sampling x from $\mathcal{D}$.

Definition 1 $((s, \epsilon)$-Indistinguishability). *We say that two ensembles $\mathcal{X} = \{\mathcal{X}_\lambda\}_{\lambda \in \mathbb{N}}$ and $\mathcal{Y} = \{\mathcal{Y}_\lambda\}_{\lambda \in \mathbb{N}}$ are (s, ϵ)-indistinguishable if for any adversary $\mathcal{A}$ of size s,*

$$\left| \Pr_{x \leftarrow \mathcal{X}_\lambda} [\mathcal{A}(1^\lambda, x)] - \Pr_{y \leftarrow \mathcal{Y}_\lambda} [\mathcal{A}(1^\lambda, y)] \right| \leq \epsilon$$

for sufficiently large $\lambda \in \mathbb{N}$.

Notation. We will say that ensembles satisfy $(\mathsf{poly}(\lambda) \cdot s, \epsilon)$-indistinguishability if the ensembles satisfy $(p(\lambda) \cdot s, \epsilon)$-indistinguishability for every polynomial $p(\lambda)$.

We will make use of the following Chernoff bound in our analysis.

Definition 2 (Chernoff Bound). *Let $X_1, X_2, \ldots, X_n$ be independent and identically distributed Boolean random variables. Let $X = \sum_{i \in [n]} X_i$ and let $\mu = \mathbb{E}[X]$. Then, for $\delta \geq 1$,*

$$\Pr[X \geq (1 + \delta)\mu] \leq e^{-\frac{\delta\mu}{3}}.$$

We define a measure.

Definition 3. *A measure is a function $\mathcal{M} : \{0,1\}^k \to [0,1]$.*

- *The size of a measure is $|\mathcal{M}| = \sum_{x \in \{0,1\}^k} \mathcal{M}(x)$.*
- *The density of a measure is $\mu(\mathcal{M}) = |\mathcal{M}|2^{-k}$.*
- *The distribution defined by a measure (denoted by $\mathcal{D}_\mathcal{M}$) is a distribution over $\{0,1\}^k$, where for every $x \in \{0,1\}^k$, $\Pr_{X \leftarrow \mathcal{D}_\mathcal{M}}[X = x] = \mathcal{M}(x)/|\mathcal{M}|$.*
- *A scaled version of a measure for a constant $0 < c < 1$ is $\mathcal{M}_c = c\mathcal{M}$. Note that $\mathcal{M}_c$ induces the same distribution as $\mathcal{M}$.*
- *The complement of a measure is $\overline{\mathcal{M}} = 1 - \mathcal{M}$.*

3.1   Useful Lemmas

We defer this section to the full version.

4   Functional Encryption

We define the notion of a (secret key) functional encryption scheme.

Syntax of a Functional Encryption Scheme. A functional encryption (FE) scheme FE for a class of circuits $\mathcal{C} = \{\mathcal{C}_\lambda\}_{\lambda \in \mathbb{N}}$ consists of four polynomial time algorithms (Setup, Enc, KeyGen, Dec) defined as follows. Let $\mathcal{X}_\lambda$ be the input space of the circuit class $\mathcal{C}_\lambda$, and let $\mathcal{Y}_\lambda$ be the output space of $\mathcal{C}_\lambda$. We refer to $\mathcal{X}_\lambda$ and $\mathcal{Y}_\lambda$ as the input and output space of the scheme, respectively.

- **Setup, msk $\leftarrow$ FE.Setup(1^λ):** It takes as input the security parameter λ and outputs the master secret key msk.
- **Encryption, ct $\leftarrow$ FE.Enc(msk, m):** It takes as input the master secret key msk and a message $m \in \mathcal{X}_\lambda$ and outputs ct, an encryption of m.
- **Key Generation, $\mathsf{sk}_C \leftarrow$ FE.KeyGen (msk, C):** It takes as input the master secret key msk and a circuit $C \in \mathcal{C}_\lambda$ and outputs a function key sk_C.
- **Decryption, $y \leftarrow$ FE.Dec (sk_C, ct):** It takes as input a function secret key sk_C, a ciphertext ct and outputs a value $y \in \mathcal{Y}_\lambda$.

We can similarly define the notion of a public key FE scheme, and our results in this work also hold for public key FE. However, we choose to focus on secret key FE, as this is a weaker primitive.

We describe the properties associated with an FE scheme.

Correctness.

Definition 4 (Approximate Correctness). *A functional encryption scheme* FE = (Setup, KeyGen, Enc, Dec) *is said to be μ-correct if it satisfies the following property: for every $C : \mathcal{X}_\lambda \to \mathcal{Y}_\lambda \in \mathcal{C}_\lambda, m \in \mathcal{X}_\lambda$ it holds that:*

$$\Pr \left[\begin{array}{c} \mathsf{msk} \leftarrow \mathsf{FE.Setup}(1^\lambda) \\ \mathsf{ct} \leftarrow \mathsf{FE.Enc}(\mathsf{msk}, m) \\ \mathsf{sk}_C \leftarrow \mathsf{FE.KeyGen}(\mathsf{msk}, C) \\ C(m) \leftarrow \mathsf{FE.Dec}(\mathsf{sk}_C, \mathsf{ct}) \end{array} \right] \geq \mu,$$

where the probability is taken over the coins of the algorithms.

We refer to FE schemes that satisfy the above definition of correctness with $\mu = 1 - \mathsf{negl}(\lambda)$ for a negligible function $\mathsf{negl}(\cdot)$ as correct.

Efficiency: Sublinearity and Compactness.

Definition 5 (Sublinearity and Compactness). *A functional encryption scheme* FE *for a circuit class* $\mathcal{C}$ *containing circuits of size at most* s *that take inputs of length* ℓ *is said to be sublinear if there exists some constant* $\epsilon > 0$ *such that the size of the encryption circuit is bounded by* $s^{1-\epsilon} \cdot \mathsf{poly}(\lambda, \ell)$ *for some fixed polynomial* poly. *If the above holds for* $\epsilon = 1$, *then the FE scheme is said to be* compact.

In this work, we will focus on FE schemes that are sublinear (and possibly compact).

Security. We recall indistinguishability-based super-selective security for FE. This security notion is modeled as a game between a challenger Chal and an adversary $\mathcal{A}$. The game begins with $\mathcal{A}$ submitting message queries $(x_i)_{i \in [\Gamma]}$, a challenge message query (x_0^*, x_1^*), and a function query C. Chal samples a bit b and responds with ciphertexts corresponding to $(x_i)_{i \in [\Gamma]}$ and x_b^* along with a function key sk_C corresponding to C. $\mathcal{A}$ wins the game if she can guess b with probability significantly more than $1/2$ and if $C(x_0^*) = C(x_1^*)$. That is to say, the function evaluation computable by $\mathcal{A}$ on the challenge ciphertext gives the same value regardless of b. We can define our security notion in terms of the size $s = s(\lambda)$ of adversaries against which security holds and an advantage $\epsilon = \epsilon(\lambda)$ that such adversaries can achieve. We say such a scheme is (s, ϵ)−secure.

Definition 6 ((s, ϵ)-secure FE). *A secret-key FE scheme* FE *for a class of circuits* $\mathcal{C} = \{\mathcal{C}_\lambda\}_{\lambda \in [\mathbb{N}]}$ *and message space* $\mathcal{X} = \{\mathcal{X}_\lambda\}_{\lambda \in [\mathbb{N}]}$ *is* (s, ϵ)-*secure if for any adversary* $\mathcal{A}$ *of size* s, *the advantage of* $\mathcal{A}$ *is*

$$\mathsf{Adv}_{\mathcal{A}}^{\mathsf{FE}} = \left| \Pr[\mathsf{Expt}_{\mathcal{A}}^{\mathsf{FE}}(1^\lambda, 0) = 1] - \Pr[\mathsf{Expt}_{\mathcal{A}}^{\mathsf{FE}}(1^\lambda, 1) = 1] \right| \leq \epsilon,$$

where for each $b \in \{0, 1\}$ *and* $\lambda \in \mathbb{N}$, *the experiment* $\mathsf{Expt}_{\mathcal{A}}^{\mathsf{FE}}(1^\lambda, b)$ *is defined below:*

1. ***Challenge queries:*** $\mathcal{A}$ *submits message queries* $(x_i)_{i \in [\Gamma]}$, *a challenge message query* (x_0^*, x_1^*), *and a function query* C *to the challenger* Chal, *with* $x_i \in \mathcal{X}_\lambda$ *for all* $i \in [\Gamma]$, $x_0^*, x_1^* \in \mathcal{X}_\lambda$, *and* $C \in \mathcal{C}_\lambda$ *such that* $C(x_0^*) = C(x_1^*)$. *Here,* Γ *is an arbitrary (a priori unbounded) polynomial in* λ.
2. Chal *computes* $\mathsf{msk} \leftarrow \mathsf{FE.Setup}(1^\lambda)$ *and then computes* $\mathsf{ct}_i \leftarrow \mathsf{FE.Enc}(\mathsf{msk}, x_i)$ *for all* $i \in [\Gamma]$. *It then computes* $\mathsf{ct}^* \leftarrow \mathsf{FE.Enc}(\mathsf{msk}, x_b^*)$ *and* $\mathsf{sk}_C \leftarrow \mathsf{FE.KeyGen}(\mathsf{msk}, C)$. *It sends* $((\mathsf{ct}_i)_{i \in [\Gamma]}, \mathsf{ct}^*, \mathsf{sk}_C)$ *to* $\mathcal{A}$.
3. *The output of the experiment is set to* b', *where* b' *is the output of* $\mathcal{A}$.

Adaptive Security and Collusions. The above security notion is referred to as *super-selective security* in the literature. One can consider a stronger notion of security, called *adaptive security with unbounded collusions*, where the adversary can make an unbounded (polynomial) number of function secret key queries and can interleave the challenge messages and the function queries in any arbitrary order. In this paper, we only deal with super-selectively secure FE schemes. However, it holds for any fully-secure sublinear FE scheme that these notions are equivalent [4, 42], and therefore, we only focus on super-selective security in this work, as it is a simpler starting place.

4.1 Semi-functional FE

In this work, to simplify some constructions and proofs, we will consider the notion of semi-functional FE (sFE). Semi-functional FE is simply a functional encryption scheme with two auxiliary algorithms. We defer the definition to the full version.

5   Set Homomorphic Secret Sharing Schemes

In [40], as an intermediate step in their construction of an FE combiner, they define and construct what they call a combiner-friendly homomorphic secret sharing scheme (CFHSS). We defer the definition to the full version. [40] show the following.

Theorem 5 ([40]). *Assuming one-way functions, there exists a combiner-friendly homomorphic secret sharing scheme for* P/poly *for* $n = O(\mathsf{poly}(\lambda))$ *candidates.*

Moreover, [40] also show the following extension of the above theorem, when the underlying OWF is $(O(s), O(s^{-1}))$-secure for $s = \omega(\mathsf{poly}(\lambda))$.

Theorem 6 ([40]). *Assuming an* $(O(s), O(s^{-1}))$-*secure one-way function, there exists an* $(O(s), \mathsf{poly}(\lambda) \cdot O(s^{-1}))$-*secure combiner-friendly homomorphic secret sharing scheme for* P/poly *for* $n = O(\mathsf{poly}(\lambda))$ *candidates. Moreover, the size of* InpEncode *is independent of the size of the circuit class and the size of any* $C_{i,j,k}$ *is bounded by* $|C| \cdot \mathsf{poly}(\lambda, n)$ *for some fixed polynomial.*

In this work, we extend the notion of a combiner-friendly homomorphic secret sharing scheme [40] to a more general setting, which will be useful for amplification. The CFHSS scheme of [40] implicitly restricts the shares to correspond to all subsets $T \subseteq [n]$ with $|T| = 3$. This is clear by simply noting that we can think of the share $s_{i,j,k}$ as corresponding to the set $T = \{i, j, k\}$ (the construction in [40] does not care about the ordering of i, j, k, so there are only $\binom{n}{3}$ shares in their construction, not n^3). For amplification, we will need to use a more general approach, where we allow the sets to be arbitrary and given as input to the scheme.

Definition 7. *A set homomorphic secret sharing scheme,* SetHSS $=$ (InpEncode, FuncEncode, Decode), *for* $n \in \mathbb{N}$ *candidates,* $m \in \mathbb{N}$ *sets* $\{T_i\}_{i \in [m]}$, *where each set* $T_i \subseteq [n]$, *and a class of circuits* $\mathcal{C} = \{\mathcal{C}_\lambda\}_{\lambda \in \mathbb{N}}$ *with input space* $\mathcal{X}_\lambda$ *and output space* $\mathcal{Y}_\lambda$ *consists of the following polynomial time algorithms:*

- **Input Encoding,** $\mathsf{InpEncode}(1^\lambda, 1^n, \{T_i\}_{i \in [m]}, x)$: *It takes as input the security parameter* λ, *the number of candidates* n, *a collection of* m *sets* $\{T_i\}_{i \in [m]}$, *where each set* $T_i \subseteq [n]$, *and an input* $x \in \mathcal{X}_\lambda$ *and outputs a set of input shares* $\{s_i\}_{i \in [m]}$.
- **Function Encoding,** $\mathsf{FuncEncode}(1^\lambda, 1^n, \{T_i\}_{i \in [m]}, C)$: *It takes as input the security parameter* λ, *the number of candidates* n, *a collection of* m *sets* $\{T_i\}_{i \in [m]}$, *where each set* $T_i \subseteq [n]$, *and a circuit* $C \in \mathcal{C}$ *and outputs a set of function shares* $\{C_i\}_{i \in [m]}$.
- **Decoding,** $\mathsf{Decode}(\{C_i(s_i)\}_{i \in [m]}, \{T_i\}_{i \in [m]})$: *It takes as input a set of evaluations of function shares on their respective input shares and* m *sets and outputs a value* $y \in \mathcal{Y}_\lambda \cup \{\bot\}$.

A set homomorphic secret sharing scheme, SetHSS, *for sets* $\{T_i\}_{i \in [m]}$ *has the following properties:*

- **Correctness**: *For every* $\lambda \in \mathbb{N}$, *circuit* $C \in \mathcal{C}_\lambda$, *and input* $x \in \mathcal{X}_\lambda$, *it holds that:*

$$\Pr \left[\begin{array}{c} \{s_i\}_{i \in [m]} \leftarrow \mathsf{InpEncode}(1^\lambda, 1^n, \{T_i\}_{i \in [m]}, x) \\ \{C_i\}_{i \in [m]} \leftarrow \mathsf{FuncEncode}(1^\lambda, 1^n, \{T_i\}_{i \in [m]}, C) \\ C(x) \leftarrow \mathsf{Decode}(\{C_i(s_i)\}_{i \in [m]}, \{T_i\}_{i \in [m]}) \end{array} \right] \geq 1 - \mathsf{negl}(\lambda),$$

where the probability is taken over the coins of the algorithms and $\mathsf{negl}(\lambda)$ *is a negligible function in* λ.
- **Security**:

Definition 8 (IND-secure SetHSS). *A set homomorphic secret sharing scheme* SetHSS *for a class of circuits* $\mathcal{C} = \{\mathcal{C}_\lambda\}_{\lambda \in [\mathbb{N}]}$ *with input space* $\mathcal{X} = \{\mathcal{X}_\lambda\}_{\lambda \in [\mathbb{N}]}$ *and sets* $\{T_i\}_{i \in [m]}$ *is selectively secure if for any PPT adversary* $\mathcal{A}$, *there exists a negligible function* $\mu(\cdot)$ *such that for all sufficiently large* $\lambda \in \mathbb{N}$, *the advantage of* $\mathcal{A}$ *is*

$$\mathsf{Adv}_{\mathcal{A}}^{\mathsf{SetHSS}} = \left| \Pr[\mathsf{Expt}_{\mathcal{A}}^{\mathsf{SetHSS}}(1^\lambda, 1^n, 0) = 1] - \Pr[\mathsf{Expt}_{\mathcal{A}}^{\mathsf{SetHSS}}(1^\lambda, 1^n, 1) = 1] \right| \leq \mu(\lambda),$$

where for each $b \in \{0, 1\}$ *and* $\lambda \in \mathbb{N}$ *and* $n \in \mathbb{N}$, *the experiment* $\mathsf{Expt}_{\mathcal{A}}^{\mathsf{SetHSS}}(1^\lambda, 1^n, b)$ *is defined below:*

$\mathsf{Expt}_{\mathcal{A}}^{\mathsf{SetHSS}}(1^\lambda, 1^n, b)$

1. **Secure share:** $\mathcal{A}$ *submits an index* $i^* \in [n]$ *that it will not learn the input shares for.*
2. **Challenge input queries:** $\mathcal{A}$ *submits input queries,*

$$\left(x_0^\ell, x_1^\ell \right)_{\ell \in [L]}$$

with $x_0^\ell, x_1^\ell \in \mathcal{X}_\lambda$ *to the challenger* Chal, *where* $L = \mathsf{poly}(\lambda)$ *is chosen by* $\mathcal{A}$.
3. *For all* ℓ, Chal *computes* $\{s_i^\ell\}_{i \in [m]} \leftarrow \mathsf{InpEncode}(1^\lambda, 1^n, \{T_i\}_{i \in [m]}, x_b^\ell)$. *For all* ℓ, *the challenger* Chal *then sends* $\{s_i^\ell\}_{i \in [m], i^* \notin T_i}$, *the input shares that do not correspond to a set containing* i^*, *to the adversary* $\mathcal{A}$.

4. **Function queries**: *The following is repeated an at most polynomial number of times: $\mathcal{A}$ submits a function query $C \in \mathcal{C}_\lambda$ to Chal. The challenger Chal computes function shares $\{C_i\}_{i \in [m]} \leftarrow$ FuncEncode($1^\lambda, 1^n, \{T_i\}_{i \in [m]}, C)$ and sends them to $\mathcal{A}$ along with all evaluations $\{C_i(s_i^\ell)\}_{i \in [m]}$ for all $\ell \in [L]$.*

5. *If there exists a function query C and challenge message queries (x_0^ℓ, x_1^ℓ) such that $C(x_0^\ell) \neq C(x_1^\ell)$, then the output of the experiment is set to $\bot$. Otherwise, the output of the experiment is set to b', where b' is the output of $\mathcal{A}$.*

We refer to a SetHSS scheme that satisfies the correctness and security properties as a correct and secure SetHSS scheme, respectively.

5.1   SetHSS from CFHSS

Given the CFHSS scheme from [40], we can construct a correct SetHSS scheme for sets $T_1, T_2, \ldots, T_m$ provided that $\{T_i\}_{i \in [m]}$ covers all subsets of size 3 (formally defined in Definition 9). Looking ahead, our SetHSS scheme will remain secure if the corruption pattern on the T_i's is such that some element $j \in [n]$ is not in any corrupted set. This is exactly the unmarked element condition in Sect. 6.

Formally, we show the following.

Theorem 7. *Assuming one-way functions, there exists a set homomorphic secret sharing scheme for P/poly for $n = O(\mathsf{poly}(\lambda))$ candidates for sets $T_1, T_2, \ldots, T_m$ that cover all subsets of size 3. Moreover, security holds regardless of the sets $T_1, T_2, \ldots, T_m$.*

We simultaneously also show the following for $s = \omega(\mathsf{poly}(\lambda))$.

Theorem 8. *Assuming an $(O(s), O(s^{-1}))$-secure one-way function, there exists an $(O(s), \mathsf{poly}(\lambda) \cdot O(s^{-1}))$-secure set homomorphic secret sharing scheme for P/poly for $n = O(\mathsf{poly}(\lambda))$ candidates for sets $T_1, T_2, \ldots, T_m$ that cover all subsets of size 3. Security holds regardless of the sets $T_1, T_2, \ldots, T_m$. Moreover, the size of the circuit $\mathsf{InpEncode}(\cdot)$ is independent of the size of the circuit class and the size of any function encoding C_i has size bounded by $|C| \cdot \mathsf{poly}(\lambda, n, m)$ for some fixed polynomial.*

We defer the proofs of these theorems to the full version.

6   Covering Sets

In this section, we will define some properties of covering sets that will be useful in our FE construction. Informally, covering sets are a collection of sets (X_i) such that some other collection of sets (Y_j) are covered by the X_i's. By this, we mean that every Y_j is a subset of some X_i. As discussed previously, our overall plan for constructing an amplified FE is to use a set homomorphic secret sharing scheme, which will allow us to secret share the message into n shares and then encrypt m sets, each which contains some of the n shares. Thus, we can think of the X_i's as subsets of $[n]$. However, we only know how to construct such set homomorphic secret sharing schemes if the sets cover all subsets of size 3. Furthermore, these set homomorphic secret sharing schemes have a specific security property defined in Sect. 5. In this section, we analyze the probability that randomly sampled sets will cover all size t subsets and the probability that the security property is satisfied when the sets are randomly corrupted. These probabilities will be instrumental in analyzing the correctness and security properties of our amplified FE construction in Sect. 8.1.

Definition 9 (Set t-Covering). *We say that a collection of sets $T_1, T_2, \ldots, T_m$ over $[n]$ covers all subsets of size t if for every $T' \subseteq [n]$ with $|T'| = t$, there exists some $i \in [m]$ such that $T' \subseteq T_i$.*

Definition 10 (Unmarked Element). *Let $f : [m] \to \{0,1\}$ be a marking function, where we say an index $i \in [n]$ is "marked" if $f(i) = 1$ and "unmarked" if $f(i) = 0$. A collection of sets $T_1, T_2, \ldots, T_m$ over $[n]$ has an unmarked element with respect to f if there exists an index $i \in [n]$ such that for all sets T_j with $i \in T_j$, $f(j) = 0$.*

Lemma 1. *Consider sampling m sets $T_1, T_2, \ldots, T_m$, where each set is chosen by independently including each element in $[n]$ with probability q. Then, with probability $\geq 1 - n^t(1 - q^t)^m$, $T_1, T_2, \ldots, T_m$ is a $t-$covering.*

Proof. Let $S_1, \ldots, S_{\binom{n}{t}}$ be all subsets of $[n]$ of size t. For any $i \in [\binom{n}{t}]$ and $j \in [m]$, then

$$\Pr[S_i \not\subseteq T_j] = (1 - q^t).$$

Therefore,

$$\Pr[\forall j \in [m], S_i \not\subseteq T_j] = (1 - q^t)^m.$$

By the union bound,

$$\Pr\left[\exists i \in \left[\binom{n}{t}\right], \forall j \in [m], S_i \not\subseteq T_j\right] \leq n^t(1 - q^t)^m,$$

giving the desired result.

Lemma 2. *Consider sampling m sets $T_1, T_2, \ldots, T_m$, where each set is chosen by independently including each element in $[n]$ with probability q. Define the marking function $f : [m] \to \{0,1\}$ by setting, independently at random for each $i \in [m]$, $f(i) = 1$ with probability p. Then, for any $\delta \geq 1$, with probability at least $(1 - e^{-\frac{\delta pm}{3}})(1 - (1 - (1 - q)^{(1+\delta)pm})^n)$, the sets have an unmarked element with respect to f.*

Proof. Let $S \subseteq [m]$. Define B_S to be the event that $\forall u \in S, f(u) = 1$, and $\forall v \notin S, f(v) = 0$. Since any distinct $i, j \in [n]$ are independently included in each set, observe that for any $S \subseteq [m]$, the event that i is unmarked given B_S is independent of the event that j is unmarked given B_S. Therefore, since i is included in each marked set (a set T_u with $f(u) = 1$) with probability $1 - q$, then

$$\Pr\left[i \text{ unmarked} \mid B_S\right] = (1 - q)^{|S|}$$
$$\Pr[\forall i \in [n], i \text{ marked} \mid B_S] = (1 - (1 - q)^{|S|})^n$$
$$\Pr[\exists i \in [n], i \text{ unmarked} \mid B_S] = 1 - (1 - (1 - q)^{|S|})^n.$$

Then,

$$\Pr\left[\exists i \in [n], i \text{ unmarked}\right] = \sum_{S_j \subseteq [m]} \Pr[B_{S_j}](1 - (1 - (1 - q)^{|S_j|})^n)$$

$$= \sum_{k=0}^{n} \sum_{S_j, |S_j| = k} \Pr\left[B_{S_j}\right](1 - (1 - (1 - q)^k)^n)$$

$$= \sum_{k=0}^{n} \Pr[k \text{ sets are marked}](1 - (1 - (1 - q)^k)^n)$$

$$\geq \Pr[\text{at most } k \text{ sets are marked}](1 - (1 - (1 - q)^k)^n).$$

for every $k \in [n]$. Let X_i be the event that set T_i is marked (in other words, $f(i) = 1$). Let $X = \sum_{i \in [m]} X_i$. Note that $\mathbb{E}[X] = pm$. Then, by the Chernoff bound (Definition 2) for any $\delta \geq 1$,

$$\Pr[X \geq (1 + \delta)pm] \leq e^{-\frac{\delta pm}{3}}.$$

Therefore,

$$\Pr[\exists i \in [n], i \text{ unmarked}] \geq (1 - e^{-\frac{\delta pm}{3}})(1 - (1 - (1 - q)^{(1+\delta)pm})^n).$$

7   Probabilistic Replacement Theorem

Please refer to the technical overview (Sect. 2.2) for the high level overview and motivation of this theorem as well as an introduction to hardcore measures.

Our Theorem: Suppose there are two randomized functions E and F that are weakly indistinguishable over their randomness and the randomness of the distinguisher. Then, our theorem below shows indistinguishability between the following two experiments: In one experiment, the adversary gets n independent evaluations of E on n inputs. In the other experiment, we probabilistically replace some of the instances of E with F. Then, we give the adversary evaluations of these instances of E and F using randomness generated by some bounded time function h. Essentially, we show that one can replace some of the instances of E with instances of F while still maintaining overall efficiency.

We also include some other details. First, we need to determine which inputs to evaluate E and F on. As such, we define Gen to be any randomized circuit that produces these inputs, and evaluate E and F on the output of Gen. Second, we also allow for the adversary to receive additionally auxiliary input, which can also be output by Gen. Lastly, we allow some control over which inputs of E and F the bounded time function h will depend upon. We can achieve this by modifying our first experiment to also output a commitment Z of the inputs we wish to remain hidden. Then, the simulator h produced in the second experiment will only depend on some of the hidden values, namely the values needed to compute the instances of E and F that are actually output. (In contrast, h could have been dependent upon on all of the potential inputs of both E and F in every instance.)

Finally, we note that our introduction of a commitment into the theorem is not a significant problem when using this theorem to prove the security of some game that did not originally contain commitments. Rather than proving directly that an adversary cannot break a security game, one can instead prove a stronger notion of security in which the adversary is unable to break the security game even when additionally given a commitment of some secret information. Since, an adversary can only have a smaller advantage in differentiating these experiments when this commitment is not given (an adversary that can break security without the commitment can break security with the commitment by ignoring the commitment), regular security trivially follows. In fact, we use this exact technique in our FE amplification. Note that if the adversary is not strong enough to break the commitment, then giving them a commitment of the secret information will not significantly impact security.

Remark 1. We wrote our theorem in a very general form in order to facilitate potential reuse in other research. As such, the security parameters in the theorem statement are quite complex. However, we have also included three corollaries that use much simpler and more natural parameters. We refer the reader to these corollaries rather than the actual theorem when fine-grained tuning of the parameters is not necessary.

Theorem 9 (Probabilistic Replacement Theorem). *Let λ be a parameter. Let $E : \mathcal{S} \times \mathcal{X} \times \{0,1\}^{\ell} \to \mathcal{W}$ and $F : \mathcal{T} \times \mathcal{Y} \times \{0,1\}^{\ell} \to \mathcal{W}$ be deterministic $O(\mathsf{poly}(\lambda))$-time computable functions, with $\ell = O(\mathsf{poly}(\lambda))$. Let $n = O(\mathsf{poly}(\lambda))$. Then, if*

- *Com is any commitment with $(\mathsf{size}_{\mathsf{HIDE}}, \mathsf{adv}_{\mathsf{HIDE}})$-computational hiding and $(\mathsf{stat}_{\mathsf{BIND}})$-statistical binding,*
- *Gen is any randomized circuit of size $O(\mathsf{poly}(\lambda))$ with range $(\mathcal{S} \times \mathcal{X} \times \mathcal{T} \times \mathcal{Y})^n \times \mathsf{AUX}$ such that for all $((s_i, x_i, t_i, y_i)_{i \in [n]}, \mathsf{aux})$ output by $\mathsf{Gen}(1^{\lambda}, 1^n)$ for all $i \in [n]$ and for all size_{EF} algorithms $\mathcal{A}$,*

$$\left| \Pr_{r_i \leftarrow \{0,1\}^{\ell}}[\mathcal{A}(E(s_i, x_i, r_i)) = 1] - \Pr_{r_i \leftarrow \{0,1\}^{\ell}}[\mathcal{A}(F(t_i, y_i, r_i)) = 1] \right| \leq \mathsf{adv}_{EF},$$

there exists a randomized function h of size size_h such that for all algorithms $\mathcal{A}'$ of size size^*,

$$|\Pr[\mathcal{A}'(\mathsf{EXP}_0) = 1] - \Pr[\mathcal{A}'(\mathsf{EXP}_1) = 1]| \leq \mathsf{adv}^*,$$

where we define

EXP$_0$:
1. *Compute* $((s_i, x_i, t_i, y_i)_{i \in [n]}, \text{aux}) \leftarrow \text{Gen}(1^\lambda, 1^n)$.
2. *Compute* $Z \leftarrow \text{Com}((s_i, t_i)_{i \in [n]})$.
3. *Sample* r_i *from* $\{0, 1\}^\ell$ *for* $i \in [n]$.
4. *Compute* $w_i = E(s_i, x_i, r_i)$ *for* $i \in [n]$.
5. *Output* $(Z, (w_i)_{i \in [n]}, \text{aux})$.

EXP$_1$:
1. *Compute* $((s_i, x_i, t_i, y_i)_{i \in [n]}, \text{aux}) \leftarrow \text{Gen}(1^\lambda, 1^n)$.
2. *Compute* $Z \leftarrow \text{Com}(0^{\ell_Z})$ *where* $\ell_Z = |(s_i, t_i)_{i \in [n]}|$.
3. *Sample a string* $\alpha \in \{0, 1\}^n$ *such that for each* $i \in [n]$, *we set* $\alpha_i = 1$ *with probability* $(1 - \text{adv}_{EF})$ *and set* $\alpha_i = 0$ *with probability* adv_{EF}.
4. *Compute* $(r_i)_{i \in [n]} \leftarrow h(\alpha, Z, (s_i)_{i \in A_0}, (t_i)_{i \in A_1}, (x_i, y_i)_{i \in [n]}, \text{aux})$ *where* $A_0 = \{i \mid \alpha_i = 0\}$ *and* $A_1 = \{i \mid \alpha_i = 1\}$.
5. *For every* $i \in [n]$, *if* $\alpha_i = 1$, *compute* $w_i = F(t_i, y_i, r_i)$; *otherwise, compute* $w_i = E(s_i, x_i, r_i)$.
6. *Output* $(Z, (w_i)_{i \in [n]}, \text{aux})$.

---

and for any parameters $\text{size}_{\text{SIM}} > 0$ *and* $\text{adv}_{\text{SIM}}, \text{adv}_{\text{HCM}} \in (0, 1)$ *and for* $\text{adv}_{min} = \min(\text{adv}_{EF}, 1 - \text{adv}_{EF})$,

- $\text{size}_h = O(\text{poly}(\lambda) \cdot \text{size}_{\text{SIM}} 2^{2n \log(\text{adv}_{min}^{-1})} \text{adv}_{\text{SIM}}^{-5})$.
- size^* *is the minimum of the following:*

  - $\frac{\text{size}_{EF} \text{adv}_{\text{HCM}}^2}{128(2\ell+1)} - \text{poly}(\lambda)$
  - $\text{size}_{\text{SIM}} - \text{poly}(\lambda)$
  - $\text{size}_{\text{HIDE}} - \text{size}_h - \text{poly}(\lambda)$

- $\text{adv}^* \leq n \cdot \text{adv}_{\text{HCM}} + \text{stat}_{\text{BIND}} + \text{adv}_{\text{SIM}} + \text{adv}_{\text{HIDE}}$.

Theorem 9 immediately gives rise to two corollaries: one where we assume that E and F are weakly indistinguishable against polynomial sized adversaries, and one where they are weakly indistinguishable against subexponential sized adversaries. These corollaries are deferred to the full version.

Furthermore, using a more fine-grained approach, it is possible to prove a variant of the probabilistic replacement theorem that allows us to lower the size of h at the cost of increasing the distinguishing advantage of the adversary. We will need to use this fine-grained approach when proving security against polynomial time adversaries. We state the resulting corollary here and provide a proof after the proof of the main theorem at the end of this section. We defer this corollary to the full version.

We defer the proof of this theorem and the corollaries to the full version.

8   Amplification via Secret Sharing and Parallel Repetition

In this section, we prove our main amplification results. As discussed previously, this is done by building an FE scheme using our set homomorphic secret sharing scheme SetHSS. In our construction, we encrypt each share in our set homomorphic secret sharing scheme under an instantiation of a weakly secure FE scheme. (To simplify the proof, we will actually use a weakly secure semi-functional FE scheme, which can be built from a weakly secure FE scheme assuming OWFs). For key generation, we first generate function encodings corresponding to each share using SetHSS.FuncEncode and then generate function keys for each of these function encodings using the appropriate weakly secure FE instantiation. Recall from Sect. 5 that SetHSS is parameterized by n "elements" and m sets $(T_i)_{i \in [m]}$ that are subsets of $[n]$. We will let n and m be parameters of our FE construction. To generate the sets $(T_i)_{i \in [m]}$ used by SetHSS, we will sample each set by including each element in $[n]$ independently with probability q, where q is a parameter of our construction. Recall that in Sect. 6, we proved various properties of such sets when sampled in this manner. These lemmas will come in handy when analyzing the correctness and security of our FE construction. Once we have analyzed correctness and security as functions of the parameters n, m, and q, we will set these parameters to obtain our results. We will apply our construction twice. The first application will amplify a weakly secure FE where an adversary has advantage $\epsilon = c$ for some small constant c to one where an adversary has advantage $\epsilon = 1/\mathsf{poly}(\lambda)$. On the second application, we amplify an FE scheme with $\epsilon = 1/\mathsf{poly}(\lambda)$ to one with $\epsilon = \mathsf{negl}(\lambda)$ (or $2^{-\lambda^c}$ for some constant $c > 0$ when dealing with subexponential adversaries).

Recall the following notation:

Notation. We say that ensembles satisfy $(\mathsf{poly}(\lambda) \cdot s, \epsilon)$-indistinguishability if the ensembles satisfy $(p(\lambda) \cdot s, \epsilon)$-indistinguishability for every polynomial $p(\lambda)$.

Our main results in this section are the following.

Theorem 10. *Assuming a $(\mathsf{poly}(\lambda), \epsilon)$-secure FE scheme for P/poly for some constant $\epsilon < 1/6$, there exists a $(\mathsf{poly}(\lambda), \mathsf{negl}(\lambda))$-secure FE scheme for P/poly. Moreover, this transformation preserves sublinearity/compactness.*

Theorem 11. *Assuming a $(2^{O(\lambda^c)}, \epsilon)$-secure FE scheme for P/poly for some constant $\epsilon < 1/6$ and some constant $c > 0$, there exists a $(2^{O(\lambda^{c'})}, 2^{-O(\lambda^{c'})})$-secure FE scheme for P/poly for some constant $0 < c' < c$. Moreover, this transformation preserves sublinearity/compactness.*

8.1   Construction

Our FE construction makes use of the following primitives.

- Let   sFE   =   (sFE.Setup, sFE.Enc, sFE.KeyGen, sFE.Dec, sFE.SFEnc, sFE.SFKeyGen) be an (s, ν, ϵ)-secure semi-functional encryption scheme, where $\frac{1}{p(\lambda)} \leq \epsilon < 1 - \frac{1}{p(\lambda)}$ for some polynomial $p(\lambda)$. Such a scheme is implied by an (s, ϵ)-secure FE scheme assuming an (s, ν)-secure one-way function and this transformation preserves sublinearity/compactness.
- Let SetGen$(1^n, 1^m, q)$ be an algorithm that outputs $(T_i)_{i \in [m]}$, where for each $T_i \subseteq [n]$, we include each element of $[n]$ in T_i independently with probability q.
- Let SetHSS = (SetHSS.InpEncode, SetHSS.FuncEncode, SetHSS.Decode) be a set homomorphic secret sharing scheme.
- Let Com be a statistically binding, computationally hiding commitment scheme. (Com does not show up in the construction and is only used in the security proof.)

Our FE scheme is defined, with respect to parameters $n, m \in \mathbb{N}$ where $n, m = O(\text{poly}(\lambda))$ and a probability $q \in [0, 1]$, as follows:

- FE.Setup(1^λ) : Setup proceeds as follows:
  1. Compute $(T_i)_{i \in [m]} \leftarrow$ SetGen$(1^n, 1^m, q)$
  2. For each $i \in [m]$, generate msk$_i \leftarrow$ sFE.Setup(1^λ).
  3. Output MSK $= ((\text{msk}_i)_{i \in [m]}, (T_i)_{i \in [m]})$.
- FE.Enc(MSK, msg) : Encryption proceeds as follows:
  1. Parse MSK as $((\text{msk}_i)_{i \in [m]}, (T_i)_{i \in [m]})$.
  2. Compute $(s_i)_{i \in [m]} \leftarrow$ SetHSS.InpEncode$(1^\lambda, 1^n, (T_i)_{i \in [m]}, \text{msg})$.
  3. For $i \in [m]$, compute ct$_i \leftarrow$ sFE.Enc(msk$_i, s_i$).
  4. Output CT $= (\text{ct}_i)_{i \in [m]}$.
- FE.KeyGen(MSK, C) : Key generation proceeds as follows:
  1. Parse MSK as $((\text{msk}_i)_{i \in [m]}, (T_i)_{i \in [m]})$.
  2. Compute $(C_i)_{i \in [m]} \leftarrow$ SetHSS.FuncEncode$(1^\lambda, 1^n, (T_i)_{i \in [m]}, C)$.
  3. For $i \in [m]$, compute sk$_{C_i} \leftarrow$ sFE.KeyGen(msk$_i, C_i$).
  4. Output sk$_C = (\text{sk}_{C_i})_{i \in [m]}$.
- FE.Dec(sk$_C$, CT) : Decryption proceeds as follows:
  1. Parse sk$_C$ as $(\text{sk}_{C_i})_{i \in [m]}$ and CT as $(\text{ct}_i)_{i \in [m]}$.
  2. For $i \in [m]$, compute $y_i = $ sFE.Dec(sk$_{C_i}$, ct$_i$).
  3. Output SetHSS.Decode$((y_i)_{i \in [m]})$.

Correctness. Correctness holds provided that sFE is correct and that SetHSS is a correct set homomorphic secret sharing scheme with respect to the sets $(T_i)_{i \in [m]}$ sampled by the setup algorithm. To see this, observe that sFE.Dec(sk$_{C_i}$, ct$_i$) $= C_i(s_i)$ since ct$_i$ is an encryption of s_i. Thus, the output of decryption is SetHSS.Decode$((C_i(s_i))_{i \in [m]}) = C(\text{msg})$ by correctness of SetHSS.

If we instantiate SetHSS with the scheme constructed in Sect. 5, we see that SetHSS is correct provided that $(T_i)_{i \in [m]}$ cover all subsets of $[n]$ of size 3 (Theorem 7). For parameters $n, m \in \mathbb{N}$ and probability $q \in [0, 1]$, the probability of $(T_i)_{i \in [m]}$ covering all subsets of size 3 when sampled in this manner was calculated in Lemma 1 to be

$$\geq 1 - n^3(1 - q^3)^m.$$

By a union bound and the correctness of sFE, the probability that one of the m copies of sFE is incorrect is $\leq m \cdot \mathsf{negl}(\lambda)$. Therefore, the constructed scheme is correct with probability

$$\geq 1 - n^3(1 - q^3)^m - m \cdot \mathsf{negl}(\lambda).$$

Sublinearity/Compactness. Let $\beta \in (0,1]$ denote the sublinearity/compactness parameter of sFE. Sublinearity/compactness follows from observing that the size of the encryption circuit is bounded by $\mathsf{poly}(\lambda, n, m) + |\mathsf{SetHSS.InpEncode}| + m \cdot |C_i|^{1-\beta} \cdot \mathsf{poly}(\lambda, |s_i|)$ for fixed polynomials independent of the size of the circuit class. Since each $|C_i| \leq |C| \cdot \mathsf{poly}(\lambda, n, m)$ and $n, m = \mathsf{poly}(\lambda)$, and $|s_i|$ and $|\mathsf{SetHSS.InpEncode}|$ are both $\mathsf{poly}(\lambda, n, m)$, it follows that the size of the encryption circuit is $\leq |C|^{1-\beta} \cdot \mathsf{poly}(\lambda)$ for some fixed polynomial independent of C.

Please refer to the full version for the proof of security. We also defer the instantiation of parameters to prove Theorems 10 and 11.

9 Amplification via Nesting

In this section, we amplify a secret key FE scheme that is secure with some constant probability $(1 - \epsilon)$ to another secret key FE scheme that is secure with some larger constant probability (in the neighborhood of $(1 - \epsilon^2)$). In this way, we can create an ϵ' secure FE scheme for any arbitrarily small constant ϵ' from any constantly secure FE scheme by repeating this transformation a constant number of times. We show that this amplification preserves compactness and note that although we consider the secret key variant, our proofs extend to the case of public key FE.

Our main results in this section are the following:

Theorem 12. *If there exists a $(\mathsf{poly}(\lambda), \epsilon)$-secure functional encryption scheme for P/poly for some constant $\epsilon \in (0,1)$, then there exists a $(\mathsf{poly}(\lambda), \epsilon')$-secure functional encryption scheme for P/poly for any constant $\epsilon' \in (0,1)$. Moreover, the transformation preserves compactness.*

Theorem 13. *If there exists a $(2^{\lambda^c}, \epsilon)$-secure functional encryption scheme for P/poly for some constant $\epsilon \in (0,1)$ and some constant $c > 0$, then there exists a $(2^{\lambda^{c'}}, \epsilon')$-secure functional encryption scheme for P/poly for any constant $\epsilon' \in (0,1)$ and any constant $c' < c$. Moreover, the transformation preserves compactness.*

9.1   Construction

Let $\mathsf{FE} = (\mathsf{FE.Setup}, \mathsf{FE.Enc}, \mathsf{FE.KeyGen}, \mathsf{FE.Dec})$ be a secret key functional encryption scheme for $\mathsf{P/poly}$ that satisfies $(s, \epsilon)-$security (as described in Definition 6) for some constant $\epsilon \in (0, 1)$.

We now construct an amplified functional encryption scheme FE^* as described below. Essentially, FE^* works by nesting the original functional encryption FE. Intuitively, the idea is that as long as one layer of FE is secure, then the nested FE^* is secure. Therefore, we can get amplification since our nested FE^* is broken only when all layers of FE are broken. We formalize this notion in the security proof.

We will use a two-layer nesting where we have an "inner" and "outer" FE. To encrypt a message, we first encrypt using the "inner" FE and then encrypt the result using the "outer" FE. To create a function key for C, we first create a normal function key for C using the "inner" FE. Then, our final function key for C is the function key for the "outer" FE of the function that decrypts the input with the "inner" function key.

FE^* (Amplified Functional Encryption)

- $\mathsf{Setup}(1^\lambda)$:
  1. Generate $\mathsf{msk}_1 \leftarrow \mathsf{FE.Setup}(1^\lambda)$ and $\mathsf{msk}_2 \leftarrow \mathsf{FE.Setup}(1^\lambda)$.
  2. Output $\mathsf{MSK} = (\mathsf{msk}_1, \mathsf{msk}_2)$.
- $\mathsf{Enc}(\mathsf{MSK}, m)$:
  1. Parse MSK as $(\mathsf{msk}_1, \mathsf{msk}_2)$.
  2. Compute $\mathsf{ct}_1 \leftarrow \mathsf{FE.Enc}(\mathsf{msk}_1, m)$.
  3. Compute $\mathsf{ct}_2 \leftarrow \mathsf{FE.Enc}(\mathsf{msk}_2, \mathsf{ct}_1)$.
  4. Output $\mathsf{CT} = \mathsf{ct}_2$.
- $\mathsf{KeyGen}(\mathsf{MSK}, C)$:
  1. Parse MSK as $(\mathsf{msk}_1, \mathsf{msk}_2)$.
  2. Compute $\mathsf{sk}_{C,1} \leftarrow \mathsf{FE.KeyGen}(\mathsf{msk}_1, C)$.
  3. Compute $\mathsf{sk}_{C,2} \leftarrow \mathsf{FE.KeyGen}(\mathsf{msk}_2, G)$ where
     $G(x) = \mathsf{FE.Dec}(\mathsf{sk}_{C,1}, x)$.
  4. Output $\mathsf{sk}_C = \mathsf{sk}_{C,2}$.
- $\mathsf{Dec}(\mathsf{sk}_C, \mathsf{CT})$:
  1. Output $y = \mathsf{FE.Dec}(\mathsf{sk}_C, \mathsf{CT})$.

Correctness: If the underlying FE is correct, then so is the scheme FE^*. This is because for any function C, message m, honestly generated ciphertext $\mathsf{CT} \leftarrow \mathsf{FE.Enc}(\mathsf{msk}_2, \mathsf{FE.Enc}(\mathsf{msk}_1, m))$ and key $\mathsf{sk}_C \leftarrow \mathsf{FE.KeyGen}$ (msk_2, G) where $G(x) = \mathsf{FE.Dec}(\mathsf{FE.KeyGen}(\mathsf{msk}_1, C), x)$, then $\mathsf{FE.Dec}$ $(\mathsf{sk}_C, \mathsf{CT}) = G(\mathsf{FE.Enc}(\mathsf{msk}_1, m)) = \mathsf{FE.Dec}(\mathsf{FE.KeyGen}(\mathsf{msk}_1, C), \mathsf{FE.Enc}(\mathsf{msk}_1, m)) = C(m)$. Thus, correctness holds with probability 1.

Preserving Compactness: It follows immediately that if FE satisfies compactness, then so does FE^*. If the running time needed to compute an FE ciphertext is independent of the function size, then so is the running time needed to compute an FE^* encryption of a message.

9.2   Security

We will prove the following two lemmas.

Lemma 3. *For any constant $\epsilon \in (0,1)$ if*

- FE *is a* $(\mathsf{poly}(\lambda), \epsilon)$*-secure functional encryption scheme for* P/poly,
- Com *is any commitment with* $(\mathsf{poly}(\lambda), \mathsf{negl}(\lambda))$*-computational hiding and* $\mathsf{negl}(\lambda)$*-statistical binding,*

then FE* *is a* $(\mathsf{poly}(\lambda), \epsilon^2 + \mathsf{negl}(\lambda))$*-secure functional encryption scheme.*

Lemma 4. *For any constant $\epsilon \in (0,1)$, any constant $c' > 0$, and any constant $c > c'$, if*

- FE *is a* $(2^{\lambda^c}, \epsilon)$*-secure functional encryption scheme for* P/poly,
- Com *is any commitment with* $(2^{\lambda^c}, \mathsf{negl}(\lambda))$*-computational hiding and* $\mathsf{negl}(\lambda)$*-statistical binding,*

then FE* *is a* $(2^{\lambda^{c'}}, \epsilon^2 + \mathsf{negl}(\lambda))$*-secure functional encryption scheme.*

Since weakly-secure FE implies a weakly-secure OWF (which can then be amplified to a fully secure OWF via [38]), Theorems 12 and 13 immediately follow from Lemmas 3 and 4 by instantiating Com using this OWF and repeating the transformation a constant number of times.

We defer the proofs to the full version.

10   Amplification of Nested Public-Key Encryption

Our amplification techniques for nested functional encryption can also be easily extended to prove amplification for nested public-key encryption. We assume familiarity with public-key encryption (PKE). Our main results in this section are the following:

Theorem 14. *If there exists a* $(\mathsf{poly}(\lambda), \epsilon)$*- indistinguishability of encryption secure public-key encryption scheme* PKE *for message space $\{0,1\}^\lambda$ and for some constant $\epsilon \in (0,1)$, then there exists a* $(\mathsf{poly}(\lambda), \epsilon')$*-indistinguishability of encryption secure public-key encryption scheme* PKE* *for any constant $\epsilon' \in (0,1)$, where* PKE* *is obtained by nesting* PKE *a constant number of times.*

Theorem 15. *If there exists a* $(2^{\lambda^c}, \epsilon)$*- indistinguishability of encryption secure public-key encryption scheme* PKE *for message space $\{0,1\}^\lambda$ and for some constants $\epsilon \in (0,1)$ and $c > 0$, then there exists a* $(2^{\lambda^{c'}}, \epsilon')$*-indistinguishability of encryption secure public-key encryption scheme* PKE* *for any constants $\epsilon' \in (0,1)$ and $c' < c$, where* PKE* *is obtained by nesting* PKE *a constant number of times.*

We defer this section to the full version.

11 Final Amplification Results

By combining the main results of Sects. 8 and 9, we immediately obtain our final amplification results.

Theorem 16. *Assuming a* $(\mathsf{poly}(\lambda), \epsilon)$*-secure FE scheme for* $\mathsf{P/poly}$ *for some constant* $\epsilon \in (0, 1)$*, there exists a* $(\mathsf{poly}(\lambda), \mathsf{negl}(\lambda))$*-secure FE scheme for* $\mathsf{P/poly}$*. Moreover, this transformation preserves compactness.*

Theorem 17. *Assuming a* $(2^{O(\lambda^c)}, \epsilon)$*-secure FE scheme for* $\mathsf{P/poly}$ *for some constant* $\epsilon \in (0, 1)$ *and some constant* $c > 0$*, there exists a* $(2^{O(\lambda^{c'})}, 2^{-O(\lambda^{c'})})$*-secure FE scheme for* $\mathsf{P/poly}$ *for some constant* $0 < c' < c$*. Moreover, this transformation preserves compactness.*

Acknowledgements. We thank the anonymous CRYPTO reviewers for their helpful feedback regarding this work. We also thank Maciej Skórski for useful discussions about [57,58].

This research is supported in part from DARPA SAFEWARE and SIEVE awards, NTT Research, NSF Frontier Award 1413955, and NSF grant 1619348, BSF grant 2012378, a Xerox Faculty Research Award, a Google Faculty Research Award, an equipment grant from Intel, and an Okawa Foundation Research Grant. This material is based upon work supported by the Defense Advanced Research Projects Agency through Award HR00112020024 and the ARL under Contract W911NF-15-C- 0205. The views expressed are those of the authors and do not reflect the official policy or position of the Department of Defense, the National Science Foundation, NTT Research, or the U.S. Government.

We would also like to thank A.K.'s cat, Mr. Floof, for emotional support during the research process, despite his complete apathy towards the research process and our existence in general.

References

1. Agrawal, S.: Indistinguishability obfuscation without multilinear maps: new methods for bootstrapping and instantiation. In: Ishai, Y., Rijmen, V. (eds.) EUROCRYPT 2019, Part I. LNCS, vol. 11476, pp. 191–225. Springer, Cham (2019). https://doi.org/10.1007/978-3-030-17653-2_7
2. Ananth, P., Badrinarayanan, S., Jain, A., Manohar, N., Sahai, A.: From FE combiners to secure MPC and back. In: Hofheinz, D., Rosen, A. (eds.) TCC 2019. LNCS, vol. 11891, pp. 199–228. Springer, Cham (2019). https://doi.org/10.1007/978-3-030-36030-6_9
3. Ananth, P., Brakerski, Z., Segev, G., Vaikuntanathan, V.: From selective to adaptive security in functional encryption. In: Gennaro, R., Robshaw, M. (eds.) CRYPTO 2015, Part II. LNCS, vol. 9216, pp. 657–677. Springer, Heidelberg (2015). https://doi.org/10.1007/978-3-662-48000-7_32
4. Ananth, P., Brakerski, Z., Segev, G., Vaikuntanathan, V.: From selective to adaptive security in functional encryption. In: Gennaro, R., Robshaw, M. (eds.) CRYPTO 2015. LNCS, vol. 9216, pp. 657–677. Springer, Heidelberg (2015). https://doi.org/10.1007/978-3-662-48000-7_32

5. Ananth, P., Jain, A., Lin, H., Matt, C., Sahai, A.: Indistinguishability obfuscation without multilinear maps: new paradigms via low degree weak pseudorandomness and security amplification. In: Boldyreva, A., Micciancio, D. (eds.) CRYPTO 2019, Part III. LNCS, vol. 11694, pp. 284–332. Springer, Cham (2019). https://doi.org/10.1007/978-3-030-26954-8_10

6. Ananth, P., Jain, A., Naor, M., Sahai, A., Yogev, E.: Universal constructions and robust combiners for indistinguishability obfuscation and witness encryption. In: Robshaw, M., Katz, J. (eds.) CRYPTO 2016, Part II. LNCS, vol. 9815, pp. 491–520. Springer, Heidelberg (2016). https://doi.org/10.1007/978-3-662-53008-5_17

7. Ananth, P., Jain, A., Sahai, A.: Robust transforming combiners from indistinguishability obfuscation to functional encryption. In: Coron, J.-S., Nielsen, J.B. (eds.) EUROCRYPT 2017, Part I. LNCS, vol. 10210, pp. 91–121. Springer, Cham (2017). https://doi.org/10.1007/978-3-319-56620-7_4

8. Ananth, P., Jain, A., Sahai, A.: Indistinguishability obfuscation without multilinear maps: iO from LWE, bilinear maps, and weak pseudorandomness. IACR Cryptology ePrint Archive 2018/615 (2018)

9. Ananth, P., Jain, A.: Indistinguishability obfuscation from compact functional encryption. In: Gennaro, R., Robshaw, M. (eds.) CRYPTO 2015, Part I. LNCS, vol. 9215, pp. 308–326. Springer, Heidelberg (2015). https://doi.org/10.1007/978-3-662-47989-6_15

10. Ananth, P., Sahai, A.: Projective arithmetic functional encryption and indistinguishability obfuscation from degree-5 multilinear maps. In: Coron, J.-S., Nielsen, J.B. (eds.) EUROCRYPT 2017, Part I. LNCS, vol. 10210, pp. 152–181. Springer, Cham (2017). https://doi.org/10.1007/978-3-319-56620-7_6

11. Badrinarayanan, S., Goyal, V., Jain, A., Sahai, A.: A note on VRFs from verifiable functional encryption. IACR Cryptology ePrint Archive 2017/51 (2017)

12. Barak, B., Hardt, M., Kale, S.: The uniform hardcore lemma via approximate Bregman projections. In: SODA, pp. 1193–1200 (2009)

13. Bellare, M., Impagliazzo, R., Naor, M.: Does parallel repetition lower the error in computationally sound protocols? In: FOCS, pp. 374–383 (1997)

14. Bitansky, N.: Verifiable random functions from non-interactive witness-indistinguishable proofs. In: Kalai, Y., Reyzin, L. (eds.) TCC 2017, Part II. LNCS, vol. 10678, pp. 567–594. Springer, Cham (2017). https://doi.org/10.1007/978-3-319-70503-3_19

15. Bitansky, N., Nishimaki, R., Passelègue, A., Wichs, D.: From cryptomania to obfustopia through secret-key functional encryption. In: Hirt, M., Smith, A. (eds.) TCC 2016, Part II. LNCS, vol. 9986, pp. 391–418. Springer, Heidelberg (2016). https://doi.org/10.1007/978-3-662-53644-5_15

16. Bitansky, N., Vaikuntanathan, V.: Indistinguishability obfuscation from functional encryption. In: Guruswami, V. (ed.) 56th FOCS, pp. 171–190. IEEE Computer Society Press, October 2015

17. Boneh, D., et al.: Fully key-homomorphic encryption, arithmetic circuit ABE and compact garbled circuits. In: Nguyen, P.Q., Oswald, E. (eds.) EUROCRYPT 2014. LNCS, vol. 8441, pp. 533–556. Springer, Heidelberg (2014). https://doi.org/10.1007/978-3-642-55220-5_30

18. Boneh, D., Sahai, A., Waters, B.: Functional encryption: definitions and challenges. In: Ishai, Y. (ed.) TCC 2011. LNCS, vol. 6597, pp. 253–273. Springer, Heidelberg (2011). https://doi.org/10.1007/978-3-642-19571-6_16

19. Canetti, R., Halevi, S., Steiner, M.: Hardness amplification of weakly verifiable puzzles. In: Kilian, J. (ed.) TCC 2005. LNCS, vol. 3378, pp. 17–33. Springer, Heidelberg (2005). https://doi.org/10.1007/978-3-540-30576-7_2

20. Chen, Y.-H., Chung, K.-M., Liao, J.-J.: On the complexity of simulating auxiliary input. In: Nielsen, J.B., Rijmen, V. (eds.) EUROCRYPT 2018. LNCS, vol. 10822, pp. 371–390. Springer, Cham (2018). https://doi.org/10.1007/978-3-319-78372-7_12

21. Damgård, I., Kilian, J., Salvail, L.: On the (im)possibility of basing oblivious transfer and bit commitment on weakened security assumptions. In: Stern, J. (ed.) EUROCRYPT 1999. LNCS, vol. 1592, pp. 56–73. Springer, Heidelberg (1999). https://doi.org/10.1007/3-540-48910-X_5

22. Dwork, C., Naor, M., Reingold, O.: Immunizing encryption schemes from decryption errors. In: Cachin, C., Camenisch, J.L. (eds.) EUROCRYPT 2004. LNCS, vol. 3027, pp. 342–360. Springer, Heidelberg (2004). https://doi.org/10.1007/978-3-540-24676-3_21

23. Fischlin, M., Herzberg, A., Bin-Noon, H., Shulman, H.: Obfuscation combiners. In: Robshaw, M., Katz, J. (eds.) CRYPTO 2016, Part II. LNCS, vol. 9815, pp. 521–550. Springer, Heidelberg (2016). https://doi.org/10.1007/978-3-662-53008-5_18

24. Garg, S., Gentry, C., Halevi, S., Raykova, M., Sahai, A., Waters, B.: Candidate indistinguishability obfuscation and functional encryption for all circuits. In: 54th FOCS, pp. 40–49. IEEE Computer Society Press, October 2013

25. Garg, S., Gentry, C., Halevi, S., Zhandry, M.: Functional encryption without obfuscation. In: Kushilevitz, E., Malkin, T. (eds.) TCC 2016-A, Part II. LNCS, vol. 9563, pp. 480–511. Springer, Heidelberg (2016). https://doi.org/10.1007/978-3-662-49099-0_18

26. Garg, S., Pandey, O., Srinivasan, A.: Revisiting the cryptographic hardness of finding a nash equilibrium. In: Robshaw, M., Katz, J. (eds.) CRYPTO 2016, Part II. LNCS, vol. 9815, pp. 579–604. Springer, Heidelberg (2016). https://doi.org/10.1007/978-3-662-53008-5_20

27. Garg, S., Pandey, O., Srinivasan, A., Zhandry, M.: Breaking the sub-exponential barrier in obfustopia. In: Coron, J.-S., Nielsen, J.B. (eds.) EUROCRYPT 2017, Part III. LNCS, vol. 10212, pp. 156–181. Springer, Cham (2017). https://doi.org/10.1007/978-3-319-56617-7_6

28. Goldwasser, S., Kalai, Y.T., Popa, R.A., Vaikuntanathan, V., Zeldovich, N.: Reusable garbled circuits and succinct functional encryption. In: Boneh, D., Roughgarden, T., Feigenbaum, J. (eds.) 45th ACM STOC, pp. 555–564. ACM Press, June 2013

29. Gorbunov, S., Vaikuntanathan, V., Wee, H.: Predicate encryption for circuits from LWE. In: Gennaro, R., Robshaw, M. (eds.) CRYPTO 2015, Part II. LNCS, vol. 9216, pp. 503–523. Springer, Heidelberg (2015). https://doi.org/10.1007/978-3-662-48000-7_25

30. Goyal, R., Hohenberger, S., Koppula, V., Waters, B.: A generic approach to constructing and proving verifiable random functions. In: Kalai, Y., Reyzin, L. (eds.) TCC 2017, Part II. LNCS, vol. 10678, pp. 537–566. Springer, Cham (2017). https://doi.org/10.1007/978-3-319-70503-3_18

31. Goyal, V., Jain, A., Sahai, A.: Simultaneous amplification: the case of non-interactive zero-knowledge. In: Boldyreva, A., Micciancio, D. (eds.) CRYPTO 2019, Part II. LNCS, vol. 11693, pp. 608–637. Springer, Cham (2019). https://doi.org/10.1007/978-3-030-26951-7_21

32. Harnik, D., Ishai, Y., Kushilevitz, E., Nielsen, J.B.: OT-combiners via secure computation. In: Canetti, R. (ed.) TCC 2008. LNCS, vol. 4948, pp. 393–411. Springer, Heidelberg (2008). https://doi.org/10.1007/978-3-540-78524-8_22

33. Håstad, J., Pass, R., Wikström, D., Pietrzak, K.: An efficient parallel repetition theorem. In: Micciancio, D. (ed.) TCC 2010. LNCS, vol. 5978, pp. 1–18. Springer, Heidelberg (2010). https://doi.org/10.1007/978-3-642-11799-2_1

34. Hemenway, B., Jafargholi, Z., Ostrovsky, R., Scafuro, A., Wichs, D.: Adaptively secure garbled circuits from one-way functions. In: Robshaw, M., Katz, J. (eds.) CRYPTO 2016, Part III. LNCS, vol. 9816, pp. 149–178. Springer, Heidelberg (2016). https://doi.org/10.1007/978-3-662-53015-3_6

35. Holenstein, T.: Key agreement from weak bit agreement. In: Gabow, H.N., Fagin, R. (eds.) 37th ACM STOC, pp. 664–673. ACM Press, May 2005

36. Holenstein, T.: Strengthening key agreement using hard-core sets. Ph.D. thesis, ETH Zurich (2006)

37. Holenstein, T., Renner, R.: One-way secret-key agreement and applications to circuit polarization and immunization of public-key encryption. In: Shoup, V. (ed.) CRYPTO 2005. LNCS, vol. 3621, pp. 478–493. Springer, Heidelberg (2005). https://doi.org/10.1007/11535218_29

38. Impagliazzo, R.: Hard-core distributions for somewhat hard problems. In: FOCS, pp. 538–545 (1995)

39. Jain, A., Lin, H., Matt, C., Sahai, A.: How to leverage hardness of constant-degree expanding polynomials over $\mathbb{R}$ to build $i\mathcal{O}$. In: Ishai, Y., Rijmen, V. (eds.) EUROCRYPT 2019, Part I. LNCS, vol. 11476, pp. 251–281. Springer, Cham (2019). https://doi.org/10.1007/978-3-030-17653-2_9

40. Jain, A., Manohar, N., Sahai, A.: Combiners for functional encryption, unconditionally. In: Canteaut, A., Ishai, Y. (eds.) EUROCRYPT 2020. LNCS, vol. 12105, pp. 141–168. Springer, Cham (2020). https://doi.org/10.1007/978-3-030-45721-1_6

41. Jetchev, D., Pietrzak, K.: How to fake auxiliary input. In: Lindell, Y. (ed.) TCC 2014. LNCS, vol. 8349, pp. 566–590. Springer, Heidelberg (2014). https://doi.org/10.1007/978-3-642-54242-8_24

42. Kitagawa, F., Nishimaki, R., Tanaka, K.: Obfustopia built on secret-key functional encryption. In: Nielsen, J.B., Rijmen, V. (eds.) EUROCRYPT 2018, Part II. LNCS, vol. 10821, pp. 603–648. Springer, Cham (2018). https://doi.org/10.1007/978-3-319-78375-8_20

43. Klivans, A., Servedio, R.: Boosting and hard-core set construction. Mach. Learn. 51, 217–238 (2003)

44. Komargodski, I., Segev, G.: From minicrypt to obfustopia via private-key functional encryption. In: Coron, J.-S., Nielsen, J.B. (eds.) EUROCRYPT 2017, Part I. LNCS, vol. 10210, pp. 122–151. Springer, Cham (2017). https://doi.org/10.1007/978-3-319-56620-7_5

45. Lin, H.: Indistinguishability obfuscation from constant-degree graded encoding schemes. In: Fischlin, M., Coron, J.-S. (eds.) EUROCRYPT 2016, Part I. LNCS, vol. 9665, pp. 28–57. Springer, Heidelberg (2016). https://doi.org/10.1007/978-3-662-49890-3_2

46. Lin, H.: Indistinguishability obfuscation from SXDH on 5-linear maps and locality-5 PRGs. In: Katz, J., Shacham, H. (eds.) CRYPTO 2017, Part I. LNCS, vol. 10401, pp. 599–629. Springer, Cham (2017). https://doi.org/10.1007/978-3-319-63688-7_20

47. Lin, H., Tessaro, S.: Amplification of chosen-ciphertext security. In: Johansson, T., Nguyen, P.Q. (eds.) EUROCRYPT 2013. LNCS, vol. 7881, pp. 503–519. Springer, Heidelberg (2013). https://doi.org/10.1007/978-3-642-38348-9_30

48. Lin, H., Tessaro, S.: Indistinguishability obfuscation from trilinear maps and block-wise local PRGs. In: Katz, J., Shacham, H. (eds.) CRYPTO 2017, Part I. LNCS, vol. 10401, pp. 630–660. Springer, Cham (2017). https://doi.org/10.1007/978-3-319-63688-7_21

49. Lin, H., Vaikuntanathan, V.: Indistinguishability obfuscation from DDH-like assumptions on constant-degree graded encodings. In: Dinur, I. (ed.) 57th FOCS, pp. 11–20. IEEE Computer Society Press, October 2016

50. Maurer, U., Tessaro, S.: Computational indistinguishability amplification: tight product theorems for system composition. In: Halevi, S. (ed.) CRYPTO 2009. LNCS, vol. 5677, pp. 355–373. Springer, Heidelberg (2009). https://doi.org/10.1007/978-3-642-03356-8_21

51. Maurer, U., Tessaro, S.: A hardcore lemma for computational indistinguishability: security amplification for arbitrarily weak PRGs with optimal stretch. In: Micciancio, D. (ed.) TCC 2010. LNCS, vol. 5978, pp. 237–254. Springer, Heidelberg (2010). https://doi.org/10.1007/978-3-642-11799-2_15

52. Meier, R., Przydatek, B., Wullschleger, J.: Robuster combiners for oblivious transfer. In: Vadhan, S.P. (ed.) TCC 2007. LNCS, vol. 4392, pp. 404–418. Springer, Heidelberg (2007). https://doi.org/10.1007/978-3-540-70936-7_22

53. O'Neill, A.: Definitional issues in functional encryption. IACR Cryptology ePrint Archive 2010/556 (2010). http://eprint.iacr.org/2010/556

54. Pass, R., Venkitasubramaniam, M.: An efficient parallel repetition theorem for Arthur-Merlin games. In: STOC, pp. 420–429 (2007)

55. Sahai, A., Waters, B.: How to use indistinguishability obfuscation: deniable encryption, and more. In: Shmoys, D.B. (ed.) 46th ACM STOC, pp. 475–484. ACM Press, May/Jun 2014

56. Sahai, A., Waters, B.: Fuzzy identity-based encryption. In: Cramer, R. (ed.) EURO-CRYPT 2005. LNCS, vol. 3494, pp. 457–473. Springer, Heidelberg (2005). https://doi.org/10.1007/11426639_27

57. Skórski, M.: Efficiently simulating high min-entropy sources in the presence of side information. In: Biryukov, A., Goyal, V. (eds.) INDOCRYPT 2015. LNCS, vol. 9462, pp. 312–325. Springer, Cham (2015). https://doi.org/10.1007/978-3-319-26617-6_17

58. Skórski, M.: A subgradient algorithm for computational distances and applications to cryptography. IACR Cryptology ePrint Archive 2016/158 (2016). http://eprint.iacr.org/2016/158

59. Tessaro, S.: Security amplification for the cascade of arbitrarily weak PRPs: tight bounds via the interactive hardcore lemma. In: Ishai, Y. (ed.) TCC 2011. LNCS, vol. 6597, pp. 37–54. Springer, Heidelberg (2011). https://doi.org/10.1007/978-3-642-19571-6_3

60. Trevisan, L., Tulsiani, M., Vadhan, S.: Regularity, boosting, and efficiently simulating every high-entropy distribution. In: CCC, pp. 126–136 (2009)

61. Vadhan, S., Zheng, C.J.: A uniform min-max theorem with applications in cryptography. In: Canetti, R., Garay, J.A. (eds.) CRYPTO 2013, Part I. LNCS, vol. 8042, pp. 93–110. Springer, Heidelberg (2013). https://doi.org/10.1007/978-3-642-40041-4_6

62. Wullschleger, J.: Oblivious-transfer amplification. In: Naor, M. (ed.) EUROCRYPT 2007. LNCS, vol. 4515, pp. 555–572. Springer, Heidelberg (2007). https://doi.org/10.1007/978-3-540-72540-4_32

63. Wullschleger, J.: Oblivious transfer from weak noisy channels. In: Reingold, O. (ed.) TCC 2009. LNCS, vol. 5444, pp. 332–349. Springer, Heidelberg (2009). https://doi.org/10.1007/978-3-642-00457-5_20

Dynamic Decentralized Functional Encryption

Jérémy Chotard[1,2,3], Edouard Dufour-Sans[2,3,4(✉)], Romain Gay[5(✉)],
Duong Hieu Phan[1], and David Pointcheval[2,3(✉)]

[1] XLIM, University of Limoges, CNRS, Limoges, France
[2] DIENS, École Normale Supérieure, CNRS, PSL University, Paris, France
e.dufoursans@gmail.com,david.pointcheval@ens.fr
[3] Inria, Paris, France
[4] Carnegie Mellon University, Pittsburgh, USA
[5] Cornell Tech, New York, USA
romain.rgay@gmail.com

Abstract. We introduce Dynamic Decentralized Functional Encryption (DDFE), a generalization of Functional Encryption which allows multiple users to join the system dynamically, without relying on a trusted third party or on expensive and interactive Multi-Party Computation protocols.

This notion subsumes existing multi-user extensions of Functional Encryption, such as Multi-Input, Multi-Client, and Ad Hoc Multi-Input Functional Encryption.

We define and construct schemes for various functionalities which serve as building-blocks for latter primitives and may be useful in their own right, such as a scheme for dynamically computing sums in any Abelian group. These constructions build upon simple primitives in a modular way, and have instantiations from well-studied assumptions, such as DDH or LWE.

Our constructions culminate in an Inner-Product scheme for computing weighted sums on aggregated encrypted data, from standard assumptions in prime-order groups in the Random Oracle Model.

Keywords: Dynamic · Decentralized · Functional Encryption · Inner product

1 Introduction

At TCC'11, Boneh, Sahai, and Waters [11] formalized Functional Encryption (FE), a new paradigm of Public-Key Encryption that allows the owner of the secret key to generate restricted keys, enabling third parties to recover *function evaluations* of the plaintext from a ciphertext. The formalization of FE gave many researchers a common framework in which to consider their schemes: the nuances between Identity-Based Encryption (IBE), Hierarchical IBE, Fuzzy IBE, and different forms of Attribute-Based Encryption (ABE) [9,10,27,32] could

© International Association for Cryptologic Research 2020
D. Micciancio and T. Ristenpart (Eds.): CRYPTO 2020, LNCS 12170, pp. 747–775, 2020.
https://doi.org/10.1007/978-3-030-56784-2_25

now be captured simply by specifying which functionality the scheme aims to implement. The set of algorithms to be implemented and the indistinguishability game in which to prove security were now standard.

But for all its successes, Functional Encryption has two, somewhat related, important limitations: (1) In many contexts, FE encourages centralization. In his 2015 position paper *The Moral Character of Cryptographic Work*, Rogaway pointed out that a switch from Public-Key Encryption to Identity-Based Encryption would represent "a radical change in the trust model", as the authority with knowledge of the master secret key would have the ability to fully recover every message encrypted under its public key, even though those messages would be intended for a variety of parties. This criticism can be extended to many other functionalities of Functional Encryption. (2) The kind of controlled computation enabled by Functional Encryption does not extend to computations involving data from multiple parties. This is limiting because a significant component of the public's privacy concerns today is related to data being made available to a third-party for the advertised purpose of retrieving some form of intelligence of the public's needs, from the computation of simple statistics to the training of advanced machine learning models. This means FE is not an appropriate framework for addressing this pressing issue.

1.1 Our Contributions

1. First, we fill the gap left by the definition of FE by introducing a new primitive we term Dynamic Decentralized Functional Encryption (DDFE). DDFE allows aggregating data coming from different parties, does not require a trusted party with a master secret key, and accounts for participants wanting to join at various stages during the lifetime of a system. Previous extensions of FE, which we review in more detail in Sect. 1.2, either failed to address the concerns we raised above, or partially forwent the generality that made the success of FE as a framework for describing cryptographic schemes. We give a formal definition of DDFE as well as a security definition.
2. We define All-or-Nothing Encapsulation (AoNE), a functionality of DDFE which we found to be a critical building-block when constructing useful DDFE schemes later in this work. AoNE allows a participant to send its data to be aggregated with other data coming from a group of participants agreeing on a label ℓ. Only if all those participants choose to send data for aggregation with the same group under the same label will the data of all participants be revealed, otherwise, nothing is revealed. We provide two constructions of AoNE. The first one is generic from any IBE, but has individual ciphertexts that grow linearly in the number of participants in an aggregation, which is not ideal. The second construction is specific and achieves constant size ciphertexts. It relies on bilinear maps, and we prove its security under the DBDH assumption in the Random Oracle Model (ROM).
3. We define and provide a construction of DSum, a functionality of DDFE which is both interesting in its own right and a useful building-block for other constructions. DSum operates over any Abelian group and allows multiple parties

to send an element from that group for aggregation with a set of participants agreeing on a label ℓ. Once every participant has sent data for aggregation with that set and that label, the sum (or rather the repeated group operation) of the data is revealed. We provide a generic construction of DSum from Non-Interactive Key Exchange (NIKE), AoNE DDFE and Pseudo-Random Functions (PRF).

4. We define and provide a construction of Inner-Product DDFE (IP-DDFE), which allows for more complex patterns of aggregation than DSum. In IP-DDFE, participants can contribute to the generation of functional decryption keys that enable individuals to compute weighted sums of plaintext data, with the weights being encoded in the key. Our construction relies on AoNE, DSum, Single-Input Inner-Product Functional Encryption, and PRFs, and we prove that it is selectively secure under the DDH assumption in the ROM.

1.2   Related Work

Fully Homomorphic Encryption (FHE) [23] is a commonly cited as a cryptographic solution to issues involving computations on encrypted data at large. We stress here that FHE shines when computation delegation is intended. That is, it is useful when a client, owning some data it wishes to protect the confidentiality of, wants a server to perform computations on their data without seeing the data. This scenario arises when the computation depends on parameters known only to the server (as in the case of Information Retrieval), or when the client wants to leverage the computational power of the server.

In the scenarii we are concerned with, however, the server directly learns something about the aggregated data, without interacting with them. This stands in contrast with FHE, where the parties need to engage in extra rounds of interaction to perform a joint decryption of the encrypted data.

FE enables the server to recover information as controlled by the client through key delegation, while FHE does not limit the types of computations the server can perform, but prevents the server from accessing any data. Given these advantages, we naturally focus on extending the line of works involving FE.

Note that FHE was also initially defined for a single data owner, and was later extended to multiple users under the name Multi-Key FHE [31].

Private Stream Aggregation (PSA). This notion, initially termed Privacy-Preserving Aggregation of Time-Series Data, is an early primitive for non-interactive aggregation of multi-party data introduced by Shi *et al.* [34]. Unlike our DDFE schemes, PSA, under its standard definitions, relies on a trusted third-party distributing the participant's secret keys, cannot accommodate new participants, and does not allow the participants to choose which functions can be computed by whom via functional decryption key derivation. Most PSA schemes in the literature focus on computing (non-weighted) sums of the participants' data [8,14,28]. Note that Private Stream Aggregation usually relies on a Differential Privacy component as an added privacy protection, while we leave the addition of a Differential Privacy layer in DDFE for future work.

Multi-Authority Functional Encryption (MAFE) was introduced by Chandran *et al.* [15]. Like DDFE, it is a strongly decentralized variant of Functional Encryption. It allows for encrypting messages for sets of authorities along with an access policy. These authorities can then generate keys for individual identities. Armed with a single ciphertext and a set of functional decryption keys from the appropriate authorities, the decrypter can recover a function of the plaintext that is specified by the access policy on the identities for which the functional keys were computed. Unlike DDFE, MAFE does not account for the possibility of multiple ciphertexts being decrypted together, and having their data interact with one another.

Multi-Client Functional Encryption (MCFE) was defined in [25,26] along with Multi-Input Functional Encryption (MIFE), and also enables computing functions of multiple parties' data in the presence of a trusted third-party distributing both the parties' secret keys and functional decryption keys. That is, both MIFE and MCFE extend Functional Encryption to a setting where the input is spread across different sources. Each source can encrypt its data independently, and the ciphertexts can then be aggregated and decrypted with functional decryption keys. Generation of the latter still requires a trusted authority, which owns a so-called master secret key: a single point of failure for the cryptosystem.

As opposed to MIFE, the encryption algorithm of an MCFE takes an additional input, referred to as a label, which enforces a finer-grained control on access to the encrypted data. Unlike in MIFE, where individual ciphertexts can be arbitrarily combined, in MCFE, only ciphertexts generated for the same label can be used together to decrypt. This limits how much information is revealed by each functional decryption key, thereby strengthening security. Typically, labels are used as timestamps. In this context, a functional decryption key can only compute, say, statistics on aggregated data *for the same time frame*.

Any MCFE for a given functionality directly implies an MIFE for the same functionality, by simply using a fixed label for all encryptions[1]. Reciprocally, an MIFE for general functions would directly imply an MCFE for general functions, since the label can be part of the plaintext, and the function can check that every slot used the same label. However, this is not true for the case of smaller classes of functions for which there are practical schemes, such as Inner-Products.

The first construction of MIFE for inner products was given in [5], from standard assumptions in pairing groups. This was later improved by [4], which gave a generic construction from any single-input FE for inner products. The first construction of MCFE from standard assumptions was given by Chotard *et al.* [17] for computing inner products, although the security they achieved admits several limitations compared to the standard MCFE security definition.

Decentralized Multi-Client Functional Encryption (DMCFE). Chotard *et al.* [17] also defined a new variant of MCFE, called Decentralized MCFE

---

[1] Note that this was not true for MCFE as originally defined in [25], as that definition had strictly increasing timestamps for labels. But followup works on MCFE have usually allowed any bitstring to be used as a label, opening the primitive to the possibility of repetitions.

(DMCFE), for which they gave Inner-Product instantiations from pairings. The DMCFE variant did away with the trusted third-party, as it enabled participants to choose their own secret keys and generate functional decryption keys non-interactively. However, it still had an interactive setup, with no easy way of adding new participants, and it suffered from the same security caveats as the MCFE it was a variant of.

In a follow-up work, [30] provided a construction in the standard model from the LWE assumption, which still suffers from the same security restrictions as [17]. The works [1,2] improved the security guarantees obtained, the former using the DDH assumption in the ROM, the latter using a generic construction from any single-input FE for inner products. Both schemes however have individual ciphertexts of size proportional to the total number of users. Thus, we use different techniques to obtain the desirable security notion without having asymptotically large ciphertexts.

Ad Hoc Multi-Input Functional Encryption. In [6], the authors define the notion of Ad Hoc Multi-Input Functional Encryption, where users can join the system on-the-fly, and functional decryption keys can be generated in a decentralized way, by each client, without interaction. They give a feasibility result for all functions, and a practical construction for inner products.

The definition of DDFE we put forth is more general than [6]. For instance, in our definition, the algorithm that generates functional decryption key does not necessarily require a specified group of users: schemes with potentially more flexibility than Ad Hoc MIFE can be captured by our definition.

Moreover, their scheme for inner product cannot handle labels, which implies that ciphertexts computed by each client individually can be mix and matched arbitrarily. As explained above, this implies that each functional decryption key reveals large amounts of information on the encrypted values, and renders the security vacuous whenever sufficiently many keys are issued. Labels help mitigate this leakage by enforcing a better granularity on the way the encrypted data is accessed.

Besides, the security model of [6] does not explicitly address the information that can be leaked when decrypting partial ciphertexts, that is, ciphertexts coming from an incomplete group of users. Preventing the adversary from recovering information on partial ciphertexts is made more challenging in our construction, which handles labels.

1.3 Outline

We first provide a definition of DDFE in Sect. 2, along with a security definition and functionalities of interest. In Sect. 3, we recall some useful preliminaries and definitions. We then showcase our constructions: a generic construction of AoNE is presented in Sect. 4, while a specific instantiation is studied in Sect. 5. We use it modularly in Sect. 6 to construct a DSum scheme. In Sect. 7, we capitalize on both those primitives to construct a DDFE scheme for the Inner-Product functionality.

2   Definitions and Security Models

In this section, we provide the formal definition of our new primitive of *Dynamic Decentralized Functional Encryption* (DDFE), together with several security models. Then, we list a few instantiations with some concrete functionalities.

2.1   Notations

In the following, $[n]$ will denote the set of integers $\{1, \ldots, n\}$. For any set $\mathcal{A}$, $\mathcal{L}(\mathcal{A})$ will denote the set of finite lists of elements of $\mathcal{A}$, while $\mathcal{S}(\mathcal{A})$ will denote the set of finite subsets of $\mathcal{A}$. Unlike sets, lists are ordered and may contain repeated elements.

2.2   Dynamic Decentralized Functional Encryption

In defining DDFE, one of our key concerns is generality: we want to achieve for multi-user primitives what Functional Encryption did for single-user primitives. We resist as much as possible the temptation to let the idiosyncrasies of the functionalities we present and implement in this work leak into the definition of DDFE itself. Perhaps the best example of this is in the role of the label. We believe labels, as used in MCFE, are useful for practical use, because in limiting what can be decrypted, they limit data leakage and make it possible to consider using the same primitive over a long time. However, we recognize that some primitives which are of practical use without labels may arise, that some schemes using labels may want to have them interact in more complex ways than perfect matching, and that there is value in our definitions being able to capture existing work. In Sect. 2.3, we give more details on how our umbrella notion captures a large set of existing primitives, ranging from Public-Key Encryption to Ad Hoc Multi-Input Function Encryption as introduced in Agrawal *et al.* [6].

Definition 1 (Dynamic Decentralized Functional Encryption). *A dynamic decentralized functional encryption scheme over a set of public keys $\mathcal{PK}$ for functionality $\mathcal{F} : \mathcal{L}(\mathcal{PK} \times \mathcal{K}) \times \mathcal{L}(\mathcal{PK} \times \mathcal{M}) \to \{0,1\}^*$ consists of five algorithms:*

- Setup(λ): *Generates and outputs public parameters* pp. *Those parameters are implicit arguments to all the other algorithms;*
- KeyGen(): *Generates and outputs a party's public key* pk $\in \mathcal{PK}$ *and the corresponding secret key* $\mathsf{sk}_{\mathsf{pk}}$;
- Encrypt($\mathsf{sk}_{\mathsf{pk}}, m$): *Takes as input a party's secret key* $\mathsf{sk}_{\mathsf{pk}}$, *a value* $m \in \mathcal{M}$ *to encrypt, and outputs a ciphertext* $\mathsf{ct}_{\mathsf{pk}}$;
- DKeyGen($\mathsf{sk}_{\mathsf{pk}}, k$): *Takes as input a party's secret key* sk, *a key space object* k, *and outputs a functional decryption key* $\mathsf{dk}_{\mathsf{pk},k}$;
- Decrypt$\big((\mathsf{dk}_{\mathsf{pk},k_{\mathsf{pk}}})_{\mathsf{pk} \in \mathcal{U}_K}, (\mathsf{ct}_{\mathsf{pk}})_{\mathsf{pk} \in \mathcal{U}_M} \big)$: *Takes as input a finite list of functional decryption keys* $(\mathsf{dk}_{\mathsf{pk},k_{\mathsf{pk}}})_{\mathsf{pk} \in \mathcal{U}_K}$, *a finite list of ciphertexts* $(\mathsf{ct}_{\mathsf{pk}})_{\mathsf{pk} \in \mathcal{U}_M}$, *where* $\mathcal{U}_M, \mathcal{U}_K \in \mathcal{L}(\mathcal{PK})$ *are the lists of senders and receivers, respectively. It outputs a value* $y \in \{0,1\}^*$.

We call a DDFE scheme Public-Key if its encryption algorithm does not make use of the secret key $\mathsf{sk_{pk}}$.

Correctness: We require that, for all security parameters $\lambda \in \mathbb{N}$, for all polynomial size lists $\mathcal{U}_M, \mathcal{U}_K \in \mathcal{L}(\mathcal{PK})$ of public keys issued by $\mathsf{KeyGen()}$, $(\mathsf{pk}, k_{\mathsf{pk}})_{\mathsf{pk}\in\mathcal{U}_K} \in \mathcal{L}(\mathcal{PK}\times\mathcal{K})$ and $(\mathsf{pk}, m_{\mathsf{pk}})_{\mathsf{pk}\in\mathcal{U}_M} \in \mathcal{L}(\mathcal{PK}\times\mathcal{M})$, it holds that the probability for

$$\mathsf{Decrypt}((\mathsf{dk}_{\mathsf{pk},k_{\mathsf{pk}}})_{\mathsf{pk}\in\mathcal{U}_K}, (\mathsf{ct}_{\mathsf{pk}})_{\mathsf{pk}\in\mathcal{U}_M}) = F((\mathsf{pk}, k_{\mathsf{pk}})_{\mathsf{pk}\in\mathcal{U}_K}, (\mathsf{pk}, m_{\mathsf{pk}})_{\mathsf{pk}\in\mathcal{U}_M})$$

is 1, taken over $\mathsf{pp} \leftarrow \mathsf{Setup}(\lambda)$, $\mathsf{dk}_{\mathsf{pk},k_{\mathsf{pk}}} \leftarrow \mathsf{DKeyGen}(\mathsf{sk_{pk}}, k_{\mathsf{pk}})$ for all $\mathsf{pk} \in \mathcal{U}_K$, $\mathsf{ct_{pk}} \leftarrow \mathsf{Encrypt}(\mathsf{sk_{pk}}, m_{\mathsf{pk}})$ for all $\mathsf{pk} \in \mathcal{U}_M$.

We stress that each user is identified by a public key pk, which it can generate on its on with the associated secret key, using KeyGen. Anyone can thus dynamically join the system, by publishing its public key.

Remark 2 (Empty keys). Note that, unlike with standard, Single-Input FE, we do not require the empty key ϵ to be in $\mathcal{K}$, because we operate over lists of elements of $\mathcal{PK} \times \mathcal{K}$, so we simply define ϵ as the empty list.

In both Single-Input Functional Encryption and DDFE, the empty key serves to capture all the information about the plaintext that intentionally leaks from every ciphertext (see [11, Section 2]). In Single-Input FE, this is typically only used to highlight the fact that encryption leaks the length of the message.

It is crucial to the security of any Functional Encryption scheme which accepts messages of variable lengths and leaks the length of the message, for otherwise it would be easy to win the IND security game by querying $\mathsf{QLeftRight}$ for two messages of different lengths (see Definition 17). With the leakage clearly stated in the functionality of the scheme, such a query would trigger the condition in the game's Finalize, and it would cause the adversary's guess to be discarded.

But in the case of DDFE, more information is usually publicly associated with a ciphertext that simply its length. For instance, the set of users the data should be aggregated with, or the aggregation label, are typically public. Besides, it happens that the leakage of a set of ciphertexts is more than the cumulative leakage of the individual ciphertexts. Our AoNE and DSum schemes have this property, and it is expressed by their functionality outputting the relevant information when evaluated on the empty key with a (possibly non-singleton) list of ciphertexts.

Definition 3 (IND-Security Game for DDFE). *Let us consider a DDFE scheme. No adversary $\mathcal{A}$ should be able to win the following security game against a challenger $\mathcal{C}$, with unlimited and adaptive access to the oracles $\mathsf{QNewHonest}$, $\mathsf{QEncrypt}$, $\mathsf{QLeftRight}$, $\mathsf{QDKeyGen}$, and $\mathsf{QCorrupt}$ described below:*

- *Initialize: the challenger $\mathcal{C}$ runs the setup algorithm $\mathsf{pp} \leftarrow \mathsf{Setup}(\lambda)$ and chooses a random bit $b \xleftarrow{\$} \{0,1\}$. It provides pp to the adversary $\mathcal{A}$;*

- *Participant creation queries* QNewHonest: *the challenger $\mathcal{C}$ runs the key generation algorithm* $(\mathsf{pk}, \mathsf{sk}_{\mathsf{pk}}) \leftarrow \mathsf{KeyGen}()$ *to simulate a new participant, stores the association* $(\mathsf{pk}, \mathsf{sk}_{\mathsf{pk}})$ *and returns* pk *to the adversary;*
- *Encryption queries* QEncrypt(pk, m): *Recovers the secret key* sk *associated to* pk *and outputs the ciphertext* $\mathsf{ct} \leftarrow \mathsf{Encrypt}(\mathsf{sk}, m)$. *If* pk *is not associated with any secret key, nothing is returned;*
- *Challenge queries* QLeftRight(pk, m^0, m^1): *runs and forwards the output of* QEncrypt(pk, m^b). *Wlog. we assume* $m^0 \neq m^1$.
- *Functional decryption key queries* QDKeyGen(pk, k): *Recovers the secret key* sk *associated to* pk *and outputs the functional decryption key* $\mathsf{dk}_k \leftarrow$ DKeyGen(sk, k). *If* pk *is not associated with any secret key, nothing is returned;*
- *Corruption queries* QCorrupt(pk): *Recovers the secret key* sk *associated to* pk *and outputs it. If* pk *is not associated with any secret key, nothing is returned;*
- *Finalize:* $\mathcal{A}$ *provides its guess* b' *on the bit* b, *and this procedure outputs the result* β *of the security game, according to the analysis given below.*

The output β *of the game depends on some conditions, where* $\mathcal{HS}$ *is the set of honest participants at the end of the game (the set of public keys generated via* QNewHonest-*queries and not corrupted via* QCorrupt*). Finalize outputs the bit* $\beta = (b' = b)$, *unless the following condition (*) is satisfied, in which case Finalize outputs a random bit* β.

The condition (*) is true if there exist two lists of public keys $\mathcal{U}_M, \mathcal{U}_K \in \mathcal{L}(\mathcal{PK})$, *two lists of messages* $(\boldsymbol{m}^0 = (\mathsf{pk}, m^0_{\mathsf{pk}})_{\mathsf{pk} \in \mathcal{U}_M}, \boldsymbol{m}^1 = (\mathsf{pk}, m^1_{\mathsf{pk}})_{\mathsf{pk} \in \mathcal{U}_M})$, *and a list of keys* $\boldsymbol{k} = (\mathsf{pk}, k_{\mathsf{pk}})_{\mathsf{pk} \in \mathcal{U}_K}$, *such that* $F(\boldsymbol{k}, \boldsymbol{m}^0) \neq F(\boldsymbol{k}, \boldsymbol{m}^1)$, *with*

- $m^0_{\mathsf{pk}} = m^1_{\mathsf{pk}}$, *for all* $\mathsf{pk} \in \mathcal{U}_M$ *such that* $\mathsf{pk} \notin \mathcal{HS}$;
- QLeftRight$(\mathsf{pk}, m^0_{\mathsf{pk}}, m^1_{\mathsf{pk}})$ *or* QEncrypt$(\mathsf{pk}, m_{\mathsf{pk}})$-*queries have been asked for all* $\mathsf{pk} \in \mathcal{U}_M \cap \mathcal{HS}$;
- QDKeyGen$(\mathsf{pk}, k_{\mathsf{pk}})$-*queries have been asked for all* $\mathsf{pk} \in \mathcal{U}_K \cap \mathcal{HS}$.

We say DDFE *is* IND-*secure if for any adversary* $\mathcal{A}$,

$$\mathsf{Adv}^{IND}_{DDFE}(\mathcal{A}) = |2 \times \Pr[\beta = 1] - 1|$$

is negligible.

Intuitively, condition (*) means that the adversary can trivially recover b and win the game, which is thus not a real attack, hence a meaningless output with a random bit. Otherwise, $\beta = 0$ is a wrong guess and $\beta = 1$ is a correct guess during a meaningful attack. As usual, we are interested in adversaries with non-negligible advantage. Note however that the condition of trivial win cannot, in general, be checked in polynomial time. This is because there are exponentially many choices that can be made for the various lists, including the participant public keys and the values of the messages. Even if we impose strict requirements on the functionality, such as the presence of a label and a set of participants, it might not be possible to guarantee that the condition can be checked in polynomial time without a direct analysis of the structure of the functionality. There may exist functionalities for which such a check is a computationally hard problem. The issue of how to efficiently check for violations is thus left to the cryptosystem designers and provers. In the following, we will consider functionalities for which this condition can be efficiently checked.

Now we present several weaker variants of the above security notion.

Definition 4 (sym-IND-Security Game for DDFE). *We define a symmetric-key variant of the above security game in which the Finalize procedure outputs 0 if the adversary makes a query of the form* (pk, m_0, m_1) *to* QLeftRight *and queries the same* pk *to* QCorrupt. *This means that the secret key* $\mathsf{sk}_{\mathsf{pk}}$ *not only allows users to encrypt on behalf of party* pk, *but also empowers them to decrypt the ciphertext generated by party* pk. *Thus, the challenge messages* m_0 *and* m_1 *have to be the same to avoid the adversary trivially recovering the random bit* β. *That is, the oracle* QEncrypt *should be used instead of* QLeftRight.

Definition 5 (sel-IND-Security Game for DDFE). *We define a selective variant of the above security game in which the adversary is forced to send all its queries to* QNewHonest, *upon which it receives the corresponding public keys. Then it sends all its queries to the oracles* QEncrypt, QLeftRight, QDKeyGen *and* QCorrupt *in one shot, and receives all of the outputs at once.*

Note that our security notions is strong, in the sense that it allows the adversary to generate malicious public keys on its own. The challenger does not know the corresponding secret keys (which may not exist) for such public keys. More precisely, we allow dishonest key registrations, as originally introduced in [13] in the context of NIKE.

2.3   Versatility of the Notion of DDFE

The notion of DDFE captures many existing primitives. We go over some such primitives and provide details here.

We first show that the notion of public-key encryption is captured by DDFE. That is, we can cast the former as a DDFE for a specific functionality that we present here. Apart from being a warm-up before delving into more advanced primitives, this shows that DDFE is not fundamentally restricted to secret-key primitives.

Public-Key Encryption. Here, the message space $\mathcal{M} = \{0,1\}^* \times \mathcal{PK}$ comprises pairs of plaintext and public keys. The key space is restricted to the identity function over the plaintexts: $\{f_{\mathsf{id}}\}$. The functionality takes as input the list of pairs $(\mathsf{pk}, m_{\mathsf{pk}})$ from all senders $\mathsf{pk} \in \mathcal{U}_M$. In our case, the list $\mathcal{U}_M$ will contain only one user pk_1 who wishes to send the plaintext $\mathsf{pt} \in \{0,1\}^*$ to user pk_2. This information is contained in the message $m_{\mathsf{pk}_1} = (\mathsf{pt}, \mathsf{pk}_2)$.

The functionality also takes the list of pairs $(\mathsf{pk}, k_{\mathsf{pk}})$ from all receivers $\mathsf{pk} \in \mathcal{U}_K$. In our case, the list $\mathcal{U}_K$ only contains the recipient pk_2'. The associated key space object is the identity function f_{id}, which is the only function available here.

The functionality outputs the plaintext if the intended recipient is the actual recipient. That is $F\big((\mathsf{pk}_2', f_{\mathsf{id}}), (\mathsf{pk}_1, (\mathsf{pt}, \mathsf{pk}_2))\big) = \mathsf{pt}$ if $\mathsf{pk}_2 = \mathsf{pk}_2'$, $\bot$ otherwise. On any input that does not have that format (for instance on lists $\mathcal{U}_M$ and $\mathcal{U}_K$ of more than one element), the functionality will also output $\bot$.

The above example can be generalized straightforwardly to capture single-input Functional Encryption [11], by considering a larger key space $\{f\}$ that is not only restricted to the identity function.

Decentralized Attribute-Based Encryption. The notion of DDFE can also capture existing decentralized primitives, such as the notion of decentralized Attribute-Based Encryption introduced in [29], as shown below. It also captures the more general Multi-Authority Functional Encryption [15].

Here, the message space $\mathcal{M} = \{0, 1\}^* \times \mathcal{P} \times \mathcal{L}(\mathcal{PK})$ comprises tuples, each of which contains a plaintext, a predicate, and a list of public keys. The key space $\mathcal{K} = \mathcal{A} \times \mathcal{ID}$ comprises pairs of an attribute and an identifier.

The functionality takes as input the list of pairs $(\mathsf{pk}, m_{\mathsf{pk}})$ from all senders $\mathsf{pk} \in \mathcal{U}_M$. In our case, the list $\mathcal{U}_M$ will contain only one user pk who wishes to send the plaintext $\mathsf{pt} \in \{0, 1\}^*$ to any user with proper credentials, that is, whose attributes satisfy an access policy expressed by a predicate $\mathsf{P} \in \mathcal{P}$. This predicate takes as inputs attributes that are handled by different authorities, listed in $\mathcal{U}$. All of this information is contained in the message $m_{\mathsf{pk}} = (\mathsf{pt}, \mathsf{P}, \mathcal{U})$.

The functionality also takes the list of pairs $(\mathsf{pk}, k_{\mathsf{pk}})$ from all receivers $\mathsf{pk} \in \mathcal{U}_K$. In our case, the list $\mathcal{U}_K$ contains the authorities involved. For each authority, the associated key space object is an attribute, and a global identifier.

The functionality is defined as $F\big((\mathsf{pk}_i, (\mathsf{att}_i, \mathsf{GID}_i))_{\mathsf{pk}_i \in \mathcal{U}_K}, (\mathsf{pk}, (\mathsf{pt}, \mathsf{P}, \mathcal{U}))\big) = \mathsf{pt}$ if $\mathcal{U} = \mathcal{U}_K$, all the identifiers GID_i are the same, and the predicate P on the attributes att_i evaluates to true. If these conditions are not met, or if the input does not have the right syntax (e.g. the list $\mathcal{U}_M$ has more than one element), the functionality outputs $\bot$.

Ad Hoc Multi-Input FE. We now show that DDFE captures more advanced decentralized primitives, such as Ad Hoc Multi-Input FE, introduced in [6].

Here, the message space $\mathcal{M} = \{0, 1\}^*$, the key space $\mathcal{K}$ comprises pairs $(f, \mathcal{U})$ where $f : \{0, 1\}^\ell \to \{0, 1\}^*$ is an ℓ-ary function for arbitrary $\ell \in \mathbb{N}$, and $\mathcal{U}$ is a list of ℓ users.

The functionality takes as input the list of pairs $(\mathsf{pk}, m_{\mathsf{pk}})$ from all senders $\mathsf{pk} \in \mathcal{U}_M$, and the list of pairs $(\mathsf{pk}, k_{\mathsf{pk}})$ from all receivers $\mathsf{pk} \in \mathcal{U}_K$. If all the key space objects agree on a function on the inputs of the list of users $\mathcal{U}_M$, the functionality outputs the evaluation of the function: $F\big((\mathsf{pk}_i, (f_i, \mathcal{U}_i))_{\mathsf{pk}_i \in \mathcal{U}_K}, (\mathsf{pk}_j, m_j)_{\mathsf{pk}_j \in \mathcal{U}_M}\big) = f(m_1, \ldots, m_\ell)$ if $f_i = f$ and $\mathcal{U}_i = \mathcal{U}_M$ for all i, and $|\mathcal{U}_M| = \ell$. It outputs $\bot$ otherwise.

Limitations of DDFE. Whereas the notion of DDFE is a strong generalization of preexisting decentralized variants of Functional Encryption, capturing functionalities not covered by Ad Hoc MIFE or MAFE, it does not cover everything. Function Private [12] and Delegatable [15] variants of Functional Encryption have been introduced, and our definitions leave room for similar variants of DDFE. Some important cryptographic protocols, such as Private Information Retrieval, Oblivious Pseudo Random Functions, or Non-Interactive Key Exchange, similarly cannot be written as DDFE functionalities. DDFE fails to capture key exchange because its definition doesn't allow us to express cryptographic properties of a function evaluation: the idea that the result of an evaluation would "look random" cannot be written as a functionality. It also cannot capture the aforementioned two party interactive protocols because it is non-interactive by nature, while interactivity is a core requirement for PIR and OPRFs, to ensure the protocol is not run more times than any party wishes for.

2.4 DDFE Functionalities

We now give some examples of concrete functionalities. The first two will be of independent interest, but also layers to improve the security and the functionalities of the later Inner-Product DDFE constructions.

All-or-Nothing Encapsulation (AoNE) allows several parties of a group to encapsulate individual messages, that can all be extracted by anybody if and only if all the parties of this group have sent their contributions. Otherwise, the messages remain hidden. The set $\mathcal{U}_M$ of public keys describes the group of parties and the label ℓ imposes a constraint on which encapsulations can be considered together: if for a given pair $(\mathcal{U}_M, \ell)$ all the parties in $\mathcal{U}_M$ send their encapsulations, all the messages can be recovered by anybody, otherwise the messages remain hidden. Note that all the players have to agree on the pair $(\mathcal{U}_M, \ell)$ for their encapsulation, and any encapsulation naturally leaks that pair $(\mathcal{U}_M, \ell)$.

Definition 6 (All-or-Nothing Encapsulation). *AoNE is defined on messages of length L as follows:*

$$\mathcal{K} = \emptyset \qquad\qquad \mathcal{M} = \{0,1\}^L \times \mathcal{S}(\mathcal{PK}) \times \{0,1\}^*.$$

Then, $F(\epsilon, (\mathsf{pk}, (x, \mathcal{U}, \ell))) = (\mathcal{U}, \ell)$ and

$$F(\epsilon, (\mathsf{pk}, m_{\mathsf{pk}})_{\mathsf{pk} \in \mathcal{U}_M}) = \begin{cases} (\mathsf{pk}, x_{\mathsf{pk}})_{\mathsf{pk} \in \mathcal{U}_M} & \text{if condition } (\ast) \\ \bot & \text{otherwise.} \end{cases}$$

and AoNE condition (*) is: $\exists \ell \in \{0,1\}^*, \forall \mathsf{pk} \in \mathcal{U}_M, m_{\mathsf{pk}} = (x_{\mathsf{pk}}, \mathcal{U}_M, \ell)$.

Decentralized Sum (DSum) allows several parties of a group to commit to values, so that their sum is automatically revealed when all the parties of this group have sent their contributions. Otherwise, the values remain hidden. The set $\mathcal{U}_M$ of public keys describes the group of parties and the label ℓ imposes a constraint on which values can be added together: if for a given pair $(\mathcal{U}_M, \ell)$ all the parties in $\mathcal{U}_M$ send their values, the sum can be recovered by anybody, otherwise the individual values remain hidden. As above, all the players have to agree on the pair $(\mathcal{U}_M, \ell)$ for their encryption, and any encryption naturally leaks that pair $(\mathcal{U}_M, \ell)$. The terminology *sum* is an abuse, as it works for any Abelian group.

Definition 7 ($(\mathbb{A}, +)$-Decentralized Sum). *DSum is defined for any Abelian group $(\mathbb{A}, +)$ as follows:*

$$\mathcal{K} = \emptyset \qquad\qquad \mathcal{M} = \mathbb{A} \times \mathcal{S}(\mathcal{PK}) \times \{0,1\}^*.$$

Then, $F(\epsilon, (\mathsf{pk}, (x, \mathcal{U}, \ell))) = (\mathcal{U}, \ell)$ and

$$F(\epsilon, (\mathsf{pk}, m_{\mathsf{pk}})_{\mathsf{pk} \in \mathcal{U}_M}) = \begin{cases} \sum_{\mathsf{pk} \in \mathcal{U}_M} x_{\mathsf{pk}} & \text{if condition (*)} \\ \perp & \text{otherwise.} \end{cases}$$

and DSum condition (*) is: $\exists \ell \in \{0,1\}^*, \forall \mathsf{pk} \in \mathcal{U}_M, m_{\mathsf{pk}} = (x_{\mathsf{pk}}, \mathcal{U}_M, \ell)$.

Inner-Product DDFE (IP-DDFE). We now present a more advanced functionality for Inner Products. It allows senders with public key pk, as part of a group $\mathcal{U}_M$, to encrypt inputs x_{pk} under a label ℓ. But they maintain control on which computations will be performed on their inputs, as they all have to agree on the weights y_{pk} to produce the functional decryption key that allows the inner-product. The set $\mathcal{U}_M$ of public keys describes the group of parties and the label ℓ imposes a constraint on which values can be aggregated together, the set $\mathcal{U}_K$ of public keys describes the support of the inner-product, and $(y_{\mathsf{pk}})_{\mathsf{pk}}$ specifies the weights. If $\mathcal{U}_M = \mathcal{U}_K$ and all the ciphertexts are provided (by all the senders on the same pair $(\mathcal{U}_M, \ell)$), with the appropriate functional decryption key (with the same $(\mathcal{U}_K, (y_{\mathsf{pk}})_{\mathsf{pk}})$, one can get the inner-product value, otherwise the individual values remain hidden. As above, all the players have to agree on the pair $(\mathcal{U}_M, \ell)$ for their encryption, and any encryption naturally leaks that pair $(\mathcal{U}_M, \ell)$. Similarly, all the players have to agree on $(\mathcal{U}_K, (y_{\mathsf{pk}})_{\mathsf{pk}})$ for the functional decryption key, otherwise they are useless.

Because our construction is based on prime-order groups, we need to impose a bound on the messages and the keys to guarantee that we can perform the discrete logarithm efficiently and recover the result of the functional evaluation in polynomial time.

Definition 8 (Inner-Product DDFE). *IP-DDFE is defined for a dimension $d \in \mathbb{N}$ and a bound $B \in \mathbb{N}$, and the sets $\mathcal{U}_M$ and $\mathcal{U}_K$ must perfectly match:*

$$\mathcal{K} = \{(y_{\mathsf{pk}}, \mathsf{pk})_{\mathsf{pk} \in \mathcal{U}_K} \text{ where } y_{\mathsf{pk}} \in [-B, B]^d \text{ and } \mathcal{U}_K \in \mathcal{S}(\mathcal{PK})\}$$
$$\mathcal{M} = [-B, B]^d \times \mathcal{S}(\mathcal{PK}) \times \{0,1\}^*.$$

Then, $F(\epsilon, (\mathsf{pk}, (x, \mathcal{U}, \ell))) = (\mathcal{U}, \ell)$ and

$$F((\mathsf{pk}, k_{\mathsf{pk}})_{\mathsf{pk} \in \mathcal{U}_K}, (\mathsf{pk}, m_{\mathsf{pk}})_{\mathsf{pk} \in \mathcal{U}_M}) = \begin{cases} \sum_{\mathsf{pk} \in \mathcal{U}_K} x_{\mathsf{pk}}^\top y_{\mathsf{pk}} & \text{if condition (*)} \\ \perp & \text{otherwise.} \end{cases}$$

and IP-DDFE condition (*) is:

- $\mathcal{U}_K = \mathcal{U}_M$
- $\exists (\boldsymbol{y}_{\mathsf{pk}})_{\mathsf{pk} \in \mathcal{U}_K} \in \mathcal{S}([-B, B]^d), \forall \mathsf{pk'} \in \mathcal{U}_K, k_{\mathsf{pk'}} = (\boldsymbol{y}_{\mathsf{pk}}, \mathsf{pk})_{\mathsf{pk} \in \mathcal{U}_K}$
- $\exists \ell \in \{0, 1\}^*, \forall \mathsf{pk} \in \mathcal{U}_K, m_{\mathsf{pk}} = (\boldsymbol{x}_{\mathsf{pk}}, \mathcal{U}_M, \ell)$

We stress that in all the above definition, F should always be understood to be equal to $\perp$ on inputs on which it was not explicitly defined above.

3 Notations and Assumptions

3.1 Groups

Prime Order Groups. We use a prime-order group generator GGen, a probabilistic polynomial time (PPT) algorithm that on input the security parameter 1^λ returns a description $\mathcal{G} = (\mathbb{G}, p, P)$ of an additive cyclic group $\mathbb{G}$ of order p for a 2λ-bit prime p, whose generator is P.

We use implicit representations of group elements as introduced in [21]. For $a \in \mathbb{Z}_p$, define $[a] = aP \in \mathbb{G}$ as the *implicit representation* of a in $\mathbb{G}$. More generally, for a matrix $\mathbf{A} = (a_{ij}) \in \mathbb{Z}_p^{n \times m}$ we define $[\mathbf{A}]$ as the implicit representation of $\mathbf{A}$ in $\mathbb{G}$:

$$[\mathbf{A}] := \begin{pmatrix} a_{11}P & \dots & a_{1m}P \\ a_{n1}P & \dots & a_{nm}P \end{pmatrix} \in \mathbb{G}^{n \times m}$$

We will always use this implicit notation of elements in $\mathbb{G}$, i.e., we let $[a] \in \mathbb{G}$ be an element in $\mathbb{G}$. Note that from a random $[a] \in \mathbb{G}$, it is generally hard to compute the value a (discrete logarithm problem in $\mathbb{G}$). Obviously, given $[a], [b] \in \mathbb{G}$ and a scalar $x \in \mathbb{Z}_p$, one can efficiently compute $[ax] \in \mathbb{G}$ and $[a + b] = [a] + [b] \in \mathbb{G}$.

Pairing-Friendly Groups. We also use a pairing-friendly group generator PGGen, a PPT algorithm that on input 1^λ returns $\mathcal{PG} = (\mathbb{G}_1, \mathbb{G}_2, \mathbb{G}_T, p, P_1, P_2, e)$, a description of asymmetric pairing-friendly groups where $\mathbb{G}_1$, $\mathbb{G}_2$, $\mathbb{G}_T$ are additive cyclic groups of order p for a 2λ-bit prime p, P_1 and P_2 are generators of $\mathbb{G}_1$ and $\mathbb{G}_2$, respectively, and $e : \mathbb{G}_1 \times \mathbb{G}_2 \to \mathbb{G}_T$ is an efficiently computable (non-degenerate) bilinear map. Define $P_T := e(P_1, P_2)$, which is a generator of $\mathbb{G}_T$. We again use implicit representation of group elements. For $s \in \{1, 2, T\}$ and $a \in \mathbb{Z}_p$, define $[a]_s = aP_s \in \mathbb{G}_s$ as the implicit representation of a in G_s. Given $[a]_1$, $[b]_2$, one can efficiently compute $[ab]_T$ using the pairing e. For two matrices $\mathbf{A}, \mathbf{B}$ with matching dimensions define $e([\mathbf{A}]_1, [\mathbf{B}]_2) := [\mathbf{AB}]_T \in \mathbb{G}_T$.

3.2 Intractability Assumptions

Definition 9 (Computational Diffie-Hellman Assumption). *The CDH assumption states that, in a prime-order group $\mathcal{G} \xleftarrow{\$} \mathsf{GGen}(1^\lambda)$, no PPT adversary can compute $[xy]$, from $[x]$ and $[y]$ for $x, y \xleftarrow{\$} \mathbb{Z}_p$, with non-negligible success probability.*

Equivalently, this assumption states it is hard to compute $[a^2]$ from $[a]$ for $a \xleftarrow{\$} \mathbb{Z}_p$. This comes from the fact that $4[xy] = [(x+y)^2] - [(x-y)^2]$.

Definition 10 (Decisional Diffie-Hellman Assumption). *The DDH assumption states that, in a group $\mathcal{G} \xleftarrow{\$} \mathsf{GGen}(1^\lambda)$, no PPT adversary can distinguish between the two following distributions with non-negligible advantage:* $\{([a],[r],[ar]) \mid a,r \xleftarrow{\$} \mathbb{Z}_p\}$ *and* $\{([a],[r],[s]) \mid a,r,s \xleftarrow{\$} \mathbb{Z}_p\}$.

Equivalently, this assumption states it is hard to distinguish, knowing $[a]$, a random element from the span of $[\boldsymbol{a}]$ for $\boldsymbol{a} = \binom{1}{a}$, from a random element in $\mathbb{G}^2$: $[\boldsymbol{a}] \cdot r = [ar] = \binom{[r]}{[ar]} \approx \binom{[r]}{[s]}$.

Definition 11 (Decisional Bilinear Diffie Hellman Assumption). *The DBDH assumption states that, in a pairing group $\mathcal{PG} \xleftarrow{\$} \mathsf{PGGen}(1^\lambda)$, for any PPT adversary, the following advantage is negligible, where the probability distribution is over $a,b,c,s \xleftarrow{\$} \mathbb{Z}_p$:*

$$\mathsf{Adv}^{DBDH}_{\mathcal{PG}}(\mathcal{A}) = \; | \Pr[1 \leftarrow \mathcal{A}(\mathcal{PG}, [a]_1, [b]_1, [b]_2, [c]_2, [abc]_T)]$$
$$- \Pr[1 \leftarrow \mathcal{A}(\mathcal{PG}, [a]_1, [b]_1, [b]_2, [c]_2, [s]_T)]|.$$

Definition 12 (Q-fold DBDH). *For any integer Q, the Q-fold DBDH assumption states for any PPT adversary, the following advantage is negligible, where the probability distribution is over $a,b,c_i,s_i \xleftarrow{\$} \mathbb{Z}_p$:*

$$\mathsf{Adv}^{Q\text{-}DBDH}_{\mathcal{PG}}(\mathcal{A}) = \; | \Pr[1 \leftarrow \mathcal{A}(\mathcal{PG}, [a]_1, [b]_1, [b]_2, \{[c_i]_2, [abc_i]_T\}_{i \in [Q]})]$$
$$- \Pr[1 \leftarrow \mathcal{A}(\mathcal{PG}, [a]_1, [b]_1, [b]_2, \{[c_i]_2, [s_i]_T\}_{i \in [Q]})]|.$$

This Q-fold DBDH assumption is equivalent to classical DBDH assumption:

Lemma 13 (Random Self Reducibility of DBDH). *For any adversary $\mathcal{A}$ against the Q-fold DBDH, running within time t, there exists an adversary $\mathcal{B}$ running within time $t + 2Q(t_{\mathbb{G}_T} + t_{\mathbb{G}_2})$, where $t_{\mathbb{G}_T}$ and $t_{\mathbb{G}_2}$ denote respectively the time for an exponentiation in $\mathbb{G}_T$ and $\mathbb{G}_2$ (we only take into account the time for exponentiations here), such that*

$$\mathsf{Adv}^{Q\text{-}DBDH}_{\mathcal{PG}}(\mathcal{A}) \leq \mathsf{Adv}^{DBDH}_{\mathcal{PG}}(\mathcal{B}).$$

Proof. Upon receiving a DBDH challenge $(\mathcal{PG}, [a]_1, [b]_1, [b]_2, [c]_2, [s]_T)$, $\mathcal{B}$ samples $\alpha_i, c'_i \xleftarrow{\$} \mathbb{Z}_p$ computes $[c_i]_2 := [\alpha_i \cdot c]_2 + [c'_i]_2$, $[s_i]_T := [\alpha_i \cdot s]_T + [c_i \cdot ab]_T$ for all $i \in [Q]$, and gives the challenge $(\mathcal{PG}, [a]_1, [b]_1, [b]_2, \{[c_i]_2, [s_i]_T\}_{i \in [Q]})$ to $\mathcal{A}$. $\square$

3.3   Non-Interactive Key Exchange

We give a definition of Non-Interactive Key Exchange below. This a rephrasing of the m-CKS-heavy model (with dishonest key registrations) as originally introduced in [13] and further refined in [22].

Definition 14 (Non-Interactive Key Exchange). *A NIKE scheme consists of three PPT algorithms:*

- Setup(λ): *Generates and outputs public parameters* pp. *Those parameters are implicit arguments to all the other algorithms;*
- KeyGen(): *Generates and outputs a party's public key* pk $\in \mathcal{PK}$ *and the corresponding secret key* sk_{pk};
- SharedKey(pk, $\text{sk}_{\text{pk}'}$): *Takes as input a public key and a secret key corresponding to a different public key. Deterministically outputs a shared key K.*

Correctness: We require that, for all security parameters $\lambda \in \mathbb{N}$, it holds that:

$$\Pr\left[\mathsf{SharedKey}(\mathsf{pk}, \mathsf{sk}_{\mathsf{pk}'}) = \mathsf{SharedKey}(\mathsf{pk}', \mathsf{sk}_{\mathsf{pk}})\right] = 1,$$

where the probability is taken over pp $\leftarrow$ Setup(λ), (pk, sk_{pk}) $\leftarrow$ KeyGen(), (pk', $\text{sk}_{\text{pk}'}$) $\leftarrow$ KeyGen().

Definition 15 (Security Game for NIKE). *Let us consider a NIKE scheme. No adversary $\mathcal{A}$ should be able to win the following security game against a challenger $\mathcal{C}$, with unlimited and adaptive access to the oracles* QNewHonest, QReveal, QTest, *and* QCorrupt *described below:*

- *Initialize: the challenger $\mathcal{C}$ runs the setup algorithm* pp $\leftarrow$ Setup(λ) *and chooses a random bit $b \xleftarrow{\$} \{0,1\}$. It initializes the set $\mathcal{H}$ of honest participants to $\emptyset$. It provides* pp *to the adversary $\mathcal{A}$;*
- *Participant creation queries* QNewHonest(): *the challenger $\mathcal{C}$ runs the* KeyGen *algorithm* (pk, sk_{pk}) $\leftarrow$ KeyGen() *to simulate a new participant, stores the association* (pk, sk_{pk}) *in the set $\mathcal{H}$ of honest keys, and returns* pk *to the adversary;*
- *Reveal queries* QReveal(pk, pk'): *Requires that at least one of* pk *and* pk' *be in $\mathcal{H}$. Without loss of generality assume it is* pk. *The challenger returns* SharedKey(pk', sk_{pk});
- *Test queries* QTest(pk, pk'): *Requires that both* pk *and* pk' *were generated via* QNewHonest.
  - *If $b = 0$, the challenger returns* SharedKey(pk', sk_{pk});
  - *If $b = 1$, the challenger returns a (uniformly) random value, which it stores so it can consistently answer further queries to* QTest(pk, pk') *or* QTest(pk', pk)
- *Corruption queries* QCorrupt(pk): *Recovers the secret key* sk *associated to* pk *from $\mathcal{H}$ and outputs it, then removes the key-pair from $\mathcal{H}$. If* pk *is not associated with any secret key (i.e. it is not in $\mathcal{H}$), then nothing is returned;*
- *Finalize: $\mathcal{A}$ provides its guess b' on the bit b, and this procedure outputs the result β of the security game, according to the analysis given below which aims at preventing trivial wins.*

Finalize outputs the bit $\beta = (b' = b)$ unless a QCorrupt *query was made for any public key which was involved in a query to* QTest, *or a* QReveal *query was made for a pair of public keys which was also involved in a* QTest *query, in which case a random bit β is returned.*

We say NIKE *is secure if for any adversary* $\mathcal{A}$, *the following advantage is negligible:*

$$\mathsf{Adv}_{NIKE}(\mathcal{A}) = 2 \times |\Pr[\beta = 1] - 1/2|.$$

Definition 16 (Static Security Game for NIKE). *We define a static variant of the security game above in which the adversary does not have access to the* QCorrupt *oracle, which means all parties created by the challenger will remain honest, and the only corrupt parties are entirely managed by the adversary.*

3.4   Definition of Symmetric Key Encryption

A symmetric key encryption SKE $=$ (SEnc, SDec) with key space $\mathcal{K}$ is defined as:

- SEnc(K, m): given a key K and a message m, outputs a ciphertext ct;
- SDec(K, ct): given a key K and a ciphertext ct, outputs a plaintext.

Correctness. For all m in the message space and all K in the key space, we must have SDec$(K, \mathsf{SEnc}(K, m)) = m$.

Security. We say SKE is secure if for any PPT adversary $\mathcal{A}$, the following advantage is negligible:

$$\mathsf{Adv}_{\mathsf{SKE}}(\mathcal{A}) = \left| 2 \times \Pr\left[b' = b : \begin{array}{c} K \xleftarrow{\$} \mathcal{K}, b \xleftarrow{\$} \{0, 1\} \\ b' \leftarrow \mathcal{A}(1^{\lambda})^{\mathsf{QLeftRight}(\cdot, \cdot)} \end{array} \right] - 1 \right|,$$

where the oracle QLeftRight, when queried on m_0, m_1, returns SEnc(K, m_b).

One-Time Security. We say SKE is One-Time Secure if the above security holds for only one QLeftRight-oracle query. Note that if the key space is larger than the message space, on can simply use the one-time pad to build a One-Time Secure symmetric encryption. Otherwise, a pseudo-random generator can stretch the key to the right length.

3.5   Single-Input Functional Encryption

For some of our constructions, we will need a instantiations of single-input Functional Encryption (for a specific functionalities). A Functional encryption scheme for a family of functions $\mathcal{F}$ consists of the following PPT algorithms:

- KeyGen(λ): on input a security parameter, it outputs a master secret key msk and a public key pk.
- Encrypt(pk, m): outputs a ciphertext ct.
- DKeyGen(msk, f): on input the master secret key and a function $f \in \mathcal{F}$, it outputs a decryption key dk$_f$.
- Dec$(\mathsf{ct}, \mathsf{dk}_f)$: deterministic algorithm that returns a message or a rejection symbol $\perp$ if it fails.

Correctness. For any message m, and any function f in the family $\mathcal{F}$, we have: $\Pr[\mathsf{Dec}(\mathsf{ct}, \mathsf{dk}_f) = f(m)] = 1$, where the probability is taken over $(\mathsf{msk}, \mathsf{mpk}) \leftarrow \mathsf{Setup}(\lambda)$, $\mathsf{ct} \leftarrow \mathsf{Encrypt}(\mathsf{msk}, m)$, and $\mathsf{dk}_f \leftarrow \mathsf{DKeyGen}(\mathsf{msk}, f)$.

Indistinguishability. The security notion is defined by a classical indistinguishability game:

Definition 17 (IND-Security Game for FE). *Let* FE *be a functional encryption scheme. No adversary $\mathcal{A}$ should be able to win the following security game:*

- *Initialize: runs* $(\mathsf{msk}, \mathsf{mpk}) \leftarrow \mathsf{Setup}(\lambda)$, *choose a random bit* $b \xleftarrow{\$} \{0,1\}$ *and returns* mpk *to $\mathcal{A}$.*
- *QLeftRight(m_0, m_1): on input two messages (m_0, m_1), returns* $\mathsf{Enc}(\mathsf{msk}, m_b)$.
- *QDKeyGen(f): on input a function $f \in \mathcal{F}$, returns* $\mathsf{DKeyGen}(\mathsf{msk}, f)$.
- *Finalize: from the guess b' of $\mathcal{A}$ on the bit b, it outputs the bit $\beta = (b' = b)$ unless some f was queried to* QDKeyGen *and (m_0, m_1) was queried to* QLeftRight *such that $f(m_0) \neq f(m_1)$, in which case it outputs a uniformly random bit β.*

The adversary $\mathcal{A}$ has unlimited and adaptive access to the left-right encryption oracle QLeftRight, *and to the key generation oracle* QDKeyGen. *We say* FE *is IND-secure if for any adversary $\mathcal{A}$, $\mathsf{Adv}_{\mathsf{FE}}^{\mathsf{IND}}(\mathcal{A}) = |2 \times \Pr[\beta = 1] - 1|$ is negligible.*

We can also define a weaker selective variant, where pairs (m_0, m_1) to QLeftRight-queries are known from the beginning.

Identity-Based Encryption. Here we define the functionality that corresponds to Identity-Based Encryption, originally envisioned in [33], and first realized in [10,19]. The functionality is described by an identity space $\mathcal{I}$, which can be of exponential size. Each function is described by an identity $\mathsf{id} \in \mathcal{I}$, and given as input a pair (m, id') where m is a payload, and $\mathsf{id}' \in \mathcal{I}$ is an identity, the function outputs m if $\mathsf{id} = \mathsf{id}'$, nothing otherwise.

Inner Product Functionality. For any dimension $d \in \mathbb{N}$ and cyclic group $\mathbb{G}$ of prime order p, the inner product functionality corresponds to the set of functions described by a vector $\boldsymbol{y} \in \mathbb{Z}_p^d$ that on input a vector $[\boldsymbol{x}] \in \mathbb{G}^d$, outputs $[\boldsymbol{x}^\top \boldsymbol{y}]$. FE schemes for the inner-product functionality were originally introduced in [3], later in [7] with adaptive security.

We will make use of the following property, satisfied by several FE schemes, including [3,7]. For concreteness we recall the scheme from [7] in Appendix A.

Property 18 (Linear Homomorphism). An FE for inner products (IP-FE.Setup, IP-FE.Encrypt, IP-FE.DKeyGen, IP-FE.Dec) satisfies the linear homomorphism property if there exists a PPT algorithm Add such that for all $\boldsymbol{x}, \boldsymbol{x}' \in \mathbb{Z}_p^d$, the following are identically distributed:

$$\Big(\mathsf{IP\text{-}FE.Encrypt}(\mathsf{IP\text{-}FE.pk}, \boldsymbol{x}), \ \mathsf{IP\text{-}FE.Encrypt}(\mathsf{IP\text{-}FE.pk}, \boldsymbol{x} + \boldsymbol{x}')\Big)$$

and

$$\Big(\mathsf{IP\text{-}FE.Encrypt}(\mathsf{IP\text{-}FE.pk}, \boldsymbol{x}), \ \mathsf{Add}\big(\mathsf{IP\text{-}FE.Encrypt}(\mathsf{IP\text{-}FE.pk}, \boldsymbol{x}), \boldsymbol{x}'\big)\Big),$$

where $(\mathsf{IP\text{-}FE.pk}, \mathsf{IP\text{-}FE.sk}) \leftarrow \mathsf{IP\text{-}FE.Setup}(\lambda)$.

4   All-or-Nothing Encapsulation from IBE

4.1   Technical Overview

Our generic construction only requires an IBE. Messages are encrypted under the public key of each member of the group successively, using the set of participants $\mathcal{U}_M$ and the label ℓ as the identity. The $|\mathcal{U}_M|$-layers deep encryption is accompanied by the functional decryption key of the IBE for the encrypting participant and the same identity. The only way to recover the messages is to gather all the decryption keys in order to decrypt all layers of IBE encryption: this requires having access to all the ciphertexts. IBE is a well-studied primitive, which admits constructions from multiple hardness assumptions, including pairings [10], LWE [24], or more recently the CDH assumption [20]. This directly implies feasibility of AoNE from these assumptions. To keep the size of the ciphertext polynomial in the number of users, we use rate-1 IBE, using hybrid encryption. In Sect. 5 we give a more efficient construction directly from pairings, inspired by the IBE from [10].

4.2   A Generic Construction of All-or-Nothing Encapsulation

Our construction uses an Identity-Based encryption scheme IBE.

- $\mathsf{Setup}(\lambda)$: Return $pp \leftarrow \mathsf{IBE.Setup}(\lambda)$
- $\mathsf{KeyGen}()$: Return $(\mathsf{pk}, \mathsf{sk}_{\mathsf{pk}}) \leftarrow \mathsf{IBE.KeyGen}()$.
- $\mathsf{Encrypt}(\mathsf{sk}_{\mathsf{pk}}, m)$: Parse $m = (x_{\mathsf{pk}}, \mathcal{U}_M, \ell)$ where $x_{\mathsf{pk}} \in \{0,1\}^L$, $\mathcal{U}_M \in \mathcal{S}(\mathcal{PK})$, and $\ell \in \{0,1\}^*$. If $\mathsf{pk} \notin \mathcal{U}_M$, return $\perp$. Let $n = |\mathcal{U}_M|$ be the cardinal of $\mathcal{U}_M$, and, for some universally accepted order, number the elements in $\mathcal{U}_M$ as $\mathcal{U}_M = \{\mathsf{pk}_1, \ldots, \mathsf{pk}_n\}$.
  Let $\alpha_{\mathsf{pk},0} = x_{\mathsf{pk}}$, and for i going from 1 to n, compute

$$\alpha_{\mathsf{pk},i} := \mathsf{IBE.Encrypt}(\mathsf{pk}_i, (\alpha_{\mathsf{pk},i-1}, \mathcal{U}_M \| \ell)).$$

  We write $\alpha_{\mathsf{pk},\mathcal{U}_M,\ell} = \alpha_{\mathsf{pk},n}$. Compute $\gamma_{\mathsf{pk},\mathcal{U}_M,\ell} = \mathsf{IBE.DKeyGen}(\mathsf{sk}_{\mathsf{pk}}, \mathcal{U}_M \| \ell)$. Return $(\alpha_{\mathsf{pk},\mathcal{U}_M,\ell}, \gamma_{\mathsf{pk},\mathcal{U}_M,\ell}, \mathcal{U}_M, \ell)$.
- $\mathsf{DKeyGen}(\mathsf{sk}, k)$: There are no keys in this functionality, so no $\mathsf{DKeyGen}$;
- $\mathsf{Decrypt}(\epsilon, (\mathsf{ct}_{\mathsf{pk}})_{\mathsf{pk} \in \mathcal{U}_M})$: Parse the ciphertexts, for all $\mathsf{pk} \in \mathcal{U}_M$, as

$$\mathsf{ct}_{\mathsf{pk}} = (\alpha_{\mathsf{pk},\mathcal{U}_M,\ell}, \gamma_{\mathsf{pk},\mathcal{U}_M,\ell}, \mathcal{U}_M, \ell),$$

  with common $(\mathcal{U}_M, \ell)$ (otherwise return $\perp$). For each $\mathsf{pk} \in \mathcal{U}_M$, we recover x_{pk} as follows: with $\mathcal{U}_M = \{\mathsf{pk}_1, \ldots, \mathsf{pk}_n\}$, recompute the $\alpha_{\mathsf{pk},i}$ for i going from n to 0 as $\alpha_{\mathsf{pk},n} = \alpha_{\mathsf{pk},\mathcal{U}_M,\ell}$ and $\alpha_{\mathsf{pk},i} = \mathsf{IBE.Decrypt}(\gamma_{\mathsf{pk}_i,\mathcal{U}_M,\ell}, \alpha_{\mathsf{pk},i+1})$. Output $(\mathsf{pk}, x_{\mathsf{pk}})_{\mathsf{pk} \in \mathcal{U}_M}$.

Correctness: Correctness follows immediately from the correctness of IBE.

Remark 19 (Rate-1 IBE). To avoid ciphertexts having length exponential in $|\mathcal{U}_M|$, we require that IBE has rate-1 encryption. That is, the ciphertext has the same size as the plaintext plus a polynomial in the security parameter. This can be obtained generically via hybrid encryption: the IBE is used to encrypt a symmetric key, that is used to encrypt the actual message. Assuming such properties of the IBE scheme, our ciphertexts have length linear in $|\mathcal{U}_M|$.

Remark 20. The astute reader will have noticed that the $\gamma_{\mathsf{pk},\mathcal{U}_M,\ell}$ seem to be playing the role of a Functional Decryption Key. Indeed, AoNE could have been defined with keys allowing decryption of the ciphertext if the appropriate key shares (i.e., for that pair $(\mathcal{U}_M, \ell)$) are contributed by all parties. However, our applications of AoNE are such that we would always end up giving out the key share with the corresponding ciphertext, so we gave a definition which is more practical for our uses and may allow constructions in settings where the alternative with keys would be harder to design.

Remark 21. Note that while we show here how to construct AoNE from IBE, it's also possible to construct IBE from AoNE. A possible construction uses only two AoNE identities, one of which creates AoNE ciphertexts that serve as IBE ciphertexts, while the other creates AoNE ciphertexts that serve as IBE functional keys. The secret key for the first identity is made public (it is part of the IBE's public key) while that for the latter remains private. Identities are encoded as labels, and groups are always chosen as the pair of identities. Now to recover the message behind a ciphertext, even generated with the known AoNE secret key of the first identity, one needs an AoNE ciphertext from the second identity for the same label/identity, which effectively acts as an IBE secret key.

4.3 Security Proof

Theorem 22 (IND-Security of AoNE). *The All-or-Nothing Encapsulation scheme described in Sect. 4.2 is IND-secure (as per Definition 3) assuming the IBE scheme is IND-secure (as per Definition 17).*

The proof can be found in Appendix B.

5 All-or-Nothing Encapsulation from Bilinear Maps

5.1 Technical Overview

This construction is essentially an instantiation of the generic construction given in Sect. 4.2 using Boneh and Franklin's IBE [10]. However, we make a few optimizations exploiting the structure of the Boneh-Franklin IBE (BF) to achieve short ciphertexts. First, we use the IBE as a Key-Encapsulation Mechanism to generate a symmetric key, which we then use to encrypt the message. Second, we exploit the randomness reusability of El Gamal-like schemes, from which BF benefits, to only commit to a randomness once. The size difference between the message and the ciphertext in BF comes entirely from that commitment to randomness, so sharing it across all encryptions removes the dependence on the size of the set of participants in the size of the ciphertext.

We provide a direct security analysis of the resulting scheme in Sect. 5.3.

5.2 A Construction of All-or-Nothing Encapsulation from Bilinear Maps

Our construction uses pairing-friendly groups, a hash function modeled as a random oracle in the security analysis, and a (One-Time Secure) symmetric encryption scheme.

- Setup(λ): Generate $\mathcal{PG} = (\mathbb{G}_1, \mathbb{G}_2, \mathbb{G}_T, p, P_1, P_2, e) \xleftarrow{\$} \mathsf{PGGen}(1^\lambda)$, a full domain hash function $\mathcal{H}$ from $\{0,1\}^*$ into $\mathbb{G}_1$, and return $\mathsf{pp} = (\mathcal{PG}, \mathcal{H})$. For the sake of clarity, for any input x, we will denote $\mathcal{H}(x) = h_x P_1 = [h_x]_1$, where h_x is the unknown discrete logarithm.
- KeyGen(): Sample $t_{\mathsf{pk}} \xleftarrow{\$} \mathbb{Z}_p$ and return $(\mathsf{pk}, \mathsf{sk}_{\mathsf{pk}}) = ([t_{\mathsf{pk}}]_2, t_{\mathsf{pk}})$.
- Encrypt($\mathsf{sk}_{\mathsf{pk}}, m$): Parse $\mathsf{sk}_{\mathsf{pk}} = t_{\mathsf{pk}} \in \mathbb{Z}_p$ and $m = (x_{\mathsf{pk}}, \mathcal{U}_M, \ell)$ where $x_{\mathsf{pk}} \in \{0,1\}^L$, $\mathcal{U}_M \in \mathcal{S}(\mathcal{PK})$, and $\ell \in \{0,1\}^*$. If $\mathsf{pk} \notin \mathcal{U}_M$, return $\bot$. Otherwise, sample $r_{\mathsf{pk}} \xleftarrow{\$} \mathbb{Z}_p$ and compute the symmetric key $K_{\mathsf{pk}, \mathcal{U}_M, \ell}$ as

$$e\left(\mathcal{H}(\mathcal{U}_M \| \ell), r_{\mathsf{pk}} \cdot \left(\sum_{\mathsf{pk}' \in \mathcal{U}_M} \mathsf{pk}'\right)\right) = \left[h_{\mathcal{U}_M \| \ell} \cdot r_{\mathsf{pk}} \cdot \sum_{\mathsf{pk}' \in \mathcal{U}_M} t_{\mathsf{pk}'}\right]_T,$$

and use it to encrypt x_{pk} as $c_{\mathsf{pk}} = \mathsf{SEnc}(K_{\mathsf{pk}, \mathcal{U}_M, \ell}, x_{\mathsf{pk}})$. Compute its share $S_{\mathsf{pk}, \mathcal{U}_M, \ell} = t_{\mathsf{pk}} \cdot \mathcal{H}(\mathcal{U}_M \| \ell) = [t_{\mathsf{pk}} \cdot h_{\mathcal{U}_M \| \ell}]_1$, and output the ciphertext $\mathsf{ct}_{\mathsf{pk}} = (c_{\mathsf{pk}}, [r_{\mathsf{pk}}]_2, S_{\mathsf{pk}, \mathcal{U}_M, \ell}, \mathcal{U}_M, \ell)$.
- DKeyGen(sk, k): There are no keys in this functionality, so no DKeyGen;
- Decrypt($\epsilon, (\mathsf{ct}_{\mathsf{pk}})_{\mathsf{pk} \in \mathcal{U}_M}$): Parse the ciphertexts, for all $\mathsf{pk} \in \mathcal{U}_M$, as $\mathsf{ct}_{\mathsf{pk}} = (c_{\mathsf{pk}}, [r_{\mathsf{pk}}]_2, S_{\mathsf{pk}, \mathcal{U}_M, \ell}, \mathcal{U}_M, \ell)$, with common $(\mathcal{U}_M, \ell)$. For each $\mathsf{pk} \in \mathcal{U}_M$, compute

$$K_{\mathsf{pk}, \mathcal{U}_M, \ell} = e\left(\sum_{\mathsf{pk}' \in \mathcal{U}_M} S_{\mathsf{pk}', \mathcal{U}_M, \ell}, [r_{\mathsf{pk}}]_2\right) = \left[h_{\mathcal{U}_M \| \ell} \cdot r_{\mathsf{pk}} \cdot \sum_{\mathsf{pk}' \in \mathcal{U}_M} t_{\mathsf{pk}'}\right]_T$$

and recover x_{pk} as $x_{\mathsf{pk}} = \mathsf{SDec}(K_{\mathsf{pk}, \mathcal{U}_M, \ell}, c_{\mathsf{pk}})$.

Correctness: First, note that the use of $K_{\mathsf{pk}, \mathcal{U}_M, \ell}$ is consistent across Encrypt and Decrypt. Then, the two evaluations correspond to $\left[h_{\mathcal{U}_M \| \ell} \cdot r_{\mathsf{pk}} \cdot \sum_{\mathsf{pk}' \in \mathcal{U}_M} t_{\mathsf{pk}'}\right]_T$. Now correctness immediately follows from the correctness of the underlying symmetric encryption scheme.

Remark 23. Note that the sum $\sum_{\mathsf{pk}' \in \mathcal{U}_M} S_{\mathsf{pk}', \mathcal{U}_M, \ell}$ is common to all ciphertexts for the same pair $(\mathcal{U}_M, \ell)$ and can thus be precomputed and reused, such that n messages can be recovered in time $\mathcal{O}(n)$.

5.3   Security Proof

Theorem 24 (IND-Security of AoNE). *The All-or-Nothing Encapsulation scheme described in Sect. 5.2 is IND-secure (as per Definition 3) under the DBDH assumption, in the random oracle model.*

The proof can be found in the full version [18].

6   Decentralized Sum

6.1   Technical Overview

The starting point of our construction is the "Sum-of-PRFs" technique used by Chase and Chow [16]. The technique aims to enable a set of parties to evaluate local PRFs for a common label ℓ, such that the sum of their local PRFs is zero. It relies on shared seeds between each pair of participants, that are computed on-the-fly using Non-Interactive Key Exchange. Those PRFs can then be added to each participant's input, masking the individual contribution but revealing their sum, because adding the masked ciphertexts causes the PRF evaluation to cancel out.

Remarkably, this is not enough to achieve IND security in the DDFE setting. As such, the random mask would be a deterministic function of the set of participants $\mathcal{U}_M$ and the label ℓ. So, repeated QLeftRight queries to the same pair $(\mathcal{U}_M, \ell)$ with different messages would enable an adversary to break security, simply by subtracting two ciphertexts associated with the same pair $(\mathcal{U}_M, \ell)$ so as to remove the identical masks. This issue can be addressed with a layer of AoNE encryption. Since our AoNE construction is asymmetric and its encryption is randomized, the layer prevents the adversary from combining ciphertexts for the same pair $(\mathcal{U}_M, \ell)$ in a meaningful way. Only when all the ciphertexts are revealed can the adversary remove the AoNE layer, and get access to the underlying ciphertexts. In that case however, the information recovered by the adversary is part of the information revealed by the functionality. For instance, the adversary can subtract two deterministic ciphertexts to obtain the different of the underlying messages. This information can also be learnt by subtracting two sums that are revealed by correctness of the scheme. In general, we show that when the AoNE layer can be removed, the Finalize condition imposes sufficient constraints on the adversary's queries that trivial attacks are no longer on the table.

Moreover, the AoNE layer that lets us achieve full IND security, instead of having to settle for sym-IND security, since, as explained, the AoNE is an asymmetric form of encryption.

6.2   A Generic Construction of Decentralized Sum DDFE for $(\mathbb{A}, +)$

For our construction, we assume a NIKE scheme NIKE, an All-or-Nothing Encapsulation scheme AoNE for messages of length the size of an element of $\mathbb{A}$, and a PRF family $(\mathcal{F}_K)_K$ that takes keys from the NIKE and messages from $\{0,1\}^*$ and outputs pseudo-random elements in $\mathbb{A}$.

- Setup(λ): Run NIKE.pp $\leftarrow$ NIKE.Setup(λ), AoNE.pp $\leftarrow$ AoNE.Setup(λ), and output pp $=$ (NIKE.pp, AoNE.pp);
- KeyGen(): Run the KeyGen algorithms from the NIKE and the AoNE:

$$(\mathsf{NIKE.pk}, \mathsf{NIKE.sk_{pk}}) \leftarrow \mathsf{NIKE.KeyGen}(),$$

$$(\mathsf{AoNE.pk}, \mathsf{AoNE.sk_{pk}}) \leftarrow \mathsf{AoNE.KeyGen}(),$$

and output the key pair

$$(\mathsf{pk}, \mathsf{sk_{pk}}) = ((\mathsf{NIKE.pk}, \mathsf{AoNE.pk}), (\mathsf{NIKE.sk_{pk}}, \mathsf{AoNE.sk_{pk}}));$$

- Encrypt($\mathsf{sk_{pk}}, m$): Parse m as $(x, \mathcal{U}_M, \ell)$, with $x \in \mathbb{A}$, $\mathcal{U}_M \in \mathcal{S}(\mathcal{PK})$, and $\ell \in \{0,1\}^*$. Let pk be our encryptor's public key[2]. If $\mathsf{pk} \notin \mathcal{U}_M$, then return $\bot$. Otherwise, for all $\mathsf{pk'} = (\mathsf{NIKE.pk'}, \mathsf{AoNE.pk'}) \in \mathcal{U}_M$ such that $\mathsf{pk'} \neq \mathsf{pk}$, compute $K_{\mathsf{pk},\mathsf{pk'}} = \mathsf{NIKE.SharedKey}(\mathsf{NIKE.sk_{pk}}, \mathsf{NIKE.pk'})$ and $r_{\mathsf{pk},\mathsf{pk'},\mathcal{U}_M,\ell} = \mathcal{F}_{K_{\mathsf{pk},\mathsf{pk'}}}(\mathcal{U}_M \| \ell)$. Compute $c_{\mathsf{pk}} = x + \sum_{\mathsf{pk'} < \mathsf{pk}} r_{\mathsf{pk},\mathsf{pk'},\mathcal{U}_M,\ell} - \sum_{\mathsf{pk'} > \mathsf{pk}} r_{\mathsf{pk},\mathsf{pk'},\mathcal{U}_M,\ell}$, where the sums are on $\mathsf{pk'} \in \mathcal{U}_M$, on which a total ordering is defined. Return

$$\mathsf{ct_{pk}} = (\mathsf{AoNE.Encrypt}(\mathsf{AoNE.sk_{pk}}, (c_{\mathsf{pk}}, \mathcal{U}_M, \ell)), \mathcal{U}_M, \ell);$$

- DKeyGen(sk, k): There are no keys in this functionality, so no DKeyGen;
- Decrypt($\epsilon, (\mathsf{ct_{pk}})_{\mathsf{pk} \in \mathcal{U}_M}$): Get $(c_{\mathsf{pk}})_{\mathsf{pk} \in \mathcal{U}_M} = \mathsf{AoNE.Decrypt}(\epsilon, (\mathsf{ct_{pk}})_{\mathsf{pk} \in \mathcal{U}_M})$, and return $\sum_{\mathsf{pk} \in \mathcal{U}_M} c_{\mathsf{pk}}$.

Correctness: The (c_{pk}) should be consistent between Encrypt and Decrypt by correctness of AoNE. Besides:

$$\sum_{\mathsf{pk} \in \mathcal{U}_M} \mathsf{ct_{pk}} = \sum_{\mathsf{pk} \in \mathcal{U}_M} \left(x_{\mathsf{pk}} + \sum_{\mathsf{pk'} < \mathsf{pk}, \mathsf{pk'} \in \mathcal{U}_M} r_{\mathsf{pk},\mathsf{pk'},\mathcal{U}_M,\ell} - \sum_{\mathsf{pk'} > \mathsf{pk}} r_{\mathsf{pk},\mathsf{pk'},\mathcal{U}_M,\ell} \right)$$

$$= \sum_{\mathsf{pk} \in \mathcal{U}_M} x_{\mathsf{pk}} + \sum_{\substack{\mathsf{pk},\mathsf{pk'} \in \mathcal{U}_M \\ \mathsf{pk'} < \mathsf{pk}}} r_{\mathsf{pk},\mathsf{pk'},\mathcal{U}_M,\ell} - r_{\mathsf{pk},\mathsf{pk'},\mathcal{U}_M,\ell} = \sum_{\mathsf{pk} \in \mathcal{U}_M} x_{\mathsf{pk}}$$

by correctness of NIKE.

6.3 Security Proof

Theorem 25 (IND-Security of DSum). *The Decentralized Sum scheme described in Sect. 6.2 is IND-secure (as per Definition 3) so long as NIKE is IND-secure (as per Definition 15) and $(\mathcal{F}_K)_K$ is a secure PRF family.*

The proof can be found in the full version [18].

---

[2] Depending on the details of NIKE and AoNE it may be necessary to explicitly include pk in $\mathsf{sk_{pk}}$ to ensure the following check can be performed.

7   Inner-Product DDFE

7.1   Technical Overview

Our starting point is Chotard *et al.*'s Inner-Product MCFE [17]: as they do, we use a Random Oracle to generate shared randomness across participants for a given label ℓ (in our case a $(\mathcal{U}_M, \ell)$ pair). However, their construction has several drawbacks, which we overcome:

1. Their security game requires that if one ciphertext is queried for a label ℓ, all such ciphertexts must be queried (for the same label ℓ and for all other honest parties). We lift this requirement by protecting ciphertexts with a layer of AoNE.
2. Their Encrypt algorithm is a deterministic function of the message and the label ℓ, and thus they do not tolerate repeated queries to the same participant for the same label. We address this by adding a layer of IP-FE, which randomizes ciphertexts. IP-FE keys are provided in our KeyGen algorithm, and they are protected by an AoNE layer to ensure ciphertexts can only be decrypted once the all the partial functional decryption keys are present.
3. Their scheme, being MCFE, only works in the context of a fixed group. We show how using a PRF to dynamically generate independent secret keys for different groups removes this constraint.
4. To enable non-interactive generation of functional decryption keys in DMCFE, they introduce pairings, and perform message-related operations in $\mathbb{G}_1$ while key-related operations take place in $\mathbb{G}_2$. Instead, we use our DSum to enforce proper key aggregation, which simplifies the scheme to a pairing-free group[3]. DSum has the added benefit that it is a DDFE functionality and thus non-interactive, meaning our Inner-Product scheme is also non-interactive, while their DMCFE has an interactive setup.

7.2   A Construction of IP-DDFE

To build our IP-DDFE, we use a cyclic group $\mathbb{G}$ of prime order p where DDH holds, a random oracle $\mathcal{H} : \{0,1\}^* \to \mathbb{G}$, an single-input FE for the inner product functionality, where each function is described by a vector $\boldsymbol{y} \in \mathbb{Z}_p^d$, and on input a vector $[\boldsymbol{x}] \in \mathbb{G}^d$, outputs $[\boldsymbol{x}^\top \boldsymbol{y}]$. We require that IP-FE is IND secure, and satisfies Property 18. We also use an All-or-Nothing Encapsulation scheme AoNE, a Distributed Sum DSum over $(\mathbb{Z}_p, +)$, and a PRF family $(\mathcal{F}_K)_K$ that outputs in $\mathbb{Z}_p^d$.

– Setup(λ): Generate $\mathcal{G} = (\mathbb{G}, p, P) \xleftarrow{\$} \mathsf{GGen}(1^\lambda)$. Generate a full domain hash function $\mathcal{H} : \{0,1\}^* \to \mathbb{G}$. Compute AoNE.pp $\leftarrow$ AoNE.Setup(λ) and DSum.pp $\leftarrow$ DSum.Setup(λ). Return:

$$\mathsf{pp} = (\mathcal{G}, \mathcal{H}, \mathsf{NIKE.pp}, \mathsf{AoNE.pp}).$$

---

[3] Of course, our DSum and our IP-DDFE themselves use AoNE, which may rely on pairings if instantiated with our construction from Sect. 5.

- KeyGen(): Sample the keys
  - a PRF key K,
  - IP-FE keys $(\mathsf{IP\text{-}FE.pk}, \mathsf{IP\text{-}FE.sk}_{\mathsf{pk}}) \leftarrow \mathsf{IP\text{-}FE.KeyGen}(\mathbb{G}, d)$,
  - AoNE keys $(\mathsf{AoNE.pk}, \mathsf{AoNE.sk}_{\mathsf{pk}}) \leftarrow \mathsf{AoNE.KeyGen}()$,
  - and DSum keys $(\mathsf{DSum.pk}, \mathsf{DSum.sk}_{\mathsf{pk}}) \leftarrow \mathsf{DSum.KeyGen}()$.

  Set the public key $\mathsf{pk} = (\mathsf{IP\text{-}FE.pk}, \mathsf{AoNE.pk}, \mathsf{DSum.pk})$ and the secret key $\mathsf{sk}_{\mathsf{pk}} = (K, \mathsf{IP\text{-}FE.sk}_{\mathsf{pk}}, \mathsf{AoNE.sk}, \mathsf{DSum.sk})$. Return the key pair $(\mathsf{pk}, \mathsf{sk}_{\mathsf{pk}})$.
- Encrypt($\mathsf{sk}_{\mathsf{pk}}, m$): Parse m as $(\boldsymbol{x}, \mathcal{U}_M, \ell)$, where $\boldsymbol{x} \in \mathbb{Z}_p^d$, $\mathcal{U}_M \in \mathcal{S}(\mathcal{PK})$, $\ell \in \{0,1\}^*$, $\boldsymbol{s}_{\mathsf{pk},\mathcal{U}_M} = \mathcal{F}_K(\mathcal{U}_M) \in \mathbb{Z}_p^d$, $[h_\ell] = \mathcal{H}(\ell) \in \mathbb{G}$, and

$$c_{\mathsf{pk}} \leftarrow \mathsf{IP\text{-}FE.Encrypt}(\mathsf{IP\text{-}FE.sk}_{\mathsf{pk}}, [\boldsymbol{x}] + \boldsymbol{s}_{\mathsf{pk},\mathcal{U}_M} \cdot [h_\ell]).$$

Return

$$\mathsf{ct}_{\mathsf{pk}} = (\mathsf{AoNE.Encrypt}(\mathsf{AoNE.sk}_{\mathsf{pk}}, (c_{\mathsf{pk}}, (\mathsf{AoNE.pk}')_{\mathsf{pk}' \in \mathcal{U}_M}, "ct" \| \ell)), \mathcal{U}_M, \ell) ;$$

- DKeyGen($\mathsf{sk}_{\mathsf{pk}}, k$): Parse k as $(\boldsymbol{y}_{\mathsf{pk}'}, \mathsf{pk}')_{\mathsf{pk}' \in \mathcal{U}_K}$. Compute $\boldsymbol{s}_{\mathsf{pk},\mathcal{U}_K} = \mathcal{F}_K(\mathcal{U}_K) \in \mathbb{Z}_p^d$ and

$$d_{\mathsf{pk},k} = \mathsf{DSum.Encrypt}(\mathsf{DSum.sk}_{\mathsf{pk}}, (\boldsymbol{y}_{\mathsf{pk}}^T \boldsymbol{s}_{\mathsf{pk},\mathcal{U}_K}, (\mathsf{DSum.pk}')_{\mathsf{pk}' \in \mathcal{U}_K}, k)).$$

Compute $d''_{\mathsf{pk},k} = \mathsf{IP\text{-}FE.DKeyGen}(\mathsf{IP\text{-}FE.sk}_{\mathsf{pk}}, \boldsymbol{y}_{\mathsf{pk}})$ and

$$d'_{\mathsf{pk},k} \leftarrow \mathsf{AoNE.Encrypt}(\mathsf{AoNE.sk}_{\mathsf{pk}}, (d''_{\mathsf{pk},k}, (\mathsf{AoNE.pk}')_{\mathsf{pk}' \in \mathcal{U}_K}, "key" \| k))$$

and return $\mathsf{dk}_{\mathsf{pk},k} = (d_{\mathsf{pk},k}, d'_{\mathsf{pk},k})$;
- Decrypt($(\mathsf{dk}_{\mathsf{pk}',k_{\mathsf{pk}'}})_{\mathsf{pk}' \in \mathcal{U}_K}, (\mathsf{ct}_{\mathsf{pk}})_{\mathsf{pk} \in \mathcal{U}_M}$): If $\mathcal{U}_M \neq \mathcal{U}_K$ return $\bot$. Now let $\mathcal{U} = \mathcal{U}_M = \mathcal{U}_K$. Let $k \in \mathcal{K}$ be such that $k = k_{\mathsf{pk}}$ for all $\mathsf{pk} \in \mathcal{U}$. If there is no such k return $\bot$. Parse $\mathsf{dk}_{\mathsf{pk},k}$ as $(d_{\mathsf{pk},k}, d'_{\mathsf{pk},k})$ for all $\mathsf{pk} \in \mathcal{U}$.
  Get

$$(c_{\mathsf{pk}})_{\mathsf{pk} \in \mathcal{U}} = \mathsf{AoNE.Decrypt}(\epsilon, (\mathsf{ct}_{\mathsf{pk}})_{\mathsf{pk} \in \mathcal{U}})$$

and

$$(d''_{\mathsf{pk},k})_{\mathsf{pk} \in \mathcal{U}} = \mathsf{AoNE.Decrypt}(\epsilon, (d'_{\mathsf{pk},k})_{\mathsf{pk} \in \mathcal{U}}).$$

Then compute $s_k = \sum_{\mathsf{pk} \in \mathcal{U}} \boldsymbol{y}_{\mathsf{pk}}^T \boldsymbol{s}_{\mathsf{pk},\mathcal{U}} = \mathsf{DSum.Decrypt}(\epsilon, (d_{\mathsf{pk},k})_{\mathsf{pk} \in \mathcal{U}})$.
For all $\mathsf{pk} \in \mathcal{U}$, compute $z_{\mathsf{pk}} \in \mathbb{G}$ as

$$z_{\mathsf{pk}} \leftarrow \mathsf{IP\text{-}FE.Decrypt}(d''_{\mathsf{pk},k}, c_{\mathsf{pk}}).$$

Let $\ell \in \{0,1\}^*$ such that all $\mathsf{ct}_{\mathsf{pk}}$ for $\mathsf{pk} \in \mathcal{U}$ contain ℓ. If there is no such ℓ, return $\bot$. Otherwise, compute $[h_\ell] = \mathcal{H}(\ell) \in \mathbb{G}$ and return the discrete logarithm in base $[1]$ of

$$\left(\sum_{\mathsf{pk} \in \mathcal{U}} z_{\mathsf{pk}} \right) - s_k \cdot [h_\ell].$$

Correctness: We write $s_{\text{pk},\mathcal{U}} = \mathcal{F}_{K_{\text{pk}}}(\mathcal{U})$. By correctness of AoNE, the use of c_{pk} in Encrypt and in Decrypt is consistent, as well as the use of $d''_{\text{pk},k}$ in DKeyGen and Decrypt; By correctness of DSum, we have $s_k = \sum_{\text{pk}\in\mathcal{U}} \boldsymbol{y}_{\text{pk}}^T \boldsymbol{s}_{\text{pk},\mathcal{U}}$; By correctness property of IP-FE, we have $z_{\text{pk}} = [\boldsymbol{y}_{\text{pk}}^T \boldsymbol{x}_{\text{pk}} + \boldsymbol{y}_{\text{pk}}^T \boldsymbol{s}_{\text{pk},\mathcal{U}} h_\ell]$. Thus we eventually compute and return the discrete logarithm of

$$\left(\sum_{\text{pk}\in\mathcal{U}} z_{\text{pk}}\right) - s_k \cdot [h_\ell] = \left(\sum_{\text{pk}\in\mathcal{U}} [\boldsymbol{y}_{\text{pk}}^T \boldsymbol{x}_{\text{pk}} + \boldsymbol{y}_{\text{pk}}^T \boldsymbol{s}_{\text{pk},\mathcal{U}} h_\ell]\right) - \left(\sum_{\text{pk}\in\mathcal{U}} \boldsymbol{y}_{\text{pk}}^T \boldsymbol{s}_{\text{pk},\mathcal{U}}\right) \cdot [h_\ell]$$

$$= \left[\sum_{\text{pk}\in\mathcal{U}} \boldsymbol{y}_{\text{pk}}^T \boldsymbol{x}_{\text{pk}} + \boldsymbol{y}_{\text{pk}}^T \boldsymbol{s}_{\text{pk},\mathcal{U}} h_\ell\right] - \left[\sum_{\text{pk}\in\mathcal{U}} \boldsymbol{y}_{\text{pk}}^T \boldsymbol{s}_{\text{pk},\mathcal{U}} h_\ell\right] = \left[\sum_{\text{pk}\in\mathcal{U}} \boldsymbol{y}_{\text{pk}}^T \boldsymbol{x}_{\text{pk}}\right]$$

7.3   Security Proof

Theorem 26 (sel-sym-IND-Security of our IP-DDFE). *The Inner-Product DDFE scheme described in Sect. 7.2 is sel-sym-IND-secure (as per Definition 5) under the DDH assumption, assuming IP-FE is sel-IND secure, the AoNE scheme is sel-sym-IND-secure, the DSum scheme is sel-sym-IND-secure, and $(\mathcal{F}_K)_K$ is a secure PRF family.*

The proof can be found in the full version [18].

Acknowledgments. This work was supported in part by the European Community's Seventh Framework Programme (FP7/2007-2013 Grant Agreement no. 339563 – CryptoCloud), the European Community's Horizon 2020 Project FENTEC (Grant Agreement no. 780108), the Google PhD fellowship, and the French FUI ANBLIC Project. This work was partially done while the third author was visiting ENS, Paris, and UC Berkeley, California.

A   Single-Input FE for Inner Products

Here we recall the IPFE from [7] on a cyclic group $\mathbb{G}$. Its IND security is proven in [7], under the DDH assumption in $\mathbb{G}$.

- IP-FE.KeyGen($\mathbb{G}, d \in \mathbb{N}$): $\boldsymbol{a} \xleftarrow{\$} \text{DDH}$, $\mathbf{U} \xleftarrow{\$} \mathbb{Z}_p^{d\times 2}$, pk $= ([\boldsymbol{a}], [\mathbf{U}\boldsymbol{a}])$, msk $= \mathbf{U}$. Return (pk, msk).
- IP-FE.Enc(pk, $\boldsymbol{x} \in \mathbb{Z}_p^d$): $r \xleftarrow{\$} \mathbb{Z}_p$, return $\begin{bmatrix} \boldsymbol{a}r \\ \boldsymbol{x} + \mathbf{U}\boldsymbol{a}r \end{bmatrix} \in \mathbb{G}^{d+2}$.
- IP-FE.DKeyGen(msk, $\boldsymbol{y} \in \mathbb{Z}_p^d$): return $\begin{pmatrix} -\mathbf{U}^\top \boldsymbol{y} \\ \boldsymbol{y} \end{pmatrix} \in \mathbb{Z}_p^{d+2}$.
- IP-FE.Dec(pk, $[\boldsymbol{c}], \boldsymbol{k}$): return $[\boldsymbol{c}]^\top \boldsymbol{k} \in \mathbb{G}$.

B   Security Proof: Theorem 22 (IND-Security of AoNE)

The All-or-Nothing Encapsulation scheme described in Sect. 4.2 is IND-secure (as per Definition 3) assuming the IBE scheme is IND-secure (as per Definition 17).

Proof. Let q_p, q_c denote (polynomial) upper bounds on the number of adversary queries to the QNewHonest oracle, and the number of *unique* pairs $(\mathcal{U}_M, \ell)$ for which the adversary sends at least one QEncrypt or QLeftRight query, respectively. We define the following games for $i \in \{0, \ldots, q_c\}$:

Game $\mathbf{G}_i$: The challenger does as specified in Definition 3, except for queries to QLeftRight. Queries to QLeftRight take as arguments a public key pk and two messages $m_0 = (x_0, \mathcal{U}_{M,0}, \ell_0)$ and $m_1 = (x_1, \mathcal{U}_{M,1}, \ell_1)$. Note that by functionality and by description of the scheme, the response reveals $\mathcal{U}_{M,b}, \ell_b$, so if the adversary wants to avoid the Finalize condition ignoring its guess, it must have $\ell_0 = \ell_1 = \ell$ and $\mathcal{U}_{M,0} = \mathcal{U}_{M,1} = \mathcal{U}_M$. Now let $(\mathcal{U}_{M,j}, \ell_j)$ be the j'th such pair queried to QEncrypt or QLeftRight. In $\mathbf{G}_i$, the challenger will respond to QLeftRight queries by encrypting m_0 if $i < j$ and m_b otherwise, where $b \xleftarrow{\$} \{0,1\}$ is the random bit chosen by the challenger.

Note that in $\mathbf{G}_0$, all challenge ciphertexts contain the left message, while in $\mathbf{G}_{q_c}$ all challenge ciphertexts contain the right message. Thus we only need to show that $\mathbf{G}_{i-1} \sim_c \mathbf{G}_i$ for all $i \in [q_c]$.

$\mathbf{G}_{i-1} \sim_c \mathbf{G}_i$: We proceed by contradiction, and, from a PPT adversary $\mathcal{A}$ which can distinguish between $\mathbf{G}_{i-1}$ and $\mathbf{G}_i$ with noticeable advantage, we construct a PPT algorithm $\mathcal{B}$ which breaks the IND-security of IBE with noticeable advantage.

$\mathcal{B}$ starts playing the IBE IND-security game and gets a public key IBE.pk. We need to choose the participant whose AoNE public key will be AoNE.pk = IBE.pk carefully, because we wont be able to answer QDKeyGen requests for them. The key is to notice that if the adversary is going to distinguish between $\mathbf{G}_{i-1}$ and $\mathbf{G}_i$, the two need to be different, meaning the adversary $\mathcal{A}$ needs to make at least one query to QLeftRight on $(\mathcal{U}_{M,i}, \ell_i)$ with $x_0' \neq x_1'$ with noticeable probability, and that, conditioned on that event, $\mathcal{A}$ retains noticeable advantage. We can thus safely assume that $\mathcal{A}$ will make such a query, and abort otherwise. From then on, if it were the case that for every $\mathsf{pk} \in \mathcal{U}_M$, the adversary either makes a QEncrypt or QLeftRight query on $(\mathcal{U}_M, \ell)$ or pk is eventually not honest[4], then the condition in the Finalize part of the security game (see Definition 3) would notice that $x_0' \neq x_1'$ and set the adversary's guess at random, rendering the adversary's efforts fruitless. We can thus safely assume that there is a $\mathsf{pk}^* \in \mathcal{U}_M$ such that pk^* will be created via QNewHonest[5], and the adversary will not query QEncrypt or QLeftRight on $(\mathcal{U}_M, \ell)$ for pk^* or query QCorrupt on pk^*.

---

[4] Note that here there are two ways for pk to be dishonest: either the adversary has the challenger create pk via QNewHonest and later corrupts it via QCorrupt, or the adversary generates pk on its own.

[5] Note that here, and in subsequent proofs, we implicitly ignore the very real possibility that the adversary sends a query for a set $\mathcal{U}_M$ for which a *later* query to QNewHonest generates a $\mathsf{pk} \in \mathcal{U}_M$. Because this happens with negligible probability it is safe to abort when this situation materializes.

We proceed by guessing which query to QNewHonest will eventually be pk^*. We cannot simply guess a member of $\mathcal{U}_M$ because we do not know anything about $\mathcal{U}_M$ during the initialization phase of the game, and by the time the ith $(\mathcal{U}_M, \ell)$ pair is queried, it is possible that many queries have been made to the QNewHonest oracle, and at that point it would be too late to embed the IBE public key in the adversary's view. Instead, we guess the index $t^* \in [q_p]$ of the query to QNewHonest which eventually yields a public key pk_{t^*} which we hope matches pk^*. At that index, we respond with $\mathsf{pk}_{t^*} = \mathsf{IBE.pk}$. Because the adversary will only make polynomially many queries to QNewHonest, our advantage is only polynomially degraded by this guess and the reduction remains valid.

Having done this, we can naturally answer most queries involving pk_{t^*} by using the oracles of the IND security game of IBE and the fact that our IBE is public key. That is, we answer all QEncrypt and most (see below) QLeftRight queries by running IBE.Encrypt ourselves and making IBE.QDKeyGen queries.

The exceptions are QLeftRight queries to any $\mathsf{pk} \in \mathcal{U}_M$ for $(\mathcal{U}_M, \ell)$. Let $n = |\mathcal{U}_M|$ and $\zeta \in [n]$ be such that pk^* is the ζth public key in $\mathcal{U}_M$ for the universally agreed upon order. In responding to $\mathsf{QLeftRight}(\mathsf{pk}, (x_0, \mathcal{U}_M, \ell), (x_1, \mathcal{U}_M, \ell))$, we will compute two sequences of α's as follows: for $s \in \{0, 1\}$, $k \in [\zeta - 1]$, let $\alpha^s_{\mathsf{pk},0} = x_s$ and $\alpha_{\mathsf{pk},k} = \mathsf{IBE.Encrypt}(\mathsf{pk}_k, (\alpha_{\mathsf{pk},k-1}, \mathcal{U}_M || \ell))$. Now compute $\alpha_{\mathsf{pk},\zeta} = \mathsf{IBE.QLeftRight}((\alpha^0_{\mathsf{pk},\zeta-1}, \mathcal{U}_M || \ell), (\alpha^1_{\mathsf{pk},\zeta-1}, \mathcal{U}_M || \ell))$, and compute the rest of the α's and the resulting ciphertext as per AoNE.Encrypt.

When $\mathsf{IBE}.b = 0$, the adversary $\mathcal{A}$ is playing $\mathbf{G}_{i-1}$. When $\mathsf{IBE}.b = 1$, the adversary $\mathcal{A}$ is playing $\mathbf{G}_i$. We only need to check that we do not violate the Finalize condition of the IBE IND-security game. But this is clear because the only IBE.QLeftRight query we make is for $(\mathcal{U}_M, \ell)$, and for that pair we never get a AoNE.QLeftRight or AoNE.QEncrypt query so we never make an IBE.QDKeyGen query. This concludes our proof. $\square$

References

1. Abdalla, M., Benhamouda, F., Gay, R.: From single-input to multi-client inner-product functional encryption. In: Galbraith, S.D., Moriai, S. (eds.) ASIACRYPT 2019, Part III. LNCS, vol. 11923, pp. 552–582. Springer, Cham (2019). https://doi.org/10.1007/978-3-030-34618-8_19

2. Abdalla, M., Benhamouda, F., Kohlweiss, M., Waldner, H.: Decentralizing inner-product functional encryption. In: Lin, D., Sako, K. (eds.) PKC 2019, Part II. LNCS, vol. 11443, pp. 128–157. Springer, Cham (2019). https://doi.org/10.1007/978-3-030-17259-6_5

3. Abdalla, M., Bourse, F., De Caro, A., Pointcheval, D.: Simple functional encryption schemes for inner products. In: Katz, J. (ed.) PKC 2015. LNCS, vol. 9020, pp. 733–751. Springer, Heidelberg (2015). https://doi.org/10.1007/978-3-662-46447-2_33

4. Abdalla, M., Catalano, D., Fiore, D., Gay, R., Ursu, B.: Multi-input functional encryption for inner products: function-hiding realizations and constructions without pairings. In: Shacham, H., Boldyreva, A. (eds.) CRYPTO 2018, Part I. LNCS, vol. 10991, pp. 597–627. Springer, Cham (2018). https://doi.org/10.1007/978-3-319-96884-1_20

5. Abdalla, M., Gay, R., Raykova, M., Wee, H.: Multi-input inner-product functional encryption from pairings. In: Coron, J.-S., Nielsen, J.B. (eds.) EUROCRYPT 2017, Part I. LNCS, vol. 10210, pp. 601–626. Springer, Cham (2017). https://doi.org/10.1007/978-3-319-56620-7_21

6. Agrawal, S., Clear, M., Frieder, O., Garg, S., O'Neill, A., Thaler, J.: Ad hoc multi-input functional encryption. In: 11th Innovations in Theoretical Computer Science Conference (ITCS 2020). Schloss Dagstuhl-Leibniz-Zentrum für Informatik (2020)

7. Agrawal, S., Libert, B., Stehlé, D.: Fully secure functional encryption for inner products, from standard assumptions. In: Robshaw, M., Katz, J. (eds.) CRYPTO 2016, Part III. LNCS, vol. 9816, pp. 333–362. Springer, Heidelberg (2016). https://doi.org/10.1007/978-3-662-53015-3_12

8. Benhamouda, F., Joye, M., Libert, B.: A new framework for privacy-preserving aggregation of time-series data. ACM Trans. Inf. Syst. Secur. **18**(3), 10:1–10:21 (2016)

9. Boneh, D., Boyen, X., Goh, E.-J.: Hierarchical identity based encryption with constant size ciphertext. In: Cramer, R. (ed.) EUROCRYPT 2005. LNCS, vol. 3494, pp. 440–456. Springer, Heidelberg (2005). https://doi.org/10.1007/11426639_26

10. Boneh, D., Franklin, M.: Identity-based encryption from the Weil pairing. In: Kilian, J. (ed.) CRYPTO 2001. LNCS, vol. 2139, pp. 213–229. Springer, Heidelberg (2001). https://doi.org/10.1007/3-540-44647-8_13

11. Boneh, D., Sahai, A., Waters, B.: Functional encryption: definitions and challenges. In: Ishai, Y. (ed.) TCC 2011. LNCS, vol. 6597, pp. 253–273. Springer, Heidelberg (2011). https://doi.org/10.1007/978-3-642-19571-6_16

12. Brakerski, Z., Segev, G.: Function-private functional encryption in the private-key setting. In: Dodis, Y., Nielsen, J.B. (eds.) TCC 2015, Part II. LNCS, vol. 9015, pp. 306–324. Springer, Heidelberg (2015). https://doi.org/10.1007/978-3-662-46497-7_12

13. Cash, D., Kiltz, E., Shoup, V.: The twin Diffie-Hellman problem and applications. In: Smart, N. (ed.) EUROCRYPT 2008. LNCS, vol. 4965, pp. 127–145. Springer, Heidelberg (2008). https://doi.org/10.1007/978-3-540-78967-3_8

14. Chan, T.-H.H., Shi, E., Song, D.: Privacy-preserving stream aggregation with fault tolerance. In: Keromytis, A.D. (ed.) FC 2012. LNCS, vol. 7397, pp. 200–214. Springer, Heidelberg (2012). https://doi.org/10.1007/978-3-642-32946-3_15

15. Chandran, N., Goyal, V., Jain, A., Sahai, A.: Functional encryption: decentralised and delegatable. Cryptology ePrint Archive, Report 2015/1017 (2015). http://eprint.iacr.org/2015/1017

16. Chase, M., Chow, S.S.M.: Improving privacy and security in multi-authority attribute-based encryption. In: Al-Shaer, E., Jha, S., Keromytis, A.D. (eds.) ACM CCS 2009, pp. 121–130. ACM Press, New York (2009)

17. Chotard, J., Dufour Sans, E., Gay, R., Phan, D.H., Pointcheval, D.: Decentralized multi-client functional encryption for inner product. In: Peyrin, T., Galbraith, S. (eds.) ASIACRYPT 2018, Part II. LNCS, vol. 11273, pp. 703–732. Springer, Cham (2018). https://doi.org/10.1007/978-3-030-03329-3_24

18. Chotard, J., Dufour-Sans, E., Gay, R., Phan, D.H., Pointcheval, D.: Dynamic decentralized functional encryption. Cryptology ePrint Archive, Report 2020/197 (2020). https://eprint.iacr.org/2020/197

19. Cocks, C.: An identity based encryption scheme based on quadratic residues. In: Honary, B. (ed.) Cryptography and Coding 2001. LNCS, vol. 2260, pp. 360–363. Springer, Heidelberg (2001). https://doi.org/10.1007/3-540-45325-3_32

20. Döttling, N., Garg, S.: Identity-based encryption from the Diffie-Hellman assumption. In: Katz, J., Shacham, H. (eds.) CRYPTO 2017, Part I. LNCS, vol. 10401, pp. 537–569. Springer, Cham (2017). https://doi.org/10.1007/978-3-319-63688-7_18

21. Escala, A., Herold, G., Kiltz, E., Ràfols, C., Villar, J.: An algebraic framework for Diffie-Hellman assumptions. In: Canetti, R., Garay, J.A. (eds.) CRYPTO 2013, Part II. LNCS, vol. 8043, pp. 129–147. Springer, Heidelberg (2013). https://doi.org/10.1007/978-3-642-40084-1_8

22. Freire, E.S.V., Hofheinz, D., Kiltz, E., Paterson, K.G.: Non-interactive key exchange. In: Kurosawa, K., Hanaoka, G. (eds.) PKC 2013. LNCS, vol. 7778, pp. 254–271. Springer, Heidelberg (2013). https://doi.org/10.1007/978-3-642-36362-7_17

23. Gentry, C.: Fully homomorphic encryption using ideal lattices. In: Mitzenmacher, M. (ed.) 41st ACM STOC, pp. 169–178. ACM Press, New York (2009)

24. Gentry, C., Peikert, C., Vaikuntanathan, V.: Trapdoors for hard lattices and new cryptographic constructions. In: Ladner, R.E., Dwork, C. (eds.) 40th ACM STOC, pp. 197–206. ACM Press, New York (2008)

25. Goldwasser, S., et al.: Multi-input functional encryption. In: Nguyen, P.Q., Oswald, E. (eds.) EUROCRYPT 2014. LNCS, vol. 8441, pp. 578–602. Springer, Heidelberg (2014). https://doi.org/10.1007/978-3-642-55220-5_32

26. Gordon, S.D., Katz, J., Liu, F.H., Shi, E., Zhou, H.S.: Multi-input functional encryption. Cryptology ePrint Archive, Report 2013/774 (2013). http://eprint.iacr.org/2013/774

27. Goyal, V., Pandey, O., Sahai, A., Waters, B.: Attribute-based encryption for fine-grained access control of encrypted data. In: Juels, A., Wright, R.N., De Capitani di Vimercati, S. (eds.) ACM CCS 2006, pp. 89–98. ACM Press, New York (2006). Available as Cryptology ePrint Archive Report 2006/309

28. Joye, M., Libert, B.: A scalable scheme for privacy-preserving aggregation of time-series data. In: Sadeghi, A.-R. (ed.) FC 2013. LNCS, vol. 7859, pp. 111–125. Springer, Heidelberg (2013). https://doi.org/10.1007/978-3-642-39884-1_10

29. Lewko, A., Waters, B.: Decentralizing attribute-based encryption. In: Paterson, K.G. (ed.) EUROCRYPT 2011. LNCS, vol. 6632, pp. 568–588. Springer, Heidelberg (2011). https://doi.org/10.1007/978-3-642-20465-4_31

30. Libert, B., Ţiţiu, R.: Multi-client functional encryption for linear functions in the standard model from LWE. In: Galbraith, S.D., Moriai, S. (eds.) ASIACRYPT 2019, Part III. LNCS, vol. 11923, pp. 520–551. Springer, Cham (2019). https://doi.org/10.1007/978-3-030-34618-8_18

31. López-Alt, A., Tromer, E., Vaikuntanathan, V.: On-the-fly multiparty computation on the cloud via multikey fully homomorphic encryption. In: Karloff, H.J., Pitassi, T. (eds.) 44th ACM STOC, pp. 1219–1234. ACM Press, New York (2012)

32. Sahai, A., Waters, B.: Fuzzy identity-based encryption. In: Cramer, R. (ed.) EUROCRYPT 2005. LNCS, vol. 3494, pp. 457–473. Springer, Heidelberg (2005). https://doi.org/10.1007/11426639_27

33. Shamir, A.: Identity-based cryptosystems and signature schemes. In: Blakley, G.R., Chaum, D. (eds.) CRYPTO 1984. LNCS, vol. 196, pp. 47–53. Springer, Heidelberg (1985). https://doi.org/10.1007/3-540-39568-7_5

34. Shi, E., Chan, T.H.H., Rieffel, E.G., Chow, R., Song, D.: Privacy-preserving aggregation of time-series data. In: NDSS 2011. The Internet Society, February 2011

On Succinct Arguments and Witness Encryption from Groups

Ohad Barta[1]([⊠]), Yuval Ishai[1]([⊠]), Rafail Ostrovsky[2]([⊠]), and David J. Wu[3]([⊠])

[1] Technion, Haifa, Israel
{ohadba,yuvali}@cs.technion.ac.il
[2] UCLA, Los Angeles, CA, USA
rafail@cs.ucla.edu
[3] University of Virginia, Charlottesville, VA, USA
dwu4@virginia.edu

Abstract. Succinct non-interactive arguments (SNARGs) enable proofs of NP statements with very low communication. Recently, there has been significant work in both theory and practice on constructing SNARGs with very short proofs. Currently, the state-of-the-art in succinctness is due to Groth (Eurocrypt 2016) who constructed a SNARG from *bilinear* maps where the proof consists of just 3 group elements.

In this work, we first construct a concretely-efficient designated-verifier (preprocessing) SNARG with inverse polynomial soundness, where the proof consists of just 2 group elements in a *standard* (generic) group. This leads to a 50% reduction in concrete proof size compared to Groth's construction. We follow the approach of Bitansky et al. (TCC 2013) who describe a compiler from linear PCPs to SNARGs in the preprocessing model. Our improvement is based on a new *linear PCP packing* technique that allows us to construct 1-query linear PCPs which can then be compiled into a SNARG (using ElGamal encryption over a generic group). An appealing feature of our new SNARG is that the verifier can precompute a *statement-independent* lookup table in an offline

O. Barta—Supported by ERC Project NTSC (742754).
Y. Ishai—Supported by ERC Project NTSC (742754), NSF-BSF grant 2015782, BSF grant 2018393, and a joint Israel-India grant. Part of this work was done while visiting the Simons Institute for the Theory of Computing.
R. Ostrovsky—Supported in part by DARPA under Cooperative Agreement No. HR0011-20-2-0025, NSF-BSF Grant 1619348, US-Israel BSF grant 2012366, Google Faculty Award, JP Morgan Faculty Award, IBM Faculty Research Award, Xerox Faculty Research Award, OKAWA Foundation Research Award, B. John Garrick Foundation Award, Teradata Research Award, and Lockheed-Martin Corporation Research Award. The views and conclusions contained herein are those of the authors and should not be interpreted as necessarily representing the official policies, either expressed or implied, of DARPA, the Department of Defense, or the U.S. Government. The U.S. Government is authorized to reproduce and distribute reprints for governmental purposes not withstanding any copyright annotation therein.
D. J. Wu—Supported by NSF CNS-1917414 and a University of Virginia SEAS Research Innovation Award. Part of this work was done while visiting the Simons Institute for the Theory of Computing.

D. Micciancio and T. Ristenpart (Eds.): CRYPTO 2020, LNCS 12170, pp. 776–806, 2020.
https://doi.org/10.1007/978-3-030-56784-2_26

phase; verifying proofs then only requires 2 exponentiations and a single table lookup. This makes our new designated-verifier SNARG appealing in settings that demand fast verification and minimal communication.

We then turn to the question of constructing arguments where the proof consists of a *single* group element. Here, we first show that any (possibly interactive) argument for a language $\mathcal{L}$ where the verification algorithm is "generic" (i.e., only performs generic group operations) and the proof consists of a single group element, implies a *witness encryption* scheme for $\mathcal{L}$. We then show that under a yet-unproven, but highly plausible, hypothesis on the hardness of approximating the minimal distance of linear codes, we can construct a 2-message laconic argument for NP where the proof consists of a single group element. Under the same hypothesis, we obtain a witness encryption scheme for NP in the generic group model. Along the way, we show that under a conceptually-similar but *proven* hardness of approximation result, there is a 2-message laconic argument for NP with negligible soundness error where the prover's message consists of just 2 group elements. In both settings, we obtain laconic arguments (and linear PCPs) with *linear* decision procedures. Our constructions circumvent a previous lower bound by Groth on such argument systems with linear decision procedures by relying on *imperfect completeness*. Namely, our constructions have vanishing but not negligible completeness error, while the lower bound of Groth implicitly assumes negligible completeness error of the underlying argument. Our techniques thus highlight new avenues for designing linear PCPs, succinct arguments, and witness encryption schemes.

1   Introduction

Interactive proof systems [GMR85] provide a general framework that allows a verifier to efficiently check claims made by a (possibly malicious) prover. The two properties we require from an interactive proof system are completeness, which says that an honest prover should successfully convince an honest verifier of a true statement, and soundness, which says that a malicious prover should not be able to convince an honest verifier of a false statement, except perhaps with small probability.

An important metric in the design of interactive proof systems is the *communication complexity*, and specifically, the amount of communication from the prover to the verifier. For an NP language, an interactive proof system is said to be *laconic* or *succinct* if the total communication from the prover to the verifier is *sublinear* in the size of the NP witness. In the setting of general NP languages, non-trivial savings in the prover-to-verifier communication (beyond sending the classic NP witness) are unlikely if we require the proof system to be statistically sound (i.e., sound even against an unbounded prover) [BHZ87,GH98,GVW01,Wee05]. If we relax the requirements and only consider proof systems with computational soundness (known as "argument systems" [BCC88]), significant efficiency improvements are possible. Starting from the seminal work of Kilian [Kil92] who gave the first construction of an interactive laconic argument from probabilistically check-able proofs (PCPs) and collision-resistant hash functions, a long sequence of works have constructed interactive laconic arguments and succinct non-interactive arguments ("SNARGs" [GW11]) for general NP languages where the communication is polylogarithmic in the size of the classic NP wit-ness (cf. [Mic00, Mie08, CL08, Gro10, BCCT12, Lip12, BC12, GGPR13, BCI+13, DFGK14, Gro16, BCC+16, BCC+17, BISW17, BBB+18, BISW18, BBHR19] and the references therein).

Minimizing proof size. A long sequence of works, beginning with Groth's con-struction of a succinct argument with a *constant* number of bilinear group elements [Gro10], has sought to minimize the proof size in SNARGs for NP. Groth's initial construction had proofs with 42 group elements; this was later reduced to 39 elements by Lipmaa [Lip12]. In both constructions, the prover complexity was quadratic in the size of the NP verification circuit. Subse-quently, using a new characterization of NP based on quadratic span programs, Gennaro et al. [GGPR13] showed how to construct SNARGs where the proof con-sists of just 7 group elements and where the prover computation is quasi-linear in the size of the verification circuit. Bitansky et al. [BCI+13] introduced a more abstract view of quadratic span programs as implying a "linear PCP," where a verifier can make a small number of inner product queries to a proof vector, and described a general compiler from linear PCPs to SNARGs using a notion called linear-only encryption. A similar compiler was implicit in [GGPR13], and both of these works follow the high-level blueprint introduced in [IKO07, Gro10]. Danezis et al. [DFGK14] subsequently refined quadratic span programs to square span programs and showed how to construct succinct arguments with just 4 group elements. This line of work culminated with [Gro16], which showed how to construct succinct arguments with just 3 group elements and with very effi-cient verification. These advances in constructing highly succinct arguments with lightweight verification have served as the basis for a number of efficient imple-mentations [PHGR13, BCG+13, BCG+14, BBFR15]. The work of Groth [Gro16] raises the following natural question on the possibility of even shorter proofs:

Can we construct succinct arguments where
the proof consists of just one or two group elements?

Bitansky et al. [BCI+13] previously showed that by instantiating their com-piler with a linear PCP built from classic PCPs (e.g., [ALM+98]) and with the ElGamal encryption scheme [ElG84], one can obtain a designated-verifier SNARG in which the proof consists of just two group elements. (Note that in the designated-verifier setting, the verifier possesses a *secret* key that it uses to check proofs [KMO89].) A limitation of the construction from [BCI+13] is the inherent reliance on "classic" PCPs, where the verifier is restricted to read individual symbols of the proof instead of the inner-product queries of a linear PCP. This greatly reduces the concrete efficiency of the resulting construction in comparison to alternative pairing-based constructions and implementations.

This work. In this work, we develop new techniques for constructing designated-verifier SNARGs[1] (and laconic arguments) where the proof size consists of just two group elements. In particular, we provide the following new constructions:

- **Concretely-efficient SNARGs with 2 group elements:** We introduce a new "packing" technique for constructing *1-query* linear PCPs from k-query linear PCPs. We then apply the compiler from [BCI+13], in conjunction with ElGamal encryption,[2] to obtain a designated-verifier SNARG where the proofs consist of two group elements (in a *pairing-free* group). Compared to the pairing-based SNARGs of [Gro16], our arguments are *half* as long (64 bytes vs. 127 bytes), and moreover, with a precomputed verification table, the verification complexity of our SNARG requires only 2 group exponentiations (and 2 multiplications), which is faster than that of [Gro16], which requires 3 pairing operations and multiple exponentiations/multiplications. Compared to [BCI+13], our SNARGs are based on *linear PCPs* rather than classical PCPs, so they also enjoy concretely-efficient prover complexities for small circuits. At the same time, compared to [Gro16], our constructions are in the designated-verifier setting, have a quadratic-size CRS (as opposed to a linear-size CRS), and provide inverse polynomial soundness (as opposed to negligible soundness). However, the fast verification time and shorter proof size make our construction naturally suited for a number of scenarios (see Sect. 1.1).

- **Laconic arguments with 2 group elements and negligible soundness:** The SNARGs obtained by combining a 1-query linear PCP in conjunction with ElGamal encryption have inverse polynomial soundness error. This limitation is due to two factors: (1) the linear PCP verification procedure is *non-linear* in the responses (for both the original [BCI+13] proposal based on standard PCPs as well as the linear PCPs obtained via our packing transformation); and (2) decryption in the (additively homomorphic variant of) ElGamal encryption requires computing a discrete log. If however we can construct a 1-query linear PCP with negligible soundness error and where the decision procedure is *linear*, then we can apply the [BCI+13] compiler (with ElGamal) to obtain a 2-element SNARG with negligible soundness error. On the one hand, [Gro16] previously showed a lower bound that such a linear PCP *cannot* exist. However, this previous lower bound only applies if the underlying linear PCP has sufficiently small completeness error (see the full version of this paper). In this work, by relying on hardness of approximation for problems related to linear codes, we obtain a 1-query linear PCP with a linear decision procedure, negligible soundness error, and $o(1)$ completeness error. The linear PCP we obtain has the property that the verifier's

---

[1] As we discuss in greater detail in Sect. 1.1, our constructions naturally extend via standard techniques to provide *zero-knowledge* and *arguments of knowledge* (namely, they are "zkSNARKs"). For simplicity of exposition, we just focus on SNARGs here.

[2] Specifically, we rely on the assumption that the ElGamal encryption scheme satisfies linear targeted malleability [BSW12, BCI+13]. We show in the full version of this paper that this holds in the standard generic group model [Nec94, Sho97].

queries depend on the statement, and as such, we do not obtain a SNARG via the [BCI+13] compiler. Instead, we obtain the first laconic argument for NP where the prover's message consists of just 2 group elements and has negligible soundness error (either unconditionally in the generic group model or assuming linear targeted malleability of ElGamal).

– **Laconic arguments with 1 group element:** We then turn to the question of whether we can *further* reduce the communication complexity. Here, under a yet-unproven, but highly plausible, hypothesis on the hardness of approximating the minimal distance of linear codes (Hypothesis 5.2), we construct a 2-message laconic argument for NP where the prover's message consists of just a single group element. We note that while there is a linear PCP associated with this language, our 1-element laconic argument construction does not follow the [BCI+13] compiler, and it is not clear how to leverage the [BCI+13] compiler to obtain an argument system where the proof is a single group element. Instead, we give a direct construction of a 1-element laconic argument that is provably secure in the generic group model.

We summarize our main new constructions of SNARGs and laconic arguments in Table 1 and also compare against existing results.

From laconic arguments to witness encryption. Several works [FNV17, BISW18, BDRV18] have studied the connection between laconic arguments and different types of encryption schemes. Notably, Faonio et al. [FNV17] show that any (even non-laconic) argument of knowledge for a language $\mathcal{L}$ where the verifier can *predict* in advance the prover's message implies an extractable *witness encryption* [GGSW13] scheme for $\mathcal{L}$. As noted in [FNV17], their construction also shows an equivalence between predictable arguments (*without* knowledge) and (non-extractable) witness encryption.

Boneh et al. [BISW18] subsequently showed that any 1-bit argument system is predictable for languages that are hard on average. In this work, we show that a conceptually-similar result holds for argument systems where the proof consists of a *single* group element. In particular, we show that any such argument system that has negligible soundness error, and where the verification algorithm can be implemented by a "generic" algorithm (i.e., it only performs generic group operations on the proof), must also be predictable. By [FNV17], such an argument system for a language $\mathcal{L}$ implies a witness encryption scheme for $\mathcal{L}$.

As noted above, if our hypothesis on the hardness of approximation for the minimal distance of linear codes holds, then we obtain a laconic argument for NP with negligible soundness error and where the proof consists of a single group element in the generic group model. Appealing now to the results above, this implies a witness encryption scheme for NP in the generic group model. We stress that, in the generic group model, this result does *not* rely on any cryptographic assumptions; it only relies on a plausible hardness of approximation result that may be *unconditionally* proved in the future. Indeed, there are no known barriers for strengthening the current hardness results to this more demanding parameter regime [Kho20]. Existing constructions of witness encryption all rely on conjectures related to indistinguishability obfuscation [GGH+13],

Table 1. Comparison of our group-based arguments to previous related results. In the "Proof Type" column, SNARG and dvSNARG refer to publicly-verifiable and designated-verifier SNARGs, respectively, and LA refers to 2-message laconic arguments where the verifier's initial message depends on the statement being proved. Verifier time counts group operations as a function of the size s of the classic NP verifier, ignoring polylogarithmic factors, and excluding quasilinear-time preprocessing of the input. An ε-subscript treats the soundness error ε as constant. In the last column, LPCP refers to proof systems obtained from any *linear* PCP whereas PCP refers to proof systems that are based on classical PCPs. The latter do not enjoy reusable soundness and have a very high concrete cost.

	Group Type	Number of Elements	Completeness Error	Soundness Error	Proof Type	Verifier Time	PCP vs. LPCP
[Gro16]	bilinear	$2\mathbb{G}_1, 1\mathbb{G}_2$	0	negl	SNARG	$O(1)$	LPCP
[BCI+13]	linear	8	0	1/poly	dvSNARG	$O_\varepsilon(s)$	LPCP
[BCI+13]	linear	2	0	1/poly	dvSNARG	$O_\varepsilon(1)$	PCP
Cor. 3.6	linear	2	0	1/poly	dvSNARG	$O_\varepsilon(s)$	LPCP
Cor. 3.7	linear	2	negl	1/poly	dvSNARG	$O_\varepsilon(\sqrt{s})$	LPCP
Cor. 3.8	linear	2	negl	1/poly	dvSNARG	$O_\varepsilon(1)^*$	LPCP
Sect. 4	linear	2	$o(1)$	negl	LA	$O(1)$	PCP
Sect. 5[†]	linear	1	$o(1)$	negl	LA	$O(1)$	PCP

[*] Using reusable statement-independent prepossessing with $O_\varepsilon(\sqrt{s})$ bits of storage.
[†] This is a conditional result that relies on a plausible (but yet unproven) hypothesis about hardness of approximation of minimal distance of codes (Hypothesis 5.2).

multilinear maps [GGSW13, GLW14, CVW18], or new and yet unexplored algebraic structures [BIJ+20]; thus, a construction in the generic group model would be considered a major development in this area.

Another intriguing implication of this result is that it effectively rules out negative results for constructing witness encryption unconditionally in the generic group model. Such negative results (or barriers) are not only known for powerful primitives such as indistinguishability obfuscation [MMN+16a, MMN+16b], but also for conceptually-simpler primitives such as identity-based encryption [PRV12]. Note that even though identity-based encryption can be built from witness encryption for NP (together with a unique signature scheme) [GGSW13], the resulting construction makes non-black-box use of the group. Thus, a construction of witness encryption in the generic group model does not conflict with existing lower bounds. Indeed, an impossibility result for constructing witness encryption in the generic group model would falsify our hypothesis.

1.1 Concretely-Efficient SNARGs with 2 Group Elements

In this section, we provide an overview of our concretely-efficient SNARGs where the proof consists of 2 group elements. Our starting point in this work is the compiler from [BCI+13] (also implicit in [GGPR13]) that compiles a linear PCP into a SNARG in the preprocessing model using a "linear-only" encryption scheme (i.e., an additively-homomorphic encryption scheme that only supports affine operations on ciphertexts).[3] Here, the preprocessing model refers to a SNARG where the running time of the setup algorithm is allowed to depend polynomially in the size of the classic NP verifier. We begin with a brief overview of this compiler.

Linear PCPs. A linear PCP for an NP language $\mathcal{L}$ over a finite field $\mathbb{F}$ is defined by a linear oracle $\boldsymbol{\pi} \colon \mathbb{F}^\ell \to \mathbb{F}$. On a query $\mathbf{q} \in \mathbb{F}^\ell$, the linear PCP oracle responds with the inner product $\mathbf{q}^\mathsf{T} \boldsymbol{\pi}$. More generally, we can view the linear PCP queries as the columns of a query matrix $\mathbf{Q} \in \mathbb{F}^{\ell \times k}$ and the oracle's operation as computing $\mathbf{Q}^\mathsf{T} \boldsymbol{\pi}$. To verify a proof of a statement $\mathbf{x}$, the verifier submits a query matrix $\mathbf{Q}$ to the oracle and receives back a set of responses $\mathbf{Q}^\mathsf{T} \boldsymbol{\pi}$. In this case, k denotes the number of linear PCP queries the verifier makes. For the language of Boolean circuit satisfiability, there exist efficient 3-query linear PCPs based on the quadratic span programs of [GGPR13] with query length $\ell = O(s)$, where s is the size of the Boolean circuit. We can also construct 2-query linear PCPs based on the Walsh-Hadamard code where $\ell = O(s^2)$. This improves the 3-query construction from [ALM+98,IKO07].

The Bitansky et al. compiler. The Bitansky et al. [BCI+13] compiler takes any linear PCP and a linear-only encryption scheme and outputs a preprocessing SNARG. If the linear PCP satisfies additional properties such as zero-knowledge or knowledge soundness, then the resulting SNARG also inherits those properties (i.e., we can obtain a "zkSNARK"). The idea behind the [BCI+13] compiler is the following: first, they compile a linear PCP into a two-message linear interactive proof (LIP) by introducing an additional consistency check. In this model, the prover is allowed to compute any *affine* function of the verifier's queries (the linear PCP model is more constrained in the sense that the prover has to apply the *same* linear function to each of the verifier's queries). To go from a LIP to a preprocessing SNARG, [BCI+13] has the verifier encrypt its queries using a linear-only encryption scheme and publish the ciphertexts as part of the common reference string (CRS). To construct a proof, the prover takes its statement and witness, computes the linear function $\boldsymbol{\pi}$, and homomorphically evaluates $\boldsymbol{\pi}$ on the encrypted queries (this is possible since the prover's strategy is linear). The proof is the encrypted set of responses. In the designated-verifier model, the verifier decrypts the responses and applies the standard LIP verification procedure (if the verifier's decision procedure is quadratic, a pairing can be used to perform the verification check "in the exponent," yielding a publicly-verifiable SNARG). Overall, the [BCI+13] compiler takes any k-query linear PCP and compiles it into a preprocessing SNARG where the proofs consist of $(k + 1)$ ciphertexts of

---

[3] Technically, a weaker property called linear targeted malleability [BSW12] suffices for a basic version of the compiler. For ease of exposition, we present everything here using the concept of linear-only encryption. We formally define linear targeted malleability in the full version of this paper.

the underlying linear-only encryption scheme. Under the assumption that the classic ElGamal encryption scheme [ElG84] is linear-only (when the message is encrypted in the exponent), this framework can be used to obtain a SNARG where the proof size consists of $(k + 1)$ ElGamal ciphertexts, or equivalently, $2(k + 1)$ group elements.

1-query linear PCPs. First, we note that any 1-query linear PCP is itself a 2-message linear interactive proof, and hence, can be directly compiled into a preprocessing SNARG via the [BCI+13] compiler where the proof consists of just a *single* ciphertext (i.e., 2 group elements in the case of ElGamal). However, as noted above, efficient instantiations of linear PCPs based on the Hadamard PCP [ALM+98, IKO07], quadratic span programs [GGPR13] or square span programs [DFGK14, Gro16] all require *at least 2 queries*, and thus, cannot be directly compiled into a preprocessing SNARG with 2 group elements. If we start instead from a traditional PCP, then [BCI+13] shows how to construct a 1-query linear PCP, which in conjunction with ElGamal encryption, yields a SNARG with 2-group elements (and inverse polynomial soundness). However, the use of traditional PCPs in this construction incurs a high *concrete* cost, and as a result, the concrete efficiency of the resulting SNARG is not competitive with existing pairing-based constructions based on efficient linear PCPs. Furthermore, the low entropy of the queries in the PCP-based construction from [BCI+13] prevents the scheme from achieving reusable soundness.[4] In this work, we introduce a new approach to constructing 1-query linear PCPs *without* relying on traditional PCPs. The resulting 1-query linear PCP has reusable soundness.

Linear PCP packing. Our first result in this work is a method to *pack* a k-query linear PCP into a 1-query linear PCP. Our packing construction is most naturally viewed by considering a linear PCP *over the integers*.[5] Namely, consider a linear PCP where both the query matrix $\mathbf{Q} \in \mathbb{Z}^{\ell \times k}$ and the proof $\boldsymbol{\pi} \in \mathbb{Z}^\ell$ consist of vectors over the integers. Clearly, any linear PCP over a finite field $\mathbb{F}_p$ yields a linear PCP over the integers $\mathbb{Z}$. We now say that a linear PCP is B-bounded if for an honestly-generated query matrix $\mathbf{Q} \in \mathbb{Z}^{\ell \times k}$ and proof vector $\boldsymbol{\pi} \in \mathbb{Z}^\ell$, it follows that $\|\mathbf{Q}^\mathsf{T}\boldsymbol{\pi}\|_\infty < B$ (i.e., the magnitude of every response is less than B). Let $\mathbf{q}_1, \ldots, \mathbf{q}_k \in \mathbb{Z}^\ell$ be the individual queries (i.e., the columns of $\mathbf{Q}$). Consider the vector $\mathbf{q}_{\text{packed}} = \sum_{i \in [k]} B^{i-1}\mathbf{q}_i \in \mathbb{Z}^\ell$. Then,

$$a = \mathbf{q}_{\text{packed}}^\mathsf{T}\boldsymbol{\pi} = \sum_{i \in [k]} B^{i-1}\mathbf{q}_i^\mathsf{T}\boldsymbol{\pi} \in \mathbb{Z}.$$

If $|\mathbf{q}_i^\mathsf{T}\boldsymbol{\pi}| < B$, then a represents an integer in base B where the ith digit is the ith response $\mathbf{q}_i^\mathsf{T}\boldsymbol{\pi}$. Thus, by making a single query $\mathbf{q}_{\text{packed}}$ (with much *larger*

---

[4] Indeed, by flipping one bit of an honestly-generated PCP, a malicious prover can mount a selective failure attack that makes the verifier reject with high probability if this bit is being queried.

[5] While we present the general ideas using linear PCPs over the integers, the construction in Sect. 3 embeds the integer operations over a large finite field $\mathbb{F}_p$.

coefficients), the verifier is able to decode all k responses and implement the verification procedure for the underlying linear PCP. As described, the above approach is not sound: namely, an adversary can choose a malicious proof vector $\boldsymbol{\pi}$ such that $\mathbf{Q}^\mathsf{T}\boldsymbol{\pi}$ is not B-bounded: then, the tuple of responses decoded using the above procedure would yield a tuple that is not consistent with applying a single consistent linear strategy to all of the query vectors. We solve this problem by *randomizing* the query-packing procedure. Namely, instead of using a fixed scaling factor B, the verifier sets $r_1 = 1$ and samples $r_2, \ldots, r_k$ from a sufficiently-large interval and computes the packed query vector as $\mathbf{q}_{\text{packed}} = \sum_{i \in [k]} \mathbf{q}_i \prod_{j \leq i} r_j$. We can now argue that over the verifier's randomness, any adversarial strategy that exceeds the bound will cause the verifier to reject with high probability. We give the construction and analysis in Sect. 3.

We have now shown how to pack a k-query linear PCP over the integers to obtain a 1-query linear PCP over the integers. To apply the [BCI+13] compiler, we require a linear PCP over a finite field $\mathbb{F}$. Here, we note that we can directly embed the operations over the integers into a sufficiently large finite field (e.g., if B_{packed} is a bound on $\mathbf{q}_{\text{packed}}^\mathsf{T}\boldsymbol{\pi}$, it suffices to work over a field $\mathbb{F}_p$ where $p > 2B_{\text{packed}}$). If we start with a linear PCP over $\mathbb{F}_p$ and desire a packed linear PCP over the *same* field $\mathbb{F}_p$, then the linear PCP responses should be small.[6] We refer to the resulting linear PCP as a "bounded" linear PCP over $\mathbb{F}_p$. The Hadamard linear PCP has this property, so using our basic query-packing transformation, we obtain a 1-query bounded linear PCP over $\mathbb{F}_p$ with query length $\ell = O(s^2)$, where s is the size of the NP verification circuit. A natural question is whether we can obtain a 1-query linear PCP with query length $O(s)$ starting from the quadratic span programs of [GGPR13]. As we explain in the full version of this paper, we are not able to leverage our packing transformation because the queries in those constructions have large coefficients, and thus, do not seem directly amenable to our packing approach.

Concretely-efficient 2-element SNARGs. Starting from our 1-query linear PCP above, we directly invoke the [BCI+13] compiler with ElGamal encryption to obtain a designated-verifier SNARG in the preprocessing model where the proof consists of 2 group elements. One caveat with ElGamal is that the scheme encodes the message in the *exponent* (i.e., the decryption algorithm recovers g^a rather than a). In the context of the [BCI+13] compiler, this means the linear PCP response is in the exponent, and the verifier has to solve discrete log in order to verify the proofs; if the size of the response is B-bounded, this can be done in time $\widetilde{O}(\sqrt{B})$ using Pollard's kangaroo algorithm [Pol78]. For this to be efficient, we thus require that the responses are in a polynomial-size interval. Of course, this means that the soundness achievable using the ElGamal instantiation will be inverse polynomial in the security parameter (rather than negligible). This is because there are now only polynomially-many possible values that causes the verifier to accept, so a malicious prover can guess an accepting value with $1/\mathsf{poly}$

---

[6] If the packing transformation requires the use of a larger field than that of the underlying linear PCP, this can negate the benefit of the packing.

probability. This yields a trade-off between the soundness error ε and the verifier's time complexity (namely, smaller soundness error means that the responses have to be drawn from a larger interval, which increases the running time of the discrete log algorithm). Thus, when compiling linear PCPs to SNARGs using ElGamal, it is natural to consider bounded linear PCPs, which provide a direct trade-off between soundness error and the bound (see Corollary 3.4).

The bound on our 1-query linear PCP based on the Hadamard construction scales with $O(s^4)$, which means the resulting ElGamal-based SNARG will have verification complexity that scales *quadratically* with the circuit size. This is both undesirable and impractical for real scenarios. However, by taking advantage of the structure of the Hadamard linear PCP, we can reduce the verification complexity to $\widetilde{O}(\sqrt{s}/\varepsilon)$ if we allow for a negligible completeness error (as opposed to perfect completeness). The high-level idea here is that in the Hadamard linear PCP, one of the (unpacked) query responses is small and lies in an interval of size $\widetilde{O}(\sqrt{s}/\varepsilon)$ with overwhelming probability. This means that instead of having the verifier solve the discrete log to obtain the full linear PCP response, the verifier can instead check whether the decrypted response corresponds to one of the (polynomially-many) accepting values of the Hadamard linear PCP. Thus, we obtain a designated-verifier SNARG with 1/poly soundness where the proof consists of exactly 2 group elements and the verifier runs in time $\widetilde{O}(\sqrt{s}/\varepsilon)$. We provide the details in Sect. 3.2.

Preprocessing to achieve constant running time. Our approach for reducing the verification time in the ElGamal-based SNARG described above relies on there only being a small number of accepting values (that depend on the statement and the verifier's secret key). In Sect. 3.2, we show that at setup time, the verifier can perform a *statement-independent* preprocessing step (which only depends on the verifier's secret verification state) and prepare a lookup table of size $\widetilde{O}(\sqrt{s}/\varepsilon)$. With this lookup table, the verification procedure reduces to performing 2 exponentiations and 2 group multiplications, followed by a single table lookup. This yields a *much faster* verification procedure compared to even the SNARG from [Gro16], which requires computing 3 pairing relations (in addition to multiple exponentiations and group multiplications). In this model, we obtain SNARGs that are both *50% shorter* than those from [Gro16] (64 bytes for our construction vs. 127 bytes for [Gro16, SCI20]) and significantly faster to verify. Based on timings provided in `libsnark` [SCI20], the verifier's running time in [Gro16] is 1.2 ms, while based on our estimates, two group exponentiations and two multiplications would take 0.1 ms, which is over 10x faster (see Sect. 3.3 for details on our performance estimates). This makes our designated-verifier SNARGs well-suited for environments that demand very succinct proofs and low-latency or low-energy verification.

Concrete efficiency estimates. In Table 2, we provide estimates on the size of the CRS, the prover complexity, and the verification complexity. With preprocessing, the primary cost for the verifier is the storage of the lookup table and without preprocessing, the primary cost is the verification time. Here, we apply the additional (standard) transformation to obtain a zkSNARK (described in Sect. 3.2 and Remark 3.9). We describe our methodology for computing these estimates in Sect. 3.3.

The main appeal of our new designated-verifier zkSNARKs is that with preprocessing, it has extremely lightweight verification. The proofs consist of just two group elements and with a modestly-sized lookup table (e.g., for circuits with over 15,000 wires and soundness 1/128, a lookup table of size just over 20 MB suffices). Our schemes are well suited in scenarios where the verifier has a modest amount of memory, but is otherwise low energy or computationally constrained. They are also well-suited in settings where the verifier might be receiving and authenticating requests from a large number of provers.

One appealing application is to combine the zkSNARK with a one-way function to construct an identification scheme. Here, a user's secret key is a random element in the domain of a one-way function and the public key is its image under the one-way function. To authenticate, the user would provide a zkSNARK proving knowledge of their secret key (i.e., the pre-image under the one-way function) associated with their public key. One way to instantiate the required one-way function is to use Goldreich's simple one-way function based on expander graphs [Gol00], which can be computed by a Boolean circuit with just 1200 gates [BIJ+20] (or 1500 wires). In this case, the CRS size is around 34 MB and the prover's computation would take just a few seconds of computation. With a moderate soundness level of 1/128, the verifier only needs to maintain a table with just over 6 MB of storage. If the bottleneck in the system is sending proofs and authenticating credentials, then our construction offers a compelling solution. Moreover, the expressive nature of zkSNARKs lends itself naturally towards implementing more complex authentication policies (e.g., the user's credential is valid and moreover, satisfies some simple Boolean predicate).

While our construction achieves a lower level of soundness compared to pairing-based alternatives, scenarios where there are severe out-of-band consequences for getting caught cheating (even once) can provide strong incentives for honest behavior. This is conceptually similar to the notion of covert security in multiparty computation [CO99, AL07]. Similarly, while our constructions do not provide perfect zero-knowledge, the effects of any potential leakage can be mitigated (in the above setting with an identification scheme) by using a leakage-resilient one-way function. Moreover, in the setting of short-lived tokens or credentials, the user can simply *refresh* their credential after a certain number of requests (based on the zero-knowledge parameter of the system).

More broadly, we believe that our new preprocessing zkSNARKs are appealing in terms of proof size and verifier complexity. It is interesting to further optimize our methods to support more complex circuits. In the full version of this paper, we describe one approach based on constructing specially-designed circuits that are "Hadamard-friendly," which can then be efficiently-checked using a linear PCP (with small amortized query size), and correspondingly, enable a more concretely efficient zkSNARK.

Table 2. Concrete efficiency estimates for our designated-verifier zkSNARK based on ElGamal (see Sect. 3.2 and Remark 3.9 for details on how to extend the basic SNARG to a zkSNARK). For different circuits sizes (number of wires in a Boolean circuits with fan-in 2 gates) and soundness levels, we measure the CRS size (in group elements), the prover complexity (in number of group operations), and the verifier cost (with preprocessing, this corresponds to the size of the lookup table and without preprocessing, this corresponds to the number of group operations needed for online verification). The proof size for *all* of the parameter settings consists of just *two group elements* (64 bytes), and with preprocessing, the verification cost is just 2 exponentiations (and 2 multiplications). We set the completeness error to 2^{-40} and the zero-knowledge parameter to achieve 0.1-statistical zero knowledge. Without zero-knowledge, we can reduce the size of the verifier's lookup table and the verification time by 8x. For the concrete timing estimates, we base them on measurements taken using the `libsodium` implementation of the Curve25519 elliptic curve [Ber06] (see Sect. 3.3 for further details).

Circuit Size	CRS Size	Prover Time	Soundness Error	Verifier Space (with Preproc.)	Verifier Time (without Preproc.)
2^{10}	16 MB	262K (3.6 s)	2^{-1}	58 KB	23K (0.33 s)
			2^{-7}	5.3 MB	1.5M (21.28 s)
			2^{-14}	923.4 MB	194M (45 m 21 s)
2^{12}	256 MB	4.2M (58 s)	2^{-1}	126 KB	47K (0.66 s)
			2^{-7}	11.2 MB	3M (42.57 s)
			2^{-14}	1.9 GB	389M (1 h 30 m)
2^{14}	4 GB	67M (15 m 40 s)	2^{-1}	270 KB	95K (1.33 s)
			2^{-7}	23.5 MB	6M (1 m 25 s)
			2^{-14}	3.9 GB	778M (3 h 1 m)

1.2 From Hardness of Approximation to Witness Encryption

A limitation of the SNARG constructions based on instantiating the [BCI+13] compiler with ElGamal is that they only provide 1/poly soundness. Part of this stems from the inherent challenge that recovering the linear PCP responses from an ElGamal ciphertext requires computing discrete log, which restricts us to linear PCPs whose responses lie in a polynomial-size set (and correspondingly, yields SNARGs with inverse polynomial soundness error). However, Bitansky et al. [BCI+13] point out that if we had a linear PCP with a *linear* decision procedure and if we apply the compiler using ElGamal encryption, the verifier no longer needs to decrypt the responses. Instead, it can simply check the verification procedure "in the exponent." This provides a general template for constructing a succinct argument based on ElGamal that can achieve negligible soundness error. While Bitansky et al. motivate the search for a linear PCP with a linear decision procedure, they do not suggest a candidate.

1-query linear PCP with negligible soundness from hardness of approximation.
In this work, we introduce a new approach for constructing linear PCPs based
on the hardness of approximating problems related to decoding linear codes.
Specifically, we construct a 1-query linear PCP with a linear decision procedure and negligible soundness error. Our construction *affirmatively* answers the
above question posed by Bitansky et al. on whether there exists a linear interactive proof with a linear decision procedure. We note, however, that the linear
PCP we construct is *instance-dependent* (i.e., the verifier's query depends on
the statement being verified). As such, applying the [BCI+13] compiler yields
a 2-message laconic argument where the prover's message consists of 2 group
elements.

Previously, Groth [Gro16] ruled out the possibility of 2-message linear interactive proofs with a linear decision procedure for languages that are hard on
average. Implicit in his lower bound is the assumption that the underlying proof
satisfies perfect completeness (or more generally, has sufficiently small completeness error). Our 1-query linear PCP construction has a small, but noticeable,
$o(1)$ completeness error which avoids this lower bound. We discuss this in greater
detail in the full version of this paper.

Our linear PCP construction relies on the hardness of approximation for the
gap minimum weight solution problem (GapMWSP) [KPV12]. At a high level, a
problem instance for GapMWSP$_\beta$ is a triple $(\mathbf{A}, \mathbf{b}, d)$ where $\mathbf{A} \in \mathbb{F}^{\ell \times n}$, $\mathbf{b} \in \mathbb{F}^\ell$,
$d \in \mathbb{N}$, and $\mathbb{F}$ is a finite field. The goal is to decide whether there exists a solution
$\mathbf{x} \in \mathbb{F}^n$ with Hamming weight at most d such that $\mathbf{Ax} = \mathbf{b}$, or, alternatively,
if all solutions $\mathbf{x} \in \mathbb{F}^n$ to the linear system $\mathbf{Ax} = \mathbf{b}$ have Hamming weight at
least $\beta \cdot d$, where $\beta = \mathsf{polylog}(n)$ is the approximation factor. While this problem
is traditionally formulated over the binary field $\mathbb{F}_2$, we show that the same NP-
hardness reduction (from the GapLabelCover problem [Raz95]) extends to general
finite fields.

We can construct a linear PCP for the GapMWSP problem in a straightforward manner (this in turn yields a linear PCP for NP by first applying a
Karp-Levin reduction to GapMWSP). The linear PCP query for an instance
$(\mathbf{A}, \mathbf{b}, d)$ consists of a random vector $\mathbf{r} \xleftarrow{\text{R}} \mathbb{F}^\ell$ and a *sparse* vector $\mathbf{e} \in \mathbb{F}^n$ where
each component of $\mathbf{e}$ is either uniform over $\mathbb{F}$ or 0. The query is the vector
$\mathbf{q}^\mathsf{T} = \mathbf{r}^\mathsf{T} \mathbf{A} + \mathbf{e}^\mathsf{T} \in \mathbb{F}^n$. The proof for an instance $(\mathbf{A}, \mathbf{b}, d)$ is a vector $\boldsymbol{\pi} \in \mathbb{F}^n$
where $\mathbf{A}\boldsymbol{\pi} = \mathbf{b}$ and $\boldsymbol{\pi}$ has small Hamming weight $\mathsf{wt}(\boldsymbol{\pi}) \leq d$. Finally, given
a response $a \in \mathbb{F}$, the verifier simply checks whether $a = \mathbf{r}^\mathsf{T} \mathbf{b}$. Suppose that
$\mathbf{A}\boldsymbol{\pi} = \mathbf{b}$. Then, $\mathbf{q}^\mathsf{T}\boldsymbol{\pi} = \mathbf{r}^\mathsf{T}\mathbf{A}\boldsymbol{\pi} + \mathbf{e}^\mathsf{T}\boldsymbol{\pi} = \mathbf{r}^\mathsf{T}\mathbf{b} + \mathbf{e}^\mathsf{T}\boldsymbol{\pi}$. Completeness follows as long
as $\mathbf{e}^\mathsf{T}\boldsymbol{\pi} = 0$. This happens with $1 - o(1)$ probability since both $\mathbf{e}$ and $\boldsymbol{\pi}$ are *sparse*
(i.e., $\mathbf{e}^\mathsf{T}\boldsymbol{\pi}$ is nonzero only if *both* $\mathbf{e}$ and $\boldsymbol{\pi}$ have a nonzero component in the same
coordinate, which happens with small, but noticeable, probability over the ran-
domness of $\mathbf{e}$). Conversely, for a NO instance, all solutions to the linear system
$\mathbf{Ax} = \mathbf{b}$ have Hamming weight at least βd. In this case, for any proof vector $\boldsymbol{\pi}$,
either $\mathbf{A}\boldsymbol{\pi} \neq \mathbf{b}$ (in which case, the verifier rejects except with probability $1/|\mathbb{F}|$
over the randomness of $\mathbf{r}$) or if $\mathbf{A}\boldsymbol{\pi} = \mathbf{b}$, then $\boldsymbol{\pi}$ has large Hamming weight and
$\mathbf{e}^\mathsf{T}\boldsymbol{\pi}$ will be nonzero with overwhelming probability over the choice of $\mathbf{e}$. Hence,

we obtain an instance-dependent 1-query linear PCP with a linear decision procedure from the GapMWSP problem, and correspondingly, a 2-message laconic argument with negligible soundness and where the proof size consist of just 2 group elements by invoking the [BCI+13] compiler with ElGamal encryption. We provide the full description and analysis in Sect. 4.

From laconic arguments to witness encryption. Given a laconic argument where the proof consists of just two group elements, a natural question to ask is whether we can have an argument that is *even shorter*: namely, a laconic argument with just a *single* group element. From a conceptual perspective, this question has a similar flavor to the notion of a "1-bit SNARG" introduced in [BISW18]. There, they showed that a 1-bit SNARG for a hard language is in fact "predictable" (i.e., the verifier can predict the value of an accepting proof), and by leveraging the result from [FNV17], implies a *witness encryption*[7] scheme for the underlying language. As it turns out, laconic arguments where the prover's message is a single group element and where the verification algorithm only consists of *generic group* operations are similarly powerful. As we show in the full version of this paper, *any* 1-element laconic argument that has negligible soundness error and a "generic" verification algorithm (i.e., it only performs algebraic operations over group elements) implies witness encryption for the underlying language. This means that improving our 2-element laconic argument to a 1-element laconic argument provides a promising new path towards realizing witness encryption from more traditional and well-understood cryptographic assumptions.

1-element laconic argument from hardness of approximation. It is not clear how to leverage our 1-query linear PCP from the GapMWSP problem to obtain a laconic argument where the proof consists of just a single group element. Indeed, any application of the [BCI+13] compiler with ElGamal would yield an argument system where the proof consists of at least 2 group elements (since the proof will contain at least one ElGamal ciphertext). However, we show that assuming a conceptually-similar, but yet-unproven hypothesis on the hardness of approximating the minimal distance of linear codes, we can leverage similar ideas used to construct our linear PCP from GapMWSP to *directly* construct a 1-element laconic argument with negligible soundness in the generic group model. The resulting argument is predictable in the sense of [FNV17] (even without applying our generic transformation above), and thus, implies a witness encryption scheme for NP in the generic group model. While the hypothesis we rely on is unproven, there are no known barriers for extending the current hardness of approximation results for the minimal distance problem to the more challenging parameter regime needed for our construction [Kho20].

---

[7] In a witness encryption scheme [GGSW13], the prover can encrypt a message to an NP statement x such that anyone with knowledge of the witness w is able to decrypt and recover the message. This is a very powerful notion of encryption whose only instantiations rely on conjectures related to indistinguishability obfuscation [GGH+13], multilinear maps [GGSW13, GLW14, CVW18], or new and relatively unexplored algebraic structures [BIJ+20].

Our 1-element laconic argument relies on the hardness of approximating the minimal distance of a linear code (GapMDP). For an approximation factor $\beta > 0$, a GapMDP_β instance $(\mathbf{A}, d)$ consists of a matrix $\mathbf{A}$ (over a finite field $\mathbb{F}$) and a distance $d \in \mathbb{N}$ and the problem is to decide whether the minimum distance (under the Hamming metric) of the code generated by $\mathbf{A}$ is less than d or greater than $\beta \cdot d$. Equivalently, we can formulate the problem as distinguishing between the following two possibilities with respect to the parity-check matrix $\mathbf{H} \in \mathbb{F}^{\ell \times k}$ of the code generated by $\mathbf{A}$.

- There exists a nonzero vector $\mathbf{0} \neq \mathbf{v} \in \mathbb{F}_p^\ell$ with Hamming weight at most d such that $\mathbf{H}\mathbf{v} = \mathbf{0}$.
- For all nonzero vectors $\mathbf{0} \neq \mathbf{v} \in \mathbb{F}_p^\ell$ with Hamming weight up to $\beta \cdot d$, $\mathbf{H}\mathbf{v} \neq \mathbf{0}$.

When $\beta = \omega(\log n)$, it is not difficult to construct a 1-element laconic argument for the GapMDP_β language with negligible soundness. We use the same principles we used to construct the 1-query linear PCP for $\mathsf{GapMWSP}_\beta$. The construction operates over a group $\mathbb{G}$ of prime order p with generator g (which we will model as a generic group for the security analysis). The construction works as follows:

- **Query generation:** The verifier samples random vectors $\mathbf{c} \xleftarrow{\mathrm{R}} \mathbb{F}_p^k$ $\mathbf{r} \xleftarrow{\mathrm{R}} \mathbb{F}_p^k$ and a scalar $s \xleftarrow{\mathrm{R}} \mathbb{F}_p$. It also samples a noise vector $\mathbf{e} \in \mathbb{F}_p^k$, where the entries of $\mathbf{e}$ are either 0 or uniform over $\mathbb{F}_p$. The density of $\mathbf{e}$ is chosen to balance the completeness and soundness requirements. The verifier computes $\mathbf{z}^\mathsf{T} = \mathbf{r}^\mathsf{T}\mathbf{H} + s\mathbf{c}^\mathsf{T} + \mathbf{e}^\mathsf{T} \in \mathbb{F}_p^k$. The query is the pair $(\mathbf{c}, g^\mathbf{z})$ where $g^\mathbf{z}$ denotes the vector of group elements $g^{z_1}, \ldots, g^{z_k}$, and $\mathbf{z} = (z_1, \ldots, z_k)$.
- **Prover's response:** For an YES instance to the GapMDP problem, the witness is a vector $\mathbf{v} \in \mathbb{F}_p^k$ such that $\mathbf{H}\mathbf{v} = \mathbf{0}$ and $\mathbf{v}$ has low Hamming weight. On input the query $\mathbf{c}$ and $g^\mathbf{z}$ and the witness $\mathbf{v} \in \mathbb{F}_p^k$, the prover computes $t = (\mathbf{c}^\mathsf{T}\mathbf{v})^{-1}$ and replies with the single group element $g^{t \cdot \mathbf{z}^\mathsf{T}\mathbf{v}}$.
- **Verification:** To verify the proof π, the verifier checks that $\pi = g^s$.

We now informally describe the completeness and soundness analysis:

- **Completeness:** For a YES instance, the witness $\mathbf{v}$ satisfies $\mathbf{H}\mathbf{v} = \mathbf{0}$ and moreover $\mathbf{v}$ has low Hamming weight. If the noise vector $\mathbf{e}$ is sufficiently sparse, then with high probability, $\mathbf{e}^\mathsf{T}\mathbf{v} = 0$. Thus,

$$\mathbf{z}^\mathsf{T}\mathbf{v} = \mathbf{r}^\mathsf{T}\mathbf{H}\mathbf{v} + s\mathbf{c}^\mathsf{T}\mathbf{v} + \mathbf{e}^\mathsf{T}\mathbf{v} = s\mathbf{c}^\mathsf{T}\mathbf{v}.$$

In this case, $g^{t \cdot \mathbf{z}^\mathsf{T}\mathbf{v}} = g^s$ since $t = (\mathbf{c}^\mathsf{T}\mathbf{v})^{-1}$. Note that $\mathbf{c}$ is uniform (and independent of $\mathbf{v}$), so the quantity $\mathbf{c}^\mathsf{T}\mathbf{v}$ is nonzero with overwhelming probability (and thus, invertible).
- **Soundness:** For the soundness analysis, we model the group as a generic group. Since the prover only has an encoding $g^\mathbf{z}$ of $\mathbf{z} \in \mathbb{F}_p^k$, in the generic group model, the only components that it can construct are of the form $g^{\mathbf{z}^\mathsf{T}\boldsymbol{\alpha} + \beta}$ for some choice of $\boldsymbol{\alpha} \in \mathbb{F}_p^k$ and $\beta \in \mathbb{F}_p$. The prover succeeds if it is able to find $\boldsymbol{\alpha}, \beta$ such that $\mathbf{z}^\mathsf{T}\boldsymbol{\alpha} + \beta = \mathbf{r}^\mathsf{T}\mathbf{H}\boldsymbol{\alpha} + s\mathbf{c}^\mathsf{T}\boldsymbol{\alpha} + \mathbf{e}^\mathsf{T}\boldsymbol{\alpha} = s$. We consider two possibilities:

- If the Hamming weight of $\boldsymbol{\alpha}$ is less than $\beta \cdot d$ and we have a NO instance, then $\mathbf{H}\boldsymbol{\alpha} \neq \mathbf{0}$. In this case, over the randomness of $\mathbf{r}$, the value of $\mathbf{r}^\top \mathbf{H}\boldsymbol{\alpha} \neq 0$ is uniform over $\mathbb{F}_p$.
- Alternatively, if $\boldsymbol{\alpha}$ has Hamming weight larger than $\beta \cdot d$, and $\mathbf{e}$ is sufficiently dense, then with overwhelming probability, there is some component e_i such that $e_i \alpha_i \neq 0$, and so $\mathbf{e}^\top \boldsymbol{\alpha} \neq 0$. In this case, the value of $\mathbf{e}^\top \boldsymbol{\alpha}$ is uniform over $\mathbb{F}_p$.

This means that for any choice of $\boldsymbol{\alpha}, \beta$ that the prover chooses, with overwhelming probability, either $\mathbf{r}^\top \mathbf{H}\boldsymbol{\alpha}$ or $\mathbf{e}^\top \boldsymbol{\alpha}$ is uniform over $\mathbb{F}_p$ (and independent of s). The probability that $\mathbf{z}^\top \boldsymbol{\alpha} + \beta = s$ is negligible.

Observe that in the above analysis, we require $\mathbf{e}$ to be sufficiently sparse for completeness to hold with high probability and sufficiently dense for soundness to hold with overwhelming probability. For this reason, we require that the gap β be large enough so as to satisfy both constraints. In particular, taking $\beta = \omega(\log n)$ suffices for our analysis. We provide the full description of the scheme and its analysis in Sect. 5.1.

To obtain a 1-element laconic argument for NP (and correspondingly, a witness encryption scheme for all of NP), we need to assume that the above GapMDP_β problem is NP-hard for some choice of $\beta = \omega(\log n)$ and $\mathbb{F}_p$ is a finite field of super-polynomial size. More precisely, we require that there is a deterministic polynomial-time Karp-Levin reduction from NP to GapMDP_β. Existing hardness of approximation results show that over polynomial-size fields, the GapMDP problem is NP-hard for constant approximation factors $\beta = O(1)$, and NP-hard under a deterministic *quasi-polynomial* time reduction for "almost-polynomial" approximation factors $\beta = 2^{\log^{1-\varepsilon}(n)}$. Thus, proving our hypothesis (Hypothesis 5.2) requires strengthening existing hardness results in two directions: (1) arguing NP-hardness for some $\beta = \omega(\log n)$ under a polynomial-time reduction; and (2) extending the hardness result to exponential-size prime order fields. As mentioned above, while our existing techniques do not seem sufficient, there are also no known barriers to showing the hardness of approximation results we require [Kho20]. If our hypothesis is true, then we obtain an *unconditional* construction of witness encryption for NP in the generic group model.

2 Preliminaries

For a positive integer $n \in \mathbb{N}$, we write $[n]$ to denote the set $\{1, \dots, n\}$. We write $\mathbb{F}$ to denote a finite field. We will use bold lowercase letters (e.g., $\mathbf{v}, \mathbf{w}$) to denote vectors and bold uppercase letters (e.g., $\mathbf{A}, \mathbf{B}$) to denote matrices. For a vector $\mathbf{v} \in \mathbb{F}^n$, $\mathsf{wt}(\mathbf{v})$ denotes the Hamming weight of $\mathbf{v}$ (i.e., the number of nonzero entries in $\mathbf{v}$). For a matrix $\mathbf{A} \in \mathbb{F}^{n \times m}$, we write $\mathsf{dist}(\mathbf{A})$ to denote the minimum distance of the code generated by $\mathbf{A}$. (i.e., the minimum Hamming weight of a nonzero codeword generated by $\mathbf{A}$).

We write λ to denote a security parameter. We say that a function f is negligible in λ, denoted $\mathsf{negl}(\lambda)$ if $f(\lambda) = o(1/\lambda^c)$ for all $c \in \mathbb{N}$. We say an event happens with negligible probability if the probability of the event happening is negligible, and that it happens with overwhelming probability if its complement occurs with overwhelming probability. We say an algorithm is efficient if it runs in probabilistic polynomial time in the length of its input. We write $\mathsf{poly}(\lambda)$ to denote a function that is bounded by a fixed polynomial in λ and $\mathsf{polylog}(\lambda)$ to denote a function that is bounded by $\mathsf{poly}(\log \lambda)$. We say that two families of distributions $\mathcal{D}_1 = \{\mathcal{D}_{1,\lambda}\}_{\lambda \in \mathbb{N}}$ and $\mathcal{D}_2 = \{\mathcal{D}_{2,\lambda}\}_{\lambda \in \mathbb{N}}$ are computationally indistinguishable (denoted $\mathcal{D}_1 \overset{c}{\approx} \mathcal{D}_2$) if no efficient adversary can distinguish samples from $\mathcal{D}_1$ and $\mathcal{D}_2$ except with negligible probability. We say that $\mathcal{D}_1$ and $\mathcal{D}_2$ are statistically indistinguishable (denoted $\mathcal{D}_1 \overset{s}{\approx} \mathcal{D}_2$) if the statistical distance between $\mathcal{D}_1$ and $\mathcal{D}_2$ is negligible. We review additional preliminaries in the full version of this paper.

Arithmetic circuit satisfiability. A central part of this work is constructing succinct argument systems for the language of Boolean circuit satisfiability. When describing some of our constructions however, it will oftentimes be more natural to consider the more *general* language of *arithmetic circuit satisfiability* which we recall formally below. Throughout this paper, an arithmetic circuit $C \colon \mathbb{F}^n \times \mathbb{F}^h \to \mathbb{F}^\ell$ over a finite field $\mathbb{F}$ consists of a collection of addition gates with unbounded fan-in and multiplication gates with fan-in 2. Both types of gates can have unbounded fan-out. As noted in [BCI+13], Boolean circuit satisfiability can be reduced to arithmetic circuit satisfiability over any finite field $\mathbb{F}$ with constant overhead.

Definition 2.1 (Arithmetic Circuit Satisfiability). *Let $\mathbb{F}$ be a finite field. For an arithmetic circuit $C \colon \mathbb{F}^n \times \mathbb{F}^h \to \mathbb{F}^t$ over $\mathbb{F}$, the arithmetic circuit satisfiability problem is defined by the relation $\mathcal{R}_C = \{(\mathbf{x}, \mathbf{w}) \in \mathbb{F}^n \times \mathbb{F}^h : C(\mathbf{x}, \mathbf{w}) = 0^t\}$. We write $\mathcal{L}_C$ to denote the corresponding language. For a family of arithmetic circuits $\mathcal{C} = \{C_\ell \colon \mathbb{F}^{n(\ell)} \times \mathbb{F}^{h(\ell)} \to \mathbb{F}^{t(\ell)}\}_{\ell \in \mathbb{N}}$, we write $\mathcal{R}_\mathcal{C}$ and $\mathcal{L}_\mathcal{C}$ to denote the infinite relation $\mathcal{R}_\mathcal{C} = \bigcup_{\ell \in \mathbb{N}} \mathcal{R}_{C_\ell}$ and infinite language $\mathcal{L}_\mathcal{C} = \bigcup_{\ell \in \mathbb{N}} \mathcal{L}_{C_\ell}$. The special case of Boolean circuit satisfiability is the problem of arithmetic circuit satisfiability over the binary field $\mathbb{F} = \mathbb{F}_2$ (in this case, the output of C can be taken to be a single bit (i.e., $\ell = 1$) without loss of generality).*

2.1   Linear PCPs

We begin by recalling the definition of linear PCPs (LPCP) from [BCI+13]. Our definition combines features from a "fully linear PCP" introduced in [BBC+19] with the traditional notion of a linear PCP. First, recall that in a fully linear PCP, the verifier does not have direct access to the statement $\mathbf{x} \in \mathbb{F}^n$ and instead is given linear query access to the vector $[\boldsymbol{\pi}, \mathbf{x}]$ that includes the proof $\boldsymbol{\pi}$ together with the statement $\mathbf{x}$. To simplify the definition (and still capture existing constructions of linear PCPs), in a k-query linear PCP, we allow the verifier to make a single "free" linear query to the statement $\mathbf{x}$ and up to k linear queries to the proof vector $\boldsymbol{\pi}$. We give our definition below:

Definition 2.2 (Linear PCP [BCI+13,BBC+19, **adapted]).** *Let* $\mathcal{R}\colon \mathbb{F}^n \times \mathbb{F}^h \to \{0,1\}$ *be a binary relation*[8] *(with associated language $\mathcal{L}$) over a finite field $\mathbb{F}$. A k-query linear PCP for $\mathcal{R}$ with query length ℓ and soundness error ε is a tuple of algorithms $\Pi_{\mathsf{LPCP}} = (\mathcal{Q}_{\mathsf{LPCP}}, \mathcal{P}_{\mathsf{LPCP}}, \mathcal{D}_{\mathsf{LPCP}})$ with the following properties:*

- *The verifier's query algorithm $\mathcal{Q}_{\mathsf{LPCP}}$ outputs a query $\mathbf{q}_{\mathsf{inp}} \in \mathbb{F}^n$, a query matrix $\mathbf{Q} \in \mathbb{F}^{\ell \times k}$, and a verification state st. We can also consider an input-dependent linear PCP where the query algorithm also takes as input a statement $\mathbf{x} \in \mathbb{F}^n$.*
- *The prover algorithm $\mathcal{P}_{\mathsf{LPCP}}$ takes a statement $\mathbf{x} \in \mathbb{F}^n$ and a witness $\mathbf{w} \in \mathbb{F}^h$ as input and outputs a proof $\boldsymbol{\pi} \in \mathbb{F}^\ell$.*
- *The verifier's decision algorithm $\mathcal{D}_{\mathsf{LPCP}}$ takes as input the verification state st, an input-dependent response $a_{\mathsf{inp}} \in \mathbb{F}$, and a vector of responses $\mathbf{a} \in \mathbb{F}^k$, and outputs a bit $b \in \{0,1\}$.*

In addition, Π_{LPCP} should satisfy the following properties:

- ***Completeness:*** *For all $\mathbf{x} \in \mathbb{F}^n$ and $\mathbf{w} \in \mathbb{F}^h$ where $\mathcal{R}(\mathbf{x}, \mathbf{w}) = 1$,*

$$\Pr[\mathcal{D}_{\mathsf{LPCP}}(\mathsf{st}, \mathbf{q}_{\mathsf{inp}}^\top \mathbf{x}, \mathbf{Q}^\top \boldsymbol{\pi}) = 1 \mid (\mathsf{st}, \mathbf{q}_{\mathsf{inp}}, \mathbf{Q}) \leftarrow \mathcal{Q}_{\mathsf{LPCP}}, \boldsymbol{\pi} \leftarrow \mathcal{P}_{\mathsf{LPCP}}(\mathbf{x}, \mathbf{w})] = 1$$

- ***Soundness:*** *For every $\mathbf{x} \notin \mathcal{L}$ and every $\boldsymbol{\pi}^* \in \mathbb{F}^\ell$, $\boldsymbol{\delta}^* \in \mathbb{F}^k$,*

$$\Pr[\mathcal{D}_{\mathsf{LPCP}}(\mathsf{st}, \mathbf{q}_{\mathsf{inp}}^\top \mathbf{x}, \mathbf{Q}^\top \boldsymbol{\pi}^* + \boldsymbol{\delta}^*) = 1 \mid (\mathsf{st}, \mathbf{q}_{\mathsf{inp}}, \mathbf{Q}) \leftarrow \mathcal{Q}_{\mathsf{LPCP}}] \leq \varepsilon.$$

- ***δ-Honest-verifier zero-knowledge (δ-HVZK):*** *There exists an efficient simulator $\mathcal{S}_{\mathsf{LPCP}}$ such that for all $\mathbf{x} \in \mathcal{L}$, the following distributions are δ-close (i.e., their statistical distance is at most δ):*

$$\{\mathcal{S}_{\mathsf{LPCP}}(\mathbf{x})\} \ and \ \left\{ (\mathsf{st}, \mathbf{q}_{\mathsf{inp}}, \mathbf{Q}, \mathbf{q}_{\mathsf{inp}}^\top \mathbf{x}, \mathbf{Q}^\top \boldsymbol{\pi}) \ \middle| \ \begin{matrix} (\mathsf{st}, \mathbf{q}_{\mathsf{inp}}, \mathbf{Q}) \leftarrow \mathcal{Q}_{\mathsf{LPCP}}; \\ \boldsymbol{\pi} \leftarrow \mathcal{P}_{\mathsf{LPCP}}(\mathbf{x}, \mathbf{w}) \end{matrix} \right\}.$$

If these two distributions are identically distributed, we say that LPCP satisfies perfect honest-verifier zero-knowledge.[9]

In the full version of this paper, we recall additional properties on linear PCPs.

---

[8] We can also define integer linear PCPs for an (infinite) family of relations $\mathcal{R} = \bigcup_{\kappa \in \mathbb{N}} \mathcal{R}_\kappa$. In this case, the inputs to the query-generation and proving algorithms would additionally take the relation index 1^κ as input, and the parameters $n, h, k, \ell, B, \varepsilon$ can all be functions of κ.

[9] We can consider a stronger notion of zero-knowledge where the simulator does not have access to the statement $\mathbf{x}$. This is the setting considered in fully linear PCPs [BBC+19] and has applications to constructing proofs on committed values or secret-shared values. This stronger notion can also be relevant in our setting where a verifier is checking proofs from multiple provers (who may each hold a secret share of a distributed database), and the goal is to minimize proof size or verifier complexity.

3   1-Query Linear PCPs via Packing

In this section, we begin by introducing the notion of a bounded linear PCP over the finite field $\mathbb{F}_p$. Throughout this section, we will view elements $x \in \mathbb{F}_p$ as both field elements over $\mathbb{F}_p$ as well as integers in the interval $[-p/2, p/2]$. We first show in Construction 3.2 how to pack k-query bounded linear PCPs into a 1-query linear PCP. In the full version of this paper, we describe how to construct a 2-query linear PCP based on the Hadamard linear PCP [ALM+98,IKO07]. In conjunction with our query-packing transformation, we obtain 1-query linear PCPs for NP. Then, by invoking the compiler from [BCI+13] with the ElGamal encryption scheme, we obtain a SNARG where the proof consists of a single ElGamal ciphertext (i.e., two group elements). Then, in Sects. 3.2 and 3.3, we show how to optimize the *concrete efficiency* of our ElGamal-based SNARG (by leveraging structural properties of our 1-query linear PCP).

Definition 3.1 (Bounded Linear PCP). *A k-query linear PCP $\Pi_{\mathsf{LPCP}} = (\mathcal{Q}_{\mathsf{LPCP}}, \mathcal{P}_{\mathsf{LPCP}}, \mathcal{D}_{\mathsf{LPCP}})$ for a relation $\mathcal{R} \colon \mathbb{F}_p^n \times \mathbb{F}_p^h \to \{0,1\}$ over a finite field $\mathbb{F}_p$ is bounded with respect to bound functions $b_1, \ldots, b_k \colon \mathbb{N} \to \mathbb{N}$ if $\mathcal{Q}_{\mathsf{LPCP}}$ and $\mathcal{P}_{\mathsf{LPCP}}$ take as input an additional bound parameter $\tau \in \mathbb{N}$ and for any $\mathbf{x}, \mathbf{w}$ where $\mathcal{R}(\mathbf{x}, \mathbf{w}) = 1$, we have for all $i \in [k]$,*

$$\Pr[\mathbf{q}_i^\top \boldsymbol{\pi} \in [-b_i(\tau), b_i(\tau)] \mid (\mathsf{st}, \mathbf{q}_{\mathsf{inp}}, \mathbf{Q}) \leftarrow \mathcal{Q}_{\mathsf{LPCP}}(\tau), \boldsymbol{\pi} \leftarrow \mathcal{P}_{\mathsf{LPCP}}(\tau, \mathbf{x}, \mathbf{w})] = 1, \tag{3.1}$$

where $\mathbf{q}_i$ denotes the ith column on $\mathbf{Q}$ and the inner product is computed over the integers. We say that Π_{LPCP} is bounded with respect to bound functions $b_1, \ldots, b_k$ with probability ε if Eq. (3.1) holds with probability ε. Moreover, when defining δ-HVZK for bounded linear PCPs, we additionally provide the bound parameter τ as input to $\mathcal{Q}_{\mathsf{LPCP}}$ and $\mathcal{P}_{\mathsf{LPCP}}$ in the real distribution and the simulator $\mathcal{S}_{\mathsf{LPCP}}$ in the simulated distribution (in addition to the input x). In this case, we also allow the bound function to depend on both the bound parameter τ as well as the zero-knowledge parameter δ.

We refer to the full version of this paper for the definition of strong soundness as it pertains to bounded linear PCPs.

Construction 3.2 (Bounded Linear PCP Packing). Let $\Pi'_{\mathsf{LPCP}} = (\mathcal{Q}'_{\mathsf{LPCP}}, \mathcal{P}'_{\mathsf{LPCP}}, \mathcal{D}'_{\mathsf{LPCP}})$ be a k-query bounded LPCP for a binary relation $\mathcal{R} \colon \mathbb{F}_p^n \times \mathbb{F}_p^h \to \{0,1\}$ over $\mathbb{F}_p$ with bound functions $b'_1, \ldots, b'_k \colon \mathbb{N} \to \mathbb{N}$ and soundness error ε'. We will assume that $\mathcal{D}'_{\mathsf{LPCP}}$ strictly enforces the bound on the responses (namely, given a set of responses $a_1, \ldots, a_k$, $\mathcal{D}'_{\mathsf{LPCP}}$ accepts only if $a_i \in [-b'_i(\tau), b'_i(\tau)]$ for each $i \in [k]$; see the full version of this paper for more discussion). We construct a 1-query bounded LPCP $\Pi_{\mathsf{LPCP}} = (\mathcal{Q}_{\mathsf{LPCP}}, \mathcal{P}_{\mathsf{LPCP}}, \mathcal{D}_{\mathsf{LPCP}})$ as follows:

- $\mathcal{Q}_{\mathsf{LPCP}}(\tau)$: On input the bound parameter τ, $\mathcal{Q}_{\mathsf{LPCP}}$ proceeds as follows:
  1. Run $(\mathsf{st}', \mathbf{q}'_{\mathsf{inp}}, \mathbf{Q}') \leftarrow \mathcal{Q}'_{\mathsf{LPCP}}(\tau)$. Set $\mathbf{q}_{\mathsf{inp}} = \mathbf{q}'_{\mathsf{inp}}$.

2. Define $B_{\mathsf{min}} = \min_{i \in [k]} b'_i(\tau)$, $B_{\mathsf{max}} = \max_{i \in [k]} b'_i(\tau)$, and $B_{\mathsf{mul}} = \prod_{i \in [k]} b'_i(\tau)$. Set $r_1 = 1$ and sample $r_2, \ldots, r_k \xleftarrow{\text{R}} [4B_{\mathsf{max}} + 1, B_{\mathsf{mul}} \cdot 2^{k+2}/\varepsilon']$. Without loss of generality, we will assume that $B_{\mathsf{min}} = b'_k(\tau)$.

3. Compute $\mathsf{st} \leftarrow (\mathsf{st}', b'_1(\tau), \ldots, b'_k(\tau), r_1, \ldots, r_k)$, and compute the query vector $\mathbf{q} \in \mathbb{F}_p^\ell$ as

$$\mathbf{q} = \sum_{i \in [k]} \mathbf{q}'_i \left(\prod_{j \in [i]} r_j \right) \in \mathbb{F}_p^\ell,$$

where $\mathbf{q}'_1, \ldots, \mathbf{q}'_k \in \mathbb{Z}^\ell$ denote the k columns of $\mathbf{Q}'$.
Output $(\mathsf{st}, \mathbf{q}_{\mathsf{inp}}, \mathbf{q})$.

- $\mathcal{P}_{\mathsf{LPCP}}(\tau, \mathbf{x}, \mathbf{w})$: On input a statement $\mathbf{x} \in \mathbb{F}_p^n$ and a witness $\mathbf{w} \in \mathbb{F}_p^h$, output the proof $\boldsymbol{\pi} \leftarrow \mathcal{P}'_{\mathsf{LPCP}}(\tau, \mathbf{x}, \mathbf{w})$.
- $\mathcal{D}_{\mathsf{LPCP}}(\mathsf{st}, a_{\mathsf{inp}}, a)$: On input the state $\mathsf{st} = (\mathsf{st}', b'_1, \ldots, b'_k, r_1, \ldots, r_k)$, an input-dependent response $a_{\mathsf{inp}} \in \mathbb{F}_p$, and a response $a \in \mathbb{F}_p$, compute $a'_1, \ldots, a'_k \in \mathbb{F}_p$ so that $a = \sum_{i \in [k]} a'_i \prod_{j \in [i]} r_j$ and each a'_i satisfies $a'_i \in [-b'_i, b'_i]$. This can be done as follows:
  - For each $i = k, k-1, \ldots, 1$, compute $a'_i \leftarrow \lfloor a/\prod_{j \in [i]} r_j \rfloor$ and update $a \leftarrow a - a'_i \cdot \prod_{j \in [i]} r_j$, where all of these operations happen *over the integers* (namely, the algorithm interprets the values a and $a'_1, \ldots, a'_k$ as integers in the interval $[-p/2, p/2]$).
  If the above procedure does not produce $a'_1, \ldots, a'_k \in \mathbb{F}_p$ satisfying the above requirements, output 0. Otherwise, output $\mathcal{D}'_{\mathsf{LPCP}}(\mathsf{st}', a_{\mathsf{inp}}, (a'_1, \ldots, a'_k))$.

We argue completeness, soundness, and zero-knowledge of Construction 3.2 in the full version of this paper and just state the main corollary below.

Corollary 3.3 (Linear PCP Packing). *Let Π'_{LPCP} be a k-query bounded LPCP over $\mathbb{F}_p$ for a binary relation $\mathcal{R}$ with bound functions $b'_1, \ldots, b'_k$, soundness error (resp., strong soundness error) ε', and which satisfies δ-HVZK. Let $B'_{\mathsf{min}} = \min_{i \in [k]} b'_i$, $B'_{\mathsf{mul}} = \prod_{i \in [k]} b'_i$, and $B = 2B'_{\mathsf{min}} \left(B'_{\mathsf{mul}} 2^{k+2}/\varepsilon\right)^{k-1}$. If $p > 2B$, then there exists a 1-query bounded LPCP over $\mathbb{F}_p$ for $\mathcal{R}$ with bound B, soundness error (resp., strong soundness error) $(k+1)/2\varepsilon'$, and which satisfies δ-HVZK.*

3.1 Constructing 1-Query Bounded Linear PCPs

As noted in [BCI+13], a simple extension of the Hadamard PCP from [ALM+98, IKO07] to arbitrary finite fields $\mathbb{F}$ yields a 3-query linear PCP for arithmetic circuit satisfiability over $\mathbb{F}$. In the full version of this paper, we note that a simple adaptation of the construction yields a 2-query linear PCP. Then, applying our linear PCP packing construction (Corollary 3.3), we obtain the following construction of a 1-query linear PCP:

Corollary 3.4 (1-Query Bounded LPCP). *Let $C: \{0,1\}^n \times \{0,1\}^h \to \{0,1\}$ be a Boolean circuit of size s, and let $\mathbb{F}_p$ be a finite field. Let $\tau \in \mathbb{N}$ be a bound parameter and $\delta > 0$ be a zero-knowledge parameter. There exist 1-query bounded linear PCPs over $\mathbb{F}_p$ for $\mathcal{R}_C$ with the following properties:*

– *Perfect completeness, strong soundness error* $3/\tau$, *query length* $(s^2 + 3s)/2$, *and bound function* $b(\tau) = 4s^4\tau^5/3$, *provided that* $p > 2b(\tau)$; *and*
– *Perfect completeness, soundness error* $3/\tau$, *query length* $(s^2 + 3s)/2$, δ-*honest-verifier zero knowledge, and bound function* $b(\tau, \delta) = 64\tau(s\tau/2 + 2\tau\sqrt{s/2\ln(4/\delta)}/\delta)^4/3$, *provided that* $p > 2b(\tau, \delta)$.

Additionally, the query-generation algorithm $\mathcal{Q}_{\mathsf{LPCP}}$ *and the prover algorithm* $\mathcal{P}_{\mathsf{LPCP}}$ *runs in time* $O(s^2) \cdot \mathsf{polylog}(p)$. *The verifier's decision algorithm* $\mathcal{D}_{\mathsf{LPCP}}$ *runs in time* $\mathsf{polylog}(p)$.

3.2 SNARGs Based on ElGamal

In this section, we describe how to efficiently compile our 1-query bounded linear PCP from Corollary 3.4 to obtain a designated-verifier SNARG in the preprocessing model where the proof size consists of 2 group elements and where the verification complexity is sublinear in the cost of the classic NP verifier. While it is possible to directly invoke the [BCI+13] compiler on our 1-query bounded linear PCP together with ElGamal encryption, the verification complexity of the resulting scheme is *quadratic* in the size of the classic NP verifier. This is because the additively-homomorphic version of ElGamal encryption scheme encodes the messages in the exponent, and decryption requires solving a discrete log. When the responses are bounded in an interval of size B, this can be done in time $O(\sqrt{B})$ using generic algorithms (e.g., [Pol78]). While a bounded linear PCP seems like a natural choice to use in conjunction with ElGamal, the bounds in Corollary 3.4 scale with s^4, where s is the circuit size of the classic NP verifier. Instantiating with ElGamal then yields an unacceptable verification complexity that is quadratic in the circuit size. In this section, we will leverage the structure of our packed 2-query bounded linear PCP to obtain an asymptotically-faster (worst-case verification complexity that scales with $\widetilde{O}(\sqrt{s})$) and concretely-efficient designated-verifier SNARG based on ElGamal. Compared with a direct instantiation of the [BCI+13] compiler with ElGamal encryption, our proofs are either 4 times more succinct (2 group elements vs. 8 group elements) or much more concretely efficient (relying on linear PCPs rather than classic PCPs).

The ElGamal instantiation. Before describing how we optimize the verification procedure for our ElGamal-based SNARG, we begin with an explicit description of the construction. We assume a 1-query bounded linear PCP, in which case we obtain a *direct* construction from any linear-only encryption scheme:

Construction 3.5 (SNARG based on ElGamal). Let $C: \{0,1\}^n \times \{0,1\}^h \to \{0,1\}$ be a Boolean circuit of size s. Let $\mathsf{GroupGen}$ be a prime-order group generator that outputs a group $\mathbb{G}$ of prime order p. Let $\Pi_{\mathsf{LPCP}} = (\mathcal{Q}_{\mathsf{LPCP}}, \mathcal{P}_{\mathsf{LPCP}}, \mathcal{D}_{\mathsf{LPCP}})$ be a 1-query bounded linear PCP with bound $B = B(\tau)$ and bound parameter τ for the relation $\mathcal{R}_C$ over $\mathbb{F}_p$. We construct a SNARG $\Pi_{\mathsf{SNARG}} = (\mathcal{S}_{\mathsf{SNARG}}, \mathcal{P}_{\mathsf{SNARG}}, \mathcal{V}_{\mathsf{SNARG}})$

- $\mathcal{S}_{\mathsf{SNARG}}(1^\lambda)$: On input the security parameter λ, the setup algorithm samples a group description $(\mathbb{G}, p, g) \leftarrow \mathsf{GroupGen}(1^\lambda)$ and a linear PCP query $(\mathsf{st}', \mathbf{q}_{\mathsf{inp}}, \mathbf{q}) \leftarrow \mathcal{Q}_{\mathsf{LPCP}}(\tau) \in \mathbb{F}_p^\ell$. The setup algorithm samples a secret key $\alpha \overset{\mathrm{R}}{\leftarrow} \mathbb{F}_p$, and computes the ElGamal public key $h \leftarrow g^\alpha$. The setup algorithm samples $\mathbf{r} \overset{\mathrm{R}}{\leftarrow} \mathbb{F}_p^\ell$, and computes the ciphertexts $(g^\mathbf{r}, h^\mathbf{r} g^\mathbf{q})$, where for a vector $\mathbf{r}$, we write $g^\mathbf{r}$ to denote the vector of group elements $(g^{r_1}, \ldots, g^{r_\ell})$. The setup algorithm outputs the common reference string crs and verification state st:

$$\mathsf{crs} = \big((\mathbb{G}, p, g), h, (g^\mathbf{r}, h^\mathbf{r} g^\mathbf{q}), \tau\big) \text{ and } \mathsf{st} = (\mathsf{st}', \alpha).$$

- $\mathcal{P}_{\mathsf{SNARG}}(\mathsf{crs}, x, w)$: On input a common reference string $\mathsf{crs} = \big((\mathbb{G}, p, g), h, (g^\mathbf{r}, g^\mathbf{s}), \tau\big)$, a statement $x \in \{0, 1\}^\ell$, and a witness $w \in \{0, 1\}^h$, the prover algorithm computes a proof $\pi \leftarrow \mathcal{P}_{\mathsf{LPCP}}(\tau, x, w) \in \mathbb{F}_p^\ell$. It computes the proof as $\pi = (g^{\mathbf{r}^\mathsf{T} \pi}, g^{\mathbf{s}^\mathsf{T} \pi})$.

- $\mathcal{V}_{\mathsf{SNARG}}(\mathsf{st}, x, \pi)$: On input the verification state $\mathsf{st} = (\mathsf{st}', \mathbf{q}_{\mathsf{inp}}, \alpha)$, the statement $x \in \{0, 1\}^n$, and a proof $\pi = (g_1, g_2)$, the verifier computes $h' = g_2 / g_1^\alpha$, and checks if there exists $a \in [-B, B]$ such that $h' = g^a$. It outputs $\mathcal{D}_{\mathsf{LPCP}}(\mathsf{st}', \mathbf{q}_{\mathsf{inp}}^\mathsf{T} x, a)$.

Assuming that the ElGamal encryption scheme satisfies linear targeted malleability with respect to the target set $[-B, B]$, then Construction 3.5 is a designated-verifier SNARG in the preprocessing model where the proof size consists of exactly 2 group elements. The bottleneck is the expensive verification procedure. As stated, the verification algorithm has to compute the discrete log of $h' = g^a$ where a is the linear PCP response. This can be computed in time $\widetilde{O}(\sqrt{B})$, which for the linear PCP from Corollary 3.4, is *quadratic* in the circuit size s.

Optimizing the verification procedure. We now describe how to more efficiently implement the verification procedure in Construction 3.5 to obtain a SNARG whose worst-case verification complexity is $O(s)$. Moreover, if we allow for a negligible completeness error (as opposed to *perfect* completeness), we give a procedure whose worst-case verification complexity is $\widetilde{O}(\sqrt{s})$. Our optimization will rely on specific properties of the linear PCP from Corollary 3.4. Namely, the 1-query linear PCP from Corollary 3.4 was obtained by packing together a 2-query linear PCP.

- The 2-query linear PCP has the property that the verifier accepts a response $(a_1, a_2) \in \mathbb{F}_p^2$ only if $a_1^2 + a_2 = a_{\mathsf{inp}} + u_C$, where $a_{\mathsf{inp}}, u_C \in \mathbb{F}_p$ are scalars that are known to the verifier.
- If $\mathbf{q}_1, \mathbf{q}_2 \in \mathbb{F}_p^\ell$ are the two queries the verifier makes, then the packed query in Construction 3.2 satisfies $\mathbf{q} = \mathbf{q}_1 + r \cdot \mathbf{q}_2$ for some $r \in \mathbb{F}_p$ known to the verifier. This means that the honest prover's response satisfies $a = \mathbf{q}^\mathsf{T} \pi = \mathbf{q}_1^\mathsf{T} \pi + r \cdot \mathbf{q}_2^\mathsf{T} \pi = a_1 + r \cdot a_2$.
- Finally, for an accepting proof, the first response a_1 satisfies $a_1 \in [-b_1(\tau), b_1(\tau)] = [-s\tau/2, s\tau/2]$.

Equivalently, this means the linear PCP verifier accepts only if there exists $a_1 \in [-b_1(\tau), b_1(\tau)]$ such that the following two relations hold:

$$a_2 = a_{\mathsf{inp}} + u_C - a_1^2 \text{ and } a = a_1 + r \cdot a_2,$$

or equivalently, if there exists $a_1 \in [-b_1(\tau), b_1(\tau)]$ such that

$$a = a_1 + r \cdot (a_{\mathsf{inp}} + u_C - a_1^2).$$

In the SNARG from Construction 3.5, the verifier first computes g^a. Now, instead of recovering a by solving discrete log, the verifier instead checks whether there exists $a_1 \in [-b_1(\tau), b_1(\tau)]$ where

$$g^a = g^{a_1 + r(a_{\mathsf{inp}} + u_C - a_1^2)}. \tag{3.2}$$

This can be done by performing a brute force search over all of the possible $2b_1(\tau)$ values for a_1 and seeing if Eq. (3.2) holds. We can also rewrite Eq. (3.2) as checking whether there exists a_1 where

$$g^a \cdot g^{-r(a_{\mathsf{inp}} + u_C)} = g^{a_1 - r a_1^2}. \tag{3.3}$$

Observe now that the right-hand side of the expression depends only on the value of a_1 and r, and in particular, is *independent* of the statement. Since r is sampled by the setup algorithm $\mathcal{S}_{\mathsf{SNARG}}$, the verifier can actually *precompute* a table of values $g^{a_1 - r a_1^2}$ for each possible value of a_1. Then, to verify a proof $\pi = (g_1, g_2)$, the verifier computes $u = g^a g^{-r(a_{\mathsf{inp}} + u_C)}$, which requires a *constant* number of group operations, and finally, checks to see whether u is contained in the table or not. This yields a substantially faster verification procedure. Even without this optimization, we obtain a SNARG where the verification complexity is $O(s)$. We summarize this in the following corollary:

Corollary 3.6 (SNARG from ElGamal with Perfect Completeness). *Let $C: \{0,1\}^n \times \{0,1\}^h \to \{0,1\}$ be a Boolean circuit of size s. Let $\varepsilon > 0$ be a soundness parameter and $\delta > 0$ be a zero-knowledge parameter. Assuming the ElGamal encryption scheme (over a prime order group $\mathbb{G}$ of order p) satisfies linear targeted malleability with respect to a target message space $[-B, B]$ for $B = \mathsf{poly}(s, 1/\varepsilon, 1/\delta)$, there exist a designated-verifier SNARGs for $\mathcal{R}_C$ with perfect completeness, non-adaptive soundness error ε, and proofs of size $2 \log |\mathbb{G}|$. The CRS has size $O(s^2)$. The setup algorithm and prover run in time $O(s^2)$ and the verifier runs in time $O(s/\varepsilon)$. Moreover, the SNARG can be extended to satisfy δ-HVZK. In this case, the verifier runs in time $O(\sqrt{s}/\varepsilon \cdot (\sqrt{s} + \sqrt{\log(1/\delta)}/\delta))$; the setup and prover complexity remain unchanged. All of the running times are up to $\mathsf{polylog}(p)$ factors.*

Sublinear verification. We can further reduce the verification complexity by having the verifier only *accept* proofs where the first response a_1 is contained in a much shorter interval. In the full version of this paper, we show that with overwhelming probability, $a_1 \in [-b'_1(\tau), b'_1(\tau)]$ where $b'_1(\tau) = \widetilde{O}(\tau\sqrt{s})$. We now modify the verification procedure $\mathcal{V}_{\mathsf{SNARG}}$ to only accept if there exists $a_1 \in [-b'_1(\tau), b'_1(\tau)]$ such that Eq. (3.3) holds. Since the subset of proofs the verifier accepts is now a strict *subset* of the proofs it accepted in the original scheme, (single-theorem) soundness is preserved. The trade-off is that the verifier may now reject some honestly-generated proofs, but this can only happen with negligible probability over the verifier's randomness. This yields the following theorem:

Corollary 3.7 (SNARG from ElGamal with Sublinear Verification). *Let $C \colon \{0,1\}^n \times \{0,1\}^h \to \{0,1\}$ be a Boolean circuit of size s. Let $\varepsilon > 0$ be a soundness parameter and $\delta > 0$ be a zero-knowledge parameter. Assuming the ElGamal encryption scheme (over a prime order group $\mathbb{G}$ of order p) satisfies linear targeted malleability with respect to a target message space $[-B, B]$ for $B = \mathsf{poly}(s, 1/\varepsilon, 1/\delta)$, there exists a designated-verifier SNARG for $\mathcal{R}_C$ with statistical completeness and non-adaptive soundness error ε, and proofs of size $2\log|\mathbb{G}|$. The CRS has size $O(s^2)$. The setup algorithm and prover run in time $O(s^2)$ and the verifier runs in time $\widetilde{O}(\sqrt{s}/\varepsilon)$. Moreover, the SNARG can be extended to satisfy δ-HVZK. In this case, the verifier runs in time $\widetilde{O}(\sqrt{s\log(1/\delta)}/(\delta\varepsilon))$; the setup and prover complexity remain unchanged. All of the running times are up to $\mathsf{polylog}(p)$ factors.*

A preprocessing variant. As mentioned above, the verification relation in Eq. (3.3) is very amenable to preprocessing. Namely, the verifier can perform a one-time setup and precompute all of the accepting values of $g^{a_1 - ra_1^2}$ and store them in a table. Applying the sublinear verification approach described above, this will only require $\widetilde{O}(\sqrt{s})$ space when verifying circuits of size s. In the online phase, to check a proof, the verifier needs to perform a single ElGamal decryption, followed by computing the left-hand side of Eq. (3.3), and finally, a single table lookup. The overall computation comes out to just 2 exponentiations and 2 multiplications, followed by the table lookup. This yields the following corollary:

Corollary 3.8 (SNARG from ElGamal with Preprocessing). *Let $C \colon \{0,1\}^n \times \{0,1\}^h \to \{0,1\}$ be a Boolean circuit of size s. Let $\varepsilon > 0$ be a soundness parameter and $\delta > 0$ be a zero-knowledge parameter. Assuming the ElGamal encryption scheme (over a prime order group $\mathbb{G}$ of order p) satisfies linear targeted malleability with respect to a target message space $[-B, B]$ for $B = \mathsf{poly}(s, 1/\varepsilon, 1/\delta)$, there exists a designated-verifier SNARG for $\mathcal{R}_C$ with statistical completeness, non-adaptive soundness error ε, and proofs of size $2\log|\mathbb{G}|$. The CRS has size $O(s^2)$. The setup algorithm runs in time $\widetilde{O}(s^2 + \sqrt{s}/\varepsilon)$ and outputs a table T of size $\widetilde{O}(\sqrt{s}/\varepsilon)$. The prover runs in time $O(s^2)$ and the verifier runs in time $\widetilde{O}(1)$ given access to the precomputed table T. If we extend the SNARG to provide δ-HVZK, the setup algorithm now runs in time $O(s^2 + \sqrt{s\log(1/\delta)}/(\delta\varepsilon))$ and outputs a table T of size $O(\sqrt{s\log(1/\delta)}/(\delta\varepsilon))$. Given access to the precomputed table, the verifier's runtime is $\widetilde{O}(1)$. All of the running times and table sizes are up to $\mathsf{polylog}(p)$ factors.*

Remark 3.9 (Arguments of Knowledge). The SNARG constructions in Corollaries 3.6 to 3.8 are all arguments of knowledge (i.e., "SNARKs") since the underlying linear PCPs provide knowledge soundness and Construction 3.2 preserves the knowledge soundness of the underlying linear PCP.

3.3 Concrete Efficiency of the ElGamal-Based SNARG

In the full version of this paper, we provide an overview of our methodology for estimating the concrete efficient of our ElGamal-based SNARG. A summary of the main results is provided in Table 2.

4   1-Query Linear PCP from Hardness of Approximation

In the full version of this paper, we show how to construct a 1-query *instance-dependent* linear PCP with a linear decision procedure and *negligible* soundness error. Combined with the compiler from [BCI+13], and assuming linear targeted malleability of ElGamal encryption, we obtain the first laconic argument with negligible soundness error where the proof consists of a *single* ElGamal ciphertext. Note that we do *not* obtain a SNARG because the verifier's first message (i.e., the verifier's query) depends on the statement. We refer to Sect. 1.2 for a high-level overview of the construction.

5   1-Element Laconic Arguments and Witness Encryption

In the full version of this paper, we show that any laconic argument system for an NP language $\mathcal{L}$ (with negligible soundness error) where the proof consists of a single group element (i.e., a "1-element laconic argument") and where the verification algorithm can be modeled as a "generic" algorithm implies a witness encryption scheme for $\mathcal{L}$. Note that since the prover is restricted to sending a single group element, this effectively restricts the prover to sending at most one message in the protocol. Thus, it suffices to just consider *2-message* laconic arguments here. Our construction of witness encryption proceeds in two steps. We first show that any laconic argument satisfying the above properties must be *predictable* [FNV17]. We then invoke the Faonio et al. [FNV17] compiler on the predictable argument to obtain a witness encryption scheme.

Next, we show that under a new hypothesis on the hardness of approximating the minimum distance of a linear code [DMS99] (Hypothesis 5.2), we can construct a laconic element for NP where the proof consists of a single group element in the generic group model. Thus, under our hypothesis, we obtain a witness encryption scheme for NP in the generic group model.

5.1   1-Element Laconic Argument from Hardness of Approximation

In this section, we show that under a hardness of approximation hypothesis for the minimum distance problem [DMS99], we can construct a 1-element laconic argument for general NP languages. We begin by recalling the minimum distance problem and then stating our hardness of approximation hypothesis.

Definition 5.1 (Gap Minimum Distance Problem (GapMDP) [DMS99, Definition 1]). *For an approximation factor β, an instance of GapMDP_β is a pair $(\mathbf{A}, d)$ where $\mathbf{A} \in \mathbb{F}^{n \times k}$ for some finite field $\mathbb{F}$ and $d \in \mathbb{N}$ such that*

- *$(\mathbf{A}, d)$ is a* YES *instance if $\mathsf{dist}(\mathbf{A}) \leq d$.*
- *$(\mathbf{A}, d)$ is a* NO *instance if $\mathsf{dist}(\mathbf{A}) \geq \beta \cdot d$.*

Here, $\mathsf{dist}(\mathbf{A})$ is the minimum distance (under the Hamming metric) of the code generated by $\mathbf{A}$. A witness for a YES *instance $(\mathbf{A}, d)$ is a nonzero codeword $\mathbf{0} \neq \mathbf{v} \in \mathbb{F}^k$ (in the code generated by $\mathbf{A}$) where $\mathsf{wt}(\mathbf{v}) \leq d$.*

Hypothesis 5.2 (Hardness of Approximation for GapMDP).   For some $\beta = \omega(\log n)$, the GapMDP_β problem is NP-hard for any choice of finite field $\mathbb{F}$ where $|\mathbb{F}| = 2^{O(n)}$. Specifically, there exists a deterministic Karp-Levin reduction from SAT to GapMDP_β, where the reduction algorithm takes a target field $\mathbb{F}$ as an *explicit* input and outputs an instance $(\mathbf{A}, d)$ over $\mathbb{F}$ in time $\mathsf{poly}(n, \log|\mathbb{F}|)$.

Existing hardness results on GapMDP. Dumer et al. [DMS99] showed that the GapMDP was NP-hard for any constant approximation factor $\beta = O(1)$ (over any polynomial-size field) via a randomized reduction. Subsequently, Cheng and Wan [CW09] as well as Austrin and Khot [AK14] gave a deterministic reduction for the same parameter regimes. The latter results additionally give a deterministic *quasi-polynomial* time reduction from NP to the GapMDP_β for any $\beta = 2^{\log^{1-\varepsilon}(n)}$ (i.e., unless $\mathsf{NP} \subseteq \mathsf{DTIME}(2^{\mathsf{polylog}(n)})$, there is no polynomial-time algorithm for GapMDP_β). In our setting, we need to strengthen the existing hardness of approximation results in two different directions: (1) Hypothesis 5.2 requires a deterministic *polynomial* time reduction to GapMDP while the existing reductions in the super-constant regime are all quasi-polynomial; and (2) we require that the reduction applies to large prime characteristic fields (i.e., fields that are super-polynomial in the instance size). While existing reductions are agnostic about the choice of the field, the running time of existing reductions scale polynomially in the characteristic of the field, so they do not directly generalize to super-polynomial size fields.[10] While existing techniques do not suffice for proving Hypothesis 5.2, there are no known barriers to doing so [Kho20]

Construction 5.3 (Laconic Argument for GapMDP).   Let λ be a security parameter, $\varepsilon > 0$ be a completeness parameter, and $\beta > 0$ be the approximation factor. Let GroupGen be a prime-order group generator, and let $p = p(\lambda)$ be the

---

[10] We formulate the hypothesis for $|\mathbb{F}| = 2^{O(n)}$, although any field of super-polynomial size would also suffice.

order of the group output by GroupGen. We construct a two-message laconic argument $\Pi_{\mathsf{LA}} = (\mathcal{Q}_{\mathsf{LA}}, \mathcal{P}_{\mathsf{LA}}, \mathcal{V}_{\mathsf{LA}})$ for GapMDP_β (for instances over $\mathbb{F}_p$):

- $\mathcal{Q}_{\mathsf{LA}}(1^\lambda, (\mathbf{A}, d))$: On input the security parameter λ and an GapMDP_β instance $(\mathbf{A}, d)$ over $\mathbb{F}_p$, the query algorithm samples $(\mathbb{G}, p, g) \leftarrow \mathsf{GroupGen}(1^\lambda)$. Let $\mathbf{H} \in \mathbb{F}_p^{\ell \times k}$ be the parity check matrix for the code generated by $\mathbf{A}$. Then the verifier constructs the following components:
  - Sample a random vector $\mathbf{e} \in \mathbb{F}_p^k$ where each component $e_i = 0$ with probability $1 - \varepsilon/d$ and $e_i \xleftarrow{\text{R}} \mathbb{F}_p$ otherwise.
  - Sample $\mathbf{c} \xleftarrow{\text{R}} \mathbb{F}_p^k$, $\mathbf{r} \xleftarrow{\text{R}} \mathbb{F}_p^\ell$, $s \xleftarrow{\text{R}} \mathbb{F}_p$ and compute $\mathbf{z}^\mathsf{T} = \mathbf{r}^\mathsf{T} \mathbf{H} + s\mathbf{c}^\mathsf{T} + \mathbf{e}^\mathsf{T} \in \mathbb{F}_p^k$. The algorithm outputs $((\mathbb{G}, p, g), \mathbf{c}, g^\mathbf{z})$ as its query and $\mathsf{st} = g^s$ as its state. Here, we write $g^\mathbf{z}$ to denote the vector of group elements $(g^{z_1}, \ldots, g^{z_k})$, where $z_1, \ldots, z_k$ are the components of $\mathbf{z}$.
- $\mathcal{P}_{\mathsf{LA}}(q, x, w)$: On input a query $q = ((\mathbb{G}, p, g), \mathbf{c}, g^\mathbf{z})$, a GapMDP instance $(\mathbf{A}, d)$ and a witness $\mathbf{v} \in \mathbb{F}_p^k$, the prover algorithm does the following:
  - If $\mathbf{c}^\mathsf{T} \mathbf{v} = 0$, then the prover aborts with output $\bot$. Otherwise, let $t = (\mathbf{c}^\mathsf{T} \mathbf{v})^{-1}$.
  - Output the proof $\pi = g^{t \cdot \mathbf{z}^\mathsf{T} \mathbf{v}}$ (which can be computed from t, $\mathbf{v}$, and $g^\mathbf{z}$).
- $\mathcal{V}_{\mathsf{LA}}(\mathsf{st}, \pi)$: On input the verification state $\mathsf{st} \in \mathbb{G}$ and a proof $\pi \in \mathbb{G}$, output 1 if $\mathsf{st} = \pi$, and 0 otherwise.

Completeness and soundness analysis. We now state the completeness and soundness theorems for Construction 5.3 as well as the resulting implication to 1-element laconic arguments and witness encryption for NP in the generic group model. We defer the completeness and soundness proofs to the full version of this paper.

Theorem 5.4 (Completeness). *Construction 5.3 has completeness error ε.*

Theorem 5.5 (Soundness). *If $\varepsilon\beta = \omega(\log n)$ and GroupGen is modeled as a generic group, then Construction 5.3 has soundness error $\mathsf{negl}(\lambda)$.*

Corollary 5.6 (1-Element Laconic Argument for NP). *Let λ be a security parameter. Under Hypothesis 5.2, there exists a predictable laconic argument for NP in the generic group model with completeness error $o(1)$ and soundness error $\mathsf{negl}(\lambda)$ and where the prover's message consists of a single group element.*

Proof. Let $\beta(\lambda) = f(\lambda) \log \lambda$ where $f(\lambda) = \omega(1)$ for which Hypothesis 5.2 holds. Take $\varepsilon = 1/\sqrt{f(\lambda)} = o(1)$. By instantiating Construction 5.3 with this choice of β, ε and appealing to Theorems 5.4 and 5.5, we obtain a laconic argument for GapMDP_β with completeness error $\varepsilon = o(1)$ and soundness error $\mathsf{negl}(\lambda)$. In addition, Construction 5.3 is predictable by construction. Finally, by Hypothesis 5.2, there exists a deterministic polynomial-time Karp-Levin reduction from NP to GapMDP_β, and so we can use our laconic argument for GapMDP_β to obtain a laconic argument for any NP language.

Corollary 5.7 (Hypothetical Witness Encryption for NP in the Generic Group Model). *Under Hypothesis 5.2, there exists a witness encryption scheme for* NP *in the generic group model.*

Proof. Follows by instantiating the general compiler from [FNV17] with the predictable laconic argument from Corollary 5.6. We provide more details in the full version of this paper.

Acknowledgments. We thank Henry Corrigan-Gibbs, Subhash Khot, and Sam Kim for insightful discussions and pointers. We thank the anonymous reviewers for helpful feedback on the presentation.

References

[AK14] Austrin, P., Khot, S.: A simple deterministic reduction for the gap minimum distance of code problem. IEEE Trans. Inf. Theory **60**(10), 6636–6645 (2014)

[AL07] Aumann, Y., Lindell, Y.: Security against covert adversaries: efficient protocols for realistic adversaries. In: Vadhan, S.P. (ed.) TCC 2007. LNCS, vol. 4392, pp. 137–156. Springer, Heidelberg (2007). https://doi.org/10.1007/978-3-540-70936-7_8

[ALM+98] Arora, S., Lund, C., Motwani, R., Sudan, M., Szegedy, M.: Proof verification and the hardness of approximation problems. J. ACM **45**(3), 501–555 (1998)

[BBB+18] Bünz, B., Bootle, J., Boneh, D., Poelstra, A., Wuille, P., Maxwell, G.: Bulletproofs: short proofs for confidential transactions and more. In: IEEE SP (2018)

[BBC+19] Boneh, D., Boyle, E., Corrigan-Gibbs, H., Gilboa, N., Ishai, Y.: Zero-knowledge proofs on secret-shared data via fully linear PCPs. In: Boldyreva, A., Micciancio, D. (eds.) CRYPTO 2019. LNCS, vol. 11694, pp. 67–97. Springer, Cham (2019). https://doi.org/10.1007/978-3-030-26954-8_3

[BBFR15] Backes, M., Barbosa, M., Fiore, D., Reischuk, R.M.: ADSNARK: nearly practical and privacy-preserving proofs on authenticated data. In: IEEE SP (2015)

[BBHR19] Ben-Sasson, E., Bentov, I., Horesh, Y., Riabzev, M.: Scalable zero knowledge with no trusted setup. In: Boldyreva, A., Micciancio, D. (eds.) CRYPTO 2019. LNCS, vol. 11694, pp. 701–732. Springer, Cham (2019). https://doi.org/10.1007/978-3-030-26954-8_23

[BC12] Bitansky, N., Chiesa, A.: Succinct arguments from multi-prover interactive proofs and their efficiency benefits. In: Safavi-Naini, R., Canetti, R. (eds.) CRYPTO 2012. LNCS, vol. 7417, pp. 255–272. Springer, Heidelberg (2012). https://doi.org/10.1007/978-3-642-32009-5_16

[BCC88] Brassard, G., Chaum, D., Crépeau, C.: Minimum disclosure proofs of knowledge. J. Comput. Syst. Sci. **37**(2), 156–189 (1988)

[BCC+16] Bootle, J., Cerulli, A., Chaidos, P., Groth, J., Petit, C.: Efficient zero-knowledge arguments for arithmetic circuits in the discrete log setting. In: Fischlin, M., Coron, J.-S. (eds.) EUROCRYPT 2016. LNCS, vol. 9666, pp. 327–357. Springer, Heidelberg (2016). https://doi.org/10.1007/978-3-662-49896-5_12

[BCC+17] Bitansky, N., et al.: The hunting of the SNARK. J. Cryptol. **30**(4), 989–1066 (2017)

[BCCT12] Bitansky, N., Canetti, R., Chiesa, A., Tromer, E.: From extractable collision resistance to succinct non-interactive arguments of knowledge, and back again. In: ITCS (2012)

[BCG+13] Ben-Sasson, E., Chiesa, A., Genkin, D., Tromer, E., Virza, M.: SNARKs for C: verifying program executions succinctly and in zero knowledge. In: Canetti, R., Garay, J.A. (eds.) CRYPTO 2013. LNCS, vol. 8043, pp. 90–108. Springer, Heidelberg (2013). https://doi.org/10.1007/978-3-642-40084-1_6

[BCG+14] Ben-Sasson, E., et al.: Zerocash: decentralized anonymous payments from bitcoin. In: IEEE SP (2014)

[BCI+13] Bitansky, N., Chiesa, A., Ishai, Y., Paneth, O., Ostrovsky, R.: Succinct non-interactive arguments via linear interactive proofs. In: Sahai, A. (ed.) TCC 2013. LNCS, vol. 7785, pp. 315–333. Springer, Heidelberg (2013). https://doi.org/10.1007/978-3-642-36594-2_18

[BDRV18] Berman, I., Degwekar, A., Rothblum, R.D., Vasudevan, P.N.: From laconic zero-knowledge to public-key cryptography. In: Shacham, H., Boldyreva, A. (eds.) CRYPTO 2018. LNCS, vol. 10993, pp. 674–697. Springer, Cham (2018). https://doi.org/10.1007/978-3-319-96878-0_23

[Ber06] Bernstein, D.J.: Curve25519: new Diffie-Hellman speed records. In: Yung, M., Dodis, Y., Kiayias, A., Malkin, T. (eds.) PKC 2006. LNCS, vol. 3958, pp. 207–228. Springer, Heidelberg (2006). https://doi.org/10.1007/11745853_14

[BHZ87] Boppana, R.B., Håstad, J., Zachos, S.: Does co-NP have short interactive proofs? Inf. Process. Lett. **25**(2), 127–132 (1987)

[BIJ+20] Bartusek, J., Ishai, Y., Jain, A., Ma, F., Sahai, A., Zhandry, M.: Affine determinant programs: a framework for obfuscation and witness encryption. In: ITCS (2020)

[BISW17] Boneh, D., Ishai, Y., Sahai, A., Wu, D.J.: Lattice-based SNARGs and their application to more efficient obfuscation. In: Coron, J.-S., Nielsen, J.B. (eds.) EUROCRYPT 2017. LNCS, vol. 10212, pp. 247–277. Springer, Cham (2017). https://doi.org/10.1007/978-3-319-56617-7_9

[BISW18] Boneh, D., Ishai, Y., Sahai, A., Wu, D.J.: Quasi-optimal SNARGs via linear multi-prover interactive proofs. In: Nielsen, J.B., Rijmen, V. (eds.) EUROCRYPT 2018. LNCS, vol. 10822, pp. 222–255. Springer, Cham (2018). https://doi.org/10.1007/978-3-319-78372-7_8

[BSW12] Boneh, D., Segev, G., Waters, B.: Targeted malleability: homomorphic encryption for restricted computations. In: ITCS (2012)

[CL08] Di Crescenzo, G., Lipmaa, H.: Succinct NP Proofs from an extractability assumption. In: Beckmann, A., Dimitracopoulos, C., Löwe, B. (eds.) CiE 2008. LNCS, vol. 5028, pp. 175–185. Springer, Heidelberg (2008). https://doi.org/10.1007/978-3-540-69407-6_21

[CO99] Canetti, R., Ostrovsky, R.: Secure computation with honest-looking parties: what if nobody is truly honest? In: STOC (1999)

[CVW18] Chen, Y., Vaikuntanathan, V., Wee, H.: GGH15 beyond permutation branching programs: proofs, attacks, and candidates. In: Shacham, H., Boldyreva, A. (eds.) CRYPTO 2018. LNCS, vol. 10992, pp. 577–607. Springer, Cham (2018). https://doi.org/10.1007/978-3-319-96881-0_20

[CW09] Cheng, Q., Wan, D.: A deterministic reduction for the gap minimum distance problem: [extended abstract]. In: STOC (2009)

[DFGK14] Danezis, G., Fournet, C., Groth, J., Kohlweiss, M.: Square span programs with applications to succinct NIZK arguments. In: Sarkar, P., Iwata, T. (eds.) ASIACRYPT 2014. LNCS, vol. 8873, pp. 532–550. Springer, Heidelberg (2014). https://doi.org/10.1007/978-3-662-45611-8_28

[DMS99] Dumer, I., Micciancio, D., Sudan, M.: Hardness of approximating the minimum distance of a linear code. In: FOCS (1999)

[ElG84] ElGamal, T.: A public key cryptosystem and a signature scheme based on discrete logarithms. In: Blakley, G.R., Chaum, D. (eds.) CRYPTO 1984. LNCS, vol. 196, pp. 10–18. Springer, Heidelberg (1985). https://doi.org/10.1007/3-540-39568-7_2

[FNV17] Faonio, A., Nielsen, J.B., Venturi, D.: Predictable arguments of knowledge. In: PKC (2017)

[GGH+13] Garg, S., Gentry, C., Halevi, S., Raykova, M., Sahai, A., Waters, B.: Candidate indistinguishability obfuscation and functional encryption for all circuits. In: FOCS (2013)

[GGPR13] Gennaro, R., Gentry, C., Parno, B., Raykova, M.: Quadratic span programs and succinct NIZKs without PCPs. In: Johansson, T., Nguyen, P.Q. (eds.) EUROCRYPT 2013. LNCS, vol. 7881, pp. 626–645. Springer, Heidelberg (2013). https://doi.org/10.1007/978-3-642-38348-9_37

[GGSW13] Garg, S., Gentry, C., Sahai, A., Waters, B.: Witness encryption and its applications. In: STOC (2013)

[GH98] Goldreich, O., Håstad, J.: On the complexity of interactive proofs with bounded communication. Inf. Process. Lett. $67(4)$, 205–214 (1998)

[GLW14] Gentry, C., Lewko, A., Waters, B.: Witness encryption from instance independent assumptions. In: Garay, J.A., Gennaro, R. (eds.) CRYPTO 2014. LNCS, vol. 8616, pp. 426–443. Springer, Heidelberg (2014). https://doi.org/10.1007/978-3-662-44371-2_24

[GMR85] Goldwasser, S., Micali, S., Rackoff, C.: The knowledge complexity of interactive proof-systems (extended abstract). In: STOC (1985)

[Gol00] Goldreich, O.: Candidate one-way functions based on expander graphs. Electron. Colloquium Comput. Complex. (ECCC) $7(90)$ (2000)

[Gro10] Groth, J.: Short pairing-based non-interactive zero-knowledge arguments. In: Abe, M. (ed.) ASIACRYPT 2010. LNCS, vol. 6477, pp. 321–340. Springer, Heidelberg (2010). https://doi.org/10.1007/978-3-642-17373-8_19

[Gro16] Groth, J.: On the size of pairing-based non-interactive arguments. In: Fischlin, M., Coron, J.-S. (eds.) EUROCRYPT 2016. LNCS, vol. 9666, pp. 305–326. Springer, Heidelberg (2016). https://doi.org/10.1007/978-3-662-49896-5_11

[GVW01] Goldreich, O., Vadhan, S., Wigderson, A.: On interactive proofs with a laconic prover. In: Orejas, F., Spirakis, P.G., van Leeuwen, J. (eds.) ICALP 2001. LNCS, vol. 2076, pp. 334–345. Springer, Heidelberg (2001). https://doi.org/10.1007/3-540-48224-5_28

[GW11] Gentry, C., Wichs, D.: Separating succinct non-interactive arguments from all falsifiable assumptions. In: STOC (2011)

[IKO07] Ishai, Y., Kushilevitz, E., Ostrovsky, R.: Efficient arguments without short PCPs. In: CCC (2007)

[Kho20] Khot, S.: Personal communication (2020)

[Kil92]   Kilian, J.: A note on efficient zero-knowledge proofs and arguments. In: STOC (1992)

[KMO89]   Kilian, J., Micali, S., Ostrovsky, R.: Minimum resource zero-knowledge proofs. In: FOCS (1989)

[KPV12]   Khot, S., Popat, P., Vishnoi, N.K.: $2^{\log^{1-\varepsilon} n}$ hardness for the closest vector problem with preprocessing. In: STOC (2012)

[Lip12]   Lipmaa, H.: Progression-free sets and sublinear pairing-based non-interactive zero-knowledge arguments. In: Cramer, R. (ed.) TCC 2012. LNCS, vol. 7194, pp. 169–189. Springer, Heidelberg (2012). https://doi.org/10.1007/978-3-642-28914-9_10

[Mic00]   Micali, S.: Computationally sound proofs. SIAM J. Comput. **30**(4), 1253–1298 (2000)

[Mie08]   Mie, T.: Polylogarithmic two-round argument systems. J. Math. Cryptol. **2**(4), 343–363 (2008)

[MMN+16a]   Mahmoody, M., Mohammed, A., Nematihaji, S., Pass, R., Shelat, A.: Lower bounds on assumptions behind indistinguishability obfuscation. In: Kushilevitz, E., Malkin, T. (eds.) TCC 2016. LNCS, vol. 9562, pp. 49–66. Springer, Heidelberg (2016). https://doi.org/10.1007/978-3-662-49096-9_3

[MMN+16b]   Mahmoody, M., Mohammed, A., Nematihaji, S., Pass, R., Shelat, A.: A note on black-box complexity of indistinguishability obfuscation. IACR Cryptol. ePrint Arch., 2016, 316 (2016)

[Nec94]   Nechaev, V.I.: Complexity of a determinate algorithm for the discrete logarithm. Math. Notes **55**, 165–172 (1994)

[PHGR13]   Parno, B., Howell, J., Gentry, C., Raykova, M.: Pinocchio: nearly practical verifiable computation. In: IEEE SP (2013)

[Pol78]   Pollard, J.M.: Monte carlo methods for index computation (mod p). Math. Comput. **32**(143), 918–924 (1978)

[PRV12]   Papakonstantinou, P.A., Rackoff, C., Vahlis, Y.: How powerful are the DDH hard groups? IACR Cryptol. ePrint Arch., 2012 (2012)

[Raz95]   Raz, R.: A parallel repetition theorem. In: STOC, pp. 447–456 (1995)

[SCI20]   SCIPR Lab. libsnark: a C++ library for zkSNARK proofs (2020). https://github.com/scipr-lab/libsnark

[Sho97]   Shoup, V.: Lower bounds for discrete logarithms and related problems. In: Fumy, W. (ed.) EUROCRYPT 1997. LNCS, vol. 1233, pp. 256–266. Springer, Heidelberg (1997). https://doi.org/10.1007/3-540-69053-0_18

[Wee05]   Wee, H.: On round-efficient argument systems. In: Caires, L., Italiano, G.F., Monteiro, L., Palamidessi, C., Yung, M. (eds.) ICALP 2005. LNCS, vol. 3580, pp. 140–152. Springer, Heidelberg (2005). https://doi.org/10.1007/11523468_12

Fully Deniable Interactive Encryption

Ran Canetti[1]([✉]), Sunoo Park[2]([✉]), and Oxana Poburinnaya[3]([✉])

[1] Boston University, Boston, USA
canetti@bu.edu
[2] MIT and Harvard, Cambridge, USA
sunoo@csail.mit.edu
[3] University of Rochester, Rochester, USA
oxanapob@bu.edu

Abstract. Deniable encryption (Canetti *et al.*, Crypto 1996) enhances secret communication over public channels, providing the additional guarantee that the secrecy of communication is protected even if the parties are later coerced (or willingly bribed) to expose their entire internal states: plaintexts, keys and randomness. To date, constructions of deniable encryption—and more generally, interactive deniable communication—only address restricted cases where only *one* party is compromised (Sahai and Waters, STOC 2014). The main question—whether deniable communication is at all possible if *both* parties are coerced at once—has remained open.

We resolve this question in the affirmative, presenting a communication protocol that is *fully deniable* under coercion of both parties. Our scheme has three rounds, assumes subexponentially secure indistinguishability obfuscation and one-way functions, and uses a short global reference string that is generated once at system set-up and suffices for an unbounded number of encryptions and decryptions.

Of independent interest, we introduce a new notion called *off-the-record deniability*, which protects parties even when their claimed internal states are inconsistent (a case not covered by prior definitions). Our scheme satisfies both standard deniability and off-the-record deniability.

1 Introduction

The ability to communicate secret information without having any prior shared secrets is a central pillar of modern cryptography [DH76, RSA78, GM84]. However, standard definitions and existing algorithms for secure communication only guarantee security if the parties' local randomness remains hidden. If the parties' secret keys or randomness are exposed, say as a result of coercion or bribery, secrecy is no longer guaranteed. Moreover, the transcript in common encryption and key exchange schemes often "commits" the sender to the plaintext, in that each transcript is consistent with only one plaintext and randomness.

To address this issue, Canetti, Dwork, Naor and Ostrovsky [CDNO96] introduced the notion of *deniable encryption*, which provides a mechanism for

ⓒ International Association for Cryptologic Research 2020
D. Micciancio and T. Ristenpart (Eds.): CRYPTO 2020, LNCS 12170, pp. 807–835, 2020.
https://doi.org/10.1007/978-3-030-56784-2_27

preserving the secrecy of communicated plaintexts even in the face of post-communication coercion or bribery.[1] Specifically, deniable encryption (or, more generally, deniable interactive communication) introduces additional algorithms, called *faking algorithms*, that are not present in standard secure communication definitions. The faking algorithms allow the communicating parties to present fake internal states (including keys and randomness) that make any communication transcript appear consistent with any plaintext of the parties' choice. Concretely, an adversary should not be able to tell whether the sender and the receiver gave it the true keys, randomness, and plaintext, or fake ones.

When the communicating parties have a secret key that was shared ahead of time, deniable encryption can be simple. The classic one-time-pad scheme is perfectly deniable: having sent $c = k \oplus m$, the parties can claim that they sent any plaintext m' by claiming that $k' = c \oplus m'$ is their true key. However, shared-key deniable schemes fail to address the crucial question of how to deniably agree on a shared key in the first place. Indeed, existing key exchange protocols are "committing" in a way that precludes deniability. For instance, in Diffie-Hellman key exchange, there exists only one key consistent with any given transcript, so it is impossible to equivocate a one-time pad key generated using Diffie-Hellman key exchange. Thus, the core question here is how to deniably transmit a value (or equivalently, to establish a shared key) *without any pre-shared secrets.*

This setting turns out to be much more challenging. Even the restricted case where only the *sender* is coerced (or bribed) was fully resolved only much later, assuming indistinguishability obfuscation, in the breakthrough work of Sahai and Waters [SW14].[2] The case where only the *receiver* is coerced or bribed follows from the sender-only case via a general transformation, at the cost of an additional message [CDNO96]; hence, the [SW14] scheme implies a 3-round receiver-deniable protocol. This transformation can also be extended to handle the case where the adversary may coerce either party, *but only one of the two*. Furthermore, as demonstrated by Bendlin, Nielsen, Nordholt, and Orlandi [BNNO11], *any* receiver-deniable encryption protocol must take at least three rounds of communication.

Constructing *bideniable* encryption protocols, namely encryption protocols that guarantee deniability in the unrestricted case where both the sender and the receiver can be simultaneously coerced or bribed, has remained open:

Do there exist bideniable encryption protocols, with any number of rounds?

Bideniability is a significantly stronger property than any of the restricted variants above, where the adversary only learns the internal state of either the

---

[1] While our results address both bribery and coercion, bribery might be the better setting to keep in mind. Indeed, protecting against bribery is more challenging in that the parties are *incentivized* to disclose all internal state, including all random choices.

[2] Prior to [SW14], we only had the partial solution of [CDNO96], where the adversary's distinguishing advantage decreases linearly with ciphertext size; in particular, to get indistinguishability with negligibly small advantage, one has to send super-polynomially long ciphertexts.

sender or the receiver.[3] Indeed, when both parties are coerced, the adversary obtains a complete transcript of an execution, including all the random choices, inputs and outputs of both parties. This means that the adversary can now fully run this execution, step by step, and compare it against the recorded communication. Even so, as long as the sender and receiver follow the protocol during the actual exchange of messages, bideniability guarantees that any (real or fake) internal state provided by the parties looks just as plausible as any other (real or fake) one.

Off-the-record deniability. When the attacker bribes or coerces *both* parties, a new concern emerges: what happens if the plaintext claimed by the sender is different from that claimed by the receiver? This could arise in various scenarios: the parties might simply not have the chance to coordinate a story in advance (e.g., if they are separated and interrogated); or the parties might be incentivized to tell different stories (e.g., to protect themselves or those close to them); or the parties might find themselves incentivized to "defect" on each other as in a prisoner's dilemma. Still, standard bideniability (as defined by [CDNO96]) provides no guarantees for these cases.

1.1   Our Contributions

Our first contribution is defining a security guarantee, called *off-the-record deniability*, that holds even in the above setting, where the coerced (or bribed) parties' responses are inconsistent with each other.[4] Off-the-record deniability achieves protection akin to an ideal, physically protected communication channel where the communication leaves no trace behind. That is, off-the-record deniability guarantees that the communication transcript does not help the attacker to determine which of the two parties is telling the truth, if any. This holds even if the parties deviate from the protocol—as long as the deviation happens after the actual protocol execution completes. In other words, off-the-record deniability guarantees protection for each party *independently of the other party's actions.* This contrasts with standard bideniability where, for the security guarantee to hold, *both parties must lie, and their claims must be consistent.*

Our second and main contribution is the first encryption protocol that is both bideniable and off-the-record deniable. We call such protocols *fully deniable.* A fully deniable protocol provides protection akin to an ideal channel, in that after message transmission, each party can claim that the message was any value whatsoever (say, from a pre-specified domain) and the attacker has no way to tell which party, if any, is telling the truth.

---

[3] We note that a related but different concept, *multi-distributional bideniability*, has previously been considered in a setting where both parties are attacked [OPW11]; see Sect. 1.4 and the full version of this paper [CPP18] for more details.

[4] The *off-the-record messaging protocol* [BGB04] is a messaging protocol that shares our motivation of enabling encrypted communications as close as possible to an ideal private channel, but is otherwise unrelated to our off-the-record deniability notion.

We stress that, prior to this work, even the existence of bideniable encryption (without the additional off-the-record property) was an open question.

Theorem 1. *Assuming subexponentially secure indistinguishability obfuscation and subexponentially secure one-way functions, there exists a 3-message interactive bit encryption scheme that is **fully deniable** (i.e., both **bideniable** and **off-the-record-deniable**) in the common reference string model. In addition, the receiver's deniability is public (i.e., the true random coins of the receiver are not required to compute fake randomness of the receiver).*

Our common reference string (CRS) consists of six obfuscated programs: three for the sender (programs P1 and P3 for generating the first and third messages, respectively, and the sender faking program SFake) and three for the receiver (programs P2 for generating the second message, the decryption program Dec, and the receiver faking program RFake). The scheme instructs the parties to run the obfuscated programs on their relevant inputs and uniformly chosen random inputs.

Designing the scheme requires addressing two main classes of challenges. First, the operation of the six programs should follow a certain "internal logic" - which ends up being necessary even in an idealized model where parties only have *oracle access* to the encryption scheme programs. We make this logic explicit by constructing and proving security of a fully deniable encryption scheme in this idealized model. While this construction is not used directly in the full-fledged scheme, it highlights key design difficulties. Interestingly, while many cryptographic primitives are trivial to construct in this idealized model, deniable encryption is still highly non-trivial; indeed, *our technical overview (Sect. 2) is fully devoted to building deniable encryption in the idealized model.*

The next challenge lies in translating this idealized protocol to one that is provably secure when the programs are (a) actual programs and (b) protected only by indistinguishability obfuscation (IO), not ideal obfuscation. Here, we use the sophisticated tools developed in [KLW15, CHJV14, BPR15, BPW16] that were developed for dealing with obfuscated programs that are designed to be repeatedly run on inputs that were generated earlier by the program itself. Our situation is however significantly more complex: We have several programs that are designed to take inputs from each other with a specific and context-dependent set of constraints. We thus develop additional tools and abstractions that allow us to deal with this more complicated setting.

We now turn to discussing our definitions and constructions in more detail.

1.2 Fully Deniable Interactive Encryption: Definition in a Nutshell

Deniable interactive encryption is equipped with algorithms to generate protocol messages, to decrypt, and to generate fake randomness. We present the definition for the three-message case, since our protocol has three messages.

We start with syntax. A scheme consists of six programs: P1, P2, P3, Dec, SFake, and RFake. Program P1, run by the sender, takes as input a message m and sender random string s, and outputs a first message μ_1. Program P2, run by the receiver, takes as input a message μ_1 and receiver random string r, and outputs second message μ_2. Program P3, run by the sender, takes s, m, μ_1, μ_2 and outputs a third message μ_3. Program Dec, run by the receiver, takes input r, μ_1, μ_2, μ_3 and outputs plaintext $\tilde{m}$. Program SFake takes as input the public transcript of the protocol (namely messages μ_1, μ_2, μ_3), the sender randomness s, the message m, a fake message m', and potentially some additional random input ρ_S, and outputs a fake random string $s_{m'}$ that is intended to explain the transcript as an encryption of m'. Program RFake takes as input the public transcript, the receiver randomness r, the message m, a fake message m', and potentially some additional random input ρ_R, and outputs a fake random string $r_{m'}$ that is intended to explain the transcript as decrypting to m'.

We define *correctness* in the natural way: if the sender runs P1, P3 with plaintext m and uniformly chosen s, and the receiver runs P2, Dec with uniformly chosen r, the receiver must decrypt $\tilde{m} = m$ except with negligible probability.

Bideniability requires that no PPT adversary can distinguish the following two distributions: (1) a protocol transcript for plaintext m', and both parties' true random coins for that transcript; and (2) a protocol transcript for plaintext m and fake random coins which make that transcript decrypt to m'. That is,

$$(\mathsf{tr}(s, r, m'), s, r) \approx_c (\mathsf{tr}(s, r, m), s_{m'}, r_{m'}) ,\tag{1}$$

where s, r are uniformly random, $\mathsf{tr}(s, r, m)$ is the transcript from running the protocol to transmit m with random inputs s for the sender and r for the receiver, $s_{m'} = \mathsf{SFake}(s, m, m', \mathsf{tr}(s, r, m); \rho_S), r_{m'} = \mathsf{RFake}(r, m, m', \mathsf{tr}(s, r, m); \rho_R)$, and $\approx_c$ denotes computational indistinguishability.

Off-the-record deniability requires that no PPT adversary can distinguish between the following three cases:

- **The sender tells the truth** and **the receiver lies**. That is, the adversary sees a transcript for plaintext m, the sender's true random coins, and fake random coins from the receiver consistent with m'.
- **The sender lies** and **the receiver tells the truth**. That is, the adversary sees a transcript for plaintext m', fake random coins from the sender consistent with m, and the receiver's true random coins.
- **Both the sender and the receiver lie**. That is, the adversary sees a transcript for plaintext m'', fake random coins from the sender consistent with m, and fake random coins from the receiver consistent with m'.

That is,

$$(\mathsf{tr}(s, r, m), s, r_{m'}) \approx_c (\mathsf{tr}(s, r, m'), s_m, r) \approx_c (\mathsf{tr}(s, r, m''), s_m, r_{m'}) ,\tag{2}$$

where s, r, tr are defined as in (1), and $s_m, r_{m'}$ are fake coins produced by running faking algorithms on the corresponding transcript.

Observe that bideniability implies that $\mathsf{tr}(s, r, m) \approx_c \mathsf{tr}(s, r, m')$, so a bideniable scheme is also semantically secure. Similarly, off-the-record deniable schemes are also semantically secure.

Full deniability. A scheme is **fully deniable** if it is both bideniable and off-the-record deniable. Full deniability provides protection akin to an ideal secure channel in that the parties can freely claim any plaintext was sent or received, and which guarantees protection even when parties' claims do not match.

1.3   A Very Brief Overview of the Construction

Our starting point is an elegant technique from [SW14] that transforms any randomized algorithm A (with domain X and range Y) into a "deniable version" using IO. The technique creates two obfuscated programs A' and F, where: A' is the "deniable version" of A; and F is a "faking algorithm" that, for any input $(x, y) \in X \times Y$, outputs randomness ρ such that $A'(x; \rho) = y$. Using this technique, for any protocol, we can equip parties with a way to "explain" any given protocol message sent: that is, to produce fake randomness which makes that protocol message consistent with any plaintext of the parties' choice.

Based on this, a first attempt at a bideniable scheme might be to apply the [SW14] technique to an arbitrary public-key encryption scheme to create obfuscated programs for encryption, decryption, sender-fake and receiver-fake—and then use the sender-fake and receiver-fake programs to "explain" the protocol messages one by one. However, this does not yield a bideniable encryption scheme: the [SW14] technique is guaranteed to work only when applied to independent algorithm executions, but here the algorithms are run on the same keys and randomness, protocol messages are interrelated, and any convincing overall explanation must consist of a sequence of *consistent* explanations across the algorithms.[5] The problem in a nutshell is that although the [SW14] technique could create a deniable version of any single program, applying the technique separately to the key generation, encryption, and decryption programs fails to achieve deniability with respect to the programs' *joint* behavior.

More concretely, it is problematic that the adversary can manipulate any given transcript and randomness to generate certain "related" transcripts and randomness, and then try running the decryption algorithm on different combinations of them. Next, we give some intuition as to why this is a problem.

The Accumulating Attack. A fake r (i.e., receiver randomness) can be viewed as a string which "encodes" or "remembers", explicitly or implicitly, an instruction to decrypt a certain transcript to a certain fake plaintext. An adversary can run RFake iteratively on a given r (and a series of related transcripts) to successively obtain $r_1, r_2, \ldots$, hoping that each new application of RFake will add a new (ith) instruction into the "memory" of r_i in addition to all the preceding instructions.

---

[5] Indeed, if this approach worked, it would yield two-message bideniable encryption, which is impossible [BNNO11].

Since r_i is a bounded-length string which, information-theoretically, can carry only a fixed amount of information, sooner or later, one of the instructions will be lost from the "memory" of r_{i*} for some i^*. It can be shown that, assuming r was fake, an adversary running RFake many times can obtain some r_i which does not carry the original r's instruction, and thus decrypts the original transcript honestly. (This attack first appeared in [BNNO11] in the two-message setting and was used to demonstrate impossibility of two-message receiver-deniable encryption.)

While the above attack does not carry over to the three-message case generically, it stills remains valid for many protocols: namely, for those protocols where it is easy, given the challenge transcript tr*, to find transcripts "related" to tr*. Here "related" means that these transcripts can be successfully decrypted using the same true randomness r that was used to generate tr*. (In particular, in the two-message case, it is always easy to generate related transcripts (pk, c) by setting $pk = pk^*$ and setting c to be a fresh ciphertext with respect to pk.)

Therefore our approach, based on the above ideas, involves: (1) designing a protocol that prevents the adversary from computing related transcripts that force receiver randomness to "accumulate" information as described above, and then (2) applying the [SW14] technique to the algorithms for generating each message of this protocol. For the first step, we design such a protocol in the *oracle-access model*, where everyone (parties and adversaries) has only oracle access to the programs for computing protocol messages. Then, we adapt the construction to the setting where everyone has access to program code, obfuscated under IO.

Step 1 of our plan—designing a protocol resistant to the Accumulating Attack—itself consists of two key steps, further detailed below: (1a) design a "Base Protocol" that resists only some attacks, then (1b) augment the base protocol using the ideas of a *level system* and *comparison-based decryption*, to obtain a protocol secure in the oracle-access model (the "Idealized Protocol") (Fig.1).

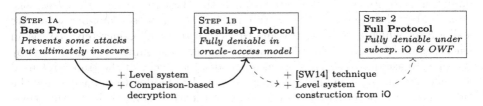

Fig. 1. The construction, step by step. The second arrow is dashed because while *conceptually* the Idealized Protocol is a stepping-stone to the Full Protocol, *technically* the Full Protocol requires very different techniques, and must be proven from scratch rather than "building on" the Idealized Protocol.

STEP 1A: We design the Base Protocol in the oracle-access model as follows. The first message μ_1 is a PRF output for input (s, m) where s is the sender randomness s and m is the plaintext. The second message μ_2 is a PRF output for input (r, μ_1) where r is the receiver randomness r. The third message μ_3 is an encryption of (m, μ_1, μ_2). All keys for PRFs and encryption are hidden inside these programs (and not known to anyone, including parties). After exchanging μ_1, μ_2, μ_3 with the sender, the receiver runs Dec, which decrypts the ciphertext μ_3 and outputs m. In addition, the programs contain certain consistency checks: Dec returns an output only if it gets the correct r (i.e., consistent with μ_2), and P3 only returns an output if it gets the correct s (i.e., consistent with μ_1).

The intuition for this design is as follows. The first two messages serve as "hashes" of the parties' internal state so far, and the next two programs—P3 and Dec—produce output only if the parties "prove" to the programs (by giving randomness consistent with these "hashes") that they are continuing to execute the protocol on the same inputs used to generate these hashes. This design aims to prevent the adversary from computing related transcripts (and thus prevent the Accumulating Attack): for instance, an adversary must not be able to reuse μ_1, μ_2 from a transcript (μ_1, μ_2, μ_3) to compute a new μ_3' such that (μ_1, μ_2, μ_3') is also a valid transcript with respect to the same r. Sect. 2 gives more intuition about this.

STEP 1B: Unfortunately, the intuition from Step 1a is only partially correct: it turns out that it is still possible to generate related transcripts, although the design above indeed protects against "most" ways of generating them. Concretely, we describe a method Ω (detailed in Sect. 2.1) to compute a series of related transcripts differing only in the third message. Importantly, Ω is generic: it works for *any* three-message bideniable encryption scheme. Ω takes any transcript (μ_1, μ_2, μ_3) and, applied iteratively, produces a "chain" of valid transcripts $\mathsf{tr}_1 = (\mu_1, \mu_2, \mu_3^{(1)}), \mathsf{tr}_2 = (\mu_1, \mu_2, \mu_3^{(2)})$, and so on. However, the scheme from Step 1a importantly ensures that Ω is the *only* way to compute valid related transcripts: this is crucial for the security proof.

It remains to ensure that the adversary cannot learn the true plaintext from the chain of related transcripts produced using Ω (e.g., by performing the Accumulating Attack). To do this, we augment the Base Protocol with a *level system*, under which each $\mu_3^{(i)}$, generated using Ω, encodes a number which we call a *level*, which is set to that transcript's own *index* i.[6] Concretely, $\mu_3^{(i)}$ is an encryption of (m, μ_1, μ_2, i). Additionally, any fake randomness r_i—generated by running RFake on $(\mu_1, \mu_2, \mu_3^{(i)})$—also encodes the level i of the transcript used to generate this r_i. The level i is encrypted, and so hidden from parties and the adversary, but the programs can decrypt and learn i using their internal keys. To complete the Idealized Protocol, we modify the decryption algorithm such that any fake r_i associated with level i may be used to decrypt transcripts with $\mu_3^{(j)}$ where $j > i$ ("correctness forward"), but decryption will fail (i.e., output $\perp$) if attempted with respect to r_i and $\mu_3^{(j)}$ where $j < i$ ("oblivious past"). We call this *comparison-based decryption behavior* (Fig. 2).

---

[6] Since Ω is inherently applied sequentially, the index i of each transcript produced by Ω is well defined.

$$\text{tr} \xrightarrow{\Omega} \text{tr}_1 \xrightarrow{\Omega} \cdots \xrightarrow{\Omega} \text{tr}_{i-1} \xrightarrow{\Omega} \text{tr}_i \xrightarrow{\Omega} \text{tr}_{i+1} \xrightarrow{\Omega} \text{tr}_{i+2} \xrightarrow{\Omega} \cdots$$

Oblivious past:
decrypting with r_i fails

RFake
r_i

Correctness forward:
decrypting with r_i succeeds

Fig. 2. Comparison-based decryption behavior

The Idealized Protocol, just described, is fully deniable in the oracle-access model. In particular, it prevents the Accumulating Attack: intuitively, this is because comparison-based decryption ensures that an iteratively faked r only encodes the most recent faked plaintext, rather than accumulating a sequence of past fake plaintexts.

STEP 2: We obtain the Full Protocol by applying the [SW14] technique to the Idealized Protocol, which enables the parties to use *obfuscated programs* (not oracle access) to compute protocol messages and to generate fake randomness. Proving security of the resulting protocol based on IO presents a number of challenges. To start with, the security argument in the oracle-access model relies heavily on certain outputs of programs being hard to find provided the corresponding inputs are hard to find. To make the analogous argument with respect to IO, we need to show that such inputs *don't exist* (rather than being hard to find). Furthermore, as part of our construction, we introduce and construct a special primitive that could be called "deterministic order-revealing encryption": a variant of deterministic encryption where $\mathsf{Enc}(0)$ and $\mathsf{Enc}(1)$ must be indistinguishable, even given programs which homomorphically increment ciphertexts (producing $\mathsf{Enc}(2), \mathsf{Enc}(3)$ and so on up to some superpolynomial bound) *and* homomorphically compare them. (Intuitively, homomorphic comparison enables the comparison-based decryption behavior; see Sect. 2). To argue security of this special deterministic encryption, we employ different primitives and techniques from the literature, including the *asymmetrically constrained encryption* from [CHJV14], and the proof techniques from [BPR15] to argue unreachability of the end of a superpolynomially-long chain.

This concludes the brief overview of our scheme. An in-depth technical overview of the scheme, including the intuition for the construction and the proof, can be found in Sect. 2 (technical overview). Impatient readers may wish to jump ahead to the Idealized Protocol program descriptions in Figs. 6 and 7 or refer to the Full Protocol in the full version of this paper [CPP18].

1.4 Variants of Deniable Encryption and Other Related Concepts

Next, we overview some variants of deniable encryption, deniable communication, and surrounding concepts. While they are not directly relevant to this work, clarifying these concepts may prevent confusion.

- **Post-execution vs. adaptive coercion.** This paper considers coercion that happens after protocol execution. A broader definition, *adaptive* coercion, would capture coercion at some (arbitrary) point during the protocol execution (with uncoerced parties possibly unaware of the coercion).

- **Private vs. public deniability.** The deniability of the sender (or receiver, or both) is *public* [SW14] if the corresponding faking algorithm does not require the true randomness or the true plaintext as input. Our scheme has public receiver deniability (our RFake has syntax RFake(m', tr; ρ_R)). This means that anyone, not just the receiver, can produce fake random coins for the receiver. Note that any publicly deniable faking algorithm must be randomized: otherwise, the adversary could easily check if a claimed r is fake by comparing it to RFake(m', tr).

- **"Coordinated" schemes.** One can also consider "coordinated" schemes [OPW11] where a single faking algorithm takes as input the true coins of *both the sender and the receiver* at the same time. Such schemes require coordination between the sender and the receiver in order to compute fake randomness. Our scheme does not require coordination, but we note that prior to this work, even coordinated fully bideniable schemes were not known.

Deniable encryption is related to a number of other cryptographic concepts:

- **Incoercible key exchange** is equivalent to deniable encryption. The former can be used to establish deniable one-time-pad keys for encryption. The latter enables a sender to pick a random key and transmit it deniably to a receiver.

- **Flexible deniability.** [CDNO96] also proposed a weaker deniability notion, variously called *flexible deniability*, *multi-distributional deniability* [OPW11, BNNO11, Dac12, AFL16, CIO16], or *dual-scheme deniability* [GKW17]. In a nutshell, this notion considers a setting where the coercer does not know which scheme is actually in use, and the coerced party has the freedom to "lie" in an undetectable way regarding the scheme that was actually used. (Equivalently, this notion assumes that the coercer does not expect to see some of the randomness used by the coerced party.) We note that none of the schemes in [OPW11, BNNO11, Dac12, AFL16, CIO16] are deniable in a setting where the coercer knows the scheme used in full and expects to see all the random coins of the coerced party.

- **Non-committing (adaptively secure) encryption (NCE, [CFGN96])** is weaker than deniable encryption, and designed for a different purpose. NCE requires that a simulator can generate dummy ciphertexts that can later be opened to any plaintext. The differences with deniable encryption are twofold. First, deniable encryption enables faking of real ciphertexts (that carry plaintexts), while NCE ciphertexts can *either* be faked (if simulated) *or* carry a plaintext (if real). Thus, in NCE, parties cannot fake; only the simulator can. Secondly, fake opening on behalf of all parties in NCE is done by the same entity, the simulator, while in deniable encryption the sender and the receiver fake independently of each other.

Bideniable encryption is strictly stronger than NCE: any bideniable encryption is also an NCE [CDNO96], but two-message NCE (e.g., [CDMW09]) is provably not bideniable, due to the three-message lower bound of [BNNO11].

– **Deniable authentication.** Deniable encryption is incomparable to deniable authentication. Deniable authentication allows the receiver of a message to authenticate the message's origin and contents, while preventing the receiver from convincing a third party who did not directly witness the communication that the message came from the sender (see, e.g., [DKSW09]). In contrast, in deniable encryption, the third party (adversary) may directly witness the communicated ciphertext and learn whether the parties have communicated with each other. The goal of deniable encryption is not to hide *whether* a party participated in a communication, but rather to preserve secrecy of the communication *contents*—even when parties are coerced (separately or jointly) to reveal their internal secrets.

1.5   Prior Work on Deniable Encryption

The definition of deniable encryption was introduced in 1996 by [CDNO96]. However, the techniques of that time fell short of achieving deniability: in fact, [CDNO96] presented a construction where the distinguishing advantage between real and fake opening was inversely proportional to the length of the ciphertext, thus requiring superpolynomially long ciphertexts in order to achieve cryptographic deniability. It was not until 2014 that Sahai and Waters presented the first (and, to date, the only) construction of sender-deniable encryption [SW14]. Their construction is based on indistinguishability obfuscation.

The [SW14] scheme can be transformed into a three-message *receiver-deniable* protocol using a generic transformation from sender- to receiver-deniable encryption (due to [CDNO96]) at the cost of one additional round, as follows: the *receiver* first deniably sends a random bit b to the *sender* deniably using the sender-deniable protocol, then the sender sends $b \oplus m$ to the receiver in the final round. Furthermore, if the sender sends $b \oplus m$ using the sender-deniable protocol rather than in the clear, the resulting scheme will be *sender-or-receiver-deniable*: that is, deniable against adversaries that coerce either one but not both of the parties. This final step incurs no additional rounds if (as in [SW14]) the message needs not be decided until the last round of the sender-deniable protocol. However, all these constructions rely heavily on the fact one of the parties' internal states remains hidden, and therefore fail to achieve bideniability.

Several prior works have focused on proving lower bounds for deniable encryption. [CDNO96] showed that a certain class of schemes cannot achieve better distinguishing advantage than inverse polynomial. [Dac12] extended this result to a broader class of constructions, showing that the same holds for *any* black-box construction of sender-deniable encryption from simulatable encryption. [Nie02] showed that any non-committing encryption, including bideniable encryption, can only reuse its public key an *a priori* bounded number of times; and therefore deniable communication must be interactive, even if two messages. Using different techniques, [BNNO11] showed that two-message receiver-deniable schemes, and hence also bideniable schemes, do not exist.

1.6   Organization of the Paper

The rest of the paper is organized as follows. Section 2 gives an informal yet almost complete description of the scheme, and outlines the main proof steps.

Due to space constraints, the rest of the paper (definitions, the level system, full description of the deniable encryption scheme both in oracle-access and the CRS model, and formal proofs) is in the full version [CPP18].

2   Towards the Scheme: Technical Overview

This section provides an informal yet almost complete overview of our construction. The primary purpose of this section is to guide the reader through the process of designing the scheme, outlining concrete attacks and corresponding protection mechanisms. This should be helpful for readers who want to gain some intuition about the scheme and its security, but are not willing to read the whole 250-page full version [CPP18], and for readers seeking to design a scheme from weaker assumptions (several issues described in this overview inhere in any 3-round deniable encryption, and could arise in schemes with more rounds too).

In this overview we describe the scheme in the oracle-access model. That is, we assume that all parties and the adversary have oracle access to programs P1, P2, P3 (which generate the three messages of the protocol), decryption program Dec, and faking programs SFake, RFake.

We build our scheme in two main steps. As a first attempt, we try to avoid the known attacks on the 2-message case by considering a 3-message scheme. Next, we discuss some attacks and augment our scheme with levels and comparison-based decryption behavior, which yields our final scheme.

2.1   A First Attempt

Recall the [SW14] technique, mentioned above, that transforms any algorithm into a deniable version using indistinguishability obfuscation. Given this, a natural attempt to build deniable encryption is to take any (2-message) public-key encryption scheme and use the [SW14] technique to make each of its algorithms Gen, Enc, and Dec deniable. Concretely, the [SW14] technique takes any randomized algorithm A (with domain X and range Y) and outputs two obfuscated programs A' and F, where: A' is the "deniable version" of A; and F is a "faking algorithm" that, for any input $(x, y) \in X \times Y$, outputs randomness ρ such that $A'(x; \rho) = y$. Using this technique, we can take any protocol and equip parties with a way to "explain" any given protocol message they send: that is, to produce fake randomness which makes that protocol message consistent with any plaintext of the parties' choice.

This approach would allow, for example, the receiver to create a fake sk' decrypting a given ciphertext c to any plaintext of its choice. This sk' would even be indistinguishable from the real sk, to an adversary that only sees the purported secret key. But the problem is that the adversary sees other related information: e.g., it has the public key, so can run the encryption algorithm and generate outputs related to sk. The [SW14] technique does not work when applied to multiple programs with interrelated outputs: such as Gen, Enc and Dec.

Let us now outline the result of [BNNO11]: impossibility of bideniable encryption in 2 messages. This will give us insight on how to construct a 3-message bideniable encryption scheme while "avoiding" the impossibility. Also, the [BNNO11] result yields a concrete attack on the first-attempt scheme outlined above.

Impossibility of the 2-message case [BNNO11]. [BNNO11] shows that even receiver-deniable (as opposed to bideniable) schemes are impossible with two messages. Their result is unconditional. Their proof shows that any 2-message receiver-deniable encryption scheme, even for a single-bit plaintext, can be used to deniably send any polynomial number of plaintexts, simply by reusing the first message (pk) and sending multiple second messages $c_1, \ldots, c_N$ (where N is arbitrarily, but polynomially, large); then they show that all these ciphertexts can be faked *simultaneously* using a *single* fake decryption key. This implies a method for compressing an arbitrary string beyond what is information-theoretically possible, as follows. To compress a string $b_1, \ldots, b_N$ from N bits (where N is larger than $|\mathsf{sk}|$) to $|\mathsf{sk}|$ bits: (1) prepare N encryptions of 0 under a single pk (call them $c_1, \ldots, c_N$);[7] (2) compute $\mathsf{sk}^{(1)} \leftarrow \mathsf{RFake}(\mathsf{sk}, c_1, b_1)$, $\mathsf{sk}^{(2)} \leftarrow \mathsf{RFake}(\mathsf{sk}^{(1)}, c_2, b_2)$, $\ldots$, $\mathsf{sk}^{(N)} \leftarrow \mathsf{RFake}(\mathsf{sk}^{(N-1)}, c_N, b_N)$. The final string $\mathsf{sk}^{(N)}$ is a compressed description of $b_1, \ldots, b_N$, since it is shorter than N and since the original string can be recovered by decrypting each b_i as $\mathsf{Dec}(sk^{(N)}, c_i)$. Since most strings cannot be compressed, we have a contradiction.

Stated differently, this impossibility says that a secret key which was faked multiple times to lie about different ciphertexts has to "remember" or store information about each lie; but information-theoretically, it cannot remember more information than its length allows. Thus, at some point, such a secret key has to "forget" previous lies, and then it can be used to decrypt the original ciphertext to its real plaintext. That is, there is always an attack on any 2-message scheme, which roughly goes as follows. Assume the adversary sees a ciphertext c, claimed to encrypt plaintext m', together with a fake sk' that decrypts c to m'; but in reality, c encrypts m. The adversary can generate $N > |\mathsf{sk}|$ ciphertexts $c_1, \ldots, c_N$ as above, and run RFake iteratively to compute $\mathsf{sk}^{(N)}$ as above, and then compute $\mathsf{Dec}(\mathsf{sk}^{(N)}; c) = m$ to learn the true plaintext.

In summary, the core issue with the 2-message schemes is that for a single receiver message (i.e., pk) it is possible to efficiently generate many different sender messages (i.e., ciphertexts), such that all these ciphertexts are valid ciphertexts with respect to the same receiver key; this, in turn, means we must be able to use a single secret key to fake all the ciphertexts at once, which is information-theoretically impossible.

---

[7] These ciphertexts do not depend on the string to be compressed and thus can be thought of as public parameters of the compression protocol.

What would be the analogous argument in the 3-message case? Consider a 3-message scheme with messages (μ_1, μ_2, μ_3). If the scheme has the property that, given a receiver message μ_2, one can efficiently generate many different sender messages $\mu_1^{(i)}, \mu_3^{(i)}$ yielding valid transcripts $(\mu_1^{(i)}, \mu_2, \mu_3^{(i)})$, then the scheme is subject to the [BNNO11] impossibility. For example, consider a 3-message scheme where the third message is a fresh encryption under freshly sampled random coins: this enables generating many third messages $\mu_3^{(i)}$ for any given μ_1, μ_2, and applying the [BNNO11] argument shows that any fake receiver randomness must remember a lie for each $\mu_3^{(i)}$, so this scheme is susceptible to the same attack as two-message schemes.

Base Protocol. Now we present our Base Protocol, which is insecure but will be augmented later to achieve a secure version. The scheme has parties first exchange two PRF values, then has the sender encrypt its plaintext m into a ciphertext μ_3 using program P3, which the receiver can decrypt using program Dec. Before presenting the scheme formally, we give motivation for the design.

With the [BNNO11] impossibility in mind, a natural approach to building a 3-message scheme is to ensure that for any given first two messages μ_1, μ_2, only one consistent third message μ_3 can be efficiently computed. The Base Protocol achieves this using the following ideas.

1. The first message μ_1 "commits" to the sender's coins s and message m.
2. The third message μ_3 is a deterministic, symmetric-key encryption of m under a key K that is hardwired in programs P3 and Dec and is unknown to parties.
3. $\mathsf{P3}(s, m, \mu_1, \mu_2)$ does a validity check before its output: if μ_1 is indeed a "commitment" to s and m, P3 outputs μ_3; otherwise, it outputs $\perp$.

In other words, the only way for the sender to generate a valid μ_3 is to "prove" to P3 that it is running P3 on the same s, m used to compute μ_1. Thus, as long as K remains secret and the ciphertexts are sufficiently sparse, for any μ_1, μ_2, there is only one (efficiently computable) consistent μ_3.

So far, since μ_3 is computed under the same key K in each execution and it is not randomized, all executions with the same m yield the same μ_3, which is clearly insecure. To fix this, we let μ_3 encrypt not only m, but the first two messages μ_1, μ_2 as well, forcing different executions to have different third messages.

We have not yet discussed how the second message μ_2 should be computed, which actually depends on an extension of the attack based on [BNNO11], described above. Recall that we wanted it to be hard to compute multiple transcripts with the same μ_2: say, $(\mu_1^{(i)}, \mu_2, \mu_3^{(i)})$. In fact, we also want it to be hard to convert a transcript (μ_1, μ_2, μ_3) with receiver randomness r into a different transcript (μ_1', μ_2', μ_3') consistent with the same r, since it is possible to extend the attack to this case as well. With this in mind, we design the protocol as follows.

1. The second message μ_2 is a pseudorandom function output $\mathsf{PRF}(r, \mu_1)$, for a PRF key that is hardwired into P2 and Dec and not known to the parties.[8] The PRF inputs are the receiver randomness r and the first message μ_1.
2. $\mathsf{Dec}(r, \mu_1, \mu_2, \mu_3)$ does a validity check before decryption: if μ_2 is the correct PRF output for input (r, μ_1), Dec outputs m; otherwise, it outputs $\perp$.

Thus, the only way for the receiver to decrypt is to "prove" to Dec that it is running Dec on a valid r (consistent with μ_2). This ensures that it is hard to transform a transcript (μ_1, μ_2, μ_3) into a different (μ_1', μ_2', μ_3') consistent with the same receiver randomness r, since that would require finding μ_1', μ_2' such that $\mu_2' = \mathsf{PRF}(r, \mu_1')$, for an unknown r and an unknown PRF key.

We conclude this protocol design with a couple of final notes. First, we instantiate our "commitment" using a PRF as well, with its key hardwired into programs P1, P3 and not known to parties (thus, both μ_1 and μ_2 are PRF outputs). Secondly, we augment each program P1, P2, P3, Dec with a "trapdoor step" which makes each of these programs separately deniable, in the spirit of the [SW14] technique. Finally, we make the validity check inside Dec accept if $\mathsf{P2}(r, \mu_1) = \mu_2$, rather than if $\mathsf{PRF}(r, \mu_1) = \mu_2$; the difference is that P2 also accepts "fake" values which are not real preimages of the PRF. We make a similar modification to P3: its validity check verifies that $\mathsf{P1}(s, m) = \mu_1$ and therefore would also accept fake s which is not a real opening of the "commitment". These changes are necessary because without them, an adversary could use the validity check to test whether a given s is a real (PRF) preimage of μ_1 or a fake one.

We present the programs P1, P2, P3, Dec, SFake, RFake as described so far, in Fig. 3. For readability, the program includes comments to explain what the code is doing. Despite the somewhat dense code, the programs are very structured, and in a nutshell they behave as follows.

- Each program has a main step which is triggered when the program is run on uniformly random s or r (which is the case during an honest execution);
- Programs P1, P2, P3, Dec each have a trapdoor step which is triggered when the programs are given fake randomness (which has a special format recognizable to the programs). The set of fake randomness is sufficiently sparse that the trapdoor steps are almost never triggered on uniform s or r. Fake randomness contains an "instruction" of how the program should behave.
- Programs P3 and Dec run validity checks, as described and motivated above.
- Programs SFake and RFake generate fake randomness which can be recognized by other programs.

In particular, during an honest execution with uniformly random s and r and plaintext m, the parties exchange messages μ_1, μ_2, μ_3 (computed by programs

---

[8] In this high-level description we omit PRF keys to simplify notation.

P1, P2, P3, respectively), as follows: $\mu_1 = \mathsf{PRF}(s, m)$, $\mu_2 = \mathsf{PRF}(r, \mu_1)$, $\mu_3 = \mathsf{Enc}_K(m, \mu_1, \mu_2)$.[9] The receiver decrypts (μ_1, μ_2, μ_3) by running $\mathsf{Dec}(r, \mu_1, \mu_2, \mu_3)$, which verifies that $\mathsf{PRF}(r, \mu_1) = \mu_2$, then decrypts μ_3 and outputs m.

Base Protocol programs: first attempt at deniable encryption.

Program P1(s, m)
1. **Trapdoor step:** if $\mathsf{Dec}_{K_S}(s) = (m', \mu_1', \mu_2', \mu_3')$ and $m' = m$, then return μ_1' //if s is fake and encodes m, output encoded μ_1'
2. **Main step:** Return $\mu_1 \leftarrow \mathsf{PRF}(s, m)$. //otherwise output $\mathsf{PRF}(s, m)$

Program P2(r, μ_1)
1. **Trapdoor step:** if $\mathsf{Dec}_{K_R}(r) = (m', \mu_1', \mu_2', \mu_3')$ and $\mu_1' = \mu_1$, then return μ_2'. //if r is fake and encodes μ_1, output encoded μ_2'
2. **Normal step:** else return $\mathsf{PRF}(r, \mu_1)$. //otherwise output $\mathsf{PRF}(r, \mu_1)$

Program P3(s, m, μ_1, μ_2)
1. **Validity check:** if P1$(s, m) \neq \mu_1$, then abort;
2. **Trapdoor step:** if $\mathsf{Dec}_{K_S}(s) = (m', \mu_1', \mu_2', \mu_3')$ and $(m', \mu_1', \mu_2') = (m, \mu_1, \mu_2)$, then return μ_3'. //if s is fake and encodes correct (m, μ_1, μ_2), output encoded μ_3'
3. **Normal step:** else return $\mathsf{Enc}_K(m, \mu_1, \mu_2)$.//otherwise encrypt m

Program Dec(r, μ_1, μ_2, μ_3)
1. **Validity check:** if P2$(r, \mu_1) \neq \mu_2$, then abort;
2. **Trapdoor step:** if $\mathsf{Dec}_{K_R}(r) = (m', \mu_1', \mu_2', \mu_3')$ and $(\mu_1', \mu_2', \mu_3') = (\mu_1, \mu_2, \mu_3)$, then return m'. //if r is fake and encodes correct (μ_1, μ_2, μ_3), output encoded m'
3. **Normal step:** else decrypt $(m'', \mu_1'', \mu_2'') \leftarrow \mathsf{Dec}_K(\mu_3)$. If $(\mu_1'', \mu_2'') = \mu_1, \mu_2$ then output m'', else abort. //otherwise decrypt honestly

Program SFake$(s, m, \hat{m}, \mu_1, \mu_2, \mu_3; \rho_S)$
1. **Validity check:** if P1$(s, m) \neq \mu_1$, then abort;
2. **Normal step:** else return $\mathsf{Enc}_{K_S}(\hat{m}, \mu_1, \mu_2, \mu_3, \rho_S)$ // output fake s with fake plaintext and the transcript inside.

Program RFake$(\hat{m}, \mu_1, \mu_2, \mu_3; \rho_R)$
1. **Normal step:** return $\mathsf{Enc}_{K_R}(\hat{m}, \mu_1, \mu_2, \mu_3, \rho_R)$ // output fake r with fake plaintext and the transcript inside

---

Fig. 3. Base Protocol programs: first attempt at deniable encryption. P1, P2, P3, Dec are deterministic; SFake, RFake are randomized. (We treat s, r as non-random inputs, even though they are supposed to be uniformly chosen, since they are reused across different programs.)

If the parties want to claim to a coercing adversary that they transmitted a different plaintext $\hat{m}$, they can use SFake, RFake to compute fake s' and r', which are random-looking strings with $\hat{m}$, μ_1, μ_2, and μ_3 encrypted inside. If the adversary decrypts the transcript (μ_1, μ_2, μ_3) with fake $r' = \mathsf{Enc}_{K_R}(\hat{m}, \mu_1, \mu_2, \mu_3, \rho_R)$, it will get $\hat{m}$ as a result (via the trapdoor step of the decryption program).

---

[9] Note that s, m (and r, μ_1) are both *inputs* to the PRF, not keys; we omit PRF keys for simplicity of notation.

Similarly, the other programs, when given fake s' or r' as input, employ their trapdoor steps as well, making each protocol message appear consistent with $\hat{m}$.

The problem with the Base Protocol. We designed our scheme above with specific attacks in mind, but is it secure against all attacks? The answer is "almost": it is relatively easy to show security of the scheme in an idealized model where parties (and the adversary) have only oracle access to the programs, *but only as long as the adversary cannot query the* SFake *oracle*. Concretely, the adversary can use SFake to mount a certain attack Ω on the scheme, but this turns out to be the *only* possible type of attack. In Sect. 2.2, we describe a special protection mechanism—comparison-based decryption behavior—which, when added to the protocol, prevents this type of attack and yields a scheme that is fully deniable even if the adversary has an access to *all* oracles including SFake. (And in the full version [CPP18], we prove this result even when the adversary can see *the code* of all programs, obfuscated under IO).

Let's unpack why the protocol described so far is insecure. Recall that we wanted μ_1 to serve as a "commitment", and we wanted P3 to output μ_3 only if the sender uses the same s and m in the commitment and as input to P3. This was important to make sure that for any μ_1, μ_2, at most one consistent μ_3 is efficiently computable. Then, however, we said that P3 should perform its validity check with respect to the whole program P1 and not just the commitment; in particular, the validity check in P3 accepts not only the true opening of the commitment, but also fake s. The problem is that P1, due to its trapdoor step, is not binding: given any $\mu_1^* = \text{PRF}(s^*, m_0)$ and $m_1 \neq m_0$, it is easy to generate a different s_1 that passes the verification check. In fact, SFake does exactly that: given $(s^*, m_0, m_1, \mu_1^*, \mu_2, \mu_3)$ for some μ_2, μ_3, it outputs s_1 such that $\text{P1}(s_1, m_1) = \mu_1^*$.

While this is not yet a concrete attack, it exposes a problem with our initial hope of a committing first message: sender deniability guarantees the first message is easily invertible, potentially with respect to inconsistent plaintexts m, so μ_1 cannot be committing. Thus, it is easy to create many fake s_i consistent with μ_1, and therefore many third messages $\mu_3^{(1)}, \mu_3^{(2)}, \ldots$, all consistent with a given (μ_1^*, μ_2^*). A procedure Ω that does this is detailed in Fig. 4. For our purposes, the key features of the attack Ω are as follows.

- To generate such a $\mu_3^{(i)}$, encrypting some m_1 for a given (μ_1^*, μ_2^*), one has to run P3 on certain fake sender randomness s_i.
- P3 can recognize when it is being used to generate such a $\mu_3^{(i)}$. (This is because P3 will be run on a "mixed input": that is, P3 should be run on s, m, μ_1^*, μ_2^*, and a fake s_i that encodes the same μ_1^* but different $\tilde{\mu}_2 \neq \mu_2^*$.)
- The only way to generate such fake s_i efficiently is to run SFake (on a transcript *different* from the one being attacked: specifically, with a different second message).

Since it is easy to generate many third messages, our scheme is subject to the same attack as all 2-message schemes: namely, the adversary can generate many

---

A procedure Ω to generate a new third message encrypting m_1 and consistent with given first and second messages μ_1, μ_2.

Inputs to $\Omega(\mu_1{}^*, \mu_2{}^*, \mu_3{}^*, s^*, m^*, m_1)$ are: transcript $(\mu_1{}^*, \mu_2{}^*, \mu_3{}^*)$, sender randomness s^* (which could be real or fake), plaintext m^*, and new desired plaintext m_1:

1. Compute an auxiliary transcript $\tilde{tr} = (\mu_1{}^*, \tilde{\mu}_2, \tilde{\mu}_3)$ with the same first message $\mu_1{}^*$, but different second message $\tilde{\mu}_2$, by choosing fresh receiver randomness $\tilde{r}$ and setting $\tilde{tr} \leftarrow tr(s^*, \tilde{r}, m^*)$. Note that the first message of this transcript is $\mathsf{P1}(s^*, m^*) = \mu_1{}^*$.
2. Compute $s_1 \leftarrow \mathsf{SFake}(s^*, m^*, m_1, \mu_1{}^*, \tilde{\mu}_2, \tilde{\mu}_3)$. Note that s_1 is fake randomness which remembers $m_1, \mu_1{}^*$ and a new $\tilde{\mu}_2 \neq \mu_2{}^*$.
3. Compute $\mu_3{}^{(1)} \leftarrow \mathsf{P3}(s_1, m_1, \mu_1{}^*, \mu_2{}^*)$.

Ω can now be repeated on input $\mu_1{}^*, \mu_2{}^*, \mu_3{}^{(1)}, s_1, m_1, m_2$ to generate $\mu_3{}^{(2)}$, and so on.

Fig. 4. Procedure Ω to compute many third messages consistent with given μ_1, μ_2.

ciphertexts $\mu_3{}^{(i)}$, fake each of them to compute an N-times-faked $r^{(N)}$, and then use it to correctly decrypt the original $\mu_3{}^*$. While this attack inheres in all 2-message schemes [BNNO11], in the 3-message case we can fix it. We do so by introducing *levels* and *comparison-based decryption behavior*, which specify how the decryption program should behave when the adversary tries to use such $r^{(N)}$ to decrypt a transcript $(\mu_1{}^*, \mu_2{}^*, \mu_3{}^{(i)})$ or a challenge transcript $(\mu_1{}^*, \mu_2{}^*, \mu_3{}^*)$.

2.2   Levels, Comparison-Based Decryption, and the Final Scheme

Comparison-based decryption behavior. Let $(\mu_1{}^*, \mu_2{}^*, \mu_3{}^*)$ be a challenge transcript. For any superpolynomial T and $j \in \{0, \ldots, T\}$, let r_j be the output of RFake on transcript $(\mu_1{}^*, \mu_2{}^*, \mu_3{}^{(j)})$, where $\mu_3{}^{(j)}$ is computed by j iterations of Ω. Let $\mu_3{}^{(0)}$ denote the challenge $\mu_3{}^*$. When Dec is run on r_j and $\mu_3{}^{(i)}$, for $i, j \in \{0, \ldots, T\}$, *comparison-based decryption behavior* requires the following.

1. *Oblivious past:* When $j > i$, Dec outputs $\bot$.
2. *Correctness forward:* When $j < i$, Dec decrypts $\mu_3{}^{(i)}$ correctly (as long as consistency checks pass).
3. When $j = i$, Dec should decrypt $\mu_3{}^{(i)}$ according to the instruction in fake r_j.

That is, if an adversary creates fake r_j using $\mu_3{}^{(j)}$, the jth in the sequence of ciphertexts, this r_j can be used to honestly decrypt ciphertexts "after" $\mu_3{}^{(j)}$, but cannot be used to decrypt ciphertexts "before" $\mu_3{}^{(j)}$; and naturally, r_j decrypts $\mu_3{}^{(j)}$ itself according to the instruction inside fake r_j (Fig. 5).

$$tr \xrightarrow{\ \Omega\ } tr_1 \xrightarrow{\ \Omega\ } \cdots \xrightarrow{\ \Omega\ } tr_{i-1} \xrightarrow{\ \Omega\ } tr_i \xrightarrow{\ \Omega\ } tr_{i+1} \xrightarrow{\ \Omega\ } tr_{i+2} \xrightarrow{\ \Omega\ } \cdots$$

Oblivious past: decrypting with r_i fails $\downarrow$ RFake   *Correctness forward:* decrypting with r_i succeeds
r_i

Fig. 5. Comparison-based decryption behavior

Comparison-based decryption behavior prevents the attack described above, despite the fact that Ω enables the adversary to generate many third messages. Next, we give some intuition as to why. Recall that the attack had the adversary generate a fake r_j (by faking a ciphertext sequence $\mu_3^{(1)}, \mu_3^{(2)}, \ldots$) and then return to the challenge μ_3^* and decrypt it. Thus, a natural idea to mitigate this attack is to make Dec output $\bot$ whenever fake r_j is used to try to decrypt the initial $\mu_3^* = \mu_3^{(0)}$.[10] This simple modification indeed stops the attack, but introducing it alone would break security. To maintain security, we need to make sure that Dec on inputs r_j, $\mu_3^{(i)}$ should output $\bot$ for *all* $j > i$, and not just $j > i = 0$.[11] In other words, the "oblivious past" rule is the "minimum" modification which prevents fake r_j from decrypting $\mu_3^* = \mu_3^{(0)}$ *and* maintains security of the scheme.

Finally, the "correctness forward" rule *must* hold as well, since it is implied by sender-deniability. As a result, the behavior of the decryption program depends on the comparison of "indices" of the transcript and the receiver randomness; therefore, we call this comparison-based decryption behavior.

Implementing comparison-based decryption behavior: levels.

Next, we consider how to construct our programs such that comparison-based decryption behavior holds. When we run Dec on some μ_3 and some r, how does it know whether μ_3 is "forward" of r in the chain (meaning Dec should decrypt honestly), or "in the past" with respect to r (meaning Dec should output $\bot$)?

To this end, we introduce *levels*. That is, we have all fake sender randomness, all fake receiver randomness, and all third message $\mu_3^{(i)}$ also encrypt a number ℓ between 0 and some superpolynomial T, as follows.

- Fake sender randomness encrypts, among other things, a level ℓ which is *how many times this randomness was faked*. (E.g., to compute fake randomness, the sender would normally run SFake once, so the level ℓ of the resulting fake randomness is 1. If it runs SFake on the resulting randomness again, its level ℓ will be 2, and so on).
- Each potential third message $\mu_3^{(i)}$ also encrypts, in addition to m and μ_1, μ_2, its level, which is *its index i in the chain*. Note that the algorithm Ω which computes $\mu_3^{(i)}$ outputs $\mu_3^{(1)}, \mu_3^{(2)}, \ldots$ sequentially, and therefore their index i is well defined. In an honest execution, the level of μ_3 is always set to 0.

---

[10] Such a restriction is not possible in the 2-message case, in contrast to the 3-message case. This relates to the fact that our procedure Ω which generates $\mu_3^{(i)}$ is "one way", i.e., it is easy to generate $\mu_3^{(i+1)}$ from $\mu_3^{(i)}$, but it could be hard—and *is* hard, in our scheme—to generate $\mu_3^{(i)}$ from $\mu_3^{(i+1)}$. In contrast, in any 2-message scheme, there is no order on the ciphertexts; they are always easy to generate.

[11] To see this, suppose Dec outputs $\bot$ whenever $r_j, j > 0$ is used to decrypt $\mu_3^* = \mu_3^{(0)}$. Now consider trying to decrypt some $\mu_3^{(i)}$ with, say, r_{i+3}. r_3 does not decrypt $\mu_3^{(0)}$, and the difference between $(\mu_3^{(0)}, r_3)$ and $(\mu_3^{(i)}, r_{i+3})$ is that $\mu_3^{(0)}$ was generated with truly random s whereas $\mu_3^{(i)}$ used s_i which was faked i times. Sender deniability requires these two cases be indistinguishable, so $\mu_3^{(i)}$ must not be decrypted by r_{i+3}.

- Fake receiver randomness encrypts, among other things, a level ℓ which is *the level of its "parent" transcript* (i.e., the transcript which was used as input to RFake). (E.g., to compute fake randomness, the receiver would normally run RFake on the honest transcript, which has level 0, so the resulting fake randomness would have level 0 too).

We claim that storing this "level" information in fake randomness and third messages is enough for the scheme to maintain the level information accurately and follow comparison-based decryption behavior. For instance, Dec can decide its output behavior by comparing the levels inside r and μ_3. RFake can record the correct level of r by copying the level of its parent ciphertext. SFake can maintain the correct number of times something was faked, by reading the level in its input s and incrementing it. P3, as discussed above, can detect when it is being run within Ω, and it can put inside its output third message the level it copied from input s; since generating each new μ_3 requires once-more fake s, the level in s—i.e., the number of times it was faked—corresponds to the index of μ_3 in the chain.

Our final protocol in the oracle-access model. We present our final protocol (albeit still in the oracle model) in Figs. 6 and 7. This scheme is a provably secure deniable encryption scheme in the oracle access model. A proof outline follows the program descriptions, and a complete proof is given in the full version [CPP18].

The structure of the final protocol programs is summarized below.

- Each program has a main step which is triggered when the program is run on uniformly random s or r, which is the case during an honest execution.
- Programs P1, P2, P3, and Dec also have a trapdoor step which is triggered when the programs receive fake randomness (which has a special format recognizable to the programs). The set of fake randomness is sufficiently sparse that the trapdoor step is almost never triggered on uniformly chosen s or r. Fake randomness contains an "instruction" of how the program should behave on some particular input.
- Programs P3 and Dec also have a "mixed input" step which serves to prevent attacks using Ω to generate many third messages μ_3. P3's mixed input step copies the level from its input s into the third message μ_3, ensuring μ_3 encrypts its own index in the sequence. Dec's mixed input step implements comparison-based decryption behavior by comparing the levels of μ_3 and r. The mixed input steps are triggered when the programs receive fake s (or r) as input, but the program's other inputs do not match the inputs in the instruction inside s (or r). P3 enters its mixed input step when its input and fake s contain the same μ_1 but different second messages, and Dec enters its mixed input step when its input and fake r contain the same μ_1, μ_2 but different third messages.
- Programs P3 and Dec's output behavior depends on validity checks, as in the Base Protocol (and for the same reasons as in the Base Protocol).

– Programs SFake and RFake generate fake randomness that is recognizable to the other programs, and maintain accurate level information inside the fake randomness as follows: SFake increments the level of sender randomness with respect to its input sender randomness (unless the latter is honest, in which case SFake sets the level to 0); and RFake copies the level from the parent transcript into fake randomness.

Programs P1, P3, SFake.

Program P1(s, m)

1. **Trapdoor step:**
   (a) out $\leftarrow$ Dec$_{K_S}(s)$; if out $=$ 'fail' goto main step, else parse out as $(m', \mu_1', \mu_2', \mu_3', \ell')$;
   (b) If $m = m'$ then return μ_1'; //if s is fake and encodes m, output encoded μ_1'
2. **Main step:**
   (a) Return $\mu_1 \leftarrow$ PRF$_{k_S}(s, m)$. //otherwise output PRF(s, m)

Program P3(s, m, μ_1, μ_2)

1. **Validity check:** if P1$(s, m) \neq \mu_1$ then abort;
2. **Trapdoor step:**
   (a) out $\leftarrow$ Dec$_{K_S}(s)$; if out $=$ 'fail' goto main step, else parse out as $(m', \mu_1', \mu_2', \mu_3', \ell')$;
   (b) If $m, \mu_1, \mu_2 = m', \mu_1', \mu_2'$ then return μ_3'; //if s is fake and encodes correct (m, μ_1, μ_2), output encoded μ_3'
3. **Mixed input step:** If $m, \mu_1 = m', \mu_1'$ but $\mu_2 \neq \mu_2'$ then return $\mu_3 \leftarrow$ Enc$_K(m, \mu_1, \mu_2, \ell')$; //if s is fake and encodes correct (m, μ_1) but incorrect μ_2', encrypt m with level copied from s
4. **Main step:**
   (a) Return $\mu_3 \leftarrow$ Enc$_K(m, \mu_1, \mu_2, 0)$. //otherwise encrypt m with level 0

Program SFake$(s, m, \hat{m}, \mu_1, \mu_2, \mu_3)$

1. **Validity check:** if P1$(s, m) \neq \mu_1$ then abort;
2. **Trapdoor step:**
   (a) out $\leftarrow$ Dec$_{K_S}(s)$; if out $=$ 'fail' goto main step, else parse out as $(m', \mu_1', \mu_2', \mu_3', \ell')$;
   (b) If $m, \mu_1 = m', \mu_1'$ then
      i. If $\ell \geq T$ then abort;
      ii. Return Enc$_{K_S}(\hat{m}, \mu_1, \mu_2, \mu_3, \ell + 1)$. //if input s is already fake then output new fake s with fake plaintext, the transcript, and incremented level
3. **Main step:**
   (a) Return Enc$_{K_S}(\hat{m}, \mu_1, \mu_2, \mu_3, 1)$. //otherwise output fake s with fake plaintext, the transcript, and level 1

Fig. 6. Programs P2, Dec, RFake.

The interesting cases of protocol execution are summarized next.

Programs P2, Dec, RFake.

Program $P2(r, \mu_1)$

1. **Trapdoor step:**
   (a) out $\leftarrow \mathsf{Dec}_{K_R}(r)$; if out $=$ 'fail' then goto main step, else parse out as $(m', \mu_1', \mu_2', \mu_3', L', \hat{\rho})$;
   (b) If $\mu_1 = \mu_1'$ then return μ_2'; //if r is fake and encodes μ_1, output encoded μ_2'

2. **Main step:**
   (a) Return $\mu_2 \leftarrow \mathsf{PRF}_{k_R}(r, \mu_1)$. //otherwise output $\mathsf{PRF}(r, \mu_1)$

Program $\mathsf{Dec}(r, \mu_1, \mu_2, \mu_3)$

1. **Validity check:** if $P2(r, \mu_1) \neq \mu_2$ then abort;
2. **Trapdoor step:**
   (a) out $\leftarrow \mathsf{Dec}_{K_R}(r)$; if out' $=$ 'fail' then goto main step; else parse out' as $(m', \mu_1', \mu_2', \mu_3', \ell', \hat{\rho})$;
   (b) if $\mu_1, \mu_2, \mu_3 = \mu_1', \mu_2', \mu_3'$ then return m'; //if r is fake and encodes correct (μ_1, μ_2, μ_3), output encoded m'
   (c) out $\leftarrow \mathsf{Dec}_K(\mu_3)$; if out'' $=$ 'fail' then abort, else parse out'' as $(m'', \mu_1'', \mu_2'', \ell'')$;

3. **Mixed input step:** If $\mu_1, \mu_2 = \mu_1', \mu_2'$ but $\mu_3 \neq \mu_3'$ then
   (a) If $(\mu_1', \mu_2') = (\mu_1'', \mu_2'')$ and $\ell' < \ell''$ then return m''; //if r is fake and encodes correct (μ_1, μ_2) but incorrect μ_3', decrypt honestly or abort, depending on whether the level in r is smaller than in μ_3 or not
   (b) Else abort.

4. **Main step:**
   (a) out $\leftarrow \mathsf{Dec}_K(\mu_3)$; if out $=$ 'fail' then abort, else parse out as $(m'', \mu_1'', \mu_2'', \ell'')$;
   (b) If $(\mu_1, \mu_2) = (\mu_1'', \mu_2'')$ then return m''; //otherwise decrypt honestly
   (c) Else abort.

Program $\mathsf{RFake}(\hat{m}, \mu_1, \mu_2, \mu_3; \rho)$

1. out $\leftarrow \mathsf{Dec}_K(\mu_3)$; if out $=$ 'fail' then abort, else parse out as $(m'', \mu_1'', \mu_2'', \ell'')$;
2. Return $r' \leftarrow \mathsf{Enc}_{K_R}(\hat{m}, \mu_1, \mu_2, \mu_3, \ell'', \mathsf{prg}(\rho))$. // output fake r with fake plaintext, the transcript, and the level copied from μ_3

Fig. 7. Programs P2, Dec, RFake.

- **Normal protocol execution.** Executing the programs on randomly chosen s^*, r^* and plaintext m_0^* triggers the main step, yielding outputs $\mu_1^* = \mathsf{PRF}(s^*, m_0^*)$, $\mu_2^* = \mathsf{PRF}(r^*, \mu_1^*)$, and $\mu_3^* = \mathsf{Enc}_K(m_0^*, \mu_1^*, \mu_2^*, 0)$, where the last 0 is the level. Dec, given the resulting transcript as input, outputs m_0^* via its main step.

- **Fake randomness of parties.** A sender wishing to claim that it sent plaintext $m_1^* \neq m_0^*$ can run SFake to obtain fake s' encoding $(m_1^*, \mu_1^*, \mu_2^*, \mu_3^*, 1)$, where the last 1 is the level. A receiver wishing to claim that it received $m_1^* \neq m_0^*$ can run RFake to obtain fake r' encoding $(m_1^*, \mu_1^*, \mu_2^*, \mu_3^*, 0)$, where the last 0 is the level. Executing programs on fake s' or fake r' and m_1^* triggers the trapdoor step, so programs will output the values hardwired into the fake s' or r'. Thus, P1 will output μ_1^*, P2 will output μ_2^*, P3 will output μ_3^*, and Dec will output m_1^* via their trapdoor steps, making the transcript, originally for plaintext m_0^*, appear consistent with m_1^*.

- **Efficiently computable related transcripts.** It is only possible to compute related transcripts of the form $(\mu_1{}^*, \mu_2{}^*, \mu_3)$, where $\mu_3 = \mathsf{Enc}_K(m, \mu_1{}^*, \mu_2{}^*, \ell)$, $\ell \geq 1$; moreover, the only way of doing so is to use the procedure Ω described above (which invokes SFake). Trying to compute μ_3 a for such transcript will cause program $\mathsf{P3}$ to execute its "mixed input step", ensuring that such μ_3 receives level $\ell \geq 1$; for this, it is important that SFake increments the level inside s. Trying to decrypt such a related transcript $(\mu_1{}^*, \mu_2{}^*, \mu_3)$ will cause program Dec to execute its "mixed input step", ensuring that the requisite decryption behavior is observed (that fake r decrypts correctly transcripts with larger level, but fails to decrypt transcripts with smaller level); for this, it is important that RFake copies the level from the transcript to r.

Outline of security proof in oracle-access model. Since the proof even in this simpler (oracle-access) model is somewhat lengthy, we only outline the main steps here, with intuition for each. The proof proceeds in four main hybrid steps. We start with a real execution corresponding to plaintext m_0^*, where the adversary receives real randomness s^*, r^*.

- **Step I: indistinguishability of sender explanations.** Instead of giving the adversary real s^*, we give it $s' = \mathsf{Enc}_{K_S}(m_0^*, \mu_1{}^*, \mu_2{}^*, \mu_3{}^*, \ell = 0)$ (note that this s' contains level 0, unlike fake randomness produced by SFake which contains level at least 1).
  Intuitively, the reason why we can switch from s^* to s' indistinguishably is because all programs treat s^* and s' indistinguishably. That is:
  • either the programs output the same value, possibly via different branches of execution (e.g., $\mathsf{P1}$ on input (s^*, m_0^*) outputs $\mu_1{}^*$ via its main step and on input (s', m_0^*) outputs $\mu_1{}^*$ via its trapdoor step);
  • or the programs execute the same code, possibly outputting different results (e.g., $\mathsf{P1}$, on input (s^*, m_1^*) or (s', m_1^*), evaluates a PRF on its input and outputs the result).

The above, and the fact that s' is pseudorandom, allow us to change s^* to s' (similarly to the [SW14] proof for sender-deniable encryption).

- **Step II: indistinguishability of receiver explanations.** Instead of giving the adversary real r^*, we give it fake r', i.e., $r' = \mathsf{Enc}_{K_R}(m_0^*, \mu_1{}^*, \mu_2{}^*, \mu_3{}^*, \ell = 0, \rho_R)$. Unlike in Step I, here there is a transcript with respect to which the decryption program treats r^* and r' distinguishably.
  Recall that r^* honestly decrypts *all* related transcripts, while r' only honestly decrypts "forward", i.e., for related transcripts with level $\ell \geq 1$. Thus, the two programs may treat level-0 transcripts differently. Consider a transcript $(\mu_1{}^*, \mu_2{}^*, \overline{\mu_3{}^*})$, where $\overline{\mu_3{}^*} = \mathsf{Enc}_K(m_1^*, \mu_1{}^*, \mu_2{}^*, \ell = 0)$ is like $\mu_3{}^*$ except that it encrypts the wrong plaintext m_1^*. This transcript decrypts correctly to m_1^* with r^*, but decrypting it with r' returns $\perp$ due to the level comparison logic. This single transcript makes r^* and r' distinguishable. As a result, the proof of Step I does not work here. Therefore, we first move to a hybrid where this "differing" transcript doesn't exist, as follows. First, since s^* (the preimage of

PRF output $\mu_1{}^*$) is not part of the distribution anymore, we can move $\mu_1{}^*$ outside the PRF image. Then we argue that P3 never outputs $\overline{\mu_3{}^*}$:

- *The main step cannot output* $\overline{\mu_3{}^*}$, since it is executed only if the validity check passes *via a correct PRF preimage*, which now does not exist.
- *The mixed step cannot output* $\overline{\mu_3{}^*}$, since P3 can only output a ciphertext with level 0 (like $\overline{\mu_3{}^*}$) via the mixed step if its input randomness has level 0, and such input randomness is hard to find since SFake never outputs randomness with level 0.
- *The trapdoor step cannot output* $\overline{\mu_3{}^*}$, since P3 can only output $\overline{\mu_3{}^*}$ via the trapdoor step if it receives as input fake randomness that has $\overline{\mu_3{}^*}$ inside to begin with. Since there are no other means of computing $\overline{\mu_3{}^*}$, such randomness is also hard to find.

Once the differing transcript $(\mu_1{}^*, \mu_2{}^*, \overline{\mu_3{}^*})$ is eliminated, we can switch r^* to r' similarly to Step I.

- **Step III: indistinguishability of plaintexts.** The next step is to switch $\mu_3{}^*$ from encrypting m_0^* to encrypting m_1^*. This is done by "detaching" $\mu_3{}^*$ from its key K in programs P3 and Dec. Concretely:

  - P3 can only output $\mu_3{}^*$ via the trapdoor thread (which does not use the key K). The reason is very similar to the case-by-case analysis of P3 in Step II: the main step requires a PRF preimage, which does not exist, and the mixed step requires level-0 sender randomness, which is hard to find.
  - Dec can only "decrypt" $\mu_3{}^*$ via the trapdoor thread (which, again, does not use K). To guarantee this, we first move $\mu_2{}^*$ outside of the PRF image (this is possible since r^* is no longer part of the distribution). Then $\mu_3{}^*$ is never decrypted via the main step because the preimage for $\mu_2{}^*$ does not exist. Further, $\mu_3{}^*$ cannot be decrypted via the mixed step either, because the "correctness forward" decryption rule outputs $\perp$ unless the input receiver randomness has level smaller than the level in $\mu_3{}^*$, and this is not possible since $\mu_3{}^*$ has the smallest possible level, 0.

In other words, neither P3 nor Dec need to use K to encrypt or decrypt $\mu_3{}^*$. Therefore we can "detach" K and $\mu_3{}^*$ and change the plaintext to m_1^*.

Note that the transcript now contains m_1^*, and both sender and receiver randomness s', r' are consistent with m_0^*. However, the proof is not finished yet, since parties cannot produce such s' themselves (since s' has level 0).

- **Step IV: indistinguishability of levels.** The last step is to change the level inside s' from 0 to 1, i.e., let $s' = \mathsf{Enc}_{K_S}(m_0^*, \mu_1{}^*, \mu_2{}^*, \mu_3{}^*, \ell = 1)$. To understand the challenge of this step, it is instructive to take a "level-centric" perspective: let's put aside that the scheme is about transmitting plaintexts, and instead think of fake s as an encryption of level (0 or 1), think of $\mu_3{}^*$ as an encryption of level 0, and think of the programs of deniable encryption as implementing homomorphic operations on encrypted levels. For example, program SFake outputs fake randomness which is an encryption of incremented level, and thus implements a homomorphic Increment operation on levels. Program Dec compares levels inside μ_3 and r and, based on that, decrypts or outputs $\perp$, and thus it implements a homomorphic isLess function on levels, which reveals (in the clear) if one level is smaller than the other.

From this perspective, step IV essentially requires switching s' from an encryption of 0 to an encryption of 1, while the adversary has access to homomorphic functions Increment and isLess.[12] In the oracle-access model, it can be easily shown that polynomially bounded adversaries cannot distinguish between Enc(0) and Enc(1), even given oracle access to isLess and Increment, as long as the largest allowed level T is superpolynomial: this is because the adversary can only generate polynomial-length sequences of encryptions— Enc(1), Enc(2), ... or Enc(2), Enc(3), ... (depending on whether the challenge ciphertext was Enc(0) or Enc(1))—and the oracles' behavior will be identical on both sequences.

This concludes the proof outline in the oracle-access model. We underline that in the actual construction we need special types of PRFs, encryption schemes, and a special *level system* primitive in order to prove security with iO. The proofs of steps I-III in the final construction roughly follow the same outline (sometimes with several hybrids per each logical step), but the proof of the step IV (indistinguishability of levels) requires substantial additional work when the adversary possesses the code of the programs.

3 Defining Bideniable and Off-the-Record Deniable Encryption

We present the definition of interactive deniable encryption, or, more formally, interactive bideniable message transmission, in the CRS model.

Syntax. An interactive deniable encryption scheme π consists of seven algorithms $\pi = (\mathsf{Setup}, \mathsf{P1}, \mathsf{P2}, \mathsf{P3}, \mathsf{Dec}, \mathsf{SFake}, \mathsf{RFake})$, where Setup is used to generate the public programs (i.e., the CRS), programs P1, P3 and SFake are used by the sender, and programs P2, Dec and RFake are used by the receiver. Let $\mathsf{tr} = \pi(s, r, m)$ denote the transcript of a protocol execution on input plaintext m, sender randomness s, and receiver randomness r, i.e., the sequence of three messages sent in the protocol execution. That is, $\pi(s, r, m) = \mathsf{tr} = (\mu_1, \mu_2, \mu_3)$, where $\mu_1 = \mathsf{P1}(s, m)$, $\mu_2 = \mathsf{P2}(r, \mu_1)$, and $\mu_3 = \mathsf{P3}(s, m, \mu_1, \mu_2)$.

The faking algorithms have the following syntax: $\mathsf{SFake}(s, m, m', \mathsf{tr}; \rho)$ expects to take as input a transcript tr along with the true random coins s and true plaintext m which were used to compute tr, and a desired fake plaintext m'. SFake is randomized and ρ denotes its randomness. RFake has the same syntax except that it expects receiver randomness r instead of sender randomness s.

Bideniable and off-the-record-deniable encryption in the CRS model. Next, we define standard and off-the-record deniability for interactive deniable

---

[12] Recall that the adversary also has $\mu_3{}^*$ which is an encryption of level 0. For simplicity, we ignore this fact in this high-level overview.

encryption in the CRS model. For simplicity, we focus on bit encryption. The definitions are naturally extensible to multi-bit plaintexts.

Formally, the deniable encryption algorithms should take the CRS as input. We omit this for notational simplicity as it is unnecessary in our construction (where the CRS contains the programs, and the programs do not take the CRS as input).

Definition 1 Bideniable bit encryption in the CRS model. $\pi =$ (Setup, P1, P2, P3, Dec, SFake, RFake) *is a 3-message bideniable interactive encryption scheme for message space* $\mathcal{M} = \{0,1\}$, *if it satisfies the following correctness and bideniability properties.*

- **Correctness:** *There exists a negligible function* $\nu(\lambda)$ *such that for at least a* $(1 - \nu)$ *fraction of randomness* $r_{\mathsf{Setup}} \in \{0,1\}^{|r_{\mathsf{Setup}}|}$, *for any* $m \in \mathcal{M}$,

$$\Pr\left[m' \neq m \; : \; \begin{array}{l} \mathsf{CRS} \leftarrow \mathsf{Setup}(r_{\mathsf{Setup}}) \\ s \leftarrow \{0,1\}^{|s|} \\ r \leftarrow \{0,1\}^{|r|} \\ \mathsf{tr} \leftarrow \pi(s,r,m) \\ m' \leftarrow \mathsf{Dec}(r,\mathsf{tr}) \end{array} \right] \leq \nu(\lambda) \; .$$

- **Bideniability:** *No PPT adversary* Adv *has more than negligible advantage in the following game, for any* $m_0, m_1 \in \mathcal{M}$:
    1. *The challenger chooses random* r_{Setup} *and generates* $\mathsf{CRS} \leftarrow \mathsf{Setup}(r_{\mathsf{Setup}})$. *It also chooses a bit* b *at random.*
    2. *If* $b = 0$, *then the challenger behaves as follows:*
        (a) *It chooses random* s^*, r^* *and computes* $\mathsf{tr}^* = \pi(s^*, r^*, m_0)$.
        (b) *It gives the adversary* $(\mathsf{CRS}, m_0, m_1, s^*, r^*, \mathsf{tr}^*)$.
    3. *If* $b = 1$, *then the challenger behaves as follows:*
        (a) *It chooses random* s^*, r^* *and computes* $\mathsf{tr}^* \leftarrow \pi(s^*, r^*, m_1)$.
        (b) *It sets* $s' \leftarrow \mathsf{SFake}(s^*, m_1, m_0, \mathsf{tr}^*; \rho_S)$ *for random* ρ_S.
        (c) *It sets* $r' \leftarrow \mathsf{RFake}(r^*, m_1, m_0, \mathsf{tr}^*; \rho_R)$ *for random* ρ_R.
        (d) *It gives the adversary* $(\mathsf{CRS}, m_0, m_1, s', r', \mathsf{tr}^*)$.
    4. Adv *outputs* b' *and wins if* $b = b'$.

Next, we define off-the-record deniability. We define it for an arbitrary message space instead of bit encryption, since having $|\mathcal{M}| > 2$ allows for an extra case when plaintexts claimed by the sender, by the receiver, and the real plaintext are three different strings (case $b = 2$ in the definition below).

Definition 2 Off-the-record deniable encryption in the CRS model. *We say that a scheme is off-the-record deniable, if it satisfies correctness as above and also has the following property.*

Off-the-record deniability: No PPT adversary Adv wins with more than negligible advantage in the following game, for any $m_0, m_1, m_2 \in \mathcal{M}$:

1. The challenger chooses random r_{Setup} and generates $\mathsf{CRS} \leftarrow \mathsf{Setup}(r_{\mathsf{Setup}})$. It also chooses random $b \in \{0, 1, 2\}$.
2. If $b = 0$, then the challenger generates the following variables:
   (a) The challenger chooses random s^*, r^* and computes $\mathsf{tr}^* \leftarrow \pi(s^*, r^*, m_0)$;
   (b) It sets $r' \leftarrow \mathsf{RFake}(r^*, m_0, m_1, \mathsf{tr}^*; \rho_R)$ for randomly chosen ρ_R.
   (c) It gives the adversary $(\mathsf{CRS}, m_0, m_1, m_2, s^*, r', \mathsf{tr}^*)$.
3. If $b = 1$, then the challenger generates the following variables:
   (a) The challenger chooses random s^*, r^* and computes $\mathsf{tr}^* \leftarrow \pi(s^*, r^*, m_1)$;
   (b) It sets $s' \leftarrow \mathsf{SFake}(s^*, m_1, m_0, \mathsf{tr}^*; \rho_S)$ for randomly chosen ρ_S.
   (c) It gives the adversary $(\mathsf{CRS}, m_0, m_1, m_2, s', r^*, \mathsf{tr}^*)$.
4. If $b = 2$, then the challenger generates the following variables:
   (a) The challenger chooses random s^*, r^* and computes $\mathsf{tr}^* \leftarrow \pi(s^*, r^*, m_2)$;
   (b) It sets $s' \leftarrow \mathsf{SFake}(s^*, m_2, m_0, \mathsf{tr}^*; \rho_S)$ for randomly chosen ρ_S.
   (c) It sets $r' \leftarrow \mathsf{RFake}(r^*, m_2, m_1, \mathsf{tr}^*; \rho_R)$ for randomly chosen ρ_R.
   (d) It gives the adversary $(\mathsf{CRS}, m_0, m_1, m_2, s', r', \mathsf{tr}^*)$.
5. Adv outputs b' and wins if $b = b'$.

We say that an encryption scheme is bideniable (resp., off-the-record deniable) with (t, ε)-security, if the distinguishing advantage of any size-t adversary in the bideniability (resp., off-the-record deniability) game is at most ε.

Single-execution security implies multi-execution security. In Definitions 1 and 2, the CRS is global (i.e., non-programmable). These definitions do not involve simulation and the same set of programs is used throughout. Furthermore, even though Definitions 1 and 2 consider a single protocol execution, a simple hybrid argument shows that security of a single execution implies security of arbitrarily polynomially many executions with the same set of programs.[13]

Definition 3 Public receiver deniability. *A deniable scheme has* public receiver-deniability *if* RFake *takes as input only the transcript* tr *and fake plaintext* m' *(not true random coins of the receiver* r^* *and true plaintext* m*).*

This concludes the informal scheme description, proof intuition, and full definitions. We have overviewed the key ideas underlying the full construction. Please see the full version [CPP18] for complete details and proofs.

Acknowledgements. RC is a member of the Check Point Institute for Information Security. Supported by the NSF MACS project. SP's research is supported by the MIT Media Lab's Digital Currency Initiative and its funders, and earlier, was supported by the following grants: NSF MACS (CNS-1413920), DARPA IBM (W911NF-15-C-0236), Simons Investigator award agreement dated June 5th, 2012, and the Center for Science of Information (CSoI), an NSF Science & Technology Center, under grant agreement CCF-0939370.

---

[13] We can change all executions from real to fake one by one, where the reduction from a single-execution security will generate other executions on its own, since knowing the CRS (but not its generation randomness) suffices to run all programs.

References

[AFL16]   Apon, D., Fan, X., Liu, F.-H.: Deniable attribute based encryption for branching programs from LWE. In: Hirt, M., Smith, A. (eds.) TCC 2016-B, Part II. LNCS, vol. 9986, pp. 299–329. Springer, Heidelberg (2016). https://doi.org/10.1007/978-3-662-53644-5_12

[BGB04]   Borisov, N., Goldberg, I., Brewer, E.A.: Off-the-record communication, or, why not to use PGP. In: Atluri, V., Syverson, P.F., De Capitanidi Vimercati, S. (eds.) Workshop on Privacy in the Electronic Society (WPES 2004), Proceedings, pp. 77–84. ACM (2004)

[BNNO11]   Bendlin, R., Nielsen, J.B., Nordholt, P.S., Orlandi, C.: Lower and upper bounds for deniable public-key encryption. In: Lee, D.H., Wang, X. (eds.) ASIACRYPT 2011. LNCS, vol. 7073, pp. 125–142. Springer, Heidelberg (2011). https://doi.org/10.1007/978-3-642-25385-0_7

[BPR15]   Bitansky, N., Paneth, O., Rosen, A.: On the cryptographic hardness of finding a nash equilibrium. Electron. Colloquium Comput. Complex. (ECCC) **22**, 1 (2015)

[BPW16]   Bitansky, N., Paneth, O., Wichs, D.: Perfect structure on the edge of chaos - trapdoor permutations from indistinguishability obfuscation. In: Kushilevitz, E., Malkin, T. (eds.) TCC 2016-A, Part I. LNCS, vol. 9562, pp. 474–502. Springer, Heidelberg (2016). https://doi.org/10.1007/978-3-662-49096-9_20

[CDMW09]   Choi, S.G., Dachman-Soled, D., Malkin, T., Wee, H.: Improved non-committing encryption with applications to adaptively secure protocols. In: Matsui, M. (ed.) ASIACRYPT 2009. LNCS, vol. 5912, pp. 287–302. Springer, Heidelberg (2009). https://doi.org/10.1007/978-3-642-10366-7_17

[CDNO96]   Canetti, R., Dwork, C., Naor, M., Ostrovsky, R.: Deniable encryption. IACR Cryptology ePrint Archive 1996:2 (1996)

[CFGN96]   Canetti, R., Feige, U., Goldreich, O., Naor, M.: Adaptively secure multi-party computation. In: STOC 1996, Proceedings, pp. 639–648 (1996)

[CHJV14]   Canetti, R., Holmgren, J., Jain, A., Vaikuntanathan, V.: Indistinguishability obfuscation of iterated circuits and RAM programs. IACR Cryptology ePrint Archive, 2014:769 (2014)

[CIO16]   De Caro, A., Iovino, V., O'Neill, A.: Deniable functional encryption. In: Cheng, C.-M., Chung, K.-M., Persiano, G., Yang, B.-Y. (eds.) PKC 2016, Part I. LNCS, vol. 9614, pp. 196–222. Springer, Heidelberg (2016). https://doi.org/10.1007/978-3-662-49384-7_8

[CPP18]   Canetti, R., Park, S., Poburinnaya, O.: Fully bideniable interactive encryption. IACR Cryptol. ePrint Arch. 2018:1244 (2018)

[Dac12]   Dachman-Soled, D.: On the impossibility of sender-deniable public key encryption. IACR Cryptology ePrint Archive, 2012:727 (2012)

[DH76]   Diffie, W., Hellman, M.E.: New directions in cryptography. IEEE Trans. Inf. Theory **22**(6), 644–654 (1976)

[DKSW09]   Dodis, Y., Katz, J., Smith, A., Walfish, S.: Composability and on-line deniability of authentication. In: Reingold, O. (ed.) TCC 2009. LNCS, vol. 5444, pp. 146–162. Springer, Heidelberg (2009)

[GKW17]   Goldwasser, S., Klein, S., Wichs, D.: The edited truth. In: Kalai, Y., Reyzin, L. (eds.) TCC 2017, Part I. LNCS, vol. 10677, pp. 305–340. Springer, Cham (2017). https://doi.org/10.1007/978-3-319-70500-2_11

[GM84] Goldwasser, S., Micali, S.: Probabilistic encryption. J. Comput. Syst. Sci. **28**(2), 270–299 (1984)

[KLW15] Koppula, V., Lewko, A.B., Waters, B.: Indistinguishability obfuscation for turing machines with unbounded memory. In: STOC 2015, Proceedings, pp. 419–428 (2015)

[Nie02] Nielsen, J.B.: Separating random oracle proofs from complexity theoretic proofs: the non-committing encryption case. In: Yung, M. (ed.) CRYPTO 2002. LNCS, vol. 2442, pp. 111–126. Springer, Heidelberg (2002). https://doi.org/10.1007/3-540-45708-9_8

[OPW11] O'Neill, A., Peikert, C., Waters, B.: Bi-deniable public-key encryption. In: Rogaway, P. (ed.) CRYPTO 2011. LNCS, vol. 6841, pp. 525–542. Springer, Heidelberg (2011). https://doi.org/10.1007/978-3-642-22792-9_30

[RSA78] Rivest, R.L., Shamir, A., Adleman, L.M.: A method for obtaining digital signatures and public-keycryptosystems. Commun. ACM **21**(2), 120–126 (1978)

[SW14] Sahai, A., Waters, B.: How to use indistinguishability obfuscation: deniable encryption, and more. In: STOC 2014, Proceedings, pp. 475–484 (2014)

Chosen Ciphertext Security
from Injective Trapdoor Functions

Susan Hohenberger[1(✉)], Venkata Koppula[2(✉)], and Brent Waters[3,4(✉)]

[1] Johns Hopkins University, Baltimore, MD, USA
susan@cs.jhu.edu
[2] Weizmann Institute of Science, Rehovot, Israel
venkata.koppula@weizmann.ac.il
[3] University of Texas, Austin, TX, USA
bwaters@cs.utexas.edu
[4] NTT Research, Palo Alto, CA, USA

Abstract. We provide a construction of chosen ciphertext secure public-key encryption from (injective) trapdoor functions. Our construction is black box and assumes no special properties (e.g. "lossy", "correlated product secure") of the trapdoor function.

1   Introduction

A public-key encryption system is said to be chosen ciphertext attack (CCA) secure [7,31,34] if no polynomial-time attacker can distinguish whether a challenge ciphertext ct^* is an encryption of m_0 or m_1 *even* when given access to a decryption oracle for all ciphertexts except ct^*. In most deployed encryptions systems, CCA security is necessary to protect against an active attacker that might induce a user to decrypt messages of its choosing or even gain leverage from just the knowledge that an attempted decryption failed. See Shoup [37] for an excellent discussion on the importance of CCA security.

Over time the cryptographic community has become rather adept at achieving CCA security from many of the same assumptions that can be used to achieve chosen plaintext attack (CPA) security for public-key encryption, where the adversary is not given access to a decryption oracle. For instance we now have practical CCA secure encryption schemes from the Decisional [5,6] and

Susan Hohenberger is supported by NFS CNS-1414023, NSF CNS-1908181, the Office of Naval Research N00014-19-1-2294, and a Packard Foundation Subaward via UT Austin. Venkata Koppula is supported by the Binational Science Foundation (Grant No. 2016726), and by the European Union Horizon 2020 Research and Innovation Program via ERC Project REACT (Grant 756482) and via Project PROMETHEUS (Grant 780701). This work was done in part while the author was visiting the Simons Institute for the Theory of Computing. Brent Waters is supported in part by NSF CNS-1414082, NSF CNS-1908611, a Simons Investigator Award and a Packard Foundation Fellowship.

© International Association for Cryptologic Research 2020
D. Micciancio and T. Ristenpart (Eds.): CRYPTO 2020, LNCS 12170, pp. 836–866, 2020.
https://doi.org/10.1007/978-3-030-56784-2_28

Search [3] Diffie-Hellman, the difficulty of factoring [20,23], Learning with Errors (LWE) [33] and Learning Parity with Noise (LPN) [11,25] assumptions.

Despite the success in these ad-hoc number-theoretic rooted approaches, there is a strong drive to be able to understand CCA security from the perspective of general assumptions with an ultimate goal of showing that the existence of CPA secure public-key encryption implies CCA secure public-key encryption. In this work we make significant progress in this direction by showing that CCA secure public-key encryption can be built from any (injective) trapdoor function. Recall that a trapdoor function is a primitive in which any user given a public key tdf.pk can evaluate the input $\mathbf{x}$ by calling TDF.Eval(tdf.pk, $\mathbf{x}$) $\rightarrow$ $\mathbf{y}$. And a user with the secret key tdf.sk can recover $\mathbf{x}$ from $\mathbf{y}$ as TDF.Invert(tdf.sk, $\mathbf{y}$) $\rightarrow$ $\mathbf{x}$. However, a polynomial-time attacker without the secret key should not be able to output $\mathbf{x}$ given $\mathbf{y}$ = TDF.Eval(tdf.pk, $\mathbf{x}$) for a randomly chosen $\mathbf{x}$. By injective, we require a one-to-one mapping of the function input and evaluation spaces.

There is a strong lineage connecting trapdoor functions with chosen ciphertext security. Fujisaki and Okamoto [13] showed how in the random oracle model any CPA secure encryption scheme can be transformed into a CCA secure scheme. Their transformation implicitly creates a trapdoor function (in a spirit similar to the random oracle based TDF construction of [1]) where the decryption algorithm recovers encryption randomness and re-encrypts to test ciphertext validity. If we allow the trapdoor function to be a "doubly enhanced" permutation [17], then they can be used to create non-interactive zero knowledge proofs which are known to give chosen ciphertext security via non-black box constructions [7,31]. Peikert and Waters [33] introduced the notion of lossy trapdoor functions and showed that this primitive also gives rise to chosen ciphertext secure public-key encryption. Other works (e.g., [22,29]) extended and generalized this notion including Rosen and Segev [36] who showed that a "correlated product secure" TDF gives rise to CCA security. In each of these (standard model) cases an additional property of the trapdoor function (i.e., permutation and doubly enhanced, lossy, correlated product secure) was required and critical for achieving chosen ciphertext security leaving open the problem of building chosen ciphertext secure encryption by only assuming injective trapdoor functions.

Finally, Koppula and Waters [27] recently showed how to achieve chosen ciphertext security from CPA secure public-key encryption and a newly introduced "Hinting PRG" which is a pseudorandom generator that has a special form of circular security.[1] Their construction can be viewed as a "partial trapdoor" where the decryption process recovers some, but not all of the randomness used to encrypt the ciphertext and re-encrypts parts of the ciphertext to check for validity. They show how Hinting PRGs can be constructed from number theoretic assumptions such as CDH and LWE using techniques similar to [2,4,8–10,15].

---

[1] Kitagawa and Matsuda [26] show how the Hinting PRG assumption can alternatively be replaced with the assumption of symmetric key encryption with key-dependent security.

Our Results

In this work we show a black box approach to construct chosen ciphertext security using just injective trapdoor functions (in addition to primitives known to be implied by TDFs.) We outline our approach, which begins with two abstractions that we will use as building blocks in our construction. These abstractions are called (1) encryption with randomness recovery, and (2) tagged set commitments. We build the first generically from injective trapdoor functions and the latter from pseudorandom generators, which are known to be implied by TDFs. These abstractions are intentionally simple, but useful for building intuition.

Encryption with Randomness Recovery. The "Encryption with Randomness Recovery" abstraction is simply an IND-CPA secure public-key encryption where (1) the decryption algorithm recovers both the message and the encryption randomness r and (2) where there is also a Recover algorithm which can recover the message from a ciphertext given the encryption randomness r. That is, when $\mathsf{Enc}(\mathsf{pk}, m, r) \to \mathsf{ct}$, then $\mathsf{Dec}(\mathsf{sk}, \mathsf{ct}) \to (m, r)$ and $\mathsf{Recover}(\mathsf{pk}, \mathsf{ct}, r) \to m$. We formally define this abstraction in Sect. 3, followed by an immediate construction of Encryption with Randomness Recovery from injective trapdoor functions. Notably Yao's method [38] of achieving encryption from trapdoor functions is actually Encryption with Randomness Recovery for 1-bit messages, where many such ciphertexts can be concatenated together to encrypt many bits.

Tagged Set Commitments. The "Tagged Set Commitment" abstraction is a commitment scheme that commits to a B-sized set of indices $S \in [N]$ with a tag tg (where N and B are inputs to a trusted setup algorithm) by producing a commitment together with a membership proof for each $i \in S$; that is, $\mathsf{Commit}(\mathsf{pp}, S, \mathsf{tg}) \to (\mathsf{com}, (\sigma_i)_{i \in S})$. The verification algorithm checks the membership proof to verify that $i \in S$ under tag tg. These algorithms take in a set of public parameters pp generated by a Setup algorithm with a bound B that enforces (the maximum) size of S. Additionally, for proof purposes, the scheme must support an alternative setup algorithm AltSetup that takes in a tag tg and produces public parameters together with a special commitment and a proof of membership for this commitment for *every* element in the committing domain (which will exceed the bound B that all other commitments must abide by). In addition to the regular soundness property, we will require that no polynomial-time adversary can distinguish between when the parameters were generated by the regular or the alternative setup algorithm. We formally define this abstraction in Sect. 4, followed by a construction from pseudorandom generators. This abstraction is related to a number of prior works. It can be viewed as a generalization of the commitment scheme used in [27] to achieve a generic CCA compiler for attribute-based encryption schemes, which was itself related to Naor's commitment from pseudorandom generators [30].

Our CCA Construction. Our construction uses three building blocks: a one-time signature scheme, a CPA-secure encryption scheme with randomness recovery and tagged set commitments. Our construction will create a CCA key that includes N CPA keys. To encrypt a message a user will encrypt it to a subset of the keys. Decryption will then follow the paradigm of recovering randomness from (some of) the CPA encryptions and then re-encrypting to check for validity. Conceptually, it is critical for us to perform a type of balancing act when encrypting the ciphertexts in order to prove security. At one step in the proof we want to have enough redundancy in the way randomness is chosen so that one can decrypt given any $N - 1$ of the private keys. However, at a later stage in the proof we want the fact that we choose any redundancy at all to statistically wash away. We sketch our construction below and show how we find this balance.

We begin by noting the parameterization of our scheme. The driving factor will be the length of randomness $\ell_{\mathrm{rnd}} = \ell_{\mathrm{rnd}}(\lambda)$ of the underlying encryption with randomness recovery scheme for security parameter λ. We will choose integers N, B such that $N > B$ and $\binom{N}{B} > 2^{\ell_{\mathrm{rnd}}+\lambda}$. For example, we could let $N = 2(\ell_{\mathrm{rnd}} + \lambda)$ and $B = N/2$.

The CCA setup algorithm initially chooses N key pairs from the CPA with randomness recovery scheme as $(\mathsf{cpa.pk}_i, \mathsf{cpa.sk}_i) \leftarrow \mathsf{CPA.Setup}(1^\lambda)$. In addition, it samples the tagged set commitment as $\mathsf{tsc.pp} \leftarrow \mathsf{TSC.Setup}(1^\lambda, 1^N, 1^B, 1^t)$ where t is the length of a verification key in the one-time signature scheme.

To encrypt one first chooses a uniformly random B-size subset $S \subset [N]$. Next, choose a signing/verification key $(\mathsf{sig.sk}, \mathsf{sig.vk}) \leftarrow \mathsf{Sig.Setup}(1^\lambda)$. And then get a commitment to the set elements as $(\mathsf{tsc.com}, (\mathsf{tsc.\sigma}_i)_{i \in S}) \leftarrow \mathsf{TSC.Commit}(\mathsf{tsc.pp}, S, \mathsf{sig.vk})$. At this point the encryptor will select the randomness used for encryption. For all $i \in S$ choose $r_i \in \{0,1\}^{\ell_{\mathrm{rnd}}}$ uniformly at random with the constraint that these values XOR to $0^{\ell_{\mathrm{rnd}}}$. Observe that this slight redundancy implies that for a correctly formed ciphertext if we are given the set S along with the r_i values for $B - 1$ of the indices in S, then we can derive the last one by simply XORing all the others together. For $i \notin S$ simply choose r_i at random.

To finalize encryption for $i \in [N]$, if $i \in S$ encrypt the message along with proof for index i as $\mathsf{cpa.ct}_i = \mathsf{CPA.Enc}(\mathsf{cpa.pk}_i, 1|\mathsf{tsc.\sigma}_i|m; r_i)$. Otherwise for $i \notin S$ encrypt the all 0's string as $\mathsf{cpa.ct}_i = \mathsf{CPA.Enc}(\mathsf{cpa.pk}_i, 0^{\ell_{\mathrm{cpa}}}; r_i)$. Finally, sign $\left(\mathsf{tsc.com}, (\mathsf{cpa.ct}_i)_{i \in [N]}\right)$ with $\mathsf{sig.sk}$ to get $\mathsf{sig.\sigma}$ and output the ciphertext ct as $\left(\mathsf{sig.vk}, \mathsf{sig.\sigma}, \mathsf{tsc.com}, (\mathsf{cpa.ct}_i)_{i \in [N]}\right)$.

The decryption algorithm on $\mathsf{ct} = \left(\mathsf{sig.vk}, \mathsf{sig.\sigma}, \mathsf{tsc.com}, (\mathsf{cpa.ct}_i)_{i \in [N]}\right)$ will first verify the signature and reject if that fails. Next, it will initialize a set $U = \emptyset$ and use the $\mathsf{cpa.sk}_i$ to decrypt all $\mathsf{cpa.ct}_i$ using the respective $\mathsf{cpa.sk}_i$. For each $i \in [N]$, it gets a message y_i which is parsed as $g_i|\sigma_i|m_i$ and randomness r_i. The decryption algorithm adds (i, y_i) to U if decryption is successful and (1) $\mathsf{TSC.Verify}(\mathsf{tsc.pp}, \mathsf{tsc.com}, i, \mathsf{tsc.\sigma}_i, \mathsf{sig.vk}) = 1$ and (2) $\mathsf{cpa.ct}_i = \mathsf{CPA.Enc}(\mathsf{cpa.pk}_i, y_i; r_i)$. It then checks that there are exactly B entries in the set U, they all encrypt the same message and that $\oplus_{(i,y_i) \in U} r_i = 0^\ell$. If so, it outputs the message. We emphasize that the decryption algorithm both checks the well formness of ciphertext components in U via re-encryption and checks for the redundancy in randomness via the XOR operation. However, ciphertext components outside of the set U are not verified in this way. Indeed, the algorithm will allow decryption to proceed even it "knows" some components outside of U were malformed.

Our proof is given as a sequence of games where we show that for any poly-time attacker the advantage of the attacker must be negligibly close in successive games. We sketch the proof at a high level here and refer the reader to the main body for details.

1. In the first step of our proof the decryption algorithm rejects all ciphertexts that come with a signature under sig.vk* where sig.vk* is the signing key of the challenge ciphertext. This step is proven via a standard reduction to a *strongly* secure one-time signature scheme.
2. In the next security game the set commitment parameters are chosen via alternate setup: $\left(\text{tsc.com}^*, (\text{tsc.}\sigma_i)_{i \in [N]}\right) \leftarrow \text{AltSetup}(1^\lambda, 1^N, 1^B, 1^t, \text{sig.vk}^*)$.
   This means that for the tag sig.vk* (and only the tag sig.vk*) proof values exist for every single index in $[N]$. However, in the challenge ciphertext tsc.σ_i are only used for $i \in S^*$ where S^* is the set used in creating the challenge ciphertext.
3. In our proof for all indices $i \notin S^*$ we will want to change cpa.ct$_i$ from an encryption of the all 0's string to an encryption of $1|\text{tsc.}\sigma_i^*|m_b$. We will change these one at a time. Suppose we want to argue that no attacker can detect such a change on the j-th index. To prove this we need a reduction that will not have access to the j-th secret key cpa.sk$_j$, but will still be able to decrypt in an equivalent (but not identical) manner to the original decryption algorithm. To do this the alternative decryption algorithm uses all $N-1$ secret keys that it has to build a partial set U as in the actual decryption algorithm above. It then branches its behavior on the size of U: (1) If $|U| > B$, then reject. In this case the missing j-th component can only add to the size of U which is already too big and will be rejected. (2) If $|U| < B - 1$, then reject. The missing j-th component can make the set size at most $B-1$ which is too small and will be rejected. (3) If $|U| = B$, then proceed with the remaining checks of decryption using the set U and ignore the j-th component. By soundness of the tagged set commitment scheme, this could not have contained tsc.σ_j for a tag sig.vk $\neq$ sig.vk* so we can safely ignore the j-th component. (4) If $|U| = B - 1$, compute $r_j = \oplus_{i \in U} r_i$ and use this candidate randomness to decrypt cpa.ct$_j$ in lieu of the key cpa.sk$_j$. Once this step is done, the result can be added (or not) to the set U and the rest of decryption proceeds as before. We can show that the required redundancy checks make this decryption case equivalent to the original as well.
   Once this proof step has occurred for all $j \in [N]$ we have that each message is $1|\text{tsc.}\sigma_i^*|m_b$, but that the challenge ciphertext has the redundancy in the randomness $\oplus_{i \in S^*} r_i = 0^{\ell_{\text{rnd}}}$.
4. For the next game we want to remove the redundancy in the randomness so that r_i is chosen uniformly at random for all indices i. It turns out that by the setting of our parameters this is statistically already done! A random set of r_i variables will have a $\frac{1}{2^{\ell_{\text{rnd}}}}$ chance of XORing to 0^ℓ_{rnd}. Thus, we could then expect there will be approximately $\binom{N}{B} \cdot \frac{1}{2^{\ell_{\text{rnd}}}}$ sets of size B that satisfy this

condition if all r_i are chosen randomly. Recall that since we set $\binom{N}{B} > 2^{\ell_{\mathrm{rnd}}+\lambda}$ we might then expect there to be an exponential amount of sets meeting this condition. Therefore we would intuitively expect that planting a single set S^* with this condition and choosing all r_i randomly will be statistically close. In the main body, we formalize this intuition by applying the Leftover Hash Lemma [21].

5. Now that the randomness in the challenge ciphertext is uncorrelated we want to change all encryptions from $1|\mathsf{tsc}.\sigma_i^*|m_b$ to 0_{rnd}^ℓ. This can be done by a hybrid over all j from 1 to N. (At this point in the security game there is no set S^*.) This is done by again using an alternative decryption algorithm that can decrypt using all but the j-th secret key.

Stepping back we can see that the XORing to 0_{rnd}^ℓ condition on S gave enough redundancy where one could decrypt with all but one of the keys allowing Steps 3 and 5 of the proof above to proceed. However, the redundant condition was limited enough where it could be statistically washed away in Step 4 of the proof.

A Further Comparison to Koppula-Waters (CRYPTO 2019). We provide a closer comparison between our work and that of Koppula and Waters [27]. To do so we will imagine modifying our scheme above and arrive at something analogous to [27]. Suppose that instead of choosing the values r_i in the set S at random with $\oplus_{i \in S^*} r_i = 0^{\ell_{\mathrm{rnd}}}$, we instead ran a pseudorandom generator (of output length $B \cdot \ell_{\mathrm{rnd}}$) on S as $\mathsf{PRG}(S)$ to determine the r_i values for $i \in S$. The r_i for $i \notin S$ are random as before.

Using this encryption algorithm, one can create an analogous decryption algorithm that first recovers a candidate set U almost as before. However, instead of getting the random coins r_i from decryption once it has U, the decryption algorithm can run $\mathsf{PRG}(U)$ to determine the candidate set of r_i values. At this point it can perform the same re-encryption and other checks as we outlined above. Indeed, the underlying encryption system does not even need to have randomness recovery and thus is not necessarily trapdoor based.

If we try to prove this system secure, we can mostly march along the same steps as above, but we hit a roadblock at Step 4. In our construction we argue that choosing random r_i is statistically close to embedding the XOR condition. Is this true in the modified construction? Let's imagine an arbitrary B-sized subset S of indices with randomly chosen r_i. The probability that $\mathsf{PRG}(S)$ outputs these r_i values is $2^{-\ell_{\mathrm{rnd}}\cdot B}$. Even though there are $\binom{N}{B}$ sets of size B, the chances of there being just one of these subsets that meets this condition is still negligibly small. Thus we cannot make a statistical argument.

To get past Step 4 in the modified construction then, we will be forced to contrive an assumption that these two distributions are computationally indistinguishable. Conceptually, this assumption is very analogous to the "Hinting PRG" assumption introduced by Koppula and Waters. Altogether, our techniques address the main limitation of [27] which was the need for a "Hinting PRG" by creating an encryption scheme with less redundancy in the randomness. This allows us to bridge over a critical proof step with a statistical argument.

1.1 Context on Trapdoor Functions

We conclude by providing some more context on trapdoor functions.

Constructions. For many years the only known standard model technique for getting trapdoor functions was to use an assumption like RSA [35] that immediately gives a trapdoor function. Peikert and Waters [33] gave the first standard model constructions for trapdoor functions from the DDH and the LWE assumptions. More recently, Garg and Hajiabadi [15] and Garg, Gay and Hajiabadi [14] gave constructions from the Computational Diffie-Hellman assumption.

On (Im)Perfect Correctness. We observe that our security argument above relies on the trapdoor function to be perfectly correct when switching from the original decryption algorithm to the alternative decryption algorithm. Otherwise, an attacker could potentially detect the change by constructing a ciphertext component which is well formed, but does not decrypt correctly. (Even if the encryption with randomness recovery correctness error is negligible for randomly sampled coins, it might be easy to adversarially discover bad ciphertexts.) This creates an issue for schemes such as [14,15] that are not perfectly correct.

To address this issue, we recall the notion of almost-all-keys perfect correctness in encryption schemes, introduced by Dwork et al. [12]. In an almost-all-keys perfectly correct scheme, the key generation algorithm $\mathsf{Setup}(1^\lambda)$ will sample a public, private key pair $(\mathsf{pk}, \mathsf{sk})$ such that, with all but negligible probability, these particular keys will work perfectly. That is, any message m and coins r used for encryption by pk will decrypt to m using sk. (This is a stronger notion of (imperfect) correctness than the usual one where potentially every public, secret key pair has a messages and coin pairs that cause decryption failures.) We observe that almost-all-keys correctness is sufficient for our proof of security to go through. Since the attacker has no influence on the key generation algorithm, with all but negligible probability, he/she will be stuck with a keypair that has perfect correctness.

The CDH based scheme of Garg, Gay and Hajiabadi [14] satisfies almost-all-keys perfect correctness. However, for the scheme of Garg and Hajiabadi [15], it is not clear if the above approach can directly work.[2] One might hope to use the transformation of [12] to go from an imperfectly correct encryption scheme to one that satisfies almost-all-keys perfect correctness. Unfortunately this does not appear to work as we require encryption *with randomness recovery*.

TDFs with a Sample Algorithm. The work of Bellare et al. [1] as well as the Katz-Lindell [24] textbook provide an alternative definition of trapdoor functions. In the standard definition the domain is simply all the strings of length ℓ_{inp} and the security experiment chooses $\mathbf{x} \in \{0,1\}^{\ell_{\mathsf{inp}}}$ to evaluate the trapdoor

---

[2] In [15], it appears that it is computationally difficult for an attacker to discover a TDF input $\mathbf{x}$ where $\mathbf{y} = \mathsf{TDF.Eval}(\mathsf{tdf.pk}, \mathbf{x})$ and $\mathsf{TDF.Invert}(\mathsf{tdf.sk}, \mathbf{y}) \neq \mathbf{x}$. We believe this property is also sufficient for our CCA transformation, but do not show this formally.

function on. In the alternative "sampling" definition there is an additional algorithm Sample that takes the public key along with random coins and outputs an element $\mathbf{x}$ in the domain. The TDF evaluation algorithm can then be run on $\mathbf{x}$ to give TDF.Eval(tdf.pk, $\mathbf{x}$) $\rightarrow \mathbf{y}$. Notably, the domain can depend on the public key and while correctness stipulates that TDF.Invert(tdf.sk, $\mathbf{y}$) $\rightarrow \mathbf{x}$, there is *no requirement to recover the coins of the* Sample *algorithm*.

At first glance it might appear that the differences in these two definitions is conceptually minor. However, these nuances are actually very important. As observed by Pandey [32] there exists a trivial construction of the sampling form of trapdoor functions from public key encryption. The public and secret key of the trapdoor function will just come from the PKE key generation algorithm. For a given public key pk, the domain consists of all (ct, m) pairs such that $\mathsf{ct} = \mathsf{Enc}(\mathsf{pk}, m; r)$ for some randomness r. The Sample algorithm will choose a random message m of sufficient length and output an encryption ct of m under the public key to give $\mathbf{x} = (\mathsf{ct}, m)$. The TDF.Eval algorithm can simply drop m. That is TDF.Eval(tdf.pk, $\mathbf{x} = (\mathsf{ct}, m)) \rightarrow \mathsf{ct}$. And the inversion algorithm can recover (ct, m) from ct by simply decrypting. Security follows immediately from the IND-CPA security of the underlying encryption scheme.

If we want the Sample algorithm to sample uniformly in the domain, we will need two additional properties of the encryption algorithm. First, that for every public key pk and every pair of messages (m_1, m_2) the number of distinct ciphertexts that can be generated from encrypting m_1 under pk is the same as the number that can be generated by encrypting m_2 under pk. And that for any pk and message m the likelihood of any ciphertext that it is in the support of encrypting m under pk is the same.

This construction feels like a cheat as it does not match our intuitive concept of what a trapdoor function is. It takes advantage of the fact that one is not required to recover the random coins used in the Sample algorithm. Thus the definition essentially allows for one to dispense with the recovery of coins requirement and seems to lose the spirit of trapdoor functions. An interesting question is whether such a transformation could be done in a definition where the Sample algorithm only took as input the security parameter and not the TDF's public key.

Looking Forward. It is interesting to think what implications our work might have on the ultimate question of whether chosen plaintext security implies chosen ciphertext security. An immediate barrier is that there are black box separations on building TDFs from PKE [16]. However, it might be possible to leverage our construction or lessons from it into an abstraction that delivers "most" of the properties of a TDF.

2   Preliminaries

For any positive integer n, let $[n]$ denote the set of integers $\{1, 2, \ldots, n\}$. For any prime p and positive integer ℓ, let $\mathbb{F}_{p^\ell}$ denote the (unique) field of order

p^ℓ. We will use bold letters to denote a vector/array of elements, and subscript i denotes the ith element (e.g. if $\mathbf{w} \in \{0,1\}^n$, then w_i denotes the ith bit). Given two distributions $\mathcal{D}_1, \mathcal{D}_2$ over finite domain $\mathcal{X}$, let $\mathsf{SD}(\mathcal{D}_1, \mathcal{D}_2)$ denote the statistical distance between $\mathcal{D}_1$ and $\mathcal{D}_2$.

Definition 1 (Pseudorandom Generator). *Let $n, \ell \in \mathbb{N}$ and let* PRG *be a deterministic polynomial-time algorithm such that for any $s \in \{0,1\}^n$,* $\mathsf{PRG}(s, 1^\ell)$ *outputs a string of length ℓ. (Here, we will not require that ℓ be polynomial in n.) We say that* PRG *is a* pseudorandom generator *if for all probabilistic polynomial-time distinguishers D, there exists a negligible function* $\mathsf{negl}(\cdot)$ *such that for all $n, \ell, \lambda \in \mathbb{N}$,*

$$| \Pr[D(r) = 1] - \Pr[D(\mathsf{PRG}(s, 1^\ell)) = 1] | \leq \mathsf{negl}(\lambda),$$

where r is chosen uniformly at random from $\{0,1\}^\ell$, s is chosen uniformly at random from $\{0,1\}^n$, and the probabilities are taken over the choice of r and s and the coins of D.

Definition 2 (Strongly Unforgeable One-Time Signature) [28]. *Let $\Sigma = (\mathsf{KeyGen}, \mathsf{Sign}, \mathsf{Verify})$ be a one-time signature scheme for the message space M. Consider the following probabilistic experiment SU-OTS($\Sigma, \mathcal{A}, \lambda$) with $\mathcal{A} = (\mathcal{A}_1, \mathcal{A}_2)$ and $\lambda \in \mathbb{N}$:*

> SU-OTS($\Pi, \mathcal{A}, \lambda$)
> $(\mathsf{pk}, \mathsf{sk}) \leftarrow \mathsf{KeyGen}(1^\lambda)$
> $(m, z) \leftarrow \mathcal{A}_1(\mathsf{pk})$ *s.t.* $m \in M$
> $\sigma \leftarrow \mathsf{Sign}(\mathsf{sk}, m)$
> $(m^*, \sigma^*) \leftarrow \mathcal{A}_2(\sigma, z)$
> *Output 1 iff ($m \neq m^*$ and* $\mathsf{Verify}(\mathsf{pk}, m^*, \sigma^*) = 1$*) or*
> $\qquad$ *($\sigma \neq \sigma^*$ and* $\mathsf{Verify}(\mathsf{pk}, m, \sigma^*) = 1$*).*

Signature scheme Σ is SU-OTS-secure if $\forall$ p.p.t. algorithms $\mathcal{A}$, there exists a negligible function $\mathsf{negl}(\cdot)$ such that

$$\Pr[SU\text{-}OTS(\Pi, \mathcal{A}, \lambda) = 1] \leq \mathsf{negl}(\lambda),$$

where this probability is taken over all random coins used in the experiment.

Definition 3 (IND-CPA) [19]. *Let $\Pi = (\mathsf{KeyGen}, \mathsf{Enc}, \mathsf{Dec})$ be an encryption scheme for the message space M. Consider the following probabilistic experiment IND-CPA($\Pi, \mathcal{A}, \lambda$) with $\mathcal{A} = (\mathcal{A}_1, \mathcal{A}_2)$ and $\lambda \in \mathbb{N}$:*

> IND-CPA($\Pi, \mathcal{A}, \lambda$)
> $(\mathsf{pk}, \mathsf{sk}) \leftarrow \mathsf{KeyGen}(1^\lambda)$
> $(m_0, m_1, z) \leftarrow \mathcal{A}_1(\mathsf{pk})$ *s.t.* $m_0, m_1 \in M$
> $y \leftarrow \mathsf{Enc}(\mathsf{pk}, m_b)$
> $b' \leftarrow \mathcal{A}_2(y, z)$
> *Output 1 if $b' = b$ and 0 otherwise.*

Encryption scheme Π is IND-CPA-secure if $\forall$ p.p.t. algorithms $\mathcal{A}$, there exists a negligible function $\mathsf{negl}(\cdot)$ such that

$$\Pr\left[IND\text{-}CPA(\Pi, \mathcal{A}, \lambda) = 1\right] \leq \frac{1}{2} + \mathsf{negl}(\lambda),$$

where this probability is taken over all random coins used in the experiment.

Definition 4 (IND-CCA [7,31,34]). *Let $\Pi = (\mathsf{KeyGen}, \mathsf{Enc}, \mathsf{Dec})$ be an encryption scheme for the message space M and let experiment $IND\text{-}CCA(\Pi, \mathcal{A}, \lambda)$ be identical to $IND\text{-}CPA(\Pi, \mathcal{A}, \lambda)$ except that both $\mathcal{A}_1$ and $\mathcal{A}_2$ have access to an oracle $\mathsf{Dec}(\mathsf{sk}, \cdot)$ that returns the output of the decryption algorithm and $\mathcal{A}_2$ cannot query this oracle on input y. Encryption scheme Π is IND-CCA-secure if $\forall$ p.p.t. algorithms $\mathcal{A}$, there exists a negligible function $\mathsf{negl}(\cdot)$ such that*

$$\Pr\left[IND\text{-}CCA(\Pi, \mathcal{A}, \lambda) = 1\right] \leq \frac{1}{2} + \mathsf{negl}(\lambda),$$

where this probability is taken over all random coins used in the experiment.

Injective Trapdoor Functions. An injective trapdoor function family $\mathcal{T}$ with input space $\{0,1\}^{\ell_{\mathsf{inp}}}$ and output space $\{0,1\}^{\ell_{\mathsf{out}}}$, where ℓ_{inp} and ℓ_{out} are polynomial functions of the security parameter λ, consists of three PPT algorithms with syntax:

$\mathsf{TDF.Setup}(1^\lambda) \rightarrow (\mathsf{tdf.pk}, \mathsf{tdf.sk})$: The setup algorithm takes as input security parameter λ and outputs a public key $\mathsf{tdf.pk}$ and secret key $\mathsf{tdf.sk}$.

$\mathsf{TDF.Eval}(\mathsf{tdf.pk}, x \in \{0,1\}^{\ell_{\mathsf{inp}}},) \rightarrow y$: The evaluation algorithm takes as input an input $x \in \{0,1\}^{\ell_{\mathsf{inp}}}$ and public key $\mathsf{tdf.pk}$, and outputs $y \in \{0,1\}^{\ell_{\mathsf{out}}}$.

$\mathsf{TDF.Invert}(\mathsf{tdf.sk}, y \in \{0,1\}^{\ell_{\mathsf{out}}}) \rightarrow x \in \{0,1\}^{\ell_{\mathsf{inp}}} \cup \{\bot\}$: The inversion algorithm takes as input $y \in \{0,1\}^{\ell_{\mathsf{out}}}$ and secret key $\mathsf{tdf.sk}$, and outputs x, which is either $\bot$ or a ℓ_{inp}-bit string.

Almost-All-Keys Injectivity. We require that for nearly all public/secret keys, inversion works for all inputs. More formally, there exists a negligible function $\mathsf{negl}(\cdot)$ such that for all $\lambda \in \mathbb{N}$,

$$\Pr\left[\exists\ x \text{ s.t. } \mathsf{TDF.Invert}(\mathsf{TDF.Eval}(\mathsf{tdf.pk}, x), \mathsf{tdf.sk}) \neq x\right] \leq \mathsf{negl}(\lambda),$$

where this probability is over the choice of $(\mathsf{tdf.pk}, \mathsf{tdf.sk}) \leftarrow \mathsf{TDF.Setup}(1^\lambda)$.

Definition 5. *An injective trapdoor family is hard-to-invert if for any PPT adversary $\mathcal{A}$, there exists a negligible function $\mathsf{negl}(\cdot)$ such that for all $\lambda \in \mathbb{N}$,*

$$\Pr\left[x \leftarrow \mathcal{A}(\mathsf{tdf.pk}, y) : \begin{array}{l} (\mathsf{tdf.pk}, \mathsf{tdf.sk}) \leftarrow \mathsf{TDF.Setup}(1^\lambda) \\ x \leftarrow \{0,1\}^{\ell_{\mathsf{inp}}}, y = \mathsf{TDF.Eval}(\mathsf{tdf.pk}, x) \end{array}\right] \leq \mathsf{negl}(\lambda).$$

Define $(r \cdot x) = \oplus_{i=1}^n r_i \cdot x_i$ where $r = r_1 \ldots r_n$ and $x = x_1 \ldots x_n$. The Goldreich-Levin theorem for hard-core predicates [18] states that no polynomial time algorithm can compute $(r \cdot x)$ given a random r, the TDF public key $\mathsf{tdf.pk}$ and evaluation $\mathsf{TDF.Eval}(\mathsf{tdf.pk}, x)$ on random input x, where $|r| = |x|$.

Theorem 1 (Goldreich-Levin Hardcore Bit [18]**).** *Assuming* TDF *is an injective trapdoor family, for any PPT adversary* $\mathcal{A}$, *there exists a negligible function* negl$(\cdot)$ *such that for all* $\lambda \in \mathbb{N}$, *the following holds:*

$$\left| \Pr \left[b \leftarrow \mathcal{A}(\mathsf{tdf.pk}, s, y, z_b) : \begin{array}{l} (\mathsf{tdf.pk}, \mathsf{tdf.sk}) \leftarrow \mathsf{TDF.Setup}(1^\lambda) \\ x, s \leftarrow \{0,1\}^{\ell_{\mathrm{inp}}}, \\ y = \mathsf{TDF.Eval}(\mathsf{tdf.pk}, x) \\ z_0 = s \cdot x, z_1 \leftarrow \{0,1\}, b \leftarrow \{0,1\} \end{array} \right] - \frac{1}{2} \right| \leq \mathsf{negl}(\lambda).$$

3   Encryption Scheme with Randomness Recovery

An encryption scheme with randomness recovery is an IND-CPA secure encryption scheme with two additional properties: (a) the decryption algorithm can be used to recover the message as well as the randomness used for encryption (b) the randomness used for encryption can be used to decrypt the ciphertext. Formally, it consists of four PPT algorithms with the following syntax. Here the message length ℓ_{msg} and the length of the randomness ℓ_{rnd} are polynomial functions of the security parameter λ.

Setup$(1^\lambda) \rightarrow (\mathsf{pk}, \mathsf{sk})$: The setup algorithm takes as input the security parameter λ and outputs a public key pk and secret key sk.
Enc$(\mathsf{pk}, m) \rightarrow \mathsf{ct}$: The encryption algorithm is randomized; it takes as input a public key pk and a message m, uses ℓ_{rnd} bits of randomness and outputs a ciphertext ct. We will sometimes write Enc$(\mathsf{pk}, m; r)$, which runs Enc(pk, m) using r as the randomness.
Dec$(\mathsf{sk}, \mathsf{ct}) \rightarrow z \in (\{0,1\}^{\ell_{\mathrm{msg}}} \times \{0,1\}^{\ell_{\mathrm{rnd}}}) \cup \{\bot\}$: The decryption algorithm takes as input a secret key sk and a ciphertext ct, and either outputs $z = \bot$ or $z = (m, r)$ where $m \in \{0,1\}^{\ell_{\mathrm{msg}}}$, $r \in \{0,1\}^{\ell_{\mathrm{rnd}}}$.
Recover$(\mathsf{pk}, \mathsf{ct}, r) \rightarrow z \in \{0,1\}^{\ell_{\mathrm{msg}}} \cup \{\bot\}$: The recovery algorithm takes as input a public key pk, a ciphertext ct and string $r \in \{0,1\}^{\ell_{\mathrm{rnd}}}$. It either outputs $\bot$ or a message $m \in \{0,1\}^{\ell_{\mathrm{msg}}}$.

These algorithms must satisfy the following almost-all-keys perfect correctness property.

Almost-All-Keys Perfect Correctness. We require perfect correctness of decryption and recovery for all but a negligible fraction of $(\mathsf{pk}, \mathsf{sk})$ pairs. More formally, there exists a negligible function negl$(\cdot)$ such that for any security parameter λ,

$$\Pr\left[\exists\ m, r \text{ s.t. } \mathsf{Dec}(\mathsf{sk}, \mathsf{Enc}(\mathsf{pk}, m; r)) \neq (m, r)\right] \leq \mathsf{negl}(\lambda) \text{ and}$$
$$\Pr\left[\exists\ m, r \text{ s.t. } \mathsf{Recover}(\mathsf{pk}, \mathsf{Enc}(\mathsf{pk}, m; r), r) \neq m\right] \leq \mathsf{negl}(\lambda)$$

where $m \in \{0,1\}^{\ell_{\mathrm{cpa}}}$, $r \in \{0,1\}^{\ell_{\mathrm{rnd}}}$, and the probability is over the choice of $(\mathsf{pk}, \mathsf{sk}) \leftarrow \mathsf{Setup}(1^\lambda)$.

Koppula and Waters [27] defined a notion of "recovery *from* randomness" which has the above almost-all-keys perfect correctness requirement on the Recover algorithm, but not also on the Dec algorithm.

3.1 Construction: Encryption Scheme with Randomness Recovery from Injective TDFs

We show an IND-CPA secure encryption scheme with randomness recovery for messages of length ℓ_{msg} where encryption uses ℓ_{rnd}-bits of randomness based on injective trapdoor functions. This construction is closely related to the CPA-secure encryption scheme of Yao [38]. Let $\mathsf{tdf} = (\mathsf{TDF.Setup}, \mathsf{TDF.Eval}, \mathsf{TDF.Invert})$ be an injective trapdoor function (see Sect. 2) with input space $\{0,1\}^{\ell_{\mathrm{inp}}}$ and output space $\{0,1\}^{\ell_{\mathrm{out}}}$. Here $\ell_{\mathrm{inp}}, \ell_{\mathrm{out}}, \ell_{\mathrm{msg}}$ and $\ell_{\mathrm{rnd}} = \ell_{\mathrm{msg}} \cdot \ell_{\mathrm{inp}}$ are polynomial functions in the security parameter λ.

$\mathsf{Setup}(1^\lambda) \rightarrow (\mathsf{pk}, \mathsf{sk})$: The setup algorithm chooses $(\mathsf{tdf.pk}, \mathsf{tdf.sk}) \leftarrow \mathsf{TDF.Setup}(1^\lambda)$. Next, it choses a uniformly random string $t \leftarrow \{0,1\}^{\ell_{\mathrm{inp}}}$. The public key is set to be $\mathsf{pk} = (\mathsf{tdf.pk}, t)$ and the secret key is $\mathsf{sk} = (\mathsf{tdf.sk}, t)$.

$\mathsf{Enc}\big(\mathsf{pk} = (\mathsf{tdf.pk}, t), \mathbf{m} = (m_1, \ldots, m_{\ell_{\mathrm{msg}}})\big) \rightarrow \mathsf{ct}$: For each $i \in [\ell_{\mathrm{msg}}]$, the encryption algorithm:
- chooses a random string $r_i \leftarrow \{0,1\}^{\ell_{\mathrm{inp}}}$.
- sets $\mathsf{ct}_{1,i} = (r_i \cdot t) + m_i$ and $\mathsf{ct}_{2,i} = \mathsf{TDF.Eval}(\mathsf{tdf.pk}, r_i)$.

For $w \in \{0,1\}$, it sets $\mathbf{ct}_w = (\mathsf{ct}_{w,1}, \ldots, \mathsf{ct}_{w,\ell_{\mathrm{msg}}})$ and outputs $(\mathbf{ct}_1, \mathbf{ct}_2)$.

$\mathsf{Dec}\big(\mathsf{sk} = (\mathsf{tdf.sk}, t), \mathsf{ct} = (\mathbf{ct}_1, \mathbf{ct}_2)\big) \rightarrow z$: For each $i \in [\ell_{\mathrm{msg}}]$, the decryption algorithm computes $r_i = \mathsf{TDF.Invert}(\mathsf{tdf.sk}, \mathsf{ct}_{2,i})$. If $r_i = \perp$, it outputs $\perp$ and aborts. Else, it sets $m_i = \mathsf{ct}_{1,i} + (r_i \cdot t) \pmod 2$.

Finally, it outputs $\mathbf{m} = (m_1, \ldots, m_{\ell_{\mathrm{msg}}})$ and $\mathbf{r} = (r_1, \ldots, r_{\ell_{\mathrm{msg}}})$.

$\mathsf{Recover}\big(\mathsf{pk} = (\mathsf{tdf.pk}, t), \mathsf{ct} = (\mathbf{ct}_1, \mathbf{ct}_2), \mathbf{r}\big) \rightarrow z$: The recovery algorithm performs the following for each $i \in [\ell_{\mathrm{msg}}]$: it computes $z_i = \mathsf{TDF.Eval}(\mathsf{tdf.pk}, r_i)$. If $z_i \neq \mathsf{ct}_{2,i}$, it outputs $\perp$ and aborts. Else it sets $m_i = \mathsf{ct}_{1,i} + z_i \pmod 2$.

Finally it outputs $\mathbf{m} = (m_1, \ldots, m_{\ell_{\mathrm{msg}}})$.

Almost-all-keys perfect correctness follows from the almost-all-keys perfect injectivity TDFs.

Encrypting Long Messages. In the construction above the number of random bits, ℓ_{rnd} required by encryption grows linearly in the message size as $\ell_{\mathrm{rnd}} = \ell_{\mathrm{msg}} \cdot \ell_{\mathrm{inp}}$. We observe that to encrypt long messages we could instead use the system above to encrypt a PRG seed $k \in \{0,1\}^\lambda$ and then encrypt the message itself as $\mathsf{PRG}(k) \oplus m$ for a pseudorandom generator of appropriate output length. This hybrid encryption method would maintain the randomness recovery property, but the growth of the random coins would be independent of the message length.

IND-CPA Security

Theorem 2. *The Sect. 3.1 construction is IND-CPA-secure (per Definition 3) assuming TDF is a hard-to-invert injective trapdoor family (per Definition 5).*

The proof of security follows via a simple sequence of hybrid experiments $\{H_j\}_{j \in \{0, \ldots, \ell_{\mathrm{msg}}+1\}}$ defined as follows. H_0 corresponds to the IND-CPA experiment of the construction in Sect. 3.1, While in hybrid $H_{\ell_{\mathrm{msg}}+1}$, the adversary will have advantage 0.

Hybrid H_j with security parameter λ, for $j \in \{1, \ldots, \ell_{\mathrm{msg}} + 1\}$:

- The challenger chooses $(\mathsf{tdf.pk}, \mathsf{tdf.sk}) \leftarrow \mathsf{TDF.Setup}(1^\lambda)$ and a random string $t \leftarrow \{0,1\}^{\ell_{\mathsf{inp}}}$. It sends $(\mathsf{tdf.pk}, t)$ to the adversary.
- On receiving challenge messages $\mathbf{m_0}, \mathbf{m_1} \in \{0,1\}^{\ell_{\mathsf{msg}}}$ from the adversary, the challenger chooses $b \leftarrow \{0,1\}$. Next, it chooses $r_i \leftarrow \{0,1\}^{\ell_{\mathsf{inp}}}$ for all $i \in [\ell_{\mathsf{msg}}]$. For $i < j$, it sets $\mathsf{ct}_{1,i}$ uniformly at random. For $i \geq j$, it sets $\mathsf{ct}_{1,i} = (r_i \cdot t) + m_{b,i}$. In either case, it sets $\mathsf{ct}_{2,i} = \mathsf{TDF.Eval}(\mathsf{tdf.pk}, r_i)$. It sends $(\mathbf{ct_1}, \mathbf{ct_2})$ to the adversary and receives guess b'. Adversary wins if $b = b'$.

Analysis: For any PPT adversary $\mathcal{A}$, let $\mathsf{adv}_{\mathcal{A},j}(\lambda)$ denote the advantage of $\mathcal{A}$ in H_j (with sec. par. λ).

Claim. Assuming the hard-to-invert property of the injective TDF family $\mathcal{T}$ (see Definition 5), for any PPT adversary $\mathcal{A}$, there exists a negligible function $\mathsf{negl}(\cdot)$ such that for all $\lambda \in \mathbb{N}$ and $j \in [0, \ell_{\mathsf{msg}}]$, $\mathsf{adv}_{\mathcal{A},j}(\lambda) - \mathsf{adv}_{\mathcal{A},j+1}(\lambda) \leq \mathsf{negl}(\lambda)$.

Proof. Suppose there exists a PPT adversary $\mathcal{A}$ and $0 \leq j \leq \ell_{\mathsf{msg}}$ such that $\mathsf{adv}_{\mathcal{A},j} - \mathsf{adv}_{\mathcal{A},j+1} = \epsilon$, where ϵ is non-negligible.[3] Then there exists a PPT algorithm $\mathcal{B}$ that breaks the hardcore bit property of $\mathcal{T}$, since this property follows from the hard-to-invert property of $\mathcal{T}$ and Theorem 1, we have a contradiction. The algorithm $\mathcal{B}$ receives $(\mathsf{tdf.pk}, s, y, z)$ from the challenger, where $y = \mathsf{TDF.Eval}(\mathsf{tdf.pk}, x)$ for a uniformly random $x \in \{0,1\}^{\ell_{\mathsf{inp}}}$, and z is either $(s \cdot x)$ or a uniformly random bit. $\mathcal{B}$ sets $t = s$ and sends $(\mathsf{tdf.pk}, t)$ to $\mathcal{A}$, and receives challenge messages $\mathbf{m_0}, \mathbf{m_1}$. The reduction then chooses $w \leftarrow \{0,1\}$. For all $i \neq j$, the challenge ciphertext components $\mathsf{ct}_{1,i}, \mathsf{ct}_{2,i}$ are identically distributed, and the reduction algorithm can compute them using $\mathsf{tdf.pk}$ and t. It sets $\mathsf{ct}_{j,1} = z + m_{w,j}$ and $\mathsf{ct}_{j,2} = y$, and sends $(\mathbf{ct_1}, \mathbf{ct_2})$ to $\mathcal{A}$. The adversary sends its guess w'. If $w = w'$, then the reduction $\mathcal{B}$ outputs 0 (indicating that $z = s \cdot x$), else it outputs 1 (indicating that z is uniformly random).

Note that if $y = \mathsf{TDF.Eval}(\mathsf{tdf.pk}, x)$ and $z = (s \cdot x)$, then this corresponds to H_j; if z is uniformly random, then this corresponds to H_{j+1}. Let $\mathsf{adv}_{\mathcal{B}}^{\mathcal{T}}$ denote $\mathcal{B}$'s advantage in the hardcore bit experiment against $\mathcal{T}$.

$$\mathsf{adv}_{\mathcal{B}}^{\mathcal{T}} = \Pr[\mathcal{B} \text{ outputs } 0 \mid z = (s \cdot x)] - \Pr[\mathcal{B} \text{ outputs } 0 \mid z \text{ is random}]$$
$$= \Pr[\mathcal{A} \text{ wins in } H_j] - \Pr[\mathcal{A} \text{ wins in } H_{j+1}] = \epsilon.$$

4   Tagged Set Commitment

We introduce an abstraction called a "tagged set commitment" and show that it can be constructed generically from a pseudorandom generator. We employ this abstraction shortly in our Sect. 5 construction.

$\mathsf{Setup}(1^\lambda, 1^N, 1^B, 1^t) \to \mathsf{pp}$: The setup algorithm takes as input the security parameter λ, the universe size N, bound B on committed sets and tag length t, and outputs public parameters pp.

---

[3] We drop dependence on λ for notational convenience.

Commit(pp, $S \subseteq [N]$, tg $\in \{0,1\}^t$) $\to$ (com, $(\sigma_i)_{i \in S}$): The commit algorithm is randomized; it takes as input the public parameters pp, set S of size B and string tg, and outputs a commitment com together with 'proofs' σ_i for each $i \in S$.[4]

Verify(pp, com, $i \in [N], \sigma_i$, tg $\in \{0,1\}^t$) $\to$ $\{0,1\}$: The verification algorithm takes as input the public parameters, an index i, a proof σ_i, and tg. It outputs 0/1.

AltSetup($1^\lambda, 1^N, 1^B, 1^t$, tg) $\to$ (pp, com, $(\sigma_i)_{i \in [N]}$): The scheme also has an 'alternate setup' which is used in the proof. It takes the same inputs as Setup together with a special tag tg, and outputs public parameters pp, commitment com together with proofs σ_i for all $i \in [N]$.

These algorithms must satisfy the following perfect correctness requirements:

Correctness of Setup *and* Commit*:* For all λ, N, $B \leq N$, t, tg $\in \{0,1\}^t$ and set $S \subseteq [N]$ of size B, if pp $\leftarrow$ Setup($1^\lambda, 1^N, 1^B, 1^t$) and (com, $(\sigma_i)_{i \in S}$) $\leftarrow$ Commit(pp, S, tg), then for all $i \in S$, Verify(pp, com, i, σ_i, tg) $= 1$.

Correctness of AltSetup*:* For all λ, N, $B \leq N$, t, tg $\in \{0,1\}^t$, if (pp, com, $(\sigma_i)_{i \in [N]}$) $\leftarrow$ AltSetup($1^\lambda, 1^N, 1^B, 1^t$, tg), then for all $i \in [N]$, Verify(pp, com, i, σ_i, tg) $= 1$.

Security. We require two security properties of a tag set commitment.

Indistinguishability of Setup: In this experiment, the adversary chooses a tag tg, set S and receives either public parameters, together with commitments for (S, tg), or receives public parameters and commitment/proofs (corresponding to set S) generated by AltSetup (for tag tg). The scheme satisfies indistinguishability of setup if no PPT adversary can distinguish between the two scenarios. This experiment is formally defined below.

Definition 6. *A tagged set commitment scheme* Com $=$ (Setup, Commit, Verify, AltSetup) *satisfies indistinguishability of setup if for any PPT adversary* $\mathcal{A}$, *there exists a negligible function* negl($\cdot$) *such that for all* $\lambda \in \mathbb{N}$, $|\Pr[1 \leftarrow$ Expt-Ind-Setup$_{\mathcal{A}}(\lambda)] - 1/2| \leq$ negl(λ), *where* Expt-Ind-Setup$_{\mathcal{A}}$ *is defined in Fig. 1.*

Soundness Security: The soundness property informally states that if public parameters are generated for bound B (using either regular setup or AltSetup), then no PPT adversary can produce a commitment with greater than B 'proofs'. However, for our CCA application, we need a stronger guarantee: if the challenger generates the public parameters for a tag tg using AltSetup and the adversary gets all N proofs, even then it cannot generate a commitment with $B + 1$ proofs for a different tag tg$'$.

---

[4] We require S to be of size exactly B for simplicity of presentation, however, one could generalize this to allow S to be of size at most B.

Expt-Ind-Setup$_\mathcal{A}(\lambda)$

1. Adversary $\mathcal{A}$ receives input 1^λ and sends $1^N, 1^B, 1^t, \text{tg}, S$ such that $B \leq N$, $\text{tg} \in \{0,1\}^t$ and $|S| = B$.
2. Challenger chooses $b \leftarrow \{0,1\}$. It computes $\text{pp}^0 \leftarrow \text{Setup}(1^\lambda, 1^N, 1^B, 1^t)$ and $(\text{com}^0, (\sigma_i^0)_{i \in S}) \leftarrow \text{Commit}(\text{pp}, S, \text{tg})$, and $(\text{pp}^1, \text{com}^1, (\sigma_i^1)_{i \in [N]}) \leftarrow \text{AltSetup}(1^\lambda, 1^N, 1^B, 1^t, \text{tg})$. It sends $(\text{pp}^b, \text{com}^b, (\sigma_i^b)_{i \in S})$ to $\mathcal{A}$.
3. $\mathcal{A}$ outputs its guess b'. The experiment outputs 1 iff $b = b'$.

Fig. 1. Experiment for indistinguishability of setup

Definition 7. *A tagged set commitment scheme* Com = (Setup, Commit, Verify, AltSetup) *satisfies soundness security if for any PPT adversary $\mathcal{A}$, there exists a negligible function* $\text{negl}(\cdot)$ *such that for all* $\lambda \in \mathbb{N}$, $\Pr[1 \leftarrow \text{Expt-Sound}_\mathcal{A}(\lambda)] \leq \text{negl}(\lambda)$, *where* Expt-Sound$_\mathcal{A}$ *is defined in Fig. 2.*

Expt-Sound$_\mathcal{A}(\lambda)$

1. Adversary $\mathcal{A}$ receives input 1^λ, sends $1^N, 1^B, 1^t, \text{tg}$ such that $B \leq N$, $\text{tg} \in \{0,1\}^t$.
2. Challenger computes $(\text{pp}, \text{com}, (\sigma_i)_{i \in [N]}) \leftarrow \text{AltSetup}(1^\lambda, 1^N, 1^B, 1^t, \text{tg})$, sends $(\text{pp}, \text{com}, (\sigma_i)_{i \in [N]})$ to $\mathcal{A}$.
3. $\mathcal{A}$ outputs $\text{tg}' \neq \text{tg}$, set $S \subseteq [N]$ of size greater than B, commitment com' and proofs $(\sigma_i')_{i \in S}$. The experiment outputs 1 iff for all $i \in S$, $\text{Verify}(\text{pp}, \text{com}', i, \sigma_i', \text{tg}') = 1$.

Fig. 2. Experiment for soundness security

4.1 Construction of Tagged Set Commitment

In this section, we will present a Tagged Set Commitment scheme TSC whose security is based on PRG security. Let PRG : $(\{0,1\}^\lambda, 1^\ell) \rightarrow \mathbb{F}_{2^\ell}$ be a pseudorandom generator. Let emb be an injective and efficiently-computable function that maps strings in $\{0,1\}^t$ (tags) to elements in $\mathbb{F}_{2^\ell}$. Below the notation $p \leftarrow \mathbb{F}_{2^\ell}[x]^{B-1}$ means that p is set to be a random degree $B-1$ polynomial over variable x, where p is represented in canonical form with B randomly chosen coefficients in $\mathbb{F}_{2^\ell}$.

Setup($1^\lambda, 1^N, 1^B, 1^t$): The setup algorithm sets $\ell = 2t + (B+1) \cdot \log N + \lambda \cdot (B + 1) + \lambda$. Next it chooses N random elements $A_i, D_i \leftarrow \mathbb{F}_{2^\ell}$ for all $i \in [N]$. The public parameters is set to be $\text{pp} = (1^\ell, (A_i, D_i)_{i \in [N]})$.

Commit(pp $= (1^\ell, (A_i, D_i)_i), S \subseteq [N], \mathsf{tg})$: The commitment algorithm first
chooses $s_i \leftarrow \{0,1\}^\lambda$ for each $i \in S$. Next, it chooses the degree $B-1$ polyno-
mial $p(\cdot)$ over $\mathbb{F}_{2^\ell}$ such that for all $i \in S$, $p(i) = \mathsf{PRG}(s_i, 1^\ell) + A_i + D_i \cdot \mathsf{emb}(\mathsf{tg})$.
(Since we fix B points, there is a unique degree $B-1$ polynomial p, which
is described in canonical form using B coefficients in $\mathbb{F}_{2^\ell}$.) The commitment
com is the polynomial p, and the proof $\sigma_i = s_i$ for each $i \in S$.
Verify(pp $= (1^\ell, (A_i, D_i)_i), \mathsf{com} = p, i, \sigma_i, \mathsf{tg})$: The verification algorithm outputs
1 iff $p(i) = \mathsf{PRG}(\sigma_i, 1^\ell) + A_i + D_i \cdot \mathsf{emb}(\mathsf{tg})$.
AltSetup($1^\lambda, 1^N, 1^B, 1^t, \mathsf{tg}$): The alternate setup algorithm chooses random
strings $s_i \leftarrow \{0,1\}^\lambda$, $D_i \leftarrow \mathbb{F}_{2^\ell}$ for each $i \in [N]$, $p \leftarrow \mathbb{F}_{2^\ell}[x]^{B-1}$ and sets
$A_i = p(i) - \mathsf{PRG}(s_i, 1^\ell) - D_i \cdot \mathsf{emb}(\mathsf{tg})$.

The correctness properties follow immediately from the construction.

Security Proofs. We need to show that the scheme satisfies indistinguishability
of setup and soundness security (Definition 7). Due to space constraints, the
proofs are included in the full version of our paper.

5 Our CCA Secure Encryption Scheme

In this section, we will present a CCA secure encryption scheme with message
space $\{0,1\}^{\ell_{\mathsf{cca}}}$ satisfying almost-all-keys perfect correctness. We require the following parameters/notations for our construction.

- λ: security parameter
- N: number of ciphertext components of underlying CPA scheme
- B: size of set for 'selected' ciphertext components
- $\ell_{\mathsf{tsc}.\sigma}$: size of proofs output by tagged set commitment scheme
- ℓ_{cpa}: message space for underlying CPA scheme
- ℓ_{rnd}: number of random bits used by CPA scheme to encrypt ℓ_{cpa} bit message
- ℓ_{vk}: size of verification key of signature scheme

The construction uses the following primitives, which are defined in Sects. 2,
3 and 4 respectively:

- A Strongly Unforgeable One-Time Signature Scheme $P_1 = (\mathsf{Sig.Setup},$
$\mathsf{Sig.Sign}, \mathsf{Sig.Verify})$.
- A CPA Secure almost-all-keys perfectly correct Encryption Scheme with
Randomness Recovery $P_2 = (\mathsf{CPA.Setup}, \mathsf{CPA.Enc}, \mathsf{CPA.Dec}, \mathsf{CPA.Recover})$,
parameterized by polynomials ℓ_{cpa} (denoting the message space) and ℓ_{rnd}
(denoting the number of random bits used for encryption).[5]

---

[5] For security parameter λ, the scheme will support $\ell_{\mathsf{cpa}}(\lambda)$ bit messages, and the
encryption algorithm will use $\ell_{\mathsf{rnd}}(\lambda)$ bits of randomness. We will drop the dependence on λ when it is clear from context.

- A Tagged Set Commitment Scheme P_3 = (TSC.Setup, TSC.Commit, TSC.Verify, TSC.AltSetup), parameterized by polynomials $\ell_{\mathsf{tsc}.\sigma}$ (denoting the length of proof for each index) and ℓ_{com} (denoting the length of commitment).

These parameters must satisfy the following constraints:

- $\ell_{\mathsf{cpa}} = 1 + \ell_{\mathsf{tsc}.\sigma} + \ell_{\mathsf{cca}}$
- $\log\left(\binom{N-1}{B-1}\right) > \ell_{\mathsf{rnd}} + 2\lambda$

$\mathsf{Setup}(1^\lambda)$: The setup algorithm performs the following steps:
1. It first chooses public parameters for the commitment scheme. Let $\mathsf{tsc.pp} \leftarrow \mathsf{TSC.Setup}(1^\lambda, 1^N, 1^B, 1^{\ell_{\mathsf{vk}}})$.
2. Next, it chooses N public/secret keys for the encryption scheme. Let $(\mathsf{cpa.pk}_i, \mathsf{cpa.sk}_i) \leftarrow \mathsf{CPA.Setup}(1^\lambda)$.
3. It sets $\mathsf{pk} = \left(\mathsf{tsc.pp}, (\mathsf{cpa.pk}_i)_{i \in [N]}\right)$ and $\mathsf{sk} = (\mathsf{cpa.sk}_i)_{i \in [N]}$.

$\mathsf{Enc}(\mathsf{pk}, m)$: The encryption algorithm takes as input $\mathsf{pk} = \left(\mathsf{tsc.pp}, (\mathsf{cpa.pk}_i)_{i \in [N]}\right)$ and $m \in \{0, 1\}^{\ell_{\mathsf{cca}}}$, and performs the following steps:
1. It chooses a uniformly random B size subset $S \subset [N]$. Let $S = \{i_1, i_2, \ldots, i_B\}$ where $i_1 < i_2 < \ldots < i_B$.
2. Next, it chooses a signing/verification key $(\mathsf{sig.sk}, \mathsf{sig.vk}) \leftarrow \mathsf{Sig.Setup}(1^\lambda)$.
3. It commits to the set S using $\mathsf{sig.vk}$ as tag. It computes $(\mathsf{tsc.com}, (\mathsf{tsc}.\sigma_i)_{i \in S}) \leftarrow \mathsf{TSC.Commit}(\mathsf{tsc.pp}, S, \mathsf{sig.vk})$.
4. For all $i \neq i_B$, it chooses random values $r_i \leftarrow \{0, 1\}^\ell_{\mathsf{rnd}}$, and sets $r_{i_B} = \oplus_{j<B}\, r_{i_j}$.
5. Using the r_i values, the encryption algorithm computes N ciphertext components. For $i \in S$, it computes $\mathsf{cpa.ct}_i = \mathsf{CPA.Enc}(\mathsf{cpa.pk}_i, 1|\mathsf{tsc}.\sigma_i|m; r_i)$. Else it sets $\mathsf{cpa.ct}_i = \mathsf{CPA.Enc}(\mathsf{cpa.pk}_i, 0^{\ell_{\mathsf{cpa}}}; r_i)$.
6. Finally, it computes $\mathsf{sig}.\sigma \leftarrow \mathsf{Sig.Sign}\left(\mathsf{sig.sk}, \left(\mathsf{tsc.com}, (\mathsf{cpa.ct}_i)_{i \in [N]}\right)\right)$ and outputs $\left(\mathsf{sig.vk}, \mathsf{sig}.\sigma, \mathsf{tsc.com}, (\mathsf{cpa.ct}_i)_{i \in [N]}\right)$.

$\mathsf{Dec}(\mathsf{sk}, \mathsf{ct})$: Let $\mathsf{sk} = (\mathsf{cpa.sk}_i)_{i \in [N]}$ and $\mathsf{ct} = \left(\mathsf{sig.vk}, \mathsf{sig}.\sigma, \mathsf{tsc.com}, (\mathsf{cpa.ct}_i)_{i \in [N]}\right)$. The decryption algorithm performs the following steps:
1. It first verifies $\mathsf{sig}.\sigma$. If $0 \leftarrow \mathsf{Sig.Verify}\left(\mathsf{sig.vk}, \mathsf{sig}.\sigma, \left(\mathsf{tsc.com}, (\mathsf{cpa.ct}_i)_{i \in [N]}\right)\right)$ then decryption outputs $\perp$.
2. Next, it initializes a set U to be $\emptyset$. For each $i \in [N]$ it does the following:
   (a) Let $(y_i, r_i) = \mathsf{CPA.Dec}(\mathsf{cpa.sk}_i, \mathsf{cpa.ct}_i)$.[6] The decryption algorithm adds (i, y_i) to U if $\mathsf{Check}(i, y_i, r_i) = 1$, where Check is defined in Fig. 3.
3. If the set U does not have exactly B elements then the decryption algorithm outputs $\perp$.

---

[6] Recall the decryption algorithm also recovers the randomness used for encryption.

4. If $\oplus_{(i,y_i)\in U} r_i \neq 0^{\ell_{\mathrm{rnd}}}$, it outputs $\bot$.
5. Finally, the decryption algorithm checks that for all $(i, r_i) \in U$, the m_i values recovered from y_i are the same. If not, it outputs $\bot$. Else it outputs this common m_i value as the decryption.

Check

Hardwired: pk, ct
Input: $i \in [N], y \in (\{0,1\} \times \{0,1\}^{\ell_{\mathrm{tsc}.\sigma}} \times \{0,1\}^{\ell_{\mathrm{cca}}}) \cup \{\bot\}, r \in \{0,1\}^{\ell_{\mathrm{rnd}}}$
Output: 0/1.

Output 1 if and only if the following conditions are satisfied:

- $y \neq \bot$. Parse $y = (g, \mathsf{tsc}.\sigma, m)$
- $g = 1$.
- $\mathsf{TSC.Verify}(\mathsf{tsc.pp}, \mathsf{tsc.com}, i, \mathsf{tsc}.\sigma, \mathsf{sig.vk}) = 1$.
- $\mathsf{cpa.ct}_i = \mathsf{CPA.Enc}(\mathsf{cpa.pk}_i, y; r)$.

Fig. 3. Routine Check for checking if tuple (i, y) should be added to set U

Perfect Correctness. The message space is $\{0,1\}^{\ell_{\mathrm{cca}}}$, where ℓ_{cca} is a polynomial function in the security parameter λ. There exists a negligible function $\mathsf{negl}(\cdot)$ such that for any security parameter λ,

$$\Pr\left[\exists\, m, r \in \{0,1\}^{\ell_{\mathrm{cca}}} \text{ s.t. } \mathsf{Dec}(\mathsf{sk}, \mathsf{Enc}(\mathsf{pk}, m)) \neq m\right] \leq \mathsf{negl}(\lambda)$$

where the probability is over the choice of $(\mathsf{pk}, \mathsf{sk}) \leftarrow \mathsf{Setup}(1^\lambda)$ and the random coins of Enc.

The almost-all-keys perfect correctness of the CCA scheme follows from the almost-all-keys perfect correctness of the CPA scheme and the (perfect) correctness of the signature and tagged set commitment schemes.

Remark 1. Any signature or tagged set commitment scheme with negligible correctness error can be transformed into one with perfect correctness. A signer or committer can check whether the respective signature or commitment verifies using the public verification algorithm. If it does not, the signing algorithm can fall back to a trivial signature that is perfectly correct, but has no security against forgeries. In the case of commitments use a trivial scheme that is binding, but is not hiding. Since the correctness error is negligible, this will only happen with negligible probability in the security argument.

5.1   Proof of Security

Theorem 3. *The above construction is IND-CCA-secure (per Definition 4) and almost-all-keys perfectly correct, assuming P_1 is a strongly unforgeable one-time signature scheme (Definition 2), P_2 is an IND-CPA-secure encryption scheme (Definition 3) with randomness recovery with almost-all-keys perfect correctness (Sect. 3) and P_3 is a secure tagged set commitment scheme (Definitions 6 and 7).*

The following result follows immediately from the above theorem and known constructions of other building blocks from injective trapdoor functions.

Corollary 1 (IND-CCA -secure Public-Key Encryption is Implied by (Injective) Trapdoor Functions). *The above construction is IND-CCA-secure (per Definition 4) assuming injective trapdoor functions.*

Proof of the main theorem proceeds via a sequence of hybrid experiments.

Hybrid H_0: This experiment corresponds to the CCA experiment. Here, we spell out the setup and encryption algorithms again in order to set up notations for the proof.

- Setup phase: This is identical to the scheme's setup.
    1. The challenger first chooses $\mathsf{tsc.pp} \leftarrow \mathsf{TSC.Setup}(1^\lambda, 1^N, 1^B, 1^t)$.
    2. Next, it chooses $(\mathsf{cpa.pk}_i, \mathsf{cpa.sk}_i) \leftarrow \mathsf{CPA.Setup}(1^\lambda)$ for all $i \in [N]$.
    3. It sends $\mathsf{pk} = \left(\mathsf{tsc.pp}, (\mathsf{cpa.pk}_i)_{i \in [N]}\right)$ to $\mathcal{A}$ and uses $\mathsf{sk} = (\mathsf{cpa.sk}_i)_{i \in [N]}$ for handling decryption queries.
- Pre-challenge decryption queries: The adversary makes polynomially many decryption queries. For each query $\mathsf{ct} = \left(\mathsf{sig.vk}, \mathsf{sig.}\sigma, \mathsf{tsc.com}, (\mathsf{cpa.ct}_i)_{i \in [N]}\right)$, the challenger outputs $\mathsf{Dec}(\mathsf{sk}, \mathsf{ct})$.
- Challenge ciphertext: The adversary sends two challenge messages $m_0, m_1 \in \{0,1\}^{\ell_{\mathsf{cca}}}$. The challenger chooses a bit b and does the following.
    1. It chooses a uniformly random B size subset $S^* = \{i_j\}_{j \in [B]} \subset [N]$.
    2. Next, it chooses a signing/verification key $(\mathsf{sig.sk}^*, \mathsf{sig.vk}^*) \leftarrow \mathsf{Sig.Setup}(1^\lambda)$.
    3. It then commits to the set S using $\mathsf{sig.vk}^*$ as the tag. It computes $(\mathsf{tsc.com}^*, (\mathsf{tsc.}\sigma_i^*)_{i \in S}) \leftarrow \mathsf{TSC.Commit}(\mathsf{tsc.pp}, S^*, \mathsf{sig.vk}^*)$.
    4. For all $i \neq i_B$, it chooses $r_i \leftarrow \{0,1\}^{\ell_{\mathsf{rnd}}}$, and sets $r_{i_B} = \oplus_{j < B}\, r_{i_j}$.
    5. Using the r_i values, the encryption algorithm computes N ciphertexts. If $i \in S$, it computes $\mathsf{cpa.ct}_i^* = \mathsf{CPA.Enc}(\mathsf{cpa.pk}_i, 1|\mathsf{tsc.}\sigma_i^*|m_b; r_i)$. Else it sets $\mathsf{cpa.ct}_i^* = \mathsf{CPA.Enc}(\mathsf{cpa.pk}_i, 0^{\ell_{\mathsf{cpa}}}; r_i)$.
    6. Finally, it computes $\mathsf{sig.}\sigma^* \leftarrow \mathsf{Sig.Sign}\left(\mathsf{sig.sk}^*, \left(\mathsf{tsc.com}^*, (\mathsf{cpa.ct}_i^*)_{i \in [N]}\right)\right)$ and outputs $\left(\mathsf{sig.vk}^*, \mathsf{sig.}\sigma^*, \mathsf{tsc.com}^*, (\mathsf{cpa.ct}_i^*)_{i \in [N]}\right)$.
- Post-challenge decryption queries: Same as pre-challenge decryption queries, but challenge ciphertext not allowed as a decryption query.
- Guess: The adversary sends bit b' and wins if $b = b'$.

Hybrid H_1: This experiment is identical to the previous one except that the challenger chooses sig.vk* and S^* during setup, and uses these to compute the challenge ciphertext.

- Setup phase:
  1. The challenger first chooses tsc.pp $\leftarrow$ TSC.Setup($1^\lambda, 1^N, 1^B, 1^t$).
  2. Next, it chooses (cpa.pk$_i$, cpa.sk$_i$) $\leftarrow$ CPA.Setup(1^λ) for all $i \in [N]$.
  3. Then it chooses a uniformly random B size subset $S^* = \{i_j\}_{j \in [B]} \subset [N]$ and (sig.sk*, sig.vk*) $\leftarrow$ Sig.Setup(1^λ).
  4. It sends pk $= \Big($tsc.pp, (cpa.pk$_i$)$_{i \in [N]}\Big)$ to $\mathcal{A}$ and uses sk $=$ (cpa.sk$_i$)$_{i \in [N]}$ for handling decryption queries.

Hybrid H_2: In this experiment, the challenger outputs $\bot$ during the decryption queries if the queried ciphertext ct $= \Big($sig.vk, sig.σ, tsc.com, (cpa.ct$_i$)$_{i \in [N]}\Big)$ is such that sig.vk $=$ sig.vk*.

- Pre-challenge decryption queries: The adversary makes polynomially many decryption queries. For each query ct $= \Big($sig.vk, sig.σ, tsc.com, (cpa.ct$_i$)$_{i \in [N]}\Big)$, if sig.vk $=$ sig.vk*, then the challenger outputs $\bot$, else it outputs Dec(sk, ct).
- Post-challenge decryption queries: Same as pre-challenge decryption queries, but challenge ciphertext not allowed as a decryption query.

Hybrid H_3: Here, the challenger runs TSC.AltSetup instead of TSC.Setup during the setup phase. During the challenge phase, it uses the commitment and proofs generated by TSC.AltSetup instead of computing them using TSC.Commit.

- Setup phase:
  1. The challenger first chooses (cpa.pk$_i$, cpa.sk$_i$) $\leftarrow$ CPA.Setup(1^λ) for all $i \in [N]$.
  2. Next, it chooses a uniformly random B size subset $S^* \subset [N]$ and (sig.sk*, sig.vk*) $\leftarrow$ Sig.Setup(1^λ).
  3. It chooses $\Big($tsc.com*, (tsc.σ_i)$_{i \in [N]}\Big)$ $\leftarrow$ TSC.AltSetup($1^\lambda, 1^N, 1^B, 1^t$, sig.vk*).
  4. It sends pk $= \Big($tsc.pp, (cpa.pk$_i$)$_{i \in [N]}\Big)$ to $\mathcal{A}$ and uses sk $=$ (cpa.sk$_i$)$_{i \in [N]}$ for handling decryption queries.
- Challenge phase: Note that the signature keys (sig.sk*, sig.vk*), set S^* and commitment tsc.com* together with proofs (tsc.σ_i)$_{i \in [N]}$ were chosen during setup. Below we include the full challenge phase for readability.
  1. For all $i \neq i_B$, it chooses $r_i \leftarrow \{0, 1\}^{\ell_{\text{rnd}}}$, and sets $r_{i_B} = \oplus_{j < B} r_{i_j}$.
  2. Using the r_i values, the encryption algorithm computes N ciphertexts. If $i \in S$, it computes cpa.ct$_i^*$ = CPA.Enc(cpa.pk$_i$, $1|$tsc.$\sigma_i^*|m_b$; r_i). Else it sets cpa.ct$_i^*$ = CPA.Enc(cpa.pk$_i$, $0^{\ell_{\text{cpa}}}$; r_i).
  3. Finally, it computes sig.σ^* $\leftarrow$ Sig.Sign $\Big($sig.sk*, $\Big($tsc.com*, (cpa.ct$_i^*$)$_{i \in [N]}\Big)\Big)$ and outputs $\Big($sig.vk*, sig.σ^*, tsc.com*, (cpa.ct$_i^*$)$_{i \in [N]}\Big)$.

Hybrid H_4: In this experiment, the challenger modifies the challenge ciphertext. Instead of encrypting $0^{\ell_{\text{cpa}}}$ at $N - B$ positions, the challenger encrypts $1|\text{tsc}.\sigma_i|m_b$ at position i for all $i \in [N]$.

- Challenge phase:
    1. For all $i \neq i_B$, it chooses $r_i \leftarrow \{0,1\}^{\ell_{\text{rnd}}}$, and sets $r_{i_B} = \oplus_{j<B}\, r_{i_j}$.
    2. Using the r_i values, the encryption algorithm computes N ciphertexts. For all $i \in [N]$, it computes $\text{cpa.ct}_i^* = \text{CPA.Enc}(\text{cpa.pk}_i, 1|\text{tsc}.\sigma_i^*|m_b; r_i)$.
    3. Finally, it computes $\text{sig}.\sigma^* \leftarrow \text{Sig.Sign}\left(\text{sig.sk}^*, \left(\text{tsc.com}^*, (\text{cpa.ct}_i^*)_{i\in[N]}\right)\right)$
       and outputs $\left(\text{sig.vk}^*, \text{sig}.\sigma^*, \text{tsc.com}^*, (\text{cpa.ct}_i^*)_{i\in[N]}\right)$.

Hybrid H_5: In this experiment, the challenger encrypts at all positions using true randomness.

- Challenge phase:
    1. For all $i \in [N]$, the challenger chooses $r_i \leftarrow \{0,1\}^{\ell_{\text{rnd}}}$.
    2. Using the r_i values, the encryption algorithm computes N ciphertexts. For all $i \in [N]$, it computes $\text{cpa.ct}_i^* = \text{CPA.Enc}(\text{cpa.pk}_i, 1|\text{tsc}.\sigma_i^*|m_b; r_i)$.
    3. Finally, it computes $\text{sig}.\sigma^* \leftarrow \text{Sig.Sign}\left(\text{sig.sk}^*, \left(\text{tsc.com}^*, (\text{cpa.ct}_i^*)_{i\in[N]}\right)\right)$
       and outputs $\left(\text{sig.vk}^*, \text{sig}.\sigma^*, \text{tsc.com}^*, (\text{cpa.ct}_i^*)_{i\in[N]}\right)$.

Hybrid H_6: In the final hybrid experiment, the challenger switches all challenge ciphertext components to encryptions of $0^{\ell_{\text{cpa}}}$. As a result, in this hybrid, the adversary has advantage 0.

- Challenge phase:
    1. For all $i \in [N]$, it chooses $r_i \leftarrow \{0,1\}^{\ell_{\text{rnd}}}$.
    2. Using the r_i values, the encryption algorithm computes N ciphertexts. For all $i \in [N]$, it computes $\text{cpa.ct}_i^* = \text{CPA.Enc}(\text{cpa.pk}_i, 0^{\ell_{\text{cpa}}}; r_i)$.
    3. Finally, it computes $\text{sig}.\sigma^* \leftarrow \text{Sig.Sign}\left(\text{sig.sk}^*, \left(\text{tsc.com}^*, (\text{cpa.ct}_i^*)_{i\in[N]}\right)\right)$
       and outputs $\left(\text{sig.vk}^*, \text{sig}.\sigma^*, \text{tsc.com}^*, (\text{cpa.ct}_i^*)_{i\in[N]}\right)$.

Analysis

Lemma 1. *For all $\lambda \in \mathbb{N}$, and any adversary $\mathcal{A}$, $\text{pr}_{\mathcal{A},0}(\lambda) - \text{pr}_{\mathcal{A},1}(\lambda) = 0$.*

Proof. In game H_0 the challenge phase is used to choose a random $S^* = \{i_j\}_{j\in[B]} \subset [N]$ and sample $(\text{sig.sk}^*, \text{sig.vk}^*) \leftarrow \text{Sig.Setup}(1^\lambda)$. Both of these samplings will use a fresh set of coins and their distribution will be completely independent of any attacker actions including the challenge messages selected by the attacker. Therefore the attacker's sampling them in the challenge phase as in H_0 or earlier as in H_1 is identical.

Lemma 2. *Assuming that P_1 is a strongly-unforgeable one-time signature scheme, there exists a negligible function $\mathsf{negl}(\cdot)$ s.t. for all $\lambda \in \mathbb{N}$, and any ppt. adversary $\mathcal{A}$, $\mathsf{pr}_{\mathcal{A},1}(\lambda) - \mathsf{pr}_{\mathcal{A},2}(\lambda) \leq \mathsf{negl}(\lambda)$.*

Proof. In game H_1, the challenger answers all decryption queries, except when queried on the challenge ciphertext $\mathsf{ct}^* = \left(\mathsf{sig.vk}^*, \mathsf{sig.\sigma}^*, \mathsf{tsc.com}^*, (\mathsf{cpa.ct}_i^*)_{i \in [N]}\right)$. In game H_2, the challenger will not respond to decryption queries on ct^* and returns $\perp$ on any decryption query for $\mathsf{ct} = \left(\mathsf{sig.vk}, \mathsf{sig.\sigma}, \mathsf{tsc.com}, (\mathsf{cpa.ct}_i)_{i \in [N]}\right)$ where $\mathsf{ct} \neq \mathsf{ct}^*$ and $\mathsf{sig.vk} = \mathsf{sig.vk}^*$. However, there are two cases to explore. First, if $\mathsf{ct} \neq \mathsf{ct}^*$ and $\mathsf{sig.vk} = \mathsf{sig.vk}^*$ but the signature $\mathsf{sig.\sigma}$ does not verify under $\mathsf{sig.vk}$ on message $(\mathsf{tsc.com}, (\mathsf{cpa.ct}_i)_{i \in [N]})$, then the challenger of game H_2 immediately outputs $\perp$ and the challenger of game H_1 would also have returned $\perp$ (via rejection of this ciphertext by the regular decryption algorithm) and the two responses are identical.

Second if $\mathsf{ct} \neq \mathsf{ct}^*$ and $\mathsf{sig.vk} = \mathsf{sig.vk}^*$, but the signature *does* verify, then the adversary's view of these two games differ, but we argue that due to the strong unforgeability of the one-time signature scheme P_1, this case occurs with only negligible probability. To see this, we argue that any adversary with non-negligible $\mathsf{pr}_{\mathcal{A},1}(\lambda) - \mathsf{pr}_{\mathcal{A},2}(\lambda)$ can be used to break P_1 as follows. The reduction generates $(\mathsf{pk}, \mathsf{sk}) \leftarrow \mathsf{Setup}(1^\lambda)$ and sends pk to $\mathcal{A}$. It receives $\mathsf{sig.vk}^*$ from the SU-OTS challenger. If $\mathsf{sig.vk}^*$ appears as the signing key in any phase I decryption query, then it aborts. Since $\mathcal{A}$ has no information about $\mathsf{sig.vk}^*$ at this point, this can happen with probability at most the number of decryption queries (polynomial) divided by the size of the public key space for the signature scheme (exponential), so with negligible probability. Once $\mathcal{A}$ outputs challenge messages m_0, m_1, the reduction selects one of these messages randomly and encrypts it according to the normal encryption algorithm, except it uses $\mathsf{sig.vk}^*$ as the verification key and obtains the corresponding signature $\mathsf{sig.\sigma}^*$ by calling the SU-OTS challenger to sign the message $(\mathsf{tsc.com}^*, (\mathsf{cpa.ct}_i^*)_{i \in [N]})$ (this message is computed according to the normal encryption algorithm). It passes this properly-distributed ciphertext $\mathsf{ct}^* = \left(\mathsf{sig.vk}^*, \mathsf{sig.\sigma}^*, \mathsf{tsc.com}^*, (\mathsf{cpa.ct}_i^*)_{i \in [N]}\right)$ back to $\mathcal{A}$. When $\mathcal{A}$ issues a Phase II decryption query $\mathsf{ct} = \left(\mathsf{sig.vk}, \mathsf{sig.\sigma}, \mathsf{tsc.com}, (\mathsf{cpa.ct}_i)_{i \in [N]}\right)$ where $\mathsf{ct} \neq \mathsf{ct}^*$, $\mathsf{sig.vk} = \mathsf{sig.vk}^*$ and $\mathsf{sig.\sigma}$ verifies, then the reduction outputs $((\mathsf{tsc.com}, (\mathsf{cpa.ct}_i)_{i \in [N]}), \mathsf{sig.\sigma})$ to win the SU-OTS challenge.

Lemma 3. *Assuming that P_3 is a tagged set commitment scheme with indistinguishability of setup (Definition 6), there exists a negligible function $\mathsf{negl}(\cdot)$ s.t. for all $\lambda \in \mathbb{N}$, and any ppt. adversary $\mathcal{A}$, $\mathsf{pr}_{\mathcal{A},2}(\lambda) - \mathsf{pr}_{\mathcal{A},3}(\lambda) \leq \mathsf{negl}(\lambda)$.*

Proof. In game H_2, the challenger uses TSC.Setup to generate the public commitment parameters and TSC.Commit to generate the commitment and proofs of membership (for the B items in $S \subseteq [N]$), whereas in game H_3, the challenger uses TSC.AltSetup to generate the public parameters, commitment and proofs of membership (for all items in $[N]$). Otherwise, these games are identical. If there exists an efficient $\mathcal{A}$ that can distinguish between H_2 and H_3, then we can use this $\mathcal{A}$ to attack the indistinguishability of setup of P_3. The reduction works as follows. In both games, a random set $S^* \subset [N]$ and a signing/verification key $(\text{sig.sk}^*, \text{sig.vk}^*) \leftarrow \text{Sig.Setup}(1^\lambda)$ are chosen at the start of the game. The reduction sets $\text{tg} = \text{sig.vk}^*$. It sends $(1^\lambda, 1^B, 1^t, \text{tg}, S^*)$ to the Expt-Ind-Setup challenger, who responds with $(\text{pp}^*, \text{com}^*, (\sigma_i^*)_{i \in S})$, which are either generated by TSC.Setup (making this equivalent to H_2 or TSC.AltSetup (making this equivalent to H_3). The reduction uses $\text{CPA.Setup}(1^\lambda, 1^{\text{CPA}})$ to generate N public/secret key pairs. It sets $\text{pk} = \left(\text{pp}^*, (\text{cpa.pk}_i)_{i \in [N]}\right)$ and $\text{sk} = (\text{cpa.sk}_i)_{i \in [N]}$. It sends pk to $\mathcal{A}$. It answers each decryption query by running the normal decryption algorithm using sk. (In both games, we already have that if any decryption (pre or post challenge) query $\text{sig.vk} = \text{sig.vk}^*$, then the response is $\perp$, so if this somehow happens the response would be identical in both games.) Upon receiving challenge messages m_0, m_1, it chooses a random bit b and encrypts m_b, using S^* (which it chose randomly earlier) in step 1 of the encryption algorithm, setting $(\text{sig.sk}^*, \text{sig.vk}^*)$ as the signing/verification key in step 2 (instead of generating a new pair), using the commitment/proofs $(\text{com}^*, (\sigma_i^*)_{i \in S})$ (obtained earlier) in step 3, instead of computing them using TSC.Commit, and then following steps 3–5 as normal to generate ct^*. It sends this challenge ciphertext ct^* to $\mathcal{A}$. It continues to answer decryption queries for $\mathcal{A}$ using sk. Once $\mathcal{A}$ outputs a guess b' if $b = b'$, then it outputs 0 (guessing H_2) and otherwise outputs 1 (guessing H_3). Since our assumption is that $\mathcal{A}$ has a non-negligible advantage in Game H_2 over Game H_3, then this reduction will have a non-negligible advantage in the indistinguishability of setup experiment for the tagged commitment scheme. Thus, we have a contradiction.

Lemma 4. *Assuming encryption scheme with randomness recovery P_2 is an IND-CPA secure encryption scheme and the tagged set commitment scheme P_3 satisfies statistical soundness (Definition 7), for any PPT adversary $\mathcal{A}$, there exists a negligible function $\text{negl}(\cdot)$ such that for all $\lambda \in \mathbb{N}$, $\text{adv}_{\mathcal{A},3}(\lambda) - \text{adv}_{\mathcal{A},4}(\lambda) \leq \text{negl}(\lambda)$.*

Proof. First, we define the alternate decryption routine which works without the jth decryption key.

$\text{Dec-Alt}_j(\text{sk}_{-j}, \text{ct})$: Let the secret key $\text{sk} = (\text{cpa.sk}_i)_{i \neq j}$ and the ciphertext $\text{ct} = \left(\text{sig.vk}, \text{sig.}\sigma, \text{tsc.com}, (\text{cpa.ct}_i)_{i \in [N]}\right)$. The 'alternate' decryption oracle performs the following steps:

1. If $0 \leftarrow \text{Sig.Verify}\left(\text{sig.vk}, \text{sig.}\sigma, \left(\text{tsc.com}, (\text{cpa.ct}_i)_{i \in [N]}\right)\right)$ then decryption outputs $\perp$.

2. Next, it initializes a set U' to be $\emptyset$. For each $i \neq j$ it computes $(y_i, r_i) = $ CPA.Dec(cpa.sk$_i$, cpa.ct$_i$). Parse y_i as $g_i | \sigma_i | m_i$. It adds (i, y_i) to U' if Check$(i, y_i, r_i) = 1$.[7]
3. If the set U' has $B - 1$ elements, then set $r_j = \oplus_{(i, y_i) \in U'} r_i$. Use r_j to recover the message from cpa.ct$_j$. Let $y_j = $ CPA.Recover(cpa.pk$_j$, cpa.ct$_j$, r_j). If $y_j \neq \perp$ and Check$(j, y_j, r_j) = 1$, then add (j, y_j) to U'.
4. If the set U' does not have exactly B elements then the decryption algorithm outputs $\perp$.
5. If $\oplus_{(i, y_i) \in U'} r_i \neq 0^\ell$, it outputs $\perp$.
6. Finally, the decryption algorithm checks that for all $(i, r_i) \in U'$, the m_i values recovered from y_i are the same. If not, it outputs $\perp$. Else it outputs this common m_i value as the decryption.

We will now show that with overwhelming probability (over the choice of the CPA keys and the output of TSC.AltSetup) there does not exist a ciphertext ct $= \Big($ sig.vk, sig.σ, tsc.com, $($ cpa.ct$_i)_{i \in [N]} \Big)$ with sig.vk $\neq$ sig.vk* such that Dec(sk, ct) $\neq$ Dec-Alt$_j$(sk$_{-j}$, ct).

Claim. There exists a negligible function negl$(\cdot)$ such that for all $\lambda \in \mathbb{N}$ and $j \in [N]$,

$$\Pr \left[\begin{array}{l} \exists \mathsf{ct} = \Big(\mathsf{sig.vk}, \mathsf{sig}.\sigma, \mathsf{tsc.com}, (\mathsf{cpa.ct}_i)_{i \in [N]} \Big) \text{ s.t.} \\ \mathsf{sig.vk} \neq \mathsf{sig.vk}^* \text{ and} \\ \mathsf{Dec}(\mathsf{sk}, \mathsf{ct}) \neq \mathsf{Dec\text{-}Alt}_j(\mathsf{sk}_{-j}, \mathsf{ct}) \end{array} \right] \leq \mathsf{negl}(\lambda)$$

where the probability is over the choice of CPA keys[8] and output of TSC.AltSetup.

Proof. We consider the following cases:

1. Both decryptions output non-bot but distinct messages.

$$\Pr \left[\begin{array}{l} \exists \mathsf{ct} = \Big(\mathsf{sig.vk}, \mathsf{sig}.\sigma, \mathsf{tsc.com}, (\mathsf{cpa.ct}_i)_{i \in [N]} \Big) \text{ s.t.} \\ \mathsf{sig.vk} \neq \mathsf{sig.vk}^* \text{ and} \\ \mathsf{Dec}(\mathsf{sk}, \mathsf{ct}) \neq \mathsf{Dec\text{-}Alt}_j(\mathsf{sk}_{-j}, \mathsf{ct}) \text{ and} \\ (\mathsf{Dec}(\mathsf{sk}, \mathsf{ct}), \mathsf{Dec\text{-}Alt}_j(\mathsf{sk}_{-j}, \mathsf{ct})) \neq (\perp, \perp) \end{array} \right] = 0.$$

This follows directly from the construction of our scheme. Note that Dec and Dec-Alt$_j$ agree on $N - 1$ of the sub-decryptions. Hence the message recovered must be the same if the output message is non-bot.

---

[7] Recall, Check was defined in Sect. 5. It outputs 1 if $y_i \neq \perp$, $g_i = 1$, the commitment verifies and encryption of y_i using public key cpa.pk$_i$ and randomness r_i outputs cpa.ct$_i$.

[8] For simplicity, we are assuming that the underlying PKE scheme is perfectly correct, instead of almost-all-keys perfect correctness. Note that in an almost-all-keys perfect scheme, there is a negligible probability that the (pk, sk) output by setup does not satisfy correct decryption on all messages. However, since only a negligible fraction of the keys are 'bad', it suffices to focus our attention on perfectly correct encryption schemes.

2. Decryption using sk outputs $\perp$ but decryption using sk_{-j} outputs non-bot message.

$$\Pr\left[\begin{array}{l} \exists \mathsf{ct} = \Big(\mathsf{sig.vk}, \mathsf{sig.}\sigma, \mathsf{tsc.com}, (\mathsf{cpa.ct}_i)_{i\in[N]}\Big) \text{ s.t.} \\ \mathsf{sig.vk} \neq \mathsf{sig.vk}^* \text{ and} \\ \mathsf{Dec}(\mathsf{sk}, \mathsf{ct}) \neq \mathsf{Dec\text{-}Alt}_j(\mathsf{sk}_{-j}, \mathsf{ct}) \text{ and} \\ \mathsf{Dec}(\mathsf{sk}, \mathsf{ct}) = \perp \end{array}\right] \leq \mathsf{negl}(\lambda)$$

Here we have the following sub-cases, depending on which step of the decryption outputs $\perp$. For each of the sub-cases, we show that $\mathsf{Dec\text{-}Alt}_j$ also outputs $\perp$.

(a) Step 1 of Dec outputs $\perp$ (that is, signature does not verify). Then Step 1 of $\mathsf{Dec\text{-}Alt}_j$ also outputs $\perp$.

(b) Step 3 of Dec outputs $\perp$ (that is, the set U constructed by Dec has size not equal to B). If $|U| < B - 1$, then Step 4 of $\mathsf{Dec\text{-}Alt}_j$ outputs $\perp$ since the set U' after Step 3 in $\mathsf{Dec\text{-}Alt}_j$ also has size less than B.

If $|U| > B$, then this can be used to break the statistical soundness security of TSC (see Definition 7) because this ciphertext can produce at least $B + 1$ commitments for tag $\mathsf{sig.vk} \neq \mathsf{sig.vk}^*$.

If $|U| = B - 1$, then we will show that the size of set U' after Step 3 in $\mathsf{Dec\text{-}Alt}_j$ is also $B - 1$, hence $\mathsf{Dec\text{-}Alt}_j$ rejects in Step 4. Suppose on the contrary, the set U' has size B after Step 3. This means (j, y_j) was not added to U in Dec (Step 2), but the same tuple was added to U' in $\mathsf{Dec\text{-}Alt}_j$ (Step 3). Note that this implies $\mathsf{Check}(j, y_j, r_j) = 1$ and therefore, $\mathsf{CPA.Enc}(\mathsf{cpa.pk}_j, y_j; r_j) = \mathsf{cpa.ct}_j$. Using the perfect correctness of the encryption scheme, $\mathsf{CPA.Dec}(\mathsf{cpa.sk}_j, \mathsf{cpa.ct}_j) = (y_j, r_j)$. This leads to a contradiction (as $(j, y_j) \notin U$).

(c) Step 4 outputs $\perp$. In this case, Step 5 of $\mathsf{Dec\text{-}Alt}_j$ also outputs $\perp$ since the set U recovered by Dec is identical to the set U' recovered by $\mathsf{Dec\text{-}Alt}_j$.

(d) Step 5 outputs $\perp$. Here again, since the set U recovered by Dec is identical to the set U' recovered by $\mathsf{Dec\text{-}Alt}_j$, Step 6 of $\mathsf{Dec\text{-}Alt}_j$ also rejects here.

3. Decryption using sk_{-j} outputs $\perp$ but decryption using sk outputs non-bot message.

$$\Pr\left[\begin{array}{l} \exists \mathsf{ct} = \Big(\mathsf{sig.vk}, \mathsf{sig.}\sigma, \mathsf{tsc.com}, (\mathsf{cpa.ct}_i)_{i\in[N]}\Big) \text{ s.t.} \\ \mathsf{sig.vk} \neq \mathsf{sig.vk}^* \text{ and} \\ \mathsf{Dec}(\mathsf{sk}, \mathsf{ct}) \neq \mathsf{Dec\text{-}Alt}_j(\mathsf{sk}_{-j}, \mathsf{ct}) \text{ and} \\ \mathsf{Dec\text{-}Alt}_j(\mathsf{sk}_{-j}, \mathsf{ct}) = \perp \end{array}\right] \leq \mathsf{negl}(\lambda)$$

Here we have the following sub-cases, depending on which step of $\mathsf{Dec\text{-}Alt}_j$ outputs $\perp$. For each of the sub-cases, we show that Dec also outputs $\perp$.

(a) Step 1 of $\mathsf{Dec\text{-}Alt}_j$ outputs $\perp \implies$ Step 1 of Dec outputs $\perp$.

(b) Step 4 of $\mathsf{Dec\text{-}Alt}_j$ outputs $\perp$. Let U' be the set after Step 3 in $\mathsf{Dec\text{-}Alt}_j$, and U the set after Step 2 in Dec. If $|U'| > B$, then Step 3 of Dec outputs $\perp$ since U also has size larger than B.

If $|U'| < B - 1$, then $|U| < B$, hence Step 3 of Dec outputs $\perp$.

We will now show that if $|U'| = B - 1$, then either $|U|$ is $B - 1$, or Step 4 of Dec outputs $\bot$. Since $|U'| = B - 1$, this means the (j, y'_j, r'_j) tuple[9] extracted in Step 3 does not satisfy $\mathsf{Check}(j, y'_j, r'_j) = 1$. Let us now consider the implications of $|U| = B$ and $\oplus_{(i,y_i)\in U} r_i = 0^{\ell_{\mathrm{rnd}}}$. First, note that $U = U' \cup \{(j, y_j)\}$, and hence $r_j = \oplus_{(i,y_i)\in U} r_i = r'_j$. Since $\mathsf{Check}(j, y_j, r_j) = 1$, encryption of y_j using randomness r_j outputs $\mathsf{cpa.ct}_j$. Using the perfect correctness of the encryption scheme, it follows that $y'_j = y_j$, but this leads to a contradiction.

(c) Step 5 of $\mathsf{Dec\text{-}Alt}_j$ outputs $\bot \implies$ Step 4 of Dec outputs $\bot$ (the set U' recovered by $\mathsf{Dec\text{-}Alt}_j$ is identical to the set U recovered by Dec).

(d) Step 6 of $\mathsf{Dec\text{-}Alt}_j$ outputs $\bot \implies$ Step 5 of Dec outputs $\bot$ (same reasoning as above).

We will now use the alternate decryption algorithm to show that hybrids H_3 and H_4 are computationally indistinguishable. We will first define intermediate hybrid experiments $H_{3,j}$ for $0 \le j \le N$, where $H_{3,0}$ corresponds to H_3 and $H_{3,N}$ corresponds to H_4. In hybrid $H_{3,j}$, for each $i \le j$, the ith challenge ciphertext component $\mathsf{cpa.ct}_i$ is an encryption of $1|\mathsf{tsc}.\sigma_i^*|m_b$. Therefore, it suffices to show that for all $j \in [N]$, $H_{3,j}$ and $H_{3,j-1}$ are computationally indistinguishable.

In order to prove $H_{3,j-1} \approx_c H_{3,j}$, we will introduce two more intermediate hybrid experiments: $H_{\mathsf{alt},j,0}$ and $H_{\mathsf{alt},j,1}$. The experiment $H_{\mathsf{alt},j,0}$ is identical to $H_{3,j-1}$, except that the challenger uses $\mathsf{Dec\text{-}Alt}_j$ instead of Dec for answering decryption queries. Similarly, the experiment $H_{\mathsf{alt},j,1}$ is identical to $H_{3,j}$, except that the challenger uses $\mathsf{Dec\text{-}Alt}_j$ instead of Dec for answering decryption queries. (Note that in both these experiments, the challenger still rejects decryption queries corresponding to $\mathsf{sig.vk}^*$). We will show that $H_{3,j-1} \approx_c H_{\mathsf{alt},j,0}$, $H_{\mathsf{alt},j,0} \approx_c H_{\mathsf{alt},j,1}$ and $H_{\mathsf{alt},j,1} \approx_c H_{3,j}$.

As before, let $\mathsf{adv}_{\mathcal{A},x}$ denote the advantage of adversary $\mathcal{A}$ in hybrid H_x.

Claim. There exists a negligible function $\mathsf{negl}(\cdot)$ such that for any $\lambda \in \mathbb{N}$ and any adversary $\mathcal{A}$, $\mathsf{adv}_{\mathcal{A},3,j-1}(\lambda) - \mathsf{adv}_{\mathcal{A},\mathsf{alt},j,0}(\lambda) \le \mathsf{negl}(\lambda)$.

Proof. The proof of this claim follows from Claim 5.1.

Claim. Assuming the encryption scheme P_1 is IND-CPA secure, for any ppt. adversary $\mathcal{A}$, there exists a negligible function $\mathsf{negl}(\cdot)$ such that for all $\lambda \in \mathbb{N}$, $\mathsf{adv}_{\mathcal{A},\mathsf{alt},j,0}(\lambda) - \mathsf{adv}_{\mathcal{A},\mathsf{alt},j,1}(\lambda) \le \mathsf{negl}(\lambda)$.

Proof. Suppose there exists a ppt. adversary $\mathcal{A}$ such that $\mathsf{adv}_{\mathcal{A},\mathsf{alt},j,0} - \mathsf{adv}_{\mathcal{A},\mathsf{alt},j,1} \le \mathsf{negl}(\lambda)$. We can use this adversary to build a reduction algorithm $\mathcal{B}$ that breaks the IND-CPA security of the encryption scheme P_1. The main observation here is that in $H_{\mathsf{alt},j,0}$ and $H_{\mathsf{alt},j,1}$, the only component that possibly changes is the jth ciphertext component $\mathsf{cpa.ct}_j$, and we can reduce the computational indistinguishability of these hybrids to the IND-CPA security because both these hybrids do not use the jth secret key $\mathsf{cpa.sk}_j$.

---

[9] We use y'_j, r'_j here to distinguish it from y_j, r_j which are computed in Step 2 of Dec.

The reduction algorithm receives the public key $\mathsf{cpa.pk}_j$ from the challenger; it chooses a uniformly random B size set S, signing keys $(\mathsf{sig.sk}^*, \mathsf{sig.vk}^*)$, CPA scheme's keys $(\mathsf{cpa.pk}_i, \mathsf{cpa.sk}_i)_{i \neq j}$, runs $\mathsf{TSC.AltSetup}$ and sends pk to $\mathcal{A}$. The decryption queries are handled using $(\mathsf{cpa.sk}_i)_{i \neq j}$ since both hybrids use $\mathsf{Dec\text{-}Alt}_j$. The adversary sends its challenge messages m_0, m_1, and the reduction algorithm chooses $b \leftarrow \{0,1\}$. If $j \notin S$,[10] the reduction algorithm sends $0^{\ell_{\mathsf{cpa}}}, 1|\mathsf{tsc}.\sigma_j^*|m_b$ to the challenger as challenge messages, and receives $\mathsf{cpa.ct}_j$. It then computes the remaining ciphertext components and sends the ciphertext ct to $\mathcal{A}$. The adversary then makes polynomially many post-challenge decryption queries, and finally sends its guess b'. The reduction algorithm guesses that $\mathsf{cpa.ct}_j$ is encryption of $0^{\ell_{\mathsf{cpa}}}$ iff $b = b'$.

Claim. There exists a negligible function $\mathsf{negl}(\cdot)$ such that for any $\lambda \in \mathbb{N}$ and any adversary $\mathcal{A}$, $\mathsf{adv}_{\mathcal{A},\mathsf{alt},j,1}(\lambda) - \mathsf{adv}_{\mathcal{A},3,j}(\lambda) \leq \mathsf{negl}(\lambda)$.

Proof. The proof of this claim follows from Claim 5.1.

Lemma 5. *There exists a negligible function* $\mathsf{negl}(\cdot)$ *s.t. for all* $\lambda \in \mathbb{N}$, *and any adversary* $\mathcal{A}$, $\mathsf{pr}_{\mathcal{A},4}(\lambda) - \mathsf{pr}_{\mathcal{A},5}(\lambda) \leq \mathsf{negl}(\lambda)$.

Proof. First, let us consider the distribution $\mathcal{D}$ defined by the following experiment:

- choose a random vector $\mathbf{x} = (x_1, x_2, \ldots, x_{N-1}) \leftarrow \left(\{0,1\}^{\ell_{\mathsf{rnd}}}\right)^{N-1}$.
- choose a random vector $\mathbf{z} \leftarrow \{0,1\}^{N-1}$ of Hamming weight $B - 1$.
- output $(\mathbf{x}, \oplus_{i:z_i=1} x_i)$.

Let $\mathcal{U}$ be the uniform distribution over $\left(\{0,1\}^{\ell_{\mathsf{rnd}}}\right)^N$.

Claim.
$$\mathsf{SD}(\mathcal{D}, \mathcal{U}) \leq 2^{-\lambda}.$$

Proof. This follows from the Leftover Hash Lemma [21]. Let $h_{\mathbf{x}}$ be a hash function defined by $\mathbf{x} = (x_1, \ldots, x_{N-1})$ which maps $N - 1$ bits to ℓ_{rnd} bits as follows: $h_{\mathbf{x}}(z) = \oplus_{i:z_i=1} x_i$. Let $\mathcal{Y}$ denote the uniform distribution over all $N - 1$ bit strings of Hamming weight $B - 1$. This distribution has min-entropy $H_\infty(\mathcal{Y}) = \log\left(\binom{N-1}{B-1}\right)$. Since the hash function family $\{h_{\mathbf{x}}\}_{\mathbf{x} \in (\{0,1\}^{\ell_{\mathsf{rnd}}})^{N-1}}$ is a pairwise-independent hash function family and $H_\infty(\mathcal{Y}) > \ell_{\mathsf{rnd}} + 2\lambda$, $\mathsf{SD}(\mathcal{D}, \mathcal{U}) \leq 2^{-\lambda}$.

As a corollary, it follows that the following distribution $\mathcal{D}'$ is also close to uniform:

- choose a random vector $\mathbf{z}' \leftarrow \{0,1\}^N$ of Hamming weight B. Let $i_1 < i_2 < \ldots < i_B$ denote the indices such that $z'_{i_j} = 1$.
- for each $i \neq i_B$, choose $x'_i \leftarrow \{0,1\}^{\ell_{\mathsf{rnd}}}$.
- set $x'_{i_B} = \oplus_{j<B} x'_{i_j}$ and output $\mathbf{x}'$.

---

[10] If $j \in S$, then these two hybrids are identical.

Corollary 2.
$$SD(\mathcal{D}', U) \leq 2^{-\lambda}.$$

Proof. Given a sample $\mathbf{x}$ which is either from $\mathcal{D}$ or $\mathcal{U}$, one can generate a sample from either $\mathcal{D}'$ or U as follows: choose a random permutation $\pi : [N] \rightarrow [N]$, and permute the components of $\mathbf{x}$ according to π; that is, set $x_i' = x_{\pi(i)}$ for all $i \in [N]$. Clearly, if $\mathbf{x}$ is a uniformly random sample from $(\{0, 1\}^{\ell_{rnd}})^N$, then the resulting vector $\mathbf{x}'$ is also a uniformly random sample.

Suppose $\mathbf{x}$ is a sample from $\mathcal{D}$, and let $\mathbf{z} \in \{0, 1\}^{N-1}$ be the random $B - 1$ weight vector chosen by $\mathcal{D}$ sampler with 1 at positions $\{i_1, \dots, i_{B-1}\}$. Let $\mathbf{z}' \in \{0, 1\}^N$ be a B weight vector which has 1 at positions $\{\pi(i_1), \dots, \pi(i_{B-1}), \pi(N)\}$ and 0 elsewhere. Since π is a uniformly random permutation, the vector $\mathbf{z}'$ is a uniformly random B weight vector and the resulting vector $\mathbf{x}'$ is from distribution $\mathcal{D}'$.

Using this corollary, we can now prove our lemma. Note that the only difference between the two hybrid experiments is the choice of randomness for encryptions. In Hybrid H_4, the challenger chooses a B-size set $S = \{i_1, \dots, i_B\}$, chooses $r_i \leftarrow \{0, 1\}^{\ell_{rnd}}$ for all $i \neq i_B$ and sets $r_{i_B} = \oplus_{j \in [B]} r_{i_j}$. This corresponds to the distribution $\mathcal{D}'$. In Hybrid H_5, all r_i are chosen uniformly at random.

Lemma 6. *Assuming encryption scheme with randomness recovery P_2 is an IND-CPA secure encryption scheme and the tagged set commitment scheme P_3 satisfies statistical soundness (Definition 7), for any PPT adversary $\mathcal{A}$, there exists a negligible function $\mathsf{negl}(\cdot)$ such that for all $\lambda \in \mathbb{N}$, $\mathsf{adv}_{\mathcal{A},5}(\lambda) - \mathsf{adv}_{\mathcal{A},6}(\lambda) \leq \mathsf{negl}(\lambda)$.*

Proof. The proof of this lemma is very similar to the proof of Lemma 4, the only difference being that there is no set S^* here (that is, we switch all ciphertexts to being encryptions of $0^{\ell_{cpa}}$; in Lemma 4, the ciphertext components corresponding to indices in set S^* were not altered). We include the proof in the full version of our paper.

References

1. Bellare, M., Halevi, S., Sahai, A., Vadhan, S.: Many-to-one trapdoor functions and their relation to public-key cryptosystems. In: Krawczyk, H. (ed.) CRYPTO 1998. LNCS, vol. 1462, pp. 283–298. Springer, Heidelberg (1998). https://doi.org/10.1007/BFb0055735
2. Brakerski, Z., Lombardi, A., Segev, G., Vaikuntanathan, V.: Anonymous IBE, leakage resilience and circular security from new assumptions. In: Nielsen, J.B., Rijmen, V. (eds.) EUROCRYPT 2018. LNCS, vol. 10820, pp. 535–564. Springer, Cham (2018). https://doi.org/10.1007/978-3-319-78381-9_20
3. Cash, D., Kiltz, E., Shoup, V.: The twin Diffie–Hellman problem and applications. J. Cryptol. 22(4), 470–504 (2009). https://doi.org/10.1007/s00145-009-9041-6

4. Cho, C., Döttling, N., Garg, S., Gupta, D., Miao, P., Polychroniadou, A.: Laconic oblivious transfer and its applications. In: Katz, J., Shacham, H. (eds.) CRYPTO 2017. LNCS, vol. 10402, pp. 33–65. Springer, Cham (2017). https://doi.org/10.1007/978-3-319-63715-0_2

5. Cramer, R., Shoup, V.: A practical public key cryptosystem provably secure against adaptive chosen ciphertext attack. In: Krawczyk, H. (ed.) CRYPTO 1998. LNCS, vol. 1462, pp. 13–25. Springer, Heidelberg (1998). https://doi.org/10.1007/BFb0055717

6. Cramer, R., Shoup, V.: Universal hash proofs and a paradigm for adaptive chosen ciphertext secure public-key encryption. In: Knudsen, L.R. (ed.) EUROCRYPT 2002. LNCS, vol. 2332, pp. 45–64. Springer, Heidelberg (2002). https://doi.org/10.1007/3-540-46035-7_4

7. Dolev, D., Dwork, C., Naor, M.: Nonmalleable cryptography. SIAM J. Comput. **30**(2), 391–437 (2000)

8. Döttling, N., Garg, S.: From selective IBE to full IBE and selective HIBE. In: Kalai, Y., Reyzin, L. (eds.) TCC 2017. LNCS, vol. 10677, pp. 372–408. Springer, Cham (2017). https://doi.org/10.1007/978-3-319-70500-2_13

9. Döttling, N., Garg, S.: Identity-based encryption from the Diffie-Hellman assumption. In: Katz, J., Shacham, H. (eds.) CRYPTO 2017. LNCS, vol. 10401, pp. 537–569. Springer, Cham (2017). https://doi.org/10.1007/978-3-319-63688-7_18

10. Döttling, N., Garg, S., Hajiabadi, M., Masny, D.: New constructions of identity-based and key-dependent message secure encryption schemes. In: Abdalla, M., Dahab, R. (eds.) PKC 2018. LNCS, vol. 10769, pp. 3–31. Springer, Cham (2018). https://doi.org/10.1007/978-3-319-76578-5_1

11. Döttling, N., Müller-Quade, J., Nascimento, A.C.A.: IND-CCA secure cryptography based on a variant of the LPN problem. In: Wang, X., Sako, K. (eds.) ASIACRYPT 2012. LNCS, vol. 7658, pp. 485–503. Springer, Heidelberg (2012). https://doi.org/10.1007/978-3-642-34961-4_30

12. Dwork, C., Naor, M., Reingold, O.: Immunizing encryption schemes from decryption errors. In: Cachin, C., Camenisch, J.L. (eds.) EUROCRYPT 2004. LNCS, vol. 3027, pp. 342–360. Springer, Heidelberg (2004). https://doi.org/10.1007/978-3-540-24676-3_21

13. Fujisaki, E., Okamoto, T.: How to enhance the security of public-key encryption at minimum cost. In: Imai, H., Zheng, Y. (eds.) PKC 1999. LNCS, vol. 1560, pp. 53–68. Springer, Heidelberg (1999). https://doi.org/10.1007/3-540-49162-7_5

14. Garg, S., Gay, R., Hajiabadi, M.: New techniques for efficient trapdoor functions and applications. In: Ishai, Y., Rijmen, V. (eds.) EUROCRYPT 2019, Part III. LNCS, vol. 11478, pp. 33–63. Springer, Cham (2019). https://doi.org/10.1007/978-3-030-17659-4_2

15. Garg, S., Hajiabadi, M.: Trapdoor functions from the computational Diffie-Hellman assumption. In: Shacham, H., Boldyreva, A. (eds.) CRYPTO 2018, Part II. LNCS, vol. 10992, pp. 362–391. Springer, Cham (2018). https://doi.org/10.1007/978-3-319-96881-0_13

16. Gertner, Y., Malkin, T., Reingold, O.: On the impossibility of basing trapdoor functions on trapdoor predicates. In: 42nd Annual Symposium on Foundations of Computer Science, FOCS 2001, Las Vegas, Nevada, USA, 14–17 October 2001, pp. 126–135. IEEE Computer Society (2001)

17. Goldreich, O.: Basing non-interactive zero-knowledge on (enhanced) trapdoor permutations: the state of the art. In: Goldreich, O. (ed.) Studies in Complexity and Cryptography. Miscellanea on the Interplay Between Randomness and Computation. LNCS, vol. 6650, pp. 406–421. Springer, Heidelberg (2011). https://doi.org/10.1007/978-3-642-22670-0_28

18. Goldreich, O., Levin, L.A.: A hard-core predicate for all one-way functions. In: Proceedings of the 21st Annual ACM Symposium on Theory of Computing, pp. 25–32 (1989)

19. Goldwasser, S., Micali, S.: Probabilistic encryption. J. Comput. Syst. Sci. **28**(2), 270–299 (1984)

20. Hanaoka, G., Kurosawa, K.: Efficient chosen ciphertext secure public key encryption under the computational Diffie-Hellman assumption. In: Pieprzyk, J. (ed.) ASIACRYPT 2008. LNCS, vol. 5350, pp. 308–325. Springer, Heidelberg (2008). https://doi.org/10.1007/978-3-540-89255-7_19

21. Håstad, J., Impagliazzo, R., Levin, L.A., Luby, M.: A pseudorandom generator from any one-way function. SIAM J. Comput. **28**(4), 1364–1396 (1999)

22. Hemenway, B., Ostrovsky, R.: Lossy trapdoor functions from smooth homomorphic hash proof systems. In: Electronic Colloquium on Computational Complexity (ECCC), vol. 16, p. 127 (2009)

23. Hofheinz, D., Kiltz, E.: Practical chosen ciphertext secure encryption from factoring. In: Joux, A. (ed.) EUROCRYPT 2009. LNCS, vol. 5479, pp. 313–332. Springer, Heidelberg (2009). https://doi.org/10.1007/978-3-642-01001-9_18

24. Katz, J., Lindell, Y.: Introduction to Modern Cryptography. Chapman & Hall/CRC, Boca Raton (2008)

25. Kiltz, E., Masny, D., Pietrzak, K.: Simple chosen-ciphertext security from low-noise LPN. In: Krawczyk, H. (ed.) PKC 2014. LNCS, vol. 8383, pp. 1–18. Springer, Heidelberg (2014). https://doi.org/10.1007/978-3-642-54631-0_1

26. Kitagawa, F., Matsuda, T.: CPA-to-CCA transformation for KDM security. In: Hofheinz, D., Rosen, A. (eds.) TCC 2019. LNCS, vol. 11892, pp. 118–148. Springer, Cham (2019). https://doi.org/10.1007/978-3-030-36033-7_5

27. Koppula, V., Waters, B.: Realizing chosen ciphertext security generically in attribute-based encryption and predicate encryption. In: Boldyreva, A., Micciancio, D. (eds.) CRYPTO 2019. LNCS, vol. 11693, pp. 671–700. Springer, Cham (2019). https://doi.org/10.1007/978-3-030-26951-7_23

28. Lamport, L.: Constructing digital signatures from a one-way function. Technical report, SRI International Computer Science Laboratory (1979)

29. Mol, P., Yilek, S.: Chosen-ciphertext security from slightly lossy trapdoor functions. In: Nguyen, P.Q., Pointcheval, D. (eds.) PKC 2010. LNCS, vol. 6056, pp. 296–311. Springer, Heidelberg (2010). https://doi.org/10.1007/978-3-642-13013-7_18

30. Naor, M.: Bit commitment using pseudo-randomness. In: Brassard, G. (ed.) CRYPTO 1989. LNCS, vol. 435, pp. 128–136. Springer, New York (1990). https://doi.org/10.1007/0-387-34805-0_13

31. Naor, M., Yung, M.: Public-key cryptosystems provably secure against chosen ciphertext attacks. In: Proceedings of the 22nd Annual ACM Symposium on Theory of Computing, Baltimore, Maryland, USA, 13–17 May 1990, pp. 427–437 (1990)

32. Pandey, O.: Personal communication (2013)

33. Peikert, C., Waters, B.: Lossy trapdoor functions and their applications. In: Proceedings of the 40th Annual ACM Symposium on Theory of Computing, Victoria, British Columbia, Canada, 7–20 May 2008, pp. 187–196 (2008)

34. Rackoff, C., Simon, D.R.: Non-interactive zero-knowledge proof of knowledge and chosen ciphertext attack. In: Feigenbaum, J. (ed.) CRYPTO 1991. LNCS, vol. 576, pp. 433–444. Springer, Heidelberg (1992). https://doi.org/10.1007/3-540-46766-1_35
35. Rivest, R.L., Shamir, A., Adleman, L.M.: A method for obtaining digital signatures and public-key cryptosystems. Commun. ACM 21(2), 120–126 (1978)
36. Rosen, A., Segev, G.: Chosen-ciphertext security via correlated products. SIAM J. Comput. 39(7), 3058–3088 (2010)
37. Shoup, V.: Why chosen ciphertext security matters. IBM TJ Watson Research Center (1998)
38. Yao, A.C.: Theory and applications of trapdoor functions (extended abstract). In: 23rd Annual Symposium on Foundations of Computer Science, pp. 80–91 (1982)

Author Index

Printed in the United States
By Bookmasters